HAVING 55% OF THE WEIGHT DISTRIBUTION OVER THE REAR WHEELS GIVES THE MGF A LOWER POLAR MOMENT OF INERTIA WHICH MEANS MORE RESPONSIVE HANDLING, SUPERB GRIP AND AN EXHILARATING DRIVE. THAT'S WHY WE PUT THE 1.8 K-SERIES ENGINE BEHIND YOU. AND A GREAT BADGE BEHIND THAT. TO EXPERIENCE THE MGF FOR YOURSELF CALL 0645 251 251.

MG
DRIVE YOUR AMBITION.

**YOU CAN ONLY DO THIS
WITH A GREAT ENGINE BEHIND YOU.**

9 INCHES BEHIND YOU.

THE UNTOLD STORY

THE UNTOLD STORY

DAVID KNOWLES

Motorbooks International
Publishers & Wholesalers ®

This edition first published in 1997 by
Motorbooks International Publishers & Wholesalers,
729 Prospect Avenue, PO Box 1, Osceola, WI 54020 USA

Previously published by Windrow & Greene Ltd, London

Library of Congress Cataloging-in-Publication Data Available.

ISBN 0-7603-0408-4

Printed and bound in the UK

Contents

Foreword by Nick Stephenson, Rover Group

It has long been the intention of the Rover Group to create a brand-new sports car worthy of the world-famous MG badge: with the MGF, we believe that we have succeeded in our aim. Just a few years ago, this ambition might not have been possible to realize, but with the radical changes that have taken place in Rover's business and product strategies, the company can now deliver a class leading range of vehicles that is the envy of our peers.

We are very conscious of the strong traditions and heritage that lie behind the MG name. In designing the MGF, we have, of course, respected those values, allowing them to enrich the car where appropriate, but at the same time, the MGF is a contemporary, rather than retrospective, statement. The RV8 pointed the way forward and clearly demonstrated that we were serious about returning to lead a market that we have dominated in the past; the MGF is the next step in that process.

From the time that former chief executive John Towers and I drove the very first 'Pocket Rocket' prototype at Gaydon, we could see that its mid-engined layout was the obvious formula to enable us to return to the forefront of the sports car market. I would even argue that the MGF could be regarded as one of the most dramatic MG sports cars that the company has produced since the pre-war K3 Magnette.

This book tells, in remarkable detail, how the MG marque has evolved over the last 75 years, taking in the background of such famous cars as the TC Midget and the MGB, not to mention a few

less familiar ones, and brings the story right up to date with the development of the MGF. I can assure you that the story is far from over yet.

NICK STEPHENSON
Director of Group Design and Engineering, Rover Group

Introduction

The subject of motor cars, and sports car in particular, has been one of the major obsessions of the 20th century. Small boys of all ages have been fascinated by cars ever since Kenneth Grahame's Mr Toad first went 'Poop, poop!' Within the sports car clique, there are a select few marques that command an obsession greater than all the rest: at the top of the heap must surely lie MG. Why this should be is a matter that fascinates historians and enthusiasts alike, but perhaps the key is that MG sports cars have always been desirable, yet affordable—never unattainable.

One man was at the heart of the MG marque, Cecil Kimber, who drew around him, like moths to a flame, a corps of men who seemed to dedicate their very souls to working for MG. With Kimber's enforced departure in 1941, and tragic death just four years later, his mantle was passed to others. Over the years, the fortunes of the marque have waxed and waned with the tides of mergers and reorganization—mostly away from the heart of MG affairs, but always with a governing influence—and for a while in the last decade, it looked as though the days of the octagon were numbered. Thankfully, recent events have proved that not to be the case, and MG seems to be faced with an exciting future.

Of course, many books have been written about MG, but in this volume, I have tried to capture a sense of not only the cars (including many that were still-born), but also an inkling of the spirit of the people who made MG what it was. I hope that reading it gives you at least half as much pleasure as it has given me during the 12 years that I have spent researching and writing it.

I would like to express my gratitude to the following people, many of whom have patiently listened to my questions over a long period of time and have poured forth a wealth of information:
Martin Abba (Rover), Doug Adams (Austin/BMC/BL), Geoff Allen (MG), Mike Allison (MG), Greg Allport (Rover Group), John Ashford (BL), Roy Axe (BL), Geoff Barron (MGCC MGA Register), Ian Beech (BL), David Bishop (British Motor Heritage), David Blume (BL/Rover Japan), Cliff Bray (MG), Roy Brocklehurst (MG), Richard Brotherton (BMIHT), David Browne (BL), John Browne (MG), Bruce Bryant (Rover Group), Don Butler (MG), Richard Carter (Rover Group), Mike Carver (BL), John Chasemore (Rover), Denis Chick (Rover Group), Jeff Clarke (MG), Anders Clausager (BMIHT), Jean Cook (Cecil Kimber's daughter), John Cooper (Rover), Ken Costello (Costello Engineering), Jimmy Cox (MG), Nick Cox (MGCC Twin Cam Group), Steve Cox (Rover Group), Alan Curtis (Aston Martin), John Daly (DCA), Jack Daniels (MG and Morris), John Dugdale, Andy Duthie (Rover Group), Tony Dyson (Triumph), Alan Edis (Rover Group), Sir Michael Edwardes (BL), Ian Elliott (BL), Norman Ewing, Nick Fell (Rover Group), Mike Ferguson (Rover Group), Phil Gillam (Rover Group), Malcolm Green, John Gregory (Rover), Brian Griffin (Rover Group), Charles Griffin (BMC/BL), Tom Haig (MG), Richard Hamblin (Rover/RSP), Vic Hammond (BL Styling), Malcolm Harbour (BL), Mike Hawke (MG Car Club), Roy Haynes (BL), Don Hayter (MG), Jack Hayward (MG), Rob Higgins (MGCC), Maureen Hil, (Rover Group), Brian Hillier (MG), Frank 'Dutchy' Holland (MG), Richard Howard (ADO35), Paul Hughes (BL Styling), Martin Ince (BL/Rover), Justin Isles (Roversport), Des Jones (MG), Kevin Jones (Rover Group), Bryan Kennedy, Michael Kennedy (Rover), 'Spen' King (Triumph/BL), Mike Kinnear (Rover Group), Jim Lambert (Morris Motors), Rod Lyne (MG), Thora Malone, Harris Mann (BL Styling), Tim Martin (Mayflower Group), Gerry McGovern (Rover Group), Bruce McWilliams (BLMI), Terry Mitchell (MG), Wynne Mitchell (Rover), Norman Morris (BL), Mike Moseley (BL/Rover), Brian Moylan (MG), Harold Musgrove (BL), Peter Neal (MG), Bob Neville (MG), Jeremy Newman (Rover/DRA), Robin Nickless (Rover), Jim O'Neill (MG), Robin Owen (BL), Gerald Palmer (MG), Dave Peers (Rover Group), Ian Penberthy, Tom Penny (BL), Tony Pond, John Pressnell, Geoff Purkis (Rover Group), Syd Purves (MG), Paul Ragbourne (BMC/BL/Rover), Karam Ram (BMIHT), Pat Rees (BMC), Leigh Richardson (Rover), Alan Roberts (BL/Rover), Andrew Roberts, Graham Robson, Norman Rose (Triumph), Steve Schlemmer (Rover Group), Dave Seymour (BMC/MG/Rover), John Sibbit (Rover Group), David Sims (6R4 Register), Gordon Sked (Rover Group), Bob Staniland (MG), John Stark (BL/Rover), John Stephenson (BL/Rover/RSP), Nick Stephenson (Rover), Jim Stimson (MG), Wyn Thomas (Rover Group), John Thornley (MG), Peter Thornley (son of John), John Towers (Rover), Stuart Turner (BMC 'Comps'), Bill Wallis (MG Car Club), Bob Ward (MG), Bob West (owner of SRX 210), Julian Whitehead (Rover Group), Janet Wilkinson (SMMT), Denis Williams (MG), Paddy Willmer (MG Car Club), Dickie Wright (MG), Don Wyatt (Rover Group), Masatoshi Yamashita (Rover Japan), John Yea (Rover Group).

DAVID A. KNOWLES
Hayes,
1997

1 The pre-war years

The story of the first MG—even allowing for the inevitable debate as to what exactly that means—is firmly rooted in the early 1920s. But to appreciate how the MG marque came about at all, one needs to delve further back, and to consider in particular the background of two men: William Morris and Cecil Kimber. The former gave his name and financial support to the birth of the Morris Garages, while the latter steered the business from 1922 and did much to shape the early years of MG.

At the turn of the 19th century, recognizing the importance of the petrol engine, William Morris began looking for a means of entering the motor cycle and motor car field. In 1901, at the age of 23, he went into partnership with a bicycle dealer named Joseph Cooper, and together they established Morris & Cooper at 48 High Street, Oxford, selling bicycles. Unfortunately, the partnership did not last, and Morris soon bought out Cooper. The two men obviously remained on reasonably good terms, however, for Cooper would later return to work for his former partner, helping develop the prototype Morris Oxford and remaining in Morris' employ until his retirement.

In need of finances for expansion, Morris secured the backing of F. G. (Frank) Barton (who already had premises in Abingdon, Bicester and Oxford, dealing in bicycles and motor cars) and a wealthy Oxford student. Together, the three partners formed the Oxford Automobile & Cycle Agency in 1903, producing the Morris motor cycle. However, this venture was also short-lived, due to financial mismanagement; Miles Thomas would later recall in his autobiography, *Out On a Wing*, that 'young Morris had the mortification of having to stand in the rain at an auction sale of the assets of the partnership; he had to borrow £50 to buy back his own kit of tools, which to him were his stock-in-trade. With this £50 debt hung round his neck like an albatross, he had to start again from the bottom rung of the ladder. The experience determined him never to go into partnership with anyone.' Licking his wounds, Morris retreated to his original cycle business.

By now older and wiser, but undaunted, Morris began formulating ambitious plans to enter the emergent motor car manufacturing business, and decided to expand his enterprise further. In 1907, as his fortunes recovered, he acquired premises at Longwall Garage Yard, and although these were little more than a collection of wooden sheds, over the following three years, they were dismantled and purpose-built workshops erected. In 1908, Morris disposed of the High Street shop and acquired more premises at St Cross Road as his empire grew.

In the autumn of 1912, as the next string to his bow, Morris formed WRM Motors Ltd with a view to manufacturing his own cars, and exhibited drawings of his proposed Morris Oxford at the London Motor Show at Olympia in November. Fortune smiled when Gordon Stewart—later to form the well-known Stewart and Arden vehicle distributors—agreed to buy 400 Morris Oxfords, largely one presumes on the strength of the drawings, a handful of prototype patterns and Morris' sales patter. The Morris Oxford, with its distinctive 'bull-nose' radiator grille (made by Doherty Motor Components of Coventry), first appeared in March 1913 and was priced at £175.

Whereas many of his rivals set out to manufacture nearly everything themselves, Morris was a more canny operator, buying in as many of the critical components as possible. In due course, his financial acumen allowed him to acquire many of the companies that supplied him. The bodies of the bull-nose Oxfords were built by Raworths, the Oxford based coachbuilders, while the 10hp engines, carburettors and three-speed gearboxes were specially designed and manufactured by the Coventry firm of White & Poppe, to whom Morris had to pay £50 per car—a considerable proportion of the overall cost.

In 1913, the business became known as The Morris Garages—Proprietor W. R. Morris and grew yet again as premises were acquired in Queen Street for a head office and showrooms. Then, in 1914, Morris acquired a courtyard alongside the Clarendon Hotel in Cornmarket, roofed it over and established a workshop. By this time, he had also taken on an agency for Sunbeam motor cycles at Queen Street, the machines themselves being stored down in the basement.

In April of the same year, Morris went on the first of a number of fact finding missions, visiting the USA to learn more about the production techniques employed there. To his surprise, he found that the Continental Motor Manufacturing Company had designed a small-capacity engine (1495cc)—for which there was little demand locally—that they could supply in conjunction with a gearbox from the Detroit Gear Machine Company for about half the cost of the White & Poppe units. Naturally, he became very interested in the Continental engines, and soon signed a contract for them to be supplied.

Meanwhile, within a year of the Oxford's launch, Morris had offered a more sporting variant, featuring a single seat and a more highly tuned engine, which retailed for £20 more than the basic Oxford. If nothing else, this early—rather ungainly—Morris 'sports car' demonstrates that Morris could see the merit in offering something a little more rakish for the less impecunious customer. Although it achieved relatively meagre sales, no doubt the sporting Oxford attracted welcome attention—and customers—into the Morris showrooms.

For the Continental engine, Morris developed a new cheaper model, the Morris Cowley. This was introduced in 1915 and was fitted with a body built by Hollick & Pratt. By now, however, war had intervened: in September 1915, the British Chancellor of the Exchequer, Reginald McKenna, imposed a punitive 33⅓ per cent import tax on American goods; then in March 1916, the government banned the carriage of non-essential supplies on shipping, since this was the lifeline of the nation. Both actions would have had a serious effect on Morris had it not been for the fact that he, too, was busily engaged in war work.

To overcome the restrictions imposed on imported goods, Morris sought a local manufacturer who could build the Continental engines under licence. Eventually, the contract went to the British factory of the French company Hotchkiss et Cie, which had been set up in Coventry in 1915 when it was feared that the company's Paris operation would be overrun by the Germans. Even so, it was not until late 1919 that Morris Cowleys began to be seen in any significant number, the first Hotchkiss engine having been delivered in July, production getting under way in September. By this time, Morris had found himself entangled in some unwelcome contractual arrangements with his distributing agents, so in June 1919,

CECIL KIMBER

Cecil Kimber was born at West Norwood, South London, on 12 April, 1888, into a world that was only just beginning to discover the internal combustion engine and the possibilities it offered. His stern father owned a printing business, which was Cecil's first place of employment, by which time, the family had relocated to Manchester. Kimber's real interest, however, lay in motor cycles, encouraged by the purchase of his first—a Rex—in 1906. According to his daughter, Jean Cook, he soon began participating in events with the Warrington and District Motor Cycle Club, through which he learned how to save money by making his own repairs. In 1909, he traded up to a 1907 Twin Rex, and continued his competitive endeavours. In the following year, he was involved in a serious accident, as a result of which, his right knee was smashed. Two years on crutches followed, while the surgeons agonized over whether or not his leg could be saved. Jean Cook recalls, 'Eventually, as they were thinking of amputating, the bones began to knit. He could walk, he could even dance and learn to skate, but above all he could drive.'

With the aid of the compensation money he received after the accident, Kimber bought a Singer 10, which he used to help sell his father's printing ink. When his father asked for the compensation money to be ploughed into the printing business, however, Kimber refused, and father and son fell out. Cecil left the business behind in 1914, to pursue his own choice of career, and the resulting family rift was never healed. His father was so bitter that he died without ever speaking to his son again.

In the second year of the so-called 'Great War', Kimber joined Sheffield-Simplex, where he became assistant to the chief engineer. During his time with that company, he acquired a 14hp Singer, which had been raced at Brooklands, where reputedly it had lapped at 80mph (128.74km/h). Later, he would recall that 'needless to say at the time (it) was the joy of my heart.' In 1916, he moved to AC Cars at Thames Ditton, although he did not stay very long. Jean Cook remembers a time, years later, when her father recalled his frustration at AC: 'He told me that he was so angry—he'd drawn up a plan to reorganize the AC works, and the director had written on his plan "What's this? See me." Father was furious!' From AC Cars, Kimber—by now married—went to Martynside Aircraft at Weybridge, Surrey, living in a hotel nearby. In 1919, the Kimbers moved to Birmingham, where Cecil worked at E. G. Wrigley. There, he met Frank Woollard, who would later help in his efforts to establish MG as a marque in its own right. Kimber's job at Wrigley's was works organizer, and his daughter Jean recalls that her uncle told her, 'You could have eaten your dinner under the machines when he had finished with the place.' Undoubtedly, it was through the Wrigley connection that Kimber first came upon William Morris, for the latter bought axles for his Morris cars from the company; later, in 1923, he bought the whole company!

Eventually, Cecil Kimber joined Morris Garages and went on to inspire so many people who worked with him. Jean Cook was told by John Browne that her father had 'the magical ability to make an ordinary exercise into a magical expedition.' She adds, 'He had a lack of engineering training, but boundless enthusiasm.' He also had a methodical mind, exemplified by the smart and purposeful way he organized the factory: Jean Cook's step-sister told her how she had noticed that all the services—gas, electricity and so on—had been colour-coded, an idea ahead of its time.

Of course, Kimber was passionately interested in racing as a means of gaining valuable publicity and 'improving the breed': Jean Cook says, 'My

(Rover)

father believed that success in racing, particularly on the Continent, helped a small manufacturer become known world-wide.' She also points out that he was rather less interested when customers, who tried to emulate the race cars, came unstuck and brought their wounded charges to the factory for repair, which would be when others, like John Thornley, came into their own.

All honeymoons must come to an end and, in due course, this would be the fate of the independent MG Car Company. Jean Cook found it interesting that her father seemed to take the Morris Motors take-over in his stride, but there were other, more personal, matters for him to deal with. In 1937, he separated from his wife (Jean's mother), who was suffering from a terminal illness. Kimber's affections lay with a divorcée, Muriel 'Gillie' Dewar, whom Jean says her father had loved since 1933. When Jean's mother died in the spring of 1938, her father became free to marry Gillie. Jean is sure that the outwardly prim and proper Lord and Lady Nuffield were unhappy about this state of affairs, which may have been a decisive factor in Kimber and Nuffield's eventual parting of the ways. Jack Daniels also believes that this was the case. The story of Kimber's departure is covered in Chapter 2. His tragic, and unnecessary, death, just before the end of the war, robbed the motor industry of one of its most capable scions, and we can only wonder at how he would have viewed the post-war development of the marque he loved so much.

WRM Motors had been liquidated and Morris Motors Ltd had come into being.

Morris Garages and Cecil Kimber

As the Morris Motors business expanded, William Morris found himself less able to devote time to Morris Garages, and he sought to delegate that responsibility to a manager. His choice for the position was Frank Barton, who had supported him in the short-lived partnership of 1903. Morris appears to have attached little blame to Barton for the failure of their business, the fault having lain with the profligate third member of the partnership, so they had remained on good terms. Barton—of whom it was said 'He could sell sand in the Sahara'—occupied this position until he resigned in March 1919 due, we are told, to ill health. Later, he would become one of the first agents for Morris cars, based in Plymouth, Devon.

Barton's place was taken by Edward Armstead, another acquain-

tance of Morris, who had bought the High Street premises in 1908. In the year following Armstead's arrival, a 15-year-old messenger boy was taken on at the Queen Street showrooms, fresh from school. Within the year, this bright lad—Albert Sydney Enever—began working at the Clarendon Yard workshop, where he soon found himself under the wing of Cecil Cousins, who had been tuning motor cycles and doing other work there since January.

In 1921, Cecil Kimber was employed as sales manager at Morris Garages, but in March of the following year, Edward Armstead suddenly left—apparently suffering from considerable personal problems, as he committed suicide by gassing himself barely two months later. As a consequence, at the age of 34, Kimber found himself in charge of the Morris Garages business.

Before long, Kimber was itching to offer specially modified versions of his patron's cars, presumably encouraged by Morris himself, who had already dabbled in 'improved' Morris Oxfords. One type of body popular at the time was known as the Chummy, this title being derived from the cosy nature of its two-seat interior, with all-encompassing hood and occasional rear seating. It was this slightly more 'personal' model that Kimber saw as the potential basis for a sporting conversion of the Morris Cowley, rather than the four-seater Oxford.

There is a commonly held romantic notion that Morris and Kimber found a ready clientele among the Oxford undergraduates, but this was not the case. The problem was not so much financial nor lack of interest—few Oxford undergraduates came from impoverished backgrounds, and motor cars were certainly becoming *de rigueur*—but rather a case of rules imposed by the colleges themselves. According to John Browne, who worked in Oxford's City Motors at the time, restrictions were tight: 'All vehicles had to be kept in a registered garage, and were required to carry a green-fronted lamp, about 2in (5.08cm) square, on the front, although this was not really legal.' As a result, few undergraduates kept cars at Oxford, preferring to rent them when required. 'Undergraduates in Essex College could hire cars from Macs Garage at the Randolph Hotel for £2 per day, and this obviously suited the needs of most,' concludes Browne.

In the spring of 1923, Morris acquired a number of his suppliers, including Osberton Radiators (which he had helped establish at Osberton Road, Summertown, in 1919, later adding premises at nearby Bainton Road), Hotchkiss and Hollick & Pratt. He kept them as part of his growing portfolio of personal businesses until June 1926, when they were sold to Morris Motors. With their incorporation into the main business, these companies became, respectively, Morris Radiators Branch, Morris Engines Branch and Morris Bodies Branch. However, The Morris Garages, including the various operations managed by Kimber, remained William Morris' personal property throughout these upheavals.

While his employer was engaged in making these acquisitions, Cecil Kimber was planning his move into the arena of more individually styled sporting motor cars. He entered a modified Chummy in the 1923 Land's End Trial, and did well enough to qualify for a medal, although he elected to take a pair of cuff links instead.

When Kimber began experimenting with his special Morrises, some of his more enthusiastic employees would work on the 'specials' outside normal working hours. This group was not restricted purely to Morris Garages' staff, as John Browne, who was attending the same night school as Cecil Cousins and George Morris for his 'improvership' (with City Motors of Oxford), also became a willing, unpaid volunteer during the evenings and weekends: 'I picked up with Cecil and George. Like me, they were mad keen on motor cycles—I could build, dismantle and tune motor bikes—and we shared an interest in racing motor cycles. I was in digs nearby, and they said to me, "Come round to Morris Garages (where they worked). Our boss Cecil Kimber is mad on tuning, and we're building a chassis up at the Clarendon (hotel yard). Why don't you come over and give us a hand?" and so I did.'

However, this out-of-hours work soon drew the unwelcome attention of the workshop manager, for whom the presence of these unfamiliar 'hooligans', as he saw them, was the last straw: '...so we got kicked out of the Clarendon Yard, and the chassis work went to Longwall, where we carried on. Then a similar thing happened there: they decided that they wanted to close up earlier at night, closing at six, and the managers and so on wanted to lock up by seven. We were sure that Longwall had been tipped off by the Clarendon about us "ruffians"!'

Thus, in February 1923, Cousins, Browne, George Morris and their work moved a second time: 'Kimber took over a little mews off Beaumont Street, a little dead-end; it was a coach house to one of the big houses. I remember it had big black-painted double doors opening outward. It had obviously been used in some car related capacity before we arrived, since there was a rudimentary wooden test body stuck up in the roof, which remained there whilst we were there, and was still in place some time after we left!' Work soon got under way again in this garage, in what was then Alfred Lane, converting the Morris chassis to form the basis for the Morris Garages Chummy. This work included resetting the springs. Soon, Kimber decided to experiment with entirely special coachwork to complement the modified chassis. In these cases, the reworked chassis would be sent off to Raworths, the coachbuilders, for their bodies to be fitted. Six cars are known to have been built in this way. At Raworths, situated in St Aldates, just below and opposite Christchurch College, Browne recalls that there was a foreman called Pittam 'who gave us a lot of help in forming the body lines and structure.'

Cecil Kimber would often pop around to Alfred Lane during the evening to see how things were getting on: 'He would make suggestions and tell us what to do,' says Browne. 'Then he would send one of us off with half-a-crown to get some fish and chips and bottles of beer—we'd work on until ten or eleven at night. There was no pay—I wasn't an employee—I just did it out of interest!' The cars that were converted were based on both Morris Oxford and Cowley chassis: 'We'd have one in at the Alfred Lane lock-up, take it down to Raworths and then finally go round to the Park End Street showroom and head offices. Cecil Kimber would then use it to drive round to the agents in order to drum up interest in his "specials". He might then sell that one to the distributor, who would order more, and so demand built up.'

Clearly, this was quite a modest success: 'Then it got so busy that there would be orders for two or three at a time, and so work had to shift back to the Clarendon Yard, but these conversions were less experimental or individual in nature.' The problem lay with the price, for the Raworth-bodied Morris Garages Cowleys were sold at £350, twice the price of the chassis itself. As a result, the 'night shift' no longer found themselves building complete cars, but rather carrying out occasional work on them: 'George Morris would take one of these cars out from the Clarendon Yard for test-

CECIL COUSINS

(Rover/BMIHT)

Henry Edward Cecil Cousins was born in Oxford on 14 April, 1902. From school, he entered an apprenticeship with a local agricultural engineering firm, T. G. West, but having completed his apprenticeship in 1919, he decided to look elsewhere for his improvership—the follow-on stage, which brought with it experience in a number of fields not covered by a normal apprenticeship, such as car sales and office work. At the beginning of January 1920, he began work for Morris Garages at the Clarendon Yard service facility, working on motor cycles brought in for service, repair and tuning.

Known by his colleagues as either 'Cis' or, less kindly, 'nitchy knackers' (on account of his unfortunate habit of absent mindedly scratching the crotch of his trousers), Cecil Cousins was, by all accounts, a character full of bluster, keen to have a go, with an enthusiasm that sometimes exceeded his abilities. John Browne, who attended night school with Cousins and George Morris, recalls that Cousins was 'a tall chap with a stoop, quite a mop of hair and slightly protruding teeth. At Edmund Road, one time, we had a visit from an actress on a sales visit; she was appearing in an advertisement for an MG car, and so she came to see the works. We were all busily working away when she came, but someone had said to Cecil Cousins, "You mustn't scratch your balls when she's here!" Cecil replied that he didn't know he was doing it, and so Jack Lowndes said that he would stand by the hooter and, if he saw Cecil putting his hands in his pockets, he would give two blasts!'

In 1928, Cousins became involved in the creation of Kimber's new baby, the Morris Six-engined MG Six, or the 'Quick Six', as it became known at the factory. He had been asked by Kimber to step in as proxy draughtsman to draw up the basic chassis. Later, he became involved in the creation of the R-type Midget, taking out the chassis patent with H. N. Charles and the MG Car Company in December 1934.

Cousins went on to become foreman of the experimental department, eventually retiring in 1967 as MG's assistant general manager.

ing, and would come to us on "reject", so we were working as an unofficial rectification department!'

Browne also remembers how the springs were modified to give the cars a more sporting, lower stance: 'They'd get two or three sets of springs from Cowley, take them to Grants at Princes Street, where a wonderful old blacksmith would reset them cold: he would make chalk marks on the floor, and by striking the springs with glancing blows from his hammer, he would stretch the metal and reshape them, often doing this straight away while I waited. He would then check them in a special wooden template box to ensure that the shackle bolts would fit.'

For a while, the future of Kimber's Morrises looked uncertain. This situation was not helped by the fact that Morris Motors had brought out their own Occasional Four, which was too close to the Morris Garages Chummy for comfort, especially as it undercut the latter on price. Seeking a way forward, Kimber toyed with a number of one-off ideas, including an Oxford-based Chummy. A rather less sporting upright saloon, with an aluminium body, was also built on the Oxford 14/28 chassis, being advertised as the MG vee-front saloon. There were other experiments, too, but the most successful was a sporting four-seat tourer, also on the Morris 14/28 chassis. This was built along the lines of the 30/98 Vauxhall, and had a rakish body of highly polished aluminium. Wilson McComb tells us, in his book *MG by McComb*, that Kimber was inspired by seeing a special-bodied Morris Oxford 14/28 owned by an employee of Sunbeam motor cycles, which is quite feasible given that Morris Garages held a Sunbeam agency.

Then, during 1924, Jack Gardiner—a salesman at Morris Garages who, later in life, would become the MG personnel manager—decided to have a similar car built for him by the MG team. Before long, this was followed by an improved, somewhat lower, version for Billy Cooper, a well-known trials driver of the day. This car had a polished body (by Coventry Car Bodies Ltd—better known as Carbodies) with the wings and interior picked out in blue.

It soon became clear that Raworths, who were coachbuilding individual bodies, could not keep up the pace, despite the cajoling of Mr Pittam, so Carbodies became involved in building semi-mass-produced bodies, using some pressings. Many of these pressings were the products of a sort of cottage industry, staffed by employees and their families working from home, says Browne: 'The pressings would often be produced in a shed in someone's garden, and on a Sunday, vans would go down the back streets, behind the houses, to collect their output! Wives could often braze and weld, but then many of them had done that sort of thing during the "Great War".'

This cottage industry, situated in the back streets of Coventry and Birmingham, was one of many things that would be lost within a few years, once the German bombs had done their worst to reshape the cities. In due course, to keep Raworths going, perhaps two chassis would be sent there and six might go to Carbodies, the latter involving a long drive on a bare chassis with no real protection from the elements, although this didn't seem to worry most of the men, according to Browne: 'We motor cycle blokes were okay, as we had our rubberized ponchos and so could stay dry in our motor cycle gear, which we sometimes loaned to the other fellows if they were taking the cars to Coventry.'

In September 1924, Morris Motors announced improvements to their Oxford, including better brakes and the availability of a longer chassis. Kimber latched on to this very quickly and, taking the 'Cooper' car as his inspiration, introduced the MG Super Sports Model, better known to some enthusiasts as the MG 14/28 Mark I. This featured very attractive, two-tone alloy bodywork, the lower portion having a polished bare-metal finish.

Next, Morris introduced a six-cylinder version of the Oxford, which he called the F-type, and naturally Kimber was soon examining it to see if he could produce an MG version. However, the Morris did not prove successful, largely because of its unfortunate engine which, recalls Browne, 'effectively comprised a Cowley block with two extra cylinders, and suffered from a sand trap in the front of the block, which caused the camshaft to overheat.' Consequently, what would have been the first six-cylinder MG was abandoned at an early stage.

THE MG NAME

There has been much debate about the derivation of the MG name, and even discussion as to whether or not one should include full stops after each letter, to render it M.G. or simply MG (Kimber preferred them in). In 1929, Cecil Kimber included the following statement in some of his advertising: 'Out of compliment to Sir William R. Morris, Bt., we named our production the M.G. Sports, the letters being the initial letters of his original business undertaking, "The Morris Garages", from which has sprung the vast group of separate enterprises including the M.G. Car Company.' One could take this to be proof—if any was needed—that MG stands for Morris Garages. However, Kimber's daughter, Jean Cook, recalls her father saying, 'MG doesn't stand for Morris Garages, it just stands for itself.' Proponents of this distancing of MG from The Morris Garages suggest that it was to avoid confusion between the two separate businesses and to reduce Sir William's vulnerability to the dreaded super-tax. Jean Cook points out that these arguments have some validity, since Lord Nuffield's papers show that his accountant recommended that the MG Car Company should be separated entirely from the Morris Garages to avoid tax problems. Of greater significance, perhaps, is that apparently Kimber really wanted MG to be divorced from Morris Garages. However, it is possible that in the end, he tried too hard to achieve this.

THE MG OCTAGON

The MG logo first appeared in Morris Garages advertisements in the autumn of 1923, the earliest known being that in the November 1923 issue of the Oxford magazine *The Isis*. The logo was omitted from the Morris Garages advertisements in Miles Thomas' *Morris Owner* magazine of March and April 1924, but appeared in the advertisement in the May issue; perhaps Kimber was wary of upsetting his patron. Over the years, various fanciful stories have evolved concerning the inspiration for the MG logo, but one thing is certain: it was not copied from the octagonal shape of Abingdon gaol, since in those days, the Abingdon factory was not even a glimmer in Kimber's eye. Credit for the idea was taken by Ted Lee, an accountant at Morris Garages. According to Jonathan Wood, in an article for *Thoroughbred & Classic Cars*, Lee claimed that he took it upon himself to draw the octagonal logo and show it to Kimber: 'I drew out this badge with a little ruler I'd bought from High School—I was good at art... Kimber saw it and said, "That's just the thing."' Then, Lee told Wood, the badge was shown to Morris, who said it was 'the best thing to come out of the company...and it will never go out of it.'

At first, the MG badge appeared in advertising literature, at each end of the door sill tread strips, and as the centre-piece to the round Morris Oxford badge fitted to conversions. The process of change was fairly gradual, however, as undoubtedly Kimber remained cautious about upsetting the apple-cart by throwing out the Morris name too quickly. MG letters in German silver, bereft of the octagon itself, began to appear on the face of the grilles of the flat-radiator 1927 MGs, and Kimber was soon carried away with 'octagon fever'. Before long, possibly early in 1928, the first enamelled MG badges were fitted in place of the Morris Oxford MG badges, but it was not until Kimber started using the unique radiator grille that the new badge was given pride of place. A final note of caution for historians comes from John Browne: 'Badges themselves are nothing to go by when dating a car. We would change a badge for anyone, and often even gave them away for free.'

While the definition of what truly constituted an MG was evolving, the famous octagonal logo began to creep into advertising for the Morris Garages cars, and by 1925, the 14/28 featured the octagon on its door tread plates, although it had yet to achieve pride of place, which is what Kimber really wanted. His ambitions lay in the manufacture of a car that he could regard as his own, and it was in 1924 that he began to formulate the next stage in his plan to achieve this.

The story of 'Old Number One'

The car known as 'Old Number One' has probably been the subject of most debate in the MG world. On the one hand are those who insist that it is futile to refer to this car as the first MG, since cars identified as MGs had been built for at least two years before the

Cecil Kimber seated in 'Old Number One', in which he entered the Land's End Trial in 1925. This car, based on a modified Cowley chassis with a special Hotchkiss engine, could be considered the first proper MG sports car, rather than being simply a sporty Morris. (Rover/BMIHT)

one-off special was constructed for Kimber himself to use competitively. On the other hand there are those who claim that Kimber regarded 'Old Number One' as his first MG, and that his word is good enough for them. Cecil Cousins, who has often been described as 'MG's first employee', expressed his views on this many times in his usual forthright manner, telling Wilson McComb that as far as he was concerned, 'Old Number One' was 'a one-off bastard. I argued until I got so unpopular that I gave up.' Ever the self-publicist, however, Kimber was keen to reinforce the pedigree of the MG line and left people in no doubt that as far as he was concerned, 'Old Number One' marked the true beginning of what he wanted for MG: a sports car identity of its own, rather than being little more than a prettily rebodied Morris. And who can blame him for that?

The story of 'Old Number One' itself is fascinating and bears repeating briefly here. Frank Stevens, one of the Longwall employees, was given the task of modifying a Morris Cowley chassis to Kimber's instructions, while Stevens' colleague, Charlie Martin, prepared a special Hotchkiss engine for the car. Although work proceeded somewhat slowly at first, Kimber's desire to compete in the Land's End Trial of Easter 1925 led to renewed impetus during March. With the unique and delicate Carbodies coachwork in place, and the car registered on 27 March, there followed some preliminary testing, as a result of which the chassis frame fractured at the rear. At this stage, Cecil Cousins was called in to carry out last-minute repairs to the cracked chassis during the Thursday and Friday before the race.

The author Barré Lyndon graphically described the creation and racing début of 'Old Number One' in his book *Combat*, published in 1933, and even though he omits to mention Kimber's passenger, Wilfrid Mathews, it is worth quoting the relevant part of Lyndon's text in full: 'On the way to the start at Slough, Kim pushed the speedometer needle past 75mph (120.70km/h), just to satisfy himself that the car was now sound, and at midnight Number One became a unit in a long line of cars headed westward. Dawn brought mist which froze on the windscreen, and he became a little uneasy about the stays which held the rakish wings, but the first hill put his heart at ease. He had given the steering a lock like that of a London Taxi-cab, solely to cope with hair-pin bends. It should have

then run without a hitch, but it did nothing of the kind. Plug trouble and obscure difficulties with the carburettor brought delays which culminated in a puncture at the top of Beggar's Roost Hill. The resultant check made really hectic driving necessary to the next control, and Kim picked up a full hour over the fifty-odd miles which lay between the summit of the hill and Launceston. That effort was a climax to an almost super-human work between the controls, and brought its reward when the car eventually reached the hostelry which marked Land's End—bringing a "gold."'

The Bainton Road factory

Before long, increasing MG sales made Cecil Kimber realize that more premises were needed, as the tiny mews at Alfred Lane could not cope with the demand for cars, so in the autumn of 1925, he rented a section of Morris Motors' Osberton Radiators subsidiary in Bainton Road. Production at the new site began in September 1925, and shortly after that, 18-year-old Syd Purves joined the small group of employees: 'I had been working for an ironmongers in Oxford, but had a disagreement with the manager and left. I can't recall exactly how I came across the job at Morris Garages, but I do recall that it was a long cycle ride from my home at Cowley Road to Bainton Road!'

Purves found himself one of a staff of little more than a dozen, comprising works manager George Propert; Cecil Cousins, in charge of engines; Jack Lowndes, in charge of chassis; George Hamilton on paintwork; Jim Prickett, an electrician; George Morris, who had been a mechanic at Longwall; Albert Eustace (stores); Pat Wright (test driver); Alec Hounslow and Frank King (both apprentices or improvers); a second test driver and a cleaner (probably Stan Saunders and Fred Hemmings respectively). John Browne was still an unpaid 'volunteer' at this stage, but before long, he would also join the full-time staff at Bainton Road.

Syd Purves reported to Jack Lowndes and soon became involved in converting six chassis a week to take the sporting MG bodywork: 'I was paid about ten old pence (just under 5p) an hour for this, with a theoretical bonus if we managed seven cars, not that I can recall that ever happening!' Before he could start work, he had to buy his own tools: a set of three Whitworth spanners and a pair of small pliers. Every Monday morning, six chassis—usually bull-nose 14/28 Oxfords, but occasionally Cowleys—would be delivered down the ramp into the first of the two bays at Bainton Road.

The engines were given special treatment, having their heads removed and polished with flexible grinders before being reassembled and taken to the engine shed, which had a corrugated-iron roof. There, they were connected to the gas main, started with the aid of a little petrol in the carburettor, and were operated on Town Gas for about a week to run them in. The engines never left their chassis during this rebuilding process, unless rejected during running-in or road testing.

Purves' job was to convert the chassis themselves, which required a variety of tasks. First, the standard Morris Oxford gear-box cover was removed, complete with gear-lever and brake lever. The gearbox cover was sent away for modification, but the gear-lever itself was Syd's responsibility. In the standard Morris Oxford, the lever was straight and upright, but this would have caused a problem in the lower, more sporting MG body. Therefore, Purves took the oval-cross-section gear-lever, which had already been nickel plated, and carefully heated it in a small hand-pumped forge. Once heated, the lever was cranked over. This was done entirely by eye—with no jig—and in such a manner that the plating remained virtually undamaged! Once bent, the lever would be quenched in oil and rebuffed. Purves was also responsible for fixing a special aluminium bracket to the right of the chassis for the brake pedal, which was 'a bit of a crude job,' he recalls.

At the rear of the chassis, the standard well-radiused Oxford lower springs were removed and sent away for flattening. On their return, it fell to Syd Purves to fit them. The rear springs comprised two parts: the semi-elliptic lower spring, which was sent for straightening, and upper quarter-elliptics attached to the chassis frame. To make the lowered assembly fit, Purves had to carefully measure an offset for the new quarter-elliptic mounting position in the chassis, mark it with a hole punch, start the hole with a small hand drill, then drill through with a ½in (1.27cm) bit in an electric drill, which he vividly remembers gave him an electric shock on at least one occasion!

Before refitting, the springs were smeared with yellow cart grease and were shod with leather gaiters, a job that Purves recalls with little relish. A servo for the brake was mounted to the side of the chassis to increase the effectiveness of the brake rods, the latter being cut and reworked by Purves to suit. André friction shock absorbers were also installed at this stage. The standard Morris artillery wheels were replaced by wire wheels, and the completed chassis were sent out on test with 'soapbox' seats prior to despatch to Carbodies at Coventry for their bodywork.

Syd Purves recalls road tester Pat Wright returning from one such run with the comment, 'I got 86mph (138.40km/h) on that one,' which, in the rather unlikely event that this was anywhere near the truth, was not bad going for 1925, but it must have been a hair-raising experience in a car with no body! A new feature at Bainton Road was the 'comparator', a device akin to the rolling-road of later years, which allowed the rolling chassis to be run-in under load inside the factory. The creation of this device has been credited to H. N. Charles, friend of the Kimbers and later to become chief engineer at MG.

The bodies themselves were finished in a choice of two colours: blue or what Purves recalls as 'a lovely ruby red'. Prior to 1926, virtually every car was based upon the distinctive bull-nosed Morris, but in September of that year, the first of the flat-radiator cars began to appear. However, at this stage, even the flat grille was basically that of the Morris Oxford: Kimber had yet to establish a unique grille for the MG marque.

George 'Pop' Propert, who lived in Leopold Street at the time with his wife and two daughters, worked at Bainton Road in a small wooden office on stilts,which was reached by a short set of steps. This was situated inside one of the two bays that had been set aside for MG production. Like Purves, Propert had only recently joined

MG, having come from the Bean company. The bays used for MG production at Bainton Road were each about 160ft (48.77m) long and 20ft (6.10m) wide, and the site is used today by Unipart.

There was an old clay pit nearby, full of water, and during their lunch break, the men would often sit outside to eat their sandwiches and drink from their flasks (there was no canteen). Sometimes in the summer, they would have a swim in the pit. One day, Syd Purves was called into Propert's office and asked if he would consider an office job, recording on tickets the time and costs against each chassis which, it seems, had been allowed to get out of hand and needed chasing up. Two months of this were enough for Syd Purves, and in late 1926, he decided to leave, accepting an offer of employment at Coopers Ironmongers in Oxford.

Syd Purves' father told him that he was mad to go—his earnings dropped by 10s (50p) a week from the 37s 6d (£1.87) he had received at MG - but he wanted to move back into the ironmongery trade. So ended his brief, but memorable, association with MG.

In October 1926, just after Syd Purves left, John Browne finally joined the Morris Garages at Bainton Road as a paid employee: 'I'd finished my improvership, and although the prospects were good at City Motors, I was more interested in tuning up cars rather than simply servicing them, and so both Sam Nash and George Morris encouraged me to join Morris Garages.' Browne's wasn't the most auspicious start: 'They were all shut out at the time, as all the stocks of the old models had been sold out, and they were waiting until after the Motor Show to bring in orders for the new season.'

At around this time, a Morris Garages brochure was produced that effectively was an enhanced Morris Motors catalogue with additional MG material. It stated that a special factory had been built to cope with demand for the MG models, which was being rather economical with the truth. Browne says that the catalogue 'showed a picture of the complete line of units, but omitted to say which were ours.'

Like Purves, Browne also remembers clearly the manner in which the cars were readied: 'Outside in a shed, chassis were run-in on Town Gas (coal gas) under load; a lethal place to be when I think about it now, with six engines running at once! We towed six chassis at a time from Cowley, over Magdalen Bridge, Long Wall and Broad Street, all in the middle of town like a long snake: quite a thrill if you were the last man!' According to Browne, the most in tow would be eight, and there would be a single set of limited trade plates fitted: one at the very front of the line, the other at the back. The police took an active interest in this process: 'They made us sit on the spare wheel; standing up, you could only stamp on the brake rod or use the handbrake in order to stop!'

Browne started as a charge-hand on the Number One line at Bainton Road: 'My section—just inside the door—took the cars after they had been run-in, and we'd change the springs, and the back brake operating bars.' This would be followed by knocking off some of the superfluous Morris bracketry, and fixing MG brackets: for example, there was a special fitting for the Salonette.

This process brought to light the limitations of some of the equipment provided for the men to use, including those 'leaking' drills (Browne says that an electric shock was most likely if the operator stood on a drainage grid): 'We'd drill holes by clamping on the new bracket and then drilling through. The trouble was that the drills were very slow-revving, so I brought my own Black-and-Decker drill and used that instead. In order to make it even more effective, I would chain down a piece of two-by-two timber at one end, then use it to lever the drill down, to the extent that it would go straight through the metal like cheese.' Needless to say, neither drill nor drill bits reacted very favourably to this treatment in the long term! So impressed were Cecil Cousins, Jack Lowndes and George Morris with Browne's drilling technique that they decided to carry out a time and motion study. However, Browne was not keen to play along with this: 'I insisted that they use the standard factory drill, and so they soon got fed up. Jack Lowndes said that the standard drill was hopeless and he had got much better things to do with his time!'

The production-line work continued with the removal of the cylinder head, grinding-in the inlet valves, grinding off the tops of the valve guides, then streamlining the ports and inlet tract with the aid of grinding wheels on a flexible shaft. The engines were rebuilt with Terry valve springs, a little extra valve clearance, and a polished cylinder head. Finally, a racing Lucas magneto and Solex carburettor were fitted.

At this point, the rolling chassis would move on to the Number Two line, where, recalls Browne, 'a chap called Robinson, who started in my section (on the Number One line), eventually took charge.' Work on this line involved the removal of the running-board brackets, cross-shaft, servo pipes and steering column. 'They also had to move the steering box back about 2in (5cm), whilst on the Salonettes, the rear wings would be fitted at Carbodies rather than at Bainton Road.' It was also necessary to shear off the rivets holding the shock-absorber brackets, and bolt on new phosphor-bronze brackets with friction-type André shock absorbers.

After road testing, for about 40-60 miles, any defects were rectified and most chassis were driven on trade plates (costing £5 per annum!) to Carbodies, where the bodies were built and fitted. The remaining chassis were delivered to Raworths at nearby St Aldates in Oxford.

The 1926 Olympia Motor Show, held in November, was the showcase for most manufacturers to exhibit their wares and solicit sales for the coming year. Naturally, Morris and Kimber followed suit, MGs being displayed on the Morris stand. According to Browne, however, these particular MGs were not quite kosher: 'The show models were just ordinary Morris Oxford chassis taken straight to Carbodies to have highly finished show bodies fitted. They weren't properly converted: the engines were fitted with MG carburettor set-ups, but the chassis were untouched.'

One of the most effective improvements that Browne and his colleagues made to the Morris chassis was to the brakes, which were regarded universally as being quite dreadful in standard form. 'There was a big fear in those days about loading up the front brakes,' claims Browne. 'Many people believed that four-wheel brakes were, in fact, dangerous, and often refused to have them fitted if they had a choice. Much of the trouble with the Morris system lay in the actuating mechanism, which suffered from wear problems where the rod slotted through a slit in the actuator cam. By a process of experimentation, we came up with a better arrangement which didn't need such a slit, although our experimental cam was so full of holes—which we had made by trial and error—that it looked like a Swiss cheese.'

The back brakes were subject to a simple alteration, too: 'We'd take the drums off, take the shoes out, and change over from two shoes at the top to two at the bottom by the expedient of swopping the shoes and spindles, left to right, after turning them upside-down to bring the levers underneath.' This provided more space for the floor of the body, as the levers worked below the floor instead of above it.

The demand generated by the Motor Show was sufficient to push up production to about 23 cars per week, just as Kimber had planned. 'Some orders were in fact transferred over from Morris sales, as a customer decided to have an MG version instead,' says Browne. The 1927 models of both Morris and MG formed quite a radical departure from their predecessors, for in place of the distinctive bull-nose, Morris had switched to a much plainer, more conventional flat radiator. 'There was a lot of advance publicity for this,' recalls Browne, 'with advertisements saying things like, "See the new Morris at the show" and "Better cooling—more area." They really went to town with the adverts.'

There were modifications to the chassis, too: 'There were different springs on the '27 cars to the '26 ones.' In fact, this was not the only change, for Morris had produced a wider, more substantial—and therefore heavier—chassis with a shorter wheelbase. The natural consequence of this was that the special bodies fitted to the MGs had to be reworked completely. At the front, a German Silver plate was soldered to the base of the radiator grille, in an effort to make it look less tall. Full-depth doors were fitted to the body, making access much easier, and the two-tone colour scheme was modified slightly, the rather impractical highly-polished aluminium lower panels being replaced by an attractive engine-turned finish. The treatment suffered much less from reflections and was easier to maintain.

The steering of the standard Morris chassis was discarded in favour of a more effective Marles set-up, complete with a René Thomas sprung steering wheel. At one point, these suffered some kind of transport problem: 'The René Thomas steering wheels were dropped in by aircraft for a while;' recalls Browne, adding wryly, 'not many survived!' By now, the wheels were wire types with large-diameter, five-stud hubs, known as Magna wheels. Modern balloon tyres were fitted for the first time.

Whereas the fledgling MG enterprise had not been large enough to warrant a proper development department, relying instead upon Cousins and his cronies tinkering with individual cars, the beginnings of what would become such a department emerged at Bainton Road. 'We did some experimenting at Bainton Road,' claims Browne. 'WRM bought Wolseley Motors (in February 1927), and a chassis came down from Wolseley. We were asked to see what we could get out of it. The engine was the small 10hp, overhead-cam Wolseley four, with the dynamo at the front.'

A road test of the chassis, as delivered, soon led to the brakes being condemned, and the men at Bainton Road set to work to improve matters: 'We tried various things,' says Browne. 'We raised the compression ratio, we modified the camshaft drive (creating an offset key on the end of the camshaft), but we soon found that the valves were bouncing, so we fitted motor cycle-style Terry springs, and this upset the timing adjustment (by eccentric cam), which we found simply wouldn't stay on whatever settings we used. We got only so far with it—not touching the distributor, for example—and then we wrote a report, and off it went.' Browne contends that the engine required wider springs and various other modifications, but these could not be tried before the chassis was taken away.

Other experiments were carried out on the products of William Morris' other acquisitions: 'Morris had bought Léon Bollée, and we had one of those in on a "look, but don't touch" basis. It had a very heavy body on it, but mechanically it had much potential. But because we couldn't fiddle with it, we couldn't learn much. Old "nitchy knackers" (Cecil Cousins) had a good scratch and sent us out to road test it.'

At this stage, William Morris appeared to be keeping his nose out of MG affairs, although Browne recalls that he would turn up from time to time and 'chat to his old cronies, who were given jobs on his instructions—mostly cleaning cars!' Morris would then call out to Cecil Cousins, saying, 'Sorry, Cousins, can't stop. I'm in a hurry,' before going off again in his Wolseley 12. There are many similar recorded instances in Morris' life, which demonstrate that he was more at ease talking to men 'at the coal face' than he was to his own managers, something that would lead him into many painful conflicts, Kimber being no exception.

It would appear that Mrs Morris also managed to upset Browne and his colleagues at MG: 'We built a special two-seater for her in 1927—they were living at Huntercombe by this stage—and we checked everything to the finest degree imaginable, over and over again so that it was perfect. They took the car over to Huntercombe Lodge, and Mrs Morris took one look at it and said, "I don't want that thing, take it away." As you can imagine, we were ever so disappointed.'

In the spring of 1927, to encourage maximum output, a bonus was offered for production of more than 15 cars per week. According to Browne, this bonus amounted to 15s 10d (79p), which he felt was not very much for the effort involved. Before long, poor delivery of the chassis from Morris Motors at Cowley caused the bonus threshold to be lowered to ten cars per week. In the midst of all this, Radiators Branch decided that they needed to use the area that had been leased to MG for their own purposes, so a rapid change-around was called for, over the space of a single weekend. 'After working all weekend,' says Browne, 'getting the bays changed over, and counting up all the overtime we would be getting, we were told that the company had decided to hold an extra day's money in hand, payable to us when we left.'

One of the last jobs to be carried out at Bainton Road was the preparation of an MG 14/40 chassis for display on the Morris stand at the 1927 Motor Show. This was given the highly finished state that would become typical of such exhibits: 'We took a cylinder-head grinder and polished up the block, and then sprayed it. The end result gleamed as beautifully as a body! Eventually, that chassis went to the Science Museum, where I saw it post-war. It is at Wroughton now.' While Browne worked on that chassis during this period, most of the rest of the work-force had been laid off as usual around show time. By this stage, the 14/28 had given way to the 14/40, the full title of the MG offering being 14/40 MG Mark IV.

The Morris Garages Ltd

As business at Bainton Road developed, it was obvious that The Morris Garages would need to be incorporated within William Morris' portfolio company, which remained separate from Morris Motors. In December 1926, Morris had bought the SU company from its founders, the Skinner brothers, and created a limited company. Earlier still, in July 1923, he had formed The Morris Company Ltd in an effort to consolidate his various business interests, but now it was becoming apparent that further action was necessary. Also looming were various so-called 'super-tax' issues, which would require some smart corporate footwork.

In June and July of 1927, therefore, Morris Industries Ltd and The Morris Garages Ltd were formed. In the spring of the following year, activities on the MG front had increased to the extent that The MG Car Co.—proprietors The Morris Garages Ltd was founded to assume full responsibility for MG manufacture.

The Edmund Road factory

Just as the MG team had outgrown its previous homes, before long Bainton Road became too cramped, so Kimber took the bold step of persuading Bill Morris to finance the erection of a brand-new factory at Edmund Road, just off the Cowley Road, at an estimated cost of £10,000. Construction of the factory, which ultimately cost 60 per cent more than estimated, was carried out over a six-month period by Kingerlee & Company (Carl Kingerlee was William Morris' personal secretary for many years after he became Lord Nuffield.) Browne remembers the involvement of the Kingerlee family well: 'Carl Kingerlee's son had been manager before Propert for a short time, but he didn't prove suitable for the job and so left. His father's company was a building concern, and as old man Kingerlee and Billy Morris had grown up together, it wasn't too surprising that he got the job of building the new factory.'

Work continued at Bainton Road while the new factory was being made ready and, in fact, Browne was one of those who helped with the preparations: 'I went to Edmund Road whilst the factory was being built in order to help Sam Nash and George Morris plan out the layout—where the various stations would go and so forth. During this process, we decided to break down the running-in period into a more manageable stage.'

The dabbling with the Wolseley and Léon Bollée at Bainton Road made it clear that more experimental work would be carried out at Edmund Road. 'There, in addition to production space, we had experimental room,' recalls Browne. 'We converted the 18hp engine and the Minor engine for the Midget, including hotting up the engines in all kinds of ways.' It was during this period that the MG logo seems to have usurped the Morris badge on the cars. This appears to have been a gradual process, since the famous octagonal MG badge had already been in existence for three years, and Cecil Kimber wasted no opportunity to use it wherever he could. At first, the octagon had appeared subtly on the door tread plates, but in 1927, the badge was applied as cut-out German Silver letters to the flat mesh of the radiator grille. Then, at around the end of 1927, an enamelled MG badge began to replace the special Morris Oxford—MG emblem.

'Edmund Road was set up with two lines, although because of a lack of length, we had to bend one of the lines around the end of the factory at a right-angle,' says Browne. At this end of the line, the German Silver MG motifs were soldered on to the grille, and the standard Morris badges replaced with MG versions: 'The men would heat up the area around the Morris badge on the radiator top with a flame, moving round and round the badge very gently, then hook the badge off, often splashing a little solder on the radiator in the process. Any splashed solder would be carefully removed using the flattened end of a piece of copper pipe with the aid of the flame,

followed by a very careful application of the finest grade of emery cloth. Then the new MG badge—initially the Morris Garages MG type, and later the familiar MG badge—would be carefully positioned with the aid of the sucker used for grinding in valves, and soldered in place.' The earlier badges in particular would occasionally turn up on cars for which they were not originally intended: 'Sometimes we would fit these badges on early cars when they came in for servicing, and sometimes the lads would even fit the badge to ordinary Morrises!'

Kimber was a keen stylist and had a penchant for saloon bodies. Bearing in mind the flexible nature of the chassis, he experimented with a fabric covered timber body, announcing it as the MG Featherweight Fabric Saloon, the coachwork of which was produced by Gordon England. However, the experiment was not a success, for sales were poor. The prototype was used as a factory hack for some years. Having a rather peculiar mottled finish, it became known as 'Old Speckly Hen'.

A new face at Edmund Road was that of Jack Daniels, taken on as MG's first apprentice: 'Someone from MG came to my school and offered a place; I am sure that the headmaster thought that the offer was for something in the commercial line, and so he told me to go along.' Daniels duly called at the new factory, which was then about a month old, to see George Propert and was told that the offer was for an apprenticeship: 'Without consulting my headmaster, I straight away said yes. My father said that he was happy, but when the headmaster found out, he was hopping mad. But as far as I was concerned, that was too bad!' Ironically, on the very day that Daniels started at Edmund Road, a letter came from a railway company, which had been his first choice, offering him a second interview in London.

Daniels senior was happy because his son's apprenticeship was not indentured—where the apprentice (or, more usually, his family) had to pay for the privilege. As MG's first un-indentured apprentice, the young Daniels was paid the princely sum of 10s (50p) per week, 'although soon after that, 1s 8d (8p) a week was deducted for health and insurance.' Every six months, there would be an automatic 2s 6d (12.5p) rise, so the amount gradually built into a modest, but respectable, wage. Naturally, Jack Daniels' first day is etched upon his mind: 'I was taken first of all to the part of the factory where the chassis (for the flat-radiator MG Mark IV 14/40) were brought in from the Morris works at Cowley. I was fascinated by how they did this: there was one tow vehicle at the front, drawing five wheeled chassis behind it, each with a man standing on a board on the chassis, steering with the wheel and operating the rod brakes. That was quite something to see!'

Once the five chassis were inside the factory, the doors would be shut and the fun would begin: 'My boss was John Bull, an ex-sergeant-major, and he showed me how to knock out various rivets, take out the engine and strip it right down, and to cut off certain brackets on the Morris chassis which were not required.' Stores control was strict, Daniels recalls: 'We had to write up in a book every little bit which we took off. Some bits had to be modified whilst others, which were surplus to requirements, would be taken back to the Morris factory.' In this way, the 16-year-old Daniels received a good grounding in how a car was constructed.

Once removed, the engine would be transformed from a humble mass-produced Morris to a carefully remanufactured MG unit: 'There were five chaps with benches: one would do the valves and polish the ports; another would polish the cylinder-head combustion chambers, after it had been skimmed elsewhere to raise the compression ratio; another would carefully lap each individual piston into its cylinder bore; whilst the last would hand fit the white-metal bearings.' While the engine work was taking place, the chassis would be moving slowly along the line, bits and pieces being built back on to them, or modified as required: 'On the Morris, the brake mechanism used two concentric tubes: one tube worked the foot brake, and the other the handbrake. MG decided to split this, but cleverly used the same pieces; just two more brackets were required. This certainly improved the brakes noticeably, especially the adjustments, which were much easier.'

John Browne remembers that running-in of new cars at Bainton Road had been carried out on a rolling-road, and for Edmund Road,

THE MG RADIATOR GRILLE

Despite the increasing application of the octagonal badge to early MG models, Kimber was not content; any 1920s schoolboy worth his salt knew that all proper car makers had their own distinctive radiator grilles, and Kimber wanted MG to have its own grille, too. John Browne and his colleagues suggested that this would be difficult, but Kimber was insistent. Browne recalls, 'There was a general carpenter employed by Morris Garages at the new Morris Garages place at St Aldates, opposite the police station by Speedwell Street. We all called him "Chippy", so I don't remember his name. Kimber told him to get a block of beech and to mount it on a plinth. As soon as "Chippy" had squared the block up, Kimber drew lines on the wooden block in pencil, and then instructed the carpenter to chamfer the wood to the shape he had defined.'

Kimber spent some time trying to achieve the effect he wanted: 'He made a cardboard template, and would go away and come back after a couple of days and do a little more.' Eventually, Kimber believed that he had obtained the result he was seeking, but he valued the opinion of the men at Edmund Road: 'He asked us what we thought, and so we fiddled with it, using a rasp. In order to make it fit the 18/80 chassis, we cut off the plinth and sat the block on to the chassis. However, we found that the wooden "grille" was far too high for the bonnet, and so we had to cut some off. Unfortunately, we cut too much off, and so a bit had to go back on again.' The process of refining the shape was, Browne remembers, one in which several people took part: 'Jack Lowndes, who was a quiet sort of chap, had a go, followed by Cecil Cousins, who was more blustery and would tend to hack too much off, so that a bit would have to be put back!'

In the end, it seems that Kimber became a little tired of this process and settled upon a shape so that work could proceed: 'The block was taken down to Cudds, where a tinsmith made a metal shell, and very nice it looked, too. I went down on a chassis to collect the shell, wrapped it up in a sack and brought it back to Edmund Road, where we proceeded to fit it on to the prototype 18/80 chassis.' Osberton Radiators—which had been Morris Radiators Branch since June 1926—provided the radiator core, the design of which was largely the responsibility of Ron Goddard.

The first public appearance of Kimber's new grille was on the 18/80, which was announced in August 1928. The same basic shape would last well into the 1950s as a distinctive hallmark of the MG car.

a new machine was designed, using similar basic principles: 'We used a big fan with adjustable paddle-type blades, linked to the rolling road by a shaft mounted sprocket and chain, and this would be used to provide a load for the engine to drive.' At the end of the line, the modified engines would be reunited with their respective chassis, which would be lined up two abreast on the first of the series of five sets of rolling roads: 'This was in a bay off to one side,' Daniels recalls, 'and Pat Riley had the knack of being able to crank the engines—which were still very tight after rebuilding, remember—and the two cars would sit there side by side, ticking over on petrol.'

After a while, each pair of cars would be moved on to the next set of rollers, where the carburettors would be substituted for units suitable for running on Town Gas: 'One car would be running and driving the other in a coasting mode; the loading would gradually be increased, and then on the next set of rollers, the two cars would be swapped over so that the second car would drive the first.' For the remainder of the testing regime, the cars would be run on Town Gas (just as they had been at Bainton Road), the fourth and fifth sets of rollers being used to run the pairs of cars faster and faster still. 'We did five cars a day,' remembers Daniels, 'and the rollers would take a whole five-day week for the complete series of running-in operations. Cars would be running all day Monday to Friday during the daytime, with Saturday morning left to square-up the week.'

Running-in completed, the chassis would be taken to the assembly line, prior to despatch to meet up with their bodies. The foreman on the chassis assembly line was Jack Lowndes, as had been the case at Bainton Road. At the end of the line, each car would be taken out on road test, followed by any rectifications required, then it was given a second road test. George Morris was in charge of rec-

tification and testing with Sam Nash ('one of his best test drivers,' says Daniels).

Overseeing all of this was Cecil 'Cis' Cousins—by now works manager—not to mention general manager 'Pop' Propert and managing director Cecil Kimber. Daniels, however, still only a callow youth, did not see Mr Kimber very often. Other noteworthy people of whom Jack Daniels has many memories include Alec Hounslow, Frankie Taylor and Reg Jackson; Frank Stevens was another notable, as was Jack Reed in charge of the stores.

As an apprentice, Daniels not only received his six-monthly rise of half-a-crown, but he also moved between departments. Furthermore, he enjoyed other special benefits: 'At that time, the work patterns were very much like Morris Motors: there would be two or three months during the summer when virtually all of the men would be laid off, except for the apprentices. One time, I had to build a road round from the front of the factory to the back, and during the second year, I installed the first compressed-air line right through the factory itself, from front to back.' It was during the latter operation that Daniels got to hear of the imminent arrival of a new face at Edmund Road: 'I was up a ladder, over the door to Propert's office, installing the compressed-air line, when I heard Kimber's voice. He said, "Propert, there's a chap named Enever at Morris Garages in Cornmarket. I want him brought into the factory here.' I thought to myself, 'I wonder who he is?' And shortly after, he came over. It was obvious that Kimber thought very highly of him.'

The MG marque comes of age: the 18/80

One of Kimber's former colleagues from his days at E. G. Wrigley and Company was Frank Griffiths Woollard, who had been chief designer there before leaving in 1922. In the autumn of that year, Morris invited Woollard to look over the Hotchkiss engine factory in Coventry, and on the basis of Woollard's report, he bought the works, installing Woollard as works manager.

In his autobiography, Miles Thomas states that he regarded Woollard as being 'the father of mass production machining in England.' Working under Woollard was his chief engineer, Pendrell, and among the staff was a promising young Yorkshireman by the name of Leonard Lord.

Somehow, Kimber managed to persuade Woollard to develop a sophisticated and quite sporting, overhead-camshaft straight-six engine of 2468cc, without Sir William being directly aware of the project, probably because he was on one of his customary extended overseas trips. Miles Thomas said that 'Morris never gave this engine his blessing, and his only half-hearted enthusiasm caused it to be mounted in three particularly unsuitable forms of chassis. First, it was put into an elongated Morris Oxford chassis and called the Morris Major. The longer chassis made it whippy, particularly at the front end, and although the car was light and had a good speed performance, it was an absolute bitch to hold on the road.' Subsequent attempts—the Morris Six of 1928 (with a wider chassis) and the Morris Isis of 1929—were also quite uninspiring. The latter was a steel-bodied saloon that was too heavy for the engine.

Kimber seemed to have the knack of recognizing the latent talents in many of his staff, and Cecil Cousins was no exception. With the Morris Light Six-engined MG needing a special chassis, it was obvious that the usual 'suck it and see' approach would no longer be good enough. Drawings would have to be prepared so that parts could be manufactured, and components brought in from outside as necessary. However, although some drawing work was carried out at Queen Street, in 1928, MG had no engineering drawing office to speak of. Kimber called in Cousins and asked if he could draw. Cousins admitted that he had done some technical drawing at school, so Kimber passed him drawings of the new engine and Morris axles that were to be used, and told him to draw up a chassis, which would be the basis of the first Mark I 18/80. Cousins' improvised drawing board was nothing more sophisticated than a sheet of plywood.

Thus, in December 1927, Kimber and his men began to construct a prototype of the car that would help to secure MG's position as a manufacturer in its own right. They acquired a Morris Light Six and installed its engine into their new chassis. Of necessity, the track width, at 4ft (1.22m), remained the same as the 1928 Morris Six, because of the use of the Morris rear axle. However, in most other respects, the chassis was unique to MG, its manufacture being under the direction of Jack Lowndes. For this first prototype, the Morris engine was left virtually untouched, but for the production version, both the block and cylinder head were extensively reworked to make a much more sporting twin-carburettor unit. One of the most unusual features of the MG Six chassis was the striking bulkhead with substantial cast-aluminium brackets incorporating the MG motif. Considering that they could not be seen beneath the bodywork of the finished car, these may be regarded as a typically stylish, but extravagant, gesture by Kimber.

Meanwhile, The MG Car Company had come into being and took over responsibility for MG manufacture in readiness for the August launch of the MG 18/80 Six. Having been personally approved by Morris, the new car was announced in *The Autocar* on 17 August, 1928, and made its début at the Olympia Motor Show alongside another newcomer, the MG Midget.

The MG drawing office

In 1928, the MG hierarchy also decided that they needed a proper draughting section of their own, and Jack Daniels soon found himself involved: 'This was after the first six-cylinder (the 18/80), and they brought in a fellow called Keith Smith, who became the first MG draughtsman.' It soon became obvious that Smith needed an assistant, and as there were no less than six apprentices by this time, they were the natural candidates for the job: 'Propert called us all into his office and asked us if any of us wanted to do the job. Nobody was particularly keen, but I asked if I could try it on the condition that I could come back to the shop floor if I didn't like it. Propert agreed to this, although in retrospect he needn't have.'

As Daniels' technical drawing experience was virtually nil, he had to learn the ropes quickly: 'Keith Smith started me off in the old-fashioned way—tracing drawings—which I found that I could do very quickly, and so my experience built up.' It was not very long, however, before Smith and The MG Car Company had a parting of the ways: 'He got into the factory one weekend and borrowed a car ('Old Speckly Hen'). There was then some trouble with his car and his passenger and, as a result, he was instantly dismissed.' For a while, Daniels was the sole draughtsman, but then a replacement for Smith was appointed in the person of George Gibson, who had recently been involved with the R100 airship.

A sports car for the masses: the M-type Midget

Prior to the appearance of the famous MG Midget, MGs had been cars for the reasonably well-heeled. Whereas the standard

SYD ENEVER

Albert Sydney Enever was born at Colden Common, near Winchester, in 1906. When he was only three years old, his parents separated, and he went with his mother, and seven brothers and sisters, to live in Oxford. School was in South Oxford, where the young Enever's practical bent soon came to the attention of his headmaster, who helped him secure a job as an errand boy at Morris Garages. Through his enthusiasm and mechanical aptitude, however,

(Rover/BMIHT)

he soon gravitated to other, more interesting, work. While at the Clarendon Yard, he built his own three-wheel car, and no doubt it was this, coupled with his outstanding intuitive mechanical abilities, that brought him to the attention of Cecil Kimber. Accordingly, Kimber told Propert to employ Enever at the new Abingdon factory, where he was placed under the wing of Cecil Cousins in the experimental department. It was not long before Enever was spearheading some of the bolder projects in this department and, in due course, he would lead it, remaining at Abingdon as liaison man when the rest of the design team left for Cowley in 1935.

In 1938, Enever became chief planning engineer at Abingdon, and he was deeply involved in the company's war work. After the war, he went on to even greater things, helping to shape a future for MG that would lead to a radical departure from its traditional heritage. Throughout, he never lost the edge of his keen mind and earned the respect of his colleagues.

Jimmy Cox, who joined as a tea-boy after the war, remembers that 'Syd was a brilliant engineer with an excellent memory. He always knew exactly what you were supposed to be doing, whether or not you were actually doing it. I remember that we had three special camshafts for some purpose, and five years later, he came to see me and said, "I think we've got one left," to which I replied that I didn't think we had. Syd said to go and check, and of course when I did, he was absolutely right.'

In later years, Syd Enever would be responsible for fathering some memorable cars, notably the MGA, MGB and the post-war record breakers. He retired in 1971, after 50 years of working with the cars he loved. How many people can claim to have been so fortunate?

The diminutive MG M-type Midget; this is actually an all-metal-bodied car from late 1932. The view out with the hood erected, as here, was rather restricted. (Rover/BMIHT)

Morrises, upon which Kimber based his early specials, were bought by moderately well-off, middle-class professionals, the MG conversions could cost up to twice as much and, therefore, appealed to a more affluent clientele. It was the emergence of the Morris 8 (more familiarly the Morris Minor)—largely in response to Austin's seminal Seven of 1923—that paved the way for an 'MG for the masses'. The Morris Minor featured an unusually sophisticated overhead-camshaft engine, designed by the Wolseley company, which Sir William had acquired in 1927. This was married to an all-new, lightweight chassis of diminutive proportions. The Minor made its début at the end of August 1928, ahead of the autumn Motor Show at Olympia. John Browne and his colleagues at MG had already studied the Wolseley, which had spawned the Morris Minor, so obviously Kimber was well aware of the potential of its potent power unit.

However, the engine was rather delicate and gave Morris Motors many headaches. As a result, it would not remain in the Minor for very long, as a new, more conventional side-valve 8hp engine was

JOHN THORNLEY

John William Yates Thornley was born in 1909, and it would be fair to say that his early home life was less than idyllic: his parents were involved in a messy and public divorce that led to young John being brought up by his three maiden aunts, although his father lived with them, too. Thornley senior set his son on the steady path to becoming an accountant, for which he trained at the City of London firm of Peat Marwick and Mitchell.

(Rover/BMIHT)

However, like so many young men of his era, John Thornley became passionately interested in motor cycles, but by the time he had reached his early twenties, encouraged by his father, that interest had switched to sports cars. On the occasion of his 21st birthday, in June 1930, Thornley changed his Brough Superior motor bike for a new MG M-type Midget, and thus began his long association with the marque. Within four months, he had responded to a letter in *The Light Car* magazine suggesting the formation of the MG Car Club, and quickly found himself drawn into its birth—he became the club's first secretary in 1930. Within the year, work at Abingdon itself beckoned, partly as a result of his own persuasive arguments to Kimber. Turning his back on accountancy, he began working at Abingdon in November 1931.

In 1934, Thornley became service manager, whereupon he found himself dealing with the occasionally vociferous complaints of customers who were disappointed that *their* MG sports cars couldn't quite do everything that those on the race track or in road tests could. This was an area of the business in which Kimber had hardly any interest at all, and it is to his eternal credit that Thornley did so much to help maintain and build customer loyalty. During the latter part of the decade, Thornley also found himself managing and supporting various racing teams, giving him a well rounded involvement in the affairs of the marque.

Wartime service in the Royal Army Ordnance Corps was followed by a return to an Abingdon without Kimber. There, Thornley's efficiency, dedication and loyalty would result in him being rewarded with the job of general manager in 1952, a position he retained until his retirement in June 1969. During those post-war years, he oversaw MG's return to the competition and record breaking arenas, before the company gradually began to be submerged within the BMC and, eventually, BL combine. His OBE—awarded in 1964—was not for his work at MG, however, but rather for his service to the Air Training Corps. Although ten years into retirement when MG sports car production at Abingdon was threatened with discontinuation, Thornley was galvanized into action, and he championed the cause of the battle to save the factory. His son Peter believes that one of his father's greatest achievements was to oversee the increase in production from 70 vehicles per week to 1100, using the same basic floorspace.

developed under the auspices of Len Lord at Wolseley, but this did not deter Kimber. Less than a month after the Morris Minor was announced in *The Motor*, the same magazine stated that there would shortly be a new 'Morris Midget, to be built by the MG Car Company of Oxford.' Cecil Kimber must have been somewhat affronted that *The Motor* should have dubbed the car a Morris, but of course, in some respects, they were not far off the mark. Kimber had gone to Carbodies with one of the prototype Minors, and had had it fitted with a neat little two-seater, fabric and plywood sports body. To give the Midget a more sporting stance, the suspension was lowered and the steering column raked, while MG hub-caps were fitted to the Morris Minor wheels. However, the basis of the car remained very much Morris Minor—a return in philosophy to MG's roots.

In the first Minor prototypes, the Wolseley engine had been considered too fast for its purpose, so for the production models, it was detuned. As far as MG was concerned, however, the more sporting nature of the original version was just what they wanted. After a great deal of interest at Olympia, production got under way in the spring of 1929 at Edmund Road, while the bodies were mated with the running chassis at Leopold Street. By the summer of 1929, the new Edmund Road factory was bursting at the seams with 14/40, 18/80 Mark I and Midget production.

Developing the Six

As far as Kimber was concerned, the original 18/80 of 1928 was but the first stage in an ambitious programme to push MG further into thoroughbred territory. Accordingly, with the MG Six Mark I in production, work swiftly got under way to develop a Mark II version, with a 4in (10.16cm) wider and substantially stronger chassis, the four-speed gearbox, which the earlier car had lacked, and better brakes. This new chassis was regarded as being sufficiently MG in identity that it was given a type letter—A—thus beginning a long tradition for MGs to be designated in this way. Although 501 Mark I 18/80s were built between 1928 and 1931, the Mark II, being a more expensive and sophisticated car, was somewhat rarer: only 236 were built between 1929 and 1932.

The Abingdon works

The new decade would see further expansion for The MG Car Company and, as well as another move, there would soon be more changes to the structure of the company itself. With the success of the new M-type Midget, MG found that even the purpose-built factory at Edmund Road was not big enough to cope with production. Kimber cast around and found that there was a large vacant area of the Pavlova Leather Works at Abingdon-on-Thames. This had been established by Robert Fraser in 1912 and expanded during World War 1 to produce leather flying helmets and other equipment. Understandably, the demand for such items had contracted after the end of the war. In 1929, therefore, Kimber persuaded Sir William to lease the larger part of the Pavlova site, and work began on adapting the empty buildings to their new purpose. It is often not appreciated that the Abingdon works was not actually owned by the company until 1939.

Among the first to arrive, in the autumn of 1929, were the members of the two-man drawing office, George Gibson and Jack Daniels: 'George and I were the first two MG people to go there, whilst the clearing of the site was still under way, and we were put in an office downstairs in what is now Larkhill House.' Daniels is quite certain of the time: 'There was a rather nice apple orchard right alongside the offices, and the apples were just ripe...'

The building and alteration works went on for some time: 'At one stage, the builders had an office in Larkhill House, right next to us.' However, as the work drew nearer completion, more and more faces from Edmund Road began to appear at Abingdon: 'Propert and Cousins, and some of the secretaries, moved into the downstairs portion of a newly-built office block inside the factory proper, and we moved into a drawing office upstairs.' About this time, too, Hubert Charles, a friend of Kimber, arrived as chief designer: 'He became the boss in charge of the drawing office, and had his own office alongside the others downstairs.' With Charles in charge, Gibson and Daniels soon found themselves designing and detailing two complete cars each year—one racing and one production—which was no mean feat for such a small team.

By January 1930, the new factory was ready, and on the 20th Kimber hosted an inaugural luncheon to celebrate the beginnings of the proud venture. In the issue immediately following this, *The Autocar* congratulated Kimber on his new factory, and reported, 'At a very largely attended lunch Sir William Morris, Bart., made a characteristic and vigorous speech on the outlook for the motor industry and MG sports cars in particular... Sir William paid warm tribute to the keenness and loyalty of the staff and workmen engaged in the production of the cars.' In the same issue, the magazine also reported that 'there is no truth in the rumour that Sir William Morris has authorized the MG Car Company to enter for races in the coming season,' but that on the other hand, private entries were expected for an MG 18/80 Mark II (to be driven by L. G. Callingham and H. D. Parker) and a team of three Midgets ('probably under the leadership of C. J. Randall') in the Brooklands Double-Twelve. It was clear that Morris, who despised motor racing, had no desire to be seen supporting factory backed enterprises.

Production at Abingdon majored on the still quite new M-type Midget, which was built at a rate of up to 30 per week and would be joined in due course by more specialized models. The 18/80, of course, was also a fairly recent model, which still had some life left in it, so during the autumn, new versions of both the Mark I and II appeared, including a Speed version of the former and a Deluxe Saloon version of the latter. Unbeknown to the men of Abingdon, in June 1930, a 21-year-old trainee accountant, with a passion for motor bikes, switched his allegiance to an M-type Midget and thus began a chain of events that would shortly align his destiny with that of the factory: his name was John Thornley.

Racing, the expensive pursuit of glory

Kimber himself records that the first victory for an MG in a race was on 10 October, 1927, in a 100km (62.14-mile) event at a brand-new, concrete-surfaced racing circuit at the San Martín autodrome, near Buenos Aires, Argentina. The race was won outright at the modest speed of 62mph (99.78km/h) by local man Alberto Sanchiz Cires, in the unlikely choice of an MG 14/40, which was not known for its ability to stand up to endurance running of this sort.

The first purpose-designed MG racing car was a large, rakish six-cylinder, based on the 18/80 Mark II, and known as the 18/100

FROM 'FASTER THAN MOST' TO 'SAFETY FAST!'

One of the first slogans that Kimber adopted for the MG marque was 'It Passes—and Surpasses', but before long, this was replaced by the more stirring, 'Faster Than Most'. However, the slogan that has come to be associated universally with the marque is 'Safety Fast!' This is still in use today as the title of the MG Car Club's monthly magazine.

Ted Colegrove was MG's first publicity manager, and the story of the origins of the 'Safety Fast!' slogan was related to South African MG enthusiast Norman Ewing by Colegrove's successor, George Tuck: 'Ted Colgrove was driving through Oxford—probably in October or November 1929—behind a new bus. To warn people behind it that it could stop quicker than the old buses, because it had brakes fitted to all wheels, a new innovation in those days, it had a triangle painted on the back and a slogan which read "Safety First!" Ted thought that if it was changed to "Safety Fast!" it would make a great slogan, and he rushed back to tell Kimber. When he arrived, Kimber was fuming as he had, in front of him, an ad with the old slogan "Faster than Most" on to which someone had added the word "bicycles" so that it read "Faster than most bicycles." Kimber saw that "Safety Fast!" could not be tampered with and changed it immediately to become the new slogan.'

'Safety Fast!' remained the main slogan for MG cars for many years, and in 1959, it was adopted as the title for the monthly BMC magazine for the MG Car Club and Austin-Healey Club. After independence was foisted upon them in 1969, the MG Car Club retained the name, and *Safety Fast!* is still a thriving club magazine, almost 70 years after Ted Colegrove spotted that new bus. There might also have been another element to the story: in an article in *The Motor* of 12 March, 1929, it was suggested that MG could consider 'Safety with Speed' as their slogan. Who is to say today that both the bus slogan and magazine article might not have been common sources of inspiration?

The 18/100 Mark III, known as the Tiger or Tigress, carried Kimber's hopes of competing against the more powerful thoroughbreds. Sadly, its début was ignominious and, as a result, its career short-lived. Note the substantial headlamp stays referred to in the text, and the lovely leaping-tiger mascot fixed to the headlamp bar—does it look familiar? (Rover/BMIHT)

Above *Rather more successful than the Tiger in the 1930 Brooklands Double-Twelve was the team of MG M-type Midgets. Victoria Worsley is shown alongside the example she drove to seventh place. (Rover/BMIHT)*

Below *Norman Black takes his winning supercharged C-type (with conventional grille) on a lap of honour at the end of the 1931 Ulster TT, during which he broke the existing lap record. (Rover/BMIHT)*

Syd Enever (in driving seat) and Jack Crooke pose with a Brooklands Double-Twelve C-type in the spring of 1931. (courtesy Jimmy Cox)

B-type or Tiger, through which Kimber undoubtedly nurtured ambitions to produce a junior-league Bentley. Few contemporaries of the car—with the honourable exception of Cecil Kimber—seem to have called it a Tigress or, even less commonly, Tigresse. However, both names have gained popularity with enthusiasts over the years, and Tigress may have been coined to avoid confusion with Sir Henry Seagrave's Sunbeam Tiger land speed record breaker of 1926. Although a clue that an MG Six was to be raced appeared in *The Autocar* immediately after the Abingdon factory was opened, the reality was that Kimber had planned a far more potent machine than merely a hotted up 18/80 Mark II. Preliminary details of the Tiger appeared in *The Motor* in February, but before long, it became known that the actual début was to be at the two-day Brooklands Double-Twelve of Friday 9 and Saturday 10 May, 1930. The driver would be Shell Petroleum's Leslie Callingham, as *The Autocar* had prophesied in January.

As number-two draughtsman, Daniels was naturally involved with the Tiger: 'I remember in particular that I drew up the substantial stay which went across between the headlamps; we had to make that bar as an aerofoil section.' Mention of the stay brings another anecdote to light: 'There was a test driver called Freddie Kindell, who had been recruited to Abingdon and would later feature alongside Jackson and Hounslow during the thirties' racing exploits. He was an ex-Mercedes racing mechanic and had a reputation as a bit of a "toughie"—he was known to wrap a bit of cloth around his hand and proceed to bash 6in (15cm) nails into a wooden work-bench with one blow. I remember that another of his party pieces was to lift the front of the Tiger up by my headlamp stay whilst the mechanics changed the wheels!'

Sadly, the engine of the Callingham car ran its bearings, barely two hours into the race at Brooklands, which proved to be the last serious competitive outing for the Tiger. Nevertheless, a great deal of effort continued to be expended at the factory in the hope that it would show the way forward for the marque, and although a small number found their way into private hands, MG soon abandoned the project. There were several more problems with the Tiger, not least the price, which was quite high at £895. However, the crux of the problem lay with the engine. The 'production' version of the

18/100 never lived up to the implied 100bhp (74.57kW) output, barely achieving 83bhp (61.89kW), and although further development pushed this to 96bhp (71.59kW), it soon became apparent that there was little point in carrying on.

Kimber himself recollected the chain of events in a paper he prepared in early 1945, but sadly never presented. He recalled how he had managed to interest Morris Engines in the idea of a special racing engine, but said that they were jealous of their knowledge of the engine, refusing to listen to MG's suggestion that the crankshaft should be fully balanced: 'We did timidly suggest to the Engine Works that this might be necessary,' Kimber recorded, 'but we were told to run away and look after the chassis we were building; but the fact remained that owing to the crankshaft being unbalanced, the throw-out loads at high speed were so great that when eventually taken down after the race, the crankshaft main journals were actually blued from the heat that had been generated.'

Although the factory effort for the Double-Twelve was concentrated on the Tiger, the race itself was notable chiefly for the success of the many M-type Midgets that had been entered, the highest placed being third in class and 14th overall. In the wake of this triumph, Kimber announced a limited series of replicas of the race cars, claiming them to be identical in every respect to those run at Brooklands. *Motor Sport* drove Victoria Worsley's actual race car soon after the race, and were most impressed with the high-speed road-holding, describing it as giving the little car a 'big car feel'. One of the few differences on the road-going replicas was the substitution of a more civilized Vortex silencer for the standard Brooklands unit, which was a silencer in name only.

Kimber and Charles plan their future

On 31 July, 1930, The MG Car Company Ltd was formed, separating it from The Morris Garages, and Cecil Kimber was made managing director. To form the company, 19,000 £1 shares were issued, 18,995 of which were bought by Morris Industries Ltd, while five were retained by William Morris himself, Cecil Kimber, Morris'

H. N. CHARLES

Hubert Noel Charles was a little younger than Cecil Kimber, having been born eight years later in 1896, and the fact that they were contemporaries undoubtedly helped to cement their friendship. At the age of 18, upon the outbreak of the 'Great War', Charles joined the Royal Naval Air Service as an aircraft designer, before being commissioned into the Royal Flying Corps as a captain in 56 Fighter Squadron. He remained with that squadron for the duration, twice being mentioned in dispatches. After the armistice in 1918, he worked for Zenith Carburettors, before moving to Automotive Products. Through his work at the latter company, Charles came into contact with William Morris in 1924. Clearly, he made an impression, since he was soon offered a job at Cowley as a roaming troubleshooter on the assembly line.

Before long, Charles met Cecil Kimber, and the two became good friends, the former helping with the design of the first bull-nose MGs. In 1930, with the MG Car Company firmly established at Abingdon, Charles was taken on as senior designer. Once, he remarked to Wilson McComb, 'Kimber and I, we were Gilbert and Sullivan: he wrote the words, and I set them to music.' However, Charles did not share Kimber's enthusiasm for the 18/100 Tiger, although while working on that project, he took an interest in the celebrated Midget known as 'Shinio', so-called because of the copious quantities of metal polish of that name that had been used to smooth the internals of its engine.

As senior designer, Charles' aircraft work stood him in good stead when it came to designing MG chassis, the ultimate expression of which would be the 'wishbone' chassis of the 1935 R-type Midget. It is also worth noting that he took the 20hp, 847cc Wolseley engine of the Morris Minor/M-type Midget and turned it into a screaming 746cc unit, complete with Zoller supercharger, from which he was able to wring 146bhp (108.87kW) at 7000rpm—an incredible 196bhp (146.15kW) per litre.

With the sale of MG to Morris in July 1935, followed immediately by the closure of the Abingdon design office, Charles found that his 'baby', the R-type, was abandoned before he could put his ideas into practice to cure the shortcomings of its suspension, and he was transferred to Cowley. With little enthusiasm, he worked on the TA Midget, but left in 1938, returning for a while to the aviation industry at the famous Rotol company, where he redesigned the variable-pitch airscrew. Those who were at Cowley at the time remember that there was friction between Charles and Issigonis, and in the end, there was room for only one genius, as others who came up against Issigonis would also discover. After World War 2, Charles joined Austin and played a part in the development of the Austin A40 engine, although in 1946, he fell out with Leonard Lord and left, setting himself up as an engineering consultant, and carrying out work for Norton Motorcycles and Cam Gears among others.

H. N. Charles was highly regarded by all who worked with him. Jack Daniels, who joined MG before Charles and transferred to Cowley with him in 1935, recalls, 'I respected him very much, and although I attended night school, it was Charles who really got me going.' John Thornley, in his obituary of Charles in *Safety Fast*, had this to say: 'Charles was a jolly man. However serious the subject under discussion, however grim the prospect, laughter was never far away. And when he laughed, the whole of him laughed from tip to toe, and we laughed with him. Naturally, in the course of the years, there were many crises. The boys would work long hours, days, weeks, but on test—bang! Morale would be shattered... And then the door would open, and "Papa" would come in—we called him "Papa" among ourselves, albeit he was only 40 years of age at the time—a rotund figure with a beaming smile and twinkling blue eyes, and he would clap his hands and rub them together, saying, "Oh well. We'll get it right next time, chaps, won't we?"' Hubert Charles died on 18 January, 1982.

---

secretary, his solicitor and his accountant. Clearly, the course had been set towards an increasingly independent MG business.

The remarkable success of the Minor-based M-type Midget prompted Kimber to contemplate his own uniquely MG interpretation of the concept. It was clear that while the M-type was light and sporting, its Morris chassis would prove as limiting to further development as had been the case with every previous Morris-based MG. In the 1920s, a small French company had begun to produce sporting cycle-cars with Harley-Davidson and SCAP engines. These Rally cars were developed into successful sports cars and offered with a variety of engines throughout the decade. Somehow, Kimber managed to get hold of one, and both he and Charles were clearly impressed by the straight-through chassis members, which were unlike the conventional 'up-and-over' layout of the Minor.

The EX-Register records 21 drawings against EX115, probably dating from the summer of 1930, for 'Frame and Suspension—Midget 1931', and it seems likely that these relate to the first chassis frame built at Abingdon using ideas gleaned from the Rally. H. N. Charles had gained invaluable experience in the aircraft industry, where he learned how to combine lightness with rigidity, while preventing heavy components, such as engines, from setting up oscillations that could literally shake a structure to bits. This knowledge was put to good use in ensuring that the new Midget chassis was far more stable than that of the delicate Morris and, consequently, better able to handle much greater reserves of power. Before long, however, the work on EX115 would be largely overtaken by the need to develop a chassis for the first of a long line of record breaking MGs, EX120.

On 3 March, 1931, in the excitement that followed the success of EX120 at Montlhéry in February, Kimber announced to a group of racing drivers and journalists that MG would be producing a limited-production racing model, the Montlhéry Midget Mark II, better known to MG enthusiasts as the C-type. This car—offered in both unsupercharged and supercharged variants—featured a 746cc version of the MG engine, which was quite different to the unique 743cc unit fitted to EX120. For the first time, the double-humped scuttle, which would become a hallmark of MG Midgets for the next 25 years, was featured, albeit as a separate, riveted on piece rather than an integral part of the body. The nose of the C-type also featured a distinctive curved cowling, which largely enclosed the

normal radiator grille, giving a better aerodynamic shape and reinforcing the association with EX120.

Kimber was determined that the C-type would be ready in time for the next Double-Twelve of 8 and 9 May, 1931, so no effort was spared at the factory in completing the rapid development and limited testing of the new car, with Jack Daniels producing many drawings for the 750 engine under the code EX125. Preliminary details of the car appeared in *The Autocar* of 6 March, 1931, accompanied by drawings by F. Gordon Crosby, but a clue that certain details had yet to be finalized is apparent from a reference in the text to the fact that 'the battery will probably be placed either low down in the tail or under the floor-boards.' On the same day as the piece in *The Autocar*, the rival magazine *The Light Car and Cyclecar* published a three-page article about the car, with a number of photographs taken of the original development chassis, which had been put together for the press to examine.

In the event, no less than 14 C-types were ready for the Double-Twelve, Kimber being determined to ensure a strong result and to capitalize on the interest that his press launch had generated. Although one of the cars did not start the race, his reward was to watch seven of the new Midgets finish, five of them in the first five places. The winner was the Earl of March, who also won the team prize. There could have been no doubt among motor enthusiasts that the MG marque had well and truly arrived.

New small MGs: the D-type Midget and F-type Magna

While the M-type—in open and Salonette versions—catered for the market for small two-seaters, there remained a significant step up to the large 18/80 models. It was clear that it would be worth plugging this gap, and Kimber decided that he could enjoy two bites of the cherry by offering a four-cylinder, four-seater Midget on a 7ft (2.13m), later 7ft 2in (2.64m), chassis and a 10in (25.4cm) longer six-cylinder version, which he dubbed the Magna. These two models were launched in September 1931, and both used—for the first time—a regular production version of the Kimber/Charles chassis. The D-type engine was not the special C-type unit, but instead exactly the same as that used in the M-type, so it struggled to propel the heavier coachwork of the four-seat body. To squeeze the four seats into the car, it was necessary for the rear passengers to sit well behind the axle, so they would have had an interesting

MG'S FIRST RECORD BREAKER: EX120

In the summer of 1930, a Wimbledon MG dealer, J. A. 'Jimmy' Palmes, and an old Cambridge college chum, Captain George Edward Thomas Eyston, called upon Cecil Kimber to ask if he would be prepared to support them in an attempt to achieve the magic figure of 100mph (160.93km/h) with a 750cc Class 'H' car. Eyston had already been experimenting with other record-breaking ideas, with varying degrees of promise, and Kimber readily agreed to help, seeing the obvious attraction of succeeding at such an endeavour. He initiated work to adapt the H. N. Charles chassis design to the task.

The chassis of EX120—based upon the work already done under the code EX115—took the classic straight-through form that would become the hallmark of MG Midgets for many years to come: two parallel, steel-channel side-members swept gently over the front axle and straight under the rear. The cross-bracing took the form of tubes, which were brazed to the chassis sides in the manner of cycle frame construction. The engine—a very special 743cc unit with a bore and stroke of 54x81mm—was fixed to the chassis at three points, while the radiator was rigidly fixed to a bracket on the engine itself.

Eyston retained the services of Ernest Eldridge as his consultant. Eldridge was a distinguished record breaker in his own right, having driven a monstrous Fiat, nicknamed 'Mephistopheles', to take the land speed record at 146mph (234.96km/h), and later a Miller 91 at Montlhéry to gain a number of 1500cc class records. As a result of an injury resulting from a crash during one of his runs in the Miller, Eldridge wore a patch over his right eye, and presumably had decided that self-preservation was wiser than the active pursuit of further glory. Eldridge, together with Syd Enever and Reg 'Jacko' Jackson, developed the engine, eventually mating it to a Powerplus supercharger. Initially, however, the car ran unsupercharged, in which form it was sent on a lorry to the Montlhéry race track, near Paris, on Boxing Day, 1930. The entourage was determined to capture the 100mph record before the year's end.

On 30 December, Eyston set off around the track, the engine running on potent RD1 ethylene-glycol-based racing fuel. Even so, the power produced was not sufficient to take him to the magic 'ton'; instead, he had to be satisfied with three Class 'H' records at lower speeds. EX120 returned to Abingdon, but in the meantime, it was learned that Sir Malcolm Campbell had taken a 750cc Austin to Florida with his 'Bluebird' world land speed record car. He had made it known that he intended to make an attempt on the 100mph record—almost as light relief, one imagines! Of course, once 100mph had been achieved from 750cc, the record would confer everlasting fame on both the driver and the vehicle, something that was not lost on Kimber and Eyston. On 6 February, 1931, Campbell drove his Austin at Daytona Beach, covering the flying mile at 94mph (151.27km/h), giving the MG team added impetus.

Within days, Eyston and the men from MG were back at Montlhéry, despite the freezing weather, and they struggled gamely to beat Campbell. Before long, Kimber despatched Cecil Cousins and Gordon Phillips to France, to relieve Eyston's exhausted crew of Jackson and Kindell. Problems were being experienced with carburettor icing, but Cousins managed to reduce this problem by enclosing the carburettor and ducting warm air to it from the radiator. However, the radiator itself was proving too efficient, so to reduce the frontal area—and provide a crude form of streamlining—Cecil Cousins quickly improvised a shroud for the radiator by cutting a piece of steel from a 5gal (22.73l) oil drum and bashing it to shape in the curved concrete gullies alongside the garage area, which lay under the track itself. Thus equipped, and looking, one imagines, like the battle-scarred veteran of a long and arduous campaign, EX120 was taken out again. As the light faded on the evening of a very wet, cold and windy Monday, 16 February, victory was grasped at last.

During 1931, EX120 was given several outings, being fitted with a more carefully fashioned cowling, and even though it would be usurped by a new record breaker, EX127, it still excelled at certain events. The end of EX120 was dramatic when it came. In the early afternoon of 25 September, 1931, Eyston squeezed his considerable bulk into EX120 and set off around the Montlhéry track, determined to secure the one-hour record for an average of 100mph. Having successfully achieved 101.1 miles (162.70km) in the hour, he continued for another lap, but to the consternation of his mechanics—Jackson and 'Nobby' Marney—he failed to reappear. Then they noticed that the engine noise had ceased, and quickly set off to look for him, only to come across the horrifying sight of EX120 fiercely ablaze by the side of the track. Rushing to the car, they tried desperately to kick away the bodywork and prise Eyston free. Then, they realized that he was not there, so they retraced their steps to discover what had become of the big man, finding no trace of him anywhere.

It transpired that, with flames licking around his feet and the car still bowling along at about 60mph (96.56km/h), Eyston had somehow extricated himself, sat on the bodywork behind the cockpit, steered the wheel with his feet, then jumped clear and rolled to the side of the track. A Citroën test driver, circling the track behind him, had seen Eyston and had managed to pick him up—itself no mean feat—place him in the back of his car and cart him straight into the nearest hospital. There, he was found to be suffering from a broken collar bone, severe burns and, one imagines, shock!

The remains of EX120 were shipped back to Abingdon and eventually cut up. The car had proved what could be done, paving the way for a generation of MG Midgets. It also led to further record breaking exploits with EX127 and other, even more exciting, record cars.

EX120 came to an end during a record attempt at Montlhéry, when it caught fire while George Eyston was driving. Here, Propert (left), Eyston, Jackson, Kimber and Marney survey the remains. (Rover/BMIHT)

EX127: THE 'MAGIC MIDGET'

Once EX120 had shown what could be achieved with the remarkable Wolseley-based engine, it was obvious that a newer, better car would push the frontiers even further. Reg Jackson was partly responsible for the sleek shape of what would become EX127—better known as the 'Magic Midget'. Although EX120 had started life as a relatively conventional looking race car, the true purpose of the new car, with its fully faired-in radiator and long tail, was obvious from the outset. Jackson is said to have used the nose of Kaye Don's 'Silver Bullet', the centre of Campbell's 'Bluebird', and the tail of Sir Henry Seagrave's 'Golden Arrow' for inspiration—an impressive array of land speed record cars. To refine the shape, he built a quarter-scale model at home, then showed it to Kimber. Jack Daniels, as assistant draughtsman, was also involved: 'I was the chassis man on EX127 and did all the drawings for it. EX127 had an inclined drive line, at an angle of 7 degrees in plan, to allow it to become a single-seater, with a full "Charles-type" chassis.' As a result, the driver sat really low in the chassis. To mate with the angled propshaft, both the differential and crown wheel had to be specially made.

Whereas EX120 had been able to crack the magic 100mph (160.93km/h) mark, EX127 was intended to capture the next psychological barrier of 120mph (193.12km), or 2 miles (3.22km) a minute. While Eyston recuperated from his injuries caused by the unfortunate demise of EX120, his confidant, Ernest Eldridge, managed to take the 'Magic Midget' to just over 110mph (177km/h) in October 1931, at Montlhéry. However, a burst radiator (ironically, one of the few non-MG parts, having been commissioned in France by Eldridge himself) foiled his attempt to reach the elusive 120mph.

By December, Eyston was well enough to make a fresh attempt, although this time, for safety, he would wear a special fireproof asbestos suit. Three days before Christmas, driving with slick tyres on sheet ice at the Montlhéry track, he raised the ante by securing four records at speeds up to 114.77mph (184.70km/h). Shortly after this, the international motor-sport bodies that adjudicated on record breaking attempts dropped a bombshell: with immediate effect, all records had to be established as the average of two runs in opposite directions. Obviously, this could not be achieved unless the path of the record attempt was kept clear. In the case of Montlhéry, the authorities were not prepared to close the track for exclusive use by one car (a ruling that had benefited Eyston when EX120 expired!), while the Brooklands track was closed for winter maintenance. As a last resort, therefore, Kimber took a leaf

from Sir Malcolm Campbell's book and decided to use the 7-mile (11.27km) stretch of beach at Pendine Sands near Tenby, South Wales. Although not as exotic as Daytona Beach, it was somewhat closer to home!

By January 1932, Eyston was ready to run at Pendine. Accordingly, a party, including Cecil Kimber, set off for South Wales, with the press in tow. After a period of acclimatization to running on sand in a C-type practice car, taking advice from a local man, Wilfred Morgan, Eyston felt happy about making a record attempt over the weekend of 6-7 February. Preparations began on the previous Monday morning, the necessary work including setting up the complicated RAC timing equipment, with its miles of cable (no radio links!) that had to be laid in the sand, while the beach was laboriously cleared of shells, stones and other obstacles. On his first run, it was found that the salt water had caused a short-circuit in the cables lying on the sand, so this had to be traced before the attempt could proceed. With the fault rectified, Eyston made another run, which was timed by a stop-watch at 122mph (196.33km/h), only to find that the tracer-pen in the RAC equipment had run out of ink. By the time that this had been rectified, the tide was on the turn, so on his third and final attempt, Eyston had to make do with 116.48mph (187.45km/h) in one direction, and 117.30mph (188.77km/h) on the return leg.

EX127 would go on to appear at Brooklands, and before long, it was fitted with the new AB-type cylinder head, introduced for the Mark III C-type. Thus equipped, it returned with Eyston to Montlhéry, in December 1932. There, in freezing, wet conditions, as before, he finally achieved the 120mph record he had sought. In the following year, EX127 was out again, mopping up records left, right and centre. Then, in October, with a slimmer body and driven by Eyston's diminutive mechanic, Bert Denly, it was used to recapture records that had been taken by Austin.

In May 1934, Cecil Kimber was persuaded to sell EX127 to Bobby Kohlrausch, a celebrated racing driver, with a good track record in German Grands Prix, who also happened to be an MG distributor in Germany. It has been suggested that George Eyston felt affronted by this. If true, his sense of insult could only have been compounded when Kohlrausch used the car to raise the 750cc record first to 130.48mph (209.98km/h) over the flying mile, in May 1935, and ultimately to 140.6mph (226.27km/h) on 10 October of the following year.

George Eyston in EX 127, the 'Magic Midget', is wheeled on to the beach at Pendine for his record attempt in January 1932. (Rover/BMIHT)

journey on rough roads. The four-seat Midget sold reasonably well during its fairly short life (it was dropped in June 1932), and another four-seater Midget succeeded it, but in truth, the concept was not one of Kimber's best.

The Magna, on the other hand, was greeted with great excitement among the motor-sporting fraternity, as on paper its specification—including a 1271cc six-cylinder with four-speed gearbox—was very promising. In reality, however, the engine was little more than one-and-a-half M-type units, and was already in use in the Wolseley Hornet. In an attempt to make this less obvious to the untrained eye and disguise its origins, Kimber had pieces of sheet metal fixed to the unit.

In October 1931, the MG M-type came in for some attention at last. The body was made completely of metal, and the wings were modified to a more angular cross-section, but although these changes were important, they amounted to little more than a mild make-over. While Abingdon was out racing exotic Midgets, such as C-types, EX120 and EX127, the humble M-type was beginning to look comparatively tame. While racing and record breaking brought great kudos to the marque, sales were not so successful. This was due, in part, to the depression, which affected the sales of all motor cars. It must be said, however, that while much effort had been expended on 'maintaining the breed' on the track, rather less had been devoted to the bread-and-butter road cars that, in theory, helped subsidize such exploits.

In the meantime, MG was developing the racing C-type even further. *The Motor* magazine of 31 May, 1932, announced a new version of the Montlhéry Midget, and followed this a week later by a description of the engine developments that justified its Mark III designation. At the rear of the bodywork, a slab-shaped fuel tank was fitted in place of the Mark II's boat-tail, and at the front, the nose cowl was dispensed with.

Building upon the successful basis of the 746cc engine, MG had developed an all-new, cross-flow cylinder head, with four separate exhaust ports on the near side and equivalent inlet ports on the opposite side. The inlet and exhaust valves were inclined towards each other, allowing shorter and lighter rockers, while the spark-plug size was reduced from 18 to 14mm diameter. This was the so-called AB-type engine, recorded in the EX-Register as EX130.

Jack Daniels became involved in this project, liaising with Wolseley engines concerning Abingdon's requirements. In the process, he made contact with Wolseley's A. V. Oak, which would prove very useful to him later.

Occasionally, in those days, MG test drivers would take a fellow member of staff along as passenger to combine a test run with an errand, and Jack Daniels experienced this on more than one occasion: 'Having just drawn up the initial Midget eight-port cylinder head, I was instructed to take the drawing to Stirling Metals in Birmingham. Freddie Kindell, driving a car fitted with an extra ball-bearing on the forward crankshaft extension (i.e. an outboard third bearing), had instructions to test the engine to failure, and take me up to Birmingham in the process. We made it in one-and-a-quarter hours, door to door, and if you happen to know the twisty road via Warwick, you will recognize a real feat. As a passenger, I have certainly never forgotten it. And then, exactly a week later, we did that journey again, and I collected a specimen of the new cylinder head—still warm from the foundry—which indicates the speed and efficiency available from our keen suppliers!'

Jack Daniels also accompanied Alec Hounslow and Frankie Taylor on a number of occasions, but one particular journey with Alec, in 1933, is etched on his mind: 'Following an MG win at Brooklands, where I had been doing timing at the pits, I joined Alec Hounslow on the journey back home in the winning vehicle, carrying the laurels. Alec reckoned to be home within the hour, and proceeded to drive accordingly. Around half-way home, we shot past H. N. Charles, our boss, and gave him a wave. Later, at Sutton Courtenay, just 5 miles (8km) from Oxford, with five minutes to go before the hour, we came up to a car ditherer, which caused Alec to brake heavily on a freshly showered road surface. The outcome was that we landed up at 90 degrees to the road, with the front wheels locked in the ditch. Thanks to no personal damage to either car occupant, and the assistance of passers by, the vehicle was pulled back on to the road, at which point Charles arrived, looked

The J1 Midget was nominally a four-seater, although considering the small size of the rear compartment, and the proximity of the rear seat to the axle, long journeys must have been endured stoically, rather than pleasurably. (Rover/BMIHT)

The L1 four-seater Magna of March 1933, with its elegantly raked radiator grille, low body line and shallow windscreen, was one of the most desirable sports cars of its day. (Rover)

at the scene, but continued driving past. The front wheels of the car were splayed so wide that stability was next to nil, but somehow Alec managed to drive on, with tyres screaming, to a garage at Iffley, where he parked it up for the night. The next morning, he acquired another complete axle and wheels, which he then fitted to the car, and had it fully mobile again and back at the factory.'

It was obvious by now that MG Midgets on the track were far removed from the road-going versions—a fact that undoubtedly caused little pleasure to Sir William—and there was pressure for action to redress this imbalance.

New Midgets, Magnas and Magnettes

In August 1932, well in advance of the Olympia show, the last remnants of the M- and D-types were swept away, with the much more specialized C-type following shortly after. They were replaced by the pretty J-type family, available in J1 four-seater guise at £220, the more popular two-seater J2 for £199 10s, and a closed Salonette version at £255. At Kimber's direction, the styling of the J-type drew heavily upon that of the racing Midgets: the humped scuttle

of the C-type, the flat tank strapped to the rear of the diminutive body, and the cut-away doors. Here was the answer to every young man's prayers for a relatively affordable sports car with obvious pedigree. The styling of the J2 would form the basis of MG Midgets for many years to come, traces surviving into the post-war years until eventually swept away by the MGA.

Mechanically, the J-type engine had moved on a long way from its humble roots in the Morris Minor and M-type: through experience with the C-type, the cylinder head now had inlet and exhaust ports on opposing sides. The engine was used by no other companies in the Morris family, the side-valve Morris 8 having quickly usurped the overhead-cam Morris Minor in 1931-32. Before long, however, the four-cylinder MG engine would become the basis of a six-cylinder unit.

The Magnette KA pillarless saloon was a popular body style on the K1 chassis, easy access to the interior being a virtue of the lack of a central door pillar. This is a 1933 model; the same basic body would later be offered as the KN saloon from September 1934. (Rover/BMIHT)

A racing version of the J-type arrived around the end of 1932. It took the form of a supercharged J2, which was christened the J3. At the Olympia show, which opened on 13 October, 1932, the new Midget was shown on the Magna chassis. In this form, and in both two- and four-seat guise, it became known as the F2, although this was changed later so that the F2 tag related solely to the two-seater, while the four-seater became the F3. However, of even more interest on the company's stand was yet another new range of MGs. Like the Magnas, these had six-cylinder engines, but of smaller capacity, from which they drew the name Magnette.

The Magnette family

The heart of the new Magnette was a brand-new, 57x71mm, 1086cc six-cylinder engine, derived from the MG four and designed by Wolseley at Ward End, with input from MG's H. N. Charles, who was newly ensconced at Abingdon. The EX-Register records work on this project against the code number EX131. To complicate matters, this engine was ultimately made available in no less than five variants: KA, KB, K3, KC and, subsequently, KD, although the last had a greater cubic capacity. The KA and KB versions appeared at the 1932 Olympia show, the former being fitted to a pillarless saloon on the 9ft (2.74m) K1 chassis.

The pillarless saloon had doors that were hinged from opposite ends of the passenger compartment, making access to the interior remarkably easy. It was a very elegant car and would remain a popular mainstay of the range for some time, even surviving the demise of the rest of the K-type Magnette range, and evolving into the KN saloon, which was related mechanically to the N-type Magnette of 1934.

In the open cars, the KB engine was made available in a choice of two chassis lengths: 9ft (2.74m) for the four-seater K1 and just over 7ft 10in (2.39m) for the two-seat K2. In all cases, the track was 4ft (1.22m), some 4in (10.16cm) wider than the Magna. The KC engine appeared in 1933, not in a K-type Magnette, but in the L-type Magna, launched in March of that year as a replacement for the earlier F2 and F3. The MG range was becoming far too complicated for its own good.

The K1 saloon, at £445, came with a Wilson patent self-changing, or pre-selector, gearbox. The equivalent K1 tourer, at £385, was provided with a conventional four-speed gearbox as standard, but with the Wilson unit as a £25 option. The K2 was fitted with the conventional gearbox, and was offered as a rolling chassis (for the customer to have his own coachwork fitted) at £315, or with a standard two-seater body at £360.

Perhaps the most interesting K1 was the unique open tourer built for Kimber himself, in which he covered almost 50,000 miles. This elegant car, with bodywork by Corsica of King's Cross, London, combined sleek looks with a Rootes-blown Magnette engine (with normal rather than reduced compression ratio) that allowed it to exceed 104mph (167.37km/h) at a heady 6500rpm. Finished in black, JB 3717 could accelerate from as little as 4mph (6.44km/h) in top gear and, therefore, was an extremely tractable car, especially so considering its 1087cc engine.

The K2 two-seater featured a body that was, to all intents and purposes, identical to that already seen on the larger-engined F2 Magna. Inside, the speedometer and tachometer were combined in one instrument, a slightly dubious feature that would be seen on a number of MG models during the next two years. Having established the Magna as a 1300 six, and the Magnette as an 1100 six, MG upset the apple-cart in March 1933 by replacing the F-type Magna with the L-type. This was fitted with the new 1086cc unit from the K-type Magnette. Rationalization of components meant that the two-seater L2 shared its basic body with that of the J2 Midget, while the four-seater L1 was similarly related to the J1.

The glory days: J4, K3 and Q-type

Ask any moderately knowledgeable enthusiast of pre-war cars to name the archetypal small sports car, and the answer is likely to be the K3 Magnette. One look at the car and its history will be enough to see why this is so.

The K3 was the *pièce de résistance* of the confusingly complex Magnette family, almost the only instance where engine type and

car name matched exactly, a consequence of its highly specialized nature. What became EX132 in the development shop began to take shape as two prototypes shortly after the Christmas break, in January 1933. One of these, registered JB 1046, made a promising, if unexpected, début at Monte Carlo, where James Wright used it to break the class record for the Monte des Mules hillclimb. The other (chassis K3752, registered JB 1269) was fitted with a sloping nose, not wholly unlike that of the R-type of two years later, and despatched with Reg 'Jacko' Jackson to Italy, in the first week of January, for five weeks of testing in preparation for the 1000-mile (1609.3km) Mille Miglia road race on 8-9 April. An MG team was to be entered for this event by Earl Howe and managed by Hugh McConnell, whose normal job was chief scrutineer at Brooklands.

Howe accompanied Jackson and the prototype K3 in his ex-Caracciola Mercedes, while Count Giovanni 'Johnny' Lurani joined the troupe with his own Alfa Romeo in Milan. The convoy visited Scuderia Ferrari (where Enzo Ferrari and the great Italian racing driver Tazio Nuvolari were able to inspect the car) and the Bugatti factory at Molsheim. Monsieur Bugatti studied the car with interest and, according to John Thornley in *Maintaining The Breed*, 'declared that the front axle wasn't strong enough... Jackson telephoned back to Abingdon and, as a result, the design was modified in time for the race.'

Three K3s were entered for the Mille Miglia, the drivers comprising Count Lurani partnered by George Eyston, Sir Henry 'Tim' Birkin accompanied by his friend and Bentley team-mate Bernard Rubin, and Earl Howe with University Motors salesman Hugh Hamilton. A series of last-minute problems cropped up before the race, which necessitated round-the-clock work by the MG mechanics, and during the race itself, fouled plugs caused difficulties. Thornley claims that 'Eyston and Lurani fitted 157 spark plugs in the course of a thousand miles,' largely due to oil problems caused by the Powerplus supercharger, although Lurani would later deny that there were quite so many stoppages en route. Despite this, the MGs acquitted themselves with honour, two of the three finishing to win both their class and the team prize, the Gran Premio Brescia—a promising start indeed.

Stripped for action: the purposeful lines of the K3 Magnette were never bettered. (Rover/BMIHT)

Like a British hare to the Italian hounds, the unmerciful Birkin drove his K3 at ten-tenths all the way, forcing the Maserati opposition to follow suit. In the process, he broke the Brescia-to-Bologna record at 89mph (143.23km/h), but this treatment took a toll on his engine and he was forced to retire at Siena with a broken valve. Much of the opposition, however, especially the crucial Maseratis, had also suffered, leaving the coast virtually clear for his team-mates, who finished first and second in class.

Such was the interest in the MG team's entry (only five of the 98 cars in the race were not Italian) that they were even met in Rome by the King of Italy and *Il Duce*, Mussolini himself. There is little doubt that Tazio Nuvolari—who had been outright winner of the Mille Miglia in his Alfa Romeo—was persuaded to drive a K3 in September 1933 partly on the strength of his brief inspection in January and the little car's stirling performance on his home ground in April. There followed a less auspicious outing at Mannin Beg in the Isle of Man, in May, when none of the eight cars entered managed to finish. A useful lesson was learned, however, since a weakness in the rear axle had been exposed. With the necessary changes made, the K3 staged a comeback in subsequent races.

Meanwhile, the K3's junior counterpart, the J4 Midget, was also under development. The basic building blocks were the J2 chassis, larger 12in (30.48cm) diameter brakes from the six-cylinder L-type, and the engine and gearbox from the C-type. The engine was supercharged, a Powerplus unit being employed to boost pressure to 18lb/sq.in (1.27kg/sq.cm), and before long the J4 began to compete with distinction, particularly in the hands of Hugh Hamilton. A fact sometimes overlooked by historians is that when MG announced the J4 in March 1933—at £445 with a normal gearbox, or £480 with the pre-selector unit, and with an optional, detachable streamlined tail for an extra £35—they also offered an unsupercharged version, the J5, at £50 less. Not surprisingly, there were no takers; as it was, only nine J4s were built.

September was always the month of the Ulster TT race, and in 1933, the event received probably its most famous pre-war MG entry: Tazio Nuvolari, who drove a K3, accompanied by Alec Hounslow as his riding mechanic. In later years, Alec would record how his first laps with Nuvolari, who was unused to the K3's unusual pre-selector gearbox, nearly caused him heart failure on more than one occasion. An indisputable sign of Nuvolari's skill as a driver, however, was that he soon mastered the K3 and proceeded to wear out a complete set of tyres within the first eight practice laps. During the race itself, Nuvolari drove as a man inspired, although Hugh 'Hammy' Hamilton also worked wonders with his J4 Midget, and might have eclipsed Nuvolari had it not been for a bungled pit stop. As it was, Nuvolari crossed the line just 40 seconds ahead of Hamilton. It had been a stunning race for both the Midget and Magnette.

Later the same month came another success for a K3, this time a single-seater (chassis K3006), in the hands of E. R. 'Eddie' Hall in the 500-mile (804.65km) handicap race at Brooklands. Against formidable, albeit handicapped, opposition, Hall brought in his K3 ahead of the field, gaining another victory for Abingdon's finest.

Back at Abingdon, in the wake of the TT, the designers and mechanics were working on a plethora of projects: improving the K3 for the 1934 season, and developing the new P-type Midget, the N-type Magnette and the KN saloon. Also being worked on was a replacement for the J4, as an offshoot of a new road-going car. By the October 1933 Motor Show, the J3 had been dropped, as had reference to the mythical J5, but the J4 was still listed at £495. The J1 four-seater Midget had also been discontinued, leaving the J2 as the sole survivor of the J-type Midgets. This had been given a facelift with new sweeping wings in place of the cycle-type originals. By March 1934, however, the J2 had been replaced by the new P-type, the racing offshoot of which was the exotic Q-type, which took the place of the J4.

The Mannin Beg race of 30 May, 1934, was dominated by MGs. Norman Black's K3 came first, while other K3s took second, third, fourth, fifth and seventh places; Bill Everitt (like Hugh Hamilton, a salesman at University Motors) trailed them in one of the new Q-types. Third place was taken by Captain George Eyston in an off-set single-seater K3 that, before long, would form the basis of the

famous Magic Magnette EX135 record breaker, and later (in 1937) yet another record breaker.

The Q-type was very much a racing MG—only eight were built—and it proved to be something of a 'curate's egg'. The remarkable 746cc racing version of the four-cylinder engine produced over 100bhp (74.57kW) at 7300rpm (later, in its final form, this would be increased to 147bhp/109.62kW), aided by a Zoller supercharger. However, the chassis, which was derived from that of the J4, being 8in (20.32cm) longer and wider in track by 3in (7.62cm), could not cope with this prodigious power output. Drivers capable of extracting the best from the Q-type were few and far between, and it was clear that the conventional semi-elliptic front and rear suspension set-ups would have to be reconsidered.

Running changes

Meanwhile, back in the mainstream of production, the sheer complexity of the range was causing headaches, so for the 1933 Motor Show, the range was slimmed from 16 to ten cars, the 18/80 finally being pensioned off. In addition to the revised J2 was a newcomer—a Kimber aberration in the eyes of some—the unusually styled L-type Magna Continental Coupé. Strictly speaking, the Continental was a two-seater, but there was sufficient space behind the driver and passenger to accommodate two small children, rather like the MGB GT 30 years later.

Normally finished in all-over black, or a striking combination of black wings, roof and bonnet with a canary yellow body, the Continental Coupé was certainly distinctive, if not to everyone's taste. A notable customer was Earl Howe, president of the British Racing Drivers' Club, who kept his Continental in a garage in Curzon Street, London.

The two-seater, six-cylinder K2 Magnette and L2 Magna (and the Continental Coupé) featured the 1271cc KD and 1087cc KC engines respectively. Thus, the engine capacities of the Magna and Magnette ranges had been swopped in the space of a year!

The KD unit was quite different to the relatively uninspiring Wolseley Hornet engine, which had made its début in the F-type Magna: MG had thoroughly redesigned the engine, to the extent that it bore scant resemblance to the original. However, Kimber was concerned that moderately knowledgeable enthusiasts, armed with 'a little knowledge', would assume the worst about the new engine, so he and his men resorted to a slight subterfuge, adding a fictional extra millimetre to the stroke to give a capacity of 1286cc. This deliberate misinformation would persist in MG literature for some time after the L2 had passed into history.

The P-type Midget and N-type Magnette

By the beginning of 1934, despite having pruned its range, MG was still feeling the consequences of a panoply of Midgets, Magnettes and Magnas, so development of the old J-type Midgets, L-type Magnas and K-type Magnettes was curtailed. On 2 March, the first of the new wave—the P-type Midget—made its appearance, followed at the end of the month by the N-type Magnette, with a 1271cc six-cylinder engine, which was derived from the KD, still specified by the factory as a 1286cc unit! The wheelbases of both Midget and Magnette had grown slightly, to 7ft 3⅜in (2.22m) and 8ft (2.44m) respectively, while each chassis was extended at the rear to support the petrol tank and spare wheel.

The P-type featured a heavily revised version of the, by now, classic 847cc four, with a three-bearing crankshaft and improved cylinder head. Behind the engine was a new four-speed gearbox with a low bottom gear suitable for competition use. The body shape was in the characteristic MG mould: neat swept wings flanking a narrow, tapered, but fairly square-sided, engine compartment; the familiar double-humped cowl; cut-away doors; and a pert tail, complete with upright spare wheel. This basic shape would be the hallmark of MG sports cars for the next 20 years. However, whereas Kimber had enjoyed a cordial relationship with a number of coachbuilders over the years—particularly Carbodies—for the bulk of P-type production, he would utilize the services of Morris Bodies Branch.

Although the P-type was not an out-and-out racing car, as an effective development of the tried-and-tested J-type formula, it was eminently suitable as the basis of a competition vehicle. P-types soon proved to be favoured entries in minor sporting events, particularly trials, which were becoming increasingly popular. Their performance could be boosted with the aid of superchargers, such as the Marshall unit, which could be supplied and fitted for around £69 in the spring of 1935. Kimber, however, had his sights set on grander prizes for the P-type. In *Maintaining The Breed*, John Thornley tells us that he 'had had his eyes on the Rudge-Whitworth Trophy for a long time, but this was a biennial award, it being necessary to compete in one year to be able to compete for the cup in the succeeding year.'

No doubt, Kimber reasoned that a relatively safe and steady entry in one year could be a precursor to something more spectacular in year two, or maybe he wanted to capitalize on Anne Itier's success in the 1934 race, so he decided to enter a team of three specially prepared, supercharged P-types for the June 1935 Le Mans 24-hour endurance race. Ever the showmen, Kimber and George Eyston engineered a highly successful publicity coup by entering an all-female team, comprising Barbara Skinner, Margaret Allan, Doreen Evans, Colleen Eaton, Joan Richmond and Margaret Simpson, who became known in the press as 'Eyston's Dancing Daughters'. Because the entry was so well planned, and the goal was to last the course and qualify, rather than attempt to grasp victory, all the entrants finished, albeit well behind the class-winning, larger-engined (972cc) Singer opposition.

In the wake of the P-type, of course, there had been further developments at the top of the MG range, with the introduction of the N-type Magnette, which was announced in *The Autocar* of 30 March, 1934. The existing 1271cc KD six-cylinder engine, mated to a Wolseley gearbox similar to that used in the L-type, benefited from many improvements, in line with those applied to the related four-cylinder unit. The chassis was new and featured substantial sub-frames, to which the body was attached with the aid of flexible mounts. Both the track (at 3ft 9in/1.14m) and wheelbase (8ft/2.44m) were greater than those of the Magna, which the new Magnette would gradually supplant. New to the Magnette was a Bishop cam-type steering unit in place of the Marles-Weller version used previously.

The L-type Magna survived solely in the form of the Continental Coupé, complete with the 1087cc engine, which sold for £350,

some £15 more than the four-seater version of the new N-type. Adding confusion, the longer-chassis KN Magnette was also on offer as the £399 pillarless saloon, an evolution of the pillarless K1. The KN was wittily dubbed 'hot stuff' by *Motor Sport*, and with some 57bhp (42.50kW) at its disposal (the original K1 had had to make do with 39bhp/29.08kW), this was not far off the mark. A few cars were built using surplus K2 bodies on the N-type chassis, being known variously as NK or KD (not to be confused with the engine designation, although the KD engine was actually used); most were intended for hillclimb use and trials events.

The rationalization of the MG range that the N- and P-types promised should have brought great economies of scale, and with them improved sales and profits, but sadly the production ledgers painted a different picture. In 1932, production had reached a high of 2400 vehicles, but this had declined steadily during 1933 and 1934 to 2100, before plummeting to less than 1300 in 1935. Clearly, something would have to be done to redress the situation, and when measures were finally taken, they hit the men at Abingdon very hard.

The Airline Coupé: a 1930s MGB GT

At the October 1934 Motor Show, three versions of the P-type were displayed: the conventional two-seater, at £222; a rather cramped four-seater, at £240; and a new design, the smoothly styled Airline Coupé, at £290. The latter, resplendent in its grey finish with silver cellulosed wheels, was a very elegant closed car with a neat sliding roof that incorporated transparent panels. Production versions were frequently finished in an attractive two-tone scheme. The Airline Coupé appealed to a subtly different person to the traditional MG sports car buyer, to whom the idea of a sports car with a fixed roof was anathema, and the sports car roots of the Airline were all too obvious beneath the surface. As a result, sales undoubtedly suffered. Only 28 Airline Coupés were built on the PA chassis, and 14 on the later PB.

Such was the attractive appearance of the Airline Coupé that the experiment was repeated with the larger N-type, the coachwork—like that of the smaller car—being the responsibility of Kimber's

The 1934 PA Airline Coupé was a sleek evocation of the 1930's obsession with streamlining. (Rover/BMIHT)

The revolutionary R-type Midget united the advanced Q-type engine with a lightweight chassis and all-independent suspension. This view of the chassis emphasizes the delicate suspension wishbones, which petrified the drivers and had to be beefed up as a result. With further development, this chassis could have formed the basis of a formidable racing machine. (Rover/BMIHT)

old friends at Carbodies. This was advertised at £385, which seemed reasonable value alongside the Continental L-type and KN pillarless saloon; even so, only seven are known to have been built.

Another good looking variant on the N-type chassis was the open-topped H. W. Allingham Coupé, with bodywork by Whittington J. Mitchell. This appeared in September 1934 and featured two seats supplemented by a neat occasional 'dickey' seat concealed beneath a panel behind the hood. Attractive features notwithstanding, less than a dozen Allingham Coupés were built. A further variant was the Cresta-bodied 2/3-seater Magnette, of which about 20 examples were produced by the Cresta Motor Company Ltd of Worthing, run by Charlie Martin and Ian

---

EXTRACT FROM *MG MAGAZINE*

The company's in-house publication, *MG Magazine*, of March 1935, carried the following statement:

'As in the past, any MGs that race will be a standard product that anyone can purchase, except for modifications their respective owners subsequently may have carried out. Both the existing Q-type Midget and the K3 Magnette, which have been so successful during the past season, will be considerably modified and improved, and instead of being produced as a two-seater road-racing model, as for the 24 Hours Race at Le Mans, will appear with monoposto or single-seater bodies. At this juncture it is not considered advisable to release any further information, but provisional orders will be accepted for delivery in strict rotation commencing April of:

-MG Monoposto Midget 750cc   - approximate price £600
-MG Monoposto Magnette 1100cc   - approximate price £950

Needless to say, they are being designed and produced worthily to maintain the great reputation MGs have already established.'

Clearly, this refers to the R-type Midget and the proposed S-type Magnette.

MacLachlan. The aluminium-panelled bodywork was by E. Bertelli Ltd at Feltham, Middlesex.

The last of the racing Sixes: the NE Magnette

While the K3 Magnette continued to perform with distinction at major events, it began to face increasingly stiffer competition as other manufacturers developed their own race cars. However, of even greater significance was the outright ban on superchargers announced for the 1934 RAC Tourist Trophy, a consequence of the small supercharged cars trouncing the larger-engined opposition. Initially, MG was in something of a quandary as to how to deal with this significant hurdle, but fortunately had an ace up its sleeve.

The previous October, an L-type Magna had been taken to Montlhéry in company with the Magic Midget and employed to take a number of Class 'G' speed records in the process. The work that had gone into preparing and developing this car was put to good use in developing a racing derivative of the N-type Magnette. Kimber also sent a standard Magnette to Brooklands. He discussed this foray in his 1945 paper, *Motor Racing*: 'The results were at first disappointing and speeds in the neighbourhood of 80mph (128.74km/h) were all that could be achieved. Then Cousins, who was a tower of strength in these matters, had a look at the pistons after running and found traces of uneven burning. As we could not alter the head shape, he had the bright idea of tilting the crown, and by a process of trial and error found a certain inclination of the crown not only gave even burning, but put the speed up to over 100mph (160.93km/h).' Other improvements included a better camshaft and larger carburettors to compensate for the lack of supercharging.

To the race modified N-type chassis was grafted a special lightweight alloy bodyshell, which was made much narrower than the production car by staggering the driver and passenger seats. The result, a splendid pinnacle of pre-war, six-cylinder racing MG design, was christened the NE Magnette. On its first outing, a relay race organized by the Light Car Club, it took third place. A team of six cars was entered for the TT itself, on 1 September, 1934. Formidable opposition notwithstanding, Charlie Dodson—in his first season racing on four wheels—brought his NE home just seconds ahead of E. R. Hall's Bentley, at a speed merely 3mph

(4.83km/h) slower than Nuvolari had achieved with his K3 in the previous year. Fired by such success, Kimber and his engineers were keen to develop what they hoped would be the ultimate six-cylinder race car, in time for their next visit to the TT.

Technical *tour de force*: the R-type Midget

The Q-type was a remarkable car, but it was also dramatic proof of the limitations within the classic MG chassis design. This simply could not cope with the 113bhp (84.26kW) pumped out by its tiny 746cc engine at 7200rpm. Obviously, any further advances in the engine department would have to be matched by a considerable overhaul of the chassis design.

In the March 1935 issue of *MG Magazine*, Cecil Kimber released preliminary details of two forthcoming racing specials with single-seater bodies, describing them as the 750cc MG Monoposto Midget and the 1100cc MG Monoposto Magnette. The former would become the R-type Midget, while the latter was the so-called S-type, possibly EX149, although the Register describes this number as 'not taken'. At about the same time as the magazine article appeared, Kimber wrote to the motoring press, attempting to solicit support for changes to the racing formulae that would benefit his new cars. 'But the Magnette version never happened,' recalls Jack Daniels. 'It was just Kimber's dream.'

On the other hand, the R-type was real, and undoubtedly it constituted the technical peak of pre-war MG design, the brilliance of which was mainly attributable to Charles, albeit supplemented by other talents: 'Most of the work was done before we were joined by Bill Renwick,' relates Daniels, 'who was a clever mathematician, who had been involved with Aston Martin—and in fact, Reid Railton came in as a consultant on the R-type, a fact which few people seem to be aware of.' Renwick is remembered as an interesting character by Daniels: 'When he had left Aston Martin, he had disappeared for a while: he told me that he had spent some time as a "hobo", travelling across America on trains! He also loved playing poker; he got himself into Frilford Golf Club to play poker, and would get me to pick him up in his car and drop him there. I would then have the use of his car for the whole weekend, and I just had to pick him up on the Sunday evening after he had spent the whole weekend playing poker!'

Daniels remembers working on the R-type drawings in late 1934 and early 1935: 'The car was drawn up by me as a half-scale on a vertical board.' Bill Renwick's analytical skills were used to determine the details of the suspension: 'There were parallel forged wishbones for the front suspension, and the top ones—at 3/8in (0.9cm) diameter—looked like little more than a couple of knitting needles. The drivers saw them and said no way were they going to drive the car with such thin wishbone arms, and so we made them thicker just to keep the drivers happy!' As is well documented, the R-type went around the track far faster than any previous MG, but the roll experienced in the process was alarming. The design team soon began working on solutions, but as we shall see, events overtook them.

As if independent suspension all round and the legendary 746cc engine were not enough, Charles insisted that for these to perform in harmony, the chassis had to be far more rigid than the traditional flexible forms of construction. It had taken considerable courage and skill to drive cars like the J4 and Q-type, but with the R-type, things would be different. To achieve the structural strength he demanded, Charles resorted to a box-section wishbone chassis, the prototype of which was fabricated by Frank Stevens, who had been responsible for modifying the chassis of Kimber's 'Old Number One' ten years earlier. As a consequence of the lightweight chassis and minimal bodywork, the R-type Midget tipped the scales at 1421lb (644.57kg).

Kimber and Charles were concerned about the possibility of infringing patents with the R-type's novel suspension, so they employed a patent agent named Eric Walford to study existing patents. That which caused the most concern was a patent held by Roesch and Clement Talbot for an independent suspension system, but in the end, Walford concluded that there was no need to worry. Some time later, MG's research into these patents would prove useful groundwork in the design of the post-war Morris Minor.

EXTRACT FROM *THE SPORTS CAR*

Within a matter of weeks of the transfer of MG from Lord Nuffield to Morris Motors, the August 1935 edition of the company's publication *The Sports Car*, sub-titled *The MG Owners' Magazine*, carried the following announcement:

'Lord Nuffield has said that there are to be no more MG racing cars. This announcement came as a shock to all and sundry connected with or interested in the sport, for since 1931 one or other of the highly successful MG racing types has either won outright, or most certainly been well in the picture, in almost every British and Continental event for which the cars have been eligible. In fact, if the upholding of British prestige abroad can be laid at the door of any one marque, that surely is MG. Why this decision? Some of those who assume the wisdom of experience have said, "What has happened to every other manufacturer who has raced to any extent? Why, of course, their financial resources are at and end!" This reason can be discounted right away when it is explained that as a company we have never raced. Racing has always been left to the enterprise of the private enthusiast. Also our last balance sheet would satisfy the most critical shareholder. The real reasons for discontinuing the building of racing machines are as follows: first of all, the Directors have decided that, at all events for the present time, racing for the purpose of development has, in our case, served its useful purpose. Another reason, rather more obscure, purely concerns racing itself and has no bearing on the commercial aspect, namely that we are handicapped out of British racing, through no real fault of the handicapper. It is simply a case of carrying a fundamentally unsatisfactory system to its logical conclusion. It stands to reason that a car which very frequently wins must inevitably have its handicapped speeds increased to a greater amount than the "also rans", whose development and speed capabilities are to the handicapper far more nebulous. This attitude can better be understood when it is appreciated that MG racing cars are securing first places in almost all the Continental events in which they compete and which are run on a class basis without handicap systems. This is briefly the true state of affairs with MG racing and we are going, so to speak, to rest on our laurels. We intend to let the production type catch up with the extremely advanced ideas incorporated in the present racing car, which is highly specialized and years ahead of its time when regarded from the point of view of applying its design to standard machines. There are many MG cars competing in races at present and they are likely to do so for several seasons, so the name will continue to appear in racing programmes until such times as we may be ready again to use the field once more for development.'

John Thornley has suggested that a hidden reason behind the cessation of factory backed racing was a private truce between Morris and Austin, since both companies were spending large sums on 750cc cars. However, if this was the intention, Austin would renege on the agreement.

Once the first R-type had been built, a rather embarrassing problem came to light, as Jack Daniels remembers: 'Following the build of the first car, we found, to our discomfiture, that the cam of the specially designed steering mechanism was in the wrong hand. However, it was essential that some initial vehicle testing was conducted. To this end, we were staggered to see Sam Nash driving with abandon up and down the length of the workshop, and turning in and out of the line of stanchions by steering the wheel in the opposite direction: it was great to watch! Thankfully, Cam Gears came up with the appropriate cam very quickly.'

The racing début of the R-type occurred at Brooklands on 6 May, 1935, in the Junior Car Club International Trophy Race. A team of four R-types was entered, and while the independent suspension was indeed a revelation, that body roll was not at all appreciated by drivers more familiar with traditional rock-hard racing suspension. For this Brooklands race, the engine remained essentially Q-type in specification, but despite the problems, Bill Everitt and Malcolm Campbell managed to bring home RA 0260 to a well deserved class win, with Doreen Evans immediately behind in RA 0255.

Encouraged by this success, the team's next outing took place at the end of the month, at the Isle of Man Mannin Beg race. Here, however, success eluded them, problems being caused by broken drive-shafts as a consequence of overheated (and, therefore, ineffectual) hydraulic shock absorbers, which must have made the ride even more peculiar. With the knowledge gained from the failures at Mannin Beg, the design team at Abingdon set out to rectify the problem, H. N. Charles scheming an ingenious hydraulically assisted set-up.

In due course, several private entrants would achieve successes with R-types, but in the United Kingdom, competition from the double-overhead-cam 750cc Austins was formidable. In an attempt to combat this, Laurence Pomeroy, of *The Motor*, and Michael McEvoy came up with a special dohc head for the R-type engine, and managed to persuade the Evans family, of the famous Bellevue Garage in Battersea, South London, to acquire three such heads. However, technically interesting though the enterprise undoubtedly was, ultimately it would prove to be of no avail without factory involvement.

EX150: the T-type independent saloon

In the wake of the R-type, work began at Abingdon on a saloon car with suspension based on similar principles. Jack Daniels worked on this project, which is recorded in the EX-Register as EX150, 3½-litre independent car. Common sense would dictate that the first choice for its engine should have been from within the Nuffield Organization, and if it was to have been a 3.5-litre unit, as the title of EX150 suggests, the obvious candidate would have been a Wolseley engine. In 1935-36, the top-of-the-line Wolseley was the 25hp Super Six, which was powered by a 3485cc (82x110mm) straight-six. This might have been a heavy and unsporting engine, developed from a Morris truck unit, but it would have made commercial sense for Kimber to have adopted it, particularly since it was not far removed—in terms of engine size, if not of pedigree—from the Bentley's 3669cc unit.

Certainly, Kimber was ambitious to drive the MG marque ever further from its humble origins, and it is quite conceivable that he would have been tempted to look outside the Nuffield family: stories have circulated to the effect that the engine was a special V8, which Kimber had commissioned, while others suggest that it was a Blackburne straight-six. Daniels drew up the chassis of this saloon, but cannot remember anything about the engine, which is a pity, since its identity has been the subject of much debate in the past. If it did come from outside the Nuffield Organization, its selection was either a brave or a foolhardy gesture by Kimber, depending upon your point of view.

Daniels believes that, in fact, the car was originally intended to have a 2-litre engine: 'We built one,' he recalls, 'and it was scheduled for the 1935 Motor Show at Olympia. The car was built on the lines of the R-type, but to overcome the problem of the roll angle, Bill Renwick sat down and designed a pre-loaded anti-roll bar—which I drew up for him—which had a torsion bar concentric with a torsion tube, with 100lb (45.36kg) pre-loading, so that when the car went into roll mode, there was already a force restraining the roll action.' Sadly, although no less than 1106 drawings relating to the car were recorded, none of these survive. As to the styling, Daniels simply remembers that it had a 'classy, typically MG look.'

Kimber did his best to salvage some of the work that he had put into this project, although the result was quite different under the skin. The idea of a 3.5-litre MG, however, would resurface briefly in the future.

Nuffield sells out: the end of MG's independence

Few people outside the company could have been prepared for the news of 1 July, 1935, when Lord Nuffield announced that he was relinquishing his personal hold of MG and Wolseley, and passing them to Morris Motors. Activities at Abingdon had been watched from Cowley with a mixture of concern and envy, and as Lord Nuffield himself began to be convinced that his remaining personal portfolio of businesses should be amalgamated with the core, the end of independence became inevitable. One of the keenest exponents of this was Leonard Lord, who had personally recommended to Nuffield that he should not privately own Wolseley Motors, which supplied most of the axles and steering gear for the public

company, Morris Motors. The idea of merging MG with Morris Motors was a natural extension of this philosophy.

Changes were swiftly announced: design responsibility would pass to the Cowley drawing office, with a nominal liaison capability retained at Abingdon, and there would be numerous other changes in personnel and procedures as MG adapted to Cowley's way of doing things. There would be changes on the shop floor, of course, but the development and racing activities would bear the brunt of the take-over. One of the first reactions in print, to the announcement that MG racing activities would cease, appeared in *The Autocar*, which reported, 'The decision that the MG company is to cease racing forthwith has come as quite a shock to a lot of people.' It went on to speculate that the cessation of racing was likely to have a knock-on effect upon factory support for private racing of MG sports cars.

On 10 July, 1935, the shares in MG were formally transferred from Morris Industries Ltd to Morris Motors Ltd. While Cecil Kimber became a director of Morris Motors, he was given the title of general manager at MG, Leonard Lord taking the position of managing director. This arrangement must have made Kimber uneasy, but he did not take long to adapt to the new regime, and he soon became an active contributor to the development of future MG proposals at Cowley.

The move of the design office to Cowley was swift and uneventful, according to Jack Daniels: 'We just got called in and together given the instruction that we were going to Cowley. There was me and George Cooper, together with Eric Selway, Geoff White and another named Lewis. We just transferred; only George and I stayed together, and the others were dispersed throughout Cowley, although I don't think many lasted there long.' Of course, H. N. Charles also moved, leaving Bill Renwick behind, along with Syd Enever as head of the experimental department.

A powerful reason behind the decision to terminate Abingdon's racing activities may have been the unfortunate publicity surrounding a tragic accident that occurred on 29 May, 1934, just before the second Isle of Man RAC Mannin Beg race. This involved Kaye Don and his mechanic, the popular Frankie Taylor. Don (allegedly suffering from the side-effects of enthusiastic partying) and Taylor were testing their car on the public highway during the night before the race and, in the process, collided with a Buick taxi with a number of passengers on board. They veered off the road and up a bank, before crashing back on to the road, facing the wrong way. Don was hospitalized by his injuries, but poor Frankie Taylor died as a result of his.

Until that time, no MG had been involved in a fatal, racing related accident; after all, the company's motto was 'Safety Fast!', so when Don was brought to court, for once, public interest in the marque was very unwelcome. From then on, Morris—by now Lord Nuffield—became resolved that MG should have nothing further to do with racing, an activity that he regarded as being of dubious value anyway.

The end of autonomy for Abingdon

At the time of the Morris Motors take-over, virtually all of the exciting projects that Kimber had sanctioned were either abandoned or modified so heavily as to be virtually unrecognizable. The R-type racing car, with H. N. Charles' novel all-independent suspension was one of the better known casualties, but other, equally ambitious designs were also chopped at the insistence of the mercurial Leonard Lord. He shared Nuffield's antipathy towards motor racing, and felt that the luxury of largely unique MG sports cars was something that the company could not afford. His expressed preference was for future MGs to be 'tarted up Morrises and Wolseleys.' In fact, if he had been allowed his way, both the Wolseleys and MGs of the late 1930s would have been little more than Morris cars with different radiator grilles and nominal specification changes.

MG production had fallen prior to the Morris takeover, and Lord stated that he wanted to see production reaching 100 cars per week, which would have necessitated a fourfold increase of MG's 1935 output. From 1935, therefore, MG was tied tightly to Cowley's apron strings, a state of affairs that persisted well into the 1950s.

During that period, all production MGs were designed at Cowley rather than Abingdon.

All change: Cowley design takes over

When Jack Daniels reached Cowley, he found many differences in working practice. At the time, the technical director was Robert Boyle, who had come from Rover (Vic Oak would take his place in 1937). Under Boyle was chief designer Bill Seddon. Soon after, the young Alec Issigonis arrived to work on suspension, with Tom Brown on engines and Cordey on axles: 'For about a year, that was the set-up, and then Boyle was sacked; Tom Brown went back to Morris Engines, Cordey disappeared, and in came A. V. Oak, the new chief engineer, brought in from Wolseley.' In fact, Oak had followed Miles Thomas to Cowley, becoming the technical director (chief engineer) with overall responsibility for Morris, Wolseley and MG cars.

It may come as no surprise that the talented Charles and Issigonis—both keenly interested in advanced suspension design— did not always see eye to eye. Daniels, who later would work closely with Issigonis on the Mosquito, which eventually led to the 1948 Morris Minor, recalls the friction between them: 'Charles resigned and went to Rotol, where he redesigned the variable-pitch airscrew.' With Charles gone, only two of the old Abingdon design team were left at Cowley working on MG design, Daniels and George Cooper: 'We were put on new MG design work under the guidance of Jack Grimes, who called himself "Section Leader for MG" and who did virtually bugger all!'

Work proceeded, during 1935-36, on the T-type Midget, both Daniels and Cooper being surprised at the sluggish pace compared to their days at Abingdon: 'George and I just got on with our work to incorporate Cowley materials. At Cowley, there were whole teams working on specific vehicles, whereas at Abingdon, we had been involved with all their cars!' Grimes helped Daniels and Cooper to identify suitable Morris components for the project, with Daniels operating as the chassis man: 'George Cooper was the body man—he was good at flared wings and such-like—and he did much of the TA, but somewhere along the line, L. P. Hall's body section must have become involved.' Although Daniels and Cooper worked on the new Midget ('Our bread and butter,' as

Despite the end of official racing activity, several loyal privateers kept the MG flag flying, none more so than the Evans family—Denis, Doreen and Kenneth—owners of the Bellevue Garage near London's Wandsworth Common. Here, they pose with (left to right) the ex-Eyston EX135 with 'coal scuttle' road-racing body, Doreen's R-type, and Kenneth's special-bodied Q-type, all finished in the Bellevue colour scheme of Oxford Blue with white stripes. (Rover/BMIHT)

Daniels calls it), they played no part in the development of the Two-Litre, or SA, model.

Daniels recalls being involved in an event that led to Jack Grimes leaving the company: 'He and I were going over to MG's in a Wolseley 25, and he let me drive. Losing control, we went through a telegraph pole. The tension of the wire was such that when I touched it, it went "twang" right along the road. We both got bumped on the head and, whilst I returned to the works, Grimes somehow got himself sent to the Nuffield Rehabilitation Centre at Bournemouth on company expense to recuperate. At the same time, the boss of Hillman's was also in residence. The next thing we knew, Grimes had gone to work for Hillman, although I don't think he stayed there very long!'

Then, in 1937, Daniels began working with Issigonis, while George continued to concentrate on MG design. Daniels believes that Vic Oak teamed him with Issigonis to give the latter an anchor in the real world: 'I had met up with A. V. Oak in the past, when he had been chief engineer at Wolseley: I used to go there on mechanical objectives, mainly pertaining to the Midget—including, of course, the cross-flow cylinder head for the Montlhéry Midget— and so he was aware of my potential. Oak could see that Issigonis had a gift, but needed someone experienced in practical issues, and I was his choice.'

Before the all-new, Cowley designed Midget appeared, however, a facelifted version of the P-type, known as the PB, was introduced, as was a new MG saloon, the first sight of which caused sharp intakes of breath among MG enthusiasts. Announced in October 1935, and making its show début at Olympia soon afterwards, the MG SA-type, or Two-Litre, was quite the largest and most luxurious MG that there had ever been, having a massive wheelbase of 10ft 3in (3.12m). A styling exercise, almost certainly for the

EX150 described previously, had been commissioned from Mulliners by Kimber, and a proposal remarkably like the car that eventually emerged as the SA was drawn up in late June 1935, just before the take-over was announced. This may go some way towards explaining why, in reality, the SA was rather over-bodied for a 2-litre car.

The PB Midget and NB Magnette

At first, the PB Midget supplemented, rather than replaced, the previous P-type, which became known as the PA. The engine size was increased from 847cc to 939cc by increasing the bore by 3mm to 60mm, thus reducing the handicap that the car had faced against the 972cc Singer opposition, and raising the RAC tax rating from 8.05 to 8.9hp. The last added 15s (75p) to the PA's annual tax of £6. A closer-ratio gearbox was fitted, but the most obvious change was to the radiator grille, which featured the painted vertical slats previously seen on the 18/80. Inside, the dashboard instrumentation was revised and regrouped, and for the first time, a 30mph (48.28km/h) warning light was fitted. The light came on at speeds over 20mph (32.19km/h) and was intended to give guidance to the motorist when driving through built-up areas, where the new 30mph speed limits were coming into force.

The PA was still listed, at a lower price of £199 10s (£199.50)—the PB retailed at £222—but few of them were sold. Consequently, by the end of the year, the final 27 PAs had been converted into PBs at the factory.

For the 1936 model year, the N-type Magnette also came in for a number of revisions, most noticeably to the bodywork and grille, the former being lower in profile, while the latter received vertical slats similar to those of the PB. The doors were hinged from the front rather than the rear, having distinctive, long, plated spear-like hinges, while inside the combined speedometer and tachometer of the earlier model gave way to separate instruments. The NB proved to be a desirable sports car, but it was soon overshadowed by the new six-cylinder SA which, while displaying a poorer pedigree and fewer sporting pretentions, arguably offered better value for money. By the autumn of 1936, the last of the NB variants were passing down the production line; the classic MG overhead-cam six was no more.

Luxury motoring: the Two-Litre, or SA

The Autocar magazine of 4 October, 1935, carried an article on the new MG Two-Litre, which began, 'Rumour has had much to say of the MG Car Company's eve of show surprise. It would be this, and it would be that. It would have this feature and that feature.'

Clearly, there had been much speculation in the wake of the dramatic events of the previous summer, and enthusiasts were apprehensive about what the men of Cowley had planned for the MG marque. For those who expected MG saloons to be light in weight and fleet of foot, there was much cause for concern, but for most people, the MG Two-Litre represented a very elegant, close-coupled sports saloon. It provided quite luxurious accommodation for four, and was offered with a good standard of equipment, which extended to Jackall four-wheel hydraulic jacks and powerful twin Lucas pass lights.

The prototype had been fitted with a conventional overhead-valve Morris/Wolseley engine of 2062cc, derived from a bore and stroke of 65.5 and 102mm respectively, the RAC horsepower rating being 15.96. The engine belonged to a family of Morris side-valve and Wolseley overhead-valve powerplants; a 2062cc side-valve unit had already seen service in the Morris Oxford Sixteen. The truth, however, was that this engine was far too feeble for the SA, so by the time the car reached production, in the spring of the following year, the capacity had been raised to 2288cc by increasing the bore to 69mm. Before long, the capacity would be increased again, to 2322cc, when the engine was rationalized as the QPHG with the closely related Wolseley 18 unit, which had a bore that was a mere 0.5mm greater. As a result, the Two-Litre tag became a bit of a misnomer.

Unfortunately, the gap between the appearance of the SA and the first deliveries to customers was at least six months, during which time a formidable rival appeared in the form of William Lyons' 2.6-litre SS Jaguar, first shown to dealers on 21 September, 1935, a little over two weeks before the SA was featured in *The Autocar*. Lyons was not afflicted by protracted development delays, so his first customers were able to take delivery of their cars much sooner after its public début at the same Olympia Show as the MG. The fact that the SA took inordinately long to reach production is illustrated by the fact that Kimber took a black SA to the Geneva show in March 1936, along with three passengers: his friend Russell Chiesman, M. F. N. Gouvy of Morris Continental Soc. An., and 'The Scribe' from *The Autocar*. The resulting two-part article, written by the last, was published in April, under the title 'Trial Trip' and sub-titled: 'The New Two-Litre MG has its final test on a run

The SA, or Two-Litre, saloon was quite unlike any MG that had preceded it, and its arrival in September 1935 was greeted with very mixed feelings by most MG sports car enthusiasts. The styling is believed to have been closely based upon a proposal by Mulliner, drawn by that company's James Wignall. (Rover/BMIHT)

The prototype T-type (TA) Midget of 1936. The fictitious number-plate refers to the fact that the car was an 'MGT' and that the intended retail price was £222. (Rover/BMIHT)

to Geneva.' Obviously, Cecil Kimber intended the journey to maintain public interest in a car that was, as yet, unavailable.

Despite the delays, the SA went on to become a popular car, not least in the equally elegant Tickford and Charlesworth drophead versions, which were announced in April and July 1936 respectively. An SA saloon (registration BRM 70; race number 148) was even entered in the 1937 Mille Miglia by Tommy Wisdom and his wife, Elsie, although their race came to an early end on a wet road near Florence.

The chassis of the SA followed conventional Morris practice, with substantial steel box-section side-members and tubular cross-bracing. At the rear, it swept up and over the axle rather than underneath, while the suspension was entirely conventional. This latter point did not prevent subsequent experimentation with an independent front suspension set-up, listed in the EX-Register as EX162, which describes 'front independent suspension designed by Mr Girling of Pratt and Manley.' It may be that this was the SA in

which Cecil Kimber had one of his few accidents, when experimental suspension came adrift during a fast journey from Southampton to Fareham in May 1938.

Cowley's Midget: the T-type

During the protracted period that the SA was being developed into its production form, work was also proceeding on the T-type Midget. If the two cars had been designed by the same team, that might have explained the delay with the SA, but this was not the case. With the discontinuation of the overhead-camshaft, Wolseley-based engine used in the PB, and no prospect of a highly specialized overhead-cam unit being produced to take its place, it was

The elegant Tickford T-type Midget, with coachwork by Salmons of Newport Pagnell. This car is the prototype with smoothly fared-in rear bodywork; production versions retained the conventional external T-series fuel tank. (Rover/BMIHT)

THE 'MAGIC MAGNETTE': THE EARLY YEARS OF EX135

By the end of the 1930s, MG's record breaking exploits were already legendary: EX120 and EX127—'The Magic Midget'— had fired the imagination of British sports car enthusiasts. Having proved the mettle of the Midget, Kimber and Eyston were determined to do the same thing with the Magnette, drawing upon the experience of EX127 as much as possible. This time, however, the car would have two interchangeable bodies: a narrow record breaking, or track, body and a broader, more conventional road body for racing. Eyston ordered the special car to be based upon the new K3, and it was given the next number in the book, EX135.

In its first guise, as built in 1934, EX135 could be fitted with a choice of two bodies. Shown above is the track body, in which form the car was known officially as 'Magic Magnette', but unofficially as the 'Humbug'. (Rover/BMIHT)

Like EX127, the new car had an offset drive-line, and the wheelbase was stretched by a little over 4in (10.16cm). The track body was finished in the MG colours of brown and cream, applied as stripes from front to back, and although the MG publicity people dubbed it the 'Magic Magnette', the popular press christened the car the 'Humbug'. The road racing body was a somewhat cruder effort, known at the factory as the 'Coal Scuttle', and in this form, EX135 would be raced by Eyston alongside more conventional K3s—notably in the 1934 Mannin Beg race.

Before long, plans were being laid to crack new records with the 'Magic Magnette' and, in October 1934, Kimber managed to upset Eyston by instructing that a Zoller supercharger be fitted to the engine to allow a crack at the world hour record. Since Eyston had a commercial interest in Powerplus superchargers and, even more importantly, because EX135 was *his* car, not MG's, he was understandably annoyed. The record attempt failed, ironically due to the supercharger expiring dramatically. Before long, however, the car had been repaired and a Powerplus supercharger installed, permitting Eyston to crack the Class 'G' records. He did not use EX135 for record breaking again, for the Morris Motors take-over of 1935 temporarily put paid to factory backed record attempts.

At this point, Ronnie Horton enters the story. Horton owned a special offset single-seater K3, which had held the one-hour Class 'G' record that Eyston shattered with EX135. When Horton retired from racing, he sold this car to someone who would follow in Eyston's footsteps as a record breaking schoolboy hero—Major (later Lieutenant-Colonel) Arthur Thomas 'Goldie' Gardner, known (inaccurately) in the press as the 'One-legged Major' on account of his lame right leg. Gardner took his new toy to Brooklands at the beginning of August 1936 and, according to John Thornley, 'managed to rekindle Kimber's enthusiasm... He (Kimber) agreed with Gardner to prepare the car at the factory.' Obviously, this required the sanction of Lord Nuffield, which Kimber carefully sought, and before long MG found itself back in the record breaking business.

In October 1936, the Horton/Gardner car ran at Frankfurt, breaking Gardner's own records for the mile and kilometre. The MG attracted the attention of Auto Union's Eberan von Eberhorst, who suggested that it needed a streamlined body similar to the record breaking Auto Union. Consequently, Kimber secured Lord Nuffield's backing and acquired EX135 as the basis for a new car along these lines. The body was designed by Reid Railton, who had also been responsible for John Cobb's world land speed record car. It was a smooth, futuristic looking alloy envelope, which enclosed the wheels and looked as though it was doing 200mph (321.86km/h) standing still.

Since the new car was so highly modified compared to the original upon which it was based, it could be argued that it should no longer have been called EX135. Indeed, it was popularly known as the 'Gardner-MG Record Car', largely because EX135 would have meant nothing to the public. However, at the factory, it was still thought of as EX135, and no less an authority than John Thornley himself continued to refer to the car as EX135.

Gardner took the car back to Frankfurt in October 1937, pushing the Class 'G' record for 1100cc cars to 148.8mph (239.46km/h), which was faster than the record for the next class up! In the following year, he was back on German soil again, coming tantalizingly close to the psychological 200mph barrier, at 187.616mph (301.93km/h) for the flying mile and 186.567mph (300.24km/h) for the flying kilometre, with a highest one-way speed of 194.386mph (312.83km/h). The agenda for 1939 was abundantly clear: to smash the

200mph barrier and, Goldie Gardner being the person he was, to smash it by a considerable margin if possible. The aim was to take the 1100cc record, quickly rebore the car on site, then break the 1500cc record immediately after. In May 1939, these ambitions were realized at Dessau, the 1100cc records being taken on 31 May, and the 1500cc records two days later. The highest speed achieved was a remarkable one-way best of 207.37mph (333.72km/h) in 1100cc guise. Despite Gardner's desire to return, however, his plans were scuppered by the outbreak of war in September.

With its new body, EX135 looked out of this world. Always immaculately prepared, the record breaker would go on to take many records both before and after World War 2, in the hands of Goldie Gardner. (Rover/BMIHT)

The MG One-and-a-Half-Litre, or VA, saloon was a personal favourite of Cecil Kimber. (Rover/BMIHT)

obvious that MG enthusiasts would have to swallow their pride and accept—for the time being at least—that any new Midget would have to employ a humbler overhead-valve powerplant from the Morris stable.

The chassis, designed by Daniels and his colleagues, followed traditional MG practice in having under-slung side-members at the rear, which ensured a low centre of gravity. However, its size had been scaled up substantially to almost Magnette proportions: at 7ft 10in (2.39m), the wheelbase of the TA was 6.5in (16.5cm) greater than that of the PB; while the track, at 3ft 9in (1.14m), was 3in (7.62cm) wider. There were other changes, too, brought about by the need to fit in with Nuffield policies which, in some cases, were alien to Kimber and his men. Thus, for the first time, an MG sports car was equipped with hydraulic brakes—which Kimber distrusted—and the engine was no longer mounted rigidly, being isolated by rubber mountings, which meant that the chassis itself needed beefing up.

The engine was derived from that of the Wolseley 10/40 and had a capacity of 1292cc. Unfortunately, this was a typical long-stroke unit of the period, a consequence of the ridiculous British RAC horsepower rating, which determined the tax class of the vehicle by using a formula that dated from 1906, and which was based solely on the cylinder bore and the number of cylinders. The formula used was $D^2n/2.5$ (where D = cylinder diameter in inches, and n = number of cylinders), and it followed that by combining a long stroke with narrow bores, a manufacturer could squeeze the maximum cubic capacity from a given horsepower class. Calculation of the horsepower of the TA engine shows that, with its bore of 63.5mm (2.5in), the horsepower worked out at exactly 10. To achieve 1292cc, but remain within the 10hp class, required a stroke of 102mm, which limited the engine's ability to rev.

The new T-type Midget made its début in June 1936, when it appeared in an article in the 19 June issue of *The Autocar*, which

proclaimed the '27 special features in the new design' beneath a photograph of CJO 617. The writer was able to inspect a prototype at the factory, but was not given the opportunity of driving it, although he was able to say that it had a 'very smooth and silent-running engine.' In fact, the engine had a distinctly unsporting exhaust note, which resulted in rare criticism in *The Autocar* road test report of 18 September, which said, 'It was odd to be without the familiar exhaust burble, for there was no real sound to the exhaust pipe.' As a result, the exhaust note was quickly 'tuned' to provide a more sporting character, testing being carried out by no more scientific means than a series of drive-bys while Kimber stood and judged whether or not the efforts had been a success. In the same article in *The Autocar*, the writer reported that 'the same car was tried a second time with this change effected.'

Although a four-seater version of the T-type was not planned, other two-seater variants were. Much was hoped of the Airline Coupé, advertised at £295, although this barely got off the ground (only two were built). However, the Tickford drophead coupé version, with elegant coachwork by Salmons of Newport Pagnell, was more successful at £269 10s. (£269.50) The prototype TA Tickford dispensed with the normal T-type external slab tank, enclosing it within smoothly faired rear bodywork, but the production versions retained the standard tank, looking none the worse for that.

The One-and-a-Half-Litre, or VA

By mid 1936, when the N-type Magnette was nearing the end of its production life, Kimber was keen to see a successor plug the considerable gap between the TA and the SA. There was no prospect of a four-seat version of the T-type: most previous attempts at creating four-seater Midgets had produced cramped, uncomfortable and relatively unpopular affairs. The answer was a new car, which was designed around a 9ft (2.74m) wheelbase and given a Wolseley Twelve-based, 1548cc, four-cylinder engine. It was known as the VA. There was added impetus for the development of this car, in that William Lyons, who had partly stolen the march on Nuffield and the MG SA with his 2.6-litre SS, also had a very attractive, four-cylinder, 1.5-litre, Standard-engined SS on sale. Before long, Cowley's prototype for the VA was nearly ready, but as John Thornley later recalled, Cecil Kimber was determined to make his mark on the car: 'Kimber was obsessed with octagons... He put no less than 47 on to the VA: special handles, instruments, horn pushes, etc, and so the cost of the VA went up until it was no match for the SS car.'

The story of the VA actually began in 1935, when three prototypes were built at Cowley: EX/VA/11, 12 and 13. Records show that by September 1936, the first of these, EX/VA/11, had become the VA development prototype, having the characteristic Abingdon chassis number of 0251 and experimental engine number 6303/1. In his paper, *The Trend of Aesthetic Design in Motor Cars*, presented in 1944, Cecil Kimber had the following to say about the VA, which he regarded with some pride: 'This car was designed around the seating accommodation for four persons, and the first drawing was produced in September 1935. No less than four sample bodies were built before the design was finalized and it follows this author's ideas on design as set out briefly in this paper.' Is it mere coincidence that Mulliners produced four renderings for an MG saloon in June 1935?

In the summer of 1936, as production of the new Midget was getting under way at Abingdon, and development of the VA was being completed at Cowley, the ambitious and fiery Leonard Lord fell out with Lord Nuffield. He had asked for what he felt would be just reward for his dramatic and sweeping overhaul of the Nuffield Group, but Nuffield was not prepared to accede to his managing director's demands, so the two parted company in August. Lord left feeling very embittered and espousing vengeance. In his place, Oliver Boden, managing director at Wolseley, became the vice chairman of Morris Motors Ltd.

Shortly afterwards, Miles Thomas, who had shrewdly moved from Cowley to the Birmingham Wolseley works in 1935 to avoid clashing with Leonard Lord, returned to Oxford to take up the post of managing director of Morris Motors. Meanwhile, Kimber had become so enamoured of the VA that he was using one as his personal car, although the engine was bored out to 73mm (the same size as the 2.6-litre WA of 1938), giving a capacity of 1708cc. The same basic engine was also fitted to the Cream Cracker TA Midget trial cars for 1938, as well as a few police-specification VAs, and it may be speculated that a 1.75-litre MG might have been added to the range had the war not intervened, with the One-and-a-Half-Litre perhaps being discontinued to make way for the planned all-new 1.25-litre car.

A new saloon for the 1940s: the MG Ten

By 1937, Jack Daniels found himself working with Alec Issigonis on, among other things, an independent front suspension design, which was proposed for the 1938 Morris 10 Series M. In the event, introduction of the independent set-up was postponed, the Morris M appearing with a conventional beam front axle suspended from leaf springs.

According to Daniels, 'Barring the war, both Morris and MG would have had independent front suspension vehicles for the 1939 Motor Show, but of course the show was abandoned and the cars were delayed or destined never to appear.' Issigonis is usually given credit for the design of the independent suspension arrangement, but as is so often the case in these situations, engineering responsibility was shared by more than one person. Jack Daniels was an experienced draughtsman whose talents complemented Issigonis' engineering genius perfectly. Thus, the independent front suspension was, in Daniels' words, 'Issigonis' inspiration and my perspiration!'

In 1938-39, further rationalization was planned at Cowley, the proposed independent-front-suspension MG and a Wolseley-badged sister car being intended to share many components with the all-new Morris 10. Consequently, the MG has become known among MG historians as the MG Ten, although there is no certainty that it would have been so named had it reached production. The car shown in Chapter 2 was a full-size prototype model. According to Jack Daniels, it was produced using Morris 8 Series E body panels, by the simple expedient of pulling out the bottom panels to produce a turned-out shape instead of the characteristic turn-in of the Morris E.

Despite the fact that Morris Motors at Cowley were very much in charge of all new-model development, the men at Abingdon were very anxious to achieve some input into any car that ultimately they would be expected to produce. Cecil Kimber visited Cowley on an almost daily basis, monitoring progress on the new MG saloon, while Syd Enever provided engineering liaison at the Abingdon plant.

The longer wheelbase of the MG chassis was balanced by extending the rear bodywork with longer rear wings and a larger boot. This work was the responsibility of Tom Ramsay, a body draughtsman in the Cowley production body drawing office, who reported to chief body draughtsman Stan Westby and chief body engineer Les Hall. With the exception of the Wolseley-style wheels, the result looks remarkably similar to the MG Y-type, which emerged after the war.

Gerald Palmer lends a hand

In 1938, with his ambitious Deroy sports car venture stalled through a lack of funds, Gerald Palmer began to look elsewhere in the hope of realizing his sports car ambitions: 'I was introduced to Cecil Kimber through Brian Robbins, the secretary of the Institution of Automobile Engineers, which I had first joined when I came to England in 1928. I brought my Deroy down to Abingdon for him to see, and he seemed quite interested, sending me over to Cowley to meet Vic Oak.' Oak must have been suitably impressed, for he quickly offered Palmer—aged 27—the opportunity of taking over the MG drawing office at Cowley: 'Prior to me, there hadn't really been a special MG chief at Cowley; any MG work required was done in the Morris drawing offices. Previously, of course, sports car design had been done by H. N. Charles and Syd Enever at Abingdon, but when it came to saloons, Abingdon were not as experienced as Cowley, which is why they wanted me there.'

Palmer's first project at Cowley was given to him by Vic Oak: 'He was uncertain about independent front suspension due to costs, and so he wanted to see a car with half-elliptic springs. I came up with a set-up based upon the existing Morris 10 ideas. It had an anti-roll bar and a parallelogram arrangement with the leaf springs.' Palmer's scheme effectively adapted H. N. Charles' front roll-bar in conjunction with softer front springs. This set-up was intended to serve as an interim measure until the independent design was approved for production. In the event, the Morris 10 Series M, Cowley's first production car featuring monocoque construction, was only built pre-war (with the cheaper front axle), since the all-new Morris Minor displaced it in the post-war line-up. Thus, when the independent front suspension eventually appeared, it was restricted to the MG.

I am indebted to MG Y-type expert and author John Lawson, who sorted out the chronological sequence and design responsibility for the front suspension that eventually emerged after the war. The steering gear and radius rods were the joint responsibility of former MG designer H. N. Charles, whose patent 502028 was registered on 9 September, 1937, and Alec Issigonis, whose patents 527468 and 539083 are dated 7 September, 1939, and 7 June, 1940, respectively. On the same day as H. N. Charles' patent was registered, Issigonis registered the independent front suspension as three separate patents, 509029-509031. Of course, all these patents were jointly registered by the designers and their employers, Morris Motors Ltd.

The production version of the so-called MG Ten, as originally conceived, could have featured a version of the 1140cc Morris XPJM engine. However, with the introduction of the longer-stroke, 1250cc XPAG version of this engine in the TB Midget, in May 1939, it was obvious that the MG Ten would be similarly equipped. At least one running prototype was built and, according to Paul

The WA was available in this elegant Tickford-bodied four-seater Foursome version. (Rover)

Skilleter in his excellent *Morris Minor*, was used during the war years by the Nuffield Organization's vice chairman, Miles Thomas.

Jack Daniels certainly remembers that there were two independent-front-suspension prototypes running in 1939: one as a Morris 12 and the other as an MG, and he recalls driving the Morris prototype on a number of occasions: 'The prototype was run throughout the war, normally by Stanley Westby, the chief draughtsman, and I was permitted to use it for visits to the Wolseley factory in the latter stages of the war.' Gerald Palmer believes that it was the MG that Westby drove, but Daniels is positive that it was the Morris: after a period of more than 50 years, memories have undoubtedly begun to fade!

Twilight of the 1930s: the WA and TB

The end of the pre-war MG story is very much a matter of 'might-have-beens': the last two models launched in 1938-39 were the TB, an improved T-series Midget with a new engine, and the WA, a 2.6-litre derivative of the SA. It had been apparent from the outset that the SA, or Two-Litre, was underpowered, even though the engine capacity of production models had grown to 2322cc. This fact was underlined by the unexpected competition provided by the 2.6-litre SS Jaguar.

So it was that the Cowley design team considered the Wolseley 25hp Super Six engine for a 3.5-litre conversion, but this heavy unit was found to be as ill-suited to the SA derivative as it would have been to the abortive, pre-Cowley, all-independent MG saloon of 1935. Abingdon's EX-Register records a '3½-litre car designed at Cowley' as EX160, but before long, this had been abandoned in favour of EX161, which became the MG 2.6-Litre, or WA-type. In fact, the WA was very closely based upon the SA, but the engine had a counterbalanced crankshaft and had been bored out from 69.5 to 73mm, increasing capacity to 2561cc, the same as the side-valve Morris Oxford 20. Of equal significance to the fact that MG now had a 2.6 to sell against Bill Lyons' Jaguar—with its Standard-based 2663cc engine—was that power output had been increased usefully by 20bhp (14.91kW) to 95.5bhp (71.21kW), and the RAC rating was within the 20hp class at 19.8hp.

Other refinements exclusive to the 2.6-Litre included 14in (35.56cm) brakes in place of 12in (30.48cm) units, and a rear track that was about 3in (7.62cm) wider than the front, which remained the same as on the SA. External features that distinguished the WA from the SA, which remained in production, included a neat dress guard. In effect, this was an extension of the rear door, which overlapped and shrouded the rear wing, keeping it clean and preventing clothing from being soiled on wet days. Finally, there was a reshaped, more voluptuous front apron, and a vee'd front bumper—similar to the characteristic Wolseley front bumper—with a central MG motif that was hinged to conceal the starting-handle hole. Inside, the dashboard resembled that of the SA, but featured four octagonal instruments in place of round gauges.

With the appearance of the WA, various improvements were made to the companion SA and VA models: the latter received a fully-counterbalanced crankshaft, a new camshaft and a dry-plate clutch; while a rear bumper became standard equipment on the former. Like the SA, the WA was offered as a four-door saloon (£442), a Tickford Foursome drophead coupé (£468), and a Charlesworth tourer (£450), although the last was short-lived, as the Charlesworth company went out of business.

The war years, however, would see the end of the road for the S-V-W series as the men at Abingdon directed their energies elsewhere, and the post-war climate would not be conducive to such a diverse range. Production of the SA, VA and WA models ceased in the autumn of 1939, by which time a total of 5524 had been built, the WA accounting for a mere 369. Given time, however, it might have become the best seller of them all.

The story of the TB Midget was also one of great promise, but unlike the S-V-W range, the T-series would have a place in the post-war scene. Whereas the TA had used the 1292cc MPJG engine, based upon the Wolseley Ten, the TB had been given a new 1250cc XPAG unit, which in less highly tuned form had appeared in the Morris 10. The TB slipped quietly into production in May 1939, but as MG production stopped soon after war broke out in September, it became even more short-lived than the WA. The factory demonstrator, CJB 59, was tested in *The Autocar* of 28 June, 1940, decked out with the obligatory Hartley headlamp mask and white paint on the leading edges of the wings and the running boards. That car would reappear a little under five years later when the first post-war MG—the TC—was being designed. For the moment, however, attention turned to other matters: the coming decade would see a dramatic sequence of events that would steer the marque on to a new course.

2 The 1940s

Cecil Kimber had become so strongly identified with the MG marque that his departure, in 1941, came as a shock, even allowing for the fact that both the motor industry and the country at large had other things on their minds. Perhaps Kimber had become too closely identified with the company for his own good; when the manager and his specialized products become better known than the owner and his more mundane, mainstream products, there are bound to be problems. The story has often been told of how Lord Nuffield discovered that Kimber and MG had found greater fame abroad than he and his Morris cars could ever have hoped to achieve, to the extent than an Australian to whom Nuffield was introduced did not believe that the 'thoroughbred' MG could be related to the humble Morris product.

Of course, the warning signs could be seen in 1935, with the sale of MG to Morris Motors, followed immediately by the increase of Cowley's influence. The senior management, in the form of Leonard Lord and, latterly, Miles Thomas, felt that subsidiary companies should have a defined role within the overall framework of the company, and they frowned upon individuals who tried to run their own shows. In 1941, Cecil Kimber secured a contract for the

Instrumental in securing Kimber's resignation, in November 1941, was Miles Thomas, the high flying Nuffield executive who would himself fall out with Lord Nuffield some six years later. (Rover/BMIHT)

assembly of the cockpit of the Albemarle bomber aircraft. This MG factory took over the complete fabrication and fitting out of the cockpit from General Aircraft, following a period of intensive training for MG staff.

Kimber's reward for displaying this initiative was his dismissal in the autumn of 1941. According to Jean Cook, however, her father's association with Lord Beaverbrook, who was in charge of aircraft production, and his friendship with John Howlett, chairman of the Southern Area Emergency Services, made some form of subterfuge necessary: 'My father said that a directive came from Morris Motors to centralize the issuing of unemployment and insurance stamps, which would have meant sacking a faithful employee, a single woman who supported her widowed mother. My father refused, and next day Miles Thomas arrived to demand his resignation.'

Miles Thomas suggested to Kimber that he should 'direct his energies elsewhere', so after 19 years with Morris Garages, suddenly Kimber was out. Jean Cook, 15 at the time, clearly recalls that the work-force at Abingdon was so incensed that they wanted to go on strike, but her father would hear none of it, insisting that they had important war work to do. Behind the façade, however, Jean recalls that her father was shattered: 'The official present was a set of silver candelabras, but the jig and tool makers made a tobacco cabinet for him. He ran his fingers over the beautiful joinery, and there were tears in his eyes.'

Kimber soon found work in Gloucester at Charlesworth, the coachbuilders that had produced open bodies for the S-V-W cars. Subsequently, he became works director at Specialloid Pistons in London, where he came upon militant shop-floor attitudes that had been completely alien to MG. Sadly, however, he never worked in peacetime again: he was killed on Sunday 4 February, 1945, in an accident involving an overloaded train on which he was a passenger. Kimber was one of only two who died; he was 56. Jean Cook admits that she has never really recovered from the loss. She had just begun to get to know her father, but war service in the WRAF meant that she had seen little of him at that time: 'I went to the crematorium at Edgware—I'd never been to such a place before—and I felt that I hadn't been able to say goodbye.'

Meanwhile at Cowley, in 1942, Gerald Palmer, who had played an important part in the design of the MG Ten prototype, found himself involved in the design of innovative medical equipment, as a result of Lord Nuffield's interest in medicine; there was little automotive engineering to occupy him during the war. Against this background, it is easy to see why—following a series of determined approaches, and the offer of a much higher salary—the 31-year-old was persuaded to join the small, but innovative, Bradford based Jowett company, where he was given a free hand to plan their post-war range. The result was the Jowett Javelin, an attractive saloon powered by the distinctive Jowett flat-four engine.

Post-war beginnings: theTC Midget
The loss of Cecil Kimber was not only a major shock, but also a sobering event for the MG team. Kimber's influence had been all-pervading throughout MG's history, and although his departure was overshadowed by the more pressing concerns and worries of war, the morale of the work-force suffered accordingly. Despite this,

WAR WORK AT ABINGDON

With the declaration of war in September 1939, production was halted at Abingdon, as it was in car factories everywhere, and plans were formulated to take in work to aid the war effort. The Allies had not been as prodigious in producing weapons of war as the Axis countries, so all the stops had to be pulled out to get production of guns, tanks, military vehicles and aircraft under way. EX135 was stored away at the St Helen's Clothing factory in Abingdon, along with most of MG's stock of car spares, and the factory cleared ready for its new role. At the same time, Cecil Kimber issued a series of patriotic advertisements based on the theme, 'It reminds me of my MG', with stirring drawings of Spitfires and other machinery of war. While this was going on, however, the men at Abingdon were idle.

Before long, Kimber and Propert began to look for work for the factory. They secured contracts for the maintenance and repair of Matilda tanks (which took place in the rectification area), and the transformation of cars into light trucks, but Kimber really wanted something more substantial. However, the factory was soon equipped with new plant to cope with the massive tank structures, while outside, both dry and wet test areas were established. Some of the men in the development section built an experimental tractor, using a T-type chassis, and because it was made from bits and pieces, it became known

as 'Bitsy'. It even received the honour of an EX number—EX167—and is recorded in the EX-Register as having engine number XPAG 529, a TB unit.

Meanwhile, the Kimbers had to give up their rented home at the Millers House. John Howlett, a friend of the family, owned Fyfield Manor, a few miles from Abingdon, so they moved there. Howlett had become chairman of the Southern Area Emergency Services, a position of some influence, and it was through him that Kimber was able to secure the sort of contract for which he felt that his men were truly suited. The Albemarle bomber featured a complex nose cone, with the added complication of the forward leg of a tricycle undercarriage, and Kimber managed to obtain the contract to build the nose cones. Eventually, MG built over 900 of them. Unfortunately, by taking this initiative, Kimber sealed his fate as far as Morris Motors' top management were concerned, and by the end of November 1941, he had been forced out.

With Kimber gone, MG continued with other contracts—secured, one imagines, with greater reference to the powers-that-be at Cowley—for tank and aircraft work, including equipping the legendary Rolls-Royce Merlin aero engines with mounting frames. By the summer of 1944, it was obvious that the end of the war could not be too far away, so thoughts at Abingdon gravitated back towards cars. While the first MG of the post-war era would draw heavily upon the last of the pre-war period, it would achieve unprecedented success in markets that had hardly been dreamt of by Kimber.

---

vitally important war work had to continue, so a new manager was appointed in his place. The new man was H. A. Ryder, the no-nonsense manager who had run Morris Radiators since 1919. Ryder soon earned the respect of the Abingdon work-force, even though, like many of his Cowley colleagues, he disapproved of motor racing. Despite this lack of interest in the competitive activities that had helped to bring universal fame to the MG marque, Ryder was instrumental in steering MG back into the sports car business barely weeks after the end of World War 2.

Although Ryder knew little about car production, he was a good engineer and a sound businessman. Sensibly, he sought the advice of Syd Enever and Cecil Cousins when considering what Abingdon should build. Clearly, a totally new car, so soon after the cessation of hostilities, was out of the question for MG, as it was with most other manufacturers. Consequently, it was necessary to draw upon the pre-war parts bins to restart car production quickly. Thus, in the

late spring of 1945, the bare bones of what would become the TC Midget were laid out. Looking through their pre-war service records enabled Cousins and his men to discover the few weaknesses inherent in the TA and TB, ensuring that the new car got off to a good start with some of the 'bugs' removed at the outset.

Of course, the design authority for MG still lay at Cowley, so production development of the TC Midget was carried out there, with minimal authority vested in the Abingdon team. Responsible for producing a quarter-scale, general-arrangement drawing of the TC was Jim Stimson, one the original team who worked on the Morris Minor, and who would become part of the exodus from Cowley many years later. He remembers, 'I produced the quarter scale for the TC to Syd Enever's requirements, using the general arrangement of the TB Midget as the basis.' In the early post-war

The so-called MG Ten prototype of 1939-40, pictured at Cowley. (Rover)

BUILDING THE TC MIDGET

Jimmy Cox began work at MG shortly before the TC production line was started, so he has a good recollection of the staff and their roles at each stage of production. At this time, the factory was still making Neptune amphibious tanks (which were built, inspected, tested and duly scrapped—mainly because the contract had not run its course!), bren-gun carriers and Rolls-Royce engine frames. The charge-hand on the TC line, Jack Lewis, was known as 'Ugly' Lewis on account of an unsightly scar on his face. He was, Jimmy remembers, quite strict: 'I remember one time when we had run out of shockers, and it was nearing the end of the day, getting on for six. I had started to wash up, and Jack made me go back to the line at two minutes to six to finish off.'

Jimmy's first job, after transferring from messenger boy to the chassis line, should have been a two-week spell in the tool stores to learn all about the various tools in use. However, because his messenger-boy role had lasted longer than normal, he missed out on this. Thus, he went straight to the line— still relatively clean and smartly dressed, fresh from delivering messages—to help Fred Saunders and Arthur Hazel with the TC suspension: 'My first job was to put the front springs on the beam axle. I was wearing a sports jacket and had no overalls (workers had to supply these themselves), so I got absolutely plastered with grease. I can remember going home proudly sporting greasy marks on my face and clothes, feeling that I had finally done something worthwhile.' In those days, there were staff canteens for lunches away from the production line, but Jimmy did not use these: 'You stayed on the track and ate your sandwiches, or whatever, at break time. I would stay with an operator each day, in that way ending up as a relief who could double-up for anyone's job if, for example, they were off sick.'

Fred Saunders and Arthur Hazel—both of whom were 'old boys' compared to young Jimmy—had the task of attaching the front axle and wheels to the TC chassis, followed by the rear axle and wheels. 'After this,' recalls Jimmy, 'the rolling chassis was lifted on to the track, where Reg Topless put some fittings inside the engine bay area, such as engine mountings and so forth, followed by the engine itself.' After Reg Topless' ministrations, the chassis was pushed along the line to the next stage, where it was received by Harry Carter: 'Harry was a very hard worker—he lived at Sutton Courtenay—who never drove a car, but always rode a bike. He used to fit the exhaust, pedals, brake pipes, etc, and would then push the car on again to the next stage.' At this point, two men, Cecil Wheeler and 'Dutchy' Holland, fitted the distinctive grey scuttle: '"Dutchy" was one of the younger men, but Cecil was getting on a bit and had started to get rheumatism in his hands. "Dutchy" used to work extra hard to help Cecil get his job done.' Holland and Wheeler's job included sub-assembling the scuttle, fixing the fuse-box and petrol pump in place, the block in the tool-box, the battery-box, and so on. Installing the scuttle on to the TC chassis was not without its own problems: 'They had to juggle with the two bolts in the chassis, which were fiddly and difficult to fit. This was on account of reinforcement, which had been added to the chassis frame after early testing on the shaker rig had shown a tendency for the original chassis to fracture. The reinforcement came just where the holes were and, as a result, it was very difficult to get the bolts in.' Comments from present-day TC restorers would be welcome, I am sure!

With the scuttle in place, the TC rolling chassis was wheeled down the line

to Bill Rennie: 'Bill was a classical music buff. I remember he loaned me some of his records, which to me, as a teenager, didn't have much appeal. Bill's job was to fit the air cleaner 'kidney', the shock absorbers and steering column, after which he did the initial lining-up of the steering wheel in the straight-ahead position.' The latter was rather difficult to do, but in due course someone on the line came up with the idea of using two parallel lengths of girder in which the tyres were a tight fit, thus ensuring that the steering wheel could be fitted 'square'. Next along the line was Archie Brown, a real character according to Jimmy: 'Archie was a Londoner, and he carried out a few small jobs and fitted the radiator and stays. Archie's final task was to bleed the brakes before pushing the chassis into the paint booth. There was a platform above the paint booth via an awkward staircase, up which you had to carry 5gal (22.73 litres) of brake fluid, which would then be tipped into overhead containers.' Later, Jack Matthews invented a clever device, powered by the air line, which automatically pushed the brake pedal up and down, thus freeing an operative from the brake bleeding operation.

The last person on the chassis line was Sam Peach, who had arrived from Bournemouth during the war: 'He would mask over the wheels and mask-up various other components before spraying the chassis. He would then start up the engine and warm it up, setting the tappets, checking the oil and water, and then running the chassis on to the "weaver" to check the tracking.' At this point, there was no petrol tank, so Peach would use a small can of petrol containing enough to run the car on test and over to the body line: 'They would pull the wires to stop the engine, and sometimes it wouldn't stop. As a naïve youngster, I initially tried to disconnect the petrol supply and wondered why the engine didn't stop straight away!'

On the body line, Jimmy Cox's tea-boy counterpart was Fred Knight, who would go on to run a successful ironmongers and model shop in Abingdon (Knight & Sons). The ironmongers is still trading, incidentally, although the model shop—which sometimes I frequented in my youth—has long gone. Also on the body line were 'Sailor' Berry and George Harvey from Drayton, whose job included mating the body tub to the chassis, an operation that involved quite a number of bolts, Jimmy recalls. After this, the rear wings and petrol tank were fitted by Neville Mott. Next, Arthur Belcher would make up the fascia, fitting the electrics, clocks and switches and installing the complete unit in the car. Later, this operation was taken over by Dick Stephens.

One of the most remarkable operations was carried out by 'Maggie' Buckle (often easy to pick out in production-line photographs due to his distinctive trilby hat) and 'Polly': 'They would fit the bonnet frame on to the front of the car, and would then take the pre-painted bonnet sections and cut them to fit using a band-saw and jig. Having done this, they would simply file the cut edges and then touch them in with the aid of a brush and would fit the bonnet halves to the car!'

In the beginning, Jimmy says, production was about eight TCs per day, but in due course, this was increased to a breathtaking 12 a day. Although these are small numbers in terms of later Abingdon output, they are substantial given the labour-intensive production methods used.

Nowhere was the impact of the post-war MG sports car more apparent than in North America. This Californian billboard advertisement likens the appeal of the TC Midget to that of the Stutz Bearcat of 30 years before. (Rover/BMIHT)

The MG TC was an instant hit in the company's export markets, where the vast majority were sold. (Rover)

days, he was often called upon by Syd Enever to produce drawings at Cowley, '...and although Syd would have liked me to transfer over to Abingdon when the drawing office was established, Cowley wouldn't let me go, and so it wasn't until the start of the sixties that I made it to Abingdon.'

In the six-month development process that followed, many changes were made to the pre-war TB Midget, resulting in a car that was clearly much improved, but little different to the untrained eye. The TC retained the traditional MG timber-framed body, but to improve interior space, that body was widened by 4in (10.16cm) across the seats, taking its cue from the pre-war Tickford TA. Other significant alterations included abandoning the pre-war, sliding-trunnion leaf-spring mounting—which had been vulnerable to the effects of inadequate greasing—changing the type of shock absorbers, and replacing the twin 6-volt batteries in front of the rear axle with a single 12-volt battery on the scuttle. Essentially, the engine remained unchanged, being the 1250cc XPAG unit that had been introduced in the TB Midget in 1939. Before long, this engine would find a home in Abingdon's second new post-war model.

The first pre-production TC, number 0251 ('Abingdon 251' was the MG plant's telephone number), was completed in September 1945, and soon the first batch of cars was rolling off the production line. Even at this stage, before the government led export drive, MG was forced to seek overseas sales through Nuffield's export division, as there were few customers at home. There is a popular romantic notion that the TC Midget was sold in astonishing numbers in North America, having been taken there by returning GIs. However, while it is true that the TC did a great deal to establish the affectionate position held by the marque in American hearts, it was the TC's successor, the all-new TD of 1950, that would fuel MG's remarkable North American success story. In fact, no TCs were officially exported to the USA until 1947, and even then, only six cars crossed the Atlantic. Having said that, Nuffield Exports statistics show that 20 cars made it to the USA in 1946, and 234 in the following year, proving that interest there was growing rapidly.

At first, the most profitable export markets were found in the old 'Empire' countries, such as Australia and South Africa, and it was not until 1948 that US sales significantly outstripped these areas. In December of that year, Abingdon finally produced an official US-specification TC Midget—the EX-U model—with a few concessions to American demands, such as twin wind-tone horns, modified lighting, and front and rear bumpers that were similar in con-

cept to those of the subsequent TD. The steering wheel, however, remained resolutely aligned on the right-hand side of the dashboard. Two significant events occurred in 1948 and 1949 that did much to shape MG's destiny, as they did many other British car manufacturers. In February 1948, George Strauss, the Labour Government's Minister for Supply, announced that steel would only be allocated to car manufacturers who exported over 75 per cent of their output. Then, in September 1949, the government devalued the pound sterling, from $4.03 to $2.80, giving British exports to the USA a dramatic boost: 1949 sales were double those of 1946 as a result.

In the meantime, however, events at Abingdon and Cowley led to MG struggling to maintain its very existence, just as the American markets were beginning to open up. Had the TC in particular, and the YA and TD that followed, not been the successes they proved to be, the Abingdon flame might have been snuffed out three years after the end of the war.

Second post-war MG: the Y-type saloon

The outbreak of World War 2 had led to MG shelving plans for a new small saloon, so it was almost inevitable that the company would carry on with this project from where it had left off. The larger pre-war MG saloons—the SA, VA and WA—had no place in the Nuffield scheme of things post-war, so they were dropped, along with the last vestiges of Cecil Kimber's influence, since he had had a hand in their design. For the immediate post-war period at least, it was decided that there would only be scope for a single MG saloon, and that would be a development of the MG Ten, which had been abandoned in 1939. For the production MG Y-type, as it was christened, the Wolseley-like wheels of the pre-war prototype were discarded, and the engine was rationalized with the XPAG unit of the contemporary TC Midget.

The EX-Register refers to a 1.25-litre MG saloon under the code number EX166, and includes an entry for a car with the Cowley experimental chassis number EX/MG/76, together with a 'guarantee plate' dated 7 January, 1945. It is possible that this car was the pre-war MG Ten prototype, supposedly driven throughout the war by Sir Miles Thomas, and thereafter used as the basis of the design of the MG Y-type. Also listed in the EX-Register are three further

THE ZAGATO AND CASTAGNA Y-TYPES

Before World War 2, there had been a proliferation of coachbuilders offering special bodywork on proprietary chassis, but when hostilities ceased, this practice never took off to the same degree. In Britain, at least, new cars for the home market were something of a rare commodity, while the gradual move away from separate chassis frames for small cars meant that coachbuilt cars, usually on Rolls-Royce or Daimler chassis, became the exclusive province of the very rich.

On the Continent, however, some of the well-known coachbuilders remained in business, even if their financial status was not always particularly strong. They were able to take advantage of skilled work-forces, low costs and loopholes in import tax legislation, which meant that chassis could be imported with fewer penalties than complete cars.

During this period, a number of those coachbuilders experimented with MG chassis—notably from the TD and YA models—and exhibited their work at the various European 'salons' in the hope of securing orders. One of the more unusual examples was the Zagato-bodied YA shown below, which was displayed at the Lugano Salon in 1949, and of which, unfortunately, only one example was built.

Also produced at around the same time was the rather more elegant, one-off YA drophead by Castagna of Milan, which bore some resemblance to the later Bertone-bodied Arnolt-MG. This car survives in the USA, but the whereabouts of the Zagato-bodied car are not known.

Below and bottom An unusual attempt to produce a 'modern' coupé on the Y-type chassis, built by Zagato. Note the curved glass, a rarity in the 1940s, and the lack of an external luggage compartment lid. (Rover)

entries: EX168, EX169 and EX170, which bore the respective chassis numbers EX/MG/125, 126 and 127. It is worth noting that these EX chassis numbers fall within a Cowley scheme, rather than an Abingdon system: Morris Motors commonly used EX-prefixed numbers as prototype chassis numbers, and it is easy to confuse the Cowley numbers with the quite unrelated EX-Register. Jimmy Cox remembers a pre-production Y-type, possibly an MG Ten, being used at Abingdon well in advance of production: 'It was a black car, registered KWL 200, and was run by "Tubby" Reid as a "garage car", Tubby being in charge of the garage.'

Abingdon was still regarded by Cowley as little more than a satellite factory, so it is hardly surprising that the definitive project code for what became the Y-type saloon was the Cowley code DO914. Sadly, large parts of the original DO list have either been lost or are insufficiently detailed to allow precise identification of dates, but the fact that DO920 and 921 were codes for the post-war Morris Oxford and Wolseley 4/50 leads one to suspect that DO914 dates from the 1945-46 period, some time before the launch of the production car.

As described earlier, the styling of the MG Y-type was governed largely by economic expediency, and its humble Morris Series E origins were difficult to disguise. Kimber's influence was barely discernible, but despite the fact that the car lacked the undeniable grace of its illustrious forebears, the result had an understated, conventional appearance that was ideal for the conservative, post-war Empire. Unlike its near contemporaries, the state-of-the-art Standard Vanguard and Morris Minor, with their flowing wings and full-width body styling, the Y-type clearly displayed its pre-war roots. It had separate headlamps, a narrow upright body and a tall, square imposing radiator grille. Of course, an MG saloon with modern styling would have looked strange alongside the decidedly pre-war styling of the TC sports car, so the Y-type saloon was given a warm, if hardly ecstatic, reception when it first appeared in public in May 1947.

The Y-type was quite a departure for MG, in that the bodies arrived at the factory almost totally bare, unlike those of the TC, which came trimmed. Fortunately, in 1942, Jack Hayward—a trimmer by trade—had arrived at the factory to teach women workers to weld, and he had stayed on after the war. When Cecil Cousins found out that he was a trimmer, he was asked to help with the Y-type. 'The TC came in trimmed, but the saloons didn't,' remembers Hayward. 'To start with, "Cis" Cousins wanted to keep the girls separate on the upper deck, and so I was charged with teaching them how to trim the cars—everything which had to be fitted to the car before mounting the body on the chassis—which included fitting the lights and window glass, etc.'

As men who had been away in the forces started returning to MG, some of the company's more recent employees, including many of the women, were forced to leave, as these men had been guaranteed jobs upon their return. Jimmy Cox also recalls the difficult times caused by the infamous winter of 1947, when severe weather combined with a shortage of fuel led to many being laid off for quite a long time—without pay, of course: 'Everybody was laid off except the tea-boys, who were kept on to keep the plant going for several weeks.'

Developments at Morris Motors: the Mosquito project

Although the roots of the MG Y-type were very much grounded in the pre-war Morris 10, the Nuffield Organization had bold plans for their post-war model range. The most significant model within this range would be the Morris Minor, the origins of which lay in 1941 proposals that led to the Mosquito prototypes. These were developed from 1943 onwards by a small team comprising Alec Issigonis, Jack Daniels and Reg Job, under the watchful eye of Miles Thomas. However, Lord Nuffield soon became an arch opponent of the car, which from the start dispensed with the traditional upright radiator grille and tall, narrow bodywork that were typical of most pre-war British cars.

Several lessons learned from pre-war MG designs were incorporated into the Mosquito—such as independent front suspension using torsion bars for springing—and, of course, Jack Daniels had been at Abingdon before transferring to Cowley. Within a year of

HOW THE R-TYPE HELPED WITH THE MORRIS MINOR

By 1943, Alec Issigonis, aided by Jack Daniels (on the chassis) and Reg Job (on the body) began working on the Mosquito, which had independent front suspension (plans for an independent rear were abandoned at an early stage). 'We were aware of a patent taken out by Maurice Olley on behalf of General Motors,' remembers Daniels, 'which talked about the roll centre being raised only marginally above ground level, then needing inclusion of an anti-roll medium. Now, with parallel wishbones, the roll centre is at the ground; that was why the R-type had rolled so badly, although we didn't know that at the time. By the time of the Mosquito/Minor, being aware of this patent, we decided to make the torsion bars stronger to avoid using anti-roll bars. Subsequently, we had a request from a number of companies—Singer, Daimler and Standard—who, with IFS vehicles in the field, were having trouble with General Motors litigation, and they paid for us to take Bill Renwick's anti-roll patent and see legal counsel for an opinion on it. GM were asking £100 per car against their patent!'

Daniels went with the Cowley patent agent to brief the top engineering lawyer, who eventually opined that the Renwick patent predated five out of the six points of the GM patent, the exception being that Renwick's patent failed to define its total function. In the meantime, GM had backed down and cut their claim to 2 cents per 100 dollars cost of each car, which was acceptable to everyone. Bill Renwick's work had saved the day.

the first ideas being formulated, the Mosquito prototype was up and running, using a Morris side-valve engine for power, pending development of an all-new, flat-four engine which, at that stage, was intended for production.

The initial Mosquito prototype, which already bore a strong resemblance to the Morris Minor that would emerge four years later, was a two door. By the beginning of 1946, however, other variants began to appear, including a four-door saloon and a convertible. Before long, there would be longer-wheelbase versions, which could have become Wolseley or MG derivatives, or both! The Wolseley version was labelled 'Wasp', while the MG variant appears to have been referred to as the MG 1100, although it is unlikely that this name would have been adopted. The Wolseley version was to have been fitted with a more conventional, in-line four-cylinder engine, which would have been used in the MG, too. In surviving photographs, the latter appears to have the same basic body as that of the Wolseley, but with an MG Y-type grille substituted for the Wolseley unit: badge engineering in its crudest and, perhaps, most cynical form.

In parallel with the Mosquito programme was the so-called Intermediate range. Eventually, this would include the Morris Oxford and Wolseley 4/50. The MG grille also appears to have been applied to prototypes of this project. Indeed, the idea appears to have resurfaced, either in 1947 or 1948, with a smooth-fronted MG proposal, the nose of which resembled that of the contemporary Midget Major sports car, of which more anon.

The MG Mosquito emerges

During 1946-47, various delays and prevarication by management were accompanied by concerns about the cost of the new car, and the need to avoid interfering with the sales of existing products. Before long, this led to some quite extraordinary ideas, which had direct implications for the MG marque. In the third edition of his excellent book, *Morris Minor—the World's Supreme Small Car*, Paul Skilleter quotes from Sir Miles Thomas' papers, uncovered in 1988, in which Sir Miles records that he suggested to the Nuffield board that the anticipated costs of the Mosquito could be covered by marketing the car as an MG: 'MG owners are not averse to paying a little more. In return, they expect novelty, which the "Mosquito" would provide.'

MG's manager, H. A. Ryder, was somewhat surprised at this suggestion, and argued that he could not easily accommodate production of the Mosquito at the Abingdon works, where the TC was being built and the launch of the Y-type was just months away.

Left *This rather ungainly proposal was an attempt to marry the longer nose of the Wolseley Wasp derivative of the Mosquito (Minor) with an 'aerodynamic' interpretation of the MG grille... (Rover)*

Below *...which was hardly any less hideous than this proposal. In this case, an ill fitting MG Y-type radiator grille has been mounted on the front. (Rover)*

Facing page, top *Cowley's stylists obviously found it difficult to marry an MG nose with the Mosquito body, as this quarter-scale model illustrates. (Rover)*

Facing page, bottom *What are we to make of this monstrosity? A Y-type radiator grille has been crudely grafted on to the nose of a Morris Oxford mock-up. Surely they weren't serious... (Rover)*

Nevertheless, Lord Nuffield's antipathy to the Mosquito in its Morris version made Sir Miles determined to push through at least one derivative of the project, so he tried another angle. Morris Motors' S. V. Smith was asked by Sir Miles whether it would be possible for the Mosquito to be built at Cowley, alongside the Morris 8, but then driven to Abingdon, where it would be road tested and marketed as an MG. Despite strong protestations from Ryder, this idea was approved, the planned introduction date being 1 January, 1948.

By June 1947, a month, incidentally, after the Y-type saloon had been launched, further prevarication resulted in a plan for rationalizing the Mosquito range. As a result, the flat-four engine was dropped, along with the Wolseley Wasp. The MG 1100 was retained, however, and was slated for launch in March 1948 as a two-door saloon with a derivative of the ZC11W in-line four-cylinder engine originally planned for the Wolseley Wasp (and which later would be considered for the Midget Major idea). It should be noted that throughout the period when the MG 1100 proposal was

being progressed, Lord Nuffield was championing his preference for a facelifted version of the pre-war Morris E instead of a Morris version of Mosquito.

In the late summer of 1947, the British government made representations to the car industry, suggesting that model ranges should be limited (by the following February, these proposals would be overtaken by the rationing of steel supplies). As a result, the Nuffield board met in September 1947 to consider the proposal, and Lord Nuffield clearly saw it as an opportunity to kill off the Mosquito project for good: accordingly, the MG 1100 was suspended, never to re-emerge.

By this stage, internal conflicts were coming to a head, and it was not long before a revised Mosquito was put forward. The fact that so much money had already been invested in the project—including a great deal of the tooling—eventually persuaded Lord Nuffield to relent and allow the Morris version to proceed. By December 1947, it had been christened Minor, a traditional Morris name, no doubt intended to placate Lord Nuffield, but also chosen because of

various other claims to the Mosquito trade mark. For the time being, therefore, MG continued much as before, many of its staff perhaps blissfully unaware of how near an MG built by Morris Motors had come to fruition.

Power struggles at Cowley

Despite his long association with Lord Nuffield—dating back to 1924—Miles Thomas, the chairman and one of the pivotal forces in the Nuffield Organization, often crossed swords with his boss after his promotion in 1940. These conflicts finally came to a head on 19 November, 1947, when he abruptly resigned. Thomas' departure caused repercussions throughout the organization, and many old faces disappeared in the first of a series of management upheavals that presaged the events of the early 1950s. With Thomas' resignation, effective control of the Nuffield Organization passed to Reginald Hanks, a long serving employee who had been head of the increasingly important Nuffield Exports business since the end of the war.

Hanks attempted to get to grips with the much needed rationalization within the company. One of the first actions of the new management was to dispense with the services of no less than eight long serving and distinguished board members, among them Victor Riley (who had joined Nuffield with Riley just before the war) and MG's H. A. Ryder, who had so recently helped the Abingdon factory to get back into production upon the cessation of hostilities. Significant among the survivors were Victor Oak and S. V. Smith, both of whom had an important part to play in the Mosquito project, and who would soon hold sway over MG affairs.

Much of the Nuffield Organization remained a loose amalgam of almost autonomous companies, a situation that would cause problems for British Leyland some 20 years later. With the requirement for British car manufacturers to export the major part of their output, coupled with the post-war climate of austerity, it was obvious that some rationalization of the group's operations was desirable. Even so, the pressure to maximize output made such a move painful to contemplate.

Cowley stumbles: the MG YT tourer

In an effort to recapture the sales success of the pre-war VA tourer, and with an eye on increased sales in the all-important export mar-

ket, it was not long before the Cowley drawing office began work on an open derivative of the Y-type saloon. The theory behind what became the YT ('T' for tourer) was all very well, but sadly its execution was bedevilled by the staunchly conservative and upright styling of the saloon upon which it was based. By fitting the more powerful twin-carburettor engine from the TC Midget, coupled with a weight saving of several hundred pounds, the YT should have been moderately successful, but the car's looks were, as Wilson McComb said, 'about as sporting in appearance as the average bath tub.' This was unfortunate, because the stylists had clearly worked hard, within almost impossible restraints, to marry elements of the VA tourer with the nose, wings and basic structure of the Y-type saloon.

That they had failed to produce a thing of great beauty, however, was in little doubt. The YT was never officially sold in the UK, and although a few found their way to enthusiastic customers in parts of the old British Empire, only 877 were built between the launch in October 1948 and the end of production in 1950. There is little

Above *The YT tourer was launched in October 1948, with export sales in mind. In the event, it proved an underwhelming success, only 877 examples being built. Note the door line: an attempt to emulate that of the pre-war VA tourer. (courtesy Graham Robson)*

Below *In 1946-47, Cowley was considering this two-seater sports car, DO926, based upon the floorpan and running gear of the forthcoming Mosquito (Morris MInor), and which might have been fitted with the still-born 1100cc overhead-cam ZC11G engine. (Rover)*

Facing page *Here, the DO926 Midget Major, with a convertible hood rather than a hardtop, as shown below, is lined up in the Cowley viewing area among the proposed Nuffield car range for 1948, between the MG YT tourer and the Morris Minor. (Rover)*

doubt that, while it was welcomed by a car-hungry market, the YT did little to strengthen Morris Motors' case for continuing to determine MG's fate.

The Nuffield ideas for MG of 1948-49

The coming of the Morris Minor, in October 1948, signalled a wave of new cars that would appear towards the end of the decade and into the next, but as part of this process of renewal came the end of several Morris and Wolseley models and, even more significantly for MG perhaps, the discontinuation of their associated engines, gearboxes and axles. This, more than any other factor, would determine the path of the MG marque in the coming years. Nevertheless, the Nuffield group, flushed with the successful reception accorded the new Morris Minor and Oxford, proceeded

with tentative plans for derivatives for the coming decade. Thankfully, thoughts of MG-badged Morris Minors and Oxfords were soon abandoned, but even so, MG cars still ranked rather low in Cowley's order of priorities: Leonard Lord's pre-war epithet of 'tarted up Morrises and Wolseleys' still echoed around the offices at Cowley. Despite this situation, serious thought was given to developing possible MGs that would be merely 'sporting', rather than the out-and-out sports cars with which the marque was more popularly associated.

Different ideas for a way forward were considered by the Cowley management, initially without any direct reference to the Abingdon management. As they saw it, any new MG would have to be based upon components that could be shared with other products of the Nuffield Organization. There were two favoured options. One was for a new MG to be designed around the Morris Minor and the planned family of related cars (largely swept away after the 1952 BMC merger). However, unlike previous proposals of this type, which called for badge engineered variants, the suggestion was for a uniquely bodied car that, presumably, could have been built at either Cowley or Abingdon. The second, fundamentally different option, involved merging MG with Riley (both had sporting traditions) to expand the use of the under-utilized, and largely unique, Riley running gear and to provide more work for Morris Bodies Branch.

The MG Midget Major

Plans were drawn up for the Mosquito related proposal, after which quarter-scale models and full-size mock-ups were built. However, with the exception of the so-called Midget Major two-seater sports car, nothing much came of them.

Undoubtedly, the Midget Major would have shared many components with the Morris Minor and the proposed Wolseley variant which, at that stage, was intended to use a new 1100cc overhead-cam engine. This was related to both the 1476cc unit of the Wolseley 4/50 and the 2215cc Morris Six/Wolseley 6/80 six-cylinder engine; sensible rationalization was obviously in hand. For the Wolseley variant of the Minor, this engine was coded ZC11W (the 'W' suffix referring to Wolseley). For the Midget Major, the engine would have been of a different, more sporting tune and would have borne the code ZC11G (the 'G' suffix relating to MG in normal Cowley engine parlance). However, there must have been grave doubts about the reception that the Midget Major was likely to receive in the increasingly important US market, and it is certain

that Abingdon must have loathed it, if indeed they were even aware of the car.

The battle of Abingdon and Foleshill

Riley had been a proud and independent company, which had run out of money shortly before World War 2. Lord Nuffield had bought the company principally as a means of preventing it from falling into the hands of his rivals, but little had changed since then, despite the departure of Victor Riley in December 1947. The company remained fiercely independent and largely self-contained, building distinctive cars with unique Riley engines, axles and chassis, the bodywork being assembled using old-fashioned coach-building techniques. The second of the two options for MG's future was for MG production to be transferred from Abingdon to the Riley factory at Foleshill, Coventry, and the Abingdon plant turned over to some other use—perhaps as a satellite to the Morris Motors facility at Cowley (presaging a similar idea that would be proposed just over 30 years later!). Both the Riley RM saloon and the MG TC Midget used timber-framed steel bodies produced by Morris Motors Bodies Branch at Coventry, which specialized in such coachwork. Consequently, there was an undeniable logic in combining both companies under one roof, in a factory not far from the body production facility.

Needless to say, as soon as they got wind of these ideas, the MG management at Abingdon mounted a strong campaign to convince their masters at Cowley of their folly. George 'Pop' Propert had become general manager at Abingdon following Cecil Kimber's departure (Ryder, and later Smith, being based at Cowley), and it fell to him and service manager John Thornley to defend Abingdon's interests. Propert put forward the argument that it would be more logical for the proposal to be reversed: to shift Riley production to Abingdon and turn the Riley factory over to Morris Engines, allowing them to expand their Coventry facilities. During this period (June to October 1948), a scheme for a possible MG family of related vehicles—coded DO963, 965 and 967—was developed by a stylist who was only at Cowley for a year or so. These proposals are all labelled as 1.5-litre cars, so it is a fair assumption that their engines would have been contemporary Riley units of that capacity.

Jim O'Neill recalls that the stylist was Stan Bletchley, and that he was ably assisted by a body layout draughtsman from Vauxhall named Welton. Gerald Palmer, who eventually returned to Cowley, recalls that the idea behind these proposals had indeed been to pro-

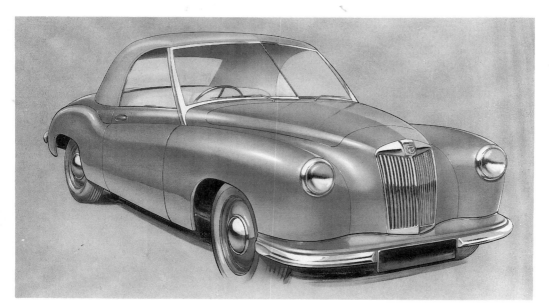

Left *This is an original styling sketch for the DO963 MG Midget, possibly intended for production alongside the Rileys at the Foleshill factory. (Rover)*

Below *The Cowley development shop produced this quarter-scale model of DO963, shown here with the hood removed. (Rover)*

duce a lower-volume 'coachbuilt' car, in the manner of the RM-series Rileys, with the intention of replacing the Y-type. Although he was not involved in its design, Palmer does recall that the two-door saloon version was built as a running prototype. Apparently, Bletchley himself used to drive around in it. This prototype was still around when Palmer returned to Cowley—he remembers driving it—and it featured a grained leathercloth finished roof, again rather like the RM Rileys. Two of Palmer's assistants, Jim O'Neill and Denis Williams, also remember this car. O'Neill recalls that it had a false wooden sill to make it look lower, and Williams that it was finished in pale metallic green with a beige roof.

By November 1948, a month after the launch of the Cowley designed, but Abingdon built, YT Tourer, matters were coming to a head. Both Abingdon and Foleshill were under close scrutiny by the Nuffield management, and a decision was imminent. One day that month, Propert's number two, Cecil Cousins, was asked to take Tom Richardson, the chief planning engineer from Morris Motors, on a guided tour of the Abingdon plant. Cousins—whose life revolved around MG—would later recall how he kept emphasizing Abingdon's successful production track record. Unbeknown to Cousins, Richardson was on a fact finding mission, and his report would have a bearing on the decision regarding Abingdon's fate: tentative plans had already been drawn up at this stage, which could have transferred MG production from Abingdon to Foleshill in March 1949. Without doubt, the favourable report that

Richardson produced, coupled with much behind-the-scenes activity by John Thornley and others, saved the day—the almost unthinkable severance of MG from Abingdon was avoided.

Before long, the Nuffield board acted almost exactly as George Propert had suggested, moving Riley production from Coventry to Abingdon (and engineering responsibility to Cowley), and turning the Foleshill factory over to engine work with effect from May 1949. In July 1949, Propert retired, being replaced by Jack Tatlow from Riley. Many of the Riley engineers found themselves transferred to Cowley, where they had to make the best of a situation that must hardly have been to their liking, particularly their chief engineer, Harry Rush. Notable among those who never moved from Foleshill to Abingdon was 39-year-old Eddie Maher, who stayed on to play an important part in the Nuffield (and later BMC) engine programme at Morris Engines at Courthouse Green.

More changes at Cowley

At some point around the end of 1948, Stan Bletchley, the stylist responsible for the 1948 Riley-based MG proposals, left the Nuffield Organization and, although he had not been an engineer, for a short time he had wielded some influence over MG design. His departure, therefore, left a gap in the Cowley design hierarchy. At the same time, Gerald Palmer learned that Nuffield were looking for a new designer and, following an interview with Reginald Hanks, he returned to Cowley from his sojourn at Jowett.

Right *Related to the smaller DO963, and sharing most of its exterior sheet metal forward of the windscreen, was this proposal—DO965— for a 1.5-litre MG two-door sports saloon with leathercloth roof. A full-size version was built based on this basic style, and was still around when Gerald Palmer returned to Cowley in 1949. (courtesy Denis Williams)*

Below *In October 1948, this third derivative was added to the proposed family of MGs. DO967 was described as an MG 1½-litre convertible coupé. (Rover)*

Gerald was asked to set up an MG design office at Cowley (still not at Abingdon, you will note), which he did, establishing it with Jim O' Neill in charge of body design and Bob Shirley overseeing chassis development. Palmer recalls his astonishment at being given almost as much free rein as he had enjoyed at Jowett, with the instruction to come up with ideas. At this point, the few Riley designers who had come to Cowley began to drift back to Coventry, leaving only Harry Rush, who was forced to share an office with Gerald Palmer. Relations between Rush and Palmer became a little strained as a result, but the arrangement did not last long, for on Christmas Eve 1949, Harry Rush was tragically killed while returning home to his family. As a consequence, responsibility for Riley design was suddenly added to Palmer's portfolio.

Abingdon proposes a TC replacement
All the while that Cowley was playing with their future, the men at Abingdon (especially people from MG's heyday, such as Syd Enever, Cecil Cousins and Alec Hounslow) felt increasingly frustrated in their ambitions to be masters of their own destiny. By 1949, however, the wind of change was sweeping through the Nuffield Organization. It may have been this, coupled with the disappointment of the YT tourer, and the abandonment of the Midget Major and Riley-MG proposals, that led to the Abingdon team being asked to submit a proposal for a new sports car.

Abingdon's simple solution was to take a Y-type saloon chassis,

shorten its wheelbase of 8ft 10in (2.69m) to the 7ft 10in (2.39m) of the TC Midget, and to crudely mount a TC body on the result. No photographs are known to survive of this rough-and-ready prototype, built in about a week in the MG experimental shop by Billy Wilkins, under the direction of Alec Hounslow and Henry Stone. However, its appearance must have been a little strange, bearing in mind the considerably wider track of the Y-type chassis compared to that of the TC. Before long, the Abingdon prototype was inspected by Victor Oak, chief engineer at Cowley, who clearly was impressed by the concept of the car, if not its execution. Within another fortnight, it had been reworked sufficiently for it to be given broad approval by the Cowley management, and the idea was adopted as the basis for a new MG sports car to replace the TC.

Jim O'Neill
One of many pivotal figures in post-war MG history is Jim O'Neill, who began his career in the car business in 1936, when he joined the Pressed Steel Company, at Cowley, as an engineering draughtsman. He worked on body designs for the many manufacturers served by Pressed Steel at the time, such as Hillman, Standard and, of course, Morris Motors, whose factory was virtually next door. Jim recalls that, in those early days, a great deal of work was necessary between receiving a client's drawings and commissioning the very expensive tooling: 'All the bodies were redrawn on 18ft (5.49m) long draughts with great accuracy, laying in highlight lines

at various angles to prove the body shape.' In later years, this method of designing tooling fell into disuse, as styling clays were measured manually and, later, electronically; today, everything is computer designed.

Jim spent his first 18 months in the die machining shop, after which he transferred to the drawing office, setting the seal on the next 50 years of his career. 'My first job there was detailing two small brackets for an MG car. Little did I realize then that most of my future career would be with the MG Car Company, rising to the position of chief body engineer.' During the war, Jim was involved in the various Morris Motors projects for the war effort, and he recalls the work done by Alec Issigonis on the Mosquito prototype. In 1948, he decided to broaden his experience and left Nuffield for

---

'GOLDIE' GARDNER AND THE EX135 RECORD BREAKER

With the coming of the war, EX135 was dismantled and stored at the St Helen's Clothing factory. When that factory was destroyed by fire, in 1944, most of the car was saved, including the 750cc engine, but the 1100cc engine was damaged beyond repair. Thus, when record breaking efforts were rekindled in 1946, a fair amount of ground had to be re-covered. Post-war Germany was hardly the most suitable venue for record attempts, so when it was suggested that there was a suitable road at Jabbeke, in Belgium, Gardner and his associates leapt at the opportunity. The local Belgian authorities were also enthusiastic, agreeing a 5km (3.11-mile) stretch for Gardner to use. On 30 October, 1946, EX135 ran with a Chris Shorrock designed supercharger and raised the Class 'H' (750cc) records to impressive heights, including no less than 159.15mph (256.12km/h) for the flying mile.

By this stage, however, 'Goldie' was not particularly happy with the top echelon of MG management. No doubt, this was partly a reaction to the shoddy way in which the Nuffield management had treated Cecil Kimber, but it was also because Harold Ryder was not interested in record attempts. Therefore, while EX135 ran with an MG engine in 1946 and 1947, these outings were without direct involvement from Abingdon, although Enever and Jackson were still permitted to help prepare the car at the factory.

During 1947, EX135 ran with two cylinders blanked off to produce a 500cc engine, opening up the possibility of an attack on the existing record of 106mph (170.59km/h), held by Count Lurani in a Nibbio. However, Gardner and MG could not agree as to how the modification should be effected, so the work was carried out away from the MG factory. In 1948, if anything, the situation became worse, as Gardner took EX135 to Jabbeke with a Jaguar engine. By the following year, however, cordial relations had been re-established—no doubt, helped by the efforts of John Thornley, who by then was assistant general manager—and EX135 flew MG's colours once more on 15 September, 1949, when it took three international class records. This time, the engine was the six-cylinder MG, but with a special crankshaft designed by Syd Enever and linked to pistons in only three cylinders. Thus equipped, EX135 added the Class 'I' (500cc) record to its portfolio, with 154.23mph (248.20km/h) over the mile.

Following an appearance at the New York Motor Show, in mid-April 1950, the car returned to Jabbeke in July, this time with only two pistons, reducing its capacity to 330cc (to attempt the 350cc Class 'J' record). At first, there were problems with the time keeping equipment, echoing George Eyston's runs at Pendine 28 years before. However, Gardner persevered and, eventually, EX135, with its remarkable, obsolete K3-based engine, added yet another string of records to its credit. Successful outings for this veteran combination of car and driver would continue in 1950 and 1951, using an XPAG engine—as fitted to contemporary production Midgets—and a six-cylinder unit derived from the Wolseley 6/80 (to attack the 2-litre Class 'E' records). Then, an unfortunate accident during a run at Bonneville, in August 1952, prompted Gardner's retirement from record breaking at the age of 67.

Before long, there would be a new record breaker—EX179—and George Eyston would return as champion of the salt flats. In later years, EX135 was bought back by MG and modified at Abingdon for display purposes. Johnny Lay cut holes in the bodywork and let in perspex panels, in which state it survives today

---

the rival Austin Motor Company at Longbridge, where he worked under Dick Burzi. 'We had an exciting programme, or so we thought at the time. Dick Burzi had produced an attractive, small coloured drawing of a convertible which was planned for the American market, which became the Austin Atlantic...'

Origins of the definitive MG TD Midget

Although happy at Austin, after about 12 months, Jim O'Neill move back to Morris Motors for financial reasons. Upon his return, he found that the company was heavily embroiled in designing new Morris and Wolseley cars, but an instruction had just come through to develop a replacement for the TC Midget, a task that largely fell to Jim. The brief from assistant chief body draughtsman Tom Ramsay (who had been responsible for both the TC and Y-type bodyshell) was to produce a body shape that was less angular than the TC and more squat, using the front suspension of the Y-type saloon with a new chassis design by Jack Daniels.

It has been suggested by others that the staff at Abingdon were responsible for engineering the TD Midget, possibly prompted by the fact that they produced the 'cut-and-shut' mock-up on a Y-type chassis. Jim O'Neill was at pains to remind me that there was no proper drawing office at Abingdon when the TD was drawn up, so all vehicle design and development was carried out at Cowley. Consequently, the project was given a Cowley experimental code in the Drawing Office series—DO968—rather than an Abingdon code in the famous EX series, and it benefited from far more comprehensive engineering development facilities than were available to the Abingdon team when hastily producing the mock-up. These led to a substantially modified chassis, which swept up and over the rear axle rather than beneath it, as was the case for the Y-type.

Jim recalls that the major priorities at Cowley were not MGs, but rather the new Morris and Wolseley cars being developed for the 1950s, and that nobody in authority ever came to enquire how the DO968 was progressing: 'Vic Oak, the technical director at Cowley, used to go around all the Morris drawing boards, but he never even stopped to look at my drawing. I concluded that Morris Motors were just not interested in MG.' Strictly speaking, of course, this was not true, for the company had dabbled with a number of serious exercises (and some surely not so serious!) while Jim was at Austin. Nevertheless, it was clear that the company's priorities lay elsewhere.

When Jim had almost finished the body layout for the TD Midget, he was told by Tom Ramsay—the only person at Cowley to take an interest—that John Thornley, at that stage still only the MG service manager, would be arriving to have a quick look at what Cowley was planning for MG. This was the first time that Jim O'Neill and John Thornley met, and Jim recalls being impressed with Thornley's genuine interest and knowledge: 'I do not know, to this day, how much he understood when looking at the complicated lines of the body layout, but he made a point of asking if we could lower the tonneau line by half an inch (1.27cm). This would reduce the height above the rear wing and give an even more squat appearance. I did this while he was still there and, sure enough, it improved the shape considerably. With a "Leave to go, Sir?", he departed.' Here at last, Jim felt, was someone interested in what he was trying to achieve.

The Cowley TD prototype

Jim O'Neill's completed body layout was shipped to Morris Motors Bodies Branch at Coventry, where a hand built prototype body was produced. This was mounted on to Jack Daniels' chassis at Cowley for road proving. Unfortunately, although the prototype looked very attractive, all was not well structurally. The first road test report stated: 'Handling good, but impossible to read instruments at any speed.' Jim O'Neill was devastated. As a 28-year-old designer, he admits that he had no idea how to overcome this rather serious problem.

Tom Ramsay came to the rescue, suggesting that a sheet of 1/8in (0.32cm) thick steel plate be welded vertically from the chassis to the body dash, with a 12in (30.48cm) square hole for the driver's feet to reach the pedals. As Jim recalls, 'It cured the scuttle shake, but I am sure that nowadays no test driver would ever expect to work under such conditions!' For the production TD Midget, which appeared at the end of 1949, the steel sheet idea was impractical, so instead a tubular steel hoop was welded to the chassis frame in line with the dashboard. Interestingly enough, the roll-over protection provided by the hoop was subsequently touted by the company as a safety feature, making a virtue out of necessity!

The first production TD went down the line on 10 November, 1949, and heralded the beginning of a new higher-volume era in MG sports car output. Soon after, the 10,000th and final TC—chassis number 10,251—left the line. Just over a fifth of production had been exported to the USA, paving the way for MG's export success of the following decades.

Running changes to the saloon: the YB

Not long after the Y-type saloon, the YA, entered production, the Cowley drawing office began to consider an improved version. Work on what would become the YB began in 1949, after the battle over Abingdon's future had been settled. The DO-Register includes two entries for the YB—DO986 and DO998—although it is probable that these numbers refer only to mechanical developments for the car, rather than the complete vehicle. Launched in late 1951, the YB differed little in appearance from the YA, and although its suspension had been improved, largely as a result of work on the TD Midget, sales were far from earth shattering. Clearly, something more modern and ambitious was needed.

In the meantime, another figure, who would prove pivotal in the fortunes of the parent company, became involved in MG affairs. Charles Griffin had joined Wolseley Motors in 1940, following a BSA apprenticeship as a draughtsman in gun design. At the end of the European hostilities, he was given the responsibility of updating the suspension and steering system designs of all the vehicles that were to be produced after the war by the Nuffield group. Upon completion of this work, Griffin became the chief experimental engineer for Wolseley Motors, being responsible for proving work, among other things.

Charles Griffin recalls that the last vehicles he was involved with at Wolseley Motors were the pilot-production 4/50 and 6/80 cars, of which 100 and 25 respectively were built. At that point, production of Wolseley cars was transferred from Birmingham to Cowley, so Griffin transferred with many of the ex-Wolseley staff, assuming the function of deputy chief experimental engineer for the whole of the Nuffield Organization. Before long, he became

Jim O'Neill, pictured in 1995.

involved with MG: 'Quite soon after my arrival at Cowley, in Easter 1949, I was involved in the proving of the MG YB saloon and the TD Midget. I compared both vehicles with their predecessors: the TD was a vast improvement over the TC in ride and handling, but was plagued with scuttle shake.' Griffin felt that the scuttle shake was ameliorated only slightly by Jim O'Neill's tubular hoop, which he called the 'towel rail'!

Even as the modifications for the YB were being finalized, it was obvious that the coming decade would bring fresh ideas and raise customer expectations; changes would soon be in the air again.

George Phillips, a Fleet Street photographer, entered this special-bodied TC in the Le Mans 24-hour race in 1949, and again in 1950. In 1949, the car was disqualified when a mechanic hitched a lift back to the pits after curing an electrical fault out on the circuit. In 1950, it finished second in its class (18th overall), and this would inspire a rather special MG backed entry for 1951. (Rover/BMIHT)

3 The 1950s

Launched on 18 January, 1950, the TD Midget was given a warm reception by sports car enthusiasts everywhere. Although most of the car was new, it retained the 1250cc XPAG engine of its predecessor and, before long, this MG unit would become the sole survivor of its pre-war Nuffield engine family. Slightly more controversial to some die-hard traditionalists were the standard bumpers (similar to those already seen on the last US-market TCs) and—horror of horrors—15in (38.10cm) disc wheels in place of the spindly 19in (48.26cm) TC wires. However, the welcome increase in width, and the lower overall height, of the new car were clearly of significant benefit to both its handling and performance. It soon became obvious that if the TC had been worthy of competition use, the TD would be even more so.

TD sales got off to a good start, and with the company still concentrating on its export drive, well over 90 per cent of the 4767 TDs built in 1950 went overseas. More than half of those cars exported went to the USA.

Variations on a theme: the TD2 and the TD Mark II

There is often understandable confusion between two similarly badged versions of the TD which, in fact, were quite different in philosophy. The TD Mark II came about as a result of early competition exploits with the TD, whereas the TD2—which began production as a running change in August 1951—amounted to a batch of improvements to the standard engine and drive-train. Of the two variants, the Mark II, distinguished by its TDC (later TD3) chassis prefix, is probably the more interesting.

After trial runs in an early TD by George Phillips and Dick Jacobs, a series of modifications were made to a TD registered FMO 885. These changes amounted to the replacement of the early solid disc wheels with perforated items (later adopted for all TDs), improvements to the suspension, and the substitution of twin bucket seats for the normal single-backrest production item. Before long, alterations to the carburetion and engine compression ratio were added to this list.

In May 1950, at a race at Blandford Camp, Dick Jacobs took FMO 885 to a class win ahead of the redoubtable HRGs. This led Abingdon to rapidly sanction a production version—the Mark II. Three of these production cars—registered FRX 941, 942 and 943—were built at Abingdon for a team comprising Dick Jacobs, George Phillips and Ted Lund. A repeat of Jacobs' Blandford success against the HRGs just eluded him and his colleagues at Silverstone in August 1950, but the team achieved a highly creditable second, third and fourth in their class, behind the inevitable HRG in first place. A month later, in torrential rain at Northern Ireland's Dundrod circuit, the team achieved first, second and third in their class in the three-hour race. The EX-Register entry for EX171 of September 1950 refers to a 'TD Midget converted to road-racing specification for Dick Jacobs.' The 44 drawings listed cover the changes that led to the TD Mark II.

The early promise shown by the TD in these races—followed by the rapid rise in popularity of the car for competition and tuning in

The production MG TD Midget. (Rover)

EX172 was a specially-bodied TD built for George Phillips to race at the 1951 Le Mans race. The influences of this design on the later EX175,

EX182 and MGA are obvious. It is shown at Abingdon with Syd Enever at the wheel and Nuffield directors S. V. Smith and A. V. Oak. (Rover)

the USA—soon led the men at Abingdon to ponder the subject of future MGs. As a result, the next entry in the EX-Register, after the Jacobs' road-racer, would have even greater significance for the future of the marque.

Palmer makes his mark: the ZA Magnette

The post-war Nuffield management had demonstrated a singular lack of direction regarding the future of the MG marque, and while the men at Abingdon had their own ideas, of course, their opinions did not hold great weight at Cowley. Various half-hearted attempts at producing MG saloons based upon the Morris Minor and Oxford had soon faded away, as had the rather more interesting Riley-based ideas of 1948. However, the changes in management seen in

1949, combined with the saving of MG's Abingdon plant from extinction and, perhaps most significantly of all, the return of Gerald Palmer heralded an exciting new decade for MG.

Palmer considered that the best way forward would be to produce a closely related family of MG and Wolseley saloons, which would utilize components from the Nuffield cupboard, but share their own, more up-market coachwork. The shake-up of 1949 had seen Riley production transferred to Abingdon (and design responsibility to Cowley, but soon under Palmer's control). It had also seen Wolseley production shift from the old Ward End Wolseley factory to Cowley, along with design. Although engineering responsibility for the larger-volume part of Nuffield's car business—Morris and Wolseley—fell to Alec Issigonis, Palmer was

The pre-production prototype MG Z-series Magnette. Note the number-plate, which refers to its DO1010 drawing office code. Production

Magnettes would feature perforated wheels (with MG-badged hub caps), paired front driving lamps and front quarterlights. (Rover)

A studio shot of an early ZA Magnette, showing the twin driving lamps missing from the pre-production example. (Rover/BMIHT)

given design authority over an important slice of Nuffield's product range.

In Palmer's opinion, the best styling at the time was that of the Italian coachbuilders, and he cited the Bertone-bodied Arnolt-MG as a typical example, along with contemporary Lancias: 'Italian styling was simply outstanding—and had been so since before the war—and, in particular, Bertone, Farina, Zagato and so forth. I couldn't help being influenced by them; we had to capture some of their artistic flair, but maintain production possibilities, and that is what I tried to achieve.'

Thus, the basic shape of what would become the Z-series Magnette was evolved in 1949, the definitive style being basically that shown in Palmer's original sketch. Subsequently, this basic shape would be scaled up for the larger Riley Pathfinder and Wolseley 6/90 luxury cars, to be built at Abingdon and Cowley respectively, but the first priority was with the mid-sized MG and Wolseley as replacements for the YB and 4/50.

To differentiate the sporting MG version from the more patrician Wolseley, Palmer's idea was to raise the latter by 2in (5.08cm). Thus, the two cars proceeded, carrying the Cowley drawing office codes DO1010 and DO1028 for the MG Magnette and Wolseley 4/44 respectively. From the outset, it was decided that both the MG and the Wolseley would utilize derivatives of the 1.25-litre XPAG engine from the TD Midget, but with the BMC merger of 1952, these plans were changed.

Working under Palmer, by this time, was Jim O'Neill, who had been largely responsible for the production version of the TD Midget. O'Neill recalls how he first became involved with the Magnette: 'Gerry presented me with one of the most detailed quarter-scale drawings that I have seen. The engine and suspension were both minutely detailed, complete with body sections. This made laying out the full-size so much easier.'

Jim O'Neill also reminded me that because the Wolseley 4/44 appeared first, people assumed incorrectly that the MG Magnette was derived from it, whereas the opposite was the case: 'It was planned that the MG Magnette would be a derivative of the Wolseley, and many still think that this is so. In fact, the opposite is true. Issigonis—at this point, Palmer's counterpart with responsibility for engineering the Morris and Wolseley ranges—was so busy on his other models that, in the end, Palmer said to me: "We cannot wait any longer. This will be the Magnette, and the Wolseley can be raised 2in (5.08cm) with a special radiator grille to give the gentlemanly appearance demanded by sales." It was Cowley's decision to put the Wolseley into production before the Magnette, which led many people to think that the MG was developed from the 4/44.'

Obviously, the common-sense aim of rationalization lay behind Palmer's proposals, but in the event, the MG and Wolseley shared only their roofs, front doors and boot lids. With the difference in height, and the distinctive grilles at the front, every other panel was different. On the mechanical front, the MG and Wolseley were intended to share the Nuffield XPAG unit, but following the merger of Austin and Nuffield, in February 1952, a different complexion was placed upon the future of the Nuffield engine range. As a consequence, it was decided to proceed with the launch of the Wolseley in October 1952, but delay the MG version until it could be adapted to take the new Austin designed 1489cc B-series unit, derived from the 1947 1200cc Austin A40 engine.

The team working on the Wolseley included Des Jones (later to participate in the MGB programme at Abingdon) and Don Butler (of whom more anon), who worked under Ron French. With the Wolseley behind him, Des recalls being given the Magnette's hockey-stick-shaped chrome side finishers to produce by Jim O'Neill, working to Gerald Palmer's drawings. On the receiving end of Jim O'Neill's Morris Motors drawings was a young Pressed Steel draughtsman by the name of Don Hayter.

When launched in September 1953, the MG Magnette became the first BMC car to use the B-series engine, heralding a wide range of models that would rely upon the same basic design for over 25 years. The Wolseley, however, retained the XPAG engine for another three years, until the B-series unit appeared in a revised Wolseley 15/50 in June 1956.

Sports car ideas

With the Austin-Nuffield merger of 1952 behind them, the men at Cowley found that they could plan their future around a much wider array of raw material. It has often been stated that the stronger partner in the union of the two industry giants was Austin, but this would be an unfair generalization, which detracts from the different strengths each had to offer. At the time of the merger, it was natural that the Cowley people were keen to keep their own engines, so it is hardly surprising that they looked at ways of extending the use of some of their more desirable units while investigating the best that their former rivals could offer.

The surviving Cowley drawing office records show that, in the period following the merger, investigations were made into a 'new small Midget with AS3 engine' (DO1035); a 'TD Midget with Austin engine' (DO1041); and a 'Midget with 1½-litre Riley engine' (DO1042). The code 'AS3' against DO1035 refers to the Austin A30 saloon, introduced in October 1951 with the original 803cc version of the A-series engine, which shows that Cowley was clearly interested in the possibilities of this versatile little unit long before the Austin-Healey Sprite was thought of. Indeed, John Thornley later found that there was much enthusiasm among senior management for a small sports car: 'We had two shots at a "buzz box", but it wasn't possible to get down to anything like a viable price. By the time that the MGA was on the way, I found myself still under pressure to consider one.'

The Austin engine referred to against DO1041 was almost certainly the twin-carburettor, 50bhp (37.29kW)—at 5000rpm—1200cc unit fitted to the Jensen-bodied Austin A40 sports, and which was the precursor of the later B-series engine. The Riley engine in DO1042 was the 1466cc, classic twin-high-camshaft unit that dated back to 1934, and which generated 55bhp (41.01kW) at 4500rpm (compared with the TD Midget's 54bhp/40.27kW at 5200rpm). This was the engine that appears to have been proposed for the 'coachbuilt' MG family (DO963, 965 and 967) contemplated in 1948. The idea of using it in the TD may have been a last-ditch effort to save the last true Riley engine from extinction.

No doubt in a quest for improved performance, the Cowley designers also investigated the use of aluminium body panels for the existing TD Midget (DO1017). Before long, however, both the Cowley and Abingdon MG people began to home in on their own interpretations of what constituted a new sports car for the 1950s.

The Palmer Midgets

With the Magnette saloon under way, the energetic and talented Gerald Palmer came up with a brilliant concept for not one, but

THE RILEY PATHFINDER

Although obviously not an MG, the Riley Pathfinder was designed and built by many of the people who were intimately involved with contemporary MGs, so its story bears some relevance here. The Pathfinder was part of Gerald Palmer's two-pronged approach to rationalizing and modernizing the up-market part of the Nuffield range: the MG Magnette and Wolseley 4/44 formed one part of this plan, while the Riley Pathfinder and Wolseley 6/90 formed the other. It is believed that, at one stage, there were tentative thoughts about producing a Riley equivalent of the Magnette, which might have become the Riley Wayfinder, but that is digressing from the story. Responsible for developing Palmer's basic ideas were Jim O'Neill on bodywork, assisted by Denis Williams, who had moved over from Morris. In June 1950, Terry Mitchell joined the Nuffield Organization and, before long, would find himself involved in chassis development for the Pathfinder.

Eventually, the full-sized prototype of the Riley Pathfinder (DO999) was ready for inspection. It was intended that this would enter production first, followed by the Wolseley variant. Attached to the design office was a viewing studio where the board of directors could examine new proposals, and it was here that the wooden Pathfinder mock-up was presented for inspection. Jim O'Neill takes up the story: 'It so happened that Lord Nuffield was handing over the chairmanship to Leonard Lord on this day. During the viewing, Lord Nuffield asked me where the radiator filler cap was. I explained that it was on the header tank, under the bonnet, which gave the radiator grille a nice clean line. He insisted he wanted it on the top, like a traditional radiator. We

hurriedly mounted a cap on some clay and, yes, he thought that was fine.' At this point, O'Neill thought that he had heard the last of the matter, and asked Gerald Palmer if he could dispense with the cap: 'He smiled and said, "If you want to," so out it went.'

A few days later, O'Neill and his colleagues heard a great tirade coming from the studio: 'Amongst the "sailor's language" we could make out, "Where is it?" Denis Williams whispered to me, "It's Nuff; he's looking for his filler cap." The unfortunate person on the receiving end of all this was the studio cleaner who, of course, had no idea what Lord Nuffield was upset about: the blank look on the cleaner's face was making Lord Nuffield even more angry.' Jim O'Neill had think quickly on his way to the studio to rescue the unfortunate cleaner and pacify Lord Nuffield: 'As soon as I entered the studio, I was asked the same question, and to my eternal shame, I had to lie and say, "Oh, I have taken it off to draw it up." Lord Nuffield immediately calmed down, and I think that he was even a bit ashamed of himself for causing such a fuss. For anyone who knew Lord Nuffield in this frame of mind, he could have easily sacked the lot of us and closed the department down. The model was approved for production, complete with its "exterior filler cap", which we were able to adapt as a bonnet safety catch release.'

There is a postscript to this story: in August 1957, when the Riley 2.6 had been announced, complete with its BMC C-series six-cylinder engine in place of the old Riley four (and without the grille mounted bonnet opening catch!), Denis Williams received an anonymous 'in memoriam' card through the post. The words on the card, which Denis still has today, simply state: 'Lord, thy will be done.'

Photographed in the Morris Motors viewing room at Cowley, this is the first full-size mock-up of the Riley Pathfinder project, DO999 (note the false RLY 999 number-plate), as shown to Lord Nuffield. Note that the celebrated 'radiator cap' (see text) is not fitted at this point. (courtesy Denis Williams)

three related MG Midget models. The basic structure was designed to be clad in two different bodies, which shared many major components. The idea was to cater for different market sectors—the traditionalist MG customer and the modern sports car enthusiast—without the considerable risk and investment associated with producing entirely different cars or, for that matter, putting all the eggs in one basket in a market where customer preferences were not that well understood.

The first version offered a choice of two similar models, and featured traditional styling with separate front and rear wings. The rear wings were fairly open, in conventional MG sports car style, on one model, while the alternative had fared-in rear wings in a more modern manner. The second option, which would have been a more radical departure from MG sports car tradition, in the manner of the 1948 Morris Motors proposals, used the same central structure, but had fully fared-in wings with a streamlined body envelope. The result was a little cigar-shaped, but quite modern for its time.

'I had my head in the clouds at the time. I wanted to do an all-steel, monocoque two-seater sports car. I had to get Vic Oak's

agreement to start off development of the twin-cam engine, although he was on the point of retirement, and it was really as a corollary of that that I did the monocoque sports car,' recalls Palmer. He was aided in this endeavour by Nuffield Metal Products, who were responsible for the body of the monocoque Morris Minor: 'I had much encouragement by getting the drafting of the monocoque done at NMP. Their director, George Dono, was very supportive. Dono had also supported me with the Pathfinder. I suppose he was empire building, and the Pathfinder bodies were actually built at NMP, who had been established to build all-steel bodies, whereas Morris Bodies were still engaged in the steel-over-timber body methods.'

Palmer is justifiably proud of his designs, and there is no doubt that they could have been very successful if produced in the early years of the decade: 'I thought that whereas the American market appeared to show a preference for the traditional styling, exemplified by the T-series Midget, the European market would prefer a more modern style, resembling the best of the Italian efforts, such as the Alfa Romeo.'

THE LAST COACHBUILT MGS

THE INSKIP MG TD FOUR-SEATER

After World War 2, MG cars were sold in the USA through a number of local distributors, one of the major companies being J. S. Inskip Inc., based in New York City. Inskip decided to produce a four-seat conversion of the TD Midget, which was achieved by lengthening the chassis by 10in (25.4cm) and fitting longer doors with superior hinges. The result was exhibited at New York's International Motor Show in 1953, where it was offered at $2925.

While undoubtedly considerably more attractive than MG's own YT Tourer, Inskip's TD-based four-seater was quite expensive and, as a result, did not sell in any great number. In fact, it is believed that no more than 12 examples were built.

THE ARNOLT-MG COUPE AND CONVERTIBLE

Another enthusiastic MG distributor was 'Wacky' Arnolt, who was based in Chicago and covered the mid-West. At the same 1953 New York show, Arnolt displayed the pretty Arnolt-MG, or Family-and-Sports Car. Like the Inskip car, this was based upon the TD Midget and was the first of a line of Bertone specials commissioned by Arnolt, among them the Arnolt-Bristol. Priced at a cool $3585 (a standard TD cost $2157), the Arnolt-MG comprised a standard Midget chassis on to which an elegant body (open or closed) had been grafted by Bertone.

The famous Italian firm of Bertone, run by father Giovanni and son Nuccio, had been in a poor financial state when it displayed examples of its work at the 1952 Turin Motor Show. At that time, the Italian car industry was finding it difficult to get back on to its feet after the war, and the show very nearly failed to go ahead. With the reduction in demand for cars based upon Italian chassis, Bertone had acquired two second-hand MG TD chassis frames and, with the aid of Franco Scaglioni, rebodied them with coachwork to his own

The Nottingham MG distributors Shipsides built this rebodied TD in 1953. (Rover)

design. The cars were exhibited by the Rome based MG distributors, Fattori and Mantani.

Visiting the Turin show was 45-year-old Stanley Harold Arnolt II, a larger-than-life character who approached Nuccio Bertone and told him that he wanted the cars, which Bertone took to mean the two on display. He was mistaken, however, for Arnolt wanted him to build 100 of each! Arnolt subsequently arranged for MG TD chassis to be shipped from Abingdon to the port of Genoa, then overland to Turin, whereupon Bertone would build the complete cars and return them to Genoa, from where they were shipped directly to Chicago.

This contract almost certainly saved Bertone's business from oblivion, and helped raise his profile on the international stage. Although the Arnolt-MG first appeared in the USA in the autumn of 1952, the first production-specification car was not seen until the 1953 New York show. Production of the Arnolt-MG continued for some time after the TD Midget was replaced by the TF, but with the introduction of the MGA, in 1955, the car's *raison d'être* diminished. The last examples appear to have been built during 1956, although they were still offered for sale for a couple of years afterwards. It is believed that half of the original quota of 200 cars were actually assembled, and of these, approximately 60 are thought to have survived.

SHIPSIDES MG TF COUPE

Perhaps inspired by the success of the Arnolt-MG, in 1953, the British Nottingham based BMC dealers of Shipsides Ltd commissioned a coupé body based upon the chassis of the TF Midget. The result was certainly far removed in appearance from the car upon which it was based, but it was neither a proper sports car, nor a practical touring car, having space for only two adults and no form of boot lid. Only one example of the car was built.

THE GHIA-AIGLE MG TD

Also in 1953, the Swiss coachbuilding company Ghia-Aigle purchased six MG TD Midgets and rebodied them all with their own design of smoothly shaped, open bodywork. This featured vestigial fins at the rear. Of the six examples built, at least two are known to have survived.

Left and above left Swiss MG distributors J. H. Keller *commissioned three specially-bodied MG TD Midgets from the coachbuilder Ghia-Aigle. These two contemporary photographs were printed from negatives originally stored in the old Cowley archives, showing that MG was interested in them as possible ways forward.* (Rover)

The car was also fitted with a folding windscreen, designed by Palmer and patented by the company. The mechanism, which can just be seen in the photographs of the vehicle, would allow the windscreen to be folded forward in a similar manner to the Austin-Healey 100, although both designs were totally independent. 'I certainly wasn't aware of the Healey design at the time,' says Palmer.

Various engine options would have been possible, including, of course, Palmer's own design for a twin-cam engine with a 90-degree valve layout, based upon the B-series block (later much modified by Coventry engines to produce the unit fitted to the MGA Twin Cam of 1958). Palmer's twin-cam could even have been fitted with fuel-injection—at least for competition purposes—

and the appeal of the basic concept was obvious. At least two prototypes of the design were built, one of which was a runner, complete with early B-series engine and a hardtop. If the car had gone into production, the bodies would have been built at Nuffield Metal Products at Birmingham, with final assembly at Abingdon.

Terry Mitchell, later to become chief chassis engineer at Abingdon, joined the Cowley team in June 1950 and began work on adapting existing Riley saloons and on the development of MG proposals. He recalls that at least six sets of body panels were made for the prototype Midget, one set presumably being used for the running prototype. The entries in the Cowley drawing office register are a little unclear, but it is possible that the relevant codes are

Above Prior to Gerald Palmer's arrival, someone made this model for a Midget proposal, which could have been produced in different versions, the most 'traditional' of which would have been a cycle-winged variant, depicted here in quarter-scale model form. (courtesy Denis Williams)

Below In this photograph, the model of the proposed MG Midget is seen in 'traditional' form, with removable fared-in wings (shades of the Jaguar XK120 perhaps?) lying alongside—a fine example of the Cowley model makers' handiwork. (courtesy Denis Williams)

A front-end view of the Midget model in 'traditional' form. (courtesy Denis Williams)

Gerald Palmer explored the same idea shown in the model above, considering up to three possible variants: a 'competition' model with cycle wings; a 'traditional' version with flowing, but separate wings; and a 'modern' variant with full bodywork. The full-size version of Gerald Palmer's 'traditional' Midget appears in this photo. Note the use of Morris Minor pull-out door handles in the traditional sports car-style rear-hinged 'suicide' doors. (Rover)

DO1048 for the streamlined version (listed as the MG Magna, a name that was certainly referred to in contemporary papers describing Palmer's car) and DO1049 for the more traditionally styled 1954 Midget.

By the end of 1952, the Cowley based MG design office was confidently predicting that the Palmer MG could be in production by March 1954. At the same time, however, John Thornley and Syd Enever were formulating their own plans for a replacement for the T-series (coded EX175), and were also making noises to the effect that they wanted more control over their own destiny—one of the more obvious results of which would be the establishment of a drawing office at Abingdon in June 1954. Understandably, therefore, there was little enthusiasm at Abingdon for pursuing Palmer's rival proposal, which would have undermined their case for autonomy, no matter how promising the car had been.

Certainly, John Thornley made it clear in a memorandum to S. V. Smith, in January 1953, that he had doubts about the wisdom of taking the bold step into monocoque sports cars, and the cost of tooling up for a monocoque sports car body would have seemed quite daunting for an operation used to building T-type Midgets in relatively low numbers. There was also the very real threat—particularly bearing in mind the recent Riley/MG battle of 1948—that production might have been shifted away from Abingdon. It is also probable that changes in management, and the limited rationalization (mostly of engines) that followed the BMC merger, meant that priorities at Cowley lay elsewhere.

Eventually, therefore, development of the Palmer Midgets was abandoned, and the prototypes were destroyed. The reason for this has always puzzled Jim O'Neill: 'I do know that Abingdon were not at all impressed. Why I will never know, because at the time I was absolutely sure that they were winners. Many years later, when I was working with Syd Enever, I asked him why Abingdon had rejected Palmer's Midget. He had no answer.'

Abingdon proposes an all-new MG

The MG team at Abingdon, led by general manager John Thornley and inspired by Syd Enever, was determined to wrest the design authority for their cars from Cowley's grasp. There is little doubt that the work-force, particularly those who had been with the MG Car Company since its heyday of the 1930s, had become extremely frustrated under what they saw as the dead hand of first the Nuffield Organization, and then the British Motor Corporation. They wished to regain at least some of the autonomy that had been

lost in 1935, and largely through the efforts of John Thornley, they would soon be successful in that aim.

Some groundwork was laid in 1951, when Syd Enever designed an aerodynamically-bodied sports racing car for George Phillips, who had raced a TD Mark II in 1950. Phillips had gained good publicity for the marque with his spirited finish in 18th place overall (and second in class) at Le Mans, in June of that year, driving his own special-bodied TC. His efforts at the famous French circuit provided MG with the nearest thing to factory racing that could be achieved under the watchful eye of Cowley. Understandably, his endeavours received enthusiastic support at Abingdon.

The 1951 Phillips car was given the project code EX172, and work began in January under the direction of Alec Hounslow. A TD Mark II chassis was chosen as its basis, Syd Enever's design for

the bodywork being largely replicated by Wally Kimpsey. By all accounts, work on the car was kept fairly quiet: every Tuesday, when S. V. Smith visited Abingdon from Cowley, EX172 would be spirited away from view. The result—registered UMG 400—featured a sleek, rubber mounted body with cutaway arm rests, no doors, and smoothly fared-in MG grille and wings. Sadly, EX172 did not distinguish itself at Le Mans, retiring after only three hours of the 24-hour race due to an engine valve failure as Phillips tried to tear past H. S. F. Hay's Bentley. Even so, it caused something of a stir among motoring enthusiasts.

It was obvious to all who saw EX172 that it could provide the basis for a modern MG sports car. While there remained a fondness for the traditional 'square rigged' lines of the old MG sports cars— and marque enthusiasts (particularly sports car marque enthusiasts)

TERRY MITCHELL

(David Knowles)

Terry Mitchell, who joined the MG drawing office at Cowley, in June 1950, is another member of the remarkable team that shaped Abingdon's products during the post-war period. He is an inventive fellow, rarely content unless he is tinkering with something mechanical. During his time at MG, he built no less than ten remarkable specials, including an Austin Westminster powered by an MGA Twin Cam engine, although like most of his specials, Terry became bored with it: 'Eventually, I sold it to a taxi driver.'

One of Terry's first specials had been a cannibalized Austin Seven, in which he was stopped once by the police. 'The poor old bobby didn't know what to make of it,' he remembers with a chuckle. Another exercise had been a low sporting two-seater coupé, which featured his own home-made chassis and suspension, some panels from one of Cowley's experimental MGs, and a Morris M10 engine and gearbox: 'I bought the engine and gearbox from Gerry Palmer, who said I could have it if I paid the cashier a tenner. Trouble was, one of the bods in experimental had wanted it too, so there was a bit of stink!' This special had been largely built in Jim O'Neill's garden, and Jim recalls how the noise of the panel beating drove the neighbours to distraction, while Terry would often be found by the night watchmen at Cowley, still working on his special at 11 at night. Terry recalls that S. V. Smith—very much of the old school—was rather disparaging about these specials: 'He told Syd Enever to sack me!' Jim O'Neill, who was present when Mitchell related this tale, countered in good humour, 'The trouble was, you were always too late!'

Like many of his contemporaries, Terry Mitchell was happy at Abingdon, and stayed with MG until the closure in 1980, by then having risen to become chief chassis engineer. The story of his involvement with Abingdon's last big-engined sports car is covered in Chapter 6.

are notoriously resistant to change—the small design team at Abingdon were both enthusiasts and realists: undoubtedly, they saw the future in a different light to their paymasters at Cowley. Thus, Enever and his men began work on a proper road car, inspired by EX172, but equipped with such essentials as doors, full lights and trim.

The prototype, EX175, used a brand-new chassis in which the side-members had been moved outwards to allow the occupants to sit much lower in the car—an objective that was impossible to achieve in EX172 with its TD chassis. Responsibility for the design of this chassis, which drew upon the Riley Pathfinder unit, was Enever's, the basic layout being worked out at his home in Westminster Way, Oxford. The detail work, however, was largely attributable to a young apprentice named Roy Brocklehurst, who had started at Abingdon in 1947, at the age of 15. For the bodyshell, Enever used the form of EX172 as his starting point, but was able to take considerable advantage of the lower driver's position, raising the sides of the cockpit to accommodate proper doors. The radiator grille was considerably better than the rather crude affair on EX172, and rectangular air vents were considered for the sides of the front wings, Aston Martin fashion.

Using Enever's sketches as a basis, Jim O'Neill (at the time, still at Cowley) produced quarter-scale drawings that were sent to the Cowley experimental shop (run by George Smith), where they were used to make an eighth-scale model. Finished in metallic maroon, and complete with the proposed engine-bay vents, the model was tested in Armstrong Whitworth's wind-tunnel. Although the scale replica of the new car was produced by George Smith's men, models were often made by MG's Harry Herring, who had joined as a carpenter in the coachbuilding section in 1930, a year after his son; he was the oldest of three generations of Herring at Abingdon.

In due course, a full-sized car was built by BMC Bodies Branch at Quinton Road, Coventry, under the direction of body engineer Eric Carter, using one of two chassis constructed by Enever. Fully finished in maroon paint and registered HMO 6, EX175 was a striking departure for an MG sports car and, in appearance, it closely resembled the MGA that eventually followed. Notably, the side vents had been abandoned in favour of small oval vents set in the top of the scuttle. These vents, which were more effective at exhausting engine-bay air than the side outlets, would become one of the distinctive hallmarks of the production MGA—but that is getting ahead of the story...

Lord rejects the EX175 prototype

While Abingdon had been beavering away on their sports car proposal, further upheavals were affecting the parent company at Cowley. Overtures had been made between the great rival Austin and Nuffield concerns during 1949, when the two companies announced that they would be co-operating on research and product development in an effort to save costs. Before long, however, it became apparent that far greater moves were afoot, so it was no great surprise when, in November 1951, Austin and Nuffield announced their intention to merge during the following year.

The story of the formation of the British Motor Corporation is fascinating, but sadly space does not permit me to do it justice. Suffice to say that the resulting conglomerate was an uneasy alliance, with Lord Nuffield as figurehead, but Leonard Lord of Austin in charge and overseeing the fortunes of the Cowley company, which he had sworn to tear down brick by brick when he left in 1936. The marriage itself took place in February 1952, after which a stressful honeymoon ensued. Against this backdrop, it is not difficult to appreciate why the affairs of Abingdon appear to have been given so little consideration at the time.

The Abingdon team presented EX175 to the management in the autumn of 1952, supported by an enthusiastic Jack Tatlow (soon to leave Abingdon in November) and confident that they would win approval to proceed towards production, albeit with Cowley's involvement, as had been the case with the TD. Unfortunately for the MG team, and no doubt unknown to them, Donald Healey had asked Leonard Lord about the possibility of buying Austin engines for a new smaller Healey sports car some time before the BMC merger. Consequently, EX175, which was intended to utilize the Nuffield XPAG unit of its TD forebear, was at a political disadvantage from the outset. It was rejected, and MG instructed to find some other means of countering the falling sales of the TD Midget. EX175 did not disappear immediately, however, as it was reworked in 1953—with a perspex bubble canopy, and cockpit and wheel arch fairings—as the potential basis of a record breaker. Unfortunately, nothing came of this idea, the purpose built EX179 record breaker making it redundant, and EX175 faded from the picture. Like UMG 400, it has not survived.

John Thornley takes charge at Abingdon

The rejection of Abingdon's proposal for an all-new MG came as a blow to the small, but dedicated, team; against the background of the vacillation and blunders of Cowley management during the previous decade, they had already demonstrated that they were best placed to determine their own destiny. Nevertheless, it should be remembered that the British Motor Corporation was still very young, and old rivalries persisted. Leonard Lord was very much in charge of the corporation, and his hostility to the company that he had left before the war was still very apparent: he often made public remarks that could be considered humiliating to the Cowley work-force and, in particular, the director, Reginald Hanks.

Given Lord's previous indifference to MG ('tarted up Morrises and Wolseleys' remember), it is not too surprising that he was not particularly interested in the concerns of Abingdon. Furthermore, the abject failure of the Austin Atlantic in North America, which had resulted in an under-utilized 2.1-litre Austin engine, was both an embarrassment and a disappointment to him. Donald Healey, let it be remembered, had proposed an Austin-engined sports car...

John Thornley became general manager at Abingdon when Jack Tatlow moved on to become the general manager of Morris

The EX175 prototype. With the exception of the bonnet bulge (needed to clear the XPAG engine) and the design of the overriders, its styling was carried over to EX182/DO1062. Note the luggage rack, the style of which would serve as the basis of a rack for the MGA, MGB and Midget. (Rover)

Commercial Cars, in November 1952. Thornley, who had been assistant general manager at Abingdon since 1948 and, therefore, had seen the saga of the BMC merger unfold, was generous in his assessment of Lord's treatment of MG. He recalled his relationship with Lord in his inimitable style: 'Whenever I see the name of Len Lord, Sir Leonard Lord, Lord Lambury in MG writings, I always sit up a bit straight. By and large, he has been much maligned in this context. Over the years, he has been depicted as the big bad wolf when, in fact, his overall attitude to us (MG)—and to me in particular—has scored above the line.'

Thornley described his feelings about some of Lord's actions, which affected MG: 'Decisions which seemed to go against Abingdon's interests were naturally resented, but there was never anything discriminatory or spiteful about them. Most of his decisions, when viewed with hindsight, are seen to have been well justified.' Thornley claimed that the Morris Motors takeover of MG, in 1935, was an example of this: 'He wrote *"finis"* to all that we have come to know as "Triple M", and all hell broke loose. But, by reverting to the old basis of quantity produced units, sales took off.'

Accordingly, Thornley was sympathetic to Lord's viewpoint

THE BIRTH OF AUSTIN-HEALEY

Donald Mitchell Healey—or 'DMH', as he was known to family and friends—began his involvement with motor-sport as a driver, and earned much respect by winning the 1931 Monte Carlo rally in a 4.5-litre S-type Invicta. Within the next three years, he had moved from his native Cornwall to Coventry and, following a brief spell at Riley, had become the chief engineer at Triumph, where he was largely responsible for the stunning, but short-lived, straight-eight Dolomite.

Following the collapse of Triumph, Healey decided to form his own company, the Donald Healey Motor Company Ltd, with the intention of building his own sports car. To do this, he used a specially designed chassis and coachwork, and called on his pre-war Riley connections to ensure a steady supply of 2.4-litre Riley engines, adapted to his own requirements by Eddie Maher, formerly of Riley, but now at Morris Engines. Before long, the Healey name became respected in motor enthusiast circles. A visit to the USA, in 1948, also helped establish awareness of the marque in that country, which would serve Healey well in the years that followed.

For 1950, the company entered into a deal with the American Nash Motors, following a chance meeting between Donald Healey and Nash's president, George Mason, on the liner Queen Elizabeth in the previous December. The resulting Nash-Healey sold well, aided by distinguished performances at Le Mans in 1950-52, but it was an exclusive and rather expensive car; a little over 500 being built between 1950 and 1954. In late 1951, Donald Healey began to lay down plans for a much lower-priced Healey sports car. The Jaguar XK120, with its thoroughbred twin-cam engine had dented Nash-Healey sales, and the Riley engines, with their distinctly pre-war origins, were thought to have an uncertain future.

With great discretion, so as not to upset his friends at Nuffield, Healey approached Leonard Lord to discuss the possibility of Austin supplying him with the 2660cc four-cylinder engine used in the Austin A90 Atlantic. Lord readily responded to Healey's overtures and, before long, Donald and his son, Geoffrey, were secretly working on the design of what was to become the

Healey 100. This featured a chassis designed by Barry Bilbie and assembled by Thompsons, and a body built to Gerry Coker's design by Tickford. One little appreciated side-effect of the new relationship was that Healey was able to help forge links between Austin and Nash, which led to the odd-ball Nash Metropolitan of 1954.

By late 1952, the prototype Healey 100 was ready, and a continental road-test was granted to *Autosport* magazine, after which a number of leading British motoring correspondents were invited the try the car before its début at the Earls Court Motor Show, in October 1952. The reception accorded the new Healey 100 was exceptional. Aware that the car was almost ready for production and employed an under-utilized Austin engine, Leonard Lord quickly arranged a meeting with Donald Healey at his hotel on the evening after the first day of the show. The two promptly agreed that Austin would take on production, market the car as the Austin-Healey 100, and aim to drop the price from Healey's anticipated figure of £850—although the actual price would not be fixed for some time.

It should be pointed out that Leonard Lord, shrewd man that he was, had already invited sports car proposals from other small companies in an effort to utilize Austin components—other offerings were an A40-engined Jensen and an A90-engined Fraser-Nash—so the equally shrewd Donald Healey would have known that his Healey 100 would be of obvious interest to Lord. Jensen was unable to complete its prototype in time for the Motor Show, but in the wake of the Healey deal, the company was able to secure a contract to build the Austin-Healey bodies, and to ensure the continued availability of the the Austin 4-litre six for its own cars.

By the spring of the following year, the Austin-Healey 100 had been shown in the USA and, before long, the Austin-Healey marque was well on the way to success, in both sales and competition terms. It is worth noting that the deal was struck well after the BMC merger: one only has to look at the timing of the announcement, and also to note the significant presence alongside the car at Earls Court—after the public announcement of the deal—of Lord Nuffield, Leonard Lord and George Harriman with Donald Healey. Three days later, MG would show Leonard Lord their EX175 prototype...

The prototype TF Midget at Abingdon. Note the louvres in the bonnet top panels, which would not reach production. (Rover)

regarding the Austin-Healey/MG sports car duel: 'When he (Lord) put his foot down on the MGA prototype, it was a perfectly rational thing for him to do. He had just "bought" the Healey 100 and, to his eyes, it and the EX175 were clearly aimed at the same market, and it didn't make sense to him to have to tool two cars. It wasn't until I had pestered the life out of him, supported strongly by the screams from the USA, that he saw the point.'

Stop-gap: the TF Midget

Faced with Lord's rejection of their proposals, the Abingdon team was compelled into a hasty reworking of the TD Midget, keeping the costs as low as possible. This they did by the simple expedient of reshaping the front panels, lowering the bonnet, and raking the radiator grille backwards. With tongue in cheek, John Thornley referred to this process as 'a knife-and-fork job.'

The prototype of the new Midget was completed inside two weeks by Freddie Wake, assisted by Bert Wirdnam and panel beat-

er Billy Wilkins. The last had joined MG from Raworths, the Oxford coachbuilders responsible for the bodies of some of Kimber's first cars. It was finished in blue cellulose for presentation to the BMC board on 8 January, 1953, by which time, it had been tentatively badged as the TF. Presumably, TE had been ruled out because it would have sounded too much like the juvenile expression, 'tee-hee'. Jimmy Cox remembers the reaction from many at Abingdon: 'We laughed at it at the time—sloping back the radiator, and so on—yet nowadays, the TF looks such a pretty car.'

Cecil Cousins and Alec Hounslow also recalled the genesis of the TF for Dick Knudson some years later. Cousins was full of

The production TF Midget; compare the bonnet louvres with those of the prototype above. (Rover)

praise for Billy Wilkins' handiwork: 'He literally handmade the first set of wings out of a sheet of metal to our idea—virtually made it; there wasn't a drawing or anything.' Hounslow added, in his inimitable style, 'We never needed drawings: half our cars were made without drawings lousing you up. We used to give it (the prototype) to the drawing office so they could draw around it with their pencil.' Before the TF was presented to the BMC board, Cousins and Hounslow gave the prototype a blast down the Marcham road, then parked it outside the managing director's office to await his return from holiday.

The result was given the EX-Register code EX177, after which, according to Terry Mitchell, it was drawn up by Keith Matthews at Cowley. Jim O'Neill, who was also still at Cowley, remembers that 'some very dark brown drawings, with barely discernible lines, came over from Abingdon, showing their requirements for the new radiator and wing lines. Taking these crude efforts as a basis, we persevered and eventually achieved what Syd Enever wanted.' Cecil Cousins who, of course, was at Abingdon, told Dick Knudson, 'It took them six months to draw the blooming thing!'

As design authority for MG was still vested in the Cowley office, EX177 became DO1047 when the production drawings and tooling designs were prepared. In creating EX177, the MG team was able to utilize components adapted from Riley products, which had been built at Abingdon since 1949. Close examination of the grille slats in a TF radiator grille reveal that they are the same as those of the Riley RM saloons, while the seat frames are cut-down Riley units.

The production TF Midget appeared at the October 1953 Earls Court Motor Show. Unfortunately, the launch of the TF not only coincided with that of Sir John Black's Triumph TR2, intended as an Austin-Healey/MG rival, but also that of the MG Magnette. Thus, MG was in the curious position of having an outdated sports car, with a virtually obsolete drive-train, alongside a modern saloon with a brand-new engine and state-of-the-art monocoque body. Little could be done, however, to counter the generally poor reception given to the TF, although it did receive a shot in the arm as a spin-off from the creation of the EX179 record breaker.

George Eyston was not only a great MG enthusiast, but also a friend of Abingdon with useful contacts at Castrol. He had many distinguished pre-war record breaking exploits to his credit, and was keen to rebuild his links with the MG marque. Accordingly, with an eye to boosting flagging sales of the TF in the USA and, no doubt, aiding the cause of those at Abingdon who wished to see their EX175 proposal yield fruit, he suggested to the management

at Cowley that a fresh record attempt should be made. EX175, by now kitted out with the fared-in wheel spats and a cockpit cover, was submitted for wind-tunnel testing in early 1954. However, the tests soon showed that EX175 was not suitable as the basis for a true record breaker, so it was agreed to clothe a spare EX175 chassis, which had been built by Enever, with a new body. The result was EX179.

Jimmy Cox and Henry Stone became involved in creating the new record breaker: 'Henry and I went to Midland Sheet Metal at Nuneaton to do the bodywork. The frame was made out of square-section tubing with alternate holes of 3/16 and 1/8in (0.48 and 0.32cm) diameter for lightness. Drilling these holes was, as you can imagine, a very, very boring job to do. Then Midland Sheet Metal, under Mr. Letchford, did the alloy body. I can remember all the wheeling machines used to shape the alloy sheet; they were doing wings for the old Princess limousine and the Morris Minor Traveller roofs.'

As the bodywork took shape, Jimmy and Henry went to do the riveting: 'They were strict union at Nuneaton, and so they wouldn't do the riveting, so we had to do it. I used to leave with Alec and Henry at six in the morning, and we would drive up the A444.' With the car finished, there remained the matter of building in the mechanical components, not least, of course, the engine: 'We used to go into the works at 6am, and run the engines for 12 hours. On one Saturday, a rod came through the block after four hours. We started again on Sunday, and we went through the same routine, running the engine from six until ten, before stopping for checks and carrying on.'

As anyone who knows the area around the factory will appreciate, all this noise, which could be heard some distance away across the town, was not very popular in Abingdon Hospital, situated next door: 'Even with earplugs in, it was terribly loud for us. Following the complaints from the hospital, we weren't allowed to do these long tests again in the same way.'

EX179 used a larger-bore (72mm instead of 66.5mm) version of the 1250cc XPAG engine, which had been developed by Morris Motors and identified by them as XPEG. With the BMC merger, this engine had been rendered virtually redundant, and it does not

THE NEW MG RECORD BREAKERS

Before World War 2, MG had been notably successful in record breaking attempts with a succession of specially built cars. These cars, particularly EX135, had continued to provide favourable publicity for MG after the war. It is hardly surprising, therefore, that the old hands at Abingdon were keen to see something new to take on the mantle of EX135. With the re-establishment of Abingdon's own design office in 1954, it did not take long for these ideas to begin to germinate.

Terry Mitchell, who eventually became MG's chief chassis engineer, recalls that the work he carried out on the first all-new record breaker, EX179, was one of the first jobs he was given after transferring from Cowley to Abingdon: 'Syd Enever said to me that he wanted the new car to look like EX135, but be different—a typical Syd remark! I drew the body up in six weeks to fit the spare EX175 chassis.' Fitted with a specially developed XPEG engine, and in left-hand-drive form, EX179 visited Bonneville in 1955. For 1956, it was fitted with a prototype MGA Twin Cam engine (by this time, Eddie Maher's unit had been adopted as the official twin-cam engine) and converted to right-hand-drive, the bubble canopy being moved to suit.

EX181 was the next, and last, completely new MG record breaker. Styled by Syd Enever, it had a smooth shape like an aircraft drop-tank or tear-drop, from which the media soon christened it the 'Roaring Rain-drop'. MG's model maker, Harry Herring, many of whose creations survive in the British Motor Heritage museum at Gaydon, produced a wind-tunnel model of EX181 that was used as an aid in refining the full-size proposal. Some weird and wonderful models of other potential record breakers also exist at Gaydon, which were three-dimensional interpretations of Syd Enever's sketches, produced directly for him by Herring.

Terry Mitchell became heavily involved once more, producing many of the 276 drawings for EX181, most of which have been saved for posterity at Gaydon, and detailing the De Dion rear suspension. Eventually, the completed car—resplendent in an attractive metallic silver-blue (later changed to the traditional EX metallic green)—was ready for testing, which was carried out by the American driver Phil Hill.

Hill made the first run on Sunday 18 August, 1957, with fine conditions on the flats. The definitive runs, however, were to be made by Stirling Moss, who flew in on the following Tuesday, fresh from his victory at Pescara, with the intention of getting under way on the following day. Unfortunately, rain delayed the action until the Thursday afternoon, when improving conditions allowed Moss to make his first attempt on the record. He recalled his feelings, 28 years on, at the MG 'Birthday Party' at Gaydon, in March 1995: 'I was thrilled to be called up, and when we got to see the salt, I was amazed at its appearance. A black line had been marked out for several miles, and the intention was that I would follow it whilst attempting the flying-mile record. The mechanic waved me in, and I just went past him, seemingly coasting for ages. Also, being sealed into the cockpit was a bit unnerving. I had been told to keep the throttle full open in order to keep the flames out of the exhaust. The tyres, which looked like inner tubes, were inflated to 70lb/sq in (4.92kg/sq cm) and had the contact area of a shilling! I simply pointed the car down that black line, and if the instruments were moving, I was happy. I had to go past the marker boards, and then back again, trying not to hit them!'

Stirling's inability to stop is partly explained by the fact that the third gear in EX181's four-speed gearbox had been damaged while accelerating on the first run, because of which he failed to achieve the target speed. As a result of this damage, on the next run, Stirling was unable to use the gearbox to slow the car, as originally intended, so he had to rely on the single brake, which acted on one of the rear half-shafts. It should be noted that, although the canopy of EX181 was sealed, there were interior release levers that, theoretically, the driver could use if necessary—albeit not very quickly.

EX181 was stripped and rebuilt by Cliff Bray for further runs in 1959, when it was driven by Phil Hill to over 254mph (408.76km/h), achieving Syd Enever's goal of cracking the 250mph (402.33km/h) mark. In fact, both Hill and Moss were to have driven EX181 at this attempt, but due to a protracted spell of bad weather, Moss had to leave to fulfil his GP commitments before getting a drive.

MG had cunningly bored out the 1498cc engine to 1506cc, making it possible to take fresh records in the 2-litre category for 1959, while retaining the 1500cc

A selection of Harry Herring's scale models for various Syd Enever schemed record breakers. Quite often, these models were produced by Harry directly from one of Syd's ideas and, consequently, were little more than flights of fancy. The two nearest the camera are obviously related to EX179, while the two at the rear are probably first (rather extreme) thoughts for EX181. (Rover)

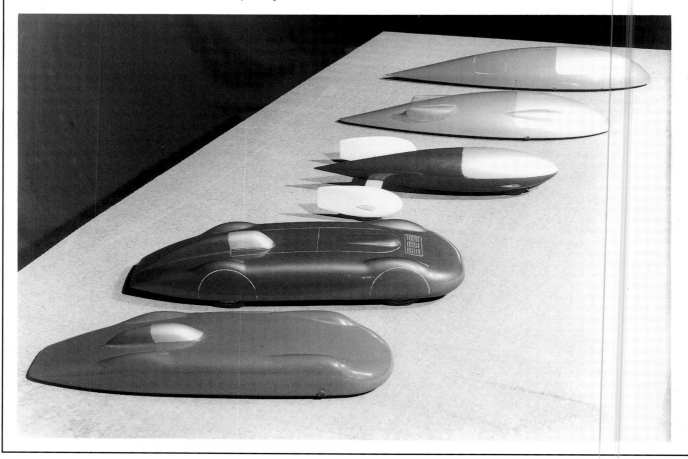

EX181 in Utah during 1959. Phil Hill (in white overalls) stands to rhe right of George Eyston, with the Castrol banner clearly visible in the background—Eyston was one of Castrol's directors. (courtesy Jimmy Cox)

records from 1957 (although there had been plans to crack these, too, had the weather permitted). For these later runs, the small tail fin, which had been featured in 1957, was removed. According to former MG apprentice Peter Neal, it had never been needed: 'George Eyston had insisted upon it, as he believed that the car would have been unstable at speed without it. Wind-tunnel tests had shown that it wasn't needed, but Syd Enever told us to keep Eyston happy and build in a tail-fin anyway.'

The other record-breaking exercise was attempted with a revitalized EX179, which stemmed from a proposal to use an ADO13 Austin-Healey Sprite as the basis of a record breaking car, coded EX219. Early wind-tunnel tests of the running prototype showed that it was hopelessly unsuitable, so instead, EX179 was repainted and fitted with a Sprite engine as a BMC record breaker (for the benefit of the press, EX179 was referred to as a Morris Minor-engined BMC development project, as the Sprite had not been announced).

One of the people who accompanied EX179 and EX181 to Utah in 1959 was MG's engine guru, Jimmy Cox, who had worked on the engines of EX135 and EX179 in the past, but never accompanied the cars on their outings prior to 1959: 'The EX181 engine had been built by Eddie Maher at Morris Engines; one of his mechanics, Brian Rees, came out with the car.' However, all was not well with the engine at first: 'On the first run, running on methanol, the Shorrock blower seized, which cost £1000 to replace.' Jimmy's first trip to the salt flats is etched upon his mind: 'Having tried to take in the spectacle of it all, I asked Captain Eyston what it was like to drive on the salt at about 300mph (483km/h). He said that to his mind, anything over 150mph (241km/h) all seemed to be much the same. There was about ⅛in (0.32cm) of water on the salt, and he said, "Oh, that's a bit of a blow; might take a month to dry out."' The only option was to play a waiting game: 'We were 68 miles (109.43km) from Wells and 110 miles (177.02km) from Salt Lake City, and in some places, you could still see the marks that the wheels of the wagons had made over a hundred years earlier.'

Eventually, the salt did dry out enough to allow the men from MG to begin their record attempts in earnest: "We ran EX179 in an enormous circle for twelve hours, and EX181 in a straight line. To do this, we had to drag the circuit with a railway sleeper, and then drove 6in (15.24cm) nails with a piece of red tape on into the salt with a hammer every 3 yd (2.74m) for 12 miles (19.31km). Every time we do a run we have to redo this; it was not the most enjoyable of jobs!' This line of nails was used to position the black line—laid with old engine oil—that Stirling Moss had to follow. It was the driver's only means of reference on the otherwise featureless plain to ensure that he stayed on course.

Phil Hill was driving when Jimmy Cox was present, and had to put up with conditions that would have put the fear of God into most of us, as Jimmy recalls: 'The engine section of the car was swimming with fuel, and the red fire warning light went on during the first timed run, but it wasn't a fire: a tube had got caught in the canopy.' At the end of that first straight run, Jimmy and Brian Rees had to turn the car around for the return leg: 'On this occasion, we just couldn't seem to restart it. It kept going "Pop, pop, pop," and we thought that that was it, and then it fired up; what a wonderful noise in all that emptiness!' Eventually, on the evening of 2 October, 1959, EX181 achieved a speed of 254.91mph (410.23km/h) and gained enduring fame as the last of the factory record breakers.

Jimmy and his colleagues had built blown and unblown 950cc engines for EX179, the latter being less troublesome than the former: 'As with EX181, the blown engine used a Shorrock blower, and we blew the first one up. A con-rod came through the side of the block, and so we had to beef up the con-rods.'

Many years later, in October 1978, EX181 was dragged out of retirement to be reunited with Stirling Moss prior to the 50-year celebrations at Abingdon, and to mark 20 years since the run of 1959. This occasion is etched vividly in Jimmy Cox's memory: 'We were going to do a run at the RAF aerodrome, where we were to be filmed by a TV crew. The CO said that we could use their main runway, and so off we went. The TV crew were supposed to wait between two hangars and were then going to run with me as I came past. I came along and found myself going slightly downhill at about 80mph (128.74km/h). I managed to turn the car round with only just enough lock and started back at about 60-70mph (97-113km/h), looking out for the TV crew in their Range Rover. Suddenly, they were right with me. I started changing down as I headed towards the end of the runway, and thought to myself that I would be okay even if I went just off the end of the runway, by this time travelling at 25-30mph (40-48km/h). What I didn't know was that the end of the runway was soft shingle, and as I came off at a slight angle, the car flipped up and over on its side before ending back on its wheels.' Needless to say, Jimmy felt terrible about this, but fortunately he was unhurt and EX181 not too badly damaged. 'The body was repaired at Midland Sheet Metal, where Litchfield and his boys were brought back from retirement. They thoroughly enjoyed themselves putting it right.' EX181 was never driven again.

appear to have been given serious consideration for any of the abortive MG exercises of the late 1940s or early 1950s. However, success with EX179, which reached nearly 154mph (247.83km/h) on the Utah salt flats, in the hands of George Eyston and Ken Miles in August 1954, appeared to vindicate BMC's decision to sanction production of the XPEG engine for an improved version of the TF. This slipped quietly into production, in July 1954, as the TF 1500, the Midget name having been dropped. It gradually displaced the TF 1250, which continued in production until September.

By now, though, BMC were listening to their dealers and MG, too. Only 3400 examples of the TF 1500 were built before something far more radical took its place.

While work was proceeding on EX179, MG was still badgering BMC at Longbridge, in the hope of producing something more modern and worthy than the old-fashioned TF. Jimmy Cox says that a special delivery arrived at Abingdon one day for Syd Enever: 'A bloke called Cordin brought a wagon down to Abingdon with sets of Austin-Healey 100 body panels. The lorry arrived and Syd was told to use as many panels as he could in a new MG—a sort of early "badge engineering" exercise. Syd never looked at any of them; he just went ahead and was determined to build his own car!' Jim O'Neill confirms this story: 'Those panels were sent from Longbridge, almost as a sop to Sydney, but he wasn't interested!'

The Abingdon men get their way
In early 1954, Alec Issigonis left BMC, having been lured away by the promise of a fairly free rein to produce an advanced, new luxury saloon for Alvis (which would come to naught). At about the same time, Victor Oak retired from his post as technical director at Cowley, while his counterpart at Austin, Johnny Rix, had also left, so something of a vacuum occurred among the senior engineering staff. To fill this gap, Gerald Palmer was promoted to the post of group chassis and body engineer, being based part-time at Longbridge and overseeing all new vehicle design. Meanwhile, Len Lord managed to stir things, often working with former Austin stylist Dick Burzi to conjure up design solutions without Palmer's knowledge. To a brilliant and justifiably proud professional like Palmer, this was intolerable. As a result, he would only remain at BMC for about another year, before departing for Vauxhall.

In the wake of Palmer's promotion, however, changes were afoot at Cowley, as Jim O'Neill recalls: 'Gerald Palmer became chief, and moved into the main Morris drawing office; we were absorbed into it, too. The boss at Morris was Les Hall, and he didn't want me to be in charge of Morris and Riley: he wanted me to report to Ron French. I threatened to leave, and when Palmer found out, he was furious, overturning it at once. Soon after, Palmer went to Longbridge full-time, and I am sure that John Thornley began to worry—with some justification—that MG would become a small backwater in BMC, and so he pushed for Abingdon to get some design autonomy.'

In the summer of 1954, around the time that the first TF 1500 was being built, the team at Abingdon finally achieved what they wanted, the good news being delivered by S. V. Smith (known irreverently to some of his staff as 'Hitler Smith', on account of his moustache). Jim O'Neill was one of those involved: 'MG had decided that it would be beneficial to have their own design team at Abingdon. With Gerry Palmer's promotion to technical director in charge of all design at Cowley, the MG design team was moved back into the main Morris drawing office. I think that perhaps John Thornley could see a repeat of the problems which we had had with the TD Midget. I approached Syd Enever, who was to become the new chief engineer, and arranged for a small team of engineers to move from Cowley to Abingdon.'

The process was not quite as simple as that, however: 'Our first task was to beg, borrow or steal as much equipment as possible. Two 18ft (5.49m) long layout tables were made up by the works carpenters, and improvised wooden sweeps were also made up in the carpenters' shop. Drawing boards were "borrowed" from Morris Motors.' Denis Williams was one of those who joined the MG team at this stage. Jim O'Neill wanted him to transfer from Morris Radiators, but there were strict company rules that forbade transfers between companies within BMC: '...but I said that if we

didn't let him come, he would leave and go to work for Ford, and so S. V. Smith agreed to waive the rule and allow Denis to join us.'

MGA: the aerodynamic sports car
Despite Leonard Lord's rejection of the aerodynamic sports car project, the MG management soon found that they had many allies, both in this country and abroad. Among them were powerful voices—such as Captain George Eyston—expressing the need for something more radical than the TF Midget. John Thornley never let the matter rest: 'It may be presumptuous of me, but I fancy that, in the period between 1952 and the time he (Lord) gave me the go-ahead, some of my enthusiasm rubbed off on him because, from that moment on, all was sweetness and light. From general conversation within BMC, I got the impression that I was just about the only senior executive in BMC who had not, at one time or another, caught the rough edge of his tongue.'

With the go-ahead for the new aerodynamic MG sports car, the Abingdon design office began work in earnest, as Jim O'Neill recalls: 'On completing the quarter-scale—based upon HMO 6—I joined Eric Carter at Morris Motors Bodies Branch in Coventry to work on the full-scale layout. This meant staying at a local hostelry for a few months, and working long hours to get the car into production. We were fortunate to have on loan from Morris Motors a young draughtsman who did all the detail drawings required by the Coventry plant: a magnificent effort by Don Butler.' The latter affectionately recalls working with Carter: 'Eric Carter was basically a one-man design team, who was joined by various members of the MG staff to do the initial design work on specific projects.'

Butler, a former Cowley body engineering apprentice, who would later transfer to Abingdon upon the closure of the Cowley drawing office in 1959, was drawn into the MGA body design because Pressed Steel were becoming involved, and also because Jim O'Neill needed to be free to maintain control of other projects at Abingdon. As part of this process, the MGA became the last MG sports car to be assigned a Cowley drawing office number, in this case DO1062 (entries dating from June 1954); the Abingdon project code EX182 seems to have been used primarily for the special Le Mans versions, which appeared prior to the launch.

After receiving the 'green light' from Cowley, in August 1954, MG intended to take about nine months to complete the development of DO1062, which meant a launch date of April 1955. For reasons that will become apparent, this was subsequently shifted to June 1955, before slipping again. Syd Enever had been allocated a total tooling budget of £80,000, which was to be split roughly 60:40 between the chassis and body. Work on developing the car rapidly got under way at Quinton Road, under Eric Carter, who received much needed help from Jim O'Neill and Don Butler. Indeed, it was mainly as a result of this work that Jim O'Neill would later press Tom Ramsay, at Cowley, to let Don move to Abingdon, his talent having been clearly recognized. The short time-scale at this stage led to much overtime working and head-scratching, with solutions to many problems—such as a means of accommodating the folding hood—being arrived at late at night.

The translation from EX175 to DO1062 involved a number of subtle changes to the body. The blunt bonnet bulge, needed in EX175 to clear the top of the XPAG engine, was not required for the production car, while the front wings were made slightly slimmer and less fulsome. At the rear, EX175 had featured a rather petite, D-shaped boot lid which, although elegant, was rather impractical. Even with a larger boot lid, however, luggage capacity would never be one of the MGA's strong suits. Also at the rear, EX175 was equipped with a raised number-plate plinth, formed in the curved bodywork at the base of the boot lid aperture and designed to take a square number-plate. For the definitive MGA, this plinth was deleted in favour of a rather less elegant, but more versatile, separate number-plate bracket.

Other detail changes included slimmer bumpers, a less prominent front valance, larger tail-lamps, and a repositioned fuel filler, which had been moved from the left side of the rear body panel to the right. The trim and dashboard differed considerably from EX175, the seats in particular being a totally new design for MG. The chassis of production MGAs were assembled at the factory from components bought in from Thompson's of Wolverhampton, while bodies came from Morris Motors Body Branch in Coventry.

Don Butler remembers that Pressed Steel's Charlie Linder became involved in the MGA, the original intention being to use so-called 'soft tools', which were suitable for low production runs and were much cheaper. Such tools were employed by Boulton & Paul, who used them to form panels for the Jensen factory, which built the 'big Healey' bodies. It is possible that Pressed Steel was keen to learn more about the practical application of this tooling, perhaps with an eye to taking over the Boulton & Paul contract.

Pressed Steel offered to create the necessary soft tools, on the understanding that if they were not successful in service, the company would provide normal tooling at no extra cost. Obviously, this was a very attractive offer, as MG could hardly lose. Another benefit, as far as MG was concerned, was the fact that work on the chassis had used up most of the £80,000 tooling allocation.

Don Butler recalls viewing the 'model stack' for the proposed MGA body tools at Cowley, based upon Syd Enever's EX175 body shape: 'We could see there were certain areas, such as around the rear wheel arch, which would have been difficult to form.' Thus, modifications were made to aid the manufacturing process before the production of the soft body tools. As a consequence, the MGA body has quite a number of flat, or softly radiused, curves, the aim being to cut costs. Even so, Jim O'Neill was not convinced that the soft tools—made of plastic—would work in practice: '...but Ken Osbourne, of Pressed Steel, assured me that they would. In the event, only about three sets of panels were pressed before the tools broke.' As a result, Pressed Steel had to cough up the cost of fabricating proper steel die tools, one of the reasons why the originally scheduled launch date of April 1955 could not be met.

In March 1955, Denis Williams joined Abingdon's new design team from Morris Radiators, where he had designed the MGA radiator grille, based upon Syd Enever's sketches and HMO 6. Morris Radiators did not want to lose him, but through Jim O'Neill's persistence, he was able to transfer and took part in the final preparation of the MGA prior to launch.

The Competitions Department: début at Le Mans
John Thornley explained to me how important the MGA was to Abingdon: 'During the two-year critical period, from 1952 until the clearance for the MGA, the car formed only the front of the argument. What was of overriding importance to me was the survival of Abingdon. Had the MGA been denied us, MG Abingdon would not have continued beyond 1960 at the latest.' Accordingly, the pressure for Abingdon to succeed with the MGA was very great, and Thornley managed to exploit the unique relationship he had established with Leonard Lord to his advantage: 'I did not have to work on him very hard to get him to see the sense of a BMC Competitions Department.' That this corporate competition unit—set up in December 1954—should be based at Abingdon was a logical move, but a typical Thornley masterstroke none the less.

At first, the Competitions Department had to experiment with vehicles that were not particularly suitable for their role, and the results that they achieved were neither spectacular nor significant. There were a few exceptions, however, occasionally in the vein of publicity coups, such as Stirling Moss' sister Pat, who drove a TF with distinction. The Magnette also came in for early attention: during the period before the Le Mans race, Jimmy Cox and his colleagues were involved in the Monte Carlo entry for the Holt brothers and Len Shaw. This comprised three of four ZA Magnettes—known as the 'Four Musketeers'—that took part in the Monte Carlo Rally: 'We had these cars in the shop,' says Jimmy, 'and we came up with a device to allow the back window of the car to be hinged open, so that the navigator could lean out from inside the car and fill up the fuel tank via the filler, without having to stop! This seemed to be a crazy idea, and I don't think it worked very well.'

Only two people from Abingdon attended the rally itself: 'This was our first outing with Marcus Chambers, who had just been appointed manager of the BMC Competitions Department, and I went as first mechanic to him—there were just the two of us. My job was to keep their cars running; Marcus drove the fourth Magnette— 'd'Artagnan'. Marcus drove, and I rode with him.' In his autobiography, Marcus Chambers makes it clear that had he arrived at 'Comps' earlier, he would not have gone ahead with the Magnette entry; the situation was certainly different in later years. At about the same time, Jimmy recalls, Linden Sims was rallying his Riley Pathfinder: 'He ran out of brakes—they were rubbing

The three EX182 entrants lined up at the Sarthe circuit prior to the 1955 Le Mans race. (courtesy Cliff Bray)

metal to metal—and I remember that he finished up grinding the side of the car along the wall, at the side of the road, as he went down the mountain in order to try to stop it.'

At this stage, there were few letters in the alphabet that had not been used to denote MG models, the most recent being 'Z', employed for the Magnette. For a while, the new sports car was referred to as the Series UA, but before long, it was decided to revert to the beginning of the alphabet, adding the letters 'MG' to the model suffix. The launch of the MG Series MGA—soon shortened to MGA—was scheduled for the summer of 1955, but in the event, this could not be achieved, as production difficulties delayed it until September.

In the meantime, however, a team of three MGA-style, alloy-bodied EX182s (together with a fourth spare car—LBL 304—which later became a popular hack at Abingdon) had been prepared for the famous Le Mans 24-hour race in June. These were powered by B-series engines fitted with special Weslake devised cylinder heads. Because of the delayed launch, it was not possible to race the MGs in the production car class, so it was decided to enter them as prototypes, probably gaining even more media attention than might have been the case had the production cars been launched. Before long, not only the enthusiast motoring press, but also the *Movietone News* crews latched on to the excitement of these prototypes, which were rumoured to be an indication of changes on the way from Abingdon.

When an Austin engine arrived at Abingdon in the wake of the BMC merger, the first reaction of Jimmy Cox and his colleagues had been to have nothing to do with it: 'However, the XPEG engine was really at its limits, and so we decided to look at the Austin engine. We put a full-flow filter on it, for which we drilled through the block, and we developed the camshaft for more lift. Then we worked with Harry Weslake on the combustion chambers and, before long, we found ourselves working on what would become the Le Mans engine specification for EX182.'

All this time, of course, the other stalwarts of the development shop—such as Cliff Bray, Tommy Wellman and Douggie Watts—were also working on the EX182 Le Mans cars. For the chassis, Jimmy recalls that the side-rails were built up from three pieces on each side: 'Harold Wiggins, Douggie Watts and Tommy Wellman

In the USA, BMC and their local agents (Hambro) were unaffected by the European backlash that followed the 1955 Le Mans race. The first endurance race had been held at Sebring in December 1950, and MGs had raced with distinction each year thereafter. In 1956, a three-car team of white MGAs was entered for the 12-hour race, held on 24 March. Nearest the camera is the car driven by David Ash and Gus Ehrman, which finished fifth in its class and 20th overall. (Rover)

used offcuts to make the chassis sides, with neat butt-welds; this is one of the ways to tell a genuine Le Mans car.'

Meanwhile, Jimmy was beavering away with the Le Mans engine: 'I started with the Weslake head and improved it. I tried sodium cooled valves, but these proved too difficult. In the end, we arrived at Stellite-tipped valves, and with all the other changes, we achieved 82.5bhp (61.52kW) at 6000.' It is no surprise that Syd Enever's ever inventive mind was always coming up with bright ideas that Jimmy would be asked to investigate: 'Syd wanted to use a cross-flow head—four or five were made—and he wanted to use two sets of carbs: one pair each side of the head. The idea was that there would be a normal pair on the conventional side, and two smaller ones—I think they were 1in (2.54cm) SUs we tried—on the opposite side. The theory was that the smaller carbs would give improved low-end power, but this didn't work, and so we finished up with a ⅝in (1.59cm) balance pipe around the back of the engine.' Other features of the race engines included blocked-off waterways and the lack of gaskets. The latter resulted in very boring work, Jimmy recalls, as the heads were lapped to the block: 'This was a very slow and tedious process, and we would take turns at it.'

Also subject to development was the exhaust—'Much work was required on the manifold to avoid any unnecessary loss of power.'—the fitting of a racing clutch 'with no take up springs, unlike a road car,' and, of course, a close-ratio gearbox. The specification more or less determined, Jimmy then set about ensuring that the engines themselves performed reliably: 'We tested them to about 7 per cent above the margin required, in order to ensure that the engines would survive on the track.'

The four EX182 cars travelled in convoy to Le Mans just prior to the race, being accompanied by the smart new BMC Competitions Department transporter and a Riley Pathfinder support car. The MG support team included Alec Hounslow, Doug Watts and Jimmy Cox who drove the three main cars, together with Cliff Bray, Harold Wiggins and Dickie Green in the transporter. Marcus Chambers and his wife took the Riley Pathfinder. The whole party—36 people in total—stayed in the decaying Château Chêne de Cœur, while Henry Stone and Tommy Wellman stayed behind to fit out a new development shop.

On the way to Le Mans, Cox experienced a heart stopping near-miss: 'We drove the four cars, and I was in the third car, Douggie Watts in the last one. We were all going down the road in convoy on the way to Dover, and the next thing I knew, the back end had gone. I was about two-thirds of the way round a left-hand bend and the car spun three times. I can remember Douggie shouting to me, "Hold on to it, Jim!", and then the car suddenly swung the other way round and shot forwards. The car went up the bank as I put the anchors on, and to our amazement there was no damage, other than a slightly bent front number plate. I don't know to this day whether or not Marcus Chambers ever got to hear about this!'

Understandably, Jimmy Cox has some vivid recollections of the 1955 Le Mans race, including the well-known tragedy involving Pierre Levegh's Mercedes: 'I saw the Levegh accident very clearly, and in my opinion, the fault appeared to lie with Mike Hawthorn. Lance Macklin was driving a Healey, and Hawthorn shot past him. In my opinion, Mike Hawthorn misjudged coming into the pits—he must have been doing about 120mph (193.12km/h)—as instead of coming in behind Macklin, he cut in front of the Healey. As a result, Macklin pulled to the left, just as Levegh was coming up behind him. The Healey was full of fuel and, therefore, riding very low. It also had that tapered rear wing line, and so Levegh's Mercedes simply rode up the Healey's wing and shot into the air, dug into the bank, and all the stuff from the wreckage flew into the crowd. Some 87 people were killed; it was a terrible thing to see.'

The reason why Jimmy is so confident of the story is because he was standing not far from where the accident happened: 'I was on the look-out for our missing EX182, driven by Dick Jacobs.' In fact, Jacobs came off the track at Maison Blanche—the 'White House'—shortly after the Levegh accident, and his car was destroyed. He suffered serious injuries that forced him to retire from motor racing.

After the tragedy of the Le Mans race, the European authorities reacted against motor racing, and the Alpine Rally was cancelled. BMC decided to withdraw from racing activities in Britain and mainland Europe, concentrating the efforts of 'Comps' on rallying, supported by North American racing exploits at Sebring. However, one exception to the no-racing rule was the Dundrod Tourist Trophy. In rallies, the MGA would enjoy some notable and memorable successes, not least at the hands of Nancy Mitchell, who achieved a particularly remarkable result in the Mille Miglia of April 1956. Driving in appallingly wet conditions, she covered a distance of 1000 miles (1609.30km) in just over 15 hours and came third in her class.

Even more remarkably, Nancy Mitchell drove all the way; her co-driver, Pat Faichney, didn't get a chance at the wheel! The MGAs were finished in bright red for the Mille Miglia, instead of the traditional British racing green, as it had been noticed in previous events that patriotic Italians would close the gates at railway crossings upon the approach of any car that wasn't painted Italian racing red. Thus began the traditional BMC red finish, which would be carried through to the 'big Healeys' and the Mini-Coopers of the following decade.

Similar success was achieved in July of the same year, when a five-car team was entered in the Alpine Rally. These cars were MGA tourers—four finished in the new team colour of red and one in white—and were all fitted with black hardtops, of a type that would go on sale to the public in the autumn. Nancy Mitchell acquired a coveted Coupe des Alpes, while John Milne and Bill Shepherd came fourth and fifth in their class respectively.

The MGA Coupé

In September 1956, a year after the introduction of the MGA, a closed coupé version was added to the range. This offered refine-

CLIFF BRAY

The formation of the Abingdon based BMC Competitions Department in 1954, under the control of Marcus Chambers, put MG back in the heart of motor-sport. Leading lights included well-known MG people like Alec Hounslow, Henry Stone, Jack Crooke, Tommy Wellman, Harold Wiggins, Douggie Watts, Jimmy Cox and Cliff Bray. Cliff had joined MG as a 16-year-old apprentice in September 1938. A year later, the war started, and he moved into the press shop on war work until February 1942.

After the war, Cliff moved into the rectification department under George Morris, where he remained for a while until the threat of cut-backs caused his transfer to the production line, where he stayed for about a year. 'Then one day, I saw George Morris and asked him if there was any chance of returning to rectification, to which he replied, "Okay,' and I worked under him for another four years.' Before long, Cliff found himself carrying out road tests (still under George Morris) until October 1954, when he joined the development team under Syd Enever. 'There we prepared TDs, the Magnettes for the 1955 Monte Carlo Rally and, of course, the four 1955 EX182 cars.'

ments that previously had been unknown on an MG sports car—wind-up windows and opening quarterlights. These transformed the nimble MGA into an all-weather sports car for those who were less hardy than the traditional sports car enthusiast. Today, the lines of the MGA Coupé are generally regarded as being very attractive, but the passage of time, nostalgia and changing fashions have altered perception of the aesthetic success of the design, rather as they have with the TF Midget. Although the idea for the MGA Coupé came from Abingdon, warranting an entry in the EX-Register as EX197, the actual design and execution were the responsibility of Eric Carter at Coventry.

Jim O'Neill recalls the genesis of the MGA Coupé well: 'I remember going to Coventry with John Thornley and Syd Enever to view the car; none of us had any idea of what we were likely to see. When I saw it, I felt that it was too round and lumpy, and I told Eric so.' However, working from the basic shape of the Alpine Rally hardtop, Morris Motors had gone ahead with the production of wooden patterns—known as bucks—without formal authorization. Jim O'Neill continues: 'Eric informed me that production tooling was already under way, although the cost had not been cleared, and implored me not to "rock the boat". In retrospect, I am sure that the MGA Coupé is a classic shape.' Don Butler was also aware of the controversy surrounding the styling of the Coupé: 'People said that the shape of the roof was designed by Eric so that he could wear his trilby inside!'

Some mystery surrounds the black MGA Coupé prototype, ULJ 426. Studio photographs of this, which were much in evidence at the time of the car's launch, show a style of rear window that is similar to that of the optional detachable Vanden Plas hardtop. However, Jim O'Neill is adamant that the prototype he and Thornley saw at Morris Bodies was virtually identical to the production car. British Motor Heritage archivist Anders Clausager kindly checked the records for ULJ 426, and found that it was listed as chassis number 13355, built in March/April 1956 and allocated to Morris Bodies Branch as a development vehicle. The studio photographs were taken on 3 May, two months before the public début of the hardtop in the Alpine Rally, and even further in advance of the Coupé's appearance in October.

Jim O'Neill points out that the tooling for the unique Coupé body panels was relatively simple: 'The roof of the Coupé was hand formed in three sections by rolling and beating over a reinforced former; likewise for the windscreen pillars.' Despite the fact that they were less expensive than fully fledged press tooling, even these relatively simple formers were quite costly, so, Jim adds, 'on MG's tight budget, questions would have been asked if they had been scrapped, hence Eric's concern.' Don Butler believes that the original intention was to build only about 50 MGA Coupés, which would explain the choice of such low-volume production techniques with their high proportion of hand work.

The MGA tourer had been designed without external door han-

Left *The MGA Coupé bodyshell required a great deal of hand finishing. Note the door window frame template being used to check the fit of the roof. (Rover.BMIHT)*

Below *KMO 326 had quite a chequered career, including use by Syd Enever as his personal development car. The paint finish was special, the lower body being finished in pearlescent gold (at one time considered for the EX181 record breaker), while the roof was white. Thankfully, the car survives in the hands of a British MG enthusiast. (Rover/BMIHT)*

dles, release cables being fitted to the interior of the doors (à la Mini) and reached through the hinged side-curtains. Obviously, this arrangement would have been impractical for the Coupé, so very neat and inconspicuous chrome-plated door catches were designed exclusively for the closed car by Eric Carter. These were mounted vertically at the tops of the door skins, and are probably the most unusual and distinctive catches ever to be seen on a British car.

Shortly before the MGA Coupé entered production, John Thornley had spoken to Vanden Plas, BMC's Kingsbury based coachbuilding wing, about the possibility of creating a cabriolet version of the MGA. The company was given the task of producing a removable aluminium hardtop (recorded as EX196 in the Ex-Register, in February 1956), which would be available as a factory accessory until replaced by a cheaper fibreglass hardtop in 1959.

The original Vanden Plas hardtop went on sale in October 1956 and was, Jim O'Neill recalls, very expensive: 'Service Department felt that there was no way that they could market the Vanden Plas top with the normal service loading. Another hardtop was exam-

ined, made by Universal Laminations, constructed of wood and fibreglass, and covered in vinyl. A fair amount of work would have been required to make this top suitable for production. However, before this could take place, the hardtop business of Universal Laminations was taken over by Dennis Ferranti. They made a quality product in double-skinned fibreglass with steel reinforcements.'

The proposed Vanden Plas cabriolet version of the MGA would have been based upon the Coupé, with its superior locks and fittings. It would have had a luxurious folding hood like the contemporary Jaguar XK140 drophead coupé. Had this idea proceeded, there would have been three basic variants of the MGA: the tourer, the more expensive Coupé, and the premium priced cabriolet. In the end, however, the idea was dropped, probably because of production problems, BMC indifference and the fact that such a car (which would have been considerably heavier than the standard MGA) would have struggled to perform adequately with the 1489cc engine.

John Thornley also related his thoughts about the MGA Coupé

Right *As an alternative to the fixed-head Coupé, those who preferred the flexibility offered by a choice of open or closed motoring could choose this Vanden Plas designed hardtop, similar to the type used on MGA rally cars during 1956. (Rover/BMIHT)*

Below *The Vanden Plas hardtop proved rather too expensive, so a cheaper glass reinforced plastic alternative was offered in 1959. (Rover/BMIHT)*

to me, and it was clear that the ideas that eventually led him towards the MGB GT were already germinating by this time: 'In the early fifties, when we were playing with George Phillips' TDs, which finally grew into the MGA, I saw, in a production car race at Silverstone, three DB2/4 Aston Martins running in line ahead, and I became obsessed with the thought that they were of the shape which we should pursue. By then, the MGA was too far down the road and, mainly because of the boot lid, the MGA Coupé bore scant relationship to the DB2/4!' By the time that Abingdon began work on the MGA's replacement, Thornley was determined to do things differently.

BMC 'Jaguars': six-cylinder Magnette and Pathfinder
Alongside the mainstream projects at Abingdon, there were always other ideas that were being investigated, either at Cowley's behest or through Abingdon's own initiative. Typical of these were the six-cylinder MG Magnette and Riley Pathfinder. In November 1955, design responsibility for the Pathfinder, at the time the sole

representative of the Riley marque (the last of the traditional styled Rileys, the RME, having been discontinued in mid-1955), passed from Cowley to the MG design office at Abingdon. It had already earned itself the unfortunate nicknames of 'Ditchfinder' and 'Hedgefinder' (see panel), and as they were responsible for its production, the Abingdon team was keen to do something to improve public perception of the car.

Ever inventive, Gerald Palmer had designed a twin-cam conversion of the 2.6-litre, six-cylinder C-series engine, the latter having made its début in the previous year in the Wolseley 6/90, sister car to the Riley Pathfinder. S. V. Smith instructed John Thornley to engineer this unit into a much improved Pathfinder, so that it could be shown in prototype form at the Earls Court Motor Show, in October 1956. Thornley and Enever took this project on board, suggesting that, at the same time, the suspension should be redesigned to produce a comfortable sporting saloon with good handling. Similar in concept and appearance to the MGA twin-cam four-cylinder unit, there is little doubt that the twin-cam C-series

The Varitone version of the ZB Magnette was distinguished by its (normally) two-tone paint scheme and larger rear window. The window aperture was enlarged manually on the production line. This car is a pre-production prototype; the lower corners of the rear window were less square on production cars. (Rover/BMIHT)

could have provided a powerful opponent to the classic Jaguar XK engine, and that the combination of the engine and a well engineered chassis would have provided a serious challenge to the Jaguar saloons.

Both the Cowley DO-Register and the Abingdon EX-Register record work carried out in connection with improving the Pathfinder: the first entry at Abingdon, against DO1067, is dated 30 November, 1954. Many references to DO1067 and EX207 are cross-related and, in due course, a prototype was built, with the experimental chassis number EX207/1. Terry Mitchell recalls that this car, equipped with disc brakes, was known at the factory as 'the barge'. Denis Williams also remembers the prototype, which had fins not unlike those of the forthcoming ADO9 MG Magnette, and was painted in three shades of blue, each colour separated by a chrome moulding: 'I was driving this car one day when, stopped at traffic lights, the man in the next car called out to me, asking where he could buy such a "marvellous car". He was crestfallen when I told him that it was only a prototype!'

By the end of March 1956, however, work on the new engine was abandoned, and the plan shifted to re-engineering the rear suspension to the more conventional Nuffield leaf-spring arrangement, and fitting the normal C-series unit in place of the Riley four. This was implemented in two stages: new suspension in late 1956, and new engine in October 1957, the car becoming the Riley Two-Point-Six. One might speculate that the twin-cam six—had it gone ahead—would have been a logical choice for the MGC some ten years later, but the significant redesign of the C-series in 1966, and the arrival of Jaguar into the fold the same year, would probably have made a twin-cam unit redundant. But it would have been interesting while it lasted!

At about the same time, the Abingdon team fitted a normal C-series six-cylinder engine in a Magnette, which gained the code EX202. Terry Mitchell recalls that, not surprisingly, it was front-heavy, but the combination of the more powerful engine in a lighter bodyshell made for a fast motor car. Don Hayter also remembers this car, with its modified front bodywork, made necessary by the bulkier engine. As he told Graham Robson, 'We built one, it was very quiet; it could out-drag Jaguars because it was so light.' The front-end lines of EX202 were laid out by Denis Williams: 'The car looked very similar to the normal Z Magnette, only it had a wider radiator grille—squarer, more like a Mercedes in appearance. The finished car was very nice to drive.'

It is not clear whether or not this project had been officially sanctioned by BMC, but without backing from the top, it would have been doomed to failure. Even had it reached production, it would

have been fairly short-lived, as BMC were already considering the future of their mid-sized and large saloons. There was also an unfortunate parallel with the Morris Oxford-based Isis, which utilized the C-series engine and had a longer wheelbase than its four-cylinder stable-mate: the Isis was not one of BMC's better cars.

Better Magnettes: the ZB, Manumatic and Varitone

Once production of the ZA Magnette was in full swing, work began on refining it for the inevitable 'mark two' version. For the ZB, which emerged in October 1956, little of significance had been altered: engine output had already been raised in the previous July by just over 8bhp (5.97kW) to 68.4bhp (51.01kW), while the final-drive ratio had been altered slightly. Externally, the distinctive chrome-plated 'hockey-stick' trims, which had distinguished the flanks of the ZA, were abandoned in favour of more conventional straight-through trims. Of more interest at the October Motor Show were two new variations on the Magnette theme: the Manumatic model with semi-automatic transmission, and the Varitone, which had a two-tone de-luxe finish. The latter was also distinguished by a wider wrap-around rear window, which had to be adapted to the bodyshell at Pressed Steel's Cowley plant by cutting out some of the metal in the roof by hand. For the Varitone—some examples of which, confusingly, were finished in a single body colour—the customer was charged a £37 premium over the £1041 price for the standard car.

The Manumatic transmission—also tried in other contemporary BMC cars—was a brave attempt at introducing a sort of 'half-way-house' automatic transmission in a sector of the market where it was relatively rare. At that stage, automatics were very much the preserve of much larger—particularly American—motor cars. The mechanism incorporated an automated clutch, which engaged at low revs and gradually released to take up drive at engine speeds above idle. A gear-lever was retained, but there was no clutch pedal. Unfortunately, the mechanism was far from smooth in operation, most noticeably at low speeds when manoeuvring, and sales were poor. Thus, before long, the option was dropped.

Another of the cars that 'got away' was the pillarless Z-series Magnette, which was an attempt at producing a more sporting variant of the Magnette that, presumably, could have commanded a higher price. There were precedents for this body style among the products of rival manufacturers: pillarless cars were popular in the USA, where the Rootes Group would enjoy some success with the Hillman Minx Californian, and some of the American styling influences were finding increasing favour in the UK. At least one running prototype was built, but in the end, the additional production costs could not be justified. The ZB Varitone, with its enlarged rear window and two-tone colour scheme, was a more viable and cost-effective alternative.

The pillarless Magnette prototype escaped from captivity and was used by Charles Griffin as family transport for a number of years. Both Charles and his son Brian (whose involvement with the MG marque is described in Chapter 6) remember this car with affection. The former told me, 'The pillarless Magnette was designed by Gerald Palmer and, initially, was duo-tone blue and cream. I bought the car and used it for some time.' Sadly, the special body was written off in an accident in about 1960, and the car was rebodied with a conventional ZB shell.

Variations on the MGA theme
No sooner had the MGA entered volume production, than the possibilities of derivatives were being explored. The first ideas centred on a special competition version, and John Thornley expressed his views on this in August 1954: 'There is no point in building five or six ultra-special cars for racing. This is very expensive, proves very little, and the competitions for which they can be entered are very few.' Thornley went on to develop his theme, suggesting that a series of 50 or 100 cars, based upon the MGA, could be built, five or six of them being kept by Abingdon to race themselves, and the remainder sold to privateers. His proposed specification boiled down to an MGA with a twin-cam engine, possibly fuel-injection, a five-speed or overdrive gearbox, disc brakes and alloy panelling. Before long, this idea sowed the seeds of the EX186 project.

Although EX186 was intended to be a limited-production road-racer, the twin-cam engine was destined for a volume-production derivative of the MGA: the MGA Twin Cam (EX187, for which entries date from June 1955). The idea of a twin-cam MGA largely stemmed from proposals for new engines made by Gerald Palmer during his tenure at BMC, and it is hardly surprising that the Abingdon engineers wholeheartedly embraced the idea of a unique, thoroughbred engine for one of their sports cars. While a completely new car would have been even better, MG had to be content with an uprated version of the MGA. For a while, the MG team referred to the twin-cam car as the MGB (for example, sketch SK7094, dated 18 October, 1955, refers to EX187 as the MGB), but by March 1957, common sense prevailed, and the car was referred to as an MGA derivative. It was hoped that it would form the basis of future MG competition cars, providing a powerful force with which to challenge the strengthening opposition from Italy and Germany.

Two entirely different engines were tried in the MGA. One was developed from Gerald Palmer's concept by the celebrated Eddie Maher of Morris Engines, at Courthouse Green, Coventry; the other was designed from scratch by Austin veteran William G. Appleby. This was exactly the sort of internal rivalry that Leonard Lord liked to foster. Bill Appleby was the chief engineer responsible for engines at Longbridge and, therefore, was Eddie Maher's boss. Like Maher, Appleby had had some competition engine experience, having been the senior draughtsman under Tom Murray Jamieson during development of the exotic twin-camshaft, 750cc Austin racing engine, which had been designed to challenge the MG Q- and R-type racing Midgets in the 1930s. In the late 1940s, he had been one of the team that designed the Austin A40 engine, which led to the B-series of 1952, so both departments were sure to produce interesting offerings.

Palmer had originally envisaged that production versions of his own sports car, described previously, would have been the principal application for his twin-cam version of the B-series. Consequently, he argued the case for development of the sports car on the back of the twin-cam engine exercise. Clearly, Palmer saw the twin-cam engine as an essential element in the battle against the European opposition, but he knew that an all-new unit was unlike-

ly to find favour in BMC, which tended to think in terms of enormous volumes for new engines: '...so I planned to use the basic B-series crankcase with virtually no alterations; the overhead-camshaft head would be a simple substitute for the normal overhead-valve head. I actually laid out the basis of the engine on my drawing board at Cowley, and got Vic Oak to agree to it. Then, Jimmy Thompson, the chief engineer at Morris Engines, took over responsibility, and Eddie Maher developed it.' In the process, some of Palmer's ideas were abandoned: 'I had envisaged that there would have been a version with fuel-injection—using a new SU fuel-injection system nestling on top of the engine—but this idea was dropped.'

The Longbridge designed unit, however, was a totally unique engine with a 66-degree angle between the plane of the camshaft cover gaskets and the block. The Austin engine would have been even more costly to produce in quantity than the 80-degree unit that Maher had schemed from Palmer's original 90-degree proposal (the reduced angle being adopted to allow the engine to fit into the MGA!). Both engines were tested in the MGA and, originally, it was intended that both should compete, alongside a standard pushrod car, in the Golden Jubilee Tourist Trophy race at Dundrod, in September 1955, just before the launch of the MGA at Frankfurt.

In the event, however, only the Eddie Maher unit was used. Alec Hounslow had received a call from Syd Enever on the night before the cars were due to travel to Liverpool, instructing him to have Appleby's engine removed and crated for return to Longbridge. This was done late at night, a normal 1500 pushrod engine being substituted for the Austin unit. As a result, the Dundrod entry comprised a single twin-cam and two pushrod cars. Bill Appleby's engine was never seen again.

At Dundrod, all sorts of problems were experienced with the twin-cam, the Abingdon team not being that familiar with its Weber carburettors: 'Ron Flockhart was driving and, after practice, he said that he wouldn't go out in the car as it was. We sat in the garage and tried to sort out what to do. We had the car in pieces with Syd Enever looking over it; we took the carburettor to pieces, and everything, but we never did really find out the problem.' In the end, a misfire was traced to a split manifold, and the twin-cam retired half-way through the race. Jimmy Cox also recalls that one of the cars at Dundrod was fitted with an experimental alloy fuel tank: 'It got split when the car went over Deer's Leap, and that was the end of that.'

The Morris Engines Branch, at Coventry, continued development of the twin-cam unit during the following three years, some testing being carried out on experimental units fitted to the EX179 record breaker, in 1956, and to the all-new EX181 in the following year. By early 1956, the basic design of the twin-cam engine had been determined, and at a meeting of the BMC engine development panel, in February, its potential uses were discussed. John Thornley's aim with the MGA Twin Cam was to tackle the burgeoning Porsche market, although he was at pains to point out to George Harriman, in a memorandum of May 1956, that 'there is no truth in the idea that I want to build a motor car like the Porsche. I am very content for some time yet with the MGA chassis as a basic design, and the only thing I covet about the Porsche is its market.'

The capacity of the twin-cam unit was raised from the 1489cc of the contemporary pushrod 1500 by increasing the bore from 73 to 75.4mm, while the 88.9mm stroke was retained to give 1558cc. The weight of the new engine was 60lb (27.22kg) greater than the pushrod unit, at 474lb (215kg), but this only slightly offset the considerable performance gains. The greater capacity came about largely as a result of MG's desire to compete in the new FIA and SCCA 1600cc racing classes, and the original intention had been for the twin-cam to be a very low-volume unit. However, this idea was overtaken by grander plans for the model, production volumes of 75 per week being talked about, although never achieved.

In addition to the MGA, John Thornley saw the potential for what he called a 'Grande Tourisme' version of the MG Magnette, equipped with the twin-cam unit and disc brakes. Had this come about, the unit cost of the engine could have been reduced, and the problems that dogged it in service might have been tackled more rapidly and effectively. Certainly, Thornley was not alone in these

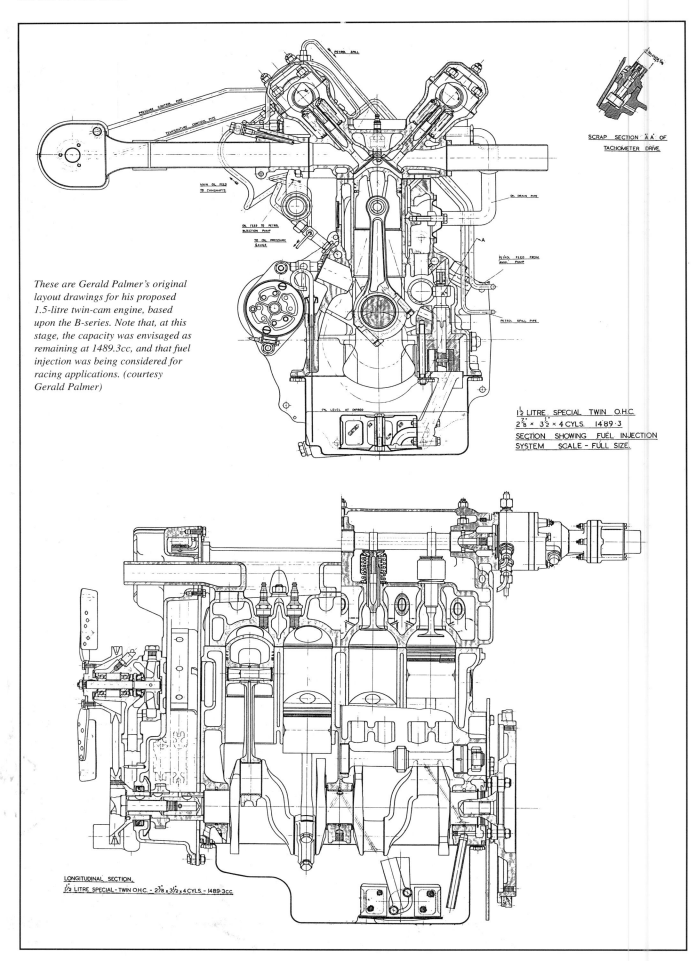

SCRAP SECTION 'A A' OF
TACHOMETER DRIVE.

*These are Gerald Palmer's original
layout drawings for his proposed
1.5-litre twin-cam engine, based
upon the B-series. Note that, at this
stage, the capacity was envisaged as
remaining at 1489.3cc, and that fuel
injection was being considered for
racing applications. (courtesy
Gerald Palmer)*

1½ LITRE, SPECIAL TWIN O.H.C.
2⅞" × 3½" × 4 CYLS. 1489·3
SECTION SHOWING FUEL INJECTION
SYSTEM SCALE - FULL SIZE.

LONGITUDINAL SECTION.
1½ LITRE SPECIAL - TWIN O.H.C. - 2⅞ × 3½ × 4 CYLS. - 1489·3cc.

The Longbridge designed 'Austin' twin-cam engine was briefly installed in an MGA, but never raced. (Rover/BMIHT)

The MGA twin-cam engine was a tight fit in the car's engine compartment. (Rover)

thoughts. Other supporters of a twin-cam Magnette included Gerald Palmer and competitions manager Marcus Chambers, who had put forward the idea not long after his arrival, but had found that no one was interested.

By the summer of 1958, the production MGA Twin Cam was ready for introduction, and it appeared in mid-July. Much testing had been carried out at MIRA, and elsewhere, by Tom Haig, who was given a single prototype, bearing the registration number ORX 855. This car features in numerous contemporary photographs. It had quite a busy time at Abingdon, since it was also used to test Jimmy Cox's engine for Ted Lund's Le Mans MGA entry of 1959.

The changes for the MGA Twin Cam were quite extensive, if not as far reaching as Abingdon might have liked. Four-wheel Dunlop disc brakes were added (quite an exotic specification for a road going sports car in the MGA class in 1958), and attractive, centre-lock disc wheels—not unlike those of the Jaguar D-type racing car—were fitted. To accommodate the much bulkier engine, the bonnet was reprofiled with a greater curvature (made common on all MGAs), and the steering rack was moved forward by 1in (2.54cm), the steering arms being modified to suit. In the engine bay, access for maintenance was more restricted than the normal MGA, so early in production (chassis number 592; September 1958), removable access panels were inserted in the inner wings; these were designed by Don Hayter. Inside, there were relatively minor trim and equipment changes. It was clear that most of the

money had been expended under the bonnet, and just as MG would find with the MGC and MGB GT V8 in subsequent decades, the lack of a different visual identity proved something of a sales handicap to the Twin Cam.

Unfortunately, the exciting new engine of the MGA Twin Cam proved to be its Achilles' heel and, ultimately, caused its downfall. The design was handicapped from the outset by the requirement that it be manufactured using existing BMC facilities. The retention of the engine block casting from the pushrod B-series allowed the basic machining operations to be carried out at Longbridge, using the existing Trans-Matic machinery. Following this process, the engines were taken to Morris Engines at Coventry for finishing and final assembly.

Because of the desire to use the car in serious competition—and to take advantage of the superior performance at high engine-speed of twin-cam engines—it was decided to make the crankshaft webs thicker than those of the pushrod unit. This meant that the main journals had to be correspondingly narrower, and although the bearings were changed to a heavier-duty type and used with a new design of competition con-rod, this led to inherent weaknesses in the engine when under load. Although not a serious problem in normal use, this proved an embarrassment in competition, where the twin-cam could prove fragile. In the Sebring race of 26 March, 1960, for example, one of the factory cars threw a con-rod through the side of its engine; it was not an isolated incident.

The Lund MGA Twin Cam Coupé at Le Mans, June 1960. (courtesy Bob West)

This MGA, photographed at Abingdon, has been painted with an experimental two-tone colour scheme. Minor Travellers (in background) were assembled at Abingdon between 1960 and 1964, which puts the date of this photograph at sometime after 1960. (Rover)

However, other problems occurred with the MGA Twin Cam engine under normal service conditions, and these probably had a greater bearing on its ultimate fate than the competition-related difficulties. Firstly, the engine had an inordinate thirst for oil (as much as 1pt/0.57 litres in every 120 miles/193.12km), which was soon tracked down to a poor piston-ring design. The second issue was pinking, or pre-ignition, to which the twin-cam engine was particularly prone. In the main, this stemmed from its high compression ratio (9.9:1 throughout most of production), which meant that it was particularly sensitive to fuel quality.

Jimmy Cox remembers that, for a while, the cause of some of the pre-ignition problems proved a mystery: 'We always had problems with that engine. I remember Laurie Hands, a big bloke from Champion, came down and tried all sorts of different plugs, gaps, cores, etc, but without any luck. We had a bloke in Cologne who kept burning holes in pistons, and for a while we couldn't replicate this. Then Tommy Haig burnt a hole in a piston on the way back from MIRA. Eventually, we reduced the compression ratio to 8.3:1 by changing the penthouse-top piston for a flatter, rounded piston.'

Partial solutions were introduced throughout production, including new pistons with twin-segment scraper rings in November 1958, and N3 spark plugs in April 1959. However, by the time the engineers had all but solved these problems, the engine had earned itself a poor service reputation, not helped by the poor engine accessibility. By the end of the decade, the future of this expensive, highly-strung unit was looking increasingly doubtful. Very late in the day, the compression ratio was lowered to 8.3:1, power output dropping as a result from 108bhp (80.54kW) to 100bhp (74.57kW).

It is not often appreciated quite how late in the Twin Cam's life

that the compression ratio change took place. The first car recorded as having the new 8.3:1 unit was car number YD1-2608 (built with engine number 2270 during April 1960), yet the last series-production Twin Cam (YD1-2610) was started down the line on the same day. A single special-order car (YD1-2611) was built for Mike Ellman-Brown on 18 May and, as a result, some people have assumed that volume production went on longer than was the case.

EX186: an MG thoroughbred for Le Mans

The EX-Register lists many MGA related exercises, which enjoyed varying degrees of success, including an idea for a tubular space-framed MGA, designated EX183. Undoubtedly, the most exciting of these ideas, however, was EX186, the proposed racing derivative of the MGA, which had a streamlined body laid out by Denis Williams at Abingdon. EX186 utilized the twin-cam engine that would appear in the MGA Twin Cam (EX187), but unlike EX183, it was based on a highly modified MGA chassis, complete with De Dion rear suspension designed by Terry Mitchell. This was the first significant project with which Dickie Wright became involved, following his arrival at Abingdon in March 1956: 'Little had been done at that stage: just odd drawings and so forth. Terry Mitchell and I set out the layout, using the normal 10in (25.4cm) grid, and although at first it was something of a spare-time job, it suddenly took on impetus and had to be finished.'

THE LAST PRODUCTION MGA TWIN CAMS OF APRIL 1960

Chassis no.	Start build	Finish build	Engine no.	Notes
YM2-2607	6 April	8 April	2264	9.9:1 compression ratio, unless modified.
YD3-2608	6 April	8 April	2270	Second engine number with 8.3:1 compression ratio.
YD1-2609	6 April	13 April	2269	First engine number with 8.3:1 compression ratio.
YD1-2610	6 April	14 April	2249	9.9:1 compression ratio, unless modified; last series-production car.
YD1-2611	18 May	14 June	2245	Built to special order for Mike Ellman-Brown.

According to factory records, the first engine with an 8.3:1 compression ratio was number 2269, which was fitted to the second from last series-production car. The previous engine in the sequence, and presumably the last 9.9:1 unit (2268), was fitted to YM1-2586, built between 11 February and 24 March. Subsequently, many twin-cams were converted to 8.3:1 in service, but this table shows that production 8.3:1 cars are very rare, even in MGA Twin Cam terms. The dates also lend credence to the story that the Twin Cam's death sentence was finally carried out after Marcus Chambers returned from the Sebring 12-hour race of 26 March, 1960.

Denis Williams was given a fairly free hand in the styling, which resembled a Mercedes SLR: 'I was given the task of laying out the full-size body lines and all the structural details required for the completed body, which was made by Midland Sheet Metal of Nuneaton, with whom I liaised closely during its construction.' In keeping with Thornley's idea of August 1954, MG planned to build a limited number of these cars—Denis Williams believes that it was just two or three; others have suggested ten—but in the event, only one was ever completed. EX186 was never raced, but Dickie Wright remembers that Tom Haig drove it once or twice.

Although the idea had begun to take shape in 1954—and it was entered in the EX-Register as 'Le Mans Car for 1956'—the early drawings date from August 1955. Before long, a model had been made by Harry Herring, but the running prototype did not take shape until 1959, at about the time that Ted Lund and Colin Escott were preparing for the first of three forays to Le Mans in SRX 210. Again, I am indebted to Cliff Bray, whose comprehensive records show how the EX186 story unfolded (see panel below right).

In fact, Ted Lund had hoped to persuade the top brass at Longbridge to allow him to race EX186, having booked himself an entry at Le Mans for June 1959. When BMC refused, Lund was offered a new racer based on EX182, his alloy-bodied 1955 car. In the intervening years, this had been run by the Fitzwilliam racing team. Bob West, the current owner of SRX 210 has evidence that proves, almost beyond a shadow of a doubt, that the body of his car is based upon a 1955 Le Mans bodyshell, fitted to an MGA Twin Cam chassis (number YD3-627S). In addition, the late Ted Lund told the second owner, Bob McElroy (who sold the car to West in 1993), that SRX 210 was definitely based upon his 1955 car.

With an engine specially built by Jimmy Cox, Ted Lund and Colin Escott made a noble effort at Le Mans, but their hopes were dashed following a high-speed collision with an Alsatian dog, 20 hours into the race. SRX 210 returned to Le Mans again in 1960, the bodywork resembling a fastback MGA Coupé (designed by Don Hayter, and coded EX212). The engine was bored out to 1762cc and fitted with twin Weber 40DCOE carburettors. Thus equipped, the car completed the race and won the 2-litre class, against a strong field. Ted Lund tried again in 1961, the racer having lost its MGA grille in favour of a smaller air intake, but this time he was unsuccessful, as the engine expired about three hours into the race when a big-end bolt failed on the Mulsanne Straight.

As far as EX186 was concerned, Terry Mitchell recalls that around Christmas 1960, the order suddenly came from John Thornley to make it disappear: 'He told us that someone at Longbridge had got wind of it, so it was crated up and shipped off to San

Hardly any photographs of EX186 have ever appeared in print, so this example, taken by Denis Williams, is a rare prize. It shows the finished prototype in the development shop at Abingdon, bearing trade plates so that it could be used unlicensed on the road. (courtesy Denis Williams)

Francisco.' The fact was that the tragic accident at Le Mans in 1955 had cast a pall over motor racing in general—and Le Mans in particular—and BMC, which had withdrawn from factory participation at Le Mans after 1955, was not prepared to sanction EX186. Dickie Wright remembers that EX186 often 'disappeared' under a dust-sheet when the Longbridge big-wigs were due, so Thornley and Enever had clearly gone out on a limb with the project.

All evidence of the existence of EX186 was carefully eradicated. Jeff Clarke remembers being told by Alec Hounslow, 'There are two De Dion MGA axles in the shop; I want you to take them out and destroy them!' Jeff duly collected these EX186 spares and proceeded to cut them up with an oxy-acetylene torch: 'We said that there would be a bloke in San Francisco who would have given his eye teeth for them, but Alec wasn't going to have an argument about it.' Apparently, EX186 was purchased in 1961 by the well-known Californian MG distributor Kjell Qvale, who later became embroiled in the Jensen-Healey affair. He kept the car for five years, before passing it on to a fellow Californian. Later, it changed

---

EX186: PROPOSED LE MANS CAR

SPECIFICATION

Twin-cam engine and special alloy body; modified MGA frame with De Dion rear suspension; engine number 16G/U/316; gearbox number 1881, with close-ratio gears; differential ratio 11/43; tyres 5.50x15 front, 6.00x15 rear; 22mph (35.40km/h) per 1000rpm

HISTORY

19/3/59	Build commenced.
09/5/59	Chassis to Midland Sheet Metal Company.
20/5/59	Returned to development shop.
26/5/59	Cancelled as a Le Mans entrant.
31/1/61	Shipped to San Francisco and acquired by Kjell Qvale
1966	Sold to Californian resident, who keeps it until 1982
1982	Seen in USA by Henry Stone; believed currently under restoration

Factory information courtesy Cliff Bray.

Left This eighth-scale model, now in the British Motor Heritage collection, features a removable rear section, which can be exchanged for the longer tail seen on the left. The intention was to provide a larger luggage compartment, but the increased length could possibly have accommodated 2+2 seating as well. (David Knowles)

Facing page This attractive four-seater MGA is owned by Richard Harvey of Wincanton. Although built to a very high standard, claims that it was converted by Eric Carter have proved impossible to verify. Nevertheless, the car is a nice demonstration of what might have been. (courtesy Richard Harvey)

hands at least once more, in 1982, and now it is rumoured to be in the course of restoration.

In the meantime, there had been changes in the management of BMC's competition department which, until the spring of 1957, had been run in conjunction with the development shop by Alec Hounslow. By all accounts, this arrangement had been less than satisfactory, not helped by a conflict of personalities between Alec and Marcus Chambers, so 'Comps' was hived off from development. Jimmy Cox went with Alec into the development department: 'Alec Hounslow had run both in the shop, but it had become too big for him to handle, so Douggie Watts, Tommy Wellman and

Doug Hamblin (who was later killed in a road accident at Bix Hill) went into a separate 'Comps' section. I stayed with Henry Stone, Bunny Hillier (Jimmy's cousin), Reg Hadden, Harold Wiggins and Cliff Bray in development.' At this stage, the development shop took in some apprentices: 'There was Terry Ward and George Bartle, and Henry Stone's son, Don, also came through the shop.'

EX195: the cheaper MGA

MG also investigated the possibility of a cheaper and lighter version of the MGA (EX195). Fitted with a single 1¾in (4.45cm) SU carburettor, Morris Minor propshaft and Austin A30 steering box,

THE AUSTIN-HEALEY SPRITE

For some time before the merger with Nuffield, the designers at Austin had been interested in producing a small, low-cost sports car based on the running gear of the AS3 Austin A30. Surviving records show that they made one or two attempts at this in the early 1950s, one of which was a curvaceous, but rather bulbous, fibreglass-bodied roadster with no doors, known as the 'Red Devil'. Little came of these ideas, however, presumably because they were thought to have comparatively little sales or profit potential compared to other projects. When the vast American sports car market had been opened up by MG, Austin-Healey and Triumph, interest returned, and the ever enthusiastic and inventive Donald Healey needed little more than the encouragement of Leonard Lord to begin investigating a sports car based on A30 components.

The 1950s had seen the growth of home-built 'specials', often using pre-war Ford parts with lightweight fibreglass bodyshells. These crude, but sporty looking, cars offered a cheap entry into the sports car market for the impecunious enthusiast. One of the better low-volume specials was produced by Turner, and this car utilized not only the new Austin A30 engine, but also the front and rear suspension: it was a clear indication of what would be possible with better resources. The Morris Motors—and indeed MG—men had also dabbled with the idea of a small car based upon the AS3 engine (see Appendix 1), but there is little doubt that Leonard Lord, who maintained an open disdain for former Nuffield employees, preferred to rely on the Austin sector, in the obvious hope of repeating the Healey 100's success. By using Healey as a consultant, no doubt he also reasoned that the exercise would be much cheaper than using BMC resources.

Thus, a prototype was built, entirely to Healey's design, for presentation to Leonard Lord at Longbridge, at the end of January 1957. In Lord's absence, this prototype—coded Q1 by Healey—was inspected by his assistant, George Harriman. Approval was soon granted, the Austin drawing office code ADO13 being assigned to the project, and production was planned to commence in the summer of 1958 at Longbridge. Initially, the car was to have been called the

Austin-Healey Imp, but the Rootes Group already had rights to this name, so the BMC 'names cupboard' was raided to produce Sprite, last used before the war on a Riley. Even then, negotiations had to be carried out with Daimler, who had also staked a claim to the Sprite name for a proposed Lanchester.

By 1958, plans for the new ADO15 Mini, which was also to be produced at Longbridge, were advanced, so it was thought more logical for the Sprite to be built at Abingdon. In fact, MG had already been involved with the project, much of the on-road development having been carried out by Tommy Haig, MG's test driver, while Syd Enever helped cure some structural deficiencies. Jim O'Neill recalls Syd Enever's involvement: 'Longbridge had given the engineering sign-off for the car, but due to the rather unusual quarter-elliptic rear springs, Syd decided to give the car the usual MG pavé test. It was found that a certain amount of extra reinforcement around the heel-board area was required. Brackets were quickly produced, virtually over the weekend by Barrett Engineering, a firm always ready to help us out in an emergency. Bodyshells already made up were modified and production was continued.'

Don Hayter was also involved with the Sprite at this stage: 'Six cars had been tested to the "Abingdon standard", loaded up with about 50lb (22.68kg) on boot mounted luggage racks; the bodies were cracking over the rear wheel arch on the pavé tests. At this time, I was working at Bodies Branch, at Quinton Road in Coventry, on the MGB, and I ran a Sprite up and down between Abingdon and Coventry every day. By the time that I had been doing this for a fortnight, there was already a noticeable crease in the body side panel, just behind the door shut line. We had produced some 5000 sets of body panels by that time—and quite a few cars—so Syd stopped production and reversed the cars up the line, necessitating ripping out of the stuck in boot trim and welding in of the reinforcements!'

By the time that the Sprite was launched, in May 1958, it had been well and truly adopted by the MG team. Don Hayter has the final word: 'We at Abingdon always thought that, had the Sprite gone into production at Longbridge, with the minimal testing done by Austin and Healey themselves, a rather nasty recall would have ensued—no further comment needed I think!'

the project was begun in November 1955. The following year, largely in response to BMC management's insistence that Abingdon should look again at the so-called 'buzz box' concept of a cheaper MG sports car, EX195 was reworked to take a 950cc A-series engine in place of the single-carburettor B-series unit. Cliff Bray, working in MG's development shop, recalls that this car was built with a 9.41 rear axle ratio and that it achieved a maximum speed of only 75mph (120.70km/h).

In fact, John Thornley had been asked by his bosses to consider a car based upon the floorpan and axles of the Morris Minor 1000, but he had countered that to do this idea justice, a new body would have been required, and he felt that this could not have been justified by the potential sales. Presumably without much enthusiasm, Abingdon allocated this project the code EX188. The idea echoed the concept that Cowley's engineers had investigated with DO1035, in 1951, but EX188 never got very far. Also, at about this time, MG looked at a number of engine options for economy vehicles: eight sketches are recorded on 28 August, 1957, for a range of engines, including a V4, a three-cylinder unit, and even V-twins.

The Suez fuel crisis of 1956 may appear to have been sufficient incentive for these proposals to be developed, but in truth, none proved to be of sufficient merit, either in terms of economy or performance. Nevertheless, work on EX195 continued, even when the arrival of the Austin-Healey Sprite at Abingdon was imminent. Among the copious entries in his notebook, Cliff Bray recorded that the 'MGA Utility Rebuild' (the A-series EX195) was built between 27 March and 24 April, 1958. This version featured 8in (20.32cm) front brakes, 7in (17.78cm) rear brakes, an 11.41 Riley 1.5 differential, a special propshaft and a Magnette gearbox. Entries were made in the EX-Register as late as 1959 for the cheap MGA, but in the end, the idea was never pursued fully.

It should be remembered that, by this stage, the vast majority of MGs went to North America, and John Thornley believed that this market had neither the need, nor the desire, for a 'buzz box' or a tiny-engined MGA that offered poorer performance than the standard car. Jim O'Neill remembers that, despite efforts to cheapen the parts, the cost saving provided by EX195 was something under £50. However, the project remained alive for some time primarily because the Abingdon team was aware that Healey was working on the Sprite and, as Thornley puts it, 'we had no intention of being left out of the race.' However, after the arrival of the Sprite, in May 1958, the importance of EX195 and EX188 evaporated.

Hindsight, of course, is wonderful, but if Abingdon had grappled with EX188, they might not have had to contend with the Sprite, nor the re-engineering that followed. As it was, Healey came up with a successful contender, which proved a commercial success,

and they sold the idea to George Harriman who, lest it be forgotten, had come from Austin like Lord and, therefore, was likely to have leaned towards Austin-Healey.

Yet another idea was for a four-seater version of the MGA which, according to John Thornley, would have been quite feasible, given the design of the chassis. As Thornley saw it, this 2+2 MGA would have been basically very similar to the two-seater version, even to the extent of retaining the same wings, scuttle, and rear body section; the extra length required would have been provided by a longer floorpan, chassis side-rails and doors. As an alternative to calling the car an MGA, Thornley even proposed fitting it with a different front end and offering it as a sporting Riley which, had it materialized, would have been the first Riley sports car since before the war. However, neither the four-seater MGA, nor an idea to provide the basic car with a much larger boot (tried in model form) made it further than the 'wish list'.

The MGA 1600

The second major change for the MGA, after the arrival of the Twin Cam in 1958, was the introduction of the 1600 in the following July. The engine size of the Twin Cam was 1588cc, so there was certainly some marketing and perhaps, to a lesser extent, production logic in rationalizing the engine capacity of its humbler pushrod brethren. However, the improvements for what was, in BMC parlance, ADO31, were not confined to the engine bay. Perhaps the most welcome change was the provision of front disc brakes, which were still regarded as fairly exotic pieces of equipment. Visible alterations were chiefly confined to larger front side-lamps with integral flashers, not unlike those that would be adopted for the MG 1100 saloon, three years later, and enlarged tail-lamp plinths fitted with separate indicators.

Genesis of the MGB: replacing the MGA

As is normal practice in the motor industry, as soon as the MGA was in production, the design team at Abingdon began to plan for its development and eventual succession. John Thornley told me that only two months after the MGA had been launched, he and Syd Enever produced a joint paper, titled 'Suggested Future Design and Development Programme for Abingdon Products', in which they attempted to set out the basis of future policy at Abingdon. Thornley recalled, with some amusement, that one of their recommendations had been that all future cars built at Abingdon should have separate chassis frames (the thought of an open monocoque body being considered extremely radical at that stage), yet by the middle of 1956, their thoughts were turning to what would become the MGB, which emerged as a monocoque-bodied car.

Above *Peter Neal produced this airbrushed illustration in 1957, based upon a sketch by Syd Enever. The intention was to produce a two-door luxury Gran Turismo MG, which could have been powered by the BMC C-series six-cylinder engine, and which was tentatively dubbed the MGC. Note the scallops beneath the headlamps, which would be a hallmark of the MGB when it emerged five years later. (courtesy Peter Neal)*

Below *The full-size Frua-bodied MGA, pictured at Abingdon. The front end, with its rather massive bumpers, was certainly very inspiring, but in general, it was felt that the car was a little 'over dressed' for an MG. Subsequently, this impressive hand-built prototype was cut up and disposed of to avoid the payment of import duties that would have been levied upon it by Customs and Excise. (Rover)*

Harry Herring's quarter-scale model of the Frua-bodied MGA, which makes an interesting comparison with the full-size car shown on the opposite page. Note the alternative coupé hardtop, which might be said to have had some influence on Jim O'Neill's EX205 coupé proposal. (Rover)

By the following year, another factor entered the equation: production of the Austin-Healey, by now in C-series-engined 100/6 guise, was transferred from Longbridge to Abingdon, along with design authority for the car. This was largely at the behest of George Harriman, who saw the obvious advantages of rationalizing sports car production to some extent. In addition, the 100/6 used a Morris Engines designed unit (and MG was more closely tied to the old Morris part of BMC), and space was needed at Longbridge for other models. Thus, MG found themselves not only looking into the replacement of the MGA—with its mid-range, four-cylinder engine and compact, relatively light sports body—but considering a larger, more powerful sports car to replace the 100/6.

Syd Enever had already sketched out some preliminary ideas for a larger, four-seater MGC sporting car (coupé and open), using the C-series engine, as Peter Neal's sketches illustrate. This concept was developed as EX210. However, the inevitable pressure on Abingdon to cut costs—as elsewhere in the BMC empire—coupled with problems with the Austin-Healey's Jensen built body, made the idea of a common successor to the MGA and 'big Healey' a logical one, even if its practical execution might not be easy. This also provided the realistic prospect, not lost on John Thornley or Syd Enever, of building the first six-cylinder MG sports car since the N-type Magnette had gone out of production in 1936. The story of the MGC, however, belongs in the following chapter.

The Frua-bodied MGA

In 1957, as MG was contemplating the form of the MGA replacement, Syd Enever sketched out what he felt was needed, and his rough drawings were used as the basis of styling sketches and the

inevitable models made by Harry Herring. These were followed by more sketches—by apprentice draughtsman Peter Neal—after which Enever took the drawings and a quarter-scale outline to show George Harriman at Longbridge. However, Harriman decided to send a complete MGA chassis to the Italian coachbuilders, Frua, and ask them to produce an alternative proposal for a new MG sports car.

The result was a smart, beautifully detailed car that looked more like a Maserati than an MG. The men at Abingdon admired its style, but were convinced that it was not right for an MG. The fact that it had been built elsewhere might also have been a factor contributing to their disapproval. They took justifiable pride in their work, and had only relatively recently regained a degree of design autonomy. There was also the fact that such a large car would have caused the contemporary 1558cc B-series engine to struggle. As Don Hayter points out, 'the car would have weighed about a ton and a half (1524.08kg), and with a separate chassis there is of course much duplication of metal—sills, "goal posts", etc—and so we began to turn our thoughts towards a monocoque body instead.' Obviously aimed at the US market, the interior of the Frua MGA had been elegantly trimmed in white leather, and the dashboard was a typically ornate Italian offering. A very attractive coupé hardtop had also been delivered with the prototype.

Sadly, BMC refused to pay the import duty on the expensive, hand built prototype once they had finished with it, so it had to be cut up with an acetylene torch while the local customs-and-excise looked on. The hardtop survived, however, and it was used as inspiration for some of Abingdon's own efforts as EX205. Now, even that has gone, the only evidence of its appearance being a quarter-

From the rear, the Frua MGA displays a resemblance to the touring styled Aston Martin DB4, which was introduced in 1959. (Rover)

scale model of the Frua car, made by Harry Herring, which survives in the British Motor Heritage collection.

Beginnings of the B: Geneva and EX205

It has often been said that the MGB was inspired by the lines of the last of the Abingdon record breakers—EX181, the 'Roaring Raindrop'. Indeed, John Thornley is on record as stating that this was Syd Enever's starting point. Needless to say, that is only part of the story. Enever's colleagues point out that he was particularly keen on very rounded shapes and, as a consequence, sometimes they had to try to temper this enthusiasm when developing his basic ideas. Peter Neal remembers Syd Enever as being 'very much a hands-on man—he didn't just leave the work to his subordinates; every part of the MGB has his stamp on it.'

If Syd Enever was the father of the MGB, Jim O'Neill and Don Hayter were surely its god parents. By the mid-1950s, O'Neill had risen to become MG's chief body engineer, and he recalled how the MGB began to evolve: 'Syd Enever and I used to visit the Geneva Motor Show. Sydney's designs were invariably started on the backs of fag packets or anything else which happened to be available, and this time was no exception.' Enever sketched out what he wanted: headlamps set back into scallops in the wings (a relatively recent European styling trait, exemplified by Pininfarina and other Italian coachbuilders), and a vertical 'prow', which would contain a lower, wider version of the traditional MG grille.

Upon their return from Geneva, O'Neill prepared a quarter-scale drawing and had a wooden model made up by the Morris Motors experimental shop. Once the model had been built, he recalls that he had little enthusiasm for this first attempt: 'The wheelbase was short and the body rounded. It looked more like a dumpy little pig

Right *Harry Herring's quarter-scale model of Jim O'Neill's proposal for a new MGA featured this removable coupé hardtop. The beginnings of the distinctive MGB rear bumper shape can be clearly seen in the outer parts of the model's bumpers, as can the vestigial rear fins. (David Knowles)*

Below *From the side, EX205 certainly had a powerful gran-turismo look about it, even if the styling was a little fussy and heavy looking. Note the door handle and boot lid handle, both of which bear a close resemblance to the push-button MGB handles of 1964 and later. (Rover)*

than a sports car. In fact, I called it the "pig".' Disappointed, but undaunted, O'Neill took the basic shape of the model and flattened the sides, giving it an appearance that was closer to the MGB we know so well. 'I remember using Austin A40 tail-lamps and a Ford bumper, which it was agreed we could use providing we paid half the tooling cost.' Thus began the development of EX205, 'MG 2 Seater', the first project register entries being dated June 1957.

Don Hayter enters the picture

Even before being given responsibility for the Austin-Healey 100/6, in 1957, the Abingdon design office had become busier, and Jim O'Neill's assistant, Denis Williams, found himself over-stretched. O'Neill told me, 'I particularly wanted a senior layout man to work on the MGB.' Thus, MG advertised for a new layout body draughtsman, a position that was soon filled by a 34-year-old

draughtsman from Aston Martin, Don Hayter, who had been working on the early development of the DB4. This was rather appropriate, given John Thornley's admiration of the Aston Martin DB2/4! Don would play a fundamental role in shaping the final lines of the MGB.

In June 1958, a year after work on EX205 had begun and, coincidentally, just before the MGA Twin Cam was launched, a new number, EX214, was allocated to the MGA replacement project. In the main, this came about because the idea of retaining a separate chassis for the car had been abandoned, but also several options were being explored that could have made the MGA replacement a much more radical design than EX205. At this point, the MG design team was able to draw upon the talents of its members: the body expertise of Jim O'Neill and Don Hayter was complemented by the chassis skills of Terry Mitchell and Roy Brocklehurst. Don

THE RENAULT FLORIDE

There is a story that Renault tried to claim that the MGB was a blatant copy—in styling terms—of their rear-engined Floride convertible of 1960. Although this was vigorously denied by BMC at the time, there was a connection between the two, albeit very tenuous.

It was, and is, common practice among motor manufacturers to check out what the opposition has to offer during motor shows, and MG was no exception. During one of their many visits to motor shows in mainland Europe—possibly the 1957 Geneva show—Jim O'Neill remembers that Syd Enever was quite taken by the styling features of some of the foreign cars, particularly the recessed headlamps that were just coming into vogue with the Italian coachbuilders (Ferrari in particular). As a result, Enever decided to feature this style on the MGB. However, as Harry Herring's surviving models show, there remained some doubt about the grille shape which, in most instances, is shown as a similar item to that of the MGA.

Then, at the Geneva show of 1959, Syd grabbed a press photograph of the new Renault Floride and proceeded, in typical fashion, to scribble on it with a soft pencil, drawing what would become the basis of the definitive MGB grille shape on the featureless front of the French car. Even so, this was not really the origin of the MGB grille, for the body shape had already been developing

The Renault Floride coupé, pictured at the Geneva Motor Show in March 1959. The shape of the nose had some influence on Syd Enever when considering the front-end treatment for the MGB. (Renault)

in that direction. Don Hayter points out that by cutting off the longer front overhang of Jim O'Neill's original proposal, the flatter front face of the MGB more or less created itself.

Hayter and Roy Brocklehurst sat down together and sketched out a sill section which, recalls Don, led to a test model: 'We made up a 4ft (1.22m) length to the design of this section, and twisted it. Syd wanted us to minimize scuttle shake—a problem with all open cars. In the end, we achieved a very stiff bodyshell.'

Even so, points out Jim O'Neill, after testing, the MGB was found to need an additional square-section steel tube, running across the car, to link the inner wings under the dashboard, with a plate connecting this tube to the transmission tunnel and concealed by the radio speaker console. When this solution was considered, no doubt, Jim was mindful of his experience with the TD Midget prototype ten years before!

Don Hayter had been refining the lines of the body, with guidance from Enever and O'Neill, and an elegant, slim sports car shape had evolved: 'Syd wanted to keep the record-breaker line used on EX181, complete with a long curvaceous nose. But to save weight, we sliced the nose off and set the headlamps into "pock-

ets", which rapidly led us to the familiar MGB nose shape.' The grille shape, recessed headlamps and delicate tail-fins, which would characterize the MGB, soon grew close to their final production appearance, and by 1959, the styling of the MGB was more or less fixed.

Far less certain than the car's styling, however, was the motive power, for MG was being encouraged to examine the planned new engine family being developed at Longbridge.

The engine options

Despite an apparent lack of progress in the rationalization of its product lines, BMC was rather more successful in the rationalization of engines. This process had stemmed from the 1952 merger, although discussions on the subject had taken place even earlier. By the middle of the 1950s, the majority of the pre-merger engines had been discontinued in favour of the 'series' units—principally A, B and C (there was a D-series, too). The first two were derived from

Left *In 1958, EX205 gave way to EX214 and, as this quarter-scale model clearly shows, the styling gradually evolved towards the familiar MGB shape. Contrast the Frua MGA and EX205 in the background. EX214 would give rise to the definitive MGB style as the decade drew to a close. (David Knowles)*

Facing page *This V4 unit was part of a family of engines planned by BMC for the 1960s. MG tried one in an MGA, but Syd Enever was not impressed.*

DON HAYTER

Don Hayter was born in 1926 and began his career, at the age of 16, by entering a five-year apprenticeship with the Pressed Steel body plant at Cowley, which began during the war, when there was very little automotive work being done. 'We worked on aircraft, the Humber scout car, and even sea mines,' recalls Don, who also remembers producing drawings for the WM2 parachute mine from some sketches by Barnes Wallis.

Peacetime in 1945 brought a return to more conventional Pressed Steel work, including adapting the rear of Rootes' Hillman Minx to incorporate a conventional boot lid, body development of the Austin GS3 Devon, and other projects for a variety of customers, many of which never saw the light of day. 'I was working on the Lanchester 12, just as Lanchester were in the throes of being taken over by Daimler,' remembers Don, adding, 'I also worked on a new chassis for the Rover 75, intended to be made from pressings which would have simplified assembly, but Rover dropped the 75 in favour of the P4.' A particular favourite of his was the Jaguar XK120: 'I worked on that with Geoff Robinson, and can well remember how marvellous it was to see the car emerge in the metal from the basis of the original scale model.'

Don Hayter first came into contact with MG in 1950, when he met with Gerald Palmer, to discuss the body of the ZA Magnette. Jim O'Neill—who later would work alongside Don at Abingdon—produced the customer's drawings at Cowley, while Don and colleague Bert Thickpenny were given the task of turning them into Pressed Steel equivalents.

By the beginning of 1954, Don felt ready to broaden his horizons: 'I realized that I never saw a project right through; I never saw a complete car. I saw a small advertisement in either *Autocar* or *Motor* for a body draughtsman

Don Hayter in 1993. (Don Hayter)

at Aston Martin at Feltham, applied and duly got the job, working for Frank Feeley.' Don enjoyed his time at Feltham, where he designed the front of the DB2/4 Mark III—'based upon a rough sketch by Frank Feeley'—before drawing the body lines for the first DB4. This car was not the DB4 that emerged in 1958, however: Hayter's DB4 was a four-seater cast more in the Lagonda mould: 'We built some prototypes, and Touring in Milan were at the same time buying chassis for one-off show cars. Of course, they built the Superleggera DB4 prototype, David Brown saw it, and that was that.'

Towards the end of 1955, Aston Martin announced that it was moving its drawing office to Newport Pagnell, but Don wasn't keen to transfer there: 'My home was still in Abingdon, and I didn't want to have to move to Newport Pagnell. So I wrote on spec. to MG, and it transpired that they had been advertising, but I hadn't seen it! I met Syd Enever and Jim O'Neill in December 1955, and started work at Abingdon on 1 February, 1956.'

When Don arrived at Abingdon, he remembers seeing the two twin-cam prototypes. He soon became involved with the definitive version: 'My first job at Abingdon was to detail the access panel under the wing of the production Twin Cam, which allowed access to the exhaust manifold.' There followed work on the Ted Lund MGA Coupé ('Syd wanted a coupé in the GT class'), the Riley 2.6 ('a reworked Wolseley') and, of course, the MGB.

recent Austin designs (from the A30 and A40), while the C-series was an all-new, six-cylinder unit designed by Morris Engines.

By the latter part of the decade, BMC's Longbridge engine designers, under Duncan Stuart, were boldly contemplating a new family of V4 and V6 engines, the design of which was masterminded at Longbridge. Although the V6 was regarded as less of a priority, development of the V4 had progressed considerably, and it was a serious candidate for production. MG, with a new sports car under development, was seen as a suitable guinea pig for the new engine. As MG's Roy Brocklehurst told me, many years later, 'We were often used by Longbridge as a sort of experimental department. We fitted a V4 engine into an MGA (EX216), and subsequently tried it in the first MGB.'

Despite the obvious potential marketing appeal of a brand-new engine in a new sports car, the Abingdon team had reservations about the V4, which was rather unrefined (even allowing for its prototype status). Don Hayter recalls that Syd Enever, as ever the

arbiter of what was acceptable at Abingdon, disliked the uneven exhaust beat created by the V4 configuration. Before long, however, the V4 and V6 engines were consigned to the history books. BMC had discovered that not only would they have been too costly to develop, but they would also have required a thorough refit of the Longbridge engine production facilities. Moreover, despite their unusually narrow V-configuration, they would not have been ideal for the short-nosed, transverse-engined, front-wheel-drive layout favoured by Alec Issigonis for his ADO15, 16 and 17 projects—and anything that fell foul of Issigonis' requirements suffered from a handicap that was difficult to overcome.

A second option, which Don Hayter recalls was favoured by many at Abingdon, was a 2-litre four, created by cutting a cylinder from each end of the C-series six. With production at Abingdon soaring (over 50,000 cars would be built in 1959—a record output for the plant), the design team clearly felt that production volumes could justify this special engine. Hayter recalls that he drew up the

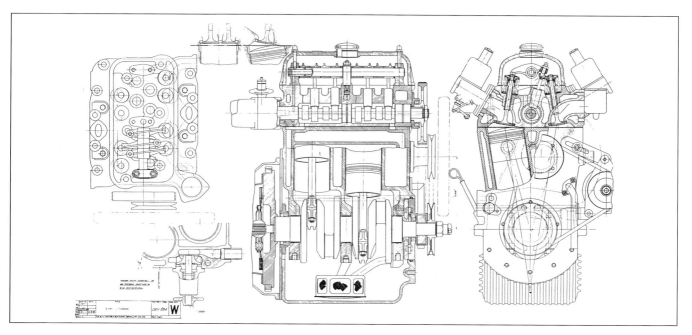

This styling illustration, almost certainly the handiwork of Longbridge stylist Dick Burzi, shows how the appearance of the ADO9G evolved. The overall shape is close to the related Morris Oxford series V, but the grille on this proposal is clearly inspired by that of the Frua-bodied MGA, dating this drawing to 1957-58. (Rover)

definitive EX214/ADO23 prototype body lines to accommodate this unit. However, enthusiasm for it was largely confined to Abingdon, and the economics of another unique MG engine made BMC agreement unlikely, so the four-cylinder C-series was abandoned, too.

The remaining options, which were regarded rather more seriously at Abingdon, were an extensively upgraded B-series engine in 1622cc guise (scheduled to appear in the MGA 1600 Mark II in 1961) and the new twin-cam unit, the latter intended primarily for competition use. The MGA 1600, of course, had entered production in July 1959, with an engine capacity of 1588cc (matching that of the Twin Cam); this should not be confused with the 1622cc unit, which was considerably re-engineered, partly with the MGA's replacement in mind.

By 1960, therefore, the decision had been made: the MGB would be launched with the trusty B-series straight-four. Although the twin-cam unit was originally intended for a higher-performance version of the MGB, it was soon abandoned due to its poor service

record and high production cost. However, while the engine choice had been settled, other important matters had yet to be resolved.

The Magnette Mark III from Cowley

On 12 November, 1958, an event occurred that seemed logical at the time, but undoubtedly caused almost as much outrage in certain quarters as the ZA Magnette had done in 1953: the MG Magnette Mark III was launched. Here was a new MG that not only had not been designed at Abingdon, but also was not even built there. John Thornley's concerns about the future that Abingdon would have faced without the MGA were obviously well founded.

The Magnette Mark III was one of a family of closely related cars, coded ADO9 (strictly speaking, the Magnette was ADO9G,

The definitive MG Magnette Mark III prototype, bearing rhe false registration ADO 9G (Austin Drawing Office project 9; G referring to MG). The grille has been toned down from the Frua-inspired rendering above. (Rover)

the equivalent Riley 4/68 being ADO9R, and the Wolseley 15/60, ADO9W). Their origins lay in BMC's decision—chiefly at the instigation of Leonard Lord—to engage Pininfarina of Turin to style the replacements for, respectively, the Austin A30 (as the Farina A40—ADO8), the Austin A55 Cambridge Mark I/Morris Oxford Series II (ADO9), and the larger Austin Westminster/Wolseley 6/99 (ADO10).

In addition to combining the mid-sized Austin Cambridge and Morris Oxford lines, the engineers at Longbridge and Cowley decided to rationalize the range further by including the more specialized MG, Riley and Wolseley models, by the simple expedient of badge engineering. BMC could argue that the principle of badge engineering had worked reasonably well with the Palmer designed MG, Riley and Wolseley models during the earlier part of the decade, but the prospect of new cars so closely related to the more mundane Austin and Morris versions was hardly exciting. An MG grille proposal featured quite early in styling renderings—at least one example displayed rather ugly, cross-barred grille openings in a pastiche of the grille of the Frua-bodied MGA (possibly produced by Dick Burzi at Longbridge)—but at least the square Farina lines seemed to marry quite well with the distinctive MG grille surround.

Although sales of the sharply styled cars took off (16,676 Magnette Mark IIIs would be sold before the model was replaced in 1961), it soon became apparent that, in common with the smaller Farina-bodied Austin A40, the ADO9 family suffered from serious deficiencies in handling and performance. Consequently, strenuous and quite expensive efforts were required to rectify the difficulties. That story, however, belongs in the following chapter.

Longbridge takes a look at MG

Although responsibility for MG design had been vested in Abingdon in 1954, this did not prevent other parts of the BMC empire from exploring possibilities for the marque. Neither the Abingdon factory nor the design team worked in isolation—the survival of both was dependent upon support from the rest of the organization—and the men from Abingdon frequently had to turn to their colleagues at Longbridge and Cowley for input. There appears to have been little in the way of properly co-ordinated product planning at BMC during the 1950s, efforts often being rather piecemeal and scattered in their approach. Therefore, it is not too surprising to learn that, in 1959, someone at Longbridge decided to look into the possibility of using the basic style of the Austin A40 to produce a Mini-based MG coupé.

'SPUTNIK': THE MINI

Few cars have been as significant to automotive history as the BMC Mini, brainchild of Sir Alec Issigonis and launched in August 1959 as the Austin Se7en. Known irreverently as 'Sputnik', after the small Soviet space satellite that had captured the world's imagination in 1957, the Mini was a revolution in car design. There had been front-wheel-drive cars before, and even tiny wheels and a transverse engine had been tried previously, but until the Mini arrived, there had never been such an innovative combination of these features in a remarkably compact car that was capable of carrying four adults.

Before long, another of the Mini's celebrated traits was discovered: the combination of fairly stiff suspension and a light, low body contributed to excellent handling, which was significantly in advance of the average car's performance at the time. An initially sceptical Alec Issigonis was eventually persuaded, by John Cooper, to sanction the development of a high-performance derivative, which duly appeared in July 1961 as the Mini Cooper. This was equipped with a 997cc version of the A-series engine. The potential of this remarkable car, which could run rings around many contemporary sports cars, was not lost on the men working at the Abingdon factory.

This took place a year before the rival Morris and Austin engineering centres, in Oxford and Birmingham, were largely rationalized under one roof at Longbridge, and it is not known what the people at Abingdon and Cowley thought of the proposal, if indeed they knew anything of it. Dave Seymour, who joined the engineering department at Longbridge in 1959, remembers seeing this car when he arrived, and that it was intended to be a 2+2. A full-size wooden model was built, most of the design and engineering being the handiwork of Jack Daniels and John Shepherd, while the wooden bodywork was created by Vic Everton under the direction of Dick Gallimore. The model was photographed for the archives in 1960. Then, however, it appears to have been shelved, re-emerging early in the following decade for a management viewing alongside later proposals.

This full-size wooden model of an MG coupé, styled by Dick Burzi and engineered by Jack Daniels, was photographed at Longbridge in March 1959. Clearly, it was inspired by the Pininfarina styled Austin A40; note the hubcaps with their revealing 'A' badges. (Rover)

4 The 1960s

Although the 1558cc MGA 1600 proved usefully faster than its predecessor, declining sales in the USA (which were afflicting all importers) meant that more improvements would be needed to maintain momentum until a successor could be made ready. The poor service performance of the Twin Cam, together with a general drop in sports car sales, led BMC to discontinue the model quite suddenly, in the spring of 1960, soon after the Sebring race. So sudden was this decision, in fact, that MG was left with a number of spare Twin Cam chassis and trim sets, including the unique four-wheel disc brake set-up and distinctive Dunlop centre-lock disc wheels. Abingdon's solution was to offer a hybrid called the MGA 1600 De Luxe which, effectively, was an MGA brought up to Twin Cam specification in terms of almost everything except the engine.

The history of MG during the BMC years shows that it was not unusual for MGs to be the first recipients of new variations of corporate engines: the ZA Magnette of 1953 had been the very first BMC car to use the B-series unit; the MGA Twin Cam of 1958 had featured a unique variant of this engine; while the MGA 1600 of 1959 featured the first capacity increase of the basic unit from 1489 to 1588cc. Thus, it was hardly surprising that, in June 1961, the MGA 1600 Mark II was launched with yet another capacity increase—this time to 1622cc, following Abingdon entries against the ADO31 project number in the previous February (ADO31/1, dated 21 February, 1961, although there had been an earlier Abingdon sketch, SK7242, dated 8 April, 1960, for the MGA De-

Luxe). Although, at first sight, this might seem to have been a rather pointless exercise, resulting in such a small capacity increase over the 1600 Mark I, in fact the engine had undergone a serious overhaul, which resulted in maximum power output being boosted by 12 per cent. This unit, intended at the time for the forthcoming MGB, would also be fitted to the revised Farina cars from the autumn of 1961.

In Mark II form, the MGA soldiered on until it was finally discontinued to make way for the MGB, the last example going down the line in July 1962. A noteworthy event was the production, in March of that year, of the 100,000th MGA, a US-export specimen, which was given a unique metallic gold finish, accompanied by gold painted wire wheels and broad whitewall tyres; apparently, these 'crimes' were rectified by Hambro upon receipt. The MGA had also achieved other production landmarks: one example, produced in May 1956, had been the 100,000th MG; while another, in December 1959, marked—for the first time—the production of 50,000 cars in one year at Abingdon. This remarkable success story would continue in the following decade.

Improvements to the Magnette: Mark IV

BMC had soon become acutely aware of the shortcomings of the Magnette Mark III, along with the rest of the ADO9 range. Accordingly, it was not long before the chassis was subject to a major overhaul, resulting in some worthwhile, if not wholly ade-

The simple and attractive interior of the MG Midget Mark I of 1961. (Rover/BMIHT)

quate, improvements. It appears that Abingdon, which had played little or no part in the gestation of the Mark III, had been involved in improving ADO9: EX226 lists two drawings that relate to this car, dated 10 April, 1961. The replacement for ADO9 was given a new code, ADO 38, and the Magnette became the Mark IV. It was given the larger 1622cc B-series engine from the MGA 1600 Mark II, a slightly longer wheelbase and wider track front and rear.

The Magnette Mark IV was launched in September 1961, followed a month later by the remainder of the Farina family. Perhaps the relative lack of enthusiasm for the Magnette and the mechanically-identical Riley 4/72 was the reason that, unlike their Morris and Wolseley counterparts, they did not receive the smaller and rather less ostentatious rear fins that were applied to their Austin, Morris and Wolseley counterparts as part of the facelift. In fact, the only visual difference between the Mark III and Mark IV—apart from the wheelbase and track—was a change in the layout of the optional duo-tone colour schemes.

John Thornley was one of those within the company who dared to voice criticism of the Magnette, and he asked MG draughtsman Don Butler to investigate means of improving its appearance. 'John Thornley got me to do quarter-scale layouts to revamp the front and rear of ADO38,' recalls Don, 'and John took these up to Dick Gallimore in the experimental body shop at Longbridge to see if he could do anything with them. Dick took my quarter-scale drawings and produced full-sized layouts, but they never got anywhere as soon as Issigonis got to hear of them.'

Already, however, fatal damage had been done to the reputation of the Magnette, and with the emergence of more modern opposition, like the Ford Corsair, sales were never particularly buoyant: only 14,320 were sold between the launch in September 1961 and the car's demise in April 1968. Few mourned its passing.

The return of the Midget; Abingdon adopts the Sprite

Although the Abingdon team had undoubtedly been disappointed to have lost out to Healey in the design of the small sports car, they were only too happy to accept responsibility for re-engineering it for the proposed 1961 facelift. Moreover, it was soon decided that it would be accompanied by a badge-engineered MG derivative. This decision was not only quite popular at Abingdon, but it was also supported at the highest level within BMC, George Harriman being one of the company's principal exponents of badge engineering. An additional incentive was the fact that the Morris/MG/Wolseley franchises were envious of the small Austin-Healey Sprite which, because of the poorly integrated BMC sales networks, was only sold in the UK through Austin dealerships.

Although the original 'frog-eye' Sprite was quite popular, and its passing would be mourned by its fans, the car's styling was to an acquired taste, and by the end of the 1950s was beginning to look rather primitive. Jim O'Neill recalls that even Donald Healey had doubts about the 'frog-eye' look: 'He felt that it was right to produce a prototype with the headlamps mounted in the wings. At the same time, it was decided that we should design an MG Midget based on the Sprite under-frame: it would be slightly up-market with a trunk lid and a more conventional bonnet.' This would also provide an opportunity to remedy the structural deficiencies of the original Sprite.

The Healeys set to work with stylists Les Ireland and Doug Thorpe to redesign the front end of the Sprite, developing a style that closely resembled the design eventually adopted for the production Austin-Healey Sprite Mark II. However, the abbreviated and shapely rear of the car—with its small rear lamps and no boot lid—was retained. The lack of a boot lid on the original Sprite caused its own special production problems. As Jim O'Neill explains, the cost advantages were largely outweighed by production problems: 'The fitting of the large rubber mat into the trunk compartment of the Mark I Sprite was a very hazardous operation, owing to the toxicity of the adhesive. The operators had to wear a mask which was fed with a fresh air line before climbing into the back of the vehicle, making them appear more like deep-sea divers than car production workers. The operation was slow and cumbersome, and obviously expensive.'

At Abingdon, meanwhile, Denis Williams was engineering the

DENIS WILLIAMS

In 1941, Denis Williams began his career with Pressed Steel, becoming involved in war work. After the war, he moved next door to Morris Motors, where he found himself working with Jim O'Neill in the MG/Riley drawing office. This was followed by a spell at Carbodies of Coventry, where he remembers being involved with the various drophead Ford Zephyrs and Hillman Minxes that the company produced, after which he moved to Morris Motors Radiators Branch in October 1953. In addition to radiators, this plant manufactured a range of car components, including exhaust systems and radiator grilles. Williams worked on most of the company's products during his stint there, including the MGA radiator grille. After about 18 months, Jim O'Neill happened to pass by one day: 'I asked him, "Do you need any good blokes?" That was 1955 and, in next to no time, I found myself with Jim at Abingdon, where I stayed right through until the closure in 1980.'

It did not take long for Williams to become heavily involved: 'At that time, the body section was in a small office, with just Jim O'Neill and myself. We had one full-size layout table and two drawing boards for detail work, although we soon moved into a new, larger office which housed all the design team. My first jobs were on the MGA, which was due for release, and this was mainly the production of a check layout for the bodyshell and the drawing of some minor trim items.'

A little over a year after his arrival, Williams was given the task of drawing up the lines for the sleek-bodied EX186 Le Mans prototype: 'I was given the task of laying out the full-size body lines and all the structural details required for the completed body. In the event, only one car was built, the body being made by Midland Sheet Metal of Nuneaton, with whom I liaised closely during its construction.' Subsequently, Williams was involved in many key projects at Abingdon, including the MGA Twin Cam, the ADO41 MG Midget, the EX220 (subsequently ADO34) front-wheel-drive Midget, the tragically short-lived EX186 project and, in the final event, the Triumph Acclaim.

revised MG rear end with its boot lid, guided by a quarter-scale drawing prepared by Jim O'Neill. Tracings of Denis Williams' drawings were sent to Coventry to allow construction of the prototype, Eric Carter acting as the liaison man. This work was begun independently of the Healey rear-end redesign, although it has to be recognized that the front-end facelift and the rear boot lid were not entirely congruent aims. Furthermore, the Healeys, as independent consultants who received royalty payments on every Austin-Healey built, clearly had their own agenda, which need not have dovetailed with that of MG. Nevertheless, Geoff Healey believed that this split effort was at least partly due to a policy laid down by Alec Issigonis, who believed that internal rivalries spurred people to greater efforts. Common sense soon prevailed, however, and the two teams compared their notes so that the result would not be a styling disaster.

The new rear end incorporated vertical tail-lamps, similar to those of the forthcoming MGB, and the tops of the round rear wheel arches were flattened to help replace the stiffness lost by opening up the rear bodywork for a boot lid. Despite the resemblance to the MGB, Jim O'Neill clearly refutes the idea that the larger car's styling inspired that of the Midget: 'The lines were perhaps influenced by my earlier MGB quarter-scale drawing. My completed Midget quarter-scale drawing was passed to Denis Williams, who was in charge of the full-size layout. It is correct to say that we didn't know what the Healeys had in mind, but we were quite confident that the Midget design would be accepted by management with whatever Healey had to run alongside.'

On the prototype, separate vertical overriders were fitted at the rear, without a horizontal bumper bar, providing a strong family resemblance to the original Sprite. Jim O'Neill recalls the reception afforded to the finished car: 'When Donald Healey viewed the facelifted Sprite alongside the new Midget, he insisted that the Sprite be similar to the MG, with badge and radiator grille changes differentiating the two.' It was also decided to adopt heavier-gauge steel for the rear bodywork to avoid any recurrence of the problems that had afflicted the 'frog-eye'. Geoff Healey subsequently noted that the cost of the tooling changes required for the facelift exceeded the original tooling cost in 1957!

In typical BMC fashion, there were two different project codes for the Austin-Healey (ADO41) and MG (ADO47) versions of what was substantially the same car; ADO47/1 was the chassis number allocated to the first Midget prototype on 23 March, 1960, the day after the equivalent Austin-Healey prototype (ADO41/6). The first drawing recorded against the 'Facelift Sprite' is ADO41/1, for a heraldic badge, dated 16 November, 1959.

Also involved with ADO41/47 was Don Butler, who used to alternate his trips to see Eric Carter at Coventry with Denis Williams. Don, of course, had already worked with Eric on the MGA in 1954, and he is full of praise for Eric's skills: 'Eric had worked at both Riley and Daimler in the past, and he could turn his hand to almost anything, working everything out from the rolled steel to the pressed sections, and all the fittings required.' Eric, don't forget, had come up with the ingenious exterior door catches for the MGA Coupé, and his genius was also applied to the design of the interior door lock release for the MG Midget. 'We had a great deal of trouble squeezing all the door mechanisms into the small and very slim Midget doors, particularly when we put the winding windows and quarterlights in,' remembers Don, 'and Eric simply copied the catches from a standard British Rail carriage door!' The mechanical side of Midget development was chiefly the responsibility of Dickie Wright, who reported to chief chassis engineer Terry Mitchell.

In the meantime, Abingdon were experimenting with a more powerful version of the Sprite (EX221), created in 1960 by squeezing in the 1588cc B-series engine from the MGA. MG development mechanic Henry Stone recalled, in his autobiography, *MG—The Insomnia Crew*, that this necessitated a reshaped gearbox cover and also moving the engine rearwards to clear the bonnet, while a cross-flow radiator took care of the cooling. So fast was the 1600 Sprite that it required 8in (20.32cm) brakes to bring it to a stop, and

there is little doubt that the prospect of a Sprite (or a Midget) that could seriously out-perform the MGA or MGB would not be countenanced. For a time, the car was used by Terry Mitchell and Dickie Wright: 'We used it to go to Longbridge, and it went like a bomb. Unfortunately, its tiny petrol tank was a liability, and so we had to carry a jerry-can of petrol in the boot!'

Launch of the new Midget

The Austin-Healey Sprite Mark II and the MG Midget were launched in May 1961, the main differences between the two cars being the grille design, stainless-steel trim and interior detailing. The Midget was heralded as 'The new MG Midget—the car that starts ahead', and retailed at £472 plus taxes (totalling £515); the Sprite was £10 cheaper. It should be noted that, at about the same time, MG introduced the MGA 1600 Mark II and was responsible for the Austin-Healey 3000 Mark II. In the background, the MGB was also being readied for production in the following year, so the men at Abingdon were obviously very busy.

It has been suggested that the MG Midget might have been called the MGD, which would have been a logical progression from the MGB (due out in 1962) and the MGC 1100 (as the MG 1100 might have been badged), but whether this idea received serious consideration is not clear. There is a reference to an MGD in the EX-Register—as EX188—which dates from the mid-1950s, and the description certainly resembles the Midget specification (an Austin A30-engined small sports car). However, this car was quite independent of the facelifted Austin-Healey Sprite, which emerged in 1961.

First thoughts on a front-wheel-drive Midget

Every year, members of the Abingdon design team visited the Paris Motor Show to see what the opposition were up to and to gain inspiration for new ideas. Always in the forefront on these trips was Syd Enever, who would often be accompanied by Jim O'Neill or Terry Mitchell. Syd was a very inventive, intuitive engineer from a similar mould as Lord Austin and Sir Alec Issigonis. Like his more famous forebears, he was notorious for sketching ideas on the back of the proverbial 'fag packet'. Many of these ideas led to production cars. Terry Mitchell remembers the late 1950s and the excitement generated by BMC's new small car, the Mini. Once the spec-

Dating from November 1960, this intriguing Longbridge archive photo of an MG-grilled coupé mock-up would appear to be based upon the ADO15 Mini. (Rover)

ification of this car became known within the BMC organization, none was more intrigued by it than Syd Enever and the crew at Abingdon, in particular Terry Mitchell: 'Before long, the Minis were running rings around everything. We felt sure that this was the way forward.'

Thus, it is hardly surprising that, before long, a number of 'fag-packet' exercises gelled into an EX project, EX220, described in the register as 'New Midget based on Sputnik FWD.' The first entry in the project register was dated 23 April, 1959, just four months before the launch of ADO15, the Austin Se7en (Mini). A great deal of thought went into a range of possible variations on the Mini theme: both MG and Austin-Healey variants were included, as was a coupé. Had it proceeded, the Abingdon proposal would undoubtedly have replaced the Austin-Healey Sprite, as well as reviving the still-dormant Midget name-tag. However, at this stage, the Mini was very much Alec Issigonis' baby, and any proposals that drew upon its components would not only need to be approved by the great engineer, but also, in all probability, masterminded by

him. The problem here was that although Issigonis had an interest in motor-sport, he also held very firm views about the role that his new small car should play. It took a persuasive John Cooper to talk Issigonis into sanctioning the Mini Cooper of 1961, and that was based upon the actual competition successes of the early Minis. Thus, Abingdon had little hope with mere paper ideas.

Nevertheless, after 14 drawings had been prepared, EX220 was given the Abingdon drawing office code ADO34. Don Butler suggests that the origins of ADO34 lay in a scale model, doubtless based upon one of Syd's sketches: 'Syd started it off really. He had Jim Oates (model shop manager) at Cowley do a scale model, and it evolved from there. We had to keep it quiet from Longbridge at first.' However, Jim O'Neill is certain that Syd Enever played no part in the creation of ADO34, even though, no doubt, he was interested in it and may have sanctioned EX220. 'I started the job off as a quarter-scale drawing,' remembers Jim, 'before handing it over to Denis Williams to work on the full-size layout. Sydney had been instructed by Issigonis that a sports-car version of the Mini was not

Above and right *The Abingdon version of ADO34 closely resembled the larger MGB. (Rover)*

Left *Enthusiast Richard Howard is in the process of painstakingly restoring the remains of what may be a missing ADO35 prototype. The construction methods and trimming materials—not to mention the 100 lire coin found in one of the sills— clearly point to Pininfarina's handiwork. (courtesy Richard Howard)*

Below *The Pininfarina styled ADO34 Mini-based MG sports car. Note the unusual integrated overriders. (Rover)*

on; even so, we managed to produce a prototype car.' Not surprisingly, the Abingdon proposal—the handiwork of Jim O'Neill, Denis Williams and Don Butler—resembled the MGB, the lines of which had been more or less finalized by this time, but the proportions were rather less successful, owing to the shorter wheelbase of the Mini van used as the basis of the prototype.

A neat tonneau panel was fitted over the rear of the passenger compartment, which could have concealed the hood or occasional rear seats, and MGA-style side screens were fitted to the doors— the luxury of wind-up windows and quarterlights still not being deemed necessary for a budget sports car. Dickie Wright was responsible for the mechanical components of the car: 'It was not a particularly pretty car,' he recalls, 'but there was a lot of enthusiasm for the concept, although there was the school of thought which said that a sports car should have rear-wheel-drive.'

Terry Mitchell recalls the fun that he and Roy Brocklehurst had

in the metallic blue prototype, hurling it down the country lanes near Abingdon. This testing demonstrated that there was a fundamental problem of body flexure, according to Jim O'Neill: 'A fair amount of work was necessary to overcome the severe scuttle shake that the car had. Although I pushed Sydney hard to let us continue to overcome this problem, he insisted that the car be cut up.' Obviously, this was extremely frustrating for the team at the time, but Jim could see Enever's reasoning: 'I can understand this decision, as Sydney had already taken a considerable risk in allowing us to make the car in the first place, against Issigonis' instruction.' Sadly, therefore, no trace remains of Abingdon's front-drive sports car.

More MG sports cars at Longbridge
The idea of a Mini-based MG sports car was obviously so good, that it is not surprising to discover that the Abingdon team were not

Right *From the rear, the lines of Richard Howard's car are pleasantly Italianate, perhaps resembling the similarly sized Fiat 850 coupé, even to the single round tail-lamps. Note the crudely cut holes in the recess for the rear number plate; these were made at Longbridge to allow access to the closed luggage compartment to wire up the rear lamps and fuel tank sender! (courtesy Richard Howard)*

Below *This is a later attempt at a Mini MG, clearly based upon the earlier Longbridge version of ADO34. The rather plain grille of this version may have been intended for an Austin-Healey derivative, but the wheel centres feature MG badges. (Rover)*

the only people seriously investigating the possibility. In 1960, as the men at Abingdon were refining EX220 into their proposal for ADO34, the designers at Longbridge were working on their own version. Jack Daniels' MG coupé, described in Chapter 3, was the first attempt at this. Despite Issigonis' general hostility to the idea of a Mini-based MG sports car—or at least one that failed to adhere to his packaging principles—the Longbridge designers clearly felt that there was merit in the concept, and more than one proposal appears to have been examined. A wooden mock-up of an MG Mini coupé was photographed for the archives in 1961, and other proposals, not necessarily ascribed official project codes, were certainly built.

In addition to Daniels' coupé and what, in due course, would become Longbridge's version of ADO34, another Mini-based MG coupé—possibly ADO35—also appeared in 1960. By remarkable coincidence, the prototype of this car has survived, having been rescued from the verge of being scrapped and since acquired by an enthusiast in Norfolk. Now being painstakingly restored, this Pininfarina-bodied car will soon be finished and demonstrates yet another frustrating missed opportunity. Pininfarina have admitted that the car is certainly their handiwork (the restorers even found a 100-lire coin inside one of the sills!), but sadly they have no records of the car.

Dave Seymour, who started at Longbridge in 1959 (he moved to Abingdon in 1968, and is still with the company today, based at Cowley), was one of those who became involved with this car, and is one of the few people who seem to recall it. He remembers that it was assessed alongside a proposal from Ogle (which was spirited into Longbridge in some secrecy) and, for comparison purposes, with the earlier Daniels/Shepherd proposal of 1959-60: 'Farina produced this coupé body in aluminium alloy, but as it was a simple metal shell, the car was not mechanised. Having viewed the car,

THE MG MINI

If it had not been for the success of the Mini Cooper, and later the restriction of the MG marque to sports cars, there might well have been an MG Mini. The Morris/Wolseley/Riley dealers of the early 1960s wanted an MG version of the Mini to sell alongside the luxury Elf and Hornet variants. Accordingly, it was planned to amalgamate the conventional short-boot Mini bodyshell with the nose panels of the Riley Elf. The engine of the Mini Cooper would have provided the motive force, giving a smart, fast and luxuriously trimmed sporting Mini.

Costing exercises were carried out and, it is believed, a running prototype built on a 1961 Mini, which survives in the hands of a Norfolk enthusiast. This particular car was found in a scrapyard near Winchester, and has the chassis number from a 1960 left-hand-drive Morris Mini Minor, which originally had been exported to Holland as a factory demonstrator. The car returned from Holland to the UK in 1961, whereupon it appears to have become a factory hack at Cowley. Little is known of its history thereafter, but the work involved in grafting on the Riley Elf front panels and fabricating the special MG grille was certainly carried out to a very high standard.

The Mini Cooper, however, was largely responsible for the MG Mini's downfall: the Cooper was so successful in competition (and was readily available in both Austin and Morris versions) that there seemed to be no need to produce an MG version, too. There, the story might have ended. However, the idea may have been reviewed at least once, in April 1967 (from which a surviving sketch dates), before the British Leyland merger, and possibly once more in 1969, when the agreement between British Leyland and John Cooper was terminated by Donald Stokes. By that time, though, the trend had moved away from adding marque badges to Austin-Morris saloons, the MG 1300 being discontinued in favour of the Austin-Morris 1300 GT which, ironically, arose from an abortive 1300 Cooper proposal. In the event, the Mini Cooper was dropped in 1971, while the concept of an MG Mini was crudely distorted into the Mini 1275 GT of 1969.

This sketch of a possible MG Mini dates from April 1967. It combines the standard short-boot Mini bodyshell with front-end panels and trim borrowed from the Riley Elf/Wolseley Hornet. (Rover)

Richard Howard, owner of the ADO35 prototype shown on the previous pages also owns this splendid Mini with an MG grille, which may have its origins in a genuine prototype. (courtesy Richard Howard)

Issigonis said, "Let's turn it into a runner." Whereas, for expediency, we could have welded Mini sub-frames on to a steel body, we couldn't do that in this case, so we fixed the sub-frames on with pop-rivets. Then, to our horror, "Issy" came down with George Harriman and said to him, "Let's go out in it," which they duly did, driving to Droitwich and back. How they ever got back...'

At the rear of the car, two horizontal oblong slots were crudely cut into the panel behind the number-plate. According to Dave Seymour, this act of apparent vandalism was carried out because Pininfarina had built the bodyshell without providing any form of access to the luggage compartment (there is no boot lid), and it was necessary to gain access to the boot area to wire-up the rear lamps and the petrol tank sender. Unlike the later ADO34 exercise, this coupé was purely Mini-based and, had it been produced, would probably have featured conventional separate Mini sub-frames, steering, etc.

Another entirely different proposal for an MG coupé was initiated by Jim O'Neill, being based upon the slightly longer floorpan of the abortive ADO16 van proposal. He remembers being very pleased with his design for this, which featured a long, elegant nose. A full-size wooden mock-up was prepared at Longbridge, but it was subjected to the unwelcome attention of BMC's chief engineer: 'Alec Issigonis came in one Friday afternoon, saw the model and ordered the front part of the nose to be cut off with a band-saw, leaving an ugly flat. A peculiar, ill-proportioned grille was then stuck on the front, in the hope, no doubt, of deliberately scuppering the idea.' Issigonis' aversion to cars that did not adhere to his policy of space-efficient, short overhangs was well known.

The matter of a new small sports car was further complicated in 1962 by the decision to investigate three entirely separate exercises, all utilizing the hydrolastic suspension system. With the approval of George Harriman, it was agreed that Longbridge (who already had the Mini and 1100 to their credit) would pursue the concept of a front-engined, front-wheel-drive sports car (ADO34); Abingdon would investigate a traditional front-engined, rear-wheel-drive car (EX229, based upon the ADO47 Midget); while the Healeys would explore the concept of a rear-engined, rear-wheel-drive car, to which they gave the title WAEC (literally 'wheel at each corner'). The EX-Register also records that MG gave some thought to a rear-engined car (EX228), but little effort went into this.

When I related this tale to Charles Griffin (from 1960, BMC's chief engineer and, from 1964, the organization's director of engineering with a seat on the Austin board), he could not remember such a competition: 'Both Sir Alec and I always believed that sports cars should be rear-wheel-drive. Sir Alec used to say that in order to have fun in driving—an essential ingredient in a sports car—two steering systems were necessary, one of which was worked with the right foot!'

EX229 was largely the responsibility of Roy Brocklehurst, according to chassis man Dickie Wright. Before long, it required so many changes to its ADO47 basis that it graduated into a completely new car, EX234, while WEAC was soon recognized as an untried and rather risky prospect, particularly in the all-important US market. The project code used henceforth by both Abingdon and Longbridge for the front-wheel-drive cars was ADO34. Jim

This is the first MGB prototype, which has several features visible in this shot that differentiate it from a production car. The side-lamp units are different (probably from a Triumph Herald), while the windscreen is not the unit that would be adopted. There is a sill trim strip with a curious upwards sweep at its forward end, clearly borrowed from the Frua-bodied MGA. Although not clear from this photograph, this car was in fact finished in a two-tone colour scheme. (Rover/BMIHT)

O'Neill is quite sure that only two running ADO34 prototypes were built: the Abingdon example and the Longbridge car. Only the latter survives, as part of the British Motor Heritage collection. 'During tests, our car suffered from scuttle shake, but there is no reason to suppose that this could not have been cured. I do believe that the powers that be had no intention of allowing this type of car into production, perhaps mainly influenced by Issigonis.'

According to Seymour, one of the people involved in the development of the Longbridge ADO34, it was created by welding two Mini sub-frames to a floor to produce a sort of rolling chassis, which could be shipped to Pininfarina in Turin for completion. Seymour recalls that the ADO34 structure itself was designed to be immensely strong: 'The strength of the floor derived from an exceptionally high floor tunnel, running between the two sub-frames. In this tunnel were the gear-lever linkage, handbrake and cable run, fuel and brake pipes.'

Another novel idea developed for ADO34 was the steering column mounting: 'The steering column was mounted in a tapering tubular structure mounted off the bulkhead. At the bulkhead end, it was oval in section with the clutch and brake pedals mounted with-

in and operating through a cut-out in the base of the oval section. At the steering wheel end, the structure was tapered to a circular section.' The entire assembly, referred to as a binnacle by Dave Seymour and his colleagues, was intended to confer production advantages, as well as structural strength: 'From a production stand-point, the steering wheel, clutch and brakes would have been a sub-assembly, mounted in one operation on to the bulkhead. In those days, there were no thoughts of such things as collapsible safety steering columns!'

According to Dave Seymour, among the 'Mini' project team, ADO34 was known as 'the wheelbarrow', and the high central tunnel, which divided the passenger compartment in two, caused some merriment: 'One wag observed that the ADO34 was an anti-social car and that whilst, in later years, there would be the advertising slogan, "You can do it in an MG," you certainly couldn't have done much in "the wheelbarrow"!'

An Austin-Healey version of ADO34 was also planned, coded ADO36. However, it appears that this would have been little more than a badge-engineering exercise. Both Longbridge and Abingdon made their own separate studies for ADO36, as surviving records

From the rear, the prototype MGB shows many differences in comparison to production versions. Note in particular the smaller rear lamp clusters (with separate square reflectors), the single rear number-plate lamp suspended over the backing place and the different boot-lid catch. Less obvious is the fact that the rear of the car, behind the rear axle line, is shorter. (Rover/BMIHT)

Left *The dashboard of the prototype MGB is like a cross between that of the MGA and MGB. On production cars, the body colour finish would be dropped in favour of crackle black paint, and the radio speaker would be transferred to a console beneath the dashboard, which would also conveniently hide additional bracing reinforcement between the gearbox tunnel and the scuttle. (Rover/BMIHT)*

Below *The MGB prototype outside Dick Burzi's Longbridge 'Glass House' studio in October 1961. (Rover)*

show, although the concept does not appear to have gone much further than the production of outline drawings.

Emergence of the MGB: the first prototype

By late spring 1960, the first recognizable MGB prototype was nearing completion (chassis number ADO23/370, dated 23 March, 1960). This formed the basis of Pressed Steel's tooling quotation, submitted in an elegant, hard-backed book format complete with hand coloured illustrations. At this stage, the prototype featured coil-sprung rear suspension.

Coil springs at the rear

During the development of EX214, it was thought that the MGA replacement should feature a more sophisticated rear suspension, using coil springs and, perhaps, a non-solid axle. There remained at

Abingdon some enthusiasm for the idea of an independent rear suspension set-up; after all, the R-type of 1935 had featured all-independent suspension. Even though independent rear suspension was still regarded as rather exotic in the saloon-car market, it was growing in popularity among the manufacturers of more exotic sports cars, against which MG increasingly found itself pitted. Unfortunately, however, there was no suitable final-drive unit for a truly independent rear end, so the next best thing was considered to be a coil-sprung live rear axle, located by radius arms and a transverse Watts linkage. The first efforts along these lines were tried in EX186, the proposed Le Mans car, which was based upon an MGA Twin Cam chassis, but fitted with a coil-sprung rear axle and trailing arms. After a great deal of experimentation with converted MGA test 'mules', the Watts linkage was abandoned on grounds of cost, and the axle restrained by a panhard rod.

It was while road-testing one of the suspension-development MGAs that Roy Brocklehurst was involved in a much celebrated accident, fortunately without injury. The coil-sprung axle permitted increased wheel travel, and on this occasion, it caused a rear wheel to jam itself in the wheel arch, with spectacular results. Shortly after the accident, an unsuspecting colleague asked Brocklehurst what he thought of the new rear suspension, to which he is reported to have replied laconically, 'Not much.' Nevertheless, MG persisted with the coil-sprung units until further testing showed that there were structural deficiencies with the panhard rod location, exacerbated by the relatively short length and consequent stiffness of the rod itself. This also produced another problem, Tommy Haig (Don Hayter refers to him as MG's 'calibrated boot') and other testers complaining of rear-wheel steer due to the short rod and generous wheel travel.

In the end, there was only one practical solution: to revert to semi-elliptic leaf springs. This necessitated lengthening the rear end of the car by 1in (2.54cm), a process carried out by Don Hayter, which involved redrawing the rear body sections and issuing them promptly to Pressed Steel. At the same time, the spare wheel, which had been mounted vertically at the front of the boot, was laid horizontally and the fuel tank was relocated under the boot floor (both alterations providing considerable benefit by lowering the car's centre of gravity).

The second and third prototypes

The reversion to semi-elliptic leaf springs, and the attendant lengthening of the body, led to the creation of two further prototypes: a red car with black trim and a black car with red trim, the latter being photographed for the archives in 1961. Des Jones, who had joined the Abingdon team in August 1960, recalls this stage of development upon his arrival: 'In August 1960, there were two prototypes; the third appeared later with a few design alterations. The bonnet inside panel was modified to suit the new locking platform, and the boot lock was all new, and had to be schemed into the boot panel.' The fascia was different too: 'The main shape was kept, but changes were made to the positions of the instruments, heater controls, glove-box and lock.' The windscreen of the third prototype was also changed: 'Don Hayter changed the windscreen layout, and although smaller than the Morris 1100, it was basically similar in style. Later, the Midget and Sprite adopted a similar windscreen construction.'

The third prototype also exhibited structural problems. Des Jones recalls how these were resolved: 'There was a problem with front-end shake, which Syd Enever solved by fitting a square-section member across the car between the A-posts, together with a substantial reinforcing panel between the cross-member and the gearbox tunnel. The steering column was then attached to a bracket welded to the cross-member. All of the heater controls, switches, instruments and glove-box had to be reworked in order to clear this cross-rail.' Further problems occurred during testing: 'Tommy Haig, our chief tester, took the car on the pavé, and with his characteristic thoroughness, the aluminium reinforcement in the bonnet front cross-member collapsed and made the lock useless. Syd Enever solved the problem by adding a steel reinforcement, which was riveted to the aluminium cross-member.'

By this stage, too, the tests were showing that the 1622cc engine would be hard pushed to provide performance that was even on a par with the out-going MGA; it would have been rather embarrassing for MG to have launched a new sports car with inferior acceleration and top speed to its predecessor. Fortunately, plans were already advanced for a further expansion of the trusty B-series unit to 1798cc. This had been necessitated by the decision to fit the engine into the Issigonis-designed, front-wheel-drive, ADO17 large family saloon, due to be launched in 1964. BMC were quite happy to use MG as a guinea pig where the new engine was concerned and, in fact, much valuable experience would be gained from the MGB application. Development of the engine continued after the MGB launch and, as a result, a new five-bearing version would be introduced into the MGB in 1964.

For the MGB, Abingdon moved away from the traditional sprung seat construction for the first time, Jim O'Neill working

DES JONES

One of the people who were instrumental in seeing the MGB through from pre-production to its final demise was Des Jones, working under Don Hayter and Jim O'Neill. Des joined Morris Motors, in August 1936, as a clerk on the production line. However, having decided to take a mechanical engineering course, he soon found himself attending the Oxford School of Technology for one day and three nights per week: 'My school reports were sent to S. V. Smith, the production director at Morris Motors. In due course, I was offered a position as a junior draughtsman in the body drawing office, where Mr. L. P. Hall was the chief body engineer.' Des took up this post in January 1939, only to be called up for war service on 16 October: 'Six years and three months later, I was back in the drawing office in January 1946.'

Being absent from Cowley during the war years, Des Jones missed out on the early development of the Morris Mosquito: 'I only became involved after the celebrated point where the width had been increased by 4in (10.16cm). The bonnet developed a shake, and so a rod each side of the centre-line was attached to the cross-member at the front of the bonnet, and the forward hinge fixing at the rear of the bonnet. Reg Job was in charge of the Morris Minor body; I was allowed a free hand to produce the Morris Minor tourer.'

Des went on to work on the Morris Oxford, under chief engineer Norman Bough, followed by the Morris Oxford Traveller. During the 1950s, he was involved with the MG Magnette/Wolesely 4/44 (working with Jim O'Neill), ADO10 and ADO16. Then, in July 1960, BMC decided to rationalize design at Longbridge, so it seemed likely that all those at Cowley would have to move to the Midlands. At this point, Syd Enever offered Des a job at Abingdon: 'He said, "Come over and see Jimmy (Jim O'Neill)." When I visited Abingdon, Don Hayter was chief draughtsman and in charge of the MGB, and Denis Williams and Don Butler were senior body designers. I was very happy to join them, so I left for Abingdon in August 1960 to work on the MGB under Don Hayter.'

Des stayed at Abingdon until it was closed, working on various aspects of the Midget and MGB. 'After the announcement of the closure of MG Abingdon, the design staff were given the Triumph Acclaim to produce. With the help of an interpreter, I was able to lay out and detail the door trim pads, and the front and rear bumpers. In December 1980, we all moved to the Cowley body facility, and I retired in June 1981.'

closely with Aeropreen Ltd of High Wycombe: 'If I remember correctly, we were the first British car manufacturer to use the German invention, polyurethane. This was first used by building the form from shaped pieces cut from a block of foam. Later, of course, the cushion and squab were moulded.' The interior trim remained fairly traditional, however, with the expected standard leather seat facings. The distinctive dashboard was largely the responsibility of Don Hayter.

Into production: early days of the MGB

With the design finalized, the lead into production began at the end of 1961. By the spring of 1962, launch plans were well in hand, and by June, the preliminary details were filtering out to dealers and distributors in advance of the launch on 20 September, just ahead of the Earls Court Motor Show in October. Even at this late stage, however, changes—albeit minor ones—were still being made to the design, as Don Hayter remembers: 'The original MGBs had saddle tanks under the boot floor, like the MGA, but we were approached by Gerry Buckman, an experimental engineer at Morris Radiators, who told us that they had just installed some very impressive deep-drawing presses and would like to do a fuel tank for us, which we did, giving us a 2gal (9.1-litre) increase in capacity to 12gal (54.55 litres) into the bargain.'

Another change was to the radiator grille badge, following comments from the police on its reflectivity. 'In response to BMC/MG requests for a one-piece grille badge, Lucas had come up with a plastic badge in Diakom, with a nice reflective red background,' remembers Don Hayter. 'Unfortunately, a red, reflective, forward facing badge contravened construction-and-use regulations, and so Lucas had to hurriedly change the badge design to a frosted backing with non-reflective red paint.'

With the Midget and MGB in production, one of Don Butler's next tasks was to help develop the optional hardtops for both models, working with various external contractors: 'I went to Ferranti in Bangor, North Wales, to develop the MGB hardtop with them, while Denis Williams did the same thing for the Midget hardtop. These hardtops were pure resin and glass—there was no filler in them—and I well remember Les Pritchard, of Ferranti, coming down to Abingdon and saying to Syd, "Would you like me to run a car over one of the hardtop shells to prove that it will spring back?" Syd agreed and, sure enough, the shell buckled and then sprang back into shape.'

These early hardtops were both light and strong, but they were also relatively expensive to produce. In the 1960s, their attraction was obviously based on competition use, where low weight and superior strength were paramount. The hardtop comprised inner and outer skins, which were bonded together around the outside edge. Normally, this was fine, but the occasional problem occurred: 'We had a letter from a BOAC pilot, who had experienced what he referred to as "temporary blindness" whilst driving his MGB to the airport. What happened was that wind pressure had caused the inner skin to balloon down and had pushed his hat over his eyes. He took it all in good humour and, of course, we provided him with a new hardtop!'

By the following decade, with MG out of serious competition in the UK, there would be pressure to cut the cost of the hardtops: 'A Mr Bennett from Watsonian Sidecars said that he could produce the hardtops much cheaper, and so Watsonian eventually took over manufacture from Ferranti. They added much more chalk to the resin to reduce the cost, which also made them much more brittle and heavier into the bargain.' Such is progress.

ADO16: the MG 1100

The story of what became the MG 1100, of course, is linked inextricably to that of the entire ADO16 project, which arose from Issigonis' concept of a family of front-wheel-drive cars, spear-

headed by the seminal ADO15 Mini. ADO16 (the 1100) and subsequent ADO17 (the 1800) grew from projects instigated in the 1950s, under the XC9000 code series, with much development being carried out by Issigonis, Jack Daniels and, later, Charles Griffin. XC9000 was a Morris Oxford-sized, rear-wheel-drive saloon that dated from 1956, and this spawned the front-wheel-drive XC9001, photographed for the archives in October 1958, while the contemporary XC9002 was a smaller car intended to supplant the Minor. Both might have made greater headway had not the Suez crisis, in 1956, prompted the accelerated development of XC9003, the 'Sputnik', which became the Mini. By the summer of 1959, XC9002 had become ADO16.

Whereas the appearance of the Mini had been almost entirely Issigonis' inspiration, Leonard Lord employed Pininfarina to refine the lines of ADO16, although the basic proportions had already been determined with XC9002. An innovation with ADO16 was the adoption of Alex Moulton's hydrolastic fluid suspension system, a much simpler and more practical alternative to the complex Citroën hydro-pneumatic suspension of 1956. Hydrolastic would become a particular favourite of BMC engineers and management in the 1960s and, subsequently, would form the basis of a number of projects with MG connections.

Charles Griffin was in charge of engineering on the ADO16 project at Cowley: 'We changed the form of the basic Morris/Austin 1100 by rotating the side panels about the front-wheel centre-line. The original Farina styling tapered inwards towards the rear and deprived the rear seat of 3½in (8.89cm) of width.' These changes to Pininfarina's design narrowed the front grille panel and arched the leading edge of the bonnet, spoiling the styling to an extent, which necessitated some reworking by the Italian company. According to Griffin, everyone was in agreement that these changes, which widened the car, were a worthwhile improvement, but other work resulted. 'The change to the basic car,' he remembers, 'necessitated the final shaping of the MG, Riley and Wolseley derivatives at Cowley, with the final approval being made by Farina at the insistence of Leonard Lord.'

Body designer Syd Goble and Reg Job, who was one of Issigonis' team on the Morris Minor, were in charge of the ADO16 body. Des Jones, who was responsible for the front-end panels, windscreen, bulkhead and side valances, remembers, 'Fisher and Ludlow did the prototype to Morris design. We were running out of time, and so some of the Fisher and Ludlow staff came to Cowley

Left *This rare preliminary information brochure dates from early 1962, and clearly refers to the MG version of ADO16 as the MGC 1100.*

Facing page *A pre-production MG 1100 two-door (export specification). Note the additional MG badge on top of the combined boot-lid handle/number-plate lamp. This rather superfluous badge would be dropped on production cars. (Rover)*

to help us out.' Subsequently, Fisher and Ludlow merged with Pressed Steel to become Pressed Steel Fisher, who took over the final design and, in due course, production of the ADO16 bodies.

There is little doubt that ADO16 was a roomy car in proportion to its exterior size, and the internal width was obviously an important factor in that. Des Jones' colleague, Jim Stimson, who had been involved with the MG TC general arrangement and, at this stage, was still at Cowley, was responsible for the doors, among other panels, of ADO16: 'These were, I believe, our first experience of curved door glasses, which allowed us to increase the internal shoulder width by 3in (7.62cm).'

The 1100 was launched in August 1962 as a Morris, followed shortly after by the MG version (October 1962). After leaving the coast clear for Morris dealerships during the first year, the inevitable Austin version appeared (September 1963), then the Vanden Plas Princess 1100 (October 1963) and, two years later, the Wolseley 1100 and Riley Kestrel.

There is evidence that, as late as the summer of 1962, the MG 1100 might have been introduced as the MGC 1100, which would have been logical, since its public début was to be alongside the MGB at Earls Court. However, there was resistance from Abingdon to this abuse of the sports car nomenclature, so the 'C' was dropped by the time the car went on sale. A preview brochure was produced, intended for issue to Morris dealers in 1962, and titled, 'Advance News of the New MGC1100,' so the idea was obviously given fairly serious consideration.

The MGC: replacing the Austin-Healey 3000
As already mentioned in Chapter 3, MG was keen to see a flagship sports tourer, perhaps with a fixed roof and four seats, that would be above their mainstream sports cars. Ideas for such a car were sketched out in 1956-57 by draughtsman Peter Neal, to the instructions of Syd Enever. When they were given responsibility for the Austin-Healey 100/6, in 1957, the MG designers naturally began to explore the possibility of developing a suitable successor, which could have been badged as an MG, an Austin-Healey, or both. Studies into a six-cylinder, four-seater sports tourer were carried out at Abingdon in 1957-58, under the code EX210; this car would have featured the 2.6-litre C-series Austin-Healey engine. It was obvious to John Thornley, however, that the prospect of BMC sanctioning two entirely different sports cars above the Sprite sector was remote. Accordingly, with the tacit agreement of George

THE MG PRINCESS VANDEN-PLAS

With the launch of the US-market version of ADO16, which was called the MG Sports Sedan, BMC's importers, Hambro Inc., became keen on expanding the range of small British saloons they could offer. On the home market, a luxury version of ADO16, specially trimmed and finished by the Vanden Plas coachbuilders in Kingsbury, North-West London, was introduced in late 1963. This car had arisen from a one-off commission by Connolly Ltd, which had been so admired that BMC decided to put it into production, equipping it with the MG 1100's twin-carburettor engine. Evidently, Hambro felt that this 'miniature Rolls-Royce' was just what Americans wanted, so a prototype was built with an MG badge mounted rather unconvincingly at the top of the standard Vanden Plas 1100 grille. Sales and service literature were printed, proclaiming, 'Today's Smart Car is the MG Princess 1100.' Potential American customers were not impressed, however, and the MG Princess 1100 quietly faded away.

Harriman and Donald Healey, he began to pursue the possibility of a shared basic structure for a common successor to both the MGA and 'big Healey'.

An obvious engine, bearing in mind the proposed V4-powered version of the MGB, would have been the related V6 unit. However, the V6 was never developed as fully as the more important V4, and no V6 was ever seen at Abingdon. Having said that, there was a non-functional V4 engine at the plant, and Don Hayter suspects that this might have been used to mock-up the packaging arrangments for the V6. Certainly, a sketch (SK7258) was drawn up at Abingdon, on 16 November, 1960, showing the V6 in the ADO23 body as a quarter-scale general arrangement.

With the final abandonment of the new engine family, at the end of 1960, the options were restricted to a range of units that were based upon existing or proposed production engines. These were the old Austin-Healey 100 four-cylinder unit, the so-called Light Six, and the trusty, but heavy and bulky, C-series six. While development proceeded, others tried their hand at a replacement for the 'big Healey', and two of the more remarkable of these projects are described elsewhere in this chapter.

The Healey proposal
By 1960, the Healeys were talking to both John Thornley and

COMPETITION IN THE 1960s: THE TURNER YEARS

The 1960s were a period of feverish activity at Abingdon, not only in the production and development departments, but also in the Competitions Department. Marcus Chambers decided to leave in the autumn of 1961, and his replacement, 27-year-old Stuart Turner, started at Abingdon on 1 October of that year. According to Turner, the fact that the Competitions Department was based at Abingdon did not mean that there was a bias towards the racing of MGs; if anything, the reverse was the case. Turner adds, 'MGs were not given the same priority as the Healey 3000 and the Mini Coopers, simply because they were not outright winners,' but, 'MGs were entered for marketing reasons to win classes or categories: those were the days when manufacturers would fill the advertisements with "first in this class" or "second in that."' Today, Turner points out, it would be impossible to run two models as different as the Mini and the Austin-Healey 3000 in the same event, let alone contend with other marques as well.

When Stuart Turner arrived at Abingdon, the Midget was new on the scene, while the MGB and MG 1100 were about a year from launch, so the range of potential MG-badged competition vehicles was broader than for some time. Needless to say, 'Comps' assessed each of these cars. 'We looked at the MGB, just as we looked at every model in the BMC range,' states Turner, 'but the Midget was regarded as an even less likely winner than the "B". Mind you, when we won a Monte class with one, the flags flew at Abingdon as much as for the outright wins with the Minis!' Another vehicle assessed was the MG 1100, with its novel hydrolastic suspension: 'The 1100 was not a competition success, although we had many happy hours, especially with Rauno Aaltonen, near Rhayader, trying to break it over the mountain tracks.'

Of the MG successes, those achieved with the MGB were more frequent and more notable, the Monte Carlo Rally being a particular instance that Turner recalls: 'The "B" on the Monte was a success because it won something and, therefore, was useful for the MG dealers, as were the Sebring efforts. We didn't always win anything, but the advertising agents in America were usually able to build things out of what we did. When we happened to do the quickest lap at Sebring during a downpour (in which the sensible people were crawling), the advertisement (for the US MGB, following the spring 1965 race) said, "Sometimes it rains when you are shopping..."'

The MGB family enjoyed a distinguished career throughout the 1960s, including gaining an impressive twelfth place at the Le Mans race of June 1963. For this event, it featured a long streamlined nose schemed by Syd Enever, drawn up by Jim Stimson and manufactured by Car Panels Ltd of Nuneaton, who also made panels for the Morris Minor Traveller. 'The lines of this front end,' remembers Jim Stimson, 'were developed from the RAF and Jacowski aerofoil section tables. We agreed that the shapes were not perfect, but we were controlled by the height of the engine and radiator.' Similarly distinguished races were run at Le Mans in 1964 and 1965, both with the Enever/Stimpson nose, while there were other notable successes at Monte Carlo and in the Sebring 12-hour race in Florida. The latter culminated in the promising, but tragically short-lived, showing of the lightweight MGC GTS. These activities are all the more impressive when one considers that the main efforts of the BMC Competitions Department were focused on Mini Coopers and the 'big' Healeys.

A peculiar diversion took place in North America during the mid-1960s, in which Abingdon took no part. This was the appearance of the MG Liquid Suspension Special, an MG-badged Indianapolis 500 single-seater race car with rear-mounted Offenhauser engine, designed for Kjell Qvale by his competition manager, Joe Huffaker of Indiana, who would go on to earn fame for race modified MGBs. The only very tenuous link with MG was the use of a hydraulic suspension system broadly similar in concept to the MG 1100's hydrolastic set-up. A team of three such cars performed unspectacularly in the 1964 and 1965 Indy 500 races. In the former, one crashed during practice (and did not race), a second retired, and the third, although dogged by fuel pump problems, struggled on to come in twelfth. In 1965, none of the three cars finished, and so ended the experiment. There is little doubt, however, that the Indy MGs provided some useful publicity for the US distributors to exploit.

In 1967, Stuart Turner left Abingdon to further his career, achieving notable success at Ford, but he remembers his time in 'Comps' with affection: 'I can honestly say that I liked all the people at Abingdon. To dine in the boardroom with people like John Thornley and Syd Enever was a great privilege. I knew Terry Mitchell, Roy Brocklehurst and Don Hayter, for example, better than Jim O'Neill or Cliff Bray, but got on with all of them. It was quite a unique atmosphere at Abingdon, and if the same spirit could have been transferred across to the whole of the motor industry...but then 20/20 vision is always easy in hindsight!'

Paddy Hopkirk (left) and Andrew Hedges at Le Mans, June 1964, with MGB BMO 541B fitted with a lengthened aerodynamic nose cone. This was the first official MG entry at the Sarthe circuit since 1955 (another 'long nose' had been entered 'privately' by Alan Hutcheson the previous year). The car finished sixth in its class and 19th overall, at an average speed of 99.95mph (160.85km/h), which possibly earned the marque more publicity than a straight 100mph (160.93km/h) would have done! (Rover/BMIHT)

George Harriman in an effort to maintain their influence over the Austin-Healey 3000's successor. No doubt, Harriman was already formulating his own, rather different, idea for a grander BMC sports car, but the Healeys' proposal would have been a rather more economical solution and might have slotted in beneath Harriman's super sports car project, so an investigation was sanctioned. The Healeys had enjoyed a long association with the 2660cc, four-cylinder Austin engine, which had been developed originally from a pre-war Austin six-cylinder truck powerplant for the ill-fated Austin Atlantic of 1949. They had adopted this engine for the Healey 100 which, in turn, Leonard Lord had taken on board as the first Austin-Healey. In the years that followed, an impressive competition record had been achieved with this engine, but the desire of BMC to increase usage of the C-series engine, had been instrumental in the development of the six-cylinder Austin-Healey 100/6 in 1955-57.

For the new sports car proposal with the old four-cylinder engine, three stages of tune were suggested. The capacity would have been reduced to 2.5 litres by the simple expedient of fitting an Austin Taxi diesel crankshaft, which had a shorter stroke, thereby extending the rev range and tuning potential. Before long, 142bhp (105.89kW) and 178bhp (132.73kW) versions were being proposed, the intention being to provide some distinction between the Austin-Healey and MG versions which, by now, had been assigned the codes ADO51 and ADO52.

A great deal of effort went into making the big four-cylinder unit fit into the MGB's engine compartment: length was not a problem, but height certainly was, and numerous modifications were required to the engine sump and the ADO23 steering set-up. Even with these alterations, bonnet bulges would have been necessary to clear the top of the engine. It became increasingly obvious that the costs involved would be too high for what, after all, would have been an almost unique engine in a highly modified MGB. The engine was still in use in the Austin Taxi and Gipsy four-wheel-

HARRIMAN'S FOLLY: THE 'FIREBALL XL-5'

In 1962, a competition was organized by the highly respected European publication *Automobile Year* for a sports car design, the prize being that Pininfarina would construct the winning design. This was submitted by three students of the Hochschule für Gestaltung in Ulm, and they were given a choice of three chassis: AC Greyhound, Bristol or Austin-Healey 3000. Although they were not directly responsible for the competition, there is little doubt that both BMC and Healey were interested in the possible outcome. The distinctive lines of the winning design included a sharp-edged fastback roof on a curvaceous lower body—styling that would be echoed in the Pininfarina MGB GT prototype of 1964. Its unusual front end featured enclosed headlamps and a grille comprising a series of horizontal slots in a shark-like nose. BMC were obviously quite taken by this last feature, since they decided to use it as the basis of the styling for a Longbridge designed sports car, coded ADO30. This project, which got under way in 1963, was a particular favourite of George Harriman's, who wanted to display BMC's advanced engineering capabilities in a flagship sports car intended to challenge the best that Jaguar could offer. Although this car is often directly linked to the story of the Austin-Healey 3000 replacement, there is little doubt that, in reality, ADO30 (also coded XC512 by BMC) was intended to sit above the existing and proposed BMC sports car range: the ADO51/ADO52 project would take care of the Austin Healey 3000 market. ADO30/XC512—christened 'Fireball XL-5' by its detractors, after a popular contemporary children's television puppet series—was developed almost entirely in-house at Longbridge, with no input from either MG or Healey. During its short and turbulent life, it is believed to have consumed about £1 million—no small sum in the mid-1960s.

Charles Griffin remembers that the engineering department was not in favour of expending much effort on anything that was not likely to sell in large numbers, and that the body for ADO30 was produced entirely in the body experimental shop, the layout and panel drawings being the work of shop foreman Dick Gallimore, assisted by Doug Adams. Alec Issigonis also provided a quarter-scale brass-plate model, which formed the basis of the full-size monocoque.

The body of ADO30 was a rigid structure with a massive central tunnel (at the insistence of Alec Issigonis), which was intended to provide very high torsional stiffness, something for which Issigonis' other recent BMC cars—notably ADO17—had established a good record. Issigonis' aim was to combine this high torsional stiffness with a relatively light overall weight, something which Griffin believes was largely achieved. Another requirement was the use of hydrolastic suspension, which would, it was hoped, reflect well upon the sales of the humbler BMC ADO16 and ADO17 saloons (and the forthcoming ADO61). The use of hydrolastic suspension incurred something of a weight penalty, but understandably, this factor was rather more significant in smaller cars. The third

ingredient in this dubious recipe was the Rolls-Royce FB 4-litre engine, which BMC were already using in the Vanden Plas 4-litre R; typically, BMC had grossly over-estimated their requirements for this engine and, consequently, were anxious to find another use for it to meet their contractual commitments.

Development proceeded in fits and starts over the next three years. Charles Griffin's son, Brian, who had just completed his apprenticeship at BMC, became involved with ADO30's front suspension design under the direction of Fred Coultas. He recalls that the engineering design office had acquired a Ferrari 3-litre V12 engine from Enzo Ferrari in exchange for a three-door Mini Cooper S, one of three built by Doug Adams in the body experimental shop: 'I don't recall the engine actually going into ADO30—I think we got it as much as anything to see what a proper sporting unit should be like.'

It soon became apparent that the prototype handled like the proverbial pig, an opinion that was not only voiced by BMC people, but also by invited test drivers, notably the highly respected journalist Paul Frère. Attempts were made to overcome this: Charles Griffin remembers converting the rear suspension to semi-trailing arms. Various events led to almost knee-jerk reactions, such as the launch of the Jaguar E-type 2+2, which led BMC to revise ADO30 to include a similar seating format. Then, in July 1966, Jaguar and BMC merged, and the reasons for producing a Jaguar beater evaporated. Apparently, ADO30 lived on for a while, various schemes for fitting Jaguar XK or even Daimler V8 engines being considered, as well as the possibility of utilizing the MGC's torsion-bar front suspension.

By the spring of 1967, the project was dead, helped on its way, no doubt, by Sir William Lyons' celebrated antipathy towards any rivals of his beloved Jaguar marque from within the company. The tragedy, as far as Austin-Healey and MG were concerned, was that this project—even though disliked by the BMC engineers involved—had consumed significant amounts of money and engineering effort, which could have been far more usefully applied, not least to more affordable and saleable sports cars.

What appears to be an ADO30 prototype taking shape at the Longbridge experimental shop, clearly based upon, but differing in detail from, the Austin-Healey-based 'Automobile Year' car of 1962. (courtesy Doug Adams)

ADO24: THE AUSTIN-HEALEY 4000

While George Harriman championed the cause of his pet sports car project, ADO30, and MG were wrestling with the intended ADO51/52 joint Austin-Healey/MG replacement for the 'big Healey', Donald and Geoffrey Healey were concentrating on their own idea for a final evolution of the 'big Healey' itself. One of the fundamental reasons behind ADO30, apart from Harriman's desire to challenge the Jaguar E-type, had been the need to find a use for the 4-litre Rolls-Royce engines that were surplus to the Vanden Plas project, but which BMC had rashly committed themselves to buying. The Healeys proposed what they believed to be a solution to both problems: they would use as much of the existing Austin-Healey 3000 structure as possible and adapt it to take the Rolls-Royce unit, thus creating an Austin-Healey 4000. This project gained official recognition and was granted the code ADO24, work being carried out at the Healeys' own Warwick premises, but with some help from Syd Enever.

The surviving MG factory records for ADO24 show that four drawings were recorded at Abingdon on 27 February, 1967, three of which were quarter-scale general arrangements, and there is a reference to drawings by both Jensen and the Healeys. That month, the newly formed British Motor Holdings sanctioned the building of six prototypes, but by April, this had been reduced to two; perhaps problems within the organization had caused them to be reluctant about the project. The prototypes were made 6in (15.24cm) wider by the time honoured technique of slicing the whole car lengthways along its centre-line and filling in the gaps. Much work was carried out to ensure that the car complied with forthcoming legislation: remember that the US safety and clean air acts had been passed, and it was known that the former would cause the end of the Austin-Healey 3000 Mark IV in January 1968, which was the projected launch date for ADO24. Rolls-Royce worked on the engine to ensure that it would meet US emissions legislation, while the interior of the car was redesigned to take account of forthcoming requirements. Within a matter of weeks, however, BMH cancelled the whole project, consigning it to the same fate as ADO30.

drive vehicle, but neither of these uses amounted to a particularly high volume, so the idea was abandoned.

The light-six engine

During the mid-1950s, the Austin engineers at Longbridge designed a six-cylinder version of the B-series, as a lighter and smaller-capacity alternative to the hefty C-series, which had been designed by Morris Engines. Problems had been experienced with the Morris designed unit which, in early development, had suffered from poor output and vibration periods. Moreover, the old rivalries between Austin and Morris added fuel to the fire. Initially, it was envisaged that the six-cylinder B-series would have used the same bore and stroke as the 1489cc four-cylinder version, resulting in a capacity of 2233cc, and have a four-main-bearing crank (the four-cylinder unit featured three main bearings at that stage).

By the end of the decade, however, the six-cylinder B-series—christened Blue Streak by its creators—was felt unlikely to have a future in the UK. However, it was adopted by BMC's Australian subsidiary, who saw it as an ideal weapon in their campaign against the local Holden and Ford competition. For the production version, the capacity was increased by using components from the 1622cc four, resulting in a 2433cc unit that, in standard form, produced 80bhp (59.66kW) at 4350rpm. For sporting applications, this could be increased to 115bhp (85.76kW) at 5200rpm, and a specimen unit was fitted to a brown MGB at Abingdon.

Pat Rees, an engineer based at Cowley, moved to Abingdon to work on this car which, according to Don Hayter, was registered BMO 340B: 'Pat fabricated a special tubular front cross-member with flanges on each end, which carried torsion-bar suspension.' Roy Brocklehurst was one of those who took the Light Six MGB out for a test run up the Oxford bypass: he was stopped for speeding at well over 120mph (193.12km/h).

The C-series engine option

The first ideas for a larger-engined MG—dating from 1957—had

centred on the use of the BMC C-series engine and, despite alternative proposals, the final decision came almost full circle, back to the C-series again. The reason was simple: as in the case of the MGB, ultimately, the choice of engine was determined by the requirements of Austin-Morris, who needed an engine to power the replacement for the Austin Westminster, Wolseley 6/110 and Vanden Plas Princess. BMC intended this car, coded ADO61, to be a technical *tour de force*, its advanced features including a special self-levelling suspension system based on hydrolastic principles, but incorporating some of the components of ADO17, the Austin-Morris 1800 saloon. Part of the reasoning behind this was a proposed joint venture between BMC and Rolls-Royce, intended to produce an up-market range of BMC luxury saloons, which would have shared many of their components with a cheaper Bentley—a project that, ultimately, came to naught.

ADO61 turned out to be large and heavy, and the only engine deemed suitable to power it was a heavily reworked version of the 2990cc C-series. Accordingly, an engine development programme was set in train, under the supervision of Alec Issigonis, the principal objectives being to refine the design (changing to seven main bearings in place of four) and reduce the weight. Improved performance was not high on the list of priorities.

In the meantime, the men at Abingdon were exploring the feasibility of squeezing the C-series engine into the MGB. The first drawing recorded against ADO51 (the Austin-Healey) was dated 6 November, 1962, and in the space of the following four months, the best part of 100 drawings were prepared. Even before that, a trial propshaft installation for ADO51 had been tried in an Austin-Healey BN7 (ADO26/30, dated 30 December, 1960), and drawings were prepared against the ADO52 (MGC) code as early as 16 January, 1961, even before the MGB had been launched. By the end of the following year, a prototype (ADO52/72, dated 20 November, 1962) had been built.

The C-series engine was massive, and although it could be accommodated lengthways in the MGB's engine bay, it was very tall, which caused problems. As a result, a complete redesign of the front inner body panels and front suspension (utilizing a neat torsion-bar set-up) was necessary, together with the addition of prominent bonnet bulges. The first two were schemed by Roy Brocklehurst, and the last by Jim O'Neill and Des Jones. The radiator was moved forwards, and numerous other expensive panel changes were made ahead of the windscreen. Ideally, given the sheer size of the engine, MG would have preferred to redesign the bulkhead, and relocate the heater and brake servo as well. This would have allowed the engine to be mounted further back, which would have helped maintain some semblance of the good balance that was a hallmark of the MGB.

However, a redesigned bulkhead and all the affected adjacent panels—expensive items to retool—would not be countenanced on grounds of cost. Financial constraints were also largely to blame for the fact that the exterior of the MGC would differ little from the MGB. Another critical factor militated against moving the engine rearwards: BMC was determined to offer the MGC with an optional Borg-Warner BW35 automatic transmission. The sheer size of this bulky unit, coupled with the fact that it would be offered in both the MGC and the Mark II MGB, meant that the position of the engine flywheel was fixed.

While the men at MG had to accept the engine with good grace, they were hopeful that, at least, its weight would be reduced as part of the redesign process. Alas, their wishes were unfulfilled, and John Thornley recalled their disappointment when the first engine arrived at the factory and was weighed. Syd Enever took his concerns to Alec Issigonis in person, hoping to persuade him, with the aid of drawings by Terry Mitchell, to reduce the stroke by about 1¼in (3.18cm), thereby decreasing the height and weight of the engine, and producing a more sweetly revving unit into the bargain. However, Issigonis, who took little genuine interest in MG affairs, was unmoved.

Don Hayter recalls that Enever also had other ideas to improve the engine: 'Based on Syd's experience of the old MG engines, he also felt that the exhaust and inlet ports could be modified to improve gas flow, but none of this was accepted.' According to

Dickie Wright, a crucial factor in this decision was, undoubtedly, the cost factor: 'Syd would have liked a bigger bore and a shorter stroke, making the engine sportier and lighter in weight, but the limitations of the transfer machinery at Longbridge put the kibosh on the idea.' The resultant engine was no more powerful than the unit it was intended to replace, and it was certainly less sporting. As the basis of a sports car, it was hardly ideal.

The MGC and the Austin-Healey 3000 Mark IV

From honourable intentions to produce separate, but related, Austin-Healey and MG designs, the paths of ADO51 and ADO52 came closer together through cost considerations. By 1966, when the Austin-Healey 3000 Mark IV was ready for viewing by the Healeys, it differed hardly at all from the MGC. The only significant differences were a Healey-style grille, which Don Hayter had styled on to the MGC nose with some difficulty (there being no budget for panel changes), different bumper overriders (from ADO17), and a chrome strip along the sill. At the same time, if the market had demanded it, there could have been an Austin-Healey 1800, too. The prototype was ADO51/182, dating from September 1964, and although intended to show the 3-litre version, it was actually built on an MGB base.

The Healeys were not impressed and refused to be associated with the car in any way. One imagines that the management at BMC had not expected this hostility from them, since parts and even publications were already in the course of production for the Austin Healey 3000 Mark IV. Whatever the rights or wrongs of Donald Healey's refusal to be associated with this car, no doubt his action helped set the scene for the termination of the long association between the Austin and Healey marques soon after Leyland came on the scene. Perhaps it was the Healeys' displeasure with the C-series engine that prompted the serious investigation of the Australian engine: a drawing recorded as ADO51/186, dated 9 February, 1965, describes the 'installation of Australian engine— six cylinder', but of course, this came to nothing.

One of the few obvious distinguishing features of the MGC was the bonnet, with its characteristic bulges. Des Jones was involved in the alterations to the bonnet and front panels: 'The prototype of the bonnet had already been done; there was an extra bulge in the bonnet to give clearance to the rear carburettor on the left side. The

This is the definitive Austin-Healey 3000 Mark IV, which differs from the MGC in only minor details: a different grille (styled by Don Hayter), relocated side-lamps, different bumper overriders and a chrome strip along the sill. (Rover)

forward sited radiator meant that the front-end panels of the body, which supported the radiator, had to be altered, and the bonnet release lever reversed. Syd Enever and I went over to Pressed Steel Fisher at Cowley, at the request of Reg White, to approve the mock-up of the bonnet prior to releasing it to the die cutting machine for the tooling.' Many years later, this same tool would be altered to form the basis of the tooling for the bonnet of the RV8.

Poor man's Aston Martin: the MGB GT

When John Thornley was inspired by the sight of three Aston Martin DB2/4s at Silverstone, during the early 1950s (see Chapter 3), it caused him to contemplate the idea of a fastback MG, and led to his much quoted concept of a 'poor man's Aston Martin'. As he explained to me, his ideas were too late for the MGA coupé: '...but when we came to work on the MGB, it was a different story. We designed the roadster with the foreknowledge that it would ultimately have an unstressed top on it, but priority was given to the open car, as this was the one which would keep the American market open.'

As early as the beginning of January 1962, the Abingdon team was planning the coupé derivative of the MGB, under the code EX227. However, their attempts never seemed to look right: the rounded shape of the MGB roadster did not appear to lend itself to a similarly rounded roof, which was necessary to provide adequate headroom. Ironically, one of Abingdon's better efforts, by Jim O'Neill, drew inspiration from the hardtop produced by Frua for his rebodied MGA, while the back end bore a passing resemblance to the Aston Martin DB4.

In 1963, Jim Stimson—another Cowley veteran, who had joined the exodus to Abingdon at the beginning of the decade—was asked by Syd Enever to draw up proposals for the MGB coupé. 'I became Syd's scribbling pad,' recalls Stimson, who produced a great many quarter-scale drawings based upon Enever's sketches: 'I did a design concept for the MGB GT for Syd, who wanted to get it sanctioned. At that time, of course, we came under the control of

Longbridge, and as we couldn't very easily take an 18ft (5.49m) long draft up to Birmingham for management viewing, we had a red painted, quarter-scale model built by Morris Bodies Branch at Coventry. The management told Syd that they retained the services of Mr Farina for that sort of thing—Syd came back quite upset, almost in tears. In the end, we sent my model to Pininfarina, along with the instruction to produce a buildable full-size prototype. They sharpened the lines, but the end result wasn't far from our concept.'

Abingdon sent Pininfarina an MGB roadster later that same year, with the instruction to rework it into a coupé prototype for evaluation. John Thornley recalled the reception accorded Pininfarina's creation: 'What came back received instant and universal approval. All along, we had been trying to retain the roadster's windscreen. Pininfarina threw it out, picked up the top rail by a couple of inches, sharpened the corners, and there we were!' Jim Stimson's version of events is slightly different, however. 'The height of the windscreen was increased at the very beginning by us, and not

The MGB GT made its show début at the 1965 Earls Court Motor Show, where it is seen here on the MG stand with optional wire wheels and Dunlop whitewall tyres. (Autocar)

Pininfarina,' he insists, adding 'I did a full-scale layout drawing of the entire body, which was sent out to Pininfarina. The only significant alteration that Pininfarina made was to add the feature line (crease) around the roof which, I must admit, improved the appearance immeasurably.'

The metallic pale green prototype, with red interior, was promptly approved and drawn up in its definitive form by the Abingdon drawing office. Few changes were made, other than those necessitated by practicalities or cost. Jim O'Neill recalls this exercise well: 'I felt the frameless glass rear quarterlights were a bit fragile, so I

When the MGC was launched, a GT version was available from the outset, seen here at the Earls Court Motor show in October 1967. (Rover)

THE COUNE MGB

The people at MG tried very hard to produce an attractive coupé version of the MGB roadster, but all their efforts looked too heavy and certainly were not as elegant as the best of the competition, especially from Italy and Germany. At almost the same time, an enterprising Belgian named Jacques Coune began to produce his own coupé conversion, which he christened the MGB Berlinette. Coune, who was an agent for Abarth, Bertone and Iso Rivolta, also had his own repair business in the Avenue de la Couronne in Brussels. No doubt due to a need for skilled men to repair such exotic cars, he employed a number of Italian craftsmen, whom he had tempted to work for him in Belgium by offering them much higher wages than they had enjoyed in Turin. To keep them gainfully employed, Coune hit upon the idea of expanding his business by modifying the coachwork of standard production cars and, before long, he turned his attention to the MGB. He succeeded in producing an elegant coupé from the basic MGB, principally because he did what Abingdon had failed to do—but which Pininfarina would also do—and that was to abandon the standard roadster windscreen in favour of a much deeper screen. This gave the finished car much better proportions than it might otherwise have had. The actual style of the body was very much of its time, with elements of the contemporary Ferrari 250GTO and even the aerodynamic Cobra Daytona coupé.

The conversion was quite expensive, involving extensive work to the basic car, and typically it added about 50 per cent to the cost of a new MGB, excluding taxes. The process of turning an MGB roadster into a Berlinette involved recessing the headlamps into the front wings behind perspex fairings, Jaguar E-type fashion, together with slight flaring of the wheel-arch lips and removal of the characteristic chrome side strip. At the rear, most of the exterior panelwork behind the doors was cut-away and replaced with a fibreglass roof and rear body structure, which was bonded to the remainder of the steel monocoque. To restore the strength lost by such drastic surgery, substantial steel reinforcements were welded into the rear of the body. To some extent, the interior of the car was tailored to the customer's specification, but most retained a basically standard MGB front cockpit, together with a distinctive quilted headlining and fully carpeted boot area. The last was reached by means of a conventional boot lid.

The MGB Berlinette received a considerable amount of publicity in the European motoring press following its début at the Brussels Motor Show in January 1964. It is not surprising, therefore, that it soon came to the attention of BMC's management. As a consequence, there was an unofficial meeting between Alec Issigonis and Jacques Coune, at which the possibility of collaboration between BMC and Coune was discussed, the idea being to adapt

his design and produce the car at Abingdon alongside the standard MGB roadster. In return for this arrangement, Coune would have been paid a royalty. The managing director of the Nuffield Press, the company's printing subsidiary responsible for manuals, brochures and stationery, was Walter Oldfield and, on a number of occasions, his taste for exotic motor cars was used by the company as an indirect means of commissioning special one-offs. It was Oldfield, therefore, who gave instructions for a standard MGB, devoid of all unnecessary trim, to be delivered straight from the production lines at Abingdon to Coune's coachworks in Brussels for conversion.

The Oldfield MGB Berlinette, resplendent in a non-standard, but extremely fetching, shade of metallic pale blue, was delivered to Cowley in June 1964. Before long, Sir George Harriman (BMC's chairman), Syd Enever, Issigonis and even Sir Leonard Lord had driven the car in a series of appraisals. Unfortunately for Jacques Coune, the Pininfarina styled MGB GT prototype had already been built by this time, and the chances of this simpler, all-steel proposal being ousted by the complex composite Coune car were slim. Issigonis is reputed to have told Coune that his car 'looked too Italian', which surely was an ironic statement given the origins of the car that did emerge as the MGB GT.

Walter Oldfield, meanwhile, had not been involved in the negotiations, his role having been simply that of intermediary. With the rejection of the Coune car, Oldfield expressed an interest in it and kept it for himself, registering it as CBW 55B. Ultimately, he passed the car to its present owner, Mike Akers (a Rover project engineer at Cowley), to whom I am grateful for relating much of the story.

Between 1964 and 1978, the Oldfield car only covered some 24,000 miles (38,623km) and was exclusively maintained at the Abingdon factory. Jacques Coune, meanwhile, continued to produce MGB Berlinettes for the Continental European market: 55 left-hand-drive models were built, the Oldfield car remaining the sole right-hand-drive example. Coune tried again, in 1966, with an oddly styled targa-top MGB conversion, exhibiting the prototype at that year's Turin Motor Show. However, this car would have been quite expensive and does not appear to have been particularly well received. Consequently, it remained unique.

At the time of writing, the ex-Walter Oldfield car has only covered a total of 31,000 miles and is currently maintained by Bob Bryant, one of the Rover engineers involved with the MG RV8 project at Cowley (Bob developed the air-conditioning installation for the Japanese-market RV8), thus maintaining the factory connection.

Mike Akers owns the MGB Berlinette converted by Jacques Coune for Walter Oldfield. It is seen here in all its glory outside Yarnton Manor, Oxford. (courtesy Mike Akers)

decided a Mini-type frame would be more suitable, although perhaps not quite so attractive. A one-piece fibre-board headlining was also prepared for speed of assembly.' There were problems, however, with the rear roof-lining header: 'The damp weather tended to make the header lose its shape; this eventually had to be changed for a much more expensive fibreglass plastic moulding.'

In the process of readying the MGB GT for production, novel, twin coil-sprung tail-gate supports were added and various interior changes made. The prototype, having served its purpose, was scheduled for destruction to avoid payment of the import duty on the expensive hand-built vehicle and, according to Roy Brocklehurst, this was carried out under the watchful eye of the local Customs and Excise officer, Mr Fishpool. However, there remains an unresolved mystery as, despite Brocklehurst's assertion,

the car has survived intact, the full story being recounted in the panel below.

The distinctive MGB GT tail-gate supports were developed from an earlier, slightly less successful, application, as Don Butler remembers: 'We had evolved a spring assisted tail-gate support at Cowley for the Morris Oxford Traveller. Someone was nearly killed by one of these when it broke, part of the mechanism shooting past his head and straight through the windscreen. This idea—made much safer—was the basis of the MGB GT tail-gate support. I did one for the MGB tourer, but in the end, a conventional prop was used instead.'

An interesting aside to this story is that Pressed Steel were convinced that gas struts could be used to support the GT tail-gate in place of the spring units. MG said that the hinges were not strong

THE PININFARINA MGB GT PROTOTYPE

The normal fate of hand-built prototypes, once they have fulfilled their purpose, is to be destroyed. This is a sad consequence of the fact that their value includes the cost of an astronomical amount of skilled labour, and these days such prototypes can be worth as much as a third of a million pounds. While they are in use, they may bear special 'experimental' chassis numbers and, if registered for road use, their tax discs are marked 'subject to excise restrictions'. Therefore, unless the money can be found, no matter how fascinating or potentially historically significant a prototype may be, it will often succumb to the acetylene torch. This should have been the fate of the MGB GT prototype, built by Pininfarina, yet from my research, it would appear that somehow this car got away.

In 1964, the destination record for a Chelsea Grey 1963 MGB roadster, chassis number GHN3-9359, was marked in the factory register as 'EXP', for experimental. In fact, it was sent to Pininfarina in Italy, where the master stylists produced a prototype of the elegant coupé proposal. The car was completed in short time and returned to Abingdon for appraisal, replete in the light metallic green traditionally favoured by Abingdon for prototypes since before the war. The car closely resembles the production version that emerged a year later, but close examination shows that a few changes were made. The roadster origins would be obvious to any MGB expert, since the wing-to-scuttle seam, in front of the windscreen, is straight rather than the distinctive dog-leg of the production MGB GT. Similarly, the rear quarterlights of the prototype were frameless glass (chrome-plated brass frames were used in production), the tailgate was crudely propped by a single stay, and the rear luggage compartment floor featured five longitudinal metal runners over red vinyl. Other interior differences on the prototype included rudimentary armrests on each side of the thinner rear seat cushion.

By the time that the MGB GT was nearing its launch, in October 1965, the Pininfarina prototype was no longer being used, yet it appears to have been saved by a fascinating turn of events. At the time, Lester Suffield was in charge of Nuffield Exports, which looked after the overseas marketing of

BMC products, and one of his senior lieutenants was Jim Malone, a man recalled with respect by North American agents for MG sports cars. Malone's wife, Thora, saw the MGB GT before its public launch and, as she told me, 'fell in love with it. I decided then and there that I wanted one.' However, there simply was no UK-specification production MGB GT available for her, so it seemed that the senior executive's wife would not have her wish granted. Then someone remembered the Pininfarina car, and it was swiftly decided that Mrs Malone could have it.

Thora Malone recalls inspecting the metallic green car and instructing that it be resprayed Porsche silver—against the advice of the paint shop, incidentally—and trimmed throughout in red leather (the seats were later changed for black examples when the original red facings cracked, but that is getting ahead of the story). The finished car was registered HBL 124D and delivered to her in time for the launch. She told me that Lester Suffield pleaded with her not to turn up at the MGB GT's launch in the silver car, saying that it would have shown up the launch car.

Over the years, the car remained in Mrs Malone's possession, appearing at an MG Car Club event in August 1984, where examination revealed visible traces of the original metallic green paint through a scratch in the otherwise immaculate silver paintwork. In the following year, it was bought by MG collector Syd Beer, who was sold the car on the strict understanding by its former owner that it would be given a good home. I questioned John Thornley about the car in 1985, and he appeared mystified about its survival: 'Where the mistake is I do not know, but there must be one somewhere,' he wrote, adding, 'When I examined the car...the sum total of the points of difference between it and a production MGB GT were such that I was convinced that it was the Italian car, quite apart from the matter of the underlying paint.' Roy Brocklehurst's assurance that he had personally witnessed the destruction of the car only adds to the mystery. Sadly, now that both John Thornley and Roy Brocklehurst are no longer with us, I shall leave the story at that...

This is the actual Pininfarina MGB GT prototype, photographed in June 1964. Note the pull-out door handles and frameless quarterlight windows. (Rover)

M.G. MIDGET.
PROPOSED NEW FRONT.

enough for this, but Pressed Steel went ahead anyway and prepared an MGB GT with the struts: 'The tail-gate closed okay, but the next day, the tail-gate had lifted right off the seals, the hinges having failed as we had forecast!'

Improving the Midget

The Abingdon engineers were never as happy about the Austin-Healey Sprite's quarter-elliptic suspension as were the Healeys, which had led Syd Enever to test the car on pavé and introduce structural reinforcements. Therefore, Enever and his men re-engineered the Mark II Sprite/Mark I Midget to accept more conventional semi-elliptic rear springs, which reduced the stresses on the monocoque considerably. At the same time, the longer springs allowed greater axle movement and softer settings, so it was possible to improve the original model's rather harsh ride. The chassis number for the prototype is recorded as ADO47/110, dated 5 February, 1963.

However, by October 1962, after the launch of the MGB, the possibility of a Midget with hydrolastic suspension was being given serious consideration. EX229 and EX231 date from October-November 1962, and April-December 1963 respectively. The fact that EX231 spawned 66 separate drawings shows how much effort went into this project, presumably after the front-wheel-drive ADO34 exercise had been virtually abandoned. Before long. EX231 was overtaken by the all-new EX234 project—the 'Hydrolastic Sports Car'.

During the 1960s, BMC considered facelifts for both the MGB and Midget and, in 1965, a proposal was drawn up to show a square MG grille, modelled upon that used for ADO16, the MG 1100. This idea does not appear to have progressed very far, however, not least because it is difficult to see how such a facelift could have been justified if the Austin-Healey Sprite front panelwork was to be retained unchanged. Financial constraints and, for once, common sense, prevailed, and the MG Midget retained its original grille until the British Leyland facelift of 1969.

More sensible, however, was the introduction of hinged front quarterlights and wind-up windows, which Des Jones remembers: 'I was given the windscreen to do by Jim O'Neill. I travelled to Coventry to work on the Midget/Sprite windscreens at Bodies

Over the years, several attempts were made to give the Midget more of an MG identity to differentiate it fromt he Austin-Healey Sprite. This proposal dates from March 1965. (Rover)

Branch. A windscreen similar to that of the MGB was designed, and a prototype produced with the help of Eric Carter. The quarterlight and door glass were then schemed, and I cut a hole in the door trim-pad and incorporated an outward bulge to give the driver more elbow room. Finally, the layout and detailed drawings were done at Abingdon. The pillar was the most difficult job, but the Cowley pattern shop did the pillar and complete windscreen assembly before issuing for production.' The surviving records—now at British Motor Heritage, Gaydon—record three prototypes for the wind-up-window cars: ADO41/165 (Sprite), ADO47/109 and ADO47/113 (both Midgets) dated, respectively, 19 November, 1962, 26 November, 1962, and 28 May, 1963.

The next development was the introduction of the larger 1275cc engine, in which form the Midget reached what was arguably its best stage of development. The engine was not the rather specialized Mini Cooper S unit, as many suppose, but in fact, a substantially redesigned version of the A-series, the block and head of which had been significantly improved for ease of production. The new engine, together with a number of other welcome improvements (such as a convertible hood), appeared in October 1966 in the MG Midget Mark III and contemporary Austin-Healey Sprite Mark IV.

In 1967, for reasons of production logistics, 489 Sprites and 476 Midgets were built at the Cowley plant instead of Abingdon. This was not too difficult to organize, since by that time, all the MG sports cars were largely assembled from brought-in components, rather than manufactured in-house near the production line. These Cowley-built cars differ only from their Abingdon-built brethren by having an 'M' suffix (for Morris) to the chassis number, in place of the normal 'G' (for MG). The exercise, however, was not a great success and was never repeated.

The emergence of the Honda S800 sports car, in 1967, with its high revving engine, excited some interest in the Healey camp and, accordingly, an example was borrowed for appraisal. As a result, the Healeys fitted a production Austin-Healey Sprite with a 1275cc

Left *The elegant lines of Pininfarina's body for the EX234 hydrolastic sports car. Note the trim strip running from the wing into the door...* (Rover)

Below *...which does not feature on the nearside.* (Rover)

A-series unit to Mini Cooper S specification, then changed this for a specially developed experimental version of the A-series, produced by Eddie Maher of Morris Engines. Despite promising test results, the discontinuation of the Honda S800 somewhat deflated the argument for the 'super Sprite', and all further development was abandoned.

At Abingdon, a similar project was born at around the time that the Healeys stopped work on theirs, as Bob Neville recalls: 'There was a proposal in about 1969 for a sort of Midget GTS, which featured flared wheel arches similar to those of the MGC GTS. A number of alloy-panelled shells were built up by Bodies Branch in 1969, with the thought of a possible racing challenge, a sort of Cooper S version of the Midget. The closure of the Competitions Department finally put paid to that idea.'

The EX-Register records a number of interesting Midget-based exercises from the mid-1960s onwards, including EX238—a

Midget with an 1800cc engine (dating from 1966), which had overtones of EX221 from 1960—and EX239, a 'competition and fuel-injection Midget' (1967-68). The latter may be the competition Midget to which Bob Neville referred. One exercise that could have borne fruit was a proposal to enlarge the space in the Midget's cockpit, long a subject of debate and an obvious source of lost sales to potential customers of large build. The exercise was carried out in late 1968, under the code EX243, as Terry Mitchell recalls: 'We tried enlarging the doors and getting the seats further back, but this was never followed through. The whole car was too short, really.'

Also investigated for the Midget was a taller windscreen, following a similar exercise carried out on the MGB after the MGB GT had been introduced. Peter Neal recalls the fate of this exercise: 'Eric Carter at Bodies Branch did it, and when Syd Enever saw the result, he told us to cut 2in (5.08cm) out of the height—and it went back to being almost the same as the original!' Ironically, as Don

The interior of the Pinifarina EX234 prototype was very neatly detailed, with an unusually wide centre console. The dashboard was cleverly designed to facilitate commonality between left- and right-hand-drive versions. Note the vestigial rear seats. (Rover)

Hayter recalls, a similar fate befell a proposal to raise the height of the MGB windscreen (originally dictated by SCCA racing regulations) to that of the MGB GT: 'Jim Oates at Cowley did it, but somehow it just didn't look right.'

Replacing the MGB: the hydrolastic sports car

Not long after the MGB entered production, the ever active Abingdon design team began to consider a means of upgrading it and, ultimately, replacing it. There was some disappointment in the design department that the sophisticated rear suspension, originally planned for the car, had not been adopted. Therefore, their first thoughts centred on the possibility of developing a truly independent rear suspension set-up for the MGB, which was not only more sophisticated, but would also behave itself in a manner appropriate to an MG. However, the original coil-sprung, live-axle set-up developed for the MGB had been poorly received by Abingdon's own testers, and it was clear that something much better would be necessary if the conventionally-sprung live axle was be improved upon significantly. The decision to retain rear-wheel-drive, but opt for independent rear suspension, posed special problems for the designers—by now, all the more advanced BMC cars featured front-wheel-drive, and there was increasing use of the new hydrolastic fluid suspension system, while the remaining rear-wheel-drive cars retained live rear axles and leaf springs.

Abingdon's only hope, it seemed, was to utilize the final-drive unit of the Austin Gipsy four-wheel-drive vehicle, which was BMC's answer to the Land Rover. Having taken the decision to combine this unit with hydrolastic suspension, the team soon realized that it would be much more sensible to develop a completely new car than butcher the MGB. At the same time, Abingdon were keen to see their own replacement for the Healey designed Sprite/Midget, and it became apparent that by offering a new car with a choice of engine sizes, they could kill two birds with one stone. Since they had already carried out studies on a hydrolastic equipped Midget, it was not long before Enever and his team turned their attention to scheming a common successor to the Midget and MGB.

In February 1964, the EX-Register records the first entry against EX234, described simply as the 'Hydrolastic sports car'. Hydrolastic suspension was still novel in 1964, but it had already been used with success in BMC's ADO16 1100 range including, of course, the Cowley-built MG 1100, which had been launched two years before. In the USA, a single-seater racing car, called the Liquid Suspension Special, helped bring the novel Moulton designed system to the attention of the American general public, despite the fact that it did not actually use hydrolastic suspension (and did not make that much of an impression in racing circles). Therefore, it was not surprising that Abingdon designed their proposed Midget/MGB replacement to accept hydrolastic suspension. Two under-frames were prepared, one of which was shipped to Pininfarina with a packaging drawing. The Turin stylists clothed it with an attractive body that, effectively, was a cross between an MGB and an Alfa Romeo Spyder.

The initial development work was carried out by a small team, led by Roy Brocklehurst and including Mike Holliday and Jim Stimson, who set themselves up in the comparative warmth and secrecy of the MG boiler house, away from prying eyes and distractions. One of those who later became involved with the work at Abingdon was Jeff Clarke: 'I recall putting all the hydrolastic suspension in, and working on the car in conjunction with Lockheed.' As delivered from Pininfarina, the trimmed bodyshell was equipped with ADO16 hydrolastic displacers. Jeff Clarke recalls that Syd Enever was not happy with these: 'Brian Hillier and I took some ADO17 displacers, fabricated some special brackets and fitted them in place of the ADO16 ones.' Jim Stimson, who also produced a quarter-scale drawing from the Pininfarina prototype, remembers that Syd continued to experiment with the hydrolastic system: 'Syd tried isolating the front and rear displacers, using domestic stop-cocks inserted in the connecting pipes.'

Also involved was Rod Lyne, who recalls that the Pininfarina body '...appeared one day, and we spent ages putting it together. It had cable operated boot and petrol filler flaps—very unusual in those days. The fascia was also designed to be easy to reverse for LHD/RHD applications, with a modular instrument unit.' Although the prototype was fitted with a standard A-series engine, it could have been equipped with either the 1275cc A-series or 1798cc B-series engine, effectively replacing both the Midget and the MGB with one car. However, Jim Stimson claims that no serious work was done on a larger-engined version: 'Our design brief for the vehicle only mentioned the A-series engine,' he says. 'We looked upon it as a replacement for the Midget, and there was never any mention of the MGB.'

Roy Brocklehurst took the EX234 prototype to Silverstone where, according to Jim Stimson, it was driven by a few trusted experts: 'I remember Roy saying that several well-known drivers who were there that day were allowed to drive it; the only name I can recall now is John Surtees. Roy said that they told him that they thought the roadholding was as good as any car they had driven.'

Despite this apparently promising start, it appears that, like so many of Abingdon's more viable projects, EX234 came to be regarded as a 'hospital job', to be worked on when there was nothing better to do. Rod Lyne recalls how EX234 was placed under wraps on at least one occasion before being brought out again.

By 1966, the Abingdon team was finding it necessary to concentrate their limited resources on the imminent US safety and emissions legislation, while the merger of BMC with Jaguar, later the same year, placed a different complexion on all BMC projects. By the time that the Leyland merger took place, in 1968, EX234 had been relegated to a corner of the development shop. It finally emerged from its resting place in the boiler room in 1976, when it was registered REW 314R (the initials of Bob Ward, MG's plant director at the time) before being passed to MG collector Syd Beer, who owns it to this day.

The last days of BMC

The decline and fall of the British Motor Corporation is a subject that would require an entire book of its own, for the problems were many and various. Any successful organization depends primarily upon strong and competent leadership, but the BMC of the 1960s was sadly lacking in that respect. Leonard Lord, by then Lord Lambury, had stepped aside in favour of his deputy, George Harriman. This gentlemanly figure undoubtedly meant well, but his actions (such as the promotion of the disastrous ADO30 project) helped cause the company's fortunes to spiral into decline. What BMC needed, but did not begin to receive until it was too late, was a drastic pruning and rationalization of its enormous and ageing product range, and its many factories. Lord had not attempted to do this, preferring to play on old rivalries throughout the period of growth in the 1950s; Harriman also failed to do it during the following decade.

John Thornley gave his opinion of the contrasting qualities of Lord and Harriman: 'Both suffered from the same delusion: that they were chief engineer as well as chairman of the company. But Lord believed that if he was right just over half the time, then he was scoring above the line. Harriman tried to do the same thing but he failed miserably—he never got it right.' Thornley was extremely blunt in summing up his views of Harriman as BMC chairman: 'I thought that he was a menace; I blame him entirely for the whole business of BMC's decline.' Another person with strong feelings about the period under Harriman's management was Geoff Healey. As he related in his book, *More Healeys*, 'Len Lord was able to

lead and keep these petty feuds under control, but George Harriman, with a life spent on production, did not have this ability, or much interest in these matters.'

Another perspective on the decline of BMC comes from Stuart Turner, the organization's competitions manager in the 1960s: 'There was no doubt that BMC were failing in the sixties. I remember telling the export director that Paddy Hopkirk wanted to rally an 1800 (ADO17). The director asked me if I could get Alec Issigonis to change the handbrake over to the other side. In other words, by then, he believed that Issigonis would be more likely to listen to the competitions people than to the sales side! By that time, the accountants were in charge.' Stuart Turner recalls George Harriman as always being a reasonable man to deal with, although he readily admits that his dealings with the chairman were mainly at meetings devoted to competition matters.

Another insider's viewpoint on BMC's downfall is that of Charles Griffin who, in the mid-1960s, was the company's director of engineering. 'I would not attach particular blame to any individual for the failure of BMC,' he says, adding, 'All one can be certain of is that it should not have happened! In the middle of the 1960s, we were holding some 43 per cent of the UK market, and were making a substantial contribution to exports; we had some 13-14 per cent of the home market with just one model range (ADO16, including the MG 1100). We knew from Ministry of Transport figures that within 15 years, the UK "vehicle park" would increase by 50 per cent, and in order to maintain our enormous share, we would have to double our production through-put.'

Griffin continues, 'We were unable to win the hearts and minds of our labour force and, coupled with the stop-and-go economic policy of the day, we had no market to expand into.' Retraction was inevitable, he believes. At this time, BMC were becoming involved with the development of ADO14 (Maxi) and ADO61 (3-Litre), which Griffin believes obstructed the more logical approach of developing second-generation versions of ADO17 and the best selling ADO16; but hindsight is a wonderful thing!

The merger with Jaguar—British Motor Holdings

The atmosphere in the British motor industry of the 1960s was one

In the USA, there were great hopes for the MGC GTS; MBL 546E (or 'Mable' as the car became known) is seen here at the Sebring 12-hour race of March 1968, in which the team of Paddy Hopkirk and Andrew Hedges came first in class and tenth overall.

This elegant sports coupé proposal was the work of Pressed Steel stylist Rob Owen in January 1967, and could, according to Rob, have been either an Austin-Healey or an MG (although it bears an MG badge on its C-pillar). Sadly, the original artwork has been damaged in storage at some point during the ensuing 28 years. (courtesy Rob Owen)

of acquisition and merger, a situation that was actively encouraged by Harold Wilson's Labour government. The aim was to create an industry that was strong enough to resist the threat of foreign ownership—a desire that would be reinforced by the take-over of the Rootes Group by Chrysler, in January 1967. It was also a decade in which the notable success of one company, Ford, was an object lesson to the others.

Ford introduced the conventional, but extremely successful, Cortina in 1962, and although BMC's ADO16 remained Britain's best selling car for most of the decade, the Cortina gradually overhauled it. In 1966, George Harriman stated that he did not intend to compete with the Cortina, preferring to concentrate on technologically more advanced cars, and many believe that at this point, he may have sealed his company's fate. Ford also introduced advanced product planning and costing techniques—almost unheard of at BMC—and it would be no coincidence that there was an influx of Ford management to BMC, BMH and later BLMC.

Merger discussions took place between a number of companies during the early 1960s. These led to BMC's acquisition of Pressed Steel in 1965, after which, Rover sought solace by merging with the recently formed Leyland Motor Corporation, which had swallowed Standard-Triumph in 1961. In fact, Leyland had turned to Jaguar before Rover, but Sir William Lyons chose to nail his colours to the BMC mast instead.

News of the BMC/Jaguar accord became public in July 1966, and the final details were announced in December. Chairman of the board of British Motor Holdings was George Harriman, and the former Pressed Steel managing director, Joe Edwards, became chief executive. Sir William retained virtual autonomy at Browns Lane, although he developed a keen interest in any projects that he saw as potential Jaguar rivals, one of them being the ADO30 'Fireball XL-5' sports car.

Exploring Jaguar's cupboard

With the union of BMC and Jaguar, Sir William Lyons brought not only his beloved Jaguar marque to the altar, but also Daimler, which he had acquired in 1960. Although most of the Daimler passenger cars in production were basically Jaguar in origin, there remained the refined and sporting Daimler V8 engines, designed by Edward Turner. There were two Daimler V8s—with capacities of 2.5 and 4.5 litres - and while it would have been impractical to fit the classic Jaguar XK straight-six into an MG, using the much more compact Daimler V8 made a deal of common sense.

Accordingly, in 1967, investigations began at Abingdon to determine if the Daimler units could be made to fit. Terry Mitchell was in charge of this exercise, but although the engine was tried for size, no running prototype was ever built. The 2.5-litre unit had various shortcomings, not least being that there was no service experience of it, either at Abingdon or, more crucially, in North America, and there were doubts about its future. The 4.5-litre engine was more powerful and potentially more attractive, but as Mike Allison told me, 'The project was doomed by the physical size of the Majestic Major unit. The idea for a V8-engined MGB probably came from the States, because I also remember a photo published in *Safety Fast* of, I think, a Chrysler-engined MGB taking part in a drag race in the USA, some time around 1965.'

Rodney Lyne was one of the team that investigated the installation of the bigger Daimler V8 in the MGB: 'We took a blue MGB tourer body and laid it on the table, whereupon we cut it in half lengthways and moved the two halves apart.' The purpose of this exercise was to try to accommodate the Daimler exhaust manifold layout, which tended to clash with the MGB chassis legs: 'We found that we had to move the two halves 6in (15.24cm) apart, which made that there was no way that the project would go ahead. The two halves were then both cut up into quarters, and the remains put into the skip.'

It is important to point out that there is a Daimler V8-engined MGB, for which an Abingdon connection has been claimed. The car in question, called 'Le Mans 51A' by its perpetrator, has been presented by some as an official joint project between Abingdon and the distinguished motor engineering consultants Ricardo, of Shoreham-by-Sea in West Sussex. My research, however, has shown that 'LeMans 51A' was no such thing: it was built in the early 1970s by a Ricardo employee in his spare time, using the company's facilities; there was no official involvement from Abingdon. Nevertheless, the car remains an interesting example of what might have been—and an object lesson in why such a car was never developed for production.

Terry Mitchell had already decided, in 1967, that what he really wanted for the MGB was neither of the bulky Daimler units, but the lightweight, ex-Buick Rover V8. At that stage, however, Rover had only recently fallen into the hands of BMH's rival, the Leyland group, and it would be another four years—after the two organizations had merged—before he would be able to test his theories.

Don Hayter also recalls a visit he made with Syd Enever to the Healeys' premises at The Cape in Warwick. There, they inspected an MGB GT with a 1.8-litre Coventry Climax V8 engine nestling low between the front chassis side-members, which necessitated

MGBs sold in the USA from late 1967 featured a particularly distinctive impact absorbing dashboard, known irreverently as the 'Abingdon pillow'. Design was the responsibility of Jim O'Neill, working with fellow MG man Des Jones and Doug Adams of the Longbridge experimental shop. Note the basket-weave vinyl trim on the seat facings and the crude centre console in this prototype. (courtesy Doug Adams)

tightly contorted exhaust manifolds. The Healey family had enjoyed a long association with the Coventry Climax concern, best known for their fork-lift trucks, but also for their expertise in the development of high-performance engines. They had also investigated the possibility of a 2.5-litre, Coventry Climax V8 powered replacement for the 'big Healey'. Sadly, though, Coventry Climax was deprived of its engine development facilities during the interregnum prior to the British Leyland merger, so both the Austin-Healey and MGB GT projects came to nothing.

Safety and emissions legislation begins to take effect

The United States' National Traffic and Motor Vehicle Safety Act, passed on 9 September, 1966, took effect from 1 January, 1968. One of the first casualties in the British sports car market was the

Austin-Healey 3000 Mark III, which was deemed uneconomical to re-engineer to comply with the new impact legislation. The act was quite radical in its demands of manufacturers, but focused mainly upon so-called secondary safety (vehicle strength, passive passenger safety and braking performance), rather than primary safety (safe handling and good performance), for which most European sports cars were noted.

According to Dave Seymour, the Act recognized three areas of vehicle safety:

Crash avoidance (brakes, lights, etc)—usually referred to as primary safety.
Crashworthiness (seat belts, seat strength, head-restraints, etc)—how the vehicle performed in the actual impact.
Post-crash safety (fuel system integrity and flammability)—making sure that the vehicle did not catch fire after impact.

The interior of the car had to be a far safer place for unrestrained passengers (seat-belts—and their use—were still something of a novelty), so at a stroke, hard fascia controls and solid steel dashboards became unacceptable. These two features were hallmarks of the MG Midget and MGB, so a programme was initiated at BMC, prior to the Leyland merger, to create some form of padded overlay for US-bound cars, which would comply with the safety requirements that took effect in 1968.

Doug Adams, by now in charge of the BMC experimental body shop at Longbridge, worked with Jim O'Neill to create the padded dashboard, subsequently known at MG as the 'Abingdon pillow'. This distinctive, curved, quilted dash padding was introduced on MGBs bound for the USA from November 1967 onwards. Adams recalls 'how impractical it was from the point of view of installing the dashboard instrumentation, but there was no better solution available at the time.' Jim O'Neill explains the reasoning: 'The head impact deceleration needed something like 4in (10.16cm) of semi-rigid foam in order to comply. This semi-rigid foam was covered with a ½in (1.27cm) thick layer of soft polyurethane foam to prevent finger indentation. The whole fascia was then covered in a leather-grain finished ABS sheet, which was vacuum formed to take instruments and switches, etc.' This ruled out any form of glove-box, and Jim O'Neill admits that the result was not attractive. All of the prototype work was carried out at VitaFoam Ltd, much of Jim O'Neill and Des Jones' time being spent at the Middleton factory.

US SAFETY AND POLLUTION LEGISLATION

Two pieces of historic American legislation were enacted in the 1960s that would shape the entire destiny of the motor industry. I am indebted to J. Bruce McWilliams, who shared his knowledge of US legislation affecting the motor industry, and to the United States' government offices for providing details of the acts themselves.

THE CLEAN AIR ACT

The Clean Air Act was passed in 1963 and included specific ultimate standards that were to be achieved for exhaust emissions. Responsibility for certification was invested in a US government agency, the Environmental Protection Agency (EPA), rather than relying on the self-certification approach subsequently adopted for the safety legislation that followed three years later.

NATIONAL HIGHWAYS TRAFFIC SAFETY ACT

The National Highways Traffic Safety Act was enacted in September 1966, and it was the beginning of an avalanche of new safety standards that would be put in place throughout the next ten years. By 1978, when MG's future was under review, no less than 50 safety standards were enforced, which were detailed in 821 pages of official text. Although safety was handled on a self-certification basis, manufacturers were constantly monitored by a US government agency, the National Highways Traffic Safety Administration (NHTSA), which was allocated an annual budget of some $60 million.

Des Jones recalls that the fascia design was tested at Longbridge: 'A special test-rig was set up under the control of Len Salkeld at Longbridge experimental, in order to test these fascias. All the fascias tested were under the required regulation of 80g for three milliseconds, at a point of impact speed of 15mph (24.14km/h). The knee-impact regulations did away with the glove-box (later relaxed), but the console under the fascia had to be padded.'

At the same time, side reflectors became mandatory on the front and rear wings (later upgraded to side marker lights), and seat head-restraints were fitted. From November 1968, all Midget, MGB and MGC roadsters sent to the USA were fitted with three windscreen wipers to comply with legislation regarding the swept area of the screen (the standard pair of wipers could not meet these requirements with the shallow MGB screen). It soon became appar-

ent that these were only the beginnings of an avalanche of regulations that would keep a team of people busy at Abingdon, working full-time on the interpretation of legislation and compliance with it.

By the time that British Motor Holdings and Leyland merged, much of this work was already under way, and the implications on future sports car production were beginning to be appreciated. Already, Abingdon's plans for a new MG sports car (EX234) had been virtually side-lined by the need to keep the MGB going in the important US market. It was against this background that the new British Leyland Motor Corporation found itself in a dilemma as the decade drew to a close: it was short of new models and of funds.

Roy Haynes and Harris Mann: new ideas from Ford

By 1967, BMH were doing their level best to recover from their

Above This is one of a series of attempt to revise the nose of the MGB, lengthening it and slimming down the grille. Note the plated Rostyle wheels, pre-dating their fitment on the 1970 model year production cars. (Rover)

Right Another longer nose on an MG, in this case an MGC, where an attempt has been made to integrate the bonnet bulges by introducing a false tear drop on the offside. (Rover)

worsening situation, and new managers were beginning a long overdue round of cut-backs and plant rationalization, under the strong leadership of former BMC and Pressed Steel employee Joe Edwards. Edwards was an effective and respected manager and, had the merger of 1968 not taken place (and given stronger finances), it would be interesting to speculate on what BMH's future might have been under his guidance. One of his actions was to establish a new styling studio at Cowley, which could work in conjunction with both the former Morris plant and the adjacent Pressed Steel Fisher body facility, where five stylists were already being employed.

To run this studio, Joe Edwards hired leading Ford designer Roy Haynes, who had been responsible for the highly successful Mark II Cortina, launched the previous year. Haynes started work at Cowley in November 1967, taking with him many of his former staff from the Ford UK design offices in Essex—the total number of ex-Ford design personnel eventually numbered about 40. In addition to the new Cowley studio, the existing studio, in the 'Glass House' at Longbridge, continued to be run by long-time Austin stylist Dick Burzi, aided by Mark Young and Fred Boobyer, all of whom were approaching retirement. Haynes recalls, 'Although I went to Longbridge at first, it was felt by Harriman that I should not be in conflict with Issigonis or Burzi, and so I went down to Pressed Steel at Cowley.'

Many people have been swayed by the British Leyland party line to the effect that the Leyland management found the BMH cupboard completely bare when they took over. Those at the heart of BMH, at the time of the takeover, have assured me that this was not

ROY HAYNES

Roy Haynes' involvement with BMH and BLMC was quite fiery and brief, but he made his most memorable mark with the Marina, conceived in 1968 and launched three years later in early 1971. Haynes joined BMH from Ford, where he had been responsible for styling the attractive and successful Cortina Mark II, having risen to become head of Ford's Medium Cars Studio in the early 1960s. His career with Ford had begun in 1954, when, at the age of 30, he went to work for Briggs Motor bodies at Dagenham. There, he soon gained a firm grounding in the American company's cost-efficient product planning techniques. In 1967, following the marvellous reception of the Cortina Mark II, Haynes responded to the siren call of Longbridge, where, in October, he became head of design for the BMC side of the business.

Haynes did not waste much time after his arrival at BMH—with nine other ex-Ford staff—before beginning to formulate a master plan for overhauling the corporation's entire car range, drawing upon his experience at Ford. Irrespective of the merits, or otherwise, of his ideas, there is little doubt that his drastic proposals won Roy Haynes few friends, and they sowed the seeds for his departure, in frustration, early in 1969. Haynes saw the future as lying in a closely integrated, yet diverse, product range, calling for a programme that would have produced four basic platforms, upon which all eight of the division's marques (Austin, Daimler, Jaguar, MG, Morris, Riley, Vanden Plas and Wolseley) could have built their ranges: 'The problem which we were faced with,' he states, 'was that there were 26 different bodies, and we desperately needed to cut costs. In comparison, Ford, where I had just come from, made do with just four basic platforms.'

The stumbling block was that the dramatic overhaul he proposed would have required virtually a clean slate. It would have called for considerable rationalization and reorganization, not only of car body and mechanical components, but also of the corporation's plants and various design centres, all of which, not surprisingly, jealously guarded their independence. Therefore, this ostensibly laudable aim rapidly came up against the dual obstacles of a reluctance to invest and the vested interests of many of the managers involved. Haynes is keen to refute the charge, publicly suggested by some of his critics, that he wanted to build an entire range of cars—from Mini to Jaguar—based solely upon the Marina: 'Each and every model would have had its own identity, far beyond the concept of badge engineering. MG alone would have had three main product lines, all produced in volume.'

Much of what Haynes told BMH would prove unpalatable to the unions and, more particularly, to those in charge: 'Sir George Harriman gave me my brief, and he was horrified when I told him that there would be a need to shed some 40,000 jobs as part of the process.' Haynes was similarly frustrated when the 'New Order' became established after the Leyland merger in 1968; there was little love lost between him and the new management: 'They took BMH—the 13th largest company in the world, outside the USA—and they destroyed it. There is a tremendous irony that today Rover have come round to the concept of a small number of basic platforms.'

Notable among the achievements of the Cowley studio, during Haynes' tenure, was the incredibly rapid development of the ADO28 Marina and the beginnings of the ADO67 Allegro. Former colleagues, such as Paul Hughes, Harris Mann and John Stark, recall the period as one of intense activity, work often continuing throughout the night. Whatever critics may say about Roy Haynes' schemes, none can deny that he brought a period of hard work and new ideas to the company.

The first major project at British Leyland under Roy Haynes was the Model C or ADO28, which became the Morris Marina of 1971. This is a prototype, tentatively badged 'Manta', photographed at Cowley in 1968. (Rover)

Right and below right *Apollo
was a proposal for a new mid-
engined MG to replace the
MGB and was styled at
Cowley in 1968-69. Note the
style of the wheels on this
quarter-scale model, which
are identical to those of one of
the full-size ADO68 Condor
proposals of the same period.
Apollo was superseded by
Harris Mann's ADO21
proposal. Apollo was
characterized by a rather long
and uninspiring nose. The
roof panels were intended to
be removable in a similar vein
to the ADO70 Mini-based
prototype. (David Knowles)*

so. In fact, BMH had many ideas, but were caught in a poverty
trap—chiefly of their own making, of course: they simply did not
have the finances or resources to proceed with further developments. The tragedy is that the people at BMH appear to have found
the way out of their troubles when the Leyland merger took place,
and the new organization promptly set off in a direction that led
towards disaster.

The MG Apollo prototype
While it was in existence, the Cowley styling studio occasionally
carried out model studies to look for ways of providing future work
for the Pressed Steel plant. One such model—built to the normal
quarter scale—was a metallic blue, square-lined two-door coupé,
which was given the name Apollo. This was probably intended as
a mid-engined MG, based upon the packaging requirements of
ADO21 (described later in this chapter). Don Hayter recalls seeing
this model, made by Jim Oates' men at Pressed Steel: 'It was one
of the "kite flying" styling exercises which they did periodically—
invariably, I am afraid, to die unseen. They were obviously interested in any follow-up to the MGB, as they had produced it for
years, once they took over from the Quinton Road body plant in
Coventry.' Fortunately, this model has survived and now forms part
of the extensive British Motor Heritage collection at Gaydon.

ADO68: The Condor prototype
One of the more remarkable exercises of the period following the

Leyland merger was the Condor project, which assumed the code
ADO68 in December 1969. This proposal was for a two-door
coupé, which was soon being touted as something in the mould of
the Ford Capri. Initially, the idea was to produce a car based upon
what would become the Marina. However, at some stage, at least
three competing versions of ADO68 were put forward, each being
given a suffix to indicate the model from which it was developed.
ADO68/67 used the running gear of the proposed successor to
ADO16 (ADO67 would become the Austin Allegro in 1973);
ADO68/28 was based upon the rear-wheel-drive Cortina chal-
lenger (the Marina, subsequently launched in 1971); and
ADO68/14 had its roots in the Austin Maxi (launched April 1969).

Three packages were presented for appraisal in April 1970 and,
as a result, three clay mock-ups were produced. As initially presented, all three were schemed to accept either the E4 or E6 engine,
even though the E4 had yet to be engineered for in-line rear-
wheeldrive. Before long, the Maxi-based project, which appears to
have been linked to a proposal to reskin the Maxi hatchback itself,
was abandoned. The remaining two versions progressed in tandem
to provide, at some stage, a choice between the two themes dictated by Harry Webster, who had been brought in by Donald Stokes
to oversee Austin-Morris: the traditional Morris rear-wheel-drive
approach or Austin high technology.

The Marina-based Condor
Without doubt, the most attractively styled version of the Condor

Above *Six early renderings by Paul Hughes for what would become the Condor project, dating from August 1968. According to Hughes, this was a brainstorming exercise in an attempt to explore as wide a variety of themes as possible in a short timescale: 'They range from the 'Berlinetta' at top right to a more 'American' approach at bottom right—we were hoping to extend our penetration in the US market—and a few variations in between.' (Rover)*

Facing page, top *There are clear overtones of the Ford Taunus coupé of 1970 in the rear of this car, demonstrating the Ford background of many of the stylists involved. (Rover)*

Facing page, centre *The completed styling model in the Longbridge exhibition hall, which was commandeered for this viewing. (Rover)*

Facing page, bottom *It may not be obvious to the naked eye, but the badge recessed into the nose of this full-size model is an MG badge. This is one of the many Condor exercises aimed at producing an MG sports coupé. (Rover)*

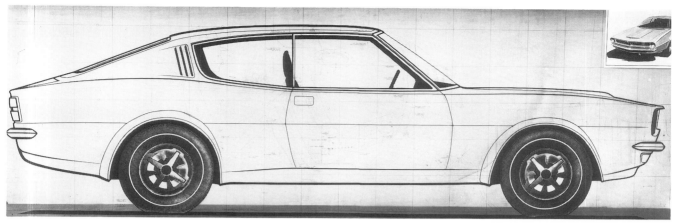

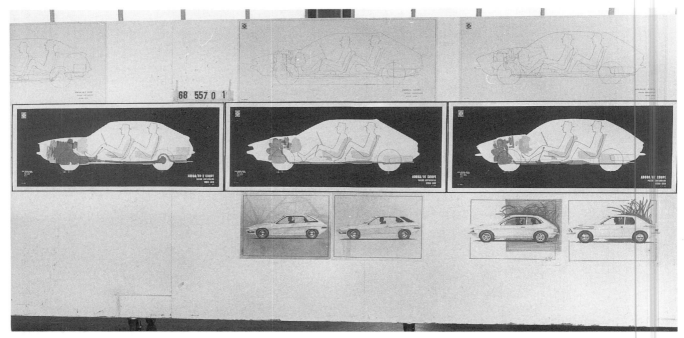

was the ADO68/28 proposal, even if it was based upon the rather less promising underpinnings of the Marina. According to Roy Haynes, however, the front suspension of the definitive Marina—derived from that of the Morris Minor—was certainly not what he had intended for ADO28 at the outset.

In fact, there were at least two variations on the theme: ADO68/28-1 and ADO68/28-2. The former was a slightly more exotic American-style concept, while the latter had a more European flavour, more closely aligned to the mainstream. Abingdon also had a stab at this, preparing ideas against their code number EX242, but theirs was never a serious project. The styling of ADO68 was given a great deal of attention, good looks being recognized as an important factor in the coupé sector. The appearance of the Ford Capri soon focused the minds of those responsible for ADO68/28's style. Various approaches were tried by Roy Haynes and his team, including some versions that were clearly inspired by contemporary North American vehicles, such as the new Pontiac Firebird.

The European look explored for ADO68/28-2 was the work of Michelotti. This MG-badged, three-door hatchback coupé propos-

Dating from March 1970, the drawings displayed in this Longbridge photograph depict package configurations for, from left to right, the ADO68/28-2 coupé (Marina-based by Michelotti), ADO68/14 coupé (Maxi-based) and ADO68/67 (Allegro-based). (Rover)

al was photographed for the archives on 10 February, 1970, and resembled a cross between a Marina coupé and a Bertone styled Fiat Dino coupé. By 17 March, the proposal had been refined to produce a clean, crisp shape, albeit somewhat conservative looking. Rather more exciting, however, was a rival version of ADO68/28, which bore a resemblance to the Fiat 124 coupé and was quite stunning—it would have been quite revolutionary for a company like British Leyland, had it been produced. Even more than 25 years later, this car has an obvious appeal. One of the prototypes was badged as an MG, featuring the famous pre-war Magna name (later, the same name would be used on TR7-based MG

This is the Maxi-based Condor proposal, ADO68/14, showing a family resemblance to Harris Mann's ADO71 Princess, then in the early stages of design. (Rover)

mock-ups), and different wheels were considered, including Rostyles and the distinctive pressed-steel wheels eventually used for the early Morris Marina TC of 1971.

Roy Haynes managed to get Syd Enever involved in the early stages of Condor. He told Haynes that the ADO28 basis would not be a problem as long as a bracket, which he had devised, could be fitted to allow improved rear-axle location: 'Syd was a very good engineer who understood what I was trying to do,' recalls Haynes. 'I asked him what he would need to make an MG out of the Marina, and he went away and came back saying that all he needed was this bracket spot-welded on the under-frame to locate a panhard rod.' Haynes' former colleague, John Stark (also ex-Ford), remembers Syd Enever as a useful and helpful engineer, whose talents Haynes recognized and wanted to utilize.

Another variant of ADO68/28 also featured American influenced styling. A full-size clay model was constructed and employed as the basis of a metallic turquoise plastic styling model, complete with four simulated adults seated inside. Harris Mann recalls that this particular model was a demonstration by Roy Haynes of a GM-style range of BLMC cars, which would have

The front end of this version of the Condor was particularly neat and simple. Note the wheels of this full-size plastic mock-up (to be adopted for the Marina 1.8TC) and the 'Magna' badging on the grille. (Rover)

been able to exploit the various names owned by the company. Budget constraints soon made this idea a non-starter, however. It is also apparent from the surviving sequence of photographs, taken during the creation of this model, that it was being used as a show-case for the talents of the British Leyland—and more particularly Pressed Steel—body designers.

By this stage, the engine options for ADO68/28 were interesting, to say the least: examples appear to have been schemed with an in-line version of the Maxi E4 (never to appear in the UK, but later adapted by Leyland Australia for their version of the Marina), or, failing that, the ubiquitous B-series; the six-cylinder E6 unit under development for the ADO17 saloon; and, finally, no less than the

The two Condor 'Magna' models. Their shapes appear very similar, but the one further from the camera is more fully finished, with door handles, windscreen wipers and simulated exhaust tail-pipes. (Rover)

Left *A fully detailed interior styling model, or seating buck, for the Condor. (Rover)*

Below *Paul Hughes' sketch for an alternative MG 'Magna' ADO28, dating from January 1970. (courtesy Paul Hughes)*

Bottom *The alternative 'Magna' proposal depicted in Paul Hughes' sketch was mocked up, with front and rear details cunningly simulated by mirrors. The highly distored reflection at the left is that of the main 'Magna' proposal. Although the photograph is undated, a 1970 calendar, just visible through a gap between the partitions gives a strong clue. (Rover)*

Triumph Stag V8, which had been saved from rationalization after the merger, despite the existence of the uncomfortably close Rover V8. The idea of using the Stag engine in the Marina family was obviously being taken seriously, for Ian Elliott, an Austin apprentice at the time, recalls seeing a Morris Marina layout drawing that showed the outline of the Stag unit. No doubt, this was seen as a possible means of justifying retention of the unique V8, which was already suffering problems (at about this time, while still under development, the Triumph V8's capacity was increased from 2.5 to 3 litres). Roy Haynes, who had left the company by the time that this idea was being mooted, was horrified at the thought of it when I told him.

One interesting spin-off from ADO28 was an investigation into how the all-synchromesh gearbox from the Marina 1.3 could be fitted into the MG Midget, which still featured a three-synchromesh, four-speed gearbox. ADO47/374, dated 20 October, 1969, was a scheme drawing for this, but little came of the exercise on this occasion. It was looked at again in December 1971 (ADO47/553), an exercise that Don Hayter recalls. In due course, however, the gearbox, which was a development of the Triumph Herald unit,

was fitted to the Midget, but only in 1974 as part of a package that included a Triumph engine.

ADO68/67—The Allegro Coupé

A number of styling proposals and full-sized models were built to explore the ADO68/67 front-wheel-drive concept, which bore a strong family resemblance to the Allegro, the latter having been approved in September 1969. Surviving sketches of ADO68/67 date from September 1970, and the definitive full-size model was photographed for the archives on 6 October, 1970, by which time most of the bodywork appears to have been almost identical to that approved for the Allegro. This clay model was badged as an Austin, suggesting that the car was seen more as an Austin Allegro coupé than as an MG. Ian Elliott recalls how remarkable the prospect of an Allegro coupé with a 2227cc, transverse straight-six engine seemed in 1970. Would it have handled 'like a small hammer?' he wondered.

By the end of 1970, however, a more realistic mood was beginning to pervade British Leyland; Roy Haynes and Harry Webster had not seen eye to eye, so Haynes parted company with British

Above *Sometime around the end of 1969, Michelotti was apparently asked to produce a version of Condor based upon the forthcoming ADO28 Marina, and this full-size model—complete with alternative front-end treatments—was the result. Vic Hammond recalls that his boss, Roy Haynes, was furious that this car had been commissioned without his knowledge. (Rover)*

Right *The Austin-Morris design studio amended the Michelotti Condor in a variety of ways. Photographed for the archives at Longbridge on 17 March, 1970, this is the final iteration of the car, ADO28-2. It had a revised rear end and straighter rear quarter-window line. (Rover)*

Surely, they couldn't have been serious—oh, but they were! The ADO68/67 coupé was photographed for the archives in October 1970, just over a year after the Allegro styling had been signed off for production. The clay model wore Austin badges, and there is no clear indication that there was any intention to produce this monstrosity as an MG, although such might have been its fate. (Rover)

Leyland in early 1969. One of the reasons for their disagreement was Haynes' resistance to design operations being transferred back from Cowley to Longbridge and elsewhere. No doubt, pressure was also applied by other styling departments in the corporation, which did not wish to become subservient to Cowley. After Roy Haynes' departure, Austin-Morris styling operations were transferred progressively to Longbridge (exterior styling moved to Dick Burzi's 'Glass House' in April 1969, and exterior styling to the 'Elephant House' in October of the same year). In the wake of this, the need to fund other, more critical, projects elsewhere in the corporation gradually led to the abandonment of the Condor programme. With the end of ADO68, all thoughts of an MG coupé faded for the time being, although a proposal for a V8-engined MG GT coupé did resurface briefly about four years later.

Sports cars: challenges in the marketplace
Even before the Condor project, British Leyland Motor Corporation had turned its thoughts to finding expedient means of updating the existing MG sports car range. The end of the 1960s saw an upsurge in the more eccentric aspects of 'youth culture', the hallmarks of which included popular art, 'flower power' and often rather dubious aesthetic taste. In North America, the principal market for all the sports cars produced by BLMC—which, of course, encompassed Austin-Healey, Jaguar and Triumph, as well as MG—there was the added problem of the newly emerging 'pony car', named after the Ford Mustang, which spearheaded a new breed of smaller, more sporting American cars aimed at the increasingly affluent youth market.

By 1967, General Motors and Chrysler had responded to the challenge presented by the Mustang, and had produced their own, broadly similar, sporting models, all based upon their mainstream compact sedan ranges—an idea that was already familiar to the fans of British sports cars. No doubt, the appeal of this concept had been behind the ADO68 Condor project. Even the comparatively small American Motors company responded by producing the AMC Javelin and AMX coupés. The more powerful of these cars could easily out-perform most contemporary British sports cars—in a straight line, at least—but there were two even more critical factors that boosted pony car sales.

Firstly, these US sporty cars were generally much cheaper, and far better specified, than the foreign competition. Such essentials as front disc brakes, bucket seats and manual gearboxes were no longer the preserve of European sports cars, while the attraction of an enormous range of options—extending to colours, trim, engine and even body styles—was something that the European sports car makers found difficult, if not impossible, to match.

The second critical factor was the emergence of emissions and safety legislation, which started to take effect in 1966-67. In the case of the 'big three'—General Motors, Ford and Chrysler—dependence on the US home market meant that they had no option, but to engineer their entire car ranges to comply with the growing mountain of new legislation. As a result, the costs and technical difficulties of compliance could be spread evenly across the board. European car manufacturers, however, did not have this luxury: there was, as yet, no legal requirement (nor, therefore, financial incentive) for them to re-engineer those models that were not sold in the USA. Consequently, the vehicles that were heavily dependent upon US sales gradually became more and more of a financial burden and engineering headache. It was hardly surprising, therefore, that one or two respected names soon faded from the North American sports cars scene altogether.

Dealing with the sports cars: Leyland's first moves
It did not take long for BLMC to appreciate that there was a problem with their overlapping sports car ranges. Consequently, a sports car advisory committee was formed to address the situation. As with later efforts along similar lines, however, it is clear that either not enough was done by this committee, or not enough notice was taken of it—perhaps because of a mixture of ignorance, indifference and vested interests on the part of management.

One of the first significant pruning actions—of mercy or vandalism, depending upon your point of view—was the discontinuation of the MGC, which had hardly covered itself in glory. The difficulties of making the MGC's engine comply with US emissions legislation, while maintaining a reasonable performance advantage over the MGB, also played a part in this decision. Late-model, US-market MGCs even had small electric fans to cool the carburettors and, according to Mike Allison (in charge of pollution control at Abingdon), some promising work had been carried out on a fuel-injection system for export cars before the MGC was abandoned.

The new year of 1968 had already seen the end of the line for the classic 'big Healey', and all plans for its direct replacement had faded with the scuppering of both the MGC-based 3000 Mark IV (ADO51) and the Healeys' own Austin-Healey 4000 project (ADO24). Ironically, later MGCs had been improved by a change of back-axle ratio and the installation of a closer-ratio gearbox, making the car more responsive. But it was a case of far too little, too late, and BLMC were left with large stocks of unwanted MGCs, which they sold off to the London based distributor University Motors, who offered them in various states of customized trim and engine tune.

Over at Triumph, the TR4A had given way to the six-cylinder

Above *Over the years, Bruce McWilliams of British Leyland's US arm produced many ideas for revitalizing MG and Triumph sports cars. Among them was this scheme for the MGC GT, dubbed GTC. It included body-colour drip rails, a side mounted filler cap, black chrome or rubber in place of chrome trim, a side stripe in 3M tape, louvres in the front wings and black sills. Note the then-fashionable, but rather pointless and impractical, high-level 'Can-Am' spoiler. (courtesy J. Bruce McWilliams)*

TR5, also reworked and 'modernized' for the North American market as the TR250. The TR5, which still owed much to the original family of TR sports cars, was a narrow-bodied car with questionable handling qualities. For the all-important US market, a styling facelift was deemed necessary to make it look less narrow-gutted and more up to date. The responsibility for this facelift rested with J. Bruce McWilliams of BLMC's Leonia, New Jersey offices. McWilliams blacked out the vertical uprights between the horizontal bars of the TR's radiator grille, contriving to make the car appear slightly wider, and applied a transfer tape across the front of the bonnet.

At the time, stripes, matt black paint and transfers were all the rage on cars in the USA, so the Triumph TR250 was clearly in tune with the period. With the addition of the BMC sports cars to the stable, it was not long before the attention of J. Bruce McWilliams and others—notably Harris Mann in Longbridge—turned to the MG family. McWilliams took a Pale Primrose MGC GT and gave it the full treatment: black side stripes, colour-co-ordinated spoked wire wheels, external 'Le Mans' filler cap, rear Can-Am style spoiler, mock louvres and bold decals. Perhaps mercifully, however, the production car was never afflicted with these features. Nevertheless, a precedent had been set, and it wasn't long before more serious attention was given to titivating the image of the MGB and Midget to counter the challenge from the US manufacturers. It is no coincidence that, around the same time, the focus of MG advertising in North America began a subtle shift away from the wealthy 'Florida set' image towards one depicting bright young things on college campuses.

Leyland's MGB facelift

Surviving photographs show that ideas for a facelift of the MGB date from almost the same time as the BMH/Leyland merger. Two of these proposals, almost certainly from 1968, show what was probably the same MGB GT with the original curved tail-lamp lenses, a lengthened nose and a shallower version of the classic MG chrome grille, giving the front some resemblance to the EX234 prototype. One version was also fitted with a bonnet that had symmetrical tear-drop bulges, presumably for the MGC; certainly, it

Above *This BL proposal for an MGB facelift dates from October 1968. It was dubbed the B-type and featured such period styling clichés as matt black paint and decal stripes. Distorted proportions are the product of a wide-angle camera lens. (Rover)*

Below *The interior of the B-type MGB facelift featured this attempt to update the traditional MG dashboard. (Rover)*

7TH JAN 1969

was not for the short-lived Daimler V8-engined MGB proposal, which never proceeded as far as a complete mock-up.

Paul Hughes, who joined BMH as a senior designer in January 1968, after seven years at Ford, recalls that some thought had already been given to updating the MGB prior to his arrival: 'A styling mock-up of a potential MGB replacement was already at Pressed Steel Fisher, at Cowley, when I joined. I believe that it came from Pininfarina and appeared to be a carry-over MGB from the A-post (windscreen) back. It looked quite sleek, but I think that it had already been dismissed, probably on the grounds of tooling cost, as I think that it would have required totally new tooling for

the wings and bonnet.' Hughes notes also that, whereas EX234 looked 'somewhat like a typical Fiat or Alfa Romeo Spyder, this car still looked distinctly MGB.' (See page 115.)

One photograph of a long-nosed MGB also shows early chrome finished Rostyle pressed-steel wheels (with a greater offset than the later Rostyle wheels adopted for production). These wheels had already been seen on the Ford Cortina 1600E, launched in 1968, and had been universally admired. Therefore, their adoption on the MGB, sponsored by former Ford design staff, is hardly surprising. By October 1968, when further photographs were taken for the archives, thoughts about a facelifted MGB had really begun to

This sketch, by Longbridge stylist Rob Owen, shows the so-called 'Leyland facelift' of the MGB in almost its definitive form: the MG badge would be reduced in size and the chrome bonnet strip deleted, while the bumper overriders would be retained. (courtesy Rob Owen)

Facing page *By early January 1969, when this photograph of the B-type proposal was taken, the seats had been changed for high-back types with integral head-restraints. (Rover)*

Right *This is the prototype that followed Rob Owen's sketch, built at Longbridge under the direction of Doug Adams. Note the hand-made grille mesh and chrome trim, the fact that the grille badge actually comprises a small MG badge mounted on top of a larger one, and the large integral seat head-restraints (as used in US-market cars during 1968-69). (courtesy Doug Adams)*

crystallize: one proposal shows an MGB GT with a satin black bonnet and tail-gate, blacked-out vertical grille bars within a chrome casing, black Mustang-style sill stripes bearing the legend 'B-Type', high-back vinyl bucket seats and a horrendous dashboard and steering wheel reminiscent of the worst excesses from Detroit.

Some of these ideas—particularly the exterior features—had already been seen on the McWilliams MGC and Triumph TR250, so it is hardly surprising that they were developed further to determine whether they had any potential. In parallel with the 'modernization' of the MG range came a new Ford inspired drive for economies, which manifested itself in the identification and attempted removal of some of the more costly components from each BLMC car.

Two of the components quickly identified on the MGB were the alloy bonnet and the attractive, but expensive, chrome radiator grille. The gradual replacement of chrome finishes with matt black, which had as much to do with fashion as with anti-dazzle legislation, ensured that the MG grille, a prominent feature of the MGB and Midget alike, was soon being targeted for removal. Thus, in 1969, Harris Mann, who had joined BMC from Ford just prior to the merger in 1968, together with his team, which included former Pressed Steel stylist Rob Owen, came up with a recessed, matt black mesh grille with a chrome trim that bore some resemblance to that of the 1968 Ford Mustang—that Ford influence again! Another ex-Ford member of the styling team was John Stark, who recalls another significant influence on himself and his colleagues: 'We had been impressed by the Fiat Coupé, and we wanted to try to give the MGB some of its character.'

Before long, Doug Adams and his team in the Longbridge experimental shop had mocked-up the new grille, and it was duly approved by senior Austin-Morris management, allowing little opportunity for objection by those at Abingdon. The fact that this facelift was done on such a limited budget is reflected by the retention of a small, square, raised moulding in the centre of the bonnet's leading edge, which had blended in with the grille badge of the original MGB.

It would probably be fair to say that John Thornley was furious about this; it may even have precipitated the incident, recalled by Terry Mitchell, when Thornley threw Austin-Morris chairman George Turnbull out of his office and told him to leave: 'He said to me, "I've told him not to come back here." I told him he couldn't

do that to Turnbull, but nevertheless he had!' Not long after this, in July 1969, John Thornley retired on health grounds, having suffered appendix problems for some time. With his departure, Les Lambourne, who had been his deputy since 1967, took effective charge of Abingdon's affairs.

By the time that the facelift was unveiled to the public, in the autumn of 1969, two months after the demise of the MGC, the dead hand of the BLMC cost accountants had been felt in other areas, too. The classic leather seats, so long a hallmark of the MG (and universally praised by the American motoring press) had been replaced by the more fashionable, and much cheaper, vinyl, while a range of 'modern' colours had been introduced to go with the insipid grin of the black grille. At some point in 1969, the alloy bonnet, which originally had been retained at Abingdon's insistence to save weight, was dropped. Its place was taken by a virtually identical steel version, which was cheaper to produce.

Poor relation: the MG Midget

Alongside the MGB, the Midget—and its near-identical twin, the Austin-Healey Sprite—gradually became the 'Cinderella' of the BLMC sports car range. Of course, several quite promising ideas to replace the Midget with Mini-based cars had already failed to gain momentum, and with the abandonment of the EX234 project, the prospect of a new MG Midget became even more remote. One of the purposes of the sports car advisory committee was to determine the best way forward for the BLMC sports cars range, and it soon became apparent that they saw little commercial merit in producing a uniquely-bodied small sports car while an MGB/TR6 replacement was needed more urgently. Various ideas had been investigated by BMC and MG prior to the Leyland merger, but with the formation of BLMC, which brought Triumph's rival Spitfire sports car into the camp, the needs of the MG Midget fell even further down the order of priorities.

In 1968, the Midget had received similar safety related modifications to the MGB: the lower price of the car did not exempt it from the new legislation, and production volumes were well above the threshold below which some smaller manufacturers were able to survive without having to comply. Thus, the Midget received a variation on the padded dashboard theme and shared numerous other safety related improvements with the MGB. Once the BLMC merger had taken place, the accountants and stylists began their

The 1970 model year Midget, with matt black radiator grille, pressed-steel wheels, back sill trim, vinyl covered seats and the short-lived black windscreen frame. (Rover)

work to facelift the Midget, in parallel with the MGB and subjecting it to similar indignities.

In an effort to enliven the Midget's appearance and, of course, save costs, its central chrome bonnet trim (which had never been fitted to the cheaper Austin-Healey Sprite) was deleted, and the sills were finished in satin black with chrome block letters reading 'Midget' or 'Sprite', as appropriate. In the cockpit, the seats were faced with vinyl instead of leather. John Stark admits that he and his ex-Ford colleagues were imbued with the cost-reduction philosophy: 'ICI had produced a deep embossed vinyl upholstery, which was, of course, much cheaper than leather, and so we went for that for the Midget as well as the MGB.'

With the introduction of this facelift alongside the equivalent MGB, in September 1969, the Austin-Healey Sprite was quietly dropped from the US market; in little more than a year, it became the Austin Sprite, before fading from the scene completely in July 1971—a sad end for the Austin-Healey marque. For a very brief period in 1970, Midgets were produced with satin black windscreen surrounds. According to Peter Neal, this was more of a styling whim (by the Austin-Morris studio) than a legislative necessity, although matt black windscreen wipers would become a requirement of anti-dazzle laws. Also fitted to the cars, from 1969 onwards, were styled steel wheels with an embossed pattern that was intended to give them the appearance of more expensive alloy wheels; wire wheels remained an option, however.

ADO21: a sports car for the 1970s

Despite the fact that they had seen the control of their own destiny move further from their grasp, the small, dedicated team at Abingdon did not lose hope that they would be permitted to design their own new MG sports car. Although they had been disappointed when the pretty and promising Pininfarina EX234 prototype had been moth-balled, they were understandably enthusiastic when it was agreed that they could explore their own ideas for a mid-engined design.

Several influential people in BLMC at the time, including Rover-Triumph engineer 'Spen' King and product planner Alan Edis, have confirmed that this was not part of an official design competition between MG and their deadly rivals, Triumph, as many have supposed, but rather it sprang from quite separate thoughts about a small sports car. A copy of the ADO21 'blue book' (a sort of brochure setting out the initial concept) survives in the hands of Don Hayter, who was kind enough to show it to me. The basic

premise for ADO21 was to produce a replacement for the MG Midget and Triumph Spitfire, rather than the MGB, so the engines suggested in the blue book were the 1275cc A-series and the two versions of the E-series.

The so-called British Leyland corporate sports car design competition came later in the day, and Abingdon were not invited to take part. Alan Edis, who oversaw Austin-Morris product planning at the time (having recently arrived from Ford), recalls talking to the people at Abingdon about what was to become ADO21 in 1969: 'MG—Roy Brocklehurst, Don Hayter, etc—were working in the boiler house and were saying, "Where do we go from here?", using available components. Although it was chiefly an Abingdon led project, it was officially recognized by the company.'

Alan Edis believes that, viewed from Longbridge, MG's situation appeared to be quite stable in 1969. However, with the changes that were taking place in both the corridors of power and the engineering sections, not to mention the growing invasion of people gamely struggling to implement Ford planning and cost-control techniques, the situation declined steadily: 'As far as MG was concerned, the MGB in particular was selling strongly in the USA, and the Triumph sports cars—the Spitfire, GT6 and TR6—were not nearly as strong there.' However, Triumph had something of a head start, since they had been planning replacements for their sports cars for some time, and had already settled upon the Les Moore styled, front-engined, rear-wheel-drive Bullet proposal as their preferred way forward.

The mid-engined ADO21 emerges

Don Hayter recalls that the BLMC planners 'decided that Triumph would work on a front-engine, rear-wheel-drive TR6/MGB replacement, and that MG would work on a mid-engined Midget/Spitfire replacement. Harry Webster asked me to come up with a packaging layout, which soon came to include both E4 and E6 engine options. I went up to Longbridge where they gave me a little office with a drawing board, just along the corridor from Harry Webster's office.' This arrangement only lasted for about six weeks, after which Don returned to Abingdon, where he continued to work on the proposals.

The E-series engine was still comparatively new and had been

developed by BMC for the Maxi. In addition, it was already planned for use in the forthcoming Austin Allegro and, in six-cylinder E6 form, in the ADO17, together with that car's intended replacement, the big Austin ADO71 Princess (at that stage, known only by its code-name, Diablo). The E-series engine was built at Cofton Hackett, in a purpose-built factory that had been constructed in 1967, at a cost of £16 million. It was one of the most modern engine plants in Europe at the time, with a production capacity of 8500 engines per week. In the light of this, doubtless it was logical for Abingdon to consider using the E-series engine.

However, the packaging requirements for the Maxi had rendered the engine less than perfect for sporting applications. The 1748cc, long-stroke E4 engine would have been mid-mounted, complete with its five-speed gearbox. Ironically, the more exotic 2227cc E6 derivative would have had to make do with the rather more prosa-

Above The Zanda styling exercise of 1969 was designed around a mid mounted Austin Maxi engine and transmission, but was never developed into a running prototype, its primary function being to demonstrate the new computer aided design facilities available to British Leyland. The full-size plastic model was exhibited at the Earls Court Motor Show and survives as part of the British Motor Heritage collection. Unfortunately, the window glass for the hollow model was so dark that it concealed the interior, making the car look like a solid mock-up. The striking shape of Zanda was a bold departure for British Leyland. The name, chosen by Don Thompson (who later moved to Ford of Australia), was derived from a fish, the Zander, the spelling being altered for effect. (David Knowles)

Below One of several renderings by Paul Hughes for ADO21, originally intended as a small mid-engined coupé to replace the MG Midget and Triumph Spitfire. (courtesy Paul Hughes)

Above *From the basis of a side elevation prepared by Harris Mann, Paul Hughes was asked by his chief to develop the three-quarter shape of the ADO21 project. This is his front three-quarter view, which displays a louvred matt black bonnet that did not make it to the full-size model. (courtesy Paul Hughes)*

Below *In this rear three-quarter rendering, the dramatic lines of ADO21 are readily apparent; note the 'MGD' badging. By this stage, ADO21 had grown from being a Midget replacement to become Abingdon's idea for an MGB replacement. In so doing, they brought ADO21 into conflict with the Triumph Bullet project. (courtesy Paul Hughes)*

ic four-speed unit, which dated back to the original ADO17 Austin 1800 of 1964. It would have been necessary to certify the engine for the US market where, of course, it was also completely untried, but according to Don Hayter, it did show promise: 'The E-series engines had the lowest warranty claims in the whole group.'

Knowledgeable enthusiasts will appreciate the fact that the 2227cc six-cylinder engine shared its bore and stroke dimensions with the smaller 1485cc Maxi 1500 four and, therefore, that a 2622cc six-cylinder unit could have been produced, using the dimensions of the larger Maxi unit. However, despite the suggestions of other authors, the 2.6-litre E6 was not suitable for transverse mounting, due to its long-stroke crank, which would have fouled the transmission. Such an engine was built, by British Leyland's Australian subsidiary, but in the event, it only saw service in in-line applications, such as the short-lived Australian Marina Six, the Leyland P76 and the later South African assembled Rover 2600 SD1.

Testing and development at Abingdon
Roy Brocklehurst was to become chief engineer at Abingdon in 1971, when Syd Enever retired, but during 1969-70, when the ADO21 project was initiated, Enever was still in control, making the mid-engined car the last project of his long career at MG. Thus, Enever oversaw development that was under the control of Terry Mitchell (chassis design) and Jim O'Neill with Don Hayter (both on body design). Don Hayter was to become largely responsible for the development of ADO21 in the MG project office. Jim Stimson, who had worked on the EX234 concept, was involved initially with the new project, but part-way through, he went into hospital, so responsibility for carrying the development forward fell to others.

Two of the people given the job of carrying out development and testing were Rodney Lyne and Jeff Clarke, of MG's development department. Jeff recalls that most of the people at Abingdon were enthusiastic about the idea, although Rod felt that Syd Enever seemed strangely disinterested at first, possibly because the impetus had come from Longbridge rather than Abingdon.

Further inspiration came from another part of the British Leyland organization, as Jeff relates: 'It got around that there was a mid-engined Rover. One of the lads—fitter Danny Lloyd—went up to Rover at Solihull, with Tommy Haig, and brought it back to Abingdon, where Terry Mitchell had a bit of a scratch around it.' Someone else who recalls the mid-engined Rover's sojourn at Abingdon is former MG apprentice Bob Neville, who had joined the company in 1966 and moved into the development department in 1968: 'We had it in the shop for a couple of months, and tested it at MIRA, trying to see how the suspension behaved.' This was obviously done surreptitiously: when, in 1994, I told 'Spen' King, creator of the car in question (the Rover P6BS), of Abingdon's tests, he said that this was the first that he had heard about it! Jeff Clarke laughed when told of 'Spen' King's surprise: 'That was typical Syd Enever: always up to tricks!'

The next thing that Rod and Jeff knew was that a 1966 US-specification, left-hand-drive MGB GT, which had already been used for previous development work, was wheeled into the development shop, and the team began work on modifying it to accept the mid-mounted Maxi unit. The first stage was the preparation of drawings (by Bob Staniland and Barry Jackson), which were used to assist fabrication and assembly on the surface table. This was vital to determine how to fit the Maxi unit in the rear of the MGB GT bodyshell, and to discover what would need to be cut out and what special fittings would need to be fabricated. At the same time, the car was converted to right-hand-drive.

Jeff remembers that 'the tail-gate was done away with and a full-depth firewall—with perspex window—was fitted behind the driver's seat, between the rear heel-board and the roof. The rear floor was cut away, and the battery and petrol tank were relocated under the bonnet.' Rod recalls that a special tank was fabricated, using two Midget tanks spot-welded along their flat flange faces, 'as per the Dick Jacobs Midget.' The double Midget tank was chosen because it was just narrow enough to fit between the front chassis rails when the original front engine mountings were removed.

The next task was to install the engine and rear suspension, the

To carry out testing of the ADO21 mechanical layout, the development shop at Abingdon made extensive modifications to an MGB GT, installing a transverse E-series four-cylinder engine in place of the rear seats. Note the firewall fitted behind the driver and passenger seats, complete with window. (courtesy Don Hayter)

latter being a specially constructed De Dion unit. For the purposes of development, it was decided to keep the front suspension basically the same as the contemporary MGB, although the fulcrum point of the spring pan was moved outwards to fix the suspension geometry. Virtually everything was fabricated in-house at Abingdon, the sole exception being the special De Dion tubing for the rear suspension. Rod and Jeff became fully involved in the project for about nine months; in Rod's case, the project absorbed virtually all of his time for the six months that it took him to build the test vehicle.

The rear track of the car was wider than standard, so it was necessary to flare the rear wheel arches. Also at the rear, 13in (33.02cm) diameter wheels were fitted in place of the normal 14in (35.56cm) MGB items. Rod recalls the evolution of ADO21's De Dion suspension arrangement, a sophisticated semi-independent system well suited to mid- and rear-engined cars, and a favourite of chief chassis engineer Terry Mitchell: 'The De Dion tube pivoted at the rear of the tunnel, level with the heel-board. Initially, this was accomplished by a rubber bush, but this was found to make the car steer at the rear, and so it was replaced with a solid universal joint.' The Watts linkage pivoted on an A-shaped bracket, supported by a specially fabricated cross-member, which ran across the car. The springs themselves were conventional helical coils, which were combined with concentric tubular shock absorbers, mounted in special turrets.

Rod Lyne remembers the problems this caused: 'The springs were very long, and tended to bend in the middle and rubbed the shock absorber when you went around corners!' For the MGB GT test car, a Maxi 1748cc E4 engine was fitted, complete with side mounted radiator, but as it was intended that a production version of ADO21 would be available with the forthcoming E6 powerplant, too, the radiator was later moved to the front of the car, with long cooling hoses being fed under the floorpan. For the initial set-up, cooling air for the radiator was fed in underneath the car, then blown out of a duct adjacent to the rear wheel arch and through the tail-gate aperture.

Once the layout of the car had been established, the next job was to adapt the Maxi transmission so that it could be actuated from a conventionally located gear-lever. This task was not easy, according to Rod: 'We used an early Maxi change—complete with three-cable operation—the later rod change unit would not have been practicable. As the engine was behind the driver, we had to have specially fabricated, extra-long cables, which we looped either side

The dramatic lines of the Paul Hughes/Harris Mann ADO21 mock-up, photographed for the archives in November 1970. What a dramatic shock for traditional MG enthusiasts this striking mid-engined car would have been if it had been launched, as originally planned, in 1971. (courtesy Graham Robson)

of the gearbox and fed underneath the car, and through to a specially fabricated housing on top of the transmission tunnel. When the cables were fitted in this way, the gear selection positions were transposed: first, third and fifth gears were down, whilst second and fourth were up!' As Rod explained to me, this arrangement made driving the vehicle something of an interesting experience for the unwary.

Terry Mitchell also looked at the possibilities of an alternative rear suspension set-up, in which the De Dion tube was routed around the back of the differential, while the springs were changed to single, long leaf springs. According to Don Hayter: 'This was a bit like similar set-ups used by Lancia, and we thought that it was a better proposition. It was cheaper, as there were less bends in the De Dion tube, and it also dispensed with the Watts linkage—doing away with the potential for problems with bush wear, which can only be prevented in the case of Watts linkages by the use of expensive Rose joints.'

The Abingdon EX-Register included details of ADO projects where they were relevant to MG developments, and the surviving document records 661 drawings relating to ADO21. These were produced between 5 November, 1969, and 29 December, 1970, soon after which, the project was cancelled.

Styling development at Longbridge

Harris Mann recalls the horrendous packaging requirements of ADO21, primarily caused by the great height of the E-series engine, which was mounted over its integral transmission in traditional Issigonis fashion. However, the idea of a mid-engined sports car, using the Austin Maxi drive-train, predated ADO21, as Mann and his team of stylists had already drawn up such a car, purely as a styling exercise. This was intended not only to show off the skills of British Leyland's stylists, but also to demonstrate the talents of the design staff at the company's Pressed Steel body division. Called the Zanda—a name chosen by stylist Don Thompson and inspired by the Zander fish—this striking, wedge-shaped car was produced as a fully finished, fibreglass mock-up and shown at the 1969 Earls Court Motor Show on the Pressed Steel stand, where it looked light years ahead of the Austin-Morris vehicles in production at the time.

The styling of ADO21 was developed from the initial Abingdon

drawings, prepared in conjunction with Don Hayter, although lessons learned from Mann's earlier Zanda concept undoubtedly had some influence: 'We started in the usual manner of the time, with quarter-scale proposals, and then full-scale tape drawings, which were then used to fashion a full-size model.' Paul Hughes prepared a number of proposals and, later, was responsible for taking Harris Mann's outline tape drawing and developing the chosen theme: 'When Harris had completed his full-size side elevation, he asked me to develop the concept into three dimensions by preparing front and rear three-quarter illustrations. Subsequently, both Harris and I supervised the model making.'

The completed model was shown to management and photographed for the archives on 4 November, 1970. Unlike the Zanda, in which Harris Mann had continued the roof rearwards to meet an abrupt, upright tail, in the case of ADO21, Mann and Hughes overcame the problem of the high engine package by sloping the engine compartment cover up to a narrow, Lotus Europa-style rear window. At the same time, they managed to hide the height by carefully shaping the flanks of the rear wings with a clearly defined shoulder line, about 4in (10.16cm) lower than the forward edge of the engine cover. Above this shoulder line, long triangular buttresses hid the differences in level, so from the side, the height of the engine and its cover became invisible.

Ian Elliott, an Austin apprentice who, later, would become involved in the external affairs department of the company, recalls seeing this wooden model in the styling studio at Longbridge, together with the quarter-scale drawings. He relates that it almost inspired him to consider building his own E6 powered, mid-engined sports car!

The final decisions

After nine months of concentrated effort on the project, Rod Lyne says that work on ADO21 simply petered out: 'I never got told that it had definitely been canned; I was simply told to leave it on one

side in order to get on with other urgent work.' The sole prototype languished in a corner of the development shop, gathering dust, until Austin-Morris engineering director Charles Griffin—who had supported the venture in the first place—paid one of his occasional visits, about 12 months after work had stopped on the vehicle. 'You might as well chop it up,' was his instruction, so the entire car was destroyed. Lyne managed to salvage the gear-knob as a small memento, but even that has gone now, the victim of a household tidying exercise.

Needless to say, this ignominious end was a source of great disappointment to the team working at Abingdon, not least, of course, to Rod Lyne and Jeff Clarke. Rod explains their feelings: 'With previous projects—such as ADO34 and EX234—there had never seemed to have been very much urgency, but with ADO21, it seemed to be different. There was clearly a great deal of pressure and enthusiasm, at first, to get the project finished.' All of a sudden, that pressure simply evaporated, and Rod's frustrations are understandable.

Roy Brocklehurst summed up why he thought ADO21 had been abandoned: 'In the end, British Leyland decided that they wanted a car with the basic style of ADO21, but the Triumph running gear. The Triumph project had the advantage of greater carry-over and more commonality with other products, and so ADO21 got the chop.' To this should be added the fact that the E-series engine, in both four- and six-cylinder versions, was also a severe handicap. Even though it was regarded as a reliable unit, it was not a particularly sporting engine, and it would not be included in the expensive emissions certification work that was already beginning at the close of the decade. With the extra handicaps of a pro-Triumph management and customer resistance to the idea of a mid-engined car, it was hardly surprising that ADO21 was dropped. Perhaps it was 20 years too early.

Of course, ADO21 was not the only mid-engined sports car project to have been investigated and subsequently abandoned by British Leyland. The Rover P6BS has already been mentioned: that exercise was terminated partly because of internal rivalries within the organization, but also because of funding priorities elsewhere. The other mid-engined project was the fabulous Jaguar XJ-13 which, although intended as a competition car, might have led to a mid-engined road Jaguar.

From the rear, the appearance of ADO21 was no less a shock. Note the very clever use of the rear buttresses that extend behind the door windows, neatly concealing the high rear engine compartment lid, made necessary by the very tall Maxi engine/transmission package. (courtesy Graham Robson)

Soon after the British Leyland merger, Lord Stokes spoke to the North American Jaguar representatives, who questioned him about the possibility of a mid-engined Jaguar. As John Dugdale relates in his fascinating account, *Jaguar in America*: 'We asked whether BL would be producing a mid-engined sports car...Stokes' comment, straight from the horse's mouth, was that they had been experimenting with the mid-engined configuration, but frankly it had been discarded, due to the additional problems it raised in meeting safety regulations (the crash factor), not to speak of luggage space limitations.' Perhaps Abingdon would have done well to have taken heed of this pronouncement from the top before proceeding with ADO21. Furthermore, the decision to move away from their original brief—to replace the Midget and Spitfire—and the creation of a car that would rival Triumph's Bullet could also be regarded as risky steps to take.

Had it been built, there is little doubt that ADO21 would have worn the MGD badge. However, it was never known as the MGD, either at Abingdon or Longbridge, and historians would be ill advised to ascribe this name-tag to ADO21. Paul Hughes agrees with this, notwithstanding the speculative 'D GT' badge that features in his rear three-quarter illustration. Remember also that ADO21 started out as a replacement for the MG Midget (and Triumph Spitfire), rather than the MGB! The MGD label had also been loosely ascribed to earlier projects—including EX188 in the 1950s and the ADO47 Midget in 1960—and even resurfaced, with equal tenuousness, in 1979-80 as a badge on the rear of a TR7-based MG prototype.

With the abandonment of ADO21, MG was left without an in-house developed replacement for either of its sports cars, so the future of the MG factory and design team became far more uncertain—despite the obvious importance of the MG marque—and lay at the mercy of BLMC's management. The coast was clear for Triumph to proceed with their own proposals, which would lead to the TR7.

5 The 1970s

One of the most universally disliked consequences of the British Leyland take-over, as far as MG was concerned, had been the facelift applied to both the Midget and MGB in 1969. It took away an attractive feature that distinguished MG sports cars from other marques—the grille. Although the intention had been to modernize the appearance of the two cars—a rather dubious motive in itself—the adverse reaction of the public and dealers alike meant that it would not be long before efforts were being made to repair the damage. However, not everyone saw all the changes as being bad. John Stark is convinced that some of the ideas from the early BL years had some merit: 'We introduced some attractive colour schemes—such as the bright orange Blaze body colour combined with navy trim, and Teal Blue with Autumn Leaf trim, both of which were quite adventurous and effective—although perhaps we went for some rather more vulgar colour schemes later on.'

The BMC/Leyland merger led to J. Bruce McWilliams, at Leonia, becoming involved with MG, and he saw the need to repair some of the damage that had been done to the MGB. As he told me, 'Given my rather heavy-duty styling involvement with the various Triumph models, but particularly the TR4, Spitfire, GT6, TR6 and Stag, and now with George Turnbull and Harry Webster at Longbridge, the slide into a similar involvement with Austins and MGs came naturally.' This is not idle talk: 'At Coventry, I had

demonstrated that largely cosmetic facelifts could have quite a powerful effect on sales.'

At first, McWilliams' work for the MG marque centred on 'their compliance with the rapidly proliferating US emissions and safety standards and, in time, identifying ways of enhancing the appeal of these ageing cars so that they remained salesworthy.' For the first time, too, the British sports cars were facing a new challenge from the Japanese: the Datsun 240Z had arrived on the scene in September 1969. As McWilliams points out, 'Technically, British sports cars had suddenly become archaic, and no one in command appreciated the degree to which they had fallen behind.'

Other improvements were necessitated by higher customer expectations, particularly in the face of stiffer competition, and by new US legislation. Thus, the heating and ventilating system came in for scrutiny for the 1971 model year, with input by Des Jones: 'The US demist legislation called for the windscreen to be demisted within a certain time. Firstly, we installed an improved tube-run from the heater to the demister, doing away with the former polypropylene tube, to give a more direct run to the demister vents, with little panel change. The larger demisters were designed with baffles inside the demisters themselves, so placed as to distribute the hot air to the correct locations. Barrett Engineering were the suppliers who were very quick in supplying the demisters for pro-

Left *This front view of the prototype for the 1971 model year MGB GT makes an interesting comparison to the prototype 1970 model year car in Chapter 4. (Rover)*

Facing page *Note the poorly fitting rear bumper on this prototype—a common problem, which even extended to some MGBs featured in brochures over the years! This example is fitted with US-market rear lamp units, which differed from contemporary UK-market equivalents by being predominantly amber lenses with red upper sections (on UK cars, this was reversed). (Rover)*

duction.' These larger demister vents were for US-market cars only at first, but subsequently were introduced on all other MGBs, too.

At the same time, the knee-impact requirement, which had resulted in Jim O'Neill's padded dashboard in 1967, was rescinded and replaced by a less onerous requirement for all interior components to comply with a specified minimum corner radius. Both Des Jones and Don Butler were involved in making the necessary changes. 'New consoles were introduced, one for the tunnel and one each below the fascia for the North American and other markets,' Des recalls.

Vic Hammond, at Longbridge, was responsible for the design of the new dashboard. The relaxation of impact standards allowed the panel to be modified to include face-level ventilation for all markets, which was a very welcome change. Again, Des Jones became involved in the process: 'Two large holes were pierced in the vertical wall of the air intake duct on the body. Shields were spot-welded around the holes to prevent the ingress of water. The vents were designed to fit into the former radio aperture in the fascia, and were joined to the two large holes by a PVC moulded tube. The radio was moved to the console, with the speaker under the dash. For the US fascia, the vents were mounted vertically.'

The Michelotti Mini: ADO70

The idea of a sports car based upon the Mini seemed so sensible that it is hardly surprising that several proposals materialized in the 1960s. In 1970, what would prove to be the last of these emerged as a neatly proportioned car with the novelty of twin lift-out roof panels. This project, coded ADO70, resulted in a single running prototype. In the main, it was the responsibility of designers Paul Hughes and Rob Owen. Shortly after Harry Webster arrived, he began to examine the model line-up. The 'Spridgets' were becoming a bit long in the tooth, and Harry said, 'I want a fun car!' However, according to Owen, who was working in the interior studio at the time, Webster couldn't or wouldn't elaborate.

Paul Hughes recalls that 'the whole of the exterior studio was invited to participate in a sketch programme, to create a suitable design for the ADO70.' This led to a 'wallpapering exercise', in which a display board was covered in sketches so that the management (on this occasion, probably only the top Austin-Morris engi-

neers, such as messrs Webster, Griffin, Bates, Dews, etc) could make a selection. At this time, the exterior studio at Longbridge comprised Harris Mann as chief designer, Paul Hughes as his number two, and three or four 'regular' designers: everyone submitted between two and four sketches each.

The sketches were based upon a specific briefing. According to Hughes, 'For ease of comparison and accuracy—in other words, to make it more difficult for the designers to cheat—all the design sketches were made over existing Mini package side-elevations to the same scale, probably one tenth.'

There were two major constraints: existing Mini 10in (25.4cm) diameter wheels had to be used; and only standard, fixed 7in (17.78cm) diameter round headlamps, set at 24in (60.96cm)—25in (63.5cm) for extra safety—above the ground could be employed. Thus, pop-up headlamps and lidded devices were precluded on grounds of cost. Neither constraint, says Hughes, was particularly conducive to achieving a sporty proportion or a desirable road hugging image on what was a rather dumpy package.

The upshot of the exercise was that one of Paul Hughes' proposals was chosen: 'Following the review, Harris asked me to prepare front and rear three-quarter perspective illustrations for Robin Owen to take with him to Turin for the guidance of those who were to build the actual prototype.' To ensure that the car was built quickly and economically, Rob Owen had been asked to take Paul Hughes' sketches and a Mini 1275GT donor car to Michelotti in Turin for a prototype to be built. (Webster and Michelotti were long standing friends from an association that began at Standard-Triumph.) This was done in some secrecy, Rob recalls, because of the powerful influence of the unions, who undoubtedly would have been hostile to the idea of such concept work being taken abroad, beyond their influence.

'I collected the drawings and a list of assumptions about the car. The proposal was that the car would have been built by Innocenti for sale in the USA. Innocenti (then a BL subsidiary) was looking for work at this time.' Next, Rob got hold of a Mini 1275GT to use as the basis of the prototype: 'It was a fairly rough, "bits 'n' pieces" development car with bouncy hydrolastic suspension. No one else seemed to be interested; I even had to make all my own travel arrangements!' Owen drove the car all the way to Turin in May

Above *To define the style of ADO70, the entire Austin-Morris exterior styling studio was asked to produce a number of side elevations, all of which were drawn to very strict guidelines to avoid too much artistic licence with regard to basic proportions. This is one of Paul Hughes' offerings; note the wheel trims styled to resemble the BLMC corporate logo. (courtesy Paul Hughes)*

Below *This proposal for ADO70 (one of three) is another of Paul Hughes' renderings and was actually selected as the basis for the prototype to be built by Michelotti. (courtesy Paul Hughes)*

Facing page, top and bottom *Once Paul Hughes' side elevation had been accepted as the basis of ADO70, he was asked to produce these front and rear three-quarter views. Rob Owen would take these to the Michelotti studios to serve as the basis of the styling of the hand-built prototype. (courtesy Paul Hughes)*

1970, stopping only twice on the journey. Upon his arrival, he met Michelotti: 'Giovanni Michelotti was really one of the nicest people in the whole motor industry: he was really easy to work with, despite the language barrier. There was a very good empathy.' Each day, Owen would prepare fresh sketches and, in next to no time, the requisite parts would be fabricated by the Michelotti craftsmen. Rob soon became used to the Turin style of driving: 'I was constantly being challenged at every traffic light and, before long, I got into the spirit and drove like a lunatic!'

Eventually, the time came to set the Mini on to a plate (a jig that would hold the parts in the correct place during disassembly and reconstruction), and to strip the car down as far as the floorpan. A wooden body, to the finished shape, had been built by a pair of local artisans, which they produced in a mere week. With the wooden body complete, Harry Webster arrived—on a Sunday afternoon, Rob Owen remembers—to look the model over and sug-

gest a couple of small changes. The next day, two panel beaters set to work to create the steel bodywork: 'They were truly amazing: they took a single sheet of steel, and by the end of the first day had transformed it into the rough shape of the rear tonneau, from the wheel arch eyebrows up the roof sides. By the end of the second day, that panel was finished.' At that rate, the whole body soon came together, while Rob busied himself with the trim proposals: 'I produced sketches utilizing the bits and pieces that were readily available at BLMC. The trimmer would set to from one of my sketches, and the trim piece would be ready in two to three days.'

In all this time, there was no word from Longbridge, which was symptomatic, says Rob Owen, of the lack of interest in anything being done outside—the so-called 'NIH' (not invented here) syndrome: 'I sent back reports every week, but never got anything back the other way.' At this point, Rob admits that he exceeded his brief somewhat by altering the steering to make it less like the

archetypal Mini 'bus driver' angle: 'Longbridge, amazingly enough, had thought that this would have been okay on a sports car, but particularly as I was going to have to drive it back, I thought otherwise.' With the aid of Michelotti, he acquired some universal joints from a factor in Turin, and inserted them into the column. Unfortunately, the finished item suffered slightly from binding, a possible consequence, Rob suggests, of a conflict between metric and imperial components.

The finished car was painted and made ready for testing, but according to Rob, it was undriveable: 'There were terrible vibrations, the hydrolastic suspension was leaking, and even with the tyre pressures inflated to 35lb/sq.in (2.46kg/sq.cm), it had a job to cope with the significant extra weight of the hand-built, heavy-gauge steel body with all its lead loading.' The suspension was pumped up at a local Innocenti distributor, then Signor Colombo, Innocenti's director of engineering, was called over to examine the

car. With his mechanics, he jacked up the car and revved the engine to about 6000rpm, in time-honoured Italian garage style, before deciding to pull the mechanical components to pieces: 'The drive-shafts were bent, perhaps as a consequence of my earlier exploits on the streets of Turin. Innocenti tweaked the engine, and by the time they had finished, it ran beautifully and smoothly.' Signor Columbo looked critically at the steering modifications and said, matter-of-factly, 'Meester Owen, I think maybe you can drive one time to Longbridge and back to Turin, but not any further!'

The car completed, Rob collected the paperwork and set off on the return journey, early one morning in October 1970, leaving Turin via the Mont Cenis Pass: 'I was just reaching the frontier, and the car was running out of puff. In my mirror was a 1904 Mercedes with GB plates, and he was gaining on me; he eventually passed me, I was so slow!' When he finally returned to Longbridge, Owen found that there was almost a total lack of interest from senior man-

agement: 'About three senior people drove it, and all they could say was, "Oh, it doesn't handle very well." They were either incredibly naïve, or stupid, if they expected a heavy hand-built car to handle properly!' However, Owens' peers—not least Paul Hughes—were keen to see what the finished car looked like. It is perhaps not sur-prising that Hughes was disappointed with the result; inevitably, compromises and changes had been made in the design—probably imposed, at least in part, by Michelotti himself—and he was quite critical of the prototype. Others, such as Ian Elliott, are more gen-erous in their opinion.

The car had been fitted with BL badges, rather than MG emblems, which many suppose suggests that BL were moving away from marque badges. However, although the car was never actually identified as a replacement for the Sprite and Midget, it would have had to be an MG if it was to be sold in the USA (even if built, as suggested, by Innocenti). However, there were already

Above *The ADO70 prototype takes shape in Turin. The young man to the right is in charge of the fabrication operations, and is seen here discussing some detail of the roof side with his craftsmen. (courtesy Rob Owen)*

Left *The ADO70 prototype survives as part of the British Motor Heritage collection. (David Knowles)*

doubts about the future of the A-series engine in the US market. Emissions legislation in that country threatened the continuation of the existing MG Midget, and there was still some resistance to the idea of a front-wheel-drive sports car, particularly in the USA. Therefore, the project, which had cost a total of £15,000, was abandoned, and for a long time the ADO70 prototype languished outside the development department and, in due course, the rain began to get in. Eventually, someone rescued the car and restored it and, today, it survives in the British Motor Heritage collection as yet another fascinating dead-end.

Bring back the grille!

Rob Owen shares his disillusionment of the time with many in the company: 'They were very frustrating days after the BL merger. There were very talented people in engineering and design, but there was not enough money and poor management.' However, Owen says that there were more serious problems: 'If only there had been a few car enthusiasts in top management, things might have been better. Syd Enever used to come up to Longbridge to see what we were doing, and he was amazed at how little we had to get by with.' The new management showed no interest in MG affairs: 'They didn't really want MG to continue—it seemed for emotive, rather than rational, reasons. Every six months or so, Bruce McWilliams would come over from Leonia with a "shopping list" of ideas to freshen up the MGB and Midget, and nobody wanted to listen to him.' Rob Owen often found himself left to talk to McWilliams and take him to lunch to discuss his ideas, knowing full well that the BL management would take no notice of them: 'The best we could offer him would be seat colour and trim changes, and this was a tragedy: McWilliams was a real enthusiast with some good ideas.'

Bruce McWilliams is equally convinced that much of the blame lay with a management whose interest in MG was, at best, margin-al: 'Either through ineptitude or disinterest, those ultimately responsible for MG turned their thoughts and commitments elsewhere. Abingdon had become an unwanted stepchild, prime attention being focused on new models with the Austin and Morris nameplates and, to some extent, the new Triumph Stag and a replacement for the ageing TR6.' The recessed grille—or 'black-hole', as it was sometimes irreverently called—was a case in point: 'As the appeal of MGs in America lessened, the need for some sort of styling or cosmetic treatments grew greater. For me, the front end of the MGB offered one place to attack. Its then empty aperture was devoid of appeal, and certainly not in keeping with the handsome grille that had distinguished the fronts of MGs almost from their earliest days.' In McWilliams' opinion, the fact that the small bulge at the leading edge of the bonnet had not been removed was demonstrative of how low regard for MG had sunk in the executive offices at Longbridge.

McWilliams put forward the idea of returning to the basic grille shape of the original, classic MGB, but with a black mesh infill instead of vertical chrome bars. This idea had two advantages: firstly, the cost of the mesh would be far less than that of the vertical bars of the original grille (remember that this was a time of extensive cost cutting); secondly, it harked back to the mesh grilles of pre-war MGs, such as the K3 Magnette. 'Fortunately, tooling for the grille casing remained available, so the change could be effected quickly and with little expense,' he says.

McWilliams' idea was taken on board by Vic Hammond, at Longbridge styling, and the mesh grille was very quickly tooled up, the only changes being to reinstate the central, shield-shaped grille badge and plinth, and to use injection moulded plastic for the mesh instead of metal. The production version appeared in the autumn of 1972, in time for the 1973 model year. McWilliams was clearly not a fan of the 'rubber' bumpers that came soon afterwards: 'Unfortunately, the extraordinarily ugly and clumsy solution,

J. BRUCE McWILLIAMS

Bruce McWilliams is a remarkable man, whose experience in the North American car import business must be almost without equal. During World War 2, he spent time in London as a cryptographer for the US Office of War Information (OWI), then moved to the US military government in Munich. After this, he spent ten years working for the United Nations in Germany, Switzerland, Korea, Italy and New York. In 1957, he left the UN and became vice president for sales and marketing of Saab USA, realizing his lifelong ambition to enter the car industry, having acted as a consultant for Saab during the year prior to leaving the UN.

The Swedish company gained a great deal of publicity when Bruce entered a team of Saabs in a local rally and won it outright. Boosted by this success, Saab's US sales took off, and Bruce moved to Europe, in 1960, to establish the company in new markets there. Then, he was headhunted by the joint company operated by Studebaker and Mercedes Benz in the USA, which he took from eighth position, in terms of imported car sales, to third, behind Volkswagen and Renault. In March 1962, Bruce visited Europe to look for other potential franchises, whereupon he met with William Martin-Hurst at Rover, who impressed Bruce with his 'enormous enthusiasm, great decency, and an intense interest in automobiles—a combination of personalities unequalled by any of the other personalities with whom I was dealing.' This meeting eventually led to Bruce accepting the offer of a job with Rover, heading their new North American sales operation, with his wife, Jimmy, joining the company as vice president in charge of sales and marketing.

There followed a fascinating period in which the Rover Gas Turbine cars were raced, and Bruce came to know people such as 'Spen' King, who would continue to play pivotal roles in shaping the future of the sports car. Then came the Leyland take-over of Rover, in 1966, whereupon the company rapidly began to lose its independence of spirit. One positive aspect was that Bruce was able to play a pivotal role in the creation of the Morgan Plus 8. With Rover and Triumph together in the Leyland family, Bruce became responsible for Triumph sales in the USA, and one of his first efforts was to sponsor the creation of the Triumph TR250.

Following the BLMC merger of 1968, Bruce found himself drawn closer into MG's affairs: he had worked with George Turnbull and Harry Webster on

J. Bruce McWilliams (left) pictured with William Martin-Hurst of Rover in 1964. (courtesy John Dugdale)

the Triumph sports cars prior to the merger, and once they were ensconced in Longbridge, it was natural that this association should continue with MG. There followed many years of involvement with most of the BL marques sold in North America. His long association with Rover, Triumph and MG finally came to an end in 1980, when he left the company to join DeLorean. Following the collapse of that ill-fated venture, in 1982, Bruce McWilliams founded his own consultancy—Galamander Ltd—which he runs with his wife Jimmy to this day.

already in the pipeline, to approaching bumper standards in the USA made this return to a more classical MG grille short lived.'

Throughout this period, efforts were still being made to cheapen everything in BLMC and, of course, MG did not escape this process. Rob Owen recalls that he and his colleagues were asked, by Harry Webster, to contribute to a chart showing how costs could be reduced for the MGB. The suggestions included the substitution of the Marina gearbox, back axle and steel wheels, the last fitted to conventional Marina hubs. Rob Owen was aghast: 'Management clearly thought that this was just the job. Thankfully, these changes never saw the light of day.' Ian Elliott remembers another of these cost saving exercises: 'The cost control people at Longbridge proposed that the MGB GT should have frameless rear quarter-windows (as per the Pininfarina prototype), but Don Hayter at Abingdon would not sanction this, and the idea was abandoned.'

More styling proposals from Leonia

Other ideas were explored at Leonia around this time, although, as McWilliams says, 'The MGB was not a car that could be easily altered without serious tooling implications. It was a well styled car, and the only low-cost opportunities lay in adding tape effects and wheel treatments. To meet these conditions, one proposal was, in fact, attempted because it only involved the boot-lid tooling, and offered a very practical advantage: an externally mounted spare wheel and tyre.' The idea was to mount the spare wheel on top of the boot lid, Rover P6 fashion, thus increasing the MGB's rather meagre boot space. Although it provided much useful space, to use McWilliams' own words, aesthetically, the idea was 'borderline, because of the scale of the spare wheel in relation to surrounding areas.' Although the external spare wheel idea was not accepted, several other less dramatic, but popular, options were proposed around this time. One of these was smartening up the wheels: 'The addition of stainless-steel rings gave the pressed wheels a good deal more sporting character, requiring only a short lead time, and costing little for the effect they achieved.'

The last Cowley MG saloon bows out

In the 1960s, an overly optimistic BMC had expected much of the MG 1100 in the USA, but by the beginning of the new decade, it was obvious that sales to North America were becoming pointless. During 1967, the MG 1300 had supplanted the 1100, while US

J. Bruce McWilliams was responsible for the production of this prototype at Leonia, which featured off-white spoked wheels (not adopted), a matt black steering wheel (subsequently used for the 750 UK-only Limited-Edition models of 1975) and a reversion to the traditional grille style, using mesh infill instead of vertical chrome bars. (courtesy J. Bruce McWilliams)

sales of the Vanden Plas Princess had been abandoned. In 1968, BLMC launched their great hope for the US market, the Austin America, a two-door saloon based upon the Austin 1300 and available for the first time with the AP four-speed automatic transmission. Clearly, the product planners saw no room for a rival MG version in the States so, before long, the MG 1300 was withdrawn from the US. However, the Austin America was singularly unsuccessful in wooing American drivers; Ian Elliott recalls seeing a pamphlet at Longbridge, which actually boasted that BMH was quite happy to lose money on the Austin America 'because it was earning foreign exchange, and BMH was public spirited!'

With the introduction of the four-door Austin and Morris 1300 GT on the home market, in 1969, springing from a proposal for Cooper-badged versions of the Austin and Morris, the MG 1300's *raison d'être* began to evaporate so, without ceremony, it was dropped in July 1971. With its demise came the end of the Cowley-built MG—for the time being—although the MG 1300 lived on in Spain for a while longer, nearly spawning a unique Spanish derivative.

Unfulfilled promise: the MGB GT V8

The sad story of the MGC might have deterred lesser men than those at Abingdon from contemplating another big-engined derivative of the MGB, but in the case of the MGB GT V8, there was great enthusiasm at all levels from the outset. Abingdon's earlier thoughts about larger engines for the MGB had not been forgotten; nevertheless, anyone who had suggested the likelihood of a V8-engined MGB surely would have been branded as naïvely optimistic, especially in the climate following the Leyland merger. Intriguingly, Roy Brocklehurst felt that a few years earlier, the MGB V8 might not have happened (even though one can argue that it should not have arrived quite so late in the MGB's career), since he felt that his predecessor, Syd Enever, who retired in May 1971, would not have sanctioned such a car.

THE MG VICTORIA

In the 1960s, BMC set up a brand-new factory at Pamplona, in Spain, encouraged by the rising economic prosperity in that country and the fact that the Spanish applied crippling import duties to non-indigenous motor vehicles. The Italian giant, Fiat, had already established a presence in the country through their licensees, Seat (Sociedad Espanola de Automoviles de Turismo), so it was understandable that BMC, and subsequently BLMC, should consider Spain for European expansion, as they did in Belgium with the Seneffe plant.

The Authi plant began production with the evergreen Mini and 1100, including an MG version of the latter, and these were joined in October 1972 by the Austin Victoria, a longer version of the 1100/1300 that had already entered production in South Africa as the Austin Apache. With its Michelotti styled front and rear ends, the Apache/Victoria resembled the contemporary Triumph saloons—in particular the similarly-sized Dolomite—but the entire centre section of the ADO16 body had been retained, which meant that the overall proportions didn't quite gel. Interestingly, the Apache/Victoria was one of the last two important BLMC projects to be styled outside the organization, the other being the Michelotti designed P76 for Leyland Australia.

At the Barcelona Motor Show, in April 1973, Authi showed an MG version of the Victoria, complete with a Downton tuned 1275cc engine developing 83bhp (61.89kW), a steel sunroof and air-conditioning (the Victoria would have been the first MG to have this facility factory fitted). The interior had been restyled with a deeply padded fascia, seats with integral head-rests and a polished alloy steering wheel with perforated spokes, which bore a faint resemblance to the wheel used on the 1970 MGB. Simulated Rostyle wheel-trims were fitted, complete with MG badges at their centres, and an MG badge was located rather awkwardly at the bottom of the front grille.

In the event, the MG Victoria never made it into production, since both Authi and British Leyland were suffering mounting problems, particularly labour-relations difficulties, and the cost of putting the MG into production simply could not be justified. Before long, Authi's short existence came to an end—largely because the Spanish unions used it as an expendable target for their wage battles—and the factory was sold to Seat, who use it to this day.

Above right The interior of the MG Victoria was considerably reworked from the contemporary Austin equivalent. (Rover)

Right The engine bay of the MG Victoria prototype, showing the air conditioning equipment and the twin-SU equipped 1275cc A-series engine. (Rover)

Below The Authi MG Victoria prototype at the 1973 Barcelona Motor Show. (Rover)

Thus, the impetus for such a scheme, when it came, derived from outside the company. Former Mini racer Ken Costello had begun converting MGBs to take the lightweight Rover V8 engine in 1969, after an MGB he converted for himself led to a flood of people demanding replicas. Costello, ever the opportunist, managed to obtain maximum publicity for the car by the simple expedient of asking the motoring correspondents of national newspapers to road-test it. Before long, business was booming, faster than Costello could cope with, and the car came to the attention of British Leyland's management.

British Leyland and Costello

Ken Costello knew that it would be only a matter of time before someone at British Leyland wanted to know more about his MGB V8 conversion, so he was not surprised when a letter arrived from Charles Griffin. As Costello told me in 1993, 'They wanted to see one of my cars, and so I took one up to Longbridge where it was looked over by Webster, Griffin and Turnbull. They were obviously very interested, because within two weeks I found myself taking one of my cars to Lord Stokes at Berkeley Square in London.' Needless to say, Stokes had already had discussions with his senior managers and was forming the opinion that a factory-built car might be a viable option.

Charles Griffin had already engineered the Rover V8 into ADO61 (which might have led to a Wolseley derivative—the Wolseley 35/150 perhaps?) and remembers trying Costello's car: 'We were looking at applications for the Rover V8, and it would fit anywhere that the B-series would go.' Therefore, the MGB was an obvious candidate. Costello recalls that Stokes asked him what would happen to his business if MG was to build its own MGB V8, to which he replied that he would keep selling his conversions for the two years that he believed it would take British Leyland to put their version into production.

By this stage, British Leyland were clearly becoming serious about the project. Consequently, they provided Costello with a brand-new, left-hand-drive, Harvest Gold MGB GT and a new Rover P6 engine, and asked him to carry out one of his conversions. Before long, the result was in the workshops at Abingdon, being pored over by the development engineers and photographed for posterity by the Cowley photographic department. The MG team clearly fell in two camps when they came to examine the car in detail: on the one hand were those who were favourably impressed by what had been achieved on a limited budget; on the other, were those who felt that some of the engineering details were not as good as they should have been.

Safety and emissions legislation takes its toll

During the 1970s, the avalanche of North American vehicle legislation gained pace, new requirements being enforced and, sometimes, withdrawn at short notice. In the main, responsibility for ensuring that the MGB and Midget complied with US legislation rested with Jim O'Neill, who was assisted by Des Jones (MGB) and Denis Williams (Midget). As O'Neill points out, 'As our major market was the USA, failure to meet any of these regulations would have meant that MG would have ceased trading. There were occasions when the American domestic car manufacturers themselves could not meet these regulations 100 per cent. A case in point was

Facing page, above *The Costello MGB V8; this is a Mark II verstion with no bonnet bulge. (courtesy Ken Costello)*

Facing page, below *MG at Abingdon was justly proud of its fine reputation in vehicle safety testing. Here, an MGB GT V8 is in the process of being crash tested at the plant's own test facility at 30mph (48.28km/h) into a solid concrete cube, the face of which is covered with 1in (2.54cm) thick steel plate. Cars were winched along the approach track with the aid of a Jaguar six-cylinder engine, and the process was filmed by a high-speed cine camera. Black triangles were added to the side of the car to provide an accurate record of horizontal position. The circular device at the bottom right of the photograph is a 'clock', driven by a specially calibrated electric motor, allowing engineers to accurately correlate time to horizontal deflection. (Rover)*

Roy Brocklehurst, Syd Enever's successor as chief engineer at MG. (courtesy Don Hayter)

a regulation which required seat-belts of the driver and any passengers in the vehicle to be fastened before the car could be driven. Peter Neal, who was responsible by now for our electrical design, developed an ingenious system of seat pressure pads and seat-belt switches, working through a black box in order to comply with the regulations. The American manufacturers had so many problems complying with this regulation that they took their own government to court, won their case and had the regulation removed. Consequently, several hundred of our cars already in the States had to be reworked to remove the system.'

The MGB GT V8 prototype

On Wednesday, 4 August, 1971, chief chassis engineer Terry Mitchell returned from holiday to be told by his boss (Roy Brocklehurst) that Longbridge had given Abingdon the go-ahead to build their own MGB V8 development prototype, no doubt using at least a few lessons learned from the Costello car. Terry had been an early exponent of adopting the Rover unit—in fact, he was probably one of the first at Abingdon to recognize its potential—so it is hardly surprising that he rose to the challenge with enormous enthusiasm. The project was assigned the number EX 249, which was described in the EX-Register as 'ADO23—Rover V8' (see Appendix 2).

The Abingdon car was based upon a Glacier White MGB GT, registered DJB 894K, and was fitted with a standard Rover P6 unit. This required two large 'blisters' on the bonnet to clear the twin SU carburettors, which were mounted between the cylinder heads on the conventional Rover inlet manifold. The engine was lowered to reduce the clearance problems under the bonnet, and many parts, such as the exhaust manifolds, were specially fabricated to suit the new application. Such was the enthusiasm and sheer hard work put in by the team (Terry Mitchell, Barry Jackson, Bob Staniland, Ron Lindars and Pat Rees) that the car was finished within the remarkably short time of four weeks.

Shortly after, Harry Webster arrived from Longbridge to take a look, and within a matter of days, approval came through to develop the car for production. At that stage, the aim was to have it on sale within a year if possible. Having been given official approval, the project's code was changed from EX249 to ADO75, and work proceeded at both Abingdon and Solihull to pave the way for production. Alec Hounslow, one of the better known names in MG folklore, was chiefly responsible for the novel carburettor manifold adopted for the production MGB GT V8. This mounted the SU HIF6 carburettors transversely across the rear of the engine, just in front of the heater unit.

Jeff Clarke remembers how this manifold came about: 'The first

While Abingdon toiled with the V8 prototype, the badging was decided upon at Longbridge. Note the rectangular US licence-plate mounting. (Rover)

THE EXPERIMENTAL SAFETY VEHICLE: SSV1

The automotive buzz-word of the late 1960s and early 1970s was 'safety', and any manufacturer who took US sales seriously regarded safety with equal seriousness. US legislators were still on a roll, introducing new and ever more stringent laws, and a nervous motor industry wanted to be certain of being, if not ahead of the game, at least at the forefront. In the spring of 1972, a major symposium—Transpo 72—was staged at Dulles Airport, in Washington, DC, and in addition to the North American domestic manufacturers, a number of European companies staged significant displays, notably Fiat, Volvo and British Leyland. MG's involvement came about as a result of a meeting between Austin-Morris engineering chief Charles Griffin and Mr Silverleaf of the British Transport and Road Research Laboratory (TRRL).

According to Don Hayter, BLMC and the TRRL had decided to mount an exhibition at Transpo 72: 'It was felt that it would be a good idea to show how European cars could be adapted to suit the proposed US safety legislation, at the same time demonstrating how ridiculous some of the standards were.' Along with Triumph, MG was chosen to be part of the BL presence and, accordingly, a special car, based upon an MGB GT and dubbed SSV1, was prepared. This was shown alongside another concept vehicle, SSV2, a Triumph 2.5 PI that featured such advanced ideas as anti-lock brakes, self levelling headlamps and a speed controlling radar system linked to the throttle and brakes. Not shown in Washington, but also developed by Austin-Morris, were a pro-pedestrian, low-nosed ADO16 (designed by Jack Daniels), a soft-nosed Mini and an ADO17. These would appear later at the Fifth International Experimental Safety Vehicle Conference in London, in 1974.

SSV1—listed in the EX-Register as EX250—incorporated many clever and advanced features. Its construction was overseen by Don Hayter: 'Charles Griffin told me that I would have to incorporate six special BL safety systems, which was hard enough, but within a fortnight, that list had grown to 12!' The suspension was quite different to the standard MGB, featuring Lockheed's highly advanced anti-roll system—also found on the Ferguson GP car and on ambulances—which was intended to keep the car upright when cornering at speed. According to Don Hayter, this made the car strange to drive: 'Bob Pitcher, Lockheed's engineer, developed the system which used a power pump pushing fluid into a sphere, which had attitude sensors. The trouble was that you need a car to roll a little—especially a sports car—in order to sense what is happening, and with the anti-roll system the handling of the car became unnaturally flat.' Charles Griffin remembers that Rover Research also contributed to the project, a similar suspension set-up having been fitted to a Rover P6.

The wheels and tyres of SSV1 were experimental Dunlop 'run-flat' units,

forerunners of the ill-fated Denovo system, which BL introduced on certain Rover P6B, Mini 1275GT, Princess and Mini Clubman models in due course. The low-level bumpers—at 12in (30.48cm) above ground level—were so-called 'pedestrian-friendly' units, made of soft polyurethane and intended to throw any unfortunate pedestrian hit by the car on to the comparative safety of the bonnet, rather than under the wheels. One wonders what the champions of this concept must make of the bull-bars seen on the front of so many of today's four-wheel-drive vehicles.

Inside, in conjunction with air-bags, there were passive seat-belts that did not require any conscious action to fasten them: they were partially fixed to the door frames, automatically retracting and tensioning themselves when the doors were closed. Don Hayter became involved in research into air-bags as a result of this project, travelling to Italy with Eaton, Yale and Towne, who wanted to become involved in the air-bag business.

The roof of SSV1 was dominated by a large, panoramic, periscope-type rear-view mirror, which must have had a detrimental effect on aerodynamic drag, while the body cavities were injected with polyurethane foam for greater impact strength. Don Hayter explains the work that went into proving the merits of this feature: 'We ran a standard MGB into the side of another at 15mph (24.14km/h), and measured the deformation upon impact. The locks and hinges held, but the inside panel moved inwards by about 4.5in (11.43cm), although it bounced back to 2in (5.08cm). We then filled the wings, door interior, etc of a similar car and tested that, and found the deflection was only 1/2in (1.27cm).'

The *pièce de résistance* of SSV1 was the British Leyland Alcohol Simulation Test, BLAST for short. This was based on a special computer, developed by Triumph, that required the driver to input a series of codes before the car could be started. It was reasoned that he would be incapable of managing this if too drunk to drive the car. It was a novel idea that was much publicized at the time. Don Hayter explains how this worked: 'When you turned the ignition on, an orange light in a thing like a car radio came on, along with the normal red ignition light. The aim then was to press eight buttons in the same sequence as this orange light and seven others like it flashed in a random sequence,' In the SSV1, the speed of this flashing could be regulated, which led to a bit of fun at the show: 'I demonstrated the BLAST device to the British ambassador, who was accompanied by the US Secretary to the Treasury and his wife. I managed to persuade the lady to sit in the car and try the device, which she duly did and succeeded with ease. She then called her husband over and I turned the speed up, and he failed, much the amusement of his wife, who winked at me knowingly!' The exhibition over, SSV1 returned to the UK. It survives today as part of the British Motor Heritage collection at Gaydon.

At the rear, the same car at Longbridge displays prototype 'MG 3.5' badging. Note the barely concealed holes on the left-hand side of the tail-gate (just below the 'V8' badge), which show that this car is a pre-October 1972 facelift MGB GT. Note also that it is a left-hand-drive model with US-style rear lamps and licence-plate mount. (Rover)

prototype had had the standard Rover pent-roof carburettor set-up, but Alec was insistent that we should avoid the need for any bonnet bulges. He told Reg Hadden to mill the basic alloy inlet manifold to his instructions, and then Brian Hillier fabricated this peculiar secondary manifold out of 16-gauge steel tube, which put the carburettors across the back of the engine.' Clarke and his colleagues were pretty sceptical about this idea, but to their amazement, it fired up first time and ran sweetly, even without the luxury of being properly set up. 'Alec got Brian to let in threads at the ends of the fabricated manifold, opposite the carburettors, and fitted screwed plugs so that he could tune the inlet manifold tract lengths. Once he was happy, Barry Jackson took the fabricated manifold and used it as the pattern for the proper alloy production version.' As a bonus, it transpired that Rover had been experiencing problems with hot spots in their pent-roof set-up: Alec Hounslow's manifold did not suffer from such drawbacks.

Other features that were unique to the MGB GT V8 included uprated brakes; stiffer, higher suspension; composite alloy/steel wheels; and standard tinted windows and head-restraints. Unfortunately, these changes were hardly sufficient to disguise the fact that the MGB GT V8 was basically an ageing (if still extremely handsome) car, which had been given a shot of steroids, but nothing significant by way of a facelift. Given the higher price compared to the humble, but visually very similar, four-cylinder MGB GT, the V8, judged in the context of its time as a brand-new car (rather than in retrospect as a classic), was perhaps not all that the customers expected it to be. Production began in December 1972, with the intention of launching the car in July 1973. During the run-up to the launch, several production-specification, export MGB GT V8s were built to examine the potential for overseas sales in Europe and the USA.

Three of these cars were sent to the USA in early 1973, one of them even making it as far as Hollywood, where it was presented to West Coast BL dealers at the Sheraton Universal hotel alongside the new Austin Marina and Jaguar XJ12, but in the end, the MGB GT V8 remained a home-market car, despite pleas from the States. One of those who was keen on the car was Bruce McWilliams: 'I liked the car because of its superior performance relative to that of the four-cylinder cars. I had, indeed, purchased the ex-Hopkirk MGC Sebring car, which had plenty of poke, and the V8 delivered this in a more relaxed manner.'

Internal rivalries cripple the V8

The question of why the production MGB GT V8 never went to the USA has often been posed and, in truth, the answer is that several factors conspired against it. Among these was the very real fact that MG was working flat out to keep the mainstream MGB and Midget models on sale in North America. Another reason was that, up to that time, the only other BL product with the ex-Buick V8 that had been exported to the USA was the Rover 3500 P6, and that had only recently been withdrawn as something of a sales disaster; there were no plans for the Rover marque to return.

In addition, there were the cost and complexity of complying with the mounting pile of certification paperwork; the limited availability of the Rover engine; the parallel development of the Rover SD1 and Triumph TR8 (which would receive new versions of the classic V8 engine); the lack of an open-topped version (in the shadow of threatened US safety legislation); and the recent ignominious retreat from North America of the ill-fated Triumph Stag. As a final nail in the coffin, there was the genuine bias of senior management in favour of Triumph sports cars. Given these all these factors, the non-appearance of the MGB V8 in the USA becomes easier to understand.

It should also be recognized that the MGB GT V8 was not significantly better equipped than its humbler brethren. As Bruce McWilliams says, 'Much as I liked the V8, I would have undoubtedly been troubled that the car offered nothing more in the way of specification enhancement, and this would have been a sticking point. It cost little to insert the V8 engine, but there would have been no support for adding the cost of other embellishments.' Had the will been there, however, surely such investment might have been made available, despite the competition from other parts of BL for funds. McWilliams concludes, 'It was a pity, at this point, MG had been relegated to virtual oblivion. As Mark Twain once said, "Reports of my death have been exaggerated." Unfortunately, this was not the case with MG.'

Soon after the MGB GT V8 was launched, on 15 August, 1973, a bitter military conflict erupted in the Middle East, precipitating an oil crisis, during which the price of crude oil soared dramatically and the threat of petrol rationing loomed. All of a sudden, any car with an engine larger than 2 litres began to be seen as a 'gas guzzler', so sales of the MGB GT V8 suffered accordingly. Although they remained buoyant for a while, during 1974 and 1975, they dropped, and by the summer of 1976, the MGB GT V8, by then equipped with the same black bumpers as the rest of the MGB range, faded from the picture just as the 1977 model facelift arrived for the four-cylinder cars. It was a sad end for what, unquestionably, had been the best derivative of the ADO23 MGB concept.

The arrival of the MGB GT V8 saw the departure of one of the mainstays of MG since the earliest days: here, Alec Hounslow (with glasses) shakes hands with Don Hayter, while the prototype MGB GT V8 (for which Alec had developed the carburettor set-up) is behind them, with the development staff in the background. (courtesy Don Hayter)

Another view on this situation comes from Dave Wall, who was Rover's chief designer in charge of development of the V8 engine at Solihull: 'My belief is that we couldn't produce enough engines, rather than there being a limit set for political reasons. It was our intention to up production to over 2000 V8s per week, but that was forestalled by the oil crisis.' Wall also discounts the rumoured objections from General Motors to a 'Buick' powered MG: 'I cannot believe that General Motors regarded their old engine being a threat to any of their production models. Indeed, GM were always slightly amused that anyone should wish to buy the rights to an outdated (to them) engine, of which they had produced three-quarters of a million examples!'

The 'rubber' bumpers

Following the publication of further federal safety standards, in 1971, it became apparent that impact protection was high on the list of priorities of the NHTSA. The legislation called for no damage whatsoever to occur to a vehicle involved in a collision at up to 5mph (8.05km/h), including exterior lighting. Consequently, work began at Abingdon and Longbridge to examine the best means of achieving this in time for the stipulated 1975 model year introduction. As an interim measure, massive overriders were designed for the early part of the 1974 model year.

The overriders themselves, comprising massive castings overlaid with black polyurethane, were nicknamed 'Sabrina overriders', in deference to a rather well endowed woman in show business, who had also, unwittingly, lent her name to an early 1960s Triumph racing engine. The 'Sabrina overriders' were exceedingly heavy, and one former Abingdon employee, Geoff Allen, vividly recalls the occasion when he dropped one on his foot.

In the case of the 1974 model year, remembers Don Hayter, the US federal motor vehicle safety legislation called for cars to be subjected to a simple test that required them to be run, head-on, into a conventional block wall without damage to the lamps or cooling system. These requirements were easily met by the 'Sabrina overriders'. However, the 1975 model year requirements were far more onerous: 'A pendulum, identical in weight to that of the test vehicle, was suspended about 16-20in (41-51cm) above the ground and was swung—both straight on and at 45 degrees—at 5mph

(8.05km/h) into the bumpers, again with no damage whatsoever to the lamps. This was virtually impossible to achieve without completely redesigning the bumpers themselves.'

Jim O'Neill was responsible for designing the impact absorbing bumpers, in partnership with Austin-Morris styling at Longbridge. He told me that designing these bumpers proved to be one of the most difficult periods of his working life: 'We were faced with the stark realization that unless we conformed to the latest US regulations, the end of MG production would be imminent.' According to O'Neill, many months were spent in trying to develop a suitable bumper system. Hydraulics, leaf springs and canvas-reinforced rubber were tried, but all proved unacceptable for one reason or another: 'It soon became apparent that a polyurethane bumper, constructed in such a way as to absorb the impact progressively, was our only hope, and even this at a temperature of -40° was proving difficult. I visited the US authorities in Washington for a clarification or easing of their temperature requirements, but to no avail. I could not help feeling that they had created a regulation and that now the tail was beginning to wag the dog.'

The solution eventually adopted utilized a special polyurethane skin, produced by Marley and similar to the Bayer Bayflex 90 polyurethane adopted for the US-market TR7. This plastic skin was riveted on to a substantial steel armature (manufactured by Willenhall). 'The MG bumper design was patented by British Leyland, and it gave us another five years of production. I have since been given to understand that the US authorities have considerably relaxed this particular requirement,' states Jim O'Neill, who is anxious to credit the various other organizations that contributed to the successful conclusion of the MG bumper design process. 'I must mention, of course, Marley Foam Ltd, who went on to manufacture the production bumpers, and also Davidson's of the USA, who helped us with the low-temperature testing.'

Des Jones also became involved in the design of the 'rubber'

THE MG GT V8 COUPE

The fact that the MGB GT V8 differed so little from the contemporary four-cylinder MGB GT was not lost on some of the people at Longbridge, so a clay mock-up of a coupé version of the V8-engined car was built, using the steel monocoque of an MGB as its basis. Clearly retaining the MGB doors and sill structure—primarily in the interest of cost saving—the clay model was given a Jaguar-like nose, with twin circular headlamps fared into the front wings, and

a choice of two rear-end styles, which differed in terms of tail-lamp proposals.

No doubt intended as a sort of 'junior' Jaguar XJ-S, this promising project did not proceed very far and soon was quietly dropped. It is unlikely that the clay model was ever completely finished, and the only surviving evidence of its existence appears to be the photographs reproduced here for the first time. They are undated, but judging by the impact-bumper proposal being modelled, and the early ADO88 'new Mini' clay models being worked on in the background, the time almost certainly must have been circa 1974.

Below *This clay model was laid over a steel MGB monocoque and sits on MGB GT V8 wheels. Note the different side-lamp treatment on each side. The basic MGB underpinnings of this MG V8 styling clay are betrayed by the sill profile and standard MGB doors. (Rover)*

Bottom *In this view, the distinctive Jaguar XJS-style rear buttresses of the Longbridge MG V8 coupé proposal are apparent. The drawings on the wall in the background appear to be early ADO88 renderings, which probably date this photograph to the summer of 1974. (Rover)*

An interim measure, ahead of the stricter requirements for the 1975 model year, MG fitted massive overriders to Midgets and MGBs bound for North America. These were the so-called 'Sabrina' bumpers (named after the well endowed actress Sabrina Duncan). This car has been set up for an impact test; note the rectangular slotted opening in the bonnet to allow filming of engine movement during impact. (Rover)

In September 1972, two rival proposals for impact absorbing bumpers on the MGB were presented for consideration by the British Leyland management. This is option 'A', featuring rubber-faced metal bumper units fronting a large rectangular grille opening. Note also the integral roll-over bar fitted to this model. (Rover)

The rear view of option 'A', as presented to BL's management in September 1972.

Option 'B' was the familiar integrated plastic-faced impact bumper, which was chosen for production. (Rover)

front bumper installation: 'On a mock-up, a 5mph (8.05km/h) impact was carried out on a car with the front longitudinal member reinforced. This was firstly achieved by welding a top-hat section across the top of the longitudinal members for about 12in (30.48cm). The resultant test showed that the top-hat section had ballooned, and so another experiment was to straighten the flanges of the longitudinal member and a U-section member was welded inside. This idea proved successful, and the information was sent to Swindon body plant for incorporation into the body.'

By September 1972, the design of the impact absorbing bumpers had been more or less finalized, but, no doubt reflecting the controversy surrounding the 'rubber-bumper' proposals, the management carried out a studio assessment towards the end of that month, when an alternative option, using square-section metal bumper units with rubber facings, was presented. This version featured a large, conventional, rectangular grille opening behind the bumper. The top of the opening resembled the infamous 'black hole' grille, which was about to be phased out from MGB production, while the lower portion extended below the bumper into the valance. An intriguing protective roll-over structure, incorporating a new windscreen, was also featured on this prototype. In the event, however, the now familiar flexible bumper design was approved, and tooling progressed accordingly.

The problems that Abingdon had to overcome are put into perspective by Jim O'Neill: 'To conform to the bumper regulations, we needed a bumper depth of approximately 6in (15.24cm).

Imagine what this looked like stuck out on a small car. The early Volvos had this sort of bumper, but were acceptable because the Volvo is a larger car. By styling the bumper up around the radiator grille area, this gave a more acceptable shape, disguising the massive 6in (15.24cm) bumper.' O'Neill is adamant that the styling of the bumper was not imposed from outside: 'I worked closely with Styling to come up with an acceptable solution. In spite of all the criticism, I feel that it was a creditable effort. Yes, there were people at MG who thought that it was an atrocity, especially with the increased weight it imposed. Nevertheless, I liked it and know what type of MGB I would prefer to be driving if unfortunately involved in an accident.'

One of the more common criticisms of the bumpers was their colour, an uncompromising satin black finish that looked fine with some body colours, but not so good with others. Jim O'Neill was acutely aware of this: 'A lot of work was carried out on coloured bumpers. For styling viewing, there was no problem: they could be painted in any colour or, indeed, could be made in wood!' However, what was suitable for a display model was not good enough for use in service: 'Obviously, for production on a flexible material, any paint developed had to be very pliable and should not crack and, of course, the keying of the paint to the bumper surface had to be 100 per cent effective and not flake.' Eventually, O'Neill recalls, a paint was produced that met these tough criteria: 'We made up six sets of the bumpers in bright orange. This distinctive colour was chosen so that they could be easily identified and would

The rear view of option 'B', clearly showing the distinctive upward sweep of the rear bumper unit, which not only neatly integrated with the vertical tail-lamp clusters, but also provided them with the necessary degree of protection. (Rover)

not "roam". The main problem with the paint was its toxicity—I think it had a cyanide base—and for this reason, there was no way that it could be used in production.'

Even though the bumpers could not be produced in colours other than black, it was intended that they should have as high a quality of finish as practical. To achieve this, Marley came up with the idea of chrome-plating the moulds for the bumper skins, providing a very smooth and moderately glossy finish. It is also important to appreciate that the skins were not solid, but hollow, with an 'egg box' arrangement of cells about 2³⁄₁₆in (5.6cm) deep, which allowed the bumper surface to deflect and absorb the minor impacts required in testing.

J. Bruce McWilliams, of course, was not a fan of the new bumpers: 'There was undoubtedly criticism by some of this solution to the US bumper requirements. I felt it was ugly, excessive and unnecessary.' To be fair, the complexities of the constantly shifting legislation were a nightmare for anyone to deal with, not least the design team at Abingdon. Although their solution might have seemed to be over-engineered, surely that had always been one of MG's traditions—it certainly had been during Syd Enever's time with the company. Obviously, disguising such alterations would have been difficult on a relatively small car. Nevertheless, other manufacturers seemed able to produce slightly less extreme solutions, even if some, such as Volvo, appeared to view such excrescences with pride.

In the MGB's shadow: the MG Midget

During the course of the 1970s, the MG Midget continued to age less gracefully than the MGB, and although it always played second fiddle to the MGB in sales and marketing terms, clearly it

---

NORTH AMERICAN BUMPER LEGISLATION

By the beginning of the 1970s, Abingdon's Dave Seymour was keeping a close watching brief on US safety legislation. He recalls that the origins of the impact absorbing bumper legislation were not wholly rooted in safety concerns: 'Around 1970-71, NHTSA were being lobbied by the insurance industry to write a "no damage" standard for bumpers. However, NHTSA had no authority from Congress to write "no damage" standards—they could only deal with safety issues.' This did not deter the NHTSA, however: 'They came out with Safety Standard 215, which required no damage to safety items, such as lights, direction indicators, steering, brakes, etc, in a barrier test.' To avoid a mis-match between the bumpers of different cars, the NHTSA later added a pendulum test: 'The "business end" of the pendulum was contoured with a forward projecting brow over the impact nose, the intention being that the brow should not strike any part of the car when the nose struck the bumper.

The net result of this was, of course, that the bumpers themselves had to project some way forward from the main body of the vehicle.'

The pendulum was set at 16-20in (40.64-50.8cm) above ground, effectively requiring a bumper 4in (10.16cm) wide. In this way, it was reasoned, all cars would have a bumper face at the same height. Meanwhile, the individual US states were passing their own legislation for 'no damage' bumpers: 'California once again led the field with a standard to be effective from September 1973. In the interests of a standard which would be uniform across the USA, Congress passed the Motor Vehicle and Cost Saving Act in 1972.' This gave the NHTSA the authority to issue a 'no damage' amendment to Safety Standard 215, although to suit the NHTSA bureaucracy, the bumper standard was later removed from the safety standards and given the title of Part 581.

Concessions were obtained for sports cars and two-seater saloons, probably, believes Dave Seymour, at the behest of Chrysler. The programme of 'no damage' bumper legislation was as follows:

FEDERAL BUMPER PROGRAMME: 1973-76

1973 model year	All vehicles: 5mph (8.05km/h) front and 2.5mph (4.02km/h) rear barrier test to Standard 215.
1974 model year	Four-seater saloon cars: 5mph (8.05km/h) front and rear barrier test. Longitudinal pendulum tests at 20in (50.8cm) and any height between 16 and 20in (40.64 and 50.8cm). Corner impact at 20in (50.8cm). Tests to Standard 215. Sports cars: 5mph (8.05km/h) front and rear barrier tests to Standard 215.

Note that, beginning with 1974 model year, several states enforce 'no damage' requirements in 5mph (8.05km/h) front and rear barrier tests. Earliest effective date is California with 1 September, 1973.

1975 model year	Four-seater saloon cars: 'No damage' criteria added to barrier tests. Sports cars: 1974 model year requirements for saloon cars applied to sports cars (i.e. corner tests, pendulum tests etc). Also, 'no damage' criteria added to barrier tests.
1976 model year	All vehicles: pendulum corner impacts between 16 and 20in (40.64 and 50.8cm) added to Standard 215. 'No damage' criteria added to pendulum tests.

In the above table (prepared with grateful thanks to Dave Seymour), the test criteria for the barrier and pendulum tests were as follows:

Barrier	No specified damage to listed safety components as a result of an impact into a fixed barrier.
Pendulum	As for the barrier test, but in addition, the vehicle should not touch the pendulum except at the impact nose or ridge of the pendulum.

To carry out development testing at Abingdon, MG built its own barrier for the 5mph (8.05km/h) tests, casting a concrete block into an earth embankment outside the development shop. As Dave Seymour recalls: 'The car to be tested would be set at a predetermined point on a slope made from trailer ramps. The speed of the vehicle at the block was measured electronically, and a remarkable 5mph (8.05km/h) consistency was obtained. Achieving a perpendicular impact with the block was most important.'

Dave Seymour recalls Bob Neville saying that he had experienced crashes on the race circuit and felt that 5mph (8.05km/h) was a mere trifle: '...so he volunteered to steer the car into the block. Strapped in and complete with his crash helmet, he made his first trip. After the impact, he emerged from the car, shaking like a leaf and vowing "Never again!" He had found the impact to have been far more severe than those he had experienced on the race circuit.'

Bob Neville remembers the occasion vividly: 'My role was simply to steer the car precisely, the aim being to hit a large concrete block outside the shop, which had been built expressly for the purpose. First, I did a run in an MGB, and then in a Midget, and then I vowed never again—and Roy Brocklehurst agreed with me!'

As a result of this first test, MG decided to take the cars to MIRA, where a more sophisticated electric sled was used to drive the cars into the barrier. In later years, MG built its own testing equipment as Abingdon became British Leyland's leading specialist department looking into North American safety and emissions requirements.

Of course, as Don Hayter points out, the bumper question was really the tip of the iceberg as far as the US market was concerned: 'Roy Brocklehurst did at least 16 trips to the NHTSA in Washington, negotiating and renegotiating practicalities along with Rover, Triumph, Ford UK, Lotus, etc. It was very painful at that time.'

An alternative chunkier style considered for the front of the US-specification MGB, featuring an attempt to integrate the licence plate into the bumper unit. (Rover)

This 'rubber-bumper' mock-up, photographed at Longbridge, differs from the production cars by having separate front indicator and side-lamp lenses, and an MG badge mounted lower on the central rib. Note the different windscreen... (Rover)

...which is even more apparent in this shot where its increased rake, body-colour finish and lack of quarterlights is readily apparent. Note also the idea for a return to the classic MGB disc wheels; perhaps this was one of the ideas for a 'cheap' MGB. (Rover)

would have benefited from rather more money being spent on it than was the case. Unfortunately, there was limited scope for doing anything significant to the car as it stood, particularly in the frantic atmosphere that surrounded the onslaught of US federal legislation and, of course, ideas to replace it—such as EX234 or ADO70—had all fallen by the wayside.

As described in Chapter 3, BL's sports car strategy group had advised against replacing the Midget, and had recommended a replacement for the MGB instead, so the Midget seemed to be hanging on by the skin of its teeth. However, perhaps this does the car something of an injustice, for with the various tuning kits available from BL Special Tuning (based at Abingdon), the Midget could be turned into a pretty rapid motor car—more easily, in fact, than the MGB. For those who were interested (and not forbidden to do so by legislation), the Midget could be transformed into quite an entertaining sports car.

By July 1971, the MG Midget had become the only small Austin-Morris sports car, the Austin-Healey Sprite having been dropped from overseas sales in September 1969, and from production altogether after a short spell as the Austin Sprite. However, the fly in the ointment was the Triumph Spitfire, a former deadly rival of the Midget, which was of similar vintage and which actually sold better in the USA. In November 1970, the Spitfire Mark IV was launched, complete with a significant number of improvements. The rear end had been restyled, to match the Michelotti designed square tail of the contemporary Triumph 2000/2500 saloon and Stag, and the rear axle had been re-engineered to tame the car's wayward handling characteristics. Initially, the engine remained at the 1296cc capacity of the Mark III, but for 1973, the engine size grew to 1493cc (for the US market only until December 1974), and the car became the Spitfire 1500. Triumph already had a larger-capacity version of their elderly four-cylinder engine, which they used in the Triumph 1500TC, so it had been comparatively simple to take this unit and make it meet US emissions legislation. This would have much significance for the MG Midget before much longer.

For 1972, a mild facelift of the MG Midget was attempted, which brought smaller versions of the MGB's Rostyle wheels—13in (33.02cm) instead of 14in (35.56cm)—and revised rear wings. The latter incorporated rounded rear wheel arches instead of the former flat-topped versions, despite some resistance to this idea from Syd Enever and Roy Brocklehurst, according to Vic Hammond. Don Hayter recalls that the rounded wheel arch was the

For the 1974 model year, the Midget had looked like this, with rounded rear wheel arches. Unlike the MGB, the Midget had not reverted to a more 'traditional' radiator grille style. For the contemporary North American versions of this Midget, overriders similar to those of the MGB were fitted; further changes, similar to those that affected the MGB, would be applied to the Midget in the following model year. (Rover)

inspiration of Ken Osborne, chief engineer at the body plant. Apparently, he agreed to implement it without reference to the team at Abingdon, who well remembered the structural problems that had afflicted the original Sprite in 1958. This resulted in a moderate improvement in appearance to what remained quite an attractive little sports car, although it was interesting that the 'black hole' grille, which had been disliked so universally on the MGB, was retained on the Midget.

Unfortunately, it soon became apparent that, although not as much of a problem as on the original Austin-Healey Sprite, the rounded wheel arches resulted in a significant reduction in strength at the rear of the monocoque which, as a consequence, could fold up more easily if subjected to a major rear impact. Although the interim 'Sabrina overrider' versions of the Midget, introduced in January 1974, retained the rounded rear wheel arches, by the time that the 'rubber-bumper' version appeared with the equivalent MGBs, later that year, the square-topped wheel arch opening had been reintroduced.

For the 1975 model year, the Midget received its last significant overhaul, in parallel with that of the MGB. A similar style of impact absorbing bumper was fitted, in this case, styled by Michael Scholey under guidance from Harris Mann. The facelift was accompanied by a 1in (2.54cm) increase in ride height. Whereas the previous Midgets had handled with reasonable competence, the combination of the heavy bumpers and greater ride height made matters worse. Almost as controversial as the bumpers, at least in the eyes of the MG purist, was the fact that the classic 1275cc A-series engine had been abandoned in favour of the 1493cc Triumph Spitfire unit, which had been introduced into the North American Spitfire in 1973.

In MG's case, however, the 1275cc A-series unit was already at the practical limit of its capacity, and it was not deemed worth certifying, which would not only have been an expensive exercise, but would also have produced an even more gutless engine than the units that did arise. In common with many of his former colleagues, Don Hayter is not a fan of the Triumph 1500 engine: 'It was tragic

when you consider that some time before, the late Stan Johnson (BL engine designer at Longbridge) had produced a smashing overhead-cam version of the A-series, which we would have dearly loved, but we got that lousy Triumph unit instead...'

The gearbox was also different, using the ex-Triumph/Morris Marina unit, which brought synchromesh on all gears to the Midget for the first time. Overdrive, which would have been of significant benefit to the short-geared Midget, was confined to the Triumph Spitfire, the cost of transmission-tunnel modifications being the official reason for this omission. Similarly, the narrow confines of the Midget's engine bay meant that it received a more restrictive exhaust manifold than the Spitfire, maximum power dropping accordingly by 2bhp (1.49kW). At first, the Midget 1500 was not available in California, which had its own, even more stringent, legislation, but for 1975, a version of the engine was made available that could run on unleaded petrol and be fitted with a catalyt-

ic converter, so the Midget became available throughout North America again.

Celebration: the 1975 anniversary MGB

In 1974, British Leyland decided to produce a limited-edition MGB to commemorate the 50th anniversary of Cecil Kimber's Old Number 1, which they confusingly described as the first MG. It was obvious that this Golden Jubilee special could not be expensive to produce, so the potential options were severely limited. Nevertheless, it was agreed that the changes could extend to special

A proposal for the Jubilee MGB, complete with Wyn Thomas' badge design. In the background are display panels featuring a variety of theme sketches for the 1977 model year facelift. (Rover)

colour schemes, decals and possibly wheels. Before long, the Longbridge studios were scheming a number of proposals, both on the open and closed MGB variants, and by the latter part of the year, the definitive Jubilee package emerged. A limited edition of 750 cars would be produced, each being finished in British Racing Green with gold side-flashes running along the tops of the wings and doors. They would be fitted with MGB GT V8 wheels, the rims being painted gold rather than having the chrome finish adopted for the V8. It was decided that the Jubilee would be available on the home-market only, although a single US-specification MGB roadster was built.

Ian Elliott recalls that the application of large gold decals proved something of a headache at first:'They needed a clean, dry atmosphere, and the only place where this could be guaranteed was the emissions lab.' The decals themselves were the work of Wyn

The final artwork for the Jubilee wing decal. (courtesy Wyn Thomas)

Thomas, nowadays a senior stylist with the Rover Group: 'The job of designing a suitable badge was given to all of the designers in the studio. All of us generally hated graphics work, because of the pin-sharp accuracy we had to work to.' Wyn deliberately set out to produce something a little cruder than everyone else, in the hope that he would get out of the job: 'I drew up a crude laurel-leaf arrangement—more of a stick with leaves on it—but then, to my horror, it was my design which was chosen!' About 1000 sets of the transfers were made up, using Wyn's design, and were promptly stolen, necessitating a second batch: 'The motif was used for the dashboard plaque, and everywhere I turned, I saw it—on T-shirts, mugs, etc—which was pretty ironic when I had set out to produce a design which I thought no one would choose!'

The final facelift

For the 1977 model year, the last significant facelift for the MGB was created. As originally planned, this should have coincided with the introduction of the O-series engine (described later), but in the event, the latter never happened. The most obvious changes were to the interior of the car, where US and UK cars alike received a comprehensive upgrade. Des Jones recalls that 'a complete new fascia was styled for the US-market cars, with integral glove-box, face-level vents and a modified lower console to take the radio, clock and heater controls. The glove-box lock was changed to a stronger specification to resist the 15mph (24.14km/h) impact requirements which came into force, and the face-level vents were mounted vertically in an escutcheon.' This fascia was styled by Wyn Thomas at Longbridge. 'There was some urgency to get this done,' he remembers, 'as it was realized that without it, the MGB would be outlawed from the USA.' Wyn worked up his initial sketches into a clay mock-up, at which point, he left the company, handing over the fascia to colleague Andy Duthie. At the same time, two black, grained moulded hardboard panels were added between the fascia and the bulkhead, the right-hand panel housing the radio speaker until twin door mounted speakers were introduced in 1978.

For the right-hand-drive cars, a black, grained moulded plastic overlay was mounted on to the surface of the existing metal dashboard panel. The original idea had been to develop a common style

Rob Owen produced this idea for a facelift of the MGB in 1975. It featured octagonal-theme alloy wheels and a fastback roof that retained

the standard windscreen and side windows from the MGB roadster. (courtesy Rob Owen)

for the left-hand-drive and right-hand-drive dashboards, but cost constraints had ruled this out. Another man on Vic Hammond's team, John Gregory, was responsible for the right-hand-drive dashboard. He remembers that the design had to be carried through on a shoe-string budget. The speedometer and tachometer were both smaller in diameter than before, so that they could still be installed through the smaller holes of the plastic overlay. In addition, the top panel (between the fascia and the windscreen) was modified to take the larger demist panels. Both the federal and home-market cars featured a new four-spoke steering wheel, which was also the work of Wyn Thomas.

An alternative offering was produced for the right-hand-drive cars by David Browne, who nowadays lectures on automotive design at Coventry University: 'My proposal, which lost out to John Gregory's, was designed from an organizational viewpoint. I figured that the dashboard would have be done on a very limited budget, and so I concentrated my efforts on reorganizing the switch-gear and using a colour break-up—getting rid of the crackle black finish in favour of a darkish mid-grey, and putting in fresh-air vents at both ends. The steering wheel I proposed had twin spokes.' In the end, John Gregory's slightly more radical approach, using the plastic overlay to disguise the original MGB instrument

This display panel features six theme sketches for the proposed 1977 model year MGB facelift, ADO76, which was thought at one stage would

accompany the introduction of the O-series engine. The two sketches on the right are by Harris Mann, the remainder by Roger Tucker. (Rover)

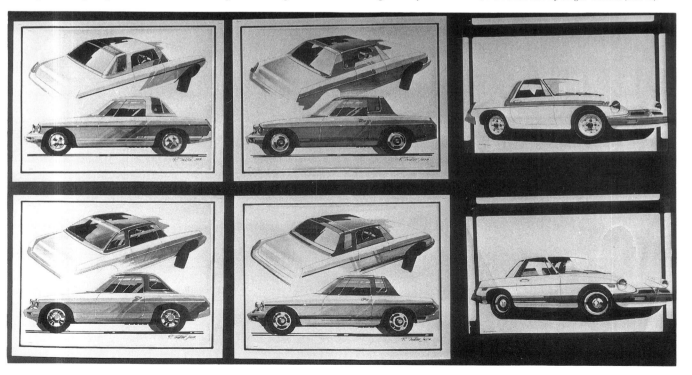

Left *Photographed on 13 November, 1974, this MGB GT has been fitted with silver painted bumpers in an attempt to integrate their appearance with a matching decal treatment along the side of the car. Note the new wheel style ideas and the modified windscreen surround trim. (Rover)*

Below left *A simpler attempt at integrating the front and rear impact absorbing bumpers of the MGB, also photographed in November 1974. (Rover)*

Below *Photographed on 17 February, 1975, this is another attempt at providing the MGB with a more modern image. Coloured bumpers were teamed with similarly coloured side decals, the idea being to provide a range of coloured bumpers that complemented rather than matched the body colours. This is probably the white MGB with orange bumpers and side strips that found its way into the hands of a Longbridge secretary. Just visible is the striped seat pattern on the head-restratint. (Rover)*

cowl, was combined with the change from the black finish to a dark grey one.

By this stage, a number of trim experiments had been carried out, including some weird and wonderful external colour and decal schemes. These efforts had also been extended to the interior. In an effort to liven up the interior, some bright seat facing fabrics were adopted, initially with the US market in mind. John Stark, a stylist who specialized in trim (and one of the nine people who had moved from Ford to BMC with Roy Haynes), remembers that the MGB's striped upholstery followed a similar experiment with the Mini: 'The idea did not originate in the USA, but was more a by-product of the fashions of the time. We saw the brightly-coloured fabric—which, in terms of production and durability, was quite a bold departure for us—and decided to assess it for possible use. In the end, the production people decided that, yes, they could adequately line up the stripes in the fabric on the seat back and squab, and we went ahead.'

These striped fabrics, nicknamed 'deck-chair material', were disliked by the people at Leonia and were, in any case, less practical in an open car than the much hardier perforated vinyl trim. In the event, therefore, the striped seats were only marketed to European customers, while the North American MGBs received a slightly improved variant of the vinyl seat facing.

At the same time, there were more thoughts about the possibili-

ty of coloured bumpers, recalls Alan Edis: 'The ADO76 facelift could have been offered with a selection of coloured bumpers: probably three colours rather than a full range. The black bumpers were a bit stark and they were difficult to disguise.' One white MGB tourer was kitted out with the striped seat trim, bright orange bumpers front and rear, and matching orange stripes along its flanks. The result was, in David Browne's words, 'pretty horrific', but the car eventually escaped into the hands of a Longbridge secretary, whom 'everyone in the office fancied.' Much nicer, in Browne's opinion, was a metallic emerald green MGB GT with a white interior, which went to the wife of the colourful and wonderfully christened Filmer Paradise, the American-born Austin-Morris sales director.

There were other minor external alterations, mainly cosmetic, that made the transition into production. Among these was a change to the front and rear valances, which previously had been finished in body colour, but now were painted satin black in an attempt to lessen the visual impact of the 'rubber' bumpers. At the C-pillar of the MGB GT (now a UK-only car), the joint with the roof had been leaded over, but there was a move to reduce lead in bodyshells (because of the health and safety implications, not to mention cost), so it was decided to simplify the finishing of this joint. First efforts left a recessed joint, which looked terrible in such a highly visible location. Accordingly, the Longbridge styling stu-

dio came up with a neat little plated casting to cover the joint, complete with an integral 'GT' logo. This finisher was designed by Gordon Sked who, 20 years later, would be the director in charge of all Rover design.

Also involved in planning at Longbridge, by this stage, was Mike Kinnear, who recalls more of the problems that thwarted attempts to 'improve' the MGB: 'Not only was the car fairly narrow-tracked—a particular handicap for the V8 version—but attempts to finish the car with metallic paints tended to be unsuccessful, added to which it was not possible to remove the bright trim strips along the side of the car because of the seam that runs along the front wing behind this strip.'

Lifeline for the MGB: the O-series engine
With the increasing emphasis on legislation to limit vehicle emissions in North America, based on a sliding scale of ever more stringent requirements over a specified period of time, it was obvious that the MGB—and beyond it, the Triumph TR7—would need a new engine in the 1970s if it was to retain its most important market. The story of the development of the O-series engine is recounted elsewhere in this chapter, but it is worth mentioning here the strangely vacillating BL product plan, which demonstrates the apparent lack of direction that the organization experienced during that decade.

As soon as the O-series became part of the engine programme, a great future began to be forecast for it. The most obvious candidate for the engine—and the most critical in terms of export sales—was the MGB, so efforts were directed towards developing the engine with that car in mind. By this time, however, the idea of a 'corporate sports car' had entered the picture, and doubts were being expressed over the future of the MGB if this new sports car was to be given a clear run in the US market. Accordingly, the MGB appears to have been shunted in and out of the forward programme during 1972 and 1973.

In February 1973, for example, the MGB was regarded as being expendable, unless the Triumph TR7 could not be made ready in time. With wild optimism, it was also forecast that the O-series engine could be ready for the MGB by April of the following year. This programme was quite impossible to achieve, however, so the date for introduction of the O-series MGB began to slip further back, various hiccups in the model programme also conspiring to delay matters.

Testing the O-series engine
Jeff Clarke and Rod Lyne, of MG's development department, were

An MGB tourer with silver bumpers, matching side decal treatment and bold 'MGB' graphic. Late in the day, it was realized that the youth market in the USA, at which this treatment was aimed, could not afford to buy the MGB, while the slightly older, traditional, clientele did not appreciate the style. In the end, the market for lurid decals was catered for by dealer fitted accessories. (Rover)

involved in the development and testing of the O-series engine. In the summer of 1975, an Aconite (purple) 'rubber-bumper' MGB GT (with V8-style forward mounted radiator) was converted by Clarke to take an early O-series development engine and prepared for endurance testing. Registered JUK 390N and decorated with the gold side stripes that had been used on the 1975 limited-edition Jubilee MGB GT, the car certainly had a very distinctive appearance, if it was not to everyone's taste. According to Jeff Clark, the engine was a very early example: 'It was still all rough sand castings—not even pre-production at that stage.' Don Butler remembers that there were two MGBs at Abingdon, at roughly the same time, which were fitted with O-series engines: 'As well as the Aconite car, there was a red one, and this led to them being nicknamed the "chocolate cars", after the wrappers on Cadbury's milk and plain chocolate!'

At around this time, another event occurred that indicated the problems with BL management, who did not know, did not care, or simply were misinformed about MG affairs. Don Butler remembers an occasion when a BL delegation visited the factory to explain why there were thoughts about closing it down: 'We had a visit from the then BL chairman, Dobson, who told us that we were going to be closed down as we couldn't fit the O-series in the MGB. Someone stood up and told Dobson that we had two cars at Abingdon, which we had done ourselves and which, if he cared to, he could inspect.'

Jeff Clarke was due to take the Aconite O-series MGB GT out to Cassenza in Italy, in June, and because the testing was to be done as part of a programme involving other Austin-Morris vehicles (Princess, Marina, Sherpa van, etc), the convoy was to start from Longbridge: 'I rolled up in the MGB GT, to find that one of the "gaffers" took a shine to it: he got to drive the "B" out to Italy, and I got lumbered with a scruffy van!' That 'gaffer' was Mike Moseley—chief engineer, testing—who nowadays is a senior engineer at Rover's Longbridge facility. Mike remembers that the cars were run on a special reference fuel supplied by BP, which was measured precisely into a small canister or 'fuel bomb' fitted under the car: 'In those days, the customs men were beginning to get quite hot on smuggling, and the French customs officers had mir-

REPLACING THE B-SERIES: THE STORY OF 'O'

The first thoughts of improving the MGB engine occurred in the early 1960s and led to the development of a 2-litre version in 1964, a batch of six engines being built. The bore was increased by 4.54mm, necessitating the rejigging of the cylinders themselves, which resulted in fully siamesed bores (the 1798cc unit had partially siamesed bores, but a water channel remained between cylinders 2 and 3). However, the engine was basically an old-fashioned, over-head-valve unit, with its roots in the 1950s, so BMC chose to concentrate their efforts on the all-new E-series unit, to be built at Cofton Hackett, which was given its own project code, ADO32.

Before long, however, it became apparent that the E-series would be a smaller engine (originally about 1200cc; later enlarged to 1485cc). Furthermore, it was intended primarily for front-wheel-drive applications, mounted Issigonis-fashion over a new five-speed gearbox. Clearly, ADO32 would be of little use for the MGB or the Marina, the latter having been added to the picture after the 1968 Leyland merger. Therefore, it was decided to reappraise the possibility of upgrading the venerable B-series. A programme was started in about 1971-72 to develop the earlier 2-litre concept further, and by the summer of 1972, a 2-litre B-series prototype was running with an alloy head. The original camshaft had become a jackshaft, operating only the oil pump and distributor, while an overhead camshaft ran in the new cylinder head. This unit showed much promise, giving an increase in power output of 10-15bhp (7.46-11.19kW) over the contemporary 1798cc B-series.

By this stage, the ADO28 Marina was being readied for export to the USA (it would be launched there as the Austin Marina in February 1973), and with plans for a revised ADO73 version in the offing (and, beyond, thoughts of its ADO77 replacement), there was extra impetus for a new engine. Added to this increasingly complex equation was the fact that the B-series production facilities were distinctly ancient and in need of major refurbishment. So urgent was this need that the new tooling was commissioned, which meant that any new engine produced from it would have to use a crankshaft closely based upon that of the B-series. However, this manufacturing facility refit did provide the opportunity to alter the engine considerably, and by September 1972, the overhead-camshaft B-series had become the O-series.

Before long, Don Hayter remembers, there was an MGB GT (OBL 50L) running around at Abingdon with an early O-series engine under the bonnet. Development proceeded, but was handicapped from the outset by the fact that BL had chosen to buy the new production machinery before the engine design had been finalized, their aim having been to acquire the equipment at a lower cost while the finance was available at favourable rates. Consequently, the engine evolved so slowly that a programme had to be instigated to 'federalize' the B-series engine—something that the new unit had been intended to render unnecessary.

Then, in 1975, the North American Marina was dropped, reducing the urgency to introduce the US certified O-series. The first cars to receive the new engine were the UK-market Marina and Princess, which were fitted with 1.7- and 2-litre versions respectively in 1978. The smaller capacity was created by using a shorter stroke, but the bore remained the same for both engines. In the meantime, the programme to make the O-series comply with US emissions legislation had been restarted in January 1977, the objective being to introduce the engine into the MGB in 1980.

During the 1970s, Dave Peers was involved in manufacturing timing, a facility that considered the overall production and planning aspects of introducing new products. At the time, he was manufacturing timing co-

ordinator for powertrains, and he recalls becoming involved in the later stages of planning the MGB application of the O-series unit: 'The UK-market specification eventually settled upon was the same as was later used in the Rover SD1 2000—in other words, 2 litres and twin SU carburettors. I remember trying it in a black MGB GT and thinking what a nice car it was.' For the US market, however, fuel-injection was considered necessary.

Sadly, of course, Abingdon's fate hung in the balance and, in the end, the Rover SD1 and Morris Ital were the only cars in which an in-line, rear-wheel-drive O-series unit appeared. The Morris Ital faded from the scene in 1984, while the Rover SD1 2000 lasted from 1982 until 1986; the transverse O-series lived on in the Princess and Austin Ambassador. It was used in the Maestro and Montego ranges of the 1980s, as well as in a low-cost derivative of the 800 series, called the 820. In all these cases, however, it was mated to a Honda designed gearbox, rather than the classic BMC gearbox in the sump, which dated from the Issigonis designed ADO17 Austin 1800 saloon of 1964.

The O-series became the O2 as a running change in 1985, the difference being a shorter block in readiness for the twin-cam M16 2-litre unit of 1986, which subsequently sired the substantially altered T-series of 1992. Another offshoot was the Rover-Perkins Prima O-series-based, direct-injection diesel which, in due course, led to the L-series diesel, launched in 1994. At the time of writing, the L- and T-series look set to continue to form part of Rover's late-1990s engine line-up. While there were private conversions of MGBs to M16 power in the late 1980s (and tentative thoughts about using the engine in MG prototypes such as the PR1), these later units form no part of MG history.

A rare photograph indeed—several people had told me that no MGB had been photographed with the O-series engine in situ. However, here, a development car has been rigged out for testing with an early O-series. (Rover)

rors on sticks. When they looked under the MGB, they saw this little canister and very nearly stripped the car!'

Rod vividly remembers taking part in the three-month trip around Italy, driving up and down the autoroutes in an endurance test for the O-series engine: 'There were about 70 people, driving the MGB, Marinas and Princesses in two eight-hour shifts per day: four in the morning until midday, then midday until eight at night. The theory was that this would achieve a thousand miles (1609.3km) a day, which would have been all right if the cars hadn't kept breaking down!' Along with the O-series-engined cars was an MG Midget—NJO 909P—which had been taken to test the Triumph 1500 engine, introduced in the Midget with the 'rubber' bumpers. Later, in 1977, Rod would become involved in fitting the Rover-Triumph '77mm' gearbox from the TR7 into the MGB, the

intention being to do away with the increasingly unique MGB unit with its heavy, expensive and old-fashioned overdrive unit.

Another person involved in developing the MGB O-series installation was Terry Mitchell, who worked in conjunction with Triumph engineers on the injection manifolding. At this stage, Terry recalls, the UK-specification MGB with the new engine would have offered around 127bhp (94.70kW), a healthy increase over the 97bhp (72.33kW) of the contemporary twin-SU equipped B-series car. The US cars would have produced around 95bhp (70.84kW), a significant improvement on the 67bhp (49.96kW) of federal-specification MGBs of the time.

Later, towards the end of MGB production, some work was also carried out on turbocharging the O-series engine (aimed at the home market and possibly Europe, too). One of the last entries in the MG register for ADO23 is for such work. Don Hayter was also involved with this: 'We got Garrett AiResearch to come in, and we built a single turbocharged car—with a fabricated mild-steel exhaust system, which kept cracking with the heat—and it produced 140bhp (104.40kW) with the potential for developing 160bhp (119.31kW).'

In the USA, cars were required to perform at a given emissions level for well beyond the normal warranty period (up to 100,000 miles/160,930km), and the difficulty of making the B-series engine comply with this, due to long-term wear problems with its distributor drive gear, had made the O-series engine project viable. In addition, the emissions legislation made it difficult to use the traditional twin SU carburettors. For the US market, therefore, it was decided that fuel-injection would be the most reliable means of guaranteeing long-term emissions compliance, and studies were instigated by John Lloyd of Triumph (Leyland Cars from September 1975), with Don Hayter and Terry Mitchell reporting to him. Hayter recalls the impetus behind this: 'The legislators in California were proposing to toughen up their emissions standards for 1976, so this increased the pressure for a fuel-injection system for the O-series.' Prior to this, BL had looked at the Chrysler 'lean burn' system, but according to Hayter, Lloyd realized that a contract with Chrysler might have been problematical: 'However, Lucas were producing their Jet-tronic fuel-injection for the V12 Jaguar engine, and so we talked to them and asked them if we could have four cylinders' worth for the O-series!'

The sports car policy committee

J. Bruce McWilliams saw the MGB's problems from the sharp end, as by the latter part of the decade, he was vice president in charge of product planning and legislative affairs. Therefore, he made an even greater contribution to the development of products that were marketed through the Leonia, New Jersey offices. Between 31 January and 10 February, 1978, a series of meetings was held by British Leyland's sports car policy committee. These meetings were intended to consider the whole question of how the company should plan its future sports car programme, with particular emphasis on sales in the USA. Sports cars accounted for 17 per cent of British Leyland's entire car production, and the vast majority of them went to the USA.

Among the papers presented to the committee was a series of reports by Bruce McWilliams, which not only outlined how the Leonia office saw the future for British sports cars, but also reviewed the current state of US legislation and how that would continue to impact upon the model programme. Interestingly, McWilliams correctly identified that the mood in American politics was gradually swinging away from passive vehicle safety towards fuel economy, the recent oil crisis having caused politicians and domestic car makers alike to rethink their ideas on the consumption of fossil fuel resources.

One of McWilliams' papers contained an analysis of three possible options facing British Leyland. The first of these was to produce an all-new sports car. For this, a minimum viable production of around 80,000 cars per annum was identified, of which, McWilliams suggested, some 50,000 would go to the USA. A second possibility was to reskin both the MGB and the TR7 (it being reasoned that neither seriously encroached on the other's share of the market), with the objective of selling around 25,000 of each per annum for much of the 1980s. The final option was to abandon sports car production altogether and suffer the attendant loss of business and plant closures, which would arise as a consequence.

For comparison, McWilliams presented the sales figures of other significant cars being sold in the USA at the time. The Datsun Z sports coupé was selling at a rate of about 50,000 per annum, often with prices (in McWilliams' words) 'padded by several hundred dollars worth of options.' Chevrolet's Corvette was selling at the rate of 40,000 per annum, often at a premium of as much as $1000 over the 'sticker price' of $9000. As no one else—with the exception of Fiat with their 124 Spider—offered a convertible, it was felt that British Leyland had a golden opportunity to exploit. Competition from the domestic manufacturers was seen as being unlikely, because they were caught up in the need to redesign their

entire model ranges, not once, but twice in some cases, to meet US federal fuel economy requirements. These were based on a sliding-scale for fleet economy fuel consumption (i.e. the average across the whole of the manufacturer's range), falling from 18mpg (7.65km/litre) in 1978 to 27.5mpg (11.69km/litre) in 1985.

In his very telling conclusion to this paper, Bruce McWilliams also highlighted the fact that, while the TR7 was seen as important, the MGB remained even more so: 'None the less, the MGB will remain a very important part of the American marketing programme. In 1977, it accounted for one third of all British Leyland Motors Incorporated's sales. Although out of date and inadequate in many ways, it remains in the eyes of many buyers, the last best example of the traditional and thoroughbred British sports car, and for these qualities, more than 22,000 people put down their money in 1977, the highest sale achieved by this model since its introduction in 1962.'

The Leonia solution

The sports car policy committee met again on 10 March, 1978, to review all the proposals that had been discussed and to make its final recommendations. Bruce McWilliams had summarized his views a week earlier: he was in favour of discontinuing the two smaller sports cars, the MG Midget and Triumph Spitfire, 'as soon as marketing and production exigencies permit.' He also urged that the imminent transfer of TR7 production from Speke to Canley be progressed with the minimum of delay, and that the car should be continued until a reskinned, or all-new, sports car could be made available.

For the MGB, he was more specific, suggesting that it should be given a facelift comprising seven fundamental elements. These were a deeper windscreen; revised hood design; new wheels; new bumpers; new boot lid and adjacent panels to update the appearance of the rear; other minor cosmetic improvements (trim, etc); and finally, the introduction of the O-series engine. Most of these specific points would form the basis of both McWilliams' own prototype and the subsequent Aston Martin prototype of 1981.

In June 1978, BL produced a product plan for the period 1979-83, which called for the following action on the MGB:

End of 1979	2-litre O-series for the UK with twin carburettors, plus an investigation into the possible reintroduction of the European specification.
Summer 1980	2-litre US version, preferably with feedback carburettor; minor facelift.
Autumn 1984	Run out MGB.

In the same product plan, there was talk of an MG coupé based upon LC10, due to be introduced in late 1984, just as it was proposed that the MGB should be run out; the story of LC10 is covered in the following chapter. Coupled with the introduction of the O-series engine would have been another facelift, recalls Alan Edis, which would have included checked cloth seats and, on right-hand-drive cars, a mirror-image version of the 1977 US-specification dashboard.

At the end of November 1978, BL's chairman, Michael Edwardes, and William Pratt-Thompson, his deputy in charge of Jaguar-Rover-Triumph (with the newly amalgamated MG), visited Leonia. Bearing in mind the recent closure of the Triumph factory at Speke, at a cost of £20 million, which had been one of Edwardes' first trials of strength with the unions, it was obviously important to reassure the staff of the company's North American subsidiary that they would continue to have a livelihood.

Both Edwardes and Pratt Thompson were at pains to point out that they saw a future for Triumph and MG and, among other things, the progress of the O-series engine installation in the MGB was discussed, including the options of turbocharging and replacing of the C-series gearbox with the Rover SD1 '77mm' five-speed unit. Triumph TR7 production had been moved to the old Standard-Triumph home of Canley, and both the long awaited TR7 convertible and TR8 were on the run-up to launch. The message from the management was clear: everything was coming together.

The nose of the Leonia MGB was an attempt to marry the necessary impact absorbing front-end structure with the appeal of the traditional MG grille form. It makes an interesting comparison with that of the Aston Martin MGB shown on page 175. (courtesy J. Bruce McWilliams)

Before long, McWilliams managed to put his paper ideas into practice, instigating what would be his last MGB facelift exercise. An MGB with the O-series engine and '77mm' gearbox was taken as the starting point, and a number of modifications put in hand. J. Bruce McWilliams himself related the story to me: 'These modifications, to a silver-coloured car, were done in 1979, prior to the demise of MG and, subsequently, various take-over efforts—Aston Martin Lagonda, for example. The most important change in the exercise involved the A-posts (windscreen pillars). By increasing their length, the car would then meet the NHTSA standards for wiped area with two wipers instead of three, as were currently necessitated by the B's very shallow windscreen. This was a particularly useful contribution to cost savings.'

Even more importantly, in McWilliams' view, 'the profile of the MGB became immensely more attractive, rather like a diminutive Mercedes 450SL. Also, cockpit height and forward visibility, par-

ticularly for looking at traffic lights, was much improved. Many American drivers, at least, had to go through a certain contortion to view an overhead traffic light with the hood raised.' The car was finished in an attractive non-MG silver colour, and the interior was trimmed in red vinyl which, no doubt, added to the 'mini Mercedes' appearance that McWilliams refers to.

The front bumper was reprofiled to allow a vestigial MG grille to be fitted, while the rear bumper was shaped to fit around the rear lamp clusters. The last were also modified, perhaps a little crudely on the prototype, but the intention was clear. McWilliams felt that a facelift inside the car was also called for: 'Numerous internal changes would be quite easily introduced without a heavy tooling commitment, most especially to seating, dashboard and instrumentation. The idea of an externally mounted wheel could have been revisited with subtle modifications to better integrate it with surrounding surfaces.'

The rear bumper of the Leonia car was altered to remove the upsweep at each end, found on the production MGB. No doubt the light units and reflectors would have needed to be better integrated if the proposal had been developed further. (courtesy J. Bruce McWilliams)

McWilliams was particularly worried about the effect that the BL bumpers had on appearance, on the Triumphs and Jaguars, as well as the MGs: 'I was so troubled by them that I investigated the problem with engineers at the big General Motors Guide Division bumper plant in Indiana. There, in the case of the TR7 bumpers, similarly ugly, I discovered that the federal standard could be met with bumpers approximately half as deep, and at rather lower cost. GM was prepared to supply such bumpers, attractively styled, at a lower cost and certified to meet the federal standards. GM was an approved government testing agency for bumper standard compliance, which would have been a considerable benefit where BL were concerned.' In fact, GM's Guide Division showed that they could produce a bumper unit that weighed 33lb (14.97kg) less than the contemporary MGB bumper, which would have cost in dollars what the MG unit cost in pounds sterling. Nothing came of this idea, however, for reasons that have never been made clear: perhaps it was too little, too late.

McWilliams was pleased with the result of his efforts: 'There was agreement that these changes would give the MGB an enormous shot in the arm, permitting sales to continue strongly for several more years while a replacement model was made ready. But no action was taken, sealing the fate of MG.' British Leyland's management saw the car, but appeared disinterested: 'A number of luminaries came from the UK to view it. One could not say that they expressed wild enthusiasm, whether because they were without understanding of what was marketable, or that internal political considerations caused them to remain non-committal.' McWilliams is clear about where he felt part of the problem lay: 'To some degree, British Leyland, at that time, was influenced by lacklustre automobile people, some of them real hacks, and men with little or no real past automobile experience. They were ill equipped to render judgement on a matter involving the life or death of one of their company's most valuable properties—MG.'

Triumph enters the equation

It might seem strange to include a section on Triumph sports cars in a book devoted to MG. However, the fortunes of both marques became so closely intertwined during the 1970s that it is necessary to consider the Triumph story in parallel with that of MG to appreciate their respective fates.

Triumph engineers, like their MG counterparts, were busily working on their proposals for the 1970s when the British Leyland Motor Corporation was formed, in 1968. In the case of Triumph, however, the plans were more advanced and gradually focusing on

the concept of an entire family of cars with a common base. Furthermore, prior to the merger, Triumph sports cars were closer to the corporate decision makers at Leyland and, thus, rather less peripheral to the core business than were MGs to the paymasters at BMH. With the wholesale replacement of former BMC managers at Longbridge, either by ex-Triumph staff or people hired from outside the organization, it soon became clear which of the two marques would have the more sympathetic ear.

Triumph's plans had centred upon two cars. One was a traditionally styled TR sports car, coded Bullet, which could have been offered with a range of engines, including the Triumph slant-head four and the venerable TR6 six-cylinder unit. The other proposal was for a slightly more up-market 2+2 coupé, coded Lynx. Incidentally, these names should not be confused with later proposals, of which more anon. The styling, which was settled upon in 1969, was squared off, but it was not unattractive, being the work of Triumph's Les Moore in conjunction with Michelotti. Thus, by the end of the 1960s, Triumph had virtually finalized its plans for the next decade.

When former Triumph supremo Harry Webster was sent to look after affairs at Longbridge, the task of masterminding engineering matters passed to Charles Spencer 'Spen' King, who was transferred from Rover, where he had played a crucial role in the design of such cars as the Rover P6 2000, of 1963, and the classic Range Rover of 1970. With his arrival at Triumph, in the spring of 1968, King soon became immersed in the business of putting the Karmann-bodied TR6 into production in 1969, doing the same thing for the Stag the following year, and starting the design of the '77mm' gearbox. Triumph was also involved in developing a new slant-head four cylinder engine for use by the Swedish Saab company, and later by the Dolomite and TR7. In addition to all this, he was responsible for progressing Triumph's planned sports car family for the coming decade.

The California trip

Bruce McWilliams, very much involved in Triumph affairs at this point, was the catalyst behind an investigation into US market requirements: 'Some time in 1970, Sir Donald called to ask that I organize a sports car oriented briefing in California for Mike

Triumph's engineering director, John Lloyd, stands behind the full-size Bullet prototype, possibly in Turin. This was the car that 'Spen' King reworked in an attempt to persuade BL's management to accept it as the corporate sports car. (courtesy Norman Rose)

Carver (of British Leyland central planning) and "Spen" King. They immediately came over and we met in Los Angeles to embark on an energetic round of meetings with automobile writers, dealers and others who could make a contribution on the probable future course of sports car design.'

The US motoring press has always had a strong enthusiast base within its cadre, as McWilliams found: 'Perhaps the most useful meeting was a round-the-table discussion I had organized with the editorial staff of *Road & Track* magazine, in Newport Beach. It was out of this meeting that the perception developed that we did not have to have anything exotic, such as a mid-engined car, but just something that was enormously competent, straightforward and attractive, essentially the very qualities that British sports cars had traditionally embodied.'

It had been thought that the layout adopted for MG's ADO21 might have found favour. After all, there was a growing enthusiasm

Closely related to Triumph's Bullet sports car was this sister project, the original Triumph Lynx. Note the badge in the centre of the grille. (courtesy Norman Rose)

for mid-engined cars in Europe and, of course, 'Spen' King himself had fathered the mid-engined Rover P6 BS sports car prototype of 1966. Prior to the Californian trip, however, British Leyland had already ascertained that the Americans were not interested in such an exotic mechanical layout: what they wanted was a conventional front-engined, rear-wheel-drive car that was sleekly styled and well appointed—in other words, an equivalent of the Datsun Z.

As McWilliams states, 'At no time, in this or any of our other meetings, was the Rover BS mid-engine car on the table. We weren't thinking in those terms: we were talking plain, old, garden-variety, inexpensive, mass-market MG and/or Triumph sports cars. The BS would cheerfully have gone up against Jaguars and, all

FMVSS 208—THE THREAT TO OPEN SPORTS CARS

The onslaught of vehicle safety legislation, which took off in North America at the close of the 1960s, reached fever pitch during the early part of the following decade. Although no doubt well-intentioned, much of it appeared to be politically driven, following publication of Ralph Nader's much publicized book, and opportunities were seized upon by those who were keen to carry forward legislation without any real comprehension of, or regard for, the practical problems or implications of their actions.

It became increasingly apparent that the future of the open sports car was in jeopardy, and this situation was confirmed, in January 1972, when the US National Highway Traffic Safety Administration (NHTSA) published its Federal Motor Vehicle Safety Standard No.208—FMVSS 208 for short. The basic tenet of this standard was that the occupants of a vehicle were to be protected if involved in an accident, without any conscious effort being required on their part: in other words, so-called passive restraints were being called for. The crucial issues, where convertibles were concerned, were the roll-over criteria. These required that the occupants remained completely within the vehicle while it was propelled sideways from a platform moving at 30mph (48.28km/h).

A few companies began to investigate the possibility of incorporating some form of reinforced targa roof arrangement in their open cars (including Austin-Morris for the MGB); the US domestic manufacturers took up the cudgels against what they saw as the core issue: passive restraint, which meant air-bags. Chrysler took the US government to court, including the convertible's

case as part of the action, and won a remarkable turn around in the legislation in December 1972.

Dave Seymour, by that time heavily involved in BLMC's efforts to comply with the legislation, points out that Chrysler's case actually centred on the test dummy that was used: 'Their concerns were the technical aspects and correlation to the human tolerance to injury. An importers' association, then known as the Automobile Importers of America (AIA), supported Chrysler's action, but took up the parallel issue of convertibles and the roll-over requirement of FMVSS 208 as part of the same hearing. MG at Abingdon were heavily supporting the AIA case and were, I suspect, one of the few manufacturers of convertibles to have actually carried out a roll-over test to the FMVSS 208 requirements. That we failed to satisfy the test requirements was no surprise to us, nor, it would seem, to the judge.'

The court found that the Highway Safety Act of 1970 did not empower the NHTSA to outlaw any existing categories of vehicle, particularly open cars. The legal opinion was that 'people knowingly accept certain risks when they choose this type of machinery over what may be a safer automobile.' For many manufacturers, however, this was a hollow victory, for during the intervening months, most of them had dropped any plans they may have had for new convertibles. It is hardly a coincidence that such cars as the Triumph TR7 and Jaguar XJS stayed with the hard-top formula, which had already been decided upon in the previous year. MG emerged from the conflict to fight another day...

Above *This dramatic sketch by Harris Mann emphasizes the strong wedge theme to the TR7's styling. (author's collection)*

Left *Taking the original Bullet as their starting point, Triumph's engineers (under 'Spen' King) together with Michelotti reworked the front and rear of the prototype to include fashionable pop-up headlamps and impact absorbing bumpers. This is the car that lost out to Harris Mann's TR7 proposal. (Rover)*

Below *Note the development of the front bumper, the raised bulges on the bonnet and the experimentation with the side crease in this photograph of the Magna styling clay. (Rover)*

things considered, more exotic, limited-production and frightfully expensive Continental high-performance models.' Furthermore, the Americans were keen on the idea of a family of related cars, with different body configurations and, as this would be much easier to achieve with a conventional front-engined car, the idea of a mid-engined vehicle was ruled out.

While Carver and King were in California, they met Pete Brock who, with Kas Kastner, had originated a concept car of their own design, called the TR250K. Kastner was Triumph's competition manager in the USA, while Brock had been involved with the Cobra, particularly the Cobra Daytona. They were hoping to persuade the Triumph engineers to adopt their design for production, but unfortunately it was not a practical proposition for BLMC to take on.

Safety legislation on the horizon
Within a few months of the Triumph visit to the USA, the US National Highway and Traffic Safety Administration (NHTSA) signalled their intention to begin implementing rigorous new vehicle safety requirements that would, it seemed, precipitate the death of the open sports car. Within another year, further details of these requirements would become apparent: a combination of onerous roll-over crush tests and the need for passive driver/passenger restraint by air-bags would cause major problems for British Leyland. Suddenly, the panic set in, as it dawned on the organization that their entire sports car range, and the proposed new Triumph in particular, would not meet these requirements—drastic action was called for.

By now, of course, the mid-engined MG ADO21 had been abandoned, but more crucially, it was clear that the front-engined, rear-wheel-drive Triumph Bullet—which was the only new sports car anywhere near production—was unlikely to comply with the impending safety legislation. Consequently, Triumph would need some rapid input to produce a vehicle that would marry the concept of the Bullet family with a body structure that was capable of meeting the imminent federal safety standards. As a result, differently styled MG and Triumph offshoots of the same basic platform were considered, although clearly Triumph would be the dominant partner in this exercise, with no clear role for Abingdon, which was still tied to the Austin-Morris sector rather than the Rover-Triumph part of the company.

The drastic efforts that had to be made to adapt the existing sports cars to the new standards have already been described. In the case of the new Triumph, however, the situation provided the opportunity to start afresh. Surely, this ought to have been a golden opportunity...

The corporate sports car emerges
Some time in 1970, a major meeting on sports car policy was held at the exhibition hall at Brown's Lane, home of the Jaguar. One of those present was Bruce McWilliams, who recalls the event: 'The meeting was organized by Mike Carver and chaired by Donald Stokes. A number of competitive cars were on view there, along with the then proposed replacement for the traditional Triumph TR line. This car had been developed at Triumph prior to "Spen" King's arrival; it had many awkwardnesses and was really quite out of date and unsatisfactory for a new-generation model. "Spen" King worked on this problem, and I helped to a limited degree because there was no time to do more. The exercise needed to be started all over again.'

Donald Stokes was particularly keen to garner opinions on the Triumph proposal. McWilliams told him that the car needed more work and, as he recalls, Sir William Lyons was asked to take on the job of determining what more could be done. McWilliams recalls another curious occurrence at this meeting: 'George Turnbull and Harry Webster arrived carrying a huge case, obviously carrying drawings or sketches. I was immediately curious to know what they had up their sleeves. None the less, the case remained firmly planted between their two chairs, it contents never revealed. At dinner that night, with "Spen" King, I speculated that another sports car scenario was evolving at Longbridge and, of course, it soon emerged in the form of Harris Mann's design.'

Apparently, the BL corporate sports car committee had decided that there should be a 'competition' to find the best styling for the new car. The principal combatants were Austin-Morris (who had styled the innovative Zanda and MG ADO21) and Triumph, both being asked to produce proposals for a closed coupé body to clothe the Bullet's mechanical package and two-seater layout. At that time, Triumph styling was still under the direction of Les Moore, who had been Mulliner's chief body designer, but who was close to retirement. The late William Towns, of Aston Martin DBS and Lagonda fame, was also retained by Triumph at this time as a consultant. Michelotti, aided by "Spen" King, developed Les Moore's earlier Bullet proposal to incorporate pop-up lamps in a revised nose, while stronger bumpers were fitted to meet the requirements of the forthcoming impact legislation.

At this point, it is important to understand that many have confused the stories of ADO21 and the TR7, suggesting that BLMC

The MG Magna styling model produced by Harris Mann and his team at Longbridge in July 1971. Note the MG badge on the bonnet, the rectangular bonnet vents, headlamp shape and the perforated bumpers, all of which would be changed by the time that the TR7 emerged four years later. (Rover)

The rear of the Magna styling clay. Note the bold 'Magna' badging on the boot lid, reviving the famous pre-war MG model name. The style of the letters themselves is the same as the Magna version of the Marina-based Condor coupé featured in Chapter 4. (Rover)

management instigated these two projects as contemporary rivals for the same role; this is not true. By the time that the results of the sports car 'competition' were being decided, the ADO21 project had already been dead for over six months, and the contenders in the corporate sports car exercise were all based upon a conventional rear-wheel-drive package. Since the future of the open sports car was in some doubt, Triumph's proposal, which featured a targa-roof arrangement (pioneered by the company on the TR4 as the Surrey Top, in 1961), had a slight head-start. In most other respects, however, it was intended to be a sports car in the classic sense and, therefore, not particularly well suited to the perceived demands of the coming decade.

Alan Edis recalls that, with no particular groundwork to go on, Harris Mann and his team were better able to meet these demands: 'From the outset, the Longbridge proposal was a closed car, and so Harris wanted to do something with an exciting sporty character to compensate for the lack of an open top.' The following parameters were defined for the car:

- Reliability problems had to be avoided, so the car had to be relatively simple.
- The car had to have a high technology appearance, belying its simple mechanical components (hence the pseudo mid-engined style that emerged).
- It had to have a large cabin to compensate for the lack of an open top.
- It had to offer a high degree of comfort, hence an efficient heater, air-conditioning, etc.
- It had to offer a high degree of safety, so it had to be structurally very sound.

The Triumph Bullet could have managed the first and last of these,

An alternative clay proposal was mocked up alongside the Magna to show a Triumph version of the corporate sports car. The two cars would have shared inner body pressings, but differed in exterior styling. The second clay showed a family resemblance to the Magna proposal, but there were many exterior modifications. Note the dramatically sculpted, colour co-ordinated front bumper with large 'nacelles', the distinctively rising and falling horizontal crease line and the silver roof roll-over bar treatment. (courtesy Harris Mann)

In this three-quarter rear view, note that Triumph badging has been applied to the left-hand edge of the boot lid. According to Harris Mann, either of the proposals could have been badged as an MG or a Triumph.

The Magna version featured a higher, shorter, stubbier look to its tail than this version, with an even more upright rear window and longer, lower boot lid. (courtesy Harris Mann)

and perhaps the fourth, too, but only the Longbridge idea was designed to take account of all of them.

The results of the 'competition' were presented to BL management in July 1971, when the Austin-Morris styling clay, badged as the MG Magna (reviving a famous pre-war MG model name), was approved. Once again, however, the Triumph marque received preferential treatment from senior management: Donald Stokes insisted that the MG Magna became the Triumph TR7.

Two basically similar styling clays had been produced at Longbridge, the intention being to build MG and Triumph derivatives from a common set of internal pressings (rather like the much later Rover-Honda collaborative efforts), although Harris Mann, who was responsible for the styling, told me that these badges were used pretty much as 'jewellery' to give the models a finished appearance. Ironically, the proposal badged as a Triumph was rejected for the TR7 and, thus, would have become an MG. In the event, the MGB received a stay of execution, and the MG offshoot

of the TR7 failed to materialize. However, the prospect of an MG-badged Triumph would resurface much later in the TR7's career.

Norman Rose recalls that 'Spen' King, reported the results of the styling 'competition' to the Canley based Triumph engineering team: 'He told us that our style hadn't won the day—Longbridge had won that battle—and, in fact, he remarked that only Bill Lyons and one other supported the Triumph styling proposal. However, Triumph retained the engineering of the car.' King confirmed this story for me: 'Bill Lyons, myself and Lyndon Mills, Triumph's sales director at the time, were the only ones to support the Triumph proposal.' This came as a surprise to the men at Triumph, who had been fairly confident that Lord Stokes would choose their proposal, which had already consumed an estimated £2 million.

Another sketch by Harris Mann of a possible MG variant of the corporate sports car. Note the MG badge on the right-hand side of the upright tailgate. (courtesy Harris Mann)

In an interview for *Classic Cars* magazine, in 1986, William Towns recalled this event: 'In order to try to save the day, the Triumph executives rushed into my studio, took out my own proposal for Bullet and dusted it off. But by this time Stokes had left, and the Longbridge TR7 came into being.' 'Spen' King recalls that he tried to persuade Lord Stokes to abandon one of the more controversial features of the TR7, the sloping side crease, but to no avail. Triumph soon set to work on the engineering of the car, which was intended to share many of its components with the planned SD2 Triumph saloon.

A year after the TR7 design had been chosen, in 1972, there was another upheaval at BLMC as the two mid-range specialist divisions, Rover and Triumph, were merged under Sir George Farmer. At this point, 'Spen' King moved to Rover, where he became involved in the important SD1 project. However, these disruptions caused few material changes in the mechanical layout and exterior styling of the TR7. Work proceeded on tooling design and manufacture, and matching the interior specification to the parameters laid down.

The TR7 coupé—replacement for the MGB?

As the corporate sports car, from the corporate sports car factory, the TR7 generated high hopes when it was launched on to the US market, in January 1975. However, there was scope for comparing the TR7 with the emperor of folklore, whose 'magnificent' clothes proved rather less than marvellous to behold. For one thing, its styling was, to say the least, controversial. Other factors exaggerated this, as Mike Carver recalls: '"Spen" King had put a great deal of wheel travel into the car, in the interests of ride quality, but this made it look even uglier. People at Leonia, especially Bruce McWilliams, were horrified at its looks, and so in due course, the suspension was lowered.' A great deal was made of the fashionable wedge theme, including faintly ridiculous US television advertisements showing a TR7 parked in a wedge-shaped garage. However, even for those who were enamoured of the car's styling, it had one major drawback as far as the traditional sports car customer was concerned: it had a roof.

There were other problems, too. The decision to fit the TR7 with the four-speed Marina gearbox was soon found to have been an error: there were many service failures, together with market resistance to a four-speed sports car when the competition were offering five-speeds. Consequently, the much sturdier '77mm' five-speed unit from the Rover SD1 was phased in instead. Ironically, at one stage, there had been a proposal to offer the TR7 with a four-speed version of the '77mm' gearbox as standard (easy enough to arrange, as fifth gear was out-rigged behind the main box), and charge a premium for an optional fifth gear. However, budget constraints had led to the adoption of the Marina unit, although the additional service costs ultimately absorbed any savings made.

At the outset, all the indications had been that convertibles would be outlawed by US safety legislation, and it had been considered probable that traditional open-topped cars, like the TR6 and MGB, would be consigned to the scrap heap. Thus, the TR7 had been designed as a closed coupé from the word go and, as there had been no thoughts of an open-topped version, it had been possible to engineer the car as a conventional closed-roof monocoque, with considerable strength and weight saving benefits. However, the abandonment of any legislation outlawing open cars led to an embarrassing situation for British Leyland: they found that the MGB, which the TR7 was largely intended to supplant, retained a major advantage over its new cousin.

This state of affairs was not easy to overcome, but Triumph gamely made an effort to provide a compromise in the form of a full-length folding fabric sunroof. This drew praise from *Road & Track* magazine in an early TR7 test, but unknown to them, it reduced the torsional stiffness of the TR7 bodyshell by as much as 50 per cent. Clearly, a more acceptable solution was required. 'Spen' King told me how he and Alan Edis first showed how a convertible TR7 would look by the simple expedient of cutting the roof off a TR7 coupé in an advertising photograph! This was about two years into TR7 production, and many believed that a soft-top TR7 would finally deal the MGB a mortal blow and allow the Speke factory to increase its output. However, there do not seem to have been any plans for an MG-badged version at this stage: the future of the

---

PRIORITIES: REPLACING THE MARINA AND DOLOMITE

During the 1970s, it became increasingly obvious that the mid-sized Morris Marina, which had been produced as a stop-gap measure to tide BLMC over, would soon need to be replaced. British Leyland had great plans for the Marina and its successor, with particular emphasis on sales in the USA—the US-specification Austin Marina had been introduced in February 1973 with a £600,000 launch programme that included advertisements in *Playboy* magazine and on the Dean Martin TV show. Unfortunately, however, there was some vacillation about the best way forward, in addition to which, two remarkably similar rival projects were competing for funds within the organization: the Austin-Morris ADO77 rear-wheel-drive saloon (roughly Cortina-sized, and intended to use a '66mm' gearbox that was similar to the '77mm' unit of the Rover SD1) and the Triumph SD2.

ADO77, the basic specification of which was laid down in 1972, was clearly intended as a direct replacement for the Marina—indeed, the styling clays bore contemporary Marina script badges—and its concept adhered to Harry Webster's Austin-Morris master plan of 1968, which specified stylish, but conventional, Morrises, and conservative, but advanced, Austins. Triumph's SD2 was intended to replace the Dolomite saloon, which had entered production at the start of the decade as a development of the front-wheel-drive 1300. Permission to go ahead with this project had been granted largely as compensation for the loss of responsibility for the corporate executive saloon (the SD1) to Rover at Solihull. SD2 began to take shape in August 1972, and it was effectively a sporty rear-wheel-drive car, utilizing components from the Rover SD1 and Triumph TR7 parts bins, that was notable for its good handling and slightly oddball styling, penned by David Bache. Engine options were in the melting pot: the three principal contenders were the O-series, the Triumph slant-four (Dolomite, TR7) and a four-cylinder engine based upon the forthcoming Triumph designed six-cylinder Rover unit (destined for the SD1).

Needless to say, there was much political infighting between the Austin-

Morris and Rover-Triumph camps concerning the relative merits of the O-series and the Triumph slant-four, but even at this stage, it was becoming increasingly obvious that the production capacity and demand for the O-series would be much greater than the lower-volume Triumph unit. After the nationalization of British Leyland, in 1974, and the Ryder report that followed, with its centralization recommendations, it was hardly surprising that, by the summer of 1975, the need for the two parallel projects was being seriously called into question. For a while, SD2 and ADO77 were effectively combined, but the trend towards front-wheel-drive cars throughout almost the entire market sector, coupled with the pressing need for funds for other, more crucial projects, led to the cancellation of this short-lived TM1 (Triumph-Morris 1) and the abandonment of the new '66mm' gearbox.

A product planning document, dated September 1975, described TM1 as a four-door notch-back Morris (and estate) and a more up-market five-door Triumph hatchback. Of possible relevance to MG affairs, perhaps, was the proposal for a coupé: 'to be evaluated, as it has considerable potential and will be evaluated as part of a review of the overall corporate coupé strategy.' Engine options were the O-series for the Morris, and the 16-valve Triumph Sprint engine for the Triumph and, presumably, the coupé.

However, the Ryder report of 1975 turned the company on its head and, as a result, it was decided that a more logical way forward, for the coming decade, was to produce a front-wheel-drive car. From this, came the seeds of the LC10 Maestro, the story of which is recounted in Chapter 6. Had TM1 proceeded, it would have been possible to rationalize components with the MGB—particularly the engine (O-series), transmission ('66mm' or '77mm') and rear axle. The cancellation of plans for a new mid-sized, rear-wheel-drive car, and the gradual abandonment of development of the existing cars of that type, reduced the economies of scale that had helped the MGB remain viable. Thus, unless it could be tied to the TR7 programme in some way, the prospects for the MGB began to look far less rosy.

MGB was still very much in flux and, before long, BL's own advisors would recommend against trying to deflect MGB customers towards the TR7.

Eventually, Alan Edis sent a TR7 coupé to Michelotti for modification into a convertible, and the result was a car that was far more attractive than the coupé, but which suffered from monumental scuttle shake. To cure this, 'Spen' King instigated suitable structural modifications and resurrected the pre-war invention of Scott Iverson, a pupil of the Danish scientist Niels Bohr. This was the so-called harmonic bumper, produced by Wilmot-Breedon, which used the principle of finely tuned weights at the vehicle's extremities to counteract scuttle shake. Harmonic bumpers had first been seen on 1930s Rovers, Daimlers, etc. Ironically, the engineering of these bumpers into the open-top TR7 fell largely to Denis Williams at MG's Abingdon plant: 'This was during a slack period at MG, and we were acting as a sort of contract office for Triumph. The harmonic bumpers were pivoted at the centre-line, with the heavy weights at each end.' This would not be the last Triumph project to be seen at Abingdon, as will be revealed in due course.

Sports car family: the TR7 Sprint, TR8 and Lynx
The Triumph TR7 was intended to be the first of a family of cars

Above and below *The Triumph Lynx prototype could have become an MG, as the badges in these photographs show. Styling was largely the work of John Ashford and David Bache. (Rover)*

that would take advantage of the impressive facilities at the Speke No.2 factory, which was equipped with its own pressing facility. The idea was to feed steel in at one end and dispatch sports cars from the other. Perhaps the most exciting prospects were the V8-engined cars: the TR8 and the sleekly styled Lynx coupé. Although the latter's name had been retained from the earlier Triumph concept, it bore no direct relationship to it.

Bruce McWilliams did not rate the Lynx very highly: 'From the beginning, the Lynx was an ungainly, primitive effort—hardly surprising, given the limited resources of the Triumph design organization, then run by Les Moore. When "Spen" King came on board at Triumph, I quite forcefully pressed my criticisms of Lynx, to which he responded in a number of ways helpful to its appearance.' The Lynx was intended to be a proper sports coupé, with reasonable 2+2 seating made possible by stretching the TR7 under-frame by 11in (27.94cm).

Various ideas were tried for the rear bodywork, including a squared-off tail, rather like the contemporary Lotus Elite. Before

BUILDING THE CORPORATE SPORTS CAR—THE SPEKE FACTORY

After the merger of 1968, the new management soon came to appreciate the problems of building so many competing models in so many different factories. With hindsight, it may appear that the unenviable task of tackling these problems was carried out less ruthlessly than might have been advisable. However, with the desperate need to maximize the returns on investment already committed prior to the merger, and to maintain sales, it is not too surprising that more drastic action was not taken. It is easy enough to form an ideal picture of where one would like to be, but the task of achieving that goal is not always so easy.

From the sports car perspective, it was obvious that sales of Triumph and MG models should have been built upon, not only because the Japanese were just beginning to make their presence felt with cars like the Datsun 240Z, but also, more importantly, because the combined sales of British Leyland sports cars accounted for such a large proportion of the company's export revenue. Following the recommendations of the BL sports car advisory committee, it was decided that the ideal situation was for all of the company's sports cars to be built at a purpose designed facility, and to be based upon a common set of components to maximize the benefits of economies of scale. In other words, this was an extension of the 'big is beautiful' philosophy that had played such a major part in the BMH/Leyland merger itself.

The purpose-built factory that resulted was at Speke, on the edge of Liverpool, where an existing Triumph plant—later known as Speke No.1—had begun operating in 1959, following its purchase from Hall Engineering. In 1960, Standard Triumph International laid plans to develop the adjacent green-field site, but with the take-over of STI by Leyland, in 1961, these plans were held in abeyance until the BLMC merger took place seven years later. A year after the merger, construction started on a massive, almost completely self-contained, plant—Speke No.2—which even included its own body panel pressing facilities.

However, despite the grand plans, the factory never achieved its potential, and it is very doubtful that the plant ever recouped the initial investment

required. It started producing bodies for the Triumph Stag (launched in 1970, and assembled at Canley), and later produced the small Triumph Toledo saloon (the rear-wheel-drive successor to the Triumph 1300) until that car was transferred to Canley, in 1974, to make way for the TR7.

By 1975, TR7 production was in full swing, and plans for the rest of the TR7 family were well advanced, but it was already apparent that these derivatives were needed urgently if the plant was to operate anywhere near its capacity. In 1977, the Triumph Stag was discontinued, and the redundant equipment was cleared away to make room for the Lynx, planned for introduction in 1978. However, the four-month strike, which began on the same day that Sir Michael Edwardes took charge of the company, sealed its fate. Within a short time of Edwardes' arrival, it became apparent that BLMC were suffering from a gross over-capacity, and the massive Speke No.2 factory, still only producing one model, was one of the first obvious casualties, closing its doors in May 1978.

There is another side to the equation, too: a legacy of the post-war expansion policies of governments of the 1950s. Triumph had been forced to build at Speke by government restrictions, when what they really wanted was to build near their existing plants in the Midlands—a problem shared by all the major British car manufacturers. The real difficulty lay in the fact that there was no tradition of car building in the Liverpool area, and although training schemes were set up, the odds against success were overwhelming. Add to that the fact that administration (from Coventry) was still remote, and the difficulties were obvious.

A story related by one of the former Triumph engineers illustrates the problem graphically: 'One of our engineers from Canley would spend three days a week at the Speke plant. One day, he was walking along the line when he saw a man applying adhesive sound-deadening pads to the toe-board. The man carefully placed the pads, and then proceeded to hit them vigorously with a lead hammer. When questioned as to why he was doing this, the reply was, "The packet says 'impact adhesive', so I'm impacting it."'

long, however, the prototypes featured a rakish, and practical, opening rear window, similar to that of the Rover SD1. John Ashford, who was largely responsible for the definitive Lynx style, recalls that work began on the TR7-based Lynx in 1971: 'I produced a model to 0.3-scale, which resembled the car which eventually appeared.' By 1973, Triumph styling had come under the direction of former Rover stylist David Bache (remember that Rover and Triumph had merged in 1972), who was also responsible for the sleek Rover SD1.

Not everything went smoothly, however, according to John Ashford: 'David Bache came over to Triumph, saw my model for Lynx and said, "That's nice." However, he wanted to make an impression, and so both he and Les Moore came up with full-sized alternative proposals. There was to be a management viewing, and at a late stage, my 0.3-size model was hidden away. Suitably miffed, I brought it out again, and it was duly chosen by management as the one to go for.' Perhaps irritated at having lost out, David Bache initially tried to kill off John Ashford's design, in favour of his own squared-off version with opera windows, which he believed were essential for sales success in the late 1970s. It seems that an argument ensued between Bache and 'Spen' King, who effectively ordered the former to become involved in the preferred option.

By the middle of 1974, five prototypes of the Lynx had been built, but at that stage, BLMC were experiencing grave financial difficulties, so the project was frozen for 12 months. Then, in the summer of 1975, the Lynx became the first project to be sanctioned by the post-Ryder-report British Leyland Ltd, with the intention of introducing the car in 1977. Subsequently, David Bache stamped his design authority on the Lynx styling, introducing his 'trademark' concave side fluting and a slight kick-up, or lip, in the roof above the rear window (worsening the aerodynamics in the process, as it happened).

By the latter part of 1977, most of the tooling had been completed (at an estimated cost of about £10 million), and although the intended launch date had slipped slightly to 1978, it seemed that

Triumph would soon achieve the original aim of an expanded TR7 family. The 16-valve TR7 Sprint, the TR8 and the Lynx were all programmed for imminent production. Studio photographs even showed a Lynx prototype badged as an MG, although in reality, this was never a serious proposal. Alongside the Lynx, plans were advanced for removing the controversial sloping crease in the flanks of the TR7. Then it all went sour... On 1 November, 1977 (the same day that British Leyland's new chairman, Michael Edwardes, was appointed), the toolmakers at the Speke factory began a strike that would last for four months. The result of this action was the cancellation of the TR7 Sprint and Lynx, and the postponement of the TR8.

Bruce McWilliams has always maintained that the Lynx, in any of its forms, was not what the Americans wanted: 'My views on Lynx continued to be vociferous and negative and, ultimately, a climactic summit meeting was organized at the "Elephant House" at Longbridge to hear them out. It was short and final: Dick Perry presided, and "Spen" King, Graham Whitehead, I and a few others attended. Dick began by asking if I believed the car to be saleable, and I said absolutely not. Then there was a sort of sucking-in-of-breath sound, and Dick said something to the effect that that was it, Lynx is cancelled. And so it was. The meeting, which lasted all of about five minutes, was immediately adjourned.'

Last-ditch efforts: the Broadside project

Once the Lynx had been cancelled, Triumph's engineers tried gamely to salvage something of their plans for a TR7-based family. In time, the MG badge was thrown into the ring again, but it is important to consider the proposals for other derivatives of the Triumph family, for it is highly likely that, had they emerged, they might have given impetus to the idea of MG-badged offshoots. Even an ardent TR7 enthusiast must recognize that the most disliked feature of the car was the controversial crease in each side, which swept up from the base of the front wing in an attempt to emphasize the wedge styling. In the case of the Lynx, with its 11in (27.94cm) longer wheelbase and 4in (10.16cm) longer doors, it had been necessary to remove this crease line, and it soon became apparent that the TR7 would benefit from its deletion, too.

The TR7 had been designed to be manufactured entirely at the purpose-built Speke factory, so the freighting component was a relatively small part of the overall cost of manufacture. The strike ended in the closure of Speke and the transfer of the TR7 to Canley, at which point, the cost of shipping components from one factory to another entered the equation. By this time, TR7 panels were pressed at Swindon, then transported to Canley for assembly; the same was true of other components that, formerly, had been sourced in-house. As a consequence, the unit cost of the car rose, and the economics of major changes to the bodywork, so early in the product cycle, militated against the facelifted sides without the economies of scale that had been foreseen originally.

By the time that the decision had been taken to move the TR7 again, from Canley to Solihull, it was clear that the future of the Triumph sports cars rested on a knife-edge, so the Triumph engineers—encouraged by BL's planning director, Alan Edis—tried to salvage something of the original TR family concept. The Lynx had been tooled up, at enormous cost, and this included the tooling for the doors, which benefited, of course, from the deletion of that sloping crease line.

The product planner in charge of the TR programme, at that time, was Tony Dyson, who recalls the creation of what became known as Project Broadside: 'Broadside was an amalgamation of Lynx front wings, Lynx doors and a TR7 chassis, which we stretched by just 4in (10.16cm) in order to match the doors. We made the car into both a convertible and a coupé, the latter with a sloping tailgate à la Lynx, and were able to squeeze in two rear "plus two" seats in the rear of the passenger compartment.' Norman Rose recalls the difficulty of accommodating the conflicting requirements of rear seating, the location of the fuel tank, and the fact that the Broadside convertible would have had a T-bar roof like the Triumph Stag, rather than the harmonic bumpers of the shorter TR7 convertible. Four prototypes were built, one of which, a metallic red coupé, survives in the British Motor Heritage collection.

Meanwhile, back at Abingdon...
Despite the adoption of the Triumph Spitfire's engine, in 1974, the MG Midget was in severe trouble as the decade drew on. Although it had some appeal as the smallest genuine sports car on sale in America, it had a cramped and crudely furnished interior, together with minimal levels of refinement, performance and handling. The MGB was universally scorned by the serious sports car enthusiasts in the American motoring press, but at least it retained some credibility; sadly, the Midget did not fare so well. The interior space was a very real problem, since the cockpit was not only narrow, but also difficult to get into or out of by the typical larger American citizen. Of course, this lack of space was not a problem for everyone, but for a little more money, they could buy an MGB or, if money was short, a Japanese hatchback with a sunroof. The latter was certainly not a sports car, but by traditional standards, the current MG Midget's claim to this title was beginning to be questioned, too.

The problems did not end with public perception of the product, either: warranty claims against the Midget in the USA were causing a considerable headache, principally in connection with the engine and its problematical anti-pollution equipment. When William Pratt-Thompson visited Leonia in March 1978, Bruce McWilliams produced one of his reports on BL's sports car range. In this paper, he recommended the discontinuation of both the Midget and the Spitfire, failing which, a drastic reduction in warranty costs was desperately needed. The sports car policy committee had suggested that a 10-16 per cent reduction in warranty costs should be the objective, but McWilliams argued that this was an unduly modest target when the prevailing warranty costs were around 50 per cent higher than the industry norm. A 30 per cent reduction in Midget warranty costs, for example, would have offered a saving of nearly $60, while still providing warranty coverage of $130 per vehicle.

It was no great surprise, therefore, when it was decided soon afterwards that the Midget should be discontinued, although the stronger selling Triumph Spitfire was allowed to soldier on for

another two years. A large batch of the last Midgets was sent to Japan, where enthusiasts had long fostered an enthusiasm for British eccentricities in car design. The very last Midget, a black home-market car, went down the line on 12 December, 1979, with a black cardboard coffin ceremoniously laid on top of it and inscribed 'RIP'.

In 1968, the sports car advisory committee had recommended that the smallest category of sports car would not be worth pursuing in the coming decade, which is why no serious replacement ever emerged, the closest perhaps being the ADO70 exercise described earlier. That the Midget—which, don't forget, had grown out of the 1958 Austin-Healey Sprite—continued in production for so long says as much about the spirit of the car, as it does the state of the company.

Sentence of death for Abingdon
Although John Thornley was nine years into retirement by the time that the sports car policy committee met in 1978, he managed to kept abreast of the developments that affected his former charge. He had seen the earlier sports car committee founder, and wasn't surprised when the latest group appeared to go unheeded: 'Both came to pretty much the same conclusions: that BLMC had the sports car market in their hands; if they couldn't make a profit on sports cars, they couldn't make a profit on anything.' They also recognized that the more valuable name, in terms of world-wide sales, was MG. Thornley suspects that the reports of these committees were stifled, at least partially because their conclusions were not what the men at the top really wanted to hear, although in fairness, it must be said that the facts they contained would have been commercially sensitive and, therefore, unlikely to be made public.

At around this time, work on the O-series-engined MGB was proceeding, with the aim of a 1981 model year launch. Don Hayter sent six cars to the USA for testing: 'They were tested at the Galveston circle, tested in the mountains, and for cooling tests, they went to New Orleans. They were very effective at complying with the emissions requirements. In fact, I was told that they were amongst the best that the testers had experienced in that regard.' Following the bombshell that was dropped in September, when it was announced that MGB production would be halted, Hayter recalls, 'We were told to take all the O-series development engines out of the test MGBs and ship the engines off to Triumph.'

In May 1979, the British General Election returned a Conservative government, led by the powerful figure of Margaret Thatcher. So popular was this change of power with the financial institutions that the pound sterling began to soar on the international markets. While this might have been good news for importers and investors, it created a dire situation for companies dependent upon exports. The MG, Triumph and Jaguar factories were firmly in the latter category, and as sterling rose against the dollar, the US prices of BL cars had to be either subsidized or raised accordingly. This all happened so quickly that, within a month, BL were forced to produce a crisis management plan to ensure the survival of the whole company.

This plan was known by the initials 'CORE', which stood for coordination of resources, and concentrated upon the LC8 and LC10 volume car programme; the sports cars were regarded as peripheral and, therefore, expendable. At the same time, members of the BL board were steeling themselves for their first formal meeting, in July 1979, with Industry Minister Sir Keith Joseph. They were sure that he would be far less happy than his Labour predecessor at the prospect of providing public money for BL. It was obvious that the Conservative government would not be prepared to provide money for the company, unless all possible efforts were being made to reduce costs, so a drastic rationalization programme was rapidly drawn up.

By this time, one of Sir Michael Edwardes' close advisors was Mike Carver, who had taken part in the fact finding mission to the USA with 'Spen' King in 1970. In 1975, Carver had left the post-Ryder British Leyland and joined the National Enterprise Board, but he returned to the company with Edwardes in 1977. He bravely admitted to me that it was at least partly on the basis of his advice that Edwardes decided to stop production of the MGB:

The MG work-force and supporters took to the streets of London to protest at the announcement that the MGB was to cease production. Here, MG Owners' Club secretary Roche Bentley (with megaphone) leads the march. (courtesy Jimmy Cox)

'Sports cars are a good thing to do if you have the basic business right, but unfortunately that wasn't the case. BL were not building cars efficiently and effectively, and it took Honda to show them how to do it.'

With monumental bad timing, the death sentence, which it certainly was, was announced on 10 September (subsequently known to MG enthusiasts as 'Black Monday'), just as people were clearing up after a week of festivities to celebrate 50 years of MG at Abingdon. The supreme irony was that a party of the leading US MG dealers had been invited to participate in the closing stages of the anniversary event, culminating in a dinner at the Connaught Rooms, where David Andrews, BL's vice chairman and the guest of honour, had the unsavoury task of breaking the news to a stunned audience.

John Thornley wasted no time in trying to galvanize support for the Abingdon factory and, in particular, its sole remaining sports car, the MGB. On Thursday 13 September, 1979, barely three days after 'Black Monday', Thornley wrote to all of the MG dealers in the USA, urging them to try to persuade Sir Michael Edwardes and the BL management to reverse their decision to close Abingdon: 'Thursday saw the Thornley and Beer families working far into the night, preparing over 400 letters—one to each dealer in the US—which, bearing US stamps, flew the Atlantic that night. And, of course, a copy went to Sir Michael Edwardes—I delivered it to Nuffield House myself!'

In the wake of the public announcement of the end of MG sports cars, there was inevitable political fall-out, and various MPs rallied to the MG cause. However, Sir Michael Edwardes assured me that, despite this, 'there was no pressure from the power base (i.e. Downing Street)—it was all peripheral public relations. Frankly, we had a thousand other things on our minds, including the survival of 100,000 jobs to worry about.' However, even the BL management could not fully have appreciated what a hornets' nest they had stirred up.

Shock waves from Abingdon

The shock accompanying the announcement that 50 years of MG

production at Abingdon were to be drawn to a close so suddenly reverberated throughout the industry. Everyone knew that Abingdon had long been grossly under-funded and that its products were suffering accordingly. Nevertheless, few expected the end of MG production to be so dramatic. No one saw this more than Alan Curtis, the charismatic and successful chairman of Aston Martin Lagonda, who had already played a leading role in saving Aston Martin itself, when that company was near bankruptcy in 1975.

Curtis saw the similarities between Abingdon and the famous Aston Martin factory at Newport Pagnell: both were relatively unautomated and benefited from skilled, dedicated work-forces. He thought that if practical support—especially money—could be found, there would be a great deal of sense in forging a link between the two well established and highly respected marques, provided, of course, that BL could be convinced and that the necessary funds could be found. On 14 October, during the course of a transatlantic telephone conversation, Curtis and his associate, Peter Sprague, agreed to proceed: during the next few weeks, they began to drum-up financial support for their proposal.

With remarkable speed, leading British businessmen joined forces with Curtis and Sprague: millionaire David Wickens (of British Car Auctions, who offered not only finance, but also UK distribution), Peter Cadbury (head of Westward Television), Lord George-Brown (who acted as broker and catalyst) and the Norwest Construction Group formed a consortium on 16 October, 1979, at the Grosvenor House Hotel. Their aim was to take over the MG factory. Lord George-Brown was particularly fascinated, according to Alan Curtis: 'He called me from Hong Kong to tell me that there was a lot of money there, and he felt sure that we could get the necessary funds.' However, taking over the factory was not the full extent of the consortium's aims: they planned to acquire all rights to the MG name, the Abingdon factory itself and the MGB sports car, and to follow up a short-term facelift of the MGB with a new range of MG sports cars to be introduced in 1983.

The consortium goes public

The consortium's proposals were made public on Thursday, 8 October, 1979, newspaper headlines proclaiming the '£30 million plan to rescue MG'. Then began six months of talks. However, BL were unconvinced of the merits of continuing to produce a car that used a large number of unique, and increasingly obsolete, components. Having decided to abandon the MGB, they did not want to be involved in the engineering work that would have been necessary to update it. Furthermore, on the day after the news of Aston Martin Lagonda's proposal broke, BL announced that neither the MG name nor the famous Abingdon factory were on offer. The only possibility that they might have been prepared to contemplate was to allow Aston Martin to produce the MGB under licence, and to supply components to them.

There ensued something of a battle of wills: the consortium would only accept the purchase of the MG factory, the rights to the MGB and the MG name; whereas BL were emphatic that this would not be possible. Alan Curtis recalls the difficulties at this point: 'Ray Horrocks of British Leyland was my first contact, and he made it clear that BL were only prepared to grant us a licence to use the name, and it took us a long time to persuade them to let us have the car and the factory.' Having full control of MG's destiny, of course, was fundamental to the consortium's plans, which were far more detailed and further reaching than many have subsequently supposed. It is worth recording Harold Musgrove's view of this stage in the negotiations (at the time he was managing director of Austin-Morris): 'Aston Martin were told right from the beginning that the MG name was not for sale, and whilst they accepted this to us, they did not, it seemed, once they were outside the door. We asked them where they were going to buy the parts if not from us— and frankly we didn't really want to supply them anyway.'

William Towns not only produced sketches of the consortium's proposed facelift for the MGB—tagged Stage I—but also drawings of an innovative Stage II rebody of the car. The latter would have retained the under-frame and major structural components, but would have featured a new set of angular exterior body panels that offered a choice of four interchangeable body styles: open-topped, coupé, fastback coupé and estate car. The publicity brochure produced by Aston Martin proclaimed that this concept offered a base vehicle that could '...provide its owner with a transition from bachelorhood, through marital bliss, to a young family and even back again.' Where one was supposed to keep all the different roof structures was not made clear, however! The engine options envisaged comprised an unspecified V6 and the four-cylinder O-series. Beyond this, there were serious thoughts about an all-new MG

Midget using, it was hoped, a suitable Toyota engine. William Towns produced some sketches, which went to Tokyo, but sadly their whereabouts is currently unknown. Chris Peacock, MG's plant director at the time, became involved in these exercises, and Curtis is confident that he would have run the plant well under the consortium's ownership if he had been given the chance.

Conflict of interest: safeguarding the TR7

However, BL were not only keen to protect their Triumph TR7 sports car—and its recently launched TR8 offshoot—but were also formulating plans for an MG-badged derivative of the Triumph as a means of maintaining their US sales levels and securing the future of the Solihull factory, where it was envisaged that the expanded TR7 family would be built. While discussions continued, BL were doing their best to placate their North American dealers, who were threatening legal action if the MGB was discontinued without an effective, and more or less immediate, replacement.

Alan Curtis met these dealers, too, both in the UK and the USA, but he stresses that he was very careful to avoid treading on BL's toes in his dealings with the Americans, who were all very supportive of his efforts to save MG. In the British House of Commons, Abingdon's MP, Tom Benyon, formed a group of Conservative MPs who began to urge BL to reverse their decision to close the Abingdon factory.

At some point during this exercise, Sir Michael Edwardes put forward the intriguing idea of a joint company, to have been called British Sports Cars Ltd, with BL and the consortium each owning 40 per cent of the shares, and the balance being offered to outside interests. Alan Curtis recalls how this came about: 'Lord George-Brown and I went over to see Sir Michael Edwardes at his flat for an informal chat, and Sir Michael said, "How about us putting Aston Martin, Jaguar and MG together, and forming a joint company?" We went away greatly enthused, but for some reason, this idea subsequently died a death.' Consequently, the primary objective of the consortium reverted to the outright acquisition of the factory, name and car.

By December 1979, nothing material had come of the consortium's proposal, and BL were actively looking for alternative means of keeping their US dealers happy. The manner in which they did this will be described in detail later, but suffice to say that a leak from within BL suggested that a new MG sports car might be in the offing, and that it might be 'built alongside the Triumph TR7 at Solihull.' Then, in January 1980, Aston Martin Lagonda announced that a formal offer would be issued before the end of the month, but the deadline came and passed with nothing having been put forward. According to Alan Curtis, the problem was that the delay in negotiations had coincided with a period of interest rate rises and fluctuating exchange rates: 'I am sure that if we had been

---

ALAN CURTIS AND ASTON MARTIN LAGONDA

To fully understand the reasoning behind Aston Martin Lagonda's interest in MG, it is necessary to take a brief look at Aston Martin's history under the chairmanship of Alan Curtis. He freely admitted to me that mistakes had been made at Aston Martin Lagonda while he was there, the principal error being the decision to proceed with the William Towns designed Lagonda saloon: 'Few of us in control had much real experience in the motor industry, but in mitigation, we recognized the fact that the existing Aston Martins were giving us horrendous warranty problems. So we decided to build a big car, where we felt that the profits would be—and I was enchanted by Bill Towns' sketches for the Lagonda.'

The Lagonda—with its very unusual styling and state-of-the-art electronics—was launched in 1976, but despite a great deal of free publicity from the considerable media attention that the car aroused, it soon became apparent that the big saloon was something of a white elephant and, clearly, not the answer to the company's problems. By 1978, Aston Martin had introduced the Volante and 'Oscar India' (uprated V8) models, but the company was stuck with the Lagonda. It was obvious that something had to be done to broaden the product range, and to do that would mean bringing in people from outside or joining forces with another company.

By this time, Alan Curtis had taken the reins at the Newport Pagnell factory: 'I knew very few people in the motor industry, and thus found it hard to recruit the right people. I tried to tempt Mike Kimberley away from Lotus, but Colin Chapman wouldn't let him go. Then I tried to persuade Colin to contemplate a merger of Aston Martin and Lotus, but by that time, he had gone off to DeLorean, and so that idea was dashed.' Then, in September 1979, the Edwardes plan for British Leyland was announced, including the discontinuation of the MGB sports car, and Curtis immediately recognized that this was an opportunity to acquire the additional business he felt that Aston Martin needed.

'My philosophy was that everyone—particularly in the UK and the USA—knew and loved the MG marque, and there was a general perception that BL were trying to run MG into the ground. I thought if we could put a bit of spice into the vehicle (MGB), we could do something worthwhile.' Curtis bounced his ideas off a few friends and contacts, and they invariably responded favourably: 'I was particularly enthused by the US dealers I went to see, who told me that they could see a synergy between Aston Martin and MG.' He also felt that there were possibilities for the future, such as Aston Martin derivatives of future MG sports cars, a sort of up-market badge engineering. From these encouraging beginnings, it was a short step to becoming involved in the maelstrom of negotiations that followed.

Above *This sketch, produced by William Towns, represents the facelift that the Aston Martin Lagonda consortium intended applying to the MGB to extend its life. Clearly, it was inspired to some extent by the prototype that had been developed by J. Bruce McWilliams in Leonia. Note the use of a cut-down bumper, a vestigial grille and a taller windscreen. (courtesy Alan Curtis)*

Below *The facelifted MGB was only the first part of Aston Martin's plan for revitalizing the marque: these sketches by William Towns show two of a proposed family of Stage II derivatives, based upon the MGB floorpan, sills and wheel arches. The idea was to have a basic open tourer with a range of removable rear body sections that would have produced the 2+2 coupé and hardtop shown, together with a sports estate. (Aston Martin)*

firmer and more positive earlier on, we could have concluded the deal more rapidly while the finance was more freely available.'

At this stage, Curtis tried to persuade Toyota to take an interest, perhaps to the extent of a 20-25 per cent stake in the venture, in return for which, they would have provided much needed new engines: 'It was never very certain in our minds whether or not the emissions certified O-series engine would be available.' Curtis hoped to be able to tap into the Japanese expertise, rather as BL did with Honda. However, Aston Martin was unable to meet Toyota's demand for a sufficiently detailed and thorough plan of how the company intended to build an MG sports car economically.

While all this was going on, BL announced their own plans for the Abingdon plant on 10 December, 1979, in the process, making it quite apparent that they doubted the likelihood of the Aston Martin bid succeeding. Harold Musgrove revealed that the company was planning to create a specialist vehicle unit at Abingdon and a CKD (completely knocked down—in other words, kit) export packing depot, the latter to be implemented by 1981. The future of one of the few areas at the factory to have received significant investment—namely the air pollution control centre and a core of engineering development—was also to be secured.

Harold Musgrove met with the staff at Abingdon and assured them that the entire site would be retained. MG's famous A-building would house the proposed CKD operation, 470 staff being transferred there from Cowley, where space was needed for the Honda-Rover joint project known as Bounty. This would have been a busy section, packing some 150,000 vehicle kits per annum for export all over the world. The B-building was to have contained the specialized build unit, thus taking advantage of the experience already gained by assembling the Vanden Plas 1500 (Allegro). This section would have employed 380 of the existing MG staff. The C-building would have continued to contain Special Tuning and the engineering section. Future work for the B-building would include performance derivatives of the Mini, Metro, Princess and the, as yet secret, LC10 (Maestro/Montego). Musgrove concluded that 'in the light of any developments emerging (from the talks with the Aston Martin consortium), then the situation would be reviewed accordingly.' Unfortunately, as the Aston Martin proposal matured, BL evidently lost patience and abandoned these plans, looking elsewhere for facilities.

The Competitions Department resurfaced, under director John Davenport, at nearby Cowley, and most of the Bounty development

---

THE ASTON MARTIN MGB

The negotiations between British Leyland and John Symonds, managing director of Aston Martin, had been going on for several months when Keith Martin suddenly got the call to start work on the Aston Martin MGB facelift proposal: 'My first direct involvement was on 19 June, 1980, when I was put in charge of the facelift project and given six days to do it; life at Aston Martin was never dull!'

At the time, Keith Martin was in charge of engineering the remarkable, but at that stage still secret, William Towns designed Aston Martin Bulldog project. He recalls that a standard MGB roadster (registered DOL 341V) was wheeled into the company's special projects workshop, whereupon he began work on it, aided by Steve Hallam as engineer (later to become a leading race engineer with the Lotus Formula One team), two fitters, two sheet-metal workers and two trimmers: 'Our skilled sheet-metal workers were set loose on it, while I rushed around chasing and collecting bits and pieces from all over the place, including the Abingdon assembly plant and the Pressed Steel Fisher Plant at Cowley.' Keith suspects that John Symonds' former position, as head of the Pressed Steel Fisher plant, may have helped to smooth things along in this regard.

The object of the exercise was to create a cosmetic facelift, as there was insufficient time in six days to engineer a proper conversion. Nevertheless, the team had been given some guidelines, so they set to work, involving a great

deal of overtime! 'All we had to work from,' says Keith Martin, 'were some styling sketches done by William Towns, in which he had changed the appearances of the front end, rear end, seats and had raised the height of the windscreen, side windows and hood.' Subsequently, it became apparent that the alterations, particularly those affecting the bumpers and the height of the windscreen, drew heavily upon the recommendations of an internal British Leyland proposal which, in turn, was related to the proposals put forward by J. Bruce McWilliams of BL's North American offshoot. It is clear that Towns was given very little leeway in this interim proposal, but his ideas for a rebodied MGB were far more radical.

Seven days after the work began, the finished article, resplendent in BL Silver Sand, was wheeled out for the press, and Keith returned to what he describes as the 'relative calm' of the Bulldog project. When the Aston Martin proposal to take over MG production eventually collapsed, the silver prototype was stored away under a dust sheet, where it remained for three years until it was sold off. Since restored, and modified as necessary to make it road legal, DOL 341V is now in the hands of an MG enthusiast.

The finished Aston Martin MGB prototype. It was finished in metallic Silver Sand paint, offset by white Wolfrace finned alloy wheels. By the time that this photograph was taken, the car had been modified to make it roadworthy: a neat fuel filler flap had been added to the offside rear wing, as originally there had been no fuel filler cap! Note the black plastic mouldings over the lower portions of the door and wings. (Aston Martin)

THE ASTON MARTIN/BL AGREEMENT

The text of the agreement made on Sunday, 31 March, 1980, between BL and Aston Martin Lagonda, read thus:

'After close and cordial discussion between BL and the Consortium headed by Aston Martin Lagonda Ltd, the two groups today reached agreement in principle for the sale to the Consortium of the MG plant at Abingdon together with a world-wide exclusive licence for the use of the MG marque. The discussions were based on an offer made by BL on March 7th. The two groups agreed to co-operate fully in implementing this agreement. In the light of this, both parties look forward to completing the agreement and thereby providing for continuity of production and employment at Abingdon.'

The deal was worth about £30 million and, according to Alan Curtis, some £7 million of this was the value ascribed to the factory, which was, to his mind, 'a good deal, even in real-estate terms alone!'

work was transferred there, too. Interestingly, some MG personnel contributed to the Bounty project during their final months at Abingdon. Under Don Hayter's direction, MG's chief body engineer, Jim O'Neill, and his assistants, Denis Williams and Des Jones, together with Jim's chassis counterpart, Terry Mitchell, and his colleagues, Barry Jackson and Bob Staniland, were subsequently engaged on the task of translating the Honda drawings into BL format. Their thoughts about the fact that the new car would be badged as the Triumph Acclaim need no explanation...

A deal is announced

Five months into negotiations, it seemed increasingly likely to most observers that the Aston Martin bid would collapse, yet on 1 April, 1980, a deal was finally announced. The protracted negotiations came to a head in a five-hour meeting with Sir Michael Edwardes,

at the end of March, when an agreement was thrashed out at last. Under the terms of this deal, BL would continue to supply the components needed to build the MGB, while Aston Martin would be allowed to buy the Abingdon factory and would be granted a licence to use the MG name.

However, the path to securing this agreement was not an easy one. Aston Martin itself was experiencing some difficulty, since high interest rates in the UK and USA, and the strong pound sterling, were wreaking havoc with all luxury car sales. The same monetary forces made it all the more difficult for the consortium to guarantee the capital required from a nervous city and increasingly reluctant backers, some of whom were also beginning to suffer problems of their own. By mid-summer, BL announced that the Abingdon factory was losing them an incredible £0.4 million per week—a figure regarded by many as the same sort of alleged 'creative accounting' that had produced the much publicized 'loss' of £900 per MGB. Then, in June 1980, Aston Martin decided to provide concrete proof of the consortium's intentions by unveiling the proposed facelift for the MGB for the 1981 model year.

Hopes fade

Nevertheless, it was clear that BL were losing patience. Within a month, it was all over: Aston Martin Lagonda found that nearly half of the British money—to the tune of £12 million—was no longer available. The consortium told BL that they could not raise the capital unless given a stay of execution, during which they hoped to persuade Japanese and Arab backers to replace the missing funds. By this time, Toyota had dropped out of the equation, and Lord George-Brown's Hong Kong source, according to one insider, was thought to be 'not very stable'.

The day after Curtis broke the news, much to his surprise, BL

Bruce McWilliams' offering for the MG Boxer styling contest was this metallic bronze car, which featured Porsche 928 pop-up headlamps, a peculiar MG grille, Rover SD1 tail-lamps and horizontal-line dashboard instrument graphics, which would appear later on the Metro. (Rover)

announced that they would be disposing of the Abingdon factory elsewhere, as they felt that the necessary funds would not become available. William Pratt-Thompson, the head of BL International, offered a glimmer of hope, however, by stating, 'BL has told the consortium that should it succeed in raising the necessary finance, we will be fully prepared to reopen discussions.' Alan Curtis told the press that he was flying out to Tokyo in a last-ditch effort to obtain the necessary funds, but the potential Japanese backers got cold feet and backed out. Before long, it became apparent that the rescue bid was not going to succeed, so a sad saga, which initially had seemed to offer so much hope, came to an end.

A few days later, BL announced that the MG factory, which they no longer planned to use, would be sold off, and that it would be closed for good on Friday, 24 October, 1980, the last cars going down the assembly line on the previous day. In his autobiography, *Back From the Brink*, Sir Michael Edwardes refers to the Aston Martin Lagonda bid with obvious frustration at what he clearly felt had been wasted effort on both sides: 'I have no reason to suspect that (Curtis') approach was other than a genuine and concerned attempt to save the MG name, but it certainly turned out to be a long running and indeed highly damaging episode, which we suspected from the start would come to nought and which in the end did come to nought.' Surely no one, however, could have doubted Alan Curtis' good intentions and sincere desire to save the MG name and factory from an undeserved fate.

Undoubtedly, the saddest outcome of the failure of the Aston Martin bid was the disbanding of the proud, loyal MG work-force and the closure of the MG factory itself. Although far less grand than the manufacture of sports cars, BL's original plans for Abingdon, after MG production had ceased, would have kept the fabric of the factory intact and allowed some of the 1030-strong work-force (930 of whom worked on MGs) to have remained in employment. As it was, the majority of them were made redundant, while a lucky few were moved to Cowley, in some cases, no doubt, carrying out the very work that they would have been employed to do at Abingdon if the Aston Martin bid had not arisen. Harold

The pop-up headlamps of the Leonia Boxer proposal certainly were distinctive. (courtesy J. Bruce McWilliams)

The rear of the Leonia car, showing the Rover SD1 tail-lamps, an alternative wheel design and, just visible, the red-striped instrument graphics. The MG badge (possibly of the type fitted to the grille of the 1970 model year MGB looks a little forlorn on the boot lid. (Rover)

Left *Triumph engineering's Triton Green offering was little better than the Leonia car, in common with which it had Rover SD1 tail-lamps. (courtesy Norman Rose)*

Below *Yet another offering for the MG Boxer. At least this version avoided any attempt to feature some form of MG grille. (Rover)*

Bottom *Close examination of the rear of the boot lid of the silver car reveals 'MG D' badging. There is still no disguising the Triumph TR7 origins of the car, however: that side crease in particular is a dead give-away. (Rover)*

The nose of a car mocked up as a Triumph TR7A featured another MG idea: in fact, those slots are simply strips of black paper. (Rover)

Musgrove points out that, as a result of plans to use the MG factory being dropped, the company had to spend a great deal of money on building a CKD unit at Cowley.

The fate of Abingdon may have been sealed, along with that of the MGB, but some minor crumbs of comfort were offered to the saddened and demoralized MG enthusiasts. BL announced that they would be retaining the MG name and, no doubt stung by the reaction that the closure had engendered, they stated, 'The MG marque is a valuable asset. We have every intention of keeping it alive.' However, even these plans were short-lived, and were soon overtaken by other, perhaps even more controversial, ideas, as will be revealed in Chapter 6.

The MG Boxer project—desperate times...

With the announcement that the MG factory was to close, there was a scramble to investigate a low-cost means of keeping the marque alive in the all-important US market. Not least was the need to pacify the US dealer network, which understandably had been so vociferous in its objection to such a large chunk of its 'bread and butter' sales being removed. The obvious solution, which had already been considered some years previously, was to use the Triumph TR7 as the basis for an MG. It was hope that this would not only secure MG sales, but also the future of the Solihull plant, which was due to take over manufacture of the Triumph sports cars.

By creating this new MG, it was reasoned that the production of TR7-based sports cars could be maintained at around 50,000 per annum for their principal market. While this would be significantly less than the combined sales of the TR7 and MGB (of the order of 60,000 per annum, of which around 35,000 were MGBs), nevertheless it would have been better than the alternative. Whereas previous suggestions that MG and Triumph should be rationalized had come to nothing, partially because MG and Triumph were tied to different parts of the BL framework, the addition of MG to the Jaguar-Rover-Triumph portfolio, in 1978, had made such matters much easier to contemplate and, of course, the end of the MGB made a decision all the more urgent.

With hindsight, J. Bruce McWilliams is thankful that the proposed idea did not succeed: 'It was a totally ill conceived plan, operating on the notion that you could sell TR7s to MG buyers if you called the car an MG. Still, from my viewpoint, it was an interesting opportunity to see to what extent a different model could be derived from only two panel changes, and a tooling bill of no more than a million pounds.' Furthermore, the manufacturing cost of the car was to be no more than £50 greater than that of the TR7, and the lead time to launch was not to exceed 11 months—in other words, the car had to be ready for the 1981 model year. The project was code-named Boxer, and a number of proposals were called for.

McWilliams admits that the Triumph TR7 was 'a particularly challenging starting point.'

...desperate measures

Having been started shortly before Christmas in 1979, the Leonia prototype was finished in four or five weeks, using a TR8 as its basis. Early in the New Year, it was flown to the UK to be shown alongside the various competing concepts. McWilliams' proposal, dubbed the MG Touring, involved the substitution of Porsche 928-style pop-up headlight units for the standard TR7 concealed lamps; a rather strange MG grille, which occupied the central portion of the nose panel; the substitution of Rover SD1 tail-lights for the ugly TR7 units; and a choice of wheels (including the ubiquitous MGB-style Rostyle steel wheels). Inside, there was a retrimmed interior and a new sporty steering wheel, while the folding hood was of high-grade mohair. Prophetically, the dashboard instrument display was reworked with horizontal graphic lines, a feature that would re-emerge on the MG Metro two years later.

Almost from a sense of embarrassment, it seems, at the reaction that BL foresaw from angry MG enthusiasts, it was decreed that the use of MG badges should be kept to a minimum, so they were only fitted discreetly to the front and rear of the car, on the steering-wheel boss and in the wheel centres. Whether or not anyone seriously thought that this would make any difference, no one can now recall, but at least it does demonstrate that BL appear to have realized the fury that they had unleashed by killing the MGB.

The other participants in the competition were Triumph Engineering (whose proposal bore a resemblance to the Leonia car, with the exception of the grille treatment and the use of Wolfrace alloy wheels), BL Styling Services (under David Bache), the Michelotti studios (Edgardo Michelotti, son of founder Giovanni), Bob Jaenkel of Panther Westwinds, and Cars and Concepts.

Following the management viewing, it was decided to pursue Leonia's MG Touring proposal, so full-scale costing and procurement research exercises were instigated. Bruce McWilliams recalls that 'Jeff Herbert, then head of Rover-Triumph, was given the job of pulling together the feasibility, which he did, and the tooling bill came out within the million pound ceiling. But then, sales forecasts for the car were, understandably, gloomy, and that was the end of this bizarre excursion in product planning.'

By then, of course, the future of the whole Triumph sports car family lay in the balance. The fate of the MG Boxer was summed up by the late Tony Hogg, of *Road & Track*, who said, 'They were undoubtedly right (to cancel it) because if you have a name like MG that has magic and mystique to it, you cannot abuse that name and misrepresent it. In fact, there is considerable truth in the old saying that you can't make a silk purse out of a sow's ear.'

6 The 1980s

Although the take-over bid by the Aston Martin led consortium had foundered by July 1980, efforts to keep the MG marque alive by some other means continued for a short time. March 1980 saw the launch of the Triumph TR7 convertible, five years after the original TR7 had been introduced, and the open car was received with general acclaim, the soft top going a long way towards ameliorating the rather awkward lines of the coupé. However, all was not well at BL Cars, and serious financial difficulties were causing the company to reign in its operations still further, with more labour cut-backs and plant closures. In April 1980, the TR7 began to be built at the Rover SD1 factory in Solihull, its third and final home; production was overlapped with Canley for five months as the old Standard Triumph production lines were run down.

The first year of the new decade was an ignominious period for British sports cars: the last MG left the hallowed portals of Abingdon in October 1980, while less publicized, but also significant, was the fact that the Triumph Spitfire also came to the end of the road, having outlasted its Midget rival by two years. In an effort to capitalize on the emotions surrounding the end of MG production, the company (by now MG was back with Austin and Morris, but under the LMC umbrella) had decided to produce a final limited edition of the MGB roadster and MGB GT for the home market (a different limited-edition MGB roadster had been available in North America since April 1979).

The MGB LE and MGB GT LE were announced on 26 January, 1981, and the advertising made great play of the fact that previous MG sports cars had proved to be such sound investments, clearly implying that these special models would prove similarly valuable in years to come. Apart from some differently coloured badges and special decals, however, there was little to distinguish the LE from the standard MGB, other than the paint colours, which were borrowed from the contemporary Austin-Morris range: Pewter metallic (MGB GT LE) and Bronze metallic (MGB LE) were more commonly seen on the Austin Princess. Even the much touted wheels (alloy on the GT; alloy or wire on the roadster) were not particularly unique: the Triumph Stag-style GKN alloy wheels, offered as standard on the MGB GT LE, were basically the same as the alloy wheels that had been optional on the MGB range since 1978.

By the spring of 1981, BL's exports were in serious difficulties. The policies of the British Conservative government, and the successful exploitation of North Sea oil, meant that the pound sterling continued to soar against the dollar on the international exchanges. Although this was good news for the country's cash reserves and financial institutions, it caused ever more serious problems for exporters, especially those British manufacturers selling into the USA. By May, BL were claiming that Jaguar was losing something like £2 million per month, a fact compounded, no doubt, by the cost of running the entire Leonia operation without the benefit of a new MG sports car and, by then, the disastrous sales figures of the TR7.

Within a matter of days, the matter came to a head: BL announced that the flagship Rover SD1 factory at Solihull, built on a green-field site in the previous decade, would be closed, and that Rover SD1 production would be transferred to the former Morris plant at Cowley. Triumph sports car production—the TR7 and recently launched TR8—would not be following the Rover to Cowley: the small BL sports car was, for the time being, well and

The very last MGB bodyshell at Stratton St Margaret on 2 October, 1980. Who would have thought, at the time, that MGB bodyshells would one day roll out of another factory only 14 miles (22.53km) down the road? (Rover)

The end of the line for the Abingdon-built MGB came with the Limited Edition or LE model of January 1981, shown here in bronze metallic roadster form (a pewter metallic GT with alloy wheels was also available). Other distinguishing features included red backgrounds to the MG badges, adhesive side stripes and a special plastic spoiler attached to the front valance. Note the fog lamp (there was one on each side)

suspended below the rear bumper, which was mandatory on UK cars from January 1980. These were made of a poor grade of plastic that tended to craze, crack and ultimately fall off should petrol, spilt when filling the tank, run down behind the bumper and dribble on to the lamp. This lack of forethought seemed typical of much of the industry during the strife-torn 1970s. (Rover/BMIHT)

truly dead. Perhaps the end of the TR7 had become inevitable, once the MGB had gone: sales of the MGB had usually exceeded those of the Triumph in the USA, but the combined sales of the two had, to a degree, helped justify the continuation of both, particularly where North America was concerned. The fact that typical US warranty costs for the MGB and TR7 had been £150 and £258 per car, at the close of the previous decade, may also have been a factor.

With this action, which took effect in October 1981, BL drastically cut the range of its products on sale in the USA and had to fall back on the Jaguar range. Within a year, many of the long serving people at Leonia had left, including vice president J. Bruce McWilliams. The creative talents of McWilliams soon resurfaced, however, in his own consultancy—Galamander Ltd—which

became involved in promoting, among other things, the structural design of the aluminium-bodied Ferrari 408 ASVT prototype and the initial Jaguar XJ220 proposal.

In the end, neither the short-lived Boxer nor the Broadside projects had succeeded in saving the TR7. The series of upheavals in BL, which had seen a succession of managers trying to wrestle with the problems, led to the Broadside project being on and off with some frequency, until it was finally buried with the rest of the Triumph sports car family by Sir Michael Edwardes as the painful march of rationalization swept on.

Ironically, the very last of these Triumph-MG exercises were perhaps the most promising: the targa-topped silver mock-up with colour co-ordinated, fared-in bumpers shown here (badged on one

The last US-specification MGB (a white car) on the line in October 1980. Geoff Allen still has that piece of card fixed to the windscreen. (Rover)

END OF THE ROAD FOR ROVER-TRIUMPH

In his book, *Back From the Brink*, Sir Michael Edwardes recognizes that when he split Leyland Cars into Austin-Morris and Jaguar-Rover-Triumph, in 1978, the problems of the former had blinded him to those of the latter. Jaguar was still largely an independent entity, but Rover and Triumph were linked by the shared components of the SD1 and TR7. Later that year, responsibility for the MG marque was moved from Austin-Morris to JRT. The problems of JRT largely stemmed from the fact that they were trying to operate with more than a modicum of independence, a luxury that the parent company could ill afford once the exchange rate began to soar in 1979. In January 1980, Rover-Triumph produced a product plan that makes interesting reading today:

December 1980	MGB run-out.
Spring 1981	TR7/8 removable hardtop with heated rear window; introduction of 'Boxer', a new model based upon the TR7 convertible with the objective of replacing the MGB initially in the US market.
Autumn 1981	2-litre O-series engine in TR7 and Boxer for the 1982 model year, with twin-carburettors.
Spring 1983	Model range replaced by Broadside.

Broadside was described, by that stage, as project RT061 and encompassed a proposed Triumph convertible and hardtop, and an MG-badged 2+2 GT. The product plan described it as 'a direct replacement for the TR7/8 model range and Boxer derivative. The vehicle will be based on the TR7/8 underbody (with longer wheelbase) and mechanicals, utilizing some new panels previously developed for the discontinued Lynx programme. Engines: 2.0-litre O-series and V8. Dependent upon Austin-Morris engine strategy, an opportunity exists to install a turbocharged version of O-series from the introduction of Broadside.'

The product plan also proposed the following further actions:

Autumn 1984	Broadside electronic facelift: instrument pack.
Autumn 1984	Rover Bravo four-door saloon to replace SD1, based on SD1 centre section and TR7 front suspension, and SD1/Lynx back axle; 2-litre O-series, 2.6-litre six-cylinder, and four-cylinder turbo-diesel.
Autumn 1985	Rover Bravo five-door hatch or wagon, with V8 engine, too.
Autumn 1987	Run-out Broadside, dependent on the future opportunity of developing a new sports car in collaboration with Honda, together with a successful launch.

In July 1980, following a top-level management meeting at the Compleat Angler Hotel in Marlow, the company was restructured again, with Light Medium Cars taking in the Austin, Morris, Rover and Triumph marques. Dominant in the new LMC structure were the Austin-Morris people; the old Rover-Triumph set-up effectively ceased to exist, and its forward programme was swept away. At the same time, it was decided that the Honda Bounty project—negotiated by Austin-Morris, but poached by Rover-Triumph as a Dolomite replacement for the Canley plant—would still be called the Triumph Acclaim. However, it would be built at the old Morris plant at Cowley. Thus, the Acclaim became the last Triumph car to be built.

Left *Towards the end of the TR7/8 family's life—and near the end of David Bache's tenure as British Leyland's design director—the Rover-Triumph studio produced this tidied-up TR7/8 proposal, featuring rear lamps similar to (but not the same as) those of the Rover SD1, and restyled colour co-ordinated bumpers. Note that this mock-up features a '2000' badge on the nearside front wing, but a 'TR8' badge on the offside of the boot lid. The car displayed different treatments for TR7 and TR8 on each side. (Rover)*

Right *This attractive proposal was the last iteration of the Broadside project; note the Triumph Lynx front wings and doors. This silver targa-roofed prototype was badged as a Triumph on the offside and as an MG on the nearside. It featured colour co-ordinated bumpers and Rover SD1 door handles. Although the photographs are undated, they are numbered and sequentially are later than the TR7/8 facelift shown above. The car is probably one of the last Rover-Triumph projects, RT061, which dates from the beginning of 1980. By the summer, Rover-Triumph was no more, and Broadside slipped into oblivion. (Rover)*

side as an MG, and on the other as a Triumph) was certainly the best looking. But it was not to be. Who is to say that a period of greater exchange-rate stability might not have seen a turn around in the fortunes of the British sports car?

Birth of the Metro: a replacement for the Mini

For the first few years after the launch of the original Mini, in 1959, little serious effort appears to have been directed towards planning a successor. Various derivatives were tried, including a number of abortive sports cars. In 1968, Sir Alec Issigonis produced his own 9X proposal for a new Mini, but with the abandonment of that innovative design, there was another hiatus until the early 1970s. In the spring of 1972, what would become ADO74 began to get under way. This was a proposal for a significantly larger, all-new Mini replacement, complete with a brand-new engine family (called the K-series, but owing nothing to the much later engine of the same name). Initially, there were three proposals, code-named Dragonfly, Ladybird and Ant, but these were soon whittled down to a single style that was slightly smaller than the Allegro.

Even before the shake-up of 1974, which accompanied the nationalization of British Leyland, ADO74 fell from favour, as the fuel crisis of the previous autumn had caused all car manufacturers to refocus their efforts on to smaller, more economical cars. Suddenly, the idea of a Mini replacement that was significantly larger and heavier than the original seemed unwise, so a new programme, ADO88, was set up.

ADO88 took shape at Longbridge, a number of styling themes being pursued by Harris Mann and his team. By 1977, a style had been chosen, and a series of styling clinics were held throughout Europe. The results of these clinics were shocking: ADO88 failed to find much support, ranking below the competition from Peugeot (104), Renault (5) and Ford (Fiesta). By the end of the year, just as Michael Edwardes arrived, there were serious worries about the sales prospects of a car that had already consumed vast amounts of money, and for which capital was committed. A crash programme

was initiated in January 1978 to tackle the main criticisms of the car and, accordingly, ADO88 became LC8, falling into the Leyland Cars numbering system already adopted for the LC10 medium-size car. Such were the pressures and demands thrust upon the British Leyland engineers, planners and designers that, out of sheer necessity, work on LC10 was slowed, delaying its launch.

The Metro launch—'A Great British Car'

The Metro—or Austin Mini Metro, to use its correct title at the time—was launched on 8 October, 1980, just over two weeks before the last MGB rolled out of the Abingdon factory. The management at Abingdon had been told to close the plant with the minimum of ceremony to avoid overshadowing the launch of BL's great white hope—a sad contrast to the marvellous celebrations of a year earlier, and a tragic end to such a glorious history. It must be recognized, however, that the success or otherwise of the Metro would have an enormous bearing on the fortunes of BL and its successors, so the pressure for a trouble-free launch was immense.

One of those who is justifiably proud of the Metro is former Austin Rover chairman Harold Musgrove: 'I was brought into cars from Leyland Trucks to ensure the successful launch of the Metro,' he recalls, 'and this must have been one of the most successful ever.' The Metro was built using an unprecedented amount of automatic machinery, to the extent that the Longbridge production facility became a place of pilgrimage for those who wanted to see what had been achieved. This was one of the keys to its very high profitability, something almost unheard of at BL for many years. Harold Musgrove points out that production soon reached over 5000 units per week: '...and each Metro had only 32 direct man-hours in it; it was a very profitable car for us.'

Musgrove is also very keen to emphasize that the Metro was a make-or-break car for the company: 'We didn't have any new

Moving towards the definitive ADO88 style, this is a utilitarian offering from the Canley studios. (Rover)

From quite early in the ADO88 programme, the idea of a separate instrument binnacle was being considered, which is hardly surprising, given design chief David Bache's enthusiasm for such a feature. This sketch, dated 28 August, 1975, is by John Gregory, who was responsible for the styling of the final home-market MGB dashboard. (Rover)

engines to offer, and we badly needed a new car. It really was a case of "back from the brink," as Sir Michael Edwardes said. I remember saying to Ray Horrocks that we would make less losses if we simply sent people home and paid them for staying there—our losses at the end of the seventies actually exceeded our wage bill!' To overcome this problem, he says, BL became much tougher with component manufacturers: 'Metro sorted out the suppliers: we had a black-list, and we even fined suppliers before the launch, but we were ruthless in order to get quality up and prices down. Strikes at the suppliers could have led to them going out of business, as we would switch to another supplier. Word soon gets around; this is largely why profits went up; much of this we learnt from Honda.'

When the Metro was being planned, inevitably, consideration had been given to a high-performance derivative; most rival manufacturers had taken a leaf from Volkswagen's book and produced 'hot' versions of their small hatchbacks (they may have also derived inspiration from the seminal Mini Cooper). Prior to the announcement of MG's demise, it was thought likely that the hot Metro would be badged as a Cooper, to rekindle the enthusiasm generated by the Mini Cooper of 1961-71. Indeed, a Cooper-badged version was proposed to BL by John Cooper, and eventually appeared, equipped with twin SU carburettors, as an after-market conversion called the Metro Monaco soon after the car's launch. However, Austin Rover considered the MG name to be

stronger and, in the light of the public outcry that ensued after the closure of Abingdon, the company decided to revive the MG badge for the Metro. Sir Michael Edwardes told me that there was another reason for this decision, too: 'We branded it (the sporting Metro) as an MG in order to keep the brand alive for a future sports car.' Even so, he admits that there were no serious sports car proposals at that stage.

The MG Metro appears

In November 1981, the then chairman (now president) of the MG Car Club, Bill Wallis, and the MG Owners' Club secretary, Roche Bentley, were invited by BL to drive a pre-production prototype of the MG Metro. At that time, according to Wallis, it was not even certain that the car would be launched. Steve Schlemmer, of the product planning department, who would play an instrumental role in the development of the MG RV8, was their host. He sought the views of the club representatives, who both pronounced themselves favourably impressed: Bill even placed an order for an MG Metro just days after his secret test session, becoming one of the first people to own one when it was launched in May 1982.

In fact, the MG Metro was developed in tandem with a luxury Vanden Plas version, which used the same basic engine, but had a slightly less sporting exhaust and, of course, the inevitable walnut trim. Once they had a chance to drive it, the press generally eulo-

A styling drawing showing the final appearance of the LC8 Metro. At this stage, while high-performance versions were being considered, the idea of using an MG badge had not been considered seriously. (Rover)

The 1982 MG Metro.

gized the MG Metro, few recalling the scorn that some of them had heaped upon the notion of an MG badge on such a car only a few months earlier, although they questioned the retention of a four-speed gearbox when five speeds had become the norm. However, the MG Metro itself was only the beginning as far as Austin Rover was concerned: even more MGs were about to emerge.

The MG Metro Turbo

At the time of the MG Metro launch, it was something of an open secret that an even more exciting derivative was waiting in the wings. The abandonment, for the time being, of any replacement for the venerable A-series engine, and the adoption of the Mini's 'transmission in the sump' layout for the Metro, meant that any performance derivatives would have to be based upon the A-series unit, which was already at the practical limit of its capacity. However, it is a strong engine with good torque characteristics—even at lower compression ratios—so it was not long before turbocharging was seen as the most cost-effective answer to the quest for more power.

Lotus engineers were brought in to help with development of the turbo Metro. Roger Parker, involved in vehicle testing for the police at the time, remembers being overtaken by a prototype Metro Turbo at the MIRA test circuit, while he was driving a very well set-up police Rover 2600 SD1 (which offered performance

equivalent to a contemporary 3500 version): 'Out on the track, we were running a maximum of 130mph (209.21km/h) indicated speeds, yet we couldn't make an impression on this matt black Metro, which maintained a half-lap head start.'

Production Metro Turbos were tamer than this, however, as it was found that too much power led to dramatic gearbox failures. Even the standard MG Metro Turbo could, apparently, have a scrap gearbox after only 30,000 miles (48,279km) if 90 per cent of the power was used constantly. Roger Parker reports that rolling-road testing of Metro Turbos indicated typical power at the wheels of between 80 and 85bhp (59.66 and 63.38kW), whereas standard MG Metros generated 48-58bhp (35.79-43.25kW). Clearly, the Turbo version was considerably more highly strung.

The Maestro and Montego

By the latter half of the 1970s, it was obvious that Austin-Morris desperately needed replacements for the ageing Morris Marina, Austin Allegro and Austin Maxi ranges. The problem was that the entire range of volume produced cars was in a parlous state, in part a legacy of the poverty trap that had led BMC to merge with Leyland during the previous decade. Work had proceeded on the Mini replacement—ADO88 and its later LC8 offshoot—but less emphasis had been placed upon the more profitable mid-range cars.

Soon after he took charge of BL, in November 1977, Michael

The Computervision Metro Turbo raced with a 200bhp (149.14kW) version of the A-series engine under the bonnet. (courtesy David Sims)

Edwardes expressed doubts about the priorities that had been decided before his arrival: he felt, understandably, that efforts should really have been concentrated on the products that would have brought higher returns—in other words, mid-range cars—rather than a replacement for the Mini. Unfortunately, very little could be done at that late stage in the programme: the intended mid-range replacement for the Allegro, Marina and Maxi was a much more expensive project, which was further from production than the Mini replacement, and it would have been impossible simply to switch from one to the other without seriously delaying both badly needed new products.

However, with the lead-in to the launch of the LC8 Metro well under way, work on the LC10 family at Longbridge gained momentum, together with an extensive overhaul programme for the E-series engine. In time honoured BMC/BL fashion, it was decided that the cars should offer outstanding space and value for their sector, and to that end, the size of the smaller derivative—the LM10 hatchback—was deliberately placed between the Ford Escort and Cortina. In many ways, this was an admirable objective, but it was dangerously reminiscent of the ADO17 'Landcrab' of 20 years previously, which had proved to be exceptionally roomy at the expense of its looks, an important consideration in the market sector at which it was aimed.

Under design director David Bache were three heads of design: Norman Morris was in charge of the exterior styling and engineering feasibility; Graham Lewis was in charge of colour and trim; and Gordon Sked oversaw interior design. Norman Morris recalls that Ian Beech's original proposal was more rounded than the finished result, 'but the management asked us to make it squarer, and so the familiar Maestro shape evolved.' Other details of the original style were also distorted out of engineering necessity: 'The original wheel-arch "eyebrows" were far less pronounced, but it was found that there were problems in finding a narrow enough gearbox, and so the wheel arches had to be flared outwards to cover the wheels.'

With the design for LM10 finalized, Norman Morris, Ian Beech and product planner Malcolm Harbour flew to the USA to visit Visioneering in Detroit, where the drawings were transformed into full-size wooden patterns. Sub-contracting the work in this way was engineering director Joe Farnham's idea, according to Harbour, due to the pressure of work at Austin-Morris on LC8, which required most of the company's engineering resources. Morris remembers being impressed by Visioneering's optical system, which was able to follow the drawings and cut straight into the wooden blocks, after which they were carved by hand to the pattern of the inscribed cuts, allowing a master pattern to be formed quickly: 'The Metro had been the world's first fully computer surfaced car, and the Maestro was, in all probability, the second.'

The original, highly ambitious plan for the LC10 family had called for a completely new engine and gearbox. The latter was described as the T-series or, more accurately, the LT80 gearbox (LT standing for Leyland Transmission; the Rover SD1/TR7 gearbox was LT77). The size of the O-series engine had been determined by its B-series roots, and it had not been designed to be used transversely with an in-line (or end-on) gearbox, so the LT80 had to be a compact unit if it was to fit sensibly in the engine bay of a mid-size car. In 1978, cost considerations led the company to consider buying in a unit from outside—quite a bold change of philosophy at the time—and they soon settled on the Volkswagen unit, which was fitted in four- and five-speed versions to the highly successful VW Golf hatchback.

Harold Musgrove, who later would be responsible for overseeing the launch of the LC10 family, was horrified when he discovered that the only engine planned for the launch was the A-series, with the O-series destined to follow: 'Then someone pointed out that we still had the E-series being produced at Cofton Hackett—the future of this engine having been more or less written off—and so we quickly decided to see if we could do something to improve it as a mid-range engine for LC10.' Thus, it was decided to fit the LC10 with the A-series and a development of the E-series unit, introduction of the O-series being deferred until later.

From early on, it was planned that, as a general rule, future Austins would comprise six basic variants: City (cheap and cheer-

THE LC10 FAMILY

In the mid-1970s, the last of the famous ADO codes to be issued—ADO99—was assigned to the vehicle that originally was intended to replace only the front-wheel-drive Allegro and Maxi. One of the engineers who became involved in its design was ex-Abingdon man Roy Brocklehurst, who worked on the project with Charles Griffin. It has been suggested that '99' stood for the length of the wheelbase, but since ADO99 followed in a direct sequence from ADO77 and ADO88, this may be a simple coincidence. Work proceeded on this project, but without a great deal of impetus, until the cancellation of TM1 made it all the more crucial.

Malcolm Harbour recalls that, with the cancellation of TM1, Gordon Bashford and 'Spen' King started sketching schemes for a simple, well-packaged, coil-sprung, front-wheel-drive car with an in-line gearbox mounted on the end of a transverse engine, rather than under it in the classic Issigonis manner of the Mini, Maxi and 1800. Harbour became involved in this project—called LC10 (LC standing for Leyland Cars) almost from the outset—in 1975: 'It was decided that we should stretch the concept from a five-door hatchback to include a four-door saloon with a boot, the latter initially envisaged to be very similar in style to the five-door. This was an ambitious project, which took in all-new engines and transmissions, too. Then, by 1976, it was felt that the four-door should be a bit more up-market, and so it gained a longer front end, too.'

Indeed, the plans for LC10 were quite grand: in 1976, it was envisaged that there would be three-, four- and five-door versions, together with a van and estate, which would be built at Longbridge and Cowley, as well as the company's Seneffe plant in Belgium. During early 1976, clinic assessments were carried out, using photographs of models, and by the end of the year, full-size models were being clinicked in Europe. Initially, several body styles evolved, but eventually they were whittled down to two, produced by Longbridge's Harris Mann and Solihulls' Ian Beech. Mann's offering was a fairly sleek, if conventional, car with overtones of the Mark II Vauxhall Cavalier, but the Beech version was a more upright, 'glassy' car, which

formed the basis of the style that eventually was chosen by Austin-Morris management for production in 1978.

On the engineering front, LC10 was developed with MacPherson-strut suspension, which was already utilized by the majority of its rivals; there were no serious thoughts of using Hydragas at this stage. The project soon embraced a family of derivatives: LM10, which went on to become the Maestro, and LM11, which became the Montego. The 1979-83 corporate product plan included a suggested forward strategy for 1984 and beyond, which proposed an LC10 coupé (possibly LM12, although not described as such), to be launched in the autumn of 1984. This was described as 'a three-door coupé based upon LC10 floor with 1.3-, 1.7- and 2.0-litre engines, and adequate styling to sustain a premium price. Possible use of the MG name.' This would have been followed by a facelift of the whole range in the autumn of 1986. The engines comprised A- and O-series units, the latter following on from the former; at this stage, neither the E-series nor the later R-series, which would be derived from it, were part of the picture.

Two different platforms were envisaged: one for the conventional 'three-box' saloon, and a 2.3in (5.84cm) shorter derivative for the hatchback version. Denis Chick, who was involved in product planning at the time, recalls that, before long, the options were narrowed down to four-door saloon, five-door hatchback and estate derivatives, 'but the volume potential for the three-door just wasn't there.' Together with thoughts of a coupé, therefore, the three-door was abandoned.

As time passed, and detailed plans for the next stages in the company's recovery emerged, two other code-numbers were added (as LM12 had been dropped): LM14 and LM15 were intended to be larger derivatives above the Montego, which would have replaced the Princess and Rover SD1. In the 1983 corporate plan, LM16 was put forward as a 'high-style sports, upper-medium sector fastback, based upon LM11, for launch in spring 1986', while LM17 was a related exercise, and LM19 became the Austin Ambassador. Eventually, the various joint projects with Honda put an end to the majority of these derivatives, most of which never got much further than paper exercises. But this is jumping ahead of the main story...

ful), HL, HLS, Vanden Plas (luxury), HPD (high-performance derivative), and VHPD (very-high-performance derivative). This policy was broadly followed with the Metro, Maestro and Montego ranges, the HPD variants carrying MG badges, and the VHPD versions becoming MG Turbos. It will be apparent that, whereas the Metro and Montego ranges received their VHPD derivatives early on, the Maestro very nearly missed out.

Initial plans for the Maestro called for the HPD version to be launched after the rest of the range, but as late as September 1982, it seems that the decision was made to badge the performance Maestro as an MG and launch it simultaneously with the Austin versions. Roger Parker learned that this shrunk the MG Maestro development time by about six months, and much engine testing was carried out on German autobahns. As Parker suggests, the latter may explain why the original MG Maestro exhibited fine top-end performance, but poor behaviour in traffic, particularly during hot weather.

Launching 'The miracle Maestro'

The LM10 Maestro range was finally unveiled to the public in March 1983, under the dubious epithet of 'The Miracle Maestro', but not without some last-minute hitches, as Ian Elliott vividly remembers: 'I was involved in the launch advertising, which included a television commercial. Filming was well under way when someone in senior management saw one of the MG Maestros and noticed that the dashboard graphics were exactly the same as the Vanden Plas Maestro—in other words, without the red lines which had been adopted for the MG Metro. The manager was insistent that the MG Maestro dash be changed, and so an order went out to the Lucas/Smith joint company to revise the specification for the MG models and to produce one double-quick for the advertisement. We incurred an additional cost of £40,000 for the reshoot required as a result.'

Although, the MG Maestro had not been part of the original launch plan, once reception of the MG Metro had been gauged, it was decided to try to repeat the exercise with the Maestro. Initial development had proceeded on a twin-SU-carburettor version of the new 1598cc R-series engine. However, judged by the performance of its peers, it soon became apparent that with such equipment the Maestro would fall well short of the mark, so more drastic action was called for. Harold Musgrove was determined that the MG Maestro would at least be on a par with the bench-mark 1.6-litre Ford Escort XR3, so it was decided to adopt a pair of twin-choke Weber 40DCNF carburettors. With the exception of the Strombergs of the late US-market MGBs, this was the first time in many years that a non-SU carburettor had been used for an MG of any description; it was all the more unusual given the family ties with the SU carburettor outfit.

As a further indication of the late stage at which this change took place, the MG version was the only Maestro not to feature the new Austin Rover electronic management system which, on lesser versions, controlled various functions such as the automatic choke and electronic idling control. This may have been a blessing in disguise, however, since in practice, the early Austin Rover electronic carburettors did not cover themselves in glory. The twin-Weber set-up provided the MG Maestro 1600 with a healthy set of performance figures: the engine produced 103bhp (76.81kW) DIN at 6000rpm, and maximum torque was 100lb/ft (148.82kg/m) at 4000rpm, giving a spirited top speed of 111mph (178.63km/h).

Unfortunately, the Weber installation was not without its problems, and the MG Maestro 1600 soon gained a notorious reputation for poor starting when the engine was hot, due to fuel vaporization. This could be particularly infuriating during, say, a shopping trip involving numerous short journeys. The problem was highlighted by *Motor* magazine, which published a number of scathing reports on the long-term test car they ran during 1983-84.

To set the MG Maestro apart from the Austin variants, Norman Morris and his team added a subtle black chin spoiler below the plastic, body-coloured front bumper. In addition, there was a distinctive black strake on each side of the tailgate, a feature shared with the economy 1.3 HLE Maestro. The MG Maestro also had an exclusive horizontal tailgate spoiler below the rear window. Alloy

wheels of an unusual finned, square-centred pattern were fitted as standard, with 180/65HR tyres.

One rather dubious benefit that the MG Maestro shared with the Vanden Plas version was an electronic 'talking' dashboard, which utilized the synthesized voice of Nicolette MacKenzie to warn of impending doom. This voice unit was manufactured in a variety of language versions by a company set up by Lucas and Smiths. At the time, much mirth was caused by the Italian version, which featured a male voice, the argument being that the average Italian man would not relish being told what to do in his car by a female!

Harold Musgrove certainly gave the impression of being proud of the Maestro, which was the type of car that was needed to lead Austin Rover back to profitability. Consequently, he was happy to defend the idea of applying the MG badge to a car that was somewhat removed from the sports cars with which the marque was more commonly associated. Musgrove told John Dugdale, in an interview for the Spring 1983 issue of the North American publication *MG Magazine*, 'In the first four months of 1983, we sold in France twice as many MGs as in any previous year since 1969.'

When I discussed this with Harold Musgrove, he laughed at the idea of being proud of the Maestro: 'It was a case of having to sell the car; I had decided that a new styling direction was needed as soon as I saw the car, but there was not much which could be done at that stage.' Musgrove's concerns further demonstrate why the MG Maestro was saddled with the task of lifting the image of the whole range, and show why—unlike the MG Metro—it was part of the original launch strategy, rather than being a later development.

At the meeting with John Dugdale, Harold Musgrove also said that the return of MG to North America formed part of Austin Rover's corporate plan. However, in subsequent discussions with the press, it soon became apparent that this return would not be with a sports car, so interim hopes were for some form of MG-badged sports saloon or coupé.

MG Montego

Whereas the LM10 and LM11 originally shared the same basis (the definitive Maestro style, produced by Ian Beech at the Solihull studio), the design eventually chosen for LM11 sprang from work by Roger Tucker. Malcolm Harbour recalls that serious work on LM11 began in 1979, after approval of LM10: 'The original style had a sloping rear window, and we also commissioned a competing style from Ogle.' Before long, a style not far from the definitive Montego began to emerge. By 1982, relations between David Bache and his superior, Harold Musgrove, had become less than harmonious, and disagreements over the appearance of the LM11 prototype only helped to speed Bache's departure.

Shortly before the launch of the LM10 Maestro range, therefore, Roy Axe took over as the new director of styling. He recalls that the appearance of the LM11 saloon offshoot was giving cause for concern: 'The Maestro was ready for production, and nothing could be done about it, but the Montego (as it became) was giving everyone the collywobbles.' At that stage, LM11 was rather more closely related to its LM10 sister than perhaps was advisable: the doors were pure Maestro, and the nose sloped down in a similar manner. Moreover, the fairly flat panels of the Maestro did not translate well into a larger car for what was, after all, a more style orientated sector of the market. Roy found that he was able to change the front and rear ends, making the car less 'spiky' in his words, but the budget and critical timing meant that little could be done to the door pressings, echoing the problems associated with the shared doors of the ADO17 1800 and ADO14 Maxi of the late 1960s!

The main problem—apart from the scallops along the flanks—was the fact that the top edges of the door skins sloped downwards, towards the rear of the car, which looked decidedly odd when married to the longer tail of the LM11 saloon. The solution—which Roy Axe admits was something of an 'Elastoplast' job—was to apply fairly substantial black plastic door cappings to the upper edges of all four door skins. Axe was responsible for starting work on the Montego estate, which was made to look less awkward than the saloon, particularly from the rear. Indeed, it is a testament to the smart looks of the Montego estate that Rover chose to keep it in production long after the saloon had been discontinued.

The LM11 duly appeared in April 1984, complete with the, by now, customary MG derivative. The R-series engine, which had been introduced for the Maestro, was suddenly superseded by another unit, the S-series. This shared only its connecting rods, valves and valve springs with its forebear. Naturally, journalists were interested to know whether problems with the R-series had precipitated this remarkably rapid change, but Austin Rover claimed that the reason had been due to development lead times preventing the S-series from being ready in time for the launch of the Maestro in the previous year. One version of the story, according to some insiders of the time, is that the government paymaster could subsidize engine modifications more easily than completely new engines, so the R-series amounted to a convenient bridge from the old E-series unit to the substantially different S-series, which was nearly called the R2. In his typically forthright manner, Harold Musgrove told me that this story was 'rubbish—it was simply a product of the fact that the R-series was a hastily reworked version of the E-series to overcome the disastrous gap between the A- and O-series units.'

The 1600 engines that had struggled to power the lighter Maestro clearly would not have been up to the task in the MG version of the Montego, so the 2-litre O-series was fitted, complete with Lucas fuel-injection using Bosch injectors, in a similar manner to the Rover SD1 Vitesse. With knock sensing mapped ignition, special pistons and a compression ratio of 9.1:1, the MG Montego produced a healthy 115bhp (85.76kW). At the design stage, once the LT80 gearbox had faded from the picture, there had been a choice between two possible gearboxes: a new Honda unit (not in use in any Honda vehicles) and a ZF gearbox. In the end, exploiting what Harold Musgrove describes as a 'marvellous opportunity', the Honda PG1 gearbox was chosen. One advantage of this was that, later, it would be produced by Austin Rover under licence from Honda for use in the Montego and other Austin Rover vehicles. For the MG Montego, a close-ratio gear set was specified, with a fifth speed ratio that equated to 20.6mph (33.15km/h) per 1000rpm.

Austin Rover was keen to point out two innovations of the MG Montego: the availability of an optional electronic dashboard incorporating a sophisticated LCD display, and a service indicator.

Left This is an early rendering by Rob Owen, which shows the propsed MG variant of the Austin Montego. The substantial under-bumper spoiler would not be featured on the basic MG variant until much later in production, and would first apear on the Montego Turbo of 1985. (courtesy Rob Owen)

Below An MG Montego EFi in the popular metallic silver finish. (Rover)

The former was not particularly popular, however, and the latter comprised little more than a device that monitored accumulated mileage and elapsed time from the last service—in other words, a much less sophisticated item than BMW's celebrated service indicator system. Another novelty of the MG Montego, in common with the rest of the range, was the adoption of metric-sized wheels with specially developed tyres that were designed to be safer in the event of sudden deflation. These were more practical than the earlier Dunlop Denovo system. On the MG Montego, these tyres (exclusively Michelin and Dunlop) were of 180/65R365 TD size on smart 365mm diameter alloy wheels, which resembled those of the MG Metro Turbo.

The MG Montego was differentiated from the Austin versions by the inevitable chin and boot spoilers, which together managed to reduce the coefficient of drag from 0.37 to 0.35. The body-coloured grille featured the obligatory red and chrome MG badge at its centre, while the area of the bootlid between the rectangular tail lights was overlaid with a red reflective plastic applique panel. In common with the other MG saloons, the theme of red striping and grey interior trim was continued, albeit in a slightly more restrained style. Herein, perhaps, lay the biggest problem of the MG Montego: the MG transformation, which had worked quite well for the Metro and Maestro, never seemed quite so appropriate for the Montego, whereas the later Vanden Plas EFi variant (with the same engine, but rather more up-market trim) appeared to provide a more mature package, which might have appealed to the 1980s equivalent of the old Z-series Magnette customer of 30 years before.

Nevertheless, the MG Montego sold well enough, even alongside other fuel-injected variants (in addition to the Vanden Plas EFi, there would be the later Si and GSi Montegos). Indeed, it remained on sale until late 1991, long after the MG Metro had been dropped.

Thoughts of facelifts

Roy Axe remembers the concerns about the styling of the Maestro and Montego that surfaced early in the decade: 'We tried a rebody around 1983 or so, which involved keeping the interior pressings, but changing all the exterior panels. The bottom edge of the scallop was blended into the lower flanks of the doors, and the end

ROYDEN AXE

Royden Axe is probably best known, in the UK at least, as the man behind the MG EX-E and Rover CCV concept cars, but his experience is far broader than that. His career stretches back to the early 1950s when, as a young man from Scarborough (where he was born in 1936), hell-bent on designing cars, he managed to get a job with the Rootes Group, probably the most dynamic British company of the period where styling was concerned. His first job was detailing the Sunbeam 90 Mark III of 1955, and he followed this up by contributing to the sleek lines of the Sunbeam Alpine of 1959.

By 1967, he had become Rootes' chief stylist and was responsible for that year's Sunbeam Rapier. Soon after, he became director of design when Chrysler UK emerged from the ashes of the Rootes empire, and in 1975, he moved to Detroit to assume overall control of the entire Chrysler design facility. Between 1975 and 1982, Roy played a major role in revitalizing the Chrysler Corporation, and one of his proudest achievements of the period is the Chrysler Minivan, which heralded a completely new sector of the market.

Roy's involvement with Rover resulted from an approach by a former colleague, Harry Sheron, who had been director of engineering for Chrysler Europe before moving on to manage Austin Rover's Gaydon Technology offshoot. Roy recalls Harry telephoning him at home in the USA and asking, 'How would you like to work for BL?', to which the response was an emphatic no! During the ensuing six months, however, he received several more transatlantic calls and, eventually, agreed to discuss BL's offer during a holiday in the UK. This led to a meeting with the Austin Rover chairman, Harold Musgrove, whom Roy describes as a 'breath of fresh air for the time'.

Musgrove, a former Austin apprentice, had been moved from Leyland Trucks to sort out the volume-car division. He was a hands-on manager who cared deeply for the company and recognized the need for a total revamp of its image. He discussed with Roy the problems as he perceived them: 'Harold thought the design side of the business was his biggest problem—and it was a problem—but I subsequently found we had major problems delivering design as a product because manufacturing was not producing Japanese levels of quality. Nowadays, of course, both are being delivered.'

Harold Musgrove offered Roy virtual *carte blanche*, as design director, to do whatever was required to rescue the company from its poor image and the low morale of its workers. This appealed to Roy, so he agreed to accept the challenge. He was assured that the facilities at Austin Rover were good, but his first visit came as a shock: 'The styling department was virtually non-existent. The facilities, such as they were, comprised the "Elephant House" (a large glass-roofed building at Longbridge), a nearby building which I likened to a railway shed, and a small building at Canley. I was so horrified that I was prepared to get on the next plane back to the States.'

Musgrove had told Roy that anything required would be provided, and he proved as good as his word, funding the construction of a new styling studio in one of the old Standard-Triumph buildings at Canley. This was completed within a year, although within six months of the work beginning, the styling department was heavily involved in the design of the Rover 800 Project XX.

Roy's other problem was building a team of stylists almost from scratch, at a time when they were relatively thin on the ground. At this point, dame for-

Roy Axe in his office at Tachbrook Park, near Warwick, in 1994. (David Knowles)

tune smiled when Peugeot suddenly announced that they were closing the former Chrysler UK design facility, at nearby Whitley, and transferring their operations to France: 'Most of the people there—many of whom I knew, since I had helped to set the operation up in the first place—did not want to transfer to France. We were able to cream off the best of the talent and swell our numbers remarkably quickly. If it hadn't been for that stroke of good fortune, I don't know how we could have coped.'

With a core of good designers—among them Roy Axe's eventual successor, Gordon Sked—the styling department began to overhaul not only the product range, but also the entire corporate image. Part of this process included the gradual abandonment of the Austin marque in favour of Rover and, to a lesser extent, MG, and the creation of a strong brand image that undoubtedly set the company on its present successful course.

In fact, there were two studios, initially catering for exterior and interior design. However, they were rationalized so that one looked after product design, headed by Gordon Sked, while the other catered for concept design, under Richard Hamblin. Staff could move between the two if a concept matured towards production. Having set this process in motion, Axe was content to step back from the limelight. The concept, or advanced design, studio eventually moved to Tachbrook Park on the outskirts of Warwick, and was given a brief to look into the requirements of the US market.

Subsequently, this division was the subject of a management buy-out, and continues to this day as an independent design consultancy, called Design Research Associates. Recent achievements of the company include a design for a new London taxi on behalf of LTI, a number of luxury aircraft interiors (including an award winning design for the BAe 125-1000), bespoke yacht concepts, and the stunning Bentley 'Java' concept car, revealed at the Geneva Motor Show, in March 1994.

Roy Axe has not lost his enthusiasm—the large motoring library and collection of models in his office testify to that—and it is good to see that his talents are still being utilized to the benefit of a wide international clientele.

result was very similar to the Vauxhall/Opel Astra of the early 1990s.' Other changes included correcting the upper profile of the door skins, but in the event, although it was clinicked, the reskin failed to materialize: 'It was decided not to go ahead, as it was planned at that stage to drop the Maestro and, therefore, it wasn't considered worth spending the money on an expensive facelift.'

Part of the problem lay in the success of the Honda-Rover Bounty joint venture—the Triumph Acclaim—which was not part of the picture when the Maestro had been conceived, and which seriously dented sales forecasts for it. As events transpired, the Maestro replacement, which would have been due in 1986-87, never materialized, being overtaken by the Honda-Rover YY project. The latter took off in June 1985, becoming the R8 Rover 200/400 range, which first appeared in October 1989. Eventually, the Maestro and Montego were largely left to fend for themselves, right through into the mid-1990s, the last Maestro being built in November 1994.

The MG Maestro 2.0

The MG Maestro 1600 had a fairly short, but eventful, life, during which its original R-series engine was replaced by the S-series unit that was introduced with the Montego range (from April 1984), and it finally faded from the scene in October 1984, being replaced by a 2-litre version using the O-series unit. The 1600 version of the Maestro had been struggling to produce the 103bhp (76.81kW) that was required of it, and this was made all the more obvious by the fuel vaporization problems. Austin Rover seriously looked at a fuel-injected version of the S-series unit for the MG Maestro (such an engine appeared in the Rover 216 EFi of June 1984), but it was found to offer little benefit over the Weber equipped engine. Thus, with the 2-litre MG Montego having been launched, the logic of fitting the O-series unit to the MG Maestro became clear. Various development Maestro HLs, bearing 'Y' and 'A' registration letters (making them 1982-83 vintage), were built with 2-litre O-series units, which were, according to Roger Parker, 'sharper than the production versions. Certainly, it was sickening at the time to experience these hacks and find that they were so much smoother, quieter, quicker and more economical than my own MG 1600!'

Malcolm Harbour, who, by 1984, had risen from the ranks of the product planners to become Austin Rover's sales and marketing director, pointed out the importance of having a good contender in the so-called hot hatchback sector, which he said had a 'great deal of visibility'. It was important, therefore, to avoid the prospect of

an MG Maestro with poorer performance than its rivals, and there is no doubt that the MG Maestro delivered the goods in a highly practical, if not stunningly stylish, package. In the new MG Maestro 2.0 EFi, the O-series engine produced the same 115bhp (85.76kW) at 5500 rpm as the MG Montego, while the torque figure of 134lb/ft (199.42kg/m) at 2800rpm was a useful increase of some 34 per cent over that of the 1600.

The Honda gearbox from the Montego was used, with a fifth-gear ratio giving 23mph (37.01km/h) per 1000rpm, compared to 19.8mph (31.86km/h) for the 1600. Top speed and acceleration were similarly improved, the former to 115mph (185.07km/h), while the 0-60mph (0-96.56km/h) time was a class leading 8.5sec. The front anti-roll bar was increased in diameter by 2mm to 22mm, the front brakes became ventilated discs, and a new 16mm anti-roll bar was added at the rear. Tyres were also upgraded, the 175/65 HR 14s chosen being the largest that could be safely fitted under the Maestro's wheel arches without alterations to the bodywork.

Cosmetic improvements included the substitution of colour keyed door handles for the black plastic items of the 1600, and an attractive, restyled, colour keyed front grille, which freshened up the nose of the car considerably and remained unique to the MG version of the Maestro. In addition, MG logos were applied to the distinctive square-pattern alloy wheels, later to be replaced by more attractive, cross-spoked alloys as part of a minor facelift resulting in the MG 2.0i, which coincided with the colour-co-ordination of some of the black plastic exterior fittings.

Almost unnoticed, the O-series engine became the O2, in 1985, as a spin-off from the new M16 twin-cam engine, which had been derived from it for the new Rover 800. The requirements of the M16 unit made it necessary to alter the O-series cylinder block, and later engines, although of identical output, were superior to their forebears. An interesting development 'mule', built in 1984-85, was based upon a dark blue 'A'-registration Maestro HL. The bodywork forward of the windscreen was longer than standard and featured fabricated panels that were reminiscent of the Montego. The result, nicknamed the 'Monstro', had the appearance of an oddly proportioned Montego hatchback.

Rover external affairs spokesman Denis Chick remembers that this car was built solely for testing the new M16 engine and Rover XX (800) front drive-train and suspension. It would be left to private enthusiasts to build their own versions of the MG Maestro and

A 1986 model year MG Maestro 2.0 EFi. (Rover)

Montego with the new M16 engine. Roger Parker recalls rumours, around late 1986, that a Montego derivative was being considered with the M16 engine, but nothing came of this, despite talk of budgeting exercises that led to an estimated cost of £1 million for such a car.

The MG Montego Turbo

From the early days of the LC10 project, the potential of a truly high-performance derivative had never been far from the minds of the product planners. The quest for power in cars that were larger than the class average made turbocharging the most cost-effective means of achieving the desired performance. It was clear that the only engine suitable for forced induction was the O-series, which had already been developed in turbocharged form for the still-born O-series MGB and an experimental Princess. Early tests were carried out with Maestro prototypes, one of which Austin Rover chairman Harold Musgrove drove.

The original plan was for two different versions of the forced-induction O-series engine: the Maestro would have been fitted with a non-intercooled version, while the more expensive and heavier Montego would have had an intercooled turbo unit, thus ensuring a ladder of performance. However, the Maestro turbo was never given a very high priority, and although prototypes were built, they were never approved for series production. As a matter of fact, Harold Musgrove was not keen on the car. When pressed by journalists for the reason why the turbo engine was not available in the Maestro body, he retorted, 'How would you stop it?'

When it was launched, in April 1985, the MG Montego Turbo was generally welcomed as a lower-priced alternative to the successful Rover 3500 Vitesse, which offered a reasonably similar combination of passenger space and performance. However, the manner in which the Montego Turbo's power was delivered to the road came in for a great deal of justified criticism: I well remember my first attempt at accelerating through a bend in an early Montego Turbo, and experiencing vividly the dubious pleasures of severe torque steer. Later versions of the car would suffer less from this trait, but the Montego Turbo was never fully tamed, and the criticisms of the early motoring magazine road-tests haunted the car, which may explain the relatively low overall production figure of less than 7300 examples in six-and-a-half years.

Austin Rover returns to motor-sport: the MG Metro 6R4

There were rumours in the rally world that Austin Rover was working on a new rally contender, based upon the Austin Metro, almost as soon as the car appeared in the showrooms. Ian Elliott recalls having dinner with BL competition director John Davenport, prior to the October 1980 launch of the Metro, and hearing him talk about tentative plans for a mid-engined Austin Rover rally supercar. Working in great secrecy (even to the extent that many of the leading lights at BL Motorsport did not know what was going on!), Davenport laid the plans for the Metro-based 6R4 in 1981.

With the co-operation of Patrick Head, of Williams Engineering at nearby Didcot, the Cowley based competitions department began to develop the Metro to such an extent that only a few of the

EXPEDITION TO AMERICA: THE STERLING

In 1985, Rover announced its intention of returning to North America in the expectation of achieving a promising future, based upon the forthcoming all-important Honda/Rover XX joint project, better known in the UK as the Rover 800. An operation was set up, with the name ARCONA (Austin Rover cars of North America), in partnership with Florida millionaire Norman Braman. Top-level local staff were recruited—such as Ray Ketchledge, formerly of VW of North America—and there was much excitement about the prospect of marrying British style with Japanese reliability.

For the North American market, Rover took the rather bold and ambitious step of creating a brand-new marque—Sterling—on the pretext that the Rover name meant little to Americans. Closer to the truth, perhaps, was the fact that Rover may have been remembered for the P6 3500 and the SD1 3500, both of which had been spectacular failures in the USA, and the company would not have wished to acknowledge that publicly at the time. In addition, Jaguar-Rover-Triumph had disentangled themselves so badly from the US market, under the threat of legal action by disenchanted former MG dealers, that there would have been legal problems in launching a new product using any of the old BL marques formerly on sale there. It would appear that the dealers might have had the legal right to sell any new products bearing those marques. From the outset, however, there was a clear intention to expand the range beyond a single model. As Rover's former export sales director, P. W. Johnson, told me, in July 1985, there was a feeling within the company that efforts to expand the Sterling range would have been better directed towards derivatives of the basic XX, and a second saloon line, before sports cars were contemplated.

Before long, Braman and his team had recruited a large number of enthusiastic dealers, who were summoned to ARCONA's first US national dealer conference, at the Marriott Hotel in Chicago. The reception accorded the pre-production prototypes on show augured well for the planned sales programme of 15,000 cars per annum. There was an optimistic aim of increasing this to 20,000 per annum if the luxury import sector grew, as predicted, during the latter part of the decade. Unfortunately, things seemed to go downhill fairly rapidly soon after this auspicious start.

Originally, deliveries were scheduled to begin in the autumn of 1986 (for the 1987 model year), but logistical problems delayed the introduction until November 1987. First-year sales were reasonably buoyant at 14,171, but in the following year, they fell dramatically by 38 per cent, to 8822. The situation was not helped by a highly publicized poor placing in the J. D. Power quality ratings, just above the bottom placed Yugo. Furthermore, the original Sterling featured a rather underpowered 2.5-litre version of Honda's V6 engine. To improve matters, a more powerful 2.7-litre engine was developed by Honda

for both the Sterling and its own Acura Legend. By this stage, there was also rather obvious friction between the UK and US members of ARCONA's management, so in May 1988, the decision was taken to buy Norman Braman's shares in the company and to establish a Rover man, Chris Woodwark, as Sterling's president in place of Ray Ketchledge.

In the meantime, the sales fortunes of the smaller, separate Range Rover of North America operation were almost the complete opposite of those at Sterling: sales of 2586 in 1987 soared to 3427 in the following year, and the upward trend continued in the years that followed. Despite the continuing problems that Rover experienced with their Sterling operation, there were plans to expand the range and, by 1988, the Rover CCV concept coupé was being used as the basis of a Sterling coupé proposal, initial development being carried out in the USA by Cars & Concepts. The resulting styling model was tested at a customer clinic in San Francisco, where the reaction was sufficiently positive for Rover's stylists to begin work on a definitive version.

In January 1989, Chris Woodwark was replaced as Sterling's president by Graham Morris, who would push hard for a new MG for Sterling to sell. Also under consideration were other models—both above and below the 800 range—and the possibility of reverting to the Rover name. A striking new luxury flagship saloon, R16, could have shared its new K-series-based V6 and V8 engines with PR5, a luxury MG sports car. In October 1989, when the Rover 200 was launched in the UK, Sterling Motor Cars of Miami issued a press release that included a 'teaser' drawing showing a rear three-quarter view of a Sterling coupé for 1992. This looked remarkably like the actual Rover 800 coupé that eventually emerged at the Geneva Motor Show in March 1992. Before long, the Rover 800 coupé was ready for introduction, with a possible convertible version in the wings (the Nightfire Red, fully finished prototype probably still lurks somewhere in the Rover Group's premises). By this stage, Sterling Motor Cars people were dropping broad hints about the possibility of a return of the MG badge.

Sterling sales, however, continued to slide: they amounted to only 4015 in 1990, despite the addition of the fastback 800 and some very bold and expensive advertising initiatives. Matters were not helped by the arrival of some powerful opposition from Japan, in the form of the new Nissan Infiniti and Toyota Lexus marques. Eventually, Rover decided to pull the plug in August 1991, barely months before the launch of the facelifted Rover 800 R17 range, complete with the grille that the Americans had demanded. Sales in 1991 had been a mere 1871 cars, although ironically, they had rallied somewhat in July—but it was too little, too late. With the death of the Sterling marque, Rover's presence in the USA and Canada was confined to the Range Rover of North America operation, and all thoughts of a new sports car for the US market were put on indefinite hold.

exterior panels bore any significant relationship to the road-going version. At an early stage, it was decided that a completely new engine would be needed for the car to be fully competitive, there being no adequate unit in the Austin Rover cupboard. However, for the purposes of development, a fairly crude, but effective, cut-down 2.5-litre V6 version of the venerable Rover alloy V8 (dubbed the V62V) was employed. This produced around 260bhp (193.88kW) and drove through a purpose designed, four-wheel-drive transmission incorporating a central differential.

Of course, it is all very well for engineers to design and develop a rally car, but without practical input from an experienced driver, all their efforts would be in vain. Consequently, BL Motorsport engaged the services of their old friend and former works driver, Tony Pond, who had extensive experience of the fiercely competitive world of rallying, and of testing and development work. Tony remembers the 6R4 with some affection: 'I sat in one of the first prototypes at Williams, and I was sufficiently interested that soon after, I was driving it to help set it up.' Rod Lyne first became involved with the 6R4 in 1983, when he made the occasional visit to Williams and attended test sessions at Chalgrove airfield and, subsequently, at Rover's own test facility at Gaydon.

Launch and competition début

The public announcement of the MG Metro 6R4—the nomenclature referring to '6 cylinders, Rally, 4-wheel-drive'—took place on Friday, 24 February, 1984, when it was revealed that the development costs amounted to £2 million. At the same time, it was announced that the car would be making its competition début in April. During the launch briefing, Austin Rover's commercial director, Mark Snowdon, said, 'Although we will not make a final commitment to international rallying until the prototype Metros have proved themselves in competition, we would not announce the car at this stage if we were not confident of its ability.' He went on to say. 'It is our ambition to win the world championship with this exciting car.'

Needless to say, it was not long before the prototype 6R4 made its first appearance at a competitive event. Tony Pond drove the car in the 1984 York Rally on 31 March, 1984. The red and white prototype easily set the fastest times for the first eight stages—in fact, Pond and navigator Rob Arthur were nearly three minutes in the

lead after 55 stage miles (88.51km), ahead of the highly-potent Audi 80 Quattro of Darryl Weidner. Unfortunately, however, they had to retire due to alternator problems. Ian Elliott also points out that Pond had to leave early in any case, as he was entered in a race at Silverstone in a Rover SD1: the 6R4 entry really was only intended to be a trial run. Nevertheless, even without its specially developed competition engine, the 6R4 had clearly demonstrated its potential, and throughout 1984 the car continued to compete effectively while the definitive version evolved.

Development for international rallying

Rod Lyne had moved to the competition department at Abingdon prior to the factory closing, so he transferred with his BL Motorsport colleagues to their new home at Cowley. John Davenport was in charge of BL Motorsport, and as soon as plans for the 6R4 had been laid, he decided that he wanted to stage a marriage of rallying and Formula One race technology. Consequently, the three prototype bodies were produced at the Williams facilities nearby. However, as Rod Lyne recalls, the resulting car was something of a compromise: 'The 6R4 suffered from a short wheelbase (a legacy of its Metro roots) and short wheel travel; Williams had effectively produced a sort of F1 rally car!'

Therefore, it fell to the engineers to develop the car gradually towards the 'production' specification (homologation regulations called for 200 copies to be produced for the car to comply), and this process led to many changes, such as a longer wheelbase, a wider track, various aerodynamic aids to increase down-force at rally speeds, and significantly increased suspension travel. The last was made all the more obvious by the rather ungainly blisters over the suspension turrets on both sides of the bonnet. At the same time, larger wheels were fitted to take advantage of the tyre improvements that Michelin had already carried out with the Peugeot team.

Development continued with extensive testing of three prototypes on a track owned by Michelin at Almeiras, in Southern Spain, the aim being to produce a car that was capable of beating the best that the Group B opposition could throw at it. At this point, in July 1984, Wynne Mitchell joined the team and found himself accom-

The central transmission, front and rear differentials and suspension of the Metro 6R4 are clearly shown in this ghosted view. (Rover)

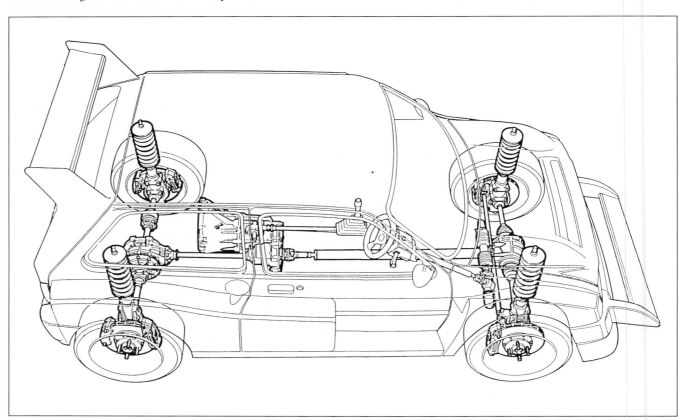

THE V6-4V ENGINE

From quite early in its history at Rover, the classic aluminium V8 engine was the subject of a number of exercises that explored ways of expanding the basic design. In addition to capacity changes (Leyland Australia used a 4.4-litre version, for example), some thought was given to a six-cylinder derivative, which could have been created quite easily by lopping off a cylinder from each bank. Indeed, there was a precedent for this: Buick, which had sold Rover the rights to the V8, developed their own V6 version, albeit with a cast-iron block. Thus, it was not such a bold step to develop a cut-down V6 version of the Rover V8 for the planned mid-engined competition Metro. 'Cut-down' is appropriate terminology, too, for, as Tony Pond recalls, 'You could even see the saw marks on the castings of the first of these engines!'

When the Metro 6R4 made its début, in February 1984, it utilized this development of the V8, but only as an interim measure, since a specially designed unit had been planned for the car's serious rally campaign. From the outset, this unique engine, probably the only engine to be designed expressly for rallying, was intended to provide high power and torque without the disadvantages and compromises seen in the engines used by most other rally teams. For example, the class leading Audi Quattro utilized a turbocharged production based engine, but Austin Rover decided to build an engine that could provide the required high outputs without resorting to forced induction. The advantages suggested for this design were almost instantaneous throttle response, far more even and massive spread of torque across the engine revolution range, and substantial engine overrun braking due to the unit's high (12:1) compression ratio (turbocharged units require reduced compression ratios to avoid self-destruction!). Unfortunately, however, turbocharger technology was not standing still—ever smaller and lighter turbochargers were being developed—and, in the end, the lack of forced induction would prove to be something of an Achilles' heel for the V6-4V.

The all-alloy engine was laid out by former Hart Engineering designer David Wood, and it was soon christened the V6-4V (V6 cylinder layout, four valves per cylinder). The total weight of the engine, with ancillaries, was 314lb (143kg), and the capacity was 2991cc, with an over-square bore/stroke ratio of 1:1.22. Twin camshafts per cylinder bank were driven by toothed belts, each of the 24 valves being operated via inverted tappets. From the outset, it was recognized that there would have to be two versions: the more tractable 250bhp (186.43kW) Clubman unit, which could be used 'straight out of the box', and the full-house International form with a dog engaged clutch and an output of up to 410bhp (305.74kW).

The Clubman engine had a single-throttle-butterfly intake system, multi-point fuel-injection and an engine limiter set to 7000rpm, at which the maximum power of 250bhp (186.43kW) was achieved. The torque curve of this version was impressively flat, remaining in the 200-250bhp (149.14-186.43kW) range from 2000rpm right up to 7000rpm. Just such a Clubman 6R4, with nothing added other than harnesses and a fire extinguisher, won the October 1985 Trossachs Rally, actually a couple of weeks prior to the car being homologated.

The International version also benefited from a flat torque curve, although the usable power was above 230bhp (171.51kW) in the principal power band from 5000 to 9000rpm, peaking at 270lb/ft (401.81kg/m). For this application, the fuel system was upgraded to a six-throttle-butterfly manifold. In addition, the engine featured special camshafts, heavy-duty con-rods and various changes to the Lucas Micos engine management system, which it shared with the Clubman version. The Micos system made use of advanced engine mapping and external sensing of such factors as air-intake temperature and barometric pressure. With these state-of-the-art features, the V6-4V was an engine of which the company could be justifiably proud.

Unfortunately, however, due to the inevitable budget constraints, the design of the V6-4V engine was something of a compromise, because it was developed from the original Rover V8 derived V6. The major drawback was the retention of the V8's crankshaft. Invariably, V8 engines have cranks that provide a firing stroke for every 90 degrees of rotation, whereas V6s and V12s have firing strokes at 60- or 120-degree intervals. The V6-4V unit, therefore, was an oddity, in that it was a V6 with a 90-degree crank. This lead to some novel solutions, such as unevenly spaced plug leads. Furthermore, the overhead camshafts were driven by unusually long belts, which often proved to be the Achilles' heel of the 6R4, particularly in the rougher rally events, where they proved especially vulnerable.

Nevertheless, the engine showed great promise as a competition unit and might well have been developed further had the end of Group B rallying not cut short the 6R4's career. Wynne Mitchell and Tony Pond both expressed their frustration with one aspect of the V6-4V's performance, which was only fixed late in the day. 'From 1000 to 4000 rpm, it would pull as clean as a whistle,' says Wynne, 'but from 4000 to 4700, there was a flat spot. The test-bed engines did not show this as much of a problem, but it was only when they commissioned a test-bed which allowed us to attach a car exhaust that they saw what we had been on about. Almost by accident, we tried a Clubman-specification long exhaust on the International-specification engine, and the problem was solved, but by this stage—1987—it was far too late in the day!' Testing also showed that a 6R4 fitted with the Clubman engine would not be far behind an International version. Tony Pond was driving prototypes 002 and 003 in the Welsh forests, just ahead of the RAC: 'We found that the Clubman car was just three seconds slower than the International car,' says Wynne, adding that it was much easier to drive.

The abandonment of the 6R4 programme, and the cessation of work on the MG EX-E, made the V6-4V engine redundant as far as its developers were concerned and, for a while, it seemed probable that it would be consigned to the museum. However, various private entrepreneurs persisted with the V6-4V, not least Will Gollop, who used the talents of former Abingdon MG man, and expert engine builder, Cliff Humphries to produce a one-off, twin-turbocharger, 2.3-litre version (taking advantage of those advances in turbocharger technology!), which generated no less than 700bhp (521.99kW). Fate finally intervened when Tom Walkinshaw expressed an interest in acquiring the rights to the engine design for another competition project on which he was working. In greatly modified form, the V6-4V engine eventually re-emerged as the motive power of the highly exclusive Jaguar XJ-220...

The V6-4V engine. (Rover, courtesy David Sims)

The definitive Metro 6R4, complete with mid-mounted V6-4V engine, is seen here on the Austin-Rover stand at the Earls Court Motor Show. (David Knowles.

panying the third prototype on the trip to Almeiras. 'I thought at first what an awful car it was,' he recalled for me some 12 years later (by which time, he was deeply involved in the MGF competition programme). 'It was some 3¾in (9.53cm) longer than the standard Metro, the back wheels were moved back 2in (5.08cm), and the front forward by ¾in (1.91cm). Initially, we used 340mm tyres, but we had to change these to the 390mm size, which Michelin were supplying to the opposition, and this affected both the set-up and the body structure.' Further work also led to a substantial widening of the rear track by 7in (17.78cm), the front being similarly extended. Before long, the definitive 6R4 emerged, looking even stranger than the first prototype.

Despite the engine development problems—only solved when it was too late—the 6R4 often proved to be remarkably sturdy, sometimes performing beyond the normal call of duty. One occasion that is vividly recalled by Wynne Mitchell was the time when the car caught fire, yet went on to win: 'Tony was driving and suddenly the car burst into flame: there were masses of flames coming out of the engine compartment, and we were sure that the car was finished. Tony got out in a hurry and ran off; we were following and used our fire extinguisher on the car, successfully putting the flames out. The whole engine bay was black—the air cleaner had melted—but we got Tony back in the car, pushed it almost half a mile (0.8km) and it started, Tony going on to achieve first place!'

Development continued apace until the time came for senior management to review what had been achieved. On 20 December, 1984, a 'ride and drive' was held at Gaydon, with Ray Horrocks and Harold Musgrove driving prototypes 002 and 003 around the test track. Wynne Mitchell remembers Harold Musgrove returning from his drive to give the thumbs-up for the car and the go-ahead for the programme: 'We then had to get the drawings ready by February and, at the same time, production got under way.' The unique V6-4V engines were built at Austin Rover's Radford, Coventry branch in Capmartin Road, where the gearbox and transmission units were also assembled. These units were taken to Longbridge, where Mike Barnett headed up the production of the 200 homologation cars.

Musgrove recalls supporting the 6R4 project: '...but you have to remember that the Metro was our life's blood: MG was very interesting, and we were delighted to put the badge on the 6R4, but as far as we were concerned, it was Metro which was crucial.'

The end of Group B rallying
The long-term career of the MG Metro 6R4 was already in doubt when it first appeared at York, but the real problem came a year later, when the Group B rally cars were banned after a series of hor-

rific accidents. In the last of these, 30-year-old Henri Toivenen (brother of Metro 6R4 driver Harri Toivenen) was killed along with his colleague, Sergio Cresto, when their Group B Lancia crashed and burst into flames in Corsica on 2 May, 1986. This prompted what was widely regarded as a 'knee-jerk' reaction by the sport's governing body, FISA, which announced on the very next day that Group B cars would be banned from the beginning of 1987, and that the plans for a new Group S to replace Group B would be abandoned. Sadly, therefore, the 6R4's promising international career was cut short, the best result being a third place on the November 1985 Lombard RAC Rally for Tony Pond.

According to Rod Lyne, the 6R4 was too little, too late in top-class rallying terms: 'The true concept of the car was laid down in 1981, but then it only made its international rally début on the Lombard RAC in November 1985, by which time it was almost out of date. In this time, for instance, Lancia had built two entirely different Group B cars. Hold-ups with the funding didn't help—John Davenport fought tooth and nail to get the money we needed—and the decision not to use a turbo engine proved to be a mistake in the end.' The latter situation arose because turbocharger technology improved to the extent that the dreaded turbo-lag became much less of a problem. As a result, the 6R4 was stuck with an engine that was bigger and heavier than the opposition's, and it produced less power into the bargain.

Following the 1986 World Rally Championship, the Austin Rover Motorsport division began to contract, and by May 1987, it had closed down completely. Upon his redundancy, Rod Lyne formed his own company, R. A. Lyne Motors of Oxford where, to this day, he specializes in the preparation of 6R4s, which still serve a useful purpose in competition. Tony Pond believes that the 6R4 showed great promise at first, but concurs with Rod Lyne's view that it was soon left behind: 'We tested the 6R4 against Stig Blomqvist's Audi, and it was a fair bit quicker; it was also quicker than the early Peugeot T16. The trouble was that the opposition weren't standing still...'

Life after Group B for the 6R4
Group B rallying may have come to an end, and the *raison d'être* of the 6R4 with it, but the car was not banned from all forms of rallying. For several years since, 6R4s have been regular participants in UK and Irish events, as well as in a few in mainland Europe, often under a five- or even seven-second handicap against humbler Group A cars, and subject to restrictions on engine capacity. So successful were the 6R4s, however, that the annual BTRDA Gold Star Championship (Britain's foremost amateur rally series) fell to 6R4 drivers on several occasions after the Group B ban.

According to the Metro 6R4 registrar, David Sims, it is believed that 233 6R4 bodies were built and, of those, at least 200 must have been built into complete cars to comply with the homologation requirements. Many examples of the 6R4 remain active in motorsport to this day, often in highly developed form, particularly on sprint circuits, where the light weight, short wheelbase and four-wheel-drive offer significant advantages. In 1988, Ted Toleman entered highly modified 6R4-based cars in the Paris-Dakar Rally, and Rod Lyne was involved in this attempt. The story was to be repeated in 1989, with an even more heavily modified car (engineered by race car builder Reynard Cars), which retained even fewer of its 6R4 origins. However, the saga of the Toleman TG89 Enduro must be left for another book! The 6R4 may have been dropped from Rover's plans long ago, but many enthusiasts continue to keep the flame burning.

The MG sports car returns

All the time that the MG versions of the Metro, Maestro and Montego were on sale, enthusiasts for the marque were asking the inevitable question: 'When, if ever, will we see a new MG sports car?' No group expressed this sentiment more vociferously than the North Americans, but of course, BL had retreated rather rapidly from that market. The company would have found it difficult to rebuild a suitable dealer network in the USA, particularly in the face of the costs and unfavourable publicity that would have accompanied the almost inevitable law suits from disgruntled former MG dealers. Many of these had threatened such an action in November 1979—with the full backing of the 416-strong Jaguar-Rover-Triumph dealer council—to the tune of £100 million against loss of business.

Rover-Triumph, which had come to the end of the road early in the decade, had already identified the potential of pursuing a joint project with Honda, and it had been planned for a still distant 1987. Harold Musgrove, as Austin Rover chairman, was characteristically forthright about the position of the company. 'Ninety per cent of MG sports cars went to the USA,' he reminded me, 'which was a market we were only thinking of going back to. Then, a sports car with anything other than an interior structure coming off a mass-production base would have been impossible. People would say, "Do one off a Metro, it'll be lovely," but they just didn't know the practicalities. Added to this, the government was a shareholder, and any plans we put forward had to be potentially profitable.'

Of course, there were thoughts about an MG sports car that could have been shared with Honda: 'We had an agreement with them,

and anything you work on with a partner has to be shared, so we could have had a closely related sports model in MG and Honda versions. MG was part of the corporate plan, but it would only have come out of the relationship with Honda.' In the event, the MG/Honda never happened, although at one time there were erroneous rumours about an MG based upon the Honda Civic.

The Austin Rover design studio: MG concepts

With the formation of the new team under Roy Axe, at Canley, work on design concepts moved up a pace. Previous design efforts within the company had tended to be somewhat fragmented, as with so many facets of its operation, the significant talent of many designers being split between different studios, which were often asked to compete with one another. While it can be argued that healthy competition is good for designers, the wisdom of such competition within a company—particularly a company in difficulties—may be questioned. The Maestro and Montego had arisen from two quite different competing designs, from different BL studios, and bits and pieces of each proposal had effectively been mixed together by the product planners.

Roy Axe's arrival changed all that and, before long, the studios at Canley were working hard on numerous concepts, some of which went no further than paper studies, while others became models, clays and even plastic bodies. Under Axe were two design directors: Gordon Sked, who dealt with exterior design, and former Ogle Transport designer Richard Hamblin, who oversaw interior design. Graham Lewis, at the time chief designer for concept design, recalls that talented young designer Gerry McGovern was responsible for creating an MG Midget as a pure concept car: 'Gerry produced an attractive red and white MG Midget concept based upon another concept, which had been done for a "glass-back" Metro. His Midget was effectively a sort of cabrio based upon the Metro concept car, but neither were pursued any further than the full-size model stage.'

Gerry remembers that he had been engaged on an exercise to look into a series of new Austins (this was well before the days of 'Roverization'), and one of them was AR6, a predecessor of R6, and known in the studio as 'Joe 90': 'AR6 was my three-door concept, which had been influenced by Guigaro's "Medusa" concept car, with its novel side section. It was simply a studio concept, and the Midget was an offshoot from it.'

Somehow, details of this car were leaked to *Motor* magazine, which published an article with very accurate illustrations, clearly based upon photos of the model, in their issue of 19 January, 1985.

Gerry McGovern's MG Midget concept model, based upon the AR6 Metro. Motor magazine ran an article in January 1985, which featured some remarkably accurate sketches, but which wrongly suggested that the car had been approved for production and that it was based upon the Honda Civic. (Rover)

The MG Midget concept model, lined up with the last MG Midget of 1979 (from the British Motor Heritage collection) in the Canley styling studio's outdoor display area. (Rover)

The magazine claimed—quite wrongly—that the car was based upon the Honda Civic CRX sports coupé, and so started a spate of rumours in the press that Austin Rover was about to return to the sports car market, five years after abandoning it. The company was quick to quench the rumours, but the real drama was yet to unfold.

MG EX-E: the star of Frankfurt

Surely, it would not be too much of an exaggeration to say that the motoring world was stunned on Tuesday, 10 September, 1985, when Austin Rover unveiled the MG EX-E concept car at the Frankfurt Motor Show. No doubt, some car-mad Britons will recall their astonishment at the sight of the stunning silver car on the slowly revolving turntable as it flashed on to their television screens during news programmes. Austin Rover had made great strides as a company, and had introduced a range of competitive mainstream cars, but it was not perceived as a particularly adventurous company, a legacy both of its unfortunate background and of public ownership. The EX-E project contrived to change all that.

Prior to the conception of the EX-E, in late 1984, the consensus of opinion within Austin Rover had been that show cars, which ultimately led nowhere, were an unnecessary distraction from the core product. There was also the thought that, as a publicly owned company, which was accountable to the British taxpayer, Austin Rover had an inherent duty not to be seen to be too frivolous or profligate with money.

Roy Axe, newly installed as the director of design, saw things differently, and he was delighted to find an ally in the chairman and chief executive, Harold Musgrove, who had appointed him as the saviour of the company's image and funded the new studio at Canley. Roy puts EX-E into context: 'Remember that there was no MG sports car at that time, and that although some thought had been given to the idea, there was nothing in the pipeline. The Rover 800 would be following on in 1986, and so the idea of EX-E was to provide a showcase of the talents within the company ahead of the new Rover. We wanted to avoid a direct conflict with the Rover 800, but we also wanted to generate some interest and excitement ahead of its launch.'

Development of the theme

The prototype that eventually emerged was, in fact, the second of three concepts, each of which was a proper sports car in its own right with no exterior panels in common with mainstream models, but in some cases, utilizing existing floorpans, running gear and so forth. Each proposal was a serious attempt at producing something that could have been built from a commercial viewpoint, but sadly all fell by the wayside, victims of cost accountancy. Roy Axe regrets that this happened: 'If you look at them purely from the point of view of profits and margins, sports cars would never get off the ground, but low-volume cars—especially open-topped ones—can provide a massive boost to the image of a company, but are unlikely to be major earners in themselves. But unfortunately, the climate at the time was not conducive to such projects.'

With the Midget concept behind them, thoughts soon turned to the fascinating idea of producing a 'supercar' based upon the MG Metro 6R4 which, at that stage, was felt to have a glowing future ahead of it. Axe discussed the basic idea with Austin Rover's director in charge of product development, Mark Snowdon and, before long, Harry Sheron of Gaydon Technology, Austin Rover's design research offshoot, took charge of the engineering aspect of the project, with former Rover engineer Spencer King and ex-MG man Roy Brocklehurst in tow. Also closely involved were engineering operations director Dr Stan Manton, business and product strategy director John Bacchus, and motor-sport director John Davenport.

A great deal of engineering and styling work went into the project during the early part of 1985. 'Spen' King, of course, had been responsible for the stunning, mid-engined Rover P6BS sports car prototype of 1967, which was cancelled largely at the behest of Sir William Lyons of Jaguar. With that experience behind him, he was a natural choice to head the engineering side of the EX-E project. Similarly, Roy Brocklehurst had been at Abingdon during the gestation of ADO21, the mid-engined MG prototype, so the collective expertise on mid-engined sports car design was formidable.

The definitive prototype emerges

Roy Axe recalls that there were many problems: 'We were frequently arguing about packaging requirements, a subject on which engineers and stylists frequently clash.' The final result illustrates this problem, notably the height of the rear deck, necessitated by the depth of the engine and transmission package—a common problem with mid-engined cars, as MG had found with ADO21. From the word go, it was agreed that the concept of EX-E should be that of a supercar and, to that end, Axe and his team sought inspiration from fighter aircraft, specifically the American F-16. He relates how, entirely by chance, the later Honda NS-X sports car was also inspired by the F-16 fighter, but he states that there was no sharing of ideas. Even so, Gerry McGovern (stylist behind the 1995 MGF, and one of the main players in the EX-E team) remembers how he gave a talk to some Honda designers about the EX-E design philosophy! Roy also strongly refutes the idea that the Pininfarina styled Honda HP-X, which preceded the public unveiling of the EX-E, was in any way related: 'There was absolutely no official dialogue between Rover and either Pininfarina or Honda on HP-X, despite what many people have supposed.'

The basic idea of the EX-E hinged upon two separate, but very important, Austin Rover projects: the specially designed V6-4V six-cylinder, four-camshaft, 24-valve, all-aluminium 3-litre engine, designed expressly for the MG 6R4 rally car; and the concept of injection moulded polypropylene body panels attached to an aluminium space frame. Since the so-called International competition form of the V6-4V engine developed a massive 410bhp

(305.74kW), it would not have been suitable for road use, so a production version of the EX-E would have been based upon the Clubman unit, which developed around 250bhp (186.43kW) at 7000rpm, coupled with torque of 225lb/ft (334.85kg/m) at 4500rpm. Projected performance figures were 0-100km/h (0-62mph) in under five seconds and a maximum speed of around 275km/h (170mph).

For the EX-E, as in the MG Metro 6R4, the engine was to have been mounted forward of the rear axle and would have provided power to all four wheels via the 6R4's permanent four-wheel-drive transmission system, complete with central viscous coupling differential and five-speed gearbox. Limited-slip differentials were fitted front and rear, and each wheel was suspended by double-wishbones. Some work was carried out on advanced suspension control, which provided an adjustable ride height that could have been selected by the driver. The wheels were 17in (43.18cm)x7J specially designed alloy units with attractive 'turbine' vanes to improve brake cooling. They were shod with ultra-low-profile 215/45VR17 tyres. Braking was by four-wheel ventilated discs with anti-lock control.

The idea of plastic body panels bonded to an aluminium frame had been developed by Gaydon Technology and had been demonstrated in the novel ECV-3 running prototype (which survives, incidentally, as part of the British Motor Heritage collection). The major advantage claimed for this method of construction was the ability to build the vehicle as a series of separate modules, which could be joined together. For the EX-E project, three modules were conceived: an engine, transmission and rear suspension module; a passenger cell, which would contain the interior trim components, such as the seats and fascia; and finally a front-end structure incorporating the front suspension, transmission and steering system. The final process, after joining the three modules together to make a rolling chassis, would have been to attach the unstressed, self-coloured polypropylene body panels and the glazed roof section. The latter was made from polychromatic plastic, having a graduated tint (dark at the roof centre and near-transparent at the waistline), with a removable targa panel in the top.

Styling and engineering

Gordon Sked, who had been with the company for many years and would go on to become Roy Axe's successor, oversaw the exterior design of the EX-E project, most of the credit being due to Gerry McGovern. Aerodynamic testing was carried out in traditional fashion, using a number of quarter-scale models and, at this stage, two styling themes were explored. A third model was used for more fundamental experiments to develop certain aerodynamic features, which were incorporated into the final full-sized model. In the process, the drag coefficient achieved for the prototype was reduced from an initial Cd of 0.31 to an impressive 0.24, a figure that has rarely been matched by any production sports car. The team was particularly proud of the fact that this was achieved, in conjunction with zero front and rear lift, without the need for spoilers. Even so, the possibility of a competition variant was catered for by the consideration of 'active' front and rear spoilers, a concept that only became a production reality on certain Porsche and VW sports cars some years afterwards.

The interior of the EX-E—design of which was led by Richard Hamblin, who credits much of the work to Gerry Newman—was not only styled to reflect the cocoon-like fighter aircraft cockpit theme, but was also used as a showcase for some of the advanced concepts that Austin Rover was working on. One idea, subsequently adopted by a number of luxury car makers, was for an interior that tailored itself to the preferred settings—seat, steering-wheel and rear-view mirror—of the individual driver once he had programmed them. This formed part of what Austin Rover called their VEMS, or Vehicle Environment Management System.

One feature that caused slight derision among a small group of former MG employees was an automatic rain sensor, which was intended to switch on the windscreen wipers automatically. Such features, they reasoned, were not worthy of a sports car to be driven by anyone with a shred of competence and, perhaps, they had a point; surely, one can have too much in the way of driver aids. Funnily enough, such an idea was not totally new: 30 years before, an American car had been shown with an optional rain sensor that could, upon detection of water on a special panel in front of the windscreen, switch on the engine, operate the wipers and raise the hood if lowered, no doubt to the consternation of passers-by.

Also considered for the EX-E interior were such features as a head-up display—also seen some years beforehand, when MG's Don Hayter had proposed such a system for his 1971 SSV-1 Safety Car—a hands-free cellular phone, a television screen display for a navigation system, and infra-red remote control for the door locks, all of which became reality in the years that followed. For the styling model, of course, the method of body construction was fairly academic, and the shell of the EX-E model was moulded from the finished clay master by Specialised Mouldings of Huntingdon. Roy Axe recalls, with a smile, that the cost of the plastic body was remarkably low, since Specialised Mouldings regarded it as a prestige exercise, so they reduced the price in return for a moderate amount of publicity gained from their association with the project.

As far as the engineering aspects were concerned, the late Roy Brocklehurst spoke to me about progress in October 1985, shortly

This dramatic rendering shows of the theme of the EX-E styling to good effect. (Rover)

Left *The interior of the EX-E in its near final state; the gear-knob would be altered for the finished version. (Rover)*

Facing page, top *Photographed against the high-tech architecture of the Cambridge Science Park, the EX-E was a dramatic statement from a company associated with family saloons. (Rover)*

Facing page, bottom *The flowing lines of the EX-E cunningly disguised the bulk occupied by the engine and transmission. The family resemblance to the MGF (also the work of EX-E stylist Gerry McGovern) is clear in this shot. (Rover)*

after the EX-E project had been made public: 'Work stopped on the project in June, with about six months' work left to be done. At that stage, we (Austin Rover) had spent about £0.5 million on the project.' Subsequently, I learned that, at this stage, there was a plan to produce a single working prototype, at an estimated cost of around £0.25 million, the idea being to create a running showcase for the company's talents. In the event, it was decided that this would be a self-defeating exercise: too many people would expect the company to put the EX-E into production, and a lot of time would be spent explaining why such an exciting project had been cancelled.

The launch at Frankfurt

Roy Brocklehurst also described how the decision to show the car to the public was very much a last-minute affair: 'It was only on the Friday before the (Frankfurt) show that they actually said yes, although there was clearly a plan to exhibit the car, due to the fact that the exhibition stand was designed for it well in advance.'

The EX-E also provided an opportunity for Austin Rover to explore the current frontiers of modern computer aided design. Nowadays, computer aided design and manufacture (CAD-CAM for short) is commonplace, but at that time, it was still largely the preserve of top-flight companies that could afford the very expensive equipment involved.

Another person who became involved in the project, principally at the promotional end, was Ian Elliott. His job, among others, was to write much of the publicity material, including the text of the brochure that the company issued at the show. He recalls that a lot of thought went into alternative engines, such as the new 2-litre Rover M16, which was being prepared for the Rover 800 XX project. The V6-4V engine was a magnificent device for competition, but it would have required an enormous amount of development for even an exotic car like the EX-E, so it was natural that more economical solutions were considered. Nevertheless, some thought appears to have been given to a competition derivative of the EX-E; indeed, the well-known monthly magazine *Cars and Car Conversions* suggested that a Group S version of EX-E was a distinct possibility. At the time, this idea was dismissed by the company as 'pure speculation'; even if true, the car would have been as short-lived as the ill-fated Group S itself.

Promise unfulfilled

Harold Musgrove played cat-and-mouse with the press when the EX-E appeared in public. 'I believe that the EX-E is a superb illustration of the talent and technology within Austin Rover, qualities upon which our future as a significant world car manufacturer depend,' he said. Then, in anticipation of the obvious question, he added rhetorically, 'Will we put the car into production?' Although

he stressed that it was a feasible exercise and not simply a fanciful dream car, Musgrove was cautious in answering his own question: 'As a car enthusiast, I would dearly love to build it. But as a businessman—well, that could be a different matter. At this moment, I don't know the answer, but it does have manufacturing feasibility. One thing I will confirm is that our future studies with the car will include further assessment of its production viability. We must consider whether to make some prototype runners.' Sadly, those prototypes were never developed enough to be shown, for although the car could have been put into production, it would have required courage to do so when there were so many demands for funds, and while the government had a tight grip on the purse strings.

Roy Axe puts the end of the story into perspective: 'The EX-E project officially died because of lack of funds, but there was more to it than that. The paymasters—the government—would, it was felt, have thought such a car frivolous, particularly when they were hoping to sell the company.' Roy regrets that there wasn't a stronger push from the top of the company to proceed with the car, but concedes that EX-E achieved its original purpose: it showed the world that Austin Rover was on the way up, demonstrating that the company in general, and the styling in particular, had been revitalized. During the following seven years, the single EX-E model was in continuous demand for company displays, and it toured the world as a showcase for Austin Rover's talents; thankfully, it survived to remain a stunning testament to what might have been.

As an interesting postscript to the story, Richard Hamblin put forward EX-E as a means of producing a positive demonstration of the much hyped synergy, which was proclaimed as the reason behind British Aerospace's surprise purchase of the Rover Group in March 1988: 'We tried to find some common ground with the people at BAe, but they were involved in small numbers of hand-built, high-budget bespoke aircraft, whereas we were involved in mass produced products. My idea—although never pursued with much effort on my part—was for a small number of EX-Es to be built by BAe to aircraft standards and technology.' Sadly, nothing came of the idea, which could have resulted in a car not unlike the later McLaren F1 in concept.

Beyond EX-E: the first MGF concept

The significance of the MG name was never lost on Austin Rover management, but unfortunately it was never quite at the top of their lengthy list of priorities. Graham Lewis remembers how the reception given to the EX-E made people in the company look at MG again: 'MG was a very emotional thing at Austin Rover; EX-E had created a great deal of publicity and euphoria, and so people said, "Let's look at it again."' As a result, Richard Carter and Gerry McGovern began work on a concept that was very loosely defined,

according to Lewis: 'It was to have a front engine, but this could have been an A-series, K-series or the 2-litre M16. None of these were particularly specified—we were just exploring the concept.' Before long, an attractive, red, fibreglass full-size model emerged, but for a while, nothing further happened.

Graham Lewis says, 'It was a very very nice little car, but it seemed almost to be the wrong time. The management at the time couldn't seem to decide what cars to build and, of course, money was fairly tight, and there were other more pressing projects.' Richard Hamblin supports this view: 'Everyone loved the car, but unfortunately, the marketing people didn't want to know at that stage.' Six months or so elapsed, and then the project was started up again. 'At this stage,' Graham Lewis remembers, 'the package proposed was the K-series, and work proceeded on scheming the proposal in more detail.' Gerry McGovern adds that, at this point, the package was pretty much R6 Metro-based, with Hydragas suspension, too. With the EX-E behind them, the team chose the name MGF. Automotive graphics were fashionable at the time, with model names and engine types emblazoned in decals over the bodywork, so the combination of the MGF title and the 16-valve engine led to the car being tagged F-16, another reference, no doubt, to that famous US fighter aircraft!

By the late summer of 1986, senior management had to give the go-ahead if the project was to progress any further. Beyond the exterior model, little work had been done, other than concept engineering, which had been carried out by Derek Anderson. Other Rover Group projects were competing for scarce funding, however, and by the autumn, priority had been given to Project Jay. This was a Land Rover proposal to produce a smaller and cheaper offshoot of the Range Rover. Project Jay was seen as a more economically viable project, since it made use of many carry-over parts and had the potential to expand Land Rover's business significantly. Thus, it was given the green light, in due course emerging as the Land Rover Discovery. The MGF model was put away and no further work was done on it.

One legacy of the F-16 almost survived, according to Graham Lewis: 'We had carried out some studies for the F-16 wheels, and come up with some "telephone-dial" pattern alloys. These were subsequently proposed for the MG Maestro Turbo, but rejected on cost grounds; the production Maestro Turbo ended up with the normal spoked alloy MG Maestro wheel instead.'

A new generation of sports cars
The British may have apparently sacrificed their sports car heritage

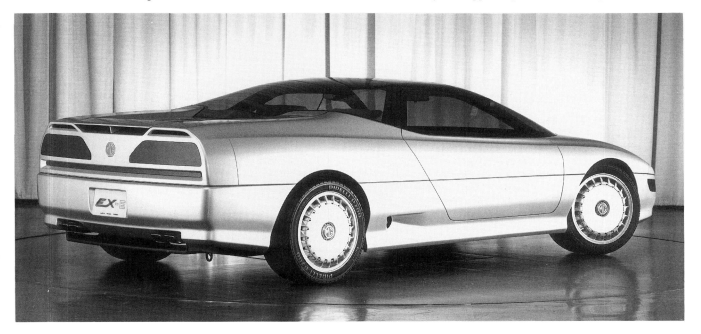

on the altar of cost efficiency, but the appeal of compact, nimble and elegantly styled open cars was not lost on the opposition. Italy clung to its remaining sports cars, including the classic Alfa Romeo Spyder and, for a time, the Fiat Spider (latterly the Pininfarina Spidereuropa) and the 'mini-Ferrari' X1/9, but this was more from expedience than through any genuine conviction. Serous interest in sports cars—in other words, interest that eventually led to cars that customers could buy—sprang primarily from Germany, Japan and North America.

The first sign of a resurgence in the sports car market came when conservative Toyota showed a fascinating concept for a small, neatly styled, mid-engined sports car—dubbed the MR-J—at the 1982 Tokyo Motor Show. Within a year, a hardly altered production version of this car, the MR2 ('midships, runabout, 2-seater'), appeared, taking most of its mechanical components from the 1.6-litre Toyota Corolla. The car was a sensation, seen in the eyes of many as a demonstration of what the promising Fiat X1/9 (and still-born MG ADO21) might have become. At about the same time, Honda used the floorpan and running gear from its immensely competent Civic to produce a sporting coupé called the CRX, and while this was not a sports car in the normal sense, it fulfilled most of the requirements of the average style-conscious customer. Both the MR2 and CRX generated healthy sales, and with the link between Austin Rover and Honda, it was understandable that, before long, there were (false) rumours of an MG-badged derivative of the CRX.

In North America, General Motors dabbled with the Pontiac Fiero, a largely unique, mid-engined two-seater that employed a steel skeleton and composite bodywork. The Fiero was quite an attractive prospect, but GM didn't seem to believe in it and, although it sold steadily for a time, it gradually faded from the picture. A similar fate befell the little-known Buick Reatta, another concept that seemed to promise a great deal, but which failed to deliver. Chrysler, meanwhile, was still fighting back from its low ebb at the beginning of the decade when it came under the control of sports car enthusiast Bob Lutz. Although this led to talk of new sports cars, the reality of Chrysler's financial position meant that Mopar enthusiasts had to be content with hotted-up versions of small Chryslers until the Dodge Viper R/T 10 (complete with V10 truck engine) appeared—initially as a concept car—at the Detroit Motor Show in January 1989.

Ford had long kept a weather eye on the sports car market, having had significant success with the Mustang and Capri sporty cars, and it should not be forgotten that sporting cars had played an important role in the development of the company's image during the 1960s (the original concept for the Mustang had been a very

European looking, lightweight sports car with a mid-mounted V4 engine, and Ford's efforts were closely allied with those of Shelby and Lola throughout that decade). The possibility of the sale of Austin Rover, in 1985, attracted Ford, not so much for the mainstream Austin products, but more for the prestige MG and Rover badges. Ford wanted to expand into the European luxury sector, and they clearly reasoned that it would be cheaper to buy established and still respected brands than attempt to create new ones.

Having failed to acquire Austin Rover in the wake of the General Motors-Land Rover fiasco of early 1986, Ford looked elsewhere and bought into Japan's Mazda car company. Meanwhile, the American company was laying plans for a small, open 2+2 that eventually would emerge as the Mercury Capri (built in Australia, chiefly for the US market, and using the Mazda 323 platform as its basis), and it is interesting to speculate whether this car might have become a Ford-MG had history panned out differently. Of far greater significance in the Ford-Mazda equation, however, was a project for a true sports car in the classic tradition, which emerged at the beginning of 1989 as the Mazda Miata.

In Germany, BMW's specialist division produced the innovative and exciting two-seater, open-topped Z1 roadster in early 1987, combining a zinc-plated steel chassis with a plastic body and what the BMW engineers called a 'mid-front' mounted, 2.5-litre, six-cylinder in-line engine. The styling of the Z1 was quite a departure from the typically elegant and restrained lines of the remainder of the Bavarian company's range, but the most remarkable features were the doors, which retracted into the massive sills at the touch of a button. The Z1 may have been a low-volume (and expensive) toy, but it sold well and did no harm whatsoever to BMW's already cast-iron image.

Although, with the exception of BMW, the sports car activities of the larger European car manufacturers were in the doldrums, the same could not be said of the small British sports car specialists. Morgans continued to be built in much the same way that they had been for 50 years, while TVR went from strength to strength, sales really taking off once the traditional curved TVR styling (redolent of the 1960s Griffith) began to usurp the squarer styling that had been adopted at the start of the decade. The small Marcos company also returned to the stage, while similar specialists, like Ginetta and Caterham, saw sales rise. Clearly, the sports car was returning to popularity, and the prospects for a new MG certainly looked brighter than they had since the end of the previous decade.

The last MG saloons: the MG Maestro Turbo
Tucked away on the Austin Rover stand at the 1988 Earls Court Motorfair was a new variation of the Maestro, yet the company did

Facing page and right The MGF that followed the EX-E was substantially different from the car that would evolve as a result of Project Phoenix in the following decade. This car was an attractive front-engine, front-wheel-drive vehicle with styling by Gerry McGovern, and clearly took a number of styling cues from the EX-E. The basic shape of this car was used later to produce three glass reinforced plastic bodyshells for the preliminary work for PR1, PR2 and PR3—see Chapter 7. (Rover)

little to trumpet its arrival. Of course, plans for a turbocharged version of the Maestro had been formulated at the same time as the Montego Turbo, but in the event, it was very late in the career of the LC10 family that the Maestro Turbo—described in its launch brochure simply as the MG Turbo—made its appearance.

It seemed very likely that the MG Maestro Turbo would not be produced at all, until it was agreed by marketing director Kevin Morley, in 1988, that a limited-edition car could provide a fillip to the Rover range, even though the company was engaged in the process of 'Roverization', which increasingly would marginalize the Maestro and Montego ranges. A particular champion of this idea was Richard Hamblin, who saw the Maestro Turbo as an expedient means of raising the street credibility of the range - especial-

ly within the youth market: 'We started the turbo programme, designed the body kit in Advanced Design, and successfully got Tickford on board.' Even so, according to Hamblin, support for the Maestro Turbo was neither unanimous nor particularly strong outside the concept studio, where it was born, which might explain the rather low-key launch that the car received.

Tickford, the famous coachbuilding and engineering offshoot of Aston Martin, was engaged to develop and manufacture a strictly limited production run on Rover's behalf, building the cars alongside the last of Ford's RS200, which had been a rival of the Metro 6R4. In the event, 505 MG Maestro Turbos were built at Tickford's Bedworth facility, near Coventry. Roger Parker, who owns one of these rare and very fast motor cars, has obtained a copy of the full

THE K-SERIES ENGINE

For many years, the problem with the A-series engine was that, although an increasingly old-fashioned unit, it was too good to justify replacement. It had always been a reasonably economical engine, in each of its many sizes, and it was capable of producing a superb balance of economy and power—particularly torque. Several attempts to convert it to overhead-camshaft operation and replace it with more modern units failed. Consequently, when the Metro arrived in 1980, it featured a significantly upgraded A-plus version of the old stager, rather than the new engine that some people expected.

During the early 1970s, when they were working on the ADO74 project, British Leyland's engineers had developed a number of new engines, dubbed the H- and K-series, although none was related to the later K-series. With the launch of the Metro, and the growing onset of emissions legislation and advancing technology, it was clear that the days of the A-series' supremacy were numbered. Therefore, work began on a brand-new engine which, from the outset, was seen as needing to be a step ahead of not only the A-series, but also the best that the opposition could muster. In addition, it had to be an engine that would last throughout the 1980s and 1990s.

Harold Musgrove had always maintained that a car company should retain the ability to design and manufacture its own engines, and this was one of reasons behind the decision to proceed with Rover's own design, rather than simply buy an engine from Honda. Musgrove remembers being asked by his political paymasters to visit Tokyo and ask three questions of Honda: would they design an engine for Austin Rover, supply one or build engines in the UK? All three questions received a negative response and, on that basis, he was able to proceed with the K-series. 'I have to give credit to Norman Tebbit, then Secretary of State for Industry,' he says, 'who was instrumental in ensuring that we got the money we needed to develop the new engine.'

So interesting was the engine project that it was one of the major factors

that encouraged Ford to discuss the possibility of acquiring Austin Rover in 1985-86, although ultimately the company's approach to the British government failed. Harold Musgrove remembers receiving a message while Norman Tebbit was still at the DTI: 'The message asked me how I would feel about a joint venture with Ford. I have always wanted to try to keep a British motor industry, so we said okay: we would have bought diesels from Ford, and they would have got the K-series from us. However, when they got the teams together and reported back on the K-series, they changed their tack—they wanted to take us over.'

The design that evolved was indeed a radical one, featuring a novel form of through-bolt construction, whereby the engine was effectively split into five layers of castings, held together by ten long bolts. These bolts withstood the considerable vertical combustion forces, distributing stresses evenly throughout the engine, and eliminating the need for separate cylinder-head bolts and main-bearing studs. Another advantage of this construction was that it allowed the use of lighter and smaller castings, thus saving weight and space. As a bonus, the coolant capacity could be much smaller than that of a conventional engine of similar size.

Ford's interest was understandable, but there was the stumbling block of Honda to overcome. Harold Musgrove recalls, 'There was a formal legal agreement that said that if Ford, or others, got a controlling interest in Austin Rover, Honda would pull out. The government went to see Honda and got a ten-minute interview, at which they made it very clear that they would not be prepared to get into bed with their main rival in the North American market.'

The K-series engine made its début in the second Rover 200, launched in October 1989, and, subsequently, was fitted to the Rover 400, Metro (Rover 100) and, of course the MGF. With the expansion of the range of capacities, in 1995, from the original 1.1 and 1.4 to include 1.6- and 1.8-litre derivatives, and the addition of the closely related 2.5-litre KV6 unit in January 1996, the future of the K-series engine seems secure for several years to come.

THE MAZDA MX-5 PHENOMENON

Like Honda, Mazda has always appeared to have a fundamentally different outlook to most of its Japanese automotive peers. The company's acceptance of, and adherence to, the Wankel rotary engine is a clear example of its independent spirit and readiness to embrace the unusual. In 1978, Mazda launched its first true sports car, the RX-7, although previously the company had dabbled with the Cosmo coupé (also with the rotary engine), which was available in Japan only. Interesting and exciting though the RX-7 undoubtedly was, it was not quite a sports car in the traditional sense, but Mazda began to explore the potential of just such a car.

By November 1983, Mazda was investigating niche products and, before long, it focused on a lightweight sports car, known by the acronym LWS. In due course, this became Project P729, which was explored as three possible engine/drive-train options. Design responsibility was shared between separate facilities in Tokyo and California. It soon transpired that while the Japanese arm of Mazda would be happy with either a front-engined, front-wheel-drive layout or a mid-engined, rear-wheel-drive design, the Californian studio was only interested in a traditional sports car layout of front engine, rear-wheel-drive. In April 1984, sketches of each of the three concepts were reviewed by Mazda's management. At first, the front-engined, front-wheel-drive car seemed favourite, but over the following months, as the concepts became full-

size models, the definitive P729 moved to the fore. This had a front mounted engine and rear-wheel-drive. Once this concept had been accepted, the project was transferred to International Automotive Design (IAD) in the UK.

Using the Californian clay, IAD produced a running prototype, called V705, which featured a plastic body mounted on a steel chassis. This was assessed in California by senior Mazda management. In January 1986, the project became part of Mazda's programme, and the task of bringing it to fruition was given to Toshihiko Hirai, who worked with IAD to produce more prototypes. Hirai was the engineer who had been in charge of the Mazda 323 family, and he was delighted to be given the task of managing the project from the concept-vehicle stage to production.

Eventually, the car was launched in the USA (at the Chicago Auto Show in the spring of 1989) as the Mazda Miata, and elsewhere as the Mazda MX-5. It was an instant hit, and all of the motoring press raved about the reincarnation of the real sports car. I remember examining the car at the 1989 London Motorfair, at Earls Court, when I was approached by Toshihiko Hirai himself, who asked if there was anything he could help with. I could not help noticing that he was wearing a small MG badge on his coat lapel...

Needless to say, when Rover began to investigate a new MG sports car, the company looked very closely at the MX-5. An early federal-specification 1.6 was acquired by Richard Hamblin, and as soon as Rover heard of the subsequent 1.8-litre MX-5, an example was acquired direct from Japan.

production records, and records that the production split was 215 in Flame Red, 149 in metallic British Racing Green, 92 in Diamond White and 49 in black. The performance was certainly electrifying for a roomy five-seater, five-door hatchback, with a claimed 0-60mph (0-96.56km/h) time of just 6.7sec, and a top speed of 128mph (205.99km/h), making it the fastest production MG to date. Only the MGF 1.8 VVC, of 1995, which has a top speed of 130mph (209.21km/h), would come near to toppling the MG Maestro Turbo from this illustrious perch.

In March 1989, Tickford—at that point part of the C. H. Industrials Group—issued a press release in which the company's managing director, John Thurston, said, 'This new model is one of the most exciting "hot hatchbacks" on the road today. We are proud to once again be working with MG and hope this marks a revival of the association between our two names.' Sadly, that bold ambition was never realized. I am indebted to Roger Parker, who is a true front-wheel-drive MG enthusiast, for providing the following break-down of MG Metro, Maestro and Montego production. The figures make an interesting comparison with the sports car output of Abingdon.

MG Metro	120,197
MG Metro Turbo	21,968
MG Maestro 1600 R	12,398
MG Maestro 1600 S	2762
MG Maestro EFi/2.0i	27,880
MG Montego EFi/2.0i	37,476
MG Maestro Turbo	505
MG Montego Turbo	7276
Total:	230,462

In the end, the Montego Turbo survived alongside the humbler 2.0i fuel-injected version until both were discontinued in late 1991. The Maestro and Montego ranges lingered on after their MG versions had been dropped, the Montego Si attempting to fill the gap left by the MG version. The last Maestro was built in November 1994, followed by the last Montegos, which were destined for Spain, just before Christmas.

An interesting story concerns the last MG Montego Turbo. Jean Parry, from Surrey, approached her local dealer in the autumn of 1991 with the intention of buying a Montego Turbo, but was disappointed when she was told that the car had been discontinued. Undaunted, she wrote to Terry Whitmore (Rover's director responsible for large cars, then based at Cowley), who asked his colleague, Martin Ince, to see if something could be done. Before long, an order was placed by the Slough Motor Company, and the very last MG Montego Turbo—a British Racing Green specimen,

registered J98 SMO—was built at Cowley and handed over to Ms Parry at the factory, following a guided tour of the plant.

The British Motor Heritage MGB

In 1983, former Cowley body engineer David Bishop joined the new British Motor Heritage organization to help with the task of preserving the company's history for posterity. Initially, he worked at Studley for Peter Mitchell, moving on to manage the Heritage Motor Museum, then at Syon Park in West London, for a while. Within a year, David was made assistant managing director of BMIHT (British Motor Industry Heritage Trust) and—as a classic car enthusiast himself—turned his attention to the important task of catering for the burgeoning classic car service industry, where an alarming number of sub-standard components were being produced as the genuine articles disappeared from the shelves. As David told me in 1987, 'We recognized the need to stop the decline in older vehicles being used; there were not many new classic cars being produced any more.' However, he was keen to emphasize that BMH were 'not in the kit car business; we are purely in the business of making parts for older cars.'

By 1986, David Bishop had realized that a substantial proportion of the MGB body tooling had survived, much of it simply stored out in the open, which was normal practice for heavy steel press tools. That year, he also learned that much of the Triumph TR7 tooling had been scrapped, and he became determined that the same fate would not befall the MGB tooling. Over Christmas, he studied the 250-page volume that listed all of the Pressed Steel/BL parts and sub-assemblies for the MGB. From this, he was able to match the part numbers with the corresponding tooling die numbers, which allowed him to locate the dies in the forests of stored press tools at Swindon and elsewhere. The search took until the end of March 1987, then permission was sought from Rover to remove the tooling and proceed, by which time April had come and gone.

'There were some 800 press tools in all, weighing over 1000 tonnes, which meant 50 lorry loads to be moved to the operation we set up at Faringdon.' Most of the tools had been stored outside and, in some cases, the older tooling that was required had been outside for 20 years. Consequently, some needed repairing, which was carried out at Faringdon and at the pressing plant. Remarkably, only four dies were found to be missing and had to be remade, while other significant finds included valuable framing jigs, which would prove invaluable for the low-volume production envisaged.

Having rescued the tooling and secured premises at Faringdon, the next tasks were to equip the facility and identify the most appropriate production procedures. Obviously, what had been necessary for a large factory assembly line, producing MGB bodies at the rate of up to 1000 per week, would have been inappropriate for

The last new MG saloon, variously christened the Maestro MG Turbo or just plain MG Turbo was launched at the October 1988 Motor Show. The alloy wheels were shared with the contemporary MG Maestro 2.0 EFi, although the 'telephone dial' wheels of the F16 prototype of 1986 were briefly considered for the car. (Rover)

a smaller, compact production facility with no automation, where the planned output was closer to 25 per week. David Bishop managed to acquire all of the overhead and floor mounted welding guns he needed from other parts of the Rover Group, which were upgrading to newer, more automated equipment. To cope with the massive electrical currents required, he located a redundant twin-turbo V8 diesel generator. The catenary power cable to the production facility was woefully inadequate, and the generator proved far cheaper to contemplate than a completely new mains supply.

Last, but not least, David needed to recruit a small, dedicated team to operate the plant, many of whom would need to be familiar with the older, manual ways of working and need to be flexible in their working practices. He persuaded former Pressed Steel supremo Jack Bellinger to come out of retirement and take charge of the facility. Jack was soon followed by old hands Alan Beckett, Bill Bailey and George Milner.

The MGB bodyshell was launched in 1988, its public début being at a classic cars exhibition at the National Exhibition Centre in Birmingham, over the Bank Holiday weekend of 30 April to 2 May. Visitors were treated to the spectacle of a team drawn from leading MG parts specialists transferring the components from a rusted-out MGB into a new British Motor Heritage bodyshell. The resulting car—registered TAX 192G, and hence known affectionately as 'Taxi'—eventually joined the BMH collection.

Subsequently, a similar car was prepared to left-hand-drive specification, and this was driven across the USA, where it was given rave reviews by motoring journalists. The seed had clearly been sown for an MG revival—the mythical phoenix rising from the ashes of Abingdon. During a visit to the Faringdon facility, I was told by David Bishop that BMH hoped to produce about 250 MGB bodies, retailing at about £1250 each (less doors, bonnet and boot lid). In the event, many thousands would be built...

Rover management sees the MGB V8

By 1989, Rover was beginning to think again about the options for future MG sports cars. There were several possible ways forward, and a high-level meeting was called at Canley in July, chaired by future Rover chairman John Towers, to discuss some of these. David Bishop took the first Heritage reshelled MGB to the meeting, while a colleague arrived in the last-of-the-line bronze MGB from the BMH collection. In a shrewd move, Bishop had invited MG enthusiast Roger Parker, together with his MGB roadster, which he had fitted with a fuel-injected Rover V8 engine.

After the main meeting was over, the dozen or so Rover staff gathered around the trio of classic MGBs on one of the factory's test roads. The cars had been assembled largely to provide inspiration, and it did not take long before interested questions about

Roger Parker's car led to him lifting the bonnet and being asked to fire-up the engine. Parker told me, 'When the engine started, all conversation stopped.' There followed a test drive, which resulted in enthusiastic discussions about the viability of producing such a car, using readily available Rover components. David Bishop was already convinced of the merits of this proposal, having also considered, and rejected, the idea of a 2-litre MGB, using the four-cylinder M16 engine; the reaction of the Rover managers was just what he had hoped for. At this meeting, the seeds of what would become the MG RV8 were undoubtedly sown.

AUSTIN ROVER DESIGN: THE CONCEPT DESIGN STUDIO

With the arrival of Roy Axe, the design function at Austin Rover underwent a major overhaul. Two studios had been established at Canley with their own directors: long-time BL stylist Gordon Sked was in charge of exterior design, while Richard Hamblin—recruited from Ogle in April 1983—was put in charge of interior design. One of the first major projects that the two teams became involved in was the Honda/Rover XX luxury car project, which eventually was launched as the Rover 800 in 1986.

In April 1986, however, in the wake of the EX-E, there was a significant realignment of the two studios. Gordon Sked's studio was charged with production design, being given responsibility for both the exteriors and interiors of production cars, while Richard Hamblin became the director of concept design, with a brief to look at more advanced projects on a 'what if?' basis. Prior to this change, Richard contributed to the EX-E and CCV interior design programmes. He recalls, 'Working for me in concept design were Gerry McGovern (responsible for exterior design), Graham Lewis (in charge of interiors), Richard Carter, Jeremy Newman, Ian Beech, Derek Anderson and an excellent team of modellers.'

The concept design studio investigated several interesting projects: 'We produced what became the Rover 200 cabriolet, a 200 coupé concept model (with a removable rear roof section), the MG F-16 and forward visions for future Rover models,' says Hamblin. In addition to the full-size models, the studio developed a number of paper studies: 'Amongst these studies was one where I noticed that the Porsche 911 had been launched at about the same time as the MGB, and yet the Porsche was still on sale. Asking myself what the MGB would look like if it, too, had stayed in production, and been continually refined, I posed this question to my designers. This produced the first concept, which I later resurrected as the basis of Adder, to fill a particular marketing need.'

Adder, and how subsequently it ran in parallel with the British Motor Heritage idea for reviving the MGB, together with other sports car ideas that began to mature at the end of the decade are described in Chapter 7.

7 The 1990s

The story of what eventually became the PR3 project really began at the close of the 1980s, its origins stemming from both the EX-E of 1985 and the F-16 MGF exercise, which had effectively died in September 1986. However, although serious sports car studies began in 1989, most of the development work would take place in the ensuing decade. The great interest shown in the idea of a new MG sports car, encouraged not least by the motoring media, led the management of what had become the Rover Group to re-examine the viability of such a vehicle. The continuous press speculation was discussed during a management conference—or 'scrum', to use the company vernacular—which took place on 18 September, 1989, and was attended by Graham Day and numerous other directors. Richard Hamblin recalls Day saying, 'If someone can show me that we could do this for £40 million, we could do it.' Richard Hamblin's response was, 'Can I take you at your word?' Day retorted that he didn't believe it could be done, particularly since a typical new-car programme could easily cost ten times that figure at the time.

Project Phoenix

Inspired by Graham Day's comment, Richard Hamblin began to consider ways of creating an MG sports car in a short time and to a very limited budget, and he soon came to the conclusion that what was needed was a carry-over base to save both development time and tooling costs: 'I set out alone to work on this idea, using Graham Day's words as authority. I needed to convince others, so I did two things: firstly, I enrolled Mike Donovan (fresh from deliv-

ering the Land Rover Discovery from the basis of the Range Rover chassis), who obviously had experience of using a carry-over base; secondly, I went to Japan where David Blume (of Rover Japan) was able—through a staff contact—to get me into the Pike Studio, which had been building low-volume niche cars (Nissan Be-1, Figaro and Pao) for Nissan.' The latter was of particular interest, since the company responsible for actual production, Takarda Togyo in Yokohama, was building cars in small batches of about 53 per day, quite unlike a typical factory production-line set-up. Back in the UK, Hamblin produced a report and persuaded Nick Stephenson, Fred Coultas and Mike Donovan of the merits of his idea for a dedicated, low-volume facility.

In October 1989, therefore, just prior to the formation of Rover Special Products—and at least partially stung into action by the stunning success of Mazda's MX-5 (launched in the USA, in February 1989, as the Mazda Miata)—Rover instigated fresh feasibility studies into a new MG sports car. The process of so-called 'Roverization' was well under way by this time, and its basic tenet was to bring the Rover name to the fore and abandon the Austin marque in the quest for lower-volume, but higher-quality products.

Towards the end of the previous decade, the idea of applying the MG badge to a derivative of the R8 Rover 200 had been considered. The MG version could have been offered as either an open car or a coupé, such as this prototype, photographed for the archives just before Christmas 1988. Before long, however, Rover's plans for the MG badge became more ambitious, and the concept of badge engineering was abandoned. (Rover)

With the removal of the Austin name from Metros, Maestros and Montegos, the MG badge appeared to be in an increasingly precarious position.

The concept design studio had briefly considered the idea of applying the MG badge to the novel coupé based upon the Project Tracer Rover 200 cabriolet, described in Chapter 6, which was a precursor of Project Tomcat, the Rover 200 coupé. A mock-up of this coupé, which featured removable rear windows over a Rover cabriolet base, was photographed with MG badges, but Gerry McGovern insists that this was never a very serious option. It began to be obvious that any future for the octagon lay with a proper sports car. There were two fundamental problems, however: the last traditional MG sports car had gone out of production ten years before; and, for various legal and technical reasons, the successful relaunch of an MG into the USA could not be taken for granted.

Under the PR code (which stood originally for Phoenix Route, but which, in the case of one of the prototypes, soon gave rise to the nickname 'Pocket Rocket'), a series of concepts was developed. As it transpired, PR1, PR2 and PR3 were all small sports cars—respectively: front-engine, front-wheel-drive; front-engine, rear-wheel-drive; and mid-engine, rear-wheel-drive—although that

need not necessarily have been the case. Brian Griffin, who was largely responsible for overseeing the small MG sports car project through to production, recalls how this came about: 'John Towers was then product development director, and I can recall him asking if we (i.e. Rover) couldn't find a way of doing a sports car again.' Griffin and his colleagues in Rover's Small Cars Division, fresh from delivering the R6 Metro with the K-series engine, were well aware of the problems of developing and producing a niche product, such as a sports car: 'We tended to think in large-volume terms, and this could have been the kiss of death for a sports car project.'

Brian Griffin is keen to emphasize that the primary purpose of Project Phoenix was as an exercise in low-volume production, the output being a sports car; it was not a project to produce a sports car at any cost: 'We were asked to see if we could come up with a viable product, both in terms of financial viability and in terms of manufacturing feasibility.' Nick Stephenson, the director in charge of Rover Small Cars, had had some dealings with Midas (a small kit car manufacturer run by the energetic and talented engineer Harold Dermott), and he suggested that Rover should try to approach the problem of building a sports car in the way that a small company would. Richard Hamblin believes that Nick

GERRY McGOVERN

Gerry McGovern set out on his career as a designer by attending what is now Coventry University and, subsequently, went to the Royal College of Art to study automotive design. He was sponsored by Chrysler—having met Roy Axe, who took him under his wing—so he spent some of his time in the company's American studios. It was during his stint in the USA that Chrysler decided to dispose of its European operations to Peugeot, by which time Roy Axe had transferred to Austin Rover. 'Roy spoke with me prior to the great exodus from Chrysler's Whitley design centre,' Gerry recalls, 'and we discussed the possibility of me coming to work with him. From my experience of working with Roy, I knew that he would be the person to get things going and, in fact, he was instrumental in laying the foundations for what is today's Rover design organization.'

One of Gerry's first tasks, when he arrived at Canley, was to review and update the design methods and presentation techniques being used: 'The Americans had developed many advanced rendering techniques, which we were keen to introduce at Austin Rover.' There followed a small amount of work on the Rover 800, although Gerry readily acknowledges that most of the work on that car should be credited to teams under Roy Axe and Gordon Sked

(including Maestro stylist Ian Beech). Before long, however, Axe created the concept studio, in which Gerry became established as the chief concept designer. His main projects at that stage were the MG EX-E and Rover coupé CCV concept cars, unveiled in 1985 and 1986 respectively

Gerry found that the reaction to these cars was excellent: '...but the press were saying, "You are playing with us; these are great designs, but you aren't putting any of them into production." Although what we were primarily doing was demonstrating that Austin Rover now had a strong design team, I did share their frustration.' After the CCV, Austin Rover decided not to display any more of their concept vehicles unless they had a good prospect of being produced. For some time afterwards, Gerry looked at various projects that never saw the light of day, including a number of MG sports car concepts (among them the original MGF of 1986), but increasingly he wanted to work on a car that would go into production. As a result, he became involved in the R17 programme (the major facelift of the Rover 800), followed by the Tomcat and Tracer derivatives of the Rover 200. From there, it was a short step to the Phoenix Project, which used one of Gerry's earlier MGF concepts as a starting point. He hasn't looked back since.

Gerry McGovern stands alongside a pre-production MGF. (Rover)

BRIAN GRIFFIN

It was largely through the effort, enthusiasm and dedication of a small group of people that the PR3 project survived from inception to production. At times, the journey was far from easy, and many people became involved to ensure that the project moved ahead. One of those who saw the entire project through, and whose peers readily acknowledge should be credited more than most for the part he played in keeping PR3 alive, is Brian Griffin, a former Austin apprentice, who rose to the rank of senior engineer in the present-day Rover Group. From childhood, Brian knew that his future lay in automotive engineering: as the son of famous Austin-Morris engineer Charles Griffin, he was exposed to experimental engineering from an early age.

Since his family lived in the Oxford area, Brian attended a local school at Cowley: 'Father usually went into work at Cowley on a Saturday morning, and as I also attended school on Saturday mornings, I used to walk into the Cowley experimental shop after school and get a lift home.' Cars at the Griffin home were rarely mundane, either: 'For a while, around 1959, we had a turquoise and cream coloured pillarless MG Magnette prototype as our family car. Following an accident, the car was rebuilt—sadly into a new standard bodyshell—resprayed Tartan Red and fitted with an MGB engine.' Another early motoring experience that sticks in Brian's mind is the time his father came home with John Gott's Austin-Healey 3000: 'I couldn't resist the temptation to try it up and down the drive, so I moved the Magnette out of the way and carefully manoeuvred the Healey past it.' Not carefully enough, however: one of the Healey's knock-off wheel nuts caught the front porch of the Griffin residence and took out six bricks: 'There was no damage to the car, but it cost me about three months pocket money to repair the porch!'

Brian began his working career at Longbridge, in September 1960, just as engineering was being consolidated at that plant at the expense of Cowley; his move actually preceded that of the rest of his family, who eventually relocated to the Birmingham area. Over the next four years, Brian moved around BMC in the time-honoured fashion of apprentices, finishing up in the chassis design drawing office. There, he worked on a number of projects, foremost among them being the front suspension of 'Fireball XL-5' (see Chapter 4), under Fred Coultas. From there, he transferred to Longbridge's South Engineering Works, where he worked on the post-prototype development of many BMC and, later, BLMC projects until 1978. Among these were the installation of the E6 engine

into the ADO17 1800; the development of the ADO71 replacement for ADO17; and the installation of the O-series engine into most of the Austin-Morris range, 'but Abingdon carried out most of the work for the MGB.'

From 1978 until 1983, Brian was responsible for building and developing prototypes for Austin-Morris, including those for the Metro and Maestro. Then followed a period of change, the cars business being reintegrated in 1983, to be followed, three years later, by the

Brian Griffin, in 1995. (Rover)

transfer of vehicle evaluation to Gaydon, under Peter Harris. At the same time, the engineering divisions were restructured, with separate directors being responsible for small cars, medium cars and large cars. Brian became the chief engineer for small cars and, from June 1987, was heavily involved in the R6 Metro facelift with the K-series engine, working under Nick Stephenson as director for small cars. By 1989, Brian and his team were looking at R6X, which might have replaced the R6 interim Metro with a significantly revised car. It was at this stage that John Towers began to ask Nick Stephenson, 'Can't you find a way of doing a small sports car again?'

The story of how Brian became involved in the MGF project is related elsewhere in this chapter, but one of his many tales concerning this period is worth repeating here. In early 1991, Nick Stephenson received a letter from a graduate trainee, asking if it would be possible to acquire an old Metro, as he and some colleagues wanted to build a mid-engined version as a college project. 'We were a bit concerned about this, for obvious reasons,' states Brian, 'and so we decided to let them have an old R6 development car, just so long as they agreed that there would be nothing about the car—or our support—in college magazines, etc. They had to build this mid-engined car in two weeks and, to our amazement, they managed it! We borrowed the car from them, as we thought that we could use it as a crash simulator.' Some Rover apprentices were duly roped in and told to use cardboard templates to fabricate steel sections to simulate the real car, removing the roof and reinforcing the sills as necessary: 'We took the resultant car and crashed it at MIRA at 30mph (48.28km/h). In effect, it was the first simulator!'

Stephenson deserves much of the credit for keeping the momentum going in the early days of the project, particularly when, from time to time, the programme seemed to be under threat: 'Nick came to my aid and convinced John Towers to find the money.'

Griffin tells the story: 'We decided to get three such companies to build us concept cars from specified parts bins inside six months. Each company was given an identical GRP shell, taken from a mould made from the earlier MGF (the F-16) done by Gerry McGovern, and they were each then told to go away and build us a running prototype, based upon the mechanical components we gave them.' Richard Hamblin explains the rationale behind this tight programme: 'In an effort to contain expenditure, I gave each contractor 27 weeks, in the proven knowledge that the longer the time, the more opportunity there is to spend money and find problems. These were planned to be—and, indeed, they were—real hands-on, no-drawings prototypes.'

Brian Griffin recalls that approval for this exercise was given quickly and decisively by John Towers: 'I was in the office with Nick Stephenson when he telephoned John, who was in his Range Rover en route to the Rover 200 launch. Nick said that the normal tender procedure would take too long, and suggested that we should offer a cash deal to each of the three companies to do the work on a "take it or leave it" basis. John agreed there and then, and so that is what we did.'

The three musketeers: PR1, PR2 and PR3

The three separate Phoenix projects were coded PR1, PR2 and PR3. PR1 was an all-steel, MGB-sized vehicle with the transversely mounted Rover M16 2-litre engine and basically Maestro chassis technology, which obviously prompted the adoption of a front-wheel-drive layout. This was given to Motor Panels to build, although the project should not be confused with the company's

later and totally different involvement in the MGF. The second car, PR2, went to Reliant and comprised a V8 engine with rear-wheel-drive, a separate chassis and polymer bodywork. The appearance of this car bore an intriguing resemblance to the restyled Reliant Sabre, which subsequently emerged in 1992! The third concept, PR3, utilized the K-series engine in 1.4-litre, MPi fuel-injected form, and was given to ADC (short for Automotive Development Centre Ltd, which was formerly part of GM-Vauxhall). The K-series engine more or less dictated the mid-engined format, although this was not a prerequisite.

From the outset, John Burton was responsible for overseeing the body engineering aspect of the Phoenix programme, while the chassis work came under engineer Robin Nickless' direction. Robin told me, 'PR1 used a Maestro floorpan, which was shortened by 70mm (2¾in) in the area of the seat.' The impressive hand-built steel prototype had a battery in the boot—to meet packaging and weight-distribution requirements—specially engineered pop-up headlamps and a well-finished interior with a Rover 200 fascia. The prototype, constructed under the direction of Alan Scholes at Motor Panels, was delivered as a very competent, drivable vehicle in July 1990. I was allowed to examine this car at Rover's Gaydon research establishment, where its impressive quality was readily apparent; it could easily have been a pre-production model. PR1 clearly remains Robin Nickless' favourite, although like his colleagues, he has no problem with the mid-engined car that eventually emerged. Richard Hamblin also felt that this option had much to recommend it: 'The wheelbase and track were almost identical to the original F-16 model. At that time, we felt that this just had to be the answer—divine providence was working and, furthermore, this would not be a difficult programme to deliver. There was one problem on the horizon, however: the Maestro was well past its sell-by date, and so the platform would not be in production much longer.'

Above *One of the three variations on the Phoenix theme was PR1, built in steel by Motor Panels, using the fibreglass copy of Gerry McGovern's 1987 F-16 as reference. It featured front-wheel-drive, using a shortened Maestro under-frame and a tranvserse 2-litre M16 engine. (Rover)*

Below *Of the three Phoenix prototypes, PR1 was perhaps the closest in styling terms to Gerry McGovern's F-16. The influence of the EX-E concept car is readily apparent in this view, particularly in the sweep of the nose. (Rover)*

Above *The second running prototype, PR2, was built by Reliant, using a chassis based upon that of the Reliant SS1, but with many tweaks to cope with the 3.9-litre V8, driving through a standard Rover '77mm' gearbox to the rear wheels. The Rover Special Products team was very impressed with this prototype: they point to the exemplary way in which the Reliant craftsmen had managed to extend the original fibreglass body with virtually invisible joins and the beautifully finished engine bay. (Rover)*

Below *From this view, the styling of the Reliant-built PR2 prototype is less successful, the long nose appearing to be at odds with the very short tail, but then styling was never the most important issue with any of these cars. Their primary purpose was to allow the packaging and the basic concepts to be assessed; any production versions that may have arisen would naturally have been subjected to much more design work and refinement. (Rover)*

Above and right *The PR3 proposal by ADC was beautifully produced as an all-steel prototype with carefully scaled proportions. Clearly, it was a concept with great potential. This photograph was taken at Canley in July 1990. (Rover Special Products)*

An attractive 'optional extra' that came with the ADC PR3 prototype was this elegant removable hardtop, which complemented the lines of the car well. Unlike some hardtops, its styling did not look as though it had been a last-minute afterthought. (Rover Special Products)

This, we felt, could have been overcome, but the anti-front-wheel-drive lobby eventually saved us the trouble.'

PR2 was built at the Tamworth based Reliant factory and utilized a Scimitar SS1 chassis, which had been adapted to accept some Maestro front suspension components and brake discs, in combination with the standard Reliant suspension, which was based on wishbones rather than the much taller MacPherson struts of the Maestro. The engine and drive-train were pure TVR in concept, the 3.9-litre fuel-injected Rover V8 being set well back in the engine bay. The entire project was overseen by Reliant's Peter Slater, and despite the fact that Reliant was experiencing problems and had only recently returned to serious development work, the car was finished ahead of time, in only four months. The bodywork, in particular, was beautifully executed: Robin Nickless and Don Wyatt (former Rover Special Products chief stylist) pointed to the well-finished engine bay, with moulded rain channels around the edges, as an example of the professionalism of Reliant's body men. The pop-up headlamps on PR2, unlike those of PR1, were not made specially, but adapted from those of the Reliant SS1, while the interior was pure Reliant. According to Don Wyatt, PR2 made 'all the right V8 noises, but does tend to overheat', a trait that will surely ring a bell with some MGB GT V8 owners! Richard Hamblin points out that the V8/rear-wheel-drive layout was an obvious choice, which would have been favoured by US customers, but as there were no suitable platforms left in the range, PR2 would have required a completely new chassis: 'I was none too keen on the styling of Reliant's Scimitar, but their chassis seemed relatively sophisticated.'

PR3 was executed by ADC at Luton, under the enthusiastic direction of Ernie Cockburn. According to Robin Nickless, 'ADC were, I felt, really trying to make a point with their car. They had only recently moved into prototype development of this sort, and they obviously wanted a good result with PR3.' The steel-bodied car was shortened by 6in (15.24cm) and narrowed by 4in (10.16cm) from the dimensions of the GRP model supplied to the company. The idea was for a cheap and cheerful sports car with the 1.4-litre K-series engine. Metro R6 sub-frames were fitted front and rear, Tony Best of Moulton becoming involved to assist in

ROVER SPECIAL PRODUCTS

In the mid-1980s, a team was formed within Land Rover, under the title Swift Group, and given the brief to explore projects from feasibility to pre-production in a reduced time-scale, drawing upon a multitude of disciplines within the company. From this group had sprung the beginnings of the Land Rover Discovery, and it gave rise to the idea of a think-tank that could be extended to cover the rest of the Rover Group.

On 28 March, 1990, a special projects group was approved by the Rover executive committee. This led to the assembly of about 40 personnel, of various disciplines, who were drawn from throughout Rover. This group, known as Rover Special Products (RSP), came under the control of four directors—Steve Schlemmer, Richard Hamblin, David Wiseman and John Stephenson—and was based at Gaydon. Schlemmer had helped set up the Swift team at Land Rover, and while he doesn't believe that this was a factor in the creation of RSP, his previous experience must have been of value. He explains the origins of RSP thus: 'The ideas for RSP came from various sources in the Rover Group, especially a number of studies by Richard Hamblin. After a three-month study by Richard, myself and John Stephenson, the idea was approved by the board in early 1990, and set up under marketing director Kevin Morley.'

RSP's brief was to explore options for niche products and take them to the point of pre-production, at which stage, if accepted, they would be taken over by the relevant business group in Rover. One of the principal objectives of RSP was to find a way of introducing a new sports car for £40 million. An early RSP project was the reintroduction of the Mini Cooper, which was followed by the limited-edition Range Rover CSK (using the initials of 'Spen' King).

The idea of a Mini Cooper had been under consideration for several years, but it took the special products division to bring the idea to fruition. RSP was also instrumental in preparing the groundwork for the relaunch of the Land

Rover marque in the USA, in the form of the Land Rover Defender and Discovery. There followed the Mini and Metro cabriolets, a limited-edition Mini Cooper Silverstone for the German market, the Rover Tourer, much of the early work on the PR1-5 prototypes and, of course, the MG RV8.

By the autumn of 1993, RSP had carried through 19 product actions, generating an extra £70 million in revenue for the Rover Group. However, the situation was not always as rosy as it seemed: what had worked very well for the more self-contained and close-knit community at Land Rover did not always succeed in the larger Rover Cars division. There were differences of opinion and, before the end of 1993, the Rover board decided that RSP had fulfilled its original purpose. Thus, the group was wound up, most of the staff being redeployed in the company, while a few moved on to pastures new.

Steve Schlemmer believes that many factors led to RSP's demise: 'I don't believe that anything went wrong with RSP. The environment in the Rover Group changed in two significant ways after RSP was set up. Firstly, a new product supply organization was formed which, in many areas, had the capabilities and the will to do niche products. Secondly, the first years of the nineties were difficult times financially; the scale of funding originally envisaged for RSP's plans was no longer justified. In 1992, I was running RSP and reporting to Graham Morris (late of Sterling); we could already see a limited future for a separate product development function in Rover Europe. We took the decision to wind it up in 1993 before BMW's purchase. I believe that BMW would have taken the same view.'

A slightly different perspective comes from Richard Hamblin: 'For the main two years of its short life, RSP had four equal directors, and no one of them was in overall charge. As such, RSP could be said to have been a slightly misconceived experiment: on occasions, it ran a bit like an ocean liner with four strong captains on the bridge, each with a different understanding of the weather, a different chart and a different port in mind...'

Left A rendering for PR3 by Rover Special Products, dating from early 1991. At this stage, a larger sports car aimed at the US market was the preferred project, but according to Don Wyatt, 'everyone who saw PR3 fell in love with the concept of the package; there were very mixed emotions at the time.' While Gerry McGovern's F-16 style looked good on the PR3 running prototype, there was a great deal of interest in how the car would look with a 'modern' style (F-16 had been styled in the mid-1980s). This sketch is an early attempt to explore this line of thought. (Rover Special Products)

adapting the Hydragas suspension system. Looking back, Richard Hamblin says that although the mid-engine configuration may seem obvious for the third design, it was not so at the time: 'This solution came to me last after struggling to find the third alternative with ADC. Moreover, it would not have been possible had the Metro not had independent sub-frames. The first prototype took a Metro sub-frame at the front with the engine removed, and another at the rear with the steering just bolted up. All we had to do was to modify a Metro floorpan to keep the two sub-frames apart and handle the torsional and bending loads.' Hamblin says that the 'quartered' F-16 bodyshell—which, like PR1 and PR2, was not a serious styling proposal—proved crude, but quite effective: 'When I left Rover two years later, there were still people telling me that this style was, for them, the best of all the options produced!'

On 27 July, 1990, Richard Hamblin produced a comprehensive report on all three options, exploring in detail the relative merits of each (referred to in the report as MGF-1, MGF-2 and MGF-3) and explaining where parts would be carried over. The report also suggested that a production car was feasible by 1993. Six months after

commissioning—by now it was August 1990—the completed PR1, PR2 and PR3 prototypes were tested by Rover management in great secrecy during a midnight session at the Gaydon test facility where, by all accounts, the cars were truly driven in anger. Richard Hamblin explains the relative merits of each car: 'PR1 was by far the easiest to deliver, being based on the Maestro, but we ran up against the anti-front-wheel-drive lobby, even though most younger drivers only knew front-wheel-drive, and the Lotus Elan was on the way. PR2 was hairy: it was frighteningly powerful and had the fun element we sought. Everyone, however, fell in love with the PR3, in particular John Towers, who emerged from it wearing a big grin.'

The Rover board came to the conclusion that they should proceed with the V8 model—in other words, a development of the PR2 concept—as it was felt that this was what the North American market needed, but there remained a great deal of interest in the small mid-engined car, too. At this stage, therefore, Rover Special Products (which had been set up earlier in the year under marketing director Kevin Morley) was asked to investigate a further

Above *At the start of the decade, a number of paper studies were made to investigate all possible permutations of the MG theme. At about this time, the Japanese produced a number of retro styled cars, and there were signs that these might be well received in the UK. Consequently,. RSP decided that they would investigate every idea, not matter how unusual it might seem. One of the more interesting was this MGX proposal, drawn by Don Wyatt. It was a modern interpretation of the MGA style, regarded by many as more classically British than the MGB. (Rover Special Products)*

Below *This rendering by Don Wyatt shows an attempt to marry the style of the MGA with the basic body structure of the MG Midget (presumably the engine would have been an in-line mounted K-series driving the rear wheels). This would have been feasible since British Motor Heritage had reintroduced the Midget bodyshell in the wake of the MGB shell. However, there is little doubt that the cramped driving position and relatively complex (and therefore expensive) Midget monocoque would have been unsuitable for a 1990s sports car. (Rover Special Products)*

option, PR4. Basically, this was similar in concept to PR2, but it was to have an all-steel bodyshell in place of the composite unit, although still on a separate chassis. PR4 never got very far, however, as it was soon overtaken by both the Adder (the RV8) and another large sports car project.

Roy Axe and DR2/PR5: the boulevard cruiser

Roy Axe (by now established in a separate advanced styling studio, called Design Research Associates, at Tachbrook Park, Warwick) produced DR2—Design Research No.2—a distinctive up-market boulevard cruiser type of sports car. This had classic styling that drew very heavily on one of Roy's favourites, the Austin-Healey 3000, and it featured the distinctive sloping side creases of that car, although it was also redolent of Jaguars and Aston Martins. Intended to feature a sophisticated chassis, this car could have shared a new V8 engine, based upon the K-series, with a boldly styled Rover flagship saloon concept, coded R16/R20. DR2 would have been an expensive project, requiring a totally new chassis and a massive investment in parts and servicing back-up in the USA if it had been sold there.

The distinctive styling of Roy Axe's DR2/PR5 (DR2 stood for Design Research No. 2) shows the influence of a number of traditional British sports cars, notably the Jaguar E-type and Austin-Healey 3000, the latter a personal favourite of Axe. Based upon the Rover V8 or proposed KV8 drive-train, this would have been quite a motor car. (Rover)

To determine if Roy Axe's design was feasible, Don Wyatt and Robin Nickless had to take a fibreglass shell from the clay and build a running prototype. They thought that the most effective way of doing this would be to cannibalize a TVR, so they went in search of suitable donor. Robin recalls, 'We went to a dealer which had a TVR 3.5S in their showroom which, it transpired, they were selling on a commission basis on behalf of its owner. We crawled all over it—underneath, over the engine, inside—much to the consternation of the lady in the showroom. Of course, we couldn't reveal who we were or the real reasons behind our interest, so she wasn't able to

This rear view shows the elegant lines of DR2/PR5 to good effect. Note the sweeping wing swage line—clearly inspired by the 'big Healey'—and neatly proportioned clean tail. (Rover)

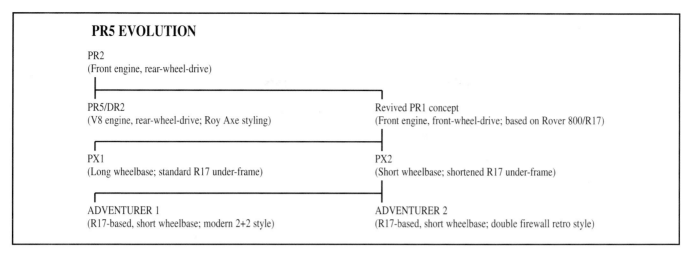

PR5 EVOLUTION

PR2
(Front engine, rear-wheel-drive)

PR5/DR2
(V8 engine, rear-wheel-drive; Roy Axe styling)

Revived PR1 concept
(Front engine, front-wheel-drive; based on Rover 800/R17)

PX1
(Long wheelbase; standard R17 under-frame)

PX2
(Short wheelbase; shortened R17 under-frame)

ADVENTURER 1
(R17-based, short wheelbase; modern 2+2 style)

ADVENTURER 2
(R17-based, short wheelbase; double firewall retro style)

tell the owner much about us. Eventually, we agreed to buy the car, and a date was agreed for us to collect it. When we arrived, the lady in the showroom told us that the owner, clearly an enthusiast, had been into the showroom, fixed the faulty car alarm and polished the car. I cannot imagine what his reaction would have been if he had seen what we did to the bodywork of his car with a chain-saw the next day, when we got it back to Gaydon...'

Before long, a running prototype had been built at Canley, with Roy Axe's DR2 bodywork grafted on to the TVR chassis. It was finished in stunning metallic green (subsequently repainted red). At this point, DR2 was officially recognized as part of the Phoenix programme, being given the code PR5/DR2. According to Don Wyatt, however, the prototype did not fully reflect Axe's original proposal: 'Roy's DR2 had a unique interior, which married to the exterior style, but because of our "old friend" timing constraints—and the complexity of developing the new style to fit over the TVR electrics (switches, gauges, etc)—we defaulted in favour of retaining the standard TVR interior for the running prototype.'

Also in contention by this point were two other RSP proposals, called Adventurer 1 and 2. An earlier idea had been to produce a convertible from the Rover 800-based CCV coupé which, in turn, led to thoughts about adapting the front-engined, front-wheel-drive PR1 concept to the Rover 800 (R17) chassis. This generated two exercises: PX1 with the standard Rover 800 wheelbase, and PX2 with a shortened wheelbase. However, neither could be considered a true sports car in concept, so the RSP team looked at ways of adapting the DR2/PR5 design to the R17 chassis.

In the case of PX1, the standard wheelbase meant that its saloon car origins were almost impossible to disguise, even with longer doors, but as Don Wyatt is keen to point out, 'Even with the same windscreen/front-wheel proportions retained from the R17, the short-wheelbase version begins to look a bit 'cheeky'; take 200mm (8in) out of the chassis behind the front seats, add a new body, and we're on our way!' PX1, the standard-wheelbase concept, was never proceeded with, but PX2 spawned Adventurer 1 and Adventurer 2. According to Don Wyatt, these were basically extensions of the front-wheel-drive PR1 component carry-over concept, using the Rover 800 floorpan with a shortened wheelbase and either modern or modern/retro styling respectively.

Adventurer 1 was built on a Sterling chassis, powered by the Honda sourced 2.7-litre V6 engine. There were only two alterations: a new windscreen and a 20cm (8in) shorter wheelbase. This, according to Don Wyatt, gave rise to an interesting 2+2 package which, in turn, generated a fairly modern design in proportion: 'Most of the work was done directly on the car, but the sketch (see page 214) shows just what this large modern car could have looked like. There were very few sketches done on this version, as we were all anxious to look at Adventurer 2.' The latter displayed more dramatic and quite innovative changes, as Don explains: 'The work was done over the original Adventurer 1 car, with the difference being that we used a double-skinned firewall. This gave us a much more interesting retro look to the front-wheel/windscreen/door-shut relationship. We now had a long bonnet and a rearward posi-

tioned cabin, much more reminiscent of the traditional British sports car.' The 2+2 seating had been dropped, the driver's seat having been moved back almost to the position of the standard R17 rear seats. However, the result was more of a sports car in appearance, akin to the RV8's proportions, but with a modern chassis.

A wire-frame model was built by Motor Panels to allow evaluation of the packaging layout for Adventurers 1 and 2. This, along with the TVR-based DR2 prototype, survives at Gaydon.

Although the mid-engined PR3 was held in high regard, particularly by those with fond memories of the EX-E concept, the larger sports car was still given higher priority. Thus, while PR5 was being developed, the Adder project, which was based on the earlier British Motor Heritage exercise and which ultimately became the RV8, was put forward by RSP. This, too, was soon given the green light. In the meantime, however, Brian Griffin recalls that John Towers kept asking Nick Stephenson about the feasibility of a small car. Needless to say, once he had been asked a few times, Stephenson wisely decided that he would have to carry out some further studies so that he could give a meaningful answer to his boss. Griffin says, 'Nick asked me—together with John Doyle and Geoff Squires—to do a concept review of PR3; to see if we could come up with a manufacturing strategy, an exercise which took us three months.' In the meantime, the other concepts, including Adder and PR5, were still being worked on.

A toe in the water: initial PR3 styling development

In January 1991, with PR3's engine packaging more or less determined, Rover decided to commission an external consultant to style the car, using the groundwork carried out by RSP's Dick Bartlam (see sketch on page 210). Primarily, this was because Rover's own team, under Gordon Sked, was too heavily involved in mainstream products to carry out the work required for the small MG concept, which was not yet part of the corporate plan. Richard Hamblin oversaw the work and, initially, this was only given to Luton based ADC, which had already built the first running PR3 prototype. However, Richard was approached by the appropriately named MGA Developments of Coventry (well-known for their prototype design and build facilities) who, according to him, 'told me that they were not very busy, and so we were able to take advantage of their services at marginal cost and let them work on a clay, too.'

In fact, both clays developed along very similar lines, being tied strictly to engineering and packaging requirements. Richard Hamblin credits John Sowden for much of the work at ADC: 'John worked on the exterior style for me at ADC, and he also produced an interior model which, in fact, was not too far off the final MGF article.' By May 1991, the ADC and MGA clays were ready to be presented to Rover's management.

In June 1991, a clinic was staged in Manchester for potential customers. Its primary purpose was to test reactions to Adder and PR5, although the PR3 clays were presented, too. According to Brian Griffin, the participants in the clinic saw the MGA clay as 'masculine' and the ADC clay as 'feminine'. Not content with gauging opinions about the various models on show, Rover was keen to

DON WYATT

American Don Wyatt was one of the Rover Special Products team charged with the exciting, but daunting, task of developing the concept of a new MG sports car. Among his accomplishments, he can list a masters degree in design from the University of Michigan, and periods spent working for General Motors, Chrysler and Toyota in the USA. He spent time both in Detroit and on the West Coast, where he was instrumental in founding Toyota's CALTY (California Toyota) studio at El Segundo. In 1981, Don moved to Europe with Peugeot-Citroën (PSA), where he became the group's director for advanced design.

Although working in France, Don maintained a home in England (where he admits to having kept a Russet brown MGB GT, complete with orange-striped seats, for use during sojourns in the UK!) and, in due course, he met and married an English girl in 1987. 'At around that time, Land Rover were starting work on the P38 Range Rover—almost called the Discovery, but that is another story—and so I joined Rover, and have been with the company ever since.' In fact, Don joined Land Rover as the advanced design manager: 'Since they were just starting P38, it was deemed an advanced programme, and George Thomson and I oversaw the first clay models of P38. Once completed, I began work on

other advanced programmes, whilst George—then production design manager—took complete charge of P38, developing the style into the final product. Land Rover and Rover had by now been reunited, and my next project resulted in my doing a 4x4 concept clay right next to Gerry McGovern's model for Tomcat (the Rover 200 coupé) in the Canley studio.' The gist of this story is that George, Gerry and Don had all worked together, between 1981 and 1983, at PSA's Whitley design studios—the car industry is a small world!

When Richard Hamblin left RSP, in August 1991, Don Wyatt assumed the position of chief stylist, but with the winding down of RSP, in 1993, he assumed other responsibilities. For some time, he has been part of a team working on a project for Rover International out of Gaydon.

Don Wyatt, at Gaydon, 1995. (Rover)

Above *This wire-frame packaging model is of Adventurer 1, one of a number of ideas that evolved from DR2/PR5 in early 1991. It clearly shows the shortened Rover 800 floorpan and 2.7-litre Honda sourced V6 engine. (Rover Special Products)*

Below *Don Wyatt's rendering depicting Adventurer 1 and showing the modern flowing lines, which neatly integrated some elements of the earlier Roy Axe DR2/PR5 design. (Rover Special Products)*

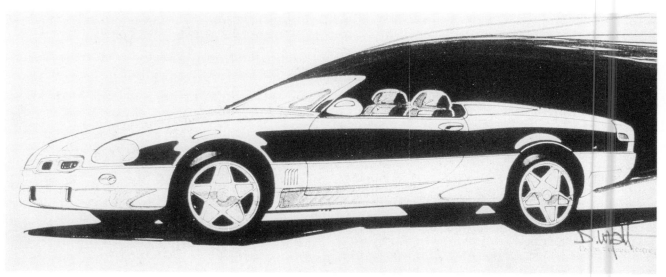

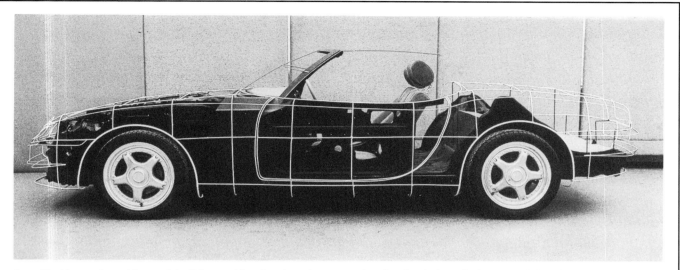

Above *After Adventurer 1 came Adventurer 2, in which a second firewall was inserted and the whole interior moved rearwards to provide a more traditional sports car balance* to the styling. *The only obvious disadvantage was the loss of the rear seat, which might have made Adventurer 1 more appropriate for the US market. (Rover Special Products)*

Above *This view probably shows Adventurer 2 at its best; the swooping rear wing line is a classic hallmark of British sports car design. (Rover Special Products)*

Below *Don Wyatt produced this rendering to show how Adventurer 2 might have looked; it remains a personal favourite of his. (Rover Special Products)*

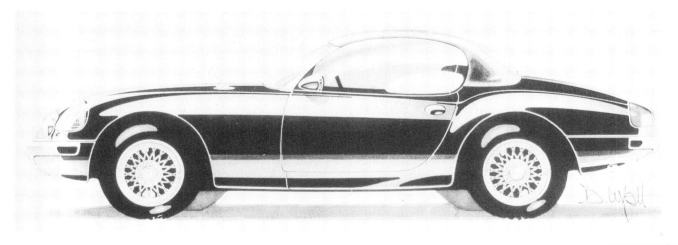

A dramatic rendering by MGF designer Gerry McGovern, featuring large 'nostrils' and narrow, slit-like headlamps. (Rover)

Below and facing page *With the mid-engine layout chosen, an external consultant was called in to develop the PR3 style, which was still not yet part of the corporate plan. Richard Hamblin oversaw the work, and this proposal—known as PR3/8300—was produced by Luton based ADC in February-May 1991. ADC had produced the lovely 'Route 3' engineering prototype and, naturally, were keen to continue their involvement with the project. Note the nondescript badge, deliberately fitted at this stage to make it difficult for prying eyes to determine the client's identity! (Rover Special Products)*

ascertain how the MG marque was perceived by the customer. In particular, the company wanted to know whether it had been damaged in any way by its decline in the 1970s and its subsequent use on the Metro, Maestro and Montego ranges. The response was overwhelmingly positive: rather than having been tarnished by recent events, if anything, MG had grown in esteem and was fondly regarded as producing the quintessential British sports car.

Ironically, the results of the clinic showed that the MG badge evoked strong sentiments and feelings of nostalgia, even in people who had never sat in an MG, let alone owned one. Furthermore, it soon became clear that the customer profile was remarkably close to that of the last MGB, which had been researched for the sports car advisory committee in 1978 (see Chapter 5). Mike Ferguson, of Rover Brand Management, recalls that people attending the clinic were asked to sum up MG in a few words; two phrases that stuck

in his mind were: 'The leading sports car brand', and 'Small, red and playful'. Clearly, the brand's image would not present any problems for the company.

However, while PR3 and Adder were largely successful, this clinic signalled problems for PR5. Although universally liked, PR5 was not perceived as an MG: it was seen as being more in the mould of a Jaguar or Aston Martin, clearly in £40,000 luxury car territory. While this was rewarding for the designers, it would have sat uneasily alongside a Rover range that peaked with the Rover Sterling at just over half that price. Furthermore, the situation in North America was deteriorating. The Sterling operation was experiencing serious difficulties: sales had fallen—in common with those of some of Rover's European rivals—and painful decisions on the future of Rover's Miami based subsidiary were imminent. With the announcement, on 9 August, 1991, that Rover was termi-

nating the Sterling sales operation with immediate effect, the need for the big US-market R16 saloon and PR5 MG sports car evaporated. Consequently, PR3 was pushed even further to the fore as PR5 was shelved.

Although there was overwhelming enthusiasm for a new MG sports car at the June 1991 clinic, opinions were strongly polarized as to the form it should take: one group was in favour of something modern and technologically exciting (in the vein of the Toyota MR2), while the other was adamant that an MG sports car should extol traditional values—such as retro styling—as exemplified by the Mazda MX-5. The two PR3 clays were both expressions of modern sports car styling, but neither was identified as an MG by the clinic visitors, which was felt to be a definite marketing handicap. That PR3 had survived this far should be credited in part to Brian Griffin and Tony Doyle, says Gerry McGovern, 'PR3 wasn't

DEVELOPING THE MG BADGE

As part of the task of reinventing the MG sports car, Rover carried out a lot of research into the public perception of the image of the MG name, and the badge in particular. It was obvious that the octagonal logo could not be altered significantly, but there was a feeling that the red and chrome badges that had been applied to the Metro, Maestro and Montego ranges lacked the class or cachet of the original brown or black and cream badges seen on the last of the MGAs in 1962.

Steve Schlemmer credits Don Wyatt as being the main influence behind the badge redesign: 'His skill and sensitivity to what was required, and his pragmatic approach to what was possible led to the result that we had on the RV8 and all associated material.' Don recalls that the origins of the new badge really sprang from a meeting with a marketing consultancy, Marketplace Design, which had been charged with the task of developing a corporate style for point-of-sale material, such as brochures and other promotional items: 'Marketplace said, "We need the badge design now," but I hadn't been able to think about it. Bear in mind that at RSP, at that time, we were working on the Mini and Metro cabriolets, a bevy of advanced concepts—including a two-seater Metro Speedster—the Rover 400 Tourer, PR1, PR2, PR3 and Adder, and there was only Richard and me to deal with it.'

All that Don could do was expound his belief that there was a need to move away from the red and chrome theme, which had been developed at the beginning of the 1960s, and to revert to the traditional MG colours of brown and cream: 'Marketplace took this idea away and literally came up with the

graphic which was used for the brochure.' The badge featured a background of horizontal lines, but retained straight sides. However, Don Wyatt felt that the new badge was not quite special enough. To develop the theme further, RSP brought in a Warwick based design consultancy, DCA Design Consultants, which had worked on previous projects for the company, such as the badge for the Mini Cabriolet. DCA was briefed to develop various ideas, including a rounded theme; they produced numerous sketches and handmade mock-ups for RSP appraisal. Don Wyatt points out that Rover has a team within its main styling group that, among other things, looks after badge design, 'but Adder was not mainstream, and so the main studio did not see the badges until they had been completed.'

Before long, the definitive new MG badge began to emerge, with its characteristic horizontally grooved setting for the chrome and bronze letters and octagon, although there was much experimentation to find the best colours. When the design had been finalized, it was adopted for publicity material, the MG RV8 and, since then, the MGF and corporate insignia. The actual badge comprises a printed aluminium substrate, which is embossed, coated in a high-gloss lacquer, then domed.

DCA also designed a chrome plinth for the badge, adding an extra sense of quality. For the boot of the RV8, a substantial black plinth had to be used to disguise the fact that the badge sits over the hole and shaped recess that had accommodated the luggage compartment lock of the MGB. For the MGF, Gerry McGovern provided the front badge with a chrome shield-shaped plinth which, in fact, forms part of the badge itself, neatly harking back to the pre-1974 MGB grille badges.

Above *This sketch by stylist Julian Quincy dates from 1991, by which time the overall theme of the PR3 styling was beginning to come together. (Rover)*

Left and below *These sketches by Julian Quincy illustrate the development of the MGF 'face'. In the event, it was decided to go for the simpler open 'nostrils'— inspired by the 'rubber-bumper' MG—and to eschew the conventional barred radiator grille. (Rover)*

The definitive PR3 styling clay takes shape at Canley under the direction of Gerry McGovern. Note the ellipsoidal headlamp shape proposed at this point. (Rover)

Side view of the 1991 Canley clay for PR3. The proportions are about right, but the head- and tail-lamps have yet to be defined in their final forms. (Rover)

even in the programme, but these guys did everything they could to keep the interest going in the concept.'

Creation of the definitive PR3 style

At this point (early summer 1991), Rover took the styling back in house at Canley, and Gordon Sked gave Gerry McGovern the task of developing the form of the definitive PR3. Brian Griffin recalls, 'We weren't going to do another early clinic on the clay model which resulted from this, because the previous clinic had already told us that we had to incorporate obvious MG styling cues.' Any similarities between the definitive MGF that eventually emerged and the proposals by external consultants should not be surprising. Principally, they are a consequence of the particular packaging and engineering requirements that had been laid down (such as the need for side air intakes of a certain size and location), coupled with a requirement to use certain vehicles for inspiration (such as EX-E).

Pop-up headlamps were a feature of the MGA clay, while the ADC design featured rather novel pop-down units, but Gerry McGovern told me, 'We found that they gave a disproportionate look at the front, and rapidly became dated.' Furthermore, he said, 'The ADC car was frankly not what we wanted.' He went on to stress that he felt the MGA clay was 'rather amorphous, with no tension. It also looked too big for its power unit.' If anything, MGA

had tried too hard to use the EX-E as a reference: 'It had a very low front end—very wedgy—and there was no obvious MG identity in the car.' This latter point was felt to be quite critical: 'The MGA car was clinicked, badgeless, alongside the ADC car, and although it was quite well received, it was not recognized as an MG.' Accordingly, it was decided to go for a look that 'had a definite link to the MGB—the combination of grille aperture and lamps was fundamental—but nevertheless, it had to be a modern interpretation.' Gerry produced a report on the MGA clay, and began to create what would become the definitive PR3 clay. While this was taking place, another fascinating project was also taking shape.

The retro MG: Project Adder

Clearly, Rover's management had been impressed by the potential of an updated MGB with the Rover V8 engine when they examined Roger Parker's home-built example at the planning meeting in July 1989 (see Chapter 6), and Richard Hamblin's concept design studio had already toyed with the idea of a revitalized MGB. There is little doubt that the visceral appeal of Parker's car went some way to encouraging the development of the PR2, PR4 and PR5 proposals. However, the story of what would eventually emerge as the MG RV8 really begins after that planning meeting in 1989.

British Motor Heritage, flushed from the success of their MGB bodyshell venture—which greatly exceeded expectations—were given the brief to build their own MGB V8, but to update it where necessary for reasons of safety, legislation and probable customer expectations. Don Wyatt, the RSP styling man, who effectively took over from Richard Hamblin in late 1991, recalls that Richard had been excited by Roger Parker's car and began to push for what, eventually, would become the Adder project. In fact, Hamblin and his staff had already produced a sketch of a possible MG based upon the BMH bodyshell, so it is hardly surprising that this idea soon began to gather momentum.

Through March, April and May 1990, British Motor Heritage's Mark Gamble beavered away in secret on the first BMH MGB V8, using a workshop at the organization's Snitterfield storage facility. The resulting crude, but effective, prototype—dubbed DEV1—was driven by Gamble, David Bishop and Rob Oldaker at Rover's Gaydon testing facility. Although quite basic, the car showed great promise, and all agreed that it warranted further development. By then, however, it became obvious that for British Motor Heritage to move into car production—with the attendant marketing, franchising, servicing and legal problems—was not viable.

It should also be remembered that Rover was already formulating grander plans for the MG marque, and a 'retrospective' MGB V8, produced by BMH, would have sat rather awkwardly in their midst. RSP had officially come into the picture in March 1990 and, with the early assessment of Project Phoenix under way, and Richard Hamblin's 'What if?' ideas for an updated MGB on record, it was decided that something more than a simple rebirth of the MGB would be required. Thus, Project Adder—named for the only poisonous snake native to the British Isles, which might loosely be compared to the Cobra—was taken on board by RSP.

Given that potential MG customers had been found to fall broadly into two camps—the traditionalists and the modernists—the Adder MGB V8 project was felt to be the ideal means of bridging the gap: it would not only pave the way for the completely new PR3, but also provide a vital link with the MGB. Richard Hamblin produced a montage from Jeremy Newman's sketch of a facelifted MGB and photographs of an original chrome-bumper MGB, a BMH bodyshell and a Porsche 911. From this, a coloured rendering was produced by Bruce Bryant and sent to Styling International, a Leamington Spa based subsidiary of prototype builders Hawtal Whiting. There, a clay was developed under Jonathan Gould's direction simply as a 'look see' exercise. The clay retained the standard MGB windscreen, although in due

course, cost and finish considerations would render it unsuitable. From the early work on the clay, it became apparent that the problems of fitting the massive Land Rover injection plenum chamber under the bonnet had yet to be appreciated.

According to Richard Hamblin, many people doubted that this idea would work: 'Everyone kept saying that the end result would be too like the old "rubber-bumper" MGB, but we persevered. There was only enough money to do the front end properly, and so that is what Styling International concentrated upon.' The headlights were borrowed from what Don Wyatt diplomatically referred to as a 'Brand-X' car, but close study reveals them to be Porsche 911 units. The wings of the Styling International car were much closer in form to those of the MGB than to the flared wings that were developed later, but even at this formative stage, according to Don Wyatt, 'the sill extensions were showing what an improvement they were in terms of the stance of the car.'

The clay was finished with red Dynoc (a surfacing film that gives a finished painted look), the finances were calculated, and the model was presented to marketing director Kevin Morley. According to Don Wyatt, 'Kevin Morley was not convinced by the proposal, and so for a while, it went on to the shelf as a dormant project—it must have been about four to five months. But Richard Hamblin, David Wiseman (RSP finance) and John Stephenson (RSP commercial) were all convinced that the project had potential, and so we had another look at it.' Richard Hamblin feels that people tended to overlook the *raison d'être* of the Adder: 'We had three aims: to keep the MG name alive, to do something as a precursor to an all-new car, and to remind people that the MGB had been the best selling British sports car ever. We needed to leap-frog the bad period of the 1970s in people's minds, and remind them of MG's heydays of the 1960s.' Another person who saw the Styling International car was David Blume, later director of Rover Japan, and Richard Hamblin remembers his support: 'Whilst some people were scornful of the idea, David saw it immediately and made some valuable input.' In fact, according to Hamblin, David Blume would remain loyal to the concept throughout, eventually selling the lion's share of the actual production car.

For the second attempt at the MGB-based concept, a bodyshell supplied by David Bishop was taken to ADC at Luton, where a design studio was being run under the direction of John Sowden. ADC, which had emerged from the former General Motors Bedford Truck operation, was keen to expand its involvement in prototype development work and to build upon the relationship

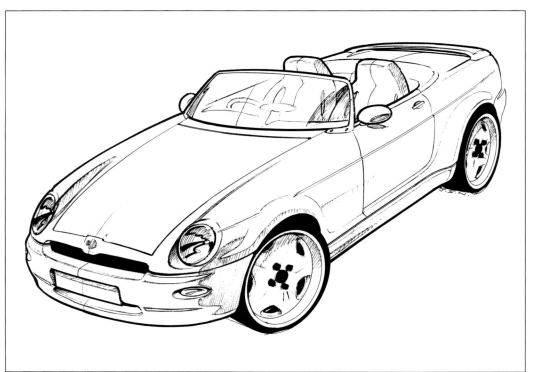

Left Jerry Newman's sketch for an updated MGB became the basis of Adder.

Facing page, top This coloured rendering by Bruce Bryant (based upon Jeremy Newman's line sketch) was to form the basis of the first RSP exercise looking into the idea of a retro MG, based upon the MGB bodyshell. (Rover)

Facing page, bottom A later sketch, by RSP's Richard Bartlam, developing the theme and illustrating the emergence of the distinctive flared wheel arches, sculpted sills and power bulge in the bonnet. (Rover Special Products)

forged with Rover through the original PR3, so the company was particularly interested in becoming involved with this project. The full-size model took shape over the MGB shell, with an alternative treatment on each side. The actual clay modelling work was carried out by John Sowden's staff at ADC, but it was supervised by Richard Hamblin, Don Wyatt and fellow RSP stylist Richard Bartlam, the last working in Luton full-time. Don is at pains to point out that Kevin Morley was still not convinced of the merits of the proposal at this stage, although he would change his mind later.

The right-hand side of the ADC car was an evolution of the Styling International design, and the actual Styling International model was stood alongside it in the ADC studio for direct comparison. However, the front end began, in Don Wyatt's words, to 'take on stronger graphics', the shape of the front bumper spoiler and auxiliary lamps receiving particular attention. Alternative head-lamp arrangements were tried: either Porsche 911 elliptical units, which eventually were approved, or conventional 7in (17.78cm) diameter units set beneath elegant glass cowls, à la Mark I Jaguar E-type. The latter were considered primarily as an insurance, in case a licence to use the Porsche units could not be obtained.

On the left-hand side, the wings were shaped differently to the Styling International car, being flared considerably to give the car much greater apparent width and presence. Eventually, this side would evolve into the familiar RV8 style. At the rear, both Jeremy Newman's sketch and the Styling International car had featured a substantial spoiler, and this was tried for the ADC clay, too, but it drew a mixed reaction. Even so, a spoiler remained a possible option until quite late in the RV8's gestation. Also at the rear, there was much experimentation with tail-lights, since a bespoke unit would have been very expensive, and the whole project was on a

The first stage of what would become Project Adder was the creation of a styling mock-up at Styling International, using Jeremy Newman's sketch as inspiration and modelling the new body features in clay directly on to a basic MGB. Note the retention at this stage (May-July 1990) of the MGB's windscreen, and the lack of a bonnet bulge. (Rover Special Products)

tight budget of around £5 million. However, none of the units that were tried looked at all attractive: I was shown attempts to blend-in late-model Metro tail-lamps and wrap-around rectangular units coupled with sloping rear wings, the latter crudely resembling the tail of a Porsche 911. It soon became apparent that there would be no alternative but to tool-up for a special rear lamp unit—a 'very expensive piece of kit,' according to Don Wyatt.

The windscreen and hood also posed problems: the hood could not be reworked significantly because of time and costs and, therefore, because of its shape, the corresponding angle and height of the windscreen remained obstinately fixed, too. The mounting height of the seats, based upon the MGB frame, was pre-determined by legislation, so many taller owners of RV8s have found that their eye-line corresponds to the top of the windscreen frame. 'We agonized about this,' says Don Wyatt, 'but the fact is that people were coming to a brand-new car, with correspondingly firmer and unworn seats; the same people were not experiencing this problem in older MGBs where, of course, the seats have been broken in.'

By this stage, says Don Wyatt, 'Kevin Morley had almost come back on board, so we were asked to do a glass-reinforced plastic model, which gives a much closer approximation to the finished article. Now doing this can often destroy the clay model: the combination of curing heat and the suction when removing the GRP moulds can pull the clay to pieces. If you have time, this can sometimes be avoided, but we didn't have the time—or the budget for

another clay—and so the original clay was destroyed. From this stage on, therefore, we had to rely upon a GRP model for all further development.' Later, this would cause further headaches.

Mark Gamble's DEV1 car was fitted with the GRP components (wings, doors, bonnet, etc) moulded from the ADC car. Then, it was completely finished as a prototype, with representative running gear, and presented to Kevin Morley, who accepted the concept. Subsequently, with British Racing Green metallic paintwork, this car was photographed (in great secrecy at the Ealing Studios) for the RV8 teaser brochure, which was issued several months ahead of the launch.

In June 1991, following a successful clinic assessment, RSP presented DEV1 as their proposal for Adder to the Rover board. Steve Schlemmer recalls, 'The clinic supported Adder as a limited edition at the right price to celebrate the MGB's 30th anniversary. Adder project funding was approved by Kevin Morley in July 1991.' By this stage, the prototype was very close to the finished article, the beautifully detailed interior being almost in its final form. Component spotters will probably have no difficulty in identifying the Jaguar XJS interior door-releases, but there were other clever adaptations, such as Vauxhall Nova door grab-handles. Particular thought had been given to the rear of the passenger compartment, and it had been hoped to provide a rigid rear tonneau cover. In the event, however, the folded hood could not be accommodated under a rigid cover, so a similarly styled flexible alternative was chosen.

The completed Styling International Adder, finished in Dinoc (a film used by clay modellers to simulate a polished painted surface) and complete with a bonnet bulge. This photograph was taken on 3 July, 1990, at Styling International's Leamington Spa premises, shortly before being shown to Rover's Kevin Morley. Note the two-piece alloy wheels; although very attractive, these were also very expensive, so the definitive RV8 would feature similar one-piece wheels made by Alloy Wheels International to Don Wyatt's design. (Rover Special Products)

For the second attempt at the Adder project, an MGB bodyshell—supplied by David Bishop of British Motor Heritage—was sent to ADC at Luton. The wings and sills were modelled on to the basic steel bodyshell, as had been the case at Styling International, but initially the ADC car featured different treatments on each side. This view clearly shows the offside, with a more subtle and delicate interpretation of Jeremy Newman's original concept. Note also the glazed headlamps, inspired by the Jaguar E-type. (Rover Special Products)

In contrast to the offside, the nearside of the ADC styling model featured a more radical departure from the earlier car. The flared wings, of a style originally seen on the Audi Quattro, gave the car a beefier, more substantial presence. It is interesting to compare this exercise of adding clay to an MGB bodyshell with the work done almost 20 years earlier—see page 147. (Rover Special Products)

As this photograph shows, a Porsche-style rear light treatment simply did not work; the Metro rear lamps looked even worse. (Rover Special Products)

By August, therefore, the Adder project was well under way, having received the green light from the Rover board and being a fully developed concept with a running prototype based on DEV1. At this stage, there was an unexpected upheaval at RSP when three of the four directors—Richard Hamblin, David Wiseman and John Stephenson—left, their places being filled effectively (although not as directors) by, respectively, Don Wyatt, John Yea and Mike O'Hara. Despite this hiccup, the project was well on the road to completion, and the new team was confident that it could deliver the programme on time.

There remained the matter of tooling for the unique panels that were needed to supplement the BMH bodyshell. 'We intended to make a master die-stack (pattern),' remembers Don Wyatt, 'and for this, we used the services of Descartes Design, a subsidiary of Abbey Panels (responsible for the RV8's unique front and rear wings). Descartes were given the task of taking the GRP-clad DEV1 and using it—in conjunction with Rover Body & Pressings and RSP—to produce the new tooling required.'

The day after DEV1 arrived at Descartes, Don Wyatt received an urgent telephone message: 'We've got a problem!' Apparently, DEV1 had been built on an ex-Florida MGB that had been involved in a traffic accident at some time during its life: 'They had set the car up on the measuring jig: it wasn't too far out at the rear end, there were a few problems in the area of the passenger compartment, but the section from the windscreen to the nose was bent by as much as 20mm (¾in)!' This was potentially disastrous, for the prototype was the only example of the car (remember that the clay had been destroyed), and it was supposed to be used for digitizing the surfaces for the new bodywork.

Nevertheless, as there was no way back, it was decided to continue with the project, and Descartes did the best that they could, attempting to correct the distortion. Following this, another Abbey Panels subsidiary, Albany Zinc (in Cannock, Staffordshire), took the digitized information and used it to mill master patterns from a hard epoxy-urethane resin—the modern counterpart of the timber used in the past. 'Unfortunately,' recalls Don Wyatt, 'the finished result looked somewhat different from the original.' As a result, over Christmas 1991, Dick Bartlam virtually lived at Albany Zinc, while Don Wyatt made regular visits: 'We restyled the car right there on the die-stack; we actually took the opportunity to improve every surface of it, altering the character lines considerably to generate a much improved surface work-out.'

According to Wyatt, failure at this stage could easily have meant abandoning the Adder project, for there was neither the time nor the money to create another clay master. In the end, the car came together, although not without some difficulty in aligning the doors and other panel problems.

The ADC car was used to form the fibreglass panels that were fitted to the MGB monocoque and finished in metallic British Racing Green. The headlamps were fitted in removable pods which, as well as simplifying manufacture, allowed two different options to be viewed and assessed. In this photograph, the glazed 'E-type' lamps have been fitted. (Rover Special Products)

The MGB doors remained largely unchanged (although so-called cheater panels for the door mirrors replaced the MGB's quarterlights), but most exterior panels were altered in some way. At the front, there was a moulded bumper unit with integral fog and indicator lights, while the simple grille opening was redolent of the 'rubber-bumper' MGB. A problem arose when the chosen driving lamps were dropped from the Land Rover programme and, consequently, they had to be re-sourced. The exact form of the grille opening caused some heart searching, recalls Don Wyatt, 'There was a removable block on DEV1, which allowed the car to be viewed with or without the central rib.' In the end, it was decided to leave out this block, thus distancing the nose a little more from the 'rubber-bumper' MGB and also following both Richard Hamblin's rendering and the Styling International car, which had been developed from it.

The bonnet was reshaped by adding a smoothly formed and very necessary bulge to cover the tall Land Rover injection plenum chamber, while the flared front and rear wings covered significantly larger-section wheels and tyres, which contributed to the more powerful stance befitting its power-train. In fact, the distinctive twin bumper mounted lamps and grille aperture of the RV8 were also tried on PR3, but they did not seem to work so well with the different proportions of the mid-engined car.

Mike O'Hara, who had been with Rover since the 1970s, subsequently summarized the ethos behind the RV8: 'We set out to create a classic British sports car with the MG RV8, and to make it very special: a car for enthusiasts—a classic car updated, but without the drawbacks.'

By the spring of 1992, the final details of the specification and styling of Adder had been determined, and the lead-up to the planned October launch was in hand. By now, the rumours in both the motoring and popular press about the imminent rebirth of the MG sports car were reaching fever pitch. Therefore, it was decided to feed this excitement by releasing a teaser brochure in June, four months ahead of the launch. This brochure, which heralded the RV8 with the legend, 'The shape of things to come', featured a few discreet detail shots and a retouched side view of the modified DEV1 prototype.

By September, it was time to repeat the exercise of 1982, when the views of MG club members had been sought prior to the launch

This view shows the Bosch headlamps (as fitted to the contemporary Porsche 911) and the nose block in place. (Rover Special Products)

Here the alternative headlamp pods have been fitted. These glazed covers were fitted over conventional round headlamps, and were considered mainly in case agreement could not be reached on the use of the preferred Bosch units. Note the lack of nose block. (Rover Special Products)

At the rear, the prototype was almost in the final form, although the boot spoiler was rejected for production. The badge mounting would also be changed, and the old-fashioned MGB boot lid latch was dropped in favour of an interior remote-release mechanism. (Rover Special Products)

of the MG Metro. Representatives of the MG Car Club, MG Owners' Club, Octagon Car Club and selected MG publications (such as *MG Enthusiast* and *MG Magazine*) were invited to Canley to view a pre-production RV8 prototype. They were welcomed by Michael Kennedy, director of external affairs, and Steve Schlemmer, who explained the philosophy and technical background to the car. Over a buffet lunch, the Rover personnel mingled with the enthusiasts and sought their views on the car. Unknown to the latter, the PR3 prototypes were secreted in a room adjacent to the one in which they were viewing the RV8!

A month later, the RV8 received its public unveiling at the 1992 Motor Show, at the National Exhibition Centre on the outskirts of Birmingham. The centre of the Rover stand was dominated by a large Perspex-walled turntable, upon which was mounted the shrouded shape of an RV8. On press day, the world's media gathered around the turntable and waited for Rover's chief executive, John Towers, to give a brief speech, emphasizing the progress that his company had made and the obvious excitement that the launch of a new sports car—albeit a celebratory limited edition—had gen-

erated. There to witness the unveiling were many of the MG club members who had been invited to inspect the car at Canley a month before, as well as former Abingdon chief engineer Don Hayter, who was intrigued to see how the MGB had been altered in its transition to the RV8.

The cover was pulled back, and the audience gave the RV8 a grand reception; all that remained now was to build the cars and sell them! The problem was that during the development of the concept, there had been significant changes in the market, and the attractiveness of classic cars as investments had diminished. The consequence of this was that sales of the RV8 in the UK were never as strong as had been hoped. Nevertheless, the *raison d'être* of the RV8—to celebrate the 30th anniversary of the MGB and to keep the MG name alive—was achieved. In October 1993, the RV8 was shown on the Rover Japan stand at the Tokyo Motor Show, and the reception it was afforded was little short of star status. Within an astonishingly short space of time, over half the planned RV8 production of 2000 cars had been snapped up by Japanese customers, and the Adder project became a resounding success. There was lit-

BUILDING THE MG RV8

Once the decision had been taken to relaunch the MG sports car, using a 'retrospective' vehicle based upon the MGB, the next step was to decide how and where it should be built. By the time that the Adder project was given the green light, in July 1991, the British Motor Heritage facility at Faringdon was already three years into production of MGB bodyshells. As the original sponsor of the concept of a 'new' MGB, it was only natural that BMH should secure the contract to build the bodyshells for what would become the RV8. Planning and preparations began fairly soon after the project had been approved, with the objective of producing the first complete bodyshells in September 1992, when 28 pre-production and development cars were built.

Much of the RV8 body structure was common to the MGB, so significant benefits would be conferred upon the bodyshells for the latter, which were still being produced at Faringdon, taking advantage of the superior finish and materials that a new Rover product needed. Some of the body components were actually pressed at Faringdon, while others were sourced elsewhere, particularly the distinctive front and rear wings, which were pressed by Abbey Panels. The components were assembled in jigs adapted from those that the BMH team had refurbished for the MGB bodyshells. The result—the 'body in white'—was meticulously examined before being transported to Cowley. This inspection process was critical, for not only had standards risen in the years since the MGB had gone out of production—ensuring that the BMH facilities were stretched to the limit—but also the RV8 bodies had to be absolutely ready for painting when they arrived at Cowley, without requiring the sort of reworking that the restorer of an old MGB might be prepared to accept.

The Cowley end of the operation, which was run in a separate facility tucked away in a corner of the giant complex, took shape at the same time as BMH was readying itself for the RV8. Starting in August 1992, and under project director Graham Irvine, assisted by plant manager Cliff Law, a new facility was created virtually from scratch, drawing largely upon redundant

plant and hardware that had become available through restructuring at Cowley. To build and operate this new facility, Irvine and Law drew together a carefully picked and flexible team, who had to adapt to the highly manual-skill-based and labour-intensive production methods that assembly of the low-volume RV8 would entail. This team not only fitted out the facility themselves, but also became deeply involved in the development of the vehicle at the pre-production stage—rather than after the final design had been signed off—thus helping to iron out as many potential problems as possible ahead of production.

The Cowley facility was laid out as a series of seven assembly stations, each of which involved a number of tasks that took considerably longer than would have been the case on a conventional car production line. The first production car was completed on 31 March, 1993—on the same day that the *Financial Times* published a report about the Rover/Mayflower deal to build PR3—and, before long, full production got under way. It was clear to anyone who was lucky enough to visit the Cowley MG facility that the work-force was justifiably proud of their endeavours. This pride even manifested itself in the floor of the facility's rest area, which had been carpeted with an MG logo, the carpet having been found and laid by the team themselves.

It is hardly a secret that UK customers for the RV8 failed to materialize in the numbers that had been hoped for, so the phenomenal reception accorded the car at the Tokyo show, in October 1993, undoubtedly saved the company a degree of embarrassment. Of about 2000 production RV8s, over 65 per cent eventually found their way to Japan, some 1300 orders having been secured soon after the show. Some cars were also exported to mainland Europe, but none to the USA. Production continued at a rate of up to 15 a week until, just over three years after the sensational Birmingham Motor Show launch, the story of the RV8 drew to a close: the final production car went down the line on 22 November, 1995. Never intended as anything more than a celebration of the MGB, the RV8 paved the way for the MGF and, undoubtedly, established a role for a more up-market MG sports car.

For the RV8, the traditional MGB metal dashboard was dispensed with in favour of a veneered fascia, the first time such a fascia had been seen in a standard MG sports car for 40 years or so. (Rover)

tle doubt that what came next would find a warm welcome in Japan, too.

On the road to production: PR3 development

From 1993, the project director for PR3 was Nick Fell, and he was under no illusion that the car should be from the same mould as the MGB: 'Whilst we respected the MG heritage,' he says, 'we were not enslaved by it.' Nevertheless, it was important that the car was clearly an MG, and not an anonymous sports car that could have worn any manufacturer's badge.

Gerry McGovern explains the difficult task of rationalizing two of the basic styling requirements that could be in conflict: 'We wanted the car to be a clear statement which recognized the MG heritage, yet in a modern proportioned car with a "cabin-forward" style and raked windscreen.' At the rear, McGovern was keen to provide a visual link to the EX-E concept car, which he had worked on under the direction of Roy Axe and Gordon Sked, and which he clearly still adores. The link with EX-E was achieved in several ways: through the similar bulk of the rear, the distinctively shaped rear lamps, the shaping of the rear deck lid, and the sweeping door-shut lines.

Brian Griffin explains that one of the challenges of the mid-engined layout was to integrate this arrangement within the overall styling of the car: 'Apart from being the first true mid-engined soft-top in its class, there was a challenging opportunity to create a modern low-fronted sports car, whereas a conventional front-engined car would have been more familiar, but a transverse-engined one could have compromised the looks.' Gerry McGovern echoes this: 'It would have been far easier to have designed an MG sports car with a front-engine, rear-wheel-drive layout; the challenge was meeting our criteria with the mid-engined package.'

According to Brian Griffin, the engineers even looked at the small projector lamps that are a feature of the new Alfa Romeo Spider: '...but we found that although they were alright on dip beam, they were pretty hopeless on main beam.' Brian adds that Rover looked at the feasibility of at least 20 different light units, seeking to balance the various parameters of cost, performance, style and practicality. The final headlamp design was seen as form-

Right *Nick Fell, project director for PR3, stands proudly in front of the MGF at the 1995 Earls Court Motor Show. (David Knowles)*

Below *Note the false number-plates on this MGF styling model, which imply that the car is an MGD. There was no doubt at this stage, however, that the car would be called MGF. Note also the rear lamp clusters, which would grow slightly larger prior to production, at Gerry McGovern's insistence. (Rover)*

ing part of a recognizable face that would contribute towards the car's unique identity. Gerry McGovern fought hard for unique front and rear lamp units. Brian Griffin told him that he might have to compromise, but 'Gerry was adamant that he needed lamps at the front which contributed to the "face" of the car, and lamps at the rear which provided a visual link with the EX-E.'

Despite the importance of the shape of the lamps, much of the car's identity comes from surface shapes, rather than features, most of which are deliberately simple and functional. One exception is the horizontal aperture at the rear of the deck lid. This was found to be unnecessary for cooling purposes, but as it was such a strong feature, it was retained and, in fact, it proved an ideal position for the high-level supplementary rear brake light that is mandatory in some markets.

As Gerry McGovern explained to me, 'We aimed for a no-non-sense look: strong and tough, but in a fun sort of way; not too macho, and yet not too feminine.' Much of the tension of the design comes from two chord lines that run from front to rear: one is clear-ly visible, while the other is more subtle, running below and almost parallel to the first. In McGovern's words, this provides a 'taut body shape'.

One feature for which past MG sports cars had earned a bad rep-utation was the soft-top hood. Both the MGA and MGB had fea-tured attractively styled hoods, which looked quite elegant when erected, but both had been difficult to raise and lower, and they were not always as weatherproof as they should have been. In stark contrast, the Italian sports cars of the 1960s had featured hoods that were not only elegant, but also easy to operate and generally more effective against the weather.

Pininfarina had been responsible for designing hoods for many European convertibles, notably from Fiat, Alfa Romeo and Peugeot, so Rover turned to the Italian company for help with the hood of PR3. Gerry McGovern remained closely involved to ensure that the result met his objectives, travelling to Italy on a number of occasions to oversee the Italian company's work. Pininfarina paid particular attention to the design of the hood lever system: when not in use, the hood is stored neatly below the waist-line, in a compartment made extremely small by the mid-engined configuration, which had to be incorporated without compromising engine access.

As an alternative to open-top motoring, and to allow PR3 to compete against conventional two-seater coupés, such as the

So determined was Rover to keep the exact form of the PR3's shape a closely guarded secret that they took the unusual step of designing special GRP disguises, which fitted closely on to the bodywork and allowed the car to be tested in daylight while concealing its appearance. This disguise was the work of Gerry McGovern, and is shown in prototype clay form, having been shaped over a plastic body mock-up. (Rover)

Mazda MX-3, from an early stage, it was decided to offer an optional hardtop. This was styled simultaneously with the car, rather than as an after-thought. The hardtop is only offered in one finish—gloss black—and it is fully lined and fitted with a heated rear window. There were two reasons for the black finish: quite apart from simplifying production of this low-volume item, Gerry McGovern was keen to maintain the smooth linearity of the PR3 design which, he felt, would have been interrupted by a colour co-ordinated hardtop. Interestingly, the optional hardtop introduced 39 years earlier for the MGA had also been in black only, as initially was the MGB hardtop of the 1960s. A useful feature is that the hood does not have to be removed when the hardtop is fitted.

Marque identity: the MG Event

Gerry McGovern recalls Rover Europe's boss, Graham Morris—fresh from his spell in Miami as head of the Sterling operation—saying in 1992, 'Let's make sure that we haven't missed any MG cues.' Morris was one of several Rover directors, including Graham Day and John Towers, who were consulted individually and asked to comment. Largely as a result of Morris' comment, McGovern and Tony Cummings, of Rover's brand management team, decided to stage a special MG Event at Canley. They invited 450 people from Rover's forward planning section and other departments within the company to examine a collection of MGs (including 'Old Number One', MGAs, MGBs and EX-E, but not the PR3 models), archive film of the Abingdon factory, and associ-ated paraphernalia. Then, the participants were asked to list items that they considered synonymous with the MG marque. Some of the features identified were clearly inappropriate for a new MG, such as wire wheels, but others, like the grille shape and MG badge, were clearly very important.

One of the ideas that came out of this session was the attractive fuel filler cap fitted to PR3. This is surrounded by a silver ring fit-ted with simulated allen-head screws, matching the appearance of fillers used on 1950s competition cars. Another feature generated

The interior of PR3 takes shape in the form of a full-size clay seating buck. Note the dashboard, which is similar to the final version with the exception of such details as the fresh-air vents. The instrument dials— conventional black and white at this stage—are from the contemporary Rover 200 (R8). (Rover)

by the MG Event was the chrome shield on which the MG badge is mounted at the front.

Keen to ensure that the PR3 styling was on target, Gerry McGovern also sought the critical assessment of his colleagues: 'We got the young designers into the design showroom on their own to walk around the car, and asked them for their honest opinions. Everyone was totally supportive.' McGovern was relieved that there was such a positive reaction to his efforts. The interior of the car is thoroughly modern, and largely unique to the MG, although it draws upon the Rover parts bin for such expensive-to-develop components as the cream-faced instrumentation (adapted from the Rover 200). McGovern was determined to give the MGF cockpit its own identity from the outset: 'We toyed with the idea of using R8 (Rover 200) door grab handles, but rejected that to maintain the unique identity.' The result is attractive and features some

clever sports car styling cues, such as the twin-cockpit theme, which harks back to the 1960s Chevrolet Corvette Stingray.

As McGovern explains, 'We deliberately went for a high tunnel and a short gear-shift, coupled with a high waistline, all of which give that sports car cocoon effect.' Sensibly, the use of MG badges was restrained, and the interior is decidedly modern, with no wood and little chrome, apart from the door releases. 'We looked at bright ashtrays, various gear-knobs and a chrome trimmed trinket tray, but came to the conclusion that these were too retro for the car,' says McGovern. The substantial windscreen surround helps provide a feeling of security while giving practical safety benefits.

In the past, some mid-engined sports cars have offered luggage space in two areas—typically between the front wheels and to the rear of the engine compartment—but it was not possible to provide luggage space in the front of PR3 because of the need to allow for

Development of the PR3 interior. Note the consideration of brightwork and a two-tone steering wheel, but neither idea made it into production. (Rover)

MG: THE UNTOLD STORY

a progressive frontal collapse under impact. Consequently, the car was given the maximum practical boot space at the rear, the design criterion being an ability to carry two sets of golf clubs. Gerry McGovern laughingly says that all his keep-fit sports bags can be accommodated, something that he had aimed to put to the test as soon as he could obtain his own production car.

PR3 engine and chassis development
In addition to having attractive styling, it was of paramount importance that PR3 met everyone's dynamic aspirations for a sports car. The team set themselves the objective of creating what they called 'the world's most enjoyable car to drive', and to establish a datum from which to work, they researched road-tests and appraisals of a wide range of cars, from the MGB to the Porsche 911, and the Peugeot 205 GTi to the Toyota MR2.

Chassis development: Hydragas and sub-frames
The original PR3 programme had called for a launch in the first quarter of 1994, which was so short that it effectively ruled out a totally new chassis set-up. According to Brian Griffin, the basic chassis alone would have taken a year to do. Thus, Griffin and his team looked at the highly regarded R6 (post-1990 Metro) suspension, which used separate sub-frames and Alex Moulton's Hydragas gas-sprung system: 'We asked ourselves, "Can we change and tune this suspension to suit our needs?", and so we consulted the established gurus, including, of course, Alex Moulton and Tony Best Dynamics, for the particular Hydragas aspects.' A party of engineers assembled at Gaydon one evening to test a running 'mule' prototype and assess the potential of the R6 set-up: 'The ride and handling of the R6 Metro had been very well received, and so we came to the conclusion that it would provide a good basis for the suspension of PR3.'

Other benefits would also arise from adopting the Metro underpinnings: the rubber mounting of the sub-frames gave excellent noise and vibration isolation from the cabin (Rover claim that the MGF is streets ahead of the established opposition in that respect) and, by adapting existing hardware, the team was increasing the use of the Metro sub-frames, which had cost £4.5 million to tool up. Nevertheless, it was not simply a matter of bolting in the Metro units: the rear suspension, in particular, had to be re-engineered to eliminate the anti-dive properties that were necessary for the front-engined Metro, but which would have been inappropriate at the rear of PR3. The changes that were made had to be engineered in such a way as to minimize potentially expensive alterations to the sub-frame production line. Those modifications that are needed are carried out on a separate low-volume production line.

By the summer of 1992, the first test 'mule', or simulator, was up and running, in the form of a converted Metro van, known as SIM-1 (and unofficially as the 'Pizza Van'). Largely built from scrounged components, this vehicle featured a K-series engine in the rear compartment and suitably modified Metro R6 sub-frames. This was just the beginning, as Brian Griffin recalls, 'We built a number of vans and pickups, which had slightly shorter wheelbases than PR3, some of which were disguised as traders' vehicles. In fact, we built 16 simulators in total, including three Toyota MR2 Mark 1s fitted with a K-series engine (for emissions testing) and four hand-built PR3 prototypes.'

Engine development
From the outset, PR3 was intended to utilize the K-series engine in some form or another, but along the way, several variations on this basic theme were explored. Initially, it was thought that the car would be powered by the MPi fuel-injected, 1.4-litre, 16-valve K-series, as fitted to the Rover Metro GTi. However, it was obvious that PR3 would not be a featherweight, so although the 1.4 might have been satisfactory for the base model, an image boosting, higher-performance version would clearly require something special. The motoring press had criticized the Mazda MX-5 for being underpowered when launched with a single 1.6-litre engine derivative; although most people do not need the extra power, image is everything with a sports car, and Rover could not afford to make the same mistake as Mazda.

The next stage was to consider two 1.6-litre versions of the K-series, that capacity being considered the maximum practical stretch for the block. For the more powerful derivative, it was planned to supercharge the engine and, to that end, experiments were carried out with both the VW G-Lader and the Sprintex superchargers. Prior to becoming involved with Project Phoenix, Brian Griffin remembers being asked by Roger Stone to try out an old-model Rover 216 Vitesse, which had been fitted with a supercharged, 1.4-litre K-series engine: 'The car was purely an ideas car with an engine producing some 200Nm torque and 150bhp (11.86kW).' Griffin drove it around the Warwickshire lanes, and quickly discovered that the chassis could not cope with such power: 'I found that I could easily get wheelspin at 90mph (144.84km/h) on the Gaydon test circuit in the wet.' Eventually, however, problems with engine reliability and in meeting ever stringent emissions legislation ruled out the supercharger option. By this stage, Rover was exploring the variable-valve-timing concept, for which AE had gained an outline patent, and this was felt to be a more viable option for the faster version of PR3.

Body engineering: a partnership of equals
From the beginning, PR3 was designed for an optimum production volume of about 12,000 cars per annum. As Brian Griffin explains, this meant choosing materials, tooling and processes that are different to those that would have been used for significantly greater volumes: 'You could possibly double up production of the MGF with the appropriate investment, but it would not have been economically viable to have gone for, say, 30,000 per annum at the outset, and then reduced it.' The decision to go for a relatively low volume also militated against US exports: 'For the US market, you need higher volumes to compete in a lower-priced market. This would have meant injection moulding more components, and many other process differences.'

When Project Phoenix effectively took off, following the go-ahead from John Towers to proceed with a paper study (a concept review) and the 1991 styling clinic, the car industry was experiencing a lean time, sales revenues dropping across the board. Clearly, it was not the time to be promoting a new venture of this type, and there was financial pressure to take projects out of the capital programme. At this point, it was decided to explore the possibility of entering into a partnership with another company, which would share the financial risks and shoulder some of the burden of development, in return for a cut of the profits. Thus, enquiries were made throughout Europe and, at the same time, the programme was delayed by a year, the planned launch slipping from 1994 to 1995.

About five potential partners were identified, of which the two front runners were Mayflower and Pininfarina. Assessments were made and recommendations presented to the Rover board in December 1992. Mayflower offered a number of significant advantages: it was a British company (with the obvious logistical and political advantages associated with that fact), it had carried out the earlier work on PR1, and it had also been joined by Terry Whitmore, Rover's former director for large cars. The Rover board duly went for the Mayflower proposal, and negotiations were entered into. Nick Fell became Rover's project director for PR3, and Tim Martin was recruited to Mayflower from Leyland DAF. Once the agreement had been finalized, Mayflower took the PR3 design and readied it for production, with support from Rover's Body Engineering Group at Cowley.

Historians might like to know that the need for secrecy when dealing with outside companies, which arose from this unique partnership, led to more project codes. For certain purposes, PR3 also became known as 8300 and, during preliminary negotiations, as EXP10 to EXP16 inclusive, a different number being quoted for each potential partner.

Final testing
Testing a top-secret vehicle usually involves playing a game of cat and mouse with the motoring press, for whom a sneak preview photograph of a new model can be very valuable. This was particularly so in the case of the first completely new MG sports car for 33 years. The simulators—including the specially converted Metro

230

THE MAYFLOWER CORPORATION

For the MGF project, Rover entered into a novel partnership with an external supplier. Most products from the company's past had used bodies designed and built by either former Nuffield or Austin body subsidiaries, or Pressed Steel at Cowley, although occasionally a few panels were sourced elsewhere. With the incorporation of Pressed Steel into BMC, in 1966, there were very few occasions when it was felt necessary to look outside the company for body supplies. One notable exception to this rule was the low-volume MG RV8 sports car, for which Rover contracted Abbey Panels to produce certain unique components. With the MGF, however, Rover went a step further, entering into a co-operative deal with Coventry based Motor Panels, a subsidiary of the giant Mayflower Corporation. Motor Panels boasts a long standing tradition of being a key supplier to major car manufacturers, having produced the bodywork for Sir Malcolm Campbell's famous Bluebird record car and a large number of significant projects in the UK and USA since that time. Until the PR3 project, however, Mayflower had always remained a supplier, without any investment in the car itself.

Until the late 1980s, Motor Panels' business had tended to concentrate on trucks rather than cars. Co-operation with the Rover Group resulted in a contract to design and produce the panelwork for the Land Rover Discovery, and other car related projects followed, including the Lotus Elan chassis, Aston Martin DB7 and the Rover 400 Tourer (code-name Tex). According to PR3 project manager Tim Martin, who moved to Motor Panels in 1993, after nine years at Freight Rover/Leyland DAF, this success was largely a result of Motor Panels' expertise in lower-volume niche products: 'If you think about it, trucks are niche products, being produced in similar volumes, and so it was quite natural for Mayflower to wish to become involved in another niche area—that of sports cars.'

In 1990, Motor Panels had been invited to produce one of the four Phoenix Route running proposals, PR1, based upon an earlier MGF exercise. From that time, the company was keen to become involved in any future MG sports car project. As described elsewhere, the Mayflower Corporation was one of a number of potential partners considered by Rover, but it clearly had a number of significant advantages. First of these was the fact that the company is British (the idea of a foreign bodyshell on an MG does not seem quite right) and has 75 years of experience behind it. Secondly, being based in Coventry, the company is at the heart of the British motor industry and, therefore, well-placed logistically. Thirdly, a key member of the Mayflower management is chief executive Terry Whitmore, who joined the company from Rover, where

he had been director for large cars and responsible for bringing the Rover R17 (800 facelift) to production.

As part of the agreement with Rover for the MGF, Mayflower invested over £20 million in preparing the Motor Panels factory at Coventry. Personnel were drawn from both Rover and Motor Panels, and simultaneous engineering techniques were used to make a bodyshell that was easy to build, yet met all the necessary safety and quality requirements. Rover's MGF project director, Nick Fell, was given a permanent office at Motor Panels, making it easier for him to divide his time between Birmingham, Gaydon and Coventry: he would often be at Motor Panels two or three times per week. According to Tim Martin, 'The partnership works well: at any one time of the day, there will be at least five or six Rover personnel on site.'

The work began at Motor Panels in early 1993, with an appraisal of the Rover PR3 design. Tim Martin became involved in the project at this point, explaining, 'We had to take all the manual data and convert it to CAD format to enable us to proceed with the tooling design.' Motor Panels has a highly sophisticated CAD set-up, based on the IBM CATIA system, and the company's facility at Coventry is regarded by IBM as a European showcase for their product. Several changes were made during this phase, too, such as a revision to the shape and position of the rear lamp units, which were moved outboard slightly to make the car look wider. The design of all the cut-lines and closing panels followed, after which the style was 'put to bed', in April 1993. As Tim Martin points out, '95 per cent of the work had already been done, but that last 5 per cent is still crucial to the whole process.'

As part of the deal, Motor Panels invested some money in Rover's Body and Pressings subsidiary at Swindon (known as RBP and managed by Trevor Giggs), which was subcontracted to produce the necessary body tooling to Motor Panels' design. In the event, RBP suddenly found themselves so busy that they had to source some of these tools from a Japanese company. As Tim Martin recalls, this meant that for about a year, there was the slightly curious situation of Motor Panels people working in Japan with Rover RBP people, while reporting back to Rover as client in the UK!

The finished press tools were installed at Coventry, where the panels are pressed and assembled into complete bodies. Then the bare shells are shipped to Rover's new paint facility at Longbridge for painting and final assembly. Speaking at the time of the MGF launch, Terry Whitmore said, 'As a partner, it is true that we share the risk to a greater extent, but we also share the benefits of success to a greater extent. Rover has been a very important customer of ours for many years, and we are delighted that the MGF project has given us the opportunity to build an even closer relationship.'

An MGF bodyshell in the process of being assembled at Motor Panels. (Motor Panels)

A black D1-build prototype MGF being tested on the inhospitable dust tracks of Arizona in November 1994. Several visits took place to Arizona and Death Valley in California, the extremes of temperature and dust being ideal for testing a vehicle to the limits of its design and beyond. The licence-plate, MT 0983, is a temporary plate issued for testing purposes and is rather similar to the UK trade plate. (courtesy Leigh Richardson)

'Pizza Van' and the Toyota MR2s—were fine up to a point, but there comes a stage in development when only the real thing will suffice. It was obvious, from an early stage, that a proper hand-built, pre-production PR3 monocoque would be needed to carry out meaningful tests on cooling, performance, emissions and NVH (noise, vibration and harshness). However, the risk of exposing PR3's distinctive styling prematurely was too great to allow testing of undisguised prototypes.

To overcome the problem, Gerry McGovern, Alan Johnson and their team of creative young modellers produced remarkable GRP disguises and colour schemes—either Nato Green or weird black and white abstract patterns—which effectively hid the true appearance of PR3, especially the nose. According to Brian Griffin, it was colleague Dave Ovens, in conjunction with the trim and hardware shop at Canley, who devised the bizarre black graphics: 'They cut out sheets of black vinyl on the trim boards at Canley, and then

For testing on public roads in the UK, Rover resorted to the Gerry McGovern designed removable GRP disguises, painted either NATO Green or, as here, in an abstract black and white pattern. (Rover)

Right *Also used for testing the mid-engine installation were a number of converted Metro vans. Note how tidily the K-series engine has been slotted in where the rear seat would normally be in the standard three-door Metro. (Rover)*

Below *The Metro test 'mules' included this so-called 'Pizza Van', offering 'Express 24-hour Delivery'. (Rover)*

applied the material to the cars.' Before long, however, celebrated scoop photographer Hans Lehmann managed to capture a photograph of one of the Nato Green' PR3 simulators, and *Carweek* even tried to 'remove' the disguise by using computer graphic techniques—without much success and to the great amusement of Rover personnel, it must be said.

Although the disguises succeeded in concealing the true appearance of PR3, they did produce weight and aerodynamic penalties, so as the final phases of testing began, a less dramatic solution was required. At this point, Brian Griffin introduced the 'bra' disguise, a black rubberized fabric nose-covering similar to those used by American classic car enthusiasts to protect their cars from stone chips. Although the shape of PR3 was less effectively concealed by this disguise, the exact detailing of the nose remained a secret while proper testing continued and, of course, Dave Oven's black vinyl graphics helped make the shape more difficult to determine.

Brian Griffin recalls driving one of the PR3 'mules' late at night through Chipping Norton: 'I was driving the simulator, which had been successfully used for a number of impact tests, including the windscreen crush test, and suddenly found that I was following a police van. I dread to think what they would have made of my car!' Brian's colleague, Paul Ragbourne (a veteran of O-series MGB development work), recalls that the early cars had no hoods: 'I feel the cold and have vivid memories of some of the winter testing we carried out!' Such are the pressures of testing that it becomes a strange experience for development engineers when they are given the opportunity to drive the car undisguised in broad daylight.

The so-called 'bra' disguise was also used for late pre-launch testing in Italy, at the Nardo test circuit (where the early DO2-build test car, driven by Rover's power train applications engineer Phil Gillam, was captured by a scoop photographer and published in a UK motoring magazine), and also in Arizona, where a D1 car was

PROTOTYPE BUILD STAGES

Code	Description
D01	First running prototype with handmade body.
D02	Vehicle development phase after Day Zero (board approval); soft-tool bodies.
D1	First prototype from tools.
QP	Quality Proving: first prototypes made almost entirely from tooling and on the production line.
QC	Quality Confirmation: second stage of proving production processes.
M	Method Build: refinements to on-line production processes prior to volume production.
AV	Advanced Volume, just ahead of full production, addressing any problems identified during the previous stage.

tested in November 1994. This testing programme continued well after the car had made its public début in Geneva, by which time, of course, all disguises could be dispensed with. A Flame Red car was taken to Canada (for a Crest climatic shaker rig test and an impromptu appearance at a local MG club meeting!), while another toured Nevada, Arizona and Death Valley, California in February, April and July 1995, with Phil Gillam on board once more: 'We were testing the air-conditioning system and to see how the engine and engine-bay would behave in extremely high ambient temperatures—looking for things like heat soak—and we did find that some additional insulation would be needed if the car were to be sold into markets where such temperatures were possible.'

Towards the launch: PR3 becomes MGF

Whereas the motoring press was convinced that PR3 would be given the name Midget, at Rover, there was never any doubt that the car was closer in spirit to the MGB. When the EX-E concept car was presented in September 1985, it was claimed that the MGD name had been attached to an earlier prototype, which had not made it into production, so clearly the EX-E was intended to be the MGE. Quite what Rover meant by the MGD is open to debate. It has been implied that this name was associated with ADO21, developed at Abingdon and Longbridge during 1969-70 (see Chapter 3), although none of the people involved with the project remembers ADO21 ever being called the MGD, even though there is little doubt that it would have become the MGD had it been put into production.

Whatever the reasoning behind the decision to adopt the MGF name—finally decided in March 1992—the fact remains that it went back further than most people realized. Of course, the MGF name predates Project Phoenix completely, having been applied to the front-wheel-drive sports car concept that Gerry McGovern had produced in 1986, in the wake of the EX-E, which is described in Chapter 6. According to Greg Allport, MG's brand manager, the 'F' can stand for many things—such as 'Fast' and 'Fun'—and, of course, it neatly pre-empts Jaguar, whose next sports car was confidently expected at that stage to be the F-type. In 1986, of course, 'F' was linked with US fighter aircraft designations; then, of course, there are the Ferrari connotations to consider...

In July 1993, John Towers initiated an MG Marque Values Day

Testing an MGF prototype in an anechoic chamber (the largest in Europe, employing 2 tonnes of sponge rubber sound insulation) to check that it complies with EC drive-by noise legislation. (Rover)

(not to be confused with the earlier MG Event), during which 30 people, from all disciplines within the company, were brought together and given the task of determining a set of core values that would describe what the MG marque represented. These were to be defined as simply as possible by single words. Subsequently, they would be used not only as a tool for outlining the form of any vehicle developed to carry the MG badge, but also as an important sales and marketing aid.

A day of discussion led to five words that were felt to describe the essence of MG. These words were 'desire' (the car had to be sexy), 'exhilaration' (in terms of performance, handling and tactile cockpit feel), 'distinctiveness' (the car had to be recognizable as an MG without the badges), 'Britishness' (British designed and built in its entirety), and 'value' (affordable to buy, run and maintain—the so-called 'whole life' expense). With these values defined, the launch programme for PR3 could get under way.

BMW on the scene

The astonishing take-over of Rover by BMW, at the beginning of 1994, inevitably precipitated a period of uncertainty within the British company, not least within the PR3 team, as the new masters took stock of their acquisition. It was common knowledge that BMW was working on its own sports car, the Z3, to be built in a new factory at Spartanburg in South Carolina from the end of 1995. Bernd Pischetsrieder, BMW's chairman, and Wolfgang Reitzle, the company's purchasing director, asked to see the entire Rover range and, more particularly, all of the projects that were being worked on. Consequently, these were assembled at Canley.

Brian Griffin recalls that, at the time, the designers were trying to find a unique colour scheme for the VVC model. At that point, they were considering a vivid pearlescent pink called Lipstick, and the fibreglass MGF styling model was on display at Canley in this rather striking colour: 'When Bernd Pischetsrieder saw the MGF in this colour, he asked to review all the activities which had gone into the MGF project.' A mass of material was collated for his next visit, when he was accompanied by BMW's styling director, Chris Bangle. By this time, the GRP model had been resprayed in metallic British Racing Green: 'BP took one look at the styling model and said, "I don't have a problem!"' After that, the proposed special colour became Volcano, a pearlescent metallic orange-bronze, known irreverently by some wags at Rover as either 'Satsuma' or 'Sarah' (after the red-haired Duchess of York).

BMW had no direct involvement in PR3, other than to offer advice when it was sought (the German company provided valuable assistance with the reinforced windscreen pillar design), and as the MG is not destined to be sold in North America, the company does not foresee any direct conflict with BMW's own sports car. In fact, an early PR3 styling model (pre-MGF) was clinicked in the USA (alongside PR5), but it was felt to be too small. Presumably, any future MG bound for the USA would have to be somewhat larger than the MGF while avoiding a head-on conflict with BMW's sports car.

Final MGF styling clinics

During the summer of 1994, Rover organized what Greg Allport describes as a 'mammoth styling clinic tour', where DO2-build (one year ahead of production) examples of the MGF were lined up with competing sports cars, such as the Mazda MX-5 and Toyota MR2. Greg recalls that one of those canvassed described the car as being 'sleek, powerful and well-balanced'. At the European venues, where many of the clinics were held, the optional hardtop and cream-faced instruments drew particular praise, the former eliciting phrases such as 'two cars in one' and 'styling enhancement'. Interestingly, the black PR3 prototype that toured the clinics was lined up with not only the MX-5 and MR2, but also a Peugeot 306 Cabriolet and a VW Golf GTi hatchback. According to Mike Ferguson, this was because of the lack of sports cars on sale at the time: 'We had to ask ourselves where PR3 sales would come from. In the seventies, there was no problem. In the eighties, former sports car customers drifted into cabrios, coupés and hot hatches, and so we included what were generally perceived as the best competitors' cabrio and hot hatch in the line up.'

Each clinic session lasted two and a half hours and was staged in a particular sequence: first, the PR3 would be revealed, devoid of any identification; then the car would be displayed with its MG badges; finally, it would be shown among the competitors, at which stage, the participants would be asked to score each car for style, practicality, etc. 'We were delighted when people guessed that it was an MG, even when there were no badges,' recalls Mike Ferguson. 'It clearly demonstrated that the styling had worked. People loved what they perceived as the Britishness of the car.' Opinions were mixed about the vivid red seats, but the option of a more restrained black and green upholstery scheme seemed to satisfy nearly everybody.

Having established that the car was on track as far as potential customers were concerned, the decision was made to launch it at the spring 1995 Geneva show, even though production cars could not be made ready until some time afterwards. Mike Ferguson and Greg Allport were clear that Geneva was right for PR3: 'It had to be a truly international event, for we had a product to shout about—a world-beater in every sense.'

Early in 1995, just a short time before the Geneva Motor Show, Rover set out to repeat the MG Metro and RV8 exercises of 1982 and 1992 respectively, and gauge the opinions of MG club officials and the leading MG dedicated publications. Therefore, in February, a group of about 20 people was invited by Rover to the British Motor Heritage museum, at Gaydon, for a special preview ahead of the motoring press, on the strict understanding that the press embargo of 7 March would not be broken.

At this stage, although some revealing scoop photographs had been published, the true appearance of the car, particularly the nose, had remained quite a well-guarded secret, and it is probably fair to say that none of those gathered at Gaydon had seen an undisguised MGF prior to the unveiling. After a briefing by Rover's external affairs director, Michael Kennedy, and MG's brand manager, Greg Allport, Mike Hawke (chairman of the MG Car Club), Roche Bentley (secretary of the MG Owners' Club) and Harry Crutchley (of the Octagon Car Club) were asked to remove the dust-covers hiding the two cars. There followed a brave move by Rover's Kevin Jones, who allowed one of the cars to be moved outside on to the large tarmac area in front of the museum, where it was screened from prying eyes by banks of Rover staff cars. This provided a marvellous opportunity to examine the MGF in daylight, rather than under artificial lighting indoors, and there is no doubt that the MGF is at its most attractive outdoors where the daylight plays on its curves.

Selling the marque: a new approach

The MGF is a prime example of that fashionable icon, the niche product. While building a largely unique vehicle obviously causes it own headaches for the production engineers, there are also potential pitfalls when it come to marketing the car. However, Rover had already moved into low-volume niche products, principally the Rover 200 convertible and coupé, so some experience had been gained of selling such vehicles.

According to MG sales executive Steve Cox, only a few Rover dealers sold these vehicles successfully, and many never sold them at all. For the MGF, therefore, it was clear that there would be little point in diluting the sales and marketing effort required to revitalize the MG marque by trying to sell the car through every Rover dealer. 'We needed to tap into the dealer's enthusiasm,' explains Cox. 'Were they actually interested in the cars themselves, as well as selling them as a business?' Furthermore, in the current climate of low dealer margins, it was felt sensible to restrict the number of dealers to maximize the profit potential and ensure continued business. Added to that, potential MG franchise holders would need to be prepared to deal in a type of car that they may not have had to deal with before as trade-ins, such as Mazda MX-5s and Toyota MR2s. It was thought that some dealers might even be prepared to move into the sale and servicing of older MGs, too.

Accordingly, a tendering programme was instigated. This did not involve money, but required the would-be MG dealer to produce a business plan and to demonstrate a clear commitment and enthusiasm for sports car sales. As a result, 120 Rover dealers were awarded MG franchises. A Rover subsidiary, MG Cars, was established to control sales and marketing, and was given its own suite of offices at the company's Longbridge headquarters.

On the international front, MG dealers have been appointed throughout Europe (about 200 in total) and in other markets, such as Singapore and South America. To present the MGF to these dealers, a special two-day symposium was held at the Gaydon museum, in February 1995. Most of the lower area of the museum was occupied by a specially constructed auditorium with a hidden 'basement'. On the first day—aptly dubbed 'drama day'—the audience sat through presentations by Mike Ferguson, Greg Allport and Nick Fell, without any cars being visible. Then, at the last minute, the floor was slid back, revealing the MGF, which was greeted by thunderous applause.

Geneva 1995: all eyes on the MGF

As the Geneva Motor Show drew near, in March 1995, the atmosphere surrounding the MG launch became electric. Rover had been remarkably successful in keeping the car's appearance a secret, even though some artists' impressions had been fairly close to the genuine article, but the company must have been surprised at the wealth of interest shown in the product. Wisely, the launch of the financially more critical Rover 400 was delayed until several weeks later to prevent it from being submerged by the attention given to the MGF.

The press embargo of Tuesday, 7 March (the Geneva show's press day) was rigidly applied by Rover, but a motoring magazine in the UK broke ranks on the previous Friday and, as a result, virtually every Saturday newspaper printed photographs of the car. To welcome the new car, a party of 30 MG Car Club members (myself among them) drove a convoy of 14 classic MGs—ranging from a 1928 18/80 to a 1993 MG Metro—the 700 miles from Abingdon to Geneva. As the first completely new MG sports car since the MGB of 1962, this was not a launch to be missed.

Towards the future

Predicting the future can be a trap for the unwary, as many have found to their cost when attempting to foretell events in the motor industry. As in politics, a week in motor industry terms can be a lifetime; surely, few pundits would have predicted, in 1993, that BMW would snatch Rover from Honda's grasp early in the following year. Nevertheless, I shall stick my neck out and make a few predictions for the rest of the decade.

For the MGF, the short-term future is clear: following UK and mainland European sales in 1995, the rate of production will be increased from the initial 15,000 per annum to as much as 30,000 per annum. This has already begun, allowing export to Japan, much to the delight of Rover Japan's Peter Woods, who expressed his enthusiasm for the car to me at its Geneva début. In July 1995, Rover announced that the MGF would be launched in Germany and Japan by the end of the year.

Sales in mainland Europe were programmed to be expanded in 1996, and other markets would be opened up after that. Sadly, for North American MG fans, the MGF is unlikely to cross the Atlantic, as it was never engineered with the US market in mind. BMW executives are keen to prevent that situation occurring with future products that bear the Rover or MG badge. Certainly, at the time of writing, moves are afoot to relaunch the Rover and MG marques in the USA—a stated aim of Bernd Pischetsrieder—but the MGF will not spearhead this return. On the other hand, it is quite likely that there will be further developments of the MGF itself, perhaps revisions to the interior trim and ancillary equipment, and the inevitable automatic transmission. Undoubtedly, the F-Heritage custom-build option, launched in June 1996, which allows customers to order leather trimmed interiors and special paint schemes, was just the beginning of this process.

BMW and Rover will work more closely together, in their own words, 'capitalizing upon the opportunities for joint development, purchasing and logistics.' Inevitably, this will influence the development of BMWs, Rovers, Land Rovers, Minis and, of course, any future MG sports cars. It is unlikely that the experiment of the 1980s, when MG badges were applied to saloons, will be repeated. Despite the fine words expressed by the company at the time, it is clear that the MG saloons were produced in a hurried manner, largely in response to the public outcry at the destruction of the MGB and the MG marque, and were all that Austin Rover could afford then. The EX-E concept car was a frustrating glimpse of what might have been, but if it had been produced, it would have sat uneasily in the showrooms alongside Metros and Maestros.

What the MGF does not do is provide a replacement for the RV8 which, although only intended as a stop-gap—pointing the way for the PR5, which never emerged—clearly demonstrated that there is a market for a more luxurious and more powerful MG with traditional touches in its styling and power-train. When BMW took charge, Rover managers must have been asked about any projects that were sitting on the shelf through lack of finance under either government or British Aerospace ownership. One of these projects, of course, was PR5/DR2, the sports car that would have been far more expensive to build than the RV8. If there is to be a new, larger MG sports car, it will not be related in any way to either PR5/DR2 or the Adventurer 2 prototypes. However, with BMW backing, there is little doubt that any car of this type that does emerge will have the potential to be even more exciting than either of these concepts.

In an interview in the North American magazine *Automobile*, Bernd Pischetsrieder told journalist Georg Kacher that he could 'see a V8 in MG's future.' Perhaps, therefore, we will see an upmarket, front-engined, rear-wheel-drive MG tourer in the Jaguar XJS/Mercedes SL class, possibly with the KV6 or BMW V8 engine. After that, there could be room for a sports coupé in the spirit of the MGB GT, a low-priced sports car in the mould of the MG Midget and, in due course, a replacement for the MGF. Hopefully, I shall be able to write another chapter for this book in the years to come...

THE MGF IN MOTORSPORT

No sooner had the MGF been launched than people began speculating about its potential for competition. The MG marque has a long and close association with serious motor-sport, so it was inevitable that thoughts would turn to the idea of revitalizing the competitive aspect of MG. For the time being, however, Rover did not want to become involved in a full-blown motor-sports campaign in the UK, preferring to concentrate on the highly successful Dunlop Rover Turbo Cup, a championship based upon the powerful Rover 2.0 litre Coupé Turbo. On the other hand, the MG Car Club welcomed the MGF with open arms, and plans were soon made to introduce the newcomer into the ranks of club racing.

It was a different story in the overseas markets, most notably Japan and France, where racing championships were announced in October 1995 and January 1996 respectively. The Japanese series comprised eight championship rounds, all of them circuit races. One of the striking features of the Japanese racing MGF is the unique hardtop, designed by Peter Stephens and larger than the normal hardtop to accommodate the full roll-cage. It is interesting to note that Peter Stephens was Gerry McGovern's tutor at the Royal College of Art, so it was a case of role reversal when Gerry found himself in a position to criticize Stephens' work: 'Peter had another very novel idea, which was to form the roll-cage on the outside of the hardtop, making it a feature, but in the end, this was probably a bit too off-the-wall, and we went for the result which you see on the car.'

For France, 11 championship rounds were planned, four of which were to be circuit races, another four rallies, and the remainder hillclimbs. Unlike the cars for the Japanese series, which was purely a racing programme (they were fitted with single seats and racing suspension), the French racers featured left-hand-drive and retained a near standard interior, complete with two seats.

An intensive development programme took place for both the Japanese and French racing series. Roversport is spread thinly throughout the company, and those involved with the MGF project included engineers Roy Ford (facilitation and liaison), Alan Reed and Wynne Mitchell at Gaydon; Vicky Steemson acted as buyer, while Andrew Vallis looked after parts and procurement. In total, seven people were dedicated to the competition development of the MGF. All the development driving was done by veteran Tony Pond, including 2431 miles (3912.21km) of hot-weather testing in South Africa, calling at Kyalami, Midvaal, Goldfields and Gerotek. According to Tony, the attraction of using South Africa for testing, apart from the climate, was the relatively low cost of hiring the circuits: 'Goldfields and Midvaal were just £20 a day,

while even Kyalami was only about £1000 a day.' The fastest laps at Kyalami were posted by Pond on the final day of testing: 'We were doing 110mph (177.02km/h), which was about a second behind the local Group 'N' cars, and we certainly interested the locals, who were impressed that the car just kept going, day after day, without breaking.'

Wynne Mitchell, who, like Tony Pond, had been a veteran of the 6R4 campaign ten years before, was also involved with the competition MGF from the outset: 'We had completed some 800 miles (1287.44km) of testing in the UK—of which 700 miles (1126.51km) had been on the rolling road in a climate chamber, to simulate the sort of conditions which we would expect in South Africa—and Japan, of course. So we went to South Africa with what we expected would be the correct specification already determined. Fortunately, the testing showed that our confidence was justified: we achieved 14.2mpg (5.03km/litre) overall and used not one drop of oil!' For competition use, the 1.8-litre K-series engine is only lightly modified: 'We converted the engines to solid tappets in place of the normal Ina hydraulic tappets used in road cars,' says Wynne, adding that considerable attention had to be paid to cooling in the high ambient temperatures of 26-30°C (79-86°F). The racing MGF uses regular 95 RON unleaded fuel (ULG) and, unlike many modern competition vehicles, retains the standard catalytic converter. This could have posed a problem in South Africa, where only 91 ULG is available. As a result, one of liaison man Roy Ford's tasks was to ensure that a supply of 95 ULG was available throughout the testing programme.

The sole test car returned from its four-week tour of South Africa on 4 February, 1996, after which it made a final track appearance at Castle Combe, on 21 February, so that a group of Japanese journalists could drive it around the Dorset circuit. Only then was the car returned to Gaydon, where it was stripped down to discover how everything had fared. Also at Castle Combe was the first of the Japanese-specification competition cars, one of 25 that were to be shipped to Japan in mid-March, ahead of the series, which was programmed to begin in May. Actual production of the cars was subcontracted to Janspeed at Salisbury. The well-known tuning company converted the Longbridge-built MGFs to Rover specification, using Rover parts. At the time of writing, Rover remained tight-lipped about the prospect of an MGF series in the UK, but the availability (since spring 1996) of special Roversport parts—shades of the old Special Tuning—must bode well for the future.

The MGF was adapted for competitive motor-sport in Japan and France during 1996, and there was talk at the end of the year of extending competition activity to other markets. (Rover)

Appendices

1 MG PROTOTYPES WITH DO CODE-NUMBERS

DO no.	Description [Author's notes in square brackets]	Approximate dates
811	10hp Midget [with independent front suspension—see Appendix 2: EX164].	10/1939
825	10hp Midget [see Appendix 2: EX165; possibly pre-war thoughts for TC].	11/1939
914	1¼-litre saloon, 1945 [believed to be the MG Ten, which became the post-war YA; see Appendix 2: EX168, 169 and 170].	?/1945
926	Midget Major [two-seater sports car based upon Morris Minor].	1946-47
963	Midget two-seater [with full-width body; both open and coupé versions considered; one of a family of three Riley-engined proposals].	6/1948
965	1½-litre saloon [styling related to DO963].	6/1948
967	1½-litre convertible [styling related to DO965].	10/1948
968	TD Midget four-seater [based upon YA chassis and suspension].	1949
986	1¼-litre YB saloon.	1950
998	1¼-litre YB saloon.	1950
999	2½-litre saloon [Riley Pathfinder].	1951
1008	1¼-litre racing programme [see Appendix 2: EX173].	1951
1009	2-litre racing programme [see Appendix 2: EX174].	1951
1010	New Magnette [ZA].	1951-52
1017	Aluminium panels for TD Midget.	-
1035	New Midget (small) with AS3 engine [AS3 was the Austin A30 saloon, launched in October 1951. This shows that Cowley gave some thought to using this engine for a true small sports car, as did Austin and, later, BMC].	-
1041	TD Midget with Austin engine [probably the 50bhp/37.27kW, twin-SU Austin A40 Sports engine, precursor of the B-series, which first appeared in the production ZA Magnette].	-
1042	Midget with 1½-litre Riley engine.	-
1047	TF Midget, modified front [see Appendix 2: EX177].	1953
1048	Magna, streamlined.	-
1049	New Midget for 1954.	1953
1060	TF Midget with larger-capacity engine [i.e. TF 1500, involving change from 1266cc XPAG to 1466cc XPEG; see Appendix 2: EX176].	1954
1062	New Midget [note annotated 'MGA'; first factory entries dated 3 June, 1954].	1954-66
1067	Riley 2½-litre Pathfinder with C-type engine [see Appendix 2: EX207 'twin-cam Pathfinder'; first MG factory entry dated 30 November, 1954].	1954-56
1071	Magnette (ex-DO1010) hardtop version [possibly the pillarless Magnette prototype, which was run by Charles Griffin; no apparent records in Abingdon files, so presumably a wholly Cowley based project].	-
1091	Magnette (ex-DO1010) restyled for 1956 Motor Show.	1955-56
1100	Riley One-Point-Five [see Appendix 2: EX208; first drawings at Abingdon dated 30 September, 1956].	1956-57

I am indebted to Richard Brotherton of British Motor Heritage, who kindly supplied some of the information given above. The DO, or Drawing Office, numbering system was the Nuffield experimental register. Its origins predate the war, as will be apparent from the dates listed, but remained in use until late in the 1950s, before succumbing to rationalization with the Austin ADO system (see Appendix 3). It is almost certain that there are earlier and later numbers of relevance to MG studies in the DO series, but at the time of writing, it would appear that the only records that have survived are those from DO920 to 1091, and even they are not comprehensive. Earlier numbers listed have been derived from cross-references in the MG EX-Register (see Appendix 2), while others, such as DO926, 963, 965 and 967, have come from other sources.

2 THE COMPLETE MG EX-REGISTER—1929-77

EX no.	Description [Author's notes in square brackets]	Approximate dates
101	Midget front wings and lamp supports [12 drawings for M-type Midget].	6/11/1929
102	Brake cross-shaft bearings and cables, Mark I [nine drawings dated 14-29/11/1929 for the 18/80].	14/11/1929
103	Brake cross-shaft bearing modification [seven drawings, undated, for the 18/80].	-
104	Mark 3 type experimental front and rear wing fittings [four drawings for the Mark III 18/100].	-
105	Mark 3 petrol tank and fittings [25 drawings for the 18/100].	-
106	Mark 3 exhaust system [seven drawings, for the 18/100].	-
107	Mark 3 headlamp assembly [seven drawings, for the 18/100].	-
108	Mark 3 miscellaneous [23 drawings for the 18/100].	-
109	Brooklands type MG Midget: exhaust and induction [six drawings for the Brooklands Double Twelve Midget].	-
110	Midget (Brooklands type) wings [one drawing].	-
111	Mark 3 controls [15 drawings for Mark III 18/100].	-
112	Mark 3 instrument panel on chassis [two drawings for 18/100].	-
113	Mark 1 and 2 miscellaneous [15 drawings for the Mark I and II 18/80].	-
114	Midget (Brooklands type) petrol tanks [two drawings for Brooklands Double Twelve Midget].	-
115	Frame and suspension, Midget 1931 [21 drawings for 1931 Midget, which saw the change-over from the Morris Minor M-type chassis to a purpose designed MG chassis].	-

238

116	Shock absorbers [six drawings for 1931 Midget].	-
117	Mark 2 close up of wings [two drawings of Mark II 18/80].	-
118	Mark 3 oil tank [two drawings for Mark III 18/100].	-
119	Mark 1 servo brakes (DeWandre servo) [two drawings for the chassis mounted brake servo on the Mark I 18/80].	-
120	Midget 750 c.c. [no less than 372 drawings listed for this car, which was Eyston's Montlhéry Midget that gained several international class records during 1930-31. It was the first car to reach over 100mph/160.93km/h on under 750cc. EX120 does not survive: following a record breaking run in September 1931, it caught fire and the remains were cut up at Abingdon soon afterwards].	
121	Midget miscellaneous (2 seater, 1931) [two drawings for 1931 Midget].	-
122	Mark 2 fan [nine drawings for the Mark II 18/80].	-
123	Midget anti-squeak [three drawings for MG M-type].	11/9/1930
124	Midget blower equipment [seven drawings for Midget supercharger].	
125	750 c.c. blower equipment [139 drawings].	
126	Midget change-speed (sliding type) [Midget gear selector].	
127	Single seat racing car [93 drawings for Eyston's second record car—the 'Magic Midget'—which achieved 120mph (193.116km/h) on less than 750cc. Bobby Kohlrausch (see also EX154) later achieved over 140mph (225.302km/h)! EX127 was eventually reworked into EX154].	-
128	'E' type [22 drawings; this appears to have been an abortive project. The D-type became the new Midget, and the F-type emerged as the Magna].	
129	'F' type chassis with three foot, ten inch [1.168m] track [16 drawings, possibly for the F-type Magna, although that car had a track of 3ft 6in/1.067m].	-
130	AB type engines [33 drawings. EX 130/32 and 33 are for J-type engine camshaft details].	
131	Experimental 'K' type engine items [11 drawings for K-type engine].	-
132	Experimental K3 type [six drawings related to the famous K3 Magnette].	-
133	Girling brakes [three drawings].	-
134	Crankshaft thrust bearings (ball type) [five drawings].	-
135	Single seat, 1,100 c.c. [233 drawings; this became the famous record breaker EX135, after a few incarnations; in original form, effectively a single-seat K3 Magnette—no. K3023].	
136	Crankshaft steady—roller bearing type [seven drawings].	-
137	Cadmium-plated big-end [one drawing].	-
138	J2 brake cross-shaft with single point adjustment [one drawing].	-
139	Reverse stop assembly [four drawings].	-
140	Reverse stop assembly [two drawings].	-
141	Laycock propeller shaft [two drawings].	-
142	Experimental brake gear [51 drawings, including proposed brake gear for K3 Magnette, designed by Cecil Cousins].	-
143	Special parts for Mille Miglia K3 cars (1934) [11 drawings].	-
144	'N' saloon [two drawings, which only depict the bonnet].	-
145	Petrol and oil sealing devices on K3 Marshall blowers [19 drawings; sealing problems with Marshall superchargers].	-
146	No title—only 'superseded by EX147' [118 drawings giving all chassis, suspension, engine mounting details for the R-type single-seater].	-
147	'R' type [106 drawings for the famous independent-suspension R-type single-seater of 1935].	-
148	'P' type sundries [13 drawings, including details of Le Mans fittings].	-
149	Not taken [in other words, not used. The following is purely conjecture on my part, but it is quite possible that EX149 was to have been the so-called S-type single-seat racing car that Cecil Kimber hoped to produce].	
150	3½ litre independent car [1106 drawings, including what is referred to as 'banana-type rear suspension'. This car was nicknamed the 'Queen Mary'. It was abandoned, along with EX147, when William Morris sold the MG Car Company Ltd to Morris Motors Ltd].	
151	10/4 engine (TA etcetera) [41 drawings detailing the engine for the TA Midget].	
152	R.A. experimental chassis (anti-roll experiments) [cancelled].	-
153	Experimental work on the Two-Litre [72 drawings for the SA].	-

154 Special car for R. Kohlrausch esq.; specification as follows: Chassis No. EX154; Engine No. 2443A; P-type chassis frame; P-type front axle; P-type rear axle; Q-type brake drums; J4 torque-reaction cables; straight-cut gears to back axle; rear axle nose-piece through-bolted with tubular distance pieces; J4 body, petrol tank and spare wheel carrier; J2 cycle type wings and P-type wing stays; three inch [7.62cm] diameter prop-shaft balanced to 8,000 r.p.m. (200 series joints, four and a half inch [11.43cm] O/D flanges, five sixteenth inch [0.79cm] bolts on a three and 61/64 inch [10.04cm] P.C.D., thirty six and 1/16 inch [91.60cm] long); Q-type engine with pre-selector box and Zoller supercharger mounted between front dumb irons; P-type steering cam gears; special road wheels and tyres supplied by Mr. Kohlrausch. [72 drawings for the special Bobby Kohlrausch car, built using some parts from EX127. EX154 was later destroyed in Germany].

155 'T'-series Midget; allocated for experimental chassis and cars [chassis no. EX155/1, engine no. 6594/1—dated 22/2/1938. The following MG Midget TA series cars were converted to competition models and fitted with 1½-litre engines:

Chassis no.	Engine no.	To EX155 chassis	New engine no.
TA 2017	MPJG 2285	EX155/2	TPBG 1383
TA 2018	MPJG 2286	EX155/3	TPBG 1373
TA 2019	MPJG 2291	EX155/4	TPBG 1397
TA 2020	MPJG 2295	EX155/5	TPBG 1384
TA 2092	MPJG 2368	EX155/6	TPBG 968

There are 20 drawings also listed, covering such items as police equipment and supercharger fixings. The chassis numbers may relate to the new Cream Cracker team cars of 1938].

156	Valve spring experiments [two drawings—cancelled].	
157	Not allotted.	-
158	SA Type Two Litre [85 drawings; including Mille Miglia car].	
159	VA Type 1½ litre [36 drawings; includes cars EX159/1, with engine 6591/1, and EX159/2, with engine TPDG 6720/2, featuring wider rear track and special body].	-
160	3½ litre car designed at Cowley [no entries; probably the proposal to produce a large Wolseley-engined MG saloon, which was abandoned in favour of the WA—EX161].	
161	2.6 litre [WA 2.6-litre saloon. 19 drawings, including three related to chassis: EX161/1 with engine QPHG 2523; EX161/2 with engine 6608/1; and EX161/3 with engine QPJG 648—described as 'working show chassis'].	
162	Two Litre—front independent suspension designed by Mr. Girling of Pratt and Manley [four drawings; cross refers negatives with EX158 MG SA; includes modified Jackall arrangements].	
163	10 H.P. XPJG engine; now 10.8 HP XPAG [five drawings of the XPAG engine exhaust valves. Cross refers to EX155 TA Midget; this is probably the TB Midget].	
164	10 H.P. Midget (DO 811) independent front suspension [one drawing; note the reference to a Cowley DO project code].	26/10/1939
165	10 H.P. Midget (DO 825) [note reference to Cowley DO code].	27/11/1939
166	1¼ litre saloon 1945 [engine no. 6946/3; EX/MG/76. Comment in register: 'Guarantee plate issued to Cowley Experimental Department 7/1/1945'].	-
167	'Bitsy' [engine no. XPAG 529. 'Bitsy' was a sort of tractor built during wartime from bits and pieces, hence its name].	-
168	1¼ litre saloon 1945 (DO 914) [engine no. 11527/1. Morris Motors experimental no. EX/MG/125].	
169	1¼ litre saloon 1945 (DO 914) [engine no. 11527/2; EX/MG/126].	
170	1¼ litre saloon 1945 (DO 914) [engine no. 11527/3; EX/MG/127].	
171	TD Midget converted to road racing specification (Dick Jacobs) [44 drawings].	25/9/1950
171A	MG 1 11.9 HP engine no. EX171/1. 69.5 mm bore, 102 mm stroke; 1,548 c.c. [this is the reregistered chassis number of 'Old Number One', allocated an EX number retrospectively in 1956.	1956

172	TD Midget for Le Mans with streamlined body. Chassis Number TD/C.5336 [16 drawings; this is the famous UMG 400 with the Syd Enever designed body that ultimately inspired the MGA].	5/1/1951
173	TD engines for Record Car—Job No. ZM.13366; Cowley DO 1008 [36 drawings—see Appendix 1].	10/1/1951
174	DO 1009 2-litre converted Wolseley 6/80 engine for Record Car [62 drawings; see Appendix 1 for DO 1009].	1/2/1951
175	1,500 c.c. streamlined Midget 2-seater [44 drawings; drawing EX175/1 is car outline; this is the second stage in the evolutionary process that led to the MGA. EX175/1—registered HMO 6—was the car shown to Leonard Lord, but rejected by him in favour of the Healey 100].	-
176	72mm bore by 90mm stroke 4-cylinder 1,466 c.c. TD engine for USA—Job No. ZM.15838 [44 drawings; presumably, this is the origin of the later TF 1500 engine. Drawings EX176/42,43 and 44 refer to a 1588cc MGA engine for Sebring in 1961, and cross-refer to EX178, although it is likely that this is a simple case of misbooking].	-
177	TF Midget [27 drawings, not all dated in register; EX177/15 is dated 7/5/1953].	May 1953
178	Austin 1,500 engine tuning [68 drawings; this was clearly involvement of MG with the Austin designed B-series, which appeared in the ZA Magnette and later in the MGA. Not all drawings are dated, but drawing EX178/63 is dated 21/3/1957, and drawings EX178/67 and 68 refer to a 1622cc version of engine and are dated 2/3/1961].	1953-61
179	Record Car for 1954 (Job No. ZM.18757) [115 drawings of this famous record breaker. Only drawings EX179/70 onwards are dated: 13/4/1956 for EX179/70 to 9/1/1959 for EX179/115].	1953-59
180	Morris Minor tuning [11 drawings, relating to valve springs, rear springs, shock absorbers, Weber 40 DCOE carburettor manifold, etc.; dated 11/3/1958 to 29/6/1960].	1958-60
181	Record Car (Special) [the famous record breaker driven by Phil Hill and Stirling Moss, and known to the media as the 'Roaring Raindrop'. Most of the 276 drawings date from 1957 to 1960, but there are later entries from EX181/273 onwards; EX 181/273, dated 10/8/1966, is for a 'radiator front duct', while EX181/274, dated 3/7/1978, is for a 'front decal showing GB and USA flags and MG emblem'—no doubt, drawn in retrospect to allow restoration. Drawings EX181/275 and 276, dated 25/10/1978 and 30/10/1978 respectively, detail the tail contours].	1957-78
182	Special parts for Series M.G.A. [note stops in MGA!] for Le Mans 1955 [68 drawings detailing parts such as oil cooler, tanks and mountings, brakes, etc. Numbers EX182/38, 39, 40 and 41 are listed as 'chassis numbers for Le Mans cars nos. 1, 2, 3 and 4 respectively', although it is not clear which car is which—see Appendix 6. The last two drawings are dated 15/3/1960].	-
183	Experimental 1956 Le Mans car (tubular chassis) [27 drawings].	-
184	Special parts for Weslake T.S.P. cylinder head [six drawings].	-
185	Special parts for competition Pathfinder [15 drawings detailing road springs, engine mountings, etc].	-
186	Twin overhead-camshaft 'Le Mans' type 1956 with MGA type chassis [202 drawings detailing 4½Jx15 alloy disc wheels, suspension, chassis reinforcements, etc. Last entry dated 3/9/1959].	?-1959
187	Twin overhead-camshaft version of MGA with disc brakes [318 drawings: 2/6/1955 to 26/11/1962].	1955-62
188	New Midget with [Austin] A30 ['A'-series] engine—MGD [no previous mention of MGB or MGC in register! No drawings or anything else listed, but this may have been related to Cowley's DO1035].	n/a
189	4-seater version of MGA—MGE [another 'kite flyer', like EX188; nothing listed in register].	n/a
190	Competition Magnette [three drawings: modifications to petrol tank to increase capacity from 9¼gal/42.05 litres to 14gal/63.64 litres, dated 16/5/1955 to 21/6/1955].	May-Jun 1955
191	Development work on production MGA [450 drawings, dated from 19/5/1955 to 7/2/1961; see ADO31, Appendix 3].	1955-61
192	Development work for rallies on Austin cars [20 drawings of such things as: EX192/1 engine no. for Le Mans type engine in Austin Cambridge, dated 28/6/1955; EX192/2 rear spring for Austin A90, dated 15/7/1955; and EX192/19 10gal/45.46-litre petrol tank for Austin A35, dated 13/6/1957. The Austin A90 was one of the early choices for rallying by the BMC Competitions Department].	1955-57
193	Magnette (for Bermuda only) [16 drawings detailing different number-plate finishers and assemblies; front wing flash; rear bumper blade, which was split in two—left and right hand; and jacking fixings on rear bumper, etc].	Sep-Oct 1955
194	MGA Police Modifications [17 drawings, detailing C-type engine dynamo and larger batteries].	-
195	MGA 'cheap version' [72 drawings, dated 11/11/1955 to 31/8/1959, detailing ideas for a low-cost MGA with Austin A30 steering box, 13 or 14in (33.02 or 35.56cm) wheels, single 1¾in SU carburettor, Morris Minor propshaft, etc].	1955-59
196	MGA Hardtop [one drawing].	7/2/1956
197	Fixed-Head Coupé MGA [no entries in register at all].	n/a
198	[Riley] Pathfinder (Mark II) Push-Rod 'C' type engine [29 drawings, dated from May 1956 to 31/7/1956, detailing the changes made to the Riley-engined Pathfinder to make it the Riley Two-Point-Six].	May-Jul 1956
199	Competition Magnette [four drawings: 13/1/1956, for ventilated brake drum, to 10/1/1958 for sump shield].	1956-58
200	Magnette facelift [no entries. Judging by date, this could be Varitone or even first thoughts about a successor to the Z-Magnette. With no entries to go on, this is pure conjecture. Note also DO1071 and DO1091: see Appendix 1].	n/a
201	[Riley] Pathfinder with semi-elliptic rear suspension [39 drawings, dated 5/3/1956 to 4/12/1957].	1956-57
202	Magnette with 'C' series engine [five drawings, of May 1956, covering rear axle scheme, rear shock absorber, scheme showing C-type rear axle, radiator casing grille and radiator block].	8&9/5/1956
203	Magnette with extra-long column [four drawings].	-
204	[Riley] Pathfinder series RMJ 6/90 modified [63 drawings, including chassis number of prototype car—EX204/56].	-
205	MG Two-Seater (ADO23) [11 drawings, all described as having been 'transferred into ADO23 book'; from June 1957 to February 1958. Includes drawing of Frua-bodied MGA].	1957-58
206	Three Litre Riley [no entries; Don Hayter recalls that this was another 'kite flyer'].	n/a
207	Twin Cam [Riley] Pathfinder (DO1067) [see Appendix 1. Note that there is reference to 'Chassis No. EX207/1—Export Car'. Presumably, drawings were done by Cowley and all booked to DO1067. The engine was designed by Gerald Palmer as a twin-cam conversion of the C-series six. Work began in November 1955, but was abandoned in March 1956].	1955-56
208	1½ litre Riley [four drawings, all relating to the Riley One-Point-Five. EX208/1 is listed as 'chassis number for runabout car', dated 12/11/1957; EX208/4 is a 4Jx13 wheel arrangement, dated 19/11/1959. This car was also DO1100: see Appendix 1].	1957-59
209	Long term development power units [no entries. This may have have been intended to include Abingdon's thoughts about a 2-litre, four-cylinder engine, 'cut down' from the six-cylinder C-series unit].	n/a
210	2.6 litre MG (4-seater sports) [six drawings; EX210/1, a quarter-scale body general arrangement, dated 28/8/1957; EX210/2, same as EX210/1, but annotated 'H. Harris' and dated 28/2/1958; EX210/3, a quarter-scale 'schematic layout', dated 28/5/1958; EX210/4, a sketch showing installation of pedals, dated 28/5/1958; EX210/5, an isometric sketch of the front end; and EX210/6, a quarter-scale frame. The last two are dated 28/5/1958. Clearly, this is a precursor of the MGC, complete with C-series engine].	1957-58
211	Anti run-on and fuel economy device [four drawings. This was an attempt to cure the common problem of running on experienced with hot engines after the ignition had been switched off].	8/2/1957
212	Fixed head coupé MGA Twin Cam [no entries in register, but this is the Don Hayter schemed coupé, built on the basis of Ted Lund's MGA twin-cam roadster, SRX 210—chassis no. YD3-627S—for Ted to race at Le Mans].	-
213	Competition [Austin-] Healey BN6 [75 drawings, ranging from EX213/1 for a 25gal/113.65-litre fuel tank, dated 20/5/1958, to EX213/75 for a shock absorber link bolt, dated 1/7/1964. The Austin-Healey 100/6 (later the 3000 Mark I, II and III) was built at Abingdon from 1957].	1958-64
214	Replacement for MGA—body facelift, wings, etc [12 drawings detailing the first thoughts for what became ADO23, the MGB—see also Appendix 3. Drawing EX214/1 is for quarter-scale body lines, dated 9/6/1958; EX214/12 is for quarter-scale body lines with a wide radiator grille—in other words, the prototype MGB with coil-sprung rear suspension—dated 1/5/1959].	1958-59
215	Competition equipment for 1.5 litre Rileys [two drawings, both detailing flexible oil cooler pipes].	3/6/1958
216	V4 power unit in MGA [13 drawings detailing modifications to front cross-member and other installation requirements. The V4 engine was one of a proposed new family of Longbridge designed BMC units, but eventually it was abandoned because of cost and balancing problems. Its demise did not cause disappointment at Abingdon. The drawings are dated 16/9/1958 to 3/12/1958].	late 1958
217	'B' type box on 'C' type engine [one drawing only, for adaptor plates].	-
218	[Austin-Healey] BN6 Development (including BN7, BN8) [50 drawings, dated from 22/7/1958 to 2/9/1960].	1958-60
219	[Austin-] Healey Sprite 24 hour record car [19 drawings from April 1959 to 16/7/1959. There is often confusion over the history of this car. Originally, EX219 was a special streamlined version of the Austin-Healey Sprite, with faired-in nose and bubble canopy.	1959

However, wind-tunnel tests showed that the body was not effective aerodynamically, so EX179 was revised instead and presented as an Austin-Healey].

220	New Midget based on Sputnik F.W.D. (Superseded ADO34) [21 drawings, dated from 23/4/1959 to 4/6/1959. Clearly, there was some thought about a number of possible variations on a theme, as both MG and Austin-Healey variants are included, together with a coupé proposal—EX220/19, dated 29/5/1959). 'Sputnik' was the code name given to the ADO15 Mini prior to its launch].	1959
221	Sprite with 1,600 'B' series engine [EX221/1 is described as 'Chassis Number for No. 1 Prototype Car'].	23/3/1960
222	ADO 10 [Austin A99 and Wolseley 6/99] and ADO 53 [Austin A110 and Wolseley 6/110] Competition [two drawings relating to rear spring modifications, dated 23/8/1960 for ADO10 (EX222/1) and 28/6/1962 for ADO53].	1960-62
223	Competition Mini Minor [162 drawings relating to the Mini Cooper and S; date from 13/10/1962 to 19/2/1973].	1962-73
224	Mini Minor ADO 15—conversion to Austin Healey sports model [no entries in register].	-
225	Mini Minor ADO 15—conversion to MG sports model [no entries].	-
226	Modifications to the ADO 9 Magnette MK. III [two drawings: EX226/1 steering wheel, dated 4/4/1961; EX226/2 engine, dated 10/4/1961. These drawings may have been part of the exercise to improve the appalling handling and performance of the ADO9 range, which culminated in the ADO38 replacement (including the Magnette Mark IV) of 1961. It is also worth noting that John Thornley sought styling improvements to ADO9 and/or ADO38, to no avail].	Apr 1961
227	1,600 GT coupé 2-seater [50 drawings, dated from 4/1/1962. EX227/2 shows a quarter-scale arrangement, dated 4/1/1962; drawings undated after EX227/34. EX227 is the MGB GT project code, although, as can be seen, Abingdon envisaged it as a 1600cc coupé, presumably because it was originally conceived to have the 1622cc engine, and only received the 1798cc engine at a fairly late stage prior to launch].	1962
228	Transverse rear-engined 'A' series car.	-
229	Midget with Hydrolastic—rear wheel drive [three drawings described as: EX229/1 steering geometry, dated 16/10/1962; EX229/2 chassis frame front end, dated 21/11/1962; and EX229/3 front sub-frame, dated 21/11/1962].	late 1962
230	ADO 15 [Mini] with integrated sub-frames [one drawing detailing under-frame scheme, dated 29/3/1963].	29/3/1963
231	Hydrolastic suspension on ADO 41/47 [66 drawings—first 1/4/1963; last dated 20/12/1963—concerning the conversion of the 'Spridget' to hydrolastic suspension; see Appendix 3].	1963
232	1,800 c.c. engine development [16 drawings, ranging from EX232/1 for a set of triple valve springs, dated 25/4/1963, to EX232/16, a scheme for a swirl-chamber induction heater, dated 17/10/1967].	1963-67
233	Record car with transverse engine [no entries].	9/9/1963
234	Hydrolastic Sports Car Prototype [136 drawings for this pretty, Pininfarina styled sports car. The prototype survives as part of Syd Beer's collection, having been bought in the 1970s after many years of 'mothballed' storage].	from 11/2/1964
235	Competition MGB [12 drawings, from 29/7/1964].	1964
236	Comps [Competition Department] ADO 17 [35 drawings, dating from 26/11/1964; ADO17 is the Austin-Morris 1800 'landcrab'; see Appendix 3].	1964
237	GT Prototype to 1965 Le Mans regulations [three drawings, dated 10/3/1965, showing body lines—EX237/1 and 2—and windscreen glass—EX237/3].	10/3/1965
238	Midget with 1,800 c.c. engine [two drawings, dated 10/7/1966 and 20/2/1967, both of propshaft].	1966-67
239	Competition and fuel injection Midget ADO 41/47 [25 drawings, ranging in date from 8/11/1967 to 9/4/1968].	1967-68
240	Mini 850 c.c. [red saloon with engine no. 8WR/U/H/4214, built by MG show shop in December 1967. After 'Comps' had finished with it, John Thornley bought EX240 for his daughter. Sadly, in his words, 'she impaled it on a Southern Electricity Board Land Rover. She survived, but EX240 did not.'].	4/1/1968
241	Competition ADO 52 [four drawings, dated 8/2/1968 to 30/7/1968, covering inlet manifolds and triple SU HS6 carburettors. EX241 is the famous MGC GTS; see Appendix 3].	1968
242	MG GT version of ADO 28; for all part numbers see sheets in Project Office Book—Don Hayter 13/11/1968 [15 drawings detailing Abingdon's proposals for a coupé based upon the forthcoming Morris Marina, on a 102in/2.59m wheelbase. Drawings date from 8/2/1968 to 30/7/1968 and detail, among other things, the E4, E6 and Rover V8 engines. This project may be related to ADO68; see Appendix 3].	1968
243	[Austin-Healey] Sprite with heel-board moved rearward.	13/12/1968
244	Triumph 2.5 P.I. for competition [ten drawings, dated 29/7/1969 to 16/2/1970. The first and only Triumph mentioned in the EX-Register! 'Comps' were preparing the fuel-injected Triumph 2.5 PI for rallies].	1969-70
245	Competition Maxi [four drawings, dated from 1/1/1970 to 27/1/71; see ADO14, Appendix 3].	1970-71
246	ADO 28 [Marina] Special Tuning. For all part numbers see sheets in Project Office Book—M. Holliday 22/2/1971.	22/2/1971
247	Mini with 12 inch wheels and larger brakes [19 drawings, dated 9/3/1971 to 3/5/1971. Interestingly, 12in/30.48cm wheels would be gradually adopted on all production Minis, starting with the Mini 1275GT later in the decade].	1971
248	Passive Restraint ADO 23 [MGB—24 drawings, dated 2/6/1971 to 14/10/1974. Passive restraint was a concept invented by the US safety legislators and meant that passengers and driver alike should be restrained inside the vehicle without the need to consciously fasten a seat belt].	1971-74
249	Installation of Rover V8 engine in MGB. [104 drawings, dated from 5/8/1971 to 14/1/1972. Cross-refers with ADO75; see Appendix 3. This is the first Abingdon prototype for the MGB GT V8, engineered by Terry Mitchell].	1971-72
250	MGB Experimental Safety Vehicle [15 drawings, dated 28/3/1972 to 24/5/1972. This was a safety concept vehicle, SSV-1, built for a vehicle safety exhibition in Washington DC, USA. The single prototype survives].	early 1972
251	Mini Project [five drawings, dated 17/3/1977 to 25/3/1977, detailing oil cooler fixings. Note the large gap in dates between EX250 and 251].	Mar 1977
252	ADO 67 [Austin Allegro] and ADO 71 [Princess] rear sub-frame mountings [two drawings detailing bush and mounting bracket; an ignominious end for such a grand list].	Mar 1977

The above information has been extracted from the original EX-Register, and is reproduced in full for the first time. There were earlier EX numbers, which predated EX101: EX1, EX2 and EX3 were the first three prototypes of the 18/80 (six) Mark I; EX4 was the 18/80 Six Mark II. Before long, this numbering system collapsed, and with the move from Oxford to Abingdon in 1929, the opportunity was taken to start afresh with EX101, code-numbers being allocated to projects rather than complete vehicles. After MG was absorbed into Morris Motors, in 1935, many MG projects were carried out at Cowley, sometimes using the Cowley drawing office (DO) numbering system (see Appendix 1). It is important to be aware that, in addition to the DO project code-numbering system, Cowley-built prototype cars were often given their own EX chassis numbers. An example of this will be noted above with EX168 to 170 inclusive, where three prototypes for the YA saloon are referred to with chassis numbers EX/MG/125 to 127. Clearly, therefore, it is essential to avoid confusion between Abingdon's EX project codes and Cowley's EX chassis numbers.

With the formation of BMC, in 1952, the DO codes continued, but there was the added complication of the Austin (or Amalgamated) drawing office—ADO—numbering system (see Appendix 3). By the 1960s, the importance of the EX-Register had diminished, and important projects were assigned ADO codes as soon as they had support from the parent company. By the 1970s, the EX-Register was hardly used at all, and the last entries were for non-MG projects. It should be noted that the much later MG EX-E concept car was in no way connected to the EX-Register.

3 THE ADO CODE-NUMBERS

ADO no.	Description	Approximate dates
6	Austin Taxi, FL 2, FL 2D, FX 4 and FX 4D; the ubiquitous London taxi.	-
8	Austin A40 Farina, later replaced by ADO44.	1958
9	MG Magnette Series III. ADO9 covers whole range; ADO9G specific to MG version.	1958-59
10	Austin A99 and Wolseley 6/99; large Pininfarina-bodied saloons.	1959

12	Austin A35 with experimental Ebert infinitely variable hydrostatic (IVH) transmission.	1956
13	Austin-Healey Sprite Mark I, the so-called 'frogeye' or 'bugeye' Sprite designed by the Healeys.	1958
14	Austin Maxi five-door saloon, launched in 1969 after BLMC merger.	1964-79
15	Mini range; no MG derivatives actually produced, but considered nevertheless.	1959
16	MG 1100. ADO16 covers whole range; ADO16G specific to MG version.	1962
17	Austin, Morris and Wolseley 1800, the so-called 'landcrab'.	1964
19	Austin Ant cross-country vehicle; prototype with BMH. Not to be confused with the ADO74 Ant proposal for a Mini replacement.	1965?
20	Mini range revised with wind-up windows and the addition of the Clubman range; basis of ADO70.	1969
21	Mid-engined MG sports car prototype; engineered at Abingdon, styled at Longbridge.	1969-70
22	New Austin-Morris 1100/1300 two- and four-door, front-wheel-drive saloon; cancelled by British Leyland and replaced by ADO67, which became the Austin Allegro. This project probably constituted little more than an extensive facelift of ADO16. It is conceivable, but not recorded, that there would have been an MG version of this car had it proceeded.	1967
23	MG MGB (see also EX-Register, Appendix 2). Launched 1962; code-number remained in use throughout the life of the MGB, although it was supplemented by ADO76 in 1975.	1958-78
24	Austin-Healey 3000-based sports car using 4-litre Rolls Royce FB60 engine; widened body, designed by Healeys with some input from Syd Enever at MG. Abingdon records date from February 1967.	1966-67
25	E6 2227cc engine derived from Maxi E4 for transverse mounting in ADO17, Australian YDO19—as X6 Kimberley/Tasman—and, later, ADO71. Like ADO32, this unit was considered for use in ADO21. A 2622cc version was engineered and built overseas for in-line applications only.	1968
26	Austin-Healey 3000 (BN7 and BN8—Marks II and III); Abingdon entries date from 27/6/1958.	1958-65
27	Two entries using the same number: (i) Riley 1.5 (ADO27R)/ Wolseley 1500 (ADO27W) update proposal with 'Farina fins'; (ii) the Australian version of ADO17, also known as YDO19.	(i)1960 (ii)1970
28	Morris Marina range; front-engine, rear-wheel-drive two- and four-door saloons, launched in 1971.	1968-71
30	New Austin-Healey sports car to replace ADO26, also coded S4 and XC5212 (see Appendix 4), and irreverently known as 'Fireball XL-5'. This was a Longbridge inspired and engineered project, which consumed millions of pounds before being abandoned. Initially, schemed with a Rolls Royce FB60 engine, later it was drawn up with a Jaguar unit. At least one running prototype was built.	1966
31	MG MGA 1600. This appears to apply to both the Mark I and Mark II versions, judging by Abingdon records, which include a sketch, SK7242, dated 8/4/1960, for the MGA De Luxe.	1959-61
32	E4 1485cc and 1748cc engine developed for ADO14 Maxi and, later, ADO67 Allegro; also re-engineered for in-line mounting in Australian and South African versions of ADO28. This engine was considered for use in ADO21 (see also ADO25).	1968
34	MG Mini-based open sports two-seater; at least two versions built: one at Abingdon, and another engineered at Longbridge. Only the latter survives.	1960
35	MG Mini-based coupé.	1960
36	Austin-Healey version of ADO34.	1960
37	Austin and Vanden Plas Princess 3-litre saloon; Farina styling.	1959
38	MG Magnette Series IV to replace ADO9. ADO38 covers whole range; ADO38G specific to MG version).	1961
39	New Metropolitan taxicab; never proceeded with.	1967
40	Austin A40 Farina (Australian).	-
41	Austin-Healey Sprite Mark II; the extensively facelifted version of ADO13, which basically was the same car as the ADO47 MG Midget Mark I.	1959-70
44	Austin Farina A40 Mark II to replace ADO8.	1961
46	Austin A60 and Morris Oxford diesel; derivatives of ADO38.	1961
47	MG Midget Mark I (see also ADO41).	1960-78
49	Siam di Tella 1500; Argentinian-built saloon and pick-up based upon body of Riley 4/68 (ADO9).	-
50	Austin and Morris Mini Cooper and S. Consideration was given to replacing the Cooper-badged cars with MG equivalents.	1961
51	Austin-Healey 3000 Mark IV; Austin-Healey version of MGC, with little more to distinguish it from ADO52 than a mock Healey grille and some minor trim differences. The Healeys were not impressed and it was cancelled in 1966.	1962-65
52	MG MGC and GT; large-engined version of ADO23 MGB, conceived for six-cylinder Blue Streak derivative of B-series engine, and later redesigned for big Austin 3-litre, shared with ADO61.	1961-69
53	Austin A110 and Wolseley 6/110 to replace ADO10.	1961
58	Short-wheelbase luxury saloon project based upon the Rolls Royce Burma T-series Bentley bodyshell, with FB60 Rolls-Royce engine.	-
59	Morris Minor 1000 with 1098cc A-series engine. A prototype was built with a chassis number that intriguingly combined Cowley and Austin practices—EX/422/ADO59—on 20/2/1962. Other ADO lists have omitted this code-number.	1962
61	Austin 3-Litre—the last large Austin saloon; used doors of ADO17 and shared engine with ADO52. Harry Webster tried to get engine replaced with Rover 3.5-litre V8 in 1969-70).	1966
66	Vanden Plas Princess 4-litre R; Rolls Royce-engined version of ADO53.	1964
67	Austin Allegro two- and four-door, front-wheel-drive saloons and estates, including Vanden Plas 1500, launched in 1973. Intended to replace ADO16 after cancellation of ADO22. Styling signed off for production in September 1969 and used as basis of ADO68/67.	1968
68	Condor two-door coupé based upon ADO14 Maxi (ADO68/14), ADO28 Marina (ADO68/28-1 and ADO68/28-2) or ADO67 Allegro (ADO68/67). Could have been badged as an MG—some styling models even badged as 'MG Magna', reviving a pre-war MG name. Engine choice, dependent upon variant, could have been the ubiquitous B-series four, E4, E6 or even the Triumph Stag V8. The idea of a V8 Marina or a six-cylinder Allegro are quite startling.	1969-70
69	New taxi cab to replace ADO6; designed 1970.	1970
70	So-called Michelotti Mini two-door sports coupé with lift-out roof panels, designed by Paul Hughes of Austin-Morris and built by Michelotti in Turin on ADO20 Mini 1275GT base. Prototype badged with BL logos, but could have been an MG if produced.	1970
71	Austin/Morris/Wolseley 18-22 series; became the Princess range barely five months after launch. Replaced ADO17 and code-named Diablo. ADO71 was styled by Harris Mann and nearly included a Vanden Plas derivative, a prototype of which survives. Used B-, E6- and later O-series engines. Superseded in 1981 by Austin Ambassador.	1975
73	Morris Marina Mark II and Ital; extensively facelifted version of ADO28, which originally would have included a North American-specification (NAS) derivative. This was killed off, which left MGB progressively more of an orphan from the components point of view. Later version saw introduction of O-series in-line, as designed for MGB.	1975-80
74	Austin Ant or Ladybird; proposed replacement for the Mini, which would have been a Metro-sized hatchback featuring an all-new OHC engine code-named the K-series. This engine is unrelated to the present day K-series engine manufactured by the Rover Group.	1972-74
75	MG MGB GT V8; the Rover V8 engine in the ADO23 MGB body (see also EX249, Appendix 2).	1971-74
76	New MG MGB, MGB GT and V8; the facelift with the so-called 'rubber' bumpers to meet US safety legislation. In the Abingdon records, this is referred to as 'MGB with Marina back axle', as there was a project to cheapen the MGB that involved a number of component changes.	1972-78
77	New Marina range to replace ADO28 and, subsequently, ADO73. All-new body, in-line engines with rear-wheel-drive (including O-series derivatives), and new '66mm' five-speed gearbox. Car and gearbox cancelled.	1972-75
88	New Mini range; front-wheel-drive small hatchback intended to replace the evergreen Mini. Project changed in 1978, slightly enlarged and renamed LC8; launched in 1980 as Metro. Some work was actually done on this project by Denis Williams at Abingdon, and records show that sketches of proposals for a hinged roof panel (i.e. a sunroof) were drawn in July 1977.	1974-78
99	Replacement for Austin Allegro/Maxi, envisaged as a 99in (2.51m) wheelbase car, which is given rather unconvincingly as the reason for the choice of code-number. Became LC10 family, leading to LM10 Maestro and LM11 Montego.	-

The ADO numbering system first came into use towards the end of the 1950s, at about the same time that the Nuffield DO numbering system came to an end (see Appendix 1). One school of thought suggested that ADO stood for Amalgamated Drawing Office, rather than the generally accepted Austin Drawing Office, although this may have been originated by the proud, independently minded, ex-Nuffield people at Cowley. Interestingly, the Cowley and Austin systems met in the case of ADO59, where the Austin drawing office code became part of a Nuffield-style EX chassis number (see also footnote to Appendix 2). As the table clearly shows, numbers were not allocated on any sequential basis, ostensibly in the interests of security: it was argued that an outsider who heard reference to ADO21, for example, would not know whether it was more recent than or earlier than, say, ADO23.

4 THE XC CODE-NUMBERS

XC no.	Description	Approximate dates
9000	Large rear-wheel-drive saloon with Moulton suspension.	1956
9001	Front-wheel-drive Morris Oxford/Austin A55 replacement, which evolved into XC9005 and eventually became ADO17 (see Appendix 3).	1958-59
9002	Front-wheel-drive replacement for the Morris Minor/Austin A40, which evolved into ADO16 (see Appendix 3).	1958-59
9003	Small front-wheel-drive car, which became the ADO15 Mini (see Appendix 3).	1958
9005	Large front-wheel-drive saloon, evolved from XC9001 and eventually identical in appearance to ADO17 (see Appendix 3), which it became in 1962-63.	1962
5212	The Issigonis project code for ADO30 (see Appendix 3), which was intended as a super BMC sports car aimed at the Jaguar E-type.	1963

The XC codes were experimental numbers applied to projects under the direct supervision of Alec Issigonis, who returned to BMC in 1955 after a spell at Alvis. Presumably, XC stood for experimental car, although this is by no means certain. The XC9000 numbers all date from the late 1950s and were precursors of the ADO15/16/17 family, whereas XC5212 is a later code taken up for the sports car christened 'Fireball XL-5'.

5 OTHER MG RELATED PROJECT CODES

Code	Description	Approximate dates
LC8	Austin and MG Metro, developed from the ADO88 proposal in 1978.	1978
LC10	Austin Maestro/Montego family, started after the Ryder Report.	1975
LM10	Austin and MG Maestro, part of the LC10 family of cars. LC = Leyland Cars; LM = Light Medium.	1980
LM11	Austin and MG Montego, the second in the LC10 family.	1980
LM12	Short-lived proposal for an MG coupé based upon the LC10 floorpan.	1980
Boxer	An attempt to produce an MG-badged derivative of the Triumph TR7, which briefly featured in the short-lived Rover-Triumph product plan of 1980.	1980
Broadside	An attempt to salvage some of the work and expenditure that had gone into the Triumph Lynx programme. Initially, Broadside was primarily a Triumph, but in the later stages, an MG version was also proposed, tentatively scheduled for a 1983 launch.	1978-80
EX-E	The mid-engined concept car based upon the running gear of the MG Metro 6R4.	1985
F-16	Although not an official title, many people used this code when referring to Gerry McGovern's first MGF proposal of 1985, due to the F-16 badges that it sported on its flanks.	1985
PR1	The first 1990 sports car concept—Phoenix Route 1: MGB size, Rover M16 engine, all-steel construction built by Motor Panels, using the bodyshell from the earlier MGF model. Running prototype survives.	1990
PR2	The second 1990 concept—Phoenix Route 2: front mounted V8 engine, rear-wheel-drive and separate chassis with composite body. Running prototype, built by Reliant using the same basic GRP shell as supplied to Motor Panels for PR1, survives.	1990
PR3	The third sports car concept—Phoenix Route 3—using a 1.4- or 1.6-litre K-series engine. This concept was given to ADC to develop. It is not strictly true that PR3 was conceived from the outset as a mid-engined car, although that is what arose, largely due to the nature of the components. PR3 was christened the 'Pocket Rocket'. In due course, it was developed into the definitive MGF launched in 1995.	1990
MGF-1	An alternative code for PR1, which featured in Richard Hamblin's report of July 1990.	1990
MGF-2	An alternative code for PR2, which featured in Richard Hamblin's report of July 1990.	1990
MGF-3	An alternative code for PR3, which featured in Richard Hamblin's report of July 1990.	1990
PR4	Added subsequently to the PR series, PR4 was basically similar to PR2, but with an all-steel body, rather than a composite shell. It was never more than a desk study.	1990
Adder	The project code title for the MG RV8, the Adder being the British equivalent of the Cobra...	1990
MGX	Not an official project code, MGX was ascribed to a sketch by Don Wyatt for a proposed MG based upon a restyled British Motor Heritage MG Midget bodyshell, fitted with an in-line K-series engine.	1990
DR2	A larger front-engined, rear-wheel-drive V8 sports car, styled by Roy Axe and resembling an amalgam of classic British sports cars, particularly the Austin-Healey 3000 (it featured a distinctive Healey-style sloping side crease). DR2, which stood for Design Research 2, eventually became the basis of PR5.	1990
PX1	This was an RSP concept for a sports tourer based upon the standard floorpan of the Rover 800 (R17). It was never pursued.	1990
PX2	Like PX1, this was based upon the Rover 800 R17, but with a shortened under-frame. PX2 lead to Adventurer 1 and Adventurer 2, both of which contributed to the PR5 programme.	1990
Adventurer 1	Evolved from PX2, this RSP concept for a large sports car comprised a modern 2+2 body over a Rover Sterling/R17 under-frame, which had been shortened by about 8in (20cm).	1991
Adventurer 2	Adventurer 2 differed from Adventurer 1 by the clever expedient of introducing a secondary firewall mounted some distance behind the main engine bay bulkhead. This allowed the dashboard, seating and door-shut lines to be moved rearward to provide more traditional sports car proportions. Abandoned with the cessation of Sterling in August 1991.	1991
PR5	A larger front-engined sports car. Various other prototypes listed above, particularly DR2 and Adventurer 2, contributed to the PR5 programme.	1990

This table only includes those projects that have become apparent at the time of writing; inevitably, there are others that have not come off the secret list, nor will they do so for some time to come. Other projects covered in the main text do not appear to have been given project codes—such as the Gerry McGovern Midget of 1985—so it has not been possible to include them here. Note that LC10, which gave rise to both the Maestro (LM10) and Montego (LM11), dates from 1975, whereas the LC8 (Metro) was not so named until 1978, when it superseded ADO88. With BMW's acquisition of the Rover Group in 1994, renewed emphasis has been placed upon the MG marque, which could not have been contemplated during British Aerospace's ownership. Hopefully, one day, it will be possible to expand this appendix considerably...

6 CHRONOLOGY OF EVENTS

10 Oct	1877	William Richard Morris born at Comer Gardens, Worcester.
12 Apr	1888	Cecil Kimber born at Dulwich.
	1891	William Morris becomes apprenticed to a bicycle repairer.
	1893	William Morris sets up his own business at James Street, Cowley St John, after his employer refuses to give him a sixpenny (2½p) rise on his salary of four shillings (20p) per week.
	1896	Hubert Noel Charles born. (died 18 Jan 1982).
	1896	Leonard Percy Lord born in Coventry.
14 Apr	1902	Henry Edward Cecil Cousins born.
	1902	Morris & Cooper, cycle dealers, opens at 48 High Street, Oxford, where Morris had already established his business. James Street ceases to be used as

		a business address. Soon afterwards, premises are also taken on at 100 Holywell Street, better known as Longwall. Before the end of the year, Cooper is bought out of the business.
	1903	Morris enters into a partnership entitled The Oxford Automobile and Cycle Agency, based at 16 George Street, with other premises at George Street Mews and New Road (Longwall and 48 High Street not used). The salesman in this enterprise is Frank Barton. Within a year, the business fails, and Morris finds himself barely solvent, having to borrow money to buy back his own tools. Morris resolves never to enter into such a partnership again.
	1904	Morris resumes business under his own name at 48 High Street, with repair and motor trade at Longwall.
Mar	1906	Albert Sydney Enever born at Colden Common, near Winchester.
	1907	Extra space at Longwall yard allows Morris to expand his garage business, construction of new premises not being completed until 1910, whereupon the local press dub them 'The Oxford Motor Palace' in recognition of their splendour.
	1908	Morris disposes of the 48 High Street premises to Edward Armstead.
11 Jun	1909	John William Yates Thornley born in London.
Oct	1912	WRM Motors Ltd established with the aid of £4000 capital from the Earl of Macclesfield.
8-16 Nov	1912	The 11th International Motor Exhibition at Olympia; during the show, Morris shows blueprints of his Morris Oxford to Gordon Stewart, who agrees to buy 400 cars.
	1913	The Morris Garages (W. R. Morris, proprietor) established as the name of the businesses in Longwall, Queen Street and St Cross Road.
29 Mar	1913	First Morris Oxford completed: body by Raworth, engine and gearbox by White & Poppe, axles by E. G. Wrigley & Co. Ltd, and the distinctive bull-nose radiator from Doherty Motor Components. Cars built in vacant buildings at Temple Cowley.
1 Jan	1914	WRM Motors lists six versions of the Morris Oxford, ranging from a standard model at £180 to a De Luxe model coupé for £255, and including a sporting model for £220.
18 Apr	1914	Morris sails for the USA on the Mauretania, accompanied by Hans 'Papa' Landstad of White & Poppe. Morris meets with the Continental Motor Manufacturing Company in Detroit, Michigan. Hans Landstad would eventually join WRM Motors in December 1914.
4 Aug	1914	Britain declares war on Germany and establishes a naval blockade of the North Sea, Channel and Mediterranean.
Apr	1915	William Morris announces the Morris Cowley two-seater with American engine and gearbox.
29 Sep	1915	Largely in response to sales in the UK by neutral USA, the British Chancellor of the Exchequer, Reginald McKenna, imposes 33⅓ per cent import duties on certain goods, including cars.
Sep	1915	First engines for Morris Cowley delivered from Continental in the USA, but supplies erratic due to enemy action in the Atlantic.
Mar	1916	Imports of engines for the Morris Cowley affected by a ban on the use of shipping during wartime for non-essential work.
	1918	Cecil Kimber joins E. G. Wrigley Ltd of Soho, Birmingham.
11 Nov	1918	Armistice between the Allies and Germany brings an end to World War 1.
Nov	1918	Production of final batch of 336 Morris Cowleys using Continental engines.
Mar	1919	The first manager of the Morris Garages, F. G. Barton, resigns due to ill health, and his place is taken by Edward Armstead. Barton would later become one of the first agents for Morris cars, founding the Barton Motor Company Ltd in Plymouth.
Jul	1919	WRM Motors is put into liquidation and, in its place, Morris forms Morris Motors Ltd. WRM Motors had been tied to a distribution agreement with an agent who was taking a considerable commission. In the same month, the first Hotchkiss engine is delivered.
Aug	1919	Morris is involved in setting up Osberton Radiators at Cowley, helping H. A. Ryder and A. L. Davies (from Doherty Motor Components) to buy the business. Earlier in the year, Morris had walked into the premises of Doherty Motor Components with a prototype radiator block, and had asked the works manager, Ryder, if he could turn out similar radiators in quantity.
Jan	1920	Cecil Cousins joins Morris Garages at Clarendon Yard.
	1920	Syd Enever, aged 15, joins Morris Garages showrooms in Queen Street, moving to the Clarendon Yard site in 1921.
	1921	Cecil Kimber joins Morris Garages as sales manager.
Mar	1922	Cecil Kimber becomes general manager of Morris Garages, following the departure of Edward Armstead (who committed suicide by gassing himself two months later). Armstead had bought the 48 High Street premises from William Morris in 1908 and continued motor cycle assembly there, although presumably without great success, as he had come to Morris Garages in 1919.
Autumn	1922	First Morris Garages Chummy produced, based upon the standard Morris Oxford equivalent, but with lowered springs, specially finished coachwork and leather trim in lieu of Rexine.
1 Jan	1923	Hollick & Pratt Ltd (coachbuilders) acquired by William Morris (later sold to Morris Motors in 1926). The company had suffered a fire on 1 August, 1922, and Morris agreed to buy it for £100,000. Osberton Radiators Ltd comes under sole ownership of William Morris. Harold Ryder of Osberton Radiators would later become a Morris Motors director and, much later in 1945, become director in charge of MG.
Feb	1923	Production of the Morris Garages Chummy transferred from Longwall to Alfred Lane; Cecil Cousins in charge.
Mar	1923	Cecil Kimber drives his own specially modified Morris Oxford Chummy in the Land's End Trial, partnered by Russell Chiesman.
May	1923	Hotchkiss et Cie factory, of Gosford Road, Coventry, bought by Morris for £349,423. F. G. Woollard becomes works manager.
16 Jul	1923	The Morris Company Ltd formed by William Morris with the intention of consolidating his various business interests.
Nov	1923	Earliest known appearance of the octagonal MG logo in a Morris Garages advertisement printed in an Oxford magazine, The Isis.
Dec	1923	Morris buys E. G. Wrigley.
Jan	1924	Miles Thomas joins W. R. Morris to launch The Morris Owner magazine in March.
May	1924	The Morris Owner magazine includes an advertisement for Morris Garages that includes the famous octagonal MG logo.
13 Mar	1925	Carbodies, the Coventry based coachbuilders, begins work on building the body of what would become 'Old Number One'. The car was registered as FC 7900 on 27 March, 1925.
10-11 Apr	1925	Cecil Kimber, partnered by Wilfred Matthews, enters FC 7900 in the Land's End Trial, gaining first in class.
Sep	1925	MG production begins at Bainton Road, alongside Osberton Radiators.
28 Apr	1926	The Pressed Steel Company is registered and begins work at Cowley.
29 Jun	1926	Morris sells some of his 'personal' businesses to Morris Motors Ltd; Osberton Radiators becomes Morris Radiators Branch, Hotchkiss becomes Morris Engines Branch, and Hollick & Pratt becomes Morris Bodies Branch. Morris Motors Ltd, as established in 1919, becomes Morris Motors (1926) Ltd.
Sep	1926	The flat-nose Morris Oxfords appear, gradually replacing the bull-nose cars.
Dec	1926	William Morris buys SU (Skinners' Union, named after the brothers who founded it) for £100,000. It continues trading as the SU Company Ltd.
23 Feb	1927	William Morris buys the bankrupt form of Wolseley Motors Ltd for £730,000.
27 Jun	1927	Morris Industries Ltd is registered and takes over the SU Company Ltd. Morris Industries also takes over from the Morris Company Ltd.
2 Jul	1927	The Morris Garages Ltd is formed as limited company.
Apr-Sep	1927	A new purpose designed factory is built for MG production at Edmund Road, Cowley, at a cost of £16,000.
10 Oct	1927	The first MG race victory is achieved in Argentina, on a new concrete track at the San Martín autodrome near Buenos Aires. The car, a 14/40, wins the 100km (62-mile) race outright. Cecil Kimber would refer to this in a paper titled The Lure of Speed, presented in 1944.
29 Dec	1927	MG acquires a Morris Light Six chassis and begins to construct a prototype on it. It features the forerunner of the definitive MG radiator, designed with the aid of Ron Goddard of Radiators Branch, and made by a tinsmith named Cudd. The car would become the basis of the MG 18/80 Six.
Spring	1928	The MG Car Company (Proprietors: the Morris Garages Ltd) formed to take over responsibility for MG manufacture.
17 Aug	1928	The MG 18/80 Six (18/80 Mark I) is announced in The Autocar. This car had a new MG designed chassis (drawn up by Cecil Cousins) and featured the new MG radiator.
31 Aug	1928	The Motor carries an announcement of the new Morris Minor, selling at very similar prices to the rival Austin Seven.
14 Sep	1928	The Motor announces that there is to be a new sports model based upon the Minor, which they refer to as 'The Morris Midget...produced by the MG Car Co., Oxford.'
11 Oct	1928	Stand 150 of the Olympia Motor Show is taken by MG, the first time that the marque appears in its own right. The new MG Midget appears alongside the 14/40 Mark IV and the new 18/80.
Mar	1929	M-type Midget production begins at Edmund Road.
Aug	1929	Morris Motors (1926) Ltd becomes plain Morris Motors Ltd.
Sep	1929	MG begins to move to the former Pavlova Leather factory at Abingdon-upon-Thames, Berkshire. Soon after, H. N. Charles, who had worked for Morris since 1924 and had grown to know the Kimber family, would become MG's chief designer.
17 Oct	1929	At the Olympia Motor Show, the MG Midget Sportsmans Coupé appears. The normal open M-type is also facelifted: the doors now open conventionally with front hinges and the brakes are improved.
6 Nov	1929	First entry in the EX-Register (see Appendix 2).
20 Jan	1930	Cecil Kimber hosts an inaugural luncheon at Abingdon to celebrate the opening of the new factory.
11 Feb	1930	The MG Car Company announces plans for a new MG Sports Six, 'in all probability to be called the MG Tiger,' reports The Motor magazine. This

		would become the 18/100 Mark III or Tigress: in the event, a very short-lived car, which made the début of its brief racing career in May.
9-10 May	1930	The Brooklands Double-Twelve 24-hour race. A number of M-type Midgets are entered alongside the factory 18/100 (the so-called Tigress). The 18/100, driven by Leslie Callingham of Shell, runs it bearings, barely two hours into the race (would-be co-driver Harold Parker does not get to drive!), but the Midgets do well (C. J. Randall/F. M. Montgomery come third in class; Lt Cdr Townend/Robin Jackson, fifth in class; G. Roberts/A. A. Pollard, sixth in class; H. H. Stisted/Norman Black, fourth in class; and Victoria Worsley/D. G. Foster, seventh in class. The highest placed, Randall, finishes 14th overall and wins the team prize.
11 Jun	1930	John Thornley part exchanges a Brough Superior motor bike for a new M-type Midget on his 21st birthday.
June	1930	Le Mans 24-hour race. First MGs appear at the Sarthe circuit, albeit as private entries by Huskinson & Fane (No. 28) and Captain F. H. B. Samuelson (No. 29). The M-type Midgets are in basically Double-Twelve form. Huskinson & Fane's car, driven by R. C. Murton-Neale and Jack Hicks, would crash early in the race, damaging the steering, and finally retire after 82 laps with a broken crankshaft (caused by over-revving the engine). The other car, driven by Samuelson and Freddie Kindell (an MG mechanic), would retire 28 laps into the race with bearing failure due to a fractured oil pipe.
21 Jul	1930	MG Car Company Ltd registered to take over the car manufacturing business of The Morris Garages Ltd. Cecil Kimber is made managing director. A total of 19,000 £1 shares are issued, of which 18,995 are bought by Morris Industries Ltd. The five remaining are held by William Morris, Cecil Kimber, Morris' secretary, his solicitor and his accountant. Meanwhile, Morris buys an old property in St Aldates, pulls it down and builds a new Morris Garages garage, incorporating his head office, at a cost of £80,000. This would open in 1932.
Autumn	1930	'Safety Fast' becomes the MG slogan.
5 Sep	1930	A letter appears in the *Light Car* magazine from Roy Marsh, suggesting the formation of an MG club.
Oct	1930	Morris Garages formally assigns the lease of the Pavlova Leather Works to the MG Car Company Ltd.
12 Oct	1930	The MG Car Club is formed, following an initial meeting in the previous month, John Thornley being elected as honorary secretary.
26 Dec	1930	EX120 leaves Abingdon on the back of a lorry, bound for Montlhéry near Paris.
30 Dec	1930	EX120 makes its first record attempt in the hands of Captain George Eyston at Montlhéry, gaining some records, but failing to achieve 100mph (160.93km/h). Instead, he takes three 750cc records at speeds of up to 87.3mph (140.49km/h).
Jan	1931	Monte Carlo Rally. Sir Frances and Mrs Samuelson enter an M-type Sportsmans Coupé.
6 Feb	1931	Malcolm Campbell takes a supercharged Austin single-seater to 94.061mph (151.37km/h) at Daytona Beach, Florida, USA, between land speed record attempts in Bluebird.
9 Feb	1931	George Eyston smashes all the Austin records in EX120, including 97.07mph (156.21km/h) over a 5km (3.11-mile) course.
16 Feb	1931	EX120 is run again at Montlhéry by Captain George Eyston, achieving 103.13mph (165.97km/h) over 5km (3.11 miles), 102.76mph (165.37km/h) over 5 miles (8.05km) and 101.87mph (163.94km/h) over 10 miles (16.09km). On the previous day, Cecil Cousins had shaped pieces of oil drum in the track-side gully to make a crude nose cowling for EX120, to cure the problem of carburettor icing.
2 Mar	1931	Henry Stone starts work at Abingdon, following an interview in the previous October.
3 Mar	1931	At a lunch at Abingdon, Cecil Kimber announces his intention of building a 750cc Montlhéry Midget. A mock-up is on show, along with EX120.
13 Mar	1931	MG fails to take the 100mph (160.93km/h) record with EX120 at Brooklands, but achieves 96.93mph (155.99km/h), still beating the Austin 750.
16 Mar	1931	MG announces the 750cc Montlhéry version of the Midget as the Midget Mark II (the C-type Midget). The engine stroke is shorter by 10mm (0.39in) than the 850cc standard engine, giving a cubic capacity of 746cc. Two versions are offered: supercharged at £345, and unsupercharged at £295.
8-9 May	1931	Brooklands Double Twelve race; 14 Montlhéry C-types are entered and, of the 13 starters, take the first five places! The factory cars are entered as four teams of three, by The Earl of March, Cecil Randall, 'Goldie' Gardner and the Hon. Mrs Chetwynd. The Earl of March/Staniland finish first; Gibson/Fell second; Hugh 'Hammy' Hamilton (no co-driver) third; Parker/Cox fourth; and Norman Black/Fiennes fifth.
Jun	1931	Le Mans 24-hour race. Two MGs (unsupercharged c-types) are entered privately: one by Francis Samuelson, driven by him and Freddie Kindell (No. 31), and the other by the Hon. Mrs Chetwynd, driven by her and Mrs H. H. Sisted (No. 32). The former would not qualify because its final lap was slower than the minimum permitted (Samuleson was nursing his car on this lap due to a broken crankshaft), while the latter would retire due to a sheared timing gear key. The Hon. Mrs Chetwynd was a relative of Sir Henry Birkin, obviously imbued with the same gung-ho spirit as her cousin.
22 Aug	1931	Ulster Tourist Trophy. Norman Black wins in a C-type Midget (No. 42), at a speed of 67.9mph (109.27km/h), 0.9mph (1.45km/h) faster than the existing lap record for any vehicle! Nine supercharged c-types and three unsupercharged versions take part; Crabtree's C-type is third.
4 Sep	1931	MG F-type Magna 12/70 Six is announced, with 1271cc six-cylinder engine. Also announced is a related low-chassis, occasional four-seater Midget (the D-type).
25 Sep	1931	During a record attempt, EX120 catches fire and is severely damaged. In the process, Captain Eyston has a very lucky escape, managing to jump from the car and being taken to a local hospital by a passing French driver. Later, the remains of EX120 would be cut up at Abingdon.
30 Sep	1931	Ernest Eldridge takes first record in EX127:International Class 'H' 5km (3.11-mile) at 110.3mph (117.51km/h) at Montlhéry.
Oct	1931	Brooklands 500-mile (804.65km) handicap race. Eddie Hall comes third overall (first in class) in his single-seater C-type, and wins the team prize.
15 Oct	1931	At the Olympia Motor Show, the revised MG M-type Midget, with all-metal bodywork, is shown and priced at £185 (the old fabric-bodied model would remain on sale for a while at £165).
17 Oct	1931	Ernest Eldridge takes the 5km (3.12-mile) record at 110mph (177.02km/h) in EX127.
3 Nov	1931	John Thornley starts work at Abingdon, as an interviewer in the service department. Cecil Kimber told him to run the MG Car Club and help in the service department, but George Propert had other ideas, telling him the exact opposite.
22 Dec	1931	EX127 takes four records up to 114.77mph (184.70km/h) at Montlhéry, on an icy track, with Captain George Eyston at the wheel. As a concession to his personal safety, Eyston wears special asbestos overalls, having learned from his experience in EX120 during the previous September.
8 Feb	1932	EX127 appears at Pendine Sands for an attempt to beat 120mph (193.12km/h). After some problems with MG's own timing equipment, Eyston achieves 122mph (196.33km/h), but the official RAC timing equipment is found to be out of ink, so the record cannot be confirmed officially!
7 Jun	1932	A Mark III version of the Montlhéry Midget is announced, still with a 746cc engine, but featuring a new cylinder head. The unsupercharged version costs £490, while the blown version, with Powerplus supercharger, costs £575. The M-type Midget is finally discontinued.
18-19 Jun	1932	Le Mans 24-hour race. A single supercharged MG C-type (No. 32) is privately entered by Francis Samuelson, being driven by him and Norman Black. A punctured fuel tank, due to fractured fixings, causes retirement after 53 laps.
5 Aug	1932	MG J2 Midget is announced in *The Autocar*, priced at £199 10s (£199.50).
Sep	1932	Ulster Tourist Trophy race. Eddie Hall takes third place in a C-type; Hamilton crashes in practice.
13 Oct	1932	MG Magnette appears on Stand 24 at the Olympia Motor Show, with 1086cc six-cylinder engine, in K1, K2 and K3 versions. Cars shown include a duo-tone blue Midget Salonette and a duo-tone green F2 (later known as F3) Magna four-seater.
26 Oct	1932	First prototype racing K Magnette (K3 prototype, chassis K3751) built at Abingdon. Second built 4 January, 1933.
13 Dec	1932	Eyston returns to Montlhéry with EX127. On a cold test track, he achieves an average of 120.56mph (194.02km/h) over the flying mile and flying kilometre. Then, over the course of the next week, aided by his mechanic Bert Denly and motoring journalist Tommy Wisdom, Eyston proceeds to break all of the remaining 750cc records, using both EX127 and a J3 Midget (chassis J3756; registration JB1047).
4 Jan	1933	The second of two prototypes (chassis K3572) for what would become the K3 Magnette begins to take shape. Soon after, on 19 January, it sets off as part of a recce trip to Italy, in preparation for the Mille Miglia in April.
Jan	1933	Monte Carlo rally. A K3 (registration JB 1046) takes part in the Mont des Mules hillclimb (driven by G. W. J. H. Wright), and not only wins its class, but also breaks the class record. In the Monte Carlo itself, the K3 comes second in the braking and acceleration tests. Overall, it finishes 64th out of 69.
Mar	1933	MG L-type Magna launched, while J4 Midget enters limited production (only nine would be built). An unsupercharged J5 version of the J4 is listed, but would not be built.
Apr	1933	Wolseley engineer Leonard Lord becomes managing director of Morris Motors Ltd, at the age of 36.
8-9 Apr	1933	Mille Miglia road race in Brescia, Italy. Three MG K3 Magnettes are entered by Earl Howe and managed by Hugh McConnell. George Eyston and Count Giovanni 'Johnny' Lurani, driving JB 1475 (No. 39, chassis K3003), come first in class; Earl Howe and Hugh Hamilton, in JB 1472 (No. 42, chassis K3001), are second in class; while Sir Henry 'Tim' Birkin and Bernard Rubin, in JB 1474 (No. 41, chassis K3002), do not finish, but set a new record for the Brescia road section of the course.
May	1933	RAC Mannin Beg race on the Isle of Man TT circuit. Mansell's Midget is one of only two finishers from 14 starters (Freddie Dixon's Riley is the winner). MG K3s include Eyston (No. 15); Hamilton (No. 16); Kaye Don (No. 18) and S. A. Crabtree (No. 19).
May	1933	First issue of *The MG Magazine*, price 6d (2½p).
Jun	1933	Le Mans 24-hour race: MGs appear for the fourth time, but on this occasion one lasts the course! A supercharged C-type Midget (No. 41), entered by John Ludovic Ford and driven by him in partnership with Maurice H. Baumer, achieves the first Le Mans finish for the marque and a very respectable sixth place overall on distance. It covers 1482.15 miles (2385.22km) in 24 hours, at an average speed of 61.7mph (99.29km/h). In addition, the MG wins the 750cc class and comes second in the Index of Performance.
Jul	1933	The last of the MG 18/80 Mark II models is built at Abingdon.
Jul	1933	Coppa Acerbo Junior race in Italy. Whitney Straight beats the local Maserati opposition in his K3 Magnette.

2 Sep	1933	Ulster Tourist Trophy race. Tazio Nuvolari in a K3 (No. 17, chassis K3003—the Eyston/Lurani Mille Miglia car) wins the race, a mere 40 seconds ahead of 'Hammy' Hamilton in a J4 (No. 25). In the process, he breaks the lap record several times.
5 Sep	1933	*The Motor* carries an announcement that the Magnette is to be revised with a number of technical changes, including an increase in engine capacity from 1087cc to 1286cc; the J2 has restyled wings; and the tourer and salonette bodies on the Magna have been discontinued, only the two-seater remaining on sale. The 1286cc capacity is incorrect, however: someone at Abingdon had discreetly added an imaginary millimetre to the 83mm (3.27in) stroke, in the hope that the enthusiast would believe that the engine was quite different from the 1271cc engine seen already in the F-type Magna. *The Autocar* had said much the same on 1 September.
14 Sep	1933	George Eyston takes three Class 'H' records in EX127 at Brooklands, at up to 106.7mph (171.71km/h) for the 50km, 50-mile and 100km (31.07-mile, 80.47km and 62.14-mile) records.
16 Sep	1933	Eddie Hall takes his single-seater K3 (chassis K3006) to victory in the Brooklands 500-mile (804.65km) handicap race.
7-8 Oct	1933	A team comprising George Eyston, Bert Denly, Tommy Wisdom and R. Yallop takes five Class 'G' records in an L2 Magna, including 80.5mph (129.55km/h) over 24 hours; Kimber was disappointed!
19 Oct	1933	Capt. Eyston's mechanic, Bert Denly, takes the rebodied EX127 to 128.62mph (206.99km/h) at Montlhéry.
20 Nov	1933	Bert Denly takes four Class 'H' records in EX127 at speeds up to 114.8mph (184.75km/h) at Montlhéry.
Jan	1934	The Magic Magnette is created at Abingdon for Capt. Eyston as EX135. It has two bodies: a single-seater for record breaking and a more conventional body for road racing.
2 Mar	1934	MG P-type Midget announced, subsequently to be known retrospectively as the PA.
Mar	1934	Cecil Kimber's special Corsica-bodied K1 is completed. It would be sold in 1936, the new owner having the bodywork modified by Corsica in 1937.
30 Mar	1934	The MG N-type Magnette is announced, with a 1271cc six-cylinder engine.
Apr	1934	Mille Miglia, Brescia, Italy. The MG team, entered by Earl Howe and managed by Hugh McConnell, returns with three K3 Magnettes (now with Roots superchargers) to attempt a second victory. The drivers are Howe and Thomas, Eddie and Joan Hall, Penn-Hughes and 'Johnny' Lurani. They would not be as successful as in 1933, however, Maserati having prepared a new car for Piero Tarufi to respond to the MG threat. Howe would crash, and the Halls retire, but Lurani and Penn-Hughes would come second in class.
30 May	1934	Second RAC Mannin Beg race held on the Isle of Man TT circuit, in which MGs dominate the opposition, finishing first (Norman Black, K3 Magnette, No. 22), second (C. J. P. Dodson, K3 Magnette), third (Capt. George Eyston, offset single-seater Magnette, chassis K3023/EX135, No. 8), fourth (C. E. C. Martin, privately owned K3 Magnette, No. 12), fifth (Roy H. Eccles, privately owned K3 Magnette), seventh (Ronnie Horton, offset single-seater K3 Magnette) and eighth (W. G. Everitt, Q-type Midget, No. 15). Both 'Wally' Handley and Hugh 'Hammy' Hamilton, in a conventional K3 (No. 9) and single-seater K3 (No. 4) respectively, fail to finish after collisions with telegraph poles. Prior to the race, Kaye Don and MG mechanic Frankie Taylor had been involved in an accident while testing Don's Magnette. Both were seriously injured, Taylor fatally.
Jun	1934	Le Mans 24-hour race. Four MGs are entered privately. Roy Eccles drives his K3 Magnette (No. 34) with Charlie Martin to come fourth on distance and first in the 1100cc class; John Ludovic Ford gives a sterling performance in his K3 Magnette (No. 33, chassis K3028) with co-driver Maurice H. Baumer, at one point lying second overall, before a holed fuel tank, caused by a crash with a 1-litre Tracta, puts paid to their chances half-way through the race; P. Maillard-Brune and co-driver Druck, in a Midget (No. 53), retire with engine problems after 30 laps; and finally, Anne Itier and her co-driver Druck, in another P-type Midget (No. 52), come 17th on distance (in a field of 23 finishers) and second in the 1000cc class.
23 Jul	1934	Ronnie Horton takes two Class 'G' records in his offset single-seater K3 (chassis K3007) at Brooklands. This car would later form the basis of EX135.
10 Aug	1934	MG Q-type racer announced for public sale, with 746cc engine good for 120mph (193.12km/h).
1 Sep	1934	The RAC TT race at Dundrod sees the racing début of the new NE Magnette. Driving one of these new MGs (No. 27), Charlie Dodson would win the 465-mile (748.32km) race on handicap at 74.65mph (120.13km/h), narrowly beating Eddie Hall's 3669cc Bentley. Other NEs are driven by G. Eyston (No. 25), 'Wally' Handley (No. 26) and Norman Black (No. 28)
19 Sep	1934	KN Magnette announced as a pillarless saloon, selling at £399 (the regular N-type Magnette continues; the KN has a chassis 12in/30.48cm longer).
14 Oct	1934	At the Circuito di Modena, Raffaelle 'Lello' Cecchini wins, just seconds ahead of a Maserati. With this victory, the culmination of series of successes, Cecchini's special-bodied K3 becomes the first non-Italian car to win the Italian 1100cc championship.
27-28 Oct	1934	Capt. George Eyston takes EX135, referred to by MG as the Magic Magnette, but better known to the general public as 'Humbug' on account of its cream and brown striped colour scheme, to capture 12 Class 'G' records at Montlhéry, at speeds of up to 128.7mph (326.90km/h).
15 Feb	1935	*The Autocar* carries news of the Cresta Magnette, based upon the N-type and with a special body produced by E. Bertelli Ltd of Feltham, Middlesex, to be sold through the Cresta Motor Company of Worthing.
Mar	1935	In the March 1935 issue of *The MG Magazine*, Cecil Kimber releases preliminary details of two forthcoming racing specials with single-seater bodies, described as the 'MG Monoposto Midget, 750 c.c.' (to be priced at about £600) and the 'MG Monoposto Magnette, 1100 c.c.' (to be priced at around £900). The former would appear in the following month as the R-type Midget, but the latter—the six-cylinder S-type—would never come to fruition. At about the same time as the *MG Magazine* article appears, Kimber writes to the motoring press to solicit support for changes to the racing formulae, which would benefit his new cars, but the events of July 1935 would render these efforts pointless.
Apr	1935	*The Sports Car* magazine replaces *The MG Magazine*.
25 Apr	1935	The all-independent-suspension R-type Midget is announced, at a price of £750.
6 May	1935	Four of the six R-types built are entered in the Junior Car Club International Trophy at Brooklands. Bill Everitt and Malcolm Campbell (RA0260) come first in class and sixth overall; Doreen Evans, in the blue Bellevue Garage car (No. 38, RA0255), takes second in class and seventh overall; Norman Black (RA0253) does not finish, neither does 'Wally' Handley (RA0252). Also in the same race, are three K3 Magnettes, driven by Hall (K3006), Manby and Colegrove (K3004), and Letts (K3023), who come third, eighth and 11th respectively.
May	1935	Third RAC Mannin Beg race sees a team of four MG R-types: George Eyston (RA0251), 'Wally' Handley (RA0252), Norman Black (RA0253) and Bobby Baird (RA0254). None would finish.
19 May	1935	Bobby Kohlrausch takes EX127 to new heights at Guyon, in Hungary, with speeds up to 130.9mph (210.66km/h).
Jun	1935	Le Mans 24-hour race. Seven MGs are entered, including George Eyston's so-called 'Dancing Daughters': six women drivers in three P-type Midgets. Doreen Evans and Barbara Skinner (No. 55) would finish 25th on distance; Joan Richmond and Mrs Simpson (No. 56) would finish 24th on distance; and Margaret Allan and Colleen Eaton (No. 57) would finish 26th on distance. Of the remaining MG entrants, the K3 Magnette (No. 39) entered by Maurice Baumer with co-driver John Ludovic Ford would retire, as would the orange K3 Magnette (No. 41, chassis K3031) of Dutchman Eddie Hertzburger, the latter after 92 laps with supercharger problems. Another K3 Magnette (No. 42), the P. Maillard-Brune/Druck car, entered on behalf of the famous *chocolatier* Jacques Menier, would finish ninth overall and win the 2-litre class. Finally, the Viale/Debille Midget (No. 58), entered by P. Maillard-Brune, would retire after 98 laps, also suffering from supercharger problems.
27 Jun	1935	James Wignall, of Mulliner, produces a number of drawings for a proposed large MG saloon, at the request of Cecil Kimber. One of these would become the basis of the SA saloon, launched in October, after the Morris Motors take-over.
1 Jul	1935	William Morris begins the process of selling the MG Car Co. Ltd and Wolseley Motors (1927) Ltd to Morris Motors Ltd. Cecil Kimber becomes a director of Morris Motors Ltd, but is now only general manager at MG, Leonard Lord taking his place as managing director. Although most of the designers at Abingdon drift to Cowley, Syd Enever remain as head of the experimental department.
5 Jul	1935	In one of the first published reactions to the announcement of 1 July, *The Autocar* expresses shock that MG is to cease racing forthwith.
10 Jul	1935	Formal transfer of shares in MG from Morris Industries Ltd to Morris Motors Ltd.
21 Sep	1935	The SS Jaguar 2.6-litre saloon is unveiled to the trade in London, just ahead of the new MG Two-Litre (SA).
17 Oct	1935	MG Two-Litre (SA) saloon (announced 4 October in *The Autocar*) appears at the Olympia Motor Show. It is a massive car with a 10ft 3in (3.12m) wheelbase. The PB Midget replaces the PA and features an enlarged (939cc) engine and altered radiator grille with vertical slats in place of mesh.
24 Apr	1936	MG SA Tickford Foursome drophead coupé advertised in *The Autocar*, with body by Salmons, price £398 (standard SA is priced at £375).
13-14 Jun	1936	This was to have been the date for the Le Mans 24-hour race, but despite attempts to reschedule, by 23 June, the race would be abandoned. MG entries had been attracted from George Eyston and Eddie Hertzberger.
19 Jun	1936	MG T-type Midget (TA) launched to replace the PB. The engine is the 1292cc MPJG unit. Price is £222.
Jul	1936	Charlesworth-bodied SA Two-Litre Tourer launched, with four seats, four doors and low-level folded hood. It features a straight-through body line at waist level. Price £375.
27 Aug	1936	Leonard Lord resigns as managing director of Morris Motors, and his place is taken by Oliver Boden. Lord had bluntly asked Morris for a share of the proceeds from his efforts, but Morris would not accede to his demands. Soon after, he would visit Miles Thomas, who would recall in his autobiography, *Out on a Wing*, that Lord said, 'Tommy, I'm going to take that business at Cowley apart brick by bloody brick.' Those who knew Lord suggest that the epithet might have been stronger than 'bloody'...
Aug	1936	At the Brooklands bank holiday meeting, Major A. T. 'Goldie' Gardner sets a new Class 'G' outer circuit track record of 124.40mph (200.20km/h) in his ex-Ronnie Horton K3 offset single-seater. In the following months, Gardner would begin to break several of the records held by Capt. Eyston. Kimber is sufficiently inspired to seek permission from Lord Nuffield to pursue record attempts again.

2 Oct	1936	MG VA One-and-a-Half-Litre, available in both saloon and open four-seater versions, is announced. The advertising slogan that Kimber uses is 'For space...for grace...for pace...', a slogan that many Jaguar enthusiasts believe was the post-war creation of Sir William Lyons. The saloon is priced at £325, the tourer at £280, and the Folding Head Foursome (Tickford) at £335.
10 Oct	1936	Bobbie Kohlrausch takes EX127 to 140.6mph (226.27km/h) over the flying mile on the Frankfurt-Darmstadt autobahn.
Feb	1937	Capt. Eyston's former Magic Magnette advertised for sale at the Bellevue Garage (price £425), including both bodies and 'many spares'. It would be acquired by Gardner and fitted with a brand-new lightweight duralumin-skinned body, designed by Reid Railton.
Jun	1937	Le Mans 24-hour race. A single privately entered MG P-type Midget (No. 54), driven by Dorothy Stanley-Turner and Enid Riddell, would finish 16th on distance, having completed 1294.08 miles (2082.56km).
Oct	1937	A modified version of the Charlesworth-bodied SA Two-Litre Tourer is announced. The front doors now feature cut-aways, similar in essence to the doors of the new VA tourer. Price of the Charlesworth is now £399, while the Tickford version is priced at £415.
25 Oct	1937	Major A. T. G. 'Goldie' Gardner uses his recently acquired offset single-seater K3 to take four International Class 'G' records at Frankfurt, reaching speeds of up to 148.8mph (239.46km/h).
Feb	1938	A receiver is appointed to take over the operation of Riley Motors.
Jun	1938	Le Mans 24-hour race. One of two private MG entries is Anne Itier's specially rebodied P-type (No. 49, Belgian registration 304797), which has a streamlined nose. With her co-driver Bonneau, she would finish 12th on distance, and fourth in class. The second MG (No. 50, British registration JB 7963) is a comparatively standard Midget entered by Dorothy Stanley-Turner, but driven by Elsie 'Bill' Wisdom and Arthur Dobson, the latter taking Stanley-Turner's place due to illness. However, they would retire after 48 laps with clutch problems.
Summer	1938	MG WA announced, with 2.6-litre engine.
19 Aug	1938	MG TA Tickford announced, with coachwork by Salmon & Sons of Newport Pagnell.
8 Sep	1938	Riley (Coventry) Ltd registered by William Morris and quickly resold to Morris Motors.
9 Nov	1938	'Goldie' Gardner takes EX135 to 186.567mph (300.24km/h) at Frankfurt, shattering two Class 'G' records: flying mile at 187.616mph (301.93km/h) and flying kilometre at 186.567mph (300.24km/h).
May	1939	MG TB Midget replaces TA, with Morris M10-based 1250cc XPAG engine.
31 May	1939	EX135, driven by 'Goldie' Gardner, achieves speeds of up to 203.5mph (327.49km/h) to take three Class 'G' records at Dessau, in Germany.
2 Jun	1939	EX135 takes two Class 'F' records at Dessau, at speeds of up to 204.2mph (328.62km/h). It will be the last pre-war record attempt.
Jun	1939	Le Mans 24-hour race—the last race before war intervenes. One of two private MG entries is a specially rebodied P-type Midget (No. 36), which has been built using parts from one of the 1935 Le Mans cars. Entered by the wealthy Collier brothers, and driven by Miles Collier and Lewis Welch, this car is christened 'Leonides'. It would retire with a leaking fuel tank after completing 63 laps and 528 miles (849.71km). The other MG is Mme Itier's rebodied Midget (No. 47), driven by Bonneau and Mathieu, which would retire after 40 laps. Mme Itier herself drives a Simca-Fiat, which would overturn during the race.
3 Sep	1939	War is declared against Germany by Great Britain and France.
Mar	1940	Oliver Boden dies, and his place as vice chairman is taken by Miles Thomas, a former journalist who has worked for Morris since the formation of the Nuffield Press, and who has been a director of Morris Motors since May 1927.
May	1940	Morris Motors is renamed the Nuffield Organization.
Nov	1941	Cecil Kimber is sacked from MG by Miles Thomas.
2 Oct	1944	Morris Garages Ltd acquires Charles Raworth & Son. Ltd, the coachbuilders responsible for some of the earliest Morris Garages specials.
4 Feb	1945	Cecil Kimber is killed in a freak railway accident, just north of London's King's Cross station.
Apr	1945	Preparations begin at Cowley for the MG TC Midget, under the direction of H. A . Ryder. The prototype is based upon the pre-war TB demonstrator.
7 May	1945	German forces surrender to the Allies; next day is VE Day (Victory in Europe).
26 Jul	1945	British general election returns a Labour government under Clement Attlee.
Sep	1945	Nuffield Metal Products Ltd formed, incorporating Morris Pressings Branch, which had been set up in 1939. The new company would eventually be responsible for producing bodies for the Morris Minor and Riley Pathfinder.
17 Sep	1945	First production MG TC (No. 0252, engine no. 1163) completed; car 0251 was the prototype.
Oct	1945	MG TC Midget launched.
Oct	1945	As part of Chancellor Hugh Dalton's first budget, the old RAC horsepower tax rating system is abolished. This had been established in 1906 and had resulted in decades of long-stroke, small-bore engines in British cars, MGs included. Initially, the RAC formula would give way to an annual tax based upon engine size, to be effective from 1 January, 1947, but a year later this would be replaced by a flat annual fee of £10.
27 Jul	1946	'Goldie' Gardner takes EX135 to 145mph (233.35km/h) over the kilometre with a 750cc engine on the Brescia-Bergamo autostrada in Italy. The next day, he exceeded 150mph (241.395km/h) in the opposite direction.
31 Oct	1946	At Jabbeke, Belgium, 'Goldie' Gardner drives EX135 to capture three Class 'H' records at speeds up to 159.2mph (256.2km/h).
May	1947	MG Y-series saloon launched, based upon the pre-war MG Ten prototype, which was a derivative of the Morris 10. It features independent front suspension, designed by Alec Issigonis and drawn up by Jack Daniels. Subsequently, this suspension would appear in the TD, TF, MGA and MGB!
24 Jul	1947	'Goldie' Gardner uses EX135 with only two cylinders running to take the Class 'I' (250-500cc) record at Jabbeke, at speeds up to an incredible 118.0mph (189.9km/h).
Aug	1947	Reginal Hanks and Sydney Smith become directors of Morris Motors.
19 Nov	1947	Sir Miles Thomas resigns his chairmanship of the Nuffield Group. Soon after, Reginald Hanks (who has worked for Morris since 1922) becomes vice chairman and is instrumental in restructuring the Nuffield board, one of the casualties being H. A. Ryder (a Morris Motors director since June 1926) in December 1947. Henceforth, Sydney Smith (known irreverently as 'Hitler Smith' because of his small black moustache) takes charge of MG affairs at Cowley and 'Pop' Propert at Abingdon.
Feb	1948	The Minister for Supply, George Strauss, announces that steel will only be allocated to car manufacturers who export over 75 per cent of their output.
Sep	1948	Austin A40 make its world début in New York. Its engine would subsequently form the basis of the B-series unit, which would feature in many MGs. Austin is the leading UK motor industry exporter to the USA in 1948, although within four years, it would slip into second place behind MG.
14 Sep	1948	'Goldie' Gardner returns to take three Class 'E' (1501-2000cc) records at up to 176.7mph (284.36km/h).
2 Oct	1948	First race at Watkins Glen, New York, in which organizer Cameron Argetsinger enters his own TC Midget. A total of 11 MGs take part, including two driven by the Collier brothers, Sam and Miles.
27 Oct	1948	MG YT open four-seater tourer appears at the Earls Court Motor Show. It is based upon the Y-type saloon, but utilizes the more highly tuned engine of the TC Midget. Intended primarily for export, it would become rare in UK.
27 Oct	1948	Morris Minor MM launched at Earls Court Motor Show. Austin and the Nuffield Organization announce that they have been holding exploratory talks about pooling information and resources. This dialogue would falter as a result of Leonard Lord's bad feeling towards Lord Nuffield, and a further announcement in July 1949 would state that exchanges of confidential information had ceased.
Nov	1948	Decision made by Nuffield board not to transfer MG production to Riley factory at Foleshill, Coventry, but to move Riley production to Abingdon and Riley design to Cowley.
Dec	1948	First official US-specification MG TC Midget built, but still right-hand-drive!
1 May	1949	Riley production transferred from Foleshill, Coventry to Abingdon (Wolseley had moved from Ward End in Birmingham to Cowley in January). The Riley factory becomes an extension of Morris Engines Branch, while the Wolseley factory is turned over to general machining work and tractor production (Tractor & Transmission Branch).
25-26 Jun	1949	First post-war Le Mans 24-hour race. George Phillips, with co-driver 'Curly' Dryden, enters a special-bodied TC Midget. However, they would be disqualified following repairs by the mechanic on the track, as Dryden would give him a lift back to the pits, which was not permissible.
20 Jul	1949	Jack Tatlow (ex-Riley) takes over from George 'Pop' Propert as MG's general manager at Abingdon. Propert joined from Beans as works manager in 1926, becoming general manager in 1930.
15 Sep	1949	'Goldie' Gardner, driving EX135 at Jabbeke, takes three international class records. It is worth noting that EX135 had been out in 1946, 1947 and 1948, but although an MG engine was used in the first two of these attempts, there was no official involvement due to a disagreement between Gardner and the factory. In 1948, EX135 had even run with a modified Jaguar engine, but for 1949, cordial relations were restored and once again EX135 carried the MG colours.
18 Sep	1949	Britain devalues the pound sterling from $4.03 to $2.80, giving UK exports to the USA a major boost. The resulting export drive is so successful that 1949's exports are double those of 1946.
10 Nov	1949	First production MG TD (chassis 0252) built. Soon after, the last TC (Serial no. 10,001, chassis 10,251) is built.
18 Jan	1950	MG TD Midget launched, based largely upon Y-series components.
15 Apr	1950	The New York Motor Sports Show opens, with EX135 as one of the star exhibits.
May	1950	First production MG TD Midget Mark II, chassis number TD/C/1123. Mark II models, offering higher performance, are identifiable by TD/C chassis

		numbers; launched in USA in January 1951.
May	1950	The prototype TD Mark II (EX171; see Appendix 2), registered FMO 885, is raced at Blandford Camp by Dick Jacobs, who would win ahead of an HRG, universally acknowledged as the car to beat.
24-25 Jun	1950	Le Mans 24-hour race. George Phillips drives a special-bodied MG TC, partnered by Eric Winterbottom. The car would finish 18th overall, averaging 72.82mph (117.19km/h).
Jun	1950	Petrol rationing is finally abandoned in Great Britain.
24 Jul	1950	'Goldie' Gardner returns to Jabbeke, Belgium, for the fifth and final run at this venue (the second with MG backing), taking three international records. Gardner also drives a tuned MG YA, KCD 698, at 104.725mph (168.53km/h).
Aug	1950	At Silverstone, three early-production MG TD Mark IIs (FRX 941, FRX 942 and FRX 943, driven by Dick Jacobs, George Phillips and Ted Lund respectively) finish second, third and fourth in their class in the production car race, behind an HRG.
Sep	1950	The three 'FRX' TD Mark IIs—with FMO 885 as a back-up—compete in the Dundrod TT three-hour race. They beat the strong HRG opposition, finishing first, second and third in their class.
Dec	1950	The 10,000th car is built at Abingdon, a Riley 2½-Litre.
31 Dec	1950	Sebring. First race at the former bomber base at Hendrick Field, Sebring, Florida—six hours long rather than the 12 hours of subsequent years. The race is won by Fritz Koster and Ralph Keshon in a Crosley Hotshot, entered by the manufacturer. Three TC and two TD Midgets take part. John Van Driel in TC No. 1 takes first in class and fifth overall, closely followed by Frank O'Hare and William Milliken in TC No. 3 (second in class and sixth overall). Rowland Keith and Robert Wilder finish second in class 'G' (ninth overall) in their TC No. 25, while D. C. Viall and Red Charlwood finish fourth in class (13th overall) in their TD No. 22. The second TD, No. 32, driven by Hubert Brundage and Hobart Cook does not finish.
Jan	1951	Work begins on EX172, a Le Mans car for George Phillips.
23-24 Jun	1951	Le Mans 24-hour race; George Phillips and co-driver Alan Rippon drive UMG 400 (No. 43), a special-bodied TD Midget (EX172), reaching speeds of 116mph (186.68km/h) on the Mulsanne Straight. The car would retire following engine problems, blamed by MG on Phillips' 'spirited' driving.
20 Aug	1951	Lt Col 'Goldie' Gardner (now aged 66) sets ten new US Class 'F' records (six international records) on the Bonneville Salt Flats, using a 1250cc XPAG engine in EX135.
17 Oct	1951	MG YB appears at the Earls Court Motor Show as an improved version of the Y-type (now known as the YA).
23 Nov	1951	Nuffield Group and Austin announce that they will be merging in 1952.
15 Mar	1952	Sebring 12-hour race. Four of eight MGs entered finish. Highest placed is a 1390cc 'MG MkII Special', No. 4, driven by David Ash and John Van Driel (second in class and sixth overall), while a trio of TD Midgets (Nos. 2, 52 and 5, driven by Dick Thompson/Bill Kinchloe, Walt Hansgen/Randy Pearsall, and Frank O'Hare/Frank Allen respectively) finish third, fourth and sixth in their class (eighth, tenth and 12th overall) and win the team prize. Other MG contenders, none of whom qualifies, are N. Patton/Bruce Bailey (TD No. 34), Paul Ramos/Tony Cummings (TC special No. 12), Jim Keeley/J. Norcross (1381cc TC No. 29) and C. Sarle (TD No. 31).
31 Mar	1952	Nuffield Motors and Austin merge to form the British Motor Corporation (BMC). Leonard Lord becomes deputy chairman and managing director of BMC, with Lord Nuffield as chairman.
16-20 Aug	1952	'Goldie' Gardner takes EX135 to Bonneville for the second and last time, capturing five more international records with the 2-litre Wolseley 6/80-based six-cylinder engine (DO1009 and EX174; see Appendices 1 and 2 respectively). During one run, he would hit a marker post, part of which would strike the canopy of EX135, injuring Gardner slightly. Although he would make plans to return in 1953, illness would scupper them, and 'Goldie' would retire at the age of 67.
21 Oct	1952	Leonard Lord sees the Healey 100 prototype on the eve of the Earls Court Motor Show and agrees to produce it as the Austin-Healey 100. Soon after, MG's EX175 proposal for a streamlined TD replacement is rejected.
3 Nov	1952	John Thornley, assistant general manager since 1948, takes over from Jack Tatlow as general manager at MG, Abingdon. Tatlow becomes the general manager of Morris Commercial Cars Ltd.
Dec	1952	As a running change, the higher-performance TD Mark II (produced since May 1950 alongside the standard TD) receives enamel 'Mark II' badges and black and white MG badges in lieu of the traditional brown and cream examples, which are retained on other TDs. With the introduction of the TF in 1953, all MG badges would become black and white, breaking a tradition that would not be reinstated until the MG RV8 of 1992!
17 Dec	1952	Lord Nuffield resigns; Leonard Lord takes over as chairman of BMC.
8 Jan	1953	MG TF prototype, EX177, is presented to BMC's joint board of management for approval.
8 Mar	1953	Sebring 12-hour race. The 1389cc MG special (No. 4) of Dave Ash and Frank Ahrens finishes second in class (13th overall); TD Midget No. 53, driven by Jim Shields and Bob McKinsley finished third in class (15th overall); TD No. 42, driven by William Wellenburg and Bill Wonder, finishes fourth in class (16th overall). Further down the field, MG specials driven by Fred Allen and Robert Longworth (No. 44), Allan Paterson and Hubert Brundage (No. 14) and Ray Leibensperger and Howard Class (No. 61) end up fifth in class (19th overall), seventh in class (28th overall) and 36th overall (unplaced).
Mar	1953	Gerald Palmer's twin-cam engine is approved for development at Morris Engines Branch.
Late Mar	1953	RAC Coronation Rally. A team of three YB saloons is entered: HMO 908 (No. 149), HMO 909 (No. 150) and HMO 910 (No.151), driven by the brothers Geoff and Reg Holt, and Len Shaw. Shaw would come first in class (for touring cars up to 1300cc) and sixth overall, while R. E. Holt would be second in class and 15th overall. Geoff Holt would be unplaced, but a privately entered Y-type saloon would come third in class.
4 Apr	1953	MG TD-based Arnolt Family-and-Sports Car displayed in open and closed coupé versions at the New York International Motor Sports Show.
17 Aug	1953	End of TD Midget production with completion of chassis number TD/29,915.
Sep	1953	First production MG TF Midget built, chassis number TF/501.
21 Oct	1953	MG Z-series Magnette appears at the Earls Court Motor Show, along with the MG TF Midget (1250). The styling of the latter would be described by those responsible as a 'knife-and-fork job'. The Triumph TR2 is exhibited at the same show, making the TF look distinctly old hat.
Dec	1953	A. V. Oak, technical director at Cowley since January 1943, retires.
7 Mar	1954	Sebring 12-hour race. Gus Ehrman and Fred Allen finish fifth in class (11th overall) in the MG 'Motto' special (No. 54). Next MGs are other specials driven respectively by Victor Herzog/Steve Lansing (No. 99), Gleb Derujinsky/Don Underwood (No. 100), and Franklin Curtis (No. 59) to 29th, 34th and 44th overall (none actually finishes).
6 Jun	1954	First drawing produced for DO1062, the MGA.
Jun	1954	Drawing office established at Abingdon, several key staff being transferred from Cowley.
Jul	1954	First production MG TF 1500 built, with 1466cc engine. Note that this would no longer be described as a Midget.
Jul	1954	Terry Mitchell starts work on the chassis of DO1062 (MGA).
Aug	1954	Syd Enever receives the go-ahead to develop EX175 into production form, the intended launch being in April 1955.
Aug	1954	The new EX179 record car, driven by George Eyston and Ken Miles, is taken to 153.69mph (247.33km/h) on the Bonneville Salt Flats in Utah. In addition, they post an average of 120mph (193.12km/h) for 12 hours.
Sep	1954	Last MG TF Midget 1250 built.
1 Dec	1954	Abingdon based BMC Competitions Department—'Comps'—opens at the MG factory under Marcus Chambers.
Jan	1955	Monte Carlo Rally. First BMC event under Marcus Chambers' direction (although planned prior to his arrival). Three MG Magnette ZAs take part: No. 49 (KJB 910, known as 'Aramis') driven by Geoff Holt, Stan Asbury and Ray Brookes, finishes 178th overall; No. 58 (KJB 908, known as 'Athos'), driven by Reg Holt, A. Collinson and Willy Cave, finishes 237th overall; No. 36 (KJB 909, 'Porthos'), driven by Len Shaw, B. Brown and Freddie Finnemore, finishes 202nd overall. A fourth ZA, 'd'Artagnan' is driven by Chambers.
Mar	1955	RAC rally, starting at Hastings and Blackpool, and finishing at Hastings. MG TF No. 193 (KRX 90) is driven by Pat Moss (sister of Stirling) and Pat Faichney through heavy snow to take third place in the Ladies' competition. Other MGs are three Magnettes: No. 200 (Reg Holt/ B. Brown), No. 198 (Geoff Holt/Ray Brookes), which achieves first in class, and No. 199 (Len Shaw/A. Collinson).
13 Mar	1955	Sebring 12-hour race. Début of the TF Midget, two of which are entered. No. 76, driven by Dave Ash and Duncan Black, finishes eighth in class (38th overall), while No. 77, driven by John Ryan and Buel Kinne, finishes next (ninth in class, 39th overall).
Apr	1955	Original launch date for the MG Series MGA (referred to as Model UA). This would slip to a proposed announcement in June, which John Thornley realized could be linked to a high-profile entry at Le Mans. Subsequent delays with Pressed Steel tooling would push the launch back to September.
Apr	1955	MG TF 1500 discontinued, the last chassis number being TF/10,100.
7 May	1955	*Daily Express* Production Touring Car Race at Silverstone. A team of three ZA Magnettes gain first, second and third place in the hands of Dick Jacobs, Alan Foster and J. R. Waller.
16 May	1955	First production MGA starts down the line at Abingdon. Early MGAs are produced using plastic tools to form the body pressings, but these would soon be changed to normal steel dies.
6 Jun	1955	The MG entourage arrives at the Château Chêne de Cœur, their base for the Le Mans race.
11-12 Jun	1955	Le Mans 24-hour race. Three EX182 prototypes are entered by MG. Two would finish in 12th (LBL 302, No. 41, Ken Miles/Johnny Lockett) and 17th

places (LBL 303, No. 64, Ted Lund/Hans Waeffler), although this achievement would be overshadowed by the tragic accident involving Pierre Levegh's Mercedes 300SLR early in the race. A third MG (LBL 301, No. 42, Dick Jacobs/Joe Flynn) would burst into flame after leaving the track near Maison Blanche at 6.39pm, just over 2½ hours into the race and minutes after the Mercedes tragedy. This effort would be the last factory enty at Le Mans until 1964.

16 Jul	1955	First production MGA leaves the factory, ahead of the September launch.
17 Sep	1955	Prototype twin-cam engine in low-headlamp version EX182 (No. 34, LBL 301 - the registration number previously carried by Dick Jacobs' Le Mans car!) runs at the Dundrod circuit in the TT race. The original plan had been to race the two competing twin-cam engine designs, but at the last minute, the Austin engine was withdrawn and never raced, contrary to popular belief. The Morris Engines twin-cam car, driven by Ron Flockhart and John Lockett, would eventually retire with ignition troubles. One of the two 1500 cars (No. 36), driven by Ted Lund and Dickie Stoop, would also retire, but the third car (No. 35, LBL 303), driven by Jack Fairman and Peter Wilson, would finish fourth in class.
22 Sep	1955	MGA launched at the Frankfurt Motor Show, being described initially as the MG Series MGA. It is powered by the 1489cc B-series engine.
19 Oct	1955	MGA makes its UK début at the Earls Court Motor Show. During the course of the show, BMC stage their Montlhéry endurance runs.
22-23 Oct	1955	Five BMC cars are taken to the Montlhéry track (in very wet conditions) for publicity endurance runs. They comprise a Riley Pathfinder, driven by Bob Porter with three passengers, which would cover 108.03 miles (173.85km) in one hour; an Austin-Healey 100, driven by Ron Flockhart, which would achieve 104.32 miles (167.88km) in one hour; a new MGA, driven by Ken Wharton, which would complete 102.54 miles (165.02km) in an hour; an Austin Westminster, driven by chief superintendent John Gott of the Hertfordshire police (101.99mph/164.13km/h); a Wolseley 6/90, also driven by Gott (101.2mph/162.86km/h); and finally, a racing MGA, again driven by John Gott, which would record 112.36mph (180.82km/h). The last's run would be memorable, since a tyre would burst three quarters of the way through it, causing Gott to start again from scratch.
Nov	1955	Alec Issigonis returns to BMC from Alvis, although he is based at Longbridge rather than Cowley.
Jan	1956	Monte Carlo Rally. Two alloy-panelled MG Magnette ZAs are entered. No. 34 (JRX 251), driven by Gregor Grant, Norman Davis and Cliff Davis, retires with electrical problems, but the other car, No. 327 (KJB 910), driven by Nancy Mitchell, Doreen Reece and Susan Hindermarsh, finishes 59th overall and third in the Ladies' class.
1 Feb	1956	Don Hayter joins the MG design office at Abingdon as senior layout draughtsman.
24 Mar	1956	Sebring 12-hour race. A three-car team of white MGAs is prepared by the BMC Competitions Department at Abingdon and driven by Americans to win the team prize. These cars are not official factory entries, BMC having withdrawn from racing at the end of the previous year, following the appalling accidents at Le Mans and Dundrod . The William Kinchloe/Steve Spittler car (No. 50) would come fourth in class and 19th overall; the Ash/Ehrman car (No.49) fifth in class and 20th overall; and the Allen/Van Driel car (No. 51) 22nd overall. David Ash and Gus Ehrman were MG racing veterans with connections to the MG sales network in North America.
28-29 Apr	1956	33rd Mille Miglia race, starting and finishing in Brescia, Northern Italy. MG enters two red MGAs: No. 227 (MBL 867), driven by Nancy Mitchell with Pat Faichney as co-driver (although Mitchell would drive all the way!), and No. 229 (MJB 167), driven by Peter Scott-Russell and Tom Haig, later to become MG chief test driver. Driving through appallingly wet conditions, Nancy Mitchell would finish third in the 1½-litre class (74th overall) and be the highest placed female driver, covering 1624km (1009.13 miles) in 15hr, 7min, 28sec. MJB 167 would also finish well, ahead of MBL 867, taking second place in class.
May	1956	Tulip Rally. The MG Magnette, No. 147 (KJB 910), of Nancy Mitchell and Doreen Reece is excluded because its alloy panels are non-standard.
16 May	1956	The 100,000th MG, a left-hand-drive MGA 1500 tourer, is built at Abingdon; not to be confused with the 100,000th MGA built in 1962.
26 Jun	1956	President Nasser of Egypt nationalizes the Suez Canal, precipitating an international crisis that would threaten a major oil crisis.
6-12 Jul	1956	28th Rallye des Alpes, a series of challenging races, in which no overall prize is awarded, only Coupes des Alpes for drivers who complete the series without penalties. MG enters a five-car team of MGAs: No. 326 (MBL 867) driven by Nancy Mitchell and Pat Faichney; No. 308 (MJB 167) driven by Bill Shephard and John R. Williamson; No. 324 (MJB 191) driven by John Gott and Ray Brookes, the only white car in an otherwise red team; No. 314 (MRX 43), driven by John Milne and Douglas Johns; No. 330 (MRX 42) driven by Jack Sears and Ken Best. Nancy Mitchell would achieve third in class, 15th overall, and win the ladies' prize; MRX 43 and MJB 167 would come fourth and fifth in class respectively, but the others would retire.
Aug	1956	EX179 is driven by Ken Miles and Johnny Lockett on Bonneville Salt Flats to take 16 international 1500cc Class 'E' speed records, including 170.15mph (273.82km/h) for 10 miles (16.09km) and 141.71mph (228.05km/h) over 12 hours.
29 Aug-2 Sep 1956		Liège-Rome-Liège rally. Four MGAs (1489cc B-series) entered. No. 15 (MRX 43), driven by John Milne and Richard 'Dickie' Benstead-Smith, finishes seventh in class (14th overall); No. 24 (MRX 42), driven by Gerry Burgess and Sam Croft-Pearson, retires following sump damage; No. 38 (MBL 867), driven by Nancy Mitchell and Anne Hall finishes 26th overall (second in the Ladies' class); and No. 75 (MJB 191), driven by John Gott and Chris Tooley, finishes sixth in class and 13th overall, just ahead of the Milne/Benstead-Smith car.
Sep	1956	MG ZB Magnette launched, the earlier version becoming known as the ZA.
Sep	1956	MG MGA coupé announced.
12 Oct	1956	Production version of Vanden Plas alloy hardtop for MGA announced (similar to type used in the Alpine Rally in July).
17 Oct	1956	The MGA Coupé and ZB Magnette make their public début at the Earls Court Motor Show. The Magnette is also available with a Manumatic (semi-automatic) transmission and as a Varitone version, which features a larger rear window and a two-tone paint finish (although, confusingly, some Varitones would be finished in single colours).
31 Jan	1957	Donald Healey shows the Q1 prototype for the Austin-Healey Sprite to George Harriman; production would begin at Abingdon in 1958.
23 Mar	1957	Sebring 12-hour race. For the second year running, a team of three MGAs is entered by Hambro Automotive and wins the team prize.No. 49, driven by Abe Miller, Ed Leavens and Rowland Keith, finishes first in class and 23rd overall; No. 51, driven by David Ash, Gus Ehrman and John Van Driel finishes second in class (27th overall); and Steve Spittler and William Kinchloe are fourth in their class (36th o/a).
11 Jul	1957	EX181 leaves Southampton on the *Queen Mary*, bound for the USA.
13/16 Aug	1957	EX179 is driven by David Ash and Tommy Wisdom in both supercharged (Shorrock supercharger) and un-supercharged form, using a 948cc A-series engine. EX179 is described as a BMC development project, and as the new 'frogeye' Sprite had not been launched, at this stage, the engine is referred to as a Morris Minor unit.
23 Aug	1957	Stirling Moss, who had won the Pescara GP on the 20th, takes EX181 to a two-way average speed of 245.64mph (395.31km/h), breaking five international Class 'F' records.
28 Aug-1 Sep 1957		Liège-Rome-Liège rally. Four MGAs are entered: No. 5 (OBL 311), driven by Nancy Mitchell and Joan Johns finishes ninth in class (16th overall), winning the Ladies' prize; No. 24 (MRX 43), driven by John Milne and Bill Shepherd, retires due to an accident; No. 48 (MJB 167), driven by John Gott and Chris Tooley, finishes eighth in class (14th overall); the fourth MGA, driven by G. Harris and G. Hacquin, does not finish.
Nov	1957	Austin-Healey 100/6 BN4 production transferred from Longbridge to Abingdon. Overall responsibility for Austin-Healey production and engineering now rests with MG, the Healeys becoming consultants.
Jan	1958	Monte Carlo Rally. There had been no rally in 1957, following the Suez crisis, although Nancy Mitchell had been entered in a Magnette. In 1958, she was entered again (with Joan Johns) in car No. 341, which retired.
20 May	1958	Austin-Healey Sprite (Mark 1), the so-called 'frogeye' Sprite, launched.
19 Jun	1958	The EX214/1 MGB prototype drawing is completed by Don Hayter.
15 Jul	1958	MGA Twin Cam launched. A demonstration day is held at the Fighting Vehicles Research and Development Establishment at Chobham, in Surrey, at which over 100 journalists are allowed to drive the new car.
27-31 Aug	1958	Liège-Rome-Liège rally. MGA Twin Cam No. 78 (PRX 707), driven by John Gott and Ray Brookes, finishes ninth overall. This was the first factory entry for a Twin Cam in international rallying.
12 Nov	1958	Pininfarina styled MG Magnette Mark III launched, related to the Morris Oxford Series V, Austin A55 Cambridge, Riley 4/68 and Wolseley 15/60. It would be built at Cowley, with no significant Abingdon input.
Dec	1958	MG ZB Magnette discontinued in favour of Magnette Mark III.
Mar	1959	Austin-Healey 3000 launched; it would be built at the MG factory.
21 Mar	1959	Sebring 12-hour race. No MGs raced at Sebring in 1958, but in 1959, a team of four MGA Twin Cams (chassis nos. YD2-931, -932, -933 and -934; all tourers converted into coupés at the factory) is entered by Hambro in conjunction with BMC Canada (who provide servicing back-up) as the first officially sanctioned BMC entry at Sebring (previous entries having been private). Gus Ehrman and Ray Saidel (No. 28) finish second in class (27th overall); Jim Parkinson and John Dalton (No. 29) finish third in class (34th overall); while Jack Flaherty, Ray Pickering and Sherman Decker (No. 30) finish fourth in class (45th overall).
Apr	1959	First issue of *Safety Fast* magazine.
20-21 Jun	1959	Le Mans 24-hour race. Ted Lund and Colin Escott drive a privately entered, aluminium-bodied MGA Twin Cam; (No. 33, chassis YD3-627 S, registration SRX 210). The body is believed to be basically that of Ted Lund's 1955 Le Mans car (LBL 303) fitted to a new Twin Cam chassis. They would eventually retire in the 21st hour of the race, following a high-speed collision with a dog.
1 Jul	1959	Austin-Healey 3000 (produced at Abingdon) is announced to replace the 100-Six.

31 Jul	1959	MGA 1600, with 1588cc B-series engine, launched, production beginning in May. The MGA 1500 had already earned BMC $60 million from exports to the USA.
26 Aug	1959	Morris Mini Minor (ADO15) launched.
Sep	1959	Tommy Wisdom, Gus Ehrman and Ed Leavens use EX219 (really EX179 dressed up as an Austin-Healey with a supercharged Sprite engine) to take 15 records at Utah, at speeds of up to 146.9mph (236.41km/h).
2 Oct	1959	Phil Hill drives EX181, fitted with 2-litre MGA twin-cam engine, to take six records up to 254.91mph (410.23km/h). This would be the last factory backed record attempt.
8 Oct	1959	British general election returns a Conservative government under Harold McMillan.
26 Mar	1960	Sebring 12-hour race. A team of three MGA Twin Cam tourers, with detachable hardtops, is entered by British Motor Car Co. of New York. Two of the three British Racing Green cars finish: No 39 (chassis YD2-2575, registration UMO 96), driven by Fred Hayes and Ed Leavens finishes third in class (24th overall): No. 40 (chassis YD1-2571, registration UMO 93), driven by Jim Parkinson and Jack Flaherty, finishes fourth in class (29th overall); while the third car, No. 38 (chassis YD2-2573, registration UMO 95), driven by Ted Lund and Colin Escott, does not finish, but is placed 63rd in the results.
Spring	1960	MGA Twin Cam discontinued. Surplus chassis, with front and rear disc brakes, would be used to create the MGA De Luxe.
May	1960	Pressed Steel begin to construct the first MGB prototype.
25-26 Jun	1960	Le Mans 24-hour race. Ted Lund and Colin Escott return with SRX 210 (No. 32), now in MGA Twin Cam Coupé form and fitted with a 1762cc engine. They would finish 12th on distance, at an average speed of 91.12mph (146.64km/h), and win the 2-litre class.
Summer	1960	A recession in the US car market causes a dramatic drop in sales of British sports cars: overall, British car exports in 1960 would be almost halved in comparison with 1959 figures, and 1961 would be even worse.
Nov	1960	Innocenti of Italy launch the 998cc Spyder, based upon the Austin-Healey Sprite, but with its own unique bodywork.
Dec	1960	Production of the Austin-Healey Sprite Mark I discontinued.
25 Mar	1961	Sebring 12-hour race. Two MGA 1600 De Luxe coupés are triumphant in their class, despite being challenged by the Sunbeam Alpine opposition. No. 44 (chassis 100148), driven by Jim Parkinson and Jack Flaherty, finishes first in class (14th overall); while No. 43 (chassis 100149), driven by Peter Riley and Sir John Whitmore, finishes second in class (16th overall).
Spring	1961	Leyland Motors acquire Standard Triumph International for £18 million.
May	1961	Austin-Healey Sprite Mark II launched.
Jun	1961	MG Midget Mark I (GAN1) launched, with 948cc A-series engine, four weeks after Austin-Healey Sprite Mark II. Both cars, derived from the original 'frogeye' Sprite, are very similar, largely due to Donald Healey's insistence that the MG's styling be adopted for the Austin-Healey. First use of a plastic, red-backed, chrome MG octagon on a black shield for the grille badge, later adopted for the MGB and MG 1100.
10-11 Jun	1961	Le Mans 24-hour race. Ted Lund, with co-driver Bob Olthoff, returns for a third and final run with SRX 210 (No. 58), now with specially streamlined nose/air intake. They would retire after 15 laps with engine trouble.
Jun	1961	MGA 1600 Mark II launched, now with 1622cc B-series engine.
Jul	1961	Mini Cooper introduced with 997cc version of the A-series engine.
26 Jul	1961	Drawing completed by Don Hayter for the revised MGB with conventional leaf-sprung rear suspension.
Sep	1961	Roy Brocklehurst becomes MG project engineer. In three years, he will become assistant chief engineer to Enever.
18 Sep	1961	MG Magnette Mark IV launched (alongside Morris Oxford Mark VI, Austin A60 Cambridge, Riley 4/68 and Wolseley 16/60) to replace poorly received first generation 'Farinas'.
30 Sep	1961	Marcus Chambers leaves 'Comps', his place being taken by Stuart Turner.
Jan	1962	Monte Carlo Rally. Two MGs entered: MGA 1600 Coupé No. 314 (151 ABL), driven by Donald and Erle Morley, finishes first in class (28th overall); while Midget No. 44 (YRX 747), driven by Peter Riley and Mike Hughes, also finishes first in its class (33rd overall).
Spring	1962	Three special coupé-bodied Midgets, each with hand beaten alloy bodywork weighing 1242lb (563.37kg), built by MG development department for Dick Jacobs and John Milne: two would go to Dick Jacobs, in whose ownership they would usually be raced by Alan Foster and Andrew Hedges. They would be returned to the factory for Sebring in March 1965.
Mar	1962	100,000th MGA produced at Abingdon; the car is finished in metallic gold with cream leather interior trim and gold painted wire wheels, then displayed at the New York Motor Show.
24 Mar	1962	Sebring 12-hour race. This is the last Sebring race for the factory MGA. A team of three MGA 1600 Mk. II De Luxe Coupés is entered by Ecurie Safety Fast. No. 51 (chassis 106073), driven by Jack Sears and Andrew Hedges finishes fourth in class (16th overall); No. 52 (chassis 106074), driven by Bob Olthoff and Sir John Whitmore, finishes sixth in class (20th overall); No. 63 (chassis 106075), driven by Jack Flaherty and Jim Parkinson, finishes fifth in class (17th overall). It becomes clear that the MGA is no longer competitive, as the Sunbeam Alpines are proving superior.
6-10 May	1962	Tulip Rally. Rauno Aaltonen and Gunnar Palm drive an MGA 1600 Coupé No. 11 (151 ABL) to 15th place overall, winning their class. This would be the last official victory for the MGA. A Midget, No. 59 (YRX 737) driven by Tommy Gold and Mike Hughes finishes third in class (38th overall).
22 May	1962	First production MGB—a left-hand-drive, Iris Blue car, GHN3-102—is built. A total of 12 production cars would be built in May (including a single right-hand-drive car, GHN3-101), and production would increase steadily for the September launch.
Jun	1962	Alpine Rally. MG Midget No. 23 (YRX 737) is driven by J. Williamson and David Hiam, but is not placed.
Jul	1962	MGA 1600 Mark II discontinued in advance of MGB launch; final chassis number is GHN2-109071.
29 Aug-2 Sep	1962	Liège-Sofia-Liège. MGA 1600 Mark II Coupé No. 49 (151 ABL), driven by John Gott and Bill Shepherd, retires due a fuel leak. This is the last outing for the MGA.
20 Sep	1962	ADO23 MG MGB launched. It features a new 1798cc version of the B-series engine, still with three main bearings (a five-bearing engine would be phased in during 1964).
2 Oct	1962	MG 1100 (ADO16G) announced, with hydrolastic suspension and twin-carburettor, 1098cc A-series engine mounted transversely.
17 Oct	1962	At the Earls Court Motor Show, the MG Midget Mark I and Austin-Healey Sprite Mark II are shown with the 1098cc engine in place of the 948cc unit. The Midget becomes GAN2. The show also marks the début of the MG 1100, MGB and Triumph Spitfire, the last intended as a rival for the small BMC sports cars.
Nov	1962	RAC Rally. Sole MG entry is an MG 1100, No. 11 (977 CBL) driven by Rev. Rupert Jones and David Seigle-Morris. A broken piston causes their retirement.
Jan	1963	Monte Carlo Rally. Two MG 1100s and an MG Midget entered. The Midget, No. 158 (YRX 747) driven by Rev. Rupert Jones and Phillip Morgan wins its class. Of the MG 1100s, No. 268 (399 CJB), driven by Raymond Baxter and Ernie McMillen, finishes fourth in its class, while the other, No. 162, driven by John Cuff, is written off when struck by another competitor's vehicle.
23 Mar	1963	Sebring 12-hour race. Ignominious début for the MGB, as neither of the two cars entered finishes. Both cars retire with engine problems due to oil surge. The cars are No. 47 (7 DBL), driven by Jim Parkinson and Jack Flaherty, and No. 48 (6 DBL), was driven by Christabel Carlisle and Denise McCluggage. A third car (8 DBL) was also built, but is not raced. After the race, 6 DBL would be sold in the USA to help defray costs, while 7 DBL would be written off in May 1964.
4 Apr	1963	Assembly of MGBs begins in Australia at BMC Australia's Zetland, New South Wales facility.
15-16 Jun	1963	Le Mans 24-hour race. An MGB (No. 31, chassis GHN3-3699, registration 7 DBL), with a long nose designed by Enever, is entered 'privately' by Alan Hutcheson, who shares the driving with Paddy Hopkirk. During the race, Hutcheson would run off the track into sand (at Mulsanne) and, as a result, would spend 1½ hours digging the car out! Despite this, they would finish 12th overall, at an average speed of 91.96mph (147.99km/h).
Sep	1963	Tour de France Automobile. MGB No. 155 (7 DBL), driven by Andrew Hedges and John Sprinzel, retires due to an accident.
Jan	1964	In the New Year's Honours List, John Thornley is awarded the Order of the British Empire (OBE) for his services to the Air Training Corps.
Jan	1964	Jacques Coune's MGB Berlinette makes its début at the Brussels Motor Show.
Jan	1964	Monte Carlo Rally. Although all eyes are on the Mini Coopers, MGs also compete. MGB No. 83 (7 DBL), driven by twin brothers Don and Erle Morley, wins the GT class (17th overall). The same car would be written off by the Morleys during the Scottish Rally in June. Also competing is an MG 1100, No. 243 (399 CJB) driven by Tommy Wisdom and J. Miles.
11 Feb	1964	Work starts on MG's design for an MGB replacement: EX234 (see Appendix 2).
9 Mar	1964	MG Midget Mark II (GAN3) launched, with new windscreen and front quarterlights, similar to MGB. Also Austin-Healey Sprite Mark III.
21 Mar	1964	Sebring 12-hour race. Three new cars are entered by Kjell Qvale, including BMO 541B, which would go on to compete at Le Mans in June. Ed Leslie and John Dalton drive car No. 47, which finishes third in class (17th overall); Jim Adams and Merle Brennan finish fourth in class (22nd overall) in BMO; while Jack Flaherty and Jim Parkinson (in No. 46) retire.
Apr	1964	Jacques Coune delivers one of his MGB Berlinette coupé conversions to Walter Oldfield for assessment by BMC as an alternative to the MGB GT.
20-21 Jun	1964	Le Mans 24-hour race. The MG factory enters a long-nosed MGB (No. 37, chassis ADO23/986, registration BMO 541B), driven by Paddy Hopkirk and Andrew Hedges. They would finish 19th overall, at an average speed of 99.95mph (160.85km/h).

Summer	1964	Studies begin on enlarging the B-series engine further, a 200cc increase to 1998cc being considered.
26-30 Aug	1964	Spa-Sofia-Liège rally. This is the last of these famous rallies in traditional road-racing form. None of the three MGBs finish: No. 38 (8 DBL) is a private entry) driven by David Hiam and Rev. Rupert Jones; No. 78 (BRX 853B) is driven by Pauline Mayman and Valerie Domleo; and BRX 854B is driven by Julien Vernaeve.
Sep	1964	Tour de France Automobile. MGB No. 153 (BMO 541B, with long nose), driven by Andrew Hedges and John Sprinzel, retires due to engine problems caused by head gasket failure.
Sep	1964	Austin 1800 (ADO17) launched with new five-bearing version of the B-series engine. The Morris 1800 would not be launched until March 1966.
Oct	1964	Five-main-bearing version of the B-series engine supersedes the three-bearing version in the MGB.
15 Oct	1964	British general election returns a Labour government under Harold Wilson.
Nov	1964	RAC Rally. MGB No. 177 (BRX 854B), driven by John Fitzpatrick and John Handley, retires following an accident; MGB No. 39 (BRX 853B), driven by Pauline Mayman and Valerie Domleo, retires due to clutch problems.
27 Mar	1965	Sebring 12-hour race. BMC enters a team of four MGs, comprising a brace each of MGBs and the special alloy-bodied MG Midgets that had been raced originally by Dick Jacobs. Untypically for Sebring, the weather turns bad during the race, but the MGs finish despite the torrential rain. MGB No. 49 (BMO 541B), drlven by Merle Brennan and Frank Morrell, finishes second in class (l0th in prototype category; 25th overall); MGB No. 48 (DRX 256C), driven by Brad Pricard and Al Pease finishes sixth in class (l0th in GT category; 32nd overall). Of the two Midgets, No. 68 (771 BJB), driven by Roger Mac and Andrew Hedges, finishes a highly respectable first in class (12th in GT category; 26th overall), while No. 82 (770 BJB), driven by Chuck Tannlund and J. Wagstaff, retires.
9 May	1965	Targa Florio. MG Midget GT 'Jacobs' coupé No. 44 (771 BJB), driven by Paddy Hopkirk and Andrew Hedges, finishes second in class (llth overall).
19-20 Jun	1965	Le Mans 24-hour race. MG enters a long-nosed MGB (No. 39, registration DRX 255C), driven by Paddy Hopkirk and Andrew Hedges. They would take 11th place (among14 finishers), with an average speed of 98.25mph (158.11km/h). This would be the last MG to compete at Le Mans.
Jul	1965	BMC make an offer for Pressed Steel, which would become effective in September 1965.
22 Jul	1965	Rover buys Alvis.
20 Oct	1965	MGB GT appears at the Earls Court Motor Show.
Jan	1966	Monte Carlo Rally. The last MG entry for 20 years is an MGB, which would fittingly become known as 'Old Faithful'—No. 183 (GRX 307D)—and is driven by Tony Fall and Ron Crellin. It retires due to a chafing oil pipe.
26 Mar	1966	Sebring 12-hour race. BMC decides to broaden its entry and, consequently, prize-winning potential by entering one of the cars as a prototype. This is 8 DBL fitted with a special bored-out 2004cc B-series engine. Sadly, it does not live up to its promise, punching a hole in the side of the block and forcing Paddy Hopkirk to retire just two hours short of the end of the race. MGB No. 59 (HBL 129D), driven by Peter Manton, Roger Mac and Emmett Brown, finishes first in class (third in GT category; 17th overall); while privately entered MGBs (Nos. 84, 85 and 86), driven by Roger West, Albert Ackerly/Arch McNeill, and Ernie Croucher/Pete Glenn, also retire.
8 May	1966	Targa Florio race: 'Old Faithful', MGB No. 64 (GRX 307D) driven by Timo Makinen and John Rhodes, wins both the 2-litre GT category and the entire GT class, finishing ninth overall. MGB No. 66 (JBL 491D), driven by Andrew Hedges and John Handley, finishes second nd in the 2-litre GT category and third in the GT class. The race is run over 450 miles, and there are 30 finishers of the 71 starters.
Jun	1966	Leonard Lord, by now Lord Lambury, retires from the BMC board. George Harriman becomes chairman and Joe Edwards managing director.
24-28 Aug	1966	Marathon de la Route 84-hour race at the Nürburgring. 'Old Faithful' MGB, No. 47 (GRX 307D), was driven by Julien Vernaeve and Andrew Hedges to finish with great distinction as outright winner after 5260 miles (8464.92km). MGB No. 46 (BRX 855B), driven by Roger Enever (son of Syd) and Alec Poole, frustratingly retires due to axle problems after Iying in second place behind 'Old Faithful' five hours from the end of the race.
11 Jul	1966	BMC and Jaguar agree a merger, which would be finalized in December.
9 Sep	1966	National Motor Vehicle and Traffic Safety Act passed by US Congress; its implications would become effective on 1 January, 1968.
19 Oct	1966	MG Midget Mark III (GAN4) launched at the Earls Court Motor Show, with 1275cc A-series engine. Also Austin-Healey Sprite Mark IV.
3 Nov	1966	Assembly of pre-production MGC begins at Abingdon, barely two months after the Healeys reject BMC's proposed Austin-Healey 3000 Mark IV equivalent. Thirteen pre-production cars would be built for development and testing.
11 Dec	1966	Leyland concludes negotiations for a merger with Rover, effective March 1967.
14 Dec	1966	British Motor Corporation and Jaguar announce their new joint holding company: British Motor Holdings. Joe Edwards becomes BMH chief executive, under Sir George Harriman.
Feb	1967	Anthony Wedgwood Benn reveals in House of Commons that Leyland and BMH are holding exploratory talks.
Mar	1967	Stuart Turner leaves the BMC Competitions Department, his place being taken by Peter Browning.
Late Mar	1967	First lightweight MGB GT racing prototype (MBL 546E) takes shape at Abingdon.
1 Apr	1967	Sebring 12-hour race. First official MGB GT entry. 'Old Faithful' MGB No. 48 (GRX 307D), fitted with a 1824cc B-series engine and driven by Timo Makinen and John Rhodes, finishes third in the GT category (12th overall); MGB GT No. 30 (LBL 591E), fitted with a 2004cc B-series engine and driven by Paddy Hopkirk and Andrew Hedges, finishes first in class (third in prototype category and 11th overall). Gary Magwood and Raymond Gray in their privately entered MGB No. 49 do not finish due to suspension problems.
14 May	1967	The lightweight MGB GT (MBL 546E), later to become the famous MGC GTS, is raced at the Targa Florio with a 2004cc B-series engine, as per Sebring, but with twin SUs helping to provide 150bhp (11.86kW) at 6000rpm. Initially, the car was sprayed red, as are all BMC competition cars, but at a late stage, it was realized that the regulations for the event demanded national racing colours, so the external panels were resprayed British Racing Green. The MGC GTS (badged 'MG GTS') was accompanied to Sicily by an MGB (MBL 547E). The former, with race number 230 and driven by Paddy Hopkirk andTimo Makinen, finished third in class (ninth overall). The MGB, driven by Alec Hedges and Alec Poole, left the road and crashed into a tree, putting it out of the race.
5 Jun	1967	Start of Six Day War between Israel and Arab states, who declare an oil embargo against Britain and the USA.
Jul	1967	First production MGCs built: G/CN-101 (MGC tourer) and G/CD-110 (MGC GT).
18 Oct	1967	MGC, MGC GT and MGB Mark II range appears at the Earls Court Motor Show.
18 Oct	1967	MG 1100 Mark II launched, alongside a facelift of the whole ADO16 range. Common features include interior improvements—notably to the dashboard—and reshaped rear fins and tail-lights.
19 Oct	1967	BMC announce that Roy Haynes would shortly be appointed director of styling at the company's Pressed Steel Fisher subsidiary at Cowley and that, henceforth, he would be responsible for all BMC styling (Dick Burzi would retain his small studio at Longbridge, but report to Haynes). Haynes had been recruited from Ford of Great Britain, where he had been largely responsible for the well received Ford Cortina Mark II of 1966.
Oct	1967	Serious discussions regarding the possibility of a merger commence between BMH and Leyland, following a meeting at Chequers between George Harriman (BMH) and Donald Stokes (Leyland), at the invitation of Prime Minister Harold Wilson.
6 Nov	1967	New design centre established at Cowley, under the direction of Roy Haynes, with the agreement of Sir George Harriman and Joe Edwards.
Nov	1967	The first cars to meet US safety and emissions requirements are built at Abingdon, complete with 'Abingdon Pillow' padded dashboards and dual-circuit brakes.
21 Dec	1967	Austin-Healey 3000 Mark III discontinued (although a single car would be built for the UK market in May 1968).
1 Jan	1968	US safety requirements come into effect.
Jan	1968	Harris Mann joins Austin-Morris styling studio from Ford.
17 Jan	1968	Announcement of £320 million merger of Leyland Motor Corporation with BMH to form British Leyland Motor Corporation (effective from 14 May). Cars to be split into Austin-Morris (including MG) and Specialist Cars (with separate Rover, Triumph and Jaguar boards). For the first few months, Donald Stokes would effectively run Austin-Morris himself.
23 Mar	1968	Sebring 12-hour race. The Sebring début of 'Mabel', the MGC GTS prototype, No. 44 (MBL 546E). Driven by Paddy Hopkirk and Andrew Hedges, it finishes first in class (third in prototype category and 10th overall); MGB GT No. 66 (LBL 591E), shared by Garry Rodriguez, Richard McDaniel and Bill Brack, finishes fifth in class (18th overall). An MG Midget (actually an Austm-Healey Sprite, LNX 628E) driven by Jerry Truitt and Randall Canfield finishes first in class (also first in sports car category and 15th overall). The Midget is a private entry by the Donald Healey Motor Company and was converted into MG guise by them at BMC's request. Subsequently, it would be converted back into an Austin-Healey and sold. A local privately entered MGB (No. 67), driven by Chris Waldron, James Gammon and Ben Scott, finishes an honourable seventh in class and 31st overall.
Mar	1968	Austin America launched in USA to replace MG version of ADO16. The new car is based on a two-door bodyshell and features a four-speed AP automatic transmission as standard.
Apr	1968	MG 1300 replaces MG 1100 Mark II.
Apr	1968	Joe Edwards resigns from BMH prior to formation of BLMC. Harry Webster and George Turnbull, both former Triumph engineers, are installed at Longbridge in charge of Austin-Morris.
8 Apr	1968	MG Magnette Mark IV dropped.
14 May	1968	British Leyland Motor Corporation Ltd comes into being.

22 May	1968	Roy Haynes writes a memo to John Barber, setting out his proposals for the ADO28 family of cars—to include an MG derivative.
Aug	1968	Harry Webster announces a plan for future Austin and Morris cars: advanced engineering and conservative styling for Austin, emphasis on style, but conservative engineering for Morris.
5 Aug	1968	BLMC board views three ADO28 prototypes: one by Pininfarina in two- and four door versions; a two-door car by Michelotti; and Roy Haynes' two- and four-door proposals, the former being a fastback coupé intended to appeal to younger customers. Haynes' basic style would be accepted.
28 Aug-1 Sep	1968	Marathon de la Route. European swansong for the stunning MGC GTS duo, also sees the end of official MG entries from Abingdon. No. 4 (MBL 546E running on wire wheels), driven by Tony Fall, Andrew Hedges and Julien Vernaeve, finishes a very respectable sixth overall; while sister car (RMO 699F running on Minilite wheels), driven by Clive Baker, Roger Enever and Alec Poole, retires with a blown head gasket after overheating.
Sep	1968	Sir George Harriman retires, leaving British Leyland largely in the control of the former Leyland management.
15 Oct	1968	At the Earls Court Motor Show press day, Sir Donald Stokes issues a statement on BLMC's future competition policy: the department at Abingdon would continue to function, but it would only concentrate its efforts on events where there was chance of winning.
16 Oct	1968	MG 1300 Mark II two-door launched at the Motor Show. From now on, MG versions of ADO16 would only have a two-door bodyshell.
22 Mar	1969	Sebring 12-hour race. The last appearance of the factory backed MGs, which sport 'British Leyland' on their wings rather than 'British Motor Corporation'. For this swansong, Abingdon prepare two of the special lightweight MGC GTS racers: No. 35 (RMO 699F), driven by the veteran team of Paddy Hopkirk and Andrew Hedges, finishes ninth in the prototype category (15th overall); No. 36 (MBL 546E), driven by Craig Hill and Bill Brack, finishes 15th in the prototype category (34th overall). MGB GT No. 62 (LBL 591E), racing on Minilite wheels and driven by Jerry Truitt and Logan Blackburn, finishes eighth in the GT category and 28th overall. Among the privateers, John Colgate and Don Parks (MGB No. 99) do well, finishing fifth in class (32nd overall; ahead of the second factory MGC GTS); Chris Waldron, Ben Scott and Dean Donley (MGB No. 64) finish sixth in class (38th overall); and Jim Gammon, Ray Mummery and Roger Houghton (MGB No. 63) retire with driveline troubles. MGs would appear as private entries in future years.
Apr	1969	The much delayed ADO14 Austin Maxi 1500 is unveiled, effectively the last 'BMC' car.
Apr	1969	Austin-Morris exterior design studio transferred from Cowley to the glass greenhouse studio, formerly occupied by Dick Burzi. The interior design studio would remain at Cowley until October.
27 Jun	1969	John Thornley retires from MG, his place being taken by Les Lambourne, the assistant general manager since 1967.
Jul	1969	Riley 1300 production discontinued, but Riley 4/72 would carry on until October.
4 Aug	1969	MGC production stopped after less than 9000 cars built. The last car would leave Abingdon on 18 September.
15 Sep	1969	Datsun 240Z sports car announced in USA, with 2.4-litre in-line straight six engine and rear-wheel-drive.
19 Sep	1969	BLMC board approves the styling of ADO67, which would become the Austin Allegro in 1973.
11 Oct	1969	British Leyland facelifted MG Midget and MGB ranges announced, all with recessed matt black grilles. Austin-Healey Sprite no longer exported.
15 Oct	1969	Mini Clubman and 1275GT appear at Earls Court Motor Show. Austin and Morris 1300 GT launched. Originally conceived as Cooper versions by BMC, they are badged GTs under the BLMC regime and finished in bright colours with fancy wheeltrims. Eventually, they would usurp the MG 1300.
Oct	1969	Austin-Morris interior design studio transferred from Cowley to the so-called 'Elephant House' in Longbridge.
24 Oct	1969	The last Riley, a 4/72, is produced.
5 Nov	1969	Work on ADO21 project commences at Abingdon.
Jan	1970	Roy Haynes leaves BLMC.
21 Mar	1970	Sebring 12-hour race. Two privately entered MGBs do quite well: No. 57, driven by John Belperche, Jim Gammon and Ray Mummery, finishes 25th overall, with Ben Scott, Lowell Lanier and Dave Houser (No. 58) in next place. Bob Kilpatrick, in MGB No. 60, does not finish. Although the parent company had withdrawn from racing after the last Sebring race, British Leyland Motors Inc., of Leonia, New Jersey, enters two MGs: No. 56 is a Midget driven by Jon Woodner and Dan O'Connor, while No. 55 is an MGB driven by Merle Brennan and Logan Blackburn. Neither finishes.
18 Jun	1970	General election results in a Conservative government led by Ted Heath.
Jun	1970	Four-wheel-drive Range Rover launched with detuned 3528cc Rover V8 engine.
Autumn	1970	Triumph engineers 'Spen' King and Mike Carver visit the USA to determine preferred customer format for new TR sports car. As a result, a competition to style a corporate sports car would be instigated, with entries from Austin-Morris styling at Longbridge, Triumph at Canley, and Michelotti. MG at Abingdon do not appear to have been invited; a mid-engined sports car is not in contention at this point, so ADO21 was probably already a dead duck!
14 Oct	1970	Austin Maxi 1750 introduced at the Earls Court Motor Show, with longer-stroke version of E4 engine, as planned for use in ADO21.
31 Oct	1970	Following an announcement in August, the Abingdon Competitions Department—'Comps'—closes after 15 years. The Special Tuning operation, started in 1964, would continue at Abingdon with a tiny competition budget.
4 Nov	1970	MG ADO21 full-size clay model viewed by British Leyland management.
29 Dec	1970	Last drawing entry in register for ADO21; work on the project would cease soon afterwards.
Jan	1971	Austin-Healey Sprite rebadged Austin, as Healey royalties discontinued.
Feb	1971	US government announces vehicle safety and emissions requirements, to take effect in 1975 model year.
20 Mar	1971	Sebring 12-hour race. Neither of the privately entered MGBs, No. 52 (Ben Scott/Lowell Lanier/Dave Houser) and No. 51 (Jim Gammon/Dean Donley), finishes.
28 Apr	1971	Morris Marina—'Beauty with Brains Behind It'—is launched in 1.3 and 1.8, two- and four-door versions. The Marina name was used previously on ADO16 models sold in Denmark.
27 May	1971	250,000th MGB, a left-hand-drive Blaze MGB GT, is completed at Abingdon. The occasion is marked by a visit from Austin-Morris director George Turnbull. The car would be given away as a national sweepstake prize in the USA in September.
May	1971	Syd Enever, 'Mr MGB', retires from his post as chief engineer at Abingdon. Roy Brocklehurst takes over.
Jul	1971	The Austin-Morris styling studios' MG Magna proposal for the new BLMC corporate sports car is approved, and promptly becomes the Triumph TR7.
Jul	1971	Last Mini Cooper in the UK, although Coopers would still be made until 1974 by Innocenti. Also the end of the road for the Austin Sprite.
4 Aug	1971	Abingdon instructed to build their own MGB GT V8 prototype, following assessment of the Costello car.
31 Aug	1971	MG 1300 Mark II dropped, ending a tradition of MG-badged saloons until the MG Metro of May 1982. However, CKD production for export would continue until 1973.
Mar	1972	Rover and Triumph merge under the control of Sir George Farmer as Rover-Triumph. The board comprises seven members from Rover and five from Triumph.
Spring	1972	MG SSV1 experimental safety vehicle, largely designed by Don Hayter and based upon an MGB GT, exhibited at a road safety exhibition in Washington DC.
23 Mar	1972	Austin and Morris 2200 and Wolseley Six launched, using ADO17 body with E6 2227cc engine. Although new to the UK, this engine had already seen service in Australia and had been considered for use in the ADO21 mid-engined MG sports car.
4 May	1972	MG Midget with round rear wheel arches launched.
Aug	1972	MGB range facelifted for 1973 model year. The grille reverts to a chrome case type, but with a mesh infill.
Sep	1972	The O-series engine emerges to produce an overhead-cam B-series engine.
Sep	1972	Design of the 'rubber' bumpers approved for the MGB.
6 Nov	1972	Final MGB is produced in Australia, the occasion being marked by a curious 'funeral' and 'wake', most notable for the liberal use of MG hexagons...
12 Dec	1972	Production of MGB GT V8 begins, for launch in the following summer.
Feb	1973	British Leyland plan for MGB to be retained as 'insurance' only, in case the TR7 is late; O-series engine programmed for April 1974.
22 Feb	1973	Austin Marina launched in the USA to replace the Austin America. High hopes would be expressed for the Marina (badged as an Austin because the Morris marque was no longer marketed in the USA), and frequently its fate would be tied to that of the MGB. The sales forecast of 10,000 cars in 1973, rising to 25,000 per annum thereafter, would never be met, however. At the time of the US launch, drivers working for British Road Services come out on strike, leading to a lay-off of 12,000 BL workers: US dealers could sell the cars, but they would not have any to sell.
24 Mar	1973	Sebring 12-hour race. Lone MGB, No. 2 of Dean Donley and Ben Scott, does not finish.
16 May	1973	Austin Allegro—'The New Driving Force From Austin'—unveiled to an underwhelmed public.
Jul	1973	Roy Brocklehurst transferred to BL Advanced Engineering; Don Hayter becomes chief engineer at Abingdon.
15 Aug	1973	The 'New 125mph (201.16km/h) MGB GT V8' unveiled to the public.
Sep	1973	So-called 'Sabrina' overriders unveiled for the MG Midget, MGB and MGB GT models sold in the USA only.
Oct	1973	Arab-Israeli War breaks out. OPEC raises price of crude oil by a factor of four, and rations supplies to Britain.
1 Jan	1974	Three-day week introduced by government, with 50mph (80.47km/h) speed limit, in an effort to conserve fuel.
Jan	1974	Work starts on ADO88, the new Mini.
28 Feb	1974	Following the miners' strike, a general election is held, but no party gains an overall majority. Prime Minister Ted Heath resigns on 4 March when

		Liberals fail to form a coalition; Harold Wilson forms a Labour government on 5 March.
Summer	1974	O-series engine now programmed for MGB and Marina by 1977 model year (i.e. autumn 1976). Within a matter of weeks, this would slip to the 1978 model year.
Jul	1974	British Leyland, in a cash crisis, meets with banks to discuss a £150 million loan.
10 Oct	1974	British general election returns a Labour government with a slim majority.
16 Oct	1974	'Rubber' bumpers for the MG Midget, MGB, MGB GT and MGB GT V8 unveiled at the Earls Court Motor Show. The Midget adopts the Triumph Spitfire's 1493cc engine in place of the 1275cc A-series unit.
27 Nov	1974	BLMC, banks and government meet to discuss state of BLMC's finances.
3 Dec	1974	Triumph Spitfire 1500 launched in the UK, with the same engine as the MG Midget 1500 and already in use for US-market Spitfires.
6 Dec	1974	Anthony Wedgwood Benn, the Industry Minister, informs Parliament that the government will guarantee BLMC's capital.
18 Dec	1974	Sir Don Ryder, the Labour government's industrial advisor, appointed to investigate BLMC.
1 Jan	1975	MGB GT withdrawn from USA, while US-specification MGB has single Stromberg instead of twin SU carburettors.
Jan	1975	Triumph TR7 two-door sports coupé announced, initially for sale only in USA.
11 Feb	1975	Margaret Thatcher becomes first woman leader of the Conservative Party; Ted Heath resigned after losing the first round of the election to Mrs Thatcher on 4 February.
26 Mar	1975	Austin/Morris/Wolseley 18-22 series (ADO71) is launched.
26 Mar	1975	Publication of the Ryder Report on British Leyland's future; recommendations include a government injection of £2.8 billion over seven years; company to be split into four divisions: cars, trucks and buses, international and special products.
May	1975	David Bache, of Rover, takes over as British Leyland's design director.
Jun	1975	Overdrive, formerly an optional extra, is made a standard feature of UK-market MGBs.
27 Jun	1975	British Leyland Motor Corporation is renamed British Leyland Ltd; government is 99.8% shareholder.
11 Aug	1975	British government nationalize British Leyland Ltd.
12 Aug	1975	The British rate of inflation peaks at 26.9 per cent.
Sep	1975	Endurance testing of prototype O-series engines in MGB, Princess and Marina.
13 Sep	1975	The Austin-Morris 18-22 series is renamed Princess as one of the first post-Ryder marque realignments. This is comparatively cheap to accomplish, as a planned Vanden Plas Princess variant of ADO71 had been cancelled after the badges had been tooled up.
16 Dec	1975	British government announces that it will secure the future of Chrysler UK with an injection of £162.5 million.
20 Mar	1976	Sebring 12-hour race. MGB No. 55, driven by Charles Kleinschmidt and Jack Andrus is placed 39th, but is not running at the finish.
19 May	1976	Triumph TR7 introduced in UK and mainland Europe.
Jun	1976	MGB withdrawn from the remaining markets in Continental Europe.
Jun	1976	Rover SD1 3500 launched, with heavily revised version of ex-Buick aluminium 3528cc V8 engine.
Jul	1976	Last two MGB GT V8s produced at Abingdon (series production had stopped in June).
Jan	1977	Work restarts on 'federalizing' the O-series engine for the MGB, aiming for introduction in 1980.
Feb	1977	Pilot-build of Triumph TR7 Sprint and TR7 V8 begins at Speke factory; it would continue until October.
19 Mar	1977	Sebring 12-hour race. MGB GT No. 52, driven by Charles Kleinschmidt and Guido Levetto, is placed 66th, but only completes 33 laps.
1 Nov	1977	Michael Edwardes joins British Leyland Ltd as chairman; on the same day, workers at the Speke Triumph factory begin what would become a four-month strike.
Dec	1977	BL consider the fate of the ADO88 Mini replacement, which has proved unsuccessful in clinic tests.
Jan	1978	ADO88 is replaced by the slightly larger LC8 project.
Feb	1978	Edwardes reveals the 1978 British Leyland corporate plan: 12,000 jobs to go and cars to be reorganized into Austin-Morris and Jaguar-Rover-Triumph, MG being part of Austin-Morris.
15 Feb	1978	British Leyland announce that the Speke factory is to close in May, and TR7 production to shift to Canley.
18 Mar	1978	Sebring 12-hour race. Long after the British seem to have given up racing the MGB, the Americans persist. MGB No. 52, driven by the redoubtable Charles Kleinschmidt, Lee Culpepper and Bill Koch (entered by Native Tan), finishes 14th in class and 30th overall with 160 laps to its credit.
1 Apr	1978	BL Motorsport at Abingdon homologates the TR7 V8 rally car.
3 Apr	1978	The government announces that it will provide £450 million of equity in British Leyland.
26 May	1978	Triumph TR7 production ends at Speke. TR7 Sprint and Lynx cancelled, and TR7 V8—which would become the TR8—delayed for two years.
1 Jul	1978	British Leyland Ltd renamed BL Ltd, the Leyland name being retained for commercial vehicles. Austin-Morris established under Ray Horrocks, and Jaguar-Rover-Triumph under William Pratt-Thompson.
Jul	1978	Development MGB with O-series engine presented to BL management. BL also approve the £275 million LC8 Metro programme.
Jul	1978	1.7- and 2-litre O-series engines introduced in revised Princess 2 range.
8 Aug	1978	John Zachary DeLorean announces that his company, the DeLorean Motor Company, will be opening a factory in Belfast, Northern Ireland, to build sports cars with the aid of government grants. This dream would eventually turn sour, and the company would end up in receivership in February 1982. MG enthusiasts would speculate on how the public money poured into DMC could have helped revitalize the MG factory.
Aug	1978	Exploratory talks begin with Honda, using an intermediary to preserve anonymity.
Sep	1978	1.7-litre O-series engine introduced in revised Marina 2 range.
Sep	1978	MG becomes part of Jaguar-Rover-Triumph.
1 Oct	1978	BL and Honda executives meet for the first time in San Francisco.
Oct	1978	Triumph TR7 production restarts at Canley after a five-month gap following the Speke closure. US dealers are unhappy with the shortfall in deliveries, which has badly affected their business.
Dec	1978	Secret ballot of 96,000 hourly paid BL workers, who vote 2:1 in favour of a BL pay and productivity deal.
1 Apr	1979	Peter Mitchell joins BL Heritage Ltd, later British Motor Heritage.
Apr	1979	US-market MGB Limited Edition (LE) model introduced at New York International Motor Show. Limited to 5000 cars, the MGB LE is black with silver side stripes, optional overdrive, special three-spoke steering wheel, alloy wheels and 185/70 SR tyres, a stainless-steel luggage rack and 'coco' footwell mats. Priced at $8550, it is $600 more expensive than a standard MGB.
3 May	1979	Conservatives, led by Margaret Thatcher, win the general election; the pound soars against the dollar.
15 May	1979	Memorandum of understanding between BL and Honda. Plan announced for a new Triumph to be built at Canley and based upon the Honda Ballade (related to the Honda Civic), with introduction planned for October 1981, half-way between the introduction of the Metro (1980) and Maestro (1983).
19 May	1979	In an article in *Autocar* magazine, a JRT spokesman is quoted as saying, 'MG? We'd be crazy to ditch it—next to Jaguar, it's the most valuable name JRT possess.' There is also reference to the MGB 'forming part of the product plan for the next five years,' and recognition that the typical TR7 and MGB customers are different.
Jun	1979	A dramatic rise in the strength of sterling affects BL's business (particularly US exports). BL formulate their CORE (Co-ordination of Resources) strategy—known as the Edwardes Plan—for maximum streamlining of the company, and to address the problem of the gap between the LC8 Metro and LC10 Maestro.
Jun	1979	Michael Edwardes accepts a knighthood from the Conservative government, having twice refused a similar honour from the previous Labour administration.
9 Jul	1979	BL meet with Industry Minister Sir Keith Joseph to discuss their proposals and the need for funding for the LC10 programme.
Jul	1979	Triumph TR7 convertible launched, five years after the TR7 coupé; initially available in the USA only.
Jul-Oct	1979	National engineering dispute.
Aug	1979	Midget production gradually run down; among the last would be a batch of 500 for Japan. Assembly of the Vanden Plas 1500 transferred to Abingdon.
1-9 Sep	1979	Special week-long programme of Golden Jubilee celebrations staged at Abingdon to celebrate 50 years of MG cars being built in the town.
10 Sep	1979	Following announcement of the closure of the AEC factory at Park Royal, and amid rumours in the press that MG might be another casualty, BL reveal plans to cease production of MG sports cars at Abingdon and to close the car manufacturing facility at Canley (the BL/Honda Bounty would be built at Cowley instead, and the TR7 would be transferred to the Rover factory at Solihull). Total redundancies amount to 25,000.
13 Sep	1979	John Thornley writes to all 445 US Jaguar-Rover-Triumph-MG dealers, pressing them to urge BL to continue MGB production at Abingdon.
26 Sep	1979	BL announce that they are losing £900 on every MGB they sell. They decline to elaborate on the basis of this figure. Austin Allegro 3 launched.
30 Sep	1979	MG clubs mount protest rally in central London.
14 Oct	1979	Alan Curtis of Aston Martin Lagonda telephones Peter Sprague in the USA and proposes a bid for MG.
16 Oct	1979	Curtis and other interested parties meet in London's Grosvenor Hotel to discuss a bid to take over the MG marque and MGB.
17 Oct	1979	Union leaders recommend to BL workers that they accept the Edwardes Plan; work-force to be balloted.

18 Oct	1979	The consortium led by Aston Martin Lagonda announces that it intends making a bid to take over the MG name and factory.
1 Nov	1979	BL work-force accept Edwardes Plan: 80 per cent actually vote, of which 87.2 per cent are in favour of acceptance.
6 Nov	1979	A group of Californian MG dealers—with the backing of the 416-strong US JRT dealer council—threatens to sue BL for £100 million if the MGB is withdrawn, since it accounts for about half their sales. Largely in an effort to placate these dealers, BL announce that MGBs will remain available until 1981, and that they wish to retain the MG marque.
10 Dec	1979	BL announce their plans for the Abingdon factory.
11 Dec	1979	*Daily Mail* announces, 'Leyland may be willing to sell MG to the AML consortium after all; if the price is right.' Harold Musgrove is quoted as saying, 'Discussions with Aston Martin are continuing'.
12 Dec	1979	The last MG Midget goes down the Abingdon production line—a black UK-specification car, destined for the British Motor Heritage collection—bringing total production to 224,817. On same day, the AML consortium says that it will present an offer 'in three weeks time'.
Dec	1979	BL briefly flirt with the MG Boxer project as a means of providing a low-cost MG offshoot from the Triumph TR7 to placate US JRT dealers. The story is 'leaked' to the press, but the idea would be abandoned early in 1980, and MG returned to Austin-Morris from JRT.
20 Dec	1979	BL Ltd announce that the British government has agreed to their recovery plan, which includes a further cash injection of £205 million.
27 Dec	1979	BL and Honda sign an agreement to produce the Bounty, including the purchase of components and tooling.
Jan	1980	500,000th MGB, a black roadster, built at Abingdon, the occasion being marked by a visit from Syd Enever.
12 Jan	1980	Aston Martin announce, '£35 million deal to save MG is due next week'. This would include the acquisition of the factory and continuing negotiations to obtain O-series engines for up to 26,000 cars per annum.
14 Jan	1980	Jaguar-Rover-Triumph issue a press release stating that 'MGBs will be produced until late 1980...available into early 1981. The MG name will be retained and there are plans to build a successor to the MGB when production ends at Abingdon.'
Jan	1980	Triumph TR8 launched (USA only). While pre-production TR8 coupés had been built, all production cars would be convertibles.
7 Mar	1980	BL make an offer to the Aston Martin consortium that would grant it rights to the MG name and permit the outright purchase of the Abingdon factory.
Mar	1980	Triumph TR7 convertible goes on sale in the UK and Europe.
31 Mar	1980	The Aston Martin consortium meets with the BL board and agrees terms for a £30 million deal for an exclusive, world-wide license to use the MG name and to acquire the Abingdon factory.
Apr	1980	Production of Triumph TR7 begins at Rover SD1 factory in Solihull, overlapping with production at Canley.
1 Jul	1980	Aston Martin announces that nearly half the £30 million has been withdrawn by the consortium's supporters; a last hope is to persuade Japanese and Arab backers to provide £12 million. On the same day, Aston Martin announces that it will be making 100 workers redundant—about a quarter of its work-force.
2 Jul	1980	BL announce their intention to dispose of the Abingdon factory. 'During the past 24 hours, we have had meetings (with the consortium) and we feel that the necessary funds are not available,' says William Pratt-Thompson, head of BL International.
4 Jul	1980	Alan Curtis enters talks with two Japanese consortia in a last-ditch effort to acquire funds for the take-over.
9 Jul	1980	BL announce that the MG factory will finally close its doors at the end of October.
Jul	1980	Morris Ital launched. This heavily facelifted Morris Marina is intended as a stop-gap until the launch of the LM11 (Montego) in 1984. Following a crisis meeting at Marlow on 4 July, it is decided to restructure BL in an effort to combat the effects of the growing strength of sterling. The car divisions are reorganized again: JRT is dissolved, and Jaguar becomes separate once more. Volume cars (Austin-Morris) absorbs Rover and Triumph to form a new division called Light Medium Cars, or LMC. A parallel organization—Cars Commercial—looks after marketing and product planning.
Aug	1980	Triumph TR7 production at Canley finishes. Triumph Spitfire discontinued. LM10 approved by BL board for 1983 launch.
2 Oct	1980	The last production-specification MGB bodyshell is produced at the Pressed Steel facility at Stratton St Margaret, on the outskirts of Swindon.
8 Oct	1980	Austin Metro launched. The three-door hatchback—'A Great British Car'—is powered by 1- and 1.3-litre A-Plus engines.
17 Oct	1980	Motor Show '80, held at the NEC, Birmingham, marks the public début of the Austin Metro.
23 Oct	1980	Towards the end of the Motor Show, while media attention is concentrated on the new Metro, the last MGB goes down the line at Abingdon.
24 Oct	1980	MG factory at Abingdon closes its doors on 50 years of history.
Jan	1981	Agreement reached for £990 million of further government funding of BL over the next two years.
26 Jan	1981	BL announce the last MGB derivative: the UK-only MGB and MGB GT LE.
Feb	1981	Henry Ford II acquires one of the last US-specification MGB LEs for the Ford Museum. It is important to note that this is not one of the last MGBs sold in North America, but simply one of the US-only limited edition models.
Mar	1981	BL reach an agreement with Volkswagen to supply gearboxes for LC10.
18/24 Mar	1981	Auction at Abingdon of contents of MG factory: 434 buyers bid for 3600 lots. The sale would realize about £100,000 for BL.
10 May	1981	BL state that, due to the unfavourable US dollar/sterling exchange rate, Jaguar is losing £2 million per month.
13 May	1981	Ray Horrocks of BL announces that the Solihull Rover factory is to close, with the exception of Land Rover work, and that the Rover SD1 will transfer to Cowley, while the TR7 and TR8 sports cars will be discontinued. A further 5000 jobs will be lost. The TR7, TR8 and Rover 3500 (SD1) are all to be withdrawn from the US market, leaving JRT selling Jaguars only.
16 May	1981	Final auction of contents of the Abingdon factory.
15 Jun	1981	BL Motorsport moves to Cowley. Shortly after, plans are formulated for what would become the MG Metro 6R4.
26 Jul	1981	*Sunday Times* carries a story that BL are planning an MG-badged version of the Metro. Other daily papers in the UK and USA follow with the story during the next week.
6 Aug	1981	Jaguar-Rover-Triumph in USA issue a statement to their dealers saying that 'there are no plans to market the Metro in the USA', and that the MG name is 'one of a number' being considered for a performance version of the Metro to be launched in the following spring.
Sep	1981	Austin Allegro discontinued, with the associated loss of 1500 jobs at Longbridge.
Oct	1981	Triumph TR7 and TR8 production suspended at Solihull. Only BL 'sports car' sold in USA now the Jaguar XJS.
7 Oct	1981	Triumph Acclaim—progeny of the BL/Honda Bounty project—is launched. Much work on the Acclaim was carried out by engineering staff at the MG factory at Abingdon, a number of whom transferred to Cowley to complete the project after Abingdon closed.
12 Nov	1981	Ray Horrocks, of BL Cars, and Honda representatives sign an agreement in Tokyo to co-operate on a new executive car, coded XX.
Jan	1982	Banks agree to lend BL Ltd £277 million over 8-10 years.
Jan	1982	David Bache resigns as design director following management disagreements, his place eventually being taken by Roy Axe, formerly of Chrysler.
5 Mar	1982	Austin Ambassador launched as a replacement for the Princess, and to act as another interim model pending launch of LM11 range (Montego).
May	1982	Austin Rover Group formed. The organization encompasses Austin, Morris, MG, Rover and Triumph. Harold J. Musgrove becomes chairman and chief executive.
5 May	1982	The MG Metro 1300 is announced.
1 Jul	1982	BL announce that the Morris name will be phased out—in two year's time!
Jul	1982	Sir Michael Edwardes announces that he is to become the chairman of Mercury, handing over to Sir Austin Bide in September.
22 Oct	1982	MG Metro Turbo announced at the Motor Show. Prototype Toyota MR-J (forerunner of the MR2) shown at the Tokyo Motor Show in the same month.
Nov	1982	Sir Michael Edwardes leaves BL Ltd. His book, *Back From The Brink*, is published soon after.
Feb	1983	First MG Metro 6R4 prototype is handed over by Williams Engineering to Austin Rover Motorsport at Cowley.
1 Mar	1983	The Austin Maestro—the 'Miracle Maestro'—is announced. The range includes the MG 1600 derivative with twin-Weber-carburettor R-series engine.
Apr	1983	Richard Hamblin is head hunted from Ogle to work at Austin Rover as director of interior design, reporting to Roy Axe. Gordon Sked is director of exterior design.
9 Jun	1983	British general election returns a Conservative government under Margaret Thatcher for a second term in office.
11 Jan	1984	Interim facelift for Metro range, including MG versions.
21 Jan	1984	General Motors confirm that they are interested in acquiring Jaguar directly from BL.
24 Feb	1984	MG Metro 6R4 is announced, initially with V6 based upon Rover V8 engine. Patrick Head, of Williams, engaged in development.
31 Mar	1984	MG Metro 6R4 makes its competition début in a rally in Yorkshire, driven by Tony Pond.
25 Apr	1984	The Austin Montego, including a 2-litre, fuel-injected MG version with the O-series engine, is announced. The 1.6-litre versions feature an extensively re-engineered S-series engine, derived from the R-series. The S-series also replaces the R-series in the MG Maestro 1600. The LC10 range has cost £210 million. BL report their first operating profit—of £4.1 million—since 1978.
9 Jun	1984	Triumph name finally discontinued with the end of the Triumph Acclaim (replaced by the Rover 213/216).
19 Jun	1984	Rover 213/216 range launched, the second Rover/Honda joint venture, based on the Honda Ballade/Civic.
19 Jun	1984	British Motor Industry Heritage Trust—BMIHT—announces the appointment of David Bishop as assistant managing director. David was formerly the materials control manager at the Austin-Morris Body Plant at Cowley.
10 Aug	1984	Jaguar privatized. British government retains a 'golden share' until the end of 1990.

Sep	1984	Austin Rover formed as LMC is integrated with Cars Commercial.
3 Oct	1984	MG Maestro 2.0 EFi launched as a replacement for the short-lived 1.6-litre S-series-engined version.
3 Apr	1985	The MG Montego Turbo is announced—'The fastest MG of all time'.
18 Jun	1985	Government approve the next BL/Honda collaborative venture—Project YY—which eventually would lead to the AR8 Rover 200/Honda Concerto.
8 May	1985	Harold Musgrove, chairman and chief executive of Austin Rover, announces the formation of Austin Rover Cars of North America—ARCONA—in partnership with Norman Braman, together with plans to launch the new Austin Rover/Honda XX joint project car in the USA in 1987.
Jun	1985	FISA announce that the current four-wheel-drive Group B cars will be banned from international rallying in 1987, replacing the class with a new Group S, with power limited to 300bhp (223.71kW).
19 Sep	1985	The MG EX-E concept car is unveiled at the Frankfurt Motor Show. British enthusiasts are given their first sight of the car in the UK at the Earls Court Motorfair in October.
1 Nov	1985	MG Metro 6R4 homologated for its international rally début on the RAC Rally. The announcements by FISA in June 1985 and May 1986 would ensure that the 6R4 had a short factory career in Group B rallying.
Dec	1985	Ford express interest in the possibility of acquiring Austin Rover. They are rumoured to be particularly interested in Austin Rover's forthcoming new and highly advanced K-series engine.
Jan	1986	Mazda's board of directors recommends that the Mazda Lightweight Sports Car should be produced; this would become the Mazda Miata or MX-5.
2 Feb	1986	Labour's Roy Hattersley breaks the news in Parliament that General Motors are in talks about buying Leyland Trucks and Land Rover.
6 Feb	1986	Government discontinue the Ford/Austin Rover dialogue.
10 Feb	1986	General Motors planning to sign a deal to acquire BL Trucks and Land Rover 'this month', with a £300 million bid to merge Leyland with their Bedford truck operation. In subsequent weeks, rival bids from Lonrho and an in-house group emerge.
24 Mar	1986	General Motors break off talks about buying Leyland Trucks and Land Rover. Other bids (including a new one from J. C. Bamford in April) will live on for a short time, but will soon be withdrawn.
Apr	1986	MG Maestro introduced in the Japanese market.
Apr	1986	The two principal design studios at Canley are reorganized: Gordon Sked, formerly director of the exterior design studio becomes director of the production design studio (exteriors and interiors), while Richard Hamblin changes from director of the interior design studio to director of the concept design studio (exteriors and interiors. Working in the latter are Graham Lewis, Richard Carter, Jeremy Newman, Ian Beech, Derek Anderson, Gerry McGovern and a team of modellers.
1 May	1986	Graham Day appointed as chairman of BL Ltd.
2 May	1986	Henri Toivonen and Sergio Cresto are killed in their Lancia Delta S4 Group B rally car.
3 May	1986	Following the tragedy of the previous day, Jean-Marie Balestre of FISA announces that Group B rally cars will be banned from January 1987, and that the planned Group S will be abandoned.
Jul	1986	BL Ltd renamed Rover Group Ltd.
15 Jul	1986	Honda/Rover joint project XX launched as the Rover 800 series.
Sep	1986	Harold Musgrove leaves the Rover Group, a casualty of Graham Day's restructuring. Musgrove's former role as chairman and chief executive is divided between Day as chairman and Les Wharton as managing director of Austin Rover.
Autumn	1986	Project Jay (Land Rover Discovery),based upon the Range Rover chassis, receives funding approval.
Dec	1986	David Bishop starts work on the British Motor Heritage MGB bodyshell project.
1 Apr	1987	British Motor Heritage facility at Faringdon is readied for producing MGB bodyshells.
18 Apr	1987	The US-market Sterling (Rover 800) is launched at the New York International Motor Show.
May	1987	The Cowley based Austin Rover Motorsport division is closed down.
11 Jun	1987	British general election returns a Conservative government under Margaret Thatcher for a third term in office.
Nov	1987	Sterling 800 range on sale in the USA.
29 Feb	1988	First MGB bodyshell produced at Faringdon.
1 Mar	1988	Announcement that British Aerospace (BAe) are in talks with the government regarding the possible acquisition of the Rover Group. Other manufacturers (at the Geneva Motor Show) express surprise.
30 Mar	1988	Announcement that Rover Group has been sold to British Aerospace for £150 million, and the government is to write off the group's £800 million debt. Since 1975, the company has received £2.98 billion in state aid.
13 Apr	1988	British Motor Heritage launch MGB bodyshell.
May	1988	Rover buys Norman Braman's shares in Sterling. Sterling's president, Ray Ketchledge, is replaced by Chris Woodwark.
22 Oct	1988	MG Maestro Turbo is announced at Birmingham Motor Show, to be built by Tickford and known officially as the MG Turbo. Surprisingly, Rover gives the car neither a launch fanfare nor very much promotion.
19 Dec	1988	A proposal for an MG-badged coupé, based upon the planned cabriolet derivative of the Rover 200 (R8), is photographed for the archives.
Jan	1989	The Rover board is restructured, Graham Day handing over most responsibility to George Simpson. The board members are reduced from 36 to 11, the principal aim being to integrate Rover and Land Rover engineering staff and to create directors of Small, Medium and Large Cars, and Four-Wheel-Drive, as well as for Petrol Engines and Diesel Engines. John Towers becomes production engineering director, and Graham Morris takes over as Sterling president from Chris Woodwark.
9 Feb	1989	Mazda Miata unveiled to the US public at the Chicago Auto Show. For Europe, the Mazda would be renamed MX-5 and make its British début in October 1989. The mid-engined Honda NSX, an exotic Ferrari-style sports car in the spirit of the MG EX-E, also makes its world début in Chicago.
Jul	1989	Planning meeting held at Canley, at which Roger Parker's home-built MGB V8 EFi roadster is displayed.
14 Jul	1989	Honda announces that it will invest £300 million in its first European assembly plant at Swindon, not far from Rover's Stratton St Margaret body plant, and will take a 20 per cent equity stake in Rover. The latter also takes a 20 per cent stake in HUM (Honda of the UK Manufacturing).
18 Sep	1989	Directors conference—known internally as a 'scrum'—at which Graham Day poses the question of whether the company could produce a new sports car. Soon after, Project Phoenix would be initiated to investigate the form of a new MG sports car. Three concepts would be explored—PR1, PR2 and PR3—with different engine/drive train configurations (see Appendix 5). Officially, 'PR' stands for Phoenix Route, but eventually PR3 would be unofficially dubbed 'Pocket Rocket'.
11 Oct	1989	New Rover 200 range—Project YY— based upon the Honda Concerto, launched at the London Motorfair. First production application of Rover's in-house designed K-series engine, in 1.4-litre guise. Mazda shows the MX-5, and Lotus unveils the new front-wheel-drive Elan sports car, with 1.6-litre Isuzu engine. Later that month, the Elan would also appear at the Tokyo show, where Toyota would unveil the second-generation MR2 sports car.
Oct	1989	Roy Axe takes charge of Rover's advanced design studio (formerly under Richard Hamblin, who is now working on Project Phoenix), with the specific task of exploring potential models for the US market. At the same time, Dr Stan Manton becomes director of concept engineering and design.
Oct	1989	Contracts placed by Richard Hamblin with subcontractors for PR1, PR2 and PR3 running prototypes.
2 Nov	1989	After 18 hours of negotiations, Ford, which had failed to acquire Rover and MG in 1985, makes an agreed cash offer for Jaguar; shareholders accept on 1 December.
28 Mar	1990	Executive committee gives approval for 'special projects' activities, which would lead to the formation of Rover Special Products—RSP—intended to carry out feasibility exercises through to running prototypes.
Mar	1990	Work starts on British Motor Heritage MGB V8 project, the prototype being built at BMH's Snitterfield storage facility by Mark Gamble. The car would be completed in May 1990.
2 May	1990	Launch of revamped Metro (Rover 100 outside UK) with 1.1- and 1.4-litre K-series engines. Top of the range badged GTi rather than MG.
Jun	1990	Rover board reviews PR1, PR2, PR3 and PR4 (the last similar to PR2, but with a steel body). PR3 increased in size.
19 Sep	1990	Graham Day tells the press at the Motor Show preview, 'We are going to do a proper MG.'
Jan	1991	Rover commissions two external consultants—MGA and ADC—to develop styling clays based upon packaging of PR3 (mid-engine) layout. In the meantime, feasibility studies into other sports car packages continue. John Towers becomes managing director in charge of product supply.
Apr	1991	Rover Special Products undertakes research to establish what the MG badge means to potential customers.
May	1991	The two styling models for PR3 are presented for appraisal by Rover. The executive committee approves PR3 vehicle concept from development through to 'D Zero'.
Jun	1991	Customer clinic to test MG sports car concepts, exhibiting early PR3 styling models, the RV8 and PR5. Feedback from this would result in abandonment of pop-up headlamps and also of the PR5 proposal, which is seen as being a Jaguar/Aston Martin type car, rather than an MG. Rover board grants approval for RV8 to proceed.
Jul	1991	PR3 proposal now features 1.6-litre K-series engine with optional supercharger.
9 Aug	1991	Rover Group announce that they are dropping the US Sterling marque with immediate effect; Range Rover not affected, and servicing back-up for Sterling models to be maintained.

Sep	1991	Gerry McGovern, at Rover's Canley studios, begins work on the exterior styling clay for the definitive PR3.
Autumn	1991	The end of MG-badged saloons, with the phasing out of the MG Maestro and Montego 2.0i.
Dec	1991	Roy Axe retires from Rover and forms his own independent consultancy. Rover design now in the charge of Gordon Sked.
Jan	1992	The MG RV8 prototype, based on DEV1, is presented at the Rover dealers conference in Birmingham.
22 Jan	1992	Exterior styling of McGovern's PR3 clay model approved.
3 Mar	1992	Rover 200 Cabriolet launched at Geneva (Project Tracer, which could almost have become an MG). Rover 800 coupé also launched at Geneva.
Mar	1992	Styling of PR3 approved, followed by style ratification: feasibility, manufacturing, design, etc.
Mar	1992	MG Design Day: an event held at Canley to which over 250 Rover staff are invited and asked to give their opinions on what they consider to be essential elements of an MG sports car.
9 Apr	1992	British general election returns a Conservative government for a fourth term in office, despite contrary predictions of opinion polls.
Jun	1992	Teaser brochure for the RV8 issued, with a retouched studio photograph of the DEV1 prototype and the legend, 'The Shape of Things to Come'.
1 Aug	1992	Graham Irvine becomes director in charge of the Adder project, and immediately begins planning production.
18 Sep	1992	MG Car Club, MG Owners' Club and others invited to a special preview of the MG RV8 at Canley.
20 Oct	1992	MG RV8 sports car unveiled by Rover chairman John Towers at the press preview of the Birmingham Motor Show, along with Rover 200 coupé.
Nov	1992	Rover board approves 1.8-litre K-series with optional VVC high-performance version.
Dec	1992	PR3 design signed off. Mayflower and Rover settle outline agreement, which calls for Mayflower to raise £24 million to invest in the project for the design, engineering and production of PR3 bodyshells.
Mar	1993	Rover board gives PR3 the green light for production, with launch planned for 1995.
31 Mar	1993	*Financial Times* reports that Mayflower will invest £24.2 million in the development of PR3 bodyshells, with delivery expected to begin in 1995. This is part of a rights issue intended to raise £34.6 million. Production expected to reach in excess of 10,000 per annum, with an annual sales value of £20 million, for a six-year contract.
31 Mar	1993	First production MG RV8 completed at Cowley (chassis no. 251, British Racing Green metallic, VIN no. SARRAWBMBMG000251) and destined for the British Motor Heritage museum. The first six customer cars would be completed on 19 April.
Oct	1993	A Woodcote Green MG RV8 makes the type's Japanese début at the Tokyo Motor Show, where Rover Japan find themselves swamped with orders.
13 Jan	1994	The first batch of 46 RV8s leaves Southampton for Japan.
31 Jan	1994	Sale of Rover Group to BMW AG announced, at a price of £800 million.
21 Feb	1994	Honda announces that it will relinquish the 20 per cent shareholding in Rover, which it took out in July 1989, thus also requiring Rover to release its 20 per cent holding in Honda's UK manufacturing subsidiary.
18 Mar	1994	Title and ownership of the Rover Group officially transferred to BMW AG. The Rover Group comprises two sub-groups: Rover Group Holdings plc, Birmingham (with 89 subsidiaries) and Rover Group USA Inc., Lanham, Maryland (with four subsidiaries).
Jun-Jul	1994	Styling clinic tours UK, France, Germany and Italy.
Jul	1994	D1-build pre-production examples of MGF, using much of the final tooling.
Sep	1994	Pilot production of MGF under way; bodies painted using water-based paints.
13 Jan	1995	Mark Blundell test drives MGF at Gaydon test track.
6 Feb	1995	Preview of MGF for MG Car Club, MG Owners' Club, Octagon Car Club and others at Gaydon.
20/24 Feb	1995	Dealer launch for the MGF at Gaydon.
7 Mar	1995	All-new, mid-engined MGF sports car launched at Geneva Motor Show. Two versions are shown: one with a standard 16-valve, 1.8-litre K-series engine, intended for sale in July, and a 1.8 VVC variable-valve-timing version to follow in October 1995.
Apr	1995	First M-build pre-production cars assembled.
16 Jun	1995	Meeting to discuss the development of a competition version of the MGF for Japan.
4 Aug	1995	First volume-production MGF built at Longbridge CAB2.
8 Sep	1995	First car available for standard run and assessment, as part of the evaluation for the Japanese racing MGF.
23 Sep	1995	First customer MGF deliveries.
Oct	1995	MGF makes its UK and Japanese Motor Show débuts. At the Tokyo show, a prototype racing MGF is shown, heralding a proposed one-make racing series in Japan in 1996.
22 Oct	1995	The first shipment of 242 MGFs leaves Southampton for Japan. A batch of 64 RV8s is also dispatched.
14 Nov	1995	Initial discussions between Roversport and subcontractors for race-specification MGFs.
22 Nov	1995	Last MG RV8—a Woodcote Green car (VIN no. SARRAWBMBMG002233) bound for Japan—goes down the production line at Cowley. Photographs taken on the day would show the work-force proudly displaying a plaque proclaiming the chassis number as '2203', which no doubt will trip up historians in the future.
23 Nov	1995	Initial feedback from subcontractors on racing MGF. This would be followed by Roversport issuing a job specification on 8 December, after which the companies would be invited to present their proposals to Roversport between 13 and 21 December.
22 Dec	1995	Letter of intent sent to successful tenderer for the Japanese racing MGF project—Janspeed of Salisbury.
22 Jan	1996	Rover makes available the first MGFs for conversion by Janspeed. Following the issue of the initial kit of components by Roversport on 1 February, Janspeed would have to ensure that the first 25 cars would be available by 24 February, an impressive feat.
1 Feb	1996	Rover announces that the MGF has been awarded the title of 'Japanese Import Car of The Year'. By this time, over 300 MGFs have been sold in Japan, and a further 1200 orders have been taken.
4 Feb	1996	Tony Pond and a team of support staff return to the UK, following four weeks of intensive racing development testing of the MGF in South Africa. They have covered 2431 miles (3912.21km) at Kyalami, Midvaal, Goldfields and Gerotek, and achieved 14.2mpg (5.03km/litre) overall, using 95 ULG petrol.
21 Feb	1996	Test session at Castle Combe for a group of mainly Japanese journalists to drive the MGF development car, fresh from its trip to South Africa and prior to strip-down. The first Janspeed car, 001, is also present, but is not run on the circuit.
22 Mar	1996	First MGF racing cars for Japan and France are exported from Southampton.
1 Jun	1996	Following a surprise announcement in April, John Towers leaves Rover. There is no immediate successor as chief executive.
1 Sep	1996	Walter Hasselkus—from BMW—becomes the new chief executive of the Rover Group.

The above table is by no means a comprehensive list of the events that have affected MG, but it includes details of the major events of significance to the marque's development. Some of the entries have no obvious MG connection, until the wider implications are considered. For example, the January 1975 launch of the Triumph TR7 in the USA coincided with the withdrawal of the MGB GT from the USA. Similarly, the European launch of the TR7 coincided with the withdrawal of the MGB from the same market. Furthermore, the events of the last years of the 1970s clearly demonstrate the tenuous position of all of the BL factories, not just the MG plant at Abingdon.

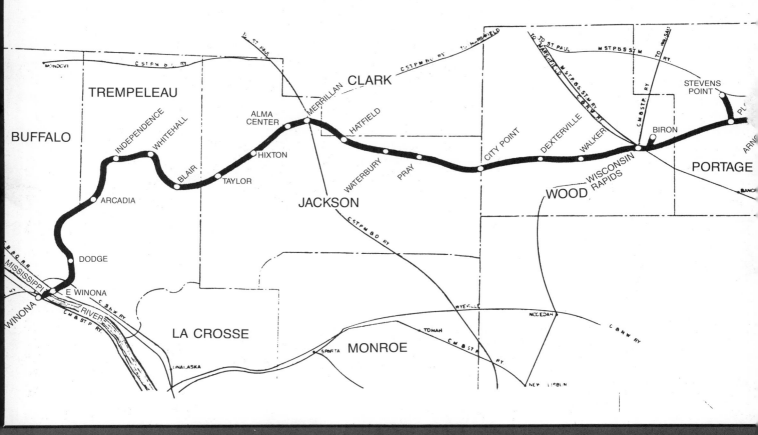

GREEN BAY ROUTE

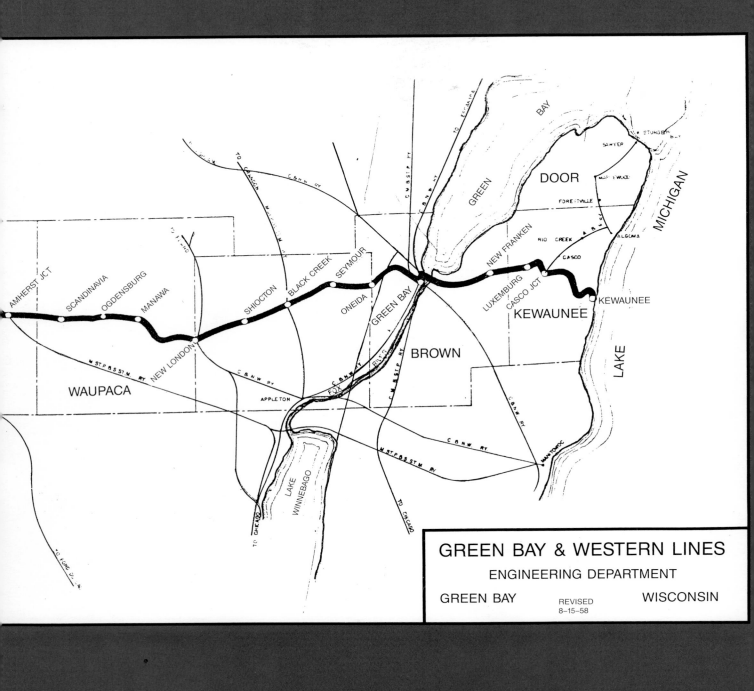

GREEN BAY & WESTERN LINES

ENGINEERING DEPARTMENT

GREEN BAY   REVISED   WISCONSIN
                   8-15-58

Green Bay & Western

The First 111 Years

By Stan Mailer

HUNDMAN PUBLISHING INC.
5115 MONTICELLO DRIVE   EDMONDS, WA 98020

Hundman Publishing, Inc.
5115 Monticello Drive
Edmonds, Washington 98020

Library of Congress No. 88-81184
ISBN No. 0-945434-01-4
Dustjacket Painting by Larry Fisher
Design by Cathy Hundman Lee
Typography by A-2-Z Graphics

DEDICATION

This history is dedicated to GB&W men and their
families since 1866, and to those who happened to take a few
photographs along the way, and to K----, and 5-28-67.

"This day is called the feast of Crispian . . ."
— HENRY V

FOREWORD

As a teenage railbuff, I often looked at a Wisconsin state map which had a thin, black line identified as "GB&W" across its midsection. During the warm days of June, our family often journeyed to the north woods, which meant crossing the GB&W at Plover, one hundred miles from our Madison home and 82 miles from Green Bay. On one 1949 day, heat "gandies" rose from GB&W's track to the east. Was there a train coming? There was! Presently, with the sorrowful moan of its steamboat whistle, Extra 402 rolled solemnly up to Plover's water tank, pushing Jordan car X-190. Unknown to me was 402's status, that of limited and fleeting magnificence, like a nightly moth, assured of imminent extinction.

Extra 402 swayed my imagination, with its green-and-white edged run boards, sleek, modern lines and decidedly new condition. One trip deserved another, which fell on the fateful day of the Scandinavia wreck scene. After the excitement, which denied my mother an otherwise boring day, we visited Wisconsin Rapids, where I saw, for the last time, steaming 400-class Mikados, just months before the end.

Over the years, I collected photos of locomotives and my interest in Green Bay & Western continued. Later photographs were an improvement over that first clumsy shot of Extra 402. I kept that photo though, which is now part of a larger group amassed in search of a book on Green Bay & Western, an ultimate growth of that fleeting day almost forty years ago when Extra 402 was alive.

Stanley H. Mailer
July 17, 1988

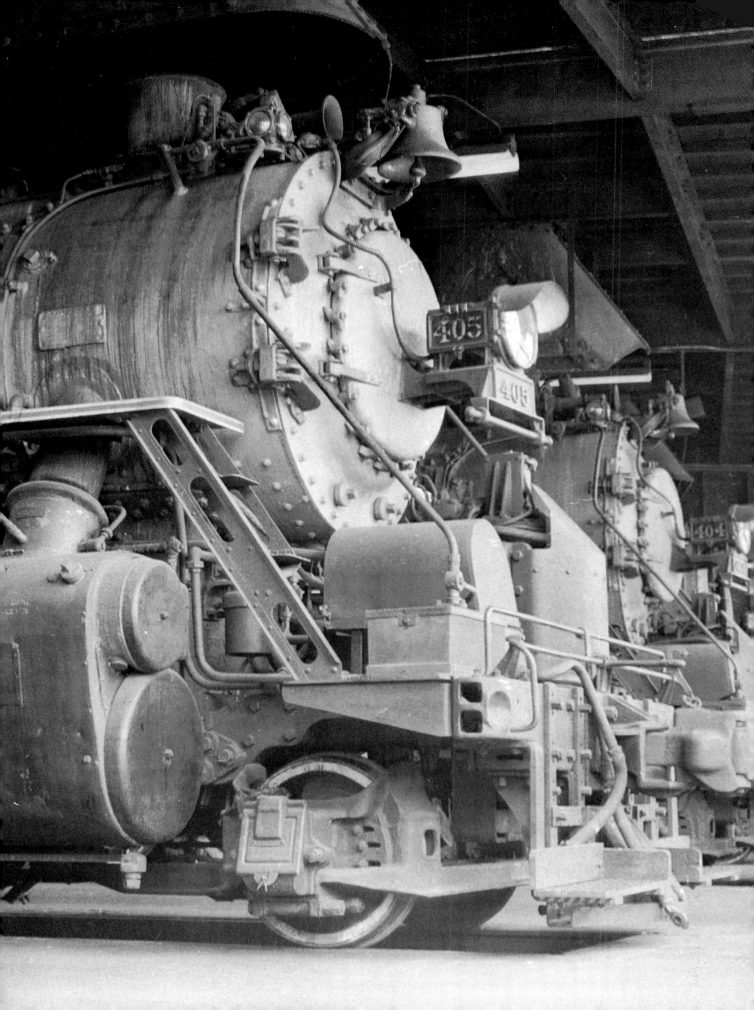

TABLE OF CONTENTS

INTRODUCTION

Thirty years of spectator interest in Wisconsin's Green Bay and Western Railroad reached a focal point in the early 1970's when a proposed magazine article grew beyond that medium's capacity. An introduction to then-President H. Weldon McGee led to a proposal for a full-scale GB&W history, which was encouraged and aided immeasurably by Mr. McGee. The timing coincided with high adventure on the financial frontier, as GB&W moved steadily toward sale to its present owner, Itel Corporation of San Francisco, California.

This book is largely the product of visits to scores of GB&W employees, active and retired, who volunteered details of its long, misty history. It involved ranking officers, their relatives, craftsmen of operations and shops, and men long separated from GB&W daily affairs. Encouraged by good friends to complete this study, I am indebted to Ray Buhrmaster, Dan Luedke, Jim Scribbins and Tom Van Dreese for their encouragement and aid, all giving generously of their time in the project.

The GB&W story took me to New York State, to Chicago's Federal Records Center, and to The State Historical Society of Wisconsin's archives. Also involved were University of Wisconsin-Green Bay's library and the good offices of Merrillan Edwards at the University of Wisconsin-Milwaukee's Microforms Service. Professor Fred I. Olson aided in research in several instances. I was fortunate enough to do extensive work in the old headquarters building of GB&W before the February 11, 1977 fire which took away many informational treasures. Generous cooperation from Winona County Historical Society and Marie Dorsch aided in the search for Winona & South-Western Railway facts. Green Bay's Neville Public Museum also aided, as did the University of Michigan's Bentley Library for Ann Arbor Railroad material. Stanley Greene, Chan Harris and Roger Schroeder of Sturgeon Bay provided valuable material on Ahnapee & Western Railway, also aided and abetted by Jim Roubal. George Huber lent letters of his grandfather, which dealt with his tragic end.

The long-time search for photos — over 15 years — led to some triumphs and tragedies. Joseph Schultz loaned his grandfather's collection, as did several other employees. Railfans proved an inadequate source until the 1980's when several fine collections yielded treasures of action shots and scenes which enriched our understanding of GB&W.

To Jim and Barbara Scribbins, and Fred Tonne who proofread the body copy, go profound thanks. Many suggestions were volunteered by all three. Jim's contribution of many fine photos to this work highlight the last days of steam on GB&W. C. C. Tinkham and Earl Ruhland also deserve credit for their photo contributions. Any errors or deletions are the fault of the author and due to the need to end the search.

Today the GB&W moves steadily toward what may be a surprising and bright future. Its personnel wrestle daily with the problem of survival in bittersweet times in which railroading seems to be rising head-up out of hard times, a hopeful new era. It is now light years from being an orphan short line and is surrounded by several others equally short, bent on continued and modest success. We wish them well in their endeavors.

1

BEGINNINGS

L.C. PORTER'S ELEVATOR, STORAGE & COMMISSION. 1877. PORTER & MOWBRAY'S FLOURING MILLS. 1874.

WINONA, MINNESOTA.

The BROOKLYN's quickstepping sternwheel beat a steady, agreeable rhythm in Lake Pepin's waters between the high bluffs of Minnesota and Wisconsin. It was June 14, 1867, and at 8 a.m. sharp, a young man of 26 and formerly of Massachusetts, David Marsh Kelly, hurriedly penned a letter in his cabin. The letter was addressed to Nathanial Marsh Edwards, also of Massachusetts, who presently resided across the state from the broad Missisippi in Appleton, Wisconsin. Smoke from the steamer's twin stacks carried eastward on the fresh morning wind as Kelly was writing of his high adventure. Even in that broadening of the Missisippi at Lake City, Minnesota, the boat pushed hard against high water's rush. BROOKLYN had left Prairie du Chien, Wisconsin on the 12th; now it steamed out of Lake City into stiff currents on the final lap to St. Paul. The new vessel and its significant cargo had made nearly half of the 1180-mile round trip from Green Bay via the Green Bay & Missisippi Canal Company's waterway across the Badger State. BROOKLYN carried symbolic trade goods and a message to the Minnesota governing body.

Kelly described the high June water en route to Wabasha, the cannon salute given them there, and the enthusiastic handshakes at dockside. The Mayor of Wabasha greeted them, as did Artemus T. Sharpe, a director of the Green Bay & Lake Pepin Railway, still a-borning over the past year. Kelly was destined for a special place in the history of both the railway and canal, for a cross-state artery of commerce would spring from Green Bay's efforts to link Great Lakes waters with the Great River. It was the underlying cause for BROOKLYN's flat bottom to be found in unfamiliar waters. Mr. Sharpe had set a fine table in his American House dining room at Wabasha, carefully thinking of his Green Bay guests. Among the guests was Kelly's companion Talbot C. Dousman, and others in the forefront of bay city commerce. Enthusiasm prevailed, causing the Wabashavians to ride BROOKLYN to Read's Landing, several miles upstream. After the steamer departed from new and old friends, it was caught in open lake by a violent summer storm which thundered for nearly six hours, forcing it to seek refuge inshore. BROOKLYN arrived in St. Paul nine days out of Green Bay, delivering forty tons of goods in what was largely a symbolic gesture designed to awaken interest in the new route. Each newspaper on the route was informed of the gesture, with few lacking details of the voyage or missing its significance; Mr. Kelly and friends made sure of that.

BROOKLYN returned to Green Bay in six days, stopping at Wabasha downbound to receive another bit of symbolism: "General" Sharpe publicly contracted for 100,000 shingles of Green Bay manufacture to be shipped to Wabasha via the next boat or by the *first train on the Green Bay & Lake Pepin Railway*. Sharpe and codirector William T. Dugan of GB&LP's first directorate had received samples of the then-important product, which was shown about Wabasha as a token of offered commerce. The triumphant boat had accomplished its public relations mission. It had called attention to the waterway dream, alive for twenty years, in which a Wisconsin canal would open the interior to economical transport on the Missisippi via Green Bay and the Great Lakes chain.

Left: The flour mills of Winona were among that city's strong young industries which caused Winona's credit to prevail over Wabasha's. Date of photo is about 1875.

The trip of the 133-foot BROOKLYN was the high point of the canal's unfortunate history, as it suffered many setbacks and pressure from the state's railroads. After the Civil War, ancestors of the Milwaukee Road held sway in Wisconsin transportation with the Chicago & North-Western Railway, the instrument of "hated Chicago commerce," close on its heels. Control of Missisippi river trade was also in Milwaukee hands, as the river packet lines had been consolidated. This development brought on the "Antimonopoly Revolt," which actively opposed the river line's tyranny. In 1866 a St. Paul convention tried to regulate rates. War taxes had taken 20% of Milwaukee & St. Paul Railway's gross earnings, which customers paid for with increased rates. Wisconsin and Minnesota delegations roasted the monopolies and advocated river improvement. In the end the postwar recession settled the matter and brought on a new era of expansion in the Missisippi Valley.

Excess products being siphoned off to the South and the long sea voyage to New York via New Orleans had controlled rates across Wisconsin up until 1860. The Civil War closed this alternative, causing the shipping of goods to become east-west. When the Erie Canal opened in 1825, New York merchants had reached out to capture the Great Lakes trade, while Lake carriers moved finished goods west and raw materials east. The Upper Missisippi Valley specialized in grain which moved east from Iowa and Minnesota, collecting at several river grain ports. Prices could be manipulated by elevators and middlemen, but mostly by railroads. By Civil War time, La Crosse and Prairie du Chien, Wisconsin, as well as Dunleith and Fulton, Illinois, were grain terminals run by railroads which hauled the crop eastward. On the other shore of Wisconsin, Milwaukee vied with Chicago for grain traffic, while other Wisconsin port cities lusted for a slice of the same loaf.

The Green Bay Advocate, a proponent of opening western commerce, rhetorically asked: "What had BROOKLYN's voyage proved?" Its answer: a permanent route eastward meant Minnesota and Northern Iowa grain could be delivered to Green Bay for less than to Chicago or Milwaukee, and Green Bay was closer to Buffalo New York, the final destination. BROOKLYN had shown interested parties the logic of a Wisconsin canal system by its June adventure. However, facts showed that support was on the wane, the canal company faced insolvency, and the real hero was high water. The *Advocate* observed that interest in the river might instead bring about the railroad, which was chartered in Spring, 1866: It was the Green Bay & Lake Pepin Railway Co.

When Captain W. W. Neff piloted BROOKLYN's 30-foot beam through June's high waters in the canal, the troubled waterway was already fading due to its troubled western portion. BROOKLYN went through only by dint of flood water. The Wisconsin River section had not received adequate attention. It was a sandy, treacherous channel which shifted quickly. Logically, the money received from stockholders was spent on the Fox River end, at population centers, which would guarantee a return on investment. Further draws upon stockholders were required. Yet, by the time of BROOKLYN's trip, the canal became only a localized system for short-haul steamers and barge traffic. Neither BROOKLYN nor any other boat tried to reach the Missisippi again. Captain Neff's sternwheeler spent its life around Oshkosh, where its keel had been laid in the Spring of 1866.

In the wake of the Civil War, a fresh desire for free, new lands in the west excited a population weary from conflict. The rush to settlements west of Wisconsin was also an opportunity for

eastern capitalists, whose view was more empirical. The canal investors and their men at the new front struggled with a white elephant which faced increasingly railroad-oriented times. It was into this climate that David M. Kelly came early in 1867, bent on finding fortune in the Badger State.

Kelly was born in Hamilton, Essex County, Massachusetts, February 11, 1841. He received his education in Haverhill, twenty miles away, near his parent's final home. Kelly's father was George Washington Kelly who had settled into a pastorate at Hamilton's Congregational Church in 1834. He married Mary Marsh in 1835 but had to resign his duties in 1849 because of illness, from which he never recovered. Thus, David and his sister Sarah lived under their maternal grandfather's roof. David studied law and was well equipped to handle a contracting career in later years. After Fort Sumpter, Kelly enlisted at age twenty. Joining the 50th Mass. Volunteers, Company F, he became Quartermaster Sergeant on November 12, 1862. Kelly served two more hitches, coming out in December 1864. By early 1865, the law firm of Merrill and Kelly appeared in Haverhill; Kelly was formally admitted to the bar at the March term of Essex County Superior Court on March 17, 1865. Kelly was eulogized as ". . . an active, industrious young man, and will promptly transact the business entrusted to him."

Kelly's partner, Henry N. Merrill, ran ads which read: "Pensions, Bounty and Back Pay secured with all possible promptness." Kelly defended a few cases in court, such as a liquor nuisance complaint. Merrill and Kelly served the Freedmen's Relief Association but, with a large number of lawyers in practice in Haverhill, Kelly sought a more active life elsewhere. In February 1867 he wrote to his cousin Nat in Appleton. An offer from one John A. Hill in a Leavenworth, Kansas wholesale paper business was turned down. After seeing Wisconsin, he considered that he would be intellectually and morally better off in Appleton than Leavenworth. Kelly soon had the intense life that he apparently wanted. He faced ten years in the forefront during the building of Green Bay & Lake Pepin Railway.

The backdrop of Kelly's early days in Wisconsin included the unfortunate farm mortgage episode. Fraud in securities, sales and exchanges of farmstead mortgages were exposed in the panic of 1857. The outcome cast a decade-long pall over railroad expansion in the state. During that time Wisconsin farmers' homes were nearly forfeited to shady dealings. They resorted to organized resistance, temporarily made legal, to thwart eviction. The result benefited Iowa and Minnesota, for money was therefore available to extend lines west of the Mississippi. This was the beginning of the Wisconsin Granger Movement.

The canal era in Wisconsin was short-lived, for it was plagued by both financial troubles and the rapid increase in railroad transportation. Several systems were promoted but only one actually approached completion. Principal transport routes led from port cities inland, east to west, from Milwaukee, Racine, Kenosha, Sheboygan and Green Bay. The Milwaukeeans managed to generate the greatest canal success just before statehood in 1848.

The Milwaukee and Rock River Canal of 1838 is best remembered for the depredations of Byron Kilbourn, whose talents included an eye for unsavory securities dealings. The Milwaukee and Mississippi Rail Road Company was incorporated in 1847 and grew to the giant controlling influence in Wisconsin commerce in the 19th Century. Milwaukee's canal began and ended as a highly localized product. The chief opposition to the Milwaukee waterway came from a far more natural route from Green Bay to the Mississippi, which gained currency and a land grant to finance it: The Fox-Wisconsin canal system.

Congress granted Wisconsin Territory 260,000 acres in 1846, which would finance the Fox-Wisconsin waterway. Nonetheless, progress on the canal lagged until Morgan L. Martin, a Green Bay lawyer and canal investor, assisted by finding outside capital

Below: Lake & River Transportation Co. sternwheeler BROOKLYN. It was this vessel that made the historic trip from Green Bay to St. Paul in 1867 with David Marsh Kelly and others from Green Bay aboard.
OSHKOSH PUBLIC MUSEUM

CANAL LOCK AT APPLETON WIS.
NO.3

Above: Lock on the lower Fox River at Appleton, Wisconsin, circa 1910. Steamer J. E. CARTER is downbound in a latter-day scene. The canal system was used locally for bulk shipments until about World War II.

to motivate the project. The Fox and Wisconsin Improvement Company was the result. In 1853 it undertook completion of the waterway in exchange for the lion's share of the land grant. The new company moved to construct necessary locks, canals and buildings, bringing investors from New York into the project. Martin involved William J. Averill, Erastus Corning and Isaac Seymour in New York City. Isaac Seymour was associated with Martin's brother in New York's Bank of North America. Locally, Otto Tank was involved. He, Martin and Corning were respective presidents until 1857 when the great panic's negative effects reduced business to dismal levels.

The improvement company twice persuaded Congress to amend the land grant which raised the acreage by 425,000, easing the concern of the investors considerably. The canal was operable to Portage, where a short connection through marshy headwaters of the Fox River put it into the larger Wisconsin and open water to the Missisippi. In November 1855 the first boat passed from Green Bay to Lake Winnebago, and there was doubt that there would be enough boats to handle the canal tonnage that was accumulating. Land was selling well; the poorest averaged $3.60 per acre, with eight percent interest on delayed payments. Erastus Corning, as president of New York Central Railroad, assured all that his railroad would "operate a regular line of propellors from Buffalo to Green Bay." This gave the new canal eastern ties needed to stimulate business. The traditional line of "Buffalo Boats," which brought many settlers to Wisconsin in the 19th Century would continue until the 1890's.

The "Panic of '57" changed business optimism. Land sales fell, foreclosures grew ominously and the stock market wilted. The canal was incomplete and efforts to save the company were in vain. According to canal authority Joseph Schafer, Morgan L. Martin had charged that, by February of 1866, New

Yorkers had maneuvered the F&WI into a compromising financial position. This forced the sale and the formation of the Green Bay & Missisippi Canal Company. There were nine purchasers; among them were Erastus Corning, Morgan Martin, Horatio and John Seymour, John Magee and Samuel Marsh. Marsh had come into the F&WI in the late 1850's and it was he who contributed $128,780 to a bidding pool which was used to claim the company. He was also an officer of the New York & Erie Railroad and owned a New York printing and dying firm on Staten Island. The assets, including the land, went to the easterners. The land amounted to about 375,000 acres in Dunn, Eau Claire, Clark, Wood, Portage, Waupaca, Marquette, Shawano, Brown and Door counties and "other of the best portion of the state." Samuel Marsh also held title to other lands in Waupaca county. The listed counties lie close to the line that was taken by the Green Bay & Lake Pepin Railway when it was built, essentially replacing the canal.

The Green Bay & Missisippi Canal Company was formed in June 1866 and Samuel Marsh served as president in his turn. The headquarters address was listed as New York City and Nat Edwards was the company's chief engineer. David Kelly served on the directorate and headed the Lake & River Transportation Company which operated sternwheelers on the lower Fox. Kelly managed the actual carrying arm of the L&RT and no doubt gained some first-hand knowledge of frontier transport problems. He lived in Appleton during the first years and frequently came to Green Bay on shipping business. It was at this time, at Kelly's direction, that BROOKLYN made its publicized run.

From its sale date, the canal steadily lost ground. The shifting sands of the Wisconsin River required far too much money to make a permanent channel. Depth ran only three and one-half feet and efforts to raise it proved ineffective. A canal convention in November 1868, at Prairie du Chien, enlisted the interest of surrounding states to raise an appropriation in Congress to allow a five-foot draught. The action failed. Coincidentally, a full engineering survey by Army General G. K. Warren proposed a full-blown canal the length of and alongside the river, estimated at a cost of $4 million. The convention, which had relied upon the Warren report as a spur to Congress, failed to receive enough support. The consensus of the convention was that they would not enter into a partnership with GB&MCCo. It instead proposed a government buy-out, effected in 1872 for $325,000. Franchises which included water power were not sold, were deemed unnecessary for navigation purposes. The GB&MCCo. remained an entity into the 1980's. Thus, "the game" had gone full circle from public works to private to public again. After substantial expenditure the Wisconsin River portion was given up as unworkable; the Fox River end remained largely intact and operated modestly into the 1950's.

Below: The well-remembered PAUL L. passes through Oshkosh upstream to Lake Butte Des Mortes. This steamer was one of the last of the grand old boats on the Fox River.

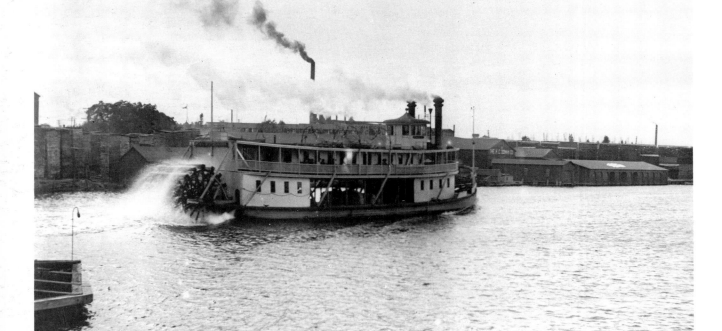

The three views above show Green Bay in 1889. In the first photo, which looks southwest, GBWSTP's depot and coal docks dominate the west side of the Fox River. The center photo shows CM&STP tracks serving industries in the foreground. C&NW tracks are on the opposite side of the river. This photo is looking west. In the final photo, the C&NW yard and depot are seen in the distance with the old Elmore & Kelly grain docks.

STATE HISTORICAL SOCIETY OF WISCONSIN COLLECTION

The competition for railroads between Lake Michigan and the Missisippi was not confined to Wisconsin. Lines west of Chicago made an all-rail connection eastward past the south shore of the lake. Eastern roads were also built west from Buffalo which shortened the time and distance to the midwest. Before the railroads linked Chicago to Buffalo, Buffalo became the "jumping off place" for the new northwest and a frontier for westbound traffic.

WALK-IN-THE-WATER, a pioneer sidewheeler, operated on Lake Erie as early as 1818 and opened upstream navigation to investors. Steamer routes reached out to Toledo, Detroit and finally to Wisconsin as navigation was improved. Buffalo evolved into a primary grain port and a junction for many eastern railroads to forward tonnage to other carriers. Between the 1830's and the 1870's, every sizable port city in Wisconsin generated interest in becoming the port to transfer traffic to the interior via canal, road or railroad. Naturally, each port felt the need to build its own railroad after the technology was proven sound.

In 1850 Milwaukee thrust its pioneer Milwaukee and Missisippi Railroad toward the Great River. Just before the "Panic of '57," it was completed to Prairie du Chien. Rival La Crosse & Milwaukee, also Milwaukee-based, was built between 1855 and 1858, merging with M&M by its completion date. During the speculative boom of the mid-1850's, Racine, Kenosha, Sheboygan and Manitowoc all started companies bent on running to the river, with varied success.

The Racine and Missisippi Railroad went to Savanna, Illinois via Beloit, Wisconsin and Freeport, Illinois, reaching the river in time for merger with the Milwaukee. Kenosha, in turn, built a line toward Rockford, Illinois to rival its neighbor Racine, which merged with C&NW about the same time. North of Mil-

The riverboats and the Green Bay-Buffalo steamers operated under David Kelly's management. The New York Central added the propellors COMET and ROCKET in May of 1867 to participate in the Green Bay trade. They were built by Peck and Masters of Cleveland, Ohio, with machinery by Cuyahoga Steam Furnace Co. Both boats were 181 feet long; COMET displaced 621 tons, while ROCKET displaced 611. Kelly personally had them in his name from November of 1867, running them in conjunction with Dousman and Elmore's dock and elevator which gave the Buffalo boats access to Oshkosh and Berlin.

In 1868 the boats were transferred to the L&RTCo. registry where they remained until 1871. While under the registry of the L&RTCo., the vessel COMET had a series of collisions in 1869. The first sank Canadian sidewheeler SILVER SPRAY off the Port Huron Lighthouse. COMET stood off and picked up the sinking steamer's fifty passengers and crew. In October Kelly wrote Nat Edwards that COMET had once again collided — this time with the steamer HUNTER, eight miles below Detroit, again sinking her opposite number.

COMET managed to steam into shallow water before she too filled and settled on a bar. Captain William Gaylord of COMET wired that it would be refloated immediately. Kelly left for Detroit to untangle the affair. Samuel Marsh showed concern in a letter to Nat Edwards stating that Mr. Kelly had much to do in looking after the steamboat accident. He seemed to have done this very well, settling the difficulties in a manner satisfactory to the L&RTCo. COMET was canvassed below, pumped out and was underway to Green Bay November 15, 1869. The cargo, all below decks, was sold off in Detroit as salvage.

As manager, Kelly was required to go to Buffalo in the winter of 1868 to ready ROCKET for spring duty. While in New York, Kelly visited with canal investor Hiram Barney regarding the future of the canal company. The meeting left him with mixed emotions concerning the canal. Kelly also had to worry about prospects for good steamers on the Fox for the 1868 season. WINNEBAGO (75 feet, 85 tons) and BERLIN CITY (110 tons) were likely candidates for the wheat trade.

The postwar recession was taking its toll and money was very tight. By now the waterway was of some value, but eastern investors were unable or unwilling to compete strongly with local railroads. The Chicago and North-Western Railway roughly paralleled the lower Fox from Oshkosh to Green Bay and offered a competing line to Chicago via Janesville. Also, the influential Milwaukee and St. Paul Railway, which ended at the Missisippi and recently had been formed of several completed cross-state railroads, provided additional competition.

By 1869 David Kelly had secured interest in Dousman and Elmore's terminal when Hercules F. Dousman's sons chose retirement. BROOKLYN and WINNEBAGO continued to call for available cargoes but trade had fallen to the extent that Kelly offered two grain barges for sale at Appleton. He eventually became more and more committed to the contest surrounding the Green Bay & Lake Pepin Railway. In the fall of 1870 Kelly's agent for L&RTCo., E. J. Shaylor, wrote to Nat Edwards, suggesting that he sell WINNEBAGO at Oshkosh for $8000. Kelly concluded the affairs of L&RTCo. in 1871 and concentrated on the commission business of Elmore and Kelly, as well as his new commitment to the building of the Green Bay & Lake Pepin Railway.

Above: C&NW local passenger train on the old Sheboy-gan & Fond du Lac line at Sheboygan Falls, Wisconsin about 1910. Sheboygan's thrust toward the Mississippi on this line failed. Engine 887 is a C-5 built by Schenectady in 1888.

waukee, Sheboygan raised a Sheboygan & Missisippi route, attracting Boston's interest, which faltered at Glenbeulah, then continued to Fond du Lac by 1869. This route terminated at Princeton, on the Fox River, far short of the Missisippi. Taken over by C&NW in 1881, it was extended just after the turn of the century, but only to Wisconsin Rapids. A Manitowoc line was a center of factional conflict and had to ally itself with Appleton in order to proceed. It too began in the 1850's, but completion didn't come until the 1870's. A short time later, it was to identify with the Milwaukee, Lake Shore & Western Railway, which in turn became C&NW property in the 1890's. Green Bay did not establish its railroad until 1866, when Green Bay & Lake Pepin Railway was chartered the same year as the GB&MCCo. incorporation.

One inland port city, Oshkosh, organized a railroad aimed at the west, assuming its position to be as favorable as any. Oshkosh & Missisippi Railroad was designed to "relieve us of miserable vassalage to Chicago & Milwaukee," and to be totally independent. O&M completed a grade to Ripon in 1856 but was only completed under new "vassalage" to the Milwaukee Road. Importantly, O&M addressed the trans-Missisippi trade. Its champions spoke of transporting lumber westward and grain eastward. Oshkosh was a major sawmill town with a supply of timber on the Wolf River to the north.

Oshkosh political power was personified in lumberman Phile-tus Sawyer, who dispensed influence statewide. When elected to Congress in 1864, he won funds for Wisconsin's internal improvements, such as rivers and harbors. It was Sawyer's politics, in alliance with Chicago lumber friends and fellow investors, that advanced the Sturgeon Bay Ship Canal. In Oshkosh, meanwhile, the goal was to push a road through Portage to Dubuque, Iowa, linking prairie lumber markets. This would be built to Mineral Point, connecting with the Mineral Point Railroad, which in turn tied into Illinois Central at Warren, Illinois. The 120-mile line never materialized, but the idea of ties to the new west remained strong. Powerful rivals in the Chicago lines protected their territory and dominated trade in lumber beyond the Missisippi. Even Sawyer routed his lumber around Wisconsin to Chicago.

A need for railroads southwest, independent of eastern capitalists and Chicago's control, was the war cry in Wisconsin in 1866. These lines would carry the treasure of northern forests to western markets and their allies in neighboring states also saw the possibilities. This need steered the state's political climate away from the "anti-investment" period to one led by the "new north" and its pro-railroad champions. The new north, which contained most of the pine forests, lay just north of a route surveyed for Green Bay & Lake Pepin Railway in the winter of 1866-67.

Mayor Charles D. Robinson of Green Bay was a fountain of enthusiasm when it came to boosting his city. He served as Mayor, investor and editor-publisher of *The Green Bay Advocate,* which was an oracle of Green Bay progress and expansion. By 1866 either a canal or a railroad westward would benefit the city of Green Bay. As Mayor, Robinson had stated that his city ". . . is better fitted than any other Lake Michigan port . . . as an outlet for . . . commerce of northern Wisconsin and Minnesota." He was sure that Green Bay's advantage of being farther "down lake" gave it a natural position to command the all-important wheat trade. Green Bay was the "natural lake port" for opening the western region and Robinson never doubted its possibilities.

Robinson, in his address, continued to detail Green Bay's chances for its prospective road. He depicted Minnesota wheat in that year running about twelve million bushels which, if handled via Green Bay's east-west short route, would yield a handsome return. And, if not a railroad, then the Green Bay &

Missisippi Canal Company's steamers. Green Bay would gain as a transshipment port and rise to prominence as a major harbor. Cargos would go aboard competitively priced Buffalo-bound steamers. A Missisippi-to-Green Bay route would shorten haulage via Chicago or Milwaukee by about 150 miles, a consideration of merit in those times. A railroad between the 44th and 45th parallels could create new prosperity for the city of Green Bay.

Part of the pressure exerted to create a Green Bay route came from Minnesota, particularly Wabasha. Railroad fever had run as high there as anywhere in the 1850's, but without success. Both Wisconsin and Minnesota had received land grants to finance roads, and Minnesota had received grants for four lines in the southern part of the state. The problem was a marked difference in land use that failed to bring the Wisconsin roads into conjunction with the Minnesota lines.

While Wisconsin was occupied with linking the north to the south, Minnesota's grant promoted its role as a wheat-growing region. Minnesota's one persevering company was Winona & St. Peter Railroad, born in 1855 as the Transit Railroad. W&SP managed to actually build westward after 1862, at which time several other land grant lines came into being: Minnesota Valley, Minnesota Central and Hastings and Dakota. Wisconsin, on the other hand, received over one-tenth of its area in two different grants (1856, 1864) of 3,750,000 acres. Wisconsin arrived at a plan for one northeast and one northwest road, over and above existing lines in Southern Wisconsin.

Badger State politics in the late 1850's, however, bathed regularly in corruption which thwarted honest railroad promotion. The northeast road was to begin at either Portage, Fond du Lac or Doty's Island (Neenah), passing to Marinette on the Michigan border. This became the Chicago & North-Western Railway. The other was to extend from Portage to Lake St. Croix, then to Superior and Bayfield. The Milwaukee Road attempted to obtain this western grant by bribing all of the state officials. In the end it went into the Omaha Road (CSTPM&ORy) and Wisconsin Central which had occupied the region closest to the grant.

The northwest grant contained some of the best pine in the state, which could be sold via the Missisippi River lumber mills to western markets. Logs from this great timberland were floated past the town of Wabasha to Winona's sawmills, from which a portion of the lumber was moved by the Winona & St. Peter Railroad. Wabasha, until 1866, could only wish for a railroad which would make it a rival of its neighbor thirty miles south. The land grants left Wabasha's and Green Bay's east-west idea "high and dry," and the excessive, monopoly-imposed steamboat rates were the bitter gall that Wabasha would swallow.

The Green Bay Advocate worked its crowd all Spring in 1866 and, in a supporting letter to Robinson, Wabasha called for a railroad to alleviate high grain rates from Minnesota. Another railroad inland from Wabasha west would be an advantage to a Green Bay line. Wabasha also took note that Winona's own road, the W&SP, was plucked in October of 1867 from local control. The C&NW Ry. had purchased it from brokers D. N. Barney and Co. If W&SP had ever been considered as a potential partner of a Green Bay route, it was not after the sale. W&SP became a supplier of Chicago-bound traffic and fully a part of C&NW after 1901.

Wabasha also noted her interesting position geographically, which was "the best and only point for making a connection" with a Green Bay route. The Missisippi River's narrow channel there made a good place for a bridge. Just above Wabasha is Lake Pepin, a widening of the Missisippi River. The Chippewa River, which enters at a right angle to the Missisippi, slows the larger river's current which tends to shoal up the Wisconsin side and produce a slackwater zone — favorable conditions for a bridge. It was called Beef Slough and later became an important log-sorting location. West of Wabasha, the Zumbro River valley slices inland to Rochester, giving easy access to the high plain of Minnesota. By mid-1866 Wabasha's several promoters, allied with Green Bay & Lake Pepin, were actively involved in proposing the Lake Pepin & Omaha Railroad Company in the towns west of Wabasha.

Artemus Sharpe, a resident of Wabasha, was at one time its mayor. Sharpe and friends wanted their LP&O to be aimed straight at Omaha and the eastern end of the Union Pacific. Their first efforts were local, with a junction planned at Faribault with the Minnesota Central (Milwaukee Road). This would give Wabasha access to St. Paul. The plan was made before the Milwaukee built its river line through Wabasha, which negated appeal for investment in a trunk line straight west. Sharpe and his son Amasa addressed railroad aid meetings in Plainview and Rochester, the latter city taking special notice. After completion of the Winona & St. Peter through Rochester, its citizens quickly found that another line would be desirable to keep rates in order, as W&SP was accused of charging exorbitantly. Between 1866 and 1876 LP&O became a Rochester-based company, its president being H. T. Horton of that city.

In the 1880's the LP&O idea gained enough support to be adopted by the Winona & South-Western Railway. W&SW would actually build southwest toward Omaha. Both hypothesized that the Wisconsin (and Winona's) pine would find available markets in the west, while grain and possibly Iowa coal from new territories would move east to market. While Green Bay's Robinson spoke of grain east to that city, Sharpe was quoting lumber rates westward. LP&O would have run some 300 miles southwesterly via Rochester, High Forest, Austin, Albert Lea, Fort Dodge and Council Bluffs, a western arm of the Green Bay route.

The bill to incorporate Green Bay & Lake Pepin Railway was introduced in Madison in January of 1866 and passed February 19th, the same year. It was one of the 33 railroads incorporated in Wisconsin between 1861 and 1867; however, most failed to find support. With its western end fixed at a Missisippi point, GB&LP was strengthened in its search for aid. The river juncture remained vague enough so that the road could be built to any point between Wabasha and Winona, determined by subscription response. It was observed that no land grant railroad had been able to progress so far in one year. This was because GB&LP was not involved in the land grant roads' political shuffle. The company negotiated with the federal government for a Missisippi bridge location which was controlled by the War Department in those times. Minnesota and Wisconsin both made unsuccessful attempts to obtain land grants for the road. Wisconsin, however, had unsettled feelings about railroads due to previous conflicts over commitment of credit from towns and counties.

GB&LP's charter is dated April 12, 1866. Its respected incorporators were Anton Klaus, Myron P. Lindsley, Morgan L. Martin, M. J. Meade, W. J. Abrams, Andrew E. Elmore, Henry D. Barron, W. J. Copp and Henry D. Kellogg. Mr. David McCartney served as president while Anton Klaus was the vice-president. Other officers included Joshua Whitney, Secretary; William J. Fisk, Treasurer; E. H. Ellis, Attorney; and

E. D. Clinton and Lewis J. Day, executive committeemen. Soon afterward, C. D. Robinson became president, and a few De Pere men joined him, including George S. Marsh, mill owner Andrew Reid and Joseph G. Lawton, who was involved in banking and business. Edward Decker, land owner and lawyer, was always active in railroad promotion and later built the Ahnapee & Western Railway to Sturgeon Bay.

W. J. Abrams, a New York State expatriate, arrived in Green Bay in 1856, and took part in railroad surveys from Green Bay to Ontonagon. He settled in Green Bay in 1861, and managed the Grand Trunk Line Steamers on the Collingwood-Sarnia-Buffalo route. Abrams was in the State Assembly from 1864 to 1867, and the Senate during 1868 and 1869. He obtained the GB&LP charter while in the Assembly. Experienced in railway surveys, Abrams' interest in the Green Bay Route continued into the 1890's.

Lastly, from the west end, Sharpe, William T. Dugan, Benjamin Allen and Henry M. Rice (of St. Paul, formerly of Wabasha) were commissioned to solicit subscriptions. On September 10, 1866 the executive board of GB&LP traveled to Wabasha to arrange for citizen's meetings on subscriptions. It was one of several junkets made at the time by Robinson and Abrams. Returning in mid-November, the party toured the Beef River Valley (now the Buffalo River) and the Chippewa bottomlands to search for a route away from the Missisippi. The Chippewa route was eventually used by a Milwaukee Road branch to Eau Claire from Read's Landing, reaching the Minnesota shore via a pontoon bridge. Another citizen's meeting was arranged at Wabasha's Wright's Hall with Sharpe, secretary John F. Rose and the Green Bay men presiding in late fall of 1866.

Northwestern Union Packet Company was criticized by the residents as being irritating, which certainly aided the cause of the railroad builders. It was not only necessary for the GB&LP to find the best route down to the Missisppi River, but also to solicit aid from communities willing to support the enterprise in sparsely settled territory. Wabasha allegedly would bond to $100,000 with a $1000 cash bonus which was required to be put before the State Legislature. The Green Bay delegation had traveled the only available route to Wabasha — passage on C&NW Green Bay to Minnesota Junction, Milwaukee Road west to La Crosse late in the same day, Northwestern Union Packet CITY OF ST. PAUL La Crosse to Winona, and finally an arrival at Wabasha via a small steamer. Not overlooked by the Green Bay men was the Zumbro Valley, located west of Wabasha, which "General" Sharpe had indicated was the LP&O route westward into Minnesota's golden wheatlands. They departed for Green Bay aboard the steamer JENNIE BALDWIN via La Crosse, confident of the future.

Artemus Sharpe wrote on March 30, 1867 from Mondovi, Wisconsin, with some difficulty: ". . . all in good health save for inflamed eyes." Sharpe had accompanied Captain W. Wellman on the arduous winter survey of GB&LP's west end, which began after Christmas, 1866. A delay in receiving surveying instruments from St. Paul set the western group behind schedule and, when Wellman's party finally got going by March, they were met by a heavy blizzard. The surveyors reached Mondovi, 26¾ miles from Wabasha, just before the 25th. The second party in the group arrived snowblinded. The survey revealed a grade of just four feet to the mile along the Beef River. Sharpe reported that the Beef's ice had broken up, "forbidding all further operations on our line." Generally they had been making ten miles a day, but when they reached Osseo, Captain Rich of the party became ill. Wellman and Sharpe continued, keeping

the river to their right all the way to its headwaters, 117 feet above the Missisippi near Strum. Wellman and Sharpe had chained a distance of 77¾ miles eastward to the Black River, at Arnold's Mill near present-day Hatfield. They stopped at a point on the west bank, opposite the halting point of Joseph Heyrmann's survey from De Pere. The party returned to the Missisippi by April 12th.

Brown County Surveyor Joseph Heyrmann was engaged to examine the route westward. Heyrmann began January 7th, escorted outward by a considerable number of citizens and the Green Bay Band. They began on a cold, clear and bright morning near the west end of the De Pere bridge. The first stake was placed in the street and the party moved off toward the Black River, 140 miles away, accompanied by music and shouts of encouragement. It was explained that the De Pere jump-off point was merely a "common point" and not the true eastern terminus. The south line of Clark County at the Black was reached, with Heyrmann reporting "generally level ground." He crossed the Wolf on January 17th near Shiocton and was well received there. A day was spent examining river crossings, after which he left for Stevens Point and Plover.

GB&LP had been chartered for nine months, and a route west looked attractive. Heyrmann found only one area in the morainal part of Waupaca County "where the country is knobby." Heyrmann's group passed on to the Wisconsin River, 1½ miles north of Plover, examining crossings on the low banks. They found unobstructed flatlands all the way to the Black River. GB&LP's original survey is interesting in retrospect, as it is a straight line nearly all the way to the Missisippi. It would have brought the road much closer to St. Paul, as well as nearly producing a road west of Wabasha. The Beef Valley might have produced less aid than the established towns along the Trempeleau. Wabasha needed heroes stronger than Artemus Sharpe and a "city-state" more powerful than Winona to prevail in the coming decade. A position farther up the Missisippi might have given the Green Bay route much greater strength, perhaps even a "native son" position for Minnesota dealings. Undaunted, Sharpe and Wabasha continued to push GB&LP and arranged meetings at Modena in 1867 and Gilmanton in 1869, while also holding gatherings for LP&O in Minnesota. The struggle continued into the mid-1870's, while Wabasha still hoped for a branch road of GB&M after it settled for Winona. A bridge bill for a Buffalo County-to-Minnesota span or pontoon crossing was authorized by February 1867, virtually assuring the road's completion.

Wabasha, Minnesota in the 1890's, which might have been the end of the Green Bay & Lake Pepin Railway. The Milwaukee Road in the foreground includes narrow-gauge cars of the absorbed Minnesota Midland Railway, which had built a Zumbro Valley route in the 1870's.

Dousman and Elmore's elevator on the Fox River bank dominated the Green Bay harbor. Built in 1862 for $80,000, the 60 × 128-foot structure stood 100 feet high and was identical to rival elevators in Chicago. Iron rods secured the solid plank walls, enabling them to hold back tons of grain. It held 300,000 bushels when loaded. Along the docks below were two flour houses and several warehouses. Dousman and Elmore were also freight and passenger agents for the New York Central propellors COMET and ROCKET and arranged cargoes for shipping. Other steamers and schooners as well crowded about the elevator in season: CUYAHOGA, LADY FRANKLIN, UNION, and side wheelers GEORGE L. DUNLAP, ARROW and QUEEN CITY were commonly seen. The business of the Onondaga Salt Company was transacted at the docks for the meat-packing trade, while lime for mortar and coal for forges passed by the dock office en route to the city, along with all manner of merchandise and niceties from New York and Boston. Green Bay and Fort Howard had become wholesaling and jobbing centers, which supplied the lumber country to the north with groceries, leather goods, iron ware, and sundries. The business extended to Lake Superior in season and also to the west, as far as transportation would reach. The city contained a sizable and growing compliment of boiler and machine shops, woodenware factories, shingle mills and dimension lumber establishments. As timber began to shrink back from Green Bay's shore in the 1860's, new industries arrived to take the place of the lumber mills. The needs of Green Bay's harbor were

Left: One of the port-to-interior railroads of Wisconsin was Sheboygan & Fond du Lac Railroad, begun before the Civil War. S&FdL was built with Massachusetts money, hence Taunton Locomotive Works built its SHE-BOYGAN 4-4-0 in the 1850's. This scene of Sheboygan Falls is from the road's early years. The building behind the locomotive still stands on the city's main street.

served by chandlers and boat works of many sizes. The pair of cities, which eventually became one several decades later, stood on the brink of change, for the new west would offer opportunity for exploitation and growth.

Colonel Robinson and Edward Decker spent the better part of June 1867, attending aid meetings in towns on either side of the GB&LP survey. On the 17th, at Plover, they addressed the Portage County assemblage requesting money for the new company. Portage was asked to put forth $100,000, which was voted down after deliberation. This was just one episode in which aid was not available due to a slackening economy and distrust. W. J. Abrams tried again in September, proposing that nothing was to be paid until grading reached the county line; then $5000 would be asked, and again $5000 for each additional five-mile graded section. This guaranteed the county at least a continuous mound of earth across its midst. Yet, once again the County balked, as did several others wary of misfortune. Only the town of Plover seemed willing and, after a tiff with Stevens Point, some five miles north, agitation bubbled around possible movement of the County Seat. Stevens Point was also interested in the land grant roads, hoping to persuade one to pass through, as it eventually did. The destiny of Stevens Point would be linked within five years to the Wisconsin Central, which built its first shop there shortly after the first WC train rolled in on November 15, 1871.

The trip to Wabasha, a 23-day outing, cost $200 for horses and carriage. Edward Decker submitted a receipt record to GB&LP, keeping his own records on money transfers between himself and Colonel Robinson. From 1867 until 1869, the struggle was a hard one for Robinson, Decker and others; however, on June 8, 1868 Robinson wrote that votes had been counted in the City of Green Bay in an aid proposition, with 450 out of 500 supporting the railroad. Colonel Robinson was positive about a large majority behind the railroad, and felt that reactionary foes were routed in such elections. On July 25, 1868 Robinson wrote about an important director's meeting in July, admonishing Decker to attend, as the treasury needed to be "recuperated." He was certain that propositions west of Green

Bay could be recruited, and advised that Abrams and himself would leave on such a mission on the 13th.

W. J. Abrams, a former senator, was asked to return to Washington in an attempt to obtain a land grant while Robinson asked Decker to invest for him to assist Abrams in his mission. The money was to come from insiders in GB&LP's "ring." Poor health of both parties impaired their activities and Decker's horse bite was to eventually remove him from the road's presidency. This was just before David Kelly came to the front of the struggling railroad.

The Town of Mukwa, west of Northport, which had voted aid of $35,000 in the fall of 1868, reneged by April 1869. The reason was the incorporation of the Village of New London which came out of Mukwa Town that year. Yet, supporters carried Brown County by that time and also Outagamie County, for $10,000. Black Creek was denied by a count of 59 against and only 15 for. Henry Ketchum, a man destined to become a driving force in the coming decade, had joined the push for the railroad. He was a lumberman-businessman, a pioneer of New London and an expatriate of Courtland County, New York. He came to New London in 1855 and bought an inn called the New London House. He then invested in lands along the Wolf River, a prime supplier of logs to Oshkosh mills. Allegedly, he was able to corner the log market, controlling prices until Oshkosh rallied against him. After that, he secured control of tugboat operations and broke the opposing combination. He also had a mercantile trade among the loggers and raftsmen, generally rounding out a frontier business career by buying grain from area producers. He may have gained some railroad expertise in New York State, and in time assumed the GB&LP presidency. He observed that his own lands and interests on the Wolf's banks would be greatly enhanced by the coming of the Green Bay & Lake Pepin Railway.

For reasons of health, C. D. Robinson wintered in Paris, France, resigning his GB&LP position by February 1869. His interest in the project he inaugurated never lagged and his letters to the officers showed that he desired to take up where he left off when home again. He still desired to have an influential position on the board, and for the April meeting gave his proxy to a trusted ally. At the Director's meeting, W. J. Abrams was given a salary of $75 per month to attend to the general business of the company, a job that would employ three-quarters of his time. Criticism of Joseph Heyrmann's survey reopened the problem of locating a competent engineer. Each board member

Right: Winona & St. Peter Railway was the subject of several stereoptican slides made from 1875 to 1880. Here W&SP No.3 is seen on the majestic climb to the Minnesota plains, a great engineering challenge at that time.
WINONA COUNTY HISTORICAL SOCIETY

Below: W&SP was a staunch Minnesota pioneer which began before the Civil War. Here W&SP No.5, a Rogers Locomotive & Machine Works product, poses in Winona, some distance from Owatonna, its namesake.
WINONA COUNTY HISTORICAL SOCIETY

agreed to pay a $200 assessment, less than enough to cover a resurvey of the Wolf River to be done in May, when mud was less of a problem. An engineer named Devry from Fond du Lac was recommended by Heyrmann, the GB&LP's chief engineer. Devry apparently had spent much of his life as an engineer on French and Belgian railroads but had no American experience. Heyrmann agreed to assist Devry through difficulties. There were also some misgivings about running the road to New London, raising further complications. Thus, countercurrents within GB&LP were many, slowing the progress toward the final goal.

GB&LP found a local competitor in Fort Howard, Shawano & Missisippi Railroad. On May 6, 1869 the FtHS&M held a meeting in Fort Howard and W. J. Fisk was appointed secretary. Mr. E. D. Clinton came up with a scheme that projected a

road to Shawano and then on to Lake Pepin. It would include lumber camps involving available timber northwest of Green Bay. GB&LP only skirted the timberlands, so this new idea would be favorable to lumbermen as a supply route. David McCartney was a would-be promoter along with Mr. Clinton, who was billed as an experienced railroad man. FtHS&M acquired options on lands of Mrs. C. L. A. Tank along the waterfront. In an evening of heated debate, GB&LP Vice-President Hercules F. Dousman Jr. angrily stormed out after a speech denouncing the literal duplicity proposed. Later, Charles Robinson informed Edward Decker, who had also left early, that the Fort Howard Road people wanted a compromise. Edward Decker wisely felt that only one road could be served at this time and that aid could not be split between the two roads. By July the tempest subsided and the newcomer's officers agreed to "merge" their interest for a unified sweep west. The Tank lands would eventually fall to GB&LP and the "lumbermen's faction" would forever rest. GB&LP was anxious to produce tangible results by early winter, despite the FtHS&M's desire to modify the route to run to Hastings and St. Paul.

On July 29, 1869, with Fort Howard's $20,000 bond vote in GB&LP's favor, the mayors of Green Bay and Fort Howard, Anton Klaus and Oscar Grey, stripped off their coats and grabbed their shovels. At 2 p.m. on a humid Thursday afternoon, the two executives topped off their wheelbarrows, dumping them in significant places on the new right-of-way. McCartney announced that thirty men would be put to work immediately, assuring that ceremony had its purpose. Also present was the Honorable T. B. Hudd, a witness to the beginning of Chicago's first railroad twenty years before. After a month of labor, GB&LP's first two miles were ready for ties, though they were somewhat disconnected by swampy stretches. Fall rains compromised the marshy earthwork but increasing numbers of men came to labor for the Lake Pepin and progress

accelerated. Shawano, observing the progress, swung in line for a bond proposal but never received the benefits. Miles away, Edward Decker's arm became bad enough to require surgery, preventing the man from actively supporting the railroad for several crucial years. Decker's interests, however, remained firmly behind the railroad, interests that would bring him back into the Green Bay picture in the future.

By year's end, Fort Howard issued bonds for three miles, $1000 for each mile graded westward. President McCartney made a second proposal in September for $100,000 bonding for Brown County to aid the road. As of September 9th, the county would issue $15,000 as soon as five miles were graded. Each subsequent five miles was covered similarly. In October the vote went against the railroad, but the Borough of Fort Howard did issue its bonds and land values rose. Shawano's pressure for the railroad continued, its offer of bonding passing in a referendum. Thus, while tangible evidence of progress was at hand, it was still a long way to the Mississippi.

Situated along the marshy banks of the Wolf River, New London lay at the disposal of the railroad. Having viewed the GB&LP as an asset which would inevitably come, the sudden reality of a Shawano route sobered New London into voting more support for the road, thus ensuring its eventual arrival. The amount was $70,000, a drastic improvement over the $20,000 figure of 1868. All that remained was for construction gangs to be in sight of the Waupaca County town. The winter of 1869-70 whistled through Wisconsin treelimbs along the Wolf River and along Duck Creek outside Fort Howard. But, after the winter had calmed and turned to delicate spring, David Marsh Kelly would begin his aggressive career to bring the railroad to completion at the Mississippi, delivering it to a cadre of some of the nation's most wealthy men, and tying it to an eastern establishment which would guide its destinies for over 100 years.

2

Construction & Completion

Moses Taylor's life was a brightly lit scene of well-orchestrated fortune. He was a merchant prince and he stood front and center on the stage of economic possibility. In 1870 his prominence in New York financial circles was unquestioned. His power was on the level of Jay Gould and it approached that of the Vanderbilt citadel in the New York Central. His world of urbane, sophisticated maneuvering covered far-reaching events in his native city, where he was born in 1806.

Taylor's father, John Jacob Astor's real estate agent, influenced him to invest his income in overseas commerce and mercantile trade. There were Cuban sugar interests, vessels to carry the trade and commercial papers handled for his Caribbean friends. By the time of his death in 1882, Moses Taylor had amassed a fortune of $45 million. Assets included coal, iron, railroads, gas and real estate.

Taylor became a director in New York City's National City Bank, one of ten original state banks chartered in 1812. Percy Rivington Pyne, an English immigrant, served as Taylor's assistant in the 1840's. He eventually rose to a partnership with Taylor and married his daughter Albertina in 1855. Taylor and Pyne established Moses Taylor & Co., financiers, which grew into a notable agency. In 1843 Taylor was elected to the board of directors of The Farmer's Loan & Trust Co., the oldest mortgage agency in the U.S. for railroads. His influence was enough to place many of his associates in corporate directorship positions, including Pyne and close friend Samuel Sloan. He advised railroad moguls such as Boston's John Thayer and James F. Joy, and also dealt with John Insley Blair, the Scranton family, Samuel Marsh and William Earle Dodge. In 1870 Moses Taylor promoted development in two of his most promising holdings, the Delaware, Lackawanna & Western Railroad and the Lackawanna Iron & Coal Co., both interested in expanding westward.

The business acumen of Moses Taylor cast a positive image over early coal and iron ventures. Just 120 miles from New York were the northern anthracite fields at the convergence of the Lackawanna River and Nay Aug (Roaring Brook) where Scranton, Pennsylvania is today. The nearby iron and coal deposits required transport, and both canal and railroad were closely competing ideas, but not for long. The New York merchant-investor community became aware of the possibilities in the 1820's when coal mushroomed from a 2000-ton annual market to two million tons in the 1850's. Anthracite, a clean heating coal, warranted attention, but any coal so close to eastern New York State prosperity was investment worth noting. It was New York investors, involved in northeast Pennsylvania, who were most able to see the needs of a Wisconsin railroad which would reach the Missisippi.

Scranton, Pennsylvania, before the time of coal and iron, was settled as Slocum's Hollow. This basic collection of frontier dwellings included a primal iron furnace that took advantage of the iron ore of Moosic Mountain as well as charcoal fuel, but was unable to fully exploit the deposit. In the early 1840's, when charcoal was becoming scarce, John F. Davis, a British immigrant, brought with him the coveted method for using anthracite to melt iron ore. Davis came from Cardiff, Wales, where the

Left: Green Bay & Minnesota's fate was harsh indeed at the time of this photo in 1876. Here, one Grant and two of the 10-12 series Dicksons stand near the original enginehouse and shop in Fort Howard.

T. VAN DREESE COLLECTION

experiment had taken place. The company formed was called Scranton's, Grant & Co., which was later changed to Scranton-Platt Co. It was George and Seldon T. Scranton, together with their cousins Joseph Hand Scranton and Edward C. Scranton, who formed the core group that eventually became Lackawanna Iron & Coal Co. The two southern cousins from Augusta, Georgia were to stay with the company through the 1860's. When English rail suppliers couldn't deliver, Scranton-Platt assured a T-rail order for the New York & Erie Railway. The British railways were consuming all British rail production so the Americans were on their own.

The family tree of Moses Taylor reflected a steady rise in management and control in some of New York's and Pennsylvania's primary industries. Noted Presbyterian theologian Edwin Hatfield married Taylor's sister and their son, Edwin F. Hatfield Jr., went into the Taylor business as a young clerk. By the 1860's he had risen to power in closely associated ventures. The carefully nurtured nephew became president of the Lackawanna Iron & Coal Company and director of distant-seeming enterprises such as Detroit & Bay City Railway, Rome, Watertown and Ogdensburg Railroad and Green Bay & Minnesota Railroad. Taylor's other daughter married Robert Winthrop, a partner in Drexel and Winthrop, a financial house similar to Taylor's own. It was the descendants of Moses Taylor and Robert Winthrop along with the John Insley Blair family who would control financial affairs of the railroad west of Green Bay, just now being organized.

John Insley Blair of Blairstown, New Jersey began building his fortune as a contemporary of Moses Taylor. Blair, the son of a Scottish immigrant farmer, was denied a full education when the death of his father required his help to support his large family. By age twenty he was involved in a Belvidere, New Jersey business and by 1821 he had his own store nearby. He quickly developed a chain of stores staffed by his relatives and one of the young Scrantons. In his stores he sold common nails which came from nearby Oxford Furnace, owned by the Scranton brothers. Blair rapidly rose to power in his territory and eventually became a Scranton-Platt partner, investing when the owners needed more money.

Seldon Scranton's father-in-law, William Henry, originally leased the Oxford Furnace in New Jersey, about 65 miles from Slocum's Hollow. Seldon was Henry's superintendent until the 1837 panic when Henry sold out and returned to Slocum's Hollow to develop his promising leasehold. There, more money was required and Joseph H. Scranton made contact with financiers John Howland & Co., the Scranton-Platt's first bridgehead into New York. It was at this time that Scranton-Platt Co., in need of a market, decided to turn to rail production and accepted the Erie T-rail order. Capital continued to be in short supply but Erie Board members and investors loaned money when the Pennsylvania iron firm agreed to take their order. The men up front were Samuel Marsh, Anson G. Phelps, Benjamin Loder and William Earle Dodge. Control of Lackawanna iron-making thus slipped into the hands and minds of New Yorkers and by 1853 Moses Taylor was counted among the financiers in Lackawanna Iron & Coal Co.

Taylor came into the investment picture through the offices of friend Marshall O. Roberts, also an Erie investor. Interest in Anthracite for the New York market was rapidly growing and Taylor held real estate, coal lands and iron prospects in the Scranton locality. Railroad transport in the area was becoming mandatory. They formed Ligett's Gap Railroad which became the pioneer part of the Delaware, Lackawanna & Western Railroad.

The fast-moving events of the 1840's produced a blizzard of possibilities for the Lackawanna group. They built roaring furnaces which made iron rails and they plunged into enterprises which became captive markets for their coal and iron. Their industries in the Lackawanna Valley also provided loadings for their own railroad. A railroad would replace primitive strap iron tram-type railroads which brought iron ore to the furnaces. Anthracite from land two miles away also required transport by rail. In contrast the Erie T-rail order had to go out via Delaware & Hudson Canal Co.'s system to the Erie. The rails in turn were brokered through Phelps, Dodge & Co., also Erie investors. The LGRR was built close to the Erie at Great Bend, due north of Scranton on the state border. It was six-foot gauge, to conform with Erie's standards, and it operated its first train on October 15, 1851.

Capitalists and capitalization gradually changed during the construction period from 1849 until 1851 and the name was changed to Lackawanna & Western Railroad. John Blair, George W. Scranton, Joseph H. Scranton, William E. Dodge and Edward Mowry acquired land for the line while watching their Scranton holdings increase in value. This group also brought in the Delaware & Cobb's Gap Railroad, whose true aim was soon clear: to bring anthracite to New York City. In 1853 the DL&W was formed, running across the territory of John I. Blair in western New Jersey. Many of the money men would occupy directorships in related companies, some eventually finding their way to Wisconsin's Green Bay Route in succeeding decades.

By the late 1860's, Moses Taylor controlled Manhattan Gas Light Co., a responsibility he shared with Samuel Sloan, Percy Pyne and Robert Winthrop. Gas was derived from coal and provided another market for Scranton's black diamonds. Taylor was on DL&W's Board of Managers and had acquired controlling interest by the time of the Civil War. He apparently held the majority interest in Lackawanna Iron & Coal Co. as well. As a result, many coal properties which he controlled became DL&W or LI&C property. Expansion of DL&W continued as smaller railroads were built, acquired or leased to the DL&W. This method freed capital to seek other opportunities, while still placing additional railroads under DL&W control. The Taylor group used National City Bank and The Farmers' Loan & Trust Co. as agencies for their endeavors. The securities of the small roads might have been used as payment for needed rails and fastenings or new locomotives. Many of Taylor's roads received power from Dickson Manufacturing Co. of Scranton. Many prominent men in the group were honored by having their names lettered on Dickson cabsides. Of the five "named-era" Dickson locomotives on the Green Bay Route, three were named for Taylor associates.

Of the Lackawanna group, John Insley Blair had perhaps the earliest travel experience westward. In 1860 he and his party were invited on a trip to Cedar Rapids, Iowa to examine both Iowa and a railroad which terminated there. Blair attended the Republican National Convention in Chicago, then traveled via Illinois Central to Dunleith, and by river steamer to Clinton, Iowa. His group traveled over the Chicago, Iowa & Nebraska Railroad to Cedar Rapids and took a good look at the state in which Blair investments were to be as important as those of the Lackawanna combine. Blair's investments spearheaded the building of the Cedar Rapids and Missouri River Railroad. In the 1860's Blair promoted and even surveyed a portion of the line across Iowa, which eventually became Chicago & North-Western's main line to the Union Pacific railhead at Omaha.

This important link in the transcontinental railway was completed in 1867. Blair headed for Nebraska in 1863 with a family group to examine the settlement conditions. He kept a record of the trip in notebooks, a report that beckoned to land and rail investors as well as farmers. Blair formed the Iowa Railway Land Co. and built the Sioux City & Pacific Railroad which linked Fremont, Nebraska and Sioux City. This gave his Fremont, Elkhorn & Missouri Valley Railroad access to the North-Western main line as well as connecting Sioux City and its region to the south. Blair's crews completed the SC&P to Sioux City and then went on to the Iowa Falls & Sioux City Railroad, showing his commitment to western Iowa.

Blair was also a promoter of the Burlington, Cedar Rapids & Northern Railroad, another Iowa line that was ultimately sold to Rock Island in June 1902. This line ran towards the northeast corner of Iowa from Cedar Rapids to Albert Lea and included various branches. Another of Blair's acquisitions, the St. Louis, Hannibal & Keokuk Railway, was an 82-mile Missouri line from Oakwood to Gilmore which was from the same period as the Green Bay route. The Hannibal road's directors included Cedar Rapids men and there were many features which the two roads shared, including bankruptcy. Blair had amassed great assets in banking, land and railroad holdings in the Iowa community. A shrewd businessman, he reputedly drove a hard bargain in selling his railroad properties to standing railroads, even those whose directorships he served.

David Kelly made contact with the Lackawanna group when he returned to Haverhill, Massachusetts for the Christmas holidays in 1869. No doubt he was full of optimism over the bright future of his plans and commitments. His correspondence with his "Uncle Samuel," president of the still-standing canal company, and his closeness to Taylor and Scranton assured that the New Yorkers would be made aware of Green Bay's needs.

GB&LP President McCartney resigned by January of 1870 in favor of newcomer Henry Ketchum. Ketchum, like McCartney, desired to have the line pass through New London. Debates over the route and the vested interests of board members initiallly slowed progress; however, by springtime Kelly was in the east negotiating for the road. He was now vice-president and Charles Robinson accompanied him to the money men's sumptuous offices. Nathanial Edwards received a letter from Mr. Whittlesey, a friend from Central Mine in Copper country, Michigan, asking for more information about the projected railroad from Green Bay to Lake Pepin. The northwestern land-grant scheme had been projected to forge an alliance across Wisconsin with the soon-to-be Northern Pacific. Duluth and Bayfield planned to be a terminus for both railroads. Whittlesey observed that the Green Bay road ought to be the real lake terminal for communications east. He also wanted to know what backing the road had, intending to invest. Whittlesey and Wisconsin observers would have to wait through another spring to discover the advancement scheme of the Lackawanna investors.

Further complications surfaced in May 1870. An engineering party was ordered into the field in response to a $150,000 bond issue, but the bond had no guarantee for iron and rolling stock. Fortunately, the money issue passed with a majority of 600, allowing Henry Ketchum to report that the means were available to complete the road to Plover by January. New London and Black Creek also fell in line with positive bonding votes the same month. In June of 1870 David Kelly found his engineer, Mr. Rice, unsatisfactory. David wrote to his cousin, Nat Edwards, telling him that he needed the canal company's engineer,

G. A. Randall, as well as his own services for two or three weeks. On June 12th Kelly informed the company that Mr. Rice would have to be discharged and pleaded for Randall's aid. Proper actions were taken and Randall stayed for the lion's share of the GB&LP surveying.

Just west of Green Bay was the Oneida Indian Reservation. GB&LP contracted to cross the tribal lands. This meant that the Indian Commission determined the route, subject to Wisconsin laws, "the same as if the land were owned by white persons." The document granting right-of-way and the customary 100-foot strip common to the rest of the road was assigned May 23, 1870, in the presence of First Lieutenant W. R. Bourne, U.S.A. Indian Department, and J. L. W. Doxtater, U.S. Interpreter. Thirteen Chiefs, President Anton Klaus and Secretary Josh Whitney signed the document. It was approved by Ulysses S. Grant on June 3, 1870. Oneida lands stretched from what is now Taylor Street, Green Bay to the Town Line of Seymour and were eventually sold by the 20th Century.

stock not already issued or to be issued for municipal or county bonds would thereby build and equip the road. Any residue would be passed to Kelly. Kelly was able to secure $533,500 of capital stock, causing quite a controversy in the years to come.

By July 23, 1870 the company had enough money to finish the first twenty miles, which entitled them to the Brown County bonds and generated enough money to grade to New London. By August 6th Engineer Randall and assistants Jacobi and Stevens returned from fieldwork in the west. David Kelly was pleased that Randall had decided to remain with GB&LP. The distance from Green Bay to the banks of the Wolf River at New London was 39 miles and a straight line from Shiocton. The Shioc River at its crossing was 100 feet wide, requiring a sizable bridge on the west side of Shiocton. The line was level with the exception of the climb out of the Duck Creek valley. The right-of-way was lined with mixed forest lands which ended at the depot grounds on the north side of New London.

Kelly went to New York to make arrangements for rail and

David Kelly resigned his position as vice-president to become GB&LP's financial agent, construction superintendent and general manager. On July 3, 1870 he signed his first contract with the company, co-signed by the new president Anton Klaus. The company's broker was Balliet, Jones & Co., with whom Kelly arranged for sale of bonds. On July 6, 1870 the bonds were deposited with The Farmer's Loan & Trust Co., to be sold at 75 cents on the dollar. They were to yield seven percent. Bonds totaling $3,200,000, dated August 1, 1870, matured August 1, 1900. Along with a bonus of $1,044,500 of the stock and another bonus of $100,000 of the city of Green Bay's stock, $1,847,000 of the company's capital stock was greatly discounted and sold for $1,220,450 cash. Balliet, Jones & Co. were to have 15 days to sell exclusively and, if $640,000 were sold in that time, they would be given exclusive rights to negotiate for all rails and fastenings, locomotives and cars. Kelly was to receive a $5000 annual salary as well as all municipal and county bonds which were received by the company in exchange for capital stock. The GB&LP's own first-mortgage bonds, at the rate of $16,000 per mile, and all of its authorized capital

Above: Only two photos of GB&LP operations survive; both show the engine JOSEPH H. SCRANTON, a Grant 4-4-0 in the 1870's. Here No. 3, which was delivered in late 1872, poses with its crew during construction days. The removable counterweights had not yet been installed.
JOHN SPURR COLLECTION

equipment. Although he stayed until September, the delay wasn't apparent in Wisconsin. Contractors Call & Farnsworth had sizable crews at work grubbing and clearing; grading went well into early winter. In October there were from 1200 to 1700 men working between Green Bay and New London. Additional laborers came from Ogdensburg, 16 miles west, to join in the toil. Soon the Shioc River Bridge was completed and ready for rails which were late in arriving. Contractors worked in the river lowlands across the Wolf, taking advantage of December's frozen boglands for filling. The grade to the Wolf was examined and accepted piecemeal by the various bonding authorities, allowing the appropriate bonds to be released to the company. So it would go across Wisconsin to the Missisippi.

27

Above: Engine No.3 pauses for photos near Arnott on eastbound passenger No.2. This cut was troublesome at the time of construction.
ISHERWOOD COLLECTION

The onrush of winter in Wisconsin allowed time to review the road's accomplishments. With each five miles accepted by commissioners, the GB&LP inched across the landscape, its 100-foot concession nearly ready for rails from the Lackawanna heartland. Three trestles had been completed and 25,000 ties were cut and piled at intervals. The Duck Creek bridge was listed as 250 feet long, Trout Creek as 300 feet, and Big Creek, ninety feet long. The long idle grade was reportedly used by farmers as a highway, a preamble to its utility as a thoroughfare in the future. Call & Farnsworth, now located 45 miles west of Green Bay in Northport, were still on the project. As weather permitted, construction continued while surveyors worked to complete the segment westward to Grand Rapids by March 1871.

The world outside continued to speculate just where the GB&LP would end. Along the Missisippi, La Crosse and Winona considered the matter still debatable, despite Wabasha's claim to the terminus. The route to La Crosse showed much promise because of the Black River's path to the Gateway City. Another option was to cross the West Wisconsin Railroad at Augusta, ultimately making an outlet to St. Paul. Meanwhile, surveyors were reported at Neillsville and Black River Falls, running two lines. The railroad favored Grand Rapids over Stevens Point as a major town, chiefly due to its river crossing prospects. There was also a $200,000 bond issue which called for trains to be operating by January 1872. Mr. S. A. Sherman allegedly offered the GB&LP $50,000 to cross the Wisconsin river at his mill. The nearby town of Grant in Portage County failed by one vote to foot an aid package.

Kelly was not completely successful in acquiring adequate capital by early 1871. He wrote again to Edwards that he was planning a fast trip to London, England in mid-March aboard the Inman Line Steamer "City of Brussels," hoping to be in Green Bay by the 25th of April. His mission was to gain rails or investors, but Kelly was unable to find success on his mission. The London and European markets were concerned about the Franco-Prussian War, which raged from July 1870 until June 1871. Kelly returned to Green Bay May 7, 1871, the doors of overseas capital locked behind him. Meanwhile, GB&LP elected Henry Ketchum as President. Its Directors were Anton Klaus, George Sommers, Conrad Krueger, M. D. Peak, Fred Ellis, W. J. Abrams and Charles D. Robinson. Kelly explained at a citizen's meeting in June that delays and disappointment from various causes, including the European conflict, had stifled attempts to raise capital. To please the crowd, he did give an estimate of potential business to be had transporting from New London to Green Bay. The new railroad had prospects of making the Wolf River Valley log production available to Green Bay. GB&LP activity slowed during the uneventful summer, punctuated by Green Bay Mayor Kimball's trip to New York to negotiate bonds in aid of GB&LP. Robinson's newspaper remained silent about the railroad, while Kelly negotiated tirelessly in New York and Boston well into August.

The absence of progress was broken in October, when Kelly returned to Green Bay, disclosing that his negotiations had been successful. A rail supply was now en route from the east, enough to lay the first forty miles. Via Buffalo, New York, the

rails would be shipped on the Erie, and from the Great Bend interchange with the Lackawanna to Green Bay, in accordance with the wishes of the Lackawanna group. Kelly's second construction contract called specifically for time-distance agreements, which compelled signatories to observe completion dates that meshed with financial aid packages. In the June 5, 1871 agreement, Kelly was to have the railroad completed to New London by January 1, 1872, but he now had only one and one half months in which to do it. Immediately, Call & Farnsworth advertised for 500 men to complete the final four miles of grading. The land to the west of Green Bay had been affected by terrible fires and they reached a climax in the Peshtigo fire of Sunday, October 8, 1871.

Peshtigo's fire occurred on the same day as the Chicago fire but it killed far more people than its grim metropolitan rival. The conflagration destroyed much of the timber north and west of Green Bay and burned south to the GB&LP right-of-way. It consumed tie piles, stacked and ready for use, causing further delays. The summer of 1871 was unusually dry and fires, fanned by hot southwest winds, ravaged many square miles. Eleven hundred or more died in the Sunday evening of searing heat, which roared through portions of Oconto and Marinette Counties. However, the fires that accounted for GB&LP's loss came in late August, meaning that Call & Farnsworth were required to replenish the shortages.

The propellors ARIZONA and CRAIG steamed out of Buffalo, New York with the sought-after rail cargo safely in lower deck compartments. The 24-foot lengths of iron made up 140 tons aboard ARIZONA and 900 tons of thirty-foot lengths were carried by CRAIG. They docked at Elmore & Kelly's wharf in Fort Howard and were unloaded in late October amid the aftermath of area fires. Their passage was uneventful but in November propellor MISSOURI, laden with 400 tons of rail, went aground on Whaleback Reef. That same month, the schooner RICHARD MOTT arrived with 278 tons and ARIZONA prepared for a second trip to bring 500 tons. CRAIG

would take another 600 tons. Kelly wrote to Nat Edwards, asking him to take charge of building the Wolf River bridge to insure its completion on schedule. If the January First deadline was not met he stood to loose all the aid from New London.

Kelly had arranged for a C&NW locomotive to handle the construction train. He also invested in a second-hand engine of foggy origin. It was named ADVANCE in newspaper accounts and was probably from the Milwaukee & St. Paul Railway. A listing of Boston & Providence engines, another indicated source, failed to divulge an ADVANCE, but buying a depleted machine 1000 miles away for brief service defies logic. The engine arrived November 20, 1871 and served less than two years. It is possible that ADVANCE was a "by-product" of the Chicago Fire, a damaged orphan at bargain-basement prices. The machine was "delivered in Chicago," intended for use on the second construction train.

GB&LP's first rails were spiked down November 2, 1871 and the feverish race was on. In December weather conditions in Green Bay forced propellors COMET and ROCKET to offload their rail cargo at Peshtigo, where it was tediously reloaded on flatcars in the ruined town. The loads were then taken south to Green Bay. The schooner FLYING MIST was frozen in the ice and her cargo was transshipped by sleigh over the surface of Green Bay. By now over ten miles had been laid with iron rail. Some reports listed the rail source as English, but most probably it was of Lackawanna Iron & Coal manufacture.

Thomas Roy took the depot construction contracts and began work on the C. L. A. Tank lands in Fort Howard's second ward, constructing a passenger and freight station. Roy also built temporary B&B shanties on flatcars, creating a set of bunk cars for housing on the front. A few miles west of Fort Howard at Duck Creek, another Depot was built by Roy. Bitter cold of

Below: GB&M's first nine engines were Grants. Here, one of them poses on No.2 at Merrillan, Wisconsin.
A. MADDY COLLECTION

minus 22 degrees impeded construction and surveying in mid-December, but the work went on as best it could. Despite the cold, Assistant Engineer F. D. Harvey managed to survey the line west of Northport. A contract for 75,000 ties, enough to build through Waupaca County, allowed the GB&LP to be completed into New London at 10 a.m. on December 19, 1871. On December 26th a train left the C&NW depot about 8 a.m. and arrived in New London a little after 11 a.m.. Kelly had succeeded in fulfilling his contract with little time to spare.

It was at the time of GB&LP's construction into New London that a 14-year old boy showed up for work among the hundreds of men and was given a job as a water boy. The lad was born in Watertown, New York in 1856, his family choosing to settle in New London toward the end of the Civil War. It was coincidence that Frank B. Seymour was born along a road 900 miles away, which was also controlled by Moses Taylor: The Rome, Watertown & Ogdensburg Railroad. Seymour later became a trainman, rising eventually to the GB&W presidency. He worked for no other company but the Green Bay Route.

In early January a semblance of regular service was opened with a mixed train using one of the new forty-foot cabooses. GB&LP received the first of eight Grant-built 4-4-0's, numbered two through nine, inclusive. No.2, the first new engine, was named SAMUEL MARSH, while No.3 became JOSEPH H. SCRANTON, named for the energetic rail selling President of LI&C.

Engineer Marvin L. Pool was assigned to the SCRANTON which went into passenger/mixed service to New London. ADVANCE allegedly handled the first train into New London in December of 1871. One unconfirmed source lists ADVANCE as an inside-connected, wood frame 4-4-0.

Grant Locomotive Works was one of three shops building steam power in Paterson, New Jersey, within cannon shot of Moses Taylor's New York premises. Significantly, David B. Grant, son of the work's President Oliver DeForest Grant, owned 100 shares of GB&LP stock. Engines 2 and 3 cost $13,000 each, and were put in service in late January of 1872.

Grant Locomotive Works enjoyed a good reputation at the time, as it produced a prize-winning exhibition engine in 1867 for the Paris Exposition. It was named AMERICA and the splendid 4-4-0 was highly decorated in German silver, brass and extra paint work. Grant advertising featured it for many years in railroad trade journals. Grant had grown out of the old Swinburne Works, also in Paterson, which crafted only 31 engines in the period from 1848 until 1851. The plant passed through the hands of the New York & Erie Railroad when Swinburne sold to them and by 1851 became the New Jersey Locomotive and Machine Co. It is probable that some of Moses Taylor's friends had financial involvements in Grant, or that it was a customer of Lackawanna Iron & Coal Co. During 1863 and 1864, the Grants purchased and reorganized the property, producing highly standardized engines built with jigs, fixtures and dies. After the Paris show, Grant began the practice of installing brass facsimiles of their Paris medal on engine cabs. The round brass casting emulated both sides of the medal — a portrait of Louis Napoleon (Napoleon III), an appropriate French inscription, plus a flip side of the company name. This left only a small space for an honorary name or engine number. It produced a "dot-dash-dot" configuration. One such medal exists in a Wisconsin museum at New London.

The Green Bay area had cause to celebrate in observing two completed railroads. Chicago & North-Western had been induced to extend its road northward toward iron and timber resources after the Civil War. One of the men most forceful in C&NW's expansion was lumberman-businessman Isaac Stephenson of Marinette, a hard-driving New Brunswick immigrant. Stephenson and his friend, William Butler Ogden of Chicago, invested in the Peshtigo Company and helped influence the C&NW Board to push north. C&NW had control of the Peninsula Railroad in Michigan but, in the 1860's, there remained a gap between Escanaba and Green Bay. This was remedied somewhat in summer by steamer service between the two ports, bringing iron from the north country to the Green Bay Furnace at DePere as well as to Fayette and Frankfort, Michigan. With the completion of the line beside Green Bay, steamers GEORGE L. DUNLAP, SARAH VAN EPPS and SAGINAW were withdrawn from C&NW service. Travel northward on the ice of Green Bay with all its hazards became history. The C&NW contractors turned their finished product over to the railroad December 27, 1871. Green Bay celebrated this new line as well as GB&LP's advance to New London. It had been the contractors of C&NW's line who were accused of creating the fire of October which destroyed Peshtigo, having carelessly set slash fires near the new railroad.

GB&LP finished their bridge over the Wolf River at New London in January of 1872 when regular service began. There were three locomotives which were used for a work extra, a freight and the mixed train. Logs transported into Fort Howard mills accounted for a large percentage of early business. Supplies for both the city and the GB&LP were badly needed in December and the propellors TRUESDALE, COMET and ROCKET again pushed up into Peshtigo Harbor to unload necessities. The Peshtigo Harbor Railroad was rebuilt after the fire, receiving a C&NW engine and rail. Business also began on the Oneida Reservation where a twelve-flatcar train of logs ran daily to the Taylor Mill. Either by plan or out of necessity, the

Below: The 1881 flood as seen from the new W&SP headquarters while under construction. The GB&M arrived from the Wisconsin side over the bridge to the left and backed its trains under the bridge in the center.

Above: A stereoptican view of GB&M's ticket office in Winona in 1881. The spring flood conditions in the Mississippi Valley that year were disastrous.
WINONA COUNTY HISTORICAL SOCIETY

Elmore & Kelly dock and warehouse office acted as a depot for all westbound freight. GB&LP passenger tickets were available at the C&NW depot in Fort Howard. Henry Ketchum presided in his office, Room 4 of the Klaus Block; a freight office was established in Room 7. Another special train began operation to the city in mid-January, stimulated by the passage and bustle of new arrivals from New London. In that wonderful first week, newlyweds from Seymour (17 miles out) journeyed to distant New London as though it were Niagara Falls, returning blissfully the next day in straw-colored coaches. The coaches were Haskell & Barker, fresh from Michigan City, Indiana.

GB&LP boxcars were showing up from H&B in quantity now. The "GB&LP" lettered modestly on their sides gave the investing city a small source of pride. Boxcars followed standard practice of even numbers only, while the accompanying flatcars received the odd numbers. Kelly delivered two certificates of 500 shares in GB&LP (1000 shares) to Green Bay's Mayor Kimball. The $100,000 of shares were exchanged for Green Bay's corporate bonds. The city treasurer duly recorded and the city clerk accepted the voucher. In spring, Green Bay held GB&LP stock at 75 cents on the dollar ($75,000) and bonds totaling $100,000 of indebtedness.

The surveyors now were dealing with the roughest part of GB&LP's territory, New London to the Wisconsin River. A survey was made from Northport to the Manawa area in an attempt to put a line several miles north. The trail passed through Manawa and crossed the Little Wolf River to Iola and Nelsonville. It crossed back through Stockton to Arnott's and finally to Plover. The surveyors crossed the Wisconsin Central 2½ miles west of Nelsonville and ran the line through to Grand Rapids on the Wisconsin. In February Randall again surveyed to the Wisconsin and compared the routes carefully. Several routes were tried through Plover, trying to avoid the Buena Vista Swamp and several side moraines between Arnott and what became Amherst Junction. Randall went back about five miles to resurvey the Waushara Ridge at an easier grade to better their survey of the previous Christmas. There were good reasons for this care — Mile 75, atop the high ridge which dominates the region, is the highest point on the road. The farm of William L. Arnott was crossed and the station there was named for him. Several people, including one Oliver Bean of Plover, had the dubious distinction of having their homes "surveyed through."

The zealous move to avoid the swamp was such that the railroad ultimately became an intimate neighbor of the Pioneer Methodist Church in Plover.

In March of 1872 Randall wrote to Nat Edwards, agreeing to take charge of a survey party headed west of Grand Rapids. Edwards was to provide his own rod and level for surveying. Randall asked him to obtain blankets for camping and meet him at Grand Rapids as soon as possible. During all this, both men were still employed by the canal company. David Kelly hoped that Edwards would become more involved in railroad work. Delayed by sickness, Edwards found a message at Grand Rapids' Raiblin House with instructions for locating the Neillsville survey party, which was already in the field.

Locating any railroad was closely related to aid votes. An energetic Henry Ketchum, bent on securing Amherst's aid, promised the on-line community instant wealth, but was still refused. Private subscriptions raised the aid package to nearly $10,000. The terrain east of Amherst Village was too rugged to accept a railroad; thus, the road passed to the north and swung toward Amherst Junction, climbing toward Mile 75. Ogdensburg fluctuated on the aid question, then voted affirmative. Eventually, Amherst became a Wisconsin Central village, the GB&LP crossing the WC at Amherst Junction, Milepost 69.8.

While pushing westward with trackwork, right-of-way clearing and surveys, GB&LP's management had to construct riverfront terminals for incoming shipments. They began on Fort Howard's dock line with an extensive 900-foot slip along the Fox River. A 500×900-foot structure was all that was planned the first year. It included a 300×100-foot warehouse and employed a sunken railroad alongside covered transfer platforms. This type of building, also found at Winona on the W&SP, was used to transship goods to river steamers. Kelly put Nat Edwards in charge of dock construction and also an economical water tank at the waterfront. Construction began in June 1872 and it later became GBWSTP's coal dock, finally passing into the hands of the C. Reiss Coal Co.

GB&LP's second construction contract was put into effect February 12, 1872, cancelling that of the previous year. The purpose of this document was to put the railroad on the banks of the Wisconsin River by the end of 1872, while Kelly's salary and incentive program remained intact. Lackawanna Iron & Coal Co. continued to advance money, rails and equipment as town and municipal bonds were surrendered to the GB&LP. The first rail shipment of the year arrived from Scranton in June. Some rail which came onto the Elmore & Kelly dockage was destined for other roads such as Wisconsin Central and St. Paul & Sioux City (Omaha Road). Some rail shipments for GB&LP had to be offloaded at Mackinaw City the previous winter and were just now arriving. At the same time, subcontractors put a grade across Plover's main street, 82 miles west of Green Bay. A settlement had to be made with Plover's Mrs. Drake for a right-of-way through her property; the luckless woman had to move her buildings. Mr. William Jones turned the first load of Plover dirt, with horsepower supplied by Mr. F. W. Halliday, a family name noted in the road's history. A contract was negotiated for Plover's depot, a 30×68-foot structure. A few miles east, graders found it difficult to work in the clay in the moraine deposits around Mile 76, yet they continued doing the dull labor of leveling the new line and preparing it for ties and rail. Throughout the summer, ties and rails were continually forwarded to the front under the piercing gaze of David Kelly and his lieutenants. Still, the work went forward at various speeds, depending on weather and soil conditions, swamp filling

episodes or creek crossings. The end product was inspected by town commissioners; valuable papers would be passed to authorities, and the railroad backed by money men would receive payments, having fulfilled its contract.

Kelly intended to complete the railroad that year to Merrillan, 148 miles from Green Bay and 110 miles west of New London's railhead. This juncture with the West Wisconsin Railroad would put the GB&LP road in contact with St. Paul grain markets and with the Northern Pacific Railroad, a connection sought by Chicago roads. West Wisconsin Railroad was completed to St. Paul in February 1872, an expansion aided by C&NW. The North Western was also on the march to the south, pushing its Baraboo Air Line northwestward from Madison, 126 miles to La Crosse. Previously, the La Crosse, Trempeleau & Prescott Railroad was built to span the 29 miles from Winona Junction (later Medary Junction) to Winona, which included the Mississippi bridge. Completion of C&NW's projects would give the W&SP an allied route to Chicago, previously effected over CM&STP via Winona Junction.

Merrillan was a scant sixty miles from the Mississippi marshlands opposite Winona. Kelly and President Ketchum went to Winona to confer with businessmen regarding a bonus. Initially, it was proposed to shift the Winona & Southwestern Railroad aid package of $150,000 to the GB&LP, but Kelly and Ketchum counterproposed a $75,000 direct commitment. The matter rested for some months, but became a thorny issue in succeeding years. While in the west, Kelly and Ketchum visited Wabasha to make a final proposal. Subsequent visits to Trempeleau Valley towns were made and proposals were set before meetings. Black River Falls was approached and surveys were made to reach the Jackson County seat. Everyone in Western Wisconsin was well informed of GB&LP's expected arrival. The Missisippi River cities continued to squabble over the issue of GB&LP's ultimate terminal and their newspapers kept a steady fire on rivals.

Late in 1872 locomotives ordered in June began to arrive, trickling in as financial arrangements were made. As track and bonds both moved positively, funds were released to the locomotive builder. Engine No.4, *MOSES TAYLOR,* a 4-4-0, arrived in September and was immediately dispatched to Merrillan via CM&STP and West Wisconsin RR to operate a construction train eastward. The TAYLOR cost $10,000 and weighed 37 tons. Rail-laden flatcars were forwarded from Milwaukee, rented from CM&STP on a six-day basis. When the two halves of the line were joined at Camp 12 on December 24, 1872, more power was available. Arriving in December were engines No.5, JOHN I. BLAIR, and No.6, GEORGE F. TALMAN, both Grant 4-4-0's. Grant was paid $10,700 for each.

Tracklaying west of New London started in August 1872, actively engaging 2000 men. Kelly's friend, Steven Kenrick, shared responsibilities. He started as a conductor and during the course of the summer was promoted, first to Master of Transportation and finally to Train Dispatcher. By mid-September rail had reached Ogdensburg. Plover was on line by October 21st and completion to Grand Rapids was accomplished by November 7th. There were still holdouts such as Joseph Carpenter, however, in the condemnation proceedings. Carpenter wanted more money, but got only $100; he resorted to court and lost. October brought problems with the cuts in the Town of Stockton. Huge glacial boulders surrounded by hard clay had to be removed from the moraine deposits. The crossing at Amherst Junction was installed while heavy work at Mile 75

Below: This 1880's view of Winona looks southeast and downstream. The W&SP freighthouse is on the extreme lower right. Eastmoor can be seen in the center distance on the Wisconsin side.
WINONA COUNTY HISTORICAL SOCIETY

continued. Work extras were constantly moving loose rock from the cuts east of Plover to the Wisconsin River Bridge site at Grand Rapids. Plover station windows rattled with the passage of Grant engines and rail flats en route to the front.

Mrs. A. C. Macrorie was the first female passenger to arrive in Plover but the depot was still unfinished and the agent, James Hall, was not yet on duty. In November the railhead was twelve miles west of Grand Rapids, moving over sandy flatland toward "Mormon Riffle," the crossing of the Black River. In September a local man, L. G. Merrill, contracted for the bridge where Hatfield is today. Gone was aid from Neillsville, 14 miles north, for the community was too far away from the chosen route. Due to conflict with the city named for Sherburne S. Merrill of Milwaukee Road, L. G. Merrill's town was named Merrillan. Merrillan had about seventy buildings and a Junction Hotel, allegedly run by a railroad agent. The original eating house burned in 1876; however, the hotel flourished into the 20th Century.

Kelly's railroad immediately required all the necessities of a north country line, including enginehouses at Green Bay and Grand Rapids. The company contracted for a four-stall round-house at Grand Rapids (64 × 62 × 56 feet). Construction began in the fall and was completed in December when the railroad arrived. The land, donated by the city, required considerable filling. Green Bay's five-stall house was begun about the same time. Its front wall was 75 feet, the rear 110 feet, and it had a sixty-foot depth. The structure had a conventional stone foundation and its walls were built of brick imported from Oshkosh.

The final days of construction into Merrillan was a frenzy of last-minute activity before winter set in. By December 17th, Kelly's forces had finished tracklaying past Mile 132, two miles west of Pray. Rail-carrying vessels such as the JAY GOULD braved Great Lakes storms to make port in Milwaukee to unload rail for the west end. A storm forced the schooner MARGARET GAFFE to return to Buffalo with a similar load. Its 388 tons of iron was later forwarded by rail. Completion to Merrillan came on January 1, 1873. GB&LP issued timetable No.2, which took effect that day. Passenger No.1 left Green Bay at 9:15 a.m., arriving at Merrillan at 8:08 p.m. No.2 left Jackson County at 5:05 a.m. and rolled into Green Bay at 4:00 p.m. The trains met at Scandinavia at 12:36 p.m. Freight service was offered only to Grand Rapids. Special instructions included a full stop at the Wolf River Bridge, west of New London. Mr. Kelly had adhered to his contract of February 12, 1872, which called for service to Grand Rapids by the first of the new year.

Wood County (Grand Rapids) had pledged $150,000 to aid the GB&LP, a major reason for the line passing through the community. Allegedly, the railroad was not finished on time and some adjustments had to be made before the Wood County bonds were released. One casualty of the new railroad was the loss of stage coach service from Grand Rapids to Stevens Point via Plover. A new age had dawned; the stage took four hours, the train 45 minutes.

Off-line observers discussed GB&LP's value to the region. Hudson (Wisconsin) observed that a West Wisconsin-GB&LP route eastward would benefit St. Croix County's wheatgrowers. They had milling interests at Menasha in mind, interested in a grain supply from the west via C&NW. The dawn of Minneapolis as the predominating grain center would bear heavily on Menasha which turned instead to paper-making. St. Paul was 282 miles from Green Bay and Hudson's paper predicted heavy traffic for the new line. In anticipation of more prosperous times, GB&LP arranged for new office space in E. J. Shaylor's

new building at Pine and Adams streets in downtown Green Bay. The road had the second story to itself, occupying the building for the balance of the 19th Century. Shaylor himself had been general freight agent, but chose to resign in favor of W. S. Mellen, who signed on from C&NW service. Mellen later returned in 1874, then he became Wisconsin Central Railway's general manager in 1886. F. L. Smith, one of the road's first dispatchers, came aboard from Northwestern Telegraph Co.

One of GB&LP's contractors in 1872 was George Hiles of Dexterville. Hiles was associated with construction from Grand Rapids to Winona, which passed through his mill town on the Yellow River. Hiles was born in Farmington, Michigan in 1829, becoming one of Baraboo, Wisconsin's first settlers. He later moved north into the Wood County wilderness to establish a lumber mill. Taking on the general contract to grade and tie the road to the Yellow, he stayed with the work to Winona. Five hundred men worked subcontracts of from five to eight miles and used 50,000 ties from the Hiles mill. Dexterville and neighboring Pittsville were the domain of "King George." He engaged in land speculation in Trempeleau Valley towns just ahead of the advancing railhead. Some of the land holdings were retained by his heirs into the 20th Century.

George Hiles eventually became involved in Chicago real estate, Florida pinelands and a 5000-acre horse ranch in Nebraska, amassing a $3,000,000 fortune. In the 1890's he moved to fashionable Farwell Avenue in Milwaukee. He died there in 1896 and his body was returned to Dexterville. The burial site was marked by a forty-foot obelisk which required a GB&W spur to be built. The landmark was perhaps the tallest object in the former townsite. Hiles' other railroad ventures included the Wisconsin, Pittsville and Superior Railway, north of Babcock, which became the property of the Milwaukee Road. He also arranged for his own logging railroad out of Dexterville to use GB&LP tracks for several miles to gain access to a timber tract.

Hiles and Henry Ketchum engaged in several businesses together, including Scranton Boom & Manufacturing Company, which supplied the railroad with much of its needed timber and ties. The trio of Kelly, Ketchum and Hiles established another mill at Scranton (Mile 121), allegedly capable of producing 40,000 board feet of lumber and 50,000 shingles on a twelve-hour day basis. In succeeding years, the firm went to court over rights to dam a stream for private purposes. Dexterville fell to ruin after Hiles Land and Lumber Company ceased operations in 1905. Many of its lumbermen moved to Washington State or to northern Wisconsin. In the end, the scrappers of World War I took whatever remained.

As GB&LP neared the Missisipi, weekly editorials were focused upon its destiny and the city that would win the end of the line. Pro-La Crosse commentaries had the road at first destined for the Black River valley, with a route through the hill country, which included tunneling a long distance. Such pipe dreams were not in keeping with the promoter's view of reality. Wabasha kept up a steady agitation and Ketchum repeatedly visited with town officials, who in turn attempted to raise aid for GB&LP and Lake Pepin & Omaha, the city's high card. All three cities kept up pressure into the mid-70's, but the financial ability of Winona was to prevail. Wabasha offered the narrow river crossing, as well as the opportunity to invest in the Minnesota line to Rochester and ample grounds, but was unable to back the scheme with adequate aid. Wabasha again sent a delegation to Green Bay to appeal. Winona lauded Kelly and company for the accomplishment of 110 miles finished in 1872,

with 18 bridges, one of which was 1492 feet long. The Republican sagely claimed GB&LP had accomplished more than any other Wisconsin road to date, expending $2 million in the process. It also stated that several routes out of Wabasha were contingent upon GB&LP arriving first. Those routes included a Milwaukee Road subsidiary to be built from the Missisippi up the Chippewa Valley to Lake Superior, obviously competing for the northwest land grant. Others were to Faribault, Owatonna and Rochester. Winona was sure that its strong railroad connections and the prospects of others would help its citizens vote an aid package in time. If more money had been available, Wabasha's future may have been different.

In mid-February Ketchum went to Wabasha, heard the position of the citizens, and then continued to Winona. The bargain was to build GB&LP to a point opposite Winona on the condition that the W&SW bonus be voted to GB&LP — or at least $100,000 of the $150,000 offered by the city. The acceptance began an extended embarrassment which was to plague the railroad for many years in Winona. Minnesota law required that such a change in a bonding vote be submitted to the State Legislature. Immediately, forces opposed to the transfer sped off to St. Paul to block the proposal. Ketchum, in meetings with leading citizens at Ely Hall, clarified that his company was not in league with C&NW, as averred in the press. He also claimed that there was no dissent on GB&LP's board as to destination, and the GB&LP would operate its trains into Winona, but not necessarily build a railroad into the city. In order to go there, Ketchum had to secure aid in the Trempeleau Valley, which was more feasible than on the less populated Wabasha route. The route to Winona was clinched when several communities came up with bonding.

In 1873 the nation slid into a situation of tightened capital and interest rates reached notable highs. It was prudent, therefore, for the new railroad to reach a strong terminal point as soon as possible, something Moses Taylor had advocated for his railroads. On May 5, 1873, GB&LP contracted for use of the La Crosse, Trempeleau & Prescott Railroad (C&NW between La Crosse and Winona), including their recently finished bridge into Winona. The contract included a wheelage plan of ten percent of one-third the cost of railroad used, plus ten percent of one-half the cost of the railroad bridge, plus any filling to be done in the first three years. There was also one-third of cost of fences, ties, piling, culvert, cattle guards and the tax assessments. Other charges included twenty cents per passenger and one cent per hundredweight on freight traffic. These costs were to be borne for twenty years. C&NW's President Martin L. Sykes signed the contract, as did Henry Ketchum for GB&LP.

GB&LP's annual meeting for 1873 reinstated Ketchum as president while Green Bay's men dominated the officers' posts. Walter Scranton was also elected, representing the easterners, along with Samuel Marsh Sr. and Samuel Marsh Jr. The elderly gentleman of the canal company and the Erie Railway passed away in November 1872. He bequeathed his shares of GB&LP (1406) be divided among several of the Marsh clan, including David Kelly's mother. Kelly traveled east upon notification of the death of his "Uncle Samuel," also informing Nat Edwards.

In late Spring, Stephen Kenrick became assistant superintendent and set out to inspect the line's condition after the first winter. His work included checking for roadway settling, washouts and erosion on the fresh, new fills. Kenrick also had to inspect the new rolling stock, including a coach and a baggage car from Haskell & Barker. The coach was finished in black walnut and birds-eye maple. The Anchor Line (Pennsylvania Railroad) sent Mr. John Blegan to confer with Kenrick regarding immigration prospects, which would include Germans to Wood County and Polish down in the Trempeleau and also Winona.

Henry Ketchum declined to comment about the final terminal city, as he was still awaiting aid-canvassing results. Surveyors began their work west of Merrillan, advancing to the Trempeleau Valley's broad, rolling entrance west of Alma Center. They moved toward the village of Whitehall and a Norwegian church, 17 miles from Galesville. There was still a chance that La Crosse would decide to aid the road. The surveyors stayed close beside the Trempeleau River as it twisted and turned down to the marshes east of Winona. At one point the railroad survey actually turned back southeast for nearly a mile, then south and finally southwest. It was far more crooked than a hypothetical Wabasha route but, because of the towering hills in the final 15 miles, there was no other choice.

Facts showed that the tightly stretched money supply nationwide was beginning to tear the fabric of the new company. Cash shortages brought about a voucher plan which helped but only until public acceptance failed. At the Black River (Hatfield) a strike occurred on a gravel train. The workers asked for $1.75 per day, claiming that the Wisconsin Valley Road paid $2.00. The prevailing rate at that time was $1.50. Station agent Stockwell telegraphed to Kenrick. At mealtime in boarding cars, Kenrick's instructions were carried out. Each of the 35 men was asked if he would work at the old wage. Those who answered in the negative were excluded from the evening meal. The matter was settled.

George Hiles began grading the last week in May of 1873, pushing the work down the Trempeleau, through Alma Center and Hixton in June. Rail was piling up at Buffalo, awaiting the plodding CANESTEO or one of the several schooners wallowing up through the lakes chain with their cargoes. Late June found the first of the vessels in, and 230 tons were slung onto flat cars and sent west. The iron trains rumbled westward over fresh new roadbed which firmed up in warmer summer days. By August George Hiles' men were working in swampy lowlands ten miles from Winona and rail was in place to Taylor, the small community named for a large investor. There were 27 medium-sized bridges in place throughout the low country as well. George Hiles and partner W. M. Dayton set up headquarters in Arcadia, planning to move down to the Missisippi by the end of August. Time was critical. Hiles advertised for 500 men and 150 teams, acquiring some of the harvest hands from Minnesota wheatfields. In October, after the "Panic of '73" and the name change to Green Bay & Minnesota Railroad, there remained only five miles to be built between the end of track and the Great River.

Excavation of a sandstone bluff, called "The Pass," slowed the pace toward the lowlands junction with the Prescott Road. Some bridges framed at Merrillan were partially floated down the Trempeleau to their positions. It was the sole instance of the treacherous river ever helping the railroad. Winona Common Council voted to allow the Green Bay road access to the public levee, giving them a single track adjacent to W&SP's. This would allow the new railroad to interchange business with both railroads and steamboat lines such as Diamond Jo Line. In early December 1873 the Green Bay route was built into a junction with the Prescott Road at what became Marshland Junction. Mr. B. P. Roberts, roadmaster, drove the final spike (he had driven the very first) on a Sunday so as not to interrupt C&NW's Winona-bound traffic. The new road was built in 25 months with only 15 actual working months. It had 24 depots, working

telegraph lines and a definite river crossing. Timetable No. 5 was issued, to take effect Thursday, December 18, 1873 and the brave new road headed into a harsh world far different than it had known in 1866.

Above: Diamond Jo Line's steamer and barges at Winona in 1875. Decline of steamboat trade was steady after 1880.
MINNESOTA HISTORICAL SOCIETY

In the mid-1870's, Diamond Jo Steamers acted as branchline connections for GB&M. They carried trade to and from Eastmoor, which was opposite Winona.
MINNESOTA HISTORICAL SOCIETY

3

TROUBLES
&
WOES

GB&M's first train ushered in an era of troubles for the new road that lasted 22 years. Pressures on capital by speculative promotion finally breached the wall of Philadelphia brokers Jay Cooke & Co., who were deeply engaged in the Northern Pacific expansion scheme. Many banks suspended payments and the shock waves hit thousands of American businesses, which were helpless against the tide. Railroads across the nation were financially embarrassed and laid aside their expansive and ambitious schemes.

In September of 1873 the Panic struck. *The Green Bay Advocate* headlines affirmed the disaster and listed the suspended banks on its pages. Manufacturing firms, including locomotive works, were shut down. Rogers in Paterson discharged 500 men due to the cancellation of three month's worth of orders; Danforth and Grant were also forced to close. Previous to the disaster, Grant had become enmeshed in a $2 million Russian government contract with a time-penalty clause; nine hundred jobs hung in the balance. Mr. Oliver D. Grant himself went to St. Petersburg to rearrange the contract and, though that disaster was averted, the company never recovered from the Panic. Its last contributions to the GB&M roster were four new locomotives. All were paid for by Edwin F. Hatfield Jr., president of Lackawanna Iron & Coal Co., at a cost of $12,250 each. The 4-4-0's (numbers seven to nine, inclusive) arrived in June 1873. The name assigned to No. 7 was CHARLES RUSSELL, but it eventually wore the name WINONA, in spite of the financial row stirred in that city. No. 7 was badly damaged in the Grand Rapids roundhouse fire of May 1879. No. 8 was named WILLIAM E. DODGE, for the prominent Phelps, Dodge & Co. partner and member of the Lackawanna group. The R. G. ROLSTON, No. 9, was named for another investor. The final Grant was No. 1, the switcher DIAMOND JO, which arrived April 22, 1874 for Fort Howard yard duty.

Formal opening of the line was celebrated with a special excursion. A train from Green Bay arrived in Winona at 9 p.m. and the crowd of visitors were taken to the Huff House, an eligible Winona hotel, where they were refreshed from their day of traveling. Some of Winona's best mingled with Colonel Robinson and bankers Decker and Lawton. C&NW officials were also present, including H. H. Porter, later Omaha Road president, Marvin Hughitt, general superintendent of C&NW, and various department heads. The party became a double celebration for, in September, the Baraboo Air Line had been completed to Winona Junction where it joined the Prescott Road and the bridge to Winona. Their line opened the route of continuous railway service from Chicago to Winona and beyond. After conferring with GB&M's representatives, the C&NW officials traveled west over the W&SP. CM&STP also used the Prescott bridge until their line on the west side of the Missippi was finished, complete with a bridge at La Crosse, in 1875.

GB&M executed a contract with W&SP, separate from the agreement covering the use of the bridge. For about one mile on the Minnesota side to the W&SP shops, GB&M could operate at a charge of $1.00 per car. W&SP agreed to do GB&M's switching and allowed GB&M to lay some track on W&SP's land. The freight charges would be 35 cents per ton. The engines of GB&M were housed and serviced for $50 each per month. The contract, dated January 1, 1874, was signed by Henry Ketchum for GB&M and J. B. Redfield for W&SP.

When the Prescott's wood bridge was completed in 1872 it was tested with a train of six flatcars loaded with rails. Each car weighed 19 tons and was pulled by a thirty-ton locomotive. Next, the rails were unloaded onto the bridge structure, putting sixty tons dead weight in the midst of each span. Three locomotives were then run on and the bridge's deflection was measured. All present were satisfied with the three-quarter-inch sag under the 140-ton load. Contractor C. C. Smith, who had built the bridge, was also responsible for the West Wisconsin's Hudson bridge and, later, the CM&STP span at La Crosse. The draw was a Post's Patent diagonal truss, 360 feet long and 36 feet high in center, with a twenty-foot entry height. Four centerposts weighing 800 pounds and 300 tons of ore iron were used in construction; the turntable was about forty tons. The first Prescott bridge collapsed on May 26, 1871, dumping a locomotive, tender first, down the swingspan deck into the water. It was recovered undamaged. The route from Winona Junction to Winona was finally reopened January 16, 1872, making C&NW's western connection.

The jinxed bridge continued to present problems. On February 27, 1874, just after GB&M's rights to use it had been established, a C&NW passenger train derailed on the low approach trestle on the Wisconsin side. The coaches landed on their roofs. The wreck was caused by spread rails but the train was traveling at slow speed and there was only one fatality.

It is interesting to note that Moses Taylor owned $101,000 of La Crosse, Trempeleau & Prescott Railroad Co. bonds. At the same time, his W&SP holdings were $115,000 and, in the 1875 Annual Report of Green Bay & Minnesota, Taylor held 50,006 shares as trustee and 1579 shares personally. This ownership could have had much to do with the Green Bay's choice of Winona as terminal, which was overseen by Taylor. Certainly the trying financial conditions in 1873 influenced the decision, capped by the September crash and the availability of town aid. Wabasha had a railroad by 1873, with CM&STP's river line to the Twin Cities nearly complete. The shadow of Lackawanna interests was stretched to the Missisippi where one could find Lackawanna anthracite coal marketed in Winona coal yards.

Green Bay & Minnesota had been reduced to paying its construction crews partly in scrip for several months after the Panic and probably for some time before that. Discontent over the scrip payments surfaced when the gangs received "50-50" wage payments in the contractor's Winona office. For several days during February 1874, labor relations deteriorated when scrip was handed out in lieu of hard currency. The incident achieved statewide notoriety when a ballasting gang spiked a sandpit switch against the main line at Camp Roberts near Dodge. Determined, the unruly mob stopped the eastbound passenger train on February 11th, allegedly armed with track tools and demanding back pay from all who would listen. Conductor Holmes, promising to contact the proper authority, finally got his train underway.

The freight was refused passage over the spiked switch the following morning. The affair magnified and a food shortage at the contractor's camp of rude huts and nightly campfires increased the threats leveled at the officials. David Kelly had left orders to finish ballasting and grading as money became available and eventually sent a telegram from the east ordering crews to procced with the the extra work. It was then that the extracur-

ricular activity broke out; the workers were not confident they would be paid in currency. Superintendent Kenrick arrived but was unable to assuage the crowd. More trains were incarcerated in the Dodge siding, the switches at either end spiked. Finally Kenrick was able to convince the ringleaders that his offer to pay them in full the next morning was sincere. Stating that it was not their intent to injure the road, the men returned to work.

Kenrick took the pay car, a caboose with covered windows, up to Camp Roberts. The laborers were let into the caboose two at a time. The names of the twenty leaders were placed on a special list and they were called in separately. There was no resistance. All of them were paid in full and ornamented with handcuffs; the leading offenders were arrested by Trempeleau County sheriff's deputies. The balance of the dissenters dispersed when they sighted their handcuffed companions alighting from the caboose. The small amount of backpay due the group was only $2000. They had drawn much of their pay in clothing and other provisions. After settling with the noisiest, it was found that he owed the company sixty cents. Judge Newman presided over Trempeleau County Court and the trial of the "Dodge 23." Nine offenders were bound over for trial to district court. They were conveyed in an omnibus sleigh over the river ice to La Crosse. The alleged charges included obstruction of the U.S. Mail aboard the GB&M passenger trains, a service which began early in 1874. The "Green Bay Nine" were found not guilty, with no malice proved by the prosecution. The press in La Crosse thought it was highly improper to use county courts to settle a dispute between company and employees.

Frank S. Halliday lived four miles west of Plover alongside the GB&LP. He went to work shortly after its arrival and eventually rose to chief engineer of the railroad; his son Frank Jr. followed in his footsteps. The elder Halliday, starting on section work, soon was promoted to foreman and eventually worked as a surveyor. It was Halliday who was responsible for locating all trackage east of Green Bay in the 1890's. In 1874 he remarked that his crew stayed with "Old Mr. Schneider, a good

old German" residing at Marshland, when there was hardly any settlement at all. Halliday also related that the railroad was not prosperous and in due time went into the hands of receivers. He once went six months without pay, finally receiving scrip. Many quit until there were barely enough men remaining to keep the road going. He decided to hang on to his scrip after others sold out. He alone received payment in the full amount.

GB&M plunged into its first operating year. Its bookkeeping for the years 1872 throuth 1874 had to be a "mixed bag" of construction accounts and income receipts because parts of the line were in regular operation. Earnings and operating expenses were held open through 1875, at which time earnings were closed into operating expenses and the deficit written off to profit and loss. Laird, Norton & Company had shipments of lumber rolling eastward to help build up the towns of the Trempeleau, perhaps competing directly with the efforts of the lumber companies owned by George Hiles and Henry Ketchum. Early in 1874 Hiles and H. M. Knowles, the latter of Winona, formed Hiles & Knowles and leased a location in Winona, selling the lumber of Dexterville and Scranton in the increasingly important Winona market. Reportedly, Wisconsin Valley Railroad, under the Joy interests and close friends of Moses Taylor, supplied special lumber to GB&M, interchanging at Centralia. Business also included a trip by Kelly to secure 200 boxcars and four new locomotives for spring delivery. Next, the company started on the Eastmoor extension, driving the first piles west of the Marshland interchange with the North-Western. It was also anticipated that Union Steamboat Co. would increase service to Green Bay in the Spring.

Grant Locomotive Works delivered just one switch engine to GB&M in April 1874. The DIAMOND JO worked the Fort Howard dock area and was occasionally seen at Grand Rapids, Wisconsin in later years. This scene was photographed about 1888 near Green Bay Junction station.

T. VAN DREESE PHOTO

GBW&STP No.1, formerly the DIAMOND JO, paused at Grand Rapids, Wisconsin in the 1890's. The switcher was a Grant Locomotive Works product.
GREEN BAY & WESTERN PHOTO

A rise of anti-railroad action and the unprecedented prominence of "new process" flour being made in Minneapolis commanded world attention in the spring of 1874. Cadwallader Colden Washburn led the anti-railroad battle in Wisconsin for many years and, while he was governor of Wisconsin, he ran against railroad interests and lost. Alexander Mitchell of the Milwaukee Road was intent upon seeing the defeat of Washburn for vetoing the Missisippi River bridge bill, which eventually joined parts of an all-Milwaukee Road Chicago-Minneapolis main line. Washburn was a La Crosse resident but heavily engaged in perfecting the flour-milling process in Minneapolis, which very shortly would influence railroad strategy across Wisconsin. Other area producers would diminish in contrast to the explosive growth in Minneapolis.

Wisconsin's Potter Law was reported March 7, 1874, modeled after an Illinois law which allegedly provided for fair and equitable rates set up by a railroad commission. It was introduced by Robert L. D. Potter of Washara County for the Republican minority and it passed as a result of inadequate vigilance by the opposition. The law classified Wisconsin lines, thereby limiting their charges on services. It was the height of Granger reform, the backlash against unbridled capitalist excess. Of the three classes, GB&M and Wisconsin Central fared only as second-class lines. Their passenger tariffs were fixed as a result and could not exceed 3½ cents per mile and set four freight classes. Kelly's partner, Andrew E. Elmore, condemned the system as a "stupid tax," while *The Milwaukee Sentinel* regarded it as "the best of its kind." The law, however, failed to take into account costs of capital or the varied conditions under which the pioneering railroads operated. It established penalties for non-compliance, a condition which guaranteed a "cornfield meet" in the state courts.

The Potter Law, reigning from 1874 to 1876, was exactly what the GB&M didn't need. High profits were needed to cover start-up costs and necessary improvements. Milwaukee Road's powerful President Alexander Mitchell chose to defy the law, as did C&NW's executive Albert Keep, both calling it impairment of contracts by the government. The hapless GB&M continued with business as usual; compliance would reduce their freight rates by thirty percent and passenger receipts by 12½ percent. David Kelly was interviewed about the Potter Law, along with Agent W. S. Mellen. Kelly, always the lawyer, stated that GB&M would do business ". . . justly and with due regard to the interests of those doing business with us." The interview outlined compliance as corporate suicide for the new company, stating that it would set railroading back five years in Wisconsin. The law was eroded away by political-railroad forces and Grangerism's decline. The new governor, Harrison Ludington, showed that such laws would impair fiscal reputations of state and local bonds in the market. The recession of the mid-1870's also contributed to its demise, leaving the law as only a rough beginning in the complex matter or railroad regulation. The Potter Law incident contributed to the numerous troubles of GB&M.

One incident put GB&M stage front. On January 6, 1874, Dr. D. L. Hays, noted arctic explorer of the time, was in need of fast transportation from Plover to Neenah. The direct route offered by Wisconsin Central Railway was unavailable and GB&M filled the breach. Superintendent Kenrick ordered

Engineer Marvin L. Pool to run No. 4 engine, the TAYLOR, on a caboose hop to Green Bay. Pool allegedly ran the 82 miles in less than two hours and the doctor made his lecture on time. The excursion east cost Hays $79.

Later that month an accident occurred as a result of winter versus the cast-iron railway wheel. Train No. 1 was delayed west of Plover with a broken flange on a locomotive pony truck. This kind of accident was a recurring nightmare of early enginemen. The hogger saw it break, managing to whistle "down brakes" before a derailment came. The truck was snubbed up to the frame rails with chain and blocked and the entire train was gingerly brought back into Plover.

Wheat traffic became comparatively heavy even before completion to Winona. In 1873 GB&M carried 46,472 tons over its line; in 1874 the total was 105,940 tons. Only 91,790 tons of wheat were carried in 1875, a reflection of that depressed year. In September of 1873 *The Green Bay Advocate* noted some fifty cars in the GB&M yard at Fort Howard. They represented Northern Pacific, St. Paul & Pacific, Lake Superior & Mississippi and Sioux City & St. Paul, all lines which were heavily into transporting Minnesota grain. The wheat loads came via the Merrillan interchange with the West Wisconsin Railway, destined for Elmore & Kelly's elevator and transshipment to Buffalo and beyond. In his "spicy memorial" on government interference in grain matters, Andrew Elmore again vented his views on the schemes accompanying the Potter Law which were aimed at regulating elevator charges. The elevator bill was struck down by the attorney general but the zeal of Granger reform had touched Fort Howard's dockside.

Coal shipments destined for St. Paul, along with salt used for meat-packing, were loaded back to the west from Green Bay. The Elmore & Kelly complex was enviably poised to deal with traffic in both directions. A contract with Union Steamboat Co. of New York, dated September 9, 1873, called for steamers PASSAIC and CANESTEO to operate between Buffalo and Green Bay, with intermediate stops at Cleveland, Detroit and Port Huron. GB&M had to guarantee the line $45,000 during a navigation season, equal to the amount of Milwaukee trade by

Union Steamboat. The boat line had to surrender all of its westbound business to GB&M; the railroad gave the boats all of its eastern trade. GB&M was to influence shippers using the road to route their commodities east of Buffalo via the Erie Railway, which was also the controller of Union Steamboat. The low rates were set at 27 cents per hundredweight. The September agreement also included the Diamond Jo Line on the Mississippi as an agent of the other participants. The river boats gathered bulk shipments into the railhead at Winona, thus acting as a branch system at the road's end. In 1874 the beginning of a dock complex on the east side further enhanced the idea. Piles driven in icy lowlands just west of Marshland Junction would bear fruit by spring in the form of Eastmoor, a landing for the Diamond Jo Line.

Joseph Reynolds was the founder of the Diamond Jo Line which had a history rooted in the Missisippi grain trade. Reynolds was a transplant who entered the flour-milling industry in Rockland, New York. After marrying Mary E. Morton in Rockland he came west to Chicago. His new business had him traveling extensively in Wisconsin and Minnesota, buying hides and furs. He left Chicago in 1860 and began buying grain at Prairie du Chien. Reynolds went into steamboating and bought his first boat, LANSING, a 123-ton sternwheeler. It went into Lansing (Iowa)-Prairie du Chien service under the nose of the powerful major lines. His success, however, was limited by the formation of Northwestern Union Packet Co., the ultimate monopoly.

Reynolds later negotiated with C&NW to deal in St. Paul-Fulton, Illinois traffic which brought Diamond Jo Lines prosperity. Diamond Jo Lines served the Chippewa River valley before railroads reached the area. By 1873 Reynolds' organiza-

GBW&STP 4-4-0 No. 5, JOHN I. BLAIR, pauses in the sparsely populated region near Hixton in the early 1880's. No. 5 is a typical Grant product of the 1870's.
T. VAN DREESE COLLECTION

tion had five steamboats and approximately twenty barges. IMPERIAL, the biggest steamer, was able to power heavy tows of barges plus a 100,000-bushel deckload. In comparison, the 100,000 bushels of 1873 is equal to 250 carloads — using 20,000-pound-capacity boxcars — or 400 bushels per car. The "standard" engines (4-4-0's) of the era could handle no more than 25 cars continuously. To move 100,000 bushels would have required ten trains of 25 cars.

In March 1874 Diamond Jo Lines began contracting Green Bay-St. Paul business, offering rates of $10 per car. This was quoted five cents per hundredweight less than any rail rate then standing. DJL would handle the sought-after western grain business, but it also handled coal traffic to St. Paul. Daily service from La Crosse and Winona to St. Paul included traffic from all Mississippi landings above Rock Island, coordinated with GB&M and W&SP railheads. The service was seasonal and IMPERIAL made ready to leave St. Louis, traditional ice-free haven for boats, in May of 1874. In one instance, GB&M started eight carloads toward St. Paul, arriving in Winona at 2 a.m. The cargo came from the east via Buffalo boats. Significantly, wheat shipments to Winona, rated as Minnesota's forth largest wheat market, peaked in 1873 with the burgeoning Minneapolis milling industry rising to eclipse all others.

A river-area wholesaler made a buying trip east in May 1874 to attend regular auctions of coffee, tea and wines. He found the New York market greatly depressed due to short money supply, favorably lowering his prices. He shipped his bargains westward via Empire Line, GB&M and DJL, which arrived in seven days at the Missisippi. DJL received a new employee from GB&M early in 1874, when Daniel Atwood was appointed DJL's general freight agent. Atwood was one of the first to leave GB&M in those troubled times. In April, however, GB&M sealed its agreement with DJL by giving the name DIAMOND JO to a new four-wheeled switch engine from Grant. The 0-4-0 arrived to work far from Eastmoor. It was numbered "1," replacing the retired ADVANCE, and remained the sole yard engine on the roster until 1892.

GB&M's winter of completion caused only a short lull. On January 26, 1874, an engineering party crossed from Winona's east-end lumber district to begin surveys for the Eastmoor extension. They found that the three-mile line to be built west of Marshland Junction would be largely pile trestle to the proposed grain elevator and dock location. Estimates called for 7000 piles to complete a straight line to the riverbank over the swampland. A curving trestle would bring the line parallel to the river for dock access. Wharf frontage would run 400 feet for steamer transfer and an island at the site would be graded some 2000 feet back from the river.

Contractor Frank Johnson began in February, bringing in three machines to drive piles for the dock. His completion date was April 1st, a tight deadline which demanded long hours. Chief Engineer J. T. Alton contracted for ties and timber, while the heavier wood came from Henry Ketchum's mill at Merrillan. Green Bay's Taylor & Duncan supplied castings and an engine of 16 × 28-inch dimensions. GB&M's Fort Howard Shops made up bolts and rods for the trestle bents and caps. Captain Sam Van Gorder of Winona, veteran contractor and riverman, had a gang of 150 stalwart Poles and Bohemians hard at work grading. Everyone was apprehensive about a sudden thaw that might flood lowland worksites and stall progress.

The grain elevator itself was designed by George M. Moulton of the Chicago firm of J. T. Moulton & Son. Moulton had been responsible for elevators at Duluth and Stillwater. The East-moor elevator would be built to a 100-foot height with a capacity of 150,000 bushels. George Moulton brought his own force to Winona since the entire contracting group was eager to meet the spring deadline. They worked well into summer and by September 1874 GB&M cars could be run out onto curving trestle work to warehouses adjacent to the river. In the fall the complex was complete, ready for DJL steamers and barges to gather in crops from Lake City and Wabasha, as well as from several down-river grain depots interested in Green Bay's terminal facility on the Great Lakes.

GB&M's arrival in Winona brought with it several years of legal and financial strife. In February of 1873 Henry Ketchum solicited aid from the many potential sources in western Wisconsin. The winning city now became, in essence, the loser. Ketchum offered to build to Winona if he could get $100,000 from the city. The conditions stipulated that he would build in 1873 and that the bonus voted by Winona to aid its own Winona & South-Western Railroad would be shifted to GB&LP, or at least $100,000 of $150,000 voted for W&SW. W&SW agreed to this. Ketchum also required that the bonds would not draw over six percent interest. The package would be ratified by a citizen's vote to back legislation as Minnesota law required such action be approved by the legislature before money could be transferred. There was a verbal agreement at that time but no documents were signed.

W&SW directors voted six-to-three to give GB&LP the desired $100,000 of their aid and the legal action to transfer bonding to GB&LP began in St. Paul. At this point other surrounding counties interested in building Lake Pepin & Omaha Railroad southwest from Wabasha opposed the measure. They were allegedly allied with lumber interests, the latter fearing competition from Wisconsin in Winona. They implied that Ketchum acted without authority from his directorate and that GB&LP's men were more interested in their C&NW holdings. A subsequent meeting of all of W&SW's interested parties produced a six-to-fifteen vote which firmed GB&LP's position and the bonus bill went for a reading in St. Paul. Later that month Winona businessmen met to redraft a citizen's proposal, strengthening the hands of St. Paul's representation.

March 13, 1873 witnessed a special meeting in which Ketchum again stressed his need for funds ($200,000) to be raised between Merrillan and the river. He then asked Winona to give $100,000 in cash in lieu of bonds, stating that he couldn't accept less and implying that no money meant no railroad. Again the city council and W&SW went into a huddle; all agreed, subject to Ketchum's referral of the deal to the GB&LP board. Winona agreed to give $50,000 cash plus the W&SW charter and franchise to GB&LP when the line was finished to Winona in 1873. The fatal catch was that the cash donations plus W&SW charter were to be returned to the city in the event that the legislature approved the arrangement. Such action could not be effected in time and was stalled until the next winter's legislation. Ketchum apparently agreed to the $50,000 amount, reflecting the road's desperate financial situation.

W&SW and its directorate (largely lumber barons of Winona) had made only preliminary plans to build its road, while the GB&LP was nearly within sight of Winona. The money and the charter was assigned to GB&LP, to be held until the city was able to issue the original $100,000. If the bonds were not delivered to GB&LP, Ketchum & Company would keep the charter and the $50,000 and build *both roads*. All agreed for the moment and the advance of money was authorized; however, there was no binding agreement for the city to repay citizens for

the loan. Those who advanced cash to the GB&LP were given a certificate with the city seal; the city looked to the State Legislature to straighten it all out.

W&SW was now having second thoughts. In a hot-tempered discussion, its board voted against surrendering the charter. Mr. J. A. Mathews of the city proposed raising $50,000 cash to be divided between GB&LP and W&SW. Ketchum was advised of this and replied that some of his directorate did not want the Green Bay road in Winona, though he did. Ketchum agreed that, if the Winona cash bonus of $50,000 could be met, he would try to raise the balance needed throughout the Trempeleau Valley. He did not want the W&SW charter at all but stressed his need for the $50,000.

Judge Wilson of Winona, a friend of GB&LP, eulogized the line's value to the city. He spoke of the extensive markets it would open for provisions, pork, beef, grain and produce of Winona's environs. Iron ore and hardwood lumber — maple, oak and black walnut — could be brought to Winona's doors from Wisconsin. He mentioned that Mr. E. P. Greeley of Nashua, Iowa recently sent a letter in reference to his proposed narrow-gauge road which would strike the river wherever the Green Bay route terminated. By spring Greeley's surveyor was working across the worst of Minnesota's topography, the southeastern corner, in order to find a route at right angles to deep valleys and steep cliff faces. Judge Wilson also thought that the GB&LP in Winona would help induce the Chicago, Dubuque & Minnesota Railroad (later CM&STP) to complete its road to Winona. The Judge stressed the GB&LP's non-land grant status and its need for bonuses to make progress.

Subscriptions for the bonus were to be deposited in Winona before July 1, 1873, to be drawn by GB&LP after completion to Marshland. A meeting of citizens resolved that, if citizens of Winona would advance $50,000, "we will work to get legislation to refund the sum." Verrazano Simpson, soon to be involved in the promotion of Winona & South-Western Railroad, wanted to see the "thousand-dollar fellows" show their hands and "come to him as one." The signers came forward and signed for $35,000, then the list was forwarded to Henry Ketchum. The city resolved to run a bond drive in May for the remaining $15,000. The arrangement was not formally accepted by the GB&LP, possibly overlooked in the press of affairs. Much of it had apparently been verbal contracting.

The bond affair deepened in January of 1874 when GB&M was ready to obtain its money. Not all of the subscribers had paid in and David Kelly and Henry Ketchum were in town to obtain the promised funds. The subscribers, many of them businessmen, were not sure that they should pay when the contract was not actually accepted by GB&M. There was a liability question. GB&M postponed its actions until the all-important legislative act was forthcoming. GB&M's rights were nearly declared in a legislative bill, but the action was tabled. It was noted that, despite a contribution of $30,000, the railroad was asking too much of the community.

The $50,000 aid package was voted down in Winona in February 1874, leaving the city aroused and defensive. Newspapers of competing towns sniped at the city and all seemed to be disillusioned with Henry Ketchum. He was seen as having treated subscribers unfairly by not formally accepting the $35,000 bonds. In addition there were further accusations regarding his conduct in 1873's summer of bartering for money.

GB&M decided to take its case to U.S. Circuit Court in St. Paul in an attempt to get its money. One person taken to task was Thomas Simpson, in which a demurrer to compel

was overruled. Simpson paid. All year verdicts were reported in the railroad's favor, strengthening GB&M's position. Many of the subscribers were later to invest in the Winona & South-Western Railroad.

Winona's financial problems were typical; bad times hung leaden on the heels of progress nationwide. With railroads being the prime expansive industry, over-expansion loomed as a specter over banking houses and brokerage firms. The pushing of new rails into virgin territory, which could not supply them with revenues until towns came up out of nowhere, was the prime cause of collapse. Rate wars, Granger laws and too much grain contributed. Traffic density was not there, certainly in relation to the high interest rates. The money, which should have flowed to securities holders, only trickled. Building programs came to a standstill. But those with disposable money made vast amounts from the shortfall of fortune.

Another source of disaster for the grain belt was the grasshopper plague of the early 1870's. In concert with the money disorder, a near-biblical natural wrath of millions of insects filled the air, descending upon newly sowed wheatfields and destroying crops. Harvests were not necessary, leaving boxcars empty. The regions hardest hit were northwest Iowa and southwest Minnesota. It required major relief efforts to fight the famine throughout grain country.

A cryptic entry in accounting logs covered a contract made with United States Rolling Stock Co., an equipment dealer located in New York. Rentals of five locomotives are recorded for April and May of 1874 to the amount of $1000 per month. The charges were for three-month periods in the year's first half, plus an additional $6000 payment in November 1874. USRSCo. contracted to deliver engines from Pennsylvania. A contract dated October 4, 1873 stated that USRSCo. would supply rolling stock in perfect order as needed. They were also to furnish the five locomotives and tenders at Meadville, Pennsylvania and GB&M "would receive them promptly upon arrival." Rates were given as $200 per month. Titles remained with USRSCo. but GB&M provided insurance. The locomotives were not to carry more than 130 pounds of steam and were required to be driven by competent engineers. They were to be surrendered in Chicago upon contractual termination at which time USRSCo.'s general master mechanic would determine the condition of the rented engines. The contract was signed by President George B. McClellan of USRSCo.

Construction contracts for boxcars and flats continued with Haskell & Barker of Michigan City, Indiana. H&B also supplied an office/paycar in April 1874, costing $4500. June of 1874 brought boxcar No. 760, the highest car number to date. Three Dickson 4-4-0's, numbered ten to twelve inclusive, also came in June. Priced at $10,000, they were purchased by Lackawanna Iron & Coal Co. for the GB&M. They were named in order: E. F. HATFIELD JR.; SAMUEL SLOAN; ARTHUR BONDON. Mr. Bondon was Moses Taylor's private secretary and Sloan was Lackawanna's president for 32 years. Sloan eventually became the Green Bay road's president and served in that capacity during the bleak years that followed. Hatfield again paid the bill for LI&CCo. on June 9, 1874. Dickson Manufacturing Co. suffered a disastrous fire shortly after the three GB&M engines were completed. Dickson did not resume full production capacity of four engines per month until 1875.

As if business conditions weren't bad enough, some of the "Mississippi River style gamblers" took to GB&M limiteds to work the crowds in 'three-card monte' games. The "pick-a-card" fleecing went on for several months before war was declared and

Above: The original LACT&P (C&NW) bridge at Winona was a wood structure built by C. C. Smith & Co. The original bridge collapsed under a train before GB&M began to use it. Smith also built CM&STP's first La Crosse bridge.
WINONA COUNTY HISTORICAL SOCIETY

the newspaper heat caused them to move on to Winona. Robert W. Nathan, general freight and passenger agent, was not above putting "wanted" posters in seven languages into cars and depots. Several months later, gamblers Backer and Shettler were "vacationing" in the state penitentiary at Waupun.

The road's pioneer conductors who dealt with the likes of the "monte men" were George W. Rose, Ed Arnold, William Monahan, N. Higbee, John Jeniger, John H. Murphy, J. H. Kinney, George Simkins and G. W. Royce. In 1875 Mr. Rose had been a conductor for 25 years and Royce for 19. Nonetheless, Rose retired as first conductor and took a position in Illinois. Rather than hire another, the company tried to get by with just two men. The regular train of 1874 had a schedule virtually the same as in 1940. It left Winona at 7 a.m., arriving in Green Bay at 6:30 p.m. The westbound train departed from Green Bay at 8:30 a.m. and arrived in Winona at 8:00 p.m. In 1874, before time zones were established nationwide, Green Bay time was 25 minutes faster than Winona time.

A New London paper complained that GB&M refused to stop regularly, choosing instead to drag through depots and harass the patrons for not responding positively to bonding issues. Such churlish writing came as a result of differences in opinion, but not at the price of safety. There were rules of operation and accusing newspaper reports were shown to be only fiction as the train would always stop properly as directed.

Adding to the manmade setbacks were acts of ill fortune. Keeping on schedule during the winter with 37-ton engines was challenging. In late February 1875 heavy snow closed Winona to both C&NW and GB&M. In twenty inches of snow the North-

Western needed twelve hours to complete the 83 miles to Elroy. GB&M train No. 1 was held in Green Bay, finally nosing into the storm at 4 p.m. and arriving at Winona at 6 a.m. the next day. The crew had just enough time to eat breakfast before starting east again, without rest. The schedule was kept. A year later GB&M train No. 2, with conductor Monahan and engineer Fitzgerald in charge, derailed near Bluff Siding on the C&NW trackage right. Fitzgerald spotted the broken rail, immediately "horsed her over," and jumped. He rolled down a 15-foot bank, sustaining minor injury. The two coaches flopped over on their sides, bruising a few passengers. Two women en route to Arcadia's Polish settlement were so frightened that they refused to ride the next train east.

GB&M fixed its lumber rates from Grand Rapids to Winona at $25 per car which was considered low. In early 1876 it abandoned its pass system and began to issue 1000-mile tickets, a boon to passengers. The change wasn't enough, however, to ward off increasing bad luck, accidents, fire and floods, which dogged the new road's fortunes. In June engine No. 16, a new Danforth, with Engineer Cook and Conductor Higbee, smashed into a bull near Hixton. Eight cars were derailed but, fortunately, there were no injuries to humankind. A mail car fire in June nearly set train No. 1 ablaze. The circus came to Winona in

43

those depressed years and Engineer Neil McKay brought it from Merrillan trouble-free to the joy of the admiring throngs.

When a two-stall enginehouse at Marshland Junction caught fire in June 1876, an engine, thought to be No. 6, was severely damaged. This and several other fires crippled engines once thought safe inside, placing severe strain on the operating and mechanical department. In addition to the fires, heavy snows caused delays and doubleheaded passenger trains each winter. One February, train No. 1 didn't reach Merrillan until 2 a.m. the next day because of fierce winds howling out of the northwest. The same train reached Winona, in temperatures below zero, at noon on the following day. The snows of 1875 turned into rushing floodwaters in spring, closing the railroad west of Whitehall, which became an all-too-familiar pattern for a century. The flooding came again in 1876, curtailing service for most of April. GB&M reopened on April 28th and the new village of Arcadia, built as a result of the land dealings of Kelly, Ketchum and Hiles, suffered repeated damage. Originally, the village was a mile south of the present community, high and dry. The promoters saw to it that the townsmen were forced to move onto parcels along the railroad which were mostly swampland. Several feet of water flooded Arcadia each spring and many edifices not built on pilings were carried away. GB&M's agent there became an adept boatman. A meal-stop called Blair House was established at Merrillan, adjacent to the depot grounds. In May 1877 C. N. Payne's mill there burned, taking 200,000 feet of lumber and twenty houses with it.

The new towns in the Trempeleau Valley experienced modest growth as a result of the railroad. Independence, also a Kelly-Ketchum-Hiles town, was the site of a Chase Patent Elevator which was erected on railroad grounds. Hixton and Sechlerville vied to develop the same area; J. R. Sechler had a post office

and lumber interests but, Mr. Hix's village predominated. Farther east, Black River Station became Hatfield, Mile 141.8; City Point at Mile 121 took Scranton's place, and Elm Lake was established at Mile 104.8. Scranton was later re-established at Mile 116. Meehan was located at Mile 86.6, a product of the Meehan brothers' mill west of Plover. P&J Meehan shared the costs of the station with the railroad. Their share of the expenses for the 22×32-foot building, constructed by the railroad, was $20 per month. Their part of the bargain was to influence business for which they would receive favorable rates.

The plat maps of both Whitehall and Arcadia indicate their further development by the troika of Kelly, Ketchum and Hiles. Streets in Whitehall to this day are still called Blair, Abrams, Dodge, Kelly, Marsh, Scranton and Hancock, the latter perhaps for W. R. Hancock. There is a Kelly's Addition in Whitehall, while Arcadia has a Hiles & Ketchum's Addition. Ketchum land is recorded in 1878 for eastern Arcadia while Blair shows a parcel remaining in 1901 for Hiles and Ketchum.

Many adjoining railroad officers came to inspect the new railroad but of interest is the scrutiny of Milwaukee, Lake Shore & Western Railway. In 1875 the Honorable George Reed, promoter of the Lake Shore Road, traveled west to examine the practicality of extending the road to Hortonville and New London, putting a strategic junction at the latter site. Conductor Rose presided over the special train which took the entourage to Winona for a Huff House meeting. Reed's companion was none other than Fredric W. Rhinelander whose name is synonymous with MLS&W's destiny. MLS&W's star was rising in Wisconsin railroading and some years later it was approached about a lease of GB&M's successor. The idea involved grain movement to Neenah-Menasha for the milling interests there, to be transferred at New London and, after processing, directed to lake steamers at Manitowoc.

Struggling to attract traffic other than lumber and grain, Robert W. Nathan, Kelly's sometime friend and passenger agent, engineered through rates in 1875 on Union Steamboat's route to Buffalo for $16. St. Louis-to-Green Bay passengers could ride GB&M from St. Paul to Milwaukee, using the new road at the Potter Law's three-cents-per-mile rate. The journey from St. Paul to Green Bay on Wisconsin Central via Amherst Junction was even cheaper in the depressed times of the mid-seventies when both roads were locked into pauper's rates.

These rates prevailed until the oppressive law was finally lifted in 1876. The message of Governor Ludington in January 1876 stated that four railroads alone paid interest on their bonds in Wisconsin during 1875; such were the crippling effects of anti-railroad legislation. A more palatable Vance Law replaced it in 1876, reducing the railroad commission bureaucracy which remained low-profile until the La Follette days of the 1900's. In that 1876 season the change was a welcome Christmas present. The office staff exchanged gifts and Superintendent Kenrick gave special ticket boxes to each of his conductors to be used on the "express trains."

Left: Although the GB&MC Co.'s canal project never was realized, Wisconsin River trade did continue. A typical sternwheeler was ELLEN HARDY, late of Minnesota River trade, calling at Prairie du Sac, Wisconsin in the 1880's.
STAN MAILER COLLECTION

Above: Diamond Jo Line steamers at Winona during the 1881 flood. Diamond Jo worked with GB&M in the grain trade, supplying Eastmoor with Minnesota shipments. (Stereoptican slide)
WINONA COUNTY HISTORICAL SOCIETY

During 1875's doldrums, Danforth Locomotive and Machine Co. supplied three 4-4-0's which became GB&M numbers 14-16 inclusive. (The thirteenth roster position, following tradition, was omitted.) Their history is clouded because renumberings and rebuildings were not fully recorded. Delivered April 30th, they carried builder's numbers 1001-1003 inclusive and were paid for by Lackawanna Iron & Coal Co. The big Danforths, which cost $8500 each, went into freight service. Of the three, No.14 was the P. R. PYNE, named for Percy Rivington Pyne, Moses Taylor's son-in-law. No.15 was THOMAS DICKSON, but No.16's name was not recorded.

Amid the Winona bonus struggle, an alternate scheme for a river terminal was raised. As the bonus trials convened in St. Paul, rival La Crosse schemed to encourage more railroads into her midst. La Crosse hoped that the Southern Minnesota Railway would strengthen the Gateway City by bridging the Missisippi and replacing the car ferry system at Grand Crossing, opposite La Crosse's south side. But the SM suffered many setbacks, including a heavy flood in the spring of 1874, and went into default the same year. In courting the GB&M, a Black River route was advanced, which would include Black River Falls and Melrose. A second idea included a line through from Blair and Galesville.

La Crosse's ambitions closely paralleled Winona's, both having a stake in lumber and grain. La Crosse wanted a series of railroads to carry its needs to and from the area. Interest in a southwestern route into Iowa generated feeble support and the Chicago, Dubuque & Minnesota Railroad remained the sole "southwestern route" via Dubuque. In Wisconsin James F. Joy's Wisconsin Valley Railroad had built northeastward from its starting point, Tomah, to Grand Rapids. The Joy road planned to build to La Crosse, producing a lumber line from the state's northern interior southwest to markets in the plains states. The WV route stood to compete directly with GB&M's proposed La Crosse branch. But in late 1875 a more positive agreement was reached between La Crosse and GB&M and President Ketchum negotiated in earnest for a La Crosse Extension.

GB&M was ready to enter La Crosse as early as February 1874, should that city vote aid. Preoccupied with the Winona decision, La Crosse's interest awaited the completion as well as the result of the negative turn of events of the bonus contest. Popular opinion indicated that GB&M would build a parallel line to the C&NW (Prescott) Road through Trempeleau and Onalaska and connect it with the Southern Minnesota Railroad on La Crosse's south side. GB&M's line curiously skirted the city on the east, made a sharp curve to the west and terminated opposite the SM's Minnesota terminal. By March 1876 a proposition for $75,000 bonding passed in La Crosse and work on the extension began. A final plan was worked out between C&NW and GB&M, which allowed GB&M to run 23 miles over the North-Western to Onalaska and six miles of its own construction to La Crosse. If C&NW had found trouble in entering La Crosse, a Milwaukee Road stronghold, it could now do so by leapfrogging into town on GB&M's back.

Surveyors began in May to locate the line from a point one-fifth mile south of Onalaska through several shallow cuts downgrade to a crossing with Milwaukee Road (present day Grand Crossing tower). Remnants of the line may still be seen east of Burlington Northern's yard at North La Crosse. GB&M next had to cross extensive swamps to enter La Crosse. Seven trestles were installed on the line, one of which was 500 feet long; another, 675 feet. A Howe Truss, 132 feet long, was in place over the La Crosse River. In later years much of this roadway was filled. It may still be seen north of the present university site. Company forces built two depots, an 80 × 24-foot freight house, a 26 × 56-foot passenger building and a 46 × 214-foot train shed. C&NW made a contract with GB&M of ten percent per annum on one-third of cash value of $17,000 per mile, plus a wheel count assessment.

Construction contracts were taken by C. C. Smith, the bridge builder of La Crosse. Captain L. Rossiter did the grading work. By July three gangs were excavating cuts and moving fill out to swamp sites. One gang worked cemetery bluff, removing 15,000 yards of fill. A short spur was immediately built at Onalaska to unload rail flats next to C&NW's line. Smith offered $3.50 a day to men with teams for grading. Street right-of-way was granted by La Crosse through what is today the University of Wisconsin-La Crosse campus, en route to the south side. C&NW's Marvin Hughitt and C. C. Wheeler joined David Kelly at La Crosse to determine station ground locations. It was perhaps the last time that the three general superintendents would meet. In September the propellor JIM FISK JR. carried 582 tons of rail to Green Bay for the La Crosse Extension. The first regular train ran September 25, 1876.

C&NW paid for fifty-percent of the station costs at La Crosse in return for its use. Both lines agreed "to connect with any bridge or ferry across the Missisippi River at said city." While interest in connecting to the Southern Minnesota Railroad and the Chicago, Dubuque & Minnesota never flagged, by the end of 1876 Milwaukee Road's trans-Mississippi bridge had made a solid connection. Transfer barges were no longer used. Some lip service was paid to the idea of a pontoon bridge for a Winona location and for La Crosse, based on the Lawler design. GB&M sought War Department permission plus state acquiescence for one, but Winona chose to alter the proposal in favor of a combination road-rail structure, which tabled the action. GB&M owned property west of their La Crosse terminal, on which a bridge might have been built.

In grim contradiction, GB&M's first La Crosse-bound rails were spiked down the day eight men rode into Northfield, Minnesota — the men of Jesse James' gang. With the La Crosse service beginnings, tiny Marshland took on the trappings of a terminal town for both river city operations. A small yard was built, angling toward the C&NW connection, which serviced the modest La Crosse mixed train, the Eastmoor switch engine (which may have been the same 4-4-0) and the passage of all Winona-bound traffic. Marshland had an enginehouse, turntable, water tank and two yard tracks. It was one of two engine terminals within about four miles of each other, operating from 1891 to 1922. It continued as a terminal until the abandonment of the La Crosse line in 1922.

In the first operating month of the La Crosse branch, Winona's newspaper tried to show GB&M service in its area as inadequate. Allegedly, the arriving train No.1 from Green Bay was compelled to terminate at Marshland, while the regular engine made the branch trip to La Crosse. Another coach and baggage car were brought in by a "freight engine," which caused an overnight delay for the main liner's passengers. Such confusion may only have been negativism due to the lawsuits then in progress. In Fort Howard, however, morale was elevated by the appearance of engine No.2, SAMUEL MARSH, which was overhauled after five hard years on the Wisconsin frontier. Master Mechanic J. H. Irwin, in charge of Fort Howard shops, also went over several others since construction had calmed down. His charges were aging quickly; accidents and normal wear had decreased the frail-looking machines' efficiency. Yet, one shining day in May 1876, the MARSH stood outside, its new lettering and striping contrasting darker colors on the tender and cab. A freshly oiled Russia Iron jacket gleamed over its drivers. It was very much the pride of all, but especially painters Ed and Jim Henderson of old Fort Howard.

There were times in which the eastern grandees came to visit and the Green Bay/Fort Howard newspapers rose to the stir of their notable passage. It was written that John Insley Blair came to explore his investment, together with sons De Witt Clinton Blair and Marcus L. Blair. Their trip to Merrillan in May 1873, via special train, was carefully tended by President Ketchum. The Blair trip was outshone by a July 1875 trip which carried Kelly, Superintendent Kenrick, Moses Taylor, Samuel Sloan, Blair and Wisconsin Central's Elijah Phillips and Gardner Colby of Boston. Taylor, late in his life, was visiting GB&M for the first time. He showed keen interest in the Wisconsin Valley road

Above: Shown is an advertisement poster for St. Paul's Winter Carnival. The event, under the stewardship of Gavin Campbell and the receivership, took place in the winter of 1887. The original color lithograph burned in the 1977 depot fire at Green Bay.

at the time, examining the business of lumber from Wausau to La Crosse. William E. Dodge also came west in June 1875 to examine GB&M in steadily darkening circumstances.

Spring of 1877 had been too dry. News of terrible eastern forest fires intensified a general fear that fire could bring on widespread destruction of towns and countryside as only a 19th Century fire could. Winona watched and waited as the days grew hotter and drier. On May 17th a small house burned in the east end near the lumber mills. Again at noon a false fire alarm set Winonans on edge and the hot, dry wind continued to whistle up the great river's valley. Five-thirty came. They noticed a thickening column of smoke rising in the east. A fire cry went out that the mills — the livelihood of all Winonans — were burning. Firemen arrived to find the smoke rising from East-moor, across the Mississippi . . . and the whole thing was burning. River steamer BELLE OF LA CROSSE lay alongside the warehouse dock at Eastmoor, doubled up against the bitts and posts of the freight house section. She had carried in 500 barrels of Minneapolis flour and loaded on seven cars of lumber and shingles for down river. Her cargo transferred. The BELLE raised steam and fire against the searing afternoon by 5 p.m. and tried to get underway, but was literally blown back into her dockspace. The steamer tried several more times to make the mainstream, with rising boiler pressure and gushing twin stacks, which shot forth sparks and black smoke from pitchy wood fuel. BELLE had run out of coal the previous day and was trying to get by on her easier southbound trip with pine knots and short logs. She filled the hot air with spark showers each time she labored out toward the river. The sparks fell on the rail-road's buildings, which were very dry, the last rain having been weeks before.

A pile of ten thousand cedar posts stacked on the river bank behind the freight house caught fire first. Elevator foreman John Flaven immediately directed men and hoses to the post pile. One man, John Towey, was detailed to extinguish a small fire on the trestlework under the freight house. Towey doused that fire but found another under the low end of the freight house nearest the river and it was moving quickly. Towey was unable to get back to the elevator. Flaven and his group saw the fire and moved their hose toward the corner. The fire ignited at several other places and suddenly the elevator itself was afire. The crew was unable to stand up to the heat.

Just before the fire was discovered, the switch engine and crew had left for Marshland, 2½ miles away, carrying Book-keeper/Clerk Wheelock to "go to beans," leaving only the four men to the shock of fire all around them. Flaven had called John Towey in early to keep a watch on a woods fire. By 2 p.m. it was already threatening the trestlework. Towey's rented house, a building worth about $400, was just north of the freighthouse on the island. His family was visiting in Winona at the time. His house caught fire but Towey himself was unable to bypass the burning freight house to save his belongings.

The Eastmoor elevator was supplied with a good steam fire-pump, complete with hose on each floor. A handpump was located in the freighthouse, along with two Babcock extinguish-ers, but they were inaccessible during the fire. In the end the hosemen were forced to abandon the dock and elevator which were both completely destroyed.

Eastmoor consisted of a curving trestle and an 800-foot-long dock. The warehouse was 250 feet long with a space between the elevator and warehouse. Eastmoor was considered one of the busiest and best on the river at the time of the fire. The elevator contained about 3500 bushels of wheat, 1200 of which had been

elevated from the barge SUSIE the day of the fire. SUSIE and her cargo also burned. Five hundred barrels of flour from another steamer, loaded at Minneapolis, were burned as well. Diamond Jo Line's steamer JOSIE was scheduled to arrive that evening to take on seven cars of lumber and staves for down-river customers, but her cargo also burned. Twenty-three boxcars were destroyed on the dock. The switch engine, which came scissoring back from Marshland, tried in vain to remove five flour-loaded boxcars from the freighthouse.

By that time, the trestle was unsafe. The BELLE had pulled up some of the pilings, loosening them extensively and denying passage to the engine above. GB&M agent C. B. Maxwell was in Winona but soon had a boatman row him back across to Eastmoor. He lost no time in getting section men to tear up some of the timber work in the path of the fire, which saved the landward end of the trestle.

Oil drippings from cars saturated ties and stringers, acceler-ating the fire in the direction of the elevator, which then burned through the bottom of the building. A draft within the tall struc-ture created a firewind which finished it. Luckily enough, some 35,000 bushels of wheat stored at Eastmoor over the winter had

Frank Seymour's administration saw to it that GB&LP's "golden spike" location and time were honored. The sign disappeared in the 1930's.
H. KNUTSON PHOTO

been shipped three weeks earlier. President Ketchum had made a contract with Weyerhauser affiliate Chancy Lamb of Clinton, Iowa that called for 10,000 cedar posts. Ketchum had stored them behind the Eastmoor dock for two years, but they went up in smoke and Lamb had to look elsewhere for his cedar posts. Eastmoor was gone. Only a portion of the $85,000 loss was insured. Such a loss before the growing season was yet another crippling blow to the railroad across Wisconsin.

Sensing a windfall, Fountain City, ten miles from Eastmoor, sent a delegation to Green Bay. GB&M was asked to build a replacement elevator there, an action seen as advantageous only to that community. A Winona alderman broached the subject to a council meeting, remarking that action to offer a site in town might be of mutual interest. The Mayor noted that GB&M's desire for a pontoon bridge into Winona might also include a new elevator there. Judge Wilson, GB&M's legal council in Winona, was approached to intervene. But, while temporary arrangements were made with C&NW, GB&M immediately planned for a replacement on the original site.

Above: Lackawanna Line steambarge WYOMING was one of few carrying twin stacks aft. The vessel often called at Green Bay in the 1880-1890 period.

Below: JOSEPH L. HURD received emergency repairs at Sturgeon Bay in the 1890's after a midlake collision. HURD was scrapped at Sturgeon Bay after its Lake Superior service. Fatalities, shipping losses and cargo damage were unfortunate facts of lake usage in the 19th Century.

Chief Engineer J. T. Alton brought Chicago's Henry I. Chase to Eastmoor to plan the replacement. Negotiations were held into June, when a contract was made. Contractors Jenkins and Johnson had crews driving new piles for the new elevator on June 27, 1877, this time a 75,000-bushel edifice. Mr. Chase made his headquarters at the Huff House, remaining for the entire season. The new 550-foot-long dock, for which 1640 piles were driven, was operational by mid-September. The first consignment of wheat came from the barge IMPERIAL — 60,000 bushels. The following day ten GB&M boxcars rolled east.

In 1877 Minnesota experienced a revival in land sales. The wheatfields were free from the grasshopper plague. Increases in lumber demand west of Winona resulted in 90,000 feet or more per day moving west over the Winona & St. Peter Railroad, threatening to deplete sawmill stocks in Winona's east end. Low water on the Missisippi slowed log movement southward to the city's mills and disrupted river transport. With Eastmoor again operational, Conductor John Kinney and Engineer Henry Harding moved 41 cars eastward, of which 33 were wheat. East of Grand Rapids, Conductor Frank Seymour was in charge of the train. Seymour would soon rise to a superintendent's position in the 1890's, the beginning of a long career in Green Bay route service. The wheat went to Elmore & Kelly's elevator and, by November 3rd, 178,000 bushels were en route to Buffalo. Over eighty cars were crowded about the elevator. *The Green Bay Advocate* indicated the fall shipment could exceed 1,000,000 bushels, a new record. Eastmoor's reconstruction was entered as a debit for $93,238.15, but wheat was moving and all bowed

The standard freighter on the Great Lakes during the late 1800's was the steambarge. Here, William H. White & Co.'s THREE BROTHERS makes port at Kewaunee, Wisconsin. White, whose business was hemlock and hardwood lumber, made his home at Boyne City, Michigan in 1906.

J. SCHULTZ PHOTO

before the golden god of Minnesota, its amber waves of grain.

After GB&M was completed, David Kelly's interest in management waned. He was building for himself a political career in Wisconsin. On September 13, 1877 Kelly was chosen for the State Assembly where he served until 1879. He later advanced to the Senate and his name was mentioned as a gubernatorial candidate. During that time, in 1880 and 1881, much of his time was spent answering to several lawsuits connected with

land acquisitions. Kelly had made extensive real estate purchases ahead of the advancing railhead in the early 1870's. It is possible that the Lackawanna group respectfully asked Kelly for his resignation, for shortly the truth came out — GB&M was in default. More importantly, the Lackawanna group predominated after board elections were held. William E. Dodge became president, Henry Ketchum moved to vice-president, and one Timothy Case became GB&M's Receiver.

Sunrise over Kewaunee harbor after great storms often found many a thankful vessel doubled up at pierside. In the distance an LMCFTCo. car float is secure, together with a "lumber hooker" and a steambarge. Kewaunee was a safe haven for Chicago-bound ships in stormy waters.

J. SCHULTZ COLLECTION

4

RECEIVERSHIP
&
GBWSTP

John Insley Blair wrote a hurried note on a yellow envelope to Samuel Sloan on January 16, 1878 from Delaware, New Jersey. Blair was unequivocal and blunt; Sloan was to let all of the foreclosure papers be drafted to make Timothy Case the Receiver for the Green Bay & Minnesota Railroad. According to reports, Blair had advanced the road $500,000 in 1877, in addition to previous substantial loans. In far away Winona a party had $50 in short-term notes returned by a Green Bay bank when the railroad was unable to pay on demand.

David Kelly put forth a letter regarding the company's affairs, stating that when his successor, Timothy Case, relieved him of his duties, the road was in good order. Although $23,209.05 was due on scrip and mercantile paper in the near future, Kelly claimed that prospects were bright and liabilities not pressing. It was earning $1000 per working day, payrolls were $11,000 per month and expenses might be carried along with ninety-day paper, the company's custom for years. Kelly stated that some of the paper "went to protest" due to the time lag in transferring books to New York, but he was assured that this would be corrected within days. Evidently the accounting transfer had turned up differing facts.

Kelly retained a considerable amount of stock — about $533,000 — his fee as construction agent for the road. GB&M had issued $8,000,000 of capital stock which was distributed as follows: $25,575 for cash; $9,500 part payment for construction work, $26,125 for other purposes; $784,000 exchanged for municipal and county bonds; $38,859.60 for $75,000 of Iowa Lumber Company's stock; $11,140.40 in settlement of various bills; $100,000 as a bonus with Brown County bonds sold; $1,471,300 as a bonus with first-mortgage bonds sold or issued in settlement of accounts; $5,000,000 issued to Lackawanna Iron & Coal Co. to settle the principal; $251,500 and interest ($41,538.11) of an account due that company, and the $533,000 issued to David Kelly. None of this stock was retired.

GB&M's first mortgage was $3,200,000 in seven-percent bonds, issued August 1, 1870, maturing in 1900. The money went for the following: $1,847,000 plus a bonus of $1,044,500 and the $100,000 in Green Bay City bonds. This amounted to a $2,991,500 face value, sold for $1,220,250. Another $1,303,000 with a $376,000 bonus in capital stock was issued, settling a $929,870 account due the Lackawanna Iron & Coal Co. Some $50,000 in capital stock accompanied another $50,000 bonus, which covered $37,500 due the Oxford Iron Company, a subsidiary of LI&CCo.'s operations in New Jersey. No part of this bond group was retired. The LI&CCo. accounts included virtually everything above the road's crossties — cars, locomotives, rails and fastenings.

A second mortgage — eight-percent bonds amounting to $2,100,000 — was dated September 9, 1873. Made at the time of the road's name change and maturing November 1, 1893, $779,860 of these bonds were issued to cover the interest on first-mortgage bonds. This issue also covered $1,320,140 deposited as collateral for unpaid advances from Lackawanna Iron & Coal Co. None of these were retired. Kelly had seen fit to release much of his stock retainer in the heat of the construction to cover certain obligations to LI&CCo. He received recognition

Left: New London Junction in the 1880's. GBW&STP engine No. 7 is eastbound with an MLS&W Rhode Island-built 4-4-0 headed south for Kaukauna. The large depot was a meal stop. The junction interchange was busy during Manitowoc's ascendency as a grain port in the 1880's.

HERBERT MOORE COLLECTION

for the action but on January 23, 1878, GB&M headed into receivership, not a unique status for the times. It defaulted on both first and second mortgages, setting the road on an austere course for the following forty years.

LI&CCo. advanced GB&M $3,093,021.06, of which $1,438,658.25 was repaid before its sale to a new company in 1881. Of this advance, $1,188,194.90 was in cash; $1,218,951.76 was for rails which came from Scranton. Often commercial papers would be transmitted through LI&CCo. to National City Bank or to any LI&CCo. security holders as interest payment. It is probable that securities were obtained at a discount by the members of the Lackawanna group. On October 14, 1881 GB&M's net loss was reported to be $913,690.26 with a net operating loss of $950,600.66.

Acting for the holders of the mortgages, Farmers' Loan & Trust Co., John I. Blair ordered the road into receivership. The affidavit stated that Blair held $319,900 in bonds, he was owner of $88,129 funded debt interest, and that he held $101,200 of the second mortgage. It was also stated that Blair, Moses Taylor and William E. Dodge, together with the LI&CCo., owned over *two-thirds* of the stock of GB&M, *one-half* of the first-mortgage bonds and *three-fourths* of the second-mortgage bonds. Blair also represented the LI&CCo, Taylor, Dodge and Henry Parrish, holder of $65,000 of the first mortgage bonds and $17,800 of the second mortgage bonds. In addition, a large amount was due the Haskell & Barker Car Company and the payrolls of November and December were largely unpaid. As Receiver, Timothy Case presided over the unfortunate railroad's plight into 1881.

Timothy Case came from the same Lackawanna group experience. Erwin C. Case, a relative, was Superintendent of the Sussex Railroad, a division of the DL&W. Timothy Case wrote about his salary to Samuel Sloan when Green Bay expenses absorbed most of his ready cash. Case then worked to drastically reduce GB&M's expenses in the time-honored way of the 1870's: wage and force reduction. He again wrote Sloan that he had reduced the section workforce from 45 to 40 men and the agents more in proportion. Engineers were cut from $3.50 to $2.75 per day. Case thought that they were most liberally paid of all GB&M men. The master mechanic had received $1,000 a year until Kelly's resignation; Kelly had promised him $1200 beginning January 1, 1878. J. H. Irwin, the respectable master mechanic, saw that such a salary couldn't be expected of an insolvent road and cheerfully took the $1,000. His men were in a different position, however; their wages were cut twenty percent. Case thought Irwin was a good man.

Conductors' and trainmen's wages were reduced in kind. Amid strike talks, Case craftily put Superintendent Kenrick ahead in salary and told him to let all the men go if necessary. The dissidents heard that they had all the earnings of the road; the owners had nothing. Case was sure that trainmen and enginemen could get along with less pay. He found that "gravel train men" used on the "wood train" in winter were receiving $1.25 per day, the sectionmen $1.24. He reduced both to $1.00 per day pay. The wood train was a fuel-gathering and distributing work extra, related to wood-burning engines. Case sought to protect the property and sent along all of his bills to Edwin F. Hatfield Jr., including lawyer's fees for receivership actions. Case, steering a neutral course, was on friendly terms with local lawyers and Kelly. He was certain that with rigid economy another year would bring solvency. Case knew some Green Bay citizens would be angered with his zeal to serve bondholders first. He wrote to Sloan after hours so that no staff member would know his answers.

51

EDWARD J. DOWLING, S.J.

Above: The steamer CUBA, a wood design by Craig of Buffalo, was built in 1872. CUBA was not a Lackawanna Line boat but frequently was seen at Green Bay's dockside.

An exodus of personnel began in 1878 and Grand Rapids telegrapher W. G. Smith, his pay reduced, left first. Engineer A. B. Brasted went over to the Wisconsin Valley road, and Daniel Atwood, general agent, resigned in favor of a Rock Island job at Leavenworth, Kansas. Lineside newspapers, wondering about management, asked if all good men were leaving. Wage reduction was not new on GB&M; Grand Rapids operator Glassford left for St. Paul in the wake of his wage reduction in summer 1874. Hogger Al Ely left for California a month later, also due to wage reductions. However, the pay car became a regular morale builder every two weeks and scrip passed into history.

The Case administration changed west-end operations by running the regular passenger train straight into Winona from Marshland Junction. The number of Winona passengers differed by a ten-to-one ratio; La Crosse was forever reduced to branch status. Other levels of decision-making were bucked up to New York, typical of Blair-Sloan management practice. By year's end GB&M's situation had improved under Case. In 1878, 550 tons of steel rail replaced worn iron rails. Six and one-half miles was to be laid near Plover. Sam Sloan notified Case that 200 tons of Illinois Central Railroad pattern rail was available; GB&M splice bars would fit the I.C. rail.

Other improvements were made for passengers, especially out of La Crosse. Fare was $7.45 to Green Bay — in carpeted coaches which in time would feature Blackstone Patent couplers and platforms. Mr. T. B. Blackstone, president of Chicago & Alton Railroad, invented the early tight-locking couplers with iron-clad timber buffers below the platform ends. The device was intended to prevent telescoping and, similar to European design, could be adjusted with screw-tensioning. The slack elimination was an improvement over link-and-pin couplers. It was intended to circumvent the Miller Platform Patent. In the Kelly administration days, Mr. J. G. Cricklair of Green Bay

invented a car coupler similar to the Miller hook, but intended for freight cars. Tested in December 1876, the Cricklair design, however, proved unsuccessful.

The Receiver's Master Mechanic was Edward Osborne, whose father, C. S. Osborne, was a Sussex Railroad veteran. Sussex was yet another railroad held by Sloan interests. The elder Osborne assisted in inventing a patented spark arrester in 1878. It was applied to engine No.3 (Scranton) which had been converted to burn coal. Unfortunately, the arrester did not prevent lineside fires, another of Case's unrelenting challenges.

Case ordered two Dickson 4-4-0's. Second No.16 and No.17 were delivered for mixed service as coal burners with Westinghouse airbrakes. The pair, named GREEN BAY and MISSISSIPPI, were in service by late May 1879. The receiver's goal was to have all airbrake-equipped passenger service by the same month. Lineside newspapers reported that, although the GB&M went through a wilderness, Attorney Case had succeeded in creating a comparatively safe railroad capable of 25 miles per hour. Some things were improving for GB&M, despite 1878's short wheat crop.

After the Civil War, grain-buying and elevator-building flourished west of the Missisippi, steadily increasing over the next thirteen years. After establishing themselves in Iowa and Minnesota, the Cargill brothers of La Crosse looked toward establishing stations in Wisconsin. Cargill and Van Valkenburg had five elevators in eastern Wisconsin, one of which was at Luxemburg, while another was at Fond du Lac. Wheat stations were established in the Trempeleau Valley and by 1879 their business relied upon the Elmore & Kelly Green Bay elevator as a collection and shipping point. Thus a relationship was created between GB&M, Green Bay and La Crosse, all having interests for grain shipments in Wisconsin. In August 1878 a grain buyer's special left La Crosse, paused first at Eastmoor, then went on to Green Bay. It was the beginning of a Cargill connection with the Green Bay route.

Respected journals commented about GB&M's stringent condition in 1879, concluding that a St. Paul line would enhance the investment. A line from Merrillan via Durand and River Falls would allow the existing 243.6-mile railroad to take advantage of the new flour-milling boom, centered on the Washburn and Pillsbury miracle. It turned Minnesota's unwanted wheat into the world's most sought-after flour. At the Green Bay end, Cargill and Van Valkenburg were appointed agents for Union Transportation Co., the regular line of propellors operating to Buffalo. Captain Gaylord represented the line, informing businesses how to request merchandise routing. Cargill and Van Valkenburg continued to receive wheat from Eastmoor, but as appointed dealers at the Green Bay Elevator.

The Report of the Railroad Commissioner of Wisconsin in 1879 included a roster of GB&M employees' salaries: four clerks, average salary $654.99; one master mechanic, $1,000; eight conductors, $708 each; eleven engineers, $891 each; 17 brakemen, $480 each; 42 station agents, $454 each; 111 section men, $396 each; 59 laborers and mechanics, $507.39 each.

Disaster struck the road in May 1879. On a Monday night at 11 p.m., the Grand Rapids enginehouse burned, resulting in the $17,000 loss of two engines. The fire started in wood fuel in a locomotive tender; an attempt was made to pull one engine out, but to no avail. The burned engines, No.2 and No.7, were repaired under contract at Wisconsin Central's Stevens Point shops and finished by September 29, 1879. Timothy Case arrived, assessed the site, and later directed an appeal to Judge Drummond for aid.

Case wrote a letter that outlined the road's pressing need for renewal of iron, ties and bridging, the Receiver's first duty. In order to save money for track work, he was practicing most rigid and unpleasant economy. The 1878-9 winter proved damaging to the line; the frost penetrated deep due to little snow-cover. He asked the judge to allow funds to maintain safety on the road.

Case noted that he had $56,838.96 in cash, needed to apply to renewals above current operating expenses. The burned locomotives at Grand Rapids were another matter. A Howe Truss bridge on the west end had burned in mid-April, further depressing his freight earnings. Twenty-five boxcars and flats were requested for current business. Case reflected that business would not improve until the autumn wheat rush. He felt that even then earnings would be insufficient to meet current operating expenses. Along with a new Grand Rapids enginehouse, twenty boxcars, intended for lumber service, were ordered from Indiana Car Co. Flat cars came from Missouri Car & Foundry Co., both groups arriving the next winter. Faced with nearly fifty-percent renewals, Case certainly had his hands full.

The Receiver's passenger coaches were improved. A special dial was placed on endwalls, indicating the next station and arrival time. New oil lamps were installed for travelers in the Trempeleau Valley. On the La Crosse branch train, Conductor Frank Seymour suffered his brother William's death while railroading on the Winona & St. Peter Road; 1879 was a hard year.

Case's request for two locomotives was met by a Danforth order which was started in October 1879. Danforth Locomotive & Machine Co.'s agent H. A. Allen wrote to Samuel Sloan (as DL&W RR president) that the recent fire at the Danforth works caused a six-week delay in delivery of the two GB&M engines.

Above: Winona's waterfront in the early GB&M years. The Diamond Jo Line's dock warehouse is at right center. Levee tracks in the foreground lead northwest toward the W&SP depot beyond the C&N-W (Prescott Road) bridge over which GB&M entered the city.

WINONA COUNTY HISTORICAL SOCIETY

Nos. 18 and 19, GRAND RAPIDS and FT. HOWARD, again 4-4-0's, were reportedly larger than previous engines. The pair involved in the roundhouse fire went back to work, sporting new woodwork and paint. GB&M was not to receive another new engine for ten years.

GB&M struggled against nature's unfair rage throughout the 1880's. On April 3, 1879 Judge Drummond of the U.S. District

Court rendered a decision in *Farmers' Loan & Trust Co. versus GB&MRRCo.*, confirming the master's report, with no objections taken. GB&M had defaulted on interest due on first-mortgage bonds, with $850,260 issued as security. It stated that Moses Taylor of New York was holder of bonds amounting to $1,052,080, William Earle Dodge held $200,740, and Lackawanna Iron & Coal held $227,800. John Blair himself held $404,020, while $2,039,620 was held by others. The suit held that LI&CCo., holder of $1,249,740 of bonds, was entitled to the security of the second-mortgage bonds held by them, amounting to $1,124,478 with interest; $4,811,976 was due the Farmers' Loan & Trust Co., trustee for the first-mortgage bonds, with $1,124,378 on second mortgage bonds plus minor charges. The road was to be sold on April 3, 1880.

Timothy Case brought other members of his family to Green Bay. Theo G. Case became assistant receiver and Munson T. Case became general passenger agent. After settling into their new environment, Munson appeared in a local production of Gilbert & Sullivan's *H.M.S. Pinafore,* but suffered vocal failure on the final night's performance. Undaunted, Munson was reportedly still singing in the spring of 1882, and dealing with passenger business in Green Bay. Theo was interviewed the same spring, indicating that earnings were up and that $60,000 worth of steel rail was ordered. Investor Charles H. Russell wrote to John Blair in March 1880 to inquire as to foreclosure proceedings. He wished to know when the road's sale was to be expected and gave his assent to unite in the proceedings against GB&M. He desired to know if he was recognized by Blair as part of the purchasing group, and that Mr. Taylor, Mr. Sloan and others of his friends were holders of considerable amounts of GB&M bonds. Blair replied that the road could not be sold for another year, or April of 1881. Meanwhile, Receiver Case was dealing with liens, right-of-way claims and generally putting the road into good shape.

George Huber had come to the GB&M from Valparaiso, Indiana, one of many men displaced by the depressed economic conditions of the 1870's. In October 1876 his employer, the Pittsburgh, Fort Wayne & Chicago Railway, laid him off and gave him a letter of introduction, signed by Master Mechanic James M. Boon. Boon's letter identified George as a man of good habits, and a first-class passenger and freight engineer. Huber became a passenger engineer, along with C. W. Case and S. W. Bennett, and regularly ran the entire 214 miles of line on Mr. Case's railroad. Usually Huber drew a Grant engine, and fireman Moses Belrose handled the wood. They took on fuel at Arcadia in the Trempeleau Valley. They did so until a dark day in July of 1880.

Huber wrote to his wife on Sundays. She maintained the family farm near Valparaiso, looking forward to the day when the Fort Wayne would again need men. On June 16th, he wrote that Winona suffered high water, rendering the railroad bridges unsafe. He wasn't sure just when trains would run again, as four to five feet of water covered the levee yards. W&SP's new station was under construction, but couldn't be approached. All North-Western trains were suspended. Huber borrowed a boat at the Mississippi House, a railroader's hotel, and rowed to the marooned train. The river had only to gain another foot and all Winona would be flooded. He thought that at least one-fourth of Winona's houses were inundated. River steamers could not land as dockage was inundated. Huber wished his family well.

Huber and Seth Champion were friends and Mrs. Champion wrote to Valparaiso about George Huber's marooned state at the time. She wrote that the engineer would be back safely

Above: In the 1880's the old CANESTEO served the route to Green Bay. In later years it served another owner out of Manistique, Michigan. Here, in 1898, it is seen with a load of shingles.
R. W. IRETON

tomorrow. George Huber brought No.2 home to Green Bay, then left for Valparaiso and a family visit. It was the last time he ever saw the rolling hills of Indiana.

The GB&M's condition was improving but it was far from perfect. Dispatcher E. C. Germond wrote train orders on plain newsprint, and one was illustrative: "Run slow over frog at Elm Lake. It is broken and in bad shape. ECG." Another read: "Notify all eastbound trains to run slow one mile west of Alma Center on account track is in bad condition. ECG." So it went.

July 9, 1880 was a stormy Friday. Wind and rain lashed the Winona area for four hours, not unusual weather for the region. Inevitably, the Trempeleau rose over its banks, flooding the lowlands. Streams took out many of Trempeleau County's road bridges. In Whitehall water rose along Scranton and Pine streets and swept into Ervin's Creek, rising eight feet. Conductor J. E. Buckman's train No.1 was running ten minutes late but had already passed several bridges safely. The rains continued as the train moved cautiously west from Whitehall toward Asylum Curve's present location. It was Sunday afternoon, shortly after 4:10 p.m.

At 4:45 p.m. a horseman came in from the west with grim news. No.1 lay jackknifed in a washout, the engine crew killed instantly. George Huber and Moses Belrose had ridden over a washed-out box culvert and in an instant the engine and tank fell into the void beneath the track, crushing the cab's occupants. Baggageman G. P. Hibbard was injured but the coaches and passengers were safe. Several washouts just ahead of the train would have denied No.1's passage.

The following Monday evening, after washouts were repaired, Huber's wrecked engine was dragged solemnly backward through Whitehall en route to Fort Howard Shops. A rail had pierced the smokebox front and it still protruded menacingly. Huber left a wife and four children in Valparaiso; Moses Belrose died short of his wedding date. Receiver Case hurried to the wreck site and later conveyed his sympathies to the families. Seth Champion and family comforted the bereaved in Indiana. Huber's passing should have caused his offspring to foreswear railroading as a career but such was not the case. His son grew up to experience the righthand side of many a Milwaukee Road locomotive out of Channing, Michigan, also helping to break in their new C-2 class engines on ore trains. The third Huber in line, George again, came to GB&W in 1927, 47 years after the tragic Friday night near Whitehall.

George Huber's death didn't terminate the affair. An assemblyman introduced a bill to inquire into GB&M's condition as Wisconsin wanted to know if managers had been lax. Ultimately a statement was issued by Commissioner Turner. He found the road to be in "fair average condition." Reports of dilapidated conditions persisted, alleged to have risen from maliciousness. Reform, however, manifested itself in a newly rebuilt combination car for the La Crosse train of Conductor Frank Seymour.

Another enemy in 1881 was the record Missisippi flood, which isolated the west end. Parties having freight in Winona's warehouses were notified of the rising waters. The river crested at ten and one-half feet above normal. In fall the Wolf River submerged trackage at New London Junction with 16 inches of water over railheads. And once again, the Trempeleau spilled over its banks to bedevil the west end of Mr. Case's beleaguered railroad.

After the April 3, 1879 foreclosure date, the Committee of Purchase and Reorganization was created. It consisted of John I. Blair, William E. Dodge and Roswell G. Rolston, the latter from The Farmers' Loan & Trust Co. The plan which they perfected was a restructuring of securities. The new company's common stock was $8,000,000 with preferred stock of $2,000,000. First-mortgage was $1,600,000 in six-percent bonds and the second-mortgage was in eight-percent bonds, set at $3,781,000. The plan was agreed to October 25, 1880 and. on January 20, 1881, John I. Blair, acting for the Committee, purchased the road for $2,000,000. The interest due on first-mortgage bonds was $10,510.02 and on the second mortgage, $289,088. Blair commented that the road never paid. Total bonded debt was $5,585,350. Again rumors flew that Blair really made the purchase for the benefit of the C&NW in which he was invested. Allegedly, Milwaukee stock brokers bought up GB&M stock for five cents on the dollar; La Crosse was a willing seller of its $75,000 block. Wood County sold out for $7,000 and Green Bay settled for $8.50 per share.

At the annual meeting John I. Blair, Samuel Sloan, Theodore Sturges, Percy Pyne, William E. Dodge, Edwin F. Hatfield Jr., Benjamin G. Clarke, Edwin C. Larned, Walter C. Larned, W. J. Abrams and R. B. Kellogg were elected to the Board of Directors for 1881. Samuel Sloan became president, Timothy Case, vice-president, and Theodore Sturges, secretary and Treasurer. Sturges had ties to Lackawanna Iron & Coal Co., the all-important supplier of cash and material to GB&M. The Larneds were Chicagoans and general solicitors for the road. Theo G. Case became assistant superintendent and general attorney. Prominent businessmen came to call upon the great men in Green Bay, especially John Insley Blair, who held forth on the "intimate connection" between GB&M and large mining and railway interests in the east. The point was made that the new company, the *Green Bay, Winona & St. Paul Railroad Company,* aimed to expand and develop coal traffic from the east to the growing northwest. To reinforce Moses Taylor's railroad properties in Wisconsin and Michigan, and to assist the Lackawanna Railroad itself to become a strong competitor, DL&W embarked upon western expansion.

Below: Deep in the Trempeleau Valley, eastbound train No. 2 pauses at The Pass curve. No. 10, a 4-4-0, is a Dickson machine, originally named E. F. HATFIELD JR. honoring the Lackawanna Iron & Coal executive and nephew of Moses Taylor. Circa 1890's.
GB&W COLLECTION

Above: The SCRANTON was a steel steamer (package freighter) built for DL&W service in 1888. Its hull was 260 feet by 39 feet by 21 feet, displacing 2015 gross tons. The vessel ran for DL&W until 1907 and, remarkably, it evaded the scrapper's torch until 1957.

EDWARD J. DOWLING, S.J.

Moses Taylor's investments in the lake states included securities in Michigan Central, Marquette, Houghton & Ontonagon (soon to be part of Duluth, South Shore & Atlantic Railway), Detroit & Bay City and Jackson, Lansing & Saginaw. Taylor had strongly favored a vital western gateway for his DL&W and, when Wabash's Jay Gould attempted to acquire control of the Lackawanna, Taylor chose an accommodation. The solution to a Gould-Wabash invasion of the East would be to jointly construct the New York, Lackawanna & Western Railroad from Binghamton to Buffalo. This would raise the status of DL&W, which leased the new company, to that of a full-traffic carrier. In 1879 Taylor sold his Michigan Central interests to the Vanderbilts and also divested interest in Rome, Watertown & Ogdensburg in New York State. RW&O had prospects for a Buffalo entry, plus an established connection with DL&W's coal port of Oswego. Loss of the RW&O property to the DL&W brought about interest in building directly to Buffalo instead of leasing existing routes to the Great Lakes. Taylor had envisaged a DL&W route to Chicago, and had planned for it without success. NYL&W, the Buffalo route, was formed in 1880 with Samuel Sloan, Percy Pyne, John Blair and William E. Dodge on its Board, balanced by Gould men. Moses Taylor died May 24, 1882, before completion of his springboard to the northwest in January of 1883.

DL&W in 1880 had a curving, mountainous line laden with slow-moving coal trains. The slack, listless period of the 1870's produced an oversupply of coal and the railroad needed other markets for its captive mines. The west was the answer and the 207-mile NYL&W became a vital necessity. A further alliance with Canada's Grand Trunk Railway allowed DL&W to take

twelve percent of westbound business without offending giant New York Central. This put DL&W connections into the greater Detroit-Toledo area. A few years later, trans-Michigan facilities developed, establishing allied rails less than one-hundred miles from Green Bay.

Green Bay, Winona & St. Paul Railroad had designs on building northwest. Receivership ended in October of 1881 and a new sense of destiny seemed to light the way toward the country beyond the Mississippi. Passenger schedules were advertised with St. Paul in mind as the ultimate destination. While the old GB&M coal dock caved in twice under new loads in 1881, the bark GEORGE M. CASE brought in 722 tons of coal to the GBWSTP dock, destined for St. Paul from Buffalo coal dealer A. H. Hedstrom. Vessels arrived from Cleveland with soft coal for the same market. *The Winona Republican* editorialized about GBWSTP building a railroad from Winona to St. Paul, not the intent of the Lackawanna men.

Formation in 1881 of the Omaha Road (Chicago, St. Paul, Minneapolis & Omaha Railway) and its control by Chicago & North-Western created GBWSTP's St. Paul gateway. GBWSTP was in no position to take on any expansion alone. Interest in a branch to Stevens Point rose in 1873 when David Kelly and Henry Ketchum approached the townsmen for $25,000 in aid. the Panic stopped the move but revival of the scheme took

Above: Robert Mills & Co. of Buffalo built the WYOMING in 1887 for the DL&W fleet. It was 241 feet by 40 feet by 15 feet. The vessel was sold in 1907 and cut down for use as a lumber steam barge.

EDWARD J. DOWLING, S.J.

place under the new regime in 1881. *Green Bay, Stevens Point & Northern Railroad Co.* was then formed to build the five-mile connection between Plover and Stevens Point with interest in an extension to Wausau. The road's cost was about $70,000, promoted by Blair-Sloan-Pyne-Dodge interests and leased upon completion to GBWSTP. The Stevens Point branch was aimed first at various wood products plants in Stevens Point, capitalizing on the town's desire to foster competition with the Wisconsin Central. When WC moved its shops and personnel away from Stevens Point to Waukesha, the irate city became more interested in shipping and traveling via GBWSTP. The Farmers'

Left: Wood package propellor SAGINAW VALLEY was built by F. W. Wheeler & Co. in 1881. W. W. Tyler of Buffalo leased it to DL&W until 1897.

EDWARD J. DOWLING, S.J.

Loan & Trust Co. held the GBSTP&N mortgage. GBWSTP assumed payment of the first-mortgage seven-percent bonds and payment of all taxes. It was also provided that the capital stock of the lessor, $35,000, should share equally with the second-mortgage bondholders in GBSTP&N. The bonds were later acquired by GBWSTP at 117.5% in exchange for its five-percent consolidated-mortgage bonds. The branch was a very good investment.

In his 1931 letter Frank Halliday stated that in 1881 conditions seemed to be improving and GBWSTP began surveying branch lines. GBSTP&N was the first to be constructed. Halliday made his survey in late summer, laid track in November and ballasting was done after freeze-up. Fires were built ahead of the steam shovel to break through the frozen ground. The Big Plover River had a 500-foot trestle which partially collapsed during construction, killing worker Jackson Blair. Halliday surveyed about six miles north of Stevens Point but that portion never materialized. The consort J. C. GODFREY brought 250 tons of steel rail for the GBSTP&N, the time-honored way. It was towed by the TOLEDO which was laden with coal for the northwest.

There were two catastrophes in 1881 which debilitated GBWSTP under Timothy Case. Engineer Anton Seims was running a ten-car immigrant train west from Grand Rapids when it plunged through a fire-weakened bridge at Hemlock Creek. The bents had charred enough to weaken one side and the engine flopped over, sliding fifty feet beyond the short bridge. Seims was injured and an immigrant boxcar caught fire due to concealed kerosene. It was asserted that the trestle was fired by an incendiary. The road lost $7,968.19.

A more serious disaster was the Fort Howard roundhouse fire in which nine locomotives were badly damaged the night of December 10, 1881. Fort Howard's fire bell sounded at 2 a.m. as a grim glow was seen over GBWSTP's shops. The Green Bay Iron Furnace and Wisconsin Leather Co. tied down their shop whistles to alarm the community. Fort Howard's and Green Bay's fire engines reached hoses to a nearby cistern but found them too short to draw water. Starting between stalls five and six and finally igniting the tarred roof, the fiery work devoured the entire building in spite of efforts of shop crews to fight the blaze.

GBW&STP had 19 engines, ten of which were west of Fort Howard. Of the nine burned, two were under repair, victims of a head-on collision. The fire was thorough enough to burn away blocking, dropping two engines into inspection pits in a vertical position, open smoke-boxes gaping at the cold sky. Engines No. 2 and No. 7 were fire-damaged a second time, the first being in the Grand Rapids fire several years before. Case thought that most were repairable and that they hadn't suffered as much as the pair caught at Grand Rapids. Water was kept off the engines which saved them to steam another day.

The building loss was estimated at $25,000. Master Mechanic Osborne, with a heavy load to bear, worked with a guest from Illinois Central and his insurance adjuster to assess damages. Insured by Commercial Union of England, a decision to raise temporary shelter preceded a new roundhouse. Case arranged to rent other locomotives from C&NW and Marquette, Houghton & Ontonagon, the latter another Taylor investment. The remaining ten locomotives were pressed to cover all work. Two burned engines were working by Christmas 1881 and the new roundhouse was well underway.

GBWSTP's holidays were less than joyous. Several lawsuits plagued the Green Bay route. In *GB&M vs. Union Steamboat*

Co. a guarantee of $45,000 per year worked against the boatline. In running steamers PASSAIC and CANESTEO to Green Bay, the traffic did not earn the steamers adequate compensation. U.S. Co. sued for $78,876.12 damages. Observers claimed the route was unprofitable, and that Green Bay was an outpost without adequate traffic.

David Kelly, Henry Ketchum and George Hiles privately speculated in lands and townsites along GB&M. But in 1881 the trio squared off against the receiver, raising an interesting legal point: should railroad officers keep land obtained for railroad purposes, whose title was secured by promises to locate the railroad and its depots on or near it? Case regarded the claims of Kelly secondary to bondholders' rights. Henry Ketchum also claimed that $60,000 of salary was due him in July 1881. Kelly's other case rose in New York (Garcia vs. David M. Kelly) regarding securities worth $90,000. A Green Bay newspaper speculated that the receivers were trying to frame Kelly. Evidently he tried to protect his investments from railroad foreclosure and had great difficulty doing so.

Kelly's personal suit against GB&M for nearly $300,000 was related to securities which Kelly surrendered to complete the ·road. He claimed that the note took precedence over the foreclosure but it was decided otherwise. Kelly's position was being pummeled by the formidable and relentless power of the Lackawanna group.

After his resignation David Kelly spent time hunting in the Black Hills and looking at future prospects. Allegedly involved in construction of Iowa's Fort Madison & Northwestern Railway, Kelly, Ketchum and Kenrick were directors. Kelly left his political adventures and tried to promote another narrow-gauge road, Wisconsin Peninsula Railroad, from Green Bay to Sturgeon Bay. Little interest was ignited by the project.

Kelly's mother, Mary Marsh Kelly, became engaged in a lawsuit against the GB&M receivership. Kelly probably was aware of the action, if not the mastermind. The case was dismissed, decidedly in favor of the bondholders. In 1882 Kelly was married in New Jersey and came back to Green Bay to live in Astor Heights. However, he spent more time in the east and finally moved to Brooklyn in the mid-1880's, listed there as an agent. He held property in Green Bay, alternately doing business in London. Kelly later moved to Boston where he practiced law in partnership (Kelly, Lincoln & Winthrop). That firm dissolved in 1902. In September 1916 a reunion of the 50th Massachusetts Volunteers, Kelly's old outfit, was saddened by the disappearance of its former president and comrade. David Marsh Kelly was never seen again; thus, the story of an exceptionally obscure man ended in even more obscurity.

George Hiles continued his lumber business but ran afoul of GB&M at trackside. Hiles made a legal case of firesetting by GB&M engines near Dexterville. Assets of Hiles' two firms, Dexterville Mfg. & Boom Co. and Scranton Mfg. & Boom Co. were destroyed by fire, allegedly set by the receiver's locomotives, a case of negligence. Master Mechanic Edward Osborne was called to testify in court about engine No. 3 (SCRANTON). The Grant carried a newly invented (1878) spark arrester, first used on Sussex Railroad, a division of DL&W. The coal-burner's arrangement was designed to prevent fires but the large $3/4 \times 6$-inch holes also helped set a few, which Hiles claimed happened frequently. No. 3 survived the Huber-Belrose wreck but its front-end arrangement did not. The cases of negligence hinged on the assumption that the lands were Hiles' which, in fact, they were not. The case boomeranged as Hiles' companies illegally claimed the land on which the fires

occurred, again tied to the claim for 400 acres of land which the trio tried to acquire. The lands were intended for the railroad and were not for those standing between railroad and the original owner.

Some of the land in question was at Seymour, Black Creek, Manawa, Merrillan Junction, Blair, Whitehall, Arcadia and Independence — about 47 acres, all outside the right-of-way. Independence's 6^7/$_{10}$ acres was decreed to be depot grounds on May 21, 1883, confirming the receiver's position.

George Hiles invested in an Arcadia lumberyard and store. During the difficult mid-1870's Hiles claimed that his yard would take farm produce in barter. His ambitions would shortly include the Arcadia Mineral Springs Co., a would-be spa "for the better health of the multitudes." He proposed a fairground and driving park with a Turkish Bath Institute near the mineral spring. Construction began August 19, 1878. Hiles shipped about 300,000 feet of lumber from his Scranton mill for the building in which he invested liberally. With his water tested and

of the Kelly case, a Green Bay news article claimed that Kelly's suits had continued until annulled by a statute of limitation.

Further actions of George Hiles and sons brought a $70,000 mill addition to Dexterville. He began the Wisconsin, Pittsville & Superior Railroad to develop Wood County and to connect several wood plants and sawmills at Vesper, Pittsville and Lynn. He purchased two engines, cars and rail in the summer of 1883 and pushed the road north from Remington (now Babcock). This line was sold late in his life to Milwaukee Road.

The St. Paul extension could not begin as a direct action of GBWSTP but plans were made in the summer of 1881 for future construction. Surveyor Halliday was again engaged to look into branch lines, one of which was considered to run to Almond in southern Portage County. Halliday's opinion of the St. Paul extension was that the plan was in earnest, not just a ploy to sell the GB&M. The Merrillan-St. Paul survey was organized in November, 1882 and hurried in the face of winter. Station "0" was placed 600 feet west of West Hall Creek bridge; then the

a prominent Winona man in charge of the building design, the man from Dexterville looked toward creation of another Saratoga Springs in the Trempeleau. The intended market included Winona, which was becoming a city capable of supporting such luxury. Most of the building was completed and enclosed by winter and justified its $20,000 building cost by spring. But, on May 15, 1879, the spa caught fire and was leveled. Rebuilding was begun immediately, the incorporators planning on a brick edifice. It reopened July 4, 1879 to the sound of a grand ball with forty couples under a handsome cupola.

Arcadia Mineral Spring Co., due to its location on railroad land, joined in the legal war between Kelly, Ketchum, Hiles and the railroad. GB&M disputed its situation and the legal action continued through the 1880's while the courts restrained sale of the land which would decide the hotel's fate. Whitehall lamented that the lawsuits tied up land which could otherwise be sold, retarding growth of such villages. In 1890, far beyond the times

Above: GBW&STP train No.1 stands at the Fort Howard (Green Bay Juction) station prior to departure for Winona, in the mid-1880's. No. 6, a Grant product, was named GEORGE F. TALMAN.
NEVILLE PUBLIC MUSEUM

survey, which required ten days' work, followed Little Tamarack Creek toward Durand. The line, practical with easy grades, crossed the Chippewa River at Round Hill, two miles south of Durand. Halliday and his crew followed up the Eau Galle Valley which he found to be an ideal route with good farms and hardwood timber. The line ascended until a summit was reached in the vicinity of Woodville or Baldwin but some rough country slowed progress. Finally, through the high country of St. Croix County, the line descended to Star Prairie alongside the Omaha Road to St. Paul. Halliday thought the line was a practical ninety-mile possibility which would have

enhanced GBW&STP significantly. The St. Paul survey cost $6,871.62.

In the early 1880's GBWSTP concentrated on building a coal business westward, with an eye to St. Paul as the main market. New hoisting engines were installed at Green Bay's GBWSTP docks to handle the expected surge, reportedly up to 75,000 tons for Minnesota. St. Paul coal dealers A. Pugh & Co. came to inspect the facility. Schooners, consorts and larger steamers would deliver the coal. The docks were repaired and the grounds between GBWSTP's station and the Fox River conditioned for coal storage. The dock face was 700 feet long and initial filling work was begun on the slough just north of GBWSTP's tracks. Material was brought in by rail. Four steam hoists were installed in a 360 × 500-foot building and a system of dump cars was installed atop the structure. Vessels reported in the coal trade were FANNIE NEAL, handling 829 tons, THREE BROTH-ERS, 662 tons, and F. Hurlbut's schooner CONSTITUTION, bringing 452 tons to GBWSTP docks. Other products unloaded were 1500 barrels of coal oil, fifty barrels lube oil, 100 barrels of gasoline, fifty barrels tar, fire brick and fire clay (for the many boilers used in local industry), plus 74 packages of merchandise for city wholesalers. Some coal schooners got into trouble. When 21 days out of Cleveland HALSTEAD put into Escanaba after battling heavy seas. The aging vessel was a peril to its ill-supplied crew. She finally limped into Green Bay with 772 tons of coal. Regular passage time from Cleveland was five days.

GBWSTP supplied charcoal from trackside ovens to the De Pere furnace and hardwood for the charcoal bound for ovens near Seymour. Charcoal iron was still an approved way of making quality iron for castings and firms such as Taylor & Duncan and John Delaney & Co. were in the business of engine-building. They also supplied GBWSTP with quality cast materials, especially for locomotives. In 1880, well before the iron and steel markets left the city, the iron furnace produced 180 tons per day. During the 1886 recession the furnace failed to go into blast for some time.

More trouble came to GBWSTP in 1885. Reports disclosed that the expected 1884 rush of coal went the way of another contractor via Superior. That port promised grain eastbound in the same hulls, whereas coal to Green Bay would have meant an empty eastbound voyage, not a good prospect for captains of coal schooners in the lean 1880's. In July 1883 President Sloan submitted a proposal to the Milwaukee, Lake Shore & Western Railway Co. to lease GBWSTP on a basis of thirty percent of gross earnings, negotiable to 35 percent, with a guarantee of interest payment on the first-mortgage bonds and on GBStP&N bonds.

GBWSTP's infancy dictated a need for interest payments on bonds due July 13, 1881. The $48,000 interest payment was met by Lackawanna Iron & Coal Co. and GBWSTP's treasurer was directed to issue a demand note with interest to LI&CCo. for the advance which constituted a first lien on the property. Notes were subsequently made out to LI&CCo. for various interest payments due through August of 1883. In January of 1885, after a deficit-ridden year, GBWSTP defaulted on interest due: $48,000. For the year ending June 30, 1884 GBWSTP showed a deficit of $17,492; the 1883 deficit was $11,500. In the calendar year of 1884 gross earnings fell off $87,500, nearly twenty percent from 1883. Farmers' Loan & Trust Co., as mortgage trustee, took possession of the railroad in the form of a receivership. Judge Dyer of U.S. Circuit Court, Milwaukee, entered an order confirming the act. The date was March 23, 1885 and Gavin Campbell became the agent for the first-mortgage bondholders. Control and custody were shifted to FL&TCo. in New York.

Gavin Campbell was born April 16, 1836 in Glasgow, Scotland. By the 1870's he was master mechanic and general super-intendent of Wisconsin Central. In the 1880's he rode herd on the Penokee Division of WC and then came to GBWSTP where he remained until 1890. This appointment led some to believe that WC would eventually take over GBWSTP but such fortune never occurred. The change was Timothy Case's "swan song" in Green Bay and on April 2, 1885 he was the center of a testi-monial which recognized his difficult days in Wisconsin. Seventy-six citizens signed an appreciative document and Case, along with his relatives, left for another commitment. Timothy Case retired in Chicago where he died in the 1890's.

Erwin C. Case's adventures were all too similar. He became receiver of another Blair-Sloan operation, the St. Louis, Hannibal & Keokuk Railroad. The Case family had drawn on experience in the DL&W and International-Great Northern Railway, in which Moses Taylor was invested; E. C. Case went to Hannibal, Missouri in March 1884. Within a decade such figures as Stephen S. Palmer and J. A. Jordan would be officers of St. Louis & Hannibal Railway after its reorganiza-tion. The same Lackawanna group investors were to be found at Hannibal. In the 1890's personnel moved between GB&W and STL&H with ease.

A prescient editorial in *The Green Bay Advocate* strangely pinpointed the plight of GBWSTP in its ever-present inability to run in the black. A link with Wisconsin Central would furnish grain and flour (if not, via Omaha Railway connections) in St. Paul, thereby strengthening the Green Bay route. The eastern connection for salvation of GBWSTP also included building a link across the peninsula to Lake Michigan's ice-free shore.

In the summer of 1885 lake trade was revived and GBWSTP's dock hosted steamers such as RUSSIA, a twelve-year-old vessel destined to become a regular visitor along the Fox River. RUSSIA would arrive with 1700 tons of coal and return east with 15,000 bushels of oats from the Cargill elevator, plus 5,000 sacks of flour from GBWSTP's docks. This traffic was down-bound for Buffalo and often markets in the old world. Another steamer, TOLEDO, brought 115 tons of rail for GBWSTP's track improvement. GBWSTP delivered about twenty carloads

Below: Few photos exist of the Arcadia Mineral Springs Co. hotel at Arcadia. Here a GB&M train pauses at the Trempeleau County village. (Engine is unknown.)
SHSW COLLECTION

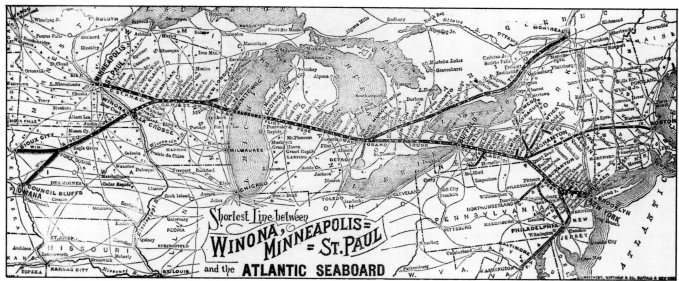

Lackawanna System in 1885.

of flour per day from Minneapolis for the propellors. TOLEDO got underway east with flour and pig iron, the latter from the Green Bay Furnace. Such items as crockery and glass arrived in great barrels via steamer, with a substantial rate saving for the wholesaling Joannes Brothers of old Green Bay. The biggest load out of Fox River's mouth to this date was carried by COLORADO — 13,500 barrels of white, pure, "new process" flour, the great hope of the northwest.

GBWSTP was never above promoting excursions, the reason for which was to draw upon the trackside west for local Green Bay exploitation. Such city guests would patronize local businesses, often climaxing their visit with a bay steamer trip. One such occasion was in the summer of 1885 aboard the KEWEENAW, a sidewheeler. The ten-car special on July 25th was switched onto C&NW and taken the mile to that company's depot for convenience. Fare was $2.00, and all were welcomed by the honorable W. J. Abrams, Green Bay's eternal railroad man. Kimball's Silver Band serenaded aboard the KEWEENAW. Some who missed the boat tagged along on the steam yacht DENESSEN, chartered by Gavin Campbell.

DL&W's control of the steamers in Green Bay was underscored by big city newspapers which asserted that an alliance between DL&W, WC and GBWSTP had been formed. It was evident to them that the Green Bay coal docks were unused for much of the 1883-4 season and one St. Paul journal was certain WC had acquired GBWSTP. The route from St. Paul to Buffalo was 1058 miles — 297 by rail and 761 by water; Chicago routings covered 1298 miles (410 by rail and 888 by water) and from Duluth, 1132 miles. The trouble with the Green Bay route was that new routes, which were strong competitors, were being opened over both water and rail. Omaha Road opened its Washburn, Wisconsin grain port during 1883, followed soon after by both Duluth, South Shore & Atlantic and Soo Line. Both of those routes were operational and hungry for the same traffic via Sault Ste. Marie. In time Soo Line's grain port at Gladstone was operational. WC also built its line to Chicago, opening up another route for northwest traffic. GBWSTP saw that its "devil" was keeping just one jump ahead of it; to expand successfully beyond the confines of Green Bay and Winona was a must.

GBWSTP's inability to lift the crushing load of interest on its bonds kept it in receivership. In 1885 a deficit of $69,543 was reported and the first-mortgage six-percent bonds were bid at

80½ with no asking figure. Finally, in January 1886, a circular proposition to bondholders asked if they would agree to fund the three defaulted coupons on first-mortgage bonds into a five-percent bond running until 1916 at which time FL&TCo. would pay the August 1, 1886 coupon in cash. The coupons aggregated $108,000 which funding would allow the FL&TCo. to return the property to the railroad company, the bond amount being $280,830. At no time were dividends paid by GBWSTP and the net operating loss during the period it was in power was $539,943.65. GBWSTP expended $214,460.72 in money, additions and betterments, emerging by fall of 1888 with a deficit of $91,436. Yet, the nation was on an upsurge and the road was having a "prosperous" year. In August of 1890 another foreclosure resulted as no coupons were paid through February 1, 1890. GBWSTP was involved in an unrelenting struggle to sort out its financial problems while a great dream of expansion took place, clearly establishing the road as part of DL&W's push for a transcontinental route.

Events of the 1880's contributed greatly to the GBWSTP's history. In summer of 1881 a shop strike was met by prompt dismissal and Master Mechanic Osborne quickly hired replacements. There was evidence of enterprise among the "news butchers" who sold ice cream on the trains as the Haskell & Barker fifty-footers swayed along toward Winona. On the way to Stevens Point construction turned to near destruction when WC's forces tried to put a crossing through GBSTP&N trackage. The row was over closeness of the Green Bay's track to WC land — six feet was not enough to cool the WC men, but the turmoil died in time. Evidently a new passenger coach . . . or a rebuild of extraordinary magnitude . . . was produced at Fort Howard shops. The car shop, under foreman William Thompson, employed seventy men in 1883, engaged in building flatcars and boxcars of increased lengths. Several of the engines damaged in the fire of December 1881 were still receiving needed work; $1,291 was spent in 1883. By late fall more passenger cars were shopped and a complete train was ready for winter service. Ominously, the elevator engine at Eastmoor was removed, together with its boiler, and placed in the car shop at Fort Howard, a move that strongly suggested the riverside dock was permanently out of the grain business.

Thomas Farrell invented a locomotive spring at Fort Howard shops. Evidenced by patent letters applicable for 1880 and 1881, the FL&TCo. was granted right and authority to make the loco-

motive springs and to use them on GBWSTP in consideration of $1.00 to Farrell. Wages were reduced twenty percent in the shop early in 1884 but hours were increased from six to eight, at least allowing for identical paychecks. Andrew Fenwick, the new master mechanic from England, managed to obtain a new steam hammer and a large hydrostatic press for wheel sets.

Nationwide economic disaster during this period accounted for 10,965 business failures. Failure was not evident in Frank Seymour's life, however; he married Miss Della M. Foote of La Crosse on Monday, August 21, 1882. The respected long-run railroader was soon to play a significant role in the Green Bay route's future.

By 1888 the lumber business was considered "exceptionally prosperous." Population increases in the western states demanded Wisconsin's pine-constructed housing far out onto the Great Plains. The Badger State enjoyed another decade of economic good fortune provided by the soft, easily worked wood before the Pacific Northwest and the South began to monopolize the industry. In 1889 Green Bay citizens were sure that "good times" were nearly there, countering reports of others who were leaving for opportunity elsewhere. Murphy Lumber Co., a Detroit firm with a mill at White Lake, Michigan, built on seventy acres on Green Bay's north side. The Murphy's came from Maine and had two supply camps at Nestoria, Michigan. They employed 125 men, helping to hold down unemployment.

In July of 1889 Joseph Walker & Sons, New York brokers, issued a circular to holders of GBWSTP securities, embodying a plan of reorganization for the railroad. The Walker firm was sure that foreclosure could be avoided by the construction of an extension southwesterly through Minnesota and Iowa to the Missouri River at Omaha. The plan was to have GBWSTP income bondholders pay a ten-percent assessment of $378,000, preferred stockholders, five percent or $100,000; and common stockholders, five percent or $400,000. The total of $878,100 would cover $152,000 GBWSTP floating debt plus pay $726,000 in cash to the Winona & South-Western Railway Co. In return, $878,100 in first-mortgage six-percent bonds and $1,053,720 of

stock would be given. The plan required five-eighths of GBWSTP securities holders to agree and, that for each $1,000 cash bond, the subscribers would receive $1,000,000 first-mortgage bonds plus twelve shares of W&SW stock. Other subscriptions would receive bonuses of six shares of W&SW stock. The New York brokers had hit on an expansion scheme which would assist GBWSTP to break out of its walled-off, Wisconsin-only world.

Winona & South-Western Railway required a large infusion of capital to lift its end of track onward to Omaha. Under the plan it would issue $6,950,000 first-mortgage bonds for a total of $18,500 per month of road, with a stock issue of $7,500,000. W&SW securities holders alleged that this plan was the only way GBWSTP could be put on a paying basis and avoid future foreclosure. If GBWSTP salvation was to come, such an outlet must be obtained. The circular went on to explain that foreclosure would not fully satisfy the first mortgage, its funded and floating debt; therefore, income bonds and stock would be worthless. Nonetheless, GBWSTP defaulted again, on the LI&CCo.-owned bonds. The brokers were successful in negotiating their plan for the expansion of the W&SW via GBWSTP securities holders.

Farmers' Loan & Trust Co. was again appointed trustee in possession of GBWSTP in August 1890. Joseph Walker Jr., Sam Sloan's son-in-law, was operating the road as FL&TCo.'s agent and the plan which included W&SW expansion. Seth W. Champion was appointed general manager for the Walker firm and FL&TCo. A GBWSTP employee since 1880, Champion stated that no changes would be made and that the future of the company was assured. FL&TCo. President Roswell G. Rolston

Below: GBW&STP 4-4-0 No.15 was a Danforth engine of greater weight than the previous engines on GB&M. Photo may have been taken at Grand Rapids after air brakes came to the road. Note cab window pin-up girl, in vogue on GBW&STP. Circa 1880's.
T. VAN DREESE COLLECTION

filed a bill of complaint, stating that the railroad constituted inadequate security for claims outstanding and that sale was necessary. It was evident that the stock was very largely held by the bondholders and they chose an expedient way of adjusting without having to "buy" a receivership. But once again, the road could not meet its interest obligation. GBWSTP went into voluntary reorganization.

By March of 1892 a Reorganization Committee proposed issuance of new securities: $2,500,000 consolidated five-percent mortgage, plus $3,781,000 second-mortgage four-percent noncumulative income bonds, $2,000,000 noncumulative preferred stock and $8,000,000 common stock. At that date the scheme, including unpaid interest, ran to $16,281,000. The committee was made up of Herbert B. Turner, Moses Taylor Pyne and Joseph Walker Jr.

In 1895 a monumental suit *(Mowry vs. Farmers' Loan & Trust Co.)* was filed by William S. Mowry, an owner of five first-mortgage bonds, who petitioned to compel foreclosure on behalf of the first-mortgage bondholders. Previous actions by the first-mortgage people were held in abeyance by the court, with an eye to reviving the road and placing it on a paying basis. In the 1890's the trust company sought to revitalize the road, which Mowry alleged was confiscation. The situation was compounded by the Panic of '93. Herbert B. Turner of New York gave a comparison of the road after the FL&T stewardship and application of $75,000 contributed by the consolidated bondholders. Mr. Henry Crawford, representing the "moneyed interests," contended that the first-mortgage people should be junior to the 1893 mortgage participants and that the road should be sold. Crawford stated that six different liens were held against the railroad, according to the FL&TCo., and he held his position of primacy for the first-mortgage group.

In April 1895 Judge Seaman ordered consolidation of complaints, which were given twenty days to serve answers. John I. Waterbury and Mark T. Cox were made defendants to protect the interests of their bond group. In November 1895 Judge Seaman granted FL&TCo. a decree to sell GBWSTP. The assenting bondholders, in agreement, were to receive six percent, the dissenters five percent. Local opinion feared that GBWSTP would give up its Green Bay headquarters and shops and become merely a division of DL&W. Having lost the case, Mowry's attorneys left town.

A plan of reorganization dated September 11th, 1895 was put forth. The committee of income bondholders and stockholders, composed of John I. Waterbury (chairman), Mayer Lehman, Edwin S. Hooley and H. Tuckerman, announced that they had entered into a tentative agreement with William J. Hunt, C. Ledyard Blair and Mark T. Cox, chairman. The committee comprised consolidated bondholders. Under its terms, the first and the consolidated mortgages were to be immediately foreclosed and the property bought, to be arranged as a new company. Securities would be as follows: Capital stock, $2,500,000; "A" debentures, $600,000; "B" debentures, $7,000,000. When 2½ percent had been paid on the "A" debentures, then 2½ percent would be paid on capital stock to share with capital stock until five percent had been paid on both. The "B" debentures were then entitled to all surplus net earnings remaining in any year after the "A" debentures and the stock had been served.

The securities provided that no mortgage would ever be placed on the road and neither could the road be leased or sold without the consent of 75 percent of capital stockholders and, if sold or reorganized, the proceeds would be distributed to "A"

debenture holders first. The stockholders would be next for payment and finally the "B" debenture holders. Gone was all long-term debt and with it fixed charges against the road's income. This meant that the first and second mortgages, money acquired at a very high cost, were virtually null and void, picked up by another form of security. The railroad, which had cost too much to build due to enormous interest charges, could now go to work and live within a framework of cost which was far more realistic for a rural, 200-mile line.

The new system required an assessment to be paid by each class of security, which would assist in paying prior legal costs and secure needed equipment. The account would be run by the Reorganization Committee, any surplus being held for betterment. Security holders had thirty days to act on the decision.

The GBWSTP sale was set for February 18, 1896 at the Green Bay Junction depot. It was then postponed until March 3rd and again to March 31st, due to efforts of the minority bondholders to establish a price below which the property could not be sold. That action ultimately caused postponement of the sale until May 12, 1896. On that date at 10:00 a.m. Special Master Hoyt faced a small crowd of important people from whom bids were requested. First came the La Crosse branch, the unwanted orphan made untenable by high rental charges from the C&NW. Mark T. Cox stepped forward to bid just $20,000 for the six-mile line. No other offers came forth. Next, the main line was brought up. Cox again stepped forward, proffering a check for $1,000,000. Mr. Cox was quite alone again, but he acted on behalf of the Reorganization Committee; in the case of the La Crosse branch he had acted for himself. The crowd representing eastern money then thinned out. Mr. Cox and Attorney George W. Wickersham (of the august firm of Cadwallader, Wickersham and Taft, the latter, William Howard Taft journeyed to Stevens Point and another special sale of the GBSTP&N. That line, in default of $34,056 interest due on $70,000 of bonds, also had been ordered sold. Most of the group went to Kewaunee to look over the installation at the lake shore. It had been a momentous day.

It was not over yet. William S. Mowry, representing $105,000 of the first-mortgage group, still fought for the full amount of their holdings with interest. Mowry filed 27 objections based on mismanagement of GBWSTP by FL&TCo. Judge Seaman in Milwaukee would once again face the dissenting side. He finally directed that Mowry et al be given a pro rata share of the proceeds, which reportedly was a victory for the Reorganization Committee. The affair continued until late 1896.

Articles of association were filed at Madison, Wisconsin on May 7, 1896 by Mark T. Cox, William J. Hunt, C. Ledyard Blair, Stephen S. Palmer and William J. Wilson. They formed a corporation, *Green Bay & Western Railroad Company,* in order to maintain GBW&STP and GBSTP&N property, with the exception of the La Crosse Branch. On June 10, 1896 the formalities of transference were completed and the new carrier began in earnest to fulfill the designs desired by the investors, the families of whom were still represented in the new railroad. Finally, Green Bay & Western was facing a more realistic future.

Right: GBW&STP 4-4-0 No.9 at Ogdensburg in another Oliver Parks photo. The polished Grant engine was named R. G. ROLSTON.
OLIVER PARKS

Above: GBW&STP's No.12, named ARTHUR BONDON, was one of three Dickson 4-4-0's which arrived in April 1874. No.12, photographed by Iola's Oliver Parks, is eastbound at Ogdensburg in the 1880's.

5

SOUTHWESTERN
LEGEND

In the rugged country along the Missisipi, hidden valleys give evidence of timeless erosion. Norton Township, Winona County, is a striking example. There, an abandoned railroad twists about in search of high ground, testifying to a struggle by engineering forces to conquer an ascending angle to Minnesota's high plain. One hundred years ago, the Winona & South-Western Railway made its way to the top of the hill, utilizing the majestic Bear Creek Valley and carrying the destiny of Green Bay, Winona & St. Paul Railroad toward the Missouri River.

The progress of 1880-style railroading is complicated, riven with brutal struggles between competitive forces for control of whole regions. The warring forces paused briefly in 1883; temporarily exhausted capital resource brought the struggling wrestlers of capitalism to a halt. The 1884 financial slump reduced railroad earnings and rates; the dividend yields shriveled in the heat of battle. Weak railroads were pushed into the mud of receiverships and GBW&STP was no exception.

New construction took a holiday, marking the end and beginning of important financial kingdoms. Villard of Northern Pacific fell, as did Jay Gould and his Wabash. Their departure only brought new energy which rose phoenix-like from the ashes. Expansion was seen as a short-run waste of capital, especially if the competition had the same goal. A critical mass was reached when Chicago, Burlington & Northern Railroad proposed its St. Paul Extension which went up the Missisipi through Eastmoor, opposite Winona. The CB&N thrust signaled America's most intensive building years, 1886 and 1887, which in the end complicated the excesses of the overbuilding from 1879 to 1883. The Burlington expansion, done in retaliation of Milwaukee Road's "invasion" of Omaha, which was deep in Burlington's territory, laid more competition on GBW&STP. Two more Chicago-Twin Cities lines west of the river became active in the 1880's — the Rock Island and Minnesota & North-Western (CGW). Wisconsin Central built to Chicago in Wisconsin and Illinois. The newer systems largely left the GBW&STP to fend for itself.

Some of the building booms of the period arose from old schemes which included old charters. One such patent was that of Winona & South-Western Railway, which would rise to divisional status in the Lackawanna Road's expansion scheme. It was the promotion of "The Great Through Route" of the DL&W system that became the Green Bay route's high-water mark.

The idea of a link between the Missisipi and Missouri Rivers was renewed and the implication of capturing open regions ripe for commercial exploitation enticed Winona's merchant princes to act. By 1886 capital demand accompanied low interest rates because of increased savings, making railroad building an attractive investment. With such low-cost loans available, small firms could again unfold fond dreams of local rail empires, controlled not by the eastern money men, but by their own closely knit circles.

Some expansion came because of the rate problem. Inequities intensified granger desires to see competitive forces slay the dragon of oppressive and exorbitant rates. Manufacturers' meetings in Winona's Board of Trade were held over rate discrimination. Allegedly, Winona paid $1,470,000 to railroads annu-

Left: Late in 1888, 4-4-0 No. 1, the WINONA, makes a triumphal march onto a new trestle for photographer Tenney. The bridge is the first Bear Creek trestle.
C. A. TENNEY, WINONA PUBLIC LIBRARY

ally. Chicago & North-Western had captured 90% of Winona's outbound traffic and 60% of the inbound traffic. Calculations outlined that one-sixteenth of C&NW's earnings came from Winona on 35,000 cars a year. Equally tyrannical was the rate structure placing Chicago-Winona rates above Chicago-St. Paul tariffs. Higher rates for westbound goods on C&NW were also grounds for Winona to consider itself a "soft touch" for the North-Western. Flour and lumber — serious business for the city — were similarly attacked. It was the dawn of debate over the long haul-short haul question that engendered the Interstate Commerce Act of 1887. It also revived the comatose idea of Winona & South-Western Railway, which could provide the regions of Iowa and Minnesota a patent medicine of lower rates for lumber and grain.

GBW&STP's Gavin Campbell led a contingent of Green Bay notables to the Winona convention in May of 1887, which was held to revive the W&SW. They were banker Rufus B. Kellogg, accompanied by businessmen Fred Hurlbut, A. C. Neville and D. W. Britton, bent on boosting Green Bay. The desire to promote GBW&STP would now assist W&SW to reach Omaha. They mingled again with Winonans like Charles Horton, Henry Lamberton, Andrew Hamilton, Earle Youmans and Thomas Simpson, the latter once involved in the GB&M bonus suit. Youmans later became president and Henry Lamberton vice-president. Thomas Simpson was secretary and Mathew G. Norton was treasurer of the W&SW. The Honorable William Windom, Minnesota's hero of Congressional rate wars, circa 1872, was also present in W&SW's councils.

Interest in the W&SW began in the peak building years of 1856 through 1872, and finally 1887. Origins are traced to the Winona & La Crosse Railroad charter, which would have connected Winona with the La Crosse & Milwaukee Rail Road, completed to La Crosse in 1858. In 1871 the charter had a base for organizing but aid faltered. Winona at length bargained away W&SW's bonus in the Ketchum-GB&M court battles, some $100,000 in bonding. It left only numerous surveys which were done to find a way up the St. Peter Sandstone in back of the city.

Lukewarm investor appeal brought about an alliance with at least one proposed Iowa narrow gauge, a Houston-Winona-Hesper-based railroad. Evidently they had in mind a line built northeast to Winona to meet the oncoming Green Bay road. Some agitation among towns west and southwest of Winona met with no commitments; Chatfield, Plainview, Lanesboro and Spring Valley were among them. The times were not right, nor would they ever be for the pink steam of narrow gauge in southeastern Minnesota.

Exploration of several routes was made by the Hilbert Brothers who located the eastern end of Winona & St. Peter Railroad nearly thirty years previous to W&SW's beginnings. The transitmen were well equipped by provisioning through Mr. Royal D. Cone's hardware emporium. Mr. Cone was another true believer in the budding railroad. Mr. William McIntire, a promoter of the W&SW, addressed the idea of construction to Omaha, lifting the road out of the short-line category. The new road was looked upon as the "salvation of Winona" and the city again voted bonding of $100,000 toward the W&SW project. The South-Western became substantial when the new offices were opened on the First National Bank's second floor.

W&SW's directors met with Mr. Frederick W. Rhinelander, of the Milwaukee, Lake Shore & Western, whose interests explored routes to the Mississippi. The Lake Shore Road, which

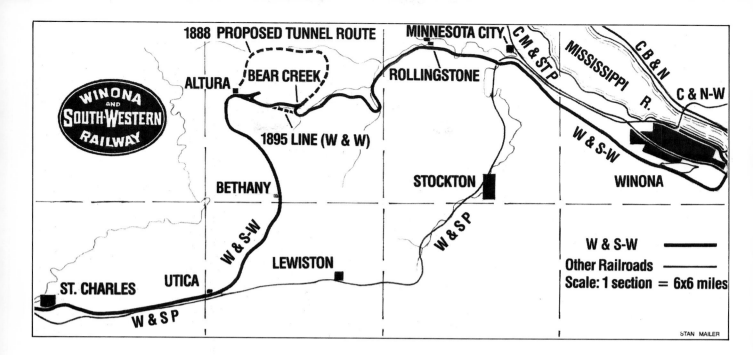

reached Wausau, Wisconsin by 1880, was interested in reaching southwest lumber markets in the "Omaha system of roads." This was again a desire to build a route away from north country forest lands to new regions. *The Winona Republican* reported that MLS&W was "finding out just as Wisconsin Central did" that a line southwest was necessary for the road's prosperity. Perhaps it was wishful thinking done to agitate for W&SW's bond issue, but MLS&W surveyors were said to be moving through Black River Falls en route to the river at La Crosse. Winona hoped for such a connection to develop, inasmuch as Washburn's Soo Line was building east from Rhinelander to Sault Ste. Marie and the Lake Shore interchanged there. It would be possible for lumber to be routed to the Mississippi if a link between Wausau and the river were built. This meant that lumbermen along the MLS&W would be freed from the exactions of roads having lumber interests of their own.

In October 1887 W&SW surveyors bound for Mason City crossed into Iowa. Their path lay farther west than the final construction, crossing the Milwaukee Road's Southern Minnesota road between Dexter and Grand Meadow, Minnesota. Surveying became infinitely easier as they reached gently rolling farm country. The aid, granted by Minnesota towns, would alter the route from a straight line bound for Mason City. The final route wound through the high country in southern Olmstead County, backtracking to Stewartville and Spring Valley. McIntire took the W&SW idea to his associates in the Twin Cities. According to *The Republican,* they "represented the interests of James J. Hill of the Manitoba" (Great Northern in 1890). Hill's associates also controlled Iowa's Mason City & Fort Dodge line, a key ninety-mile road which was to figure in the plan to reach the Missouri River.

The Mason City & Fort Dodge Railroad was incorporated in 1881 as a climax to Hill's interest in Iowa coal. Webster County, Iowa possessed the northernmost known deposits of coal, very important for locomotive fuel and heating in the north country. Webster County would also make the Hill road independent of eastern coal suppliers. Coal was later found in the Dakotas but the deposits near Fort Dodge were the prime interest in the

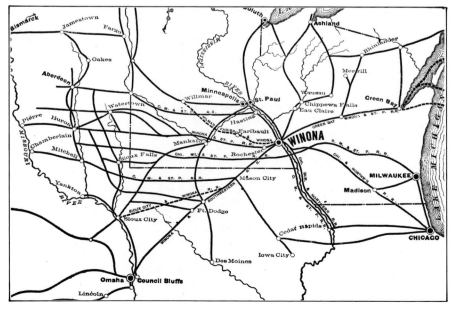

W&S-W projected routes to Sioux City and Omaha in the optimistic 1880's. The would-be "semitranscontinental" DL&W-backed thrust was illustrated in the "Winona Republican" as shown. Another connection with the Hill-controlled roads was the Willmar, Faribault & Winona, yet another "paper" railroad.

Above: This view to the south, showing the completed trestles at Bear Creek, was taken in the summer of 1889 after its completion. The first trestle is in the center. The line leads left toward Winona and to Bear Creek Station which was located in the small cut at center right.

Below: Well-wishers and board members step down from three CB&N coaches for another Bear Creek excursion photo. The W&S-W train is led by engine No. 1.

it would build a 372-mile line to Omaha through various fertile counties in rolling prairie and enjoy a satisfactory business from the outset. It stressed that lumber traffic from the timbered regions to the prairies was an aggregate business "almost beyond computation." Winona was described as one of the largest lumber milling centers with a yearly cut of 125,000,000 feet at its mills.

After the Interstate Commerce Act passed, rates were in favor of the shortest route. As a coal road the South-Western would bring both anthracite and bituminous coal to coal-less lands in the west. Bituminous coal would be supplied from Webster County, Iowa whose output in 1887 "approximated 400,000 tons," coming from Mason City & Fort Dodge Railroad lands. Anthracite coal would come "via Green Bay, Winona & St. Paul

Above: The Empire Lumber Company at Winona was one of four large lumber mills along the Mississippi. It was valued at $150,000 and employed 250 men. W&S-W boxcars used for lumber traffic are seen in the foreground.
WINONA COUNTY
HISTORICAL SOCIETY

Right: W&S-W Brooks-built 4-4-0 No. 2, the H. W. Lamberton. It is spotted for photographer Charles A. Tenney of Winona in the Bear Creek Valley in 1889.
WINONA PUBLIC LIBRARY

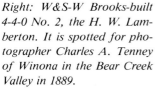

1880's. Hamilton Browne, an Iowa associate of Hill, became engrossed in developing the resource as early as the 1870's. For some years Charles H. Benedict, Hill's chief clerk, was president of the MC&Ft.D road. In September of 1887 William McIntire, representing the directors of W&SW, proposed to purchase the MC&Ft.D as a route through to Omaha. A "syndicate" which would carry the road westward, was to contact eastern financiers and seal the arrangement. William Windom would proceed to London to conclude financial affairs. Winona & South-Western would then spring forth, being established to Mason City by January 1, 1889 and to the Missouri River by January 1890.

In 1887 Mason City & Fort Dodge was completed from Mason City to Beem's Mine, Iowa (88.4 miles) with a 3.6-mile branch to Coalville. It possessed five locomotives. Hamilton Brown of Fort Dodge served as President. Its coal tonnage went to St. Paul via Rock Island road or M&STL. The coal supply proved to be marginal in character, encouraging W&SW to attempt to buy the MC&Ft.D for $1,400,000. By late 1887 W&SW was preparing to build out of Winona. The South-Western published a prospectus in *The Republican,* stating that

Railway, which was in harmony with the Delaware, Lackawanna & Western system." The route would be continuous between Green Bay on Lake Michigan and Council Bluffs and Omaha on the west. Steel steamers and barges would deliver coal from Buffalo, and from the coal mines of eastern Pennsylvania. The cheap water route to Green Bay would be a decided advantage in delivering coal west of the Missouri.

The prospectus continued to outline the system's advantages and the eight-month season of open navigation to Green Bay. The system would be assured of a competitive place between Buffalo and Green Bay. The "harmonious through line" — Omaha to New York — would also net large shipments of grain eastward to Green Bay from the lineside areas. The system would also create a direct short-line between the Canadian roads at Sault Ste. Marie and Omaha, which would adjust the rate problem.

In describing its connections, W&SW's prospectus showed the closeness of the GBW&STP alliance, as well as the fact that "the company controlled the only franchise for an additional railway bridge across the Mississippi at Winona." GBW&STP would interchange with the MLS&W, the Rhinelander System,

Above: W&S-W No. 1, the Winona, is at Bear Creek Station before the line was opened to Altura. No. 1 was a 4-4-0 of uncertain ancestry.
WINONA COUNTY HISTORICAL SOCIETY

Below: The South-Western ran many specials and promoted Bear Creek as a tourist attraction. Here a heavy train is eastbound on the second trestle.
WINONA COUNTY HISTORICAL SOCIETY

MINNESOTA HISTORICAL SOCIETY

as well as WC and Soo Line, to reach all lumbering and mining sections of Wisconsin.

Green Bay's detractors called attention to the fact that its one east-west railroad had been in bankruptcy for several years, noting that it only took two or three steamboats a week to carry away its traffic. Green Bay's *Advocate* jingoistically stated that GBW&STP was here to stay and that its traffic was increasing. With the construction of the Soo Line, plus the Duluth, South Shore & Atlantic Railway, Duluth would face a struggle for the eastbound wheat and flour trade. Minneapolis wheat would go east via the cheapest route. Soo Line's Saunder's Point grain terminal at Gladstone, Michigan was operational by 1888, ruling against both Green Bay's and Duluth-Superior's primacy in the port field.

In conjunction with the new Green Bay route, the DL&W organized the Lackawanna Transportation Co. The company was staffed by DL&W officers interested in the GBW&STP. The company allegedly ordered two steel boats of 2200 tons burden for the 1888 season, with two more to follow. In August of 1887 the steamers WESTERNER and ROANOKE made port at Green Bay laden with coal; they would return east with flour. Gone were the problems connected with rival boat lines which might buy off the Green Bay route boats. The pair made their very first trips into the Great Lakes, having been previously employed between Baltimore and Norfolk. At the time of their arrival the GBW&STP docks at Green Bay were host to seven coal-laden vessels.

By April 2, 1888 W&SW executed a mortgage with The Farmers' Loan & Trust Company for contemplated construction from Winona to Council Bluffs at a rate of $18,500 per mile. The bond issue was $6,950,000. Winona & South-Western Improvement Company was the construction agent. They would also equip the road for the railway company and complete it before December 1, 1892. In April of 1888 W&SW board members William Mitchell, John A. Mathews, W. H. Yale and John Robson resigned. They were replaced by John Insley Blair, William P. Hallstead, General Manager of DL&W,

Above, The C&N-W's yard at Winona about 1900, looking northwest. Until 1891, GBW&STP trains entered the city over the curving bridge lead in the foreground. Trains then backed under the bridge to their own station. The depot was built under W&SP ownership in 1881. C&N-W fully absorbed W&S-P in 1901.

STAN MAILER COLLECTION

Above: W&W No. 4, the M. G. Norton, at the Winona shops about 1897.

Below: Upon reorganization of the W&S-W, the engines were relettered as shown. Here No. 3, the V. Simpson, and its well-wishers gather in early afternoon. The Winona bridge is in the background.

C. J. VINCENT PHOTO

Joseph Walker, representing President Samuel Sloan of DL&W and GBW&STP, and W. H. Lyon, a New York capitalist. Earle Youmans also resigned; William Windom succeeded him as president. W&SW became a Lackawanna affair and Windom set off for Europe to enlist financial backing.

Routes were still determined by local aid and there were two finalists: one via Chatfield and Spring Valley; the other via Dover, Marion and High Forest townships. The High Forest route was the ultimate selection, following the ridgetop to Simpson, south of Rochester, while the Chatfield route encountered rough terrain. Spring Valley offered aid but it was not on a beeline southwestward. The High Forest route actually swung back southeast to accommodate that town.

The route of W&SW in Winona was a curiosity. W&SW won a line eastward along Second Street past the great lumber mills and paralleled CB&N trackage to the east end. It then described an arc of 180 degrees, which allowed the road to exit Winona against the bluffs along the south shore of Lake Winona. It was the personification of a model railroad in plan form. Originally, the citizens of Winona opposed the southshore location but in the end Chief Engineer Wheeler prevailed, wanting to prevent a crossing of the Milwaukee Road at an acute angle. The alternative northshore location would have required a nine-degree curve to maintain its approved northwest route several miles to Minnesota City. Land acquisition was finalized in the fall of 1888, in time for the first twenty miles of grading. Wheeler let contracts to Foley Brothers of St. Paul for the actual work. Some differences erupted and by July, 1888 Minnesota & Iowa Construction Co. took over. Completion was scheduled for November 1st.

After several months, right-of-way and aid questions were settled and William McIntire grumbled that, although $25,000 had been expended, only pine stakes resulted. Surveyor Wheeler had finally finished all surveys and on August 11, 1888 Mayor

Ludwig broke ground for W&SW near Winona's levee. In his speech he stated that W&SW had been awakened by passage of the 1887 Interstate Commerce Act which now regulated rates from Great Lakes terminals and made possible such roads as W&SW. He then cited the great engineering difficulties which faced the road in the first twenty miles.

Like a biblical army, contractor Donald W. Grant's force of men and mules moved overland from Faribault. They bivouacked in the Rollingstone Valley and made ready to face the enemy — St. Peter Sandstone. Their target was a lone tree, far up the grade of fifty feet to the mile, the only route on which such a grade was attainable. Grant soon had 120 teams working at three different locations. Blacksmiths were busy putting scrapers together and about forty teams worked on the first great loop in a side valley. The first of W&SW's legendary 26 trestles to Bear Creek Station was begun. Dennis Galligan from Lanesboro had the Bear Valley contract. His scrapers arrived from St. Paul aboard Diamond Jo Line's steamer MARY MORTON. Fresh off the Soo Line, Galligan's Irishmen were reunited with their equipment for a new struggle west of Winona. Their boss was strict; his crew of 500 was allowed no liquor or cards in camp. Laborers were paid $1.75 per day.

Engineer D. M. Wheeler reported to his board about the problems of the route. The Rollingstone Valley offered a one-

percent eight-mile grade to Bear Valley Station, which would require a tunnel. Wheeler's 37.8 mile route to southern Winona County was approved. Fascinating in retrospect, the tunnel would have emerged northward into the so-called Straight Valley which has a greater gradient than the valley finally utilized.

While construction in Bear Valley continued, W&SW's terminal was settled in Winona's east end. Fifty acres of land acquired on the river below the estate of Mrs. John Keyes became the nucleus of Bridge Yard. Local speculators bought half of the Keyes estate in anticipation of Burlington's crossing into the city. Winonans considered it "valuable land," while clairvoyant minds envisaged roundhouses, shops and teaming tracks built on their purchase. A Congressional bill had authorized another bridge for Winona but, before a permanent bridge was erected, CB&N put in winter bridges across the Mississippi. The Keyes home stood until the 1970's, last used as a railroader's hotel occupied by GB&W crews.

A month into construction, W&SW completed its first large trestle which stretched 705 feet just west of Minnesota City and 41 feet above the Winona & St. Peter main line. The grade west of this point was complete for five miles, including many more bridges to the mouth of Bear Valley. Piedmont was established two miles west of Rollingstone and a glowing account was given of the scenic beauty of the horseshoe curve nearby. Eventually, nine large bridges were built, six of which were fifty feet above the valley floor. Bear Valley widened out into a large natural amphitheater, which allowed construction of the great curving trestles at Bear Creek Station, one of the great scenic wonders of the northern midwest. One bridge, a wood structure 700-foot long, carried the roadway 65 feet above the valley floor. This was followed by a 600-foot structure seventy feet in the

air. Between the two, a 65-foot cut required removal of 25,000 yards of rock. The line curved through about 220 degrees, and headed eastward again before curving into the ravine tunnel site. The ravine tunnel, which put the road into Straight Valley, would have been 1800 feet long — 300 feet above Winona at this point.

Trestle timber came from Laird, Norton & Co.'s great mill on Winona's east end. The first of it was carried up to Minnesota City via W&SP. Rail was ordered from Joliet, Illinois, the first load coming in a 29-car consist over CB&N; ties were rafted in over several weeks from points above Winona. McIntire acquired a used 4-4-0 locomotive, allegedly a Rogers, from a Chicago source. Trackage in the city's east end was arranged with the CB&N to run up Second Street to the business district. This route ran through the great lumber mills of Laird — Norton & Co., Empire Lumber Co. and Youmans Brothers & Hodgins — to the CB&N terminal.

On November 23, 1888 the newly received engine, named WINONA, handled a special inspection train of five CB&N coaches. Engineer John Murphy eased the 4-4-0 over the dizzying trestles up the one-percent grade to Rollingstone. Rail was not yet in place to Bear Creek; the balance of 130 cars was still en route. Finally, on January 14th, 1889 Mayor Ludwig and his city council rode over the entire line to the high ledge near the proposed tunnel site. CB&N provided the Sunday excursionists with a dining car brought over on the car-ferry OSBORNE. The

party enjoyed the view and the meal with the Mayor, finally getting down to the finer points over cigars. Wheeler was called upon to explain his railroad, especially the proposed tunnel, and the resulting grade on its far side. Bids had been returned on the tunnel subject but no action had been taken.

W&SW had completed its first year's work on January 3, 1889. It possessed one 36-ton locomotive, over a mile of trestles and a terminal on a sandstone ledge 300 feet above the investing city. The council agreed to issue its $100,000 bonus and the incomplete road settled into an uneasy winter.

Interest in W&SW's progress into Iowa was an old adventure which was in the minds of Mason City boosters for decades. William McIntire had visited and exhorted the crowds as had Lamberton and others before him. In 1888 McIntire asked for a $20,000 subsidy. With W&SW a stirring reality, the subject became the focus of attention for Sioux City promoters. The city on the Missouri was moving into a speculator's boom in the late 1880's and a Winona committee was delegated to spur interest there in the new road. It was an attempt to bargain for a western terminal of the South-Western and generate investment at the Missouri River.

When work was completed at Bear Valley, Galligan's crew broke camp and withdrew. Winter surveys continued while the directors searched for subscriptions and bonding. The financial problem was exacerbated with a price of $35,000 per mile for the climb to Bear Creek. A report circulated in March indicated that W&SW would build a temporary track of three-percent grade over the bluff to assist tunnel construction. The next month, when workers began filtering back to Winona, they learned that no work was to begin on the road that spring. Galligan paid off his men after riprapping the Winona yard. Surveyors were discharged and the road finally settled accounts with contractors Grant, Foley Brothers, and E. C. Long & Co. William McIntire received W&SW Improvement Company stock in exchange for a $25,000 mortgage on the road's terminal grounds.

In May of 1889 Mr. Wheeler was ordered to arrange flat cars to accommodate picnic parties to Bear Creek during the summer, the only steady source of revenue for the fledgling road. The struggling road next approached Winona Deposit Bank for a $10,000 loan for four months. William Windom had returned from Europe empty-handed and an earnest search for capital began. It led to the Farmers' Loan & Trust Co. and the DL&W interests. In the midst of the GBW&STP reorganization plans, the *Walker Circular* was brought up as a method of funding the W&SW advance. This action became the Green Bay road's salvation. Joseph Walker Jr. proposed the plan to pay for "the Omaha Extension." Since the securities were closely held by directors of FL&TCo., DL&W and the GBW&STP, and the W&SW first mortgage was held by the Farmers, agreement to the plan was thought to be forthcoming.

The plan called for assessments on GBW&STP second-mortgage income bonds of ten percent, or $378,100; on preferred stock of five percent, or $100,000; and on common stock of five percent, or $400,000. Of the $878,100 available, $152,000 would be applied to liquidation of the floating debt, leaving $726,100 cash on hand for the W&SW. GBW&STP security holders would receive the following securities from W&SW: W&SW first-mortgage six-percent gold bonds of $878,100 and 10,537.2 shares of stock, amounting to $1,053,720, a total of $1,931,820; for each cash subscription of $1,000 the subscriber would receive $1,000 of first-mortgage bonds and twelve shares of W&SW stock; for each of the $500 cash subscriptions, subscribers would receive one $500 first-mortgage bond and six shares of stock. The agreement required the affirmation of five-eighths of the controlling securities of the road.

Below: CGW used McKeen motor cars on Rochester-McIntire-Osage runs. Here 1002 and baggage trailer 1025 await departure at Rochester's station. The building is now a bus terminal.
C. LAVALLEE COLLECTION

73

Left: A Mogul-powered train crosses the Bear Creek bridge, headed for Altura in the 1920's. The westbound train may fill out at the doubling siding a mile ahead before attacking the 3½-percent grade to Altura.

The plan, based on an agreement between W&SW Improvement Co. and Joseph Walker & Sons, covered the following: 1) that capital stock of W&SWICo. was $500,000, paid in full; 2) that further of the assets of said Improvement Co. were $725,000, including twenty miles of constructed road, now in operation, Winona to Norton; 3) that W&SWICo. owned and paid for the road. The Improvement Company was to agree to give $152,000 of W&SWRy. Co. first-mortgage bonds to GBW&STP to liquidate certain indebtedness and that interest accruing would be paid by the Improvement Co. until the road was turned over to the W&SW Ry. Co. It also required that the Improvement Co. agree to use the funds only for extension of the W&SW Ry. Co. It was stated that if the security holders would ever receive any return on their investments, a south-western outlet for GBW&STP must be obtained.

The proposal continued to outline the business to be interchanged along with the eastern coal business. It was absolutely

essential for the road to make such a union, so as to compete with roads that were diverting traffic from the GBW&STP. Walker thought that GBW&STP should be commanding the coal trade. With the large floating debt of the GBW&STP and its inability to meet its fixed charges, something had to be done; otherwise, the Green Bay road would suffer foreclosure and would not satisfy its first mortgage, leaving the balance of its securities valueless. Walker believed the road would show hand-some earnings after the W&SW was completed to Omaha *and* Sioux City. The GBW&STP then signed a traffic agreement with the South-Western for a mutual exchange of business to last the life of the W&SW bonds. Immediately, the W&SW's case improved drastically. The W&SW Directors were notified that the DL&W/GBW&STP security holders assented and that extension of the road in Minnesota was to be forthcoming. But before the money was available to continue, the summer turned to autumn and the Board of W&SW directed $3,000 be paid to cover interest on $100,000 of bonds due October 1, 1889.

In September a request to "purchase steel and locomotive" was made by Superintendent Wheeler. The 1100 tons of sixty-pound rail was to be ordered from Lackawanna Iron & Steel Co. at $28.50 per ton. In February of 1890 the subscription for first-mortgage bonds of W&SW Ry. Co. included the following subscribers and amounts: Lackawanna Iron & Coal Co. and Thomas Simpson for $250,000 each; B. G. Clarke, Sam Sloan, P. R. Pyne, E. F. Hatfield Jr. and H. S. Wilson, all committed for $25,000. Others in the Lackawanna community were Melissa P. Dodge, W. W. Crapo (of the Pere Marquette Road) and several brokerage houses.

Arrangements made on February 1, 1890 called for W&SWICo. to act as construction agent for W&SW Ry. Co. The Improvement Company was to receive the first-mortgage

Below: CGW 101 is a D-2 class machine which was typical of specialized power assigned to the Winona branch. Here the engine is seen at the famous shop town of Oelwein, Iowa on July 13, 1925.

bonds and stock of the railway as compensation, to be sold by the Improvement Company to generate funds for construction. The traffic alliance included DL&W, Flint & Pere Marquette Ry., MLS&W, GBW&STP and CSTPM&O. The Improvement Company had Royal D. Cone, Andrew Hamilton, Charles Horton, William McIntire, William H. Laird, H. W. Lamberton, James L. Norton, H. G. Norton, Verrazano Simpson and Earle S. Youmans as its directors. William McIntire was president and H. W. Lamberton was vice-president. Mathew G. Norton was secretary and treasurer and E. G. Hornbrooke was assistant to Norton.

In the summer of 1889 the W&SW offices were moved to the second floor of the CB&N building. The building, located on the corner of Second and Layafette Streets, would become the "station" of the Green Bay route, after it entered the city on its own accord. After settling into the new quarters, the engineers went to work on a new switchback, which would be required to ascend the steep grade out of Bear Creek. They also looked to the planned crossing of W&SP west of St. Charles. Once again, surveys were made toward Spring Valley, looking to run a narrow line between aid money and a realistic route to Omaha.

A description of the switchback operation at Bear Creek was given by a Rochester native. Regular trains came around the horseshoe curve and onto the ledge above the valley. The engine was uncoupled and turned on a turntable. It was then run to the other end of the train and coupled to the last car. Then the train moved engine first up the incline to Altura. In descending, it was observed that air brakes were a God-send, such was the attendant peril.

The money chase continued as Earle Youmans sought to enlist Winona's own in W&SW's capital stock roles. All the company officers had drawn handsomely of their personal resources; Youmans thought that others should also invest. His goal was to sell $100,000 to his fellow citizens, making it more of a local enterprise.

The men behind W&SW became involved through land and lumber. William Harris Laird and Mathew G. Norton were long associated with Laird, Norton & Co., a large Winona-based sawmilling firm with ties to the Weyerhauser group. James L.

Norton, brother of Mathew, was also in the same company. Royal D. Cone was a successful hardware merchant associated with supplying lumber camps in Wisconsin's north woods. Andrew Hamilton was a partner in Empire Lumber Company, another large mill along Winona's riverfront. Henry Lamberton started as W&SP Railroad's land commissioner, while Verrazano Simpson, another 1850's Winona pioneer, made a fortune in wheat trading and real estate. Earle Youmans was a partner in Youmans Brothers & Hodgins, yet another saw mill.

Wheeler was empowered to purchase a "40- to45-ton passenger engine," which arrived in mid-October 1889. Brooks Locomotive Works apparently completed the machine for the Davenport, Iowa and Dakota Railway in June of 1889. Renumbered No. 2 and named "H. W. LAMBERTON," it arrived over the CB&N. After storage in the Burlington's long-vanished enginehouse on the east end, it was fired up by Brooks' traveling engineer W. S. Abell, and run to Bear Creek Valley on October 12, 1889. Afterwards, Wheeler ordered two more engines, five tons heavier, costing $8,250 each. Shipped on May 15, 1890, they were named V. SIMPSON (No.3) and M. G. NORTON (No.4). The SIMPSON arrived in June, NORTON in August. One hundred boxcars costing $500 each and fifty flatcars costing $362 each arrived from Muskegon Car Co. Two cabooses arrived later and in time gondolas were made up from flat cars for rough tonnage. The initial group of cars arrived in 1890.

W&SW's annual meeting in June of 1889 underscored the costs of the road to date — $435,000. William Windom was elected president, with the slate of lumbermen largely intact. Activity dawdled into fall, and Lamberton, Verrazano and Thomas Simpson went to New York, while Mathew G. Norton vacationed in Europe. Progress on the road was leisurely at best. The Improvement Company planned the ten-mile segment

to Utica from Bear Creek in September, putting Contractor Leary onto trestle work at Bear Creek. W&SW flats were sent to handle ordered rail and fastenings. The turntable on the Bear Creek Valley's north side was removed and a water tank was built. Switchback construction progressed on the valley's north slope, west of the great horseshoe curve trestles. Wheeler put 100 men on the excavation. Other shipments of rail arrived from Green Bay via GBW&STP, feeding material to the sudden burst of activity. At the end of 1889, trackage reached to Utica Township, nearly 300 feet above Bear Creek and 600 feet above Winona.

Below: A W&W 4-4-0 drifts downgrade after an assist of a westbound train about 1897. Bear Creek Station is at the extreme left at the cut.
MINNESOTA HISTORICAL SOCIETY

Above: The CGW wreck near Rollingstone, Minnesota was in the 1920's. The 2-6-2 tends the work extra which has come up from Winona.
MRS. C. MEISCH

The achievement of reaching tableland required a celebration. It was obligingly attended by New York broker Joseph Walker Jr., Mr. A. Fell, DL&W's General Western Agent, GBW&STP's Seth Champion and Frank B. Seymour. The broker and board member was queried about the *Walker Circular* plan for welding the Green Bay road to the South-Western. Walker indicated that the money had been paid into the Trust Company but he didn't know if the Improvement Company had received its share. The Great Men left on the Bethany excursion that afternoon.

The special arrived at Bear Creek, advancing up the valley's north side on the stiff grade for nearly two miles past Switchback Junction, where the tunnel-Straight Valley route would rejoin the main line. The dignitaries were satisfied that the Lackawanna's reach would include Winona County's breathtaking scenery. Joseph Walker considered Bethany's tableland an ideal site for the World's Fair. Their enthusiasm for high adventure sharpened. Walker and Fell then left for St. Paul and other serious affairs.

The original aid packages from various townships had largely expired by January 1, 1890. This altered the route away from the hilly Chatfield-Spring Valley line to the more practical St. Charles-Marion route. W&SW paralleled W&SP's line from Utica through Dover, crossing to the south side west of St. Charles. The line then ascended a ridgetop to Simpson. Con-

twenty miles from Mason City and the coveted Mason City & Fort Dodge connection. Officers examined Osage's terminal grounds west of town, never to be crossed by their railroad. Osagians feted the Winonans, promising to hold a July 4th sham battle in their honor under new electric lights in 1891, the year of the South-Western's arrival.

In summer of 1890, Wheeler negotiated for crossing rights with W&SP for St. Charles and Plank's Crossing locations. Rail from Scranton continued to come up the lakes; 250 tons was off-loaded in July at Green Bay. The road appointed a master mechanic, R. H. Emerson, and an assistant superintendent, C. L. Stewart. Emerson came from the Maple Leaf Road, soon to be the Chicago Great Western, which would buy the South-Western a decade later. Passenger equipment was obtained through Ohio Falls Car Co., Jeffersonville, Indiana. OFCCo.

tractor Galligan excavated a 500-foot long deep cut, just east of St. Charles. At Simpson the road swung around and headed south to Stewartville, running through Racine, Spring Valley, Ostrander and Leroy. South of Spring Valley little heavy work was encountered to the Iowa Line. During 1890's summer, W&SW ran more excursions, which heavily outnumbered the freights. Some went to Winona's Woodland Cemetery in the manner of many 19th Century pilgrimages. Ironically, the distance via carriage was less from downtown than by W&SW. Decoration Day trips were followed by a Congregational Sunday School picnic train consisting of a baggage car, two coaches and two observation cars. The young people boarded at the Burlington station at 10 a.m., and enjoyed the W&SW's "commodious pavilion" and picnic ground far up in remote Bear Valley. One gentleman sojourned en familia for two weeks, inviting friends to join him there over a pan of brook trout. The South-Western issued a pronunciamento that Camp Harris was a stop for its vestibuled limiteds; at least it sounded progressive.

For the South-Western road to enter Iowa and obtain aid, a separate Iowa corporation had to be unfurled. *The Winona, Osage & South-Western* was signed into existence in May of 1891, enabling the company to proceed to Osage. Action to form the wing corporation began in early 1890 and Osage then voted $30,000 in aid. The Iowa town considered itself in line for a division point, as it lay 117 miles from Winona, but a scant

Above: Simpson, Minnesota in the days of the CGW, about 1910. The junction of the Rochester branch and the main line from Winona was located here. The Rochester branch, built in late 1890's, actually prevailed after 1900's.

had an undelivered bargain: two 54-foot combination cars and six coaches. They arrived on CB&N in October in coach green, livery, with oak and cherry interiors, with Forney-pattern seats from Scarritt Co., St. Louis. Passenger service to St. Charles opened in September 1890. The day train left Winona at 8:30 a.m., returning at 3:40 p.m. By December the village of Orion was renamed Laird and regular service was extended to Spring Valley. Laird, Norton & Co. moved their lumberyard from Chatfield to Stewartville to be on the line closely related to the Norton and Laird fortunes. Stewartville's depot was at first a boxcar, in the manner of many a beginning institution. In the same month a special train, again carrying officials, inspected all the way to Stewartville, making the brisk trip at twenty miles per hour. The stars were Joseph Walker Jr., the GBW&STP men and the Winonans; the engine V. SIMPSON was in charge. Spring Valley received the six-car special; each guest wore a red badge which read "GUEST W&SW RR, DEC. 30, 1890." Despite some sander troubles with the V. SIMPSON, the trip was awash with anticipation that next year would see progress to the Missouri.

In January 1891 Winona's newspaper reflected upon the state of affairs between W&SW and Mason City & Fort Dodge Railroads. It reported that the sale of the Iowa road to W&SW was about to be settled, as DL&W had advanced $500,000 to W&SW for Iowa construction and acquisition. Yet *The Fort Dodge Messenger* reported that the merger was suspended due to the high asking price of $1,300,000. Perhaps the Hill affiliates had chosen to keep the DL&W out of their territory, or the territory of Alpheus B. Stickney and his Chicago, St. Paul & Kansas City Railway (CGW). President Lamberton asserted that he had nothing to add. W&SW had attempted to buy MC&FtD a year previously, finding the price too high, and the bid was not renewed. Lamberton indicated that they preferred to build their own road to Omaha. Other reports stated that a stock exchange had taken place between the two roads, which was also denied.

The railroad was ready to make the final thrust to Osage. While several passenger specials ran to Spring Valley with exchanges of goodwill, W&SW's new superintendent, J. J. Mahoney, got ready to build the road up Third Street to new terminal grounds. This action was related to the new Winona Union Terminal Railway Co., which proposed to group all the lines into the W&SP station in the central part of town. W. H. Laird, R. D. Cone and H. W. Lamberton were the officers of the new company. The North-Western counterproposed the use of its own station, for which an ordinance was passed. The Second Street route was to be followed on a fifty-foot path into the C&NW yard beyond the road's depot, then only ten years old. The proposition was dropped when Milwaukee Road declined to enter Winona streets with passenger trains, thereby reducing running time.

Just beyond the meeting of W&SW and CB&N trackage in Winona lay the W&SW yard and enginehouse. Another mile beyond was the crossing with the Milwaukee Road, achieved halfway around the 180-degree swing to Sugar Loaf station. The State of Minnesota required installation of a Saxby & Farmer interlock at the junction, which included a switch point derail system. Speeds were not to exceed twelve miles per hour for

Above: The enginehouse and shop in Rochester, Minnesota in the closing days of CGW steam. Here engines 289 and 713, a 2-6-2 and a Mike (used to McIntire), doze outside the barn. The building was razed in the 1980's.

Below: Winona's river front in 1892 included W&S-W's terminal, Bridge Yard, Milwaukee Road's Wall Street transfer and the sawmill district.

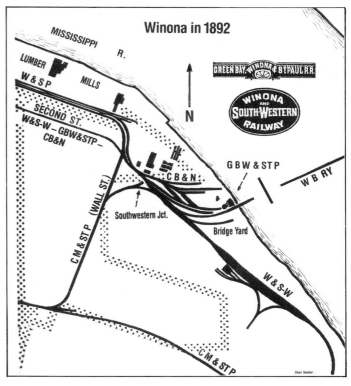

passenger trains and eight miles per hour for freight. The installation was operating by Spring 1891. At the same time Messrs. Frank and Kahn, cigarmakers of Winona, christened their fine new stogies with the South-Western's name, an honor sanctioned by President Lamberton.

The race to Osage continued into summer. Two more 4-4-0's arrived on June 16th from Brooks: W. H. LAIRD (No. 5) and E. S. YOUMANS (No. 6). Engineer John Spellman was assigned to the latter, which was dispatched immediately to the tracklaying front. Engineer A. J. Wheeler and Fireman Fred Baumann, assigned to the LAIRD, were presented with a posh set of seatboxes and cushions, complete with armrests. The LAIRD assisted the NORTON with the seven-car Old Settler's Excursion up the three-plus-percent grade in what must have

Above: CGW 1000 spent much of its time as a "yard goat" at Winona's Bridge Yard. This car was introduced to eliminate firemen and worked in the postwar era. It is preserved at North Lake, Wisconsin.

Below: F-class 2-6-2, No. 292, was one of two equipped with LFM disc drivers during World War II. Here the highest numbered CGW Prairie gets off from Bridge Yard's engine and freight terminal (yard office) across from the GB&W terminal. The roof of the old Keyes home, plus the water tank, show above the bridge lead in this 1947 view. The CGW 1000 "McKeen Switcher," another famed Winona landmark, lurks in the background to the right.

been extraordinary railroading sights and sounds. In the same month William Windom passed away, leaving behind him honors and accolades from the state he served.

Service to McIntire, Iowa on the "Kansas City Road," (later CGW) began July 8, 1891. The "South-Western Limited" left Winona at 3:40 p.m. and arrived at 7:35 p.m. Returning, the train left "Mac" at 7:49 a.m. with a 12:20 p.m. arrival at the Missisippi. On August 7, 1891 Osage's first W&SW train arrived at 8:45 p.m. On the night of the great day, the Osage band serenaded the spike maul's last blows on the sixty-acre tract. Three thousand five hundred people attended, fully expecting to win a terminal on the new road. The track people graded a short distance toward Cedar River and Mason City. In those few extra lengths of rail on fertile Iowa soil, the South-Western paused, never to gain further momentum. Gradually, freight business expanded on line and W&SW arranged tariffs to suit Winona shippers, excluding La Crosse jobbers and merchants from

W&SW territory. Incentive was enough to bring an order of 100 Haskell & Barker-built boxcars in mid-September 1891.

At year's end, Winona's newspaper speculated optimistically that South-Western extension beyond Osage was only a springtime away. W&SW still looked for support from Sioux City and a connection with the new "Pacific Short Line." PSL's speculative goal was to flank the Union Pacific to as far west as Ogden, Utah. PSL (Nebraska & Western Railway Company) had built 128 miles in 1890. By January 1, 1892, N&W Ry. Co. was a Hill road. It was renamed Sioux City, O'Neill & Western Railway Company and incorporated October 27, 1891. The presence of the W&SW was considered to be behind a thrust westward via Iowa's northern counties to Sioux City in early 1891. Receivership for the Pacific Short Line eventually put it into Great Northern's camp. In early 1892 GN-controlled Sioux City & Northern Railroad company was thought to be a possible route into the Missouri River city for the extended W&SW "system."

Winona & South-Western 4-4-0 No.2, "H. W. Lamberton," poses on the Minnesota City trestle in the late 1880's. The new road required many such structures in the deep valleys behind Winona, most of which were never filled. Brooks Locomotive Works built No.2 for the Davenport, Iowa and Dakota Railroad, but the new engine was never delivered to the Iowa road.

H. W. TENNEY PHOTO; WINONA PUBLIC LIBRARY

The effect of the Panic of 1893 began to fall heavily upon the South-Western. On June 30, 1893, the construction contract between Winona & South-Western Railway Company and W&SW Improvement Company was canceled by mutual agreement. On October 1, 1893, the railway company defaulted on interest amounting to $59,110; the trustee filed for foreclosure and requested a receivership. The Farmers' Loan & Trust Co. held the mortgage, declaring the property insufficient security, the company insolvent and the rolling stock in inadequate repair. It contended that there was a large floating debt and that the Improvement Company and the road itself was run by the same officers. It was further alleged that much of the rolling stock was returned to the ownership of the Improvement Company and then leased back to the road at exorbitant rates.

Judge Caldwell found the railway in default and ordered the road sold by May 1, 1895, unless payment was made. Further claims by the Improvement Company were to be considered; Tilden R. Selmes would be appointed Receiver.

The $400,000 sale of W&SW on September 29, 1894 was made to Harry W. Lamberton, Verrazano Simpson and Matthew G. Norton, three of the original board members and financiers of the road. Prior to the sale, attorneys for FL&TCo. asked for the sale to be reopened in ten days, when bondholders would make a bid of $500,000. The judge agreed to hold the matter open, with deposit of $100,000 necessary as a guarantee. If not, then sale would be made to the Winonans. Inasmuch as the eastern bondholders were disorganized at that point, they did not respond. Allegedly, they had become suspicious of Joseph Walker Jr.'s business methods.

When the final decree was made, W&SW bondholders received a little over 16 percent of their claims plus a judgment for the balance. The aggregate amount due was $2,354,106.68; the total realized by sale and applicable to bondholders was $384,325. The actions cleared the way for the formation of successor Winona & Western Railway Company, which considered further extensions southwestward. However, the treacherous Bear Creek switchback and the steep grade out of its canyon had to be improved first.

A new route up the hill was finished in November 1895. The two wood trestles were eliminated in favor of a steel structure constituting the chord of the bow-shaped first trestle. The excavating crews worked on the south side of the valley, eliminating the switchback trackage on the north side and a crossover

It was then evident that DL&W strength had played out at Osage, Iowa and that Mason City & Fort Dodge Railroad was not for sale to "The Great Through Route." Yet, with the opening of the Kewaunee gateway, it was likely that DL&W influence to the Missisippi was a future probability.

W&SW's limited prosperity allowed it to acquire No.7, a second hand 0-6-0, for duty in the lumber district at Winona. It arrived in December 1892. That same year, gondola cars were acquired, W&SW's shops were improved and mail service was extended to Osage. Total expenditures for 1892 were $40,000, which included a search by Engineer C. E. Scott for a better route out of Bear Creek. Yet, the end of the dream was near. General Manager C. C. Burdick of the MC&FortD announced that his company was to become part of the Chicago Great Western Railway Company and that Hamilton Browne, James J. Hill and others controlled its securities. The Winona road was left to fend for itself in increasingly difficult times.

trestle to the south side. The new line was 2½ miles long, extending from the location of Bear Creek Station westward. The small cut between the two old trestles was opened in another direction; the new line actually angled across the old track location. Ominously, the rails used on the new line had been removed from the short extension beyond Osage as well as from the old switchback. In building the new line it was claimed that a 1½-percent grade was achieved. On Sunday, November 24, 1895 the track at the short cut was changed to allow operation over the new line and Monday's inbound passenger train arrived five minutes early.

The recession of the 1890's was considered severe. Lumber prices were depressed and the new company was struggling due to lack of adequate west end interchange trade. The road was overequipped, as most of the rolling stock was to cover Mason City interchange traffic. The pine supply also changed as southern and western forests competed even more strongly with

lumber from Winona. When the road was finally sold in 1901 to Chicago Great Western Railway, the great mills and families of Winona were vacating the riverside scene. With the end of the agricultural frontier in sight in the 1880's, the growth of American plains towns slowed and the need for Wisconsin lumber dropped. The novel idea of Winona's own railroad faded before changing times along the Missisippi.

Conditions did permit the road to build a 7½-mile branch into Rochester, Minnesota, which provided that city with a second railroad. Rochester had agitated well back into the 1870's for another line, and the moribund Lake Pepin & Omaha Railway as well as Davenport & St. Paul Railroad were candidates. One route considered as practical was the extension of the Chicago Great Western via Mantorville, and even Wisconsin's Foster road (Sault Ste. Marie & Southwestern, another 1887 rate outgrowth) was listed as a candidate. W&SW had built through Simpson, south of Rochester, an appropriate junction for a

Right: On April 10, 1967 CGW operated an Alco switcher from Rochester to Osage. It was the last train service to the Iowa community.
D. L. HOFSOMMER

Below: The ICRR depot is on the left at Osage, Iowa, while the CGW terminal is on the right. Photo taken about 1910.
OSAGE HISTORICAL SOCIETY

branch. The road into Rochester was completed in the fall of 1899, having a depot and eventually a shop along the Zumbro River. The new line supplied heavier traffic southward and it was a sensible investment for the road. In time, the rectangular enginehouse became the home shop for CGW power used on the branch lines to Osage, Red Wing & Mankato. The Rochester extension cost the Winona & Western $150,000.

CGW made plans to unite its eastern Minnesota lines, connecting the Duluth, Red Wing & Southern line with Rochester via new construction to Zumbrota. It was the year of expansion for the line, which also ordered 41 new Prairie-type engines for heavy freight service. In May of 1901 W&W Ry. was offered to the larger road. CGW's President A. B. Stickney visited Winona to calm the fears of employees caught in the merger. It was also averred that CGW was soon to buy the Green Bay & Western. Stickney was closeted with the Winonans at Laird, Norton & Co.'s office on May 7, 1901 and soon the final special train set off for McIntire. The press bubbled about possible extension but the subject was never raised. On September 12, 1901 W&W became CGW and the lumbermen were relieved of their burden.

As a token peace offering, CGW brought engines 24 and 82, a 4-4-0 and a 2-6-0, to be overhauled at the W&W shops. The forty men remained on duty, their pay raised to CGW standards. The 4-4-0 No. 5 (LAIRD) was renumbered at Winona to CGW 1123 after an overhaul. It was different for middle management. Superintendent J. J. Mahoney and Mort Allen left for the Fort Smith & Western road; Master Mechanic John Mailer joined them in 1903. After 1899 CGW used the Milwaukee Road depot for passenger and freight service, leaving their Second and Lafayette building in the bleak 1890's. For a while in the early 1920's, CGW reduced the Winona line to occasional service, then put on daily service with a mixed train, departing Rochester at 6:30 a.m. and arriving at Winona at 11:00 a.m. The freight office at Center and Mark Sts. remained in service.

In 1931 CGW sought to eliminate the Bear Creek hill route in favor of trackage rights over C&NW from Utica to Winona. Altura would be served via the stub to the top of the great hill. CGW claimed that it was only able to take 450 tons up the hill in a single train and a 1200-ton train required three hours' running time to ascend to Altura. In the recession era, the wood trestles needed attention, yet the triweekly mixed train to Simpson was to be increased to two daily trains. Altura, Bethany and Rollingstone would be served as needed from either end and CMSTP&P's station at E. 4th and Adams Streets would be retained. Some opposition was raised as locals feared that CGW would then renege and withdraw altogether from the region. The road was finally abandoned June 14, 1933 after a complicated battle with shippers. Meanwhile, an enterprising lady in Altura made application for a chauffeur's license to truck, mail and freight along the route.

The monumental bridge at Bear Creek finally came down, about 35 years after Chicago Bridge & Iron Co. had raised it and the hopes of Winona & Western. In 1935 the trackage right over C&NW was expanded to include the Utica-Plank's Crossing segment, which allowed the CGW to enter the other company's property four miles south of Eyota, but service to Dover, St. Charles and Utica was retained via new turnouts to old CGW industries. The Winona end continued service to Rollingstone, until the Minnesota City trestle was considered unsafe for use in the 1930's. CGW shrank into a terminal along the Swift & Company plant near Bridge Yard which it maintained until merger with C&NW in 1964.

Thus, attrition of the "Corn Belt Route" carried away a distant cousin of the Green Bay route, which was to be its salvation. The South-Western road was a weak attempt to further the ambitions of men of vision like Moses Taylor, years after the great financier passed away. Even today in the beautiful Bear Creek valley, the concrete foundation blocks of the iron bridge bears witness to the expansion fever of a forgotten empire.

R. W. BUHRMASTER PHOTO

What might have been: CB&Q 2-6-2 1938, an R-4a class, heads for O'Neill, Nebraska in July of 1948. The former Pacific Shortline nearly made alliances with DL&W's Great Through Route, linking it with the far west.

6

WINONA BRIDGE

The bid by Delaware, Lackawanna & Western investors to push their railroad into the trans-Mississippi West was a simultaneous action which included stimulating several properties. On the eastern edge of Wisconsin, Kewaunee, Green Bay & Western Railroad was fostered from the old port city to a "warm-water port" at Kewaunee. In Michigan, Toledo, Ann Arbor & North Michigan Railway was completed to Frankfort in 1892 and agreements were made with GBWSTP afterward for traffic via the new car ferries on Lake Michigan. The Winona & South-Western road moved to continue its progress, but its eastern terminus required a solid Mississippi crossing and one dominated by the Lackawanna group, devoid of excessive charges for trackage rights.

With the reorganization of the Green Bay route in 1881, interest arose to better its contract between C&NW for the La Crosse trackage right. Negotiations focused on the entire lease of trackage, observed to be a great annual loss to GBWSTP. The isolated line was intended originally to be connected by an all-GBWSTP route to La Crosse but, in the light of the road's financial condition, extension and union could not be accommodated. The six-mile orphan continued to drain the corporate coffers and was not considered in the plan for 1890's road. Yet, operation continued through the 1880's, although rentals ran to as much as $1500 per month. And certainly, with the coming of a new business partner in W&SW, the Green Bay route looked to rid itself of costly and entangling alliances with C&NW.

By 1891 C&NW had granted GBWSTP the privilege to run one mixed train each way per day, scheduled by C&NW. However, it allowed only business transacted on GBWSTP's own line, with payment of six cents per hundredweight, and raised rates 2½ cents per hundredweight more on cargo destined for Buffalo boats at Fort Howard. Carload lots were logged at $4.00 per car of twelve or more tons, with excess charges over proportionate amounts. Passenger earnings from Onalaska to Marshland were entirely C&NW's. It was only one of many disagreeable conditions to be found at the Mississippi River's edge.

Burlington's intent to build a twin cities line was fueled by the Winona, Alma & Northern Railroad's incorporation in 1883. It began as a Chippewa River-Pepin County land aquisition, leaving C&NW opposite Winona. Grading was well advanced by 1885. A year later, CB&N's General Superintendent Holcomb met with Winona's Board of Trade, the latter anxious to secure Burlington service. Months later, CB&N resurveyed its line closer to GBWSTP's forsaken Eastmoor grain dock. In October 1885 contractors Hannan and Horrigan secured the contract to build 5000 feet of CB&N's line from the Green Bay elevator westward. The route from Dunleith (E. Dubuque) to Prescott was active with contractors and the Burlington cat was out of the bag. Milwaukee Road had cut its lumber rates into Omaha, and Burlington rivalry would spur the new route to the St. Paul gateway in retaliation.

Left: Construction of the Winona Bridge began with pile driving late in the summer of 1890. CB&N served Winona via the ferry WILLIAM OSBORNE which is shown maneuvering between clusters of piles and barges en route to its landing near the bridge site.
WINONA PUBLIC LIBRARY

Eastmoor's elevator, abandoned in the early 1880's, was hardly noticed by the advancing CB&N forces. Nearby, carloads of rail were unloaded but the structure seemed to be merely an old haunted castle of commercial decadence. Burlington built a high embankment seven miles past the site, its riprap and fill transported across winter's ice from Minnesota. Four thousand laborers, performing like ants in a linear nest, completed the road in 1885, finishing southward from Prescott past Trevino (Chippewa River) in just one year. Coincidentally, the road's surveyors took readings along Washington Street in Winona. Entry by Burlington into Winona would be congruent with the Green Bay route. Winona considered CB&N an opening into St. Louis and southwest markets, a salvation for its lumber business. Winona put forth an ordinance to permit CB&N into Winona and it was rumored that GBWSTP would pass to CB&N, allowing a line to La Crosse over friendly rails.

CB&N's general manager rode over the new line July 19, 1886. Only thirty miles remained to be completed on the Chicago-St. Paul route. The line was formally opened October 1st, but the true, grand opening occurred when "The Boston Ownership" of Messrs. John Murray Forbes, Charles E. Perkins and distinguished retinue arrived. Carriages were quietly rushed to meet the special. On Sunday, October 3, 1886 the Bostonians crossed over the Great River to Winona, now comfortably within their fiefdom.

The Burlington eventually made its way into the city via a winter bridge and a steam ferry. The ferry slip was near Bridge Yard. The transfer boat operated from dockage at a point near Eastmoor. CB&N contractors had to team their rails from Milwaukee Road's South Shore Depot because the competitor would not switch in the needed cars. Thwarting the North-Western took another Sunday special surprise party, as swiftly assembled men hauled ties all night long to secure access to the city with 1700 feet of track. CB&N acquired offices at No. 2 Ely Block; Forbes' and Perkins' grand scheme became a reality in Winona.

The CB&N strengthened its competitive position but found the competing Minnesota & North-Western, along with Wisconsin Central, was undercutting its rates. The press declared that CB&N would prevail as it had water-level grading, while M&NW and WC had to contend with grades as much as sixty feet to the mile. The famed Burlington Strike of early 1888 did not touch CB&N. Superintendent Barr stated that passenger engineers at La Crosse were paid 3¼ cents per mile and freight men 3⁷/₁₀ cents due to longer hours. Passenger men ran La Crosse to Savanna (157 miles) in six hours, earning $5.10. A freight engineer was on duty for twelve hours, making $5.80 with 143 working hours a month. The CB&N received heavy new 4-6-0's to compete with similar Ten wheelers used on the Milwaukee Road, the latest in heavy power for the fierce new competition. The engines were built in Boston by the Hinckley Locomotive Works.

The Burlington moved its transfer ferry WILLIAM OSBORNE to Winona where it first worked in the ice-free months of 1888. A switch engine employed in Winona drilled about the levee and riverside lumber mills. On schedules which coincided with east shore main line arrivals, the 0-4-0 and a coach were run down to the Keyes property ferry landing, whisked aboard the OSBORNE and carried across to East Winona, transfering about four freight cars at a time. When water levels were low in the river it was necessary to station an engine on both sides to bring off the loads. An ice bridge was built to the east shore during winter, while OSBORNE operated

between the bridge ends. Afterwards, OSBORNE was hauled out of the river on a nearby marine railway, a common practice.

The Winona Pontoon Bridge Co., projected by Winona lumbermen, was incorporated early in 1886 for rail and wagon use. A bill for either a draw or an elevated bridge was introduced in Congress. It had to be submitted to the Secretary of War, sovereign over federal waterways. Thomas Simpson, attorney for W&SW, drew up the bill in mid-1888. While the bill was progressing through Congress, Winona & South-Western was

Above: WBRy Co.'s progress was marked by photographs which were taken every two weeks. This May 18, 1891 photo was taken before the swingspan was in place. The bridge opened in August of that year.
WINONA PUBLIC LIBRARY

busy staking out its yard just east of the Keyes property. All assumed that CB&N, GBW&STP and W&SW would be tenants and the joint depot would be located at Second and Lafayette Streets, presently in use by CB&N. The bridge bill was

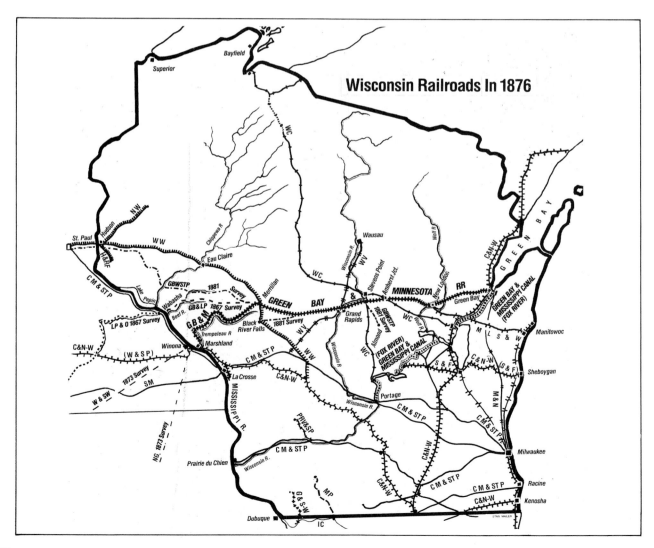

Right: This department store-like building housed original CB&N, W&S-W and GBWSTP "depots" in Winona after the summer of 1891. A CB&Q Mack bus replaced combination car service to the east side of the river in the 1930's. This building was razed by 1939 but the structure that replaced it still stands.
BEN ERICKSON PHOTO

Right: CB&Q used H-1 Moguls for switching and "stub" service from Winona to East Winona when passenger trains were run. No. 1099 was one of scores of 2-6-0's on the "Q" in pre-World War I days.
WINONA COUNTY HISTORICAL SOCIETY

Below: CB&Q's Pioneer Zephyr entered Winona just once for display in 1934. On May 28, 1936 the revolutionary silver train returned to the St. Paul line to replace one of the regulars, No. 9901 and No. 9902, seen here at La Crosse eastbound.
K. L. ZURN PHOTO

K. L. ZURN PHOTO; H. EDMONSON COLLECTION

GB&W's roundhouse at Winona is shown on August 9, 1947. The first three views show the old Keyes home, a crew layover "hotel," a four-stall house, passenger carbodies, water tank and 2-8-0 No. 398. By 1950 the roundhouse had been razed due to damage caused by a windstorm. A new building erected for diesels was completed in October. The bottom right photo looks south across the Winona Bridge after the GB&W round-house was razed; the Keyes house is on the right.

K. L. ZURN PHOTO; H. EDMONSON COLLECTION

shepherded through by Minnesota's Senator Sabin. It was to be a W&SW project with other tenants to come later. Forty-five acres of terminal lands were deeded to the new company by September 15, 1888 and a beginning point for the surveys was established.

In November of 1889 W&SW Engineer D. M. Wheeler was instructed to examine the river crossing and submit a report. He found that the cost of an iron bridge would be an estimated $315,000 for a single track, 2000-foot crossing. The cost of approaches, including connections with CB&N and the old grade of the GBWSTP, would be $27,735 for a 500-foot pile trestle. This included a 3100-foot embankment plus riprap. A pontoon bridge similar to those in place at Read's Landing, Minnesota and Prairie du Chien, Wisconsin would total $137,850. The maintenance costs would be greater on the pontoon bridge, with a shorter life span prevailing. Wheeler found that the best spot was the "upper location" which would cost $341,140. The "lower location," below the Keyes property and parallel, would have "cut in twain" the valuable terminal grounds owned by the W&SW Improvement Co.

Wheeler visited with John Lawler, proprietor of Milwaukee's Prairie du Chien bridge, to estimate the cost of constructing a similar bridge for CB&N. Lawler advised against a pontoon bridge due to variance in the water level at Winona. He pointed out that water depth at Read's Landing, a short distance from Winona, was only twelve feet — not deep enough to prevent ice damage, which occurred in 1888. Wheeler concluded his report by recommending an iron bridge for the crossing.

In early December of 1889 Henry W. Lamberton, Verrazano Simpson and M. G. Norton met with CB&N's Vice-President Harris aboard CB&N's business car. As the business car rolled over the new road toward La Crosse, the subject of discussion was the Winona Bridge. An agreement was forthcoming by midsummer 1890, which brought about incorporation of *Winona Bridge Railway Company* on July 14, 1890, for 50 years.

On July 26, 1890, WBRyCo. entered into construction contracts with Union Bridge Company for $399,000 par value of capital stock and $282,000 par value of first-mortgage bonds, for a total of $681,000. Each of the three carriers as tenants of WBRyCo. agreed to guarantee one-third its capital stock. GBWSTP acquired the same proportion of stocks and retained $133,000 par value of capital stock and sold the bonds

Right: This new steel building in Winona was used to house way-freight diesels overnight when built. After trains were moved from the west end, it was rarely used for locomotives.

to Lackawanna Iron & Coal Co. A performance bond made between WBRyCo. and Union Bridge Co. provided a $10,000 penalty for failure to make on-time completion.

Winona Bridge Railway Co.'s organization included the following officers: Mathew G. Norton, president; Joseph Walker Jr., vice-president; Henry W. Weiss, treasurer; Henry W. Lamberton, secretary. The chief engineer was D. M. Wheeler and George S. Morison was consulting engineer. Other officers of the bridge company affiliated with GBWSTP were E. F. Hatfield Jr. and Benjamin G. Clark. The bridge was to be a "substantial steel arch structure, located about where the Burlington Transfer was." The swingspan was to be 460 feet long, with the next span northward 360 feet long. This was followed by two 253-foot arches, and a trestle leading to the mainland. Monthly maintenance dues per company would be $100, while each road would be charged $4.00 per carload above fourth class and $2.50 per carload below. Individual passenger dues would be 25 cents per head.

Union Bridge Co. was located in Athens, Pennsylvania, just off the DL&W main line near Binghamton, New York. Union had built a number of bridges in northern Pennsylvania for local roads and distinguished itself by being the contractor for a Niagara bridge built in 1882-3. Some years after the Winona Bridge was built the company was responsible for erecting Merchants Bridge at St. Louis, Missouri. The works merged with American Bridge Co. in 1910. Today, one large building remains in Athens to mark the builder of at least two great Mississippi River crossings.

The construction forces began at Winona in July 1890. A machine named "Jumbo" was assigned to pile-driving. Jumbo possessed a jet pump which was used to loosen sand on the riverbed. When ready, Winona's mills supplied the pilings which were sunk 25 feet into the bottom and sawed off uniformly above the water. Work began near the Wisconsin side at Pier 4, with 17 rows of piles, five in a row, 85 in all. Piers 5 and 6, near the Minnesota side, were completed next. The swingspan pier took 121 piles; the work began September 12, 1890. September's crisp air was filled with sounds of the competing "Nasmith Steam Hammer" which took a half hour to drive home each of the 18 to 22 piles per day. "Jumbo" was shortly retired in favor

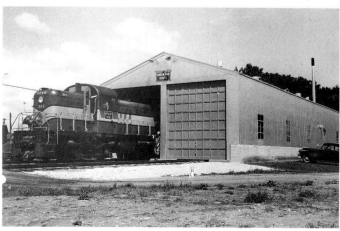

of the Nasmith, which could punch with a 5000-pound weight, against Jumbo's less than elephantine 2200 pounds.

By September 1st GBW&STP forces on the east side had begun to reconstruct its long-abandoned spur from Marshland out to the Eastmoor elevator, which would become its main line to the new bridge. All of the unsafe trestles were filled in and several new bridges were installed. In many cases new stringers were placed on old pilings to permit gravel cars to be run onto the old, decaying structures, allowing for car dumping. Locomotives were not permitted onto the work until the spots were

GB&W's way-freight No. 6 was still in steam when railfans Jim Scribbins and Ken Zurn recorded it at Bridge Yard. Above, KGB&W caboose 630 brings up the rear as the train enters the swingspan on August 9, 1947. Below, D-48 No. 401 ascends the steep grade on June 2, 1948.

PHOTOGRAPHS BY K. L. ZURN (above) AND JIM SCRIBBINS (below)

Above: BN's way-freight backs across the WBRyCo. swingspan toward East Winona in 1981.

STAN MAILER COLLECTION

properly graded. First access to the bridge site was from the Wisconsin side.

During the previous winter, a story had circulated about the Eastmoor's elevator watchman, Mr. Davis, who patrolled the old structure on horseback. Davis confronted two "marauders," who had taken up residence at Eastmoor, and came away with a severe scalp wound, while his assailants escaped. The thieves were intent upon scavanging lumber from buildings. In the end Davis succeeded in ridding Eastmoor of such elements, his wound the cost of such diligence.

The stone pier work required 78 men, as stone was laid inside a cofferdam, each member numbered. Each piece of material was dressed to fit on a barge moored alongside. The centers were filled with concrete, while the on-board steam pump kept water out of the cofferdam. The pivot pier was seventh in line and by mid-September four tiers of grillage, two open and two solid, were laid on the piles before the stonework was placed. Crossbeams were 16 feet long and one foot square. The steamer LITTLE HODIE was contracted for, which brought blocks of Gilmore Valley stone from a temporary dock. Three derricks handled the stone, brought via W&SW, while grillage was constructed at the end of an incline railway which led to W&SW's track. Blesanz and Steinbaner of Winona supplied stone.

The east approach was contracted for by McDougall & Deacon of Mankato, Minnesota. The work, entailing 1300 feet of pile trestle just beyond McD&B's contract, went to the Union Bridge Co. which dealt with a curving bridge leading up to the first arch. While completion date had been set for March 1, 1891, as of January, Union Bridge had not delivered steel to the site. The delay was short, however, and in mid-February of 1891 GBW&STP delivered the first three cars of steel for the work

from Athens, Pennsylvania. From then on the "Modified Pratt Truss" was raised steadily over the Missisippi. U.B.Co. arranged for photos to be taken every two weeks. Vice-President W. D. Searle of Farmers' Loan & Trust Co. received the certificate of the bridge company engineer, notifying them that the bridge was complete. On July 4, 1891 the great bridge was opened. At 8:30 a.m. a special bearing Engineer Morison rolled into Winona for a day of inspection. Although the negotiations surrounding the bridge would go on, CB&N ran its first scheduled train into Winona on July 15, 1891 with all of its properly designated officers aboard. Afterwards painting crews would give the great structure its designated white coat and Winona could claim a new group of railroads as its own.

Some difficulty arose before the bridge was formally accepted by WBRyCo. George S. Field of Union Bridge Co. wrote to Mathew G. Norton about bridge tests, indicating that it was the custom for purchasers to do their own testing. Field was confident that his bridge would support the heaviest load WBRyCo. could muster. He indicated interest in prompt payment and that delays in construction were not the bridge builder's fault. Field's company's profits would be very small in light of a lag in procuring materials. The WBRyCo. also looked into hand-operating gear for the new bridge, which Field considered impractical due to sheer size. As it stood, the thirty-horsepower steam engine was the only way to swing the 1400-ton span.

It was also hoped that other roads would make use of the bridge. Speculation ran high that Milwaukee, Lake Shore &

Western Railway would reach Winona via the Omaha Road to Merrillan and Marshfield, taking advantage of the W&SW outlet. This supposition would find little currency in the bleak 1890's just ahead, when MLS&W was sold to the North-Western on the eve of the end of Wisconsin's pineries.

Another prospect for Winona entry over the new bridge was the theoretical lumber traffic of the Fairchild & Missisippi River Railroad Co. Nathaniel C. Foster of Fairchild, Wisconsin organized a railroad to connect his lumber empire with the CB&N at Alma. If completed, Foster's lumber could have moved southwest from Winona into the prairie. Further ambitions of the Foster road would also put it in connection with northern Wisconsin lumber districts via a line to Rhinelander. Foster's reasoning involved rates and the long haul/short haul clause with its implications. The new road was surveyed toward Osseo and Mondovi, picking up support at lineside.

E. J. Matchett, an Osseo contractor, was F&MR's builder. He later constructed Ettrick & Northern. The fifteen-mile route from Fairchild to Osseo was graded in sixty days and right-of-way was tentatively secured to Alma.

The F&MR soon reorganized and then faltered at Mondovi. It was sold to CStPM&O Ry. in 1893, after proprietary control was in the latter's hands by March 1891. Foster's local railroad ambitions did not flag. He wound up building Wisconsin's late-blooming Fairchild & North-Eastern Railway which reached to a Wisconsin Central connection at Owen. The Foster Road was never successful, ending as a settlement railway for Foster's cut-over lands. The area was one of poor agricultural prospects and the F&NE, destitute by 1920, was finally abandoned in the late 1920's. Foster's attempt to bring CB&N influence into the Fairchild area was not acceptable to the Omaha. Fairchild was on the Omaha Road's main line and purchase of the Mondovi Line turned it into a feeder. The Mondovi branch was abandoned in 1976.

While the bridge progressed, GBWSTP also continued a process of improvement, in spite of dismal financial progress. In 1889 an agreement was reached with the Omaha Road for the movement of 10,000 to 15,000 tons of coal from Green Bay to St. Paul, Minneapolis and Stillwater or intermediate points via Merrillan Junction, at a rate equal to that published from Chicago or Milwaukee. The rate was given as $1.50 per ton, allowing GBWSTP a percentage for dockage at Green Bay. The agreement was signed by Gavin Campbell for GBWSTP and Francis B. Clarke for CStPM&O.

Three years later, the two roads renewed their agreement for a Merrillan Junction enginehouse which continued in a 99-year lease of a two stall, Omaha Road-design building just east of the Merrillan diamond. A freighthouse, water tank, and depot were also shared. The engine terminal netted GBWSTP a service point for engines and housed Merrillan-Winona duty engines. Emergency housing for engines was needed in early 1888 when heavy snows blocked Merrillan-Whitehall trackage. It took several weeks to restore service.

The opening of the 1260-foot Winona bridge signaled completion of facilities for the three tenants. GBWSTP, CB&N and W&SW brought their passenger trains to uptown Winona, 1.03 miles. In late August the first GBWSTP passenger train eased over the new bridge, dropped downgrade and around the new route to Southwestern Junction, then moved with new-comer's caution up Second Street to the depot. CB&N and GBWSTP made an agreement, operable after September 1, 1891, which involved payment by GBWSTP of one-third of

Below: No. 2 rolls slowly (six miles per hour) across the Winona Bridge Railway toward "212" or East Winona. The majority of No. 2's tonnage will come from BN at the interchange. STAN MAILER COLLECTION

Left BN's No.1601 is rolling up the age-old route used by GB&W, CB&Q and W&S-W passenger trains in Winona: Second Street. A year later the track was removed.
STAN MAILER PHOTO

six percent per annum on $177,648.72, the cost of the property CB&N used in Winona.

The press supposed that the ordinance which limited CB&N's speed in Second Street to ten m.p.h. would have to be abrogated, for a flood of traffic was confidently expected over the semi-transcontinental line. Winona Bridge Railway Co. issued its first timecard for the government of its six employees and its group of "guest" trains.

GBWSTP's depot was located in a grand arcade of a building, looking very much like a department store. The road built a street-front ticket office in the same manner of Burlington's large urban establishments. The space had formerly been occupied by Preece-Laatsch & Company, a local wholesaler. The establishment lasted into the late 1930's when a new building was built by CB&Q, also hosting GB&W.

The connecting Burlington trackage, describing an "S," curved into platforms at the rear for about one block. Burlington's "stub" train, usually a coach or combination car, lasted until the 1920's. Before 1925 the "Q" would assign a Mogul to switching and stub service at Winona, much like Galena, Illinois' branch service.

Promotion of the "Through Line" policy established rates for traffic between St. Paul, Minneapolis and intermediate points via Merrillan Junction and Green Bay. Westbound through rates were published by DL&W. Only by mutual consent would rates be lower than via Lake Superior prevail. All business to be secured by DL&W would go via Merrillan Junction and Green Bay. The reverse also held, that the Omaha Road would direct all of its Lake Erie ports business through GBWSTP and had to accept current rates at the time of shipment. Twin Cities-Chicago traffic split proceeds via their own agreement. DL&W in turn had to accept current rates from Lake Michigan to Lake Erie ports with its steamer traffic. Conditions in 1889 were subject to great fluctuation and the elaborate agreement held only for that navigational season. Mr. A. Fell signed for the DL&W rail and boat line. The freight agent employed for soliciting traffic by the "Green Bay route" and DL&W was paid thus: 50% by DL&W; 25% by GBWSTP and 25% by CStPM&O.

In 1892 after the establishment of the Winona connections, Joseph Walker Jr. again raised the question of the St. Paul extension, which he was confident would hold the key to northwest freight traffic. The old plan was dusted off, to be promoted in spring of 1893, the point of beginning again being two miles

west of Merrillan. It was reported that such confidence engendered an order for more rolling stock — 1500 "Northwestern Dispatch Fast Freight Line" boxcars and ten locomotives. If Walker referred to combined railroad orders there might have been ten new machines but in GBWSTP's case only three new engines were built in June of 1891. The 20-22 class Schenectady 4-4-0's were purchased by The Farmers' Loan & Trust Co., aggregating $20,400 and were essentially Milwaukee Road H-7b's. At the same time, the road received six new coaches ("40-class" fifty-foot cars), totaling $23,640, from Ohio Falls Car Company. The boxcar fleet was increased by sixty units, numbers 1000-1120, even numbers only. FL&TCo. made an outright loan to the beleaguered Wisconsin line to cover the indebtedness for the new equipment. In 1892 FL&TCo. also purchased switch engine No.3 for GBWSTP, which was another Milwaukee Road design, corresponding to their J-3 class Grant-built engines. The three-spot was again a Schenectady, clouding design responsibility. But from that day forward most of the Green Bay route's power orders went to Schenectady. Around 1889, the first rectangular logos for "Green Bay Line," much the same as the herald used in the 20th Century, appeared in *The Green Bay Advocate*.

Frank B. Seymour and Seth Champion were reported to have traveled over the St. Paul route, because the Merrillan-Durand section was not completely settled. The route was beset with several grades, especially west of Durand, which would require expensive construction. The Green Bay, St. Paul & Minneapolis Railway Company was incorporated August 9, 1892, developing a route some 268 miles from Green Bay to the Minnesota capital. It was claimed that a few maximum grades of one percent westbound would rule, with 85 to 100 feet per mile eastbound ruling grades. Curves ran to twenty degrees maximum. GBStP&M's chief engineer was Edward Sargent and Joseph Walker Jr. was vice-president. Its incorporators were Seth W. Champion, W. J. Abrams, Frank B. Seymour and A. Fell. The bold plan was finally arrested in late 1892, when foreclosure proceedings by William S. Mowry complicated the plans of expansion by exposing of the road's debt. On the eve of hard times the last strong attempt at extension toward the Twin Cities was snuffed out.

Improvement of the road in the form of new rail continued despite the complex financial struggle taking place in New York. Approximately 7500 tons of Lackawanna rail were replaced in

sections between Merrillan and Grand Rapids. The rail moved as expected, via Lackawanna Line boats, along with several shipments for the South-Western Road. There were also special excursions, such as the Mystical Seven Council's Lake Emily trip, handled easily by Bill Monahan, conductor. Mr. P. H. Clinton was proprietor of camp grounds and small boats at the Lake, catering to railroad-borne traffic in season. By September of 1891, GBWSTP employees sought relaxation there and again the Brotherhood of Locomotive Firemen sojourned the same fall. GBWSTP promised a small depot for the new business. Stevens Point's Amphion Musical Association went to Green Bay via an excursion, in which about 500 people took advantage of Dennessen Boat Line trips to the park. Another attempt to develop more local service came when a Merrillan-Winona train was established as a shopper. As often occurred, disadvantaged merchants whose business flew to larger cities demonstrated against the new service and it was obligingly removed. Green Bay route's bold new disturber of commerce in Wisconsin last ran November 27, 1892.

Some difficulty arose in regard to the Burlington trackage right. Adjacent residents generated a lawsuit because of excessively heavy traffic on their street. The Green Bay route and W&SW attempted to locate a new line along the south side of Third Street, northwest of the Keyes property. Some complications in right-of-way acquisition barred the new route aimed at using the new street railway. The project was shelved until spring of 1893 and then buried under the troubles of the "Panic."

Curiously enough, the terminal facility at Marshland was retained until the La Crosse branch was abandoned in 1922. The little Marshland connection with C&NW had a short yard, a water plug, a windmill-type supply system and an enginehouse. With the majority of its traffic eastbound, the La Crosse daily mixed train never tied up across the river at Bridge Yard, three miles away. Marshland's depot was actually moved 100 feet

south to the location of the diamond. The building survived into the 1940's.

Some other roads found that GBWSTP could perform useful services, transferring carloads to other parts of their empires. Milwaukee Road's Albert J. Earling, the general manager, found advantages in using GBWSTP to route carloads from Milwaukee & Northern Railroad points near Green Bay to the west and northwest, as well as to and from its Wisconsin Valley line. The cost was but $10 per car. The method was continued into the 1970's.

In July 1903 Chicago, Burlington & Quincy Railroad, the successor to CB&N in 1901, purchased W&W's one-third interest in Winona Bridge Railway Co. Annual meetings thereafter were held in Chicago. WBRyCo.'s vice-president was J. A. Jordan of the Green Bay & Western. Burlington officials made up the balance of the Board: W. W. Baldwin of Burlington, Iowa; H. W. Weiss of Chicago; T. S. Howland, and La Crosse's Superintendent D. Cunningham. After the transfer, the great white bridge of the Lackawanna was repainted red oxide in the manner of CB&Q bridges.

In 1934, when the "Q" launched its Zephyr service, the three-unit train was tested on the St. Paul Division, reaching 97 m.p.h. between La Crosse and East Winona. The Zephyr averaged 71 m.p.h. from Chicago to St. Paul. On May 29, 1934 Winona hosted the "Pioneer Zephyr," No. 9900, which crossed the Winona Bridge and eased up Second Street trackage to the depot, now old and gloomy. It remained alongside the building for all to admire, departing at 7 p.m. Imagine the revolutionary train backing out of Winona slowly and carefully, negotiating the great bridge in reverse, never to return again. It came and went in marked contrast to Green Bay & Western's small, coach green two-car train, which within the year would begin mixed service. By the late 1930's Burlington's own Zephyr connection would be a bus to Winona Junction. Zephyr service and conventional trains were no longer fed by a branchline relic.

The Mondovi branch of CSTPM&O Ry began as a proposed connection with CB&N at Alma. Built by Nathaniel C. Foster, the Fairchild & Mississippi River Railroad never got further than Mondovi in Buffalo County. It was planned as an outlet for Foster's lumber empire, centering on Fairchild. A mixed train is shown at the end of the line in 1910.

J. LONGLEY PHOTO

95

7
CARGILL & KGB&W

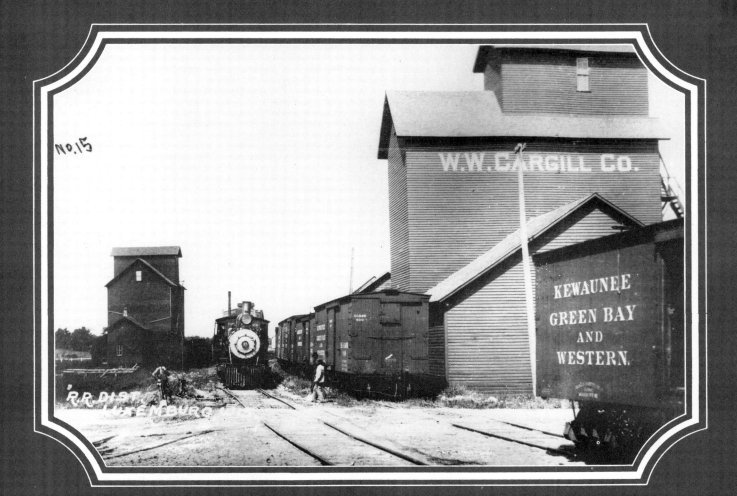

No. 15

W.W. CARGILL Co.

KEWAUNEE
GREEN BAY
AND
WESTERN.

R.R. DEPT.
LUXEMBURG

William Wallace Cargill looked up from his La Crosse office desk to a distant view. His family's grain industry stretched from Minneapolis, across Minnesota, Iowa and South Dakota and back to La Crosse via the image of trackside elevators. Cargill's world was grain and grain was the prince, if not the king, of the limitless plains. Beside the river Will Cargill and his entourage consolidated their power. They had ties to Milwaukee banking interests and a reach to the new, powerful world of Minneapolis flour milling. Growing into the 1890's, the Cargill empire of La Crosse, through various family organizations, controlled 71 elevators and 28 coal sheds at trackside, a number of them located alongside Green Bay, Winona & St. Paul Railway.

For the Cargills to have some interest in their lineside railroads was a natural condition. Their energies were concentrated upon buying and selling the product, but the next level of importance after grain was its transportation to eastern markets. The struggle for survival in the capitalist wilderness was harsh; rate wars, fleeing agreements, secret contracting and rebates were rampant. The late 1880's were also filled with cries for justice for investor and villain alike. Justice began slowly, following the Interstate Commerce Act of 1887, but for the time, the titans would brawl their final time in the marketplace. Cargill was, above all else, interested in a secure, stable route for his product and for a moment he contemplated the plight of GBWSTP. The result was largely the latter's salvation.

The great power in grain transport was James J. Hill of the St. Paul, Minneapolis & Manitoba Railway, later to become the Great Northern Railway. Hill had deftly seized control of grain and flour routes out of Duluth-Superior and his Northern Steamship Company maintained the lowest rates in season. With the flour trade rising ever higher (a major traffic for such Chicago-Minneapolis carriers as C&NW, Rock Island, Milwaukee Road, Wisconsin Central and Chicago Great Western), other methods of transport eastward were examined by shippers, entrepreneurs and distressed railroads alike. The trade reached a crescendo in the late 1880's when, well-established roads struggled with new competitors for the business. The Cargills were interested in seeing GBWSTP eventually prosper, for more than just the well-being of its trackside grain elevators in Wisconsin.

Throughout the 1880's GBWSTP participated in grain and flour movement to Manitowoc, as well as Green Bay. The Manitowoc connection was via MLS&W Ry, which interchanged with GBWSTP at New London Junction. The object was to put the product on the shore of Lake Michigan and Manitowoc's harbor, a relatively "warm water port" which allowed for break-bulk steamers to load late into the navigation season. Such was hardly ever the case at Green Bay, which had a history of freeze-up nearly every year. Manitowoc grew into a sizable grain port, and by the 1890's the Northern Grain Company had a large elevator downtown.

Traffic eastward from Manitowoc developed soon after its railroad connection to New London was realized. By 1874 Michigan's Flint & Pere Marquette Railroad had reached Ludington on Lake Michigan. Originally named Pere Marquette

Left: La Crosse grain dealer W. W. Cargill helped build KGB&W and had early holdings at Luxemburg, Wisconsin, halfway between Green Bay and Kewaunee. Here 4-4-0 No.35, the road's "super standard-type" pulls into the depot with mixed train No.12, headed for Kewaunee.
J. P. LONGLEY PHOTO

for the lake and harbor, the city was renamed for Harrison Ludington, a lumberman of prominence in both Wisconsin and Michigan. F&PM became interested in grain traffic when its timber business declined and it engaged Goodrich Transit Company, a steamship line, to solicit business on the west side of the lake. Traffic developed with the pioneer Sheboygan & Fond du Lac Railway by 1876 and was furthered with Milwaukee-Michigan trade routes. In 1883 F&PM went into the field itself when it purchased two steamers, FLINT & PERE MARQUETTE. No.1 and No.2. During the recession of 1884, F&PM's two vessels were taken out of service and lengthened about 35 feet to increase their grain-handling capacity. They were similar in appearance to the Goodrich propellors of the period with machinery and boilers aft and pilot house well forward, allowing for maximum main deck and grainhold capacity. F&PM acquired three more steamers in the late 1880's, with the No.5 boat measuring 226-foot overall. Thus the grain route was well-established, but it was only one of many which competed for the business. Fortunately for all, flour sales to European markets declined little in the 1880's. Bread for English tables was dependent on American wheat, which was shipped to Liverpool, a major world grain port.

The trade from Manitowoc continued through the winter of 1889-90. F&PM No.1, for example, carried 5000 barrels of flour to Ludington for F&PM's care eastward. In January of 1890 the propellor OSCEOLA, 787 tons capacity, was reported en route from Port Huron, Michigan to Manitowoc, to be used in the interests of the Lackawanna Line. OSCEOLA would operate Manitowoc to Ludington as part of the "Great Through Route." The distance from Minneapolis to New York was given as 1206 miles, divided thus: Minneapolis to Manitowoc, 314 miles (via CStPM&O, GBWSTP and MLS&W Ry.); Manitowoc to Ludington, 62 miles via propellor; Ludington to Port Huron, 227 miles, via F&PM; Port Huron to Buffalo, 196 miles, Grand Trunk Railway of Canada; Buffalo to New York, 409 miles via DL&W RR. OSCEOLA made port at Manitowoc on the 11th and began regular duty on the grain route, loading merchandise westbound for the wholesalers of the Northwest.

Cargill interests also established a presence in Minneapolis, becoming a member of the Minneapolis Chamber of Commerce's Grain Exchange in 1883. An office was opened in Duluth in 1888 to deal with receipts in Red River grain. The Cargill operation was at the same time integrating its Wisconsin operation and centering it on La Crosse. From Hokah and Houston (Minnesota) flour mills, Will Cargill competed in markets as far as St. Louis and via the lake ports to eastern markets through Chicago and Milwaukee. He intended to enhance his position in the field as much as possible. One of his goals was to operate a terminal elevator in Green Bay to take advantage of the short rail haul from La Crosse. The shortest distance happened to be via GBWSTP which was in financial distress at that time. With Cargill grain elevators in nearly all GBWSTP agricultural towns, a terminal elevator established in conjunction would allow export eastward from Green Bay during the ice-free months. To facilitate shipment during the winter months, Cargill became involved in the GBWSTP management-sponsored Kewaunee, Green Bay & Western Railroad Company.

The KGB&W was organized March 12, 1890 for the purpose of building a railroad "from Kewaunee, Wisconsin to a point on the Green Bay, Winona & St. Paul Railroad, about one mile west of the depot of said railroad, on the west side of the Fox River, Brown County, Wisconsin, approximately 34 miles in length." The first board of directors included W. J. Abrams of Green Bay; Seth W. Champion of GBWSTP management; Charles Joannes, a Green Bay merchant/investor; William Wallace Cargill of La Crosse, and George Grimmer, a Kewaunee merchant and investor. The new company's principal office was in Green Bay. Of authorized capital stock of $680,000, $200,000 was preferred and $480,000 common.

Kewaunee, Wisconsin, a community at the mouth of the Kewaunee River, was inhabited in the mid-1880's by Bohemian and German settlers. Kewaunee, which means "wild duck," grew to moderate prominence as an agricultural and light industrial center by 1890. The population of 1216 was served by steamers and schooners exclusively, especially those of the Goodrich Transit Co. The shrewd Bohemian population went into grain

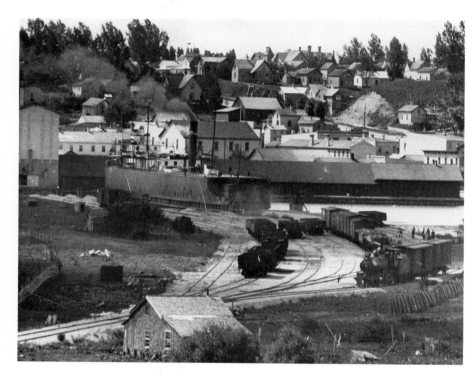

Left: The Kewaunee car ferry slip in 1908. Ann Arbor No.3 is unloaded by KGB&W 4-4-0 No.34. The Shayville residence is in the foreground, while the salthouses and the grain elevator lie across the entrance channel to the south.
J. SCHULTZ PHOTO

An agreement was reached with Joseph Walker & Sons of New York, again the chief promoters of another segment of the Green Bay-Great Through Route. The Walkers became financial agents, negotiating all bonds to the extent of $330,000 and stock to accompany the bonds (bonus) of $110,000, of which $50,000 was common and $60,000 preferred stock, at a figure satisfactory to the KGB&W. A later agreement also conferred another five-percent commission upon the Walkers to negotiate the bonds. It was expected that construction would begin in early 1890 but delays prevented the start even by fall. In January of 1891 Frank Halliday wrote to George Grimmer of Kewaunee regarding the lapse of action by the KGB&W. Halliday inquired about progress and a prospective order by Abrams to work on estimates for the new road, which was not forthcoming. The

farming and allied fields, and several elevators were raised in the 1890's. During the early 1880's, a Rivers and Harbors bill had recognized the port, and an appropriation had produced piers to allow deeper draught vessels to dock. Further appropriations enabled the city to cut through the sandbar at the river's delta so the river mouth became a true harbor. The cut allowed the construction of car ferry docks which were a neccessity if the Great Through Route was to become an all-rail, nearly all-weather traffic line.

A railroad into Kewaunee County was first suggested by Edward Decker, whose answer was to promote his own line, The Ahnapee & Western Railway. Interest in a Kewaunee connection to whatever Decker produced was strong in the 1880's. Kewaunee County was prepared for KGB&WRR's approach for town aid by 1887. Aid for the road was voted, aggregating $43,500 from on-line towns. In April of 1890, Frank S. Halliday was engaged to survey the route. Halliday considered the line "a strong one," full of heavy cuts and fills, plus one-percent grades and six-degree curves. He was able to locate the line from his preliminary survey. Halliday was on location for 28 days, after which he went onto the Ahnapee & Western survey. W. J. Abrams had recommended Halliday to locate the line from a junction with the KGB&W to Ahnapee (Algoma).

answer came in the spring of 1891, when further arrangements regarding stock bonuses were made with subscribers to the first-mortgage bonds. The amount of common stock to go with the bonds was raised to 25%; preferred stock went up to 20%, which raised the total amount to 45%.

On April 18, 1891 the Walker firm had negotiated $175,000 KGB&W first-mortgage five-percent bonds which left $155,000 to be placed. On that date The Lackawanna Iron & Coal Co. agreed to take the balance, which would be allocated as follows: $55,000 for rail purchased at the LI&CCo's Scranton mill, the price at $32 per car at Scranton; $100,000 of the bonds not to be paid for until the bonds of Winona Bridge Railway Company, Winona & South-Western Railway or GBWSTP were sold to the equivalent amount. The agreement was that GBWSTP RR guarantee a five-percent interest (2.5% semi-annually) on total bond issue in perpetuity and also to guarantee payment of up to two percent annually on KGB&W stock, payable upon completion of the KGB&W. It acted as a pact to lease the KGB&W in perpetuity. Interest would be met in advance until operation was opened by KGB&W and Joseph Walker & Sons. Edwin F. Hatfield Jr. signed for LI&CCo. On April 21, 1891 Theodore Sturges, secretary of GBWSTP, signed an agreement which was adopted by the road's executive committee. His company was to guarantee the KGB&W company interest on the entire capital stock ($680,000) of two percent per annum, payable semi-annually, first payment to be July 1st, 1892 and a guarantee of the interest on $408,000 of five percent. On May 14th KGB&W's President W. J. Abrams was notified that $330,000 in bonds was available to begin construction.

Once again, the subscribers to KGB&W bonds were familiar names: John Insley Blair, $50,000; W. W. Cargill, $5000; Samuel Sloan, $25,000; Benjamin Clarke, $25,000; E. S. Rapallo, $5000; Lackawanna Iron & Coal Co., $155,000. Other bondholders were less identified with the long, difficult history of the Green Bay Route. Calls for funds were made for construction purposes on the following dates: May 18, 1891, for 10% ($15,000); July 11, 1891, for 30% ($44,600); July 31, 1891, for 30% ($44,600). On October 1, 1891 another $29,750 was issued to complete the subscription. Ninety percent of the LI&CCo. subscription was applied to the steel rail account and vouchers were sent to LI&CCo. instead of cash, in what amounted to a revolving door of credit for the new road's rails.

The construction contract was finalized by May 14, 1891. McIntosh Brothers of Milwaukee would grade the roadbed, build the bridges and furnish all material for the work. The option was made to pay either in cash or capital stock; inasmuch as the contractor was bidding low and liberally, the company was able and willing to make the offer. KGB&W resolved to pay $105,000 in cash, plus an amount of stock (1974 shares common, 729 shares preferred) upon completion.

As the Winona Bridge neared completion, and Winona & South-Western was under construction to Spring Valley, Minnesota, KGB&W hired contractors McDougall and Beacon to start on a subcontract to grade Baird's Creek Hill. The prime contractor concentrated on the balance of the work. The grading continued through the summer of 1891 and by September ties were being distributed along the new grade. Ties from Ahnapee went by barge completely around the peninsula to Green Bay and were carried to the eastward-moving front. In one day six miles of rail were laid by a twenty-man gang and the road was completed to Luxemburg by September 30th. A major trestle, 35 feet high, was finished at Scarborough Creek, just east of Casco Junction. It remained for most of the 1890's, finally subcumbing to filling in the 20th Century. By fall KGB&W was in possession of a line which left Green Bay via a trackage right agreement. It climbed a grade of 44 feet to the mile, in several cuts 30 to 44 feet deep, up the Niagara Cuesta via Baird's Creek. From the summit the road was nearly level as far as Luxemburg. From there it descended into the Kewaunee River Valley and wound down to Lake Michigan.

A new W. W. Cargill Co. elevator was raised at Luxemburg, replacing an old Cargill and Van Valkenburgh ancestor. Mr. T. F. Ballering, visiting from Madison, claimed to be the first KGB&W passenger into the village when he rode in on a construction train in early October. A quarry operator east of Green Bay cut stone for several new buildings in Kewaunee, taking advantage of the new railroad to extend his business reach. George Duvall of Kewaunee, grain dealer and owner of the great sandbar at the Kewaunee River's mouth, considered the railroad men's offer for his land, as well as W. W. Cargill's approach for his elevator's lease. The elevator stood alongside the channel, recently dredged to a 13-foot depth, to allow for much larger steamers in the harbor. Kewaunee had its railroad, as did the men behind the Lackawanna's Great Through Route.

Improvements for the Kewaunee terminal were scheduled immediately. A trainload of timber for new salt and flour sheds

arrived at dockside. The depot was temporarily located in a former steamboat warehouse, moved east of Main Street. The first outward-bound passenger was a Miss Darbellay who faced a day-long ride to Chicago. She was one of many passengers wrested away from the Goodrich steamers, whose overnight boats also steamed down to the Windy City.

It was all in place by October 21, 1891. A grand celebration was planned for November 7th to eulogize the railroad, builders, men of substance and the local scene and future prospects. Station agent Curran was installed with ceremony to receive several special trains arriving from the west. Allegedly, a decorated locomotive, temporarily named "George Grimmer," brought the dignitaries to lakeside, delivering them to the mercy of a trombone band. Conductor for the day was GBWSTP's venerated William Monahan, while Engineer William Simms and Fireman Bert Lucas tended the "Grimmer." Carrying GBWSTP's officers, the special left Green Bay at 9:47 a.m., passing through the new stations at New Franken, Luxemburg, Casco Junction, Clyde, West Kewaunee. Manager Champion bestowed his son Clyde's name on a lonely station in the Kewaunee Valley, which served as a entrepot for Slovan's business a mile away. Several days before, the Kewaunee newspapers had recorded the number of the very first boxcar in town, GBWSTP 578, and the first grain business locally completed on KGB&W's premises.

With formalities out of the way, the system settled down to business. Five carloads of flour destined for Liverpool arrived just before Christmas, to be transferred to the steamer GRAND TRAVERSE for Ludington. While the scheme was being completed, some difficulties arose. Vanderbilt interests on both sides of the lake sought to retaliate for losses suffered. On June 1, 1891 C&NW moved to acquire Milwaukee, Lake Shore & Western Railway, completing the securities exchange in 1892. C&NW, a Vanderbilt-controlled property, was allied with Flint & Pere Marquette Railway. The Michigan road fell in line, leaving the DL&W at some disadvantage for its Ludington business. As a result F&PM steamers stayed away from Kewaunee's docks, accepting cargoes exclusively at Manitowoc.

Above: KGB&W Mogul No. 36 eases train No. 12 into Clyde, Wisconsin about 1910. The station was a rural stop for tiny Slovan, a Bohemian settlement eight miles from Kewaunee. It was named for Seth Champion's son.
KEWAUNEE COUNTY HISTORICAL SOCIETY

Above: Kewaunee Harbor as it looked about 1908. The Goodrich Liner GEORGIA steams out into the lake while lumber schooners crowd the cityside dock. KGB&W's city yard is in the foreground, while the ferry yard is in the distance.

Perhaps as a result of the Vanderbilt problem, or out of the grand plan in the minds of its founders, an agreement was forged between KGB&W, GBW&STP, Toledo, Ann Arbor & North Michigan Railway and DL&W on December 19, 1891. It called for establishment of a permanent through routing from Northwest to the Atlantic Seaboard via Kewaunee. It was to run between all points east of Manistee and Frankfort, Michigan and St. Paul-Minneapolis, Minnesota Transfer, La Crosse and Winona on the western end. TAA&NM, jointly with KGB&W and DL&W, agreed to supply the suitable steamers, guaranteeing daily service, weather permitting, between Kewaunee, Frankfort and Manistee. The Green Bay roads would be responsible for storage and handling at Kewaunee and control of territory between Kewaunee and points west of the lake. Choice of a lake line was left open as a traffic option for KGB&W. Lines east would make no higher rates to Kewaunee than from Milwaukee, Grand Haven and Ludington, the competing routes. Lines west of Kewaunee would have rates no higher than from Milwaukee west, to acquire a fair proportion of westbound traffic from eastern roads.

The agreement forged a new system and introduced a new partner in Michigan: The Toledo, Ann Arbor & North Michigan Railway. There was press comment about the possibilities of the DL&W route using a line from Manistee to a connection with the Ann Arbor. The Frankfort & South-Eastern Railway was completed to Cadillac in 1885 and, at the moment of Vanderbilt truth, became part of the new route. The sale was completed on January 8, 1892.

F&SE was a logging road of sorts, which was developed into a suitable road for the flour traffic. KGB&W's Seth Champion engaged OSCEOLA to ply between Kewaunee and Frankfort. The wood vessel arrived for the first time at Kewaunee in mid-

January, carrying a load of salt from Manistee for western points. OSCEOLA took on flour from the accumulation and began the carrying trade for the railroad.

On the 27th, OSCEOLA ran into trouble. She missed Kewaunee and made Ahnapee, ten miles off course. On her second crossing OSCEOLA was driven by a gale into the Sturgeon Bay Ship Canal where she found the bottom at the lake's entrance. Returning to Frankfort and leaking badly, the vessel was pounded against the dock by the incessant wind. A steam line burst above Engineer W. P. McDonald's cabin, fatally scalding him. OSCEOLA then proceeded to a Milwaukee drydock, limping along at six miles per hour and taking water. On February 24th she resumed her work, taking 35 carloads of flour eastward. Returning, she encountered a southwest gale which again forced her to a more northerly course. Her captain again decided to head for the ship canal, but had great difficulty in running into Sturgeon Bay and struck a pierhead in the heavy sea. Three attempts were made to enter the canal. A fire broke out to add to the terror but 24 hours later the 183-foot wood boat took advantage of fair weather and ran to Kewaunee. During the first four weeks of duty OSCEOLA was able to make only three trips against a cruel winter. On other adventures the vessel broke her propeller, was towed again to Milwaukee and was stuck fast in the ice just off Kewaunee.

With all OSCEOLA's bad luck and harrowing scrapes, the flour trains ran heavily into Kewaunee from the west. About forty cars were reported into the downtown yard in March but the same storms that ravaged the steamer's passage also closed cuts east of Green Bay with snow. An early eastbound passenger train stalled near New Franken in an eight-foot drift, remaining fast all day. Nearby Brown County residents came to its aid, supplying survival rations. A relief train arrived after passengers trudged into the city to find help and ten hours later the waiting was over. Above all, the flour had to get through to Kewaunee and the roadway was again available.

To the delight of jobbers and wholesalers in the district, KGB&W effected a new tariff for freight to Kewaunee and Green Bay, which put the ports on the same basis as Milwaukee and Chicago. Businessmen could now have shipments from New York at the same cost as from Chicago and Milwaukee. Shipping time was also reduced, when and if the savage first winter allowed OSCEOLA to land. Passenger service became acceptable, often in deference to freight extras. On March 21, 1892 mail via KGB&W put Mr. Ed Richmond and his mule out of business. Adjustments were made several times on the westbound passenger train departure from Kewaunee, but for the first few months the train departed at 4:00 a.m. from the chilly lakeside depot. An eastbound counterpart left Green Bay at 6:45 a.m., arriving at Kewaunee at 8:25 a.m. No. 13 left Kewaunee at 12:15 p.m. and No. 14 left Green Bay at 4:45 p.m. Trains connected with the steamer service for the east shore.

In March of 1892 KGB&W and Milwaukee & Northern Railroad, the latter in the hands of CM&STP, made an agreement to secure trackage through Green Bay. KGB&W trains would operate from a connecting track on Quincy Street to a point between Smith and Crooks Streets in Fort Howard. M&N also granted KGB&W rights to use its depot in the city of Green Bay, adding that KGB&W must provide its own team tracks. The price was $160 per month for the run-through, $60 per month for the passenger depot and $25 per ton for handling at M&N's freighthouse. This operation continued until the Fox River Bridge was completed in 1895.

The arrangements between TAA&NM and KGB&W were revised in the spring of 1892 as OSCEOLA's services called for improvement. Seth Champion of KGB&W hired the steamer CITY OF MARQUETTE to be operated from May 1, 1892 to April 27, 1894. The two railroad companies "will jointly assume all marine and lake risks on hull and machinery of said steamer and cargo from the furies of the sea." Rates and divisions would remain the same with Grand Trunk Railway and DL&W carrying the transfers from TAA&NM. KGB&W and TAA&NM would split the costs of operation of the CITY OF MARQUETTE. In a letter sent to Manager Champion, Joseph

Below: The steamer OSCEOLA was the first connection with KGB&W between Frankfort and Manistee. The vessel served only a short time as it had a difficulty staying afloat.

E. DOWLING, S.J.

Left: Seth Champion chartered CITY OF MAR-QUETTE for Kewaunee-Frankfort service, which continued break-bulk business after OSCEOLA's difficult days. Here the little steamer is running for its final owner, the Hill Line.
E. DOWLING, S.J.

Top Right: ANN ARBOR No.2 winds about the pilings on a summer morning just before getting underway from Kewaunee ferry yard. The cabin was lengthened in later years, while a stack was added 45 feet above the cabins. The wood car ferry was an unpopular job for its crew. The photo was taken about 1905.
J. SCHULTZ PHOTO

Bottom Right: Ann Arbor No.1 and Goodrich's CAROLINA were in Kewaunee harbor about 1900. This view faces north. CAROLINA had just backed away from cityside, preparing to make a turn out to the lake, which is to the right. Lindecker's Hill is in the distance on the right.
J. SCHULTZ PHOTO

Below: This is a rare shot of ANN ARBOR No.1 in the mid-1890's. The pioneer vessel is shown in its original configuration with tandem stacks and a short cabin. The unprotected car deck aft was later modified. The 4-4-0 No.1 switched the boat.
J. SELNER PHOTO

Above: The fine old Goodrich liner CHICAGO heads out into Lake Michigan from Kewaunee about 1905. Goodrich gave the KGB&W some competition on overnight-to-Chicago business into the early 1900's.
STAN MAILER COLLECTION

Walker, Jr. stated that TAA&NM Manager J. M. Ashley had agreed to turn over the steamer's operation to Champion, to allow the boat three cents per hundredweight, "delivered to the rail of the boat, the boat to bear expense of handling inside of the rail out of their earnings." Evidently, OSCEOLA's adventures were burdensome to the leasing companies. In the mid-1890's losses were substantial on the break-bulk steamers, both vessels costing $21,302.65.

CITY OF MARQUETTE was a new vessel, but its gross tonnage was one-third that of OSCEOLA. The steamer spent a season in Marquette, Michigan-Sault Ste. Marie trade for C. W. Andress & Sons, proving its strong, ice-breaking capabilities on Lake Superior. On April 26, 1892 Seth Champion became managing owner of the MARQUETTE, duly authorized by his employer. KGB&W agreed to charter and maintain it, paying Champion $20 per day plus wages of crew and other operating expenses. From the unspectacular performances of the break-bulk steamers, the idea of a car-ferry evolved. Initiating open-lake car ferries was a bold idea which required a new technology, one attributed to the mind of James M. Ashley of the Ann Arbor road. Undoubtedly, Samuel Sloan was aware of the revolution and he approved the measure.

News of the ferries broke in January 1892 while OSCEOLA was struggling to keep schedule on Lake Michigan. KGB&W sidings were filling up with back-logged flour cars from the Omaha Road transfers and by March 5th a Sturgeon Bay newspaper observed that a craft longer than Brunel's GREAT EASTERN would be required to transport forty cars, the ferry's supposed capacity. Exaggeration of the coming ferries' size only fed the fires of marine gossip. On June 16th a GBW&STP rate division agreement was made with TAA&NM which stated that

"the Ann Arbor Company is now building boats for the ferrying of cars, with provision made for rate division on mileage." Soon the plans for the new vessels would be published in *The Railroad Gazette,* furnished by its builder, Craig Ship Building Co., of Toledo. The 260-foot boats would carry 24 cars and the price tag for each vessel was $250,000. The first was to be launched about September 15th and the second six weeks later.

With the anticipated ferry connection, Ashley of Ann Arbor and Joseph Walker visited the proper authority in Washington to promote harbor improvements on behalf of the coming innovation. During the spring months, the pair went to Cape Charles, Virginia, to examine its ferry system in operation. Returning to Toledo, they inspected the construction at Craig's. They were certain that their system would save three days' transit time. In June, Samuel Sloan's General Manager B. A. Hegemann rode with A. Fell, Joseph Walker, Jr., James Ashley

Right: This is a photo of Shayville "city hall." The old structure was taken over by KGB&W for car inspector Tom Shay and became a social center of sorts. It was formerly part of a fishing village which stood on what became railroad land.
J. SCHULTZ PHOTO

Above: The tragic Reardon-Brown wreck of May 29, 1900 was caused by a box-culvert washout. Two such accidents occurred during the road's history. Engine No. 1 was a former PRR D-3 class, extensively rebuilt in the Raidler program of 1900-1906.

Below: The KGB&W wreck of October 6, 1899 was a prelude to the 1900 accident which took the lives of Mike Reardon and John Brown. The PRR D-3 toppled down a ten-foot embankment west of the Kewaunee Wye. Cows evidently were the cause of the mishap.

and Seth Champion on the steamer, crossing from Frankfort to a series of meetings along the busy, bullish route to the Mississippi. They were confident that the Green Bay road would spread its influence and new extensions into the west and northwest, the new traffic being a salvation. The roads all had good financial backing and were on the "highway to prosperity."

Land for the new car ferry docks at Kewaunee was acquired from George Grimmer. For the deed executed May 2, 1892, Grimmer received sixty shares of common and thirty preferred of KGB&W stock. Upon their arrival in June the officers met with Kewaunee city officials to arrange for acceptable harbor improvements. Turning space was needed and the upcoming dredging would require a new iron swing bridge located farther west. Walker submitted drawings of the new ferries to the Corps of Engineers for the excavation. While the world awaited the new ferries, Champion's little steamer MARQUETTE went safely about its business and completed 100 trips and approximately 13,000 accident-free miles out of Kewaunee. Champion ran it in general service, including excursions, salt-hauling and apple-toting through 1894.

While KGB&W tended to its maintenance-of-way and finished an enginehouse, the great steamers were completed at Craig's yard in Toledo. A steam shovel worked near Clyde to provide ballast for the Luxemburg-New Franken sector. Construction of the ferry yard trackage began in August at what became the Kewaunee Wye. Kewaunee noted that the improvement was a relief of the crowds of boxcars downtown near Main Street. Pile driving for the ferry slips continued into late summer, following the plans drawn by Ann Arbor's Assistant Chief Engineer, Mr. Augustus Torrey. While filling the trackwork eastward from the wye, several flatcars nearly turned over as the track sank heavily into the mire. Hours were spent bringing the flats to safety, as heavy rains had swelled the Kewaunee River's estuary. The apron work at the slips, which took approximately 350 piles, was completed September 30th at a cost of $20,000.

ANN ARBOR No.1 was reported moving up the St. Clair River above Detroit October 27th, marine reporters following its progress. The ferry was launched September 20th, its owners confidently expecting to have consorts (engineless barge counterparts) built for extra capacity. Several new yard tracks were competed at the ferry yard, when No.1 passed the Straits, and proceeded to Frankfort. On November 25th the thermometer stood at four degrees, foretelling another ominous, ruinous winter on the northern Great Lakes. On Sunday, November 27th all eyes were riveted on the eastern lake horizon at Kewaunee to catch the first glimpse of the newcomer's smoke above many on the busy waters. Finally, it came, tandem stacks laying a thick carpet of coal smoke, lavishly laid on by unseen coal passers, a performance of Victorian majesty. Aboard were Captain Kelley, and John Craig, of the shipbuilders, who oversaw the vessel, yet to be signed for. James Ashley, Jr., the Ann Arbor's six-foot four-inch vice-president, accompanied Captain Louis Ryersa of St. Ignace to direct fitting of the wood colossus to its apron.

The fitting at Kewaunee continued from 7 p.m. that Sunday evening until the 11 p.m. departure. Loaded one-half hour after final adjustments were made, No.1 accepted 22 carloads of Pillsbury flour bound for England from Minneapolis. Whether or not the DL&W actually had faith in the system, as detractors denied, the exceptional service was about to begin. Her first trip was a ten-mile-per-hour crossing which consumed six hours.

The second crossing proved less majestic. Steaming westward in a fog, her officers somewhat unfamiliar with the new route, the 1128-gross-ton leviathan drove full force into a gravel reef two miles north of Ahnapee. Up to the instant of collision with the bar, No.1 had logged four hours and fifty minutes for sixty miles, an otherwise commendable achievement. The ferry was stuck fast 300 feet from shore and was levered about 28 inches above her normal depth marks. Captain Kelley ordered her scuttled to prevent waves pounding the hull against the reef and signaled for tugs. The Sturgeon Bay canal lifesaving station rescued the crew who set up camp ashore to direct wrecking operations. Shortly after, the Leathem & Smith wrecking tug fleet was dispatched from Sturgeon Bay, but heavy seas kept aid away. The second day, no less than eight tugs, including FAVORITE of Sheboygan, stood off and put lines aboard No.1. Thousands of horsepower moved the ferry only three feet. The barge MARY MILLS finally came alongside and lightered off six carloads. Then, in an unforgettable display of steam-era tuggery, the eight shepherds of cold, northern waters dragged the car ferry off the bar. The tug SEAGULL, billed as a salt-water rig of great power, parted a 17-inch hawser in the ordeal. Spectators rode overland 15 miles to view the pageant but such attention and publicity was not appreciated by the Great Through Route's management. FAVORITE and SEAGULL, like distrusting parents, accompanied the errant one to Kewaunee's safe harbor, two days after her fall from grace.

No.1 was released a day later after close inspection. A diver checked for hull damage but found none. Her engines were taken down to be inspected for possible damage, while alterations were made so that two more cars could fit on the apron end. Seven days after the first trip, No.1 went back on duty. By year's end TAA&NM had employees at Kewaunee, headed by Agent L. E. Vorce. Encouraged by initial success, the ferry route faced a ghastly winter which would test the feasibility of the boat's unusual design and the innovative theory of open-water car-handling.

Passing up from Craig's after a Christmas departure, ANN ARBOR No.2 had a hard time of it in the five-inch ice which covered Lake St. Clair. Some of her steel sheathing was ripped loose and the new boat put in to Port Huron for repairs. Taking a week to reach Frankfort, she was able to make her first arrival in Kewaunee on January 4, 1893, carrying only eight loads. She returned to Frankfort with 22 loads of flour, settling into harrowing winter duty. Because of the open deck aft, there was risk of heavy seas swamping the new ferries. Stormy passages tended to open seams and caused much concern among crewmembers that first winter. The first week in January No.1 was in distress and, in a furious blizzard, inadvertently made for Ahnapee. The ferry then coasted southward in an attempt to locate Kewaunee in the white-out. Missing the harbor, the ferry continued to Manitowoc where she put in to the river. Reports from Manitowoc alleged that a number of crewmen quit upon landing. Yet, by early February the two boats were formally accepted by TAA&NM.

The all-important rate struggle loomed as a deciding factor for the new route. The cross-lake break-bulk lines were allowed a differential of two cents per hundredweight which covered cost of transshipment. With in-car transport for their portion of the Minneapolis flour, the differential would amount to extra profit for the Green Bay Route. After publishing a low rate to compete, GBW&STP found that other flour roads (Soo Line, Duluth, South Shore & Atlantic, Canadian Pacific and Grand

Above: KGB&W's venerable engine 32 rolls along with the mixed train — probably No.13 — out of Kewaunee about 1907. Rebuilt after several bad accidents, the former PRR 4-4-0 was eventually given a new Belpaire boiler. It remained in service until 1932.

Below: Bright and shiny KGB&W No.1 rolls past Casco Junction with a ferry train in mid-1897. Shortly after, the ex-PRR D-3 (No.653) would lose its Keystone-State charms, as it was wrecked several times.

CHARLES V. DEDA PHOTO

Trunk) undercut, which began a flour rate war. Chicago-Minneapolis roads clamored for a repeal of the differential, which led to ever-decreasing profits. It was difficult for *The Marine Review* to spot profitability in the cross-lake system. The Kewaunee Route refused to withdraw its differential rate; the war against the line was called off January 16th, 1893. Roads which met the rate of the cross-lake system had to advance them, leaving the Kewaunee Route with the lowest rate for flour. It remained so for at least part of 1893. Surrounding roads claimed that the forty carloads per day taken by the Kewaunee Route netted a daily loss, all things considered. It was predicted that the DL&W, behind the scheme, would be defeated in the end.

Profitability notwithstanding, a much-heralded flour train was dispatched from Minneapolis to New York in March via "The Kewaunee Short Line." The 22 cars were Northwest Dispatch Fast Freight Line or "Eureka Line" boxcars recently built for Minneapolis-Seaboard service. The car line was reported to be another Joseph Walker, Jr. constituency. Over the "mountain division" of the Omaha Road's main line in western Wisconsin, the train ran into heavy drifts which delayed it for hours. Reaching Merrillan Junction, the cars were quickly transferred to the care of a new GBW&STP 20-class 4-4-0 which had journal lids rattling in short time across the road's profile. Another hour was consumed at Green Bay when an elusive photograph was taken and the train was moved through the M&N interchange, the "alley track," onto KGB&W rails at North Quincy Street. ANN ARBOR No.2 loaded the cars at 1:30 p.m. after a carefully coordinated arrival at Kewaunee. Arriving at Frankfort, TAA&NM had the train moving shortly after the boat's 7 p.m. docking. The car-ferry route's adventure

was in contrast to the normal ten to fourteen days via Chicago. Confidently, a second train was expected in early April.

News of another freight traffic agreement on regional lines handled by C&NW and GBW&STP was published in April 1893. John B. Last of the Green Bay Route met with his C&NW counterpart in Chicago's Western Freight Association office and came away with certain rates equalized, lowering tensions between the companies. Kewaunee and Chicago became equals for entry points for east-to-west traffic. An allied decision was reached, resulting in some of C&NW's traffic crossing the lake from Kewaunee, chiefly some of C&NW's Hocking Valley coal traffic. The early 1890's were filled with day-to-day struggles over rates which alternately starved and flooded competing rail lines.

KGB&W benefited indirectly from the Chicago World's Fair of 1893 when C&NW and CM&STP were saturated with passenger traffic. It was reported that their busy facilities in the Windy City caused an overflow of freight tonnage to KGB&W, rerouted to Toledo and the LS&MS (NYC). There was speculation that TAA&NM was building two more ferries and would also lay a telegraph cable.

Early in 1893 a little-known and short-lived industry had sprouted in Kewaunee. It was based on the abundant limestone which was easily quarried near West Kewaunee. Mr. Mark English caused a stone dock to be built which loaded the vessels' iron ore dock-style. The structure was built where the present west slip now stands and boasted several pockets into which the stone was dumped, each taking 15 tons of material. The dock was completed by April 1, 1893 with ten stone pockets and a track thirty feet above the water. The 600-foot approach was an incline. Ten cars were converted from flats with wedge-shaped centers and side-traps. In June, just before the "Panic of 1893,"

the barge RICHARD MARTINI took on the first load destined for Port Washington, Wisconsin. MARTINI made one more haul after the recession. Billed as the last cargo, it departed on September 13, 1893. Dormant for two years, the dock was dismantled in spring of 1895 to provide timber for the new Fox River trestle at Green Bay which would connect the KGB&W to its parent road in Fort Howard.

Another traffic delay on KGB&W materialized when the Ann Arbor suffered an engineers strike. The road's president, Governor James M. Ashley, a former congressman and ex-governor of Montana Territory, was confronted by an organizer's committee of the Brotherhood of Locomotive Engineers who pressured Ashley to discharge two senior engineers not interested in joining the union. Ashley refused, precipitating a strike in which TAA&NM cars were refused by union crews at transfer points. The action led to an injunction against the union for interfering in interstate commerce and the strike was broken. The traffic starvation only compounded Ann Arbor's financial woes and on April 28, 1893 The Honorable Wellington R. Burt of Saginaw, Michigan was appointed receiver for the company. During the month prior to the strike the ferries made 21 trips, transporting some 70,000 barrels of flour. CITY OF MARQUETTE, held at bay by ice during the first half of February, carried 9000 barrels in five trips. At the same time, Milwaukee shipped 95,000 barrels across to Michigan railroads in 46 clearances from its docks.

During the strike the two ferries remained on the Wisconsin side, while strike-breaking engineers highballed the Michigan road's trains. In May 1893 Craig's of Toledo obtained a judgment against Ashley for unpaid amounts on the two ferries, alleging that only $151,000 was paid. TAA&NM stock fell on the market from 39 to 12 and the long night of the 1890's recession set in, chilling enterprise for many years.

Kewaunee newspapers reported that Joseph Walker, Jr. and his associates were the principal creditors of TAA&NM, who bought up the road's stock during the crash of May 1893. Traffic scarcely moved in the still spring of that year. The bottom fell out of "grain freights," the rate dropping to one cent per hundredweight for Buffalo-bound shipments. Many lakers would be laid up for months; others would be forced to run at rates tantamount to slavery for those involved.

Reorganization included Joseph Walker, Jr. and John Jacob Astor on the TAA&NM directory. The Ashleys — father and two sons — faded from the scene and the enterprise passed to the bondholders and the Farmer's Loan & Trust Co. The GBWSTP was just then facing its financial inquisition, as TAA&NM faced a struggle between the Astor Estate and Samuel Sloan. It was shortly to be further aligned "with DL&W interests," becoming Ann Arbor Railroad Co. in 1896.

KGB&W's early crews included Winford Abrams, later the mayor of Green Bay, who worked through the long recession of the mid-90's, firing regularly on the Kewaunee-based switch job. Abrams' father was the road's president. Win married Miss Ottilia Rhode, a doctor's daughter, and they settled down in rented Kewaunee rooms. He was just in time for KGB&W's first engine, an 1873 Pennsylvania D-3 purchased second-hand from New York Equipment Co. No.1 was unofficially named "Kewaunee." The forty-ton 4-4-0 found a home in the west side enginehouse at Kewaunee as its crew kept busy switching car ferries and rolling carloads away from downtown salt sheds. In time, Win was promoted and in 1899 he ran the daily mixed train out of Green Bay to Kewaunee. He continued railroading into mid-1900, even after KGB&W had its share of accidents, luckily without injuries. But on the morning of May 29, 1900, when Mike Reardon and John Brown were killed, Win Abrams left railroading for a real estate career.

Several times in the late 1890's, the strange-looking GBWSTP wrecker 01 had to be called out to clean up wrecks on the east end. Common derailments were handled by other locomotives. Once, a superannuated Grant 4-4-0 stripped itself, its siderod snapping, which cracked a cylinder head, all without personal injuries. On October 6th, 1899, No.1 was proceeding into Kewaunee with the mixed train when it unexpectedly tumbled down a bank west of Lutz's cut, coming to rest ten feet into the swampland. Mike Reardon and John Brown, engineer and fireman, escaped without injury but the accident involved the cows of Messrs. Svoboda and Streu. The mixed train's passengers obligingly walked into town. Mike and John were lucky this time.

Below: This is a view of the team track and main line at Kewaunee's city yard. Both types of Ann Arbor Corporation's lettering of the 1890's are shown on the box cars.
J. SELNER PHOTO

No. 1 was in bad shape, spending most of the month of October at Fort Howard Shops for repairs. The 1873 veteran was steadily losing its PRR profile. At that point, both No. 1 and newcomer No. 2, a 4-4-0, were laid up. The GB&W substituted numbers 18, 19 and 20 for Kewaunee duty. Built in the early 1880's, No. 2, a used machine, had come from Erie Railroad.

Once again, a heavy spring rain fell, lasting days. Side creeks were filled with the heavy run-off, raising the Kewaunee River. On the morning of May 29, 1900, Reardon and Brown were easing the rebuilt No. 1 down the Kewaunee Valley, nearing Clyde station just before 8 a.m. with nine loads and two coaches. Beyond lay a fatally washed-out box culvert.

depot was authorized. Construction began in 1900 but the signboard didn't arrive until 1902.

Passenger service to Kewaunee was always a secondary affair and never was there a pure passenger train. Early conductors were William Lake, Charles Thompson and, for a short time, "Hank" Sipes. Uniforms became de rigeur only in 1899. In the beginning years, when snow and high water halted service, trains met at the blighted sections to transfer passengers, mail and express. Trains met again when landslides blocked Baird's Creek cuts, which for years afterwards supplied sand ballast as they were widened. Earliest coaches, all converted into more practical combination baggage-passenger counterparts, were

F. W. SCHNEIDER PHOTO; GB&W COLLECTION

Too late to help themselves and their engine, men and machine fell into the gaping pit ahead. A rush of steam silenced the sounds of boxcars tearing into the broken locomotive. John Brown, a Green Bay native, was killed immediately. Reardon lived only a short time, tended by Kewaunee doctors after initial care was given at Charles Kinstetter's farmhouse. Mike Reardon, who was 35 years old, left a wife and two children. He was buried in Jackson, Michigan.

KGB&W crews hurried to replace the railroad and earnestly sought to make conditions safer after the accident. Close economics had denied the new line its share of wealth and such earnings were necessary to maintain a fresh, young line in the face of ruinous competition, such as faced the company in the closing years of the 19th Century.

Kewaunee for too long had to do without a "real" depot. Seth Champion promised that one would be built on the old Darbellay house site, then owned by Joseph Duvall. In 1896 plans for a 24 × 50-foot building were divulged, but an old warehouse persisted as accommodation. Kewaunee balked when KGB&W promoted closure of Main Street an hour before train departure to allow undisturbed train make-up. The city's press saber-rattled about money pledged and depot refused, but in time a

Above: A party of businessmen was taken to Kewaunee's ferry landing in the mid-1890's. The second ferry stands by on the far right as a Grant 4-4-0 prepares to load an empty boat at the apron. The docked vessel is probably No. 1, while No. 2 waits in the channel.

Top Right: A&W 4-4-0 No. 33 brings a KGB&W mixed train into Kewaunee about 1907.
J. SCHULTZ PHOTO / S. H. MAILER COLLECTION

Right: The road to Clyde from Slovan saw many mail wagons in its day. The steep slope led directly down to the KGB&W "halt." Today the blacktop road is known as Clyde Hill Road.

probably the old Haskell & Barker GB&M coaches rebuilt by a Master Car Builder. Help came after the GB&W was formed when in July 1896 cars No. 5 and No. 6 arrived new from Ohio Falls Car Co. The newcomers cost $3400 each. With the new, ruby red coaches in service, self-deputized critics condemned the service for its failure to be the Fast Mail of popular literature.

CHARLES V. DEDA PHOTO

West Kewaunee grew into a noticeable community in the 1890's, centralized about the West Kewaunee Roller Mill and the Nast Brothers lime kiln. Both industries received sidings and in time the roller mill became a Seyk Co. property. However, the community shriveled in the 1920's, becoming Footbridge, and the basic industries vanished. Today the kiln area is Bruemmer Park, while the mill site is overgrown and forgotten. Elsewhere, a siding was built at Scarborough to service the Trudell Mill, which also disappeared during the same period.

Interest in solving the problems of a connection through Green Bay for KGB&W began immediately after completion. Attempts to buy land on the Fort Howard side ran into political trouble and, after the economic troubles of 1893, the subject was shelved. Land for the connection was eventually acquired north of GBWSTP's Fort Howard Shops, which was swampy slough land through a residential district. When the project was raised, some aldermen were interested in putting the Kewaunee connection farther out, thus minimizing congestion. Fort Howard went against the road by one vote, while the Green Bay counterpart affirmed it. In the end the new City Common Council favored the KGB&W.

In early 1895 the $20,000 Fox River Bridge project was begun. The structure was reportedly 2370 feet long. Contractors McGrath & Anderson of Green Bay began with a pile trestle reaching westward from North Quincy Street on what was then marshland. The 800-foot-long trestle would later be filled. By February, with 58 of the 138 bents in place, the progress could be measured. Upon completion in August, fill for the east approach (the trestle) was obtained from Baird's Creek cuts under the busy maw of a Bucyrus steam shovel.

The new connection to the GBWSTP shops and yards was made later in 1895 but the first gravel extra chuffed across the newly tested swingspan in late July. Joint ownership with C&NW put the latter in position to enter the new Hoberg Paper Co. on the east side of the Fox River. Hoberg's new mill, which began operation in October 1895, was a new source of business for both railroads. The Milwaukee Road trackage-right contract was abrogated, although that road remained in the area of the paper plant; its "alley track" was a city nuisance in the age of the motor car. Rumors of a depot along the KGB&W near the plant in the Eastman addition of the city proved to be false.

Of equal significance was the building of the KGB&W trackage to the Cargill elevator, which lay along the Fox River nearly opposite the C&NW depot. It allowed the Green Bay Route access to the Cargill-leasehold when the bridge connection was finally made. The trackage was completed, only to have the entire elevator go up in flames in June of 1896. The $80,000 loss was seen as even more ominous for GBW&STP. The main line, among other things, had defaulted on lease rentals due the KGB&W to the amount of $21,000. W. W. Cargill immediately sought to have a replacement elevator built. Seth Champion and Will Cargill visited Kewaunee with the intent to arrange alternate grain facilities for fall and met with Joseph Duvall regarding a site. Such a grain terminal at Kewaunee instead of Green Bay might have changed the history of either community considerably. In August, the Green Bay Elevator Company was incorporated to operate the elevator with C&NW the primary force behind it. The new building's capacity was 300,000 bushels.

The waning years of Seth Champion's CITY OF MARQUETTE may not have been profitable ones. Catching the odd break-bulk cargo here and there while the car ferries took the lion's share, the little steamer was out of service by 1895. It had spent much of the 1890's darting about like a petrel in search of sustenance. The MARQUETTE hailed at Manistee for salt, routed to Cargill's for meat packing, a considerable market. Champion finally sold his portion and invested in Green Bay real estate with the proceeds. Champion's other investments were apparently far removed from the midwest, as he was reported to have owned the Tres Amigos Mine at Nogales, Arizona in 1900. Champion resigned from both GB&W and KGB&W on July 1, 1897 and moved his family to Pasadena, California where he died in 1910. MARQUETTE drifted back to Lake Michigan in the service of the Hill Line and was finally abandoned in the late 1920's.

Champion, W. J. Abrams, W. W. Cargill and George Grimmer sold out to the new GB&W, giving the latter controlling interest in KGB&W. President Abrams of KGB&W proposed to sell 3417 shares of common and preferred stock, plus some 150 shares of common and preferred in the treasury, amounting to a total of $356,700, for $150,000. He also proposed that present KGB&W officers resign to allow vacancies to be filled by GB&W personnel. The road would be surrendered free of all debts, except bonded debt of $408,000, the proposal to be acted upon by July 1, 1897. Joseph A. Jordan of Hannibal, Missouri replaced Champion and W. J. Abrams on the KGB&W staff. Joseph Jordan was vice-president of the St. Louis & Hannibal Railway, another Blair-Farmers Loan & Trust Co. property, splitting his time between Green Bay and Hannibal. Stephen S. Palmer of New York became president of the new Green Bay & Western, the KGB&W and the StL&H.

The building of the KGB&W from Green Bay to Kewaunee largely saved the GBW&STP from a bleak future. Will Cargill's plans to move grain eastward during winter months provided the impetus and the interest in investing in a separate road which could be bonded and paid for by separate arrangements. With GBW&STP ensnared in insurmountable financial difficulties, KGB&W, I&N and Winona Bridge invited fresh capital or fresh securities coordinated by investing officers of the GBW&STP. Cargill also routed his coal purchases through Kewaunee via car ferry and later to the extensive coal docks at Green Bay. Cargill sold coal in the many small towns of his elevator lines, which required GB&W to at least carry them westward. The arrival of Ann Arbor ferry service was the foundation which led to a stable Green Bay & Western.

Above: KGB&W's Luxemburg Station is shown about 1900. United States Express Co. and Western Union were ensconced in the agency. The depot served the major towns between Green Bay and the lake. STAN MAILER COLLECTION

8

LC&SE
THE OTHER
CARGILL ROAD

LC&SE 4-4-0 No.6 awaits another trip to Viroqua. Caboose 01 (origin unknown) was the road's sole caboose. It was destroyed in a collision at LaCrosse in 1922 when a CB&Q yard crew backed into the car. This photo was taken about 1920.

At the turn of the century, La Crosse, Wisconsin moved away from its river-borne, log-dominated ways toward the development of a modern economy. This included manufacturing and services which its well-to-do would include in their portfolios. In the past, investments in railways, steamboating, lumber and grain facilities prevailed in the city. The coming of a new age, that of electricity, offered new possibilities to the well endowed. In 1901 one of the predominant empires down by the Missisippi was that of the Cargill-MacMillan grain interests. The two families made their original ancestral home in La Crosse. Cargill-MacMillan's lines of grain elevators strung out across Iowa and Minnesota and along the railroads west of La Crosse. The Cargill, beginning in 1867, was at Conover, Iowa on the Milwaukee Road.

Interest in an interurban electric railway system, rendering La Crosse master of its surrounding territory, spawned the La Crosse & Southeastern Railway. William Wallace Cargill, capitalist, entrepreneur and respected citizen, shared his interest with Duncan MacMillan in Edison Light Co., Vote-Berger Telephone Co. and La Crosse Telephone Co., as well as newspaper enterprises. He was also the president of La Crosse & Onalaska

Left: The elevator of William Wallace Cargill's grain company stands behind the ex-Pennsylvania 4-6-0 No.2 at Viroqua, Wisconsin. No.2 operated about 16 years on the LC&SE until it was sold to Cazenovia Southern Railway. Too heavy for that road, it was scrapped at Cazenovia in 1923. Note that the engine has plain tires on No.1 drivers.
PETER HENSGEN PHOTO

Street Ry. and La Crosse City Railway. The Southeastern's counterpart, aimed toward the northeastern perimeter of La Crosse County, was La Crosse & Black River Falls Railway. Only the LC&SE came into being, while a third route to Galesville never progressed beyond the suggestive stage. LC&SE's fate was no worse than short lines with brighter prospects; LC&SE operated for 29 years. After sale to Milwaukee Road, parts of the road remained into the 1970's.

LC&SE ended its zig-zag path southeast at Viroqua in Vernon County, about 34 miles from La Crosse. Viroqua was located 700 feet higher than La Crosse in what is known as the coulee region of steep valleys. Vernon County is a tobacco-growing center, a unique west Wisconsin agriculture. Articles of Incorporation for LC&SE were filed in 1902, its first wave of management-ownership being easterners. Joseph Boschert was listed as president, David H. Palmer as vice-president, John P. Reeve, secretary-manager, and James B. Taylor was treasurer, while E. C. Higbee, F. A Cummings and J. Turneck were on the board.

Franchise and financial problems stalled progress of the new LC&SE but certainly the La Crosse electric empire could be deemed righteous, for in December 1902, La Crosse's Congregationalist Reverend Henry Faville's sermon "Christ and Inter-

115

urban Railways" pronounced the new crusade "good for God's sake." The contractors balked and money was slow in coming. Finally, in March of 1904 Will Cargill, although near the end of his business career, came aboard to bring revitalization and local thrust to the enterprise. The thorny problems of city and village franchises involving in-town right-of-way and crossing rights to CB&Q tracks were solved. Ultimately LC&SE entered La Crosse as a close neighbor of GB&W on CB&Q's city loop to the Burlington station. In time the easterners faded out of the picture and the Cargill's prevailed over their second railroad investment in fourteen years.

In early summer of 1904, citizens' elections focused on problems of extending time and money (bonds) to complete the work. The towns of Coon and Hamburg held their mass meeting which extended bonding for another year. Cargill assured everyone that men and teams would answer the affirmative vote. Will Cargill's forceful personality pushed the new road to begin its three decades of service to Wisconsin's hill country.

The decision was made to turn away from electricity and track laying started in 1904 at Stoddard, about ten miles south of La Crosse. Stoddard had its railroad war in which tracks were laid across streets on a Sunday morning, wild west fashion. Townsmen who opposed the railroad attempted to remove them and the company had to patrol its property constantly. This insurgency was traceable to shortcomings inherent in the first contractor's character, who neglected to pay local help. Such obligations were the province of the past. Ultimately trackwork continued up a coulee toward Chaseburg and Coon Valley, as roadway was widened, interurban-style standards being vacated.

LC&SE's first locomotive was a GB&W lease, probably an old Grant, which brought in ten GB&W flatcars on October 30, 1904. The train was transferred from GB&W to CB&Q trackage at Grand Crossing, run down to Stoddard and then onto the new construction. The grand work continued unabated and raced winter to the high country around Westby and Viroqua. In late November grading crews were worked seven-day weeks with steel gangs passing through Coon Valley en route to the big hill up to Westby. Three locomotives, including LC&SE No.1 and No.2, were present; one at the front, another moving material up to the railhead and a third switching at Stoddard. The two LC&SE machines came from F.M. Hicks, a used equipment dealer in Chicago and probable source of many otherwise untraceable midwestern locomotives. Both were ex-Pennsylvania Railroad 4-6-0's with Belpaire boilers. No.1's stay

Above: Former CB&Q 4-4-0 No.4 is shown with another mixed train at Viroqua, Wisconsin. No.4 allegedly went to Montana Western Ry. at Valier, Montana, along with No.3, which reportedly was a former LS&MS 4-6-0 similar to Ettrick & Northern's No.10.

Top left: LC&SE's Viroqua Depot about 1912. The trains arrived out of sight and one story below. Dexter Street is in the foreground.

Left: LC&SE mixed train No.6 is shown two miles west of Coon Valley, Wisconsin about 1920. It was headed for Chaseburg. Stalwart No.6, a former NYC engine, served the longest of any South Eastern engines. According to an eyewitness, No.6 came to the line with hard-coal grates.

was short but No. 2 was seen regularly until 1922 when it was sold for further duty on nearby Cazenovia Southern Railway.

The depots along the line, which were built by Mr. John Miller, had a distinct design reminiscent of both GB&W and CB&Q stations. They were Stoddard, Chaseburg, Coon Valley and Westby. Viroqua's depot was at right angles to the track, which ended a floor below. Excavation of the terminal's hillside location would bring trains into level ground to the rear, hidden from view of street level. Dexter Street station, looking more like a waterworks, was architecturally a very urban approach to embarking on the shortline. The building remained until the 1970's as a warehouse.

LC&SE laid its last rails to Viroqua in January 1905 but popular opinion suggested that the interurban would continue, perhaps down the steep hills toward Madison or southwestward to West Prairie, Retreat and De Soto. Ambition on the road was

Above: LC&SE operated in Spring Coulee which offers some of Wisconsin's most majestic scenery. Here, a daily passenger train nears Coon Valley in the 1920's.

Below: GB&W loaned the South Eastern its pile driver on a spring day in pre-WW I days, along with tank car TC-1.

L. THRUNE PHOTO

far from stilled. The Cargill clan settled into an uneasy posture vis-a-vis their investment, which was deemed by some of the prominent family to be less than worthy. This was substantiated by years of loss to its owners, which only worsened when autos began to arrive in the high country. From its first business of moving Sheriff Ward from Chaseburg to Viroqua, there was less than what is required to survive. Blind also was the ambition of the La Crosse & Black River Falls Railway, which never ceased to agitate its case around Melrose, with even less population density.

The Cargill connection would not have been complete had the grain dealer not built trackside grain elevators. Another plan called for hauling firewood to La Crosse, a traffic not likely to be remunerative. Elevators had been erected at Stoddard, Coon Valley and Viroqua by the spring of 1905. LC&SE's first business day came and went; with it were the first timetable and the first 250 passengers. Patent medicine, wonderful "Swedish Oil," was reaching into the highlands to cure all via LC&SE and drummers from the big city of La Crosse. The service left Viroqua at 5:00 a.m., met the CB&Q at Stoddard, returning by 6:00 p.m. The first such run, February 1, 1905, was on a typically frigid west Wisconsin morning, a Sunday which produced only eight or ten passengers. More boarded at Westby, utilizing the road's first passenger coach, another Hicks value. Not surprisingly, the steam heat malfunctioned and the coach was sent to CB&Q's North La Crosse shop for adjustment.

In Spring 1905 Southeastern construction crews finished final projects on the completed portion, experiencing the first of many snow blockades between Westby and Viroqua. The line was closed for six days that month while cuts were unburdened by hand, assisted by local Sons of Norway. Bridge construction crews went north from Stoddard with pile drivers, working just east of the CB&Q main line. Looking ahead optimistically, spring excursions were planned but a retaliatory Milwaukee Road, in defense of its traffic to Westby and Viroqua, reduced its fare from La Crosse to Viroqua via Sparta. The price was the same as Southeastern: $1.26, a rate made by the newcomer.

While the Viroqua Band rode to bring harmony to Westby, construction hands went on strike over wages. The demonstration was met in the usual way of the times: dismissal and hiring of replacements. The new workers from St. Paul carried on without further incident. Tobacco, dried and bought locally for cigars, began to appear at the LC&SE freighthouse. Mr. Alton Mills, agent for the road at Coon Valley, soon designed a cigar band for "Coon Valley Cigars." He also created a logo for his employer "The Coon Valley Route.'

LC&SE finally entered La Crosse in June of 1905 but it required an overhead crossing of the CB&Q main line, east to west. A line was then built parallel to the Q's line from South Junction into the city's south side. A junction switch, 1.8 miles

line continued until the mid-twenties, long after fortune had ceased to smile on the Coon Valley Route.

Valier insisted that LC&SE run four trains a day at the outset and in time trains left opposed terminals at about the same time, meeting at Coon Valley. Mail was handled by the locked pouch system instead of RPO's. During the first year excursions continued to acquaint area people with the wonderful new conveyance. Some 1000 La Crosse grocers made a day of it in Viroqua; one engine had to double back to assist a brother secondhander in dragging the rest of the grocers to the top of Westby Hill.

There were some interesting attempts to operate with internal

LACROSSE HISTORICAL SOCIETY

LC&SE 4-6-0 No.2 is seen on a winter day at Viroqua, Wisconsin about 1914.

away from the "Q" station at Second and Pearl Streets, surrendered the interurban to the greater company, as Cargill had given up the struggle to put his road on La Crosse streets. With its Hicks coaches, the ultimate interurban reached the Burlington station, greeted by an admiring crowd.

The LC&SE train arrived June 30, 1905 under the command of Superintendent Peter Valier. Valier had come to Cargill's La Crosse operations from Lockport, Ontario via several other positions. He was now in charge of the interurban, formerly of the street railway and soon to leave his name on a small town in Montana. Cargill's Valier-Montana Land and Water Co., a scheme which nearly ruined the Cargill business empire, carries the name of the trusted lieutenant to this day. At one point in its history, LC&SE supplied locomotives to Montana Western Railway, a short line which connected the lands to a Great Northern division. Peter Valier's stewardship of the ailing short

combustion power at the outset. Three Strang gas-electrics were reportedly summoned from a Kansas City interurban but the cars were unable to perform satisfactorily. In early 1905 CB&Q experimented with a motor car which had a 150-horsepower three-cylinder engine. It was reported that the car would exceed $15,000 in costs. The car was considered to run to Viroqua but it never happened.

The Coon Valley Route never did fulfill the aspirations of its creators. Yet, trackside natives of the area remember with fondness the daily passage of the small trains, reciting the name "The Old Southeastern" in a traceable Norwegian brogue. The regular crewmen were remembered well beyond their days of good work and more leisurely ways. Its regulars at the throttle were Morton Shirks and Henry Weber. Peter Hensgen, Henry Allen and Charley Fowell worked as firemen, conductors or brakemen, whatever was necessary. Peter Hensgen started in 1912 and

This is a rare view of the ex-Ocean Shore Meister motor car No.62. The California-built car came to Wisconsin about 1921 upon the demise of the West Coast road. This photo was taken at Viroqua, Wisconsin about 1924.

STAN MAILER COLLECTION

"About 1939"

LLOYD THRUNE

The "Coon Valley Route" survived its more humble past and became part of its competitor, Milwaukee Road. On separate occasions, 27 years apart, differing trains negotiated a trestle west of Coon Valley, Wisconsin. Both trains were powered by 4-6-0's — No.2 for LC&SE's movement and 1158 for the latter-day CMSTP&P. Note the continued existence of the building and water tower but the variation in other structures. Note as well the revisions in the trestle and abutments.

E. NOLTE

"About 1912"

retired from railroad service in 1956 after working for C&NW, GB&W and Milwaukee as well. A retiree from the last steam days on Milwaukee Road in the coulee region, Peter had the satisfaction of being headman on the branch trains which took over the LC&SE operations after sale to Milwaukee. Peter Valier, never a ramrod super in reality, would be found on the righthand side of engines, when he was needed.

Valier's daughter Edna told a story of the wonderful Unit/Stanley/Laconia steam car which was offered to the road in 1920. Her brother Ronald, assistant manager of the LC&SE, was sent east to oversee construction of the sophisticated steam-powered rail car at Laconia Car Co., in Laconia, New Hampshire. Ronald, not as avid a railroader as his father, kept some distance from the project, with good reason: car 402 had extremely high boiler pressure. After several trips in July the car was used on an outing of railroaders and their white-clad wives. While working hard up Westby Hill from the Spring Coulee, a boiler tube developed a burned flaw. Instantly the boiler blew into the firebox, spewing oily residue over the assembled multitude. The laundry bill stands unrecorded for the day's event. Ronald, the day's engineer, was blown firmly out of the engine room door, sustaining minor injuries. Car 402 was retired from the scene and, according to one source, went to a railroad in Iowa which was "on the level!"

Two other motor cars were tried after patronage had fallen to dismal levels following World War I. Ex-Ocean Shore Railway Meister car 62 was used for a while. It was an Eklund Bros. (Minneapolis) railbus which hung on long enough to be taken away by salvagers in 1933. The Eklund had a trailer which was used for express shipments. Steam was used when business at harvest time ran heavy enough to create a mixed train. After retirement, just before World War II, the Eklund was used as a fruit stand along Highway 16 east of La Crosse.

When the Great Depression came, it only added the final millstone about the neck of the beloved short line with the Norwegian accent. The road filed a finance docket with ICC, giving notice of abandonment, and on August 5, 1933 the Coon Valley Route was no more. Its sale was an even swap; Cargill accepted a 25-year lease on Elevator "E" in Milwaukee in return for the railroad. The line was abandoned from La Crosse to Chaseburg and a portion between Westby and Viroqua was removed. The balance functioned as a branch run out of Sparta until the 1970's, at which time all but a small segment of LC&SE line at Viroqua remained to mark the way of a less formal, individual way of railroading.

Below: Unit steam car No. 402 is seen at the Burlington Station in LaCrosse on the occasion of the disastrous trip in the summer of 1923. The car was remembered as being very quiet. A Stanley engine powered one pair of truck wheels. Peter Valier, superintendent, stands first left. His son, Ronald, is in the baggage door on the right.

STAN MAILER COLLECTION

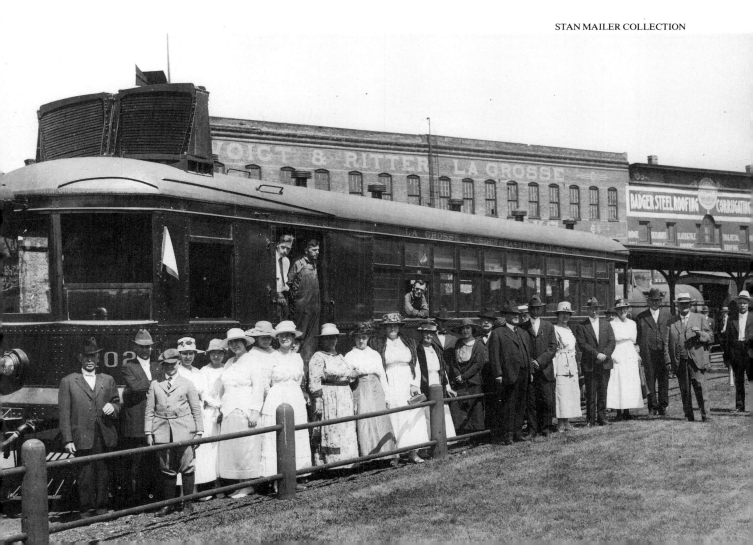

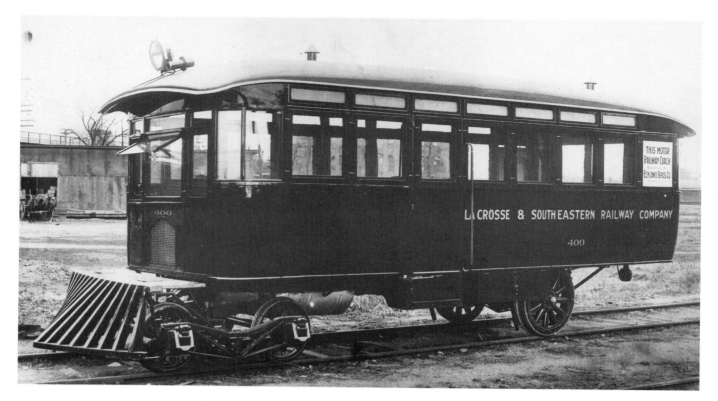

Above: This Eklund Bros. railbus, powered by a White "45" engine, was built in Minneapolis. In later years it served as a roadside fruit stand near La Crosse.
WILLIS HENDRICKS PHOTO

Top right: The last run of LC&SE was on August 5, 1933. Presiding at the CB&Q station in La Crosse is engine No.7, an ex-CB&N Hinkley 1887 product.

Right: Locomotive No.2, the former PRR 4-6-0, stood at Coon Valley Station in 1912. The train was eastbound for Viroqua.

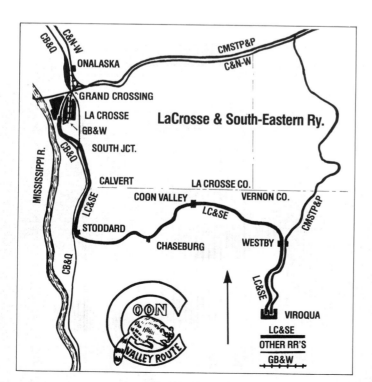

9

A&W
MR. DECKER'S
RAILROAD

Sturgeon Bay in 1968 had a population of 6776, a solid little town of willing workers and marine charm. It maintained a number of small industries which relied upon transport south to markets, and some even relied on the Ahnapee & Western Railway. East of the city, the Sturgeon Bay Ship Canal cuts through one and one-half miles of the Door County peninsula, venting the V-shaped bay off Green Bay, from which the city derived its name. From the mid-19th Century, Sturgeon Bay had traditions of waterborne commerce, which essentially stalled railroad entry until 1890. But that was 78 years before and, on May 27, 1986, Ahnapee & Western filed for abandonment out of the Door County seat.

Interest in Sturgeon Bay's canal was generated on the same internal improvement winds of change which brought Green Bay & Mississippi Canal Co. to Wisconsin, but with a more private motivating breeze. Lumber interests, allied with politician Philetus Sawyer, engaged in acquiring a 200,000-acre grant in aid of the canal during 1866 and 1867. The potential was intriguing; Chicago interests were bent on shortening and easing their lumber vessels' passage from Menominee and Peshtigo down to Chicago. "Death's Door" is the basis for Door County's name, and the perilous passage around the tip of the peninsula constituted a raw threat to navigation. There were rocks and shoals and contrary winds which stood to ruin many a voyage. The picturesque islands of Wisconsin's vacationland were deadly barriers in the 19th Century.

Chicago's William Butler Ogden, Jesse Spaulding and others had extensive timber operations along the Menominee River, while Issac Stephenson was involved with the Peshtigo Company on the namesake river. Together they formed Sturgeon Bay and Lake Michigan Ship Canal & Harbor Company. Sturgeon Bay natives E. S. Minor and Joseph Harris assisted locally. Ogden attempted to negotiate a loan of $350,000 for the canal, but faced interest charges of forty percent. The "Panic of '73" distorted the situation but by 1886 Philetus Sawyer shepherded the canal into federal ownership. A $150,000 appropriation was added to a record-breaking bill. Sturgeon Bay's economy then revolved around the canal and its attendant shipyards, chandleries and captains' homes. While the lumber boats passed

Left: A&W's Sturgeon Bay yard in the winter of 1950 shows Mogul 260 switching prior to going on the road. The tracks leading to the right went to Fruit Grower's Co-op and Peterson's Boat Works. The majority of the road's business was east of the brige.

F. BUTTS PHOTO

down to Chicago, the windy city's hold on lumbering in the north only grew stronger. Chicago's finished-wood industry held sway by the 1880's, shipping as much as fifty cars a day for example from Sawyer-Goodman yards to Iowa, Nebraska and Illinois points.

There were groups which promoted early railroads into Door County, but they were faced with entrenched marine interests. The plain fact arises that it is a peninsula, better suited for docks than railroad yards. Population was sparse, perhaps too low to support a railroad. Steamer lines touched at Sturgeon Bay and a portion of the voting population was vested in the field. Yet, several prominent names promoted Sturgeon Bay & Fond du Lac Railroad and a bill to incorporate was introduced in January 1870, an effort that was blocked by owners of piers and vessels when they were approached for subscriptions.

Outside interests bent on entering trade with Door County were then promoted and in 1880 David M. Kelly, Timothy Howe, E. H. Ellis and others from Green Bay put forth Wisconsin Peninsula Railway, a narrow-gauge idea for the thrifty-minded. However, visions of Lilliputian trains lost in deep snow prevented the wise from voting aid. WPRy carried the ultimate scheme which developed a decade later. It was David Kelly's swan song in state railroading but it emboldened other area promoters.

Fond du Lac interests tried next with the Fond du Lac, Portage and Sturgeon Bay Railroad. FdL,P&SB projected a Y-shaped line in 1881 with branches to Sturgeon Bay and Shawano. Dana C. Lamb and N. Boardman emerged as its chief promoters. Later in the decade it was Wisconsin Midland Railroad, aimed at linking L'Anse, Michigan on Lake Superior to Fond du Lac. A branch would serve Sturgeon Bay and the peninsula's interior, not too close to either shore, minimizing waterborne competition.

A third attempt was via Two Rivers and a Milwaukee, Lake Shore & Western Railway connection. The Rhinelander road surveyed northward from Two Rivers, withdrawing finally. It remained for the Green Bay entry to prevail.

The three schemes each produced surveys and, as charters expired, new names arose. By June 1885 State Senator E. S. Minor and Edward Decker of Casco were co-incorporators of Wisconsin Railway & Navigation Co., whose capital stock was $1,500,000. WR&N approached reality by projecting from the Fox River's mouth to Ahnapee via Casco, Decker's own fiefdom. WR&N's route finally evolved into Decker's anticipated railroad empire.

Sturgeon Bay's newspaper, *The Advocate,* represented a view which opposed bonding for a railway, much as periodicals in the southern half of the state had in times of the farm mortgage issue. They also knew that a railroad between two communities worked against the lesser city, draining off commerce and growth. *The Advocate* saw its trade and prosperity aimed south to Chicago and Milwaukee, no doubt arriving on fine propellors. Kelly's Wisconsin Peninsula Road was defeated on a bonding issue, *The Advocate* assisting.

The Wisconsin Railway & Navigation in 1885 also solicited local aid but was unsuccessful. *The Advocate* resorted to a subterfuge exposed by a rival paper and the wronged population backed the truth. A positive vote for bonding yielded $80,000 in aid. In 1887 Wisconsin Midland Railway, guided by an informed populace, received approval for $35,000 bonding, Dana Lamb actively soliciting. The bond amount was deposited in the Kellogg Bank at Green Bay, where Lamb tried unsuccessfully to sell the Midland. Lamb was also a special agent for

125

Above: Construction into Door County was rushed in 1894. Here, GBWSTP 4-4-0 No. 8, a Grant product, was utilized on a supply train. The scene at Naswaupee, about two miles south of Sawyer, Wisconsin, shows a train after delivery of rail produced in Buffalo.

A. T. SCOFIELD PHOTO; KRAUSS COLLECTION

Below: Ties and 52-pound rail were new on the fresh grade at Naswaupee in 1894. Immigrant labor gangs had just a few more days on the job since the bridge was nearly finished at the time.

A. T. SCOFIELD; KRAUSS COLLECTION

land and allotment to the Oneida Indians, another suit for a busy man.

Unfortunately, Fond du Lac's A. G. Ruggles, the Midland's President and strongest promoter, passed away. Locked with C&NW over crossing rights, the Midland faltered and expectations of a Sturgeon Bay branch flickered and died. The road planned to occupy the east shore of Lake Winnebago, making a junction at De Pere, Forest Junction or Green Bay. Discussions centered on the best location to ascend the Niagara Cuesta, the rock formation creating the Door County peninsula directly east of Green Bay. Arrangements were said to have been made to cross GBW&STP at Seymour and the MLS&W at Gillett and Little Chute. *The Advocate* also reported that the Midland "ring" was linked to the Illinois Central, perhaps releasing a parthian shot at the hobbled Lamb and his project. When Dana C. Lamb passed away in August 1893 the Midland's stub in Fond du Lac passed to CM&STP. Gone was the scheme to link Fond du Lac, the mineral-rich upper peninsula of Michigan and the Door County "thumb" of Wisconsin.

The father of the Ahnapee & Western Railway was Edward Decker, the long-time advocate of a line east from Green Bay. Decker had served as President of Green Bay & Lake Pepin Railway in the days before David M. Kelly had become its promoter. The man from Casco, Wisconsin had suffered a horse bite in 1868, which had cost him his arm. After his recovery, Decker lived in Kewaunee and later Casco, busy with lumbering, land speculation and town-building. He entered into law practice due to his skill in making deeds and titles to lands, which became the source of his wealth. Decker owned about 10,000 acres of land centering on Casco, which was the locus of several of his businesses.

He was born in 1827 at Casco, Maine and followed the trail of many a lumberman west to Wisconsin. Decker, at age 14, landed at Milwaukee in 1845, first going to Oshkosh and later to the Casco area. He entered a large amount of land in Kewaunee and Door County. He founded Casco, on Decker Creek, surrounded by his holdings. In the 1880's Decker went into banking as far away as Two Rivers and Chicago. He entered publishing and established a newspaper at Kewaunee, *The Enterprise*. He published the *National* magazine in connection with Bostonian Joseph Chapelle and attempted to move the *National* magazine to Casco to enhance his empire there. Decker was married four times and built a large home at the head of the street which leads down to the business district. He could also overlook the depot of Ahnapee & Western when it too arrived in Casco.

Throughout the two decades prior to 1890, Decker kept a close watch on railroad schemes in the area, corresponding with all sides, agreeing with some, opposing others. Surveys in large numbers crossed the district and always Decker noted their effect on his investments. He pushed for lines which converged on Casco and Kewaunee. He stood astride ideas, influenced bond issues and county elections, all the while watching for the main chance.

When the Kewaunee, Green Bay & Western road materialized, Decker was able to organize and incorporate his own line. His supporters were M. C. Haney, Ahnapee; C. G. Boalt,

Painesville, Ohio (who later moved to Ahnapee); W. J. Abrams, Green Bay, and GBWSTP's manager Seth W. Champion. On August 18, 1890 The Ahnapee & Western Railway Co. was a legal entity, which was "commencing at a point in Kewaunee .County, running thence to the City of Ahnapee (renamed Algoma in 1899) and thence to a point in the City of Sturgeon Bay, in Door County, Wisconsin." The beginning segment was to be 14 miles long. Capital stock was set at $100 per share to total $250,000. Decker advanced most of the funds for construction and equipment and from his own mill at Casco he would supply material to begin the task.

Two surveys had been made in June. The chosen location was to be ready when KGB&W was completed to a junction point. It required another year to vote bonds in key towns along the route and by June 1891 the towns of Ahnapee, Lincoln and Red River had complied. A grading contract emerged in September 1891 after financial moorings were secured. Grading contractors

Below: Here, A&W engine No.1 poses on the 1300-foot trestle at Casco Junction when the road was new. The Deckers were inspecting the work completed during the first winter operation. The trestle later was filled in. No.1 was formerly a GBWSTP Grant-built 4-4-0.
ED TOMJANOVICH COLLECTION

McDougall and Beacon began at Rio Creek, working both ways from the center. Brushing work was contracted to Mr. George King at what became Casco Junction, the A&W-KGB&W meeting point.

On April 30, 1892 a resolution was passed which provided capital stock of $10,000, first-mortgage bonds of $10,000 per mile of finished road and $108,000 county and municipal bonds, to be turned over to Edward Decker. He was empowered to dispose of the bonds, using the proceeds to construct and equip A&W. He then received $331,500 capital stock and first-mortgage six-percent bonds, the total being $671,000. Decker retained the capital stock and bonds, later acquiring the majority of stock issued to the counties for their bonds. The municipal and county bonds were sold for $106,000 cash.

Sturgeon Bay also was approached for aid ($50,000) to complete the road to Bay View (Sawyer) and $70,000 if the line crossed to the east side. This implied a bridge across a federal waterway, the Ship Canal. Pressure was applied by Sturgeon Bay to change the road's name to Sturgeon Bay, Ahnapee & Western, but without success.

Above: A&W engine No. 1 and its passenger train pose at Sturgeon Bay in the 1890's. The little 4-4-0, weighing less than forty tons, was no match for the cruel 1890's winters which prevailed in northeastern Wisconsin.
KEWAUNEE COUNTY HISTORICAL MUSEUM

The first construction lap was the right-of-way from Casco Junction to Ahnapee. General contractors McDougall and Beacon began by grading to, and then building, a 1300-foot bridge at the Kewaunee River. They also constructed a shorter one at Decker Creek. Both were later filled in.

Construction intensified in the summer of 1892. David Decker, Edward's son, handled rail purchases on missions to Chicago where he looked over prospects for other equipment. Illinois Steel Co. received the A&W order for rail. The work continued without labor strife, although there was a shortage of

Below: During the 1890's, the Union Pacific Railroad disposed of a number of its 4-4-0's. The engines went to used equipment dealers such as Chicago's F. M. Hicks Co. A&W No.3 was acquired from Hicks in December of 1902 and became No.33 in August of 1906. It was out of service by 1911. C. R. BLOOD PHOTO; DOOR COUNTY LIBRARY

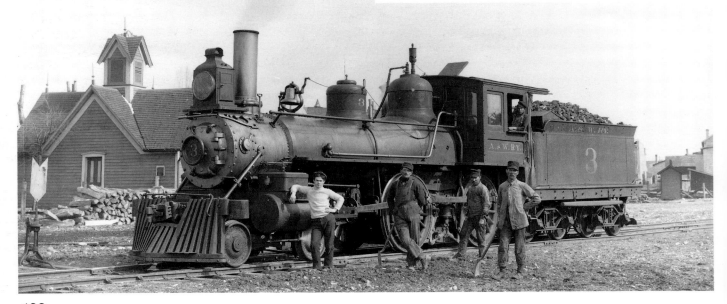

manpower and the ownership had to boost the daily pay scale to $1.50 per day.

During August a violent electrical storm toppled trees across the new roadway, while a worktrain proceeded down to Casco Junction. Patronage began with locals shipping a threshing rig outward on September 5th and receipt of a car of horses from Iowa. Construction forces finished in October, and A&W came to serve Casco, Rio Creek and Ahnapee for the next 94 years.

One of A&W's longest standing customers, Ahnapee Seating & Veneer Co., was incorporated in the spring of 1892. It replaced a sawmill, forwarding a tradition of the eternal small town-north county Wisconsin establishment, still around in 1987. A&W served the operation which modernized from time to time, changed names and product, but was always present. In

covered the tracks in springtime and the spot was an operational headache until abandonment, never really disappearing.

Decker's forces now concentrated on the road to Sturgeon Bay. In the Fall of 1892 rough-graders strove to complete as much as possible before heavy winter. Contractor George King finished grading in 1892, including rough terrain near Bay View, in sight of the canal. The pile driver worked on the Ahnapee River Crossing, a bridge location still to be seen along Highway 42. Most of the line up to Forestville was ready for rail by October.

The "old" portion of the new road began operations with "second-hand pearls" in the form of a former GBWSTP Grant-built 4-4-0 commanded by Jacob Green. A story emerged via the Halliday family that, upon instruction from management,

the beginning, the Ahnapee mill was complemented by a brother mill at Birchwood, Wisconsin and veneer logs moved between the two operations via the A&W. The business of furniture-making, depot benches predominating, continued well into the 20th Century.

GBWSTP's Chief Engineer Frank Halliday was detailed to survey the entire railway system east of Green Bay. His party established the routing of KGB&W, then went on the the A&W survey. Mr. Halliday spent much of the year handling the details of the A&W. He evened moved to Ahnapee with his family. One of the more interesting problems which confronted Halliday and the contractors north of Ahnapee was the infamous "Cranberry Marsh," a half-mile long sink hole located west of present-day Highway 'S' in southern Door County. Water often

Above: The port of Sturgeon Bay busied itself with passing lumber boats which brought Michigan's felled forests. Here a group of three masted vessels are ready to be towed through the Sturgeon Bay ship canal. A&W's bridge is on the extreme right.

C. R. BLOOD PHOTO; DOOR COUNTY LIBRARY

GBWSTP painted the drive wheels red, perhaps to differentiate between theirs and Decker's. The engine arrived on November 22, 1892. Green and his charger were said to have run off the Casco Junction-Ahnapee segment in 17 minutes. Basic buildings appeared. A&W put up a temporary enginehouse just west of 4th Street and a small depot just off 3rd, a convenient two blocks from metropolitan Ahnapee. The "Great New Scene" was marred only by an injector failure on No.1 engine which grounded the swift Grant in favor of a horse team for the inbound traveler. U.S. Express handled the small packages and with several appropriate coaches, also from GBWSTP, a bright future seemed imminent.

Joseph Walker Jr. came out to survey the empire in November with a tour of the "Great Through Route." Seth Champion, F. B. Seymour, W. J. Abrams and George Grimmer of Kewaunee plus Dispatcher Teetshorn accompanied the financier-broker to riverside in Ahnapee. Theirs was one of ten trains run on specials on November 17, 1892 when all came to experience the new service. A measure of reality set forth in the next month when, upon the first derailment, KGB&W dispatched GBWSTP engine No.9 to assist from Kewaunee. KGB&W was to operate parent road equipment until 1894, at which time its first locomotive was purchased.

In January 1893 A&W experienced its first heavy snows which closed the line for many days, a frequent winter misfortune. Engineer Green suffered serious wounds when his cab windows shattered while bucking drifts between Casco and Rio Creek. The custom was to set out the train and lunge at filled cuts which did little to maintain schedules. During the same winter GBWSTP sent in doublehead engines to clear snow and these in turn were overwhelmed. Severe weather prevailed for three weeks, producing a bumper crop of ice to be supplied to Chicago the following summer from area icehouses.

A&W's most infamous bridge, the swingspan across Sturgeon Bay, began with the city's need for a wagon bridge. Ship owners Leathem & Smith Co., also proprietors of a shipyard, were granted a charter in July 1886. The result was a toll operation run by the Commercial Bridge Co., Sturgeon Bay. Eventually the bridge was rebuilt as a combination rail-and-highway structure after Frank Halliday had made soundings for a separate bridge. The A&W engaged a large workforce in the spring of

1894 to bring the road into the port city before the bonus deadline. A&W railroaders were fearful of weather delays and the plan to build their own bridge was set back due to the federal government's failure to consent to the construction of another bridge. The government was concerned about another navigational hazard, a very justifiable position in light of the final evidence. On May 1st a plan to build into the Commercial Bridge arose, to alter the steel swingspan to accommodate rail traffic, negating the federal objection. Agreement was reached with the City of Sturgeon Bay (owner of the bridge company) and construction began May 15, 1894. Contractors Knapp & Gillen of Racine began on the trestle section, and revision of the swingspan — a 250-foot 92-ton structure — went to Milwaukee Bridge Co. Contractor Gillen opined that the time period would not allow for a train to enter the city by the appointed day. They were able to finish track only by July 13, 1894. Track laying reached the trestle's south end by July 2nd and on the 26th the triumphant first train crossed the finished swingspan. All agreements were thereby fulfilled and the aid package secured. The line opened July 23, 1894 for regular business.

Purchase of rails for the Ahnapee-Sturgeon Bay sector was made in Buffalo, while David Decker made a hurried trip east to confront the Secretary of War, the federal agency responsible for navigation. Decker had to catch up with the key men in Toledo, Ohio to get the proper signatures. The Buffalo rails were shipped to Ahnapee — 512 tons aboard PHILETUS SAWYER and 400 tons aboard FOSTER with another shipment on ANNIE LAURIE. Timing had been very close.

The combination bridge had its drawbacks. Wagonmakers and blacksmiths were kept busy repairing horse-drawn vehicles whose wheels had been wrenched off when, fully loaded, they fell into flangeways of the railroad. Ice pressure on the bridge in

Right: Here, A&W 4-4-0 No.31 brings combination cars up to Casco Junction's depot. The isolated and lonely junction at this time, about 1920, was the interchange for Kewaunee passengers en route to Green Bay.

T. VAN DREESE COLLECTION

Left: Mornings in Sturgeon Bay witnessed the arrival of A&W's daily connection with Green Bay. Here, in 1905, ex-UPRR 4-4-0 No.3 heads across the combination bridge to its final destination.

DOOR COUNTY LIBRARY

winter was serious but the railroad structure was further east and somewhat protected by the older highway section. Initial glitches included improper closures. The major problem was putting vessels safely through the openings without damage, which proved time and time again to be difficult. In November of 1907 the schooner BERTHA BARNES, downbound to Chicago from Ford River, Michigan, rammed the bridge. The vessel luffed at an indiscriminate moment, tearing into the bridge and knocking it ten feet out of plumb. It was only the first of many accidents to the unfortunate structure.

Sturgeon Bay now unlimbered a planned celebration. Some parties loosed both cannon and a quartet of beer kegs in homage to the constructors. Celebration day was bright, windy and clear and an unprecedented 2000 or more people crowded into Sturgeon Bay via all available transport. The first A&W excursion train handled 350 Ahnapee citizens, riding only one coach but several flatcars which were equipped with makeshift seats and green pine boughs for sun protection. The Hart Line steamer FANNIE C. HART arrived from Marinette-Menominee with 150 passengers, leaving behind another 300 who were fearful of the heavy sea on Green Bay. Sturgeon Bay rang with whistles, cannonades and appropriate salutes from more genteel yachts anchored out. It was perhaps the only time the city gave its railroad full honors and accolades.

Another 1000 people arrived in eleven coaches which left Green Bay at 8:30 a.m., arriving at 12:45 p.m. to deposit its crowd into the human sea. The train grew at Green Bay as car after car had to be commandeered and standing-room-only was the ultimate condition. Several hills on the KGB&W had to be doubled, the small 4-4-0 overtaxed. The De Pere band which came on the excursion found a place in the sun to perform. The crowd in Sturgeon Bay was addressed from a bandstand, the scheduled opera house being hopelessly inadequate. Management's David Decker talked of sweat and tears and difficulties in bringing the road to reality. And, on a loftier note, Reverend W. H. Thomas, vacationing in the pure air, made the appropriate observations upon the blessed occasion. The crowd, satiated with all that the city had to offer, embarked for home. On the following day, businessmen of Green Bay arrived on a special to hear how the Deckers had persevered and of how trees of late May were now sturdy piles in the 2000-foot trestle into the bay. GBWSTP's Seth Champion and Frank Seymour consulted with the Deckers and the business of serious railroading in Door County had finally begun.

While A&W put its Sturgeon Bay yard in order, David Decker met with freight agents in Chicago to establish through rates in competition with steamer service. Fares to Sturgeon Bay were fixed at $1.95 and at $1.40 to Ahnapee. Ballast trains continued to roll from Naswaupee gravel pit near Bay View to all points in need. The Ahnapee turntable, only recently installed, was moved to Sturgeon Bay and arrangements were made to build an adjacent enginehouse. By September, when the Deckers wound down contractor's work, disbanding camps along the line, smoke from northern Michigan forest fires hung in the air so thickly that A&W trains had to reduce speed and whistle frequently. Engineer Ed Kenyon now handled engine No.1 and found that the machine was less than dependable. Allegedly, the 4-4-0 still had woodburning grates and Ed pined for a new engine. Conductor W. F. Welby was having problems with wags placing obstructions on his track which only served to shorten his temper, especially as Kenyon had to run his engine tender first to Ahnapee from Sturgeon Bay. But shortly and steadily the road ironed out its glitches and the train from Sturgeon Bay began to run "head-first."

With winter just weeks away, A&W started its first Sturgeon Bay depot. The 28 × 100-foot combination building was constructed by Henry Poehler's crew, the de facto B&B gang. When finished, the depot had ash-trimmed interior and contained a telephone. Mail service came early the next year. Steamer service between Green Bay and Sturgeon Bay maintained similar rates as rail traffic began to compete. No longer did the Hart Line steamers handle the mails to the docks of Sturgeon Bay. Interchange between railroad and steamers for more northerly points was opened and service was curtailed only in severe weather and during layup of the steamers.

In December's cold, locomotive problems became more acute, enough for David Decker to finalize a Chicago purchase. Shopping in October had turned up an Illinois Central engine, one of the company's bargains. The result was engine No.2, which arrived in January 1895. C&NW handled the engine "dead in train" to Fort Howard for $55, the more costly alternative being to run the engine light. No.2's actual pedigree is unknown; probably a 4-4-0 from a non-standard shortline I.C. absorbed. What was billed as a more palatable replacement turned out to be just another troublesome affair.

At year's end, Frank Halliday completed his tour of engineering on A&W and returned with his family to his Plover home. Among others who came to the railroad was Sturgeon

Bay's first agent, F. C. Reitzel, late of Marshland on the main line. He came aboard in time to preside over A&W's first shipments of Christmas trees to Chicago. Reitzel hailed from Whitehall. Generally all of the early men of A&W were graduates of the main line, even though ownership of the road was clearly not GBWSTP.

A wreck occurred the first week of January 1895 when the mixed train derailed near Forestville. The combination car toppled over and rolled down an embankment, scattering coal of the overturned car heater which immediately started a fire. Fortunately, injuries were slight and the fire was quickly extinguished. The car derailing was blamed on a broken flange. Passengers were put aboard the locomotive and conveyed to Casco Junction for the KGB&W connection. A GBWSTP coach substituted while Fort Howard attended to the damaged car.

The Door County winter continued to show the new road little compassion, as snow-filled cuts on the south end hampered service. At best, trains were delayed hours, the small locomotives unequal to the task of winter operation. It was also clear that patronage did not require a second set of coaches, although daily runs in the spring became the rule. During winter the Casco Junction turntable was immobilized; engines again were forced to run backwards. A cut was plugged solid in January and both engines were again required to punch through hard drifts near Casco. Trains were hours off schedule and piping froze on locomotives in a glacial grip of passing storm fronts. Both engines, still woodburners, were supplied from the Decker mill at Casco. Nearby, the New Franken water tank along the KGB&W froze completely. Some drifts over tracks were seven feet deep. Winter conditions caused the A&W railroaders to halt northbound trains at the top of the grade into Bay View. Engines were run around the trains to ease the

Below: The train to Sturgeon Bay picked its way through floodwaters on Green Bay's east side in 1910. Several hazardous conditions threatened the road, including the infamous "Cranberry Marsh." In this view train No.11 is handling both fifty- and sixty-foot coaches.

STAN MAILER COLLECTION

Right: No. 11 poses at Sturgeon Bay in the 1920's. Open-platform wood cars were a common sight in this era.
A. MADDY COLLECTION

Right: Western Refrigerator Car Co. collaborated with GB&W Lines after 1928 to allow private lessors in the cherry business to place billboard advertising on the new cars. The Reynolds firm was a pioneer of Door County's cherry business.

STAN MAILER COLLECTION

Right: Caboose 020 was a former G.N. car which was rendered surplus by 1924. Renumbered 620 during World War II, the car is preserved today at Green Bay.

ERIC SWANSON PHOTO

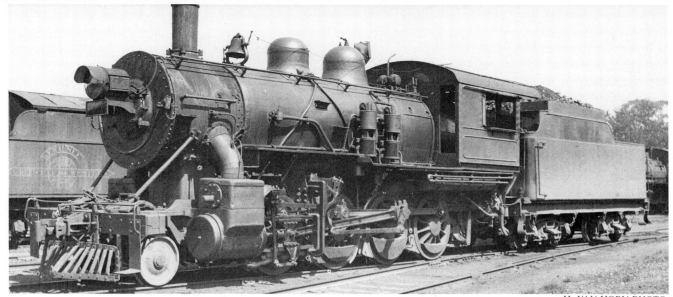

descent to Sawyer. New No.2 was promptly changed to coal fuel in March.

Depots were completed at Ahnapee and Casco Junction in 1895. Casco Junction received a small design which burned a decade later. Ahnapee had a two-story design which was the same size as Sturgeon Bay's station. It was also intended to serve Goodrich Liners for interchange business and the A&W. Ahnapee was a residence depot, located where the old city pier jutted into Lake Michigan. Trackage was extended eastward in Summer 1895 to accommodate it. It was many years before suitable depots stood at Forestville or Maplewood.

As the 1890's passed, other GBWSTP engineers replaced Ed Kenyon, a Kaukauna native, for a stint on the old engines of the new railroad. There was Bert Lucas, Steve Slattery and Fred White. Kenyon customarily laid off in summer for an 1890's equivalent of a vacation. On the rear end Frank Welby was the victim of Decker nepotism when Nat Decker became conductor, at least for several summers. Nat went off to college in the fall of 1899 as Republican prosperity returned to the nation.

In late 1898 the Deckers sought to put an end to their locomotive problems and ordered a new Baldwin 4-4-0. In the previous three years, No.1 had been sent to C&NW's Kaukauna Shops for a new firebox, while C&NW No.922 was leased for about two months. No.1 evidently was used as a spare locomotive for the balance of its A&W life, being traded to Hicks Locomotive and Car Works in 1902 for No.3. The new Baldwin was perhaps the only worthwhile machine put on the road in the first decade, for it alone survived beyond 1911.

The "cranberry marsh" of the town of Naswaupee, a bottomless pit caused by hurried construction, soon became the road's chief operating headache. Each spring ice or water would cover the roadway, often causing the rails to spread. The rush to Sturgeon Bay to claim additional bonuses ($50,000 for Bay View, $10,000 for crossing to Sturgeon Bay) was to blame. The builders had settled for a quick solution instead of bypassing the location. Even telegraph poles were affected and had to be moved closer to the track. As early as 1895 the mixed train suffered a derailment in the soft area. A wood dike was constructed of mill materials to dam the right-of-way and drain the swamp, to no avail.

In Spring 1905 it was again impossible to send a locomotive across the swamp. Coaches and boxcars were shoved over by a south end locomotive where they were handled to Sturgeon Bay by a marooned north end crew. Gravel extras were run to the site and steam shovel No.2 supplied material at Casco Junction. In the fall Milwaukee-bound State Fair passengers were delayed by another onslaught of water. In 1904 a concerted effort to build a corduroy bed of trees under the track ran the total bill to $5000 for ten years. B&B gang regular Henry Poehler estimated

Top Left: A&W No.74, a former Chicago, Peoria & St. Louis Railway secondhander, was assigned to A&W but, dut to its weight, may never have operated on that road. Later, as No.303, it was sold to Escanaba & Lake Superior Railroad, becoming ELS 18 in 1937.

Middle Left: A&W's R-class 72 is shown at Green Bay in July 1936. Locomotives of this era wore the "East-West Short Route" herald in a circle with the individual road's name in "wings."

Bottom Left: Extra 251 West is about to leave Algoma depot in the summer of 1939. The water tank and windmill were retired in 1940 and the depot was razed in 1980. Lake Michigan is one-half mile beyond.

that, even with twenty feet of timber under the line, no permanent relief was in sight. Within four years water was again over the rails and service was curtailed.

North of Algoma (nee Ahnapee) in the fall of 1910, bridges were in poor condition after the Ahnapee River rose and flooded the roadway to three feet above trackage. A northbound crew reported high water conditions and the marsh situation was equally bad, necessitating GB&W engine No.22 (marooned north of the bridge) to accept trains pushed across by a Green Bay-Algoma crew. B&B men got conditions back to normal within a week, using trainloads of gravel arriving from Casco Junction sandpits. Passage through the marsh was again possible but the quagmire still threatened to engulf the roadway at any time.

Similar conditions in September 1912 isolated Sturgeon Bay for two weeks. In 1913 Frank Seymour was determined to subdue the marsh. Sheetpiling was sunk parallel to the trackage and forty feet of material was dumped until limestone bottom was reached. Track was then moved and the void was filled. Four hundred linear feet of roadway was filled to an average depth of 31 feet. Seymour's determination reflected the days of Teddy Roosevelt and the Panama Canal: Time was not a factor, victory was. Fortunately, material was available just two miles away. Hundreds of carloads of brush, rock and gravel were dumped and trains were crossing the spot by June 1913. Another $25,000 was expended but the company had prevailed.

Forestville's depot was a product of pressure. Locals Sam Perry and Charles Plinske took their case to the State Railroad Commission, winning a new building for the town. The commission ordered adequate shelter for proffering business. The "open shed" which served in Decker times was no protection for man or merchandise in harsh Door County weather. Business out of Forestville was alleged to be $4333.58 for the past year (1906) but passenger service brought between $18,000 and $20,000 annually. Forestville was a non-agency station which could not accept C.O.D. shipments, a situation which was judged to be inadequate. The resultant depot cost $834. Further discontent surfaced in 1913 when locals found the walk to the depot excessive. Again the railroad was confronted and the residents prevailed; the depot was moved back to town. The company insisted that the village pay the costs of moving but collections only brought in $150. In time the site was improved with planted trees and businesses moved as well. The Cargill elevator, still standing in 1987, opened in 1898 and figured prominently in the depot game. The 1907 location of the depot was subservient to that business, not to the town. The advent of a "pure freight" (No.15-16) operating to Maplewood from Green Bay negated the old depot site. Now the passenger train could stop at the foot of the village, eliminating the double stop of the mixed train.

Maplewood's station followed a similar pattern. The old station allegedly was discontinued in 1902 and a platform erected, without supervision, like Forestville. A 20 × 32-foot depot built at Maplewood in late 1918 lasted until 1944. Both declining agencies were the subject of a comparison during 1943 and 1944. During that year, Forestville originated 105 cars, Maplewood 96. Maplewood was closed for a period during World War II; its freighthouse and depot were gone by 1946.

Algoma started with a small structure and graduated to the combination Goodrich Lines/A&W terminal out in the lake. In need of modernization, company forces remodeled it in 1914 in an attempt to make "the old barn" more acceptable. The city agitated for better accommodations as early as 1912 and a tug-

Above: Prisoners of war from the Afrika Korps line up on Sturgeon Bay's usually peaceful depot platform in the summer of 1945. These German soldiers went off to battle with Door County crops during their stay in Wisconisn.

W. C. SCHROEDER

of-war erupted over location of a new building. Railroaders wanted the prospective new building to be west of 4th Street, on solid ground and near the mill. Prevention of trains backing across city streets was another reason. The ice houses of Rahr Brewing Co., a Green Bay firm, were on the site. Mr. Seymour met with the brewers and arranged to dispose of the obstructions to the new depot. Ultimately this depot issue went to the Railroad Commission of Wisconsin, which pushed for the 4th Street location and a substantial brick building. Other buildings were removed from the site and, because of soft ground, piles were driven to support the 60 × 30-foot newcomer. Construction started April 1, 1917, the site costing $1000, the building $6,798. The architect was P. T. Benton of Green Bay. The old 40 × 101-foot depot remained as a warehouse until November

1922, at which time it was dismantled. Algoma's final depot was demolished in 1980.

Sturgeon Bay's original depot, erected in 1894, was destroyed by fire January 22, 1897. A 30 × 80-foot building without commendable architecture, its chief fame evolved from the fire which destroyed Mr. Leopold Goldberg's luggage. He carried the claim for damages to the courthouse and lost. It was one of A&W's small victories in an austere decade. Completed by Spring 1941, Sturgeon Bay's longest living depot still stands. The successful builder was Fabry of Green Bay. The cost of the new 33 × 56-foot building was $6338.26.

A&W passenger service from 1895 until 1906 was a leisurely affair, reflecting ways of an independent road and certainly of less hurried times. Accurate descriptions of equipment are not available but most cars came from GBWSTP. Just before the Deckers bowed out, the short line's roster was increased by one "old theatrical car" which was introduced in Summer 1906. Evidently used as an excursion or parlor car, it perhaps raised the standards for Door County in measurable quantity. Some improvements were in order, for the same year an "auto line" was started between Manitowoc and Sturgeon Bay. It operated daily passenger service with an open four-seated car for the determined and brave. Winter adventures with light rail and inadequate locomotives made desirable even the barest of improvements.

The Decker road promoted excursions to on-line parks; Sunday runs given to picnics and berrypicking and county fairs. The first ever handled a group of GAR veterans from Forestville to Green Bay. Again in 1903, a typical excursion had 550 riders on six coaches plus two boxcars outfitted with seats. This one went to Kewaunee. In 1904 seventy rode from Kewaunee to Sturgeon Bay, the first in a revival of inter-railroad operations between KGB&W and A&W. Others went from the lake port towns to Green Bay for a night on the Denessen Boat Line and Green Bay's cool waters. The fare was $1 round trip.

On July 23, 1904 A&W stockholders passed a resolution that, inasmuch as Edward Decker owned $340,000 in outstanding first-mortgage bonds of the company and that the company was indebted to him for $272,000, the company should issue Decker $612,000 of new five-percent bonds under mortgage of May 14, 1904 to retire Decker's investment. Some $425,000 of first-mortgage five-percent bonds were issued. The mortgage was dated September 1, 1906, maturing in 1936 in exchange for $612,000 first-mortgage five-percent bonds. The bonds were outstanding in public hands. The reorganization committee of GB&W acquired $434,900 of A&W capital stock and $175,000 of the new five-percent first-mortgage bonds for $181,165.65.

By 1907 summer competition with Green Bay steamers and Goodrich Lines resulted in rate-cutting. Travel became cheaper and the steamers steadily lost ground. A regularly scheduled event was a Sunday train which gave Sturgeon Bay coordination with C&NW trains at Green Bay Junction. Some of the sixty-foot Hicks Standard "50 class" coaches were assigned to this task. The budding resort trade in Door County catered to Chicago and Milwaukee clientele and, as traffic grew, sleepers were operated in interline service with Chicago & North-Western.

Conditions on the road were such that complaints regarding both passenger and freight service began to surface, chiefly because of the long route and light track. Responding to pressure, Freight Agent J. B. Call, visiting with shippers in Algoma, observed that, with added business, the daily freight would run as far north as Sturgeon Bay instead of stopping at Maplewood. Businessmen at Sturgeon Bay petitioned for operation of a freight train to separate the two services for their own benefit. Frank Seymour considered it impossible in light of sparse traffic. The object was to connect with steamers at the port which the road declined to serve. Algoma's complaints stated that the merchants there waited ten days for rail shipments from Milwaukee, only 125 miles away.

Algoma also pushed hard for a better depot. A Door County newspaper campaigned against A&W, alleging that the road made $30,626.27 from its service, proof of "a gold mine in thirty

miles of track, over which the company's wheezing donkey engines draw belated trains and passengers daily."

As early as 1905, interest in an interurban in Door County vied with a good roads movement. It was to be Sturgeon Bay & Northern Traction Co. which tried to obtain a franchise from the City Council. Fortunately for its investors, the line was never more than a paper dream.

A series of grim wrecks occurred in the teens. Adventures with cracked cylinder heads in winter's cold were commonplace. No. 13 stalled in the winter of 1910, battling its way out of Sawyer. Conductor Harry Walker was injured in a derailment in September 1911 but continued on with the train after medical aid was given. The baggage car was demolished at the Rio Creek site and Walker was on crutches for some days afterwards. The wreck was caused by a broken rail and new iron was scheduled to replace the old 52-pound originals. Seventy-two-pound rail was put down at the rate of five miles per year.

Fifteen passengers were shaken up when two trains collided at Casco Junction in October of 1912. One of the brakemen jumped, sustaining injures after landing in the turntable pit. There were also several other derailments around Algoma in 1912 which were attributed to light or worn rail. The train went on, observing a new timeworn custom of handling post-accident travelers in available empty boxcars. In several such instances the passengers whiled away the hours in local roadhouses, awaiting aid, playing "sheepshead" or commenting on snow conditions. In another incident a train which included a special coach requested for a Forestville wedding derailed; however, the dauntless couple and friends continued to their destination in a boxcar. Another more serious wreck at Forestville in September of 1913 spilled Mogul No. 36 (KGB&W No. 36) down an embankment, the culprit being spreading rails. It was a prelude to the line's worst accident, two years later.

In April 1915 Engineer Frank Buttrick and fireman Thomas Dare were assigned to the Maplewood freight train which had completed its work at the small village and was returning to Algoma. Conductor Clarence Richards was in charge as No. 15-16 with engine 36, running tender first at twenty miles per hour, approached Forestville. The train left Maplewood at 11:32 a.m. but never made it to Forestville. A mile north of town the Mogul's tender wheels climbed the rails and in an instant the engine jackknifed. Buttrick lay dead near the overturned engine. Dare came away with injuries he sustained when he was thrown out of the high side of the wreck. Fifty-year-old Buttrick was a family man and a veteran of the first train on KGB&W into Kewaunee in the 1890's. The line was cleared by 6 p.m. that day, along with the contents of a stock car — an 1800-pound bull. The big fellow was not at all happy to be tied to the wreck train's locomotive and slowly towed to Forestville to the safety of an empty boxcar.

In May of 1914, when an upsurge of business prevailed, the company launched the "Door County Special," complete with a pamphlet on "Wisconsin's Wonderland." The train made its first run June 14, 1914, leaving Green Bay at 10:00 a.m., into Algoma at 11:20 a.m. and Sturgeon Bay at 12:05 p.m. The service was coordinated with "twelve-passenger autos" which were run to all northern resorts on the peninsula. The new train returned, leaving Sturgeon Bay at 12:45 p.m. and arriving in Green Bay at 2:20 p.m. Pride in its railroad showing, the Algoma newspaper noted "the glitter and pomp of a solid Pullman train, with porters . . . Conductor Kiel, General Manager Seymour in a not too pleasant frame of mind. . ." were in attendance. Seymour's state of mind was due to a

Above: Sturgeon Bay's bridge often was the victim of collision-bound lake vessels. Here, on May 2, 1916, the steamer FLETCHER rammed the south approach but the swingspan was unscathed. STAN MAILER COLLECTION

hotbox which came to light at Algoma westbound, causing a 25-minute delay. Nevertheless, the train was pronounced a "dandy," with a smoker, day coach and a parlor car. Forty-five minutes were clipped from the old schedule on A&W. Some adjusting of schedule put the Special out ahead of the regular noon train, No.17. The newcomers were No.47-48.

Although the first service was "an expense to the company," the Special was again operated a year later. Departure time was rescheduled to 10:30 out of Green Bay, returning at 2:40 p.m. It was still touted as an asset in bringing Chicago and Milwaukee traffic to the tourist center in the north. Parlor car service was continued. Train No.14 left Green Bay at 3:15 p.m. and pulled into Sturgeon Bay at 5:35 p.m. It is probable that both trains were handled by engines No.31 and No.34 as regulars, with occasional assistance from GB&W's "20-class Standards."

Edward Decker, father of the Ahnapee & Western Railway, died in July 1914, nearly destitute. The Deckers (Edward Sr., sons Edward Jr., David B. and Nat) were involved in banking, land speculation, the Casco mill and A&W, plus various other supportive interests. After the turn of the century, the Deckers went into a Chicago bank, which drew on their assets in order to avert ruin. Decker creditors were Jay Morton (who inherited the Diamond Jo Reynolds fortune in Chicago) and the National Bank of the Republic, Chicago. In December 1902 David Decker asked the City of Sturgeon Bay for an option on its A&W stock in the amount of $320,000. Edward Decker also invested in Jackson National Bank of Chicago as a reserve for his "fleet" of Wisconsin banks.

The Jackson allegedly failed, taking the Decker empire down with it. When the old gentleman of Casco had asked his son Edward Jr. for assistance in his darkest hour, the son placed $100,000 on the senior's desk, all that he had. It was to no avail,

for the monetary outflow couldn't be stopped and the younger man was personally compromised as well. Deeply in arrears, Edward Jr. hit upon a melodramatic end to his situation. In April 1905 he boarded a Pere Marquette car ferry at Kewaunee, carefully placed his coat and shoes at the railing and disappeared. With appropriate headlines, the Kewaunee newspapers marked his passing, surely a suicide, as a major blow to the local business scene and the county's first family. Actually, the younger man had stolen away, resurfacing as a Christian Scientist in Los Angeles in the 1920's. Brother Nat had succumbed previously to typhoid fever at Ouray, Colorado after his health failed during the crisis. In 1914 David Decker put his family's affairs in order, moved to Michigan and later to Chicago. The Decker mill was dismantled the same year; thus, on the eve of World War I, all significant traces of the Deckers had disappeared.

The great family house stood in Casco until the 1940's where it was used as a rooming house and apartments in which several A&W railroaders resided.

After sale to GB&W, the Sturgeon Bay line became the main line, while secondary status was assigned to Kewaunee. In August of 1906 tangible evidence of the change was noticeable on A&W and KGB&W locomotives. To avoid confusion, Norwood Shops renumbered A&W engines to No.31 and No.33. KGB&W's next Raidler-designed super 4-4-0 rolled out in December of 1906. Scheduling of east end service had two trains out of Green Bay at 6:40 a.m. and 3:00 p.m., arriving in Sturgeon Bay at 9:50 a.m. and 6:00 p.m.; westbound trains left

Sturgeon Bay at 6:15 a.m. and 1:45 p.m., reaching Green Bay at 9:10 a.m. and 4:55 p.m. The afternoon train could thus make connections with the Grand Rapids service west on GB&W.

It was at this time that the Algoma freight was introduced, allowing passenger trains to graduate from mixed status. The freight left Green Bay at 6:50 a.m., arriving at Algoma at 10:25 a.m. The return trip departed at 12:40 p.m., arriving at Green Bay at 4:40 p.m. Provision was made to run the way freight as far as Maplewood if traffic required it and, by October 1906, the wye at Algoma was installed to accommodate the operation. In September 1906, after consolidation of KGB&W and A&W, two trains per day left Sturgeon Bay at 6:15 a.m. and 2:10 p.m. respectively; arrivals from Green Bay were 9:55 a.m. and 6:15 p.m., with some adjustments for the Sturgeon Bay layover. A&W's somewhat nondescript coach fleet went back to the parent road and newer equipment arrived from Hicks. *The Door County Advocate* was unimpressed, stating that running time was not improved and that "56 miles at average speed of 18 mph" was hardly noteworthy.

After pioneer days of logging ceased, A&W territory farmers tried various crops in the unstable north climate. Hay and peas were among the specialties and substantial crops of hay were directed by steamer to Chicago for that city's vast number of "hayburners." Next, a joint effort focused on peas and the region geared up to the task, with Kewaunee and Sturgeon Bay being the depot for much of the crop. Unfortunately, the pea louse came with damp conditions to Kewaunee and Door Counties and depressed the industry by 1909. Other attempts included fruit, a traffic for both railroad and Goodrich Liners until 1920. Reynolds Preserving Co., caught in the pea louse blight, turned to cherries, which became a major crop on the peninsula for several decades.

Goodrich boats held sway in the years before World War I. Even new boats such as the ALABAMA, built at Manitowoc, were put in service. In the summer of 1915 Kewaunee Grain Co. shipped 1250 bags of green peas to South America, which left in Goodrich holds, but it was one of the last such shipments out of the area. Goodrich boats came less frequently as a new competitor — the motor truck — gained popularity among shippers. Of

Below: New York photographer Mike Runey traveled to Sturgeon Bay in 1950 to photograph the short line A&W. He found Extra 260 West easing across the then-56-year-old swingspan. A&W's third decade was its busiest, showing short-lived promise of a good future.
H. D. (MIKE) RUNEY

interest is the fact that Goodrich's NEVADA, a two-year-old steamer, was sold to Imperial Russia in May of 1917 for a handsome price. That same year 120 lake vessels were commandeered by the government, 77 of which were cut in two to pass through the locks for war service. On the Green Bay side, the well-known FANNIE C. HART was sent to Florida in 1911. A&W's enemies grew old, only to be replaced by rubber tires and good roads. Ironically, as though biting the hand that once fed it, the steamer CITY OF MARQUETTE, which had become the property of the Hill Line, rammed the Sturgeon Bay swingspan, causing $100,000 damage. The aging vessel later loaded fish for Green Bay at the Albert C. Kalmbach dock near the A&W bridge.

With the onset of war in Europe, business in America emerged from a slump and A&W's fortunes were no exception. The road took delivery of the first of its two Moguls of ALCO class 260-S-139 in June of 1915. A&W also received an order of fifty 80,000-pound capacity boxcars from Haskell & Barker Car Co., the only order of cars to be supplied. Total cost was listed at $55,000 and the parent road also took delivery of 100 cars at this time of high demand. Mogul No.39 retained its number for only six years — all the 30-series numbers had been assigned. In 1921 A&W No.39 became No.71, clearing a slot for a new KGB&W No.39 purchased that year. In October 1922 a second 2-6-0, numbered 72, was delivered to A&W, its price tag reading $29,015. The pair of identical engines were to serve until the end of steam. A&W also received coach 86 from Central Locomotive and Car Works (the old Hicks works) in August 1914. The road had one other Hicks coach, new in March of 1909. It is clear that the teens on A&W constituted prosperous, expansive years in comparison with later times.

When war finally came to America, Door County saw its "Doughboys" off to training camps. Sturgeon Bay Battery "F" left in August of 1917 for Camp Douglas, Wisconsin. Five thousand people saw them off from the Sturgeon Bay depot at 6:15 a.m. They filled four coaches and two baggage cars. Algoma's group departed September 2, 1917, with disruptions in schedules. Another 33 with Belgian, Bohemian and German names embarked for Camp Custer, Michigan, the start of a long journey back to their ancestors' homes "over there."

Schedule changes were made the same year to accommodate C&NW and CM&STP service at Green Bay, the tourist lifeline to Chicago and Milwaukee. Train No.14 arrived in Sturgeon Bay at 6:45 p.m. with No.13 out at 6:15 a.m.; Train No.11 left the Bay at 1:45 p.m., while No.20 retained its arrival at 8:15 p.m. Sundays only. In August 1917 *The Door County Advocate* stated: "The A&W is enjoying the best business it has had since construction." A&W installed a sixty-foot turntable at Maplewood to turn the way freight locomotive in November 1917 but it was moved to Scandinavia in June 1921. The regular crew in 1918 was Engineer Russ Hollister and Conductor Richards, typically with engine No.39, the new Mogul. Other east enders included Messrs. Kuehl and Ward on No.11-12 and Harry Walker, conductor, and Steve Slattery, engineer, were usually found on No.13-14. Joe Ferris and Gus Mickelson also ran engines on the A&W.

Postwar industry required more train service in spite of motor truck competition. Two important industries came to Sturgeon Bay — Van Camp's Condensery and Reynolds Preserving Co., which would figure in the prosperity, or lack of it, in A&W's final years. Another was Fruit Grower's Co-op which reached a high point by 1928, requiring many new Western Refrigerator Line cars on GB&W Lines. Several of the local firms leased

Western cars, their names emblazoned lavishly on car sides.

A&W greeted the fall of 1920 with another derailment near Algoma. Conductor Maddy and Engineer Ferris were in charge of train No.14 when, just as it was clearing the Algoma Wye, put its tender and two of three coaches on the ground, tearing up 100 feet of track. The rear coach remained upright. Evidently, it was engine No.36 again which spread rails and dropped to the ties. Fortunately, the train was running slowly and the work extra crew arrived and rerailed the limited which made Sturgeon Bay at 2:30 a.m. Passengers had already come in via autos.

The year 1920 spelled the end for a veteran of over forty years of lakes service when wood steamer J. L. HURD was scrapped, giving up her boilers to landlocked service. One went to a local canning factory, the other went out on a special train, teetering slightly en route. The extra had considerable trouble averting a derailment under the bulky boiler. It was interchanged with Soo Line and shipped to Ladysmith's Flambeau Paper Co.

Competition in 1920 included Northern Transportation Co. The new truck line operated semi-trailers from Green Bay to Sturgeon Bay, making its first ominous run April 23, 1920. This action served to snuff out the remainder of Green Bay boat lines. Two decades later, A&W and GB&W were to enter the trucking field throughout their territories. Agitation grew for a concrete bridge at Sturgeon Bay to give motor carriers better access to the city, replacing the rail-highway crossing. This was finalized in 1931, freeing A&W to own the entire span. The toll system which had benefited the city's treasury was phased out, leaving the railroad in possession for the first time in 36 years.

A momentous ice storm in February 1922 closed the A&W between Algoma and Sturgeon Bay for four days. Forty men armed with pickaxes were required to open flangeways and free switches. The KGB&W was also iced over from Green Bay to Luxemburg, requiring the attention of hand labor. Wednesday's mail was received the following Monday morning. A party of five men from Sawyer got through after riding with section men to Luxemburg. They walked to Casco, hired a team of horses and rode to their homes.

Tourism was on a postwar rise and, in response, A&W announced sleeping car service would be inaugurated to Sturgeon Bay on June 23, 1923. Until September 3rd, the Pullman would arrive at 9:30 a.m., transferred from C&NW's train No.121, the service available on Fridays. On Sundays the car left at 5:20 p.m., arriving in Chicago on Mondays at 8:30 a.m. Tourists could travel north from Sturgeon Bay via Yellow Car and Transit Co.'s "Buick Special" service twice a day over a "smooth Macadam road" as far as Ephraim. For $3.00 the Buicks would take the traveler to the U.S. Mail boat landing at Ellison Bay on the tip of vacationland. By August 1926 business was booming. On Sunday the 26th no less than nine Pullmans

Top Right: In July 1952 A&W was on a three-day-week schedule. No.351 was often kept north of the bridge at Sturgeon Bay. Diesels joined A&W's fleet the next year.
E. WILKOMMEN PHOTO

Bottom Right: A&W's heaviest engine, No.261, switches in Sawyer on August 10, 1950. Built as KGB&W 45 in 1923, the Consolidation was renumbered 398 in May of 1937 and first ran on A&W on February 17, 1949. Too heavy for the line, No.261 made its last run on November 30, 1950 and was then sold to Michigan's Detroit, Caro & Sandusky Railroad.
W. J. HUSA JR. PHOTO

departed, handled by a doubleheader. Five Pullmans of regular tourists headed for Chicago were fully occupied, while another four carried summer camp children on "exclusive vacations" to points as far away as Cleveland, Ohio. Another run, the "Cherry Special," catered to the fruitpickers and a Luxemburg fair. Tourism helped to fill places such as Cabot's Lodge, west of Sturgeon Bay. The facility was operated by F. T. Cabot & Son and was advertised in GB&W's 1923 public timetable as a first-class resort.

Freight service was enhanced in late 1924 when A&W acquired its first and only caboose, purchased second-hand from Great Northern via Hyman-Michaels Co. The next year it received a steel underframe in accordance with new safety standards. Caboose 020, later renumbered 620, served the road for nearly fifty years. Three second-hand 2-8-0's came to GB&W lines in 1927. No. 74 was A&W but probably never ran on that road, contributing to main line power requirements instead. This purchase put four A&W engines on roster, the

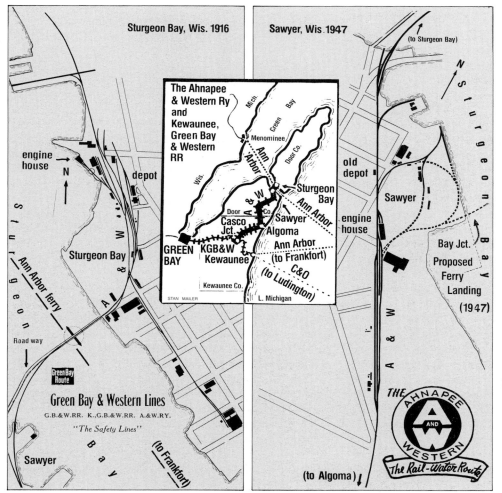

Above: Sturgeon Bay's Railroad Day in July 1894 required a maximum effort by the new railroad to cope with record crowds of passengers. Here, two 4-4-0's (separated to favor bridges) work a Green Bay-Sturgeon Bay special across the combination bridge. Sawyer can be seen in the distance in this southwest view.
A. T. SCOFIELD PHOTO / KRAUSS COLLECTION

Left: A&W's two northernmost towns were mapped in 1916, during the road's more prosperous era. The Sawyer map was revised in Ah&W times to depict the proposed Bay Junction ferry landing, the new company's great hope for increased business.
GB&W MAPS / REVISED BY STAN MAILER

most ever. Other improvements included new trackage to Fruit Grower's Co-op's dock. The expenditure request stated: "to intercept boat shipments of fruit now going to Marinette and Menominee." The Van Camp milk plant required 360 feet of track for its new trade of inbound shipments in the summer of 1926. Prosperity was surely ahead for the A&W. Clearly, Door County was becoming the proverbial land of milk and cherries, if not honey.

The dispatcher's sheet of August 1928 gives insight into A&W and GB&W operations during that busy month. A series of cherry extras was running. Bill Rude and "Roaring Ben" Billings, with engine No. 56 (GB&W Mogul), handled 22 loads of Door County cherries plus seven empties to the icing platforms of Wisconsin Rapids. On the 5th, Rushford and Erickson, with engine No. 51 (2-6-0), left Sturgeon Bay at 3:05 a.m. with seven loads and five empties, arriving at Green Bay at 6:45 a.m. Further adventures were ahead. They doubled back to Casco Junction, leaving Green Bay at 8:50 a.m. and went on to Kewaunee where they arrived at 12:05 p.m. At the ferry yard they picked up a cut of Ford autos (three loads and ten empties) and returned to Green Bay, finally making Sturgeon Bay at 4:30 p.m.

During the A&W's "Roaring Twenties" most A&W trains did not draw A&W locos, but had older GB&W/KGB&W engines. These were slide-valve, saturated steam Moguls (27-29, 36 and 37) while occasionally 71 or 72 would handle regular trains. Durable Baldwin 4-4-0 No. 31 handled passenger trains 11 and 12 up to the early 1930's. KGB&W 32, 34 and 35 (4-4-0's) worked during the Great Depression, sidelined only when enough superheated 2-6-0's were available to cover east end assignments.

Some of the August trains included sleepers Holden, Amargosa, Ogdensburg and Cabazon, which handled organized groups of cherry pickers to Door County. One hundred thirty-eight girls of the Boyce pickers were carried and another 105 of the Goldman group. Camp Wildwood required sleepers Grand Crossing and Halcyon to be picked up from the Northwestern at McDonald's, a freight interchange in Green Bay. Dispatcher H. C. Erbe specified "R" class engines for train No. 12 (Moguls were R class) to cover Labor Day traffic. In October 1928 GB&W stalwart 4-4-0 No. 18 handled trains 11 and 12, plus a trip on No. 16 which had to "double the hill" to Summit and Casco Junction. It then ran to Kewaunee light and assisted a freight (No. 25) west from the ferry landing. Freight trains managed to get in the way of passenger trains, especially when No. 13 was delayed, because No. 15 ahead stalled on Luxemburg Hill. It took No. 15 an hour and 15 minutes to make the four miles of upgrade with GB&W Mogul No. 51 pulling 19 loads and eight empties. A few days later, GB&W engine 25 broke a spring hanger at Algoma, fouling the reverse lever. The hapless old main liner had to limp in "light engine" to Green Bay.

Luxemburg Hill required more than a few assists by the conveniently located junior train crew. The crew and engine of train No. 16 gave No. 15 another lift out of Casco Junction and up Luxemburg Hill. The train included five cars of autos for Green Bay. A regular occurrence was the doubling of the Summit hill just east of Green Bay. An example was June 13, 1929 when engine 28 took a total of 23 loads and nine empties up and onto the flats east of Green Bay.

The Depression years fell heavily upon the A&W. Tourism declined to a minimum, shipments fell off and the branch was down to a mixed (No. 13-14) and a passenger (No. 11-12). Rio Creek lost its freight depot, although the passenger section handled general trade until 1943. In January 1935 the mail contract was lost and trains 11 and 12 went to mixed status, eventually becoming 34 and 35. Sturgeon Bay estimated the loss at $30,000 a year. Some 15 families were displaced. A&W complied with requests for mail delivery by 7:00 a.m. in Sturgeon Bay, only to lose their passenger trade due to 4:00 a.m. departure time. Cherryland Bus Co. reigned for the balance of the decade, taking a more direct highway route. The shippers of perishables failed in their efforts to hold onto a full and pure passenger service.

In April 1937 a GB&W yard engine still handled No. 34's combination car from the depot to Norwood Yard and a waiting and modest cut of cars, the central reason for departure. It followed the Kewaunee mixed No. 30, which went out in the same fashion, at 6:05 a.m. No. 35's crew was required to return the combination car to the depot in Green Bay, but the Kewaunee mixed unloaded its express via the Kewaunee Wye access road at Norwood. This signaled that the patronage was not overwhelming for No. 31, which was also a doomed affair.

The official end came and, as of July 4th, 1937, east end trains no longer handled passengers. Trains 30 and 34 were scheduled to depart from Norwood as freight-only assignments but on June 29th Superintendent E. V. Johnson issued a bulletin which momentarily put the old days back into effect: No. 34 would once again handle weekend sleepers from C&NW's train 121. The sleeper would be delivered to GB&W at Green Bay Junction on Saturdays, handled with dispatch to Sturgeon Bay without stops but with freight cars, for a 7:00 a.m. arrival. No. 34 would leave at 4:30 a.m. to accommodate the Pullman passengers once again. Freight work was westbound only, when the crew returned without the sleeper to Green Bay. On Sundays, an extra left Green Bay at 2:00 p.m. with available Sturgeon Bay tonnage to handle the Pullman's return trip. It left at 10:00 p.m., arriving at 12:10 a.m., and making delivery to C&NW at McDonald's for train No. 162. The schedule was to remain through September 6th.

With the slowdown of prewar conditions, the Sturgeon Bay enginehouse was razed, along with an icehouse which supplied the A&W. Maplewood became the most northerly train order station but registry remained in the larger city. Traffic rose with the declaration of war but profitability did not. On the surface the wartime bustle hid reality, a reality which was to determine GB&W's course of action for A&W in the future, spelling abandonment or sale.

As early as 1944 private and public interests in Sturgeon Bay campaigned to stay any abandonment attempts and to increase service. The person mainly responsible for this action was Sturgeon Bay native Vernon M. Bushman, president of the Bushman Dock & Terminal Co., just one of his endeavors. The terminal was the site of the Bushman Milling Co. years before, but in wartime it became a coal yard. Bushman had spent 15 years in Pere Marquette's rate department in addition to his time spent on C&NW and GB&W. Brother Erwin F. Bushman served his entire career with A&W at Sturgeon Bay. Vernon Bushman took up agitation for a new scenario with GB&W. He claimed that A&W had shown regular and substantial losses since 1940 and that interests in the city offered to purchase A&W for $55,000 free of encumbrance.

A&W's prospective buyers intended to turn nonprofitability around by conducting a heavy coal and pulpwood business out of Sturgeon Bay, challenging the Port of Green Bay itself. The new A&W would have competed with GB&W's rates beyond Green Bay, a possibility which GB&W took into account.

Right: This photo shows the interior of the Casco, Wisconsin station about 1915. At left is J. H. Koss; Agent John Kinnard is on the right.
KEWAUNEE COUNTY
HISTORICAL SOCIETY

Meanwhile, trains 11 and 12, originally old No.34-35, could still plod along A&W at thirty miles per hour over the light rail but were restricted on the swingspan to less than ten miles per hour. The aging structure whose approaches were scarred from ship collisions continued to be repaired again and again. Always the thread that held the A&W together, the 1894 bridge never had shown the road long moments of tranquillity.

GB&W counter-offered a price of $100,000 in June of 1944. By the end of 1946 Bushman's firm was claiming that GB&W carried the entire capital stock of $439,500 at a value of $1.00, that A&W first-mortgage bonds were GB&W's property as of October 30, 1939 and that GB&W carried A&W as a $90,979 investment. As a condition of purchase the new firm would form a corporation with paid-in capital of $25,000 to buy A&W securities and that all bills payable in past operations would be the assumption of GB&W. Interline accounting was to be done by KGB&W. On April 30, 1947 the directors of the new company settled the finances and GB&W retired. V. M. Bushman was chairman of the board and president, M. W. Kwapil of Algoma was vice-president and F. W. Trowbridge was director. As if to salute the accession with a flourish, Ann Arbor car ferry No.3 plunged into the Sturgeon Bay swingspan's west approach piling, the first collision in a year. The bridge was out of action for a week, requiring trucks to bring A&W's shipments across the water.

On the morning of June 1st, 1947 the great change was bulletined for the GB&W employee's benefit. The Ahnapee & Western Railway company, now a brave new venture, began with its headquarters in the Gordon Bent Building, 127 Main Street, Green Bay and its operational headquarters located in Sturgeon Bay. Employees from GB&W were invited to transfer to the new company, their rights protected in event of a compromised outcome. E. B. Nancarrow became chief engineer, Max M. Martens, auditor, and E. F. Bushman, executive vice-president. After adjustments over several months, Francis Reynard and Herb Holschuh became enginemen and Jim Roubal, M. O. Warren and Bob Ruby became trainmen.

Rolling stock assets of A&W, hereafter to be the Ah&W, included the two faithful Moguls 259 and 260. Both had received "Kirkby modernization" in 1941 and 1943, which included power reverse, foot warmers, steel pilot and pilot beam, Alemite rod fittings and renewed electrical equipment. They arrived without GB&W bolt-on heralds, along with A&W coach 84 (a fifty-foot open platform relic) and caboose 620, rebuilt in 1942 from old 020. Only the caboose and Mogul 259 received the newly designed "A&W — The Rail-Water Route" heralds in yellow and green. Coach 84 was sidetracked, never having a true assignment (observers thought it would be the business car) and acted as a "bookend" on the Evangeline Milk Co.'s siding. Somewhat the worse for wear, the car was rented to an architect, finally winding up in a Sawyer quarry. Casco Junction received an agreed-upon run-around track plus a wye to turn the Moguls. In its second year war was declared on territory trucks and Ah&W purchased two Diamond-T units to fight fire with fire.

The Summer of 1947 brought with it another plan which had far-reaching consequences for both Ann Arbor and GB&W. Ah&W's Bushman had concocted a scheme to create a junction with Ann Arbor at Sawyer. The plan had some innovative strong points which included a second interchange and a goal of increased rate divisions. That summer Green Bay engineers of the Foth & Porath Co. produced estimates for a ferry slip and apron. The drawings were completed by September and a tenacious plan was activated to make the short line a more competitive and viable investment for its new owners and a thorn in the side of established gateways in the region.

September of the first year brought a sharp dispute with GB&W over rebilling at Casco Junction. The case was carried to ICC in Washington. GB&W had refused to deliver loads and billing, claiming that Ah&W refused to honor drafts for interline settlements. GB&W issued its Embargo No.2 of September 23, 1947, requiring prepaid shipments. Waybills were taken up and accounted for at Casco Junction and rebilled to Ah&W. Ah&W countered that the action was restraint of trade which delayed car movements. The matter was settled in accordance with established rules. On October 8th the commission canceled GB&W's embargo; from then on sight drafts were to be honored and cars were to be delivered. The action was only one of many differences which erupted in the Ah&W's 25-year separation from GB&W. Ah&W also attempted to change its status from a Class I to a Class II railroad, thus cutting labor costs and creating more resistance. It happened during the road's busiest years in which crews worked six-day weeks. A heavy sugar beet business centered at Forestville grew in the fall with loads headed for Menominee and Green Bay. Hardwood logs contributed to carloads that were barged from Washington Island to Sturgeon Bay's railhead. The potato harvest which accounted for many more carloads, as did malt barley, today are only distant memories of commerce in Door County.

The struggle for a car ferry slip at Bay Junction intensified in Sturgeon Bay. Planned for Bushman Dock & Terminal Co.'s land, arrangements were made to mortgage the property of the railroad to cover installation costs estimated at $237,026. Ah&W reasoned that Ann Arbor would be required to call at Bay Junction if it was established as an interchange and the Michigan road made a point of refusing to do so. The ferry

On the way to dieselization, Ah&W bought two more ex-GB&W steam locomotives, both 2-8-0's. KGB&W 398 was available after retirement in late 1948 and Mogul 259 was out of service July 31, 1949. No. 398, which was renumbered 261 by Ah&W upon purchase, was found to be too heavy for the aging ties and light rail and derailed on several occasions. The big engine was eastbound with a train one night when a portion of the consist derailed. Such was the comparative power of the new arrival that only when the air was pulled did Engineer Reynard become aware of the catastrophe. No. 261 left the road sometime after December 1, 1950, being sold to Michigan's Detroit, Caro & Sandusky Railroad which didn't fare any better with the 100-ton engine. DC&S apparently only ran it twice. After DC&S abandoned operations July 31, 1953, 261's tender was used as a track removal car.

In the fall of 1950 GB&W offered both of its C-38 class Consolidations for sale. They had last been used that spring on work extras. Ah&W bought No. 351 on November 15, 1950 for

Above: A&W's first Algoma depot served both the steamer trade and the railroad. In this rare view KGB&W engine 34 has backed the mixed train to the waterfront which also served Goodrich Line boats. Ahnapee became Algoma in 1899. The depot was replaced and the dock removed after World War I. STAN MAILER COLLECTION

line was then placed in a defensive posture with much weight in favor of the connection locally. Ah&W claimed that its present situation was disadvantaged, that its region was economically blighted by such action, having to rely upon only one junction. Ah&W's lawyer reasoned that Ann Arbor's ferry business would be increased by the Bay Junction interchange. Without the connection the interchange could not perform its role, thereby impairing commerce. If the slip was installed Ah&W stood to increase its revenues with a better trunk line division, competing directly with KGB&W's Kewaunee-Casco Junction line. This short connection was a significant source of revenue for GB&W.

The new gateway was a potential stand-in and its opponents were well aware of it. The lengthy struggle by Ah&W lasted from 1948 through 1960 with three complaints in all. Ah&W lost the first round but appealed the case to division three in May 1960, winning an order for Ann Arbor to stop at Sawyer. Ann Arbor then went before a full ICC session and succeeded in heading off the order to put in to Door County.

$6000. The 1929 2-8-0 was the final steam purchase for the road, going into service December 8, 1950. As if to flaunt short line individuality, 351's tender was repainted bright red with yellow trim, advising all to "Route Your Freight Via Ahnapee & Western Railway, The Rail-Water Route." The blurb was clearly in response to the battle of Bay Junction, then raging about the trim engine. No. 351 bore Ah&W's duties for the balance of steam operations and it became progressively dirtier, spending most of its time stored outdoors until dieselization. Mogul 260 alternated with the bigger brother until February of 1952, then running only seven days in fall.

It was 260 which made the solemn march to Casco Junction the night of February 8, 1953 to pick up new diesels 600 and 601. The General Electric seventy-tonners had come via the contested Kewaunee gateway which was to prevail over Bay Junction's supposed economy, delivered by the same night Kewaunee freight which would always deliver Ah&W interchange cars.

One argument had won Ah&W its backing in the beginning: that a railroad into on-line towns would tend to anchor existing non-rail freight rates. This aided the small business found in Door County. Eventually the old saw about providing service versus providing carloads worked to the road's misfortune. By the early 1960's trains ran only three times a week, a factor which encouraged more trucking and magnified costs. Train speeds dipped to ten miles per hour, deferred maintenance the ruling factor. Finally the loss of key shipper Evangeline Milk Co. in Sturgeon Bay by the mid-1960's tipped the scales badly against the north end and the linchpin of Ah&W's eastside business, the bridge, became its downfall.

Inspection of the 72-year old swingspan, a regular and necessary occurrence, uncovered deterioration in floor system

Rehabilitation would have equaled the cost of a new bridge and, as a result, the line was embargoed August 8, 1968. Abandonment proceedings had been filed May 27, 1968, covering 18.65 miles of line from the Algoma Wye to Sturgeon Bay which was responsible for at least 58 percent of Ah&W's losses over the past several years. With most of its customers on the bridge's far side, traffic had dwindled to a daily average of 2.6 cars inbound and 1.2 cars outbound. ICC reached the conclusion that the financial picture could not be improved by merely reopening the bridge. Ah&W's service was "commensurate with the volume of traffic offered it." Together with other needed repairs to the line itself this opinion spelled the end for the northern portion.

Counteractions by east side shippers resulted in an option to purchase the embargoed portion but it expired 120 days later without action. ICC's safety bureau engineer pronounced the bridge unsafe when the abandonment's legality was questioned and the embargo assailed. City and state and ICC and railroad company steadily revolved around one another. The railroad's management made plans in September 1967 to sell the road without the north end to U.S.Plywood-Champion Papers, Inc.

Left: Brave New Railroad: Ah&W's two stalwart Moguls 260 and 259 pause to backstop well-wishers, officers and employees at Casco Junction, Wisconsin, just after the June 1, 1947 sale by GB&W.
Ah&W COLLECTION

girders. Unless $83,000 could be raised for repairs, the structure woule have to be abandoned. Bushman's company offered the bridge to the city for $1.00, exactly the figure of the 1931 sale. The object was to place the responsibility on the shippers and the city, both of which objected to abandonment proceedings. The old structure was the center of controversy, but little was done except cursory repairs. The deed did not stress repair, which was necessary by July 19, 1966, the date of the sale. On June 14, 1967 the scow CHEROKEE collided with the bridge. The damage was only lightly repaired and trucks once again streamed into Sturgeon Bay with the lost shipments.

A federal order to inspect all rail and highway bridges was issued after a highway bridge collapsed in May 1968 and Ah&W hired Roen Salvage Co. to inspect the entire bridge. The Roen firm called for immediate action at eight points, five on the trestle and three on the swingspan. It also recommended that a weight embargo (180,000 pounds) and a speed restriction of five miles per hour be imposed (by a GB&W engineer) and that Wisconsin Bridge & Iron Co. be retained to inspect the steel portion. WB&ICo.'s inspection sounded the final round. It recommended that the bridge be "closed to further rail traffic."

which owned the mill at Algoma. A three-man crew operated the road until the last days of 1972.

Just after the embargo of the bridge, a borrowed Trackmobile removed the last east side empties, making up the final train south. They tied up at Algoma that night, leaving one of the diesels isolated in Sawyer's quonset hut. When Hyman-Michaels Co. representative Don Starr came to inspect the line for removal a year later he received a free and final ride down to Algoma September 4, 1969. A full year after the last revenue trip, the little green, brown and orange diesel picked its way south through deep weeds, exiting Door County forever and carrying Vern Bushman away from his city by the bay.

On December 31, 1970, Ah&W was sold to California's McCloud River Railroad, a division of U.S. Plywood-Champion Papers, Inc., which continued the Algoma-Casco Junction operation. The Green Bay staff moved to Algoma where the small depot acted as headquarters. A metal enginehouse was acquired and the locomotives were repainted orange and white. Finally, No. 601 was transferred to the Moscow, Camden & San Augustine Railroad at Camden, Texas. In the fall of 1972 No.600 was sold to a Mexican operation and a train-

146

HERB REYNOLDS PHOTO

GB&W 351 was purchased to replace engine 261. It sported a red-and-yellow paint job on the tender and made its first run on December 8, 1950.

rental agreement followed with GB&W which was employed to upgrade the line the following year. Further retrenchment occurred when Champion International (the owning company's new name) closed the Algoma plant, which in 1975 had generated 1062 carloads. Yet another attempt was made to keep the plant open as Algoma Hardwoods continued the traditional work on site.

In April 1977 Itel acquired control of McCloud River Railroad and Ah&W as a direct result. ICC ordered Ah&W to issue stock as newly incorporated in Wisconsin, owned by McCRRR and controlled by Itel. The latter had acquired GB&W October 12, 1978 and the remaining 13.75-mile stub of Ah&W again became part of GB&W, completing a cycle of events. This arrangement continued, although traffic was far from lively, until the spring of 1986, when some minor damage occurred to

the Kewaunee River bridge abutment from a washout. The last train to Algoma operated March 25, 1986, in the form of Extra 323 East, GB&W's lone C-420 ALCO, on the short line from 9:10 a.m. to 1:00 p.m. The crew was Conductor Bowden, Brakemen Van Pay and P. Schultz, Engineer Scanlan and Helper Milquet. After the washout a car department Trackmobile removed stored and empty cars from the Algoma Branch in a repeat of the 1968 action at Sturgeon Bay.

The A&W as of this writing lies dormant, awaiting the inevitable. Perhaps the line will join its northern half in becoming another Ahnapee Trail segment and hikers can consider the furious winters and the labor which was needed to unburden the line in its "good old days." There are spirits afoot no doubt who would care to avoid such endeavors for an eternity.

CHAN HARRIS/"DOOR COUNTY ADVOCATE"

Right: A full year afer abandonment, the last run was made on September 3, 1969 to remove seventy-tonner No. 600 from the quonset hut enginehouse in Sawyer. Pictured left to right are: Don Starr, Hyman-Michaels Co. representative, Jim Roubal of A&W, and A&W President Vernon Bushman.

10

I & N

DEPOT, IOLA, WIS. NO. 5.

Left: Last stand of a veteran. Raidler 4-4-0 No. 11 was assigned to the Iola branch train in 1927. Formerly a passenger engine, the rebuilt Dickson was cut up in 1934.
R. BUTTOLPH PHOTO

An attempt to expand the Green Bay route's empire in difficult times produced a short branch to Iola in Waupaca County, sixty miles west of Green Bay. Iola & Northern Railroad Company was formed in May of 1893 and it was chartered to operate from Scandinavia northwest through Waupaca, Portage, Marathon, Lincoln, Taylor and Price Counties. The project included a connection with the Soo Line, 100 miles from Scandinavia, plus another link with a speculative Prentice-Superior route. Most significant and often overlooked was the fact that the I&N would cross the Wisconsin River valley at Merrill or Wausau and both cities were receptive to new and competitive rail services.

A partial survey made in 1892 billed I&N as a line "through almost unbroken timberlands" northwest of Wausau. The route very probably followed the valley of the New Wood River, later accomplished by a Milwaukee branch built in 1914. Capital stock of I&N was fixed at $1,700,000. Principals were New Yorkers Joseph Walker Jr. and B. A. Hegeman, former general freight agent for DL&WRR, Frank B. Seymour, Seth Champion and W. J. Abrams of Green Bay. Each held five shares at the outset. Initial aid was voted by Iola ($10,000), with balance of expense carried by the Walker brokerage firm. The total cost to construct and equip the road was $37,855.71.

GBWSTP Manager Seth Champion wrote to George Dale of Iola that work was to begin on the I&N May 12, 1893. A cash deposit made April 24th by 39 of Iola's citizens guaranteed a specific sum by responsible parties. Champion wanted a certificate of deposit payable to I&N's order when rails were laid. He received a telegram in late April from Dale, stating the $10,000

guarantee for I&N had been deposited with the National Bank of Waupaca, allowing the new company to begin surveying a route. Champion was anxious to arrange for rails with Illinois Steel Co. and asked Walker to confirm his cash situation, which was necessary to expedite negotiations for rail and supplies. The August 1st deadline was evidently a little close for comfort in obtaining needed Iola aid.

In another letter to Walker on the 16th, Champion said that contracts would be let that week and requested a bankdraw up to $10,000. Evidently one subscriber backed out on his I&N commitment, reducing the available funds to only $10,000. Champion went to the village on the 17th to oversee construction bids. He was interested in having McIntosh Brothers, a Milwaukee firm, build the line. They were dependable and capable of making the August deadline. McIntosh took the work, claiming that it would give employment to their workers, but they had an eye on the planned extension to Galloway's Camp as a probable reward for their diligence. The 15 miles from Iola to Galloway's Camp would constitute the second section of I&N, which would require 1000 tons of sixty-pound steel and fastenings for $10,000. Steel was on hand for the Iola portion and the manager was confident they could raise aid to grade and tie north of Iola. He indicated that any money left over from construction into Iola would pay for incidental fencing, laying steel and ballasting north of the town. Money matters were close but Champion was sure that the extension northwestward would be a real feeder for the Green Bay route.

Arranging work with McIntosh Brothers, Champion confirmed prices in a letter of May 18th: earth work, 19 cents per

Left: I&N engine No. 2, an 1875 Danforth product, is posed here at the Iola depot about 1910. The engine is headed west to run the four miles to Scandinavia.

Right: This is another view of engine No. 11 at Iola in 1927.
R. BUTTOLPH PHOTO

Above: After W-GB Ry. was built, the morning scene was busier at Scandinavia. Train No. 1 occupied the main line with Raidler 4-4-0 No. 12 on the head-end. I&N's connection arrived on the north track (left), while the W-GB connection was south (right) of the depot. The photo was taken about 1910.

Below: This photo shows Scandinavia and GB&W train No. 1. The foreground track was the Iola lead, running behind the camera to the west.

Below: Engineer Lem LaHaie oils around his stout Mogul 258 prior to a trip to Iola from Scandinavia. Service was available between Waupaca, Scandinavia and Iola via the combination car. Ironically, both 258 and combine 60 are KGB&W assets. This photo was taken in August of 1938.

Above: In this westward view, I&N engine No.2 and coach No.1 are at Scandinavia after arriving from Iola.
D. WATSON COLLECTION

ROY CAMPBELL PHOTO

yard; clearing of stations, $6; grubbing per rod, $1; loose rock, 50 cents, and solid rock, $1. By May 20th most of the right-of-way through Scandinavia had been purchased and the grading, scheduled to begin the following week, was to be completed by July 15th, leaving only two weeks to lay ties and rail before the completion date.

The financial reverses of 1893 and the plight of GBWSTP were of prime concern and Joseph Walker wanted assurances that I&N activities would not interfere with main line affairs. Walker received notice May 19th that at least $5000 should be made available to pay for ties, etc., and was to be deposited with the broker. Extension toward Galloway's Camp wasn't possible unless rails and fastenings were assured. Walker indicated that the Lackawanna didn't support the I&N scheme, something the projectors wished they did. The contractor would be paid in full upon completion to Iola and any small bills would receive prompt payment. All money subscribed would be needed by July 15th.

Significantly, Champion received a letter from the Merrill Advancement Association, stating advantages of passing through that city. Another came from W. H. Mylrea, industrial agent at Wausau, asking to meet with I&N's officials. Champion indicated that 1894 would be a satisfactory time to decide on a route through the Wisconsin Valley. Mylrea, a lawyer, was appointed industrial commissioner in January 1893 to induce manufacturing and other business to locate in Wausau. All were sure that the city in the valley was on the verge of a boom. Later W. H. Mylrea became attorney general and in 1919 his son Jack purchased the narrow gauge Robbins Railroad at Rhinelander.

One of the supply contracts for ties was taken by Samuel Perry of Door County. Thirty carloads were shipped from Ahnapee & Western territory to the I&N construction site. There is no indication that Illinois Steel Co. supplied rail to the new line. The matter was settled in favor of used rail, the source of which is unknown.

Iola's depot was an immediate addition of 20×56-foot dimensions. A survivor of the railroad, today it serves Iola as a museum. Service to Iola began July 16, 1893 and the new short line received its engine No.1, a former GBWSTP 4-4-0. The Grant-built engine was an 1872-vintage 37-ton survivor, similar in design to the engine sold to A&WRy, save for reconditioned dome casings. No.1 came without air brakes, suggesting frugal conditions on GBWSTP. I&N in turn was a level railroad and up-to-date brake systems could be postponed to better times. In

Above: This GB&W freight train was westbound from Scandinavia about 1898 with Schenectady 4-4-0 No.20 (1891). Little Wolf Creek, shown here, runs through a concrete culvert today.
D. WATSON COLLECTION

November of 1903, No.1 was exchanged for No.2, which was an 1875 Danforth veteran with a clouded history. It was returned with the entire railroad to GB&W in 1915 and renumbered second No.7, lasting until 1924. The engine saw brief service on the Ettrick & Northern Railroad during its construction days.

An ancient combination car of great durability came from the main line, serving I&N for all of its corporate life. Apparently an Ohio Falls product of June 1889, it measured 40 feet 1½ inches over sills and remained in operation on the Iola assignment until the 1930's. After a decade as a B&B car it later served as the New Franken, Wisconsin depot. To this day, at nearly 100 years old, it survives in a lonely field south of that village.

The Iola branch had potatoes, the Wipf Flour Mill, forest products and general merchandise traffic. Iola's potato commerce rivaled Waupaca's, 15 miles to the south. Early methods of shipment employed individuals who would tend an

Below: Iola & Northern Railroad's Iola's station in 1893. The Grant 4-4-0, built in 1873, was originally No.4 on the main line.
O. PARKS PHOTO

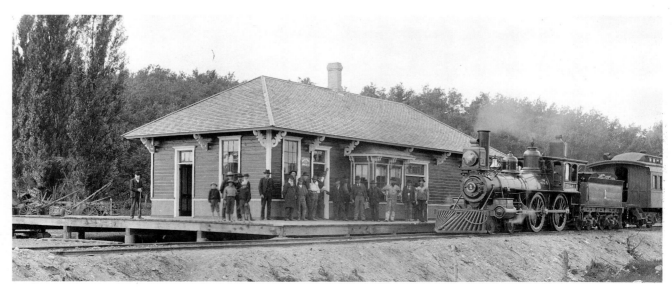

With the depressed 1930's, GB&W combined the Waupaca and Iola branch runs, retiring the ancient baggage coach No. 1 (above). At left, 4-4-0 No. 23 and KGB&W car 74 constitute Train 42. It is shown here ready to leave Scandinavia at 12:50 p.m. on November 10, 1937.

improvised car heater en route to Chicago's produce terminals. The rider would then return via passenger train to repeat the process. Potatoes became important traffic again in World War II. Large quantities of "spuds" arrived and departed from Iola, a sorting station for crops as far away as the Red River valley in North Dakota and Minnesota.

Operations consisted of up to four runs a day in the 1920's, depending on traffic demand. In the 1920's a special agreement was made to allow for a four-man crew but no more than four cars were handled in any given train. There was an enginehouse and basic coaling station, much the same as Waupaca, and a sixty-foot turntable. The Scandinavia turntable was operational though the 1930's but was removed by the spring of 1942. Iola's enginehouse, long unused, was razed by 1941. On July 8, 1938, a GB&W bulletin covered a change in crew assignment, revising mixed-train service to a six-day work week. The task remained the same in terms of passenger service offered, but emphasized way-freight work between Scandinavia and New London. The point was that Iola runs would be annulled and thereby loads could be consolidated for pick-up by main liners numbers 31 and 33 at New London. This was in the days of egg-loading at Manawa and provisions were made to deliver loaded and iced egg reefers to No.2's train.

I&N continued as a separate entity until GB&W was able to absorb it in 1914. GB&W's reorganization committee acquired the outstanding securities of the I&N, which were turned over to the main line in June 1907. A book value of $714 was placed on capital stock and $300 on construction certificates. New assets amounted to $18,737.74. On December 28, 1914 I&N was finally brought into GB&W's organization. Thus, a speculative venture launched by GBWSTP officers toward the Wisconsin Valley came to rest far short of its destination. While GB&W proved a big success when completed, I&N never reached its finished 100-mile form. However, it was able to survive and supply modest traffic to the main line.

The Iola line outlasted its southern neighbor to Waupaca by nearly ten years. While diesels never ran to Waupaca, Iola's line survived into a time of ALCO road switchers, chime horns and the regular way-freight's diversion (train No.8) from the main line. Interest in abandonment began with the decline of traffic in 1949, although a serious attempt was made to tear it out in 1935. The picture in 1956 showed that only 97 cars were handled on the branch the first six months. The final run to Iola on May 3rd took away several carloads of company materials. GB&W applied for permission to abandon operations in August of 1956 but abandonment did not go into effect until June 1, 1958.

Right: The Iola combine spent its last days in a field near New Franken, Wisconsin. The car served as a depot from August 1936 in New Franken and was later a rod-and-gun clubhouse. It is seen here in August of 1973.

STAN MAILER PHOTO

11

ON THE
FAR SIDE

The roots of the Ann Arbor Railroad pushed into Michigan soil in 1839 just after the Michigan Central completed its line through Ann Arbor. The question of overly high rates rose up to cloud the MC's progress and Ann Arbor citizenry discussed a north-south alternative. Not until August 1869 did the city activate a road southward to the state line. Grading began in the spring of 1872, but track was not laid before the economic panic in September 1873 halted Toledo & Ann Arbor Railroad entirely.

A second portion of the plan was the Toledo & State Line Railroad. It was completed from a connection with the Pennsylvania Railroad five miles to a second junction with LS&MS and MC lines through Alexis, Ohio. After the recession of the mid-1870's, Governor James M. Ashley, ex-congressman, politico and former Montana Territory executive, was the personality responsible for construction. Ashley had returned to Toledo after delving in politics and, with no vocation open to him, decided to enter the railroad field. A giant of a man, Ashley's two sons, James Jr. and Henry W. Ashley, were well over six feet as well. The trio continued with the road into the 1890's and were responsible for the innovation of the cross-lake ferries. During the 1877 winter Ashley had a road completed between Alexis (state line) and Ann Arbor, his first freight train arriving in Ann Arbor June 21, 1878. An inaugurating passenger train pulled in shortly thereafter. T&AA connected Toledo with other east-west lines, bringing another line to the college town. T&AA had three locomotives, six coaches and 31 freight cars.

The road's name reflected new ambitious plans, for it was soon changed to Toledo, Ann Arbor and Grand Trunk Railway. The scheme was to connect with Detroit, Lansing & Northern RR at South Lyon and Chicago & Grand Trunk at Pontiac. By 1884 the Grand Trunk possessed the South Lyon-Pontiac section as part of its line to Jackson. Finally, Toledo, Ann Arbor & North Michigan Railway came into being by a revision of the planned northeast line, changing it to a northwesterly heading through the center of Michigan. TAA&NM lasted as the road's name from 1884 to 1895. A blizzard of construction company names appeared for various sections, but the heavy building work took place between 1884 and 1889. The line was extended to Durand, Mount Pleasant, Cadillac and eventually to Copemish in Benzie County. The final lap into Frankfort was a logging road, Frankfort & Southeastern. In 1892 the TAA&NM purchased F&S to begin ferry and break-bulk service to Kewaunee.

In 1890 TAA&NM had 36 locomotives, 24 coaches and more than one thousand freight cars. Business had steadily increased, its passenger service carrying over 281,000 patrons. Service to Copemish included daily trains out of each end of the road,

Above: TAA&NM met the F&SE at Copemish where a basic enginehouse and coaling station were located. Engine 5 (Rogers 1886) and 26 (Pittsburgh 1884) represent original power of the first decade of service to Frankfort.
MICHIGAN HISTORICAL COLLECTION

Below: Here, the Frankfort ferry terminal is shown with the Hotel Frontenac in the distance. No.3 boat was outward bound for Lake Michigan from Lake Betsy. The hotel burned in 1912, negating some of AA's summer passenger trade.
MICHIGAN HISTORICAL COLLECTION

while Toledo-Clare business was covered by an afternoon train with a morning counterpart. TAA&NM handled 941,000 tons of freight that year but traffic ebbed during the several years following. TAA&NM in general had some steep, hilly railroading north of Cadillac and, with the original alignment, one four-percent grade at Boon. The Huron River bridge at Ann Arbor remained the road's major overpass. It was built on a four-degree, thirty-minute curve and was upgraded to a steel structure at the same time the car ferry service started.

The car ferry terminals at Kewaunee and Frankfort were operational by April of 1892 and arrangements for a branch track into Elberta (south side of Lake Betsie) were finalized. Rights were secured through the defunct Frankfort Furnace, a property partially owned by Eber Ward of Detroit. A Mr. E. G. Chambers owned land between the location of the ferry slips and the old charcoal furnace belonging to Ward. Chambers sought to block the coming of the road through his summer home property. It took a small railroad war to stop Chamber's attempt to prevent a line to the new slips, but in the late summer the Benzie County community awaited the arrival of the car ferries from Toledo. Completion of the line called for a shop location at a central point and Owosso, Michigan became the mechanical home of the Ann Arbor. Included were locomotive, car and related trades and Owosso grew up around its new industry with AA men investing in land and housing in the city. Consolidation of the shops was concurrent with Ashley's mortgage of the several incorporations, car ferries and harbor installations to Farmer's Loan & Trust Co. The 1889 Annual Report listed officers as James M. Ashley, president; A. W. Wright, first vice-president; Henry W. Ashley, second vice-president and general manager; G. B. Parks, auditor; C. F. Cook, secretary, and B. F. Jervis, treasurer.

The strike by Ann Arbor's Brotherhood of Locomotive Engineers over the question of closed shop sovereignty brought on the action which led to default by the TAA&NM. The road's receiver, Wellington R. Burt, the "Saginaw Salt King," was also Henry Ashley's father-in-law. In May of 1893 Burt had deposited his bond as receiver. The interest, due May 1st, amounted to $65,000. Craig Ship Builders Co. payments were also in arrears approximately $135,000. Reportedly, $125,000 was also due to President Ashley. At a meeting of TAA&NM security holders in Joseph Walker's New York office, an attempt was made to raise $300,000 for the road, at which time word was spread that a receiver had been appointed. A newspaper report linked Burt with the easterners in a sense, for it claimed the salt man was a DL&W stockholder.

In the years following the Ann Arbor was upgraded considerably from its promoter railroad beginnings. A reduction in ruling grades north and southbound to one percent and elimination of the four-percent Boon-Harriet hill were among the improvements. Ashley, once claiming the steam shovel a devilish piece of machinery, assented after the 1890's, stating that such improvements were required for a modern road. Ballasting and relocating other bad spots on the north end continued to the century's end. Traffic on the Ann Arbor continued to build and figures for the 1890's reflect Ashley's desire to promote eastbound business, congruent with car ferry development.

Below: By 1905 the Ann Arbor Railroad was a Gould property, linked to the Wabash. George Gould soon released the road to other ownership. Here, 4-6-0 No. 46 rumbles northward with a mixed freight for the ferry at Frankfort. It was a Pittsburgh 1900 product which was scrapped in 1940.
MICHIGAN HISTORICAL COLLECTION

Left: AA K-7 2491, on an extra, heads south from Frankfort in 1947. The K-7's weight was just under 150 tons. H. D. RUNEY PHOTO

Right: This cold day in Ann Arbor, Michigan shows L-2 class 2-10-2 No.2553 rolling easily through the university district en route to Owosso in 1938. PAUL MICHAELS PHOTO

Below: AA F-3 class 152 was one of five originally on the roster and it was the last to serve. The 1903 Baldwin 4-6-0 arrived at Ithaca, Michigan with a way freight about 1950. STEVENS/SUMNER COLLECTION

Below: In the postwar years, standard freight power for Ann Arbor was usually a Mike. No. 2490 was one of five K-7 class 2-8-2's built in 1923. It was originally an H-1 class series 183-187 and came after three others that pioneered the wheel arrangement in 1916. This photo was taken at Elberta, Michigan on July 11, 1939.

C. T. FELSTEAD

Following Page (large): Orphan Manistique & Lake Superior Railroad was a thrust of AA to enter Upper Peninsula trade. Baldwin 2-8-0 No. 2380 was built in 1901 for Atlantic & Lake Superior Railway near Houghton in Copper County in March of 1901. The engine was scrapped in 1951. The ferry is the WABASH and is seen at the Manistique slip.

H. D. RUNEY PHOTO

Frankfort Harbor is shown here in 1952 from the Elberta side. Ann Arbor No.3 was loading cars put aboard by S-3 No.7.

Left: Way-freight power for AA was a pair of RS-1 1000-HP locomotives. They wore the attractive blue-white-gray Wabash paint scheme. No.20 arrived at Ithaca, Michigan with the peddler, shortly after delivery in November of 1950.
STEVENS/SUMNER COLLECTION

Below: AA and C&O shared Manitowoc's harbor into the 1970's. Below, AA's VIKING and C&O's CITY OF MIDLAND load rail cars, autos and passengers on a bitter cold Lake Michigan night in January 1981.
STAN MAILER PHOTO

Ann Arbor possessed a locomotive roster of Pittsburgh and Rogers 4-4-0's throughout the 1880's. The final unit came in 1887 just before extension of the road into the rough country north of Cadillac. Six Moguls followed from Pittsburgh, along with a group of 4-6-0's in 1890 and 1891. After receivership some of the newest power was returned to its builders due to default on payment. Eight Baldwin 2-8-0's, four of which came in November 1892, and an additional four in spring of 1893, were surrendered and later resold to Canadian Pacific. ANN ARBOR No.1 was taken in for repairs and revision as it possessed inadequate rear clearance over the car deck. The superstructure was cut forward about sixty feet which changed its appearance. It was strengthened with new timbering at Frankfort. During its layup CITY OF MARQUETTE assisted in moving the flour traffic to Frankfort and No.2 ran continuously during the dismal 1893 summer.

Even after several bad crossings in the northern winters, Ann Arbor chose to open a route to Menominee, Michigan in 1894, extending the road to an upper peninsula port engaged in lumbering. Initially, steamers would dock at the Ludington, Wells & Van Shaik Co.'s facility at Menominee to load lumber for eastern ports. The company considered passage around Death's Door as an alternative to the Sturgeon Bay Canal, believing that the shorter route was too shallow for the ferries. The scheme was attributed to the Burt Receivership. In late April 1893 No.2 ferry made an "excursion" to Menominee with half its deck full of Kewaunee-bound cars. The work of installing a slip began and a steel apron was contracted to Detroit Bridge & Iron Works. Shortly thereafter, AA sent a supply car to Menominee via Kewaunee, together with a crew to install the slip itself.

Receiver Burt had traveled to Washington to oversee an appropriation for harbor improvements, which would aid his plan for Menominee service. AA bought a right-of-way from the harbor entrance to the C&NW and built a foundation for the steel apron and a slip. The engineers loaded a car-ferry with necessary supplies in a precise order for disembarkation at the site. Timbers last on board, would be the first used in the work. The massive steel apron was loaded amidships for better trimming of the vessel. When manager Ashley showed up to make the crossing from Frankfort with the load, he arbitrarily stated that the whole careful job preparation was all wrong. Ashley, a contrary headstrong individual, had the ferry reloaded in improper reverse order. The ferry encountered heavy seas in its crossing and the rear-loaded apron nearly went off into the lake. In Menominee, the work was hampered, the cargo had to be laboriously transferred over the apron and track materials in order to complete the work. Menominee was enthusiastic about the new service and one thousand people rode initial trips, which coincided with the July 4th celebration of "Railroad Day" at Sturgeon Bay for Ahnapee & Western.

Kewaunee considered the new AA landing competition for its own facilities, especially AA's overtures to a new shortline, Wisconsin & Michigan Railroad, and its Soo Line connection. Subsequent events prevented W&M from a direct transfer to AA ferries at first but in time a juncture was made. Winter crossings of upper Green Bay were done in the face of heavy ice conditions. The winter of 1897 built ice so heavy that Menominee and the fleeting Gladstone service was curtailed. During 1894's depressed times, AA attempted to maintain thrice-weekly service to Kewaunee and Menominee.

Interest in expansion of the yet-unproved Green Bay services included a novel scheme to serve Oconto, Wisconsin with fer-

Below: On an inaugural run between Menominee and Frankfort, AA No.2 passed Sturgeon Bay with a record crowd celebrating Railroad Day in July of 1894.
A. T. SCOFIELD PHOTO

ries. The old lumber town and its businessmen, chiefly Holt Lumber Company, had approached Ashley with a plan. Hardly more than a letter of inquiry, it failed to materialize. In summer of 1894, however, the very real plan for another Minneapolis-Frankfort route, excluding GB&W's system, surfaced with the completion of Wisconsin & Michigan Railway to Faithhorn Junction. Clearly, Ann Arbor had intentions of working outside the Lackawanna through route to develop its own traffic. The AA feeder would open a coal market in the north via Toledo and glean a sizable amount of eastbound tonnage.

In early 1895 AA attempted to serve Menominee via Death's Door but ice conditions there were too heavy. AA ordered its carloadings shipped to Kewaunee while the newspapers contended that failure of the new route was inevitable. In February 1895 No.1 and No.2 ferries were held fast in east-shore ice of Manistee after trying to return from Kewaunee to Frankfort. The ice-locked vessels were able to make Manistee but coal supplies aboard were low on the return trip. A tug and F&PM No.4 attempted to free the ferries but were unable to break a path in their location. Coal was brought out via sleighs in bags and laboriously loaded into the ferry's bunkers. Some of the coal was dumped down a ventilator shaft on No.1, and seventy tons was loaded via the hurricane deck. An attempt to blast the

Above: AA No.3 slipped into Kewaunee after a night run, a June sunrise gleaming on her new hull. No.3 was the first steel ferry of AA. This photo was taken about 1906.
J. SCHULTZ COLLECTION

163

Above: AA No.3 was switched by KGB&W Mogul No.37 at Kewaunee. No.3 served for 62 years, much longer than the 2-6-0, which worked about twenty years.
GREEN BAY WESTERN COLLECTION

Below: Ex-GB&W 301-303 were sold to Ann Arbor Railroad System for service on its southern end. Another sometime railroad, AARRS was a last-ditch effort to save the road after the 1977 takeover by Michigan Interstate Railway Company. Numbers 301-303 rolled across the Huron River bridge at Ann Arbor, Michigan on May 16, 1980.
B. A. CARLSON PHOTO

ice with dynamite also failed to free the vessel. Both were carried south and No. 2 finally broke out and headed for Ludington.

One year later, wracked by a stormy crossing, No. 1 lost seven cars to the lake. Northern Pacific's boxcar No. 8022, floated ashore in ice six miles north of the Sturgeon Bay Ship Canal entrance. Another's cargo of butter floated about the lake for weeks to the delight of feasting seagulls. No. 1 later encountered about forty barrels of flour some twenty miles off Kewaunee, a

memento of the ordeal. One ton of butter, still in good condition, reputedly made its way to Owosso, Michigan and a receiving creamery there. The butter had originated with a Minnesota consignee.

AA promoted passenger service on the west side of the lake, stopping at Sturgeon Bay en route to Menominee. The Gladstone trade also included a passenger stop at Escanaba's dock, although no ferry slip was available. Such was the case at the Soo Line's grain terminal at Gladstone. By February of 1895 No. 1's passenger cabins were extended back to the aft smokestack, giving it twelve staterooms. In summer of 1896 No. 1 went into the yard at Toledo where the bow engine and propellor were removed. Both wood ferries had been equipped with icebreaking forward wheels which proved useless against Lake Michigan ice. The two engines removed from No. 1 and No. 2 were original power for ANN ARBOR No. 3, built by the Globe Iron Works of Cleveland in fall of 1898. AA ordered 25,000-bushel grainholds put in the old forward-engine space, just ahead of coal bunkers, supposedly to make the ferry better able to deal with slack seasons. Frankfort's grain elevator would aid in the plan.

With the onset of better times and stimulation from the Spanish-American War, railroading came out of a long slump. In early 1897 the Menominee route was again sealed off by ice on Green Bay and Ann Arbor gave it up for the winter. By now Kewaunee had become a profitable route for AA. When Menominee was iced in the traffic came south to Green Bay and east via Kewaunee. Reportedly, the two overworked wooden arks carried about 350 cars in 15 days. Manitowoc became a ferry port in July of 1896 when nine cars were taken aboard No. 2 for Frankfort. She then proceeded to Kewaunee for 13 more cars. The service also reduced its rates to six cents per hundredweight, one cent less than its Wisconsin competition. Both WC and C&NW served the car ferries at separate docks as AA attempted to operate five and finally four routes by 1902.

Construction of the Manistique Railway in the 1880's led to another route to the upper peninsula's interior when, after several reorganizations, it became Manistique & Lake Superior Railway. The road's recreation from a logging road to an AA-controlled line negated the old Gladstone ferry connection which was destroyed by fire in the late 1890's. Speculators thought that AA would extend the M&LS to Munising and perhaps to Negaunee's iron district. A connection at Shingleton, Michigan put AA in direct contact with DSS&A for yet another Minneapolis-east route, plus a Duluth-Superior connection.

Ann Arbor's receivership lasted four years and two months, ending July 1, 1897, after which the road consolidated its position on the Wisconsin side of the lake. The Ashleys were shut out of the organization, reflecting again the plight of David M. Kelly in the GB&M. Young Harry Ashley continued with the road for several years and under his tutelage the expansion was made. During his years ANN ARBOR No. 3 from Cleveland made her first call at Kewaunee on November 21, 1898. No. 3 escaped the scrapper's torch until 1960.

In 1900 Ann Arbor outfitted No. 1 and No. 2 with extremely tall stacks, their final and distinctive silhouette. However, it

Below: AA's WABASH was unafraid to lay a load of coal smoke. It is seen here in a portrait of the way it used to be. It was exiting Manistique about 1947.
H. D. RUNEY PHOTO

wasn't enough, for in February of 1902 Captain Edward Williams of No. 2 resigned, following Captain Charles Moody down the gangplank. Both reasoned that the wood ferry's poor design and condition was cause for resignation. Moody was a veteran of the storm which had cleared seven cars from the deck in midlake. Williams felt that the hull was opened from too many groundings and rough landings.

The early years of the 20th Century found the road in the hands of George Gould of the Wabash. Gould was very interested in expansion and the union of the AA and Wabash helped greatly in obtaining more westbound traffic. Considerable coal traffic developed as a result of Toledo connections with Hocking Valley and other trans-Ohio coal carriers. In summer of 1902 difficulties arose between AA and C&NW, the North-Western reportedly canceling agreements with the AA for Upper Michigan trade. AA secured a somewhat better footing on the west side by arranging to deal with Wisconsin & Michigan Railway for its eastbound carloads. This included some iron ore, a tonnage which developed as a result of the Aragon Mine's opening near Iron Mountain.

After traffic increased AA ordered its No. 4 car ferry. The Cleveland-built steel vessel, a near-duplicate of No. 3, made its initial run to Manitowoc December 13, 1906. The ferry made its

Right: The Menominee route was hardly easy in the winter. An ice-caked City of Green Bay negotiates the Sturgeon Bay canal on a winter morning, bound for Menominee.
CHAN HARRIS PHOTO

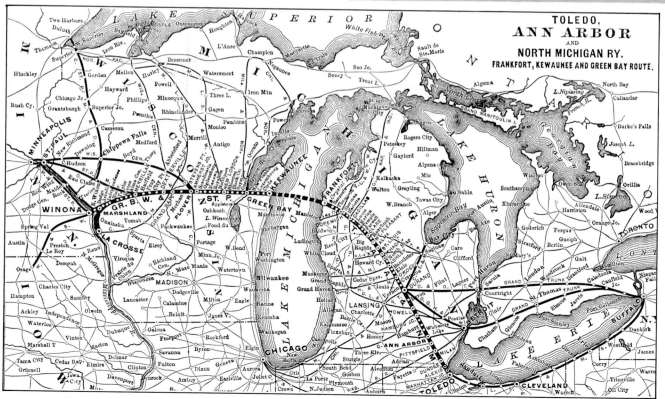

first trip through the Sturgeon Bay Ship Canal to Menominee in early January 1907. Previously, the new boat had journeyed to Menominee via Death's Door. AA traffic had increased from about 25,000 carloads in 1900 to 27,644 in 1903 and the new ferry was very much in demand. The new vessel allowed AA to withdraw No.2 for a refit which included hull strengthening. During 1903 it was reported that AA leased the big green ferry of No.1, Manistique, Marquette & Northern Railway. It was similar to the new PERE MARQUETTE 18 which began to call at Kewaunee competitively in 1903. MM&N No.1 brought an increasingly important cargo of westbound coal. The new vessel which cost $450,000 would shortly (1908) be sold to Grand Trunk Milwaukee Car Ferry Co.

Traffic into Kewaunee had its ups and downs in 1904. In February an embargo caused all tonnage to cease rolling over KGB&W. Yet, by June 1904, the yards of Kewaunee were congested with backlogs of westward-bound cars. Much of it was coal which had to await haulage by short, underpowered

consists to Green Bay. KGB&W's Kewaunee crews were charged with lifting the trains up to Luxemburg by doubling or tripling the hill west of Casco Junction.

Ann Arbor suffered the loss of ferry No.1 in a fire at Manitowoc where it had been secured at the C&NW slip. The fire was discovered about 6:30 p.m. on March 8, 1910. It consumed twenty loaded cars and by the next morning the ferry had burned to the waterline. No.1, which had to be refloated and eventually towed elsewhere, spent its declining years as a Muskegon sand scow. No.5 boat, which came in late 1910, was launched at Toledo on November 26, 1910, giving the road three steel boats. No.2 was relegated to "spare boat" status. Contrary to its pioneering spirit, AA was allegedly the last firm on the Great Lakes to receive wireless sets, so important to safety for those in peril on the merciless, cold waters. ANN ARBOR No.2 made her last trip September 29, 1912 and was dismantled to become a barge at Manistee. In 1927 she was abandoned in the St. Clair flats north of Detroit. Thus the two pioneers were

Ann Arbor dieselized in 1950 with FA-2 Alco 1500-HP cab units. A pair of two-unit locomotives stood at Owosso, Mighigan, which is still the physical head-quarters of the remains of the road.

gone, leaving in their place far more powerful and rugged designs which lasted into the diesel age.

AA competed with other carriers in December 1911 for a fast flour train which reached its ferries via Soo Line at Manitowoc. A train of 31 cars came over the former Wisconsin Central line (WC having been absorbed by Soo Line in 1909) and arrived in Frankfort five hours and four minutes later. AA then rushed it to Toledo where it continued on the New York Central Lines to New York. AA had engaged in a bidding war with Pere Marquette, its constant rival, for cross lake traffic to Manitowoc after 1897 and to Kewaunee after 1903.

Pere Marquette's entry into the cross-lake trade signaled a more difficult time for the Ann Arbor. Some sources link the old Flint & Pere Marquette Railroad to Sam Sloan's empire-building. Mark T. Cox, a GB&W Director, also had interest in both the Detroit, Grand Rapids & Western and the Chicago & West Michigan Railroads. In 1900 they were merged with F&PM to become the Pere Marquette Railway. F&PM's inter-ests had long included a west shore harbor and both Sheboygan and Manitowoc were worth consideration for their older steamer connections. After rival AA had opened ferry service to Kewaunee F&PM business fell off at Manitowoc. The poor economy in 1893 also contributed significantly to the lack of business. F&PM met with Wisconsin Central for ferry facilities connecting its main line with Manitowoc and creating a dupli-cation of the Kewaunee-Frankfort route.

On June 24, 1896 WC opened its line but had to wait until January 1897 for the maiden voyage. PERE MARQUETTE was finished at Wheeler's Bay City Michigan yard, making a visit to Milwaukee where a great crowd inspected the first steel ferry on Lake Michigan. When she came into Manitowoc can-nons were fired as a salute but tracks were found to be too close together on the car deck and several details had to be altered to fit the new aprons. C&NW took off 28 cars after the fitting at 7 a.m. on February 18, 1897. At 11:00 a.m. the newcomer went upstream to WC's slip for another fitting. PERE MAR-QUETTE was capable of 15 miles per hour and had a 350 × 56-foot beam. It could carry 32 cars and fifty passengers. General Manager Crapo's private car was carried at the time. Flour began to come back to Manitowoc, much the way grain had come over MLS&W and GBW&STP in the old days.

Wisconsin Central had several hundred cars en route which would involve the last of F&PM's break-bulk steamers, No.5, taking eighty carloads per trip. In March F&PM experienced a longshoremen's strike when they failed to raise the laborer's pay of $1.50 per day. A company detective exposed an outside agita-tor of the Longshoremen's Union and the strike was broken.

The newly organized Pere Marquette Railway was formed on January 1, 1900. Service reached Kewaunee and the KGB&W in mid-July 1903 when No.18 boat arrived. Captain Peter Kilty, who had signed on after giving up an AA commission, was in charge of taking four carloads east. Pere Marquette confidently planned to carry off dairy products of Wisconsin to eastern markets, one of the first cars being a La Crosse-to-east refrigerator. This service was to become a twice-weekly operation. Frank Seymour came over from Green Bay to inspect

the new vessel and General Manager Jordan arrived via regular train several days later. At the outset PM ferries came to Kewaunee on Wednesdays and Saturdays with numbers 15, 17 and 18 alternating. PM service rose quickly and about 27,000 cars were ferried in 1900, growing to nearly 75,000 by 1904. PM's order of four new ferries from American Ship Building Co. of Cleveland in 1901 greatly strengthened its position on Lake Michigan. From that time on regular service by two lines was the general rule at Kewaunee and continued for several decades into the 20th Century.

Above: AA's heaviest steam power was a quartet of Santa Fe types, a slow-gaited USRA Light design. The L-2's were sold to KCS in September 1942.

Below: AA succumbed to non-ALCO diesel power in the early 1960's, settling for GP-35's from EMD, which rolled on trucks salvaged from its traded ALCO cab units. AA came very close to buying ALCO C-420's, but new owner DT&I cancelled the order. Here, train TF-3 rolls through Michigan lake country at Mesick in August 1965.

12

EARLY MODERN

G.B.&W. STATION, ONEIDA, WIS.

A passenger special sped eastward on the KGB&W in July of 1896 carrying men of influence and power. President Stephen S. Palmer of New York, Joseph A. Jordan, vice-president, along with Will Cargill, Seth Champion and Superintendent Frank B. Seymour would direct the Green Bay & Western Railroad's course. The reorganization was the beginning of a time when the Green Bay route would begin to pilot a financially stable future.

GB&W began its corporate life with 21 engines, 510 freight cars and twelve coaches, plus a varied roster of headend and combination cars, numbering 13. There were ten cabooses and one remarkable hand-operated wrecker numbered 01. A decidedly medieval device, No.01 was a fixture of unknown pedigree, along with parlor car 99, which seemingly solidified from primal gases in the time of the railroad's creation. In June 1896 there was a project afoot to improve the Stevens Point branch (GBStP&N), including trestle filling and track upgrading. On the main line, 47 miles of sixty-pound rail was scheduled to be laid from Hixton to Marshland. Allegedly, that section used 4500 tons of rail.

Green Bay's Cargill Elevator fire of June 10, 1896 was a notable setback for the grain transport field. The officials aboard the special train considered the Kewaunee facilities and the loss of grain storage for that fall and were exploring alternatives. In August 1896 the Green Bay Elevator Company was established. It would rebuild on the site of the thirty-year-old complex dating to David Kelly's time. The new elevator was hurriedly completed by late October. The structure immediately received carloadings and the Lackawanna-Green Bay steamer CUBA came alongside for 20,000 bushels destined for Buffalo. A few days later, WILLIAM H. WOLF took 116,000 bushels into the bay in time to move through forming ice. WOLF's captain feared a grounding in the channel, while CUBA had gone out with scant inches under her keel. Buffalo boats were getting larger as the new 15-foot channel permitted.

Lackawanna-Green Bay Line got its start in 1886. Organized by Sam Sloan's DL&W, its first boats were RUSSIA and COLORADO. In the decade to 1896, the channel depth precluded the full use (deeply loaded) of vessels over 15,000 barrels (of flour) capacity, their principal cargo. Each vessel would seasonally make 15 trips to Buffalo; some larger boats were obliged to go down lakes half-empty. Westbound trips carried loads of coal or general merchandise. The new channel and the new elevator were expected to increase the number of larger steamers and more economical operations. In 1895 Seth Champion had arranged in Lackawanna Line's Chicago office to have CUBA, RUSSIA and GRAND TRAVERSE serve Green Bay, their combined capacity totaling 5000 tons. The three could make the run in eleven days. The vessels were also bringing supplies for new paper mills up the Fox River, a growing trade. The steamer HENRIETTA still engaged in Fox River business as far upstream as Oshkosh. She also did a business from Green Bay's dockside. The steamer movements involved the GB&W's boxcars and baggage cars being loaded for La Crosse, Winona and St. Paul consignees. The old

Left: Oneida, Wisconsin is located ten miles west of Green Bay on GB&W's main line. It was also the site of an Oneida Indian school, located on former reservation lands. Oneida's 20×40-foot depot was built in 1896.
GBW COLLECTION

Advocate was optimistic that Green Bay would find a way to compete in New York markets while rates were seasonally low.

The channel of the Fox River into Green Bay needed an appropriation, for which L.T.Co. agent M. J. McCormick labored long to secure. Wisconsin's man in Washington, Isaac Stephenson, was prominent in securing $25,000 and then an additional $66,000 for a deeper channel by early 1894. Steamers such as SAGINAW VALLEY had brought in cargoes of rail for Winona & South-Western and Winona Bridge Railway Company, but now heavier draught steamers would be able to enter the Fox's mouth in season.

While tonnage figures inched upward in the early 1890's, the road had laid about eighty miles of new 56-pound steel rails in six years' time. After the new company was formed, the list of tangible improvements began to grow. The 1896 winter brought an upsurge of traffic, which focused on the Kewaunee ferry landings. With the loss of the competing Menominee route for the ice-locked winter, KGB&W could absorb a portion of the resulting surplus. It was during the terrible winters of that period, that the wood ferries were taking punishment and business was heaviest. James J. Hill's line of great steel steamers were immobilized by the frozen lakes, freeing the cross-lake rail lines to raise their rates without the threat of competition. The Hill vessels (Great Northern Railway-controlled) commanded the rates from the port of Superior, Wisconsin on flour and grain. It brought about a backlog of cars, "wild" trains and a 4-4-0 stationed as a switch-engine at Kewaunee on a semi-permanent basis.

Green Bay's harbor scene in 1896 showed a renewal of industries. Diamond Match Company established a plant in the old Eldred mill after being burned out of Ontonagon, Michigan. The matchmakers created 400 jobs, claiming to run night and day. The short-lived Murphy mill which operated from 1887 to 1906 had a woods railroad and several of its locomotives came to Green Bay for repairs. However, Murphy voted itself out of business, much as the Winona mills did, and dismantled its physical plant. Their steamer S. J. MURPHY plied the waters between Buffalo and Green Bay, a route-mate of the grain boats. Businesses were recuperating from the 1890's recession and GB&W was beginning a series of construction improvements.

One of the road's earliest appointments was J. C. Thurman as general auditor, replacing Cashier H. A. Champion, the latter retiring with Seth Champion in mid-1897. Seth Champion's energy in the cause of GB&W was acknowledged in the annual meeting of March 1897. He was asked to remain until the summer and was unanimously re-elected. Champion was seen as a benefit to the new incorporation and a man to help the road out of the barrens of the dark past. Seth Champion left his railroad in a state of new hope, but not without renumerative rewards; his securities in KGB&W were purchased by GB&W, along with the other original incorporators.

In February 1897 Dickson Manufacturing Co. delivered two 42-ton 4-4-0's, No.23 and No.24, the first new GB&W locomotives. Fifteen months later, No.25 and No.26 arrived and the quartet joined the three FL&T-financed Schenectadys as the prime freight power for the next decade. Two orders of boxcars also came in 1897, the first since 1891. One hundred fifty arrived in January and another 150 in November.

GB&W's Annual Report for 1897 claimed a gain in earnings from $416,317.76 in 1896 to $442,319.81 for 1897, an increase of $26,002.05. It reflected December's heavy harvest rush eastward, reportedly two freight trains a day from Winona.

There were 140 cars on sidings at Kewaunee, awaiting transfer after the bay froze over. Caught in the freeze, L-GB's LACKAWANNA and RUSSIA were fast in ice until released by the ice-breaking capabilities of ALGOMAH from Mackinac. ALGOMAH was a Christmas hero, as it broke through foot-thick ice ahead of the Buffalo boats coming in with Christmas goods for Green Bay merchants.

Plans for the much needed GB&W depot were completed by April 1897. The new depot would be a 40 × 80-foot three-story building costing $10,000. The architects were Walter and Rockwell, while the construction contract went to Golueke Brothers and H. Naumann. Louis Weber of Neenah contracted for the masonry work. Excavation started August 20, 1897 on the site of the old depot which had been moved aside for warehouse use. The new facility included space for the road's general offices which were moved from their location at Pine and Adams Streets. At the same time, both C&NW and Milwaukee Road were building new stations in the city.

The railroad now needed a new shop to replace the inadequate, elderly structures; the newest was the 1881 roundhouse. The shop was begun in the summer of 1898 and Wisconsin Bridge & Iron Co. raised the steel superstructure as it arrived from Milwaukee. Along with steel workers, carpenters and masons were busily laying up stone foundations and putting in piping, sewers and steam fittings. Cars of iron arrived daily and nearby an eighty-foot smokestack was raised. While boilers were fabricated by company forces, brickwork was done by local contractors. The shop walls were completed by mid-month. Meanwhile, inspection pits were finished while several carloads of slate roofing arrived. Next, a blacksmith shop was underway, locals again doing piecework. The cost was $25,000 and the buildings were operational by November 1st, soon occupied by 25 machinists and about thirty car repairmen practicing their professions.

The next year's improvement was a six-stall roundhouse extension which started when piles were driven for a new, longer steel turntable. The plan called for a 240 × 66-foot addition. The scene, which included a late fall turnout of all locomotives while the table was being installed, provided a rare opportunity for some glass-plate photographers. The roundhouse addition was closed up for the winter, while interior work went on uninterrupted. On December 11, 1900, after the GB&W's work was completed, C&NW's turntable became disabled and at least five engines were brought to the Kewaunee Wye at Norwood for turning. Sometime later, a new coal shed went into operation and work began along the unsightly slough. The infamous slough, which was considered offensive to the community, ran southward beside KGB&W's trackage, then east to the Fox River north of Shawano Avenue. The shape and form of today's GB&W Norwood Shops was a result of the new additions and slough work.

Shortly after GB&W's new shop opened, the road began a rebuilding program to better its fleet of 25-year-old 4-4-0's. Faced with the immediate need to replace most of its older power, William P. Raidler, the new master mechanic, had to work within the constraints of rebuilding in kind, under stringent orders of the Reorganization Committee. He chose the more "promising" engines, some of which may have been stored for several years. In 1899 GB&W's heaviest power was chiefly the 20- and 23-class 4-4-0's and it was decided to create a roster of upgraded rebuilds of greater boiler capacity. It was the same year that GB&W bought its last new locomotive from Dickson which was 0-0-6 No. 4. With two second-hand machines on KGB&W's roster, Raidler and his men faced a challenge which required an unusual solution.

The first "Raidler Rebuild" was No. 12, a former 1874 Dickson named the "Arthur Bondon." The work was so complete that only the frame and minor fittings of the old machine remained. The boiler shop hammered out a Belpaire firebox equipped boiler, a relatively recent addition to U.S. locomotive practice. Raidler's knowledge of Belpaire design was inherited from Burlington practice. He had been master mechanic for the Hannibal & St. Joseph Railroad (division of Chicago, Burlington & Quincy) at Hannibal during 1895 and 1896 and filled the same post for Blair's St. Louis & Hannibal Railway in 1897 and 1898. The square-shaped firebox gave more steaming capacity to a constricted, narrow firebox which rode between driving wheels. The dark side was that Belpaires were more expensive to build and maintain. What Raidler brought forth for the GB&W very much resembled the CB&Q's 550-class "Fast Mail" 4-4-0's, although they were somewhat smaller.

Another factor which influenced GB&W's rebuilding program was the ability of the Duncan Foundry to supply castings. Fort Howard's respectable old engine-building firm was located on Broadway, near the Green Bay Junction station, where its final home was still standing in 1988. It began as Taylor & Duncan Foundry in the years after the Civil War. John Duncan apparently built Wisconsin's first locomotive in North Milwaukee at the old La Crosse shops in 1854. After migrating to Green Bay, Duncan stayed in the engine business until lumbering caught his attention and he went north to Westboro. His son bought out his old partner Taylor and opened a larger operation in the 1880's. In October 1890 J. Duncan & Co. cast a 5000-pound ship's propeller, eleven feet in diameter, the largest casting done in the north country. Duncan also built marine engines, casting an 8500-pound engine bed (for use in stationary or "Corliss" engines), and thus was skilled and equipped well

STAN MAILER COLLECTION

After reorganization, GB&W was able to build its final mechanical headquarters at Norwood Avenue, Green Bay. Built 1899-1901, the shop buildings remain in present-day service.

enough to supply GB&W with cylinders, smokestacks and drive-wheel centers, plus other minor parts needed for the rebuilding program. It was written that No. 12's smokestack was an entirely new design, unlike any other work done at Duncan's. Taylor & Duncan had made contracts with GB&W for gray iron and brass castings as early as 1877.

No. 12 was ready for first fire-up by October 10, 1900 after spending about six weeks in the backshop. It hardly resembled the old spool-domed Dickson in any way, yet it was the subject of several surviving photos. Engineer Charlie Baker was assigned the engine and he spent several days breaking in "the little 12." Baker ran No. 12 on its break-in route out to Oneida, taking it into regular service on trains 1-2 to Grand Rapids and Winona. "Little 12" went out on October 15th, returning the next day a success.

the former Pennsylvania engine had received a new tender, cab and jacket in addition to the host of other repairs required to return it to service. Over the 1900-01 winter, No. 1 again in bad order was returned to Fort Howard for extended periods. For much of 1901 more dependable engines, such as Nos. 19 and 21 of GB&W, were worked on the Kewaunee-Casco Junction mixed. In February 1902 it was reported that No. 1 was to receive a new boiler; GB&W would have the locomotive outshopped by mid-September. In the week of September 16th, Engineer Russ Hollister brought the engine back to surprised onlookers at Kewaunee. No. 1 was the fourth Raidler product with a Belpaire boiler. Only the frame and drive wheel centers remained of the Juniata product of 1873. It was billed as being much larger with an overall weight of 52 tons, the heaviest on the GB&W lines. The old one had weighed 35 tons. No. 1's new

Above: Local No. 3 leaves Taylor, Wisconsin en route to Winona from Merrillan. Photographer J. M. Colby of Wausau created many rare postcard views, recording long-extinct Wisconsin station scenes.
J. M. COLBY PHOTO

The Raidler product must have been excellent, for No. 12 was quickly followed by No. 10 which came out in April 1901. It was broken in April 10th and made its first trip westward on April 24th, again on No. 1. The new ones were not above a little freight service, for No. 10 doubleheaded with Dickson 24 on a pulpwood extra to Grand Rapids that first month. Regular men on the early runs of No. 10 and No. 12 that summer were John C. Wigman, Jake Spitzer and Baker, together with Joe Doyle and John Vandenboom, the skilled shovel artists. No. 11, the final rebuild of the "10 class," went through the program in late 1901.

The 10-class had a boiler pressure of 150 pounds and an average weight of 39 tons each. No. 12 had slightly less coal and water capacity; with overall loaded weight of 1500 pounds less than the others, it was given the nickname "little 12." Cylinders remained at 16 inches diameter and tractive effort was a mere 12,450 pounds. Yet, the "10-class" served for twenty years afterwards on trains 1-2, the first of the type on the road.

After the tragic Reardon-Brown wreck of 1900, KGB&W's engine No. 1 was in line for major boiler work. By June 30, 1900

boiler pressure was 160 pounds and it weighed 52 tons with a tractive effort at 14,025 pounds.

Duncan Foundry cast yet another cylinder saddle in October 1902, allegedly the fifth one done for GB&W and this time for a 17×24-inch locomotive. Apparently, GB&W's No. 15 was rebuilt completely and outshopped by July 1903. A faded photograph shows the big 4-4-0 to be similar. It had a tractive effort of 14,960 pounds and 160 pounds boiler pressure. No. 14, heavier yet, followed in May of 1904. Raidler finished the program with No. 18 in July 1905 and KGB&W 35 in January of 1907. All eight locomotives carried Belpaire boilers.

Some discrepancies in the roster of the Raidler period have never been resolved. The origin of engines 14 and 15 before they were rebuilt is unknown. The three Danforths of 1875 apparently were renumbered, one surfacing as Iola & Northern's

Above: GB&W's new life permitted an era of equipment modernization. One shiny example was the reboilered Dickson 4-4-0, No. 17, seen here on Train No. 1, ready to depart from Green Bay Junction. No. 17 was sold to Waupaca-Green Bay Railway on February 1, 1909. The engine apparently met its end in an enginehouse fire at Waupaca, circa 1915.
GBW COLLECTION

Below: The Kewaunee local arrives at Green Bay's new station which was begun in the summer of 1897. With additions, the historicl building remained until February 11, 1977.
SHM COLLECTION

No. 2, another as second No. 7. In a 1916 roster, 4-4-0 engines No. 2 and No. 7 carry builder's numbers which indicate their renumbered position among the three 1875 Danforths. No. 14, No. 15 and KGB&W 35 were either constructed completely from raw materials or received their frames and tenders from an unidentified source. Official roster data is unclear and carries a number of mistakes forward without mechanical or accounting records to support it. An engine 13 was reported unofficially by lineside newspapers as being in a wreck in 1899. However, no No. 13 engine was ever built, nor is it clear that it was put on the roster. All of the Grants except No. 8 vanished without record of their passing. It is possible that several of them went into the big rebuilds as parts which would account for the frames needed by the three newcomers. Both KGB&W 35 and GB&W 18 had big 18-inch cylinders, evidently cast by Duncan, which were the largest diameter until the 19×26-inch cylinders of the first Moguls.

In the first decade GB&W continued to acquire second-hand "pearls" under Raidler. A Pittsburgh 0-4-0 was purchased in April of 1904 from F. M. Hicks. This was an 1898 construction, curiously new to have fallen to an equipment dealer. Hicks also supplied a Rome-built 0-6-0 in June 1910 which was probably a former Union Pacific offering. The Hicks firm also supplied passenger cars, at first combination cars like No. 27 (October 1903), later GB&W coach 96 (March 1909) and KGB&W coach 77 and 78 (1909, 1910). When Hicks began to enter the shortline coach field in earnest, it supplied the "Hicks Standard Coach" to several companies, among them Atlanta & St. Andrews Bay, Lake Superior & Ishpeming and the GB&W. The cars were sixty feet (overall) with archwindow styling and, in many cases, were rebuilt from old Pullman and Wagner Palace cars of the 1880's. Hicks systematically acquired the old sleepers, reconstructed them along a standard plan (some were combines) and sold their attractive open-platform product to railroads in need. The big cars were designed with mixed-train operation in mind, possessing extra heavy sills, steel platform framing and an interior finish of quarter sawn oak. Hicks announced in 1908 that it had a large number in stock for early delivery, indicating that their market was possibly a slim one. GB&W seized the opportunity to equip its passenger service with the more acceptable car and from 1906 to 1911 Hicks delivered numbers 51 to 54 and 57-58 to GB&W. A&W received No. 96 coach and KGB&W its No. 74 combine. In time Hicks went into receivership, emerging as Central Locomotive and Car Works, but continued to attract GB&W purchases. Central supplied combines 50 (GB&W) and 60 (KGB&W) respectively, while A&W 86 (coach) and GB&W 106 (coach) came in July of 1914. A final round of similar coaches with nearly the same specifications came from AC&F. The AC&F cars were 107 and 108 for GB&W and 64 for KGB&W and had steel underframes. During World War II, 64 became No. 109 and it was this final group which closed out GB&W passenger service.

After initial receipts of new boxcars, groups of second-hand coal cars were introduced to GB&W to serve its on-line customers from Green Bay coal distribution points. GB&W again took advantage of bargains as roads like Hocking Valley, Virginian, Wheeling & Lake Erie and others gave up composite cars for all-steel, long-haul fifty-ton cars.

GB&W's steam shovel came from Hicks in December 1906. Many of the equipment purchases in the early 20th Century were directed by the Reorganization Committee which wisely matched its needs to the bargains offered by Hicks/Central. Things went well enough for GB&W that it began to yield the anticipated five-percent earnings by January 1905 and began earnings applications on "B" debentures by January 1908. Each year after December 1903 funds were voted as an appropriation for the purchase of new equipment, which amounted to $70,000 the first year and an average of $30,000 per year through January 22, 1908. The system, while hardly unique, reflected the policies of Samuel Sloan. The grand old man had resigned as DL&W president in 1899 but remained on its Board of Managers until his death in 1907. Back in 1883, Sloan had instituted a practice of paying for a road's improvements from current income. It became standard for his railroad's bookkeeper to charge expenditures for renewals and betterments to a "suspense account" which was charged against income at some time each year. This was done instead of crediting it to the investment account, thus building up the latter. No doubt Sam Sloan would approve of the continued policies in his protégé GB&W which, in the closing years of his life, began to show the promise and vitality all had long hoped for.

The end of the century was a signal for other personnel changes and John B. Last, general freight and passenger agent, resigned to join General Paper Co. at Chicago. Another Hannibal man, W. C. Modisett who came to Green Bay to fill the slot, had gained his experience at StL&H and CB&Q. Others of importance simply passed away. Influencing the road greatly in their time were: Percy Rivington Pyne, Moses Taylor's son-in-law, late vice-president of DL&W and Lackawanna Iron & Coal Co., who died in Rome, Italy, February 1895; John Insley Blair

KGB&W Mogul 37 pauses at Marshland with its west-end crew. Shown here about 1915, from left to right, are: William Young, Engineer J. Brey, Brakeman F. Callier, Fireman S. Manning and Conductor B. J. Cloisuit.

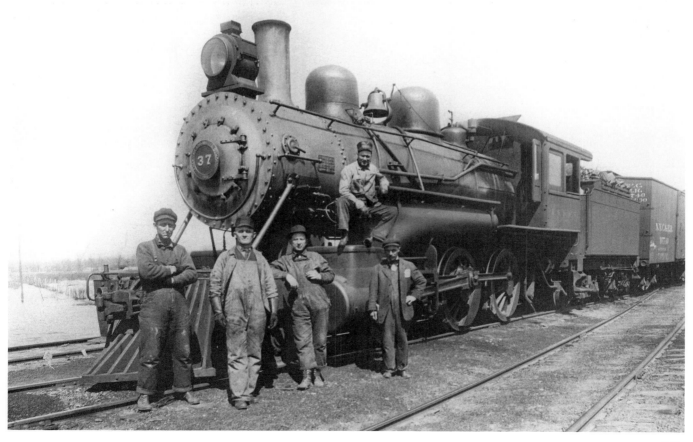

of Blairstown, New Jersey who died in 1899. Both men left behind records of achievement in railroads, industry and philanthropy, as well as the Green Bay Route in Wisconsin.

Improvements were required for the railroad's major bridges which were mostly wood. Renovations on the steel span at Hatfield began in early 1898 at a cost of $30,000. Delay of repairs to the swingspan at the Wolf River in Shiocton resulted in collapse of a pier in August 1898. It was a long wait before a new bridge could be installed but authorization finally came in a board meeting on December 12, 1913. On that date the annual appropriation covered "one Mogul engine (American Locomotive Co.) for $12,500; one first-class coach (Central Locomotive & Car Works) for $8,000; and contracts for a renewed Shiocton bridge." The $6500 bridge appropriation covered piers, abutments and new iron spans to carry the present iron drawspan. For several years GB&W followed the "one Mogul, one coach, one bridge" appropriation method. The total in 1913 was $27,000. In that same year the Waupaca-Green Bay Railway narrowly to avert receivership. GB&W acquired $36,000 worth of collateral bonds of WGB, which required further protection of what investment they had in the faltering short line. In September 1915 another expenditure covered 100 forty-ton steel underframe boxcars. The road would not receive anymore Haskell & Barker cars in the future. These were also the last double-sheath cars purchased by GB&W.

Trackwork had continued in the 1890's but another box culvert washout caused train No.2's wreck on April 8, 1899 near Royalton. No.2 was running with four cars and engine No.13, when it ran over a washout on a high fill east of the village. The 4-4-0 broke through the crust above an abyss but skidded across without jackknifing. The engine crew escaped without major injury. The head-end cars lost their trucks into the hole, the carbodies sledding across the open space. While service was arranged via other railroads, wrecker 01 was engaged to remove the wreck.

The Stevens Point branch, which also included its on-line paper mill yards, began receiving new rail in the spring of 1899. Some rail on the east end of the main line proved to be too light and it was allegedly removed for use on the branch. GB&W No.17, a Dickson 4-4-0, was assigned in May 1899. The same month, GB&W received combination cars 25 and 26, painted tuscan red; No.26 was assigned to Stevens Point. A factor which influenced GB&W's upgrading in Stevens Point was the Wisconsin Central's decision to abandon its remaining backshop there. Initially, WC moved to a new shop at Waukesha; a second move by Manager Whitcomb in 1899 to North Fond du Lac removed the remaining shop employees from the tax rolls. John Last, in his final days on GB&W, arranged a special freight train to operate between Stevens Point and New London Junction to supplant Wisconsin Central's fast freight offerings. GB&W would offer overnight-from-Chicago handling which would travel over the C&NW to New London Junction. Evidently, the new way included tie-up at Grand Rapids and fed on Stevens Point's disgruntlement with WC's cavalier methods.

Conditions on the Kewaunee end required considerable raising of the track above the Kewaunee River floodplain. In 1900 the railroad began filling the long Scarboro Creek bridge, using about 100,000 yards of material. Additional work was done on the trestlework at "Footbridge," at the time only a nickname for West Kewaunee. The fill work, along with a general ballasting and leveling, continued into freeze-up. Memories of Mike Reardon and John Brown hung in the minds of every section-

hand on the project. Weather again ravaged the right-of-way in March 1903, preventing regular train service and undermining low spots. The Scarboro bridge, now a shorter span thirty feet above the creek, was badly damaged and out of action for several days. Driftwood had jammed against pilings, threatening to push it out of line. The regular train was forced to return to Luxemburg and telegraph for aid. Dispatched back to Green Bay, the locomotive brought a B&B crew to the bridge. During the cessation, Kewaunee mail and express went via A&W to Algoma and over roads to its destination. Several days later Scarboro Bridge was passable and a short train arrived to maintain the schedule. Most of the damage had been caused by the burst dam at Trudell's Mill just west of the high bridge. Today the mill is but a trace artifact on the landscape.

On October 30th defective trucks under a boxcar derailed the Kewaunee mixed on the Scarboro Bridge. The car was the first in the train and was precariously balanced so the passengers had to cross the derailment on foot and ride the engine the eleven miles to Kewaunee. Afterwards Engineer Russ Hollister and Conductor W. E. Secord returned to the teetering car with section-hands and tools. Service was restored the next day. A year later Superintendent Seymour had plans for two steel bridges which spanned the Kewaunee and Scarboro Creeks. In time the Scarboro crossing became a high fill pierced by a concrete culvert of considerable size.

Track maintenance proved remunerative for KGB&W was then able to improve scheduling of the mixed train, putting the westbound train out of Kewaunee at 7:20 a.m. to arrive in Green Bay at 10 a.m. The next year the *Enterprise* proudly counted nine passengers westbound and twelve eastbound in one day. The limited clattered between Casco Junction and Kewaunee in just thirty minutes. Improved service meant higher tariffs and a surcharge was levied against baggage left over 24 hours at Kewaunee Union Station. For a while the press was satisfied with rail service.

When Kewaunee's new station was built in 1900 the port city was immediately concerned about just how trains would be operated through the town. The press allowed that pushing the mixed into the depot might be the ticket for backwoods places but was hardly the proper form for Kewaunee. Risk notwithstanding, KGB&W continued the practice for several years.

In July 1981 Casco's venerable Lee Metzner, who was then aged 96, remembered Kewaunee's passenger service well. Beginning at 7:00 a.m. Metzner rode away in 1904 from Lake Michigan's waters to attend University of Wisconsin classes at Madison. Metzner carried the customary lunch hamper at the ready. The limited stopped at Casco Junction, a buzz of activity when the A&W mixed arrived from Sturgeon Bay. An hour later Metzner was boarding C&NW's southbound train at Green Bay Junction. That train would leave him at Fond du Lac in care of a Janesville train to deposit him at Jefferson Junction, thirty miles east of Madison. By 8:35 student Metzner stepped off train 103 at Blair Street Station, 13½ hours from Kewaunee. Metzner also recalled that Kewaunee's language of business then was Bohemian, reflecting the region's ancestry.

Turn-of-the-century Kewaunee had its special trains and among them was an extra to the Kewaunee Fair which celebrated Republican Days in late September. KGB&W charged regular fare to hear Wisconsin's "Fightin' Bob" La Follette's speech, even though it may have ripped railroads for their inequities. In the summer Kewauneans journeyed to Green Bay

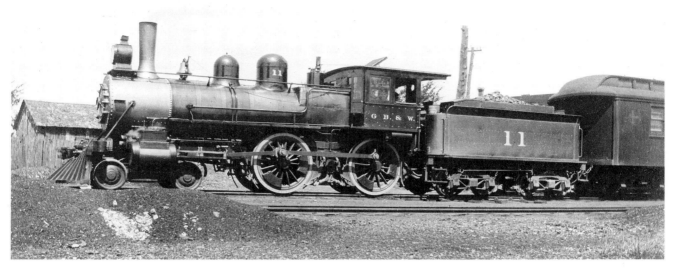

for Buffalo Bill's Wild West Show, leaving on the regularly scheduled train. KGB&W also sold tickets for the North Wisconsin Saengerfest held at Green Bay. The German-American community singalong began tragically as C&NW had a head-on collision involving the special train, killing six and injuring sixty. KGB&W's trains ran on time to the Green Bay events, maintaining a satisfactory record. But a year later the arriving mixed demolished Hans Jacobson's milk wagon while the dairyman was tending a small stove. The wagon was reportedly parked too close to the railroad.

KGB&W's freight service required its own boxcars by 1901 and seventy cars comprised the road's first order from Haskell & Barker Car Co. Delivered in November, the first such car into

Above: Raidler rebuild No. 11, a former Dickson-built 4-4-0, is shown at Merrillan, Wisconsin on August 20, 1908. No. 11's "Burlingtonesque" lines are apparent in this view.
J. F. ADAMS PHOTO; SHSW.

Below: Engineer Charlie Baker poses in his "little 12" at the GB&W-C&NW junction at Marshland, Wisconsin, shortly after No. 12's rebuilding in the Raidler mold. Baker's gleaming engine has train No. 2 in tow.
AUTHOR'S COLLECTION

Kewaunee was No. 564. The 60,000-pound capacity 34-footers were in time for the new car service rules of the following year which allowed only 48 hours to unload and free a car. KGB&W received two other boxcar groups thereafter, Nos. 800-998 (even numbers only) in September 1904 and another 100 (5000-5198, even numbers only) in January 1914, also from H&B. Once again — this time in 1902 — the late fall rush began and the Kewaunee Line had heavy traffic. An extra brought 36 empties to Casco Junction for the A&W while the KGB&W mixed labored to make three trips westbound to Luxemburg, settling out at the hilltop and running back light for more. Hollister and Secord brought the evening eastbound train with full tonnage for the car ferries after doubling the Summit grade out of Green Bay.

Also in 1902, the enginehouse at Kewaunee required a new turntable capable of handling the heavier power. Extra platforms were built at the freighthouse in time for the arrival of Pan-American Shows. GB&W engines No. 17 and No. 20 brought the show over to the roar of the Kewaunee crowd.

The previous February Russ Hollister had suffered an injury while fixing a leaking boiler flue. While calking the fizzling tube with a long bar and maul, Russ slipped and knocked out two teeth. The company telegraphed for another engine and Hollister rode it to the hospital for surgery. Hollister's accident was followed by several derailments on the east end, due chiefly to misaligned track.

The railroad worked to improve its physical plant in the following few years, after an unfortunate collapse of the new Kewaunee turntable entrapped one engine for several hours. Another engine was sent over from Green Bay and for the next few days KGB&W engines, undignified, ran tank-first. The trapped engine delayed Ann Arbor's boat for six hours until it was finally dragged out of the wreckage by the extra engine.

The year 1903 was the height of industrial growth at West Kewaunee. KGB&W put in a siding for Seyk's agricultural commerce, the new location drawing off some of Kewaunee's business. The hay dealers used the location to their advantage but eventually the city went to the Railroad Commission of Wisconsin to protest the new competition with Seyk. At the same time the pea canneries came to Kewaunee. It was a promising new trade for the area but it all ended when the pea louse brought the fledgling industry to its knees during 1907 and 1908. West Kewaunee also attracted a lime kiln which promised 15 carloads a day for the railroad, but that business was linked to old traditions and soon vanished in Kewaunee County.

Mishaps on the east end didn't vanish, even with the addition of more modern equipment. In September 1904 Engineer Hollister and his fireman experienced a side-rod failure, causing the heavy rod to flail dangerously under Hollister's seat box. The accident occurred near Clyde. A catastrophe was averted by the relatively low train speed but it held up traffic for several hours. Days later a boxcar's wheel flange snapped, putting three loaded cars onto the ties within a mile of Hollister's mishap with engine No. 1. Once again passengers rode the first empty boxcar and the locomotive to Kewaunee.

Dissatisfaction with Kewaunee accommodations rose from its mixed train-second class status. The Kewaunee newspaper opened its complaint pages to comments about punctuality as early as 1904. The main barb involved the drawback of switching en route, the downfall of many a mixed train. Other condemnations included the lamentable Casco Junction depot which, as though castigated by the gods, obligingly burned to the ground when struck by lighting on May 17, 1907. Yet, before the thunderbolt, the company was commended for putting the little building in a somewhat habitable condition. Clyde's supply shed doubled as a depot, obligating its hardy passengers to brave the valley's cold at 7:15 each morning. Eventually, a boxcar body was used as a supply depot, followed by a second which withered away in the 1930's.

After Edward Decker's retirement, neighbors A&W and KGB&W were operated more closely with a meshing of equipment numbers to maintain tranquillity in the dispatcher's office. There had been two No. 2 locomotives which roamed the rails east of Green Bay but this confusion was neutralized by the renumbering. Kewaunee continued to be served by a mixed train to Casco Junction but soon, to the satisfaction of most, a larger Hicks combination car (No. 74) costing $7000, was delivered. However, sharp comments continued. On September 14th Kewaunee's not-altogether-first-rate passenger service suffered petition circulations which reviled the ill-vented combination car. The crowded and shabby car was switched frequently and was often located behind coal cars. The city was confident that it deserved better treatment from KGB&W. As if by magic, a full coach was introduced to muffle criticism and Agent Oscar Pierpont could now look his customer straight in the eye, especially when a new two-cents-per-mile fare was being debated in the State Legislature. Further requests to put on a Sunday mail train met with silence from the company. Shortly thereafter the full coach was removed and a single combine continued to rule the route to Kewaunee.

La Crosse's quiet branch line mixed train nearly had access to a new union depot at La Crosse but, due to the coming of the interurbans, the joint station was postponed. While improvements were made, complaints continued. Among them was the frequent whistling within city limits, especially when passing the normal school (La Crosse State Teacher's College). As the city grew, GB&W's quaint branch train faced slow running and frequent grade crossings which constituted a danger. GB&W's depot and freighthouse of 1878 were remodeled by fall of 1903. The train left La Crosse at 8:30 a.m. and connected with an eastbound main line train at 9:35 a.m. at Marshland. Another attempt to run a short passenger from Merrillan to Winona, with coordinated La Crosse service, met with some popularity but the slow train was less than a star attraction.

While Kewaunee and La Crosse suffered, the A&W received better accommodations by October 1908. Trains 15 and 16, a Sturgeon Bay-Green Bay route, were under charge of Engineer R. P. Otterson and Conductor R. H. Thompson. No. 11 and No. 12 were the realm of Steve Slattery and Conductor Walker, while No. 13 and No. 14 were run by George Shequin and Conductor L. M. Dingman. Slattery transferred from Grand Rapids to make his home at Sturgeon Bay. No. 15 and No. 16 made the 58 miles in three hours ten minutes which was judged an improvement for the "super mixed" to Sturgeon Bay.

While Kewaunee settled down with its service condition, bridge reconstruction occupied engineering minds on the Green Bay & Western and by November 1898 construction began on a steel Duck Creek bridge. Good progress was also reported on the Shiocton drawbridge with new abutments raising the roadway four feet at the approaches. The two bridges would be completed by springtime. Spring also signaled a beginning of filling operations to finally close up the unsightly slough northwest of Green Bay Junction. Two work extras, led by engines 21 and 18, hauled material from the bridge site at Duck Creek. Material was also brought in to fill the coal shed frontage on the Fox River, adding a 500×600-foot section to the coal-storage docks. The last of the shabby sheds of Norwood Shops dating to GB&LP days were demolished to make way for the improvements. In 1900 Greiling Brothers took a contract for three bridge jobs which included completion at Duck Creek, the Wisconsin River bridge at Grand Rapids and the Little Wolf River crossing at Manawa. The steel work was placed at Duck Creek by October 23rd, Greilings having completed the abutments in the summer. Wisconsin Bridge & Iron Co. ironworkers finished the span, while a work extra surfaced the roadway in November.

In June of 1901 GB&W again concentrated on maintenance-of-way. A steam shovel, probably leased, was moved from the Green Bay dockside to Slovan gravel pit to provide fill for KGB&W's right-of-way. Engines 19 and 22 were dispatched with ballast cars and a "Lidgerwood Plow" for the summer's work on a reportedly clay-based railroad, largely unfilled.

Right: Traintime at Dodge, Wisconsin about 1908 shows Train No. 2 arriving at the Trempeleau County village at half past nine. It brought daily necessities to the hill-locked community, nine miles from Winona.
J. P. LONGLEY COLLECTION

Another ballasting extra left for Dodge to begin the long process of battling the Trempeleau River in terms of ballasting, washouts and bridge work. In 1901 the excavator went to Royalton with a ballasting extra, engine 21 in charge. Greiling Brothers and WB&ICo. again teamed together and completed a bridge at Ogdensburg. The two also built the Manawa bridge and worked on dock-front filling along Mason Street with Slovan gravel. Three gravel extras per day with 25 cars each began October 24, 1901. The road was to be raised 18 inches and needed 300 carloads. High water on the La Crosse Branch in 1899 and 1900 required further attention on the road's west end. Taking advantage of a good price on rail, GB&W acquired forty carloads which arrived via car ferry from the east just before a "sharp advance" in cost.

While the roadway was being improved, GB&W's new shop discovered that there were many "outside jobs" to be done for profit, thereby beginning a tradition. While scant records show locomotive repair work done for Winona & South-Western and Ahnapee & Western, during 1900 and 1901 GB&W was reported to have courted Marshfield & South-Eastern (engine No.2), Nekoosa-Edwards Paper Co., Escabana & Lake Superior (No.3) and Sagola Lumber Co. (engines 1096, 3).

While time and space were arranged for short line engines, the car shop readied baggage car 15 and coach 35 for the La Crosse branch mixed and repainted some "40 class" fifty-footers tuscan red with new goldleaf lettering. In 1901 the majestic business car, No.99, was rebuilt from a chair car, divided into compartments and painted tuscan red. The car had a mahogany interior with sage green ceiling and other "costly trimmings." In early July J. A. Jordan, Frank Seymour, William Raidler and others made the first trip on the 99 behind lace curtains and on new carpets. They stopped at major on-line towns, including La Crosse. It was a businessman's association trip which enabled jobbers and wholesalers to call on customers and open new business channels. Throughout the 1890's and into the new century GB&W officials attended social functions by rail, taking Green Bay men to races at La Crosse or to a houseboat sojourn on the broad Mississippi. W. W. Cargill kept his houseboat well-stocked for such occasions. Grain and coal interests began to show more concern for the railroad and all worked much more closely together.

Excursions in 1899 seemed to top all those recorded in previous years. Denessen's Boat Line took Grand Rapids parties onto the Green Bay waters and then there was the Odd Fellows excursion, 1000 strong, arriving at 11 a.m. on August 12th. The special was nine coaches long. People stood on the steps and the platforms and 25 climbed on a 4-4-0's tender top. Another special ran from Merrillan to Winona for Buffalo Bill and company. On Labor Day a special went to Riverside Park for a 15-cent fare, leaving at 1 p.m. And, so the stories went. In 1901 the Maccabees of Stevens Point and Grand Rapids, not to be outdone, had their "doings" at Spitzer's Hall, out from Green Bay at 2:45 p.m., back at 9 p.m. Seymour's fair required the engine and cars to be decorated with black-and-yellow bunting of the Gentlemen's Driving and Riding Club.

Below: GB&W's first 0-6-0 yard engine poses on the new steel turntable at Norwood Avenue Shop. No.4 was built by Dickson in the latter days of 1899. Few photos survive of the Scranton-built switcher which was scrapped in the 1930's.
A. MADDY COLLECTION

Pulpwood, long associated with Green Bay & Western economics, was supplied from a different source in 1897. In those days a tug brought rafts of pulpwood logs from the "Canadian Soo" to Long Tail Point. Pulpwood Supply Company, which supplied logs to GB&W, had its operation on the point well out into Green Bay. The logs were then transferred to Grand Rapids mills. C&NW ran a daily train with 35 empties to a junction with the Long Tail Point line near the village of Suamico. The loads were brought back to Green Bay and GB&W's portion found their way into an every-other-day pulpwood and tie train, often doubleheaded as far as Black Creek. There, part would be set out, while the extra locomotive returned light to Green Bay. It required a good, heavy engine such as the newer 20-class to handle this assignment. The portion set out would again travel westward with a regular movement. It was classified as "dead freight" without a time requirement.

Regular engineers on road assignments in the first years of the century were Art Coppin, Frank Buttrick, C. W. Bowen, George Ward, V. Miller, W. H. Whiting, Joe Brey and Bert Lucas. Conductors included John Seymour, Knox, Kenyon, Manning, Johnson, Glynn, Monahan, Brown, Patenick and Ellison. John Ray fired for George Ward on 1901's construction/work extras. George Shequin and L. M. Dingman were engineer and conductor on tie trains in 1900 with a very busy engine 19. Later, R. H. Thompson went on the "tie and pulp" run, which distributed ties while hauling pulpwood logs westward. When the new Dickson 0-6-0 No. 4 arrived it was assigned to R. P. Otterson. At the time, the Dickson 0-6-0 was thought by onlookers to be the largest switcher in the city. The engine, which arrived just before Christmas of 1899, had modern knuckle couplers fitted in place of the outlawed link-and-pin devices before it went to work. No. 4 weighed 45 tons.

On November 1, 1904, Train No. 1 was running with engine 10, Green Bay to Grand Rapids. No. 1 had an engine and crew change — Engineer Panke and Conductor Glynn took engine 11 to Winona. Train No. 3 with engine 22 ran off the miles with

Above: The Stevens Point Branch trains (numbers 21 through 26, inclusive) operated just 5.43 miles to Plover. The engine was kept at Stevens Point in a single-stall shed. Here, venerable Danforth-built No. 19, built in 1879 and rebuilt by Raidler, was about to leave the brick depot at Stevens Point. The combination car was either 25 or 26. The branch crew kept busy switching paper mills seven days a week.
AUTHOR'S COLLECTION

R. H. Thompson and Conductor Kenyon in charge. Train No. 7 operated with locomotive 15, while Dickson No. 23 was busy with an extra. Engineer Kona and Conductor Bigelow worked the Stevens Point job with engine 17. They made three trips to Plover in a day. Engine 8 could be found on the La Crosse mixed. Meanwhile, Art Coppin had the 26 moving an extra toward Winona in good order. It was a "4-4-0 railroad" seriously turning out the ton/miles.

In the summer of 1899 Mark T. Cox, secretary-treasurer and principal stockholder of GB&W, came west to inspect new dock construction east of the recently completed depot in Green Bay. His special car arrived from the west and, together with Messrs. Jordan and W. C. Modisett, Mr. Cox examined the newly prepared grounds, a promising addition to the road's facilities. GB&W's own coal docks and those of W. W. Cargill Co. meant an anticipated boost in GB&W traffic. Cargill's new dock would supply the La Crosse-based operation's coal needs via the Port of Green Bay. Expecting a business of 100,000 tons annually, Mr. W. C. Rassig was put in charge of the facility, moving from La Crosse for the purpose. The operation specialized in Pocahontas Coal. Greiling Brothers contracted at the same time for a 600,000-bushel addition to the new elevator downstream.

As the north country grew, so did its need for coal. Usage ranged from home-heating to mine hoists and to factory steam

181

for the hundreds of Corliss engines which provided power for the region's industries. Coal was king in 1900. Cargill also dealt in DL&W-Scranton coal which previously had been marketed through North-Western Fuel Co. in Green Bay. The DL&W's partnership with W. W. Cargill in 1903 called for coal to be brought in via Lackawanna-Green Bay Line steamers such as SCRANTON, LACKAWANNA and RUSSIA. GB&W would participate in distribution at least as far as the Missisippi. Green Bay's capacity to transship coal had increased fourfold by mid-1903.

The Cargill docks were finished in May 1903, in time for the steamer WAVERLY which arrived from Cleveland with 1700 tons of soft coal. The new steam-and-electric hoisting system was Meade clamshell-type, each with a one-ton bucket and 540-tons-per-hour capacity. A tramway system of twenty three-ton cars operated by cables to distribute coal to storage pockets which in turn loaded railroad coal cars. The pockets held 3000 tons. Statistics for the Port of Green Bay list its annual tonnage as 200,000 tons by 1902, reaching 415,000 tons by 1908.

It was observed by Kewaunee's newspaper that the new hoisting system, which came via ferry, would negate the KGB&W as a coal-shipping route for Cargill. The new coal depot was made self-sufficient by modernization but coal continued to arrive by ferry during the winter. W. W. Cargill, taken ill in 1904, suffered some reversals of fortune and in May of that year the new coal facility was sold to Peter and John Reiss. W. R. Guenzius

remained with the new owners. The Reiss firm continued to operate the facility until the present time, having added the former Cleveland-Cliffs coal yard after 1958.

GB&W published a pay scale as of March 1, 1900. Engineers with more than a year's experience received 3½ cents per mile run and firemen two cents per mile. Engineers on the four-way freights west of Green Bay were paid 3.7 cents per mile; firemen 2.2 cents per mile. Yard engines paid $2.90 and $1.60 at Green Bay for twelve hours' work. Grand Rapids yard engines paid $2.65 and $1.50 per day, also a twelve-hour day but with one hour allowed for meals. Other rates included 35 cents per hour for engineers on overtime and special rates for branch line services. The Stevens Point branch paid $3.50 per day to engineers, while the La Crosse and Iola & Northern were set at $3.00 per day. Rights in that distant time were divided between GB&W, KGB&W and Iola & Northern services. Firemen "were not required to scour or clean below the running board, but negligence on the fireman's part in not keeping their engines as clean as possible, condition of service taken into consideration, will be taken into account for promotion."

It was during GB&W's early years, after the great forests had thinned out, that paper-making came to Wisconsin and the road's neighborhood. Just as the Weyerhauser group of owners and employees left Winona's mills, many in Wisconsin followed them to the Pacific Northwest. However, some stayed behind to establish paper-making in central Wisconsin. In June 1896

One setback for the reorganized GB&W was the 1899 wreck at Ostrander, Wisconson, in which a passenger train barely escaped destruction. A box culvert washed out, causing the fill above it to collapse. Of interest are the "30 class" and "40 class" coaches, the latter purchased by FL&TCo. in the early 1890's. Ancient wrecker 01 is shown here as it handles the engine, possibly 4-4-0 No.13.

A. MADDY COLLECTION

GB&W constructed its Biron spur to the Grand Rapids Pulp & Paper Co. Soon the area around Grand Rapids (Centralia, Nekoosa, Port Edwards and Biron) became dedicated to paper-making and it remains so to this day. Paper also became a major industry at Stevens Point.

With paper mills located along the Wisconsin River relying on water power, Consolidated Water Power Company started to harness the dark river at Grand Rapids for rotary power applications. Soon George Mead of Rockford, Illinois, a relative of the founders, inherited the responsibilities of the firm. The word "paper" was added to the name and, in December 1902, a nine-acre island in the river, just below the GB&W bridge, was cleared to build a dam. In April 1903 Consolidated Water Power & Paper Co. was begun. It installed two Fordrinier paper-making machines powered by two Nordberg-Corliss engines. The industry grew to become the life blood of the city which became Wisconsin Rapids in the early 1920's.

The paper industry had its ups and downs. At first Wisconsin mills did well in newsprint, but Canadian competition came into the field in 1913, causing a scramble for specialized markets. From butcher paper to a final line of high-grade clay-coated enamel papers, "the land where paper comes from" developed not far from GB&W's brick-and-stone roundhouse and its depot on First Avenue.

Another great hope came to life 15 miles east, when Illinois promoters projected a drainage of the great Buena Vista Swamp southwest of Plover, to produce thousands of acres of land for agriculture. It was similar to a project that reclaimed land near Kankakee, Illinois. Announced in March 1903, the project was underway by May of 1905. A South Milwaukee dredging company opened the way for new croplands in 1908.

With the improvements in GB&W's financial and physical plant, rumors spread that the road would soon follow the Winona & South-Western and the Ann Arbor into either the Chicago Great Western or the Wabash camp. Evidence was amassed by lineside newspapers, assuring that GB&W's recent good show in "cleaning up its act" was an attempt to attract buyers. La Crosse merchants were reported to be conferring with A. B. Stickney, asking for service to their community. Another report of Stickney traveling in his private car on GB&W assured the press at least the merger was soon to be. The rumors persisted through the summer of 1901 while GB&W business was on the rise. Joseph A. Jordan held to the truth, denying each and every story. Next, Grand Trunk was the suitor in 1902, CGW again in 1903 and by spring of 1903, George Gould of the Wabash was supposedly interested in acquiring the road. The logic was that Ann Arbor was Gould's and a merger of both trans-Lake Michigan participants was in the best interests of both roads. The old idea of a Gould-sponsored trans-continental was reportedly raised by the *New York World* to be somehow shared by CGW and the Gould forces. Since the GB&W's reorganization it seemed logical that the line might have buyers. The same theme continued to echo throughout the next few decades but serious offers were seldom extended.

The financial reins of GB&W were gripped by its inheritors. John I. Blair's side included C. Ledyard Blair of Blair & Co., New York, and Moses Taylor's line through Robert Winthrop & Co., also of New York. Stephen S. Palmer's office was at Win-

throp's, as was Charles W. Cox's. Mark T. Cox, who was closely associated with the GB&W formation, was also a partner in Robert Winthrop & Co. and a member of the protective committee of bondholders. Cox represented the Winthrop interest in GB&W, passing the interest to Charles W. Cox. William Jay Hunt was also associated with the Cox family through Winthrop's house on Wall Street.

GB&W's first Mogul (2-6-0) engines arrived as primary freight power after November 1907. No.27 was a straightforward design from American Locomotive Co. which would continue to supply the 56-inch drivered, slide-valve power for another seven years. The new engines weighed 62 tons nominally, with a loaded engine and tender weight of just over eighty tons. Tenders of the first five Moguls carried 4000 gallons of water and ten tons of coal. No.28 followed a year later (November 1908) and in January 1910 KGB&W received its first 2-6-0 (No.36).

PERE MARQUETTE 15 delivered two more, Nos. 29 and 37, which arrived in Wisconsin the morning of Sunday, February 24, 1911. Their total empty weight was 78 tons apiece. No.37 was to spar with No.36 on the mixed, while the second went on the Green Bay-Algoma way-freight. Kewaunee again raised hope for more acceptable passenger service with the arrival of the new power and two full coaches owned by KGB&W (No.77 and No. 78) in 1909 and 1910.

A new wye at Kewaunee was installed in 1911, in addition to a steel turntable at Casco Junction, to accommodate the mixed train's heavier power. While the Moguls were in service on August 1, 1911 they were furloughed for the day. Under Engineer Ward and Conductor Kuehl, trains 11-12 had 4-4-0 No.33, the old Union Pacific veteran. No.13-14 with Steve Slattery and Conductor Walker had engine 31, the venerable Baldwin 4-4-0 from A&W. Otterson and Dingman got out with Raidler 4-4-0 No.35. On the GB&W main line Moguls 27 and 28 were operating the runs between Green Bay and Grand Rapids, No.8 (J. Hickey) and No.7 (Joe Brey and Ben Closuit). Other main liners included engines 10, 15, 18, 21, 22 and 25. La Crosse had No.14 (Art Coppin and Bill Kenyon), while Joe Doyle and Bigelow worked the Stevens Point trains, with engine No.7.

While the GB&W continued to modernize, Seth Champion passed away at his home in Alhambra, California in May of 1910, far from Green Bay. Conductor William J. Monahan, age 72, died on Sunday, February 21, 1915, in Green Bay. Monahan was a veteran of the very beginnings, having started with GB&W in the 1870's. He was a respected Elk and his friends Win Abrams, John Seymour and J. H. Flatley attended his last rites. On November 20, 1911 Charles H. Smith was appointed GB&W's trainmaster by General Manager Seymour. Mr. Smith became GB&W Lines superintendent in January 1916 and remained with the company for several decades, eventually rising to the position of assistant to the president. Replacing Smith as trainmaster was L. M. Dingman who was promoted from train service.

Joseph Dennis had a problem in 1908. He ran a small "mixed store and saloon" located on the KGB&W in Brown County at Summit, six miles east of Green Bay. Never a time-carded stop, Summit nonetheless had in Dennis an energetic petitioner who intended to make a station stop of the doubling siding, helping locals to establish a community. The locale was entered on timecards after the siding was installed; Dennis alleged that a station was therefore a desired addition. KGB&W disagreed, stating that Summit didn't enter the timecard until September 1906. Prior to the entry no actual business was done save for occasional loading on an empty siding. The railroaders were worried about stopping their trains on the hill. While roads were barely passable in season, Dennis argued that a stop would not inconvenience the railroad and would serve his locals. KGB&W operated trains averaging seven freight cars plus three coaches, winding around three curves to Summit. The one-percent grade eastbound and hazardous snowdrifts induced the railroad to argue its case vigorously. Yet, the Railroad Commission ordered a flag stop as an experiment and instructed the road to record patronage. No.11-12 was selected to make the stop. KGB&W kept tabs of ridership that fall. No.11 carried only 29 passengers, netting $5.56, while No.12 made 22 stops for 37 people, earning $7.08. The experiment ended in defeat for Dennis and the commission vacated its original position.

Another case involved the village of Luxemburg and its desire for a crossing bell on its Main Street crossing. Six trains and

GB&W's first Mogul stands on the ALCo turntable at Schenectady, New York in November 1907, prior to delivery. Straightforward No.27 began an era in which GB&W Lines 2-6-0's served every division. Engine 28 followed in November 1908. Both weighed 128,000 pounds.

switch movements constituted ten movements over the crossing. Although visibility was more than adequate, KGB&W was willing to comply with the bell suggestion. Luxemburg still wasn't content and other solutions were sought. Further west and two years later, Seymour's Business Men's Association alleged that Sunday service was desired and that such service would gain great profits for GB&W. The commission held that it could not require the service and Sunday trains did not come to Seymour in 1911.

In mid-1913 GB&W was ordered to establish a flag stop at Dooney's Siding (MP 199.5) between Arcadia and Dodge. The petitioner was located about ten miles from each station and ten miles from the CB&Q at Fountain City. The region was extremely hilly and Dooney's was most convenient for the inhabitants. Roads were seldom adequate for the sixty families living in the surrounding countryside. It was proposed that considerable cream traffic could be developed with a stop at remote Dooney's. GB&W had abandoned Dooney's as a passenger stop for No. 1 and No. 2 before, but was willing to experiment in light of the petition. No. 5 and No. 6 would not be stopped, however; the expense was considered unwarranted. The commission ordered GB&W to halt on flag and to keep a record of business at the lonely spot.

Meehan (MP 86) was another station that caught the attention of the Railroad Commission with a petition. Signed by 78 residents, the 1912 petition asked for a shelter, stating that no cover existed for passengers, nor was there a platform since the company had removed it in 1909. In August 1912 a hearing was held at Meehan. The railroad showed that it had maintained a depot there, and later, a boxcar body which provided shelter was removed three years before. All trains did stop on signal and passengers were frequently deposited at the convenience of the train crew. Travelers awaited the limited in the window of a general store or a potato warehouse. Train arrivals could only be ascertained by private use of telephones. GB&W's freight service was inconvenienced, while 255 passengers used the road in 31 days of 1912. With 118 carloads produced in the area, the commission ordered GB&W to provide a suitable structure within thirty days. Meehan received an 18×24-foot depot in 1912.

GB&W received three more slide-valve Moguls between 1912 and 1914. Numbers 30, 50 and 51, which were built in July 1912, March 1913 and January 1914 were slightly heavier than the first group. They carried 5000 gallons of water and twelve tons of coal. GB&W had to number the newest arrivals in the 50-class. No. 40, occupied by a KGB&W 0-6-0, was built in July 1912. With war clouds blowing in Europe, GB&W ordered its first superheated 2-6-0's, No. 52 and No. 38, which arrived in September and October of 1914, just as the war started. Equipped with piston valves and Walschaert Valve Gear, the new engines retained their 19×26-inch cylinders and 56-inch drivers. Their ALCO class "260-S-139" included an engine weight of 139,000 pounds, or just under seventy tons. Tractive effort remained at about 25,600 pounds but the superheater's efficient, dry steam helped considerably. Grate area was 30.2 square feet with 180 pounds of boiler pressure.

In December of 1914 GB&W's directorate proposed that GB&W acquire Iola & Northern Railroad. GB&W owned 700 shares of I&N stock of a total of 714 shares issued, $30,000 of construction certificates of indebtedness issued. The acquisition was arranged by purchase of I&N's property, except its franchise to be a corporation. GB&W agreed to surrender for cancellation the $30,000 construction certificates and assume

Above: KGB&W's Mogul 36 gets underway at New London, Wisconsin. The sturdy design was new, heavy power.
T. VAN DREESE COLLECTION

I&N debts. On December 28, 1914 the deed to I&N went to GB&W. The I&N, for all of its short life, had been dependent upon GB&W for nearly all services and would now cease its anomalous existence. I&N's 4-4-0 No. 2 came into the system roster as No. 2 of GB&W, later becoming GB&W No. 7. The I&N combination car, which was an original GB&LP selection, came back to enter B&B service. Eventually, the car became the last New Franken depot.

Passenger connections for GB&W's customers out of New London was a thorny issue in 1914. C&NW's train 153, due at New London Junction at 6:59 p.m., missed its meet with GB&W mixed train No. 3, due at 6:35. GB&W riders as far west as Scandinavia petitioned to return service to pre-1911 conditions. C&NW wouldn't budge due to arrival commitments elsewhere in its territory. GB&W insisted on keeping its schedule, citing important mail connections at Grand Rapids. The commission thought surely the two roads could agree on a common time.

C&NW's counsel advised ominously that their train 153 was an interstate run, suggesting immunity to commission action. GB&W pleaded that their mixed train No. 3 handled a few freight cars, performing way-freight work, and thus could not be held strictly to passenger schedules. No. 3 only averaged 22½ miles per hour and it was impractical to increase its speed. The commission, which did not hesitate to make requirements regarding interstate runs, ordered both roads to make the connection. In March of 1916 a revised order placed the burden of the meet requirements on GB&W as C&NW's train 153 was engaged in heavy head-end (express) business. No. 3, it was learned, generally arrived on schedule. The published time of arrival was 6:47 p.m. but trains were held to 7:02 p.m., or upon notification of the agent at New London Junction as to the lack of interchange business.

In the years prior to World War I, KGB&W continued its see-saw effort to placate its Kewaunee patrons, but by 1907 there were five automobiles in town, underscoring the imminent alternative to railroad travel. New rails came to both KGB&W and A&W in 1910 aboard the steamer VIKING to Kewaunee where they were loaded on work flats. At the tiny community of Clyde, railroad patrons allegedly made bonfires of ties and logs for warmth while they waited. On July 25, 1912 a heavy summer storm dumped 5½ inches of rain on the Kewaunee Valley, sending its runoff downriver at two or three feet above normal. West

Above: KGB&W Train No. 13 negotiates the Kewaunee Wye curve about 1906. A rebuilt GB&W 4-4-0 is on the head-end. When KGB&W engines were not available, main line power would "pinch hit." The train ran only to Casco Junction.
J. SCHULTZ COLLECTION

Below: Train time at Hixton, Wisconsin about 1910. The ladies' coach, a "50-class" Hicks Standard, came to the GB&W in the 1900's.
VAN SCHAIK COLLECTION; SHSW

Above: Wisconsin & Northern Railroad received a 4-4-0 from GB&W, one of three W&N engines to carry the number. No.2, shown here at Crandon, Wisconsin, was probably an 1870's-era GB&W rebuild, sold or leased to W&N.
SHSW

Below: Wrecker W-180 was an ancient hand-operated car. Formerly numbered 01, the car had two crane units and did heavy service in GB&W's early years. The heirloom survived until the McGee era and was photographed at Norwood in 1936.
H. LEHMAN PHOTO

Kewaunee's Seyk Mill was nearly swept away as the waters reached almost ten feet at Footbridge. Scarboro Creek's dam was nearly carried away, potentially threatening KGB&W's bridge.

Several times after its rebuilding, engine No.32 suffered mechanical failures, one of which was a mainrod end break which put a piston through a cylinder head. Raidler's big 4-4-0 limped in on one side for aid at Green Bay. Later that year, a couple spurned rail service for the adventure of their Ford and a getaway to Green Bay's ball game. Kewaunee was learning to live without the tuscan red combine.

While Casco Junction today hardly seems recreational, the Minahan family of Green Bay, who held land nearby, and the railroad were interested in development of a forty-acre park, complete with pathways. The development stalled on the eve of war, but construction in the form of a new 50,000-gallon windmill-fed watertank changed Casco Junction's "skyline" considerably.

High lime content in Kewaunee's water had much to do with a foaming incident in engine 35 as it struggled to bring No.12 into Sturgeon Bay on the A&W. Returning to Casco Junction, 35 was exchanged for GB&W Mogul 27 which brought No.11 into Green Bay. No.35's failure to make steam adequately from the alkaline water bestowed yet another delay on the railroad.

Below: This interior view of AC&F-built GB&W coach 108 was taken in January of 1918. The coach was the last one built for the road.

Casco Junction was the site of another, more serious affair as Engineer Al Zimms was running Mogul 27 slowly out of the Casco Junction gravel pit June 4, 1915. Zimms was bringing out several flatcars loaded with sand for ballasting. When he was opposite the steam shovel, Zimms felt the right rail under the engine flop over. No.27 keeled over into the sand, slightly injuring Zimms. It took the wrecker a full working day to bring No.27 up and out of the site.

The uneven freight traffic at Casco Junction proved trying for many a winter passenger. In one instance, Conductor Lake's two brakemen needed two hours to make up their 26-car train, the combine being far from the depot's warmth. The train finally got underway, passengers vowing to petition for reform. Frank Seymour, in December 1915, promised better service, thereby smothering Railroad Commission action, and created a daily Green Bay-Kewaunee train. The businessmen of Kewaunee were informed that the new limited would carry people and perishables without switching en route and would expedite mail service. In time, mixed service to the junction returned as patronage did not warrant a separate train and the age-old departure at 7:30 a.m. continued to be the acceptable norm.

Frank Halliday remembered his experiences with Joseph Jordan during his early GB&W years. Halliday related that Jordan, a veteran of the C&A and an ex-telegrapher, used to gravitate to that office at Green Bay Junction where the clacking sound of the telegraph punctuated the air. Halliday remarked that Jordan "had come from the StL&H, which was owned by

AC&F PHOTO

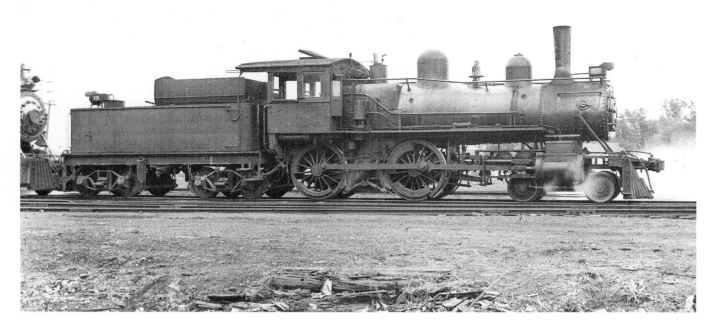

GB&W's 4-4-0 No.18, another Raidler rebuild, was completed in July of 1905. It was the last one done for the main line. The upper view was taken at Norwood in 1935. The last surviving Belpaire-boilered rebuild, well remembered as a helper engine, is shown in the lower view at Wisconsin Rapids in 1918. No.18 was withdrawn in late 1937.
BOTH PHOTOS: STAN MAILER COLLECTION

the same New York gang that owned us." While reviewing GB&W's modest earnings, Jordan asked Halliday if they shouldn't sell the GB&W. Halliday was then detailed to negotiate with the Harris Trust people to sell GB&W to CB&Q. The problem was that of the financial structure of the GB&W, which stood like a sentinel against such sales. Halliday remarked that "Mr. Cox had put George Wickersham (of the Cadwallader, Wickersham and Taft Law firm) up to the formation of the road, in the financial form it takes today." Halliday formed a sale group within the company and was none too popular at the time with his fellow officers. It was found that the road couldn't be sold, which left Halliday's group exonerated as far as his contemporaries were concerned. Halliday, who began his career with GB&W "on April Fool's Day, 1913," remained with the road and witnessed a more prosperous GB&W several decades later.

GB&W's total revenue tonnage in 1907 of 394,010 tons had fallen to 328,200 tons in 1909. The amount increased significantly by 1914, however, to 547,069 tons and revenue traffic had reached 840,264 tons by 1920. The freight tonnage of 1911 was divided as follows: 33% agricultural products, 32% coal and other mine products, while 13% was attributed to other freight. GB&W's lumber and pulpwood business fell to 9.5% of the total freight but, during the war years, coal traffic rose to the highest levels for the period, reaching 42% in 1917 and declining

only slightly thereafter. By 1920 agriculture again accounted for the major portion. Passenger density rose to its highest in 1914 and 1915. At 27,705, ridership reflected the economic buildup in American business as the European war intensified. Freight increased steadily from 152,297 tons to 349,357 tons in 1920.

President S. S. Palmer died suddenly in late February 1913 at Redlands, California. Palmer had been president for 16 years. His son, Edgar Palmer, became vice-president in 1913 and Joseph A. Jordan rose from vice-president and general manager to the president's post in the same year. Charles W. Cox became secretary and treasurer. Directors were C. Ledyard Blair, C. W. Cox, William J. Wilson, J. A. Jordan, Edgar Palmer, H. R. Taylor and F. B. Seymour. Significantly, the Blair-Taylor lineage continued to dominate GB&W's affairs. In the same time span rumors of GB&W's sale to Newman Erb-Hawley interests would have an alliance with M&StL on one side and Ann Arbor on the other. Erb was president of Ann Arbor and it was reported that an option was secured on 2500 shares of GB&W common stock and that the price paid was $100,000. Just after S. S. Palmer's death, the deal was claimed to be void. Trackside speculators settled for the next sale rumor, which was as certain as the arrival of next year's Mogul at a GB&W roundhouse.

Another significant rumor arose from the actions of the Reorganization Committee in 1906. The Green Bay & St. Paul

Railroad Company was reportedly organized to again expand the road northwestward. In October it was certain that GB&W was quietly securing terminal facilities and acquiring land in St. Paul. Mark T. Cox, a stockholder in Pere Marquette, was rumored as the force behind the new road. GB&W never realized the long-cherished drive for a St. Paul gateway, observed by many as a way out of its short line dilemma.

GB&W'S DISPATCHER SHEET
June 1, 1918

Train	Route	Eng.	Conductor	Engineer
1	Green Bay to Winona	10	Johnson	Wigman
2	Green Bay to Winona	12	Witherall	Baker
3	Gr.Bay to Gr.Rapids	18	Welby	Whiting
4	Return	18	Welby	Thompson
9	Gr. Rapids to Winona	50	Myott	Fredricks
10		30	Collier	Ray
7	Gr. Rapids to Winona	53	Manning	Hickey
8	Winona to Gr. Rapids	52	Baenen	Brey
5	Gr.Bay to Gr.Rapids	26,27	Closuit (Berg)	Millen (Lucas)
6	Return	51	Pratt	Paape
11	Kewaunee Division	34	Kuehl	Ward
12	Kewaunee Division	34	Kuehl Ward	
13	Kewaunee Division	31	Walker	Slattery
14	Kewaunee Division	31	Walker	Slattery
15	Kewaunee Division	39	Richards	Hollister
16	Kewaunee Division	39	Richards	Hollister
Extra 2	Gr.Bay to Casco Jct.*	29	Walker	Ferris
LaCrosse Mixed	On the Point	25	Kenyon	Coppin
Stevens Point		15	Reilahan	Doyle
Mixed 13	Gr.Bay to Sturg.Bay	2		
Mixed 14	Sturg.Bay to Gr.Bay	2		
Mixed 3	Gr.Bay to Gr.Rapids	35		
Mixed 4	Gr.Rapids to Gr.Bay			

*Then on to Kewaunee; then doubled a train back to Luxemburg.

In June 1915 and September 1916, GB&W received two Moguls from American Locomotive, this time one for A&W (39) and GB&W's 53, both ALCO class "260-S-139." No.53 possessed an Otis steel boiler shell, cast-steel drive wheel centers, steel driving wheel boxes, brass hub liners and Alligator cross-

heads. It was the only Mogul equipped with the garden-variety crosshead which was retained until it was scrapped in 1948. No.53's price tag was $14,475. GB&W specifications were written to cover a "saturated freight steam locomotive," but the final product carried a superheater, complete with damper control on the righthand side. The new cast-steel parts were an improvement over cast iron, the norm for most locomotives in a more leisurely era of moderate train speeds.

Nearly twenty years after the 1896 fire, the second Cargill elevator went up in flames. Grain worth "$185,000 and buildings worth $160,000" burned on August 26, 1916, at three in the afternoon. Embers soared high over Green Bay and debris rained down from a windless sky, kindling other blazes. C&NW worked quickly to clear its nearby yard of boxcars and coaches, while several cars of GB&W burned at the elevator. Cargill's 25-year lease was to end in 1921. Two years earlier, Cargill had moved its offices to Milwaukee. It would be several years before a replacement was built for grain service.

Charlie Chapman of Wisconsin Rapids, retired and living in remembrance of the old days, recalled a 1910 tornado that swept through the Winona area. Charlie, "half Irish and half Connecticut Yankee," witnessed the high wind, remaining above ground while his womenfolk went into the basement. Their home was the former Keyes estate, a longtime railroader's hotel adjacent to the GB&W Winona enginehouse. At about 4 p.m. Charlie saw train No.6 just pulling up to the bridge as the wind swept down from Winona's bluffs. Wilbur Whiting was the engineer. He stopped short of the bridge just as the wind struck. Charlie claimed that the wind bowled over coaches on the rear and the lights went out in them as they toppled over. Later, Charlie and his sisters were commandeered to energize push cars in order to convey the baggage car's contents up the Second

Below: Black Creek is located 23.5 miles west of Green Bay and passenger train No.1 was scheduled to arrive there at 7:47 a.m. Visible are the first class 50-series accommodation with the 40-series smoker coach just ahead. The depot was replaced in the McGee era. This photo was taken about 1909.

E. SHAW COLLECTION

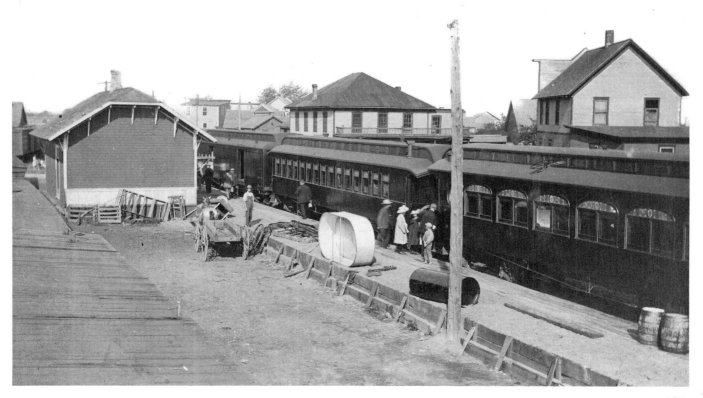

Street trackage to the depot. Chapman began his GB&W labors cleaning coaches at Bridge Yard, which were kept there after the trains arrived. He remembered well the tuscan red coaches which ran up Second Street behind the shiny little engines, no doubt numbers 10-12. When the train unloaded, it backed cautiously down to Bridge Yard and the attention of young Charlie. Chapman later worked in the Winona enginehouse and was "set up" as a fireman in 1910.

Chapman, who became an engineer in 1912, also recalled the weather signs which GB&W installed on the baggage cars as a service to rural onlookers. They were metal placards, their color denoting the predictions for the day. A storm was significantly indicated with black, while light gray meant more clement conditions. Charlie also remembered that, in those pre-war days, GB&W did its own switching near the C&NW freighthouse, back of Second Street. He also noted that the La Crosse train, on which he fired later, left its coach at Marshland in honor of the C&NW trackage right. This way, GB&W could not carry La Crosse-Winona passengers in competition. "Coal was the big business on the La Crosse branch," Charlie recalled, "which went to the Normal School." However, this business was to evaporate with the coming of barged coal to La Crosse from Southern Illinois and Kentucky. Barged coal spelled the end of the La Crosse branch in 1922. Charlie also remembered taking an engine around the Hatfield Dam destruction, via Marshfield and Neilsville, in 1911. The severing of GB&W's main line that day, which was probably the road's greatest disaster, has had repercussions to the present day.

STAN MAILER COLLECTION

J. P. LONGLEY COLLECTION

DEPOT SCENE
AMHERST JUNCTION WIS.

The depot at Amherst Junction, Wisconsin was unusual. Originally a level crossing with Wisconsin Central until 1901, WC then chose a grade separation to help reduce its heavy westbound gradient. It required the bi-level station illustrated. The new depot had a stairway, as well as an elevator for express. The depot, which burned in 1932, was replaced by a 24×40-foot structure which retained the minehoist-like express transfer. The system was removed about 1940.

13
HATFIELD

Hatfield, Wisconsin has a fine reputation among outdoors-men and get-away-from-it-all vacationers. Its cool pines rustle in clear air and warm sands are underfoot. Hatfield was named for Lackawanna Iron & Coal Company's President Edwin F. Hatfield Jr. There are agreeable bars, Vi Teeple's Thunderbird Museum and once-a-day railroad service. Hatfield hosts Lake Arbutus, held back these many years by a dam now mossy and eternal seeming, pockmarked with age. The Black River which spills gently in summer over the old concrete is hardly able to murmur the word disaster . . . except for a time in Autumn of 1911.

Waterpower was old, but electricity by waterpower was all very new in 1911. It was a new way of life; a new revenue producer. It could power trolley cars, light homes and drive industry. The La Crosse Water Power Co., envisioning economic electricity for interurban railroads out of La Crosse, created a fine dam in 1904 with an unusual power house location two miles downstream above and beside the river gorge. Even though the railroads were supposed to be the main consumers of the power, the electricity went into general use and the company settled down to hopes of profit. Fortune, however, did not look kindly at the dam on the Black River. Records show that there wasn't enough water in Lake Arbutus on two separate occasions and the two turbines merely dabbled at humming out their kilowatt hours. However, 1911 wasn't one of those years.

Summer had come, overripe with precipitation. Torrential June rains, capping an already wet spring, had inspectors frowning and sandbag crews had to be sent to the edge of swirling, thundering waters. Both the Hatfield Dam and its partner six miles upstream, the Dells Dam, were under siege. Ten miles downstream, Black River Falls was having problems with its own city dam, which had a new powerplant for local service. The lights in Black River Falls had already flickered out

once that first year and heavy rains had disabled the dam and power equipment. The townspeople were impatient to have their electricity back and uneasy about the Hatfield Dam. Many thought the dam to be a threat to a town of two thousand.

Black River Falls lay on the outer edge of a bend in the Black River. The stream emerges from a tight, rocky valley aimed straight at the heart of the business district. Water Street, then as now, is a sort of front line by the river, carrying today's Highway 12 past the business district, not far above subdued waters which rush over pre-Cambrian rocks. The river then flows to the Missisippi at La Crosse. The city was equally unhappy at the loss of the railroad main line which had crossed the narrow valley on a lacy iron bridge high above any normal waterlevel's threats. Big business spelled progress by eliminating the Omaha Railroad's sharp, curving St. Paul-Chicago main line bottleneck and bypassing the city.

Crews struggled to control the critical situation at the three dams, the Dells, the Hatfield and the Black River Falls, each straining to hold back great masses of water. The long canal to the Hatfield power plant carried all it could of the raging torrent. Inadequately protected, it transformed the current into spare electricity. The earthen dams were saturated and signs of impending catastrophe showed in the sodden embankments.

In October the condition was tense. The rains came again with October first registering better than a half-inch. On October 5th the Hatfield rain gauge read 3.12 inches. Beginning at 1 p.m. western Wisconsin's creeks and rivers were gorged with runoff and the the three dams of the Black River stood for the final assault.

The Dells and Hatfield dams were all that technology of the times (and the company's purse) could make of them. Both consisted of a concrete corewall, much like a large garden enclosure, carefully buried within compacted earthwork. There were some circles of thought that recommend better ways to build dams and better ways to control the overburdens resulting from high water. Hatfield and Dells were equipped with planks which fitted into triangular steel units atop the dam to hold back any assault beyond the capacity of the concrete spillway below. It seemed adequate; one dam protecting the other, providing the upper dam held.

Above: Dam construction at Hatfield proceeded in 1904 with ex-Rock Island 0-4-0t No.321 and tender employed by the original contractor to bring aggregate to the concrete-mixing plant. The scene includes GB&W's original bridge over the Black River's main channel and the original dam's beginning.
VAN SCHAIK PHOTO; SHSW COLLECTION

The Dells Dam was in trouble. The engineers had seen signs of overload in the summer and the dam's narrow spillway was unable to contend with the assault. The company had concentrated crews on the upstream structure each time the water rose to new heights. Wet, straining manpower tugged and shoved and packed sandbags on the narrow slippery top. Grim-faced and tired crews worked to raise the dam's height. The Dells dam, the first domino of three above Black River Falls, was never out of trouble. The work continued with dogged determination into

Below: Contractors' employees gathered around ex-Rock Island 0-4-0t with tender No.321 at Hatfield's dam construction site in 1904.
AUTHOR'S COLLECTION

the first hours of Friday, October 6th. At 4 a.m. exhausted workers watched in horror as water poured around the west end of the dam, undercutting the earthen backbrace for the concrete corewall. The waters tore at the softened earth until dawn when at last, with everybody ordered off the doomed structure, the corewall gave way and fell flat. Four hundred feet of dam disappeared in the torrent and the entire mass thundered down upon Lake Arbutus.

Dells Dam, completed in the fall of 1909, was an answer to a need for a backstop, a control for the Hatfield Dam. The company was embarrassed the next year, however, when near-drought conditions reduced the waters of the Black to a trickle. But that was 1909. On October 5, 1911 Black River Falls businessmen, uneasy with the rains and rumors of trouble at Dells Dam, began to load their business goods into wagons and move them away from Water Street "for good measure." There were those in Black River Falls who gave assurances . . . but, then again . . .

A gray, wet dawn witnessed a fire bell ringing in the distance. The downstream people were told the news and the company's chief engineer at Hatfield wasted no time in making what preparations he could for the onslaught. Black River Falls also received word of the impending disaster. People feverishly began evacuating what belongings they could. A lawyer took part of his library, banks withdrew valuables, both placing the items west of the business district. Shopkeepers gathered what they could in the morning hours. At Hatfield a force of men quickly swung into action, digging a side cut in the overburdened powerhouse canal. If left alone, the mass of water would rush through and destroy the power plant, perhaps demolishing the entire building. The side cut worked, for the water then thundered down into the original gorge of the Black River and headed for Black River Falls. By 9 a.m. the water from the Dells

Dam was upon Hatfield. Water sluiced west of the dam on level ground, tearing out the Green Bay & Western tracks.

The railroad was lucky. Train No. 9, a short freight which had left Grand Rapids at the crack of the wet dawn, reached Hatfield and the high iron bridge over the Black just after 8:00 a.m. With little to do except get out of the way, No. 9 snorted off toward Merrillan by 8:15 a.m. No. 9 was the last train to pass through Hatfield for a month or more. When the Dells gorge smashed full force into Hatfield at 8:40 a.m. water poured over the east approach to the dam and the railroad, quickly tearing it away from the embankment. The train's smoke was still hanging in the damp air as the track disappeared. Water roared through the woods west of the dam into an old gravel pit. On the east side the worst was just beginning. The torrent rushed over the spillway fully eleven feet higher than the concrete is today. As in the Dells catastrophe, the water undercut the back side of the earthen dam east of the spillway and overturned the corewall. The waters in the next hour completely stripped sand and mud from the bedrock, down about 25 feet, creating a new channel in short order. One thousand feet downstream the waters re-entered the original gorge of the Black. A wall of water no dam could stop rumbled toward Black River Falls.

Excursions to Hatfield from Winona were often made on summer Sundays with Tr. 1-2's available equipment. Here, one of the specials employed 4-4-0 No. 12 and coach 53, while a baggage car carried outing supplies to the shores of Lake Arbutus in 1912. Winona's younger set obliged the photographer on No. 12's pilot.
JACKSON COUNTY HISTORICAL SOCIETY

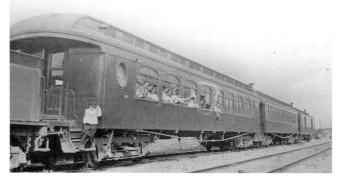

By 10:00 a.m. Black River Falls was in frantic motion to save itself. The river was rising rapidly, rumbling ominously under the Omaha Railroad bridge. The townsmen thought surely there was enough underlying hard rock in the embankments north of town opposite the restricted channel through which the waters were pouring. The city power dam was also expected to do its share of holding off the deluge, but it didn't happen that way.

By noon, a rising wave of angry water gushed past Black River Falls and shook the Omaha bridge, engulfing the newly built wall at the west end of the city dam and its spillway. The

Below: This is a 1908 view of the completed west dam at Hatfield in tranquil times.
AUTHOR'S COLLECTION

THE DAM AT HATFIELD, WIS.

Above: Hatfield's east dam location as it appeared on October 6, 1911, the day of the flood. At the center of the photograph, GB&W's rails dangle into surging waters south of the core wall's remaining portion.
SHSW COLLECTION

Below: The destruction at the west dam at Hatfield is shown in October 1911. The flume to the powerhouse is a wall-like structure in the center background. Damage to the community, seen in the distance, was extensive. GB&W's original bridge is on the left.
GREEN BAY & WESTERN COLLECTION

Above: GB&W raised a temporary trestle across the washed-out section to re-open their main line a month after the disaster. Soil overburden was carried off the bedrock — about 25 feet of thickness.
JACKSON COUNTY HISTORICAL SOCIETY

Below: Hatfield's destruction after the flood of October 6, 1911 is shown here with GB&W's depot in the distance. The photographer is on the powerhouse flume bridge in this westward view. At first, the floodwaters went around the dam's west end, carrying track off the roadbed.
AUTHOR'S COLLECTION

city's last buffer against destruction fell when men and sandbags could no longer avert the dam's destruction. The power plant crumbled into the raging swell and the water began to steadily scour everything off the bedrock at the outer edge of the bend. Worse yet, the flood followed narrow Town Creek which led up into the northern business district, allowing the torrent access to the back side of the city and buildings there began to be swept away.

One by one the small wooden shops were torn off their footings as the river, swinging in from the north, uprooted everything including many feet of earth, leaving only hard bedrock. Large brick buildings, thought able to stand, were undermined and collapsed with a roar into the torrent. Three-story buildings crumbled and fell away, their foundations disappearing in the rush. Downstream, in Mr. Bright's pine grove, deposited debris formed an island which continued to grow. The destruction continued into the night as the city dam with its destroyed spillway focused the rush into the great new wound in the earth. Bridges across the river were carried away and tossed against the wrecked buildings. Stacks of merchandise from the businesses littered the island. Chinaware in cupboards washed up unbroken and fruit jars were found intact, but the buildings they once inhabited were nonexistent.

The next day, with the water down fifteen feet from the previous noon and the torrent still eating at the city, desperate measures were taken to direct the water into the original channel. With a limited stock of dynamite available, the dam's arm was blown up, but only a small channel resulted. The waters continued to rush into the city until the next day when the Omaha Railway brought in cars of explosive which succeeded in relieving the city.

Marshal Carnahan was faced with another problem. There were not enough marshals to guard valuables, maintain order and care for the destitute. He placed a guard at the Omaha depot across from the city to prevent undesirable people from investigating the disaster area. However, some succeeded in breaching his defense and relieved the beleaguered town of valuables. On Sunday morning Sheriff Meek, who found himself with an overwhelming task, wired Governor McGovern for aid. Two troops of militia, one each from Eau Claire and Mauston, arrived to bring order and some peace of mind.

The entire state had heard of the disaster by this time. Local photographer William Heller produced some spectacular photos showing buildings collapsing in a shower of spray. Harrison Montgomery of Hartford sped to the scene, producing panoramas of the destruction. The first shipments of aid began to arrive from as far away as Superior, the earliest being a carload from Eau Claire Grocery Company. Volunteers were soon wrapping "survival rations" as a wagon rumbled into town from

nearby Alma Center on the GB&W with $60 of goods. Governor McGovern wired sympathy and aired a proclamation to all states. Floods of telegrams crowded the depot as keys clattered incessantly. Sparta voted $1000 to aid the stricken city and Milwaukee appealed to its citizens to do the same.

To the north the waters receded and the earth around Hatfield began to dry out. The four men who had dug the side cut in the powerhouse channel had reason to be proud. They had saved the powerhouse. Indeed, a barrel of oil, which had been thrown over when the waters struck the building, coated the precious generators, protecting them from extensive damage. Soon the State of Wisconsin sent investigators. The Railroad commission of Wisconsin dispatched Professor W. D. Pence of the University of Wisconsin Engineering Department to survey and photograph the scene to determine the cause of the disaster. From this examination and subsequent legal action, the conditions of the power company went from bad to worse. The company went bankrupt.

The Green Bay & Western, cut in two by the flood, fared badly. Forced to detour its trains via Marshfield, the road allegedly lost some $50,000 in the process. But within a month the road had a temporary trestle across the gap and was well into settling the matter with the dam's owners. Eventually, the railroad received a permanent free bridge across a new Taintor gate built at the site, courtesy of the unfortunate power company.

Black River Falls rebuilt itself slowly and painfully. The following year the Omaha Railroad bridge which had almost collapsed into the flood was removed in favor of a new line a mile upstream. Today you can find traces of the disaster at Hatfield below the Taintor gates of the east dam. Parts of the corewall lie on rocks south of the GB&W to this day. All of Black River Falls businesses along Water Street are post-1911 construction. Upstream, along Highway 95 and north of the bridge over the Black, stands the Dells Dam spillway. It was never rebuilt.

14

COMING
OF
AGE

The years before World War I, during which the nation witnessed the rise of government regulation and lowered profits, were trying ones for American railroads. The cause was steadily rising costs, coupled to rates held down by public reaction to monopoly. Railroad costs rose fifty percent, while rates went up only thirty percent. A series of flat spots came to railroads in the form of 1907's economic slump and 1914's downturn. In September 1915 a large number of financially shaky railroads went into receivership. Having experienced its own tempests in past decades, Green Bay & Western now showed modest gains and scant evidence of railroading's furor.

Wisconsin progressivism was personified in Robert M. La Follette who contributed to the state's regulatory policies in an era keen to usher out autocratic railroad management in favor of public control. State and federal action, including the Hepburn Act (1906), wrested control of transportation from ownership smacking of royalism. Rate hikes, many of which were officially rejected by the stronger Interstate Commerce Commission, eventually advanced at a rate lower than the corrosive costs. Railroaders finally won the eight-hour day by March 19, 1917. Labor unions had picked the best possible time to push demands. Traffic was heavy, for defense work had brought the inevitable riches of war profits to industry.

GB&W's responsibilities were extended to cover Ettrick & Northern and La Crosse & Southeastern. Rates and priorities were centralized at Green Bay, although few priority shipments other than food emerged from the two short lines. E&N's construction was somewhat endangered by the war due to manpower shortages but in April of 1917, shortly before USRA became a fact, GB&W built its interchange trackage with E&N.

As the volume of war material increased, railroads required further federal control to ensure that priority shipments got through. With much confusion reigning in the shipping of war goods, a priority act was executed in August 1917 and on December 26th President Wilson put the railroads under government operation. The Railroad Control Administration was a reality. Federal regulation guaranteed that adequate compensation would be equal to the average income of the three years prior to June 30, 1917. Director General William G. McAdoo was a competent administrator, well versed in accounting, law and public relations. McAdoo allowed each railroad's operating department to remain intact. The Federal Operating Contract between Green Bay & Western and USRA was signed after the Armistice on April 20, 1919, fixing GB&W's compensation for the period at $331,000.

The road's federal treasurer, A. H. Mongin, was headquartered at Green Bay. GB&W's net earnings from 1917 through 1919 were $202,633, $275,099 and $204,878 respectively, of which $155,000 was received July 1, 1919 from USRA. GB&W Directors on June 1, 1919 declared the regular five-percent dividend on class A debentures, five percent on capital stock and one-half of one percent on class B debentures out of 1918 earnings, nearly the same conditions which had prevailed since the early 1900's. GB&W's takeover date by USRA was fixed at

Left: GB&W built two special snowplows for east-end service. At right, Mogul 28 had the formidable 1920-era plow fitted for its dedicated operation; 4-4-0 No. 18 had the small size ready for action. The plow rivals D&RGW's wedge designs for size.

GBW PHOTO

Life on a 4-4-0, circa 1920. Engineer Charles "Chip" Dickey and Fireman Dave Dains man their small engine for a day of serious railroading.
RAY BUTTOLPH COLLECTION

noon, December 28, 1917, somewhat after the fact and before the actual legal papers came forth, reflecting the emergency aspect of the frantic war years.

Some of the problems in purchasing power came to light during the war years. When GB&W bought Mogul No. 53 in 1916, the works had problems with material allocations, especially in midyear. The GB&W board deliberated about the advance in price over A&W's 39, choosing to pass upon the matter at the annual meeting on March 8th. The agreement was based on ALCO's ability to hold the line on price to March 15, 1916. Action was nearly dropped over the increased price, but ALCO assured GB&W that money would be saved by prompt action. The 53 was a mark-up of some $800 over A&W's No. 39. In September of 1918, two Pittsburgh 2-6-0's were delivered. They were numbered 54 and 55 and cost $71,316.23.

New engines No. 54 and No. 55 were unique only in that both came from ALCO's Pittsburgh Works at a time when that smaller operation was nearing its closing. Aside from USRA 0-6-0's, 0-8-0's and Toledo Terminal 2-8-0's, the Moguls were the last road power built in Pittsburgh. No. 54 and No. 55 were 116 shop numbers from the plant's phase-out in January 1919. ALCO often would farm out small engine orders to the older shops in its group to clear the larger erecting halls for orders of heavier power. Of the superheated Moguls, this pair was scrapped nearly a decade before the others, suggesting that "Liberty steel" might have been inferior to pre-war metal.

GB&W's October 1918 USRA timetable shows that No. 1-2 were on their usual schedule, departing from Green Bay at 7:00 a.m. and arriving there at 6:00 p.m., while Winona's arrival and departure were 9:00 a.m. and 3:30 p.m. respectively. Trains 3 and 4 were carded as passenger-only, running on a local schedule as far as Grand Rapids (Wisconsin Rapids by 1920), departing Green Bay at 2:00 p.m., arriving Grand Rapids at 6:30 p.m. No. 4 left the Rapids at 6:50 a.m., getting into Green Bay at 11:10 a.m. No. 7-8 were freight trains between the two major cities, No. 7 running on the heels of No. 1. No. 8 left Grand Rapids at 5:00 a.m. for the east. Merrillan-Winona trains 5-6 constituted "shopper service," leaving Merrillan at 7:55 a.m. and returning by 6:15 p.m. This allowed a 2½-hour layover in Winona. No freight service was scheduled between Grand Rapids and Merrillan, from which No. 9-10 (freight) operated, even though it left at 8:30 a.m. from Merrillan, reaching Southwestern Junction (Bridge Yard) at 4:30 p.m. GB&W's special

instructions included the admonition that freight trains must not exceed twenty miles per hour. Speed restriction at The Pass Curve (MP 198) was a cautious six miles per hour. The curve brought the railroad around a promontory along the Trempeleau River, always requiring careful operation. Kewaunee operations returned to the Casco Junction mixed service which was increased to twice daily. This was the shape of the 1918's GB&W; it was heavily "Mogulized" and sported its last new passenger coach, an open-platform sixty-footer from AC&F.

KGB&W's 2-8-0 No.45 arrived in early 1923, one of two curiously similar to Toledo Terminal individuals. At one hundred tons each, they constituted the heaviest machines on the road until 1937. Plans survive for Toledo Terminal's engine, indicating only slight differences between GB&W's 45 and 65, TT's 47 and MAR's No.5. GB&W's 56 arrived in 1924. The renumbered ALCo is seen at lower right, double-heading with a Mayflower about 1937.

ALCo HISTORIC PHOTO

In spite of GB&W's "business as usual" condition, the road was able to budget for roadway betterments, chiefly the bridges in the Trempeleau Valley. Eight bridges were raised about 17 inches above the ever-threatening flood-plain, including extra piles and caps. Three years previously, an April flood had raised the river and damaged GB&W roadbed in the final twenty miles to the Mississippi, a condition which by 1919 was hardly unusual. But in spring of 1919 the Trempeleau River again rose dramatically, the companion railroad in its valley suffering destruction over fifty miles. Most frequently effected by floods was the sector east of Arcadia (MP 192), the village located exactly where Kelly, Ketchum and Hiles intended it to be, but which always stands with its railroad in the path of wrathful waters.

Aging depots had a habit of catching fire and certain GB&W structures were no exception. On January 17, 1923 Plover's

1898, 20 × 40-foot building burned to the ground. The culprit was a burnt-out chimney. The replacement, a 20 × 85-foot one-story frame design, was completed by July at a cost of $2805. Plover's business included the Stevens Point branch paper mill and express for Stevens Point. Soo Line's Portage branch, which was abandoned in 1945, also interchanged some business there. On April 16, 1924 Dexterville also lost its depot to fire. It was struck by lightning. The virtual abandonment of Dexterville after World War I left only a makeshift station made of two boxcar bodies placed end to end. Whitehall's newspaper observed that Dexterville, once the center of George Hiles' pine empire, would no longer be placed on the post office map.

The long, slow end of the La Crosse Branch began during the war years. A service complaint to the Railroad Commission stressed inconveniences to passengers and proposed that GB&W

R. GRAHAM PHOTO

change its westend service. At a Madison hearing July 11, 1916, the petitioner's representatives met with GB&W's Superintendent Charles H. Smith and J. B. Call, soon to be named general freight agent. It was proposed to have branch train 42 connect with trains 5-6 (Merrillan-Winona) instead of GB&W No.1-2. The gist of the argument would raise again the rivalry of La Crosse and Winona, as La Crosse wished to enjoy access to the Trempeleau Valley communities as far east as Merrillan.

Crosse in town at noon. Passengers coming into La Crosse would then have nearly four hours to shop. The commission found the GB&W's service inadequate and ordered the changes for trains 41-42. The experiment in convenience didn't last long. In June of 1917 the condition was reversed and, under USRA control, La Crosse's mixed again was ordered to depart at 7:30 a.m., arriving in Marshland at 8:55 a.m. Returning, No.41 left at 3:10 p.m. and was back in La Crosse by 4:20 p.m..

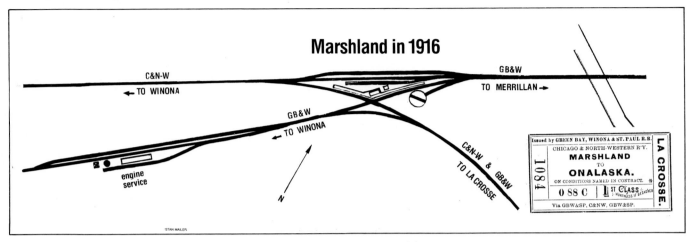

Marshland in 1916

Inasmuch as GB&W through passengers could use CB&Q or Milwaukee road service from La Crosse to Winona, La Crosse local service could be arranged for the main line local business. The mixed train's freight offerings to the main line had to await train No.10 at 5:30 the next morning at Marshland. The argument revealed the paltry number of La Crosse-to-east passengers during 1915 and 1916, totaling a mere 111, an average of only two per day. Freight from the east to La Crosse arrived with train No.9 and was left at Marshland. The southbound La Crosse mixed arrived in La Crosse under the original schedule at 4:20 p.m., too late for car delivery. The connection with No.5-6 would put GB&W's deliveries to La

The idea of a La Crosse Union Station persisted until 1920, spurred on by the burning of Milwaukee Road's depot in December 1916. The city had five roads in 1920 and clamored for a convenient central depot. GB&W appeared for several hearings but declined action due to their feeble business. La Crosse & Southeastern declined to appear at all, such was their state of affairs. The winds of abandonment began to blow in earnest by 1921. The postwar recession brought reduced railroad business and even affected river traffic, which was all but extinct after 1912. GB&W filed with ICC for abandonment March 7, 1921, but was opposed by the Railroad Commission, the City of La Crosse and its Chamber of Commerce. GB&W's rental pay-

GB&W's Plover depot burned on January 17, 1923. A new depot, which was built at a cost of $3,000, stood until February of 1959.

STAN MAILER COLLECTION

Above: Kewaunee County prepared for war as eligible young men were arranged before a group of GB&W 51-class Hicks Standard coaches at Casco Junction. They were gathered for training camps from Sturgeon Bay, Algoma and Kewaunee.

ment to C&NW of $7000 per year precluded any serious attempt to solicit business in La Crosse, while the larger road restricted GB&W to one mixed train per day. The GB&W's "considerable amount" of freight was directed as far east as Merrillan and involved jobbers' and merchants' competition in the Trempeleau Valley versus Winona. Rates favored La Crosse's participation there on a single-rate basis. The alternative after abandonment was a double-local rate basis which threatened to drive out La Crosse's trade in favor of Winona. La Crosse also reminded the public that it had invested $75,000 in the 6.38-mile orphan branch.

Much of the coal for La Crosse's State Teachers College was dock coal from Green Bay, or came via the Grand Crossing interchange. Other coal customers were the La Crosse City Waterworks' pumping station and the local gas and electric company, which used both steam and gas coal. Steam coal came up the lakes and, from 1917 until the abandonment application date, GB&W hauled $49,734.21 worth of coal traffic, based on freight charges. These and other industries were dependent upon GB&W. Essentially, the road had the exclusive business of the normal school, as the line passed through the campus, miles from competition, and the state had purchased a spur to the school in 1918 which ran off from GB&W's line.

GB&W's La Crosse branch showed a deficit for the period 1911 to 1920 of $197,476.21 so management began to search for another La Crosse railroad to acquire the line. The Railroad Commission observed that GB&W's recent years had not been all that disastrous and the operating ratio for 1920 stood at 89.63 percent. The state chose to consider the company's condition as a whole and not just for the lonely little branch in question; if the GB&W could bring about a rate situation which would not be greater than 1921's, the commission would agree to a review of the case. As it stood, the commission denied the request.

GB&W continued to operate through 1921, while rates on Illinois coal were lowered from Central Illinois points to northern states, including Wisconsin. GB&W was further motivated to reopen the branch case and, on June 7, 1922, filed another petition to ICC stating that appropriate steps had been taken to equalize rates. A contract between CB&Q and GB&W allowed the larger road access to the customers of GB&W and the establishment of joint rates with C&NW and CB&Q no

higher than single-line rates to Marshland and East Winona. Final protests came from some splinter passenger groups but, on September 25th, ICC granted GB&W the right to vacate the Gateway City.

The exit was not absolute. GB&W was quoted as being interested in renting its La Crosse landholdings to CB&Q. With the numerous trestles over swamplands north of the city, there was the problem of either rebuilding them or providing access from the southside Burlington line near the GB&W depot. CB&Q yard engines were already too heavy to operate from Grand Crossing which condemned the railroad north of the present university district.

In the midst of the 1920 postwar slump, a Railroad Labor Board was empowered to cover grievances, wage rates and other disputes. The board ordered a general advance in wages, which averaged 22 percent, effective May 1, 1920, just as USRA closed its operations. Even though the gain was substantial, relations were less than cordial between management and labor. Conditions did not improve when the business downturn in 1921 forced layoffs. Wage reductions in mid-1921 were ordered to stem the sinking operating ratios and workers began filing

Above: In the days of men and Moguls, Engineer Oscar Kallman posed with KGB&W's 39 after a wintery passage. Stalwart 2-6-0's were the backbone of GB&W lines' motive power in the 1920's.
OSCAR KALLMAN COLLECTION

grievances, one of which involved operation of unsafe equipment. In the summer of 1922 a GB&W shopmen's strike in Green Bay was led by the GB&W band.

GB&W train service was affected more by the coal strike of 1922 than by the shopmen's brief outing. Some survivors of the GB&W strike reported that they were more interested in a day off than smoothing grievances. Their wish was granted when train operation was severely reduced in August 1922. No.3-4 and No.5-6 were pulled off, while 41 and 42 to La Crosse were reduced to three-day service. Coal miners came to the table with their terms, while the rail strike spread elsewhere, lasting until

August 31st. The nature of the disruptions served to further distort the La Crosse condition but finally, by October 1922, the city made plans to pave certain city streets north of the school and widen a cut through a cemetery to accept a street. October 26, 1922 was to be the last day of service. The C&NW and CB&Q jointly took an advertisement announcing the acceptance of former GB&W traffic.

The La Crosse press scarcely noticed the passing of GB&W, stating that, on the Wednesday in question, the daily GB&W train would consist of a combine, engine and maybe a freight car, which would travel slowly southward over the rickety GB&W line to the southside depot. It was recorded that the John A. Salzer Seed Co. shipped the first car (1876) and the last (1922) over the La Crosse Branch. October 26, 1922 was fair and cool with a 7 a.m. temperature of 37 degrees which rose to 53 degrees by 10 a.m. It was one of those excellent western Wisconsin days but it failed to generate a surviving photo of the obscure ending. Business was busy surviving car, shortages nettling, coal problems looming and "Wobblies" agitating in Portland, Oregon, to ever notice a forty-ton 4-4-0 marching northward through the campus of the normal school, or overaging backwater trestles. The little train marked the last of the first GB&W trackage to be abandoned, which dutifully and finally carried northward Mr. Saltzer's seeds, to Marshland and oblivion.

GB&W ownership of lands and rights lingered while specifics of its operation on La Crosse faded away. The railroad performed grading and paving related to its ownership of the trackage, but CB&Q G-3 0-6-0's delivered coal to the old GB&W customers. Five bridges were salvaged across the backwaters in 1924 and Marshland's small engine terminal was retired. With the end of the branch, coal services were removed in favor of a new coal chute installed "up country" at Whitehall (MP-177), halfway between Merrillan and the river. The 170-ton dock was a $10,659 investment.

The Marshland abandonment was of interest, as much of the equipment was carried off to Winona and installed at Bridge Yard. This included water tank, windmill and a pumping station which had been changed from steam to gas only the summer prior to abandonment. Not removed for further service were a fifty-foot wooden turntable built in 1900, various sheds and a 492-foot coal shed track to the coaling station. The remaining yard was kept for some years, eventually obliterated by the construction of original Highway 35.

Master Mechanic Charles W. Dieman died June 13, 1919, ushering the short reign of Thomas J. McPherson over matters in the backshop and ahead of drawbars. McPherson inaugurated a campaign to acquire more and improved power, in many cases finding used engines and cars cast off by larger roads. New York Central, anxious to modernize and standardize its power, sold off large numbers of engines that were well suited to GB&W's needs. It was an example of buyer and seller awareness of an opportune moment.

In December 1920 McPherson was directed to purchase a 133,000-pound 0-6-0 from ALCO, probably a stock engine built on speculation by the works in a slack post-war period. Several others of this design were built, one of which survives to this day at Bensenville, Illinois as Chicago Gravel Co.'s No. 18. In turn, this engine had been built for Studebaker Corp. as its No. 14 months after GB&W's No. 60 arrived. GB&W's engine cost $35,040, a much higher price than the $15,000 they paid for 1915's 2-6-0. The ALCO engines of this design were piston-valve, Walschaert Valve Gear-equipped machines. Evidently, GB&W disliked No. 60's whistle and immediately re-equipped it

with a cast type. The new arrival was ready for operation February 9, 1921.

When Waupaca-Green Bay Railway came into the fold, GB&W inherited 4-4-0 No. 2, appraised at $2500, in addition to combine 24 and a lone cinder car. No. 2 was renumbered 8, continuing to the end of its days with the new number. WGB was dissolved in early 1922. In August of 1921, KGB&W's Mogul 39 was ordered, GB&W's orderform reflecting the increasing numbering problem. When completing the order, the number 72 was written, then scratched out in favor of 39. No. 72 would actually be assigned to the A&W's 39, while the newly ordered machine would be KGB&W 39. This time, the price was a deflated $28,400. With identical specifications, the new 39 went into service October 29, 1921. GB&W Lines' next-to-last new 2-6-0 was broken in for two days prior to its service date.

In McPherson's time, GB&W Lines found a need for coal service cars. It began dealing with General Equipment Co. of New York, acquiring forty 36-foot wood gondolas, second-hand from Wheeling & Lake Erie Railway. This order was followed by an additional ten cars in October which were to meet the "demand for such cars in the sugar beet, gravel and coal traffic." The "new-old" cars were all numbered in the 4200-series, odd numbers only. Other groups of the same type went to KGB&W and were numbered 4301-4339 inclusive, odd numbers only. Many cars were needed to replace those worn out under federal control. Subsequent groups came, always from General Equipment. They had been Virginian, Hocking Valley, or W&LE property, evicted to allow for modernization. The bargains were adequate for short-haul traffic. The practice continued while acquiring more freight cars, ending up with steel cars in 1930, which came from Chicago's Briggs & Turivas Co., and were numbered in the 4700 and 4800 series. Some also came from Steel Tube Co. of America, which were placed in the 4800 series.

In November of 1922 three more locomotives were brought in to cope with heavy traffic; one second-hand and two possible order cancellations. No. 80 was a 67-ton 0-6-0, ex-NYC 313, acquired via General Equipment Co., a B-2 class of 1900. No. 80 was shipped from Patterson, New Jersey and cost $9650. Considerable work was needed to prepare No. 80 for service and GECo agreed to bear part of the expense, donating $455.47. No. 80 went to work January 19, 1923.

GB&W's next engines, ordered November 1, 1922, were destined to be the heaviest until the 400 class 2-8-2's came. No. 45 (KGB&W) and No. 65 (GB&W), ALCO class 280-S-199, signified a 100-ton, 52-inch drivered Consolidation, capable of 42,000 pounds tractive effort. A mystery surrounds these capable muscle machines. Brooks built others just like them. The companions were built for Toledo Terminal Railroad over several years, both before and after the GB&W pair. Another was supplied to Magma Arizona Railroad (still intact) which differed in its tender type and minor details. GB&W's machines had the regular Laird crosshead design. Closely numbered, GB&W's and TT's orders were mates on the Brooks erecting floor in 1922-23. Further, GB&W's engines could have been a TT cancellation, later resumed by the Ohio road. Irony visited upon the MAR No. 5, which later received identical low-slung headlight bracketing, furthering their brotherly appearances, years and miles later. New or not, GB&W paid $33,450 for their powerhouses. The pair was broken in during a heavy winter coal crisis in Green Bay in late January 1923. They went to work in regular service about February 5th.

Along with the new engines, GB&W acquired a new master mechanic. Tom McPherson was succeeded by Ernest Becker

Top: Magma Arizona Railroad 5 was identical to Toledo Terminal engines, which also matched GB&W Lines' 45 and 65. Small details differed, including the Vanderbilt tank. MAR 5 still survives.

Middle & Lower: GB&W Lines bought two large Consolidations — ALCo class 280-S-199 — in late 1922. The pair, identical to Toledo Terminal engines of the same year, were generally well received.

Above: GB&W Train No.2 clattered through "Stoney" at Mile 76. Terminal moraine contained large boulders, hence the name. No.25 headed a standard consist which contained a "10-class" 39-foot mail car in this rare 1920-era photo. No.25 was an 1898 Dickson.

Below: Sphagnum moss is being loaded at City Point, Wisconsin. Moss was used to package certain perishables and contributed to GB&W tonnage in the 1920's.

who started out with Milwaukee & Northern in 1885, went with Milwaukee Road until 1895, then to GB&W's new shop in 1897. He was C&NW's master mechanic at Green Bay and Escanaba, returning to GB&W February 15, 1923. Becker continued the practice of acquiring ex-NYC switchers for yard assignments. He also introduced C&NW letter classifications to GB&W wheel arrangements, with some margin for error. The new Consolidations became Z-class, alluding to C&NW's infamous, coal-ravenous "Zulus" which were not quite the fine engines the GB&W machines were. Other classes were not so obvious; R-class was applied to the "heavy" superheated Moguls, corresponding to C&NW's successful 4-6-0's. M and M-1 covered KGB&W's 40, ex-NYC switchers, as well as No. 80. Becker's I and J classes were the older slide-valve Moguls which were split between GB&W and KGB&W examples. It would seem that

Seymour had a desk which was cut out like a cribbage board to fit his ample middle. Behind this, in his office, one of the pigeon holes in his roll-top desk contained a group of goose bones which the no-nonsense New Londoner insisted could determine weather conditions.

Fred R. Bolles, formerly general manager of Copper Range Railroad, was appointed GB&W line's traffic manager October 1, 1923 and succeeded in getting a share of the Ford Motor Company's business for GB&W. Fidelity of service was demanded by the automaker to supply his new St. Paul assembly plant and Mr. Ford insisted on a special train for his exclusive benefit. Seymour exploded at the prospect. Later, after more serious consideration of the benefits of the Ford trade, the extra runs began to crowd dispatcher Henry C. Erbe's train sheets. Several times Ford needed a single car of paint in St.

H. F. BRADEN PHOTO

Above: Doubleheading of Moguls was standard practice over the entire road in the late 1920's. In later years, however, it was restricted to the Sturgeon Bay line (A&W). Here, No. 53 and No. 72 "get their air" on the Kewaunee Wye in the mid-1930's.

some of this was tongue-in-cheek practice, for C&NW's J-class were heavy 2-8-2's, while I-class (KGB&W) related to Omaha Road's 4-6-0's.

After serving GB&W as managing superintendent for the previous 23 years, Frank B. Seymour was elected president on August 7, 1923. He succeeded Joseph A. Jordan who died August 1st. The legendary rise of "FBS" began with his walk to the railhead near New London in 1872 to offer his underage services as a waterboy to the advancing GB&LP. Frank Halliday mentioned that, in his time, the frugal old school executive did indeed save lightbulbs having a glimmer of reuse about them and knew acutely the cost of extravagance. Among other things,

Paul and GB&W dutifully complied by unleashing a venerable and somewhat dependable "Standard" type (4-4-0) to Winona with the lonely carload. Transfer was made to the Milwaukee Road in minimum time over the sand ballast and seventy-pound rail of the GB&W.

In October 1922 GB&W completed reinforcement work on the Shiocton swingspan, raising the Cooper rating from E-27 to E-55. The bridge had an interesting history, having replaced the original Wolf River span, a 230-foot wood "jack-knife" structure. The 57-foot drawspan was destroyed in a wreck in 1889 which dropped a locomotive (and Engineer Doyle) into the river. The bridge was replaced by a trestle which joined the original

173-foot pilework and remained until money was available for a replacement. During the decade of the trestle, the Wolf River was closed to navigation. The 1898 replacement was a steel-plate girder span which revolved on a cut-stone masonry pier, 137 feet long. In 1914 the balance of the pile trestle was replaced with a seventy-foot through plate girder. Greilings, an outside contractor, constructed new concrete footings for the bridge which were placed by company forces in 1914.

A report circulated in July of 1923 proclaimed that carloadings were at unprecedented levels, the highest since 1920. It was also time to retire several of the smaller, outclassed engines which were never at ease in the 20th Century. Switch engines 3 and 5, plus 4-4-0's 2, 7, 10, 12 and 19, which included two Raidler-built engines of 1900-01, were written off. Only Raidler's No. 11 escaped the purge. In need of switchers, Master Mechanic Becker received four ex-New York Central 0-6-0's of 72 tons each, the first of which came from Toledo, Ohio in June of 1924. Numbers 90, 91 and 41 were 1905 Brooks-built NYC B-56-c class, while the 42 was a B-55-a of 1902. Discards of NYC standardization, the slope-cylindered newcomers generally served until World War II. In a three-cornered trade-in, GB&W 0-6-0 No. 6, which came from Hicks, was transferred to KGB&W's accounts, then traded for a new KGB&W 41 for a credit of $4000. It was held at Green Bay until October 1924 when it was shipped to Quaker Coal Co. of Carterville, Illinois.

Improvements to cabooses were a result of the actions of the operating brotherhoods. In Wisconsin several accidents involving cabooses were attributed to failure of the wooden underframes, especially in pusher service ahead of helper locomotives.

University of Wisconsin engineering staffer P. H. Hyland, in conjunction with state railroad representatives, recommended that steel center sills be applied to all cabooses operated in Wisconsin. Compliance was to be met in stages with one-fourth of the work finished by the end of 1924, half by the next year's end and total compliance by 1927. GB&W began the project but found that several cars were beyond any repair so they began purchasing ex-Great Northern cabooses from Hyman-Michaels Co. No.08 and No.010, ex-GN 90058 and 90071, were acquired in November of 1925. KGB&W received former GN X-256 (032) which required a steel underframe to comply, a probable reason why GN disposed of the car. No.032 was the final KGB&W caboose, arriving in September 1928. The shorter line also acquired GN 90010 after purchasing a Stanley, Merrill & Phillips Railway second-hander in 1922. No.031 was acquired in October 1924. A&W's still-surviving car was GN's 90008, which cost $620 in November 1924. Lastly, GN X-153 became new 06, after a March 1929 wreck demolished the original car.

Improvements in locomotive appliances included a law to require cab curtains, a godsend for those in peril on the decks in below-zero weather. Another deliverance was the air-operated fire door applied to larger power, especially the Moguls. Consistent with safety measures were some efficiency devices, providing work for Becker's boilermakers: Thermic siphons on Moguls and 20-class 4-4-0's. Many cast-iron parts such as driving boxes were replaced with cast-steel for safety's sake.

Inconsistent with progress, perhaps, was the late-1924 order of 2-6-0 No.56, the "Coolidge Mogul." No.56 weighed a bit more than the others at 142,500 pounds (engine weight) and

Below: GB&W's Bucyrus steam shovel crew is seen at work near Casco Junction, Wisconsin in the early 1920's. The shovel was used to load sand which had been removed from the sandy flats at such locations along the railroad as Dodge, Hatfield, Summit and Casco Junction.

T. VAN DREESE COLLECTION

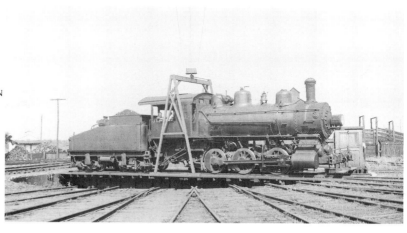

Right: Ex-NYC Brooks-built 0-6-0's were purchased at bargain prices and lasted until World War II. Here, No. 91, a Becker class M-1, rode the old Wisconsin Rapids turntable in 1934. Numbers 90 and 91 were renumbered 143 and 144, respectively.
WILLIAM MONYPENY PHOTO; AUTHOR'S COLLECTION

Below: KGB&W 42 was another NYC second-hander which was built in 1902 by Brooks. The four switchers were acquired between 1923 and 1925. No. 42, which became 142, was scrapped in 1941. This photo was taken at Green Bay Junction in 1935.
WILLIAM MONYPENY PHOTO

took ALCO class 260-S-143. Aside from higher coal sides on its tender and a modern, all-steel cab, 56 was a virtual duplicate of its precursors, the last of the type. Parenthetically, the Coolidge Mogul was very nearly the last 2-6-0 built for domestic service. The price tag read $27,391.31.

GB&W car knockers were surprised when the boxcar they were rebuilding handed them a prize. In the time of the great snowstorms of early 1923, a purse belonging to an Oakland, California doctor fell out of the car lining with $85 in war saving stamps inside. Storekeeper Ernest Juley investigated and found that the doctor had been robbed in La Crosse in 1921. The cash was gone, but the stamps inside went back to their rightful owner.

F. E. Macha encountered a problem in 1922. He had deeded a narrow strip of his farm to GB&W as a passenger stop and the company had put down old boxcar B-174 as a depot at Milepost 116. In 1947 Macha wrote to GB&W, asking the road to deed the land back to him, which he received on May 1 of that year, from Chief Engineer Frank Halliday. Macha's little station was the second location of Scranton, which came to life in a time when GBW&STP was in far worse days. The original station had been located at Milepost 118.7 at an old lumber mill location.

GB&W's star shone brightly in the days of the great Green Bay snowfall. The storms of February 1923 brought with them a coal shortage, related to strike episodes of the previous summer. In the days when big Consolidations 45 and 65 were breaking in, a night extra brought coal to the imperiled city from Kewaunee, much like the children's Christmas train fable. GB&W's coal train overcame heavy snows, reportedly tripling Luxemburg hill from Casco Junction. The extra's crew braved record snowdrifts all night, bringing much-needed bituminous to empty coal yards. Ann Arbor No. 5 made port about midnight with 14 cars destined for C. Reiss Coal Co. of Green Bay. Arriving at 8:30 a.m., the extra was nothing extraordinary to F. B. Seymour. He was quoted as "always having the best interest of Green Bay at heart and a policy foremost to render patrons efficient service." The comment was widely publicized.

GB&W's freight traffic was to receive a welcome boost from the booming auto industry, while its passenger traffic would suffer fatal blows from the same hand. Minneapolis, Northfield & Southern Railway was formed in 1918 from the financial ruin of a gas-electric interurban, the Dan Patch Line. Herbert E. Pence headed a drive to solicit subscriptions for $250,000 in capital. Shortly after the First World War, Minneapolis native Win Stephens joined Pence in a scheme to deliver automobiles to Stephens' dealerships via their own railroad. Stephens had gained experience in moving autos by rail as early as 1916 when his dealership bought a large fleet of ex-W&LE wood gondolas and converted them to special auto-carrying flats. With their ownership in MN&S solidified, Pence and Stephens engaged a banker to explore the possible purchase of GB&W as a link in its chain to Detroit. MN&S trackage was to be extended to Winona, but the approach by MN&S interests to GB&W ownership is unrecorded.

Automobiles were just then entering into GB&W's traffic picture via normal boxcar conveyance. It was the trend of the future and an important one for GB&W. Ford Motor Company's 1923 expansion called for a $10 million facility in Minneapolis for the production of its astonishingly successful "flivvers." It was also a momentous time for Harry Byram's Milwaukee Road which would build a connecting line into the new factory. Byram's Milwaukee would spend up to $4 million on the 4.45-mile link to the auto plant from Fordson to Fordson Junction. The main building was reportedly 1720×600 feet and the finished plant, which was to employ 14,000, would produce 300 cars a day. In the same year, the Whitehall paper was certain a Minneapolis & St. Louis Railway official car had been part of a train carrying high officials, and GB&W's stock was being bought up where possible, which it was not. Conductor Ben Closuit, on train No.5, was quoted as confirming that the "Hank Ford Special" had passed, assuring that the new plant spelled prosperity for GB&W. The rumor of the MN&S purchase persisted, linked in April 1924 to Chicago Great Western from Randolph to Winona, Minnesota. Was Ford seeking his own road? A Minneapolis newspaper was the source of rumors which confirmed heavy movement via GB&W to the Ford plant. Improvements on Ann Arbor lent credence to the Ford stimulation of both roads, done with auto traffic from Ford's Detroit, Toledo & Ironton Railroad.

Another rumor had MN&S petitioning authorities to build its own line into the Ford tract. It was certain that a cross-lake route would avoid the "Chicago gateway" and autos were beginning to move this way, Ford or other makes. Significantly, GB&W's new agent in Detroit was W. Stanley Hogue who joined the road March 1, 1924. Hogue was reportedly a former Ford traffic man. J. B. Dooney, "hero" of Hatfield dam, was posted at Minneapolis in March of 1920 as general agent. Jim Dooney, for whom the siding at Milepost 199 was named, stood by at Merrillan during the 1911 Hatfield disaster, to oversee the transfer of GB&W trains onto the Omaha Road. The movement had cost GB&W $12.50 per car. Dooney, a 36-year GB&W man and Winona native, died in April 1925.

ANN ARBOR No.7 was launched December 30, 1924 at Manitowoc. The event was attended by a number of Green Bay shippers and AA president Newman Erb. Five thousand people watched Miss Jane Reynolds, daughter of Marine Superintendent R. H. Reynolds, christen No.7. An independent Ann Arbor would be short-lived. Investor Jules S. Bache began acquiring AA common stock and became AA's new president shortly after Erb's death in early 1925. Walter P. Chrysler was elected to the directorate and finally Ann Arbor was purchased by Wabash.

Mogul No.30 and the Bucyrus shovel are shown here at Casco Junction. Coal was laboriously loaded into the shovel's coal bunker via a chute from No.30's tank.

RAY BUTTOLPH PHOTO

Above: Ford Motor Co. opened its important St. Paul plant in 1923. A very pleased Ford customer received his shiny dream of freedom shortly after the plant opened. GB&W benefited from the westbound traffic.

MINNESOTA HISTORICAL SOCIETY

Financial journals cited the takeover as evidence of a consolidation plan by Delaware & Hudson's L. F. Loree which would begin a new alliance with the east for the road to Frankfort. Wabash's strong Detroit-Chicago line worried Green Bay people who thought that AA's new master might adversely affect cross-lake conditions. Michigan's traffic league opposed Detroit-Chicago rates, part of a four-year rate problem which affected the ferry routes. But in 1924 Ann Arbor traffic had increased by 100 percent. The Menominee route was competition for GB&W, as short line Wisconsin & Michigan Railroad had a live-wire freight solicitor who was dutifully winning automobile carloadings to Minneapolis via the Soo Line interchange.

A conscience-struck former passenger of GB&W wrote a confession in October 1924. After yielding his life to the Lord at Pacific Bible Institute, a one-time Seymour-Green Bay easy-riding youth wrote GB&W's officialdom, telling of his misdemeanor in disguising his age behind a puny appearance. He enclosed $2.50 to cover cost of tickets and conscience, payable to the passenger department. His blessing came from several biblical passages but it was perhaps too late to save declining ridership.

Right: Three ex-Chicago, Peoria & St. Louis 2-8-0's were bought from Briggs & Turivas in 1927. There was one for each of the three GB&W Line roads. No. 44 is shown on duty at Green Bay in 1936.

ED SELINSKY PHOTO

Below: Northern Pacific rail historian, Ron V. Nixon, photographed train No. 1 at Merrillan, Wisconsin en route to Winona. Nixon was aboard an Omaha Road passenger train on this day in December of 1928. Engine 20, one of the 1891 Schenectady's, was eight years from scrapping. The 39-foot mail car was removed from service two years later.

R. V. NIXON PHOTO

Absent from Kewaunee for some time, Pere Marquette's ferry service reappeared in May 1924, strongly committed to auto commerce. Frank Seymour announced that GB&W tonnage which had been going to Manitowoc and Milwaukee would be routed again on afternoon ferries. GB&W's traffic department expanded and offices were opened in New York, Seattle, Pittsburgh and Chicago. This new action strengthened GB&W's hand in soliciting business on a large scale. When PERE MARQUETTE 18 docked at Kewaunee autos were included in the shipments; Ford alone accounted for 25 cars daily. Pere Marquette ordered two new car ferries from Manitowoc in 1924, No. 21 and No. 22, and both were in service later that year.

Down in the Trempeleau Valley, Arcadia and Blair got together to contribute further tonnage to the ferries. They shipped butter to Cleveland, Ohio, which had previously gone local freight service to Chicago. In new boom times, their butter car went to Kewaunee and Toledo. It was faster and boasted a rate reduction of 29½ cents per hundredweight. Green Bay's Association of Commerce completed a list of potential cargoes, including paper eastbound from Fox and Wisconsin Valley plants, condensed milk, canned vegetables, flour and feed

tonnage from Minneapolis eastbound and from points west of Winona. Another customer, Northwestern Milling Co. of Minneapolis, expressed their desire to move more than eight million pounds of feed via Green Bay.

GB&W began construction of a concrete elevator on its Norwood Yard property in 1918, adding to it a ten-tank reinforced complement in August 1924. The contractor was James Stewart & Co. of Chicago. Eventually, the 750,000-bushel-capacity complex was leased to Cargill Grain Co. and finally Strid Elevator Co. in 1942. Cargill also made joint plans with C&NW to build a waterfront grain elevator nearby on the location of the old structure which had burned in 1916. In October 1926 construction was again entrusted to J. Stewart & Co. for a concrete ten-tank elevator, similar to the GB&W elevator of 1924. The new riverside elevator had a capacity of 600,000 bushels. Upon completion, the structure was leased to Cargill until 1943. Green Bay was facing a heavy year in export grain and GB&W flourished in the "Coolidge Prosperity."

While grain burgeoned, coal was not far behind. C. Reiss leased the Central Dock below Mason Street, also known as the "St. Paul Dock" served by Milwaukee Road. This 100,000-ton-capacity facility was to be ready October 1, 1926. Standard Oil chose Green Bay as a storage depot for inland delivery of gasoline and oil, a product line sure to expand in the auto age of the 1920's. A producer of railway motor cars, Oneida Railway Motors, Inc., struggled to sell their motor conversion kits for elderly wood railroad coaches. Its production facilities soon merged with a motor truck manufacturer. At Green Bay, the firm's president, R. W. Melcher, later perfected roller-bearing applications to journal boxes.

Another scheme to include the GB&W in a semi-transcontinental east from Minneapolis was revealed in February 1927. Again L. F. Loree interests in Delaware & Hudson, Wabash and Ann Arbor sought to lease C&NW trackage from Winona to Rochester and Waseca, linking with the Minneapolis & St. Louis Railway at Waseca. New York Banker F. J. Lisman felt that GB&W was unable to acquire a large enough share of traffic because its original allies were steamship lines and the link was never a successful one. Lisman claimed that Wabash bought AA to gain a share of the through northwest business. Their scheme included D&H, Buffalo, Rochester & Pittsburgh Railway (later sold to B&O) Lehigh Valley (ironically a close competitor of DL&W) and M&StL. The remarkable promotion remained a windy concept except for legitimate car routings.

To handle its new prosperity, GB&W ordered 200 new boxcars patterned after a large Milwaukee Road order. General American Car Company accounted for fifty, while Western Steel Car built 150 of the single-sheath forty-footers which were equipped with Bettendorf forty-ton trucks. The cars arrived in mid-1925.

Mail service on trains 3-4 between Green Bay and Wisconsin Rapids underwent a change in January 1925. Gone were the RPO's and in their place was "pouch service" for local business. Small towns were concerned but a responsible post office saw a decline in patronage. New London was to make up sacks for the Royalton-Wisconsin Rapids territory and train No.3. Shiocton-Green Bay mail went on No.4's baggage car. Satisfaction was guaranteed.

With the growth of railroad auto-carrying came a competitive system of routing new autos by lake steamships. Minneapolis' Pence-Stephens interests pioneered transport via water to Duluth's docks, but some credit goes to Captain William Nicholson of Northern Transportation Company. In a merger between Nicholson's boat line and Universal Carloading Company, which had specialized in auto distribution, Nicholson-Universal Transportation Steamship Company began to load upbound lakers with deck loads of new autos. Some of the ore boats were actually dedicated auto haulers, as their smaller size precluded efficient participation in the bulk trade. In January 1925, 3000 autos were to be shipped to the port of Green Bay. Auto accessories such as tires from Akron, Ohio were also destined for the northwest via lakers.

Steamer traffic was not without its mishaps. The steamer LAKELAND, with a load of Wisconsin-built Kissel and Nash autos, was headed east off the Sturgeon Bay Canal entrance when it sank December 24, 1924. LAKELAND's crew, upon discovering a seam leak, began to head for the canal; the vessel sank six miles out but, fortunately, no lives were lost. In 1927 the CITY OF BANGOR went aground on Keweenaw Point in Lake Superior. Eighteen of the 232 Chryslers on deck went overboard. A wilderness road was carved out of the woods four months after the November accident and the cargo was driven out by a salvage firm. Green Bay received more than 3600 autos via steamers SPOKANE, J. T. REID and others which distributed their cargoes via C&NW and GB&W loading docks. All makes of autos arrived at Green Bay; SPOKANE brought 24 loads of 150 autos each in 1926. The cars were reloaded into "automobile cars," specially equipped boxcars with loading racks. Ramps allowed drive-off disembarkation at all ports. SPOKANE also went into Gladstone, Michigan with deckloads for upper peninsula distributors.

GB&W created special facilities in the late 1920's to receive, store and distribute autos, including extensive filling of Fox River frontage north of Mason Street. Over the years, GB&W struggled to reclaim this land, including the marshy slough bottoms. In April 1929, 1053 linear feet of frontage was filled and a 60 × 200-foot frame warehouse with ramps, platforms and 1543 feet of track was built to handle autos from the steamers. A month later, another 90 × 300-foot building of steel and timber design was authorized. Even after "Black Friday" in 1929, the beginning of the Great Depression, auto business was demanding new boxcars. Bettendorf Co. received another "tack-on" order to a Milwaukee Road transaction, covering 75 normal single-sheath cars and fifty double-door automobile cars.

The boom year of 1926 again raised demands for heavier power on GB&W, but such was not the case for an Illinois carrier headed for bankruptcy. Ten locomotives were made available by the receiver of Chicago, Peoria & St. Louis Railway and Ernest Becker picked out three, CP&StL's 70, 72 and 78. The actual vendor was scrap-dealer Briggs & Turivas, Inc. The individual price averaged $7000 before GB&W received them. The CP&StL units became the GB&W line's 74, 64 and 44, one for each of the companies. Becker requested Engineer George Thiele ride the trio, leaving on C&IM March 22, 1927 at the usual "dead-in-train" speed of twenty miles per hour. The trip took ten days. Becker christened the trio "R-1 class" after the highly successful C&NW 4-6-0's. Road crews, however, had other ideas, for the bargains were soon dubbed "Mayflowers," apparently in reference to their age and alluding to the possibility that they came over on the famed ship from England. The "Mayflowers" went to work in April of 1927. Although the CP&StL had superheated the engines, the newcomers were remembered as having a near-permanent home for firemen on their decks, such was the need for continuous firing under load. Nonetheless, the used engines were the first to carry the new tender-borne herald: "The East-West Short Route."

Traffic boomed in 1928-29 and the dispatcher's sheets reflected much of the activity. As GB&W continued to replace its lighter seventy-pound rail with its first eighty-pound rail in the 1920's, tonnage figures climbed. Imagine train No. 7 with Mayflower No. 44, Engineer Hollister and Conductor Collier, stalled on Amherst hill and having to double with "fireman about bushed." No. 74 with an extra made poor time westbound due to a hot driving box and 28 loads. Engine 54 was delayed by No. 6 at New London because the engine was foaming. The Mogul left Green Bay with 23 loads and ten empties. Extra 56 West was also delayed for cherry reefer icing at Wisconsin Rapids. Time was again lost when 4-4-0 No. 20 suffered a broken driver spring on No. 2, losing thirty minutes and annoying anxious customers.

The October 24, 1928 entry was lengthy. Train No. 9 had to double into Alma Center, engine 30 (2-6-0), with 23 loads and 21 empties. The engineer, "Roaring Ben" Billings, had a full day as he doubled into Walker and Elm Lake due to his heavy train. Billings also had to double the knobs at Hatfield and Alma Center and finally set out his dead weight cars. Arriving at Whitehall at 5:59 p.m., Billings reported his engine grates stuck open and his crew tried to right the heavy castings after pulling the fire. At 6:52 p.m. Billings went into the still-hot firebox, only to find the shaker liner broken. The grates couldn't be fixed. The crew was tied up. An eastbound extra arrived to clear the dead engine and train from the main line. Engine 56 proceeded east with Engineer Draland and retrieved the crew after the unfortunate five had been on the road from 5:55 a.m. to 8:20 p.m.

Business on October 27, 1928 was also considerable. Train No. 6 required three sections, the first leaving at 7:00 p.m. behind engine 44 with Grobb and Kroll in charge. At 10:00 p.m. a big 2-8-0, No. 65, took the second part, staffed by Paape and Welby. The final part was under George Thiele and Gus Beyers, leaving at 1:30 a.m. on the 28th behind Mogul 72. Two days later, Mogul 38 took seven loads and 13 empties out with Taylor and Newcomb leaving at 7:00 a.m. The second part departed behind Mogul 72 (Brown and Mellen) at 10 a.m., hauling 13 loads and nine empties. The final part left at 1:30 a.m. on the 30th with 14 loads and 16 empties.

Delays often were caused when cars were "set back for autos," meaning that loaded cars were coming into Norwood Yard from the boats or from ferries. Foul weather was also a factor. October 16, 1928 was a wet day and Train No. 7 stalled west of Scandinavia due to engine slippage. The train backed into town, cleared out sander pipes and stormed out again. Wet rail caused the westbound to stall again going up Amherst hill and two hours were consumed doubling into Amherst Junction. The 945-ton train, pulled by engine No. 28, had left Green Bay at 7:30 a.m. It made it into "95" (mileage for Wisconsin Rapids and its station number) at 10:25 p.m. with eleven loads and five empties; it had left Scandinavia with 17 loads and five empties.

The apple business flourished that month. Many cars were required to be on ferries the same day. Apple loads came from Arcadia and Independence and several extras were loaded for the east, occasionally handled on No. 2, the eastbound passenger train. Once Dave Myott's Extra 54 East returned to East Winona from Independence for three cars of apples for cross-lake destinations. Another time, on October 15th, train No. 5 was set back two hours and 35 minutes for autos, to 7:05 a.m., when 4-4-0 No. 18 doubleheaded Mayflower 44 out of Green Bay. No. 18 was often called as a helper engine and was equipped with a second air pump to handle the work.

Engine No. 8 also doubleheaded Third No. 6, engine 53, on the 15th of October, consisting of 21 loads and five empties. John Hickey had the 18 with Schroeder and Budd on the 53. The first section had Mogul 27 (21 loads, 13 empties) and the second section had 2-6-0 No. 72 (20 loads and 19 empties). First No. 6 had to double from "Smoky to Stony," which translates "Mile 72 to Mile 77." Mile 75 is the highest point of the GB&W and the grade westbound was a battle from Scandinavia to Arnott, even with a brief respite on flat areas. In August, however, a washout held up traffic. Extra 56 West held at Blair for Extra 25 and 72 (doublehead), which waited for help at the spot west of Highway 95 and Whitehall. Mogul 29 had doubleheaded 56 from Wisconsin Rapids, which was dropped off for Extra 25/72 East, as the old Dickson 4-4-0 No. 25 was needed for a work extra out of Merrillan to the washout. It was just another day for Dispatcher Henry Erbe.

Traffic continued unabated in 1929 and growing prosperity called for more power. As early as February 6, 1928, Frank Seymour had contacted ALCO requesting price information on one Consolidation type, a duplicate of 45 and 65. The quotation was $35,500 for a pair and ALCO's District Sales Manager N. C. Taylor pointed out that delivery could be made in early 1929. "FBS" replied that he had asked for only one engine and that confirmation could only come after GB&W's annual meeting in May. ALCO countered that they expected to become busy by then with other orders. Seymour finally replied that "we do not care to add or leave off anything now on the 65" and "we do not want a siphon on the new locomotive." Ernest Becker added minor additions in another letter, pointing out that a serious drawback on engines 45 and 65 was the crosshead guide attachment to the cylinders. Becker also thought that the engine truck on Mogul 56 was the best type he had ever seen and wanted it on the new engine. A contract was made December 27, 1928 for two 2-8-0's with 21 × 28-inch cylinders, ALCO cast-steel frames, 7000-gallon tanks and 57-inch drivers, higher than those on 45 and 65. They were ALCO class 280-S-174, a lighter 87 tons, as opposed to 100 tons for Becker's Z-class. No.49

(KGB&W) and No.69 (GB&W) were built in March of 1929 at a cost of $34,050 each. The pair were shipped March 30, 1929, arriving in Green Bay April 14th in the charge of ALCO's messenger, J. Shaughnessey. They traveled at 15 miles per hour, customary for new engines at the time, dead-in-train, via NYC, Wabash and Ann Arbor. Becker dubbed them R-2 class, out of habit, although C&NW had no such designation.

Dispatcher Erbe recorded the arrival of 49 and 69 at 7:00 p.m. on the 14th. Extra 45 celebrated the occasion by derailing on a switch at the long pass siding, tipping over a rail in the excitement. It didn't take long for the graceful Consolidations to swing into action. No. 49 went out on train No. 7 (Joe Brey and

Top Left: Famed surviving "Whaleback" METEOR once carried autos to Green Bay. The boat was named J. T. REID in the 1920's and worked for Spokane Steamship Co. into Green Bay. REID did grain service as Soo Line's WASHBURN when it was new in the 1890's. METEOR is in a museum today in Superior, Wisconsin, its birthplace.

Shown here are three scenes of auto unloading operations at the auto dock warehouse just north of Mason Street in Green Bay. Cars were disembarked, warehoused and some were reloaded into automobile cars. The dock warehouse still stands but ramps were removed during the Great Depression. The cars are Willys.

Guy Pratt) at 7:30 a.m., April 16, 1929 with 15 loads and 14 empties. It returned from the west on No. 8 the next day with 19 loads and eight empties. April 17th witnessed a meet between two brand-new Consolidations as No. 69 left on No. 7 (Russ Hollister and Callahan), shepherding 23 loads and eleven empties westward to meet No. 8 with No. 49, perhaps at Scandinavia, in a never-recorded shine contest that lit up Waupaca County. If only the world could have seen it.

It was generally true that R-2's never operated east of Green Bay in the early days. The new ones were busy with Ford Specials and extras all the way to the river, as their weight permitted such operation. No. 49 got into Winona as early as June 15th and even doubleheaded with KGB&W 4-4-0 No. 35 west from Green Bay. No. 69 went to Winona on June 8th in regular service. Shortly after, however, No. 49 broke a spring hanger. Although not a serious problem, it was necessary to apply stay braces to the R-2's saddles, according to a veteran of the times. No. 69 chalked up one delay to a truck cellar repacking job and the newness soon began to wear off. Not to be outdone in the mishap department, Mayflower 44 contracted a bad case of piston-packing blow-by. In October, engine 64, also a Mayflower, took 1428 tons up to Oneida, doubling the hill with twenty loads and ten empties and nearly stalling in the attempt.

With the R-2's, GB&W had received another landmark product, almost the last 2-8-0's built commercially for domestic service. Only Great Western Railway (Colorado) had a later Consolidation, its No. 60. Press releases in Spring 1929 spoke of two new high-speed engines for Green Bay-Winona service. They were for use on the Ford train and had bells on their fronts to warn motorists. Certainly able to sustain higher speeds than their contemporaries, the R-2's continued as the chief road power until the 400-class engines were ordered seven years later.

GB&W passenger service westward always included its quaint, 39-foot mail cars, numbers 10-12 inclusive. During 1929 and 1930, when federal regulations required steel underframes for postal cars, GB&W removed the small cars from service and built five large baggage/mail replacements with Commonwealth underframes. The five were formerly Hicks coaches 51-54 inclusive and KGB&W coach 77. It was these five cars which closed out mail and express services in 1948; today all are preserved in railroad museums.

Western Refrigerator Line Company was organized in 1929 to operate a fleet of standard forty-foot refrigerator cars placed in GB&W's service under contract. The contract stated that preference would be given the cars of Western for perishable goods destined for the longest hauls possible. Five hundred cars were built by American Car & Foundry at a cost of $1,500,000. GB&W's "trademark" was to appear on the cars, while the GB&W's car service officer would act similarly for Western. The new company was organized to provide GB&W with the service, while a minimum mileage contract with GB&W would produce revenues for the refrigerator line. Officers of the new firm were: J. Kibben Ingalls, president, also president of Northwestern Refrigerator Car Co.; E. M. Miller, vice-president, and Allin K. Ingalls, also vice-president of Northwestern Car. With increases in on-line produce destined for eastern markets, GB&W could then discard its own fleet of makeshift "reefers" which had been converted from its own boxcars. A number of Sturgeon Bay cherry growers took the opportunity to cause Western to make up "billboard" reefers for their products, along with potato, dairy and produce firms. From the outset, "WRX" cars carried a red "Green Bay Route" herald with a slate gray major color on

their sides. Both Northwestern and Western reefers were painted gray and were distinctive carriers of the GB&W and WRX name outward from Wisconsin. WRX moved into shop and operating headquarters at the east end of the Norwood Shops in Green Bay, at the corner of Oakland Avenue and Clinton Street, where it remained until relocation in the 1960's.

Coming of age for GB&W meant a steady increase in revenue freight tonnage after 1925, reaching one million tons in 1926 for the first time in the company's history. Freight traffic and tonnage figures had inched steadily upward since 1918, rising over nine of those years. Most of the traffic came from GB&W's interchanges, both at Kewaunee and at on-land locations. Green Bay Route's situation in years past had produced 70% of its traffic from on-line sources but by 1926 the figure reversed itself, representing now the "overhead" or end-to-end traffic. The awakening manufacturing districts east of Lake Michigan took into account the delays in their shipments via "Chicago's gateway" for the first time after World War I and were becoming conscious of the need to save time. World War I had changed many things and it profoundly altered the way American companies made their way. The adrenalin of the Great War filtered down to all levels of industry and speed became all-important. The "up to the minute" world of Babbitt had come to America, which now emulated the words of Calvin Coolidge: "The business of America is business." The modern nation ran faster with longer, faster trains for businesses that looked more and more at the clock.

The time-saver route included the Ann Arbor and Pere Marquette ferry systems and their attendant railroads. PM in 1926 experienced the greatest automobile tonnage in its history — 733,424 tons — which increased the average rate of ton-per-mile return. In that year, PM's coal traffic accounted for 52% of its revenue tonnage, while the high auto figure accounted for 32%. Ann Arbor in 1927 received over 80% of its tonnage from interchanges and handled its average car 166 miles, or about half its mileage. It too found itself in the time-saver field. Briefly, Ford traffic declined to 52,424 auto-tons westward, as opposed to 1925's 124,213 tons and 1926's 109,525 tons. The decline reflected the model switchover when the Model "T" bowed out in favor of later Model "A" production. This conversion, interestingly enough, took six months to implement, no doubt a cultural shock to motoring America in two ways. It deprived the country of a standard, while stopping all production and distribution. It was very evident that business lost to railroads was measurable, showing the chancy aspects of single-commodity economics. Ann Arbor did its share by running over a railroad blessed with nearly all 85-pound rail and behind heavy modern power: its 1923 H-1 Mikados. AA's 1926 figures for coal and coke traffic ran to 1,159,592 tons which represented nearly 48% of its loads, while manufactured goods comprised 26% of its traffic. Both AA and GB&W had modest agricultural traffic offerings which declined relative to the new high-rate manufactures filling boxcars.

Car ferries handling loaded cars also experienced inflated figures which climbed from 50,390 forty-ton cars in 1924 to 60,861 in 1927. While 1926's figure of 64,358 was higher, the dip was again related to Ford's model changeover. AA had organized a subsidiary, Ann Arbor Boat Company, in 1916. It was a Michigan corporation which operated its ferry fleet under a long-term lease with monthly rentals; securities included a first-mortgage on ferries No. 6 and No. 7, a combined value of $1,516,000. Ann Arbor's 1928 auto tonnage accounted for more

Right: Consol No. 49 is seen at Winona, Minnesota in 1935. For five years the pair of 1929 2-8-0's rolled the Ford Extras and No. 30 and No. 31. Here, Engineer George Manning, a Winona native, and Ernie Wanek, fireman, show off the pride of the "East-West Short Route." All engines in the "40 series" were KGB&W machines. No. 49 survives in a museum.

C. FELSTEAD COLLECTION

Right: Charlie Chapman had the 69 in Winona in the summer of 1936. The train is probably No. 30 and the engine is just seven years old. Photographer Ken Zurn was one of few to cover the Winona terminal of GB&W.

KEN L. ZURN PHOTO

HAROLD LEHMAN PHOTO

Right: GB&W 69 is shown on July 4, 1936, two years after the McGee administration began. Illinois photographer Harold Lehman caught the tall Consol on a holiday outing in Green Bay. No. 69 was sold to A&W Ry.

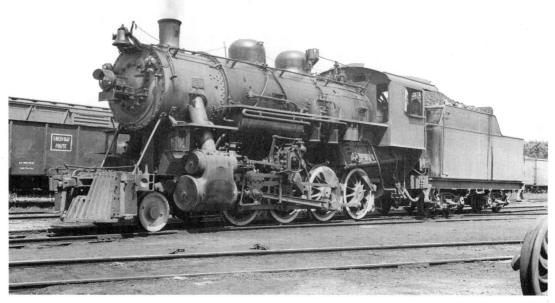

223

than 107,000 tons of a revenue tonnage of 3,337,929 for the year. The brisk trade brought about a 1926 order for the ferry WABASH, built about twenty feet longer (366 feet) than the No. 7 boat of 1925. WABASH sported a unique covered fore-castle which was a distinction of her late design. The new boat was ready for service in late June 1927. Competitor Pere Marquette launched two new ferries in August and November of 1929, namely CITY OF SAGINAW and CITY OF FLINT, which inappropriately steamed straight into the Great Depression, courtesy of their new turbo-electric drives.

GB&W's earnings continued to reflect the Ford business, which was mainly parts and supplies for the St. Paul plant. The 1928 operating ratio was 74.2% compared with 1923's pre-Ford 84.18%. The gain was attributed to a conservative maintenance program, but the lift to GB&W's cash position, the major attribute of its unique financial formula, was significant. Net income in 1923 was just $31,387; in 1928, the figure was $189,279. The "good times" paid for the five newly arrived 2-8-0's which were prominent in rolling the Fords westward.

A 1928 time book of a switchman's duties on the Stevens Point branch reflects the arrivals and departures of other significant traffic of local value. There was always coal, inbound from Green Bay in GB&W's recently acquired second-hand wood "hopper-bottom gondolas," making an 88-mile delivery. Rags arrived from off-line points for papermaking, while pulpwood came from all points north and east. Reefers carrying bananas from New Orleans usually appeared in ICRR cars. Autos also came in boxcars to local dealerships, along with bagged lime for papermaking, brick and steel for construction and sulphite pulp for the mills. There were reefers of produce, often cabbage and "spuds" from on-line stations, some of which were related to local potato-growers. It was evidence of the needs of another "up-to-date" American city with new-found industry and increasing population.

GB&W gross earnings in 1929 hit $1,996,633, a reported net profit of $531,599. With the stock market crash, a new reality set in and speculative schemes to link railroads to other transportation systems took a holiday until decades later. "The East-West Short Route" securities paid their customary 5%/5% and voted a 1% in 1930 but, for 1931, had to omit a dividend on its class "B" debentures. There were some dark days when deficits were turned in for a few months, notably in 1932 when no reserve was reported. Annual rail revenues nationwide dropped to 1915 levels, while the ICC refused the industry's request for a 15% rate increase. The road's earnings and its traffic declined in 1930 and 1931, but not as greatly as many other roads of that time, comparing well with 1921-25 levels. GB&W's working capital, while not large, was adequate; 1930's amount was $209,000, while 1931's was $234,000. GB&W originated only 20% of its traffic in 1932 and 1933 and operating revenues dipped to levels 59% below its 1929 figures. The operating ratio in 1929 was 73%, in 1930 74%, 83% in 1932 and 84% in 1933. Subsidiary KGB&W, which was owned 80% by GB&W, declined in its dividends paid in, which brought about the discontinuance of "B" debenture payments by GB&W. But special deposits of working capital, the saving grace of the GB&W's

financial picture, held over $300,000 at the end of 1933; more than that available at any time since the end of 1929. The GB&W ship was very much afloat, while much greater railroad systems were financially embarrassed and often found wallowing in a morass of court actions.

The Emergency Railroad Transportation Act, recommended in the spring of 1933 by the Interstate Commerce Commission, became law by June of that year. The act provided for a Federal Coordinator of Transportation and the man chosen was Joseph B. Eastman. One of the railroaders involved in the three-year life of the office and its activities was Homer Edgar McGee, who would soon be settling far from his last railroading position with Missouri-Kansas-Texas Railroad in the Lone Star State. McGee's exodus northward ended at the banks of the Fox River in 1934 where he was confronted by a solvent but none-too-modern short line running westward from Green Bay in the state of Wisconsin. The meeting of the small railroad with homely Badger State characteristics and the man from Texas would leave a profound impression on both sides of the equation.

These five photos show Western Refrigerator Car Line refrigerators in the 1930's in the days of billboard advertising. This type of advertising was deemed unfair competition and was outlawed in the late 1930's.

15

WGB
THE POTATO
PUSHER

The Waupaca branch of GB&W grew out of a small town's interest in furthering its own destiny through boosterism. Waupaca-Green Bay Railway was a latecomer to Wisconsin's railroad mileage, born of a home-grown corporation to help the Waupaca County Seat toward prosperity. The second line to enter the town, it connected Green Bay & Western's main line at Scandinavia with the industrial area adjacent to the Wisconsin Central main line. Self-help in Waupaca had brought it electric power and, to make use of that energy, it also promoted a five-mile electric railroad. Waupaca's chief businesses included buying and selling potatoes, while private interest in a granite quarry fostered the bootstrap W-GB Ry., which became the Waupaca branch of GB&W — a particular world of small power and quaint operations.

As early as 1886, Waupaca wanted a second railroad which would scale down excessive freight rates. GBW&STP was closest as an alternative road, but its condition ruled out action. Waupaca County's several granite outcrops attracted attention as potential building stone. Attempts were made to exploit the material but the results were marginal. The Oshkosh firm of Ripley Brothers operated a quarry four miles northeast of Waupaca, using the water power of Little Wolf Creek. Some of the product was used for ornamental work in the state capitol building in Madison. About 145 laborers worked in shops and polishing houses and were paid from $1.00 to $4.00 per day. Paving block interests also examined the granite and GBW&STP's Frank Halliday surveyed a three-mile extension to an appropriate outcrop. But again, GBW&STP found itself unable to build and the Ripley Brothers found the material too hard to develop.

Herbert Penney of Waupaca, age 99, once said of his relative A. M. Penney's interest in the W-GB: "Old A. M. built the road because he couldn't get cars from the Central." While A. M. Penney was involved, it took a larger effort by Waupaca. It was an unusual Wisconsin town which undertook to build its own railroad so late in railroading's history. In the wake of "Fightin' Bob" La Follette's progressive campaign against railroad abuses, it was interesting that investor confidence could be generated. But the dynamism of Waupaca's movers and shakers, though somewhat misguided, prevailed and the town committed itself to boost a railroad. It looked like the right thing to do.

Penney's firm engaged in potato commerce in central Wisconsin and had warehouses as far away as Rhinelander, Stevens Point and Joliet, Illinois. Chicago was a large market for "spuds" and in season they were brought in large quantity from elsewhere in Wisconsin. Other buyers were Hans Ebbe and the Starks' Co., with stations in Waupaca. Some were arranged on the Fisher and Fallgatter's rye mill spur, referred to as "South America" by GB&W crews. Starch mills were built near the spur, providing a market for potatoes. And Herb Penney, at his advanced age, recalled teaming potatoes on the brick streets of Waupaca in a horse-drawn wagon to warehouses along the new railroad.

In the 1890's Seth Champion met with prominent people from Waupaca at Green Bay's Beaumont House hotel. He saw W. B. Baker of the Waupaca bank, A. G. Nelson, mayor of Waupaca,

Left: W-GB's engine No. 2 came from the Soo Line, where it had last been No. 2007. Schenectady originally built it for Wisconsin Central as No. 65 (builder's number 2027). It weighed 89,000 pounds and was renumbered "8" when GB&W acquired the railroad in January of 1922. It was removed from service in 1932 or 1933 and was scrapped in 1936.

R. C. LOTZ PHOTO

M. C. Baldwin, potato jobber, and Irving P. Lord, attorney. Messrs. Nelson, Lord and Penney guided W-GB through its 15-year life span, delivering it into GB&W hands after World War I. GBW&STP's financial wilderness would preclude its own branch line prospects until reorganization. In their discussions Scandinavia was to be the junction, inasmuch as Iola & Northern also joined the main line there. The Wisconsin Central, evidently aware of the Green Bay meeting, adjusted Waupaca rates to meet the implied threat in 1897. The planned GBW&STP line was to pass the granite quarry halfway between Scandinavia and Waupaca.

Waupaca's self-help program brought about Waupaca Electric Light Association in 1886. The company built a water-powered 100 KW plant but it was forcibly removed by a flood the next year. In 1898 the successor, Waupaca Electric Railway and Light Company, installed a steam generator and produced electricity for Waupaca, as well as for the five-mile street railway and interurban to King.

Waupaca lawyer Irving Parish Lord headed the interurban and the power company. Mr. Lord was born in Waupaca in 1858 and, after graduating from Lawrence College, entered into business affairs in Waupaca County. Lord bought the interurban in 1916 and was sole owner until after its shutdown on July 4, 1925. It was bought finally by two Chicagoans, Messrs. Aspenes and Richardson. The interurban was modestly profitable from 1905 until 1908 but quickly fell prey to the explosive rise of auto competition after 1910. In those days one could alight from a Central local, stay overnight at a Waupaca hotel near the station and journey the next day to the Grand Army of the Republic Home at King, the chief reason for the trolley's existence. Such leisurely traveling was obsolete after World War I. All save one of the line's cars were open summer designs. The one closed four-wheel car operated during wintertime. The investment by a city of 4000 (1917) without freight business was done at great peril. Its fate was shared by the steam-powered Waupaca-Green Bay Railway.

Waupaca's Businessmen's Advancement Association strongly supported a branch road in the fall of 1906. It was observed that car shortages were hurting their business. The group looked to the possibility that C&NW might extend its line from a point on the Princeton & North-Western line, a continuation of a moribund Sheboygan and Fond du Lac road. Similarly, they considered that Milwaukee Road's stub end at Berlin might be extended further northward. No one could believe that Wisconsin had really come to the end of railroad expansion by 1906. With few exceptions, only line improvements would occupy engineering talent in the state after that date.

In January of 1907 Mr. A. Aggerbeck and Mr. W. B. Johnson purchased the old Ripley quarry and entered into the promotion and completion of W-GB Ry. They did so to provide their new investment with rail service, causing the line to have a dog-legged plan form and to increase its length to 9.8 miles. The incorporation, dated January 8, 1907, shows capitalization set at $150,000. Waupaca citizens purchased some $14,000 worth of stock in half a day, such was their ardor for the project. Right-of-way options were secured and Messrs. Aggerbeck, Johnson, A. G. Nelson (president), John Gordon and A. M. Penney were the incorporators. Aggerbeck and Johnson agreed to take the portion of stock not sold to Green Bay or Waupaca citizens. Waupaca's booster spirit hoped for a population increase to 5000 by 1909. Surely city action would unhorse the Wisconsin Central's monopoly and W-GB would never fall to WC.

Waupaca Electric Light & railway Co. had but one closed car for regular use on the five-mile line. No.16 posed at King, Wisconsin in the road's early years.

STAN MAILER COLLECTION

The city of Waupaca immersed itself in the holy waters of capitalism to the extent of having a special election to enable it to issue $15,000 in city bonds, to be exchanged for 150 shares par value W-GB. Civil engineer John Patten made a preliminary survey. The route lay initially through lowlands and marshy stretches along Little Wolf Creek; cost was estimated at $80,000. At Granite Quarry the line looped back toward the west, then northwest to a junction with GB&W a mile east of Scandinavia. After a 10% assessment on $43,000 was subscribed to, Green Bay contractor T. J. McGrath of Green Bay Cement & Construction Co. was awarded the task of locating the line. McGrath's bid was dated April 23, 1907. Another contract was negotiated with Waupaca Granite & Quarry Co. for spurs into their property, the latter doing grading and furnishing ties and rail. The quarry firm agreed to pay in capital stock at $2.00 per linear foot. Bids to supply rail were received — one from Wisconsin Central, furnishing 500 tons of 60-pound for $31 per ton. GB&W countered in March with a mix of 56- and 60-pound, F.O.B. Scandinavia, at $25 per ton. Surveys were completed by April 1908 and men and equipment crowded land north of Mill Street. W-GB began with its only depot, a former Danish Lutheran church located north of the street which remained there until the 1970's. Adjacent to the depot lay A. M. Penney's potato warehouse and A. G. Nelson Lumber Co., their location hardly coincidental.

W-GB arranged for an underpass through WC's main line a few hundred yards north of the depot, WC being quite amenable to the project. WC's own depot lay east of W-GB's on the north side of Central's high fill. Transfer and interchange tracks were alongside the fill with W-GB's first enginehouse well west of its depot. It was reached via a ninety-degree curving track to the west from the depot lead. WC spurs also crossed the depot lead to industries denied W-GB. The second enginehouse, built after a 1919 fire, backed up against the depot lead, facing west. Engines were run out of Waupaca without aid of a turning facility, the mark of a brave and true short line.

McGrath spent a year on W-GB, even employing fierce Sicilians, another group who labored for American growth. GB&W's Frank Halliday related that the Sicilians made their own bread on the site in mud ovens. Evidently the flavor wasn't enough to retain their "chieftain," for he skipped town with all their money, leaving the ranks in less than a jovial mood. The Italians were hard at work in May 1907 after a local son contracted to clear right-of- way. Their pay was $2.00 to $2.25 per day, while men and mules received $4.00. Contract deadlines would have the line to the quarry by August 15th and to Scandinavia by October 1, 1907. Miss Rose Penney, arranging a shower for a friend and bride, chose potato dressing as the highlight activity in a burst of potato fervor. The object was to dress the "Murphies" like little dolls, the goal a suitable prize. The worshipful potato was on the rise, alive and well in Waupaca County.

The Waupaca Republican regularly championed potatoes, publishing helpful accounts of shipments as far as California, freight rate problems, even an article on extracting alcohol from the touted tuber. It also publicized the Penney Company's expansion over 25 years, including four counties lying along GB&W's main line. The Advancement group took up the cause of sugar beets, another agricultural hope for post-logging lands and communities in northern Wisconsin. Waupaca's potato shippers were looking anxiously toward the fall completion of their new railroad in time for harvest. Andrew Rowe's daughter Ansea, a plucky girl who helped with team and scraper, worked to build W-GB northward. The county applauded her zeal.

The hot Waupaca summer passed to August before the first rails were slid into place and spiked. Wet weather delayed activity but tracklayers were finally advancing from the GB&W junction toward Granite and bridge builders were keeping just ahead of their progress. Steady delivery of the accepted GB&W rail was never a problem. Frank Halliday brought his son Frank Jr. to watch the building of GB&W's last extension. Bonding of the line was settled with Milwaukee Trust Co. and by August the

Here, Train No. 40 was leaving Waupaca with 4-4-0 No. 23, a Dickson product of 1898, in the lead. The combination car is next to the engine, which was a normal occurrence on the branch.

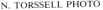

fourth 10% assessment was levied on stockholders. Among other costs, GB&W sold the company 1000 tons of rails on August 29, 1907, along with fastenings.

Money was now flowing to the contractor in quantity, only the beginning of an outpouring for the needs of such an undertaking. Irving Lord stated before a meeting of Advancement people that "some bad weather, labor's high price and a big sinkhole had retarded progress, but that cars should be running by November." The new road was also grading for yard roundhouse and arranging its station grounds. Lord also reported that

his electric road had received 2500 fares that month. Their investments in two railroads looked promising but men were still needed to aid "Bulgarians and others" on the project.

On September 13th President Nelson announced that W-GB bonds were on the market in $500 denominations, drawing six-percent interest semi-annually. Within the month, GB&W's piledriver was laboring on bottomland sites. The sinkhole continued to swallow fill, some of which was supplied by Wisconsin Central B&B forces at the underpass. W-GB was employing WEL&RCo. gravel cars to handle the WC fill material, while WC had a narrow-gauge dinky line with dump cars at the underpass. Cars of rail arrived on WC for W-GB,

Waupaca branch service featured GB&W's last 4-4-0's No. 18 and No. 23. In the summer of 1939, No. 23 readied a modest train for the 9.8-mile run to Scandinavia on the main line.

which were used in yard construction. Completion was now expected before Christmas. Previously, Waupaca had voted to bond the railroad for $60,000 to cover rail shipments, rolling stock and other costs to date. By month's end track work had been completed.

On Sundays, laborers idled about, their laundry spread carefully in appropriate places to dry. Curved pipes, firmly placed under fierce mustachios of Mediterranean fashion would appear and arguments would crackle in a tongue quite foreign to Waupaca's Danish and Yankee constituency. It was a new century and, if the "City of Potatoes" could arrange, it would be theirs to exploit.

GB&W supplied the new road with a locomotive and combination car which arrived on January 15, 1908. The engine was a 4-4-0 but some conflicting notes cloud the issue. GB&W Dickson engine No. 17 was listed as "sold to W-GB Ry. February 1, 1909," leaving a one year gap from first run to sale. It is possible that another error crept into accounting records, for the little Dickson probably went to Waupaca on Inaugural Day.

On January 15, 1908 the train arrived about 11:00 a.m. in the charge of Conductor L. M. Dingman and Engineer J. Fredericks. Passengers were A. G. Nelson, A. M. Penney, Frank Stout, T. J. McGrath and William P. Raidler and honored guests. There was the appropriate band, the crowd and last-minute adjustments. A donation by Nelson Painting Co. arrived in time; it was the gold leaf-on-black sign: WAUPACA-GREEN BAY Ry., which would hang on the depot front for the next 13 years.

The W-GB had been a two-year effort; actual construction began May 18th, with an average of 75 men per day on the job.

There had been 125,000 cubic yards of material moved and six bridges installed. The biggest cut, at 27 feet, required the removal of 11,000 cubic yards. The sink hole near Scandinavia occupied 25 men for two months and it took 500 cubic yards of rock, four acres of small Tamarack timber, twelve carloads of old ties and 8000 cubic yards of earth. Six thousand feet of timbers were used on approaches, plus many carloads of cinders. A bridge at the "Marl Mill" gave way twice due to uneven settling and required 14,000 cubic yards of earth, delaying completion by four weeks. Steel laying began October 5th and was finished by December 20, 1907 at a cost of $120,000.

The Republican ran a sizable ad which read: "NOW-USE IT" and ran W-GB's first timetable which called for a round trip starting at 7:20 a.m. and another at 3:20 p.m.. It would accommodate travelers on GB&W No. 1 and No. 2. Inevitably, the road planned an excursion but it was promptly postponed to warmer times due to many GB&W coaches being in shop that spring. GB&W's Manager Jordan also wanted to give Waupaca a welcome in more agreeable summertime weather. Finally, beginning on June 7, 1908, excursions were scheduled every Sunday, leaving Green Bay at 6:40 a.m. and arriving at Waupaca at 9:30 a.m. This was actually a seventh day for main liner No. 1, run as an extra because of the potential Waupaca trade for Green Bay's wholesale industries.

In September 1908, the year asphalt paving came to Waupaca, the Advancement Association's potato merchants sponsored an annual Potato Fest. Congressman J. H. Davidson gave a speech and presided over barbecues, balloon ascensions, a tug-of-war and the baking of "spuds" by the thousands. Four years later, the 1912 Potato Fest's crowd was guaranteed a thirty-

Chicago railfans Eric Swanson and "Doc" Yungmeyer drove to Waupaca to photograph GB&W's 4-4-0 No. 23 in July of 1939. Here, Yungmeyer asks La Haie to spot the old engine in a classic "Chicago Style" photo pose, rods down with less background. Several prominent cameramen of the Windy City made pilgrimages to Wisconsin for the purpose. Boxcars held coal that was shoveled across to the engine. Combine 60 was always left on the wye leg. This photo, looking east, shows a Soo Line tank in the distance near the depot of the Soo Line.

E. SWANSON PHOTO

minute flight in a Curtiss aeroplane and Clintonville dispatched one of its avant-garde Four Wheel Drive Auto Company products to demonstrate before the power-addicted.

Mr. A. E. Cartwright's gravel pits along the W-GB supplied twenty cars a week to customers and contributed to the area's road construction.

Above: During the winter, No. 23 was issued a plow pilot for use on the branch trains out of Scandinavia. This photo was taken in 1940.

Below: This view of No. 23 at Waupaca enginehouse was taken in July of 1939. The north track was used for coal boxcars only.

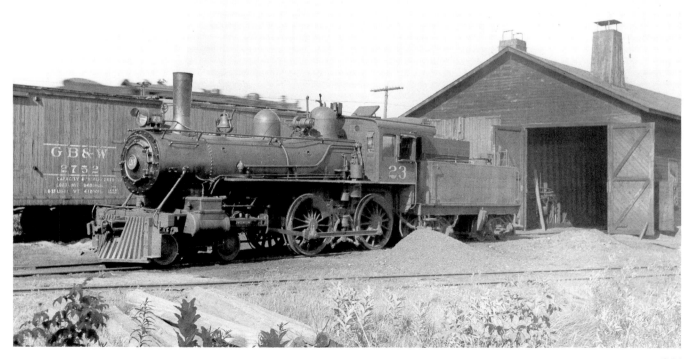

Above: Betten's scrapyard in Green Bay was the last mile for most GB&W engines. Here, the remains of 4-4-0 No. 23 and Mogul 255 are at rest in the summer of 1940.

W-GB owed $29,693.52 on March 3, 1908 and an eight-month note was secured at 6% with $36,000 first-mortgage bonding secured. Mr. Olfson, seller of the church-depot, received $1,200, just one more bill for the new company. W-GB bonds in the amount of $10,000 were sold to GB&W in November 1907, via banking interests in Green Bay, to cover construction to that date. Another $30,000 went to GB&W in January of 1908 as security on a note held by the main line, making the relationship even closer.

Ominously, automobiles reduced passenger earnings some 50% by summer of 1912. At the same time Agent M. F. Skinner left to enter Oshkosh real estate. Worse was the fact that Soo Line, which leased WC for 999 years in 1909, petitioned for a higher switching rate to handle cars to "South America," much to the consternation of the "potato people." It would be $4.00 per car to spot the box cars; double the old charge. The case went to the Railway Commissioner in Madison, producing a real crisis for W-GB.

The company had made an agreement with WC which was refuted by Soo Line after the lease date. Six Soo witnesses — all of them on that company's payroll — claimed that the charge was insufficient. The cost at the new rate, based on the 737 cars that had been switched in the preceding year, would total

Below: GB&W's 256, class B-25, prepares Train No. 40 to leave Waupaca in 1938 as Planzer and La Haie await the highball. Built in 1924, No. 256 was the last of its type for the GB&W.

$14.74 each. R. F. Whale, W-GB's Superintendant and Auditor, went before the Waupaca City Council to urge that W-GB build its own tracks to the warehouse district to offset the impending financial calamity. Any other action would break the supporting fabric of the unhealthy short line. Whale suggested an increased evaluation of W-GB for better bonding to "get on a better financial basis." Waupaca responded to the cries of its "home road" and allowed an eight-foot easement along Oborn Street. All of the warehousemen were sure their real estate values would increase agreeably.

On March 15, 1913 the commission gave Soo Line a compromise package, allowing a $2.75 per car rate for the switch. W-GB, unable to absorb the increase, objected due to only a $9.00 plus per diem charge on potato cars. The net receipt was considered too low due to frost damage losses. Finally, it would jeopardize car supply which W-GB had diligently upheld, harking back to the conditions which spawned the short line in the

Above: Mogul 257 (ex-KGB&W 38) is ready to handle train No. 40 away from the Waupaca depot. Conductor Holger Hanson is standing on the platform in this circa 1938 photo.

first place. It was a stand-off which prompted Waupaca to consider investment in the Oborn Street trackage. The city ordinance materialized in May 1913, allowing the new tracks. Twenty-five men and a steam shovel went to work, with completion scheduled for November.

The W-GB could offer second-morning delivery to Chicago and Milwaukee points and next-morning service to all GB&W points. It even offered special potato train service every Sunday morning. The community was admonished to cooperate and help keep the local line independent and solvent.

Independence never came to the W-GB due largely to money matters. In order to complete the new spurs, $15,000 was expended and a new mortgage was ordered to secure an issue of $75,000 in bonds, dated July 1, 1913, to First Savings and Trust Co. of Milwaukee. W-GB voted to reduce its capital stock to

GB&W's very first Mogul, No.27, pauses with the daily eastbound freight on the main line at Scandinavia about 1910. This view is from W-GB trackage which ran to the rear of the depot. The track ran behind the camera to Waupaca.

$100,000 for the bond issue. The GB&W received bonds of the home road in payment for the Oborn Street construction. GB&W and W-GB executed a voting trust agreement July, 17, 1913 for 308½ shares, of 614 outstanding.

Side tracks and potatoes notwithstanding, W-GB was never able to outrun its financial problems. Despite one other special excursion when Green Bay's St. Ansgar Society came to visit (the only Sunday train in 1913), W-GB's fortunes were dimming. Two small "halts" of marginal value to railroad and the public, Knutson's and Rowe's, were eventually eliminated, although farmer Andrew L. Rowe resisted. Both farmers insisted a small station be erected for their convenience as compensation for right-of-way concessions. In September 1930, the

8 × 10-foot depots at Knutson's, Rowe's and Granite were removed from the Waupaca branch. Waupaca Sand and Gravel Co. expanded, adding $5,248 to the road's revenue, but the level of growth was inadequate to address the impending actions by the trust company. WS&GCo. supplied over 100 cars for a Sheboygan County highway project.

W-GB acquired its second and final engine in 1913, a 4-4-0 purchased from Soo Line. No.2 evidently came as a result of an enginehouse fire which badly damaged No.1, the former GB&W 17. No.2 had been WC 65, a Schenectady, built in 1886. The engine cost W-GB $2,500 and was the final power on the road. No.2 survived into GB&W ownership as second No.8, finally being scrapped by Betten's in the summer of 1936. The sole com-

KGB&W No.60 was assigned to the Waupaca Branch in 1940. The car was relieved on inspection date by car 50 of the GB&W.

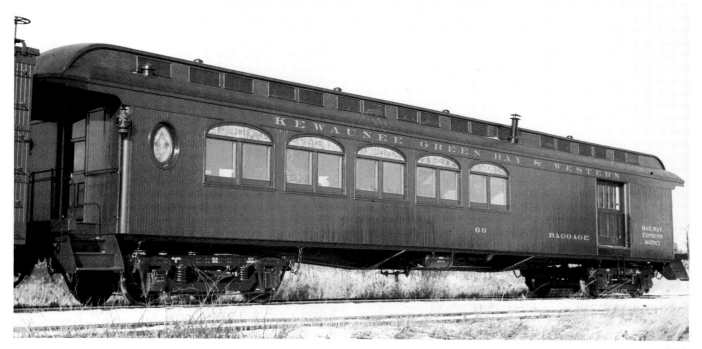

Yard engine 144 handles the assignment at Waupaca on a rare occasion in 1940. Speed wasn't everything in those days.
N. TORSSELL PHOTO

Waupaca's W-GB depot was once a Lutheran church. The building was razed in the late 1970's.
ERIC SWANSON PHOTO

Mogul 258 works the scrapping train, pulling up Waupaca branch rails in the summer of 1947.
T. VAN DREESE PHOTO

bination car came from KGB&W in February 1909. Renumbered 2, it became GB&W 24 and later was retired in 1939.

In October of 1921, after a protracted receivership of W-GB, First Savings and Trust Co., Milwaukee, foreclosed on the road and a sheriff's sale on December 15, 1921 closed the matter. GB&W was the sole bidder at $55,000; Sheriff Swenson had done his duty. GB&W's report stated that, in view of the fact that W-GB Ry. had not been able to meet its fixed charges and that GB&W was the owner of all the bonds of said railway, the only recourse left was for GB&W to foreclose and take the property at a cost of $91,000.

Adelbert Monroe Penney died January 26, 1922 in a Fond du Lac hospital, some distance from the railroad which he helped boost. His A. M. Penney Co. was a strong, nationwide organization, still thriving on potatoes and still calling Waupaca home. The railroad he hoped would make a better community had come to an end, but it would continue to operate until 1947 under GB&W ownership. As local heroes, Penney, Lord and Nelson faded away into the background but some utility came of their experiment in creating a "home road" for their home town.

If GB&W's Waupaca branch is remembered at all, it is emphatically for the small locomotive treasures of the 1930's. Chicago railfans on several occasions headed up to Wisconsin, which would have been an all-day jaunt in the 1930's, just to photograph two obscure, unlettered handmaidens of tank car and reefer at Waupaca. The pair were engines 18 and 23 which were the last of the breed to call the sooty two-stalled enginehouse home. After their demise the B-class Moguls prevailed until main line trains took over.

The Waupaca branch train No.40 would be timed to connect with main line train No.1, allowing for express and mail transfer and the very occasional passenger. After departure of No.1, the branch train would amble the 4.7 miles to Iola, arriving at 7:50, if on time. Here again was a sleepy branch line which could rise to a potato-oriented bustle in season, but which usually had a car of lumber, oil or coal as a staple. The southbound from Iola left at 8:15 a.m. with a liberal schedule allowing a return to Scandinavia by 12:15 p.m.. They were due back in Waupaca at 12:45 p.m. In years just before World War II, the Waupaca job would do way-freight work as far as New London, taking the combine from Scandinavia to New London where it arrived in the afternoon. This work included Manawa and its dairy products business, potatoes or pickles at Royalton, and coal, lumber or feed. Once at New London, the Hamilton Canning Co. absorbed some time to switch in season. Any cars for the C&NW transfer would be set out and the engine turned on the wye at the joint New London Junction depot. The trip back to Waupaca would include any C&NW pick-ups, beer and gasoline cars, empty reefers for potatos, pickles and company coal. Tie-up time was mid-afternoon at Waupaca.

A daily extra which was dispatched from Green Bay would work local business as far as New London, meeting the Waupaca job for car exchange. It ran so regularly that it was nearly "bulletined." Occasionally a 400-class would be assigned to this work until further changes were made. In GB&W's public timetable for July 1937 the Waupaca to Iola service ran twice a day and a second run was scheduled for a 12:50 departure. The final run southward (No.43), arrived in Waupaca by 3:01 p.m.

In the Great Depression year of 1933, after the Iola engine assignment was abolished, the Waupaca job ran as many as four scheduled trips (numbers 41 through 48 inclusive) between the two branch ends. In 1939's public timetable it was just trains 40 and 41, finishing the work by noon, which left time for a New

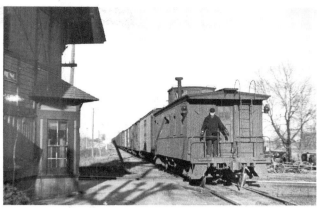

BEN ERICKSON PHOTO

GB&W freight train No.2 rumbles over the New London Junction diamond in 1938 when two depots were in service on GB&W.

BEN ERICKSON PHOTO

GB&W 4-4-0 No.23 is "on the spot for beans" at New London, Wisconsin in this 1938 or 1939 scene. The depot was moved east of Highway 45 in the summer of 1945 and the fifty-foot turntable behind the engine was removed in April of 1942.

BEN ERICKSON PHOTO

Scandinavia was the junction of the Iola and Waupaca branches. Looking eastward, a cut of cars occupied the Waupaca lead main line. By this time, No.23's days were numbered. The depot was built in 1903.

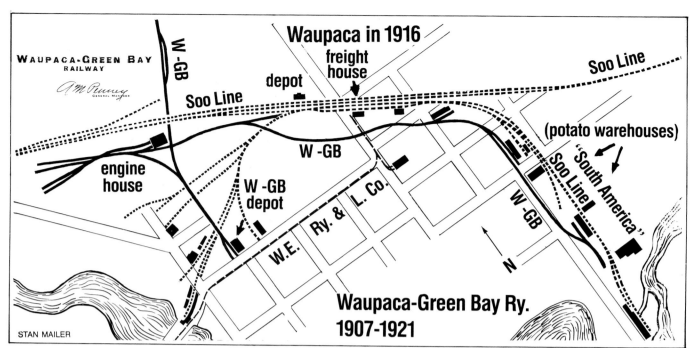

London trip. The final arrangement occurred after branch Bridge No.4.62 was rebuilt to take heavier power. Interestingly enough, it was strengthened by use of the old Wisconsin Rapids turntable. The turntable measured eighty feet three inches and made it possible for the main line way-freight No.8 to go to Waupaca by summer of 1942. The eighty-foot turntable at Scandinavia was removed; New London's turntable was taken out at the same time. In August of 1945 Norman Schaumann acquired the Waupaca enginehouse. He dismantled the structure and moved the material via flatcar to Oneida, Wisconsin. The New London Junction depot was retired in June of 1946, thus ending a little-known way-freight operation.

Engine 23, with No.18's old tender, handled the assignment out of Waupaca and had its picture taken on many occasions. Railfan Eric Swanson of Chicago found the engine several times, literally following it to its bitter end in Betten's scrapyard in Green Bay. After photographing it live at Waupaca in the summer, he returned to Green Bay in 1940 only to find it in the scrap line.

No.23's final trip was on February 26, 1940, under charge of Engineer La Haie and Conductor Holger Hanson. Lem La Haie's seniority on the Waupaca line is traceable to 1913 and Holger Hanson's to 1914, nearly as old as the line itself. They were called to work at 8:05 a.m. at Waupaca and their train arrived at Scandinavia at 8:38 a.m. With no side trip to Iola that day, No.23 ran from Scandinavia to New London, leaving at 10:15 a.m. and arriving in New London at 11:30 a.m. Extra 23 returned to Scandinavia by 12:57 p.m. where it met Extra 252 east. Engine 252 was dropped off, having come from Wisconsin Rapids, and Engineer Paul Graf with Conductor J. G. Dean made No.23's last one-way trip to Green Bay. They departed at 1:05 p.m. and tied up at Norwood at 5:00 p.m. Today the 23's whistle survives in a private collection, polished and quite able to function as a reminder of better and more colorful times in Waupaca County.

After World War II, GB&W looked further toward its bridge traffic and less to rural Wisconsin branch line operation. Impending dieselization might require lighter units to serve branches, something to be avoided for efficiency's sake. Three branches which didn't relate to the overhead traffic theory were the A&W and the two out of Scandinavia. The Stevens Point branch was endowed with paper industries and would be retained. Sale of A&W was pending in 1946 but not the two Waupaca County lines.

In November of 1946 Scandinavia became a flag stop for trains 7 and 8, which now carried the coach over the New London Division. Mail service was discontinued in 1945. Further changes included annulment of trains 3 and 4 which were replaced December 8th, 1946 with numbers 1 and 2. Mixed train No.8 arrived in Scandinavia about 11:00 a.m., while No.7 reached its destination by mid-afternoon.

Intention to abandon the 9.8 miles of the Waupaca branch was announced the first week of 1947; ICC application was made January 3rd. *The Waupaca Post* noted the long association with Waupaca County's northern parts. Coal shipments were pegged at forty to fifty per month and carloadings for 1945

were 494. In 1946 there were 671 cars of coal, oil products and potatoes, the area's leading commodities. The "coal men" voiced bitter disapproval over the abandonment. But, with spring on the way, the south branch of Little Wolf Creek again would threaten bridges and right-of-way in its predictable pattern. Since the Soo Line would take over service to industries in Waupaca, other opposition to abandonment was minimal. GB&W could make transfers at Amherst Junction, 8.8 miles west of Scandinavia and backhauling to Waupaca would solve any problems.

By March 6, 1947 the ICC had granted permission to abandon. The date was set for March 31st at 12:01 a.m., but Waupaca's Association of Commerce decided to appeal for a thirty-day stay of abandonment. The resulting June meeting at Neil's Hotel spotlighted the abandonment and the ICC hearing of July 3rd. Adjustments as to details of the Soo Line's take-over of yard trackage and service were made with all objections being therefore withdrawn. GB&W abandoned and removed the line under ICC Finance Docket 15564 in the late summer of 1947, leaving only the Iola branch in operation out of Scandinavia.

GB&W's Northwest crane was used to remove Waupaca branch trackage. Here, a bridge is dismantled and swung onto flatcars in the summer of 1947.
T. VAN DREESE COLLECTION

Left: When it came time to abandon the road, GB&W chose to do its own work. Here, Mogul 256 handles the track-removal job in her last weeks on the branch. The work continued throughout the summer and fall of 1947.
T. VAN DREESE COLLECTION

16

MOGULS, MIKES
&
McGEE

GB&W's train No. 1 strolled leisurely through the Depression-troubled landscape, maintaining the mundane but adequate schedule to Winona on November 7, 1934. The two-car consist included the legendary business car 99, long the carriage of executives bent on betterment of the road to Winona. This day, however, GB&W's new president, Homer Edgar McGee, rode westward on a tour of inspection and familiarization, accompanied by the old staff of Wisconsin men. It was a day of revelation for the man from Texas.

Aboard the 99 was General Manager Charles H. Smith, a 47-year veteran, once in GBW&STP train service and general manager since 1925. Louis P. Wohlfeil, general auditor, accompanied Chief Engineer Frank S. Halliday to advise and observe the change in corporate authority. The week prior, the ailing Frank B. Seymour had retired, at his own request, following a remarkable 64 years of continuous employment with GB&W. "FBS" finally left the railroad which had been his life's blood. He was encouraged to accept his pension at an age when most men were forgetting their careers. The mature sway of car 99 was to be counsel to the new president instead of the man from New London.

Homer Edgar McGee was born on October 15, 1885 in Alvord, Texas, about fifty miles northwest of Fort Worth, on Fort Worth & Denver Railway's main line. During his years on the farm he developed a passion for "brasspounding" on a homemade key. McGee entered a Dallas telegraphy school and shortly thereafter began railroading on Missouri-Kansas-Texas Railway. In 1906 he broke in at Holland and San Felipe, Texas and was soon promoted to dispatcher and trainmaster posts. In 1917 McGee was at Parsons, Kansas as general manager but when war broke out his offices were removed to Dallas, Texas. During USRA days, McGee was regional director of both "KATY" and Houston & Texas Central Railroads. His office was moved to St. Louis, Missouri in 1931. Although his credentials indicated lifetime KATY service, the Depression put the company on the ropes and McGee's position was forfeited in October 1931.

KATY's severe staff cutbacks placed McGee on other avenues. His next job was with Joseph Eastman's Committee of Railroad Consolidation which examined possible government-sponsored alternatives to Depression strife. In 1932 more federal work focused on Central of Georgia Railroad. In 1933 a family vacation included a Nova Scotia sojourn in which McGee and son Weldon observed well-maintained 4-6-0's still turning in a day's work on Canada's Dominion Atlantic Railway. Intrigued by the picture of antiquated, polished railroading at hand, both father and son couldn't know that their future held similar experiences on a Wisconsin road which overflowed with the same, quaint images of light rail and ancient standard-type locomotives.

In the months before McGee's first tour of the line, he had met with the New York officers, including Secretary Charles W. Cox. Cox's friend Walter Trammel introduced the man from Texas to the surviving representation of the Sloan-Taylor-Blair ownership. Mr. Cox was a partner in Robert Winthrop & Co., brokers and keepers of the GB&W flame. Other directors of the time were C. Ledyard Blair, Edward Palmer and G. H. Pyne,

Left: No. 401, on its first working trip, car 500 and a cut of cars, eased into Plover's water tank on February 11, 1937. The crew was Engineer M. Erickson and Fireman E. Jensen.

H. MANSKE/STEVENS POINT JOURNAL

In its sunset years, the Wisconsin Rapids depot was host to crewmen awaiting train No. 1's arrival and duties westward. The 1886 setpiece edifice was razed in 1959 in favor of glass-and-brick efficiency.
STAN MAILER COLLECTION

all of whom were traceable to the 19th Century Wisconsin railroad investment. Thus, for the first time, a president had been selected from well outside the usual geographic boundaries.

Engineer Halliday and President Homer McGee climbed aboard car 99 at Bridge Yard in Winona after an inspection of facilities. The Winona press was told that there were no plans for immediate changes but that GB&W was still in business to make money and looking for ways to improve its traffic. Soon enough, the new administration would swing into gear. Having been transplanted from Texas to Wisconsin soil, McGee often differed sharply from the patriarchal rule of Frank Seymour. Until "FBS" retired, his gruff but heartfelt concern for all things GB&W seeped into each transaction. The old chief had watched over lightbulbs, nuts and bolts, even coveted piles of used rail for secondary replacement. He had been certain that none in the company was fit to follow him into office, so absolute was his grasp of the reins. While GB&W wasn't doing badly during the Depression, Secretary Cox was alarmed that the old gentleman was still out in Wisconsin in charge of their holdings and hadn't appointed a successor. The president's son-in-law was secretively approached to coax Seymour into retirement, to which he allegedly snorted: "Not by a damn site!" But, in the end he relented. No longer would quotations from the Bible (inaccurate, according to witnesses) flow from the mind at the helm on Green Bay Junction's second floor. A new day had dawned on GB&W's main line.

Homer McGee was acquainted with John M. Davis (president, Lackawanna Railroad 1925-41) who served on GB&W's board from 1934 to 1944. Also a Texan, Davis' career followed SP and ATSF in the bumpy 1890's, later migrating to regions closer to GB&W's territory on Great Northern. He became involved in GN's lake carrier arm which took him to Buffalo, New York. He later returned to SP, after which he spent some time with B&O. Finally, he settled during USRA days with the DL&W presidency. Davis worked to increase service with fast-freight trains and elimination of old drag-era practices which were fast becoming a drain on company coffers. Davis also reduced marginal operations to a minimum. When McGee came aboard GB&W it was as a "Lackawanna Man" with approved experience and many friends in railroad boardrooms from Texas to New York. Perhaps the McGee hand at the telegraph key steadied his accomplished golf game, for the sport of executives was avidly pursued, enhancing championship railroading as well.

Fast-freight service arrived on GB&W with the Ford trains of the 1920's, encouraged by record auto loadings at Green Bay

Left: Whitehall's unusual depot echoed the archi-tecture of the Hicks arch-windowed coaches that once paused en route to Winona. Built in 1914, it was sold in late 1963 and still stands. In the dis-tance an eastbound train moves up to the coal dock in 1938.
BEN ERICKSON PHOTO

Right: Another business excursion eased into Whitehall behind Mogul 256 about 1938. Cars 50 and 500 conveyed management on another good-will and promotion tour of the Trempeleau Valley.
B. ERICKSON PHOTO

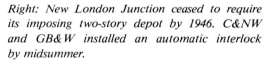

Left: GB&W's last Mogul arrived in 1924 in time for many a Ford extra. A decade later, No. 56 pauses at Arnott on train No. 1, just before the humble passenger run became a mixed in the sum-mer of 1935.
S. McDONALD PHOTO

Right: New London Junction ceased to require its imposing two-story depot by 1946. C&NW and GB&W installed an automatic interlock by midsummer.
G. STRECKERT PHOTO

through 1929. Nicholson Universal and Spokane Steamship Companies accounted for 26,000 autos carried into the port in 1929 with 84% of the new cars going out by rail, a savings of $5.00 per auto for shippers. Competitive rates were introduced by hungry eastern railroads eager to re-enter the auto-carrying trade. Nicholson and Pennsylvania Railroad were locked in a rate case in which GB&W supported its ally Nicholson. A lake-rail rate was proposed in which GB&W and the two boat lines would cooperate further, allowing GB&W to continue auto

shipments from its dockside. Green Bay stood to lose its hard-won traffic to Lake Superior ports, which finally did occur.

In September 1930 GB&W received fifty new composite box cars, again patterned after a standard Milwaukee Road design of higher vertical capacity. Another fifty were similarly designed automobile cars with the customary double-door configuration, the first on the road. Too late for the auto boom, forty were rebuilt with single doors within a few years. A third series of the

In Depression Days, 4-4-0 No. 14 had long since passed W. P. Raidler's time. The old engine's patched stack reflects GB&W's frugality in leaner years. The super 4-4-0 went to Betten's in 1935.
R. CAMPBELL PHOTO

Train No. 1 rolls westward from City Point at a leisurely pace, far less than capable 402 could deliver. The 400-class Mikes seldom were taxed, especially west of Wisconsin Rapids.

E. RUHLAND PHOTO

same 40,000-pound-capacity boxcars went to KGB&W. It was the last new order of cars until after World War II.

While the economy remained blighted, GB&W made a bid for ten-hour freight schedules by bravely announcing to lineside newspapers that coast-to-coast service was being offered. The employee timetable of October 22, 1933 detailed freight trains, with No. 3-4 billed as "Easterner" and "Westerner," while No. 27-28 became "Atlantic" and "Pacific." Westbound paper, cheese and other native shipments could be loaded as late as 6:00 p.m. at Green Bay for second-morning, 7:00 a.m. arrival at Twin Cities. KGB&W running time was "cut to a mere hour and a half," to accommodate the new service. No. 27 was due out of

In the Depression's depth, it was still Mogul and Consolidation slugging it out with deep drifts and stiff, ornery little grades such as "Stoney," "Smokey," Luxemburg and Summit. Ford extras, slim as they were, still required that operators flag railroad crossings at Black Creek or New London to save time. R. H. Thompson and W. H. Whiting were the engineers December 30, 1932 on No. 1-2, 4-4-0's 25 and 26, while Frank Welby and John Seymour were the conductors. Welby passed away only two years later. The New Londoner had 47 years' service and had presided over his passenger train since 1918. He would miss the great changes coming on GB&W. Out west, Charlie Chapman and Ben Closuit shepherded No. 9 across the

New President Homer Edgar McGee began his GB&W responsibilities in late 1934. Here, McGee and Western Refrigerator Line President E. M. Miller are engaged with a favorite pastime at French Lick Springs, Indiana in the 1930's. BEN ERICKSON COLLECTION

Green Bay ten minutes later, scheduled to arrive at East Winona (212) just before 9:00 a.m. Manager Charles H. Smith announced that points between Green Bay and Wisconsin Rapids would also benefit, as way-freight No. 5 would coordinate its 4:30 p.m. departure so as to have all cars for Winona in Wisconsin Rapids ahead of the fleet newcomer. Patriotically, the new trains would give twenty Depression-era employees work not otherwise available. Smith noted that Lake Michigan-to-Missisippi service had been a 13-hour proposition and that the eastbound counterpart would offer 9:00 a.m.-to-6:00 p.m. service for next-morning Green Bay delivery. With adjustments, No. 27-28 became trains 30-31 after Sept. 29, 1935, the fast, faithful whistle in the GB&W night, sadly bereft of classic names entrusted to distant oceans.

fifty odd miles of cutover timberland through Pray and City Point. Carl Pintsch remembered that No. 9 traditionally stopped at City Point (MP 121) for breakfast. The population, then 100, seemed more like fifty. One of Carl's relatives operated the hotel, a gathering place for GB&W people in the isolated village. Tickets were occasionally sold for the four-mile trip to Spaulding, west of town, much to Ben Closuit's consternation. Ben chose to ignore the Spaulding halt, stopping instead on a gentle rise beyond, heedless of the wild-eyed complaints. His retort to the humble patrons was that No. 9 was hardly their interurban and made them walk back, optimistically never to see them again. Soon enough, his outland customers faded away. Ben had bigger business and he often went rattling through

Spaulding with a heavy train.

Carl Pintsch started at Dodge (MP 204) in 1929, soon graduating to City Point which boasted of its Sphagnum Moss production, a florist's resource which accounted for about one carload per day in season. It was also the time of unique train order inscriptions, in which trains were named for conductors. A "flimsy" might read thus: "Myott run extra Merrillan to Pray meet Closuit extra east . . ." In the blighted years after 1930, extras bearing a person's name were seldom seen and men lucky enough to hold their jobs gave up a day so that laid-off employees could work. Another arrangement pooled ten percent of wages, given up to support those without regular income. The grim times cut back service on the Stevens Point branch which had averaged five runs to Plover daily in good times. At Iola, which like Stevens Point had a "short" or four-man crew, the potato business changed and service was reduced. Each of the branches had a one-stall enginehouse, a fifty-foot turntable and primitive coaling equipment. Water was drawn at Iola from a nearby creek via siphon hose. It was all to change further in the coming years.

The Seymour administration attempted to improve passenger service between Kewaunee and Casco with bus substitution. KGB&W's bus was a Yellow Coach, acquired from Rex Finance Corp. of Chicago in February 1932. The blue-and-white machine was driven by Sammy Roubal, required by the mail service to carry a revolver in defense of his sacred trust. Roubal promptly locked the piece, a .32-caliber Hopkins & Allen "Ranger No. 2," in the bus' safe and, when the mail inspector admonished him for not holstering the gun, Roubal retorted, "I'm not going to shoot *anybody!*" Roubal's revolver survived, but the bus achieved retirement in late 1934.

The winter of 1932 registered some sold, snappy days which didn't enhance train operation. December 9th in Green Bay was reportedly minus-twelve degrees, severely hampering steaming qualities of GB&W's small locomotives. All the slide-valve, sat-

GREEN BAY & WESTERN COLLECTION

Former President Frank B. Seymour, second from left, visited with Dispatcher Henry C. Erbe who is seated at the right. The topic was the railroad which was so deep in Seymour's blood.

urated-steam Moguls were set aside and some never again moved under their own power. The nine GB&W and three A&W-KGB&W 4-4-0's continued to work branch and passenger assignments but, one by one, their time ran out and they were retired to their stalls at Green Bay or Wisconsin Rapids as victims of deferred maintenance and frugality. The December 8th cold reduced train No. 5 to a low crawl up Oneida Hill. Mayflower 2-8-0 No. 44 was forced to double 1250 tons (23 loads, eight empties) in a brisk northwest wind. No. 5 was not through the ordeal, for ahead lay Amherst Hill, requiring yet another doubling. The hapless Consolidation took a mere 1716 tons up in the bitter cold.

GB&W announced plans to improve the entire system on

Mayflower 302 worked its last days on several assignments west of Wisconsin Rapids. Its last run was in 1939.

KEN ZURN PHOTO

*Mogul 50 is shown here after rebuilding. Piston valves and Walschaerts Valve gear
were among the improvements in the 1935 rebuild of this superheated machine. It was
renumbered 250 and later sold to MT&W.*

March 14, 1935, after a conference in Green Bay with Charles W. Cox. Expenditures would depend on improved earnings, but resumption of Ford traffic had given GB&W the needed shot in the arm. Once again the daily "Ford train" would rush auto parts westward to the St. Paul plant and with the proceeds would come reballasting. More ninety-pound rail was ordered and gravel pits were opened near Hatfield and Casco Junction. GB&W entered into a five-year contract with Winona Sand & Gravel Co. to operate a Hatfield pit of eighty acres. For rail already in place, it was electric welding of ends which received the go-ahead. The railroad through Elm Lake which required drainage and culverts, received the first of the ninety-pound steel. This area (MP 106-107) was always wet and several bridges were retired in favor of large steel pipes. By September

the new ninety-pound rail was in use from Scandinavia to Amherst Junction.

Homer McGee began to gather talent from the KATY to staff his new administration, bringing in Grover C. Byers as general manager. Byers had been superintendent at Muskogee, Oklahoma in 1927 and succeeded C. H. Smith on GB&W. His trainmaster was E. V. Johnson, also a KATY man. J. C. Hill was made general roadmaster and, finally, Theodore M. Kirkby returned to Wisconsin as superintendent of motive power and equipment. Ted Kirkby came to GB&W after ten years with KATY. Born in Olso, Norway July 4, 1886, he graduated from engineering school in the old country. He had been employed by the CM&STP as a mechanical draftsman in July 1908, rising to shop engineer in Chicago. Ambition moved him onward to

*Mogul 253 shows off its final and modern lines while switching at Sawyer (on the A&W) in
May of 1939. The Engineer is Joe Ferris.*

Above: Several days before this photo was taken, Mogul 252 had headed a Director's Special to Winona. The shine still shows. No. 252 was modernized by 1939 with distinctive front-mounted bell and all-steel pilot, pilot beam and run-boards. This photo was taken at Green Bay on September 30, 1939.

Left: KATY-ized Mogul 252 awaited the Director's pleasure at Green Bay Junction on October 18, 1940. Combine 50 and officer's car 500 were also present.

the Duluth & Iron Range Railroad as a Two Harbors shop draftsman, also returning him to CM&STP at Milwaukee. At the old 35th Street Shops, Kirkby worked under C. H. Bilty, designer of the Milwaukee's great Hudson-type 4-6-4's, and L. K. Sillcox, GSMP at Chicago as assistant. In those days Kirkby was surrounded by talent which produced the final types of CM&STP Mikado's (2-8-2's), including the L-2a class which was the basis for GB&W's 400-class 2-8-2's. With the CM&STP reorganization, Kirkby went down to Parsons, Kansas in July 1926 where he worked under H. M. Warden, KATY's motive power chief. Kirkby earnestly desired a position which would allow him to design locomotives and in April 1936 he got his wish. He came to GB&W as mechanical representative and finally became the No. 1 motive power man for GB&W that September. Kirkby was the man behind the 400-class Mikes of GB&W, the apex of the road's locomotive development.

The minds of Kirkby and McGee agreed on the plane of motive power improvement. Ernest Becker and Frank Seymour

had begun the business; it was now a question of continuity. Kirkby lost no time in organizing Norwood Shops to modernize existing power, girding itself for the future trends. This really meant getting heavier locomotives which would have the capabilities the future dictated. Kirkby's failing was that his talents didn't include diesel-electric theory, a trend which crouched specter-like in the corner of his drafting room like Poe's raven, crying "nevermore." E. V. Johnson grasped the reality, as did Frank Halliday, forming a consensus that cautioned against outlays in big steam power. Heavy steam brought with it a need to change bridges, turntables and even roundhouses. Counsel suggested a short wait until the proven diesel left the yard limits and achieved perfection in workday freight service. But there was a pressing need to act and the deliberation finally fixed on the decision which brought the greyhound-like 400-class to Norwood Avenue in Green Bay.

Albert Arcand of Green Bay served the GB&W in the boiler-making trade. He said that McGee had kept his word and per-

Ancient business car 99, which survived until World War II, was finally scrapped in 1943. The car was of unknown origin but served as a parlor car in GBWSTP days. This photo was taken in the summer of 1939.

The railroad saw fit to acquire a better business car during the McGee era. WUTCO's Morse became GB&W 500. It was built in 1904 by Pullman and sold off in 1945.

mitted the boilermakers to stay on the payroll in hard times. The two-edged act allowed GB&W to exploit this talent and, even before Kirkby's arrival, Ernest Becker had begun to upgrade several engines. Becker's first effort was to rebuild Mogul 50, formerly a saturated slide-valve machine, to superheated status. The work required Universal steam chests (piston valves), boiler reinforcement, new flue sheets and Walschaert's Valve gear, a $7,153 expenditure. Becker next embarked upon a curious project which produced a Mogul from an 0-6-0, which used to be a Mogul.

Becker journeyed to Chicago & Alton's shop at Bloomington,

Illinois to ostensibly acquire another bargain which would be used as a switch engine. Picking 0-6-0 No.49, he completed his inspection in May 1933 and purchase was made through a scrap dealer from Chicago, Iron & Steel Products Co. Becker rode the long-wheelbase oddity for five days to Green Bay. No.92 was apparently tried and found wanting as a switch engine, probably due to its long wheelbase. The preparation for service claimed the summer months of 1933 and it was ready by October 1st, the product of thankful boilermakers. But it wasn't the switcher that GB&W wanted.

The entrance of new management brought about a change for

GB&W car 500 was a wood-and-steel masterpiece which saw regular use in the upgraded years of GB&W. This photo was taken at Green Bay in August of 1939.

the unsuccessful yard goat. It was decided to convert the ugly duckling to a 2-6-0, its original configuration on the Alton road. Baldwin built it as C&A 320 in 1899 and converted it to a heavy switcher in May 1923. GB&W's reconversion was an extensive project which included sliding the boiler forward to the original position and building an engine truck. Application of a superheater, Barco reverse gear and a rebuilt tender was required. The Universal Steam Chests and thermic siphons were added later. The total cost was $14,799. No. 92 made its first road trip eastward on mixed train No. 6-8 on October 25, 1935 to Kewaunee with Russ Hollister and conductor Richards in charge of the twenty loads and four empties. For the interim period between its rebirth and the takeover by the 400-class, No. 92 sparred with 45 and 65 on east-end trains to Kewaunee, giving a reasonable return on the investment.

Kirkby and Becker later tackled switch engine 80, which received similar treatment and was completed by the spring of 1936. The economics of superheating was brought to at least two of the slope-cylindered switchers, No. 90 and No. 41, in late 1936 and early 1935 respectively. In March 1936, while improvements were made on useful power, ten obsolete engines were sold to Betten Processing Co. for scrap. The old engines followed six others scrapped in the two preceding years, some of which were cut down by GB&W forces as a Depression project.

The La Crosse branch curiosity continued into the Depression. In one of his first actions after taking office, Homer McGee moved to sell the orphan to CB&Q. It comprised some 2.65 miles, operated by CB&Q under a lease arrangement, but GB&W was not receiving any revenue from the arrangement. In early 1935 several officers went to La Crosse to determine the amount of traffic moving over the GB&W track. Its evaluation stood at $80,000, including an enginehouse and 350 tons of rail. The ICC docket stated that GB&W wished to sell the line for $27,000. As no business was interchanged with CB&Q, GB&W was not deriving any benefit. It had to grant switching service to the industries after abandonment, GB&W receiving only $1.00 per annum in return. GB&W demanded a substantial increase in rental, as examination divulged a traffic increase in CB&Q's favor. Sale was effected in July 1936 and the coal traffic to the university continued for several decades afterwards.

One ancient combination car, long the conveyance used on the Iola branch, was retired from passenger service and sold to KGB&W as a depot. While much newer cars were burned at Casco Junction, the oldster went to New Franken, retiring later to a nearby field. A worthy business car was obtained from Western Union Telegraph Co. Their car "Morse" became GB&W car 500 and cost $10,200 after remodeling. Old 99, nearing the end of its days, was demoted to J. C. Hill's office car and was eventually retired after a derailment in 1943. Several coaches remained in B&B service as homes and offices for the rail and ballast gangs of the 1930's.

The spring of 1935 witnessed several operating adventures as new management began to take root. Mogul 71 (A&W) was nearing Marshland with twelve loads and six empties when Engineer Rude heard the drawbar break and pull out between the engine and tender. With nothing else damaged, Rude eased his train into Bridge Yard at reduced speed, the safety chains performing their intended duty. In March, due to inclement weather, No. 1 was doubleheaded, engines 21 and 24 bucking the drifts. Loyal Van Dreese went out on a work extra with big 45 and a C&NW ditcher to work from Milepost 38 to Royalton on May 1st in anticipation of greater things to come in the roadway

ERIC SWANSON PHOTO

GB&W sold engine 146's tank to Oconto Co. for use on Flander's Spur logging road in Nicolet National Forest near Carter, Wisconsin. When the tender was scrapped, it still bore the Green Bay Route herald and had Fox trucks. Baldwin No. 6 2-6-2 is shown here in December of 1938.

GREEN BAY & WESTERN COLLECTION

During the closing years of the Seymour era, a Yellow Coach was substituted for mixed train service between Kewaunee and Casco. The bus met A&W's passenger run there. The blue-and-white bus didn't last long, however; it was pulled off in 1934.

T. VAN DREESE COLLECTION

GB&W rented a C&N-W Jordan ditcher for the summer of 1935. There was a crash program to turn the 25 m.p.h. track into a competitive time-saver route.

department. The informality of GB&W passenger service was reflected when No. 2 stopped to unload two cars of ties east of Hatfield for the new gravel pit siding.

Real trouble came to engine 21 and train No. 1 two miles west of Pray. The old Schenectady's eccentric cam slipped after overheating, disabling the engine. Though several bolts were missing, Engineer Thompson tried to take the eccentric down. Meanwhile, Dispatcher Erbe ordered sister 4-4-0 No.20 extra from Wisconsin Rapids to pick up the train and disabled engine and convey both to Winona. Engineer Swanson and Dave Myott arrived with No.20 and dragged the two cars and one engine onward. Thompson and Kenyon's crew were tied up at Blair due to the "hog law" (hours of service). The action further delayed train No.1, Myott's engine 20 having also been delayed before it left Wisconsin Rapids. No.1 of May 30, 1935 made Winona at 2:30 the next morning. It had not been a nice day.

Perhaps the incident was the motivation for heavier power on No.1-2 and its Merrillan-to-Winona counterpart, No.21-22, which were christened on May 13, 1935. The new west-ender was entrusted to a Mogul and it was a mixed train designed to expedite any "fast" cars. For several experimental months, train No.1 terminated at Merrillan at noon with passenger coaches entrusted to mixed service. G. C. Byers and Trainmaster E. V. Johnson worked on intricate scheduling designed to make the most of the short line's potential. No.21 left Merrillan with six cars, its crew armed with a new agreement which limited the number of cars handled and restricted trainmen's duties. By May 24, 1935 train No.1 consisted of 4-4-0 No.21, baggage car 20, coach 107 and seven loads, the majority of which was scheduled for train No.21 and East Winona delivery. Weeks later, a derailment at Elm Lake tore up 1,000 feet of track and disrupted the experimentation. The cause was a washed-out culvert. In a

short time, Moguls, often doubleheaded, were assigned to the mixed train west from Green Bay.

Weldon McGee years later recalled that an old regime veteran was aghast when the decision was made to use Moguls on No.1-2. "You're going to put those *great big freight engines* on the passenger train?" Such changes were now coming quickly and plans were made to renumber all but the short-lived 4-4-0's, to place them in series, dispensing with the disconcerting past system. Upon occasion, as though enjoying their twilight years, the 20 and 23 class 4-4-0's ran off their final hours in the service, often doubleheaded, in a display of superannuated Victorian grace. Beginning with engine 40, all 0-6-0's were renumbered from 140 to 146 exclusive. Individual road ownership identification was done by placing initials above the rear tender numerals, while new porcelain "GREEN BAY ROUTE" bolt-on heralds would grace tender sides. Lettering, previously done in red or orange, was done in white, reflecting the well-kept, snappy appearance which identified all KATY engines. Several experimental interim lettering schemes appeared in 1935. No.49 and No.69 briefly exhibited a painted tender herald, white running-board striping and white tires, also a KATY trait. In fact, the firm which made GB&W's tender heralds (Everbrite Signs, Chicago) also supplied KATY with their bright bolt-on emblems. The R-class 2-6-0's were numbered upward from old 50, which became 250, and the series ended with 92 becoming new 261. Mayflowers, the old R-1 class, became 301-303, while 1929's 2-8-0's became 350-351. Lastly, the big Z-class, 45 and 65, received numbers 398-399. Even the numerals now standing out

GB&W's Norwood Shops are shown as they appeared during the Great Depression. The line of rusting Moguls and 4-4-0's awaits the end of the Seymour era.

STATE HISTORICAL SOCIETY OF WISCONSIN

248

Above: GB&W's heaviest switcher was 146, formerly No.60. Rebuilt in the Kirkby era, 145 received the tank from Mogul 54 at Green Bay in the summer of 1939. It was sold in 1948.

Below: KGB&W 45, class Z, stood at Green Bay Junction with C. Reiss Coal Company's offices and works in the background. The 100-ton Consol was the road's heavy-weight until 1937.

distinctly on cab sides were of KATY design. Letter classification of each wheel arrangement, never too clear on C&NW and the Becker transliteration, also fell back on KATY. The 0-6-0's were A-class while Moguls went to B-class; C-class covered Consolidations and appropriate antecedents indicated tractive effort. Finally, grey graphite was applied to smokeboxes, completing new paint schemes.

The roadway rebuilding program continued into 1936 and 1937, nearly $228,000 plowed into rail in 1936 alone. All of it was ninety-pound steel. The 1937 program put another $127,000 into rail replacement and ballasting, plus nearly $40,000 into the Wolf River bridge reconstruction. The summer of 1937 also brought a crash program to install automatic flashing signals at grade crossings in accordance with state requirements. A parallel program covered rebuilding of old cabooses into bay-window designs, which continued until 1940. Roadway work achieved the majority of funding as the two years' work prepared GB&W for the heavier power which was just then being designed.

While GB&W prospered, a competitor in cross-lake traffic collapsed. Hard luck bedeviled Wisconsin & Michigan Railroad

which connected with Ann Arbor's Menominee, Michigan car ferry, finally gave up the fight June 30, 1938. Several years before, GB&W had acquired W&M's Jordan Spreader and ten Hart convertible gondolas for ballast work. Later, six "Western" air dump cars were added as W&M sold off the last of its assets. Maintaining the Lackawanna tradition, fussy accounting put the last bargains into KGB&W ownership. The cars were inspected at Menominee and brought to Norwood in December 1935. Ex-W&M Jordan 1001 cost $5,054 and became X-190 on GB&W, and to this day is an indispensable part of maintenance work, summer and winter. KGB&W also picked up fifty ex-N&W gondolas, built 1909-1913, which assisted in both coal and gravel service. The leased road was authorized to ballast its own line from Milepost 14 to Mile 23, the expenditure accounting covering the rental of Moguls 260 and 253, which were put on work extras. Casco Gravel Co. supplied material at $5.00 per yard. The new road was just in time for the coming of the 400's.

Ted Kirkby was in his element. Plans for the new Mikados were approved and specifications were developed by September

1936. The program called for an engine of average size which closely paralleled Milwaukee Road's L-2a of 287,000 pounds, but more modern, employing later techniques and details. While bids were submitted by Baldwin ($86,770 per unit) and Lima ($86,000), the company accepted ALCO's low bid of $83,425. American Locomotive's design called for flame-cut frames, Delta cast-steel trailer trucks and outside-frame cast-steel engine trucks. In keeping with higher boiler pressures, then in vogue, the 400-class would have running pressure of 245 pounds, 22 × 30-inch cylinders and a grate area of 60.4 square feet. Tractive effort would be 47,250 pounds with customary 64-inch drivers. Weight on drivers ran to 201,800 pounds which was not much more than the 1923 Consolidations; they wouldn't tax the several large bridges on line. The welded tank was a modest one with 9,000 gallons water capacity and 14 tons of coal. Total length was just over 72 feet. Once again, GB&W's locomotive purchase was close to the last of the type built for domestic service. The order covered GB&W No.401 and No.402 and KGB&W 403. They were inspected by GB&W representatives at Schenectady and Weldon McGee was impressed by the procedure which raised steam pressure to at least 500 pounds per square inch, holding the spectators at a respectful distance. Completed in January 1936, No.401 left Schenectady on Wednesday the 27th, while 402 followed on the 30th and KGB&W 403 on February 1st. All three arrived via D&H, DL&W, NYC and AA.

Handling GB&W's business in 1936 could be complicated. E. V. Johnson had to service the Hatfield gravel pit frequently in order to get out his work extra's ballast. In May he had ordered alternate way-freight service between Winona and Hat-field be started, with orders to handle all eastbound cars to points west of Pray. The opposing days had eastbounders No.2 and No.30 bring the local cars east, depositing them at "convenient places," while the LCL cars went to Merrillan to be worked back to Winona. The Merrillan and west LCL car went out of Green Bay on the Ford Train, to be set out at Merrillan on Mondays, Wednesdays and Fridays; alternate westbound trains would receive cars from No.1 at Merrillan. Under Johnson's schedule, the way-freight turned its engine at Merrillan, backed up the seven miles to Hatfield's gravel pit and brought out the westbound loads to Merrillan.

In August the way freight was discontinued, its work load taken by trains 1 and 30. No.1 handled all LCL and "shortcars" westbound. No.30 did the same chore eastbound; that train would not be held for the CGW or "other late connections." No.2 would take this tonnage. Train 30 was provided with another (head-end) caboose so that trainmen could unload LCL shipments without walking the train's length. In order to meet his schedules, Johnson had to fuss over the short cars, seeing to it that not too much work was assigned. No.30 was ordered not to do local work east of Wisconsin Rapids, other than minimal setouts at Seymour, Scandinavia, Amherst Junction and Plover, in order to keep the 5:00 a.m. Green Bay arrival. It was a time of broad business usage when local firms filled the hours and work load of scores of railroad employees, far from a later time of bulk-carrier level compromise. The system functioned well, being responsive and responsible to its territory.

In November 1936 a New London turn was established. It operated six days a week out of Green Bay at 5:00 p.m. to act as

In the grip of winter Engineer John Ray and Fireman Albert Drolland were commandeered to assist train No. 1 during a blizzard. Engine 69 ran light from Wisconsin Rapids to Scandinavia and doubleheaded the passenger train to Wisconsin Rapids. The Consol is shown back home at Rapids.

RAY BUTTOLPH

The last Schenectady 4-4-0 poses outside Norwood stall one on July 4, 1936. No.20 was last used on train 1-2, just before Moguls and mixed trains took over. The engine was purchased by The Farmer's Loan & Trust Co. for moribund GBWSTP in 1891.

H. LEHMAN PHOTO

KGB&W 40, a Becker class M, for years was considered too heavy for its duties. Renumbered 140, it was scrapped just after the second diesel 103 appeared in 1941. This photo was taken at Green Bay in the summer of 1934.

WILLIAM MONYPENY PHOTO

Mogul 92 was just in from Kewaunee and received hostler's attention. The big rebuild is shown at Green Bay on July 4, 1936.

H. LEHMAN PHOTO

GB&W 146 was formerly No. 80 (ex-NYC 313) which arrived in Green Bay in the 1920's. In a swap in the late 1930's it received the tank from engine 142 which was also a mid-30's rebuild. No.146 was scrapped in November of 1941.

ED SELINSKY PHOTO

way-freight over the forty miles west of Green Bay. The freight-house force at Green Bay had to hustle to load its cars for the Soo Line at Black Creek, while the east side yard engine had to have its cheese and paper cars into Norwood in time. Upon arrival at New London, the turn would have to perform its LCL work, pull the C&NW transfer and sort out westbound and eastbound cars. Westbound cars would go on No. 33 to New London. It was hoped that No. 33 would thereby be moved on time, leaving Green Bay at 7:00 p.m. Cars were to be pulled from the freighthouse by 4:00 p.m. The LCL cars for Seymour, Black Creek (north and south) and New London were behind yet another train's LCL merchandise car, that of No. 38. This activity kept Mogul and Consolidation busily scurrying about on relatively short trains and filled the employee timetable just before the coming of the 400-class and considerably unified train service.

ANN ARBOR NO. 6 eased into Kewaunee Friday, February 5th with a special load. It had to be an extraordinary morning for a small group of onlookers at Kewaunee Ferry Yard that gray day. No. 401 lumbered ashore backward at 8:45 a.m., as Grover Byers, Frank Halliday, E. V. Johnson and AA's O. T. Larson observed GB&W's first large engine as it was placed securely onto Wisconsin rails. ALCO representative B. S. Horton rode 401, a customary procedure. Little knots of spectators gathered at Casco Junction, Luxemburg and New Franken, marking the arrival of "the local railroad's" heavy machinery. On the 7th, 402 was unloaded, again from ANN ARBOR NO. 6, and went "dead in train" to Norwood. Newspapers covered the story of the original September 1936 order and pointed to the 25 miles of new rail already in place for the modern engines. What No. 6 boat had carried on her port center track was soon tucked into the north backshop track, while ALCO men and GB&W staff installed the heavy pistons, filled mechanical lubricators and bustled about making final

adjustments. On the 8th, 401 was fired up for the first time. Engineer Loyal Van Dreese took the engine into Norwood Yard the next day for trials. Onlookers from 12th Avenue to the west yard limit peered at the shining Mikado as it scissored back and forth, warming new rod brasses and showing off the new hope for a recovered economy as only a new locomotive could do. Many were reminded of the Diamond Jo packet on the Mississippi sixty years before by the haunting steamboat whistle which moaned at grade crossings. ALCO's A. D. Lawrence and GB&W's Ted Kirkby worked together over the final details which raised the new machine to its operational status.

Some of the other costs directly related to the 400-class surfaced by 1937. In September 1936 two stalls were lengthened at Norwood Avenue roundhouse at a cost of $5,209. Plans were made by January to purchase two Milwaukee Road turntables, after exploration of proposed new construction. The used 85-footers came from mountain helper stations on that road's western lines. This required demolition of the old sixty-foot-diameter pit which incapacitated the roundhouse for a summer. The construction of the newer larger pit also consumed considerable resources. The Wisconsin Rapids roundhouse faced the same events. That work was not completed until November 5, 1937, requiring road crews to run eastward two miles to Coyne Wye to turn engines. After June 21, 1937 engine crews no longer were required to turn their outgoing engines on the Kewaunee Wye at Norwood; however, continuous hostler service was maintained.

Bridges received major attention, partly due to the 400's. The three Mikes were initially kept on the New London division, handling trains 30-31, 32-33 and 1-2 over the hilly line west of Green Bay. With one major bridge over the Wolf River at New London now beefed up, the new engines were kept off the five major spans until they received the necessary repairs. In the spring of 1937 an AFE was floated to reinforce Bridges 95.6 and

Train No. 1 awaits its departure time at Green Bay Junction in July 1935: Nominally, 7:00 a.m. Norwood Yard, a mile west, would add several "hot shot" freight cars, destined for quick delivery to Burlington and Milwaukee Road connections. Last-minute travelers hurried to the single ACF coach, just days after "big engines" like Mogul 55 were assigned the great task.

This rare shot of Chicago & Alton 0-6-0 No.49 is shown at Bloomington, Illinois on July 25, 1926. Formerly 2-6-0 No.320, it was sold to GB&W in October of 1933 and was reconverted to Mogul No.92 and then to No.261.

95.8, both Wisconsin River spans, to bring them to Cooper's E-48 ratings. Structural steel came from Wisconsin Bridge & Iron Co. of Milwaukee at a cost of $24,708. The Yellow River bridge at Dexterville was also recommended by WB&I for E-45 or E-48 Cooper ratings "in accordance with loading diagram for the new engines." Studies were made on all four Wisconsin River spans and included the Hatfield west spans and three 100-foot Trempeleau River trestles. By April work was begun on Bridge 110.4 at Dexterville to raise it to Cooper E-48.

With the arrival of the 400's, backshopping of the four larger Consolidations could proceed. Among them, 350 was to receive exemplary attention. Both 1929 engines experienced trouble with running gear at the outset which had been diagnosed as frame flexing. An ALCO valve-setter was there and several conferences concluded that a brace from saddle to frame would cure it. In 1936 Kirkby also ordered a Sellers exhaust feedwater type applied to the 400-class. The device arrived but was never installed; it was later returned to the factory. Work authorized on 350 included the new Z-shaped rolled-steel pistons, new rings, cast-steel front cylinder heads and piston adapters for rear heads, floating mainrod bushings and a main Boxpok driver assembly. All of which indicated that some dynamic augment (rail pounding) was still present.

Locomotive work in 1937 also included backshopping of No.60 which emerged as No.145 with a "new" square tank. Some interesting deck-shuffling put scrapped Mogul 54's tank on GB&W's youngest 0-6-0. The machine received major upgrading of cab, running boards and boiler. Later, when 146 was reconditioned, it possessed 142's square tank, the latter acquiring 145's old tank. To add to the carnival, GB&W sold 146's sloping tank to the Oconto Company, a logger, for use at

Flander's Spur near Carter, Wisconsin. It was last seen in 1939 or 1940, accompanying Oconto's old Baldwin 2-6-2 No.6, deep in the woods and still sporting its painted-on "Green Bay Route" herald!

Bulletins issued in 1937 included restricting the 400-class to just four miles per hour across the Wisconsin River bridges. Johnson also required that trains handling hopper cars loaded with coal be run at only 25 miles per hour west of Green Bay. Train No.31 was scheduled to handle all Black Creek-Soo Line cars but it could not take loaded hopper cars west of that station. The first-shift yard crew brought over both Winona cheese and paper from Green Bay's east side and room had to be made on No.31 for "Rapids" gasoline loads. No.33, the way-freight, wouldn't make Soo Line connections at Black Creek but had to move along to make the Milwaukee Road connection at Wisconsin Rapids with their coal shipments. On the west end, trains 36-37 operated Merrillan to Winona, but started out of Wisconsin Rapids on Monday and returned there on Sunday with a layover at Winona. The sprint to and from "the Rapids" was done to handle ferry cars usually run on No.1-2, which didn't operate on Sunday. Upon arriving at Wisconsin Rapids, No.1 was instructed to cut off its freight cars east of the crossover and pull the coaches down to the depot. Meanwhile, the yard crew went through the crossover and tackled the cars for the city. Next, cars destined for the west were put in. Meanwhile, LCL shipments were to be "thrown in the baggage car" on trains 1-2. Such were the literal and graphic terms of E. V. Johnson.

On the KGB&W, effective December 4, 1937, No.30-31 was discontinued. When Ford traffic moved on AA boat TF-5 to Kewaunee, an extra would be called to accommodate. When no

Car 6062, a composite boxcar built in 1925, was one of 200 built for prosperous times and increased traffic. Note the white-painted "X" design on the car door, applied in the mid-1930's as a grade-crossing safety feature.
STAN MAILER COLLECTION

ACF built ten green "Freight-Saver" cushion underframe sixty-footers for Ford service in early 1964. They joined 352 cars of DT&I, PC, RDG, and had yellow lettering. Greenville also built ten.
ACF PHOTO

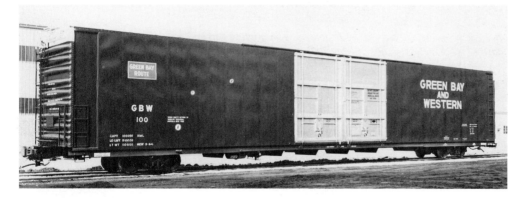

Thrall Car Co. built fourteen 86-foot "Hi-Cubes" in 1964-65 which briefly served in Ford's Buffalo stamping plant pool, toting sheet metal parts for the automaker. Some were later sold to Soo and DT&I.
THRALL PHOTO

GB&W's little red cabooses were all rebuilt between 1937 and 1940 with steel bay windows; sashes were painted gray. Two survive — 605 and 620.
R. W. BUHRMASTER PHOTO

*Above: No longer a coach, old Iola combine No.1 became New Franken's final depot,
purchased by KGB&W from GB&W for $100. It lasted as such until World War II.*

*Above: Car 600 once was the conveyance of The Prince of Wales, later oilman Joshua Cosden,
finally GB&W staffers. It was finally sold in May 1971 for preservation in Ottawa, Illinois.*

*Below: Car 600's replacement was patriotic 1776, finished in June 1973 by Kraft Steel
Fabricating Co. of Green Bay. The red-white-blue car still sees occasional service.*

255

Engine 256 crosses old Highway 12 at Merrillan with an eastbound drag of incredible proportions, probably way-freight 36 running extra. Ahead is the Omaha Road diamond.

EARL RUHLAND PHOTO

Ford traffic came across, all loads came into the port on AA's nightly TF-3 for movement on train No.39 for train No.1. On "non-Ford" days, No.31 would not operate westward; No.33 took the business instead. When 30-31 was not operating, No.1-2 took it all but, if there were too many empties, that train would have to leave some behind. Johnson ordered the use of Consolidations 350-351 on No.1-2 west of Rapids and 400-class east of the river city. This condition prevailed until the second trio of Mikes came in October 1939, together with corresponding track improvements.

GB&W's status was getting better each day. By 1935 traffic levels again reached that of 1925-26 and the showing was brighter than the national average. Resumption of auto traffic gave it a heavy boost when Ford's St. Paul plant went back to work. Coal, lumber, petroleum and manufactures were major tonnage items, while autos rose dramatically to 1929 equivalents. Operating ratios in the Depression years at 87% were

actually better than those in 1935, which had been around 78%. In 1936-37 maintenance-of-way charges rose to, perhaps, the highest in the company's history, again relating to the 400-class program and the new rail acquisitions. Reduction of "A" income debenture payments and suspension of the "B" debenture payments during the same period gave the company satisfactory working capital for the 1935-36 period. In 1937 dividends were paid out in the calendar year, while such payments previously had followed the year's end. Five percent was paid on "A" debentures and stock early in 1939. The operating ratio for 1938 was 75.39%; 1939 was 72.22% and 1940 reached 71.13%.

Comparison of GB&W's revenue categories showed soft coal as the largest commodity with a 1937 total of $300,006 versus $245,667 for 1940. Auto parts earned $103,023 and $125.687 respectively. While the main line company did well, bad boy Ahnapee & Western continued all through the 1930's to show a deficit which signaled a desire to sell the property. KGB&W on the other hand showed a 1937 operating ratio of 87.26%, going to 77.13% in 1939.

With the three 400's in service, GB&W's operating department was able to project further savings with large power and plans were made to acquire additional "D-47" Mikados at the earliest opportunity. Between the Mikado orders, however, GB&W's diesel advocates won a chance to put theory into practice. An order was placed for one 600-horsepower ALCO yard unit, under a lease agreement which involved ALCO, Guaranty Trust Co. of New York and GB&W. The order brought a black and shiny "E-1519-4" switcher which began to revolutionize yard duties in Green Bay. No.101 was available for several switching shifts and became a familiar sight in Green Bay after its delivery in October 1938. GB&W soon discovered the cost differences and began planning for diesel power in the future.

The motive power revolution also sounded the last call for the old guard in GB&W's roundhouses. Little time or sentiment was wasted on the Mayflowers; A&W's 303 was sold to Escanaba &

GB&W Dickson 4-4-0 No.26 handles some of the last "pure passenger" assignments on GB&W. Built in 1898, it worked No. 1-2 and A&W summer extras. This photo was taken at Winona in about 1935.

R. GRAHAM PHOTO

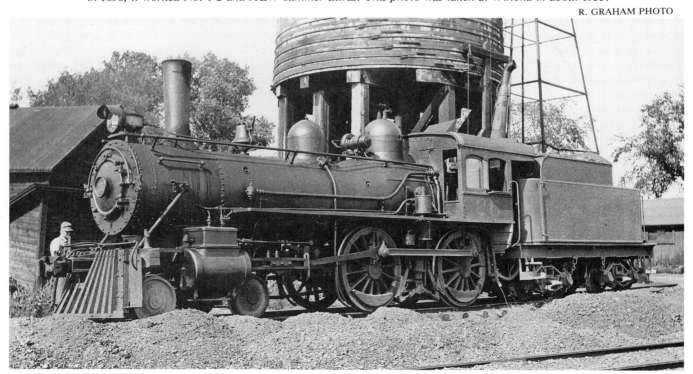

Ex-NYC 0-6-0 No. 143 was the last survivor of the "Central clan." It was a superheated engine, so equipped in the Depression years. It was scrapped in late 1947. Note the painted herald.

Lake Superior Railroad in 1937 and the other two were not far behind. KGB&W 301 last ran on September 16, 1939. GB&W 302 came in extra from Wisconsin Rapids, July 9, 1939, its final trip. Mogul 255 was last used about June 11, 1939. It suffered a crankpin failure which condemned the World War I acquisition. The surplus of small power after numbers 404-406 arrived in October 1939 prompted repairs and maintenance to be focused on superheated Moguls 252-253 and 256-260, inclusive. The 1938 program also brought 2-8-0's numbers 398-399 to more acceptable standards, as they were all equipped with Alemite fittings, mechanical lubricators and other modern devices.

One of the consequences of the fast-moving innovations was the sale of Mogul 250 only four years after it had taken up shop slack in 1935. Sold to Wisconsin's Marinette, Tomahawk & Western Railroad, it was run out of Wisconsin Rapids over the Milwaukee road under its own steam. No. 250 left the GB&W at 11:00 a.m., June 13, 1939 with a Milwaukee engine crew and pilot in charge for the 83-mile trip. It spent the next 13 years in the north woods, finally going for scrap in May 1953. The Mogul was sold for $3,000, complete "with cab curtains, flangers and snowplow and new tank drawbar." No. 250's last GB&W trip was June 10, 1939.

Frank Seymour, GB&W's retired president, was honored with the dedication of a memorial park adjacent to Norwood Yard. A crowd of over 200, many of them GB&W employees, gathered at F. B. Seymour Park in late July 1936. Formerly a slough of brackish waters, "FBS" himself had donated material, while WPA workers, under the management of WPA Director Major G. H. Boyer, provided labor to fill the lowland. A bronze tablet outlining the 64-year career of the grand old man from New London was unveiled by Miss Janet Zahorik, the former president's great-granddaughter. Afterwards, "FBS" thanked all and Mayor John V. Diener and other dignitaries spoke on behalf of the new management, pointing to the coming of large-scale main line status which would render GB&W quite different from Seymour's era. On May 6, 1938, before the first diesel arrived, Seymour passed away. The second order for Mikado types was already in process at ALCO.

In early June 1936 GB&W traffic men met at Winona's Country Club for the annual staff meeting. They came from the network of offices and, after the meeting, an inspection was conducted for their familiarization all the way to Kewaunee, they returned to Green Bay. GB&W had offices in New York, Chicago, Pittsburgh, Detroit, Minneapolis, Los Angeles and Seattle. President McGee, Traffic Manager L. C. Jorgenson and Western Refrigerator Lines Vice-President E. W. Miller headed west on business car 500 to conduct the meeting. It was one of many which would later include Minneapolis flour-milling interests and their special tours of GB&W facilities.

While the first three 400-class worked steadily on the New London division. The new management often ordered passenger specials to Winona and on September 26, 1939 Engineer Loyal Van Dreese took recently outshopped Mogul 252 westward, following No. 1 by two hours. His fireman was F. F. Lindemann. The ten-hour trip was followed the next day by an eleven-hour thirty-minute trek back to Green Bay. There were work extras, especially with Mogul 256 which was due for flues and a general overhaul in early 1939. No. 256 with Van Dreese

Above: Plover is shown here in September, 1933. Deep in the Depression years, a gaunt GB&W could muster scant polish. Train No.2 pauses for Stevens Point passengers bound for eastern points. Mogul 51 and combine 25 had just brought them to the main line, five miles south of the Portage County seat. Just beyond No.2's rear is the Soo Line crossing.

Below: KGB&W 40 and crew are busy on October 2, 1936, morning switching the auto dock area just north of Green Bay Junction. Ths crossing watchman is framed by vintage buildings along Broadway.

Above: Train No.2 has stopped at New London in July 1935 with R-class No.52 in charge. No.52 received new tires that year, inaugurating the mixed service, enabling R-class to make time.

Below: 1929's R-2 class Consols were the newest and finest until the advent of the 400's. Typically, No.69 got underway at Norwood westbound, probably on a Wisconsin Rapids run.

Below: On a goodwill tour, No. 404 poses with 400 designer T. M. Kirkby (right), Road Foreman of Engines L. J. Van Dreese, and Engineer N. Christiansen. The photo was taken at Blair.

Above: Milwaukee railfan Earl Ruhland was one of a few riders of No. 1-2 with a camera. This 1940 view shows No. 1 arriving at City Point.

handled work trains to Trempeleau Valley points such as Arcadia-Dodge and Blair-Independence, preparing the roadway for new ninety-pound rail, a scarcity on the west end. The previous May 10th Van Dreese had taken Mogul 253 to Stevens Point and Winona on yet another special.

Specifications for the second order of Mikes (No.404-406) were written by February 1939. The blueprints were completed March 17th and then revised on July 28th. Differences between the two trios included a more rakish tender side, rounded turret cover, air horns and a revised letter class: D-1-47. After its mid-October arrival, 404 made a special trip to Wisconsin Rapids on November 1, 1939. N. H. Christiansen and C. O. Budd, in charge of three coaches, were out at 7:00 a.m.. The same day, Paul Graff and "Jimmy Dean from 17" took 405 west on a

which extended stalls 5 and 6 and provided a reinforced concrete floor. The cost was $7,646.

A final round of "bridge-beefing" was performed on Bridge 141.5 at Hatfield, increasing its loading capacity to Cooper's E-45 (trusses) and E-48 (floor system) at a cost of $15,484. Other reinforcements were made at Trempeleau River crossings, especially below Arcadia. A bulletin of November 1, 1939 restricted the 400-class to six miles per hour on the Winona Bridge Railway crossing and further instructions followed regarding the Winona Bridge. The WBRy was governed by automatic signals after August 1941 and both CB&Q and GB&W conductors were required to register at East Winona or Winona. Other important crossings were now controlled via automatic devices: Black Creek (Soo Line) and Merrillan (CSTPM&O) had inter-

ALCo HISTORIC PHOTO

D-47 Mikado 404 takes shape in ALCo's Schenectady, New York erecting hall. The second order of 2-8-2's was operational in late 1939. They lasted only ten years.

freight extra. On November 3rd Schmidt and Dean ran 406 westward on its preliminary run. Shortly afterwards, the 400-class were cautiously handling trains into Winona but their duties were restricted until track standards were raised.

Useless to the new engines, the old sixty-foot turntable was condemned and removed in favor of fan tracks. A joint wye was built, running off CB&Q's main to the Milwaukee's "gold dust" lead. This work was completed in October of 1939. Winona's roundhouse received a 53-foot extension and an inspection pit revision in September to accommodate one 400-class. Other construction included an addition to the Norwood roundhouse

locking systems, while Dexterville (MILW) had a gate system. Plover's Soo Line crossing (Portage branch, abandoned in 1945) received a gate and color light for protection, set against Soo Line. The operating speed was doubled in 1936 on the C&NW crossing at Marshland which had for many years been restricted to 15 miles per hour. The adjustment was made, no doubt, to accommodate its new "Minnesota 400" service which began in mid-June. GB&W crews were admonished to look sharp for fast trains, at first a polished D-class Atlantic on a few equally clean cars, establishing the new and acclaimed passenger train.

GB&W's ex-NYC 0-6-0 No.80 (ex-NYC 313 of 1900) was rebuilt into a superheated machine by company forces in the mid-30's. The tender was later sold to an upstate logger.

By the end of 1939, GB&W operated trains 1-2 west of Green Bay as a mixed, with No.30-31 as time freight and No.46-49 between Wisconsin Rapids and Plover. As a mixed train, No.46 ran to Stevens Point, finishing out at Plover by 2:30 p.m., to arrive in Wisconsin Rapids by 3:01 p.m. The stub runs made two round trips on the branch with a combination car to service No.1 at 8:46 a.m. and No.2 at 1:13 p.m. West of Wisconsin Rapids, it was No.1-2, No.30-31 and No.36-37, a way freight, which evolved from prior experiments with a Merrillan-based operation. On the KGB&W, or Kewaunee division, No.34-35 did the A&W, while No.30-31 covered the day chores at Kewaunee. No.38-39 repeated the assignment at night.

Engine 404 made the Blair newspaper shortly after it arrived on GB&W. It was the intention of GB&W management to show off the new engines, especially down in the Trempeleau towns. Citizens made a trek to trackside to admire the design and its designer. Ted Kirkby rode on the special which was in the hands of enginemen N. H. Christensen and Paul Hochstruh, Conductor Oral Budd; Tom Budlong was brakeman. Other officials on the special were President McGee, Grover Byers, L. C. Jorgenson and L. J. Van Dreese. The train included a baggage car

rigged as a buffet car, a coach and car 500. Refreshments were served and presently the gleaming train moved on to Whitehall, Independence and Arcadia to the sound of either air horn or steamboat whistle.

In retrospect, the proponents of steam had won but several possibilities might have been substituted. In the short time between 404-406's first trips and Pearl Harbor, ALCO developed the RS-1 road switcher which might have been E. V. Johnson's choice instead. Another possibility was the rebuilding of the three Mayflowers, much as Lake Superior & Ishpeming Railway had done with the remarkably similar and equally unsuccessful narrow-firebox 2-8-0's. LS&I rebuilt seven of eight 1910 machines and produced a highly acceptable design by purchasing new fireboxes and saddles. Yet, these fine SC-4 2-8-0's were ironically replaced by RS-1 ALCO road switchers. Nonetheless, most wouldn't have had history any other way. The morale-building aspect of the big engines succeeded in conveying a serious status finally and completely, as no black, pioneering road switcher could have done. The choice made GB&W a heavy-rail, main line bridge route.

Passenger service on the branch lines was discontinued in the late 1930's, putting nearly all the familiar wood combination cars out of work. Much of the antiquated equipment was eliminated one way or another. An ancient pile driver, for instance, was lost in a derailment at Independence. Outlying enginehouses at Iola and Stevens Point were abandoned as operation of the Stevens Point line was now handled at Wisconsin Rapids. Iola's operation was combined with Waupaca's. At the roundhouse

The ugly duckling Mogul 261 managed to acquit itself well in the years just before World War II. Fitted with a pilot plow, the old Alton veteran was one of only two Baldwin locomotives ever on the GB&W. No.261, which never received a red-and-white herald, is shown leaving Norwood with a "New London turn."

another purge disposed of five more small engines in mid-1941. With them went 4-4-0 No.23, the last and best known on GB&W. It sold to Betten's for $777.26. Other small facilities such as the fifty-foot turntable at New London were removed. The lengthy short line was steadily moving toward large carrier status. Ex-Chicago & Alton Mogul No.261 was the final Depression rebuild to be condemned, having spent several months as a heater at the Norwood roundhouse. No.261 had accumulated about 102,000 miles by May of 1940, while No.23 had traveled approximately 67,000 miles since its last flue change in 1935. Since its in-service date, D-47 No.401 had clocked 165,000 miles and 403 about 171,000 miles.

During the war years, GB&W acquired a business car of princely proportions located in a pauper's environment. The stately private car "Roamer" was built by American Car & Foundry Co. in 1918 at its St. Charles, Missouri shops for oil magnate Joshua Cosden. "Roamer" allegedly cost more than $200,000. Soon after it was built, the car was host to England's Prince of Wales. Cosden sold the car to steel man William Replogle for $75,000 and it was later purchased by William Carey of New York City. In February 1944 Carey offered to sell it to GB&W for $6,000.

"Roamer" was in rough shape by 1944, having been used at Morris Run Coal Company as housing for a manager's family, but the priceless interior was still sound and fairly dry. Morris Run proposed to lease the car but Carey chose to sell it to GB&W instead. "Roamer" was billed out of Tomhicken, Pennsylvania, on March 30, 1944 via Lehigh Valley and finished its trip over Wabash and AA. GB&W President H. E. McGee inspected the car and decided to send it back to AC&F at St. Charles for restoration. "Roamer" became GB&W 600, an investment of $32,782.

With the 600's debut on GB&W, car 500 was retired and sold to Iron & Steel Products Co. of Chicago early in 1945. Later, the car was sold to Royal American Shows for use in circus trains.

GB&W's universal 2-6-0's could handle any job on the road. Here, newest "R" class No.56 was ordered out on a work extra to drop off ties in the Plover area in June 1935.

GB&W operated only one office car until 1947, when caboose 603 was converted to an officer's car and assigned to L. J. Van Dreese at Wisconsin Rapids. No.603 was painted the standard "GB&W green" which, according to a company recipe, was three parts black to one part chrome yellow.

As the war continued the railroads were increasingly convinced of the economics of dieselization, especially in yard service. GB&W authorized purchase of a second yard unit in November 1940. This time it was KGB&W's turn; the leased property acquired S-1 ALCO No.103. The engine started work

No.401 is underway west of 12th Avenue and Norwood Avenue Yard in this early 1937 view.

H. F. BRADEN PHOTO

No. 256 spent much of its final year (1948) on a work extra, which included working with a ballast plow thrown up on its pilot deck. The unit fit under the car wheels.
R. G. LEWIS PHOTO

Ex-NYC 0-6-0 No. 146 was one of three Depression-era projects of Kirkby and Becker. Roy Campbell found it on the spot at Wisconsin Rapids on April 30, 1938, shortly after it had been renumbered.

KGB&W 398 served three masters during its 31-year history, but only did well on the Green Bay Route. The C-43 heavyweight was photographed at Green Bay by Milwaukeean Ed Wilson on June 18, 1938.

January 18, 1941. It received several more white stripes, made necessary by grade crossing incidents and close work along Green Bay streets. Eventually, GB&W yard units received a group of flashing light fixtures along their frames, connected to an outside conduit. The KGB&W next disposed of 0-6-0's No. 141 and No. 142 in 1941. In 1944, No. 140 and No. 257 were cut up, although 140's boiler was a steam plant candidate for Wisconsin Rapids.

During the 1930's Green Bay's industrial area along Eastman Avenue and North Quincy Street became an important supplier of traffic to GB&W. Green Bay Paper & Fibre Co. (later Hoberg Paper Co.) began in 1902. A later development was the

Dapper Mikado 401 breaks in new rod brasses and valve packing on March 9, 1937, just west of 12th Avenue. GB&W had become an owner of first-class road power at last!

H. F. BRADEN PHOTO

Texas Company Marine Terminal and the Phillips Petroleum Marine Terminal which transshipped petroleum products from lake terminals. Farther east along the KGB&W, the cheese house district contributed a large share of carloadings to GB&W. In the 1930's Kraft and other cheese houses supplied up to thirty cars per day, typically in "WRX" reefers. Private-owner advertising on refrigerator cars, judged an unfair business practice, was outlawed in 1938. Many Western forty-foot "reefers" previously had been emblazoned with Kraft lettering in full-scale representation.

By 1940 the principal on-line towns west of Green Bay could only boast of modest population growth after 1920. Towns such as New London, Waupaca and Arcadia gained less than five percent, while Stevens Point and Wisconsin Rapids gained about 15 percent due to growth of paper mills and other industries. Winona, which actually lost population, was down about eight percent since 1920. The local scene on GB&W was, therefore, of a small depot for a small town of average population of 430 souls, not all of whom availed themselves of daily mixed train service. After the dire days of the Great Depression many younger people made their way to California, Milwaukee or Chicago for a better way of life. While still important, the small depots manned by the Al Wallers, Ben Ericksons and Harold Knutsons were soon to be uprooted. They vanished with the local trains, small steam power and open-platform coaches as the company plunged into the even faster-paced changes of the 1940's and 1950's.

Gone were the days of German-language telegrams from Algoma, sent by an overworked "brasspounder" who labored ten-hour days at fifty cents per hour and then loaded fish into the mail car. Also committed to ancient history was the first trip of fireman Glenn Smart, who swung his scoop to the clanking of a chain fire door, as engine 18 doubleheaded a road job to New Franken, up along Baird Creek to the top of the homely world that was the old era of Green Bay & Western. In 1939 the bones of No. 18 were picked over for the last time as it lay at the shop, some distance from the gleaming flanks of the 400-class, and ever so far from the muffled clanking of internal-combustion investments now mastering the business at 12th Avenue.

H. DU BAL COLLECTION

Possibly the best photo ever taken of a 400-class happened in early 1937 as Chicagoan Harold Du Bal focused his 5×7 camera on the shining greyhound at Norwood Yard.

17

ETTRICK
&
NORTHERN

ETTRICK & NORTHERN LOCOMOTIVE

Western Wisconsin has many small villages which lie isolated in the hill country known as the "Driftless Area," a region of notable midwestern scenery. Ettrick, a village in Trempeleau County, was located in the path of the GB&M's projected route to La Crosse from Blair. The town never forgot the idea of rails to the outer world; however, it waited too long and by World War I, when many short lines were withering due to highway competition, Ettrick bravely decided to foster the Ettrick & Northern Railroad Co., closing the ten-mile gap across a forbidding sandstone ridge.

E&N was incorporated June 5, 1915. It was promoted and staffed by locals H. F. Claussen, M. T. Pederson, John Raichle and former Senator John C. Gaveney of Arcadia. The Ettrick region's dairies and farmsteads were deemed prosperous enough to support a small road. Some interest was found in extension south to La Crosse and, perhaps, to North Bend, above Blair. In September 1915 bonds totalling $75,000 were voted by the Town of Ettrick. Boosters celebrated their alleged victory although, even before the road was begun, the state had plans to build a new highway through Ettrick parallel to the railroad survey.

Late in 1916 construction contracts were made and E. J. Matchett of Osseo became general contractor. The graders were Anderson Bros. of Appleton who began at 9:07 a.m. on September 7, 1916. Dirt was turned and mules and their men moved away toward the great hill which separated Ettrick's valley from Blair's. Eventually that one great scenic attraction was pierced by a curving cut more than 100 feet deep and 300 feet wide at the top with approach grades exceeding four percent. Step-cutting was done to prevent landslides in the friable rock. Contractor Anderson created a shanty town for the winter at the cut site. The noble work went on despite manpower shortages and women allegedly sought work at the site.

By May 1917 costs had risen to $40,000. An additional

Engine No.10 assaults the grade to the great cut. This photo, taken in 1924, is the only known photo of the E&N revenue train in action.
MRS. CARL SEXE PHOTO

authorization of funds in the amount of $50,000 was voted. Ettrick didn't see its first revenue train until August 1918 but twenty citizens advanced funds to acquire the sole steam locomotive owned by E&N. It was 4-6-0 No.10, ex-LS&MS 5099, built by Brooks in the 1890's. The engine rivaled GB&W's latest Mogul in weight, their largest engines at the time. Combination car No.100 came also from a used equipment dealer. Mr. Frank Wall of La Crosse became the regular engineer on E&N.

E&N was completed just in time to experience the post-World War I recession which contributed to its financial demise. Construction during inflationary times of the war had distorted costs and the "one-horse' railroad soon went into receivership (1922).

Below: E&N's first stock train is ready to leave Ettrick, Wisconsin October 18, 1918. The No.10 4-6-0 was the sole power on the road.

KITTLESON COLLECTION

Left: E&N No.10 poses with its admirers at Ettrick, Wisconsin when the line was nearly completed. The location is on the present State Highway 53, just west of Ettrick.
ERICKSON BROS. PHOTO

Several attempts were made to solicit funds for the road but selling bonds to cover operation was judged to be illegal. Mr. H. R. Mathison became receiver and a chastened management attempted to operate a railtruck or light motor car when steam was not needed as early as 1919. This was a Ford auto which pulled a two-ton trailer capable of handling mail, express and five passengers.

There were several wrecks. In August 1922 the 4-6-0 was put out of action for a month. Another accident occurred in 1926, south of the great cut. Trucks were pressed to handle the inbound carloads of stock to Ettrick during the road's immobilization. Lastly, in the late 1920's, a landslide caught the locomotive in the great cut and destroyed its tender. Eyewitnesses stated that the damaged tank lay up in the cut for years, while the engine was eventually dragged back to Ettrick.

Early in 1928 two local Ettrick men bought the line. Maurice Casey and Obel Pederson began the arduous task of tracing the paper trail and finalizing the line's obligations. Renaming their purchase the Ettrick Railroad Co., Casey and Pederson bought a thirty-ton Whitcomb Model LRX-1s four-speed gasoline locomotive which Manager C. M. Sherwood claimed "was able to pull 226 tons up the 4½% grades to the cut in second gear." The engine burned 25 to 30 gallons of gasoline on the round trip. The improvement was only enough to postpone the inevitable, for Ettrick never developed enough industry to bolster such an enterprise. Traffic was lumber, oil supplies and livestock in season, all of which fell prey to adjacent Highway 53's trucks.

On July 1, 1937 Ettrick Railroad Co. was formally abandoned and the property's physical assets were sold to Harry P. Bourke of Escanaba, Michigan for $15,100. Iron & Steel Products of Chicago bought the locomotive. GB&W had retired its interchange to ERR in September of 1936 and Trempeleau County's adventure in short line railroading came to a close.

Ettrick RR Co. No. 1, a Whitcomb 30-tonner, had less than ten years' service on the ten-mile short line when it was sold to Chicago's Iron & Steel Products. This photo was taken at Ettrick about 1936.

STAN MAILER PHOTO

Above: E&NRR's complete roster included combine No. 100 and ex-Lake Shore & Michigan Southern Ten-Wheeler No. 10. The Brooks 1890's product had been No. 5099 on the Lake Shore. Engineer Frank Wall, Fireman Carl Mason, Conductor Henry Kroll and Brakeman Palmer Peterson were on duty at Ettrick.

MRS. HELEN FOLKKEDAHL PHOTO

Right: Ruins of the great cut on the E&N are shown here. The floor of the cut had been covered with ten feet of loose material over the original alignment.

STAN MAILER COLLECTION

18

TO THE
111TH YEAR

Green Bay & Western reached 1940 in good order. Its physical plant had vastly improved over the past six years and, with 510 employees and 177 stockholders, it had established itself in the specialized niche of "time-saver railroading." It had grown from an unwanted castaway in a nearly worthless location to a lucky specialist in fast freight, dealing in traffic moving from the industrial heartland of the central states to the northwest. While 71% of its 1921 traffic was generated on-line, only 20% of 1940's tonnage came from the line itself, which worked to funnel lumber, coal, auto parts, petroleum products and agricultural goods on a path across the north country. GB&W coordinated with Chesapeake & Ohio's Pere Marquette District, Ann Arbor Railroad, Milwaukee Road and Burlington Route. During the pre-war years, coal still maintained the No.1 return, producing $245,667 in revenues, contrasted with petroleum products at $208,622, agricultural goods $142,000 and auto parts at $125,667. GB&W's operating ratio was 79.43% and the six 400-class D-47 Mikados ruled the main line.

Records of the early 1940's showed 400's dominating the operation of trains No.1-2. In charge were engineers Paul Graf, Bill Sowatzke, Charlie Chapman, Henry Burmeister and Felix Weslaski. "Heimer" Schultz, Larry Dennis, "Daisy" Weytens and Charlie Rank made sure of light fires and did their best with the poor coal of wartime. Conductors included Guy Pratt, Bill Miller, J. D. Reiter, C. O. Budd, Ben Billings, H. W. Kroll and J. A. Rude. In May 1940 the west-end way-freight, No.36-37, was run with Mogul 253, the train experiencing new competition in the Trempeleau Valley. In those days, butter, cheese and eggs were regularly loaded in reefers and transferred to the Omaha Road at Merrillan for overnight service to Wood Street Produce Terminal in Chicago. GB&W was already head-to-head with a small truck line. Its first trip on October 5, 1934 started an ominous trend for the future.

On the Kewaunee division, trains 30-31 were running behind Mike 402 on May 30, 1940 with Engineer Gus Nickelson and Conductor J. D. Reiter aboard. The big Mike trotted along easily to the lake with seven loads and as many empties, returning with eighteen loads and five empties. The other Kewaunee movement went behind Consolidation 398 which mightily lifted 35 loads and eight empties up Baird's Creek Valley to Summit. Chip Dickey and Sammy Roubal were in charge. No.34-35 to Sturgeon Bay was behind Mogul 251 with George Thiele and Otto Woods in command. No.34 left Green Bay with eight loads and one empty but filled out to eleven loads and eight empties at Casco Junction. On that day, ferries PERE MARQUETTE No.18, ANN ARBOR No.3 and WABASH called at Kewaunee. Activity on the Waupaca branch included a "dog leg" trip to New London, Mogul 252 captained by Lem La Haie and Holger Hanson. Other adventures in 1940 included Schmidt and Dean's Extra 406 East, which "reported a man lying on track just west of Milepost 20." The Seymour City Marshal was called at 4:20 p.m. to investigate on an otherwise clear, calm, 31-degree day. Freight No.30 ran with average consists of twenty loads and 23 empties but, notably, on April 4th the train ran with 29 loads and 34 empties out of Norwood.

Left: By the late 1950's, Green Bay Junction had become the old and venerated landmark it deserved to be. GB&W's home office looked eastward to C. Reiss Coal Company's storage yard whose ancestry can be traced to GBW&STP days. GB&W's occupation of downtown lands ceased when the old depot, which is shown left of center, was destroyed in the fire of February 11, 1977.
PHOTOGRAPHY INC. PHOTO

Former roundhouse foreman Clarence Stutleen, in comparison, recalled the 1920's operations. A single R-class Mogul could handle 1050 tons up Luxemburg Hill, the westbound ruling grade on the Kewaunee division. Stutleen also remembered his time behind the fireman's shovel when a crew had to be rounded up from Bob Hutz's tavern near the Green Bay Junction depot. The day's work was a cherry-picker's special to Sturgeon Bay and Stutleen won the honors. Engine 51 had a crack in a firebox side sheet and he had been shown how to bank coal against the sizzling leak to keep his steam pressure on the mark! The engine's problem had been reported but never fixed. It was different in the 1940's; the 400-class prowled a railroad now very much removed from its short line past, when Moguls were emperors.

The year 1940 did not pass without incident, however. When No.30 made its nightly processional through Dodge it hit the west-end switch at speed, about 25 miles per hour. No.30's last five cars spread the rail, tipping all at sharp angles, while caboose 609 and business car 99 made a very rough landing. The accident hastened the supreme sacrifice — 99's end in 1943.

C. C. TINKHAM PHOTO

Train No.4 eases through Lutz's Cut Just west of Kewaunee on April 14, 1947.

A year later, on April 16, 1941, an accident occurred at Milepost 128 near the location where the last spike was driven in 1872. Charlie Chapman and Dave Myott brought No.2 (Mike 406) eastward from Pray at 11:20 a.m. at about twenty miles per hour with twelve loads and eight empties, loads trailing. "Five poles east of MP 128" the train derailed, turning over an empty mid-train car. Almost immediately, ten others followed. The frost had begun to thaw under the south rail, causing it to soften, while the north rail remained firm. The cars rocked off their truck centers, pivoting on the north rail. Chapman had just released a seven-pound reduction, keeping the train stretched against 406's open throttle. The tension kept the cars from jackknifing. A work extra dispatched with the new Northwest crane (not a wrecker) had the line reopened by 3:55 a.m. next day. It was the closest call for five-month old 406. Luck also held on lading salvage; only one carload was damaged.

During the months before Mikes 404-406 arrived, the first three were equipped with force-feed lube systems, covering driving boxes and chafing irons. A 32-point lubricator was

introduced and extended to all Mikes by 1941. Air horns had to be added to the first three Mikes; the factory equipped the second order thus. During the war, some ninety-pound rail was laid, while a complete tie-plate and rail anchor program was pushed. The 400's also received speed recorders in anticipation of greater performances.

With Ford's model change in the fall of 1939 GB&W's G. C. Byers announced that 15 fifty-foot and 98 forty-foot Milwaukee Road automobile cars would be in service September 15th for station-wagon bodies. The loaded cars in question would travel GB&W with their route stencils reading: "Wagon Body Car. Return to CMSTP&P, Iron Mountain, Michigan." Byers stressed that the car group would supply bodies to various Ford assembly plants, expedited via Central States Dispatch-157. GB&W had another high-rate line haul movement to Winona for transfer Milwaukee Road and Fordson, the St. Paul assembly plant.

While GB&W's freight revenue briefly plateaued in 1943 at nearly $2,750,000, passenger service and its revenues remained

The back-burner operation was facing a systematic slide toward extinction with management's desire to do a long-haul, nonlocal business. It made sense in the light of a motoring public.

It took a fight to end the service, however. Trempeleau Valley towns began to hear the abandonment litany as early as August 1944. Mail service quietly slipped away to motor trucks and Merrillan-Arcadia contractors moved mailbags on Highway 95. Area newspaperman Merlin Hull delved into the federal mail contracts issue, alerting the citizens of the Trempeleau to the coming change. After hearings were conducted at Merrillan in March, the Public Service Commission of Wisconsin acted to block discontinuance of passenger, mail and express activity June 5, 1945. GB&W continued to press for a cut-off, citing the abilities of several bus lines to carry GB&W's business. Fox River Bus Lines, an Appleton-based firm, operated over Highway 10 (Appleton to Stevens Point), covering part of the area, while Stewart Bus Lines of Eau Claire had a "branch line" to Arcadia and Independence. Whitehall and Independence, with similar populations of about 1,000 each in 1940, maintained a

J. SCRIBBINS PHOTO

Train No.5 crosses the Wisconsin River after leaving the Wisconsin Rapids yard en route to Winona on August 16, 1947. The bridge and causeway are one of the major bridges on the line. No.5 handles the lone coach, the last vestige of passenger service. The engine is 351.

dismal. The public perceived the venerable "Hicks-AC&F" open-platform coaches to be less than inviting. Passenger revenues had fallen steadily from 1927 to 1933 but the service had been bolstered by an equally tenuous mail contract. What was promising for the freight was hardly so for the intrepid traveler to Winona from Green Bay. A journey to Merrillan and a train ride to the Twin Cities was a possibility; not possible was a close connection with CB&Q and Milwaukee speedsters at Winona. The mixed status helped the company sustain the modest service, staving off the inevitable. Wartime to 1943 netted a final high point of passenger revenues of about $8,000 for the year.

Left: KGB&W's lone Mikado No.403 rolls across Hudson Street on a westbound train — probably No.3. Signals guard the Milwaukee Road crossing.

C. B. KNISKERN PHOTO

slim hold on GB&W's RPO-baggage service through 1945.

Whitehall's City Attorney Ralph Lund represented Hixton and Taylor, while John A. Markham fielded for Independence and Clarence Fugina stood for Arcadia. GB&W argued that its service netted a loss. Its passenger revenue in 1945 was a mere $6,246.40 and daily ticket sales amounted to only $20. The combined forces of lawyers, underdeveloped roads and a snowstorm before the meeting prevented interruption of service. Thinking he had trapped his adversaries, a GB&W representative confidently asked the Trempelonians how they rode to the meeting, to which the learned opposition replied: "We rode on the GB&W!" The debate was shelved.

Among other financial struggles, GB&W's personnel, who stood to be affected by layoffs, took up the cudgel against the inevitable. In times of large advertising claiming union "featherbedding," little sympathy could be generated to sustain the green cars. Placement of coaches on No.5-6 was seen as a deliberate

Top Left: Late afternoon settles over Wisconsin Rapids as Mogul 256 clears cylinder cocks alongside 402 on August 16, 1947. Steam was nearly finished on main line assignments by this date.

J. SCRIBBINS PHOTO

Bottom Left: It's tie-up time for two crews at Norwood in 1940. No.399 and No.403 in the distance will shortly be delivered to machinists and boilermakers for inspection.

E. RUHLAND PHOTO

Below: Casco Junction from an eastbound freight harbors a Mogul and Jordan Spreader X-190 on July 5, 1947.

J. SCRIBBINS PHOTO

move to shake off patronage. The opposition claimed the dawdling way-freight's coaches slowed the never-too-speedy arrival in Winona (about 6:00 p.m.). It was the company's desire to make it a single-crew, single-locomotive way-freight-mixed, combining all needs. Employee's timetable No.71 showed No.1-2 transferring its coaches to No.5-6 at Merrillan by May 1944, scheduling the junior train out of Winona at 6:45 a.m. It returned to the river by 3:20 p.m., trailing No.1, which was thereby cleared to run non-stop to "212" and Bridge Yard. Speed restrictions west of Merrillan held all trains to 35 miles per hour on the west end's last seventy-pound rail.

GB&W readied papers to retire its passenger equipment in February 1944 in the event that no opposition was encountered. Mail car 21 was demoted to electrical supply car X-21 in February 1945, while coach 108 went to X-108 status in March 1941 as a surplus to the passenger trade. Eligible combination cars 50

and 60 went to B&B service in 1943, useful to the active track gangs. Prophetically, the two depots at Arnott and Royalton were torn down, the first on a long list to come. Ogdensburg's long-closed depot was retired in 1945 and in 1946 the rambling, two-story 1880's style residence depot at New London Junction, an architectural marvel, was razed. It was replaced by an interlock plant of no architectural significance.

With the return of peace, GB&W continued installing ninety-pound rail, a $100,400 expenditure in 1946. Summer work crews placed new rail at Black Creek and Alma Center. In the previous summer, GB&W had lost a connection of historic interest, the Soo Line's 78.6 mile Portage branch. Long a haven for short trains and the light, picturesque Brooks-built 4-6-0's of the old Wisconsin Central, the land-grant route south of Stevens Point never did well. The loss eliminated a stop at Plover's depot

Above: Mike 406 is shown here on March 18, 1950, taking water at Norwood for the last time. At that very moment, sister 404 was en route to Norwood with the last steam-powered run of train No.8. By that evening steam was history on GB&W revenue runs.
C. B. KNISKERN PHOTO

Left: Kewaunee, Green Bay & Winona Transportation Co. was GB&W's over-the-road motor service. The fleet is gathered at Broadway's freighthouse in the early 1950's.
B. ERICKSON PHOTO

Below: Train No.2 pauses at Plover in 1940, its gleaming mail/express car spotted at the junction town's station.
E. RUHLAND PHOTO

for GB&W, subtracting a trickle of interchange business. It also lost GB&W half the station agent's keep, as Soo Line's representative. The removal, a major-length post-war abandonment, was not to be the last.

Three passenger coaches (No.86, 107 and 109) were converted to "combination caboose-coaches" in 1947, evidently with some space allotted to baggage compartments. It was these outwardly unchanged cars equipped with small bay-window inserts for window slots which terminated all passenger service. No.5-6 went to every-other-day operation, while on opposing days No.1-2 took the coach, but at differing times. The scheduling discouraged ridership. A January 1949 hearing confirmed the deteriorating status and on April 14, 1949 service ended quietly. The year's passenger total was only 213 riders. The Wisconsin Rapids press claimed the coach had passed through riderless the previous day. Yet, an embarrassed crew hosted a teacher and 35 school children on a ride between Manawa and New London that week, without a coach. Thus, the wily passenger train passed away, not with a bang, but a whisper.

The whisper was the sound of a quintet of ALCO diesel-electric cab units, painted bright red with a grey sash-stripe. They would fulfill the promise of dieselization which had been under examination as far back as 1938. At the same time, the last gaps in the heavy-rail program were being closed, while the lonely green coach, just behind a 400-class Mikado, was rolling toward oblivion. In August 1947 the Blair-Arcadia program was shelved in anticipation of the purchase of three diesel road units. In 1948, due to steel shortages, GB&W's 55-man crew under

Section Foreman "Jake" Skroch began replacing the older seventy-pound steel. The gap in the heavy rail was further narrowed in 1949 when an eighty-man extra gang was hired to work under Rudy Hagen in Whitehall. Beginning April 4th, the high-priority plan called for Skroch's gang to work the Arcadia-Paso section (eight miles), while the remaining work between Blair and Taylor was Hagan's. Final parcels of trackage would be changed the following year and an 85-car siding would be built at Blair.

At the end of 1947 one more veteran retired. Blair's station agent Earl Weidemann, after 21 years' duty, was replaced by

George Leischow. Soon many of the small agencies would be closed as the scene changed to modern railroading, diesel operations and better operating ratios.

On December 18, 1946 Trainmaster and Road Foreman of Engines Loyal J. Van Dreese received a letter from Milwaukee Road Division's master mechanic at La Crosse, R. C. Hempstead. Van Dreese was advised that, when Milwaukee's Valley Division had several of its new ALCO RSC-2 road switchers in freight service, he could personally observe them hard at work on the ruling westbound grade. While four were on hand at the beginning of 1947, at least one was still assigned to passenger service on a seven-car train. The Milwaukee men suggested a ride on train 269 with two units doing the work, formerly the province of one C-2 class 2-8-0 having 42,000 pounds tractive effort. Van Dreese also visited Gulf, Mobile & Ohio to examine their ALCO freight cab units, the first of the type in operation and the choice of GB&W. He went aboard at

No.503, came on the afternoon ferry which was detained by rough seas on Lake Michigan.

Mike Schultz remembered looking back from the lefthand side of a 400-class Mike at the new fire-engine red units and the little clusters of onlookers at grade crossings in Green Bay, noting the "red revolution." Ten years and ten months before, the sleek Mike which Schultz tended had seen such a day. Perhaps a light fire and 65 pounds of stoker pressure meant less now. It wouldn't be long before the 400's would pass away slowly, moving now to secondary duty and finally to silence.

After ALCO representatives and shopmen completed delivery of the new, snobbishly classic 1500-horsepower units, No.501-502 made a trip to Kewaunee with a seventy-car train as a test, moving smoothly up the winding curves in Baird's Creek Valley, on Monday, December 15th. The day before, another Sunday inaugural was made to Wisconsin Rapids to pit the two units against the big hills at Amherst Junction and "75" for the

Consol 399 is ready to leave Wisconsin Rapids with train No.8 on
March 15, 1947. Milwaukee rail historian Jim Scribbins covered GB&W's closing steam
years. No.399 was scrapped in 1950.

Bloomington, Illinois (14 years after Becker was there to acquire No.92) and rode GM&O's trains 98-99 to Roodhouse in western Illinois. It was necessary to amass intelligence on the cab units as GB&W's order had been placed in anticipation of a November 1947 delivery.

Homer McGee wrote to his auditor, Louis P. Wohlfeil, regarding the upcoming expenditure for the three diesel road units. Although a large figure for a small road, it was agreed to pay cash for the machines, each costing $152,000. As a result Wohlfeil had to arrange the building of cash reserves. The order was placed in June 1947 for two KGB&W and one GB&W. November passed and the delayed units finally left Schenectady December 5th, KGB&W 501-502 arriving Saturday, December 13th aboard ANN ARBOR No.7. The lone GB&W unit,

very first time. No.501-503 competed for public attention against C&NW's announcement that its "Ashland Limited" would soon be dieselized and that Milwaukee Road had recently ordered 39 diesels. On New Year's Day, 1948, No.501 made a tour of the Trempeleau Valley, accompanied by what came to be called "the B unit." Superintendent Van Dreese's green caboose No.603 was remodeled to become an official car in August 1947. Much had to be learned about the diesel's habits, especially the very new "244" series V-12 engine which chuckled resolutely between the red-grey walls of the 500's. Ahead lay problems with lubrication, piston-ring composition, turbochargers and electrical propulsion, now the responsibilities of men long used to properly kept water in boiler sight glasses and large, well-polished levers, regarded as the keys to deliberate motion.

The origin of the bright-red color scheme is obscure, but KATY's ALCO freight diesels, with their eye-catching red-and-yellow side panels, may have been the source. Continuation of ALCO purchases for the head-end probably stemmed from the close association with Ford Motor Company, and not General Motors. The durability of ALCO's diesel switchers was a well-known fact, although the company had examined EMD's product line. It also explains Ann Arbor's choice of ALCO. Within a short time, the two black diesel switchers used around Green Bay received red-grey paint work to further ward off motorists at close quarters. Soon they were joined by two more yard units, No.102 and No.201, delivered in 1948 and 1949, which closed out steam on yard assignments. Finally, the two older diesels, No.101 and No.103, were moved to Wisconsin Rapids. Concerned about smoke nuisances, Wisconsin Rapids

citizens confronted GB&W in December 1948. L. J. Van Dreese assured the city attorney's office that diesel switchers were to completely supplant steam power after January 1, 1949 and any remaining steam power would be operated under a smoke ban while in town.

Part of the burden of coal smoke came from GB&W's old 0-6-0 No.145, now an asset of Consolidated Papers across the Wisconsin River. CWPPCo. bought the engine for $3,000 in May 1948 and it served until October 1950 when GB&W disposed of 2-8-0 No.350 to the mill for $9,000. The paper company received the better of the two 1929 engines; A&W purchased No.351 for $6,000 on November 15, 1950. GB&W sold its three remaining Moguls (No.253, No.256 and KGB&W 258) plus 2-8-0 No.399 for scrap in October 1948.

The last ex-NYC 0-6-0, No.143, went to the torch in Novem-

*Here, Mike 402 is attending Kewaunee's ferry yard. C&O's Pere Marquette 22 and
AA's No. 7 were in port on this morning just after the end of World War II.*

Below: Norwood roundhouse and shop, coal chute and Western Refrigerator Car Line shops are shown here in this 1940-era view.

PHOTOGRAPHY INC.

ber 1947, after the Waupaca branch and A&W were no longer a responsibility. Thus dieselization brought economy in multiples, as branches and branch engines, passengers and their coaches, spare engines, coal docks, water tanks and extra manpower could be dismissed from the fast freight trade. In a very short time, GB&W drastically changed its scope of operations and its ability to earn its keep.

After a second order for two more cab units arrived in mid-April 1949, GB&W was within a year of completing dieselization. The new pair were second KGB&W 503 and GB&W 507. Upon delivery, old GB&W 503 became new GB&W 506, which aligned number groups thus: 501-503 were KGB&W, while 506-507 were GB&W. The service date for the units was April 20, 1949. In most cases the 500's were operated singly into 1950, which covered all through train movements of No. 1-2 and No. 3-4, Kewaunee to Winona. The 400's continued on work trains and way-freights 5-6 and 7-8 west of Green Bay. Consolidations 350-351 filled in where needed, from work extras to yard jobs, covering occasional diesel inspection dates.

Disaster struck GB&W on July 29, 1949. Two 500's were wheeling train No. 1 through Scandinavia, 61 miles west of Green Bay, making a run for the hill to the west. Just as a big C&NW hopper car loaded with "Rapids coal" rumbled past the depot, the leading journal burned completely off and 26 cars reared, tearing up more than 100 feet of main line. The incident marred the fine safety record that had built over many seasons. Conductor James Dean suffered a head injury at the rear of the Friday-evening main liner. GB&W, without a wrecker, summoned the C&NW's Green Bay hook, which arrived as Extra 501 West. Soo Line sent its W-1, picked up at Plover by Extra 103 East. Many grim-faced men worked long hours attending to the wreckage; the heavy work caused a whole day's loss. Luckily, the pile-up occurred inside Scandinavia's yard limit, which allowed sectionmen to utilize the Iola branch lead and by-pass the destruction. Among the spectators that day was the author, whose entire day of trouble-free train-watching on GB&W was completely spoiled. Unspoiled, however, were the dazzling paint schemes of the well-wiped diesels at the site, anchoring the wreckers deep among the debris. One loaded pickle car and the Scandinavia water tank were also destroyed, adding to the pungent atmosphere of mid-summer heat.

Anxious to complete dieselization, an order was placed with ALCO in late 1949 for four RS-2 road switchers which would draw the final fires of GB&W steam. No. 301-304 arrived in late February 1950 to take the way-freight assignments covered by the 400-class. They were placed in operation about a week apart, allowing for staggered inspection dates. On March 7th, No. 303

handled both the day and night Kewaunee jobs (No. 1-2 and No. 3-4) while 301 repeated the exercise on March 8th. The last one, No. 302, went on duty March 18, 1950 and, after several test runs as two-unit combinations to Kewaunee, they settled into way-freight work. The new units were purchased via a conditional sales agreement with New York Trust Co., the individual price being $142,694. GB&W was allowed 120 months to pay, the same terms given individuals who bought 1950 Fords.

Each night in early March, five of the six remaining 400's brought their respective way-freights in for the last time. The 401 made its final trip on No. 8. Arriving at Green Bay the evening of February 27, 1950, Engineer Ed Wanek was accompanied by Al Campbell, fireman, and George Wheritt, conductor. No. 402, unrecorded, was possibly out of service for several months. The 403 worked in with the same crew of No. 8, March 8, 1950. The 404 finished its duties on No. 8 of March 18th with Engineer Henry Burmeister, Dick Dickey, fireman, and T. Budlong, conductor. The 405 made the trip on March 16th to Kewaunee on No. 1-4 with crewmen C. W. Hull, Morris Erickson, and H. Coniff. Engine 406, with less than 2000 miles logged since major overhauling, last ran on No. 8 March 10th with Borchers, Wanek and Campbell in the cab. It was 404 which lived the longest of the D-47's; no other runs were ever recorded. Yet, an untraceable story persists to this day that one night, after a diesel shortage developed, a 400 went off into the night to Kewaunee, expressly against orders. Some of the survivors of the times feel sure it happened. Perhaps it is only a ghost story, conjuring memories of a phantom Mikado far too young to

Mike 402 brings eastbound tonnage across First Street in Wisconsin Rapids on August 16, 1947.

Train No.1 has cut off its freight cars at Bridge Yard and forwarded the two passenger cars to Winona's joint CB&Q-GB&W station on Second Street. KGB&W 403 is checked over before the crew backs a load of varnish to Bridge Yard for the night. The depot, still standing in 1989, is to the right.

Train No. 2 halts at New London, Wisconsin on February 15, 1941. As varnish was seldom switched at Winona, the coach was always closest to the locomotive eastbound.

Often, 400-class did yeoman duties on work extras, especially on ballasting chores. Here, on April 29, 1949, No.404 labors near Summit as H. W. McGee inspects the work from a hopper car ladder.

On January 1, 1948, cab 501 had Superintendent Loyal Van Dreese's assigned office car No.603 in tow, as the new red-and-gray unit made an experimental trip to Winona. Photographer Reuben Dissmore of Blair (mile 170) made formal portraits of the Great New Way.
R. DISSMORE PHOTO

pass from the scene without one final measure of victory over the opposition.

It wasn't the end of all steam on GB&W, for a pile driver work extra was operated in March and April of 1950 with 350 and 351. With conductor Al Jerezek in charge of the train, Engineer Fred Rondou was on the 350 thumping piles into lowlands between Scandinavia and Manawa during March and later near Shiocton. The trim Consolidation finished up her days on March 20th, about 21 years old, when she rolled into Norwood on a cloudy evening. The 351 next went out with its new crew, "Daisy" Weytens and John Schmidt, and the pile driver crew (C&NW) to work on the west end. They unloaded and then, for nearly a week, drove piles at Bridge 190.7, just east of Arcadia, later working west of Dodge and near Blair. On April 21, 1950, Extra 351 East ran from Arcadia to Green Bay, tying up at 9:20 p.m., on a clear, calm day of 28 degrees.

Steam power was finished on Green Bay & Western, and 351 was the last. Probably both 350 and 351 were run under their own steam off the property in the fall of 1950 to serve several more years. While Ahnapee & Western's No.351 was last run in early 1953, No.350 served until 1955, at which time it was preserved in a Wisconsin Rapids park. In the 1980's No.350 was moved to North Freedom, Wisconsin, the sole survivor of GB&W's steam power.

Traffic in 1950 continued to show improvement. President Homer McGee's directorship now included Walton W. Cox, Robert Winthrop and C. T. Richardson of New York. Mr. Cox, by this time, was chairman, secretary and treasurer. GB&W had 244 employees, 13 locomotives and originated 286,955 tons on line (16%), while 84% came from the highest tonnage category (320,625 tons) with lumber products at 147,004 tons. The previous year showed an operating ratio of 66.4% and operating revenues of $3,816,276. Homer McGee's son Weldon, who had joined the operating staff of GB&W in 1937, began his duties with the extra track gangs on the ninety-pound rail program. After working as yardmaster in the 1940's, H. Weldon McGee became superintendent in 1946 and assistant general manager in

1951. He climbed to Vice-President-Operations in 1955 during the road's biggest year to date.

With dieselization came the inevitable great changes to the physical plant. On October 12, 1950 a violent storm removed the Winona roundhouse roof. A speedy replacement was imperative. It was about that time that Homer McGee had asked Weldon what he might get him for Christmas. The next president of GB&W replied: "I'd like a new enginehouse at Winona!" The ARMCO-built structure, a practical, useful and long-lasting building, was the younger McGee's gift. All coal and water facilities were dismantled by 1954, some unceremoniously. It took 45 pounds of dynamite to remove the coal dock at Wisconsin Rapids and a similar amount was set aside for the July 1952 destruction of Whitehall's Ogle coaling station west of town. Across the nation the same dull thump could be heard as skylines were cleansed of the once-important, massive fueling stations, now quite useless. Water tanks were irreverently pulled over by their diesel conquerors or nudged by off-road equipment, to collapse into kindling, rendering archaic the Americanisms "tank town" and "jerk water."

From the spring of 1950 to October 1, 1952, the six 400's stood silent, cold and useless with scarcely a glance from management. While fine dust settled and thin rust advanced, rumors oozed about that somewhere, somehow, there would be a market for the barely used machinery. It was thought that the Mikados would be sold to a Venezuelan road to haul iron ore in their old age. The 401 and 402 stood outside. No.401 seemed to hide under the coal chute, while the balance occupied the long "400-stalls," awaiting that certain day and "the call." The only call that did come was a settlement for all six, putting an end to all rumors. Betten's paid $6000 each for the 400's and they were lined up along Norwood Yard's north storage tracks later that month. After remaining there for all of 1955, they went in slow procession to the Milwaukee Road yard, moaning as their great thirty-inch pistons offered *a missa solemnis,* a requiem to the last of the race. The inheritors had come.

Dieselization continued in 1951 as two more road switchers

arrived. No. 305-306, the newer RS-3 type, were routed separately. No. 305 went D&H to Owego, New York; Lehigh Valley to Suspension Bridge, New York; C&O to Ludington. No. 306 went D&H to Binghamton; DL&W to Black Rock; Wabash to Milan, Michigan; AA to Frankfort. The object was to keep peace in the family. The locomotive was to be handled as near the train's head-end as possible. The price tag was $142,167.92 per unit. ALCO referred to them as "E-1662-A" types, a classification system best known to the New York-based manufacturer.

GB&W's prosperity of 1952 was outlined in a prospectus for sale of 250 shares of its capital stock. The price quoted was $70 per share with a yield of 7.14%. That year about sixty percent of GB&W traffic was overhead, manufacturers accounting for 55-60% of total revenues. Improvement expenditures for the

battle with truckers, E. F. Bushman operated the service via lease, which continued until A&W was sold in 1947.

GB&W's public relations activities since 1925 included the annual "Miller's Special," which allowed the flour merchants of Minneapolis to observe the GB&W first hand, along with the ferries and partner Ann Arbor. Through the 1950's, the special began to resemble a first-class passenger train. On July 23, 1960 diesel 503 handled Bar Car 21, Pullman "Eagle Ridge" (T&P) and business car 600 to pick up Pullman "Clifton," "Stillwater River" and "Thornapple River" which would provide adequate space for the Minneapolitans. Upon arrival at Kewaunee, the Pullmans made the crossing to Frankfort. Returning on Sunday July 24th, the special arrived at Winona's CB&Q depot later that evening. The Pullmans were placed at the head-end of

To honor working partner C&O's launching of BADGER in September 1952, GB&W spruced up at least one paper car as a backdrop for the advertising banner. The train was brought to Kewaunee by two 500's, typical of the 1950's power assigned to the Kewaunee Division.

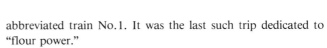

years 1946 to 1951 totaled $2,900,000, with another $100,000 slated for 1952, equaling about one-third of the road's total investment in roadway and equipment. The 1952 transportation ratio amounted to 27.8%, compared to industry averages of 36.8% for Class I railroads. Because of a protracted car ferry strike, GB&W did not surpass previous figures. But, despite the strike, their earnings were still respectable.

With reductions in local service, LCL and express, GB&W officers utilized seventy shares of capital stock to organize a trucking subsidiary, Kewaunee, Green Bay & Winona Transport, Inc. The stock was owned by Harold A. Knutson, Lawrence J. Knutson and D. J. Lardinois. The subsidiary flourished, eventually acquiring off-railroad construction equipment used in GB&W maintenance work. It became a wholly owned subsidiary of GB&W in February 1978. But in its early days small shipments went into its red-and-grey trucks. GB&W's over-the-road service dates to December 23, 1939 when Ahnapee & Western and KGB&W were granted authority to establish supplementary motor service for LCL and express. After a legal

abbreviated train No. 1. It was the last such trip dedicated to "flour power."

GB&W ton-miles inched upward during the boom year of 1955 to 265,250,000 and operating revenues climbed to $4,477,741. New auto traffic contributed a share of the good fortune, for vehicle parts made up 11.6% of the revenue. Coal destined for paper plants at Wisconsin Rapids and Stevens Point, always a substantial income-producing business, accounted for 15.4%. At the same time, KGB&W's operating ratio ran to 66.43%, while the main show carried 69.4%. Vehicle parts during 1957 reached 87,186 tons, 4.4% of GB&W revenues. Traffic in 1955 warranted the purchase of two more RS-3's, No. 307-308, which were placed in service July 12th and 13th. Routing from Schenectady was again split. GB&W traditionally equipped their diesels with steel-tired wheels and ordered careful braking by the delivering carriers. No. 307-308 were factory class E-1662-B's. In 1955 more ninety-pound rail was added through Merrillan's junction and up Oneida Hill to cope with higher speeds and heavier loads.

GB&W was steadily streamlining its plant. In 1953 trains 3-4 were re-introduced to operate westbound in daylight hours, leaving Norwood at 5:01 a.m. Way-freights No. 7-8 were reduced to every-other-day operation. The condition prevailed through the fifties, terminating by early 1962. Winona-Wisconsin Rapids way-freight 5-6 disappeared in the late 1950's and No. 3-4 began every-other-day operation by June 5, 1960. On January 14, 1962 trains 1-2 covered all traffic between Wisconsin Rapids and Winona, while No. 7-8 did the every-other-day business between Wisconsin Rapids and Green Bay. By February 1967 No. 7-8, which became the Stevens Point way-freight, was scheduled to Amherst Junction to meet No. 5-6 out of Green Bay. Until the early 1970's No. 5-6, the "Manawa Turns," would take extra cars fifty miles west where they were forwarded by other trains to Soo Line connections or for local delivery.

Runs to Kewaunee continued as No. 1-2 in daylight while No. 3-4 covered the night boats.

GB&W's car fleet required attention in post-war years, its newest boxcars being 1930-vintage. A fifteen-year lease of 200 forty-foot welded-steel boxcars from Pullman-Standard Car Mfg. Co., in connection with Equitable Life Assurance Society, brought the 700-800 series cars in late 1950. Twenty steel hopper cars had come the previous year from Pullman-Standard for paper mill coal business. Originally the cars were to be split between KGB&W and GB&W ownership; all were delivered with "KGB" report marks. Conversion of the locomotive shop to diesel requirements included a special servicing pit on the south track. Previous commitments to diesel in 1939 placed a Whiting sixty-ton drop pit facility at the shop, capable of lowering a diesel truck or a 400-class trailer. While many depots were slated for removal, GB&W built a new station at Manawa in 1951. The strictly functional architecture was of concrete-block design, hardly destined to evoke nostalgia. Although scheduled for 1954, the Wisconsin Rapids depot-office replacement didn't materialize until 1959. The new 31 × 58 foot glass-brick-concrete

Keeping the 500's going proved to be a challenge. Here, in the mid-1950's, Norwood's machinists guide an overhead craneload — a new 244-series ALCO V-12 — into the spotless and varnished carbody of 503, marking the beginning of another 600,000 miles of service.

A "Miller's Special" prepares for a trip to Winona on July 21, 1957. The polished 506 stands at Kewaunee with ROAMER in the rear of the train, behind two of GB&W's vintage passenger cars. The baggage/mail reinforced travelers with refreshments the entire 200 miles to Winona.

structure replaced an 1886 gingerbread board-and-batten architectural gem which dated to far less prosperous days. That year GB&W showed a net income of $325,894,31 with an operating ratio of 73.63%.

The needs of the Wisconsin Rapids paper mills were further served by fifty new forty-foot boxcars. The newcomers were equipped with twelve-foot doors to accommodate paper-roll-toting forklifts. The 900's were the first in bright yellow with black lettering, again a characteristic of KATY. They too were leased from Equitable Life and had fifty-ton capacity. Another 42 cars (650-691) were leased from U.S. Railway Equipment Co. They were placed in service April 1962 to handle high-quality enamel paper. The two groups were dedicated to carrying magazine papers to eastern markets. In those years, shipments were transferred to Soo Line at Amherst Junction as well as going east through Kewaunee. GB&W's first fifty-foot cars were leased from General American-Evans (No. 112000-112009) and were equipped with damage-free loading devices. The ten green cars went to work in October 1960.

The abandonment of GB&W's last rural branch line occurred in May of 1958. Often the subject of abandonment studies, the Iola branch traffic had declined considerably since 1949 and the company wanted to end it. On May 15th Messrs. Chester Krause and Alfred Langeland sought to purchase the line for $30,000 but the offer was refused. GB&W management sensed that such branch lines, either owned or separately operated, would not dovetail with their scheme. GB&W moved to abandon both lines out of Scandinavia immediately after the war and, as local business was discouraged, traffic fell almost according to plan. By mid-1956 Iola branch carloadings had dwindled to 97. In September 1957 GB&W applied to abandon the 4.73 miles of a dream railroad aimed at Northern Wisconsin, begun 66 years before. On June 1, 1958 branch operations ceased.

GB&W's progress in the early 1960's began to tax the abilities of its motive power. As trains became mile-long affairs, they required more horsepower; mere two-unit 3000-horsepower combinations were no longer efficient. Late-1950's competition among locomotive builders engendered a nationwide horsepower race. ALCO developed its newer "251" series engines, up to 1800 horsepower and finally to 2400 horsepower in a V-16 which was to be the ultimate in locomotive power. On August 12, 1960. No. 506 was retired, its useful components traded in on GB&W's — and the world's — first 2400-horsepower four-motor road switcher, which arrived via D&H-DL&W-WAB-AA routing. No. 310 cost $222,000 and was in service by December 8, 1960.

Below: Train No. 2 rolls past Whitehall and agent Ervid Erickson's message hoop is at the ready. It was 1952 and GB&W was enjoying some of its best earning years.

New 310 wasn't the first "251" on the property, for KGB&W 309 had arrived in 1956, making its first run on September 8th. No. 309 cost $163,192.80 and developed 1800 horsepower from a V-12 engine. The newer design was an improvement, but the ALCO's remained temperamental at best and the 251 was the last go-around for most railroads willing to experiment. In 1964 RS-11 No. 309 was re-equipped with a 2000-horsepower 251, generally a satisfactory performer. The new "DL-640" type, equally prone to failures, frayed the patience of ALCO users throughout 1960. Yet, 310 was the wave of the future and, temperamental or not, it was soon joined by ten other 2400-horsepower ALCO's as standard power for the long trains of the 1970's. Vindication of the big V-16's came with GB&W's first "Century" series units when No. 311 was delivered after display at a Chicago railroad trade show in the fall of 1963. Four such units were acquired from 1963 to 1965. The final one, No. 314 under KGB&W ownership, was the last locomotive to bear the initials of the smaller company. Prior to each order, a

500-class cab unit was dismantled and the parts directed to ALCO Products. The last 500-class, No. 503, was dismantled in the spring of 1965 to provide a trade-in for No. 314.

During the years of fast, heavy trains and booming automobile-building, which was the great American railroad show finale, Homer Edgar McGee passed away, leaving GB&W in its best-ever condition. On a winter visit to Phoenix, Arizona, the man from KATY succumbed while enjoying his other professional passion, a fine golf game. McGee, whose final position was chairman of the board, left a railroad about to produce an operating ratio of 65.55%. The previous spring, on May 10, 1962, his son Weldon McGee had become president.

The new president was born in Smithville, Texas on December 31, 1912 in the days when his father was tending to KATY affairs in the small south Texas town. Interest in the great game of railroading had come easily to the son and he grew to enjoy the "fine art" long before he was gainfully employed in the field. Educated at Terrill Preparatory School in Dallas, Weldon went to Washington University at St. Louis in 1931 and earned a BBA degree at the University of Texas in 1936. His early railroad experience came in the form of summer jobs on KATY track gangs and, after completing his schooling, GB&W hired him as a special apprentice.

The new staff of 1963 included Clarence H. Halvorson, General Manager; Lawrence J. Knutson, Superintendent; H. A. La Chappelle, Chief Engineer and Manager of Industrial Development; Lawrence J. Kelly, Vice-President of Traffic; L. B. Ward, Executive Assistant, and Allan S. Johnson, Superintendent of the Mechanical Department. It was during this period that GB&W received several groups of very large and revolutionary boxcars intended for automobile traffic. The Ford parts cars took on an important specialized status. Several groups acquired at Ford's own direction were used to convey automobile sheet metal in the

manufacturer's Buffalo stamping plant pool. Another car order involved 374 units, split between Reading, Pennsylvania, Detroit, Toledo & Ironton and GB&W. Still another large group went into paper service.

New equipment and heavier loads required a phase-out of lighter yard units and the new management opted to sell to local industries. Nekoosa-Edwards Paper Co. of Nekoosa, Wisconsin purchased numbers 102 and 103; the latter eventually was transferred to Arkansas. No. 102, as NEPCO 12, worked for many years at the paper plant. A decade earlier, on April 4, 1956, GB&W's first diesel No. 101, had been sold to United Electric Coal Co. at the Illinois River coal dump. It was resold to Material Service Co. of Romeoville, Illinois where it remained in service until about 1975.

GB&W's heavy traffic and higher speeds, the outcome of the soaring sixties, placed a heavy demand upon motive power. During January 1967 C&NW's four DL-640's, twins of GB&W 310, were stored at the road's Green Bay shops, the owner less than content with the units' performance. GB&W availed itself of a locomotive design which few of its buyers could keep out of repair stalls and put 902 and 903 in servicable condition for use, while the other two (900, 901) were returned to ALCO. For many months the leased pair, still in C&NW colors with a red GB&W decal on the cab sides, operated daylight runs, typically to Amherst Junction or to Plover. In the spring of 1967, GB&W chose to return 902 to ALCO. However, a Ford strike in September 1967 obviated further need for 903's services. In 1968 No. 903 was stored, its lease canceled due to a failed turbocharger on July 14th. By October 1968 No. 903 was under GB&W ownership. No. 902 was finally purchased February 21, 1969 from ALCO, which had formally closed its doors. C&NW had meanwhile traded the units, a paper shuffle; on its units

The RS-20 program was an economical way out of "sticker shock" 1975-style. RS-3's 305-308 were rebuilt with 251-C 2000-horsepower ALCo Products engines and were made into "chop-nose" short-end-ahead units. *Left:* unit 308 has the new engine in place; *below,* new 308 is two days out of the shop; *bottom,* Painter George Taylor applies vinyl reflective decals to the carbody of 308.

ALL STAN MAILER PHOTOS

Left: In her last months as an RS-3, stalwart 307 clears a long cut of cars from N. Quincy Street in January 1975. An anxious crew faced a police ticket and four throttle notches were skipped, hence the acute "turbo lag" in the paper mill district.

STAN MAILER PHOTO

Above: During GB&W's 1960's, a frequent entry on Dispatcher "Bud" Curran's train sheets was No.7 "turned extra" beyond Manawa, its often-exceeded timetable limit. "Extra 301 West" was assaulting Amherst Junction's hill, its "244" engines howling a four-cycle bel canto of raw power to an approving summer afternoon sky.
M. DUNN PHOTO

401-404, the newer and better "Century 425" type. GB&W eventually renumbered 903 to 316, and 902 to 317, after the units were repainted in GB&W red. The pair were the first used diesels on GB&W and the first to receive the all-red "austerity" paint job. The well-remembered gray stripe was beginning to bow out and ended in June 1973 with the repainting of unit 301. GB&W was now operating without the Ford business.

GB&W's annual report for 1967 stated that the road had reached a record high point in gross operating revenues for the year. Its net income was below that reported for 1966. Increases in freight car rentals and wages accounted for the difference. Nonetheless, KGB&W grossed $1,365,778.21. From a net income of $140,528.96, the parent company received $53,120 in dividend income. The operating ratio in 1967 was 68.12%. By mid-1969 GB&W was beginning to originate as much as 45% of its traffic from on-line shippers, up from 30% in the past.

The decision to stick with ALCO locomotives had its drawbacks, especially when the fortunes of the old builder began to flicker and die. In ALCO's last year of production, GB&W acquired C-430 No.315, a 3000-horsepower alternator-equipped unit, the last of only sixteen built. Delivered February 1968, 315 was the longest, heaviest and most unique of GB&W's ALCO's.

becoming ALCO Engines Division of White Motors, Inc. Boxy and ungainly looking, the 315's distinctive profile was a regular on the long, single train daily which constituted GB&W's 1970's way of life.

The end of GB&W's little red wood cabooses came in the mid-1960's. Thrall Car Co. delivered two all-steel 36-foot bay-window cars in July 1940, a design similar to C&NW's which were finished by Norwood. No.613-614 were followed in 1965 and 1966 by three differing cars (615-617) from International Car. A final pair, fabricated by Kraft Steel in Green Bay, in the interest of safety, employed fiberglass bay windows. Instead of committing the wood-body cabooses completely to scrap, small steel box hutches were built and applied to the old frames, creating small switching and transfer cabooses.

STAN MAILER PHOTO

Below: Just hours into its 27-year career on GB&W, RS-2 No.301 labors at Norwood after silencing steam power on regular assignments. The date is March 18, 1950, the same day Mike 404 brought the final edition of train No.8 to close out steam-for-profit forever. The last turn of the crank, 27 years later, on the afternoon of October 14, 1977, No.301's V-12 engine rolls to a halt. GB&W sold and shipped the road switcher to an Arizona contractor. Two years later, Michigan's AARRS had No.301 and No.303 in operation in southern Michigan.
C. B. KNISKERN PHOTO

It was equipped with "Hy-Ad" trucks, a new development in countering weight transfer in diesel locomotives. A pioneer of alternating-current application to diesels, ALCO, nonetheless, was unable to ward off the overwhelming economic onslaught of General Motors and its locomotives, which were the universal norm. ALCO became a parts supplier after 1969, in time

GB&W fortunes were increasingly being dictated by forces beyond the road's control from Green Bay. Militant restrictions about to be placed upon Lake Michigan car ferry service by new anti-pollution edicts would imperil GB&W's eastern connections, while C&O could and did offer alternative routing via Chicago, available to compete on a time-cost basis. Both ferry services were considered labor-intensive and overaged, despite improvements, and prone to high repair costs. In the 1970's GB&W's potential loss of ferry dockings would have serious consequences. After auto-loading losses in the late 1960's GB&W struggled to obtain a fair share of traffic from both overhead and on-line customers. Merger fever in the northern midwest began to take a toll on coveted gateways, some of them closely related to GB&W's fortunes. Ann Arbor's Upper Peninsula ward, Manistique & Lake Superior Railroad, fell victim to the Soo Line-DSS&A merger. The small road pulled out in October 1968. The Menominee Route, long the most costly and difficult to operate in winter, was closed March 9, 1970.

Ann Arbor settled down to operate its Kewaunee and Manitowoc lines, although its costs were steadily rising. From 1955 to 1973 ferry costs had risen 59%. Despite a lower crew count, an annual loss of 2.23% of westbound traffic continued to sap the AA's strength. AA had risen to the challenge of post-war passenger and auto-tourist business by modernizing three of its boats: ARTHUR K. ATKINSON (1959), CITY OF GREEN BAY (1963) and VIKING (1965). The problem of scheduling for passengers' benefits plus the wily boxcar proved difficult. During

Retiring President H. W. McGee confers with new President Joseph Galassi and Itel Rail Division's President Joseph Costello, November 13, 1978.
GREEN BAY PRESS-GAZETTE PHOTO

Top: Delivered in early 1980, GB&W's "Hornell Units" were just short of being mechanical disasters. Ex-L&HR 27 became GB&W's 323, which belied its less-than-perfect form, as its big 2000-horsepower "251" engine was started for the first time at Norwood. The unit was rebuilt on contract at Hornell, New York.

Bottom: ALCO's at rest in Norwood roundhouse in January 1975 included Continental Grain 207, a contract job which was finished later that year.

Top: Norwood shop housed a new 251 series V-12 on January 1, 1974. Extra traction motors replaced those shorted in the severe winter's powder snow; a set was held ready for installation, on consignment from Chandeysson Electric of St. Louis.

Bottom: Hostler Brian Goethe washes RS-27 No.318 in a "400 stall," on February 12, 1980. No.318 is ex-C&NW No.901.

the 1940's and 1950's, wages and benefits for ferry personnel rose significantly, offsetting any newly won traffic. After 1974 only two boats remained to handle business: the fast, diesel-powered 21-m.p.h. VIKING and the 18-m.p.h ATKINSON.

Ann Arbor's share of westbound auto parts, which had constituted 55% of the traffic in 1962, plummeted to only 2.8% in 1972. Automotive production-distribution methods had changed, especially with regard to the Detroit-St. Paul trade. On October 8, 1970, AA applied to the ICC to abandon its Frankfort-Manitowoc service, claiming the move was essential for profitability. ICC denied AA's request so the railroad added that it intended to apply to abandon all ferry service in its application. Upon ICC's examination of public convenience and necessity factors, a denial of the application was made on May 1, 1972, requiring AA to remain calling in Wisconsin. ICC had foreseen that abandonment at Manitowoc would accelerate curtailment of the Kewaunee service.

AA's retaliation came on June 19, 1974 when it announced its intention to abandon the entire railroad, car-ferries included. Two months later the ICC postponed any further hearings on the subject, although the railroad petitioned that little could be done to avert bankruptcy. In summer of 1973 one of the ATKINSON's two Nordberg diesels had snapped a crankshaft and the fleet was reduced to VIKING, a lone Norwegian in a threatened environment.

The Penn Central merger of 1968 produced more problems, perhaps, than it solved. One such problem was the re-routing of vital auto traffic. Further hampered by the N&W merger, the Penn Central debacle drained the cross-lake auto parts business, as AA wasn't to be a partner in PC. After the Wabash entered the N&W camp, AA was cast adrift and eventually lashed to Pennsylvania's Detroit, Toledo & Ironton in 1964. It was DT&I's $2.8 million contribution that created VIKING, a proud, fast, well-engineered, yet doomed, Kewaunee connection. VIKING was rebuilt from ANN ARBOR No.7 of 1925 with four EMD 567D1 engines at Superior, Wisconsin in 1964-65. VIKING, however, wasn't enough to stave off economic problems nor obstruct the premium traffic outpour, which now went through Chicago to the Milwaukee Road. The latter, needing traffic just before its bankruptcy, worked out rolling warehousing for Ford parts by storing shipments on Missisippi River sidings, to be called "just-in-time" to St. Paul. Now the Fords rolled straight past Winona and the Wall Street interchange. A lot of revenue disappeared with the Ford business, leaving GB&W in some trouble.

Retrenchment for GB&W included the 1971 sale of certain assets such as its landmark grain elevator and equally notable business car 600. Another move was the buy-out of Western Refrigerator Line's properties adjacent to Norwood for car repairs. The road concentrated its attention on lineside customers as never before and food products, paper, lumber and mill supplies became dominant. On June 1, 1969 Kewaunee, Green Bay & Western was merged with GB&W, the act of common directors for both roads.

By the mid-1960's C&O was operating seven boats on three routes and was encountering financial struggles similar to those of Ann Arbor. Another problem was created by the newer, longer railcars which decreased the on-board count while overland trains became longer. C&O's Kewaunee service after 1966 was unscheduled. Although carloadings through Manitowoc declined, Kewaunee deliveries remained stable through 1970. On October 8, 1970 C&O applied to ICC to abandon its Ludington-Kewaunee service. This move was contingent upon AA's similar

action to get off the lake entirely. ICC denied C&O's petition May 9, 1972, stressing the harm done to GB&W and Wisconsin industries. Impact studies conducted by the state showed that up to 1500 jobs and/or families might be lost and the ability of Wisconsin paper mills to compete in eastern markets would be severely curtailed.

Ann Arbor defaulted on its VIKING loan November 1, 1972 and was allowed by DT&I to file bankruptcy a year later. AA was then eligible for consideration in Conrail and was operated by them for 18 months beginning April 1, 1976. Michigan Interstate Railway Company next operated AA from October 1, 1977. The service, which was subsidized by state money, struggled into the 1980's but was ended by whistle-blowing legislatures, intent on suturing monetary hemorrhages. An attempt by GB&W to operate AA was refuted. At last, on April 5, 1982, the Kewaunee-Frankfort service ended amid the cries of the affected and staggering costs. VIKING, silent and cold, was towed out of Frankfort Harbor on May 11, 1983 to Sturgeon Bay where it became a floating office for a shipbuilder. On April 25, 1984 ATKINSON, after re-entering service on August 16, 1980 was also towed away to Kewaunee's mud flats to face oblivion. AA withered back to Yuma's sandpits, a final northern terminus miles away from Lake Michigan's surf. Ann Arbor became an unfortunate "has-been," redundant in an era of run-throughs and unit trains.

Concern about older motive power on GB&W prompted interest in rebuilding the aging 244-powered road switchers of the early 1950's. Initial inquiries by Diesel Supervisor Ralph Stutleen unearthed data on Portuguese ALCO's which had been re-engined with new 251 V-12's. The results from Norwood were repowered RS-3's, now called "RS-20's." Western contractor Morrison-Knudson looked into the idea in 1974 to create a new "TE-56-4R" road switcher from reclaimed RS-3's, basing their proposed product on GB&W's success. While M-K went their way, GB&W's 305 went back to work with its engine tested to 2,167-horsepower, making several road tests after June 20, 1973. It was followed by 308, 307 and 306 in succeeding years. Unable to convert the older RS-2's, all four received rebuilt 244 engines from the RS-20 program. No.302 was scrapped (frame only) by Betten's in September 1976. No.304 was sold the same month to Michigan Northern Railroad, becoming its 1501, while units 301 and 303 were sold to Railroad Builders, Inc. of Navajo, Arizona in October 1977. Both units were returned to the midwest in 1979 and sold to Ann Arbor Railroad System.

Mechanical staffers were concerned about acquiring extra power, still opting to stay with ALCOs which each day became more "GB&W custom" locomotives. Overtures were made to Soo Line for the "Dolly Sisters," two RS-27's then banished from Soo's main line. Numbers 415 and 416 were priced too high and thus they were later scrapped. Junkets to ALCO-dominated roads and dealer contacts finally turned up an acquaintance, ex-C&NW 901, leased to Canadian Pacific. The black-painted RS-27 arrived at Norwood on May 10, 1976 and was in service as No.318 by October. The price was $47,500.

GB&W continued to survey the locomotive market, even soliciting a price on the Montreal-built "M-420," a Canadian

Right: The world's first 2400-horsepower hood unit, GB&W's 310, switches in dismal weather at Broadway Tower, Green Bay, sorting cars in McDonald's yard. No. 310 was scrapped in March 1986. GB&W employed an unusual M-U hose connection with air hoses at platform level.
STAN MAILER PHOTO

development of the later ALCOs. New locomotives had reached fantastic prices and the M-420 was available for $350,000. A good chance slipped by when Erie-Lackawanna's entire fleet of C-425's rolled through East Winona en route to British Columbia Railway. With sale or merger fever looming, especially if GB&W was sold to Burlington Northern, speculation had the ALCOs banished to scrap yards. Yet GB&W solicited outside repair jobs on ALCOs, putting their expertise to work on the many industrial units brought their way. GB&W was responsible for the acquisition of Fort Howard Papers' pair of ALCO S-2 yard units and did contract work on three ex-LS&I road switchers for Continental Grain, as well as several others.

Above: H. Weldon McGee is shown in the center with Soo, C&NW and Milwaukee representatives. The group met in 1977 to discuss the proposed sale of GBW to BN.
GREEN BAY PRESS-GAZETTE PHOTO

Right: Train No.2 is operating on Milwaukee track at Tunnel City, Wisconsin on August 26, 1975 after a washout at Mile 188.
STAN MAILER COLLECTION

Below: GB&W's new headquarters at 2155 Hutson Road, Green Bay, are seen here. After the fire of February 11, 1977, the present headquarters was leased, several miles from downtown Green Bay Junction.
STAN MAILER PHOTO

Above: Single unit 311, the road's first "DL-640-a," proceeds eastward from Casco Junction after a side trip to Algoma over Ah&W in 1975.
STAN MAILER PHOTO

GB&W had considered selling out as far back as 1930, a continuation of its old short line philosophy. The Prince Plan of Consolidation had matched it with CB&Q and talks between Ralph Budd of the "Q" and Homer McGee took place in the 1940's. Again, during the high earnings period of the 1960's, Soo Line was approached. By then the obvious candidate was BN and by October 1974 actions were initiated to bring GB&W into union with the giant, the safest, life-assuring action. The majority of GB&W business was interchanged with BN at East

switching and transfer road of marginal value.

Enter the competition. In late 1975 Soo Line, C&NW and Milwaukee Road moved to counter Burlington Northern's offer, concerned that BN would compete deep in their territory. Actually, BN's office in Green Bay was soliciting traffic and was actively engaged in assuring car supply among the mills. The Three entered into a blocking position and made a counter-proposal to purchase GB&W about Christmastime 1975, while BN announced that 86% of GB&W's stockholders had tendered their shares to an offer of $100 per share; additionally, $2,514,000 of class B debentures had been tendered. An ICC hearing for BN's offer was postponed from January 12th while The Three planned a balkanization of GB&W's main line to be operated as convenience allowed off existing junctions. They pledged that GB&W's customers would have better service, that Green Bay would benefit from less duplicate rail facilities and that all would be strengthened thereby. The ICC was asked to stave off its decision while their plan was completed.

The central plan included abandonment of all trackage west of Wisconsin Rapids, the Manawa-Plover segment and Shiocton-Seymour track. C&NW would operate Kewaunee-Green Bay and Manawa-Shiocton, while Milwaukee Road would take Green Bay-Seymour. Milwaukee and C&NW would serve Green Bay industries and Soo Line would operate the Plover-Stevens Point-Rapids leftover. The process smacked of C&NW's dismemberment of CGW and M&STL. The Three offered $4 million hard currency in early March 1976, billed as a "constructive alternative" to a BN takeover.

GB&W was convinced that little save destruction of their enterprise would result and that the GB&W share of traffic would be bought off with the road's physical plant. The Three had some grounds for concern, as BN had the potential to cause revenue losses of up to $5 million and it was the largest transportation firm in the nation at the time. A representative of Consolidated Papers, Inc. testified that BN would not divert traffic from the other roads and the great mill would continue to distribute its traffic as evenly as possible. The paper company had moved about 25,000 cars the previous year, GB&W being only one carrier. Consolidated sided with the BN merger plan.

As ICC deliberated the BN takeover plan, GB&W saw its revenues drop slightly due to a construction slump which had caused lumber carloadings to fall. GB&W had a net income of $250,973 in 1975 against the previous year's $332,497. By January 1977 the Justice Department registered its opposition to the proposal of The Three on the grounds that competition would be decreased in GB&W's area. Drawing great pride from GB&W's accomplishments, President McGee allegedly stated: "I'll be damned if I'll sell it to the North Western!"

On Friday, February 11, 1977 at 2:00 a.m., a fire surged through GB&W's headquarters-depot at Green Bay Junction, gutting the structure. Green Bay's firefighters worked all night while railroad personnel attempted to salvage valuables from the stricken building. President McGee, vacationing in Texas, returned to direct the recovery. Historic documents were lost but important files were saved and moved to available space and placed under armed guard. Soon office employees were settled into space at 2155 Hutson Road in Packerland Industrial Park, a 12,000-square-foot vacancy. The old building's loss, which amounted to approximately $500,000, was the work of an incendiary.

Throughout 1977 The Three struggled to hold their ground against Burlington Northern. BN and GB&W countered with a

Winona and merger would assure shippers the service they desired. Both parties to the merger had reason to acquire jitters over the ever-threatened eastern connection. Ann Arbor and C&O were moving toward elimination of the costly ferry service. C&O tried internally to divert traffic already pledged to its car ferries. Environmental laws began to menace the boats; water and air quality standards were transgressed by the coal-burning C&O fleet. GB&W was threatened with the loss of at least 40% of its business if the boats were lost and atrophy to a joint petition to Judge A. D. O'Neal of ICC to eliminate a stay of approval of BN's acquisition, which had been a holding tactic of the other roads. Abruptly, railroad supplier A&K Materials, Inc. of Clearfield, Utah, which did business with GB&W, made an offer to buy 51% of GB&W's 18,000 common shares outstanding. The maneuver aligned GB&W's directors solidly with BN, despite a hearing alleging violation of securities laws. With a substantial percentage of GB&W shares held by its officers and employees, it was unlikely that the A&K offer would have been accepted. A&K Materials was not under ICC control, while each of the five long-suffering roads were obligated to await the commission's final decision. A&K's idea of breaking the logjam by introducing a non-railroad purchaser was the hingepoint of the ultimate GB&W sale.

GB&W's directors studied the offer for several days, choosing at first to stand by their BN cohorts as a point of honor. They were torn between the offer and an opportunity to increase their net worth by 50%.

Texido brought his formal papers to Green Bay on November 22nd after a month's deliberation by GB&W. The San Francisco firm maintained that it would keep the railroad intact, changing nothing but its ownership. A week later BN announced its withdrawal from the battle and Brae received the securities from BN's escrow depository, Kellogg-Citizen's National Bank of Green Bay. Itel, aware of BN's withdrawal, decided to enter the fray with its own offer. Itel wanted to acquire GB&W by purchase of assets or by a merger action for $5,800,000, subject to ICC consideration. Itel indicated that it might offer up to

William Texido of Itel Corporation's SSI Rail Division brought several newly created short line railroad lease car operations to his company. He was unable to interest Itel in buying GB&W so he formed Brae Corporation on August 7, 1977. While The Three had conceded to keep GB&W intact in their struggle to August 4, 1977, a ploy to ease the GB&W's concern, a non-railroad like Brae could acquire GB&W if approved by the railroad's owners alone, Weldon McGee was visited by Texido, with his firm's offer October 17, 1977. Brae offered to buy GB&W capital stock at $150 per share, the "A" debentures at $1,000 per share and the "B" debentures at $4275. Texido's offer was to expire at 5 p.m., December 2, 1977.

$225 per capital stock share, $1,000 per "A" debenture and $275 per "B" share, matching Brae's offer.

On November 29th the GB&W directorate met in New York, ultimately confirming the Brae scheme, yet aware of the Itel offer. GB&W's main concern was to move away from ICC actions which in essence had produced a stalemate. At the end of November Itel's offer to President McGee was met with concern, as Itel held firm and put its staff into action to acquire GB&W.

In early December Itel and Brae's Washington attorneys opposed each other as Itel attempted to gain ICC approval of a voting trust plan. By December 7th Brae had increased its offer

Right: When new, 310 stirred the imagination as it hissed powerfully across the GB&W landscape, its exhaust noticeably louder than attending 500-series cab units. It was the beginning of the second-generation, albeit temperamental. Here, No.310 stands at Wisconsin Rapids on October 12, 1961.
STAN MAILER PHOTO

Right: GB&W rebuilt former Long Island Rail Road unit 207 for client Little Rock & Western Railroad, controlled by Green Bay Packaging. Here, LRWN 101 tested on the Day Kewaunee Train, before shipment to Arkansas. GB&W leased two RS-20's to LRWN previously. The date is December 20, 1982.
STAN MAILER PHOTO

Left: The "day Kewaunee job" switches the carferry on July 11, 1966.
M. DUNN PHOTO

Right: A regular 1970's "herd" gets underway west of the old Milwaukee Hudson Street interchange on October 20, 1973. Units 315-305-316 had machinery grey-painted trucks. C-430 No.315 is presently on display at Green Bay's railroad museum.
STAN MAILER PHOTO

J. SCRIBBINS PHOTO

STAN MAILER COLLECTION

to partially equal Itel's last bid, raising its "A" and "B" debenture figures by $50 and $25 respectively. McGee's meeting with Itel men the next day included the report that GB&W's board had approved the Brae offer which matched Itel's. A further upward bid by Itel prevailed, however, prompting GB&W's board to stand down from its earlier recommendation of the Brae offer. By December 14th Itel had bid and won GB&W with an offer of $330 per unit of capital stock, the "A" debentures for $1050 and the "B" debentures for $325 each. Brae backed out of the contest after contending the action before the ICC to block the sale of securities. By Spring 1978 Itel and Brae had settled some of their differences, in particular an argument over monopolization of freight car leasing to short lines. Ironically, Milwaukee Road, one of the three strongmen opposing BN with a monetary offer, filed for bankruptcy December 18, 1977, a troubled and fatigued giant among mid-western roads.

In the final round GB&W's 230 shareholders accepted Itel's voting trust arrangement for about $8 million and formal application to ICC was made by late January 1978. President McGee was asked to remain at the helm during the transition period. He indicated that ICC approval would be a routine matter, as 99%

Top Left: Brand-new RS-11 No.309 switches at KGB&W's ferry yard on August 3, 1958. The unit originally was laid out with its long hood at the front end. When rebuilt in 1964, its power rating was raised to 2000 horsepower and it was changed to the chopped-nose, short-end-ahead format. No.309 was the first "251" series ALCO engine on the property.

Bottom Left: The search for motive power in the mid-1970's proved frustrating. Soo Line's 415-416 were priced too high and E-L C-425's were sold en masse to BCR. Finally, nomadic ex-C&NW RS-27 No.901 was acquired from Precision National's Canadian subsidiary at a cost of $47,500. Here, it's seen in June 1975 moving to Norwood's paint shop to become No.318.

Above Right: Running on Milwaukee tracks after a bad washout at Mile 188, GB&W's No.2 is "Extra 312 East" as far as the big road is concerned. Ironically, Extra 312 is easing past Grand Crossing tower, which also governed GB&W's La Crosse branch trains until 1922. This August 26, 1975 scene is on the east end of Milwaukee's La Crosse yard at the BN crossing.

of the 18,000 capital shares were tendered, with 6,376 of the "B" debentures. McGee was the largest individual shareholder with 3,730 shares of capital stock. The three members of the Board of Directors, Charles W. Cox, Richard B. Wilson and John Winthrop of New Jersey and New York, all descendants of the ancient capitalists, or their assigns, held 5,344 shares, about 29% of the total outstanding shares.

In the midst of the excitement GB&W incurred a near disaster on the 86-year old Winona Bridge. At 5:30 a.m. on December 9, 1977, during what had been a bitter cold winter, two diesel units moved onto the swingspan and derailed. While tow boats raced to beat sub-zero conditions and a river freeze-up below, GB&W's veteran roadmaster Leonard Wolfe and associates were required to inch their way along the outside of the track with re-railing frogs. River traffic was backed up, intent on releasing barges for the winter and making a dash for safe winter tie-up. After hours of difficulty, train No. 1 rolled safely across the span.

Itel operated a fleet of 40,000 leased box cars which dovetailed conveniently with their new investment in GB&W. The 1970's were remembered for a proliferation of new rail cars owned by lease firms which sported names of small roads too short to receive their whole car fleets. The firm moved into the field from computer leasing. A sharp decline in boxcar suppliers spawned government intervention (RAILBOX) and finally adjusted car rules in 1970. Itel moved to arrange financing of new cars for needy roads with ownership split among the designated carriers. It did so cautiously and decided to buy a few small railroads to keep surplus cars busy. Controlled were Hartford & Slocum (Alabama), McCloud River (California) and Ahnapee & Western Railroads. A&W rejoined GB&W in the 1980's.

During the sale year GB&W suffered C&O's continuing pressure to vacate the lake, citing $5 million losses at hearings held in February. Subsidies as a panacea prevailed and plans for a tug-barge project were begun June 4, 1979. Designed to reduce marine manpower to acceptable proportions, it included four barges and two tugs which were to be built by Upper Peninsula Shipbuilding Co. of Ontonagon, Michigan. The order, ironically, was partly introduced to help alleviate the north country's unemployment situation. The questionable design became entangled in contract litigation between UPSCO and the state of Michigan, the latter involved to at least $41 million. The one tug and one barge completed were sold for service elsewhere after the complete cost of discharging the old ferries was made clear.

The Day Kewaunee Job eases across the historic Fox River swingspan in Green Bay. Joint C&NW - GB&W ownership allowed Kewaunee Division's main line east and both roads access to important paper mill traffic along N. Quincy Street which is in the distance in this September 1976 photo.
STAN MAILER PHOTO

Probably the first time a General Motors locomotive ever entered Norwood Shops was the occasion of a Conrail unit's needs, a leased unit serving a feeder road. E&LS now extends to Green Bay, and the work was required on the six-motor unit on October 30, 1980.
STAN MAILER PHOTO

VIKING gets underway from Kewaunee as RS-27 No.317 begins its 36-mile trek to Green Bay in 1972.
FRED TONNE PHOTO

302

On October 31st H. Weldon McGee retired from the presidency of Green Bay & Western. He was succeeded by Joseph Galassi, a former assistant to Burlington Northern's vice-president of operations. No stranger to GB&W affairs, Galassi was involved in the ICC hearings during the BN-GB&W merger negotiations. The new man in Green Bay would pilot GB&W until June 1, 1981 when he accepted a higher position in BN at Minneapolis.

Upon his retirement, President McGee circulated a letter reflecting his life's work:

All employees:

Having been born into railroading and after completing a career of forty-three satisfying years on the Green Bay & Western, I am anticipating an interesting change in my life-style with my retirement November 1.

Amongst my experiences, I value highly the many fine friends I have made on the railroad and the great privilege I have had working with each of you as well as those who have retired. Anything worthwhile which I have accomplished was a direct result of having the support and cooperation of such an exceptional group of people. Individually and collectively, you helped make my job a pleasure, and for this I offer my sincere thanks and appreciation.

Best wishes to you and the Green Bay & Western for continued success.

— H. Weldon McGee

When Itel came to Green Bay its great fleet of boxcars immediately began to ease car shortages for GB&W customers. Succeeding years found ferry service a costly, unresolved affair as Michigan was concerned with potential loss of rail mileage due to cross-lake route abandonment. In 1979, however, Michigan Northern Railroad, a Conrail spinoff operator, managed to net several month's worth of Canadian potash trains it won away from Soo Line. MN chose to maintain lower rates which attracted Canadian shippers and the traffic came over GB&W from Plover to Kewaunee. The heavy extras taxed GB&W's Centuries, evidenced by conductors' entries of gross tonnage figures rivaling ore drags.

GB&W acquired two stop-gap ALCO locomotives, 25-year veterans, and investigated a new source of 2400-horsepower ALCO's coming from Conrail overstocks. In late 1979 GB&W acquired five Centuries, rebuilt by General Electric Apparatus, an English firm based in Hornell, New York. All were in service by March 21, 1980 but they were too late for the potash trains which ended by agreement with shippers. GB&W acquired a new customer at Taylor, Badger Mining Corporation's silica sand find, which had a large supply. A new pulpwood landing at Sechlerville (Kress) began to supply Green Bay paper mills with the raw material. GB&W appeared to be one of Itel's better investments, since it had recently suffered heavy losses from its computer business.

Reflecting on his last day in office, President Galassi in mid-1981 said GB&W's position was competitive and plans for the future included coal. GB&W was handling a twenty-car unit train to Wisconsin Rapids. Interest in developing a facility at Kewaunee for western coal continued but later was opposed by environmentalists. GB&W was studying the idea of vacating the Winona Bridge in favor of run-throughs to La Crosse over BN tracks from East Winona. Cars for Winona would be back-hauled on Milwaukee Road. Since the twelve-hour service law

Train No. 2 nears the high point of GB&W (Mile 75) east of Arnott in November of 1974.

STAN MAILER COLLECTION

might be violated in going to La Crosse, management was reluctant to use four crews west of Green Bay. Galassi indicated that $52 million was spent to date on the Michigan tug-barge effort and an additional hitch requiring another $4 million for docking aprons. GB&W was not interested in spending the same amount at Kewaunee. The oncoming Republican spending freeze would curtail any available federal monies. GB&W now felt that every car counted, no traffic downstaging any other business.

Throughout the troubled 1980's GB&W's stalwart ALCO's have continued to trace a path into the western sun, showing traditionally clean red flanks in Wisconsin pine lands. Its trains are slower now than in the 1960's, burdened with less hustle-ori-ented commodities. It relies no longer upon the Winona Bridge to deliver vital auto shipments to the old Wall Street interchange, through a now-abandoned Bridge Yard, destined to be a Winona Park. The great bridge, approaching its 100th year, stands eternally open to conquering river traffic, devoid of utility. Most of GB&W's problems of the 1970's and 1980's were legal battles, too wearying to recall, changing little the vital need for Michigan ferry service. The ferry now is ex-C&O, that company relieved of the burden of malignant cost. Michigan-Wisconsin Transportation Co., confident of success in operating the MIDLAND to Kewaunee, caters to auto-tourists in the summer, secondarily to boxcars.

Above: Former GB&W S-2 No.201, a 1000-horsepower yard unit, was sold to Wisconsin Power & Light Co. for use as a robot at their Sheboygan (Creekside) power plant to switch unit coal cars to unloaders.
STAN MAILER PHOTO

Left: Converted RS-11 No.309 and RS-20 No.305 work the ferry landing at Kewaunee in February 1974. No.309 had become a favorite of many and eventually was named H. W. McGEE. C-424 No.312 became H. E. McGEE, honoring the first of two administrations since 1934.
STAN MAILER PHOTO

Bottom Left: The Day Kewaunee Run bears down on New Franken, Wisconsin, 13 miles east of Green Bay, on October 31, 1980.
STAN MAILER PHOTO

Below: The Day Kewaunee Job has made a side trip to Algoma on the Ah&W to service the mill. The depot, at the time of this 1974 photo, was an office for the separately managed short line. It was razed several years later.
STAN MAILER PHOTO

Today, in a deregulated atmosphere, transportation companies compete vigorously. Rail empires larger and grander than GB&W have fallen apart, their entrails salvaged by short line operators happy to have the business, unmindful of the disgrace of the fallen. GB&W faces possible merger again, perhaps with pieces of dismembered rival North Western. But elements of this too await squadrons of lawyers and careful examination. Resale of GB&W is not out of the question, either. Both Burlington Northern and Soo have re-examined its case in the 1980's, feeding the eternal short line rumor mill. ALCO diesels remain in daily service, maintained expertly by a small staff of recognized professionals and suppliers. New business includes Consolidated Papers additions at Biron. But Moses Taylor, Sam Sloan and John Blair would probably join Homer Edgar McGee and H. Weldon McGee in bountiful pride, even Texas-style, in the Green Bay & Western Railroad.

Left: No. 2 clanks across C&NW (former Omaha Road) at Merrillan en route to Wisconsin Rapids on January 5, 1976.
STAN MAILER PHOTO

Below: A fast-moving "Manawa turn" (train No. 7) skates past Mile 22 in sub-zero weather, as it handles some "short cars" (local loads) to the towns east of Plover in December 1972. No. 7 made the transfers at Black Creek, New London and Amherst Junction, relieving trains 1-2 of excessive time on the road.
STAN MAILER PHOTO

Above: For nearly a year, GB&W stabled ex-C&NW 902-903, two RS-27's which were eventually purchased. The pair were regularly assigned to train No. 7 and could not be operated with other GB&W units due to the outdated GB&W MU schedule. After their purchase, the units became 316-317, receiving the changes for standardization, and were given the first all-red paint job. Under Itel ownership, the "elephant's trunk" MU schedule was changed, allowing GB&W units to "multiple" with any other road's power. No. 902-903 are shown here, westbound at Amherst Jct., on March 17, 1967.
JIM SCRIBBINS PHOTO

19

GBW PICTORIAL

Left: GB&W's C-430 No. 315 leads the way as Train No. 2 rolls eastward at Mile 47 between Manawa and Royalton in the summer of 1973.

Below: D-47's No. 401 and No. 403 were on duty at Norwood on April 14, 1947. Steam had only two more years to live on GB&W.

Above: In this 1940 scene at Merrillan, the manual gates for GB&W are protecting the Omaha Road's main line. GB&W's water tank and a joint freighthouse depict a distant mode at the junction town. The depot remains today.

Left: Under construction at ALCo's Schnectady, New York works, Mike 403 has been "wheeled" and is only weeks away from its first duty in March of 1937.
ALCo HISTORIC PHOTO

Right: Train No. 2 was stopped at Merrillan, its mail car spotted on the joint depot platform. California's Robert M. Hanft caught the new engine on November 6, 1940.
ROBERT M. HANFT PHOTO

Above: Only several days after its arrival in March 1937, Mikado 402 was photographed by Green Bay's C.B. Knistern at the Norwood penstock.

Below: Just in fron Kewaunee, 402 eases along near North Quincy Street alongside Eastman Avenue on Green Bay's east side.

H. F. BRADEN PHOTO

Above: Late in the steam game, Mike 402 races through Pamperin Park west of Green Bay on Train 8.
B. ERICKSON PHOTO

Below: In 1955, all six 400-class Mikes were banished to Milwaukee's yard in Green Bay. In early 1956, almost six years after being silenced, they were taken to steel mills in Gary, Indiana.
C. B. KNISKERN PHOTO

*A&W's Mogul 259 was pulled out in the rain for a
Chicago fan club on September 18, 1938.*

*The last Raidler rebuild, No.18, worked out its life at
Waupaca. Both Neil Torssell (above) and Chicagoan Harold Lehman (below) photographed 18 during the hot
summer of 1935.*

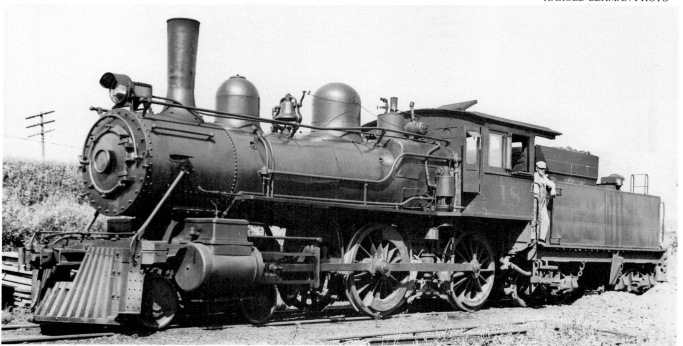

GB&W had three coaldocks. Two of them, located at Norwood (below) and Wisconsin Rapids (left), were local landmarks. Taken from the rear platform of Train No.1 in 1940, the "Rapids" structure stands above 0-6-0 No.140 as it switches the mixed train's rear portion. Below, in the fall of 1950, Mikes 401 and 402 await their fate after steam's end.

EARL RUHLAND PHOTO / STAN MAILER PHOTO

Single unit days: Beginning their road dieselization with just three ALCo FA-1 cabs, units 501-503 were utilized to the maximum. Above: Jim Scribbins photographed train No.1 (unit 501) from train No.2 (and 502) meeting June 3, 1948 at Oneida. No.2 had 57 loads and three empties, averaging forty miles per hour from Winona to Green Bay. Right: 501 and well-wishers ready No.2 at Bridge Yard in early 1948. Below: "Railway Age" editor Robert G. Lewis photographed another 500-class at Kewaunee's wye en route from the Ferry Yard the same year. Left: GBW No.4 (unit 506) is eastbound on November 22, 1959, east of Merrillan. BRUCE MEYER PHOTO

Above: VIKING's 21 m.p.h. passage in Lake Michigan is no longer a daily occurrence. This photo captured the crew in the wheelhouse during its active years.
STAN MAILER PHOTO

Right & Below: A brand-new rebuild, RS-20 No. 305, worked a regular boat just days after leaving Norwood's backshop. It did the chores at Kewaunee, pulling cars from ARTHUR K. ATKINSON. The date was July 5, 1973.
STAN MAILER PHOTOS

Above: The Day Kewaunee Train, after a side trip to Algoma in March of 1974, approaches Casco on now-abandoned trackage.

Left: On March 14, 1980 new "Hornell units" 320-321 rolled ashore for their first moments on Wisconsin's shore.

Right: Ann Arbor No.5 negotiates a heavily iced channel at Frankfort during the 1930's. The port was often jammed with ice in winter.

Below: Interurban-like running on Winona's Wall Street Milwaukee interchange by GB&W is now concluded, since Winona Bridge was vacated.

ALL STAN MAILER PHOTOS

Above: GB&W's shop crew uses A&W Mogul 72 as a backdrop in this photo taken during the Great Depression.

Below: GB&W often hosted railfan excursions. In 1948 the Railroad Club of Chicago's trip included 500's No. 403 and No. 256.

Left: One of several contract jobs done in the 1970's was an ex-LS&I RS-3 for Continental Grain Co.
STAN MAILER PHOTO

Top Right: GB&W rebuilt two C-420's for Green Bay Packaging's Little Rock & Western (Arkansas). Ex-L&N No.1309 goes to the load box at Norwood on April 25, 1983.
STAN MAILER PHOTO

Right: GB&W began the 1980's with a lease program for five rebuilt ALCo Centuries, the first ever for GB&W. Units 320 and 321 were "load-boxed" on March 19, 1980.
STAN MAILER PHOTO

322

Green Bay's Fox River swingspan was occupied by GB&W's first diesel 101, en route from eastside paper mills. Above, nearing its sale date, RS-2 No.304 idles in Green Bay's "Cheese House District."

Above: A regular meet point for Train No.1 and No.2 was Manawa, where four Centuries met on April 27, 1976. No.313 and No.314 are seen in the foreground with 312 and 315 in the distance.

Above: Reliving the great fast train days of GB&W, a "Manawa Turn" bears down on Mile 22, leaving a plume of powdered snow rising in its wake. The units this day in December of 1972 were 310-313.

Above: The first run of "the Homer" is shown here. Under ITEL ownership, two units (312 and 309) were named for presidents. The unique paint job of 312 was first shown on February 25, 1982.

No. 314 was the last new C-424 delivered to GB&W.
ALCo HISTORICAL PHOTO

Left: DL-640-A 3ll was an eyecatching display for ALCo at a Chicago trade show in 1963.

Below: No.2 crosses the Yellow River bridge at Dexterville on February 11, 1977. The unusual steel design was from Wisconsin Bridge & Iron Co.
STAN MAILER PHOTO

One of GB&W's venerable Haskell & Barker cars occupied a rail
yard in Milwaukee shortly after its construction in 1910.

After many seasons, GB&W's lone steam
survivor, No. 350, was inched out of a Wisconsin Rapids park by volunteers of Mid-
Continent Railway Museum on October 10,
1981. Backdated to No. 49, the 2-8-0 awaited
contributions to restore it at North Freedom.
Below, the survivor served Consolidated
Water Power & Paper Co. at Wisconsin
Rapids between 1950 and 1955.

Unit 305 left Kewaunee's Ferry Yard on July 5, 1973.

STAN MAILER COLLECTION

ROSTERS

WINONA   SEPT. 4, 1944   A. ROBERT JOHNSON PHOTO

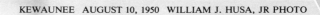

KEWAUNEE   AUGUST 10, 1950   WILLIAM J. HUSA, JR PHOTO

Iola & Northern Railroad Co.
LOCOMOTIVE ROSTER

NUMBER	NAME	WHYTE ARRANGEMENT	BUILDER	DATE	REMARKS
1		4-4-0	Grant	1872	Probably ex-GBW&STP No. 4 MOSES TAYLOR; No. 1 traded to GB&W for No. 2, date unknown.
2		4-4-0	Danforth	1875	Ex-GB&M first No. 16; to GB&M 13, to I&N 2; to GB&W 2, then GB&W 7, all at unknown dates. Scrapped 1920's.

Waupaca-Green Bay Railway
LOCOMOTIVE ROSTER

NUMBER	NAME	WHYTE ARRANGEMENT	BUILDER	DATE	REMARKS
1		4-4-0	Dickson #231	April 1879	Ex-GB&M No. 17 MISSISSIPPI; To W-GB 2/1/09; ret'd 1915.
2		4-4-0 17×24″	Schenectady #2027	1885	Sold to W-GB 10/1913; ex-Soo 2007, ex-WC 65; to GB&W second No. 8; scrapped 1936 by Betten's.

Winona & South-Western Railway
LOCOMOTIVE ROSTER

NUMBER	NAME	WHYTE ARRANGEMENT	BUILDER	DATE	REMARKS
1	WINONA	4-4-0	Rogers	?	Used engine
2	H. W. LAMBERTON	4-4-0	Brooks #1546	June 1889	Built as Davenport, Iowa & Dakota RR No. 1; to W&SW No. 2; to CGW 1120. Sold to Georgia Car & Loco. Co. in 1910 and became No. 137.
3	V. SIMPSON	4-4-0	Brooks #1665	May 1890	Built as W&SW No. 3; to CGW 1121 in 1903. Sold to GC&L 1910. To A&STAB No. 4.
4	M. G. NORTON	4-4-0	Brooks #1666	May 1890	Built as W&SW No. 4; to CGW 1122. Sold to GC&L in 1910.
5	W. H. LAIRD	4-4-0	Brooks #1901	June 1891	Built as W&SW No. 5; to CGW 1123 in 1903. Sold to GC&L in 1910.
6	E. S. YOUMANS	4-4-0	Brooks #1902	June 1891	Built as W&SW No. 6; to CGW 1124 in 1903. Sold to GC&L in 1910.
7		0-6-0	?	?	Acquired used from a Chicago equipment dealer in December 1892. Became CGW No. 410 in 1903. Scrapped in 1907.
8		4-4-0	Baldwin #3597	May 1874	Ex-STP&D No. 35; to CGW 1113 in 1903. Scrapped in 1906.

Ettrick & Northern (Ettrick Railroad Co.)
LOCOMOTIVE ROSTER

NUMBER	NAME	WHYTE ARRANGEMENT	BUILDER	DATE	REMARKS
10		4-6-0 17×24″	Brooks #2593	1895	Ex-NYCL #5099, sold via unknown dealer. 57′ drs., 10,800 lbs. wt. Scrapped Ettrick, 1930's? (Tender destroyed in landslide).
1		0-4-0 Gas-Mech.	Whitcomb LRX-1s	1928?	30-ton. Sold (?) to Iron & Steel Products, Chicago, Illinois.

La Crosse & Southeastern Railway
EQUIPMENT ROSTER

ENGINE NUMBER	WHYTE CLASS	ACQUIRED FROM	BUILDER	REMARKS
1	4-6-0(?)	Hicks/Chicago ca 4/1905	PRR (?)	Sold or traded for boxcars in Chicago
2	4-6-0	Hicks/Chicago ca 4/1905	PRR	Sold 1922/23 to Cazenovia Southern Ry. Cazenovia, Wis. Too heavy/scrapped.
3	4-6-0	Hicks? ca 4/1905	Brooks	Sent to Montana Western Ry. 1912?
4	4-4-0	CB&Q	A-2 Class	Sent to Montana Western Ry. 1912?
5	4-4-0	Union Pacific; to Hicks/Chicago; to PB&W		Sold to Pine Bluff & Western Ry. Pine Bluff, Arkansas 1910?
6	4-4-0	Central Loco & Car Works Chicago; Ex-New York Central Lines 600 series		From CL&CW 1912/13. Scrapped by CMSTP&P No. La Crosse, Wis. 1934-35.
7	4-6-0	Ex-CB&N 151, ex-CB&N 981; Ex-CB&Q 681 (1904) K-3 class; Hinkley-#1711, 1887; retired by CB&Q 2/1913.		Delivered about 1914. Scrapped by CMSTP&P No. La Crosse, Wis. 1934-35.
8	4-6-0	American Loco Co. Brooks Works #63166 Nov. 1921.		Purchased new. Scrapped by CMSTP&P No. La Crosse, Wis. 1934-35.
400	Railbus	Eklund Bros., Minneapolis Ca. 1920; White '45'.		Purchased new 1899; to CMSTP&P; scrapped N. La Crosse 1934.
402	Two-Truck Steam Car	Unit-Stanley-Laconia (Unit Ry. Car Co. Boston, Mass.) Body by Laconia Car Co.		Leased or loaned pending sale 1921 Trials 7/20 LCSE.
62	Two-Truck Gas Car	A. Meister & Sons, Sacramento, CA 1920 Type R-62; 40' 4" 31 seats; Buda SSU 60 HP gas.		Acquired from Ocean Shore RR California #62.

— PASSENGER CARS —

20, 21	Baggage	Hicks/Chicago		Single Door.
51	Combin.	Hicks/Chicago		Baggage/Smoker combination.
50, 52	Coaches	Hicks		Acquired through Hicks from Eastern Road 4/1905.
53	Parlor	Hicks?		12-wheel car; traded for freight cars.

Equipment Was Painted Pullman Green

— FREIGHT EQUIPMENT —

Flat Cars:				
Nos. 101-111, 115 (ONO)		Hicks?	40'	Wood/arch bar trucks. Convertible to gons.
Box Cars:				
Nos. 100-110 (ENO)		Hicks?	40'	Wood/40,000 Capy.
Nos. 120-138 (ENO)			40'	Wood/40,000 Capy.
No. 124			50'	Wood/50,000 Capy.
Stock Car:				
No. 126		Hicks?	?	Wood/?

Roster data from Mr. Peter Hensgen

(10/1906   3 box cars from Hicks: 36' 50M capy.)

The Ahnapee and Western Railway Company
LOCOMOTIVE ROSTER

NUMBER/CLASS			WHYTE	BUILDER/REMARKS
1			4-4-0	Grant 1872-4. Ex-GBWSTP; delivered 11-22-92. Traded to Hicks Loco & Car Works about 12-30-1902. Woodburner.
2 (1)			4-4-0	Ex-ICRR; acquired in Chicago December 1894. In service first week in 1895. Woodburner at outset. Changed to coal burner after short time. Later scrapped, traded or otherwise disposed of by 1898.
2 (2)			4-4-0	Baldwin #16334 17×24" 63" TF 14960 EX 79500 Nov. 1898. Renumbered 31 August 1906; Scrapped by Bettens November 1935.
3			4-4-0	Ex-Union Pacific, via Hicks Loco & Car Works; acquired Dec. 1902. Renumbered 33 August 1906; Out of service by 1911.
39	R		2-6-0	ALCO-Schen. 55143, June 1915; ALCO class 260-S-139; 19×26," 56," 180# 25640 TF, E&TW 182900#. Renumbered 71 1921; renumbered 259 1937; Sold with railroad to new company 6-1-47. Scrapped Chicago Jan. 1951. New class B-27.
72	R		2-6-0	ALCO-Schen. 63138, Oct. 1921; renumbered 260 4-37; sold with railroad to new company 6-1-47; scrapped Chicago April 1953. New class B-27.
74	R-1		2-8-0	ALCO #53790 July 1913; Ex-Chicago, Peoria & St. Louis Ry. #70; Purchased from Briggs & Turivas Chicago, $6450.00 (In Springfield, Ill.) Jan. 18, 1927; In service June 8, 1927. Renumbered 303 1-20-37, Class C-31. Sold 10-4-37 to Harry P. Bourke, Escanaba, Mich. "For $1.00 and other considerations." Became Escanaba & Lake Superior RR 18; Scrapped 1-53 Chicago.
261	C-43		2-8-0	Ex-KGB&W 45, class Z, 280-S-199 Alco-Brooks #64128 Jan. 1923. Renumbered 398, 5-1937; retired by GBW 10-48; renumbered 261, first operated by Ah&W Feb. 17, 1949. Last run 11-30-50. sold to Detroit Caro & Sandusky Ry., scrapped ca. 1952.
351	C-38		2-8-0	Ex-GB&W 69, class R-2, 280-S-174, ALCO-Schen. #67820, 12-1-29; Renumbered 351 June 1937 class C-38; sold Ah&W 11-15-50 $6000.00. First run 11-30-50. Last run early Feb. 1953. Scrapped after March 1956 in Chicago.
600	G-E	B-B	70-Tonner	General Electric 70-ton diesel, 600-HP Cooper-Bessemer engine; Built 12-52, #31727. Sold to Mexican firm, 1972.
601	G-E	B-B	70-Tonner	G-E 70-ton diesel, 600-HP Cooper-Bessemer engine. Built 1-53, #31728. Sold or transferred to Moscow, Camden & San Augustine RR, Camden, Texas, 1972.

STURGEON BAY   1898   STAN MAILER COLLECTION

STURGEON BAY   1952   CARL ULRICH PHOTO

PEORIA   OCT. 1925   HAROLD VOLLRATH COLLECTION

WELLS, MICHIGAN   1940   STAN MAILER COLLECTION

GREEN BAY   JULY 4, 1936   H. LEHMAN PHOTO

CAMDEN, ARKANSAS   JULY 11, 1981   W. C. BUHRMASTER

SAWYER   1960   HARMANN STUDIOS PHOTO

333

Kewaunee, Green Bay and Western Railway
LOCOMOTIVE ROSTER

NUMBER		TYPE (WHYTE)	BECKER	KIRKBY	BUILDER No.	DATE BUILT	REMARKS
1	(32)	4-4-0 17×24-63	G		Ex-PRR #653	1873	Scrap 1932. Class D-3; purch. New York Equipment Co. 3-1894, in service 4-94. Rebuilt GB&W/Raidler Belpaire boiler 1902, 52-ton engine; renumbered 32 in A&W/KGB&W merger Aug. 1906.
2	(34)	4-4-0 17×24-63	G		Brooks #731	1882	Scrap Dec. 12, 1925. Ex-Chicago & Erie 102? Sold via J. T. Gardner Co. 1896; renumbered 34 Aug. 1906.
35		4-4-0 17×24-63	G		GB&W	Dec. 1906	Scrap Jan. 3, 1936. Rebuilt from ???
36		2-6-0 19×26-56	I		ALCo-Sch. #46834	Dec. 1909	Scrap Apr. 1936
37		2-6-0 19×26-56	I		ALCo-Sch. #49688	Apr. 1911	Scrap Jan. 3, 1936
38	(257)	2-6-0 19×26-56	R	B-25	ALCo-Sch. #54888	Sep. 1914	Scrap July 1945 Engine 38 renumbered 257 4-1937.
39	(258)	2-6-0 19×26-56	R	B-25	ALCo-Sch. #63139	Aug. 1921	Scrap 1945 Engine 39 renumbered 258 5-1937.
40	(140)	0-6-0 19×26-51	M	A-28	ALCo-Sch. #51526	July 1912	Scrap May 1945. Engine 40 renumbered 140 4-1936.
41	(141)	0-6-0 20×26-51	M-1	A-31	ALCo-Brooks #37738	1905	Scrap Nov. 1941. General Equipment Co. Toledo, Ohio. $8900.00. 71 tons. Engine 41 renumbered 141 11-1935.
42	(142)	0-6-0 20×26-51	M-1	A-31	ALCo-Brooks	1902	Scrap May 1941. Ex-NYC 4382, B-55a #25532 Engine 42 renumbered 142 5-37. Purchased General Equipment Co., Cleveland, Ohio
44	(301)	2-8-0 20×26-55	R-1	C-31	ALCo #53797	Jul 1913	Scrap Sep. 1939. Purchased through Briggs & Turivas Co., from Chicago, Peoria & St. Louis (No. 78) in service 4-1927. Engine 44 renumbered 301 1-1937.
45	(398)	2-8-0 22×28-51	Z	C-43	ALCo-Brooks #64128	Jan 1923	$33,450.00. Scrap 1952. Engine 45 renumbered 398 5-1937; sold to A&WRy. 1950; sold to DC&SRy. 1951. Scrapped at Caro, Mich. 1952. Renumbered 261 on A&W.
49	(350)	2-8-0 21×28-55	R-2	C-38	ALCo-Sch. #67819		$34,000.00. Engine 49 renumbered to 350 11-1936. Sold to Consolidated Papers, Inc. Wisconsin Rapids, 11-1950, $9000.00. Preserved after 1955.
403		2-8-2 22×30-64		D-47 D-48	ALCO-Sch. #68779		First trip 2-20-37; last trip 3-8-50. Sold Betten's 11-1-52. Scrapped Chicago?.

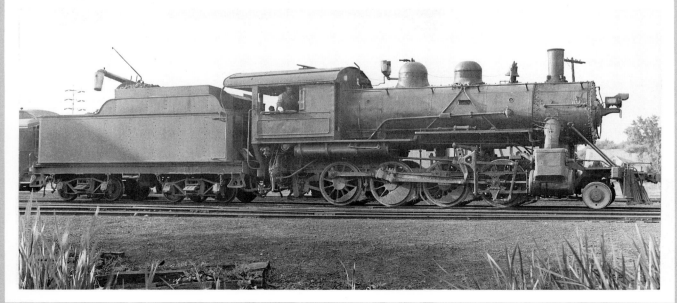

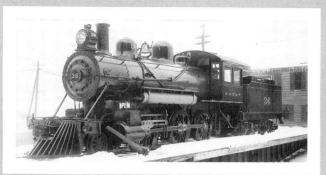

STURGEON BAY 1923 T. VAN DREESE COLLECTION

ALCo HISTORIC PHOTO

GREEN BAY 1928 STAN MAILER COLLECTION

ALCo HISTORIC PHOTO

GREEN BAY 1940 ED WILSON PHOTO

GB&M and GBW&STP
LOCOMOTIVE ROSTER to 1896

NUMBER	NAME	WHYTE ARRANGEMENT	BUILDER/NUMBER	DATE	REMARKS
1 (1)	ADVANCE	4-4-0	Lawrence?	1855?	Second hand; may have been CM&STP 11. Scrap by 1874.
1 (2)	DIAMOND JO	0-4-0	Grant	1874	Delivered 4/11/74. Scrap? $8000.00
2 (1)	SAMUEL MARSH	4-4-0	Grant	1871	$13,000.00. Rec'd 12/2/71. Scrap?
3 (1)	JOSEPH H. SCRANTON	4-4-0	Grant	1871	No. 3. Rec'd 12/2/71. Scrap?
3 (2)		0-4-0	Schenectady #3672	12/92	16×24" 50". Scrap 12/23.
4 (1)	MOSES TAYLOR	4-4-0	Grant	1872	Sold or scrap by 1899.
5 (1)	JOHN I. BLAIR	4-4-0	Grant	1872	$10,700. Sold or scrap by 1899.
6 (1)	GEORGE F. TALMAN	4-4-0	Grant	1872	Sold or scrap by 1910.
7 (1)	CHARLES RUSSELL	4-4-0	Grant	6/73	$12,325.00. Rec'd 6/11/73. Scrap?
8 (1)	WILLIAM E. DODGE	4-4-0	Grant #1068 ?	6/73	$12,250.00. Sold, scrap. Rec'd 6/13/73.
9 (1)	R. G. ROLSTON	4-4-0	Grant #1069 ?	6/73	$12,250.00. Rec'd 8/6/73. Scrap?
10 (1)	EDWIN F. HATFIELD JR.	4-4-0	Dickson #165	4/74	$10,000.00. Rebuilt 4/1901.
11 (1)	SAMUEL SLOAN	4-4-0	Dickson #166	4/74	$10,000.00. Rebuilt 11/1901.
12 (1)	ARTHUR BONDON	4-4-0	Dickson #167	4/74	$10,000.00. Rebuilt 10/1900.
13 (1)	JOSEPH C. PLATT	4-4-0	Danforth #1003	4/75	$8500.00. Formerly No. 16 (1)
14 (1)	PERCY R. PYNE	4-4-0	Danforth #1001	4/75	$8500.00. Rebuilt 5/1904.
15 (1)	THOMAS DICKSON	4-4-0	Danforth #1002	4/75	$8500.00. Rebuilt.
16 (1)	JOSEPH C. PLATT	4-4-0	Danforth #1003	4/75	$8500.00. Became No. 13 by 1879.
16 (2)	GREEN BAY	4-4-0	Dickson #230	4/79	Sold 3/9/07 to A&G Ry.
17 (1)	MISSISSIPPI	4-4-0	Dickson #231	4/79	Sold 2/1/09 to W-GB Ry.
18 (1)	GRAND RAPIDS	4-4-0	Danforth #1091 ?	10/79	$6500.00. Rebuilt.
19 (1)	FT. HOWARD	4-4-0	Danforth #1185	1879	$8386.91. Scrap 1924.
20 (1)		4-4-0	Schenectady #3507	6/91	$9304.00. Scrap 4/37.
21 (1)		4-4-0	Schenectady #3508	6/91	$9304.00. Scrap 3/36.
22 (1)		4-4-0	Schenectady #3509	6/91	$9304.00. Scrap 9/35.

— INCLUDES ALL LOCOMOTIVES ON THE ROSTER THROUGH 1896 —

Green Bay & Western Railroad
LOCOMOTIVE ROSTER (1896–1950)

NUMBER	TYPE (WHYTE)	BECKER	KIRKBY	BUILDER No.	DATE BUILT	REMARKS
1	0-4-0 16×24-48			Grant	3-1874	(Diamond Jo) Scrap ?
2 (2)	4-4-0			Danforth #1003	4-1875	Scrap 12-23. Originally 16(1); to No. 13; to I&N No. 2; to GB&W No. 2, then No. 7. Scrapped as No. 7.
3	0-4-0 16×24-50			ALCo-Sch. #3672	12-1892	Scrap 12-23.
4 (2)	0-6-0 17×24-51			Dickson #1097	12-1899	Scrap 10-34.
5 (2)	0-4-0 17×24-50			Pittsburgh	5-1898	Scrap 12-23. Purch. Hicks 4-28-04. 96,000 lbs. Origin?
6 (2)	0-6-0 19×26-52			Rome	?	Ex-UPRR? Purch. Hicks 6-1910. Sold Quacker Coal Co. 10-1924.
7 (2)	4-4-0			Danforth #1003	4-1875	See No. 2 (2).
8 (1)	4-4-0			Grant #1068	6-1873	Scrap 7-19.
8 (2)	4-4-0			Schenectady #2027	1885	Scrap 1-36. Ex-Wis. Central No. 65; to Soo Line No. 2007 in 1909; sold to W-GB (No. 2, Oct. 1913); into GB&W as No. 8 January 1922.
9	4-4-0			Grant #1069	6-1873	Scrap 12-10.
10 (2)	4-4-0 16×24-62			GB&W/Raidler	4-1901	Scrap 12-23. 77,800 lbs. GB&W/Raidler Rebuild.
11 (2)	4-4-0 16×24-62			GB&W/Raidler	11-01	Scrap 10-34. GB&W/Raidler Rebuild.
12 (2)	4-4-0 15×24-62			GB&W/Rdlr	10-1900	Scrap 12-23. 73,300 lbs. GB&W/Raidler Rebuild.
13	4-4-0			Danforth	4-1875	See No. 2 (2).
14 (2)	4-4-0 17×24-62			GB&W/Raidler	5-1904	Scrap 2-35. Raidler Rebuild.

No.	No.	Type / Cylinders	Class	Class	Builder	Date	Notes
15 (2)		4-4-0 17×24-62			GB&W/Raidler	7-1903	Scrap 1-2-34. GB&W/Raidler Rebuild.
16 (2)		4-4-0 16×24-62			Dickson #230	4-1879	Sold 3-9-1907 J. T. Gardner "A&G Ry."
17		4-4-0 16×24-62			Dickson #231	4-1879	Sold 2-1-1909 to W-GB Ry. as No. 1; scrap 1915?
18 (2)		4-4-0 18×24-62			GB&W/Raidler	7-1905	Scrap 12-39. GB&W/Raidler Rebuild.
19		4-4-0 17×24-62			Danforth #1185	10-1879	Scrap 1-24. 71,000 lbs.
20		4-4-0 17×24-63	D		Schenectady #3507	6-1891	$9304.00. Scrap 4-37.
21		4-4-0 17×24-63	D		Schenectady #3508	6-1891	$9304.00. Scrap 3-36.
22		4-4-0 17×24-63	D		Schenectady #3509	6-1891	$9304.00. Scrap 9-35.
23		4-4-0 17×24-63	D		Dickson #942	2-1897	$9488.00. Scrap 6-41.
24		4-4-0 17×24-63	D		Dickson #943	2-1897	$9488.00. Scrap 4-37.
25		4-4-0 17×24-63	D		Dickson #995	5-1898	$9695.00. Scrap 6-35.
26		4-4-0 17×24-63	D		Dickson #996	5-1898	$9695.00. Scrap 3-36.
27		2-6-0 19×26-56 (260-133)	J		ALCO-Sch. #44539	11-1907	128,000 lbs. Scrap 5-36.
28		2-6-0 19×26-56 (260-134)	J		ALCO-Sch. #45658	11-1908	128,000 lbs. Scrap 4-36.
29		2-6-0 19×26-56 (260-134)	J		ALCO-Sch. #49687	2-1911	128,000 lbs. Scrap 6-36.
30		2-6-0 19×26-56	J		ALCO-Sch. #51527	7-1912	136,000 lbs. Scrap 3-36.
50	250	2-6-0 19×26-56	J	B-27	ALCO-Sch. #52823	2-1913	136,000 lbs. Sold MT&W 5-15-39. Engine 50 rebuilt with Walschaerts Valve Gear, super-heater, universal valves, new flue sheets 4-6-35 completed, cost $7153.00. Renumbered 6-37 to 250; Sold Marinette, Tomahawk & W. for $3000. Scrap 5-53.
51	251	2-6-0 19×26-56	J	B-25	ALCO #54402	1-1914	Scrap 7-41. Engine 51 was last slide valve Mogul; renumbered 251 5-37.
52	252	2-6-0 19×26-56	R	B-27	ALCO-Sch. #54940	9-1914	141,000 lbs. Engine 52 renumbered to 252 1-37. "Modernized" 3-30-39. Scrap 10-48.
53	253	2-6-0 19×26-56	R	B-27	ALCO-Sch. #56298	9-1916	139,000 lbs. Engine 53 renumbered to 253 11-36. Scrap 10-48.
54		2-6-0 19×26-56	R		ALCO-Pitts. #59048	9-1918	139,000 lbs. Engine 54 was not renumbered; tender to engine 145. Scrap 4-37.
55	255	2-6-0 19×26-56	R	B-25	ALCO-Pitts. #59049	9-1918	139,000 lbs. Engine 55 was renumbered 3-37. Scrap 7-41.
56	256	2-6-0 19×26-56	R	B-25	ALCO-Sch. #65975	11-1924	141,000 lbs. $27,391.31. Engine 56 was renumbered 5-37; "Modernized" 4-20-39. Scrap 10-48.
60	145	0-6-0 19×26-50	M	A-28	ALCO #62632	1-1921	126,000 lbs. $35,050.00. Tender to KGB&W 142, tender from 54 Engine 60 was renumbered 2-37. "Modernized" 6-42. Sold to Consol. Water Power & Paper Co. 5-1948. Scrapped by CWPP 1951.
64	302	2-8-0 20×26-55	R-1	C-31	ALCO #53792	7-1913	$8353.00. Purch. 1927. Engine 64 was renumbered 10-36; Ex-Chicago, Peoria & St. Louis Ry. 72; purchased via Briggs & Turivas Co. Scrap 9-39.
65	399	2-8-0 22×28-51	Z	C-43	ALCO-Brooks #64127	1-1923	$33,450.00. Engine 65 was renumbered 12-36. "Modernized" 11-38. Scrap 1951.
69	351	2-8-0 21×28-56	R-2	C-38	ALCO-Sch. #67820	4-1929	Engine 69 was renumbered 6-37; sold to Ahnapee & Western as their 351, 1950. Scrapped about 1953.
80	146	0-6-0 19×26-50	M-1	A-28	Schenectady #5510	3-1900	$9650.00. Purch. 11-1922. 67 tons. Engine 80 was renumbered 1936; Ex-New York Central 313, B-2 class; Engine 80 rebuilt with superheater, Walschaerts Valve Gear, universal valves, new flue sheets, completed 1-1936; cost $6665.00. By 1937 tank from eng. 142 used, old tank sold to Oconto Co. for use on their engine 6; No. 6 scrapped at Carter, Wis. 1940. Scrap 11-41.
90	143	0-6-0	M-1	A-31	A.L.-Brooks #37726	8-1905	$8963.00. Purch. 12-1923. Engine 90 was renumbered 1937; Ex-LS&MS (New York Central) 4438, B-56-C class; Engine 90 superheated, front and rear flue sheets renewed 10-36. Power reverse. Scrap 11-47.
91	144	0-6-0	M-1	A-31	A.L.-Brooks #37737	8-1905	$8394.68. Purch. 7-24. 72 tons. Engine 91 was renumbered 1937; Ex-LS&MS (NYC) #4449, B-56-C class. Scrap 8-1941.
92	261	0-6-0/2-6-0 20½×28-56	M-1 R-1a	B-35	Baldwin #17125	10-1899	Purch. 10-1933. Engine 92 was renumbered 261 6-1935. Ex-Chicago & Alton 320 (2-6-0); rebuilt by C&A to 0-6-0 and renumbered 49, then 307. Sold to GB&W 1933; renumbered 92 as 0-6-0; Rebuilt as 2-6-0 92 and completed June 1935. Superheated with universal valves, boiler moved to original position. Renumbered 261 5-12-35. Work cost $14,800.00. Scrapped 1-1943.
401		2-8-2	D-47		ALCO	2-1937	Builder #68777
402		2-8-2	D-47		ALCO	2-1937	Builder #68778
404		2-8-2	D-47		ALCO	10-1939	Builder #69187
405		2-8-2	D-47		ALCO	10-1939	Builder #69188
406		2-8-2	D-47		ALCO	10-1939	Builder #69189

DEC. 1896 SCHENECTADY HIST. CENTER PHOTO

JAN. 1921 ALCo HISTORIC PHOTO

ALCo BUILDERS PHOTO

ALCo HISTORIC PHOTO

1935 GBW COLLECTION

SEPT. 30, 1939   ED WILSON PHOTO

NORWOOD   1936   WILLIAM MONYPENY COLLECTION

TOMAHAWK   1939   BOB HANFT PHOTO

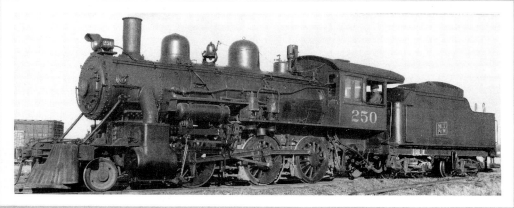

GREEN BAY   APRIL 20, 1940   ED WILSON PHOTO

Green Bay and Western Railroad
DIESEL LOCOMOTIVE ROSTER

ROAD & NUMBER		MODEL	HP	BUILDER'S NUMBER	DATE	REMARKS
GB&W	101	HH-600	600	69085	10/38	Sold United Electric Coal Corp; Liverpool, IL; resold Material Service, Corp., Romeoville, IL, No. 49-0159. Scrap 1976? Irv's Entrpr.
GB&W	102	S-1	600	76152	1/49	Sold Nekoosa-Edwards Paper Co., Pt. Edwards, WI 6/68, No. 12; Resold Cargill, Buffalo Lake, IA 1981.
KGB&W	103	S-1	600	69403	1/41	Sold Nekoosa-Edwards Paper Co., 3/68; re-#61, transferred to Ashdown, AR 2/70; Scrapped?
KGB&W	201	S-2	1000	75666	4/48	Sold after lease to Wisconsin Electric Power Co., Sheboygan, WI 6/68 Robot loco.
	301	RS-2	1500 1600	77914	2/50	Sold Railroad Builders, Inc.; Navajo, AZ 10/77. Resold Ann Arbor RR 1979.
	302	RS-2	1500 1600	77915	2/50	Scrapped 9/76. GB&W Betten's.
	303	RS-2	1500 1600	77916	2/50	Sold RRB, Inc. 1/14/78; Navajo, AZ; Resold to Ann Arbor RR 1979.
	304	RS-2	1500 1600	77917	2/50	Sold Michigan Northern (No. 1501) 10/76. Scrapped.
	305	RS-3	1500 1600	78856	5/51	Rebuilt to "RS-20" (2000 HP) 6/73. In service.
	306	RS-3	78857	1500 1600	5/51	Rebuilt to "RS-20" 2/76. In service.
	307	RS-3	1500 1600	81286	6/55	Rebuilt to "RS-20" 1/75. In service.
	308	RS-3	1500 1600	81287	6/55	Rebuilt to "RS-20" 4/74. In service.
KGB&W	309	RS-11	1800 2000	81931	8/56	Rebuilt in 1964 to 2000 HP. In service.
	310	RS-27	2400	83600	11/60	First RS-27 (DL-640). Scrapped 3/86.
	311	DL-640A	2400	84559	9/63	In service.
	312	C-424	2400	3375-01	7/64	In service.
	313	C-424	2400	3382-04	1/65	In service.
KGB&W	314	C-424	2400	3382-08	9/65	In service.
	315	C-430	3000	3498-01	2/68	Preserved 1987 (Green Bay).
	316	RS-27	2400	83604	3/62	Ex-C&N-W 903; leased, sold GB&W 10/68; ex-ALCO 640-5.
	317	RS-27	2400	83603	3/62	Ex-C&N-W 902; sold GB&W 2/21/69; scrap 11/84. ex-ALCO 640-4.
	318	RS-27	2400	83602	3/62	In service. Ex-C&NW 901; to Precision-National 901, to GB&W 5/11/76; ex-ALCO 640-2.
	319	C-424	2400	84558 Ord. No. 3358-16	9/63 2/8/80	Ex-PRR 2415, CONRAIL 2474. In service.
	320	C-424	2400	84553 Ord. No. 3358-12	6/63 3/19/80	Ex-E-L 2412, CONRAIL 2486. In service.
	321	C-424	2400	84557 Ord. No. 3358-15	6/63 3/19/80	Ex-E-L 2415, CONRAIL 2489. In service.
	322	C-424	2400	84733 Ord. No. 3367-1	10/63 3/?/80	Ex-Reading 5204, CONRAIL 2493. In service.
	323	C-420	2000	3463-1	2/66 12/18/79	Ex-Lehigh & Hudson River 27, CONRAIL 2475. In service.
KGB&W	501	FA-1	1500 1600	73679	12/47	Scrap 2/64.
KGB&W	502	FA-1	1500 1600	73680	12/47	Scrap 2/65.
KGB&W	503	FA-1	1500 1600	76836	4/49	Scrap 11/65.
GB&W	506	FA-1	1500 1600	73681	12/47	Scrap 8/60; renumbered from 503 4/49.
GB&W	507	FA-1	1500 1600	76837	4/49	Scrap 5/63.

EW	207	C-420	2000	84729	2/64 leased by GBW 10/79	1) Ex-Long Island; 2) Ex-Erie Western; 3) GBW 207; rebuilt to Little Rock & Western 101, shipped 12/26/82.
CC	1201	S-6	900	80934	Leased 4/79 to 7/79 to NEPCo.)	Ex-SP 1201; via Chrome Crankshaft Co.; resold James River Co., Green Bay.

GREEN BAY   FEB. 1948   HANK LEFEBVRE PHOTO

GREEN BAY   OCT. 29, 1938   C. B. KNISKERN PHOTO

341

GREEN BAY 1947 ROBERT G. LEWIS PHOTO

BIRON, WISCONSIN MAY 1975 STAN MAILER PHOTO

CASCO JUNCTION JULY 14, 1954 C. C. TINKHAM PHOTO

GREEN BAY   JULY 1958   R. McLEOD PHOTO

GREEN BAY   STAN MAILER PHOTO

NORWOOD   MARCH 7, 1980   STAN MAILER PHOTO

343

KEWAUNEE   JUNE 1979   STAN MAILER PHOTO

GREEN BAY   FEB. 25, 1982   STAN MAILER PHOTO

WISCONSIN RAPIDS   NOV. 1974   STAN MAILER PHOTO

344

MISCELLANEOUS CAR PHOTOS

GOLDEN VALLEY, MINN.   1963   BRUCE BLACK PHOTO

GREEN BAY   JAN. 1936   GBW COLLECTION

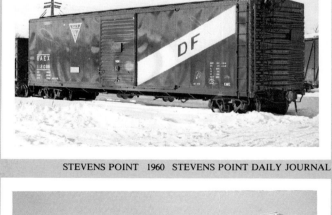

STEVENS POINT   1960   STEVENS POINT DAILY JOURNAL

STURGEON BAY   SEPT. 1950   STAN MAILER PHOTO

GREEN BAY   JULY 21, 1964   C. C. TINKHAM PHOTO

WISCONSIN RAPIDS   AUGUST 16, 1947   JIM SCRIBBINS

GREEN BAY   APRIL 22, 1939   ED WILSON PHOTO

WINONA   1949   NEIL TORSSELL

MEEHAN, WISC. 1927   JOHN L. SPURR PHOTO

NEW FRANKEN   1940   E. RUHLAND PHOTO

PRAY 1937 B. ERICKSON PHOTO

DEPOT RETIREMENT SCHEDULE
Green Bay & Western Lines

Station	MP	Type	Notes		Station	MP	Type	Notes
Sturgeon Bay	MP 57	PF	(standing)		Arnott	MP 76	PF 1912 20×36	2/57
Sawyer	MP 56	PF	(standing)		Plover	MP 82	PF 1898, 1921	1/23, 2/59
Maplewood	MP 48	PF	1946		Meehan	MP 85	PF 1912	1/35
Forestville	MP 44	PF	194★		Wisconsin Rapids	MP 95	PF 1886 24×40	1959
Algoma	MP 37	PF	1980				(Frt Hse 1912)	
Rio Creek	MP 31	P	191?		Walker	MP 104		6/54
Casco	MP 26	PF	1961		Elm Lake	MP 105	PF 1912 24×36	
Casco Junction	MP 23	PF	1940		Dexterville	MP 110	PF 18×36 Burned	6/48
Clyde	MP	P Boxcar body	192?				Boxcar bodies (2)	
Kewaunee	MP 37	PF	6/57 (standing)		Scranton	MP 116	Boxcar body	4/47
Luxemburg	MP 19	PF	1940		City Point	MP 121	PF 1898 18×40	8/61
New Franken	MP 13	PF	1935				F 1886, 16×30	
Summit	MP 10	P?	?		Spaulding	MP 125	?	
Haevers	MP	P Boxcar body	3/39		Pray	MP 130	PF 1903 18×36	6/48 (Standing)
Green Bay	MP	PF 1900, 1902, 1915	2/11/77		Waterbury	MP 135	Platform	1934
Elms	MP 6	?	?		Clay	MP 140	Platform	1934
Oneida	MP 10	P 1896 20×40	4/46		Hatfield	MP 142	PF 1909 18×36	6/47 (Standing)
Seymour	MP 17	P 1915, 1909, 1915	(standing)		Alma Center	MP 152	PF 1874 24×56	7/60 (sold, standing to 1970's)
Black Creek	MP 23	PF 1896 20×40	New 3/55 (standing)		Hixton	MP 158	PF 1874 30×60	4/63 (standing)
Black Creek Jct.	MP 24				Taylor	MP 165	PF 1903 20×50	4/46, 1/54 (moved)
Shiocton	MP 30	PF 1874 30×68	10/60		Blair	MP 171	PF 1874 30×62	1963 (standing, moved)
New London Jct.	MP 39	PF 50% ownership	6/46		Whitehall	MP 178	PF 1914 30×62	11/63 (sold, standing)
New London	MP 39	PF 1904	Moved 1945, 1970		Independence	MP 184	PF 1874 26×60	6/62
Northport	MP 42	PF 1894 16×32	1936		Arcadia	MP 192	PF 1874 30×60	(moved, standing)
Royalton	MP 46	PF 1873 24×54	1/45 (box car to 1957)		Pass Siding	MP 199		
Manawa	MP 50	PF 1898 24×64	6/51 (standing)		Dodge	MP 204	PF 1912 20×40	6/48
Ogdensburg	MP 55	PF 1872 24×40	7/45		Dooney's Siding	MP 199	Chute/runway 4×20	
Scandinavia	MP 61		11/54		Marshland	MP 209	PF 1890 20×40	6/48
Iola	MP 66	PF 1898 20×56	Standing (museum)		East Winona	MP 212	P 1889 ?	
Rowe's	MP	P 1908	1947		Winona	MP 214	1889, 1939	(standing — ex-CB&Q station)
Waupaca	MP 70	PF 1908	1947 (standing to 1980)		La Crosse	MP 239	PB 1878 26×56	in 1970's
Amherst Junction	MP 70	PF 1900 24×64	1932, 1974? (moved)				F 1878 24×80	
Lake Emily	MP 71	Box car body			Stevens Point	MP 87	PB 1896 24×56	1963
Fancher	MP	PF ? ? ?					F 1899 24×78	

Index

— Bibliography —

KOHLMEYER, F. W. *Timber Roots: The Laird, Norton Story, 1855-1905.* 1972, Winona County Historical Society
LEIPOLD, L. E. *Win Stephens: Business and Civic Leader.* 1969, T. S. Denison & Co., Inc., Minneapolis
OVERTON, R. C. *Burlington Route: A History of the Burlington Lines.* 1976, Lincoln, The University of Nebraska Press
GRODINSKY, JULIUS *Transcontinental Railway Strategy: 1869-1893.* 1962, Philadelphia, The University of Pennsylvania Press
DERLETH, AUGUST *The Milwaukee Road: Its First Hundred Years.* 1948, New York, Creative Age Press
HIDY, R. W., HILL, F. E., NEVINS, ALLAN *Timber & Men: The Weyerhaeuser Story.* 1963, New York, MacMillan & Co.
MARTIN, ROY L. *History of the Wisconsin Central.* 1941, New York, New York University Press
HODAS, DANIEL *The Business Career of Moses Taylor.* 1976, New York, New York University Press.
TABER, T. T. III *The DL&WRR In The 20th Century,* Vols. I, II, III. 1979, 1980, 1981, Muncy, Pennsylvania
HILTON, G. W. *The Great Lakes Car Ferries.* 1962, Berkeley, California. Howell-North
MERK, F. *Economic History of Wisconsin During The Civil War Decade.* 1971, Madison. The State Historical Society of Wisconsin
NESBITT, R. C. *The History of Wisconsin, Vol. III.* 1985, Madison. The State Historical Society of Wisconsin
CASEY. R. J., DOUGLAS W. A. S. *The Lackawanna Story.* 1951, New York. McGraw-Hill.
STEPHENSON, I. *Recollections of a Long Life: 1829-1915.* 1915. Chicago (privately printed)
MORGAN, DAN *Merchants of Grain.* 1980. Penguin Books
STOVER, J. F. *American Railroads.* 1961, Chicago University of Chicago Press

Periodicals: *The Winona Republican, Arcadia News-Leader, La Crosse Tribune, Green Bay Press-Gazette, Green Bay Advocate, Algoma Herald, Plover Times, Blair Press, Door County Advocate, Kewaunee Enterprise, Waupaca Post, Manitowoc Pilot, Commercial & Financial Chronicle, Wabasha Herald, La Crosse Tribune*

GREEN BAY ROUTE

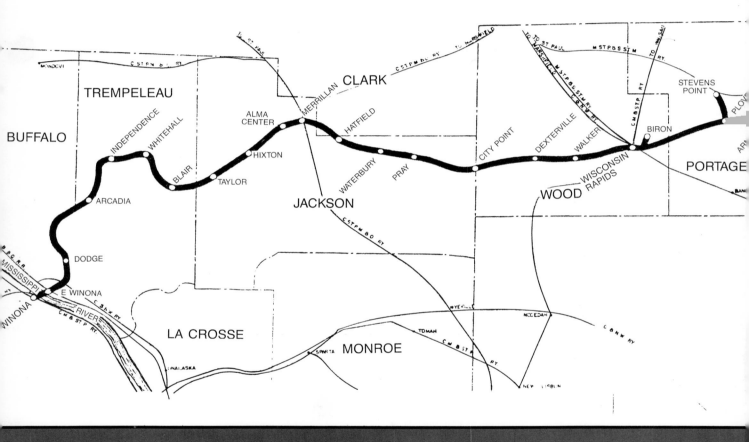

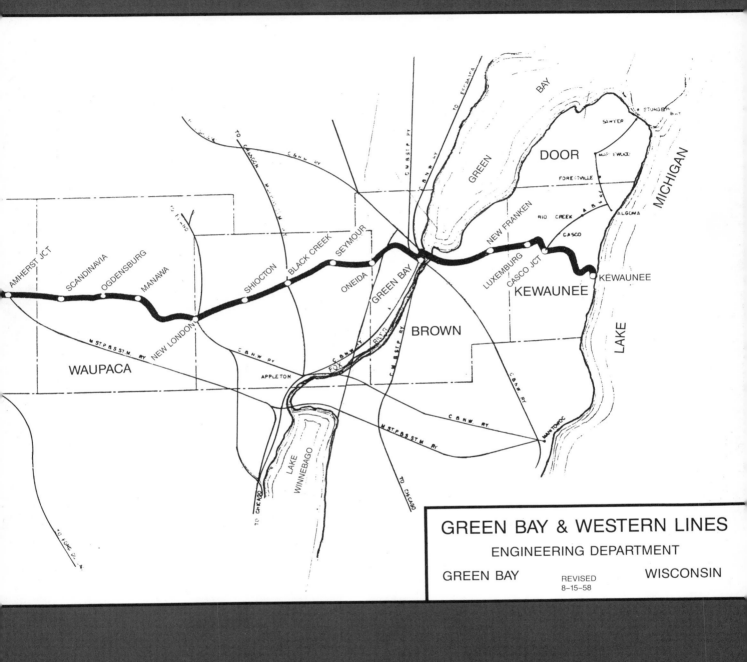

GREEN BAY & WESTERN LINES

ENGINEERING DEPARTMENT

GREEN BAY   REVISED 8-15-58   WISCONSIN